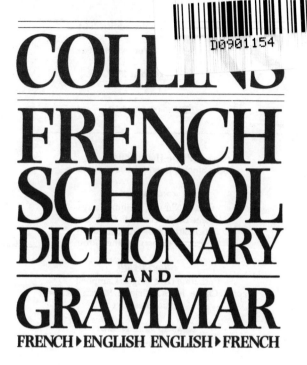

COLLINS
FRENCH
SCHOOL
DICTIONARY
AND
GRAMMAR
FRENCH ▸ ENGLISH ENGLISH ▸ FRENCH

HarperCollins*Publishers*

First published in this edition 1994

© HarperCollins Publishers 1994

Latest reprint 1997

ISBN 0 00 470389-8

Pierre-Henri Cousin
Lorna Sinclair Knight Lesley Robertson

contributors

Claude Nimmo Philippe Patry
Hélène Lewis Elizabeth Campbell
Renée Birks Jean-François Allain
Christine Penman Sabine Citron

editorial staff

Catherine Love Angela Campbell
Stephen Clarke Joyce Littlejohn Megan Thomson
Linda Chestnutt

editorial management

Vivian Marr

*A catalogue record for this book is
available from the British Library*

*Dictionary text typeset by Morton Word Processing Ltd, Scarborough
Grammar text typeset by Tradespools Ltd, Frome, Somerset*

*Printed and bound in Great Britain by Caledonian International
Book Manufacturing Ltd, Glasgow, G64*

Introduction

We are delighted you have decided to buy the **Collins French School Dictionary and Grammar**. This book is designed to give you, in one handy volume, comprehensive and authoritative answers to all your vocabulary and grammar queries.

In the Dictionary section you will find:

- in-depth vocabulary coverage which will more than meet your examination needs
- clear signposting of meanings and subject areas to guide you to the most appropriate translation
- modern, idiomatic phrases showing words in their context
- the most common words in each language are highlighted and treated in depth

The Grammar section contains further essential information on:

- all the basic rules and structures of French
- French verbs
- avoiding pitfalls in translation

We hope you will enjoy using this book and that it will be an invaluable reference tool for all your French language studies.

Contents

Using the Dictionary

The various typefaces, type sizes, symbols, abbreviations and brackets used throughout this dictionary all convey useful information. Take time to establish what they indicate and this will help you get the most out of your dictionary.

Finding the word you want

The information above the line at the top of each page helps you to locate, quickly and easily, the entry you want to consult. At the outside margin, the first and last entries on that page are shown, separated by an arrow. Information about which side of the dictionary you are using is shown at the inside margin.

above → *acknowledge*   *ENGLISH-FRENCH*   220

Headwords

The words you look up in a dictionary are called headwords and are printed in **bold** type. The phonetic spelling is given in square brackets immediately after the headword. An explanation of these symbols is given on pages viii-ix. Information about the usage or form of certain headwords is given in brackets after the phonetic spelling. This usually appears in abbreviated form and in italics eg (*fam*), (*comm*). Explanations of these are given on pages vi-vii.

Where appropriate, words related to headwords are grouped in the same entry in a slightly smaller type than the headword.

> **passion** [...] *nf* passion; **passionant, e** *adj* fascinating;...

> **explosion** [...] *n* explosion *f*; **explosive** [...] *adj* explosif (ive)...

Common expressions in which the headword appears are shown in a smaller bold type.

> **autre** [...] *adj* **1** (*différent*) other, different; **je préférerais un ~ verre** I'd prefer another *ou* a different glass

iv

Translations

Headword translations are given in ordinary type and, where more than
one meaning or usage exists, these are separated by a semicolon. You
will often find bracketed words in italics appearing before the translations. These are called "indicators" and they offer suggested contexts
in which the headword might appear or provide synonyms for the
headword to guide you to the most appropriate translation.

> **opposer** [...] *vt* (*personnes,
> armées, équipes*) to oppose; (*cou-
> leurs, termes, tons*) to contrast; ...

> **relation** [...] *n* (*person*) parent
> (e); (*link*) rapport *m*, lien *m*; ...

> **superposer** [...] *vi* (*faire che-
> vaucher*) to superimpose; ...

> **retire** [...] *vi* (*give up work*)
> prendre sa retraite; ...

Key words

Special status is given to certain French and English words which are
considered "key" words in each language. These words occur very frequently in French or English, or have several types of usage (eg **vouloir,
plus; get, that**). A combination of lozenges and numbers helps you to
distinguish different parts of speech and meanings.

Grammatical information

Parts of speech are given in abbreviated form in italics after the phonetic
spellings of headwords (eg *vt, adv, conj*). A lozenge indicates a change
in part of speech and different meanings are split into separate categor-
ies and numbered accordingly. Genders of French nouns are indicated
as follows: *nm* for a masculine and *nf* for a feminine noun. Feminine and
irregular plural forms of nouns and adjectives, along with any change in
pronunciation, are also shown.

> **directeur, trice** [ ] *nm/f*
> (*d'entreprise*) director;

> **cheval, aux** [ ] *nm* horse,

Note on trademarks

Words which we have reason to believe constitute trademarks have
been designated as such However, neither the presence nor the
absence of such designation should be regarded as affecting the legal
status of any trademark

v

Abbreviations

adjectif, locution adjective	**adj**	adjective, adjectival phrase
abréviation	**ab(b)r**	abbreviation
adverbe, locution adverbiale	**adv**	adverb, adverbial phrase
administration	ADMIN	administration
agriculture	AGR	agriculture
anatomie	ANAT	anatomy
architecture	ARCHIT	architecture
article défini	**art déf**	definite article
article indéfini	**art indéf**	indefinite article
l'automobile	AUT(O)	the motor car and motoring
auxiliaire	**aux**	auxiliary
aviation, voyages aériens	AVIAT	flying, air travel
biologie	BIO(L)	biology
botanique	BOT	botany
anglais de Grande-Bretagne	**Brit**	British English
commerce, finance, banque	COMM	commerce, finance, banking
comparatif	**compar**	comparative
informatique	COMPUT	computing
chimie	CHEM	chemistry
conjonction	**conj**	conjunction
construction	CONSTR	building
nom utilisé comme adjectif, ne peut s'employer ni comme attribut, ni après le nom qualifié	**cpd**	compound element: noun used as an adjective and which cannot follow the noun it qualifies
cuisine, art culinaire	CULIN	cookery
article défini	**def art**	definite article
diminutif	**dimin**	diminutive
économie	ECON	economics
électricité, électronique	ELEC	electricity, electronics
exclamation, interjection	**excl**	exclamation, interjection
féminin	**f**	feminine
langue familière (! emploi vulgaire)	**fam(!)**	colloquial usage (! particularly offensive)
emploi figuré	**fig**	figurative use
(verbe anglais) dont la particule est inséparable du verbe	**fus**	(phrasal verb) where the particle cannot be separated from main verb
dans la plupart des sens; généralement	**gén, gen**	in most or all senses; generally
géographie, géologie	GEO	geography, geology
géométrie	GEOM	geometry
impersonnel	**impers**	impersonal
article indéfini	**indef art**	indefinite article
langue familière (! emploi vulgaire)	**inf(!)**	colloquial usage (! particularly offensive)
infinitif	**infin**	infinitive
informatique	INFORM	computing
invariable	**inv**	invariable

vi

irrégulier	*irreg*	irregular
domaine juridique	*JUR*	law
grammaire, linguistique	*LING*	grammar, linguistics
masculin	*m*	masculine
mathématiques, algèbre	*MATH*	mathematics, calculus
médecine	*MÉD, MED*	medical term, medicine
masculin ou féminin, suivant le sexe	*m/f*	either masculine or feminine depending on sex
domaine militaire, armée	*MIL*	military matters
musique	*MUS*	music
nom	*n*	noun
navigation, nautisme	*NAVIG, NAUT*	sailing, navigation
adjectif ou nom numérique	*num*	numeral adjective or noun
	o.s.	oneself
péjoratif	*péj, pej*	derogatory, pejorative
photographie	*PHOT(O)*	photography
physiologie	*PHYSIOL*	physiology
pluriel	*pl*	plural
politique	*POL*	politics
participe passé	*pp*	past participle
préposition	*prép, prep*	preposition
pronom	*pron*	pronoun
psychologie, psychiatrie	*PSYCH*	psychology, psychiatry
temps du passé	*pt*	past tense
quelque chose	*qch*	
quelqu'un	*qn*	
religions, domaine ecclésiastique	*REL*	religions, church service
	sb	somebody
enseignement, système scolaire et universitaire	*SCOL*	schooling, schools and universities
singulier	*sg*	singular
	sth	something
subjonctif	*sub*	subjunctive
sujet (grammatical)	*su(b)j*	(grammatical) subject
superlatif	*superl*	superlative
techniques, technologie	*TECH*	technical term, technology
télécommunications	*TEL*	telecommunications
télévision	*TV*	television
typographie	*TYP(O)*	typography, printing
anglais des USA	*US*	American English
verbe	*vb*	verb
verbe ou groupe verbal à fonction intransitive	*vi*	verb or phrasal verb used intransitively
verbe ou groupe verbal à fonction transitive	*vt*	verb or phrasal verb used transitively
zoologie	*ZOOL*	zoology
marque déposée	®	registered trademark
indique une équivalence culturelle	~	introduces a cultural equivalent

Phonetic Transcription

Consonnes

NB. **p, b, t, d, k, g** sont suivis d'une aspiration en anglais.

Consonants

NB. **p, b, t, d, k, g** are not aspirated in French.

Français		Anglais
poupée	p	*puppy*
bombe	b	*baby*
tente thermal	t	*tent*
dinde	d	*daddy*
coq qui képi	k	*cork kiss chord*
gag bague	g	*gag guess*
sale ce nation	s	*so rice kiss*
zéro rose	z	*cousin buzz*
tache chat	ʃ	*sheep sugar*
gilet juge	ʒ	*pleasure beige*
	tʃ	*church*
	dʒ	*judge general*
fer phare	f	*farm raffle*
valve	v	*very rev*
	θ	*thin maths*
	ð	*that other*
lent salle	l	*little ball*
rare rentrer	ʀ	
	r	*rat rare*
maman femme	m	*mummy comb*
non nonne	n	*no ran*
agneau vigne	ɲ	
	ŋ	*singing bank*
hop!	h	*hat reheat*
yeux paille pied	j	*yet*
nouer oui	w	*wall bewail*
huile lui	ɥ	
	x	*loch*

Divers

pour l'anglais: précède la syllabe accentuée   ˈ

pour l'anglais: le r final se prononce en liaison devant une voyelle   *

Miscellaneous

in French wordlist and transcription: no liaison

Phonetic Transcription

Voyelles		*Vowels*
NB. La mise en équivalence de certains sons n'indique qu'une ressemblance approximative.		NB. The pairing of some vowel sounds only indicates approximate equivalence.
ici v*ie* l*y*re	i i:	h*ee*l b*ea*d
	ɪ	h*i*t p*i*ty
jou*er* ét*é*	e	s*e*t t*e*nt
l*ai*t jou*et* m*e*rci	ɛ	
pl*at* *a*mour	a æ	b*a*t *a*pple
b*as* p*â*te	ɑ ɑ:	*a*fter c*ar* c*a*lm
	ʌ	f*u*n c*ou*sin
l*e* pr*e*mier	ə	ov*er* *a*bove
b*eu*rre p*eu*r	œ	
p*eu* d*eu*x	ø ɜ:	*ur*n f*er*n w*or*k
*o*r h*o*mme	ɒ	w*a*sh p*o*t
m*ot* *eau* g*au*che	o ɔ:	b*or*n c*or*k
gen*ou* r*ou*e	u ʊ	f*u*ll s*oo*t
	u:	b*oo*n l*ew*d
r*ue* *u*rne	y	

Diphtongues		*Diphthongs*
	ɪə	b*eer* t*i*er
	ɛə	t*ear* f*air* th*ere*
	eɪ	d*a*te pl*ai*ce d*ay*
	aɪ	l*i*fe b*uy* cr*y*
	aʊ	*ow*l f*ou*l n*ow*
	əʊ	l*ow* n*o*
	ɔɪ	b*oi*l b*oy* *oi*ly
	ʊə	p*oor* t*our*

Nasales		*Nasal Vowels*
mat*in* pl*ein*	ɛ̃	
br*un*	œ̃	
s*an*g *an* d*ans*	ɑ̃	
n*on* p*on*t	ɔ̃	

ix

Dictionary

FRANÇAIS - ANGLAIS
FRENCH - ENGLISH

A a

A *abr* = **autoroute**

a *vb voir* **avoir**

MOT CLÉ

à [a] (*à* + *le* = **au**, *à* + *les* = **aux**) *prép* **1** (*endroit, situation*) at, in; **être ~ Paris/au Portugal** to be in Paris/Portugal; **être ~ la maison/~ l'école** to be at home/at school; **~ la campagne** in the country; **c'est ~ 10 km/~ 20 minutes (d'ici)** it's 10 km/20 minutes away

2 (*direction*) to; **aller ~ Paris/au Portugal** to go to Paris/Portugal; **aller ~ la maison/~ l'école** to go home/to school; **~ la campagne** to the country

3 (*temps*): **~ 3 heures/minuit** at 3 o'clock/midnight; **au printemps/mois de juin** in the spring/the month of June

4 (*attribution, appartenance*) to; **le livre est ~ Paul/~ lui/~ nous** this book is Paul's/his/ours; **donner qch ~ qn** to give sth to sb

5 (*moyen*) with; **se chauffer au gaz** to have gas heating; **~ bicyclette** on a *ou* by bicycle; **~ la main/machine** by hand/machine

6 (*provenance*) from; **boire ~ la bouteille** to drink from the bottle

7 (*caractérisation, manière*): **l'homme aux yeux bleus** the man with the blue eyes; **~ la russe** the Russian way

8 (*but, destination*): **tasse ~ café** coffee cup; **maison ~ vendre** house for sale

9 (*rapport, évaluation, distribution*): **100 km/unités ~ l'heure** 100 km/units per *ou* an hour; **payé ~ l'heure** paid by the hour; **cinq ~ six** five to six

abaisser [abese] *vt* to lower, bring down; (*manette*) to pull down; (*fig*) to debase; to humiliate; **s'~** *vi* to go down; (*fig*) to demean o.s.

abandon [abɑ̃dɔ̃] *nm* abandoning; giving up; withdrawal; **être à l'~** to be in a state of neglect

abandonner [abɑ̃dɔne] *vt* (*personne*) to abandon; (*projet, activité*) to abandon, give up; (*SPORT*) to retire *ou* withdraw from; (*céder*) to surrender; **s'~** *vi* to let o.s. go; **s'~ à** (*paresse, plaisirs*) to give o.s. up to

abasourdir [abazurdir] *vt* to stun, stagger

abat-jour [abaʒur] *nm inv* lampshade

abats [aba] *nmpl* (*de bœuf, porc*) offal *sg*; (*de volaille*) giblets

abattement [abatmɑ̃] *nm* (*déduction*) reduction; **~ fiscal** ≈ tax allowance

abattoir [abatwaʀ] *nm* slaughterhouse

abattre [abatʀ(ə)] *vt* (*arbre*) to cut down, fell; (*mur, maison*) to pull down; (*avion, personne*) to shoot down; (*animal*) to shoot, kill; (*fig*) to wear out, tire out; to demoralize; **s'~** *vi* to crash down; **s'~ sur** to beat down on; to rain down on

abbaye [abei] *nf* abbey

abbé [abe] *nm* priest; (*d'une abbaye*) abbot

abcès [apsɛ] *nm* abscess

abdiquer [abdike] *vi* to abdicate ♦ *vt* to renounce, give up

abeille [abɛj] *nf* bee

aberrant, e [abɛʀɑ̃, -ɑ̃t] *adj* absurd

abêtir [abetiʀ] *vt* to make morons of (*ou* a moron of)

abîme [abim] *nm* abyss, gulf

abîmer [abime] *vt* to spoil, damage; **s'~** *vi* to get spoilt *ou* damaged

ablation [ablɑsjɔ̃] *nf* removal

abois [abwa] *nmpl*: **aux ~** at bay

abolir [abɔliʀ] *vt* to abolish

abondance [abɔ̃dɑ̃s] *nf* abundance; (*richesse*) affluence

abondant, e [abɔ̃dɑ̃, -ɑ̃t] *adj* plentiful, abundant, copious

abonder [abɔ̃de] *vi* to abound, be plentiful; **~ dans le sens de qn** to concur with sb

abonné, e [abɔne] *nm/f* subscriber; season ticket holder

abonnement [abɔnmã] *nm* subscription; (*transports, concerts*) season ticket

abonner [abɔne] *vt*: **s'~ à** to subscribe to, take out a subscription to

abord [abɔʀ] *nm*: **être d'un ~ facile** to be approachable; **~s** *nmpl* (*environs*) surroundings; **au premier ~** at first sight, initially; **d'~** first

abordable [abɔʀdabl(ə)] *adj* approachable; reasonably priced

aborder [abɔʀde] *vi* to land ♦ *vt* (*sujet, difficulté*) to tackle; (*personne*) to approach; (*rivage etc*) to reach; (*NAVIG: attaquer*) to board

aboutir [abutiʀ] *vi* (*négociations etc*) to succeed; **~ à/dans/sur** to end up at/in/on

aboyer [abwaje] *vi* to bark

abrégé [abreʒe] *nm* summary

abréger [abreʒe] *vt* to shorten

abreuver [abrœve] *vt* (*fig*): **~ qn de** to shower *ou* swamp sb with; **s'~** *vi* to drink; **abreuvoir** *nm* watering place

abréviation [abrevjasjɔ̃] *nf* abbreviation

abri [abri] *nm* shelter; **à l'~** under cover; **à l'~ de** sheltered from; (*fig*) safe from

abricot [abriko] *nm* apricot

abriter [abrite] *vt* to shelter; (*loger*) to accommodate; **s'~** *vt* to shelter, take cover

abroger [abrɔʒe] *vt* to repeal

abrupt, e [abrypt] *adj* sheer, steep; (*ton*) abrupt

abrutir [abrytiʀ] *vt* to daze; to exhaust; to stupefy

absence [apsɑ̃s] *nf* absence; (*MÉD*) blackout; mental blank

absent, e [apsɑ̃, -ɑ̃t] *adj* absent; (*distrait: air*) vacant, faraway ♦ *nm/f* absentee; **s'~er** *vi* to take time off work; (*sortir*) to leave, go out

absolu, e [apsɔly] *adj* absolute; (*caractère*) rigid, uncompromising; **absolument** *adv* absolutely

absorber [apsɔʀbe] *vt* to absorb; (*gén MÉD: manger, boire*) to take

absoudre [apsudʀ(ə)] *vt* to absolve

abstenir [apstəniʀ] : **s'~** *vi* (*POL*) to abstain; **s'~ de qch/de faire** to refrain from sth/from doing

abstraction [apstraksjɔ̃] *nf* abstraction; **faire ~ de** to set *ou* leave aside

abstrait, e [apstʀɛ, -ɛt] *adj* abstract

absurde [apsyʀd(ə)] *adj* absurd

abus [aby] *nm* abuse; **~ de confiance** breach of trust

abuser [abyze] *vi* to go too far, overstep the mark ♦ *vt* to deceive, mislead; **s'~** *vi* to be mistaken; **~ de** to misuse; (*violer, duper*) to take advantage of; **abusif, ive** *adj* exorbitant; excessive; improper

acabit [akabi] *nm*: **de cet ~** of that type

académie [akademi] *nf* academy; (*ART: nu*) nude; (*SCOL: circonscription*) ≈ regional education authority

acajou [akaʒu] *nm* mahogany

acariâtre [akaʀjɑtʀ(ə)] *adj* cantankerous

accablant, e [akɑblɑ̃, -ɑ̃t] *adj* (*témoignage, preuve*) overwhelming

accablement [akɑbləmɑ̃] *nm* despondency

accabler [akɑble] *vt* to overwhelm, overcome; (*suj: témoignage*) to condemn, damn; **~ qn d'injures** to heap *ou* shower abuse on sb

accalmie [akalmi] *nf* lull

accaparer [akapaʀe] *vt* to monopolize; (*suj: travail etc*) to take up (all) the time *ou* attention of

accéder [aksede]: **~ à** *vt* (*lieu*) to reach; (*fig*) to accede to, attain; (*accorder: requête*) to grant, accede to

accélérateur [akseleʀatœʀ] *nm* accelerator

accélération [akseleʀasjɔ̃] *nf* acceleration

accélérer [akseleʀe] *vt* to speed up ♦ *vi* to accelerate

accent [aksɑ̃] *nm* accent; (*inflexions expressives*) tone (of voice); (*PHONÉTIQUE, fig*) stress; **mettre l'~ sur** (*fig*) to stress; **~ aigu/grave** acute/grave accent

accentuer [aksɑ̃tɥe] *vt* (*LING*) to accent; (*fig*) to accentuate, emphasize; **s'~** *vi* to become more marked *ou* pronounced

acceptation [akseptɑsjɔ̃] *nf* acceptance

accepter [aksepte] *vt* to accept; (*tolérer*): **~ que qn fasse** to agree to sb doing; **~ de faire** to agree to do

accès [aksɛ] *nm* (*à un lieu*) access; (*MÉD*) attack; fit, bout; outbreak ♦ *nmpl* (*routes etc*) means of access, approaches; **d'~ facile** easily accessible; **~ de colère** fit of anger

accessible [aksesibl(ə)] *adj* accessible; (*livre, sujet*): **~ à qn** within the reach of sb; (*sensible*): **~ à** open to

accessoire [akseswaʀ] *adj* secondary; incidental ♦ *nm* accessory; (*THÉÂTRE*) prop

accident [aksidɑ̃] *nm* accident; **par ~** by chance; **~ de la route** road accident; **~ du travail** industrial injury *ou* accident; **~é, e** *adj* damaged; injured; (*relief, terrain*) uneven; hilly

acclamer [aklame] *vt* to cheer, acclaim

accolade [akɔlad] *nf* (*amicale*) embrace; (*signe*) brace

accommodant, e [akɔmɔdɑ̃, -ɑ̃t] *adj* accommodating; easy-going

accommoder [akɔmɔde] *vt* (*CULIN*) to prepare; (*points de vue*) to reconcile; **s'~ de** *vt* to put up with; to make do with

accompagnateur, trice [akɔ̃paɲatœʀ, -tʀis] *nm/f* (*MUS*) accompanist; (*de voyage: guide*) guide; (: *d'enfants*) accompanying adult; (*de voyage organisé*) courier

accompagner [akɔ̃paɲe] *vt* to accompany,

be *ou* go *ou* come with; (*MUS*) to accompany

accompli, e [akɔ̃pli] *adj* accomplished

accomplir [akɔ̃pliʀ] *vt* (*tâche, projet*) to carry out; (*souhait*) to fulfil; **s'~** *vi* to be fulfilled

accord [akɔʀ] *nm* agreement; (*entre des styles, tons etc*) harmony; (*MUS*) chord; **d'~!** OK!; **se mettre d'~** to come to an agreement; **être d'~** to agree

accordéon [akɔʀdeɔ̃] *nm* (*MUS*) accordion

accorder [akɔʀde] *vt* (*faveur, délai*) to grant; (*harmoniser*) to match; (*MUS*) to tune; **s'~** *vt* to get on together; to agree

accoster [akɔste] *vt* (*NAVIG*) to draw alongside ♦ *vi* to berth

accotement [akɔtmã] *nm* verge (*BRIT*), shoulder

accouchement [akuʃmã] *nm* delivery, (child)birth; labour

accoucher [akuʃe] *vi* to give birth, have a baby; (*être en travail*) to be in labour ♦ *vt* to deliver; **~ d'un garçon** to give birth to a boy

accouder [akude]: **s'~** *vi* to rest one's elbows on/against; **accoudoir** *nm* armrest

accoupler [akuple] *vt* to couple; (*pour la reproduction*) to mate; **s'~** *vt* to mate

accourir [akuʀiʀ] *vi* to rush *ou* run up

accoutrement [akutʀəmã] (*péj*) *nm* (*tenue*) outfit

accoutumance [akutymãs] *nf* (*gén*) adaptation; (*MÉD*) addiction

accoutumé, e [akutyme] *adj* (*habituel*) customary, usual

accoutumer [akutyme] *vt*: **s'~ à** to get accustomed *ou* used to

accréditer [akʀedite] *vt* (*nouvelle*) to substantiate

accroc [akʀo] *nm* (*déchirure*) tear; (*fig*) hitch, snag

accrochage [akʀoʃaʒ] *nm* (*AUTO*) collision

accrocher [akʀoʃe] *vt* (*suspendre*): **~ qch à** to hang sth (up) on; (*attacher: remorque*): **~ qch à** to hitch sth (up) to; (*heurter*) to catch; to catch on; to hit; (*déchirer*): **~ qch (à)** to catch sth (on); (*MIL*) to engage; (*fig*) to catch, attract; **s'~** (*se disputer*) to have a clash *ou* brush; **s'~ à** (*rester pris à*) to catch on; (*agripper, fig*) to hang on *ou* cling to

accroître [akʀwatʀ(ə)] *vt* to increase; **s'~** *vi* to increase

accroupir [akʀupiʀ]: **s'~** *vi* to squat, crouch (down)

accru, e [akʀy] *pp de* **accroître**

accueil [akœj] *nm* welcome; **comité d'~** reception committee

accueillir [akœjiʀ] *vt* to welcome; (*loger*) to accommodate

acculer [akyle] *vt*: **~ qn à** *ou* **contre** to drive sb back against

accumuler [akymyle] *vt* to accumulate, amass; **s'~** *vi* to accumulate; to pile up

accusation [akyzɑsjɔ̃] *nf* (*gén*) accusation; (*JUR*) charge; (*partie*): **l'~** the prosecution; **mettre en ~** to indict

accusé, e [akyze] *nm/f* accused; defendant; **~ de réception** acknowledgement of receipt

accuser [akyze] *vt* to accuse; (*fig*) to emphasize, bring out; to show; **~ qn de** to accuse sb of; (*JUR*) to charge sb with; **~ qch de** (*rendre responsable*) to blame sth for; **~ réception de** to acknowledge receipt of

acerbe [asɛʀb(ə)] *adj* caustic, acid

acéré, e [aseʀe] *adj* sharp

achalandé, e [aʃalãde] *adj*: **bien ~** well-stocked; well-patronized

acharné, e [aʃaʀne] *adj* (*lutte, adversaire*) fierce, bitter; (*travail*) relentless, unremitting

acharner [aʃaʀne]: **s'~** *vi* to go at fiercely; **s'~ contre** to set o.s. against; to dog; **s'~ à faire** to try doggedly to do; to persist in doing

achat [aʃa] *nm* buying *no pl*; purchase; **faire des ~s** to do some shopping

acheminer [aʃmine] *vt* (*courrier*) to forward, dispatch; (*troupes*) to convey, transport; (*train*) to route; **s'~ vers** to head for

acheter [aʃte] *vt* to buy, purchase; (*soudoyer*) to buy; **~ qch à** (*marchand*) to buy *ou* purchase sth from; (*ami etc: offrir*) to buy sth for; **acheteur, euse** *nm/f* buyer; shopper; (*COMM*) buyer

achever [aʃve] *vt* to complete, finish; (*blessé*) to finish off; **s'~** *vi* to end

acide [asid] *adj* sour, sharp; (*CHIMIE*) acid(ic) ♦ *nm* acid

acier [asje] *nm* steel; **aciérie** *nf* steelworks *sg*

acné [akne] *nf* acne

acolyte [akɔlit] (*péj*) *nm* associate

acompte [akɔ̃t] *nm* deposit; (*versement régulier*) instalment; (*sur somme due*) payment on account

à-côté [akote] *nm* side-issue; (*argent*) extra

à-coup [aku] *nm* (*du moteur*) (hic)cough; (*fig*) jolt; **par ~s** by fits and starts

acoustique [akustik] *nf* (*d'une salle*) acoustics *pl*

acquéreur [akeʀœʀ] *nm* buyer, purchaser

acquérir [akeʀiʀ] *vt* to acquire

acquis, e [aki, -iz] *pp de* **acquérir** ♦ *nm* (accumulated) experience; **être ~ à** (*plan, idée*) to fully agree with; **son aide nous est ~e** we can count on her help

acquit [aki] *vb voir* **acquérir** ♦ *nm* (*quittance*) receipt; **par ~ de conscience** to set one's mind at rest

acquitter [akite] *vt* (*JUR*) to acquit; (*facture*) to pay, settle; **s'~ de** *vt* to discharge, fulfil

âcre [ɑkʀ(ə)] *adj* acrid, pungent

acrobate [akʀɔbat] *nm/f* acrobat

acte [akt(ə)] *nm* act, action; (*THÉÂTRE*) act; **~s** *nmpl* (*compte-rendu*) proceedings; **prendre ~ de** to note, take note of; **faire ~ de candidature** to apply; **faire ~ de présence** to put in an appearance; **~ de naissance** birth certificate

acteur [aktœʀ] *nm* actor

actif, ive [aktif, -iv] *adj* active ♦ *nm* (*COMM*) assets *pl*; (*fig*): **avoir à son ~ de** to have to one's credit; **population active** working population

action [aksjɔ̃] *nf* (*gén*) action; (*COMM*) share; **une bonne ~** a good deed; **~naire** *nm/f* shareholder; **~ner** *vt* to work; to activate; to operate

activer [aktive] *vt* to speed up; **s'~** *vi* to bustle about; to hurry up

activité [aktivite] *nf* activity

actrice [aktʀis] *nf* actress

actualiser [aktɥalize] *vt* to actualize; to bring up to date

actualité [aktɥalite] *nf* (*d'un problème*) topicality; (*événements*): **l'~** current events; **les ~s** *nfpl* (*CINÉMA, TV*) the news

actuel, le [aktɥɛl] *adj* (*présent*) present; (*d'actualité*) topical; **actuellement** *adv* at present; at the present time

acuité [akɥite] *nf* acuteness

adaptateur [adaptatœʀ] *nm* (*ÉLEC*) adapter

adapter [adapte] *vt* to adapt; **s'~ (à)** (*suj: personne*) to adapt (to); **~ qch à** (*approprier*) to adapt sth to (fit); **~ qch sur/dans/à** (*fixer*) to fit sth on/into/to

additif [aditif] *nm* additive

addition [adisjɔ̃] *nf* addition; (*au café*) bill; **~ner** *vt* to add (up)

adepte [adɛpt(ə)] *nm/f* follower

adéquat, e [adekwa, -at] *adj* appropriate, suitable

adhérent, e [adeʀɑ̃, -ɑ̃t] *nm/f* (*de club*) member

adhérer [adeʀe]: **~ à** *vi* (*coller*) to adhere *ou* stick to; (*se rallier à*) to join; to support; **adhésif, ive** *adj* adhesive, sticky ♦ *nm* adhesive; **adhésion** *nf* joining; membership; support

adieu, x [adjø] *excl* goodbye ♦ *nm* farewell; **dire ~ à qn** to say goodbye *ou* farewell to sb

adjectif [adʒɛktif] *nm* adjective

adjoindre [adʒwɛ̃dʀ(ə)] *vt*: **~ qch à** to attach sth to; to add sth to; **s'~** *vt* (*collaborateur etc*) to take on, appoint; **adjoint, e** *nm/f* assistant; **adjoint au maire** deputy mayor; **directeur adjoint** assistant manager

adjudant [adʒydɑ̃] *nm* (*MIL*) warrant officer

adjudication [adʒydikɑsjɔ̃] *nf* sale by auction; (*pour travaux*) invitation to tender (*BRIT*) *ou* bid (*US*)

adjuger [adʒyʒe] *vt* (*prix, récompense*) to

award; (*lors d'une vente*) to auction (off); **s'~** *vt* to take for o.s.

adjurer [adʒyʀe] *vt*: **~ qn de faire** to implore *ou* beg sb to do

admettre [admɛtʀ(ə)] *vt* (*laisser entrer*) to admit; (*candidat: SCOL*) to pass; (*tolérer*) to allow, accept; (*reconnaître*) to admit, acknowledge

administrateur, trice [administʀatœʀ, -tʀis] *nm/f* (*COMM*) director; (*ADMIN*) administrator; **~ judiciaire** receiver

administration [administʀɑsjɔ̃] *nf* administration; **l'A~** ≈ the Civil Service

administrer [administʀe] *vt* (*firme*) to manage, run; (*biens, remède, sacrement etc*) to administer

admirable [admiʀabl(ə)] *adj* admirable, wonderful

admirateur, trice [admiʀatœʀ, -tʀis] *nm/f* admirer

admiration [admiʀɑsjɔ̃] *nf* admiration

admirer [admiʀe] *vt* to admire

admis, e *pp de* **admettre**

admissible [admisibl(ə)] *adj* (*candidat*) eligible; (*comportement*) admissible, acceptable

admission [admisjɔ̃] *nf* admission; acknowledgement; **demande d'~** application for membership

adolescence [adɔlesɑ̃s] *nf* adolescence

adolescent, e [adɔlesɑ̃, -ɑ̃t] *nm/f* adolescent, teenager

adonner [adɔne]: **s'~ à** *vt* (*sport*) to devote o.s. to; (*boisson*) to give o.s. over to

adopter [adɔpte] *vt* to adopt; (*projet de loi etc*) to pass; **adoptif, ive** *adj* (*parents*) adoptive; (*fils, patrie*) adopted

adorer [adɔʀe] *vt* to adore; (*REL*) to worship

adosser [adose] *vt*: **~ qch à ou contre** to stand sth against; **s'~ à ou contre** to lean with one's back against

adoucir [adusiʀ] *vt* (*goût, température*) to make milder; (*avec du sucre*) to sweeten; (*peau, voix*) to soften; (*caractère*) to mellow

adresse [adʀɛs] *nf* (*voir adroit*) skill, dexterity; (*domicile*) address; **à l'~ de** (*pour*) for the benefit of

adresser [adʀese] *vt* (*lettre: expédier*) to send; (: *écrire l'adresse sur*) to address; (*injure, compliments*) to address; **s'~ à** (*parler à*) to speak to, address; (*s'informer auprès de*) to go and see; (: *bureau*) to enquire at; (*suj: livre, conseil*) to be aimed at; **~ la parole à** to speak to, address

adroit, e [adʀwa, -wat] *adj* skilful, skilled

adulte [adylt(ə)] *nm/f* adult, grown-up ♦ *adj* (*chien, arbre*) fully-grown, mature; (*attitude*) adult, grown-up

adultère [adyltɛʀ] *nm* (*acte*) adultery

advenir [advəniʀ] *vi* to happen

adverbe [advɛʀb(ə)] *nm* adverb

adversaire [advɛʀsɛʀ] *nm/f (SPORT, gén)* opponent, adversary; *(MIL)* adversary, enemy

adverse [advɛʀs(ə)] *adj* opposing

aération [aeʀɑsjɔ̃] *nf* airing; ventilation

aérer [aeʀe] *vt* to air; *(fig)* to lighten

aérien, ne [aeʀjɛ̃, -jɛn] *adj (AVIAT)* air *cpd*, aerial; *(câble, métro)* overhead; *(fig)* light

aéro... [aeʀɔ] *préfixe:* ~**bic** *nm* aerobics *sg;* ~**gare** *nf* airport (buildings); *(en ville)* air terminal; ~**glisseur** *nm* hovercraft; ~**naval, e** *adj* air and sea *cpd;* ~**phagie** [aeʀɔfaʒi] *nf (MÉD)* wind, aerophagia *(TECH);* ~**port** *nm* airport; ~**porté, e** *adj* airborne, airlifted; ~**sol** *nm* aerosol

affable [afabl(ə)] *adj* affable

affaiblir [afebliʀ] *vt* to weaken; **s'**~ *vi* to weaken

affaire [afɛʀ] *nf (problème, question)* matter; *(criminelle, judiciaire)* case; *(scandaleuse etc)* affair; *(entreprise)* business; *(marché, transaction)* deal; *(occasion intéressante)* bargain; ~**s** *nfpl (intérêts publics et privés)* affairs; *(activité commerciale)* business *sg;* *(effets personnels)* things, belongings; **ce sont mes** ~**s** *(cela me concerne)* that's my business; **ceci fera l'**~ this will do (nicely); **avoir** ~ **à** to be faced with; to be dealing with; **les A**~**s étrangères** Foreign Affairs; **affairer: s'affairer** *vi* to busy o.s., bustle about

affaisser [afese]: **s'**~ *vi (terrain, immeuble)* to subside, sink; *(personne)* to collapse

affaler [afale]: **s'**~ *vi:* **s'**~ **dans/sur** to collapse *ou* slump into/onto

affamé, e [afame] *adj* starving

affecter [afɛkte] *vt* to affect; *(telle ou telle forme etc)* to take on; ~ **qch à** to allocate *ou* allot sth to; ~ **qn à** to appoint sb to; *(diplomate)* to post sb to

affectif, ive [afɛktif, -iv] *adj* emotional

affection [afɛksjɔ̃] *nf* affection; *(mal)* ailment; ~**ner** *vt* to be fond of

affectueux, euse [afɛktɥø, -øz] *adj* affectionate

afférent, e [afeʀɑ̃, -ɑ̃t] *adj:* ~ **à** pertaining *ou* relating to

affermir [afɛʀmiʀ] *vt* to consolidate, strengthen

affichage [afiʃaʒ] *nm* billposting; *(électronique)* display

affiche [afiʃ] *nf* poster; *(officielle)* notice; *(THÉÂTRE)* bill; **tenir l'**~ to run

afficher [afiʃe] *vt (affiche)* to put up; *(réunion)* to put up a notice about; *(électroniquement)* to display; *(fig)* to exhibit, display

affilée [afile]: **d'**~ *adv* at a stretch

affiler [afile] *vt* to sharpen

affilier [afilje]: **s'**~ **à** *vt (club, société)* to join

affiner [afine] *vt* to refine

affirmatif, ive [afiʀmatif, -iv] *adj* affirmative

affirmation [afiʀmɑsjɔ̃] *nf* assertion

affirmer [afiʀme] *vt (prétendre)* to maintain, assert; *(autorité etc)* to assert

affligé, e [afliʒe] *adj* distressed, grieved; ~ **de** *(maladie, tare)* afflicted with

affliger [afliʒe] *vt (peiner)* to distress, grieve

affluence [aflyɑ̃s] *nf* crowds *pl;* **heures d'**~ rush hours; **jours d'**~ busiest days

affluent [aflyɑ̃] *nm* tributary

affluer [aflye] *vi (secours, biens)* to flood in, pour in; *(sang)* to rush, flow

affolement [afɔlmɑ̃] *nm* panic

affoler [afɔle] *vt* to throw into a panic; **s'**~ *vi* to panic

affranchir [afʀɑ̃ʃiʀ] *vt* to put a stamp *ou* stamps on; *(à la machine)* to frank *(BRIT),* meter *(US);* *(fig)* to free, liberate; **affranchissement** *nm* postage

affréter [afʀete] *vt* to charter

affreux, euse [afʀø, -øz] *adj* dreadful, awful

affront [afʀɔ̃] *nm* affront

affrontement [afʀɔ̃tmɑ̃] *nm* clash, confrontation

affronter [afʀɔ̃te] *vt* to confront, face

affubler [afyble] *(péj) vt:* ~ **qn de** to rig *ou* deck sb out in; *(surnom)* to attach to sb

affût [afy] *nm:* **à l'**~ **(de)** *(gibier)* lying in wait (for); *(fig)* on the look-out (for)

affûter [afyte] *vt* to sharpen, grind

afin [afɛ̃]: ~ **que** *conj* so that, in order that; ~ **de faire** in order to do, so as to do

africain, e [afʀikɛ̃, -ɛn] *adj, nm/f* African

Afrique [afʀik] *nf:* **l'**~ Africa; **l'**~ **du Sud** South Africa

agacer [agase] *vt* to pester, tease; *(involontairement)* to irritate

âge [ɑʒ] *nm* age; **quel** ~ **as-tu?** how old are you?; **prendre de l'**~ to be getting on (in years); **l'**~ **ingrat** the awkward age; ~ **mûr** maturity; **âgé, e** *adj* old, elderly; **âgé de 10 ans** 10 years old

agence [aʒɑ̃s] *nf* agency, office; *(succursale)* branch; ~ **de voyages** travel agency; ~ **immobilière** estate *(BRIT) ou* real estate *(US)* agent's (office); ~ **matrimoniale** marriage bureau

agencer [aʒɑ̃se] *vt* to put together; to arrange, lay out

agenda [aʒɛ̃da] *nm* diary

agenouiller [aʒnuje]: **s'**~ *vi* to kneel (down)

agent [aʒɑ̃] *nm (aussi:* ~ **de police)** policeman; *(ADMIN)* official, officer; *(fig: élément, facteur)* agent; ~ **d'assurances** insurance broker; ~ **de change** stockbroker

agglomération [aglɔmeʀɑsjɔ̃] *nf* town; built-up area; **l'**~ **parisienne** the urban area of Paris

aggloméré [aglɔmeʀe] *nm (bois)* chipboard; *(pierre)* conglomerate

agglomérer [aglɔmere] vt to pile up; (TECH: bois, pierre) to compress

aggraver [agrave] vt to worsen, aggravate; (JUR: peine) to increase; **s'~** vi to worsen

agile [aʒil] adj agile, nimble

agir [aʒiʀ] vi to act; **il s'agit de** it's a matter ou question of; it is about; (il importe que): **il s'agit de faire** we (ou you etc) must do

agitation [aʒitɑsjɔ̃] nf (hustle and) bustle; agitation, excitement; (politique) unrest, agitation

agité, e [aʒite] adj fidgety, restless; agitated, perturbed; (mer) rough

agiter [aʒite] vt (bouteille, chiffon) to shake; (bras, mains) to wave; (préoccuper, exciter) to perturb

agneau, x [aɲo] nm lamb

agonie [agɔni] nf mortal agony, death pangs pl; (fig) death throes pl

agrafe [agʀaf] nf (de vêtement) hook, fastener; (de bureau) staple; **agrafer** vt to fasten; to staple; **agrafeuse** nf stapler

agraire [agʀɛʀ] adj land cpd

agrandir [agʀɑ̃diʀ] vt to enlarge; (magasin, domaine) to extend, enlarge; **s'~** vi to be extended; to be enlarged; **agrandissement** nm (PHOTO) enlargement

agréable [agʀeabl(ə)] adj pleasant, nice

agréé, e [agʀee] adj: **concessionnaire ~** registered dealer

agréer [agʀee] vt (requête) to accept; **~ à** to please, suit; **veuillez ~ ...** (formule épistolaire) yours faithfully

agrégation [agʀegɑsjɔ̃] nf highest teaching diploma in France; **agrégé, e** nm/f holder of the agrégation

agrément [agʀemɑ̃] nm (accord) consent, approval; (attraits) charm, attractiveness; (plaisir) pleasure

agrémenter [agʀemɑ̃te] vt to embellish, adorn

agresser [agʀese] vt to attack

agresseur [agʀesœʀ] nm aggressor, attacker; (POL, MIL) aggressor

agressif, ive [agʀesif, -iv] adj aggressive

agricole [agʀikɔl] adj agricultural

agriculteur [agʀikyltœʀ] nm farmer

agriculture [agʀikyltyʀ] nf agriculture; farming

agripper [agʀipe] vt to grab, clutch; (pour arracher) to snatch, grab; **s'~ à** to cling (on) to, clutch, grip

agrumes [agʀym] nmpl citrus fruit(s)

aguerrir [ageʀiʀ] vt to harden

aguets [agɛ] nmpl: **être aux ~** to be on the look out

aguicher [agiʃe] vt to entice

ahuri, e [ayʀi] adj (stupéfait) flabbergasted; (idiot) dim-witted

ai vb voir **avoir**

aide [ɛd] nm/f assistant; carer ♦ nf assistance, help; (secours financier) aid; **à l'~ de** (avec) with the help ou aid of; **appeler (qn) à l'~** to call for help (from sb); **~ judiciaire** nf legal aid; **~ sociale** nf (assistance) state aid; **~-mémoire** nm inv memoranda pages pl; (key facts) handbook; **~-soignant, e** nm/f auxiliary nurse

aider [ede] vt to help; **s'~ de** (se servir de) to use, make use of; **~ à qch** (faciliter) to help (towards) with

aie etc vb voir **avoir**

aïe [aj] excl ouch

aïeul, e [ajœl] nm/f grandparent, grandfather(mother); forebear

aïeux [ajø] nmpl grandparents; forebears, forefathers

aigle [ɛgl(ə)] nm eagle

aigre [ɛgʀ(ə)] adj sour, sharp; (fig) sharp, cutting; **aigreur** nf sourness; sharpness; **aigreurs d'estomac** heartburn sg; **aigrir** vt (personne) to embitter; (caractère) to sour

aigu, ë [egy] adj (objet, arête, douleur, intelligence) sharp; (son, voix) high-pitched, shrill; (note) high (-pitched)

aiguille [eguij] nf needle; (de montre) hand; **~ à tricoter** knitting needle

aiguiller [eguije] vt (orienter) to direct

aiguilleur du ciel [eguijœʀ] nm air-traffic controller

aiguillon [eguijɔ̃] nm (d'abeille) sting; **~ner** vt to spur ou goad on

aiguiser [egize] vt to sharpen; (fig) to stimulate; to excite

ail [aj] nm garlic

aile [ɛl] nf wing; **aileron** nm (de requin) fin; **ailier** nm winger

aille etc vb voir **aller**

ailleurs [ajœʀ] adv elsewhere, somewhere else; **partout/nulle part ~** everywhere/nowhere else; **d'~** (du reste) moreover, besides; **par ~** (d'autre part) moreover, furthermore

aimable [ɛmabl(ə)] adj kind, nice

aimant [ɛmɑ̃] nm magnet

aimer [eme] vt to love; (d'amitié, affection, par goût) to like; (souhait): **j'~ais ...** I would like ...; **bien ~ qn/qch** to like sb/sth; **j'aime mieux ou autant vous dire que** I may as well tell you that; **j'~ais autant y aller maintenant** I'd rather go now; **j'~ais mieux faire** I'd much rather do

aine [ɛn] nf groin

aîné, e [ene] adj elder, older; (le plus âgé) eldest, oldest ♦ nm/f oldest child ou one, oldest boy ou son/girl ou daughter; **aînesse** nf: **droit d'aînesse** birthright

ainsi [ɛ̃si] adv (de cette façon) like this, in this way, thus; (ce faisant) thus ♦ conj thus, so; **~ que** (comme) (just) as; (et aussi) as well as; **pour ~ dire** so to speak; **et ~ de suite** and so on

air [ɛʀ] nm air; (mélodie) tune; (expression) look, air; **prendre l'~** to get some (fresh) air; (*avion*) to take off; **avoir l'~** (*sembler*) to look, appear; **avoir l'~ de** to look like; **avoir l'~ de faire** to look as though one is doing, appear to be doing

aire [ɛʀ] *nf* (*zone, fig, MATH*) area

aisance [ɛzɑ̃s] *nf* ease; (*richesse*) affluence

aise [ɛz] *nf* comfort ♦ *adj*: **être bien ~ que** to be delighted that; **être à l'~ ou à son ~** to be comfortable; (*pas embarrassé*) to be at ease; (*financièrement*) to be comfortably off; **se mettre à l'~** to make o.s. comfortable; **être mal à l'~ ou à son ~** to be uncomfortable; to be ill at ease; **en faire à son ~** to do as one likes; **aisé, e** *adj* easy; (*assez riche*) well-to-do, well-off

aisselle [ɛsɛl] *nf* armpit

ait *vb voir* **avoir**

ajonc [aʒɔ̃] *nm* gorse *no pl*

ajourner [aʒuʀne] *vt* (*réunion*) to adjourn; (*décision*) to defer, postpone

ajouter [aʒute] *vt* to add; **~ foi à** to lend *ou* give credence to

ajusté, e [aʒyste] *adj*: **bien ~** (*robe etc*) close-fitting

ajuster [aʒyste] *vt* (*régler*) to adjust; (*vêtement*) to alter; (*coup de fusil*) to aim; (*cible*) to aim at; (*TECH, gén: adapter*): **~ qch à** to fit sth to

alarme [alaʀm(ə)] *nf* alarm; **donner l'~** to give *ou* raise the alarm; **alarmer** *vt* to alarm; **s'~r** *vi* to become alarmed

album [albɔm] *nm* album

albumine [albymin] *nf* albumin; **avoir *ou* faire de l'~** to suffer from albuminuria

alcool [alkɔl] *nm*: **l'~** alcohol; **un ~** a spirit, a brandy; **~ à brûler** methylated spirits (*BRIT*), wood alcohol (*US*); **~ à 90°** surgical spirit; **~ique** *adj, nmf* alcoholic; **~isé, e** *adj* alcoholic; **~isme** *nm* alcoholism

alco(o)test (®) [alkɔtɛst] *nm* Breathalyser (®); (*test*) breath-test

aléas [alea] *nmpl* hazards; **aléatoire** *adj* uncertain; (*INFORM*) random

alentour [alɑ̃tuʀ] *adv* around (about); **~s** *nmpl* (*environs*) surroundings; **aux ~s de** in the vicinity *ou* neighbourhood of, around about; (*temps*) around about

alerte [alɛʀt(ə)] *adj* agile, nimble; brisk, lively ♦ *nf* alert; warning; **alerter** *vt* to alert

algèbre [alʒɛbʀ(ə)] *nf* algebra

Alger [alʒe] *n* Algiers

Algérie [alʒeʀi] *nf*: **l'~** Algeria; **algérien, ne** *adj, nmf* Algerian

algue [alg(ə)] *nf* (*gén*) seaweed *no pl*; (*BOT*) alga

alibi [alibi] *nm* alibi

aliéné, e [aljene] *nmf* insane person, lunatic (*péj*)

aligner [aliɲe] *vt* to align, line up; (*idées, chiffres*) to string together; (*adapter*): **~ qch sur** to bring sth into alignment with; **s'~** (*soldats etc*) to line up; **s'~ sur** (*POL*) to align o.s. on

aliment [alimɑ̃] *nm* food

alimentation [alimɑ̃tasjɔ̃] *nf* feeding; supplying; (*commerce*) food trade; (*produits*) groceries *pl*; (*régime*) diet; (*INFORM*) feed

alimenter [alimɑ̃te] *vt* to feed; (*TECH*): **~ (en)** to supply (with); to feed (with); (*fig*) to sustain, keep going

alinéa [alinea] *nm* paragraph

aliter [alite]: **s'~** *vi* to take to one's bed

allaiter [alete] *vt* to (breast-)feed, nurse; (*suj: animal*) to suckle

allant [alɑ̃] *nm* drive, go

allécher [aleʃe] *vt*: **~ qn** to make sb's mouth water; to tempt *ou* entice sb

allée [ale] *nf* (*de jardin*) path; (*en ville*) avenue, drive; **~s et venues** comings and goings

alléger [aleʒe] *vt* (*voiture*) to make lighter; (*chargement*) to lighten; (*souffrance*) to alleviate, soothe

allègre [alɛgʀ(ə)] *adj* lively, cheerful

alléguer [alege] *vt* to put forward (as proof *ou* an excuse)

Allemagne [aləmaɲ] *nf*: **l'~** Germany; **allemand, e** *adj, nmf* German ♦ *nm* (*LING*) German

aller [ale] *nm* (*trajet*) outward journey; (*billet: aussi: ~ simple*) single (*BRIT*) *ou* one-way (*US*) ticket ♦ *vi* (*gén*) to go; **~ à** (*convenir*) to suit; (*suj: forme, pointure etc*) to fit; **~ avec** (*couleurs, style etc*) to go (well) with; **je vais y ~/me fâcher** I'm going to go/to get angry; **~ voir** to go and see, go to see; **allez!** come on!; **allons!** come now!; **comment allez-vous?** how are you?; **comment ça va?** how are you?; (*affaires etc*) how are things?; **il va bien/mal** he's well/not well, he's fine/ill; **ça va bien/mal** (*affaires etc*) it's going well/not going well; **~ mieux** to be better; **cela va sans dire** that goes without saying; **il y va de leur vie** their lives are at stake; **s'en ~** (*partir*) to be off, go, leave; (*disparaître*) to go away; **~ (et) retour** return journey (*BRIT*), round trip; (*billet*) return (ticket) (*BRIT*), round trip ticket (*US*)

allergique [alɛʀʒik] *adj*: **~ à** allergic to

alliage [aljaʒ] *nm* alloy

alliance [aljɑ̃s] *nf* (*MIL, POL*) alliance; (*mariage*) marriage; (*bague*) wedding ring

allier [alje] *vt* (*métaux*) to alloy; (*POL, gén*) to ally; (*fig*) to combine; **s'~** to become allies; to combine

allô [alo] *excl* hullo, hallo

allocation [alɔkasjɔ̃] *nf* allowance; **~ (de) chômage** unemployment benefit; **~ (de) logement** rent allowance; **~s familiales** ≈ child benefit

allocution [alɔkysjɔ̃] *nf* short speech

allonger [alɔ̃ʒe] *vt* to lengthen, make longer; (*étendre: bras, jambe*) to stretch (out);

s'~ *vi* to get longer; (*se coucher*) to lie down, stretch out; ~ **le pas** to hasten one's step(s)

allouer [alwe] *vt* to allocate, allot

allumage [alymaʒ] *nm* (*AUTO*) ignition

allume-cigare [alymsigaʀ] *nm inv* cigar lighter

allumer [alyme] *vt* (*lampe, phare, radio*) to put *ou* switch on; (*pièce*) to put *ou* switch the light(s) on in; (*feu*) to light; **s'~** *vi* (*lumière, lampe*) to come *ou* go on

allumette [alymɛt] *nf* match

allure [alyʀ] *nf* (*vitesse*) speed, pace; (*démarche*) walk; (*maintien*) bearing; (*aspect, air*) look; **avoir de l'~** to have style; **à toute ~** at top speed

allusion [alyzjɔ̃] *nf* allusion; (*sous-entendu*) hint; **faire ~ à** to allude *ou* refer to; to hint at

aloi [alwa] *nm*: **de bon ~** of genuine worth *ou* quality

— MOT CLÉ —

alors [alɔʀ] *adv* **1** (*à ce moment-là*) then, at that time; **il habitait ~ à Paris** he lived in Paris at that time

2 (*par conséquent*) then; **tu as fini?** ~ **je m'en vais** have you finished? I'm going then; **et ~?** so what?

~ **que** *conj* **1** (*au moment où*) when, as; **il est arrivé alors que je partais** he arrived as I was leaving

2 (*pendant que*) while, when; ~ **qu'il était à Paris, il a visité ...** while *ou* when he was in Paris, he visited ...

3 (*tandis que*) whereas, while; ~ **que son frère travaillait dur, lui se reposait** while his brother was working hard, HE would rest

---

alouette [alwɛt] *nf* (sky)lark

alourdir [aluʀdiʀ] *vt* to weigh down, make heavy

alpage [alpaʒ] *nm* pasture

Alpes [alp(ə)] *nfpl*: **les ~** the Alps

alphabet [alfabɛ] *nm* alphabet; (*livre*) ABC (book); **alphabétiser** *vt* to teach to read and write; to eliminate illiteracy

alpinisme [alpinism(ə)] *nm* mountaineering, climbing; **alpiniste** *nm/f* mountaineer, climber

Alsace [alzas] *nf* Alsace; **alsacien, ne** *adj, nm/f* Alsatian

altercation [altɛʀkasjɑ̃] *nf* altercation

altérer [alteʀe] *vt* to falsify; to distort; to debase; to impair

alternateur [altɛʀnatœʀ] *nm* alternator

alternatif, ive [altɛʀnatif, -iv] *adj* alternating; **alternative** *nf* (*choix*) alternative; **alternativement** *adv* alternately

Altesse [altɛs] *nf* Highness

altitude [altityd] *nf* altitude, height

alto [alto] *nm* (*instrument*) viola

altruisme [altʀɥism(ə)] *nm* altruism

aluminium [alyminjɔm] *nm* aluminium (*BRIT*), aluminum (*US*)

amabilité [amabilite] *nf* kindness, amiability

amadouer [amadwe] *vt* to coax, cajole; to mollify, soothe

amaigrir [amegʀiʀ] *vt* to make thin(ner)

amalgame [amalgam] *nm* (*alliage pour les dents*) amalgam

amande [amɑ̃d] *nf* (*de l'amandier*) almond; (*de noyau de fruit*) kernel; **amandier** *nm* almond (tree)

amant [amɑ̃] *nm* lover

amarrer [amaʀe] *vt* (*NAVIG*) to moor; (*gén*) to make fast

amas [ama] *nm* heap, pile

amasser [amase] *vt* to amass

amateur [amatœʀ] *nm* amateur; **en ~** (*péj*) amateurishly; ~ **de musique/sport** *etc* music/sport *etc* lover

amazone [amazon] *nf*: **en ~** sidesaddle

ambages [ɑ̃baʒ]: **sans ~** *adv* plainly

ambassade [ɑ̃basad] *nf* embassy; (*mission*): **en ~** on a mission; **ambassadeur, drice** *nm/f* ambassador(dress)

ambiance [ɑ̃bjɑ̃s] *nf* atmosphere

ambiant, e [ɑ̃bjɑ̃, -ɑ̃t] *adj* (*air, milieu*) surrounding; (*température*) ambient

ambigu, ë [ɑ̃bigy] *adj* ambiguous

ambitieux, euse [ɑ̃bisjø, -øz] *adj* ambitious

ambition [ɑ̃bisjɔ̃] *nf* ambition

ambulance [ɑ̃bylɑ̃s] *nf* ambulance; **ambulancier, ière** *nm/f* ambulance man(woman) (*BRIT*), paramedic (*US*)

ambulant, e [ɑ̃bylɑ̃, -ɑ̃t] *adj* travelling, itinerant

âme [ɑm] *nf* soul

améliorer [ameljɔʀe] *vt* to improve; **s'~** *vi* to improve, get better

aménagements [amenaʒmɑ̃] *nmpl* developments; ~ **fiscaux** tax adjustments

aménager [amenaʒe] *vt* (*agencer, transformer*) to fit out; to lay out; (: *quartier, territoire*) to develop; (*installer*) to fix up, put in; **ferme aménagée** converted farmhouse

amende [amɑ̃d] *nf* fine; **mettre à l'~** to penalize; **faire ~ honorable** to make amends

amender [amɑ̃de] *vt* (*loi*) to amend; **s'~** *vi* to mend one's ways

amener [amne] *vt* to bring; (*causer*) to bring about; (*baisser: drapeau, voiles*) to strike; **s'~** *vi* to show up (*fam*), turn up

amenuiser [amənɥize]: **s'~** *vi* to grow slimmer, lessen; to dwindle

amer, amère [amɛʀ] *adj* bitter

américain, e [ameʀikɛ̃, -ɛn] *adj, nm/f* American

Amérique [ameʀik] *nf* America; **l'~**

centrale/latine Central/Latin America; **l'~ du Nord/du Sud** North/South America

amerrir [amerir] *vi* to land (on the sea)

amertume [amertym] *nf* bitterness

ameublement [amœbləmã] *nm* furnishing; (*meubles*) furniture

ameuter [amøte] *vt* (*badauds*) to draw a crowd of; (*peuple*) to rouse

ami, e [ami] *nm/f* friend; (*amant/maîtresse*) boyfriend/girlfriend ♦ *adj*: **pays/groupe ~** friendly country/group; **être ~ de l'ordre** to be a lover of order; **un ~ des arts** a patron of the arts

amiable [amjabl(ə)]: **à l'~** *adv* (*JUR*) out of court; (*gén*) amicably

amiante [amjɑ̃t] *nm* asbestos

amical, e, aux [amikal, -o] *adj* friendly; **amicale** *nf* (*club*) association; **amicalement** *adv* in a friendly way; (*formule épistolaire*) regards

amidon [amidɔ̃] *nm* starch

amincir [amɛ̃sir] *vt* (*objet*) to thin (down); **s'~** *vi* to get thinner *ou* slimmer; **~ qn** to make sb thinner *ou* slimmer

amincissant, e *adj*: **régime ~** (slimming) diet; **crème ~e** slenderizing cream

amiral, aux [amiral, -o] *nm* admiral

amitié [amitje] *nf* friendship; **prendre en ~** to befriend; **faire** *ou* **présenter ses ~s à qn** to send sb one's best wishes

ammoniac [amɔnjak] *nm*: **(gaz) ~** ammonia

ammoniaque [amɔnjak] *nf* ammonia (water)

amoindrir [amwɛ̃drir] *vt* to reduce

amollir [amɔlir] *vt* to soften

amonceler [amɔ̃sle] *vt* to pile *ou* heap up; **s'~** *vi* to pile *ou* heap up; (*fig*) to accumulate

amont [amɔ̃]: **en ~** *adv* upstream; (*sur une pente*) uphill

amorce [amɔrs(ə)] *nf* (*sur un hameçon*) bait; (*explosif*) cap; primer; priming; (*fig: début*) beginning(s), start

amorphe [amɔrf(ə)] *adj* passive, lifeless

amortir [amɔrtir] *vt* (*atténuer: choc*) to absorb, cushion; (*bruit, douleur*) to deaden; (*COMM: dette*) to pay off; (: *mise de fonds, matériel*) to write off; **~ un abonnement** to make a season ticket pay (for itself); **amortisseur** *nm* shock absorber

amour [amur] *nm* love; (*liaison*) love affair, love; **faire l'~** to make love; **amouracher: s'amouracher de** (*péj*) to become infatuated with; **amoureux, euse** *adj* (*regard, tempérament*) amorous; (*vie, problèmes*) love *cpd*; (*personne*): **amoureux (de qn)** in love (with sb) ♦ *nmpl* courting couple(s); **amour-propre** *nm* self-esteem, pride

amovible [amɔvibl(ə)] *adj* removable, detachable

ampère [ɑ̃per] *nm* amp(ere)

amphithéâtre [ɑ̃fiteɑtr(ə)] *nm* amphitheatre; (*d'université*) lecture hall *ou* theatre

ample [ɑ̃pl(ə)] *adj* (*vêtement*) roomy, ample; (*gestes, mouvement*) broad; (*ressources*) ample; **ampleur** *nf* (*importance*) scale, size; extent

amplificateur [ɑ̃plifikatœr] *nm* amplifier

amplifier [ɑ̃plifje] *vt* (*son, oscillation*) to amplify; (*fig*) to expand, increase

ampoule [ɑ̃pul] *nf* (*électrique*) bulb; (*de médicament*) phial; (*aux mains, pieds*) blister

ampoulé, e [ɑ̃pule] (*péj*) *adj* pompous, bombastic

amputer [ɑ̃pyte] *vt* (*MÉD*) to amputate; (*fig*) to cut *ou* reduce drastically

amusant, e [amyzɑ̃, -ɑ̃t] *adj* (*divertissant, spirituel*) entertaining, amusing; (*comique*) funny, amusing

amuse-gueule [amyzgœl] *nm inv* appetizer, snack

amusement [amyzmɑ̃] *nm* amusement; (*jeu etc*) pastime, diversion

amuser [amyze] *vt* (*divertir*) to entertain, amuse; (*égayer, faire rire*) to amuse; (*détourner l'attention de*) to distract; **s'~** *vi* (*jouer*) to amuse o.s., play; (*se divertir*) to enjoy o.s., have fun; (*fig*) to mess around

amygdale [amidal] *nf* tonsil

an [ɑ̃] *nm* year; **le jour de l'~, le premier de l'~, le nouvel ~** New Year's Day

analogique [analɔʒik] *adj* analogical; (*INFORM, montre*) analog

analogue [analɔg] *adj*: **~ (à)** analogous (to), similar (to)

analphabète [analfabɛt] *nm/f* illiterate

analyse [analiz] *nf* analysis; (*MÉD*) test; **analyser** *vt* to analyse; to test

ananas [anana] *nm* pineapple

anarchie [anarʃi] *nf* anarchy

anathème [anatɛm] *nm*: **jeter l'~ sur** to curse

anatomie [anatɔmi] *nf* anatomy

ancêtre [ɑ̃sɛtr(ə)] *nm/f* ancestor

anchois [ɑ̃ʃwa] *nm* anchovy

ancien, ne [ɑ̃sjɛ̃, -jɛn] *adj* old; (*de jadis, de l'antiquité*) ancient; (*précédent, ex-*) former, old ♦ *nm/f* (*dans une tribu*) elder; **anciennement** *adv* formerly; **ancienneté** *nf* oldness; antiquity; (*ADMIN*) (length of) service; seniority

ancre [ɑ̃kr(ə)] *nf* anchor; **jeter/lever l'~** to cast/weigh anchor; **à l'~** at anchor; **ancrer** [ɑ̃kre] *vt* (*CONSTR: câble etc*) to anchor; (*fig*) to fix firmly; **s'~r** *vi* (*NAVIG*) to (cast) anchor

Andorre [ɑ̃dɔr] *nf* Andorra

andouille [ɑ̃duj] *nf* (*CULIN*) sausage made of chitterlings; (*fam*) clot, nit

âne [ɑn] *nm* donkey, ass; (*péj*) dunce

anéantir [aneɑ̃tir] *vt* to annihilate, wipe

out; *(fig)* to obliterate, destroy; to overwhelm

anémie [anemi] *nf* anaemia; **anémique** *adj* anaemic

ânerie [ɑnʀi] *nf* stupidity; stupid *ou* idiotic comment *etc*

anesthésie [anɛstezi] *nf* anaesthesia; **faire une ~ locale/générale à qn** to give sb a local/general anaesthetic

ange [ɑ̃ʒ] *nm* angel; **être aux ~s** to be over the moon

angélus [ɑ̃ʒelys] *nm* angelus; evening bells *pl*

angine [ɑ̃ʒin] *nf* throat infection; **~ de poitrine** angina

anglais, e [ɑ̃glɛ, -ɛz] *adj* English ♦ *nm/f*: **A~, e** Englishman(woman) ♦ *nm* *(LING)* English; **les A~** the English; **filer à l'~e** to take French leave

angle [ɑ̃gl(ə)] *nm* angle; *(coin)* corner; **~ droit** right angle

Angleterre [ɑ̃glətɛʀ] *nf*: **l'~** England

anglo... [ɑ̃glɔ] *préfixe* Anglo-, anglo (-); **~phone** *adj* English-speaking

angoissé, e [ɑ̃gwase] *adj* *(personne)* full of anxieties *ou* hang-ups *(inf)*

angoisser [ɑ̃gwase] *vt* to harrow, cause anguish to ♦ *vi* to worry, fret

anguille [ɑ̃gij] *nf* eel

anicroche [anikʀɔʃ] *nf* hitch, snag

animal, e, aux [animal, -o] *adj, nm* animal

animateur, trice [animatœʀ, -tʀis] *nm/f* *(de télévision)* host; *(de groupe)* leader, organizer

animation [animɑsjɔ̃] *nf* *(voir animé)* busyness; liveliness; *(CINÉMA: technique)* animation

animé, e [anime] *adj* *(lieu)* busy, lively; *(conversation, réunion)* lively, animated; *(opposé à in~)* animate

animer [anime] *vt* *(ville, soirée)* to liven up; *(mettre en mouvement)* to drive

anis [ani] *nm* *(CULIN)* aniseed; *(BOT)* anise

ankyloser [ɑ̃kiloze]: **s'~** *vi* to get stiff

anneau, x [ano] *nm* *(de rideau, bague)* ring; *(de chaîne)* link

année [ane] *nf* year

annexe [anɛks(ə)] *adj* *(problème)* related; *(document)* appended; *(salle)* adjoining ♦ *nf* *(bâtiment)* annex(e); *(de document, ouvrage)* annex, appendix; *(jointe à une lettre)* enclosure

anniversaire [anivɛʀsɛʀ] *nm* birthday; *(d'un événement, bâtiment)* anniversary

annonce [anɔ̃s] *nf* announcement; *(signe, indice)* sign; *(aussi: ~ publicitaire)* advertisement; **les petites ~s** the classified advertisements, the small ads

annoncer [anɔ̃se] *vt* to announce; *(être le signe de)* to herald; **s'~ bien/difficile** to look promising/difficult; **annonceur, euse** *nm/f* *(TV, RADIO: speaker)* announcer;

(publicitaire) advertiser

annuaire [anɥɛʀ] *nm* yearbook, annual; **~ téléphonique** (telephone) directory, phone book

annuel, le [anɥɛl] *adj* annual, yearly

annuité [anɥite] *nf* annual instalment

annuler [anɥle] *vt* *(rendez-vous, voyage)* to cancel, call off; *(mariage)* to annul; *(jugement)* to quash *(BRIT)*, repeal *(US)*; *(résultats)* to declare void; *(MATH, PHYSIQUE)* to cancel out

anodin, e [anɔdɛ̃, -in] *adj* harmless; insignificant, trivial

anonyme [anɔnim] *adj* anonymous; *(fig)* impersonal

ANPE *sigle f* (= *Agence nationale pour l'emploi*) national employment agency

anse [ɑ̃s] *nf* *(de panier, tasse)* handle; *(GÉO)* cove

antan [ɑ̃tɑ̃]: **d'~** *adj* of long ago

antarctique [ɑ̃taʀktik] *adj* Antarctic ♦ *nm*: **l'A~** the Antarctic

antécédents [ɑ̃tesedɑ̃] *nmpl* *(MÉD etc)* past history *sg*

antenne [ɑ̃tɛn] *nf* *(de radio)* aerial; *(d'insecte)* antenna, feeler; *(poste avancé)* outpost; *(petite succursale)* sub-branch; **passer à l'~** to go on the air; **prendre l'~** to tune in; **2 heures d'~** 2 hours' broadcasting time

antérieur, e [ɑ̃teʀjœʀ] *adj* *(d'avant)* previous, earlier; *(de devant)* front

anti... [ɑ̃ti] *préfixe* anti...; **~alcoolique** *adj* anti-alcohol; **~atomique** *adj*: **abri ~atomique** fallout shelter; **~biotique** *nm* antibiotic; **~brouillard** *adj*: **phare ~brouillard** fog lamp *(BRIT)* ou light *(US)*

anticipation [ɑ̃tisipɑsjɔ̃] *nf*: **livre/film d'~** science fiction book/film

anticipé, e [ɑ̃tisipe] *adj*: **avec mes remerciements ~s** thanking you in advance *ou* anticipation

anticiper [ɑ̃tisipe] *vt* *(événement, coup)* to anticipate, foresee

anti: **~conceptionnel, le** *adj* contraceptive; **~corps** *nm* antibody; **~dote** *nm* antidote

antigel [ɑ̃tiʒɛl] *nm* antifreeze

antihistaminique [ɑ̃tiistaminik] *nm* antihistamine

Antilles [ɑ̃tij] *nfpl*: **les ~** the West Indies

antilope [ɑ̃tilɔp] *nf* antelope

anti: **~mite(s)** *adj, nm*: **(produit) ~mite(s)** mothproofer; moth repellent; **~parasite** *adj* *(RADIO, TV)*: **dispositif ~parasite** suppressor; **~pathique** *adj* unpleasant, disagreeable; **~pelliculaire** *adj* anti-dandruff

antipodes [ɑ̃tipɔd] *nmpl* *(GÉO)*: **les ~** the antipodes; *(fig)*: **être aux ~ de** to be the opposite extreme of

antiquaire [ɑ̃tikɛʀ] *nm/f* antique dealer

antique [ɑ̃tik] *adj* antique; *(très vieux)* anclient, antiquated

antiquité [ɑ̃tikite] *nf* (*objet*) antique; **l'A~** Antiquity; **magasin d'~s** antique shop

anti: **~rabique** *adj* rabies *cpd*; **~rouille** *adj inv* anti-rust *cpd*; **traitement** **~rouille** rustproofing; **~sémite** *adj* anti-Semitic; **~septique** *adj, nm* antiseptic; **~vol** *adj, nm*: (**dispositif**) **~vol** anti-theft device

antre [ɑ̃tʀ(ə)] *nm* den, lair

anxieux, euse [ɑ̃ksjø, -øz] *adj* anxious, worried

AOC *sigle f* (= *appellation d'origine contrôlée*) *label guaranteeing the quality of wine*

août [u] *nm* August

apaiser [apeze] *vt* (*colère, douleur*) to soothe; (*faim*) to appease; (*personne*) to calm (down), pacify; **s'~** *vi* (*tempête, bruit*) to die down, subside

apanage [apanaʒ] *nm*: **être l'~ de** to be the privilege *ou* prerogative of

aparté [apaʀte] *nm* (*THÉÂTRE*) aside; (*entretien*) private conversation

apathique [apatik] *adj* apathetic

apatride [apatʀid] *nm/f* stateless person

apercevoir [apɛʀsəvwaʀ] *vt* to see; **s'~ de** *vt* to notice; **s'~ que** to notice that

aperçu [apɛʀsy] *nm* (*vue d'ensemble*) general survey; (*intuition*) insight

apéritif [apeʀitif] *nm* (*boisson*) aperitif; (*réunion*) drinks *pl*

à-peu-près [apøpʀɛ] (*péj*) *nm inv* vague approximation

apeuré, e [apœʀe] *adj* frightened, scared

aphone [afɔn] *adj* voiceless

aphte [aft(ə)] *nm* mouth ulcer

apiculture [apikyltyʀ] *nf* beekeeping, apiculture

apitoyer [apitwaje] *vt* to move to pity; **s'~ (sur)** to feel pity (for)

aplanir [aplaniʀ] *vt* to level; (*fig*) to smooth away, iron out

aplatir [aplatiʀ] *vt* to flatten; **s'~** *vi* to become flatter; to be flattened; (*fig*) to lie flat on the ground

aplomb [aplɔ̃] *nm* (*équilibre*) balance, equilibrium; (*fig*) self-assurance; nerve; **d'~** steady; (*CONSTR*) plumb

apogée [apɔʒe] *nm* (*fig*) peak, apogee

apologie [apɔlɔʒi] *nf* vindication, praise

apostrophe [apɔstʀɔf] *nf* (*signe*) apostrophe

apostropher [apɔstʀɔfe] *vt* (*interpeller*) to shout at, address sharply

apothéose [apɔteoz] *nf* pinnacle (of achievement); (*MUS*) grand finale

apôtre [apotʀ(ə)] *nm* apostle

apparaître [apaʀɛtʀ(ə)] *vi* to appear

apparat [apaʀa] *nm*: **tenue/dîner d'~** ceremonial dress/dinner

appareil [apaʀɛj] *nm* (*outil, machine*) piece of apparatus, device; appliance; (*politique, syndical*) machinery; (*avion*) (aero)plane,

aircraft *inv*; (*téléphonique*) phone; (*dentier*) brace (*BRIT*), braces (*US*); **"qui est à l'~?"** "who's speaking?"; **dans le plus simple ~** in one's birthday suit; **~ler** [apaʀeje] *vi* (*NAVIG*) to cast off, get under way **♦** *vt* (*assortir*) to match up; **~(-photo)** [apaʀɛj(fɔto)] *nm* camera

apparemment [apaʀamɑ̃] *adv* apparently

apparence [apaʀɑ̃s] *nf* appearance

apparent, e [apaʀɑ̃, -ɑ̃t] *adj* visible; obvious; (*superficiel*) apparent

apparenté, e [apaʀɑ̃te] *adj*: **~ à** related to; (*fig*) similar to

apparition [apaʀisjɔ̃] *nf* appearance; (*surnaturelle*) apparition

appartement [apaʀtəmɑ̃] *nm* flat (*BRIT*), apartment (*US*)

appartenir [apaʀtəniʀ]: **~ à** *vt* to belong to; **il lui appartient de** it is up to him to, it is his duty to

apparu, e *pp de* **apparaître**

appât [apɑ] *nm* (*PÊCHE*) bait; (*fig*) lure, bait

appauvrir [apovʀiʀ] *vt* to impoverish

appel [apɛl] *nm* call; (*nominal*) roll call; (: *SCOL*) register; (*MIL: recrutement*) call-up; **faire ~ à** (*invoquer*) to appeal to; (*avoir recours à*) to call on; (*nécessiter*) to call for, require; **faire ~** (*JUR*) to appeal; **faire l'~** to call the roll; to call the register; **sans ~** (*fig*) final, irrevocable; **~ d'offres** (*COMM*) invitation to tender; **faire un ~ de phares** to flash one's headlights; **~ (téléphonique)** (tele)phone call

appelé [aple] *nm* (*MIL*) conscript

appeler [aple] *vt* to call; (*faire venir: médecin etc*) to call, send for; (*fig: nécessiter*) to call for, demand; **s'~: elle s'appelle Gabrielle** her name is Gabrielle, she's called Gabrielle; **comment ça s'appelle?** what is it called?; **être appelé à** (*fig*) to be destined to; **qn à comparaître** (*JUR*) to summon sb to appear; **en ~ à** to appeal to

appendice [apɛ̃dis] *nm* appendix; **appendicite** *nf* appendicitis

appentis [apɑ̃ti] *nm* lean-to

appesantir [apzɑ̃tiʀ]: **s'~** *vi* to grow heavier; **s'~ sur** (*fig*) to dwell on

appétissant, e [apetisɑ̃, -ɑ̃t] *adj* appetizing, mouth-watering

appétit [apeti] *nm* appetite; **bon ~!** enjoy your meal!

applaudir [aplodiʀ] *vt* to applaud **♦** *vi* to applaud, clap; **applaudissements** *nmpl* applause *sg*, clapping *sg*

application [aplikasjɔ̃] *nf* application

applique [aplik] *nf* wall lamp

appliquer [aplike] *vt* to apply; (*loi*) to enforce; **s'~** *vi* (*élève etc*) to apply o.s.

appoint [apwɛ̃] *nm* (extra) contribution *ou* help; **avoir/faire l'~** (*en payant*) to have/give the right change *ou* money; **chauffage d'~** extra heating

appointements [apwɛ̃tmɑ̃] *nmpl* salary *sg*
appointement [apɔ̃tmɑ̃] *nm* landing stage, wharf
apport [apɔʀ] *nm* supply; contribution
apporter [apɔʀte] *vt* to bring
apposer [apoze] *vt* to append; to affix
appréciable [apʀesjabl(ə)] *adj* appreciable
apprécier [apʀesje] *vt* to appreciate; (*évaluer*) to estimate, assess
appréhender [apʀeɑ̃de] *vt* (*craindre*) to dread; (*arrêter*) to apprehend
apprendre [apʀɑ̃dʀ(ə)] *vt* to learn; (*événement, résultats*) to learn of, hear of; ~ **qch à qn** (*informer*) to tell sb (of) sth; (*enseigner*) to teach sb sth; ~ **à faire qch** to learn to do sth; ~ **à qn à faire qch** to teach sb to do sth; **apprenti, e** *nm/f* apprentice; (*fig*) novice, beginner; **apprentissage** *nm* learning; (*COMM, SCOL: période*) apprenticeship
apprêté, e [apʀete] *adj* (*fig*) affected
apprêter [apʀete] *vt* to dress, finish
appris, e *pp de* **apprendre**
apprivoiser [apʀivwaze] *vt* to tame
approbation [apʀɔbasjɔ̃] *nf* approval
approche [apʀɔʃ] *nf* approaching; approach
approcher [apʀɔʃe] *vi* to approach, come near ♦ *vt* to approach; (*rapprocher*): ~ **qch (de qch)** to bring *ou* put sth near (to sth); **s'~ de** to approach, go *ou* come near to; ~ **de** to draw near to; (*quantité, moment*) to approach
approfondir [apʀɔfɔ̃diʀ] *vt* to deepen; (*question*) to go further into
approprié, e [apʀɔpʀije] *adj*: ~ **(à)** appropriate (to), suited to
approprier [apʀɔpʀije]: **s'~** *vt* to appropriate, take over
approuver [apʀuve] *vt* to agree with; (*autoriser: loi, projet*) to approve, pass; (*trouver louable*) to approve of
approvisionner [apʀɔvizjɔne] *vt* to supply; (*compte bancaire*) to pay funds into; **s'~ en** to stock up with
approximatif, ive [apʀɔksimatif, -iv] *adj* approximate, rough; vague
appui [apɥi] *nm* support; **prendre ~ sur** to lean on; to rest on; **l'~ de la fenêtre** the windowsill, the window ledge; **appui(e)-tête** *nm inv* headrest
appuyer [apɥije] *vt* (*poser*): ~ **qch sur/contre** to lean *ou* rest sth on/against; (*soutenir: personne, demande*) to support, back (up) ♦ *vi*: ~ **sur** (*bouton, frein*) to press, push; (*mot, détail*) to stress, emphasize; (*suj: chose: peser sur*) to rest (heavily) on, press against; **s'~ sur** to lean on; to rely on; ~ **à droite** to bear (to the) right
âpre [ɑpʀ(ə)] *adj* acrid, pungent; (*fig*) harsh; bitter; ~ **au gain** grasping
après [apʀe] *prép* after ♦ *adv* afterwards; **2**

heures ~ 2 hours later; ~ **qu'il est parti** after he left; ~ **avoir fait** after having done; **d'~** (*selon*) according to; ~ **coup** after the event, afterwards; ~ **tout** (*au fond*) after all; **et (puis)** ~? so what?; **après-demain** *adv* the day after tomorrow; **après-guerre** *nm* post-war years *pl*; **après-midi** *nm ou nf* (*inv*) afternoon
à-propos [apʀopo] *nm* (*d'une remarque*) aptness; **faire preuve d'~** to show presence of mind
apte [apt(ə)] *adj* capable; (*MIL*) fit
aquarelle [akwaʀɛl] *nf* (*tableau*) watercolour; (*genre*) watercolours *pl*
aquarium [akwaʀjɔm] *nm* aquarium
arabe [aʀab] *adj* Arabic; (*désert, cheval*) Arabian; (*nation, peuple*) Arab ♦ *nm/f*: **A~** Arab ♦ *nm* (*LING*) Arabic
Arabie [aʀabi] *nf*: **l'~ (Saoudite)** Saudi Arabia
arachide [aʀaʃid] *nf* (*plante*) groundnut (plant); (*graine*) peanut, groundnut
araignée [aʀɛɲe] *nf* spider
arbitraire [aʀbitʀɛʀ] *adj* arbitrary
arbitre [aʀbitʀ(ə)] *nm* (*SPORT*) referee; (: *TENNIS, CRICKET*) umpire; (*fig*) arbiter, judge; (*JUR*) arbitrator; **arbitrer** *vt* to referee; to umpire; to arbitrate
arborer [aʀbɔʀe] *vt* to bear, display
arbre [aʀbʀ(ə)] *nm* tree; (*TECH*) shaft; ~ **de transmission** (*AUTO*) driveshaft; ~ **généalogique** family tree
arbuste [aʀbyst(ə)] *nm* small shrub
arc [aʀk] *nm* (*arme*) bow; (*GÉOM*) arc; (*ARCHIT*) arch; **en ~ de cercle** semi-circular
arcade [aʀkad] *nf* arch(way); ~**s** *nfpl* (*série*) arcade *sg*, arches
arcanes [aʀkan] *nmpl* mysteries
arc-boutant [aʀkbutɑ̃] *nm* flying buttress
arceau, x [aʀso] *nm* (*métallique etc*) hoop
arc-en-ciel [aʀkɑ̃sjɛl] *nm* rainbow
arche [aʀʃ(ə)] *nf* arch; ~ **de Noé** Noah's Ark
archéologie [aʀkeɔlɔʒi] *nf* archeology; **archéologue** *nm/f* arch(a)eologist
archet [aʀʃɛ] *nm* bow
archevêque [aʀʃəvɛk] *nm* archbishop
archipel [aʀʃipɛl] *nm* archipelago
architecte [aʀʃitɛkt(ə)] *nm* architect
architecture [aʀʃitɛktyʀ] *nf* architecture
archive [aʀʃiv] *nf* file; ~**s** *nfpl* (*collection*) archives
arctique [aʀktik] *adj* Arctic ♦ *nm*: **l'A~** the Arctic
ardemment [aʀdamɑ̃] *adv* ardently, fervently
ardent, e [aʀdɑ̃, -ɑ̃t] *adj* (*soleil*) blazing; (*fièvre*) raging; (*amour*) ardent, passionate; (*prière*) fervent
ardoise [aʀdwaz] *nf* slate
ardt *abr* = **arrondissement**
ardu, e [aʀdy] *adj* (*travail*) arduous; (*pro-*

blème) difficult; (*pente*) steep

arène [aʀɛn] *nf* arena; **~s** *nfpl* (*amphithéâtre*) bull-ring *sg*

arête [aʀɛt] *nf* (*de poisson*) bone; (*d'une montagne*) ridge; (GÉOM *etc*) edge

argent [aʀʒɑ̃] *nm* (*métal*) silver; (*monnaie*) money; **~ de poche** pocket money; **~ liquide** ready money, (ready) cash; **argenterie** *nf* silverware; silver plate

argentin, e [aʀʒɑ̃tɛ̃, -in] *adj* (*son*) silvery; (*d'Argentine*) Argentinian, Argentine

Argentine [aʀʒɑ̃tin] *nf*: **l'~** Argentina, the Argentine

argile [aʀʒil] *nf* clay

argot [aʀɡo] *nm* slang; **argotique** *adj* slang *cpd*; slangy

arguer [aʀɡye]: **~ de** *vt* to put forward as a pretext *ou* reason

argument [aʀɡymɑ̃] *nm* argument

argumentaire [aʀɡymɑ̃tɛʀ] *nm* sales leaflet

argumenter [aʀɡymɑ̃te] *vi* to argue

argus [aʀɡys] *nm* guide to second-hand car *etc* prices

aristocratique [aʀistɔkʀatik] *adj* aristocratic

arithmétique [aʀitmetik] *adj* arithmetic(al) ♦ *nf* arithmetic

armateur [aʀmatœʀ] *nm* shipowner

armature [aʀmatyʀ] *nf* framework; (*de tente etc*) frame

arme [aʀm(ə)] *nf* weapon; (*section de l'armée*) arm; **~s** *nfpl* (*armement*) weapons, arms; (*blason*) (coat of) arms; **~ à feu** firearm

armée [aʀme] *nf* army; **~ de l'air** Air Force; **~ de terre** Army

armement [aʀməmɑ̃] *nm* (*matériel*) arms *pl*, weapons *pl*; (: *d'un pays*) arms *pl*, armament

armer [aʀme] *vt* to arm; (*arme à feu*) to cock; (*appareil-photo*) to wind on; **~ qch de** to fit sth with; to reinforce sth with

armistice [aʀmistis] *nm* armistice; **l'A~** ≈ Remembrance (BRIT) *ou* Veterans (US) Day

armoire [aʀmwaʀ] *nf* (tall) cupboard; (*penderie*) wardrobe (BRIT), closet (US)

armoiries [aʀmwaʀi] *nfpl* coat *sg* of arms

armure [aʀmyʀ] *nf* armour *no pl*, suit of armour; **armurier** [aʀmyʀje] *nm* gunsmith; armourer

arnaquer [aʀnake] *vt* to swindle

aromates [aʀɔmat] *nmpl* seasoning *sg*, herbs (and spices)

aromatisé, e [aʀɔmatize] *adj* flavoured

arôme [aʀom] *nm* aroma; fragrance

arpenter [aʀpɑ̃te] *vt* (*salle, couloir*) to pace up and down

arpenteur [aʀpɑ̃tœʀ] *nm* surveyor

arqué, e [aʀke] *adj* bandy; arched

arrache-pied [aʀaʃpje]: **d'~** *adv* relentlessly

arracher [aʀaʃe] *vt* to pull out; (*page etc*) to tear off, tear out; (*légumes, herbe*) to pull up; (*bras etc*) to tear off; **~** *vt* (*article recherché*) to fight over; **~ qch à qn** to snatch sth from sb; (*fig*) to wring sth out of sb

arraisonner [aʀɛzɔne] *vt* (*bateau*) to board and search

arrangeant, e [aʀɑ̃ʒɑ̃, -ɑ̃t] *adj* accommodating, obliging

arrangement [aʀɑ̃ʒmɑ̃] *nm* agreement, arrangement

arranger [aʀɑ̃ʒe] *vt* (*gén*) to arrange; (*réparer*) to fix, put right; (*régler*) to settle, sort out; (*convenir à*) to suit, be convenient for; **s'~** *vi* (*se mettre d'accord*) to come to an agreement; **je vais m'~** I'll manage; **ça va s'~** it'll sort itself out

arrestation [aʀɛstasjɔ̃] *nf* arrest

arrêt [aʀɛ] *nm* stopping; (*de bus etc*) stop; (JUR) judgment, decision; **rester** *ou* **tomber en ~ devant** to stop short in front of; **sans ~** non-stop; continually; **~ de mort** capital sentence; **~ de travail** stoppage (of work)

arrêté [aʀete] *nm* order, decree

arrêter [aʀete] *vt* to stop; (*chauffage etc*) to turn off, switch off; (*fixer: date etc*) to appoint, decide on; (*criminel, suspect*) to arrest; **s'~** *vi* to stop; **~ de faire** to stop doing

arrhes [aʀ] *nfpl* deposit *sg*

arrière [aʀjɛʀ] *nm* back; (SPORT) fullback ♦ *adj inv*: **siège/roue ~** back *ou* rear seat/wheel; **à l'~** behind, at the back; **en ~** behind; (*regarder*) back, behind; (*tomber, aller*) backwards; **arriéré, e** *adj* (*péj*) backward ♦ *nm* (*d'argent*) arrears *pl*; **~-goût** *nm* aftertaste; **~-grand-mère** *nf* great-grandmother; **~-grand-père** *nm* great-grandfather; **~-pays** *nm inv* hinterland; **~-pensée** *nf* ulterior motive; mental reservation; **~-plan** *nm* background; **~-saison** *nf* late autumn; **~-train** *nm* hindquarters *pl*

arrimer [aʀime] *vt* to stow; to secure

arrivage [aʀivaʒ] *nm* arrival

arrivée [aʀive] *nf* arrival; (*ligne d'~*) finish; **~ d'air** air inlet

arriver [aʀive] *vi* to arrive; (*survenir*) to happen, occur; **il arrive à Paris à 8h** he gets *ou* arrives in Paris at 8; **~ à** (*atteindre*) to reach; **~ à faire qch** to succeed in doing sth; **il arrive que** it happens that; **il lui arrive de faire** he sometimes does; **arriviste** *nm/f* go-getter

arrogant, e [aʀɔɡɑ̃, -ɑ̃t] *adj* arrogant

arroger [aʀɔʒe]: **s'~** *vt* to assume (without right)

arrondir [aʀɔ̃diʀ] *vt* (*forme, objet*) to round; (*somme*) to round off; **s'~** *vi* to become round(ed)

arrondissement [aʀɔ̃dismɑ̃] *nm* (ADMIN) ≈ district

arroser [aʀoze] *vt* to water; (*victoire*) to celebrate (over a drink); (*CULIN*) to baste; **ar-rosoir** *nm* watering can

arsenal, aux [aʀsɔnal, -o] *nm* (*NAVIG*) naval dockyard; (*MIL*) arsenal; (*fig*) gear, paraphernalia

art [aʀ] *nm* art; ~**s ménagers** home economics *sg*

artère [aʀtɛʀ] *nf* (*ANAT*) artery; (*rue*) main road

arthrite [aʀtʀit] *nf* arthritis

artichaut [aʀtiʃo] *nm* artichoke

article [aʀtikl(ə)] *nm* article; (*COMM*) item, article; **à l'~ de la mort** at the point of death; ~ **de fond** (*PRESSE*) feature article

articulation [aʀtikylasjɔ̃] *nf* articulation; (*ANAT*) joint

articuler [aʀtikyle] *vt* to articulate

artifice [aʀtifis] *nm* device, trick

artificiel, le [aʀtifisjɛl] *adj* artificial

artificieux, euse [aʀtifisjø, -øz] *adj* guileful, deceitful

artisan [aʀtizɑ̃] *nm* artisan, (self-employed) craftsman; **artisanal, e, aux** *adj* of *ou* made by craftsmen; (*péj*) cottage industry *cpd*, unsophisticated; **artisanat** *nm* arts and crafts *pl*

artiste [aʀtist(ə)] *nm/f* artist; (*de variétés*) entertainer; performer; **artistique** *adj* artistic

as[1] [a] *vb voir* **avoir**

as[2] [as] *nm* ace

ascendance [asɑ̃dɑ̃s] *nf* (*origine*) ancestry

ascendant, e [asɑ̃dɑ̃, -ɑ̃t] *adj* upward ♦ *nm* influence

ascenseur [asɑ̃sœʀ] *nm* lift (*BRIT*), elevator (*US*)

ascension [asɑ̃sjɔ̃] *nf* ascent; climb; **l'A~** (*REL*) the Ascension

aseptiser [asɛptize] *vt* to sterilize; to disinfect

asiatique [azjatik] *adj, nm/f* Asiatic, Asian

Asie [azi] *nf*: **l'~** Asia

asile [azil] *nm* (*refuge*) refuge, sanctuary; (*POL*) droit d'~ (political) asylum; (*pour malades etc*) home

aspect [aspɛ] *nm* appearance, look; (*fig*) aspect, side; **à l'~ de** at the sight of

asperge [aspɛʀʒ(ə)] *nf* asparagus *no pl*

asperger [aspɛʀʒe] *vt* to spray, sprinkle

aspérité [aspeʀite] *nf* excrescence, protruding bit (of rock *etc*)

asphalte [asfalt(ə)] *nm* asphalt

asphyxier [asfiksje] *vt* to suffocate, asphyxiate; (*fig*) to stifle

aspirateur [aspiʀatœʀ] *nm* vacuum cleaner

aspirer [aspiʀe] *vt* (*air*) to inhale; (*liquide*) to suck (up); (*suj: appareil*) to suck up; ~ **à** to aspire to

aspirine [aspiʀin] *nf* aspirin

assagir [asaʒiʀ] *vt* to quieten down; **s'~** *vi* to quieten down, sober down

assaillir [asajiʀ] *vt* to assail, attack

assainir [aseniʀ] *vt* to clean up; to purify

assaisonner [asɛzɔne] *vt* to season

assassin [asasɛ̃] *nm* murderer; assassin; ~**er** [asasine] *vt* to murder; (*esp POL*) to assassinate

assaut [aso] *nm* assault, attack; **prendre d'~** to storm, assault; **donner l'~** to attack; **faire ~ de** (*rivaliser*) to vie with each other in

assécher [aseʃe] *vt* to drain

assemblée [asɑ̃ble] *nf* (*réunion*) meeting; (*public, assistance*) gathering; assembled people; (*POL*) assembly

assembler [asɑ̃ble] *vt* (*joindre, monter*) to assemble, put together; (*amasser*) to gather (together), collect (together); **s'~** *vi* to gather

assener [asene] *vt*: ~ **un coup à qn** to deal sb a blow

asséner [asene] *vt* = **assener**

assentiment [asɑ̃timɑ̃] *nm* assent, consent; approval

asseoir [aswaʀ] *vt* (*malade, bébé*) to sit up; to sit down; (*autorité, réputation*) to establish; **s'~** *vi* to sit (o.s.) down

assermenté, e [asɛʀmɑ̃te] *adj* sworn, on oath

asservir [asɛʀviʀ] *vt* to subjugate, enslave

assez [ase] *adv* (*suffisamment*) enough, sufficiently; (*passablement*) rather, quite, fairly; ~ **de pain/livres** enough *ou* sufficient bread/books; **vous en avez ~?** have you got enough?

assidu, e [asidy] *adj* assiduous, painstaking; regular; **assiduités** *nfpl* assiduous attentions

assied *etc vb voir* **asseoir**

assiéger [asjeʒe] *vt* to besiege

assiérai *etc vb voir* **asseoir**

assiette [asjɛt] *nf* plate; (*contenu*) plate(ful); ~ **à dessert** dessert plate; ~ **anglaise** assorted cold meats; ~ **creuse** (soup) dish, soup plate; ~ **de l'impôt** basis of (tax) assessment; ~ **plate** (dinner) plate

assigner [asine] *vt*: ~ **qch à** (*poste, part, travail*) to assign sth to; (*limites*) to set sth to; (*cause, effet*) to ascribe sth to; ~ **qn à** to assign sb to

assimiler [asimile] *vt* to assimilate, absorb; (*comparer*): ~ **qch/qn à** to liken *ou* compare sth/sb to; **s'~** *vi* (*s'intégrer*) to be assimilated *ou* absorbed

assis, e [asi, -iz] *pp de* **asseoir** ♦ *adj* sitting (down), seated; **assise** *nf* (*fig*) basis, foundation; ~**es** *nfpl* (*JUR*) assizes; (*congrès*) (annual) conference

assistance [asistɑ̃s] *nf* (*public*) audience; (*aide*) assistance

assistant, e [asistɑ̃, -ɑ̃t] *nm/f* assistant; (*d'université*) probationary lecturer; ~**e sociale** social worker

assisté, e [asiste] *adj* (*AUTO*) power assisted

assister [asiste] vt to assist; ~ **à** (scène, événement) to witness; (conférence, séminaire) to attend, be at; (spectacle, match) to be at, see

association [asɔsjasjɔ̃] nf association

associé, e [asɔsje] nm/f associate; partner

associer [asɔsje] vt to associate; **s'~** vi (collaborateur) to join together ♦ vt (collaborateur) to take on (as a partner); **s'~ à qn pour faire** to join (forces) with sb to do; **s'~ à** to be combined with; (opinions, joie de qn) to share in; ~ **qn à** (profits) to give sb a share of; (affaire) to make sb a partner in; (joie, triomphe) to include sb in; ~ **qch à** (joindre, allier) to combine sth with

assoiffé, e [aswafe] adj thirsty

assombrir [asɔ̃bʀiʀ] vt to darken; (fig) to fill with gloom

assommer [asɔme] vt to batter to death; (étourdir, abrutir) to knock out; to stun

Assomption [asɔ̃psjɔ̃] nf: **l'~** the Assumption

assorti, e [asɔʀti] adj matched, matching; (varié) assorted; ~ **à** matching

assortiment [asɔʀtimɑ̃] nm assortment, selection

assortir [asɔʀtiʀ] vt to match; **s'~ de** to be accompanied by; ~ **qch à** to match sth with; ~ **qch de** to accompany sth with

assoupi, e [asupi] adj dozing, sleeping; (fig) (be)numbed; dulled; stilled

assouplir [asupliʀ] vt to make supple; (fig) to relax

assourdir [asuʀdiʀ] vt (bruit) to deaden, muffle; (suj: bruit) to deafen

assouvir [asuviʀ] vt to satisfy, appease

assujettir [asyʒetiʀ] vt to subject

assumer [asyme] vt (fonction, emploi) to assume, take on

assurance [asyʀɑ̃s] nf (certitude) assurance; (confiance en soi) (self-) confidence; (contrat) insurance (policy); (secteur commercial) insurance; ~ **maladie** health insurance; ~ **tous risques** (AUTO) comprehensive insurance; ~**s sociales** ≈ National Insurance (BRIT); ≈ Social Security (US); ~**vie** nf life assurance ou insurance

assuré, e [asyʀe] adj (certain): ~ **de** confident of ♦ nm/f insured (person); **assurément** adv assuredly, most certainly

assurer [asyʀe] vt to insure; (stabiliser) to steady; to stabilize; (victoire etc) to ensure; (frontières, pouvoir) to make secure; (service, garde) to provide; to operate; **s'~** (contre) (COMM) to insure o.s. (against); **s'~ de/que** (vérifier) to make sure of/that; **s'~ (de)** (aide de qn) to secure; ~ **qch à qn** (garantir) to secure sth for sb; (certifier) to assure sb of sth; ~ **à qn que** to assure sb that; ~ **qn de** to assure sb of

asthme [asm(ə)] nm asthma

asticot [astiko] nm maggot

astiquer [astike] vt to polish, shine

astre [astʀ(ə)] nm star

astreignant, e [astʀɛɲɑ̃, -ɑ̃t] adj demanding

astreindre [astʀɛ̃dʀ(ə)] vt: ~ **qn à qch** to force sth upon sb; ~ **qn à faire** to compel ou force sb to do

astrologie [astʀɔlɔʒi] nf astrology

astronaute [astʀɔnot] nm/f astronaut

astronomie [astʀɔnɔmi] nf astronomy

astuce [astys] nf shrewdness, astuteness; (truc) trick, clever way; (plaisanterie) wisecrack; **astucieux, euse** adj clever

atelier [atəlje] nm workshop; (de peintre) studio

athée [ate] adj atheistic ♦ nm/f atheist

Athènes [atɛn] n Athens

athlète [atlɛt] nm/f (SPORT) athlete; **athlétisme** nm athletics sg

atlantique [atlɑ̃tik] adj Atlantic ♦ nm: **l'(océan) A~** the Atlantic (Ocean)

atlas [atlɑs] nm atlas

atmosphère [atmɔsfɛʀ] nf atmosphere

atome [atom] nm atom; **atomique** adj atomic, nuclear; (nombre, masse) atomic

atomiseur [atɔmizœʀ] nm atomizer

atone [atɔn] adj lifeless

atours [atuʀ] nmpl attire sg, finery sg

atout [atu] nm trump; (fig) asset; trump card

âtre [ɑtʀ(ə)] nm hearth

atroce [atʀɔs] adj atrocious

attabler [atable] : **s'~** vi to sit down at (the) table

attachant, e [ataʃɑ̃, -ɑ̃t] adj engaging, lovable, likeable

attache [ataʃ] nf clip, fastener; (fig) tie

attacher [ataʃe] vt to tie up; (étiquette) to attach, tie on; (souliers) to do up ♦ vi (poêle, riz) to stick; **s'~ à** (par affection) to become attached to; **s'~ à faire** to endeavour to do; ~ **qch à** to tie ou attach sth to

attaque [atak] nf attack; (cérébrale) stroke; (d'épilepsie) fit

attaquer [atake] vt to attack; (en justice) to bring an action against, sue; (travail) to tackle, set about ♦ vi to attack

attardé, e [ataʀde] adj (passants) late; (enfant) backward; (conceptions) old-fashioned

attarder [ataʀde]: **s'~** vi to linger; to stay on

atteindre [atɛ̃dʀ(ə)] vt to reach; (blesser) to hit; (émouvoir) to affect

atteint, e [atɛ̃, -ɛ̃t] adj (MÉD): **être ~ de** to be suffering from; **atteinte** nf attack; **hors d'atteinte** out of reach; **porter atteinte à** to strike a blow at; to undermine

atteler [atle] vt (cheval, bœufs) to hitch up; (wagons) to couple; **s'~ à** (travail) to buckle down to

attelle [atɛl] nf splint

attenant, e [atnã, -ãt] adj: ~ **(à)** adjoining
attendant [atãdã] adv: **en** ~ meanwhile, in the meantime
attendre [atãdʀ(ə)] vt (gén) to wait for; (être destiné ou réservé à) to await, be in store for ♦ vi to wait; **s'**~ **à (ce que)** to expect (that); ~ **un enfant** to be expecting a baby; ~ **de faire/d'être** to wait until one does/is; ~ **que** to wait until; ~ **qch de** to expect sth of; **en attendant** meanwhile, in the meantime; be that as it may
attendrir [atãdʀiʀ] vt to move (to pity); (viande) to tenderize
attendu, e [atãdy] adj (visiteur) expected; ~ **que** considering that, since
attentat [atãta] nm assassination attempt; ~ **à la bombe** bomb attack; ~ **à la pudeur** indecent exposure no pl; indecent assault no pl
attente [atãt] nf wait; (espérance) expectation
attenter [atãte] : ~ **à** vt (liberté) to violate; ~ **à la vie de qn** to make an attempt on sb's life
attentif, ive [atãtif, -iv] adj (auditeur) attentive; (travail) scrupulous; careful; ~ **à** mindful of; careful to
attention [atãsjɔ̃] nf attention; (prévenance) attention, thoughtfulness no pl; **à l'**~ **de** for the attention of; **faire** ~ **(à)** to be careful (of); **faire** ~ **(à ce) que** to be ou make sure that; ~**!** careful!, watch out!; **attentionné, e** adj thoughtful, considerate
atténuer [atenɥe] vt to alleviate, ease; to lessen
atterrer [atere] vt to dismay, appal
atterrir [ateʀiʀ] vi to land; **atterrissage** nm landing
attestation [atɛstɑsjɔ̃] nf certificate
attester [atɛste] vt to testify to
attirail [atiʀaj] nm gear; (péj) paraphernalia
attirant, e [atiʀã, -ãt] adj attractive, appealing
attirer [atiʀe] vt to attract; (appâter) to lure, entice; ~ **qn dans un coin/vers soi** to draw sb into a corner/towards one; ~ **l'attention de qn (sur)** to attract sb's attention (to); to draw sb's attention (to); **s'**~ **des ennuis** to bring trouble upon o.s., get into trouble
attiser [atize] vt (feu) to poke (up)
attitré, e [atitʀe] adj qualified; accredited; appointed
attitude [atityd] nf attitude; (position du corps) bearing
attouchements [atuʃmã] nmpl touching sg; (sexuels) fondling sg
attraction [atʀaksjɔ̃] nf (gén) attraction; (de cabaret, cirque) number
attrait [atʀɛ] nm appeal, attraction; lure
attrape-nigaud [atʀapnigo] nm con
attraper [atʀape] vt (gén) to catch; (habi-

tude, amende) to get, pick up; (fam: duper) to con
attrayant, e [atʀɛjã, -ãt] adj attractive
attribuer [atʀibɥe] vt (prix) to award; (rôle, tâche) to allocate, assign; (imputer): ~ **qch à** to attribute sth to; **s'**~ vt (s'approprier) to claim for o.s.
attribut [atʀiby] nm attribute; (LING) complement
attrister [atʀiste] vt to sadden
attroupement [atʀupmã] nm crowd, mob
attrouper [atʀupe]: **s'**~ vi to gather
au [o] prép +dét = **à** +**le**
aubade [obad] nf dawn serenade
aubaine [obɛn] nf godsend; (financière) windfall
aube [ob] nf dawn, daybreak; **à l'**~ at dawn ou daybreak
aubépine [obepin] nf hawthorn
auberge [obɛʀʒ(ə)] nf inn; ~ **de jeunesse** youth hostel
aubergine [obɛʀʒin] nf aubergine
aubergiste [obɛʀʒist(ə)] nm/f inn-keeper, hotel-keeper
aucun, e [okœ̃, -yn] dét no, tournure négative +any; (positif) any ♦ pron none, tournure négative +any; one(any); **sans** ~ **doute** without any doubt; **plus qu'**~ **autre** more than any other; ~ **des deux** neither of the two; ~ **d'entre eux** none of them; **d'**~**s** (certains) some; **aucunement** adv in no way, not in the least
audace [odas] nf daring, boldness; (péj) audacity; **audacieux, euse** adj daring, bold
au-delà [odla] adv beyond ♦ nm: **l'**~ the hereafter; ~ **de** beyond
au-dessous [odsu] adv underneath; below; ~ **de** under(neath), below; (limite, somme etc) below, under; (dignité, condition) below
au-dessus [odsy] adv above; ~ **de** above
au-devant [odvã] : ~ **de** prép: **aller** ~ **de** (personne, danger) to go (out) and meet; (souhaits de qn) to anticipate
audience [odjãs] nf audience; (JUR: séance) hearing
audio-visuel, le [odjovizɥɛl] adj audio-visual
auditeur, trice [oditœʀ, -tʀis] nm/f listener
audition [odisjɔ̃] nf (ouïe, écoute) hearing; (JUR: de témoins) examination; (MUS, THÉÂTRE: épreuve) audition
auditoire [oditwaʀ] nm audience
auge [oʒ] nf trough
augmentation [ɔgmãtɑsjɔ̃] nf: ~ **(de salaire)** rise (in salary) (BRIT), (pay) raise (US)
augmenter [ɔgmãte] vt (gén) to increase; (salaire, prix) to increase, raise, put up; (employé) to increase the salary of ♦ vi to increase
augure [ɔgyʀ] nm soothsayer, oracle; **de bon/mauvais** ~ of good/ill omen; ~**r** [ɔgyʀe] vt: ~**r bien de** to augur well for

aujourd'hui [oʒuʀdμi] *adv* today
aumône [omon] *nf inv* alms *sg*; **faire l'~ (à qn)** to give alms (to sb)
aumônier [omonje] *nm* chaplain
auparavant [oparavã] *adv* before(hand)
auprès [opʀɛ]: **~ de** *prép* next to, close to; (*recourir, s'adresser*) to; (*en comparaison de*) compared with
auquel [okɛl] *prép* +*pron* = **à** +**lequel**
aurai *etc vb voir* **avoir**
auréole [oʀeol] *nf* halo; (*tache*) ring
auriculaire [oʀikylɛʀ] *nm* little finger
aurons *etc vb voir* **avoir**
aurore [oʀoʀ] *nf* dawn, daybreak
ausculter [oskylte] *vt* to sound
aussi [osi] *adv* (*également*) also, too; (*de comparaison*) as ♦ *conj* therefore, consequently; **~ fort que** as strong as; **moi ~** me too; **~ bien que** (*de même que*) as well as
aussitôt [osito] *adv* straight away, immediately; **~ que** as soon as
austère [ostɛʀ] *adj* austere; stern
austral, e [ostʀal] *adj* southern
Australie [ostʀali] *nf*: **l'~** Australia; **australien, ne** *adj, nm/f* Australian
autant [otã] *adv* so much; (*comparatif*): **~ (que)** as much (as); (*nombre*) as many (as); **~ (de)** so much (*ou* many); as much (*ou* many); **~ partir** we (*ou* you *etc*) may as well leave; **~ dire que** ... one might as well say that ...; **pour ~** for all that; **pour ~ que** assuming, as long as; **d'~ plus/mieux (que)** all the more/the better (since)
autel [otɛl] *nm* altar
auteur [otœʀ] *nm* author
authentique [otãtik] *adj* authentic, genuine
auto [oto] *nf* car
auto: **~biographie** *nf* autobiography; **~bus** *nm* bus; **~car** *nm* coach
autochtone [otokton] *nm/f* native
auto: **~collant, e** *adj* self-adhesive; (*enveloppe*) self-seal ♦ *nm* sticker; **~couchettes** *adj*: **train ~couchettes** car sleeper train; **~cuiseur** *nm* pressure cooker; **~défense** *nf* self-defence; **groupe d'~défense** vigilante committee; **~didacte** *nm/f* self-taught person; **~école** *nf* driving school; **~gestion** *nf* self-management; **~graphe** *nm* autograph
automate [otomat] *nm* (*machine*) (automatic) machine
automatique [otomatik] *adj* automatic ♦ *nm*: **l'~** direct dialling; **automatiser** *vt* to automate
automne [oton] *nm* autumn (*BRIT*), fall (*US*)
automobile [otomobil] *adj* motor *cpd* ♦ *nf* (motor) car; **~ motoring; the car industry; **automobiliste** *nm/f* motorist
autonome [otonom] *adj* autonomous; **autonomie** *nf* autonomy; (*POL*) self-

government, autonomy
autopsie [otopsi] *nf* post-mortem (examination), autopsy
autoradio [otoʀadjo] *nm* car radio
autorisation [otoʀizasjɔ̃] *nf* permission, authorization; (*papiers*) permit
autorisé, e [otoʀize] *adj* (*opinion, sources*) authoritative
autoriser [otoʀize] *vt* to give permission for, authorize; (*fig*) to allow (of), sanction
autoritaire [otoʀitɛʀ] *adj* authoritarian
autorité [otoʀite] *nf* authority; **faire ~** to be authoritative
autoroute [otoʀut] *nf* motorway (*BRIT*), highway (*US*)
auto-stop [otostop] *nm*: **faire de l'~** to hitch-hike; **auto-stoppeur, euse** *nm/f* hitch-hiker
autour [otuʀ] *adv* around; **~ de** around; **tout ~** all around

────────── MOT CLÉ

autre [otʀ(ə)] *adj* **1** (*différent*) other, different; **je préférerais un ~ verre** I'd prefer another *ou* a different glass
2 (*supplémentaire*) other; **je voudrais un ~ verre d'eau** I'd like another glass of water
3: **~ chose** something else; **~ part** somewhere else; **d'~ part** on the other hand
♦ *pron*: **un ~** another (one); **nous/vous ~s** us/you; **d'~s** others; **l'~** the other (one); **les ~s** the others; (*autrui*) others; **l'un et l'~** both of them; **se détester l'un l'~/les uns les ~s** to hate each other *ou* one another; **d'une semaine à l'~** from one week to the next; (*incessamment*) any week now; **entre ~s** among other things

autrefois [otʀəfwa] *adv* in the past
autrement [otʀəmã] *adv* differently; in another way; (*sinon*) otherwise; **~ dit** in other words
Autriche [otʀiʃ] *nf*: **l'~** Austria; **autrichien, ne** *adj, nm/f* Austrian
autruche [otʀyʃ] *nf* ostrich
autrui [otʀμi] *pron* others
auvent [ovã] *nm* canopy
aux [o] *prép* +*dét* = **à** +**les**
auxiliaire [oksiljɛʀ] *adj, nm/f* auxiliary
auxquelles [okɛl] *prép* +*pron* = **à** +**lesquelles**
auxquels [okɛl] *prép* +*pron* = **à** +**lesquels**
avachi, e [avaʃi] *adj* limp, flabby
aval [aval] *nm* (*accord*) endorsement, backing; (*GÉO*): **en ~** downstream, downriver; (*sur une pente*) downhill
avalanche [avalãʃ] *nf* avalanche
avaler [avale] *vt* to swallow
avance [avãs] *nf* (*de troupes etc*) advance; progress; (*d'argent*) advance; (*opposé à retard*) lead; being ahead of schedule; **~s** *nfpl* (*ouvertures*) overtures; (*amoureuses*) ad-

vances; **(être) en** ~ (to be) early; (*sur un programme*) (to be) ahead of schedule; **à l'**~, **d'**~ in advance

avancé, e [avɑ̃se] *adj* advanced; well on, well under way

avancement [avɑ̃smɑ̃] *nm* (*professionnel*) promotion

avancer [avɑ̃se] *vi* to move forward, advance; (*projet, travail*) to make progress; (*être en saillie*) to overhang; to jut out; (*montre, réveil*) to be fast; to gain ♦ *vt* to move forward, advance; (*argent*) to advance; (*montre, pendule*) to put forward; **s'**~ *vi* to move forward, advance; (*fig*) to commit o.s.; to overhang; to jut out

avant [avɑ̃] *prép* before ♦ *adv*: **trop/plus** ~ too far/further forward ♦ *adj inv*: **siège/roue** ~ front seat/wheel ♦ *nm* (*d'un véhicule, bâtiment*) front; (*SPORT: joueur*) forward; ~ **qu'il parte/de faire** before he leaves/doing; ~ **tout** (*surtout*) above all; **à l'**~ (*dans un véhicule*) in (the) front; **en** ~ forward(s); **en** ~ **de** in front of

avantage [avɑ̃taʒ] *nm* advantage; ~**s sociaux** fringe benefits; **avantager** *vt* (*favoriser*) to favour; (*embellir*) to flatter; **avantageux, euse** *adj* attractive; attractively priced

avant: ~**-bras** *nm inv* forearm; ~**coureur** *adj inv*: **signe** ~**coureur** advance indication *ou* sign; ~**-dernier, ière** *adj, nm/f* next to last, last but one; ~**-goût** *nm* foretaste; ~**-hier** *adv* the day before yesterday; ~**première** *nf* (*de film*) preview; ~**-projet** *nm* (preliminary) draft; ~**-propos** *nm* foreword; ~**-veille** *nf*; **l'**~ two days before

avare [avaʁ] *adj* miserly, avaricious ♦ *nm/f* miser; ~ **de** (*compliments etc*) sparing of

avarié, e [avaʁje] *adj* rotting

avaries [avaʁi] *nfpl* (*NAVIG*) damage *sg*

avec [avɛk] *prép* with; (*à l'égard de*) to(wards), with

avenant, e [avnɑ̃, -ɑ̃t] *adj* pleasant; **à l'**~ in keeping

avènement [avɛnmɑ̃] *nm* (*d'un roi*) accession, succession; (*d'un changement*) advent, coming

avenir [avniʁ] *nm* future; **à l'**~ in future; **politicien d'**~ politician with prospects *ou* a future

Avent [avɑ̃] *nm*: **l'**~ Advent

aventure [avɑ̃tyʁ] *nf* adventure; (*amoureuse*) affair; **aventurer**: **s'aventurer** *vi* to venture; **aventureux, euse** *adj* adventurous, venturesome; (*projet*) risky, chancy

avenue [avny] *nf* avenue

avérer [aveʁe]: **s'**~ *vb +attrib* to prove (to be)

averse [avɛʁs(ə)] *nf* shower

averti, e [avɛʁti] *adj* (well-)informed

avertir [avɛʁtiʁ] *vt*: ~ **qn (de qch/que)** to warn sb (of sth/that); (*renseigner*) to in-

form sb (of sth/that); **avertissement** *nm* warning; **avertisseur** *nm* horn, siren

aveu, x [avø] *nm* confession

aveugle [avœgl(ə)] *adj* blind; **aveuglément** *adv* blindly; ~**r** *vt* to blind

aviateur, trice [avjatœʁ, -tʁis] *nm/f* aviator, pilot

aviation [avjɑsjɔ̃] *nf* aviation; (*sport*) flying; (*MIL*) air force

avide [avid] *adj* eager; (*péj*) greedy, grasping

avilir [aviliʁ] *vt* to debase

avion [avjɔ̃] *nm* (aero)plane (*BRIT*), (air)plane (*US*); **aller (quelque part) en** ~ to go (somewhere) by plane, fly (somewhere); **par** ~ by airmail; ~ **à réaction** jet (plane)

aviron [aviʁɔ̃] *nm* oar; (*sport*): **l'**~ rowing

avis [avi] *nm* opinion; (*notification*) notice; **changer d'**~ to change one's mind; **jusqu'à nouvel** ~ until further notice

avisé, e [avize] *adj* sensible, wise

aviser [avize] *vt* (*voir*) to notice, catch sight of; (*informer*): ~ **qn de/que** to advise *ou* inform sb of/that ♦ *vi* to think about things, assess the situation; **s'**~ **de qch/que** to become suddenly aware of sth/that; **s'**~ **de faire** to take it into one's head to do

avocat, e [avɔka, -at] *nm/f* (*JUR*) barrister (*BRIT*), lawyer ♦ *nm* (*CULIN*) avocado (pear); ~ **général** assistant public prosecutor

avoine [avwan] *nf* oats *pl*

MOT CLÉ

avoir [avwaʁ] *nm* assets *pl*, resources *pl*; (*COMM*) credit

♦ *vt* **1** (*posséder*) to have; **elle a 2 enfants/une belle maison** she has (got) 2 children/a lovely house; **il a les yeux bleus** he has (got) blue eyes

2 (*âge, dimensions*) to be; **il a 3 ans** he is 3 (years old); **le mur a 3 mètres de haut** the wall is 3 metres high; *voir aussi* **faim**; **peur** *etc*

3 (*fam: duper*) to do, have; **on vous a eu!** you've been done *ou* had!

4: **en** ~ **contre qn** to have a grudge against sb; **en** ~ **assez** to be fed up; **j'en ai pour une demi-heure** it'll take me half an hour

♦ *vb aux* **1** to have; ~ **mangé/dormi** to have eaten/slept

2 (*avoir +à +infinitif*): ~ **à faire qch** to have to do sth; **vous n'avez qu'à lui demander** you only have to ask him

♦ *vb impers* **1**: **il y a** (+ *singulier*) there is; (+ *pluriel*) there are; **qu'y-a-t-il?, qu'est-ce qu'il y a?** what's the matter?, what is it?; **il doit y avoir une explication** there must be an explanation; **il n'y a qu'à ...** we (*ou* you *etc*) will just have to ...

2 (*temporel*): **il y a 10 ans** 10 years ago; **il**

y a **10 ans/longtemps que je le sais** I've known it for 10 years/a long time; **il y a 10 ans qu'il est arrivé** it's 10 years since he arrived

avoisiner [avwazine] *vt* to be near *ou* close to; (*fig*) to border *ou* verge on

avortement [avɔʀtəmɑ̃] *nm* abortion

avorter [avɔʀte] *vi* (*MÉD*) to have an abortion; (*fig*) to fail

avoué, e [avwe] *adj* avowed ♦ *nm* (*JUR*) ≈ solicitor

avouer [avwe] *vt* (*crime, défaut*) to confess (to); ~ **avoir fait/que** to admit *ou* confess to having done/that

avril [avʀil] *nm* April

axe [aks(ə)] *nm* axis; (*de roue etc*) axle; (*fig*) main line; ~ **routier** main road, trunk road; **axer** *vt*: **axer qch sur** to centre sth on

ayons *etc vb voir* **avoir**

azote [azɔt] *nm* nitrogen

B b

babines [babin] *nfpl* chops

babiole [babjɔl] *nf* (*bibelot*) trinket; (*vétille*) trifle

bâbord [babɔʀ] *nm*: **à** *ou* **par** ~ to port, on the port side

baby-foot [babifut] *nm* table football

bac [bak] *abr m* = **baccalauréat**; ♦ *nm* (*bateau*) ferry; (*récipient*) tub; tray; tank

baccalauréat [bakalɔʀea] *nm* high school diploma

bachelier, ière [baʃəlje, -jɛʀ] *nm/f* holder of the baccalauréat

bachoter [baʃɔte] (*fam*) *vi* to cram (for an exam)

bâcler [bɑkle] *vt* to botch (up)

badaud, e [bado, -od] *nm/f* idle onlooker, stroller

badigeonner [badiʒɔne] *vt* to distemper; to colourwash; (*barbouiller*) to daub

badin, e [badɛ̃, -in] *adj* playful

badiner [badine] *vi*: ~ **avec qch** to treat sth lightly

baffe [baf] (*fam*) *nf* slap, clout

bafouer [bafwe] *vt* to deride, ridicule

bafouiller [bafuje] *vi, vt* to stammer

bagage [bagaʒ] *nm*: ~**s** luggage *sg*; ~**s à main** hand-luggage

bagarre [bagaʀ] *nf* fight, brawl; **bagarrer:**

se bagarrer *vi* to have a fight *ou* scuffle, fight

bagatelle [bagatɛl] *nf* trifle

bagne [baɲ] *nm* penal colony

bagnole [baɲɔl] (*fam*) *nf* car

bagout [bagu] *nm*: **avoir du** ~ to have the gift of the gab

bague [bag] *nf* ring; ~ **de fiançailles** engagement ring; ~ **de serrage** clip

baguette [bagɛt] *nf* stick; (*cuisine chinoise*) chopstick; (*de chef d'orchestre*) baton; (*pain*) stick of (French) bread; ~ **magique** magic wand

baie [bɛ] *nf* (*GÉO*) bay; (*fruit*) berry; ~ (**vitrée**) picture window

baignade [beɲad] *nf* bathing

baigner [beɲe] *vt* (*bébé*) to bath; **se** ~ *vi* to have a swim, go swimming *ou* bathing; **baignoire** *nf* bath(tub)

bail [baj] (*pl* **baux**) *nm* lease

bâiller [bɑje] *vi* to yawn; (*être ouvert*) to gape

bâillon [bɑjɔ̃] *nm* gag; **bâillonner** *vt* to gag

bain [bɛ̃] *nm* bath; **prendre un** ~ to have a bath; **se mettre dans le** ~ (*fig*) to get into it *ou* things; ~ **de foule** walkabout; ~ **de soleil: prendre un** ~ **de soleil** to sunbathe; ~**s de mer** sea bathing *sg*; **bain-marie** *nm*: **faire chauffer au bain-marie** (*boîte etc*) to immerse in boiling water

baiser [beze] *nm* kiss ♦ *vt* (*main, front*) to kiss; (*fam!*) to screw (*!*)

baisse [bɛs] *nf* fall, drop; "~ **sur la viande**" "meat prices down"

baisser [bese] *vt* to lower; (*radio, chauffage*) to turn down; (*AUTO: phares*) to dip (*BRIT*), lower (*US*) ♦ *vi* to fall, drop, go down; **se** ~ *vi* to bend down

bal [bal] *nm* dance; (*grande soirée*) ball; ~ **costumé** fancy-dress ball

balader [balade] *vt* (*traîner*) to trail round; **se** ~ *vi* to go for a walk *ou* stroll; to go for a drive

baladeur [baladœʀ] *nm* personal stereo, Walkman (®)

balafre [balafʀ(ə)] *nf* gash, slash; (*cicatrice*) scar

balai [balɛ] *nm* broom, brush; **balai-brosse** *nm* (long-handled) scrubbing brush

balance [balɑ̃s] *nf* scales *pl*; (*de précision*) balance; (*signe*): **la B**~ Libra

balancer [balɑ̃se] *vt* to swing; (*lancer*) to fling, chuck; (*renvoyer, jeter*) to chuck out ♦ *vi* to swing; **se** ~ *vi* to swing; to rock; to sway; **se** ~ **de** (*fam*) not to care about; **balancier** *nm* (*de pendule*) pendulum; (*perche*) (balancing) pole; **balançoire** *nf* swing; (*sur pivot*) seesaw

balayer [baleje] *vt* (*feuilles etc*) to sweep up, brush up; (*pièce*) to sweep; (*chasser*) to sweep away; to sweep aside; (*suj: radar*) to scan; **balayeur, euse** *nm/f* roadsweeper;

balayeuse nf (machine) roadsweeper
balbutier [balbysje] vi, vt to stammer
balcon [balkɔ̃] nm balcony; (THÉÂTRE) dress circle
baleine [balɛn] nf whale; (de parapluie, corset) rib; **baleinière** nf whaleboat
balise [baliz] nf (NAVIG) beacon; (marker) buoy; (AVIAT) runway light, beacon; (AUTO, SKI) sign, marker; **baliser** vt to mark out (with lights etc)
balivernes [balivɛrn(ə)] nfpl nonsense sg
ballant, e [balɑ̃, -ɑ̃t] adj dangling
balle [bal] nf (de fusil) bullet; (de sport) ball; (paquet) bale; (fam: franc) franc; ~ **perdue** stray bullet
ballerine [balrin] nf ballet dancer
ballet [balɛ] nm ballet
ballon [balɔ̃] nm (de sport) ball; (jouet, AVIAT) balloon; (de vin) glass; ~ **de football** football
ballot [balo] nm bundle; (péj) nitwit
ballottage [balɔtaʒ] nm (POL) second ballot
ballotter [balɔte] vi to roll around; to toss ♦ vt to shake about; to toss
balnéaire [balneɛr] adj seaside cpd
balourd, e [balur, -urd(ə)] adj clumsy ♦ nm/f clodhopper
balustrade [balystrad] nf railings pl, handrail
bambin [bɑ̃bɛ̃] nm little child
ban [bɑ̃] nm cheer; ~**s** nmpl (de mariage) banns; **mettre au** ~ **de** to outlaw from
banal, e [banal] adj banal, commonplace; (péj) trite
banane [banan] nf banana
banc [bɑ̃] nm seat, bench; (de poissons) shoal; ~ **d'essai** (fig) testing ground; ~ **de sable** sandbank
bancaire [bɑ̃kɛr] adj banking, bank cpd
bancal, e [bɑ̃kal] adj wobbly; bow-legged
bandage [bɑ̃daʒ] nm bandage
bande [bɑ̃d] nf (de tissu etc) strip; (MÉD) bandage; (motif) stripe; (magnétique etc) tape; (groupe) band; (: péj) bunch; **par la** ~ in a roundabout way; **faire** ~ **à part** to keep to o.s.; ~ **dessinée** comic strip; ~ **sonore** sound track
bandeau, x [bɑ̃do] nm headband; (sur les yeux) blindfold; (MÉD) head bandage
bander [bɑ̃de] vt (blessure) to bandage; (muscle) to tense; ~ **les yeux à qn** to blindfold sb
banderole [bɑ̃drɔl] nf banner, streamer
bandit [bɑ̃di] nm bandit; **banditisme** nm violent crime, armed robberies pl
bandoulière [bɑ̃duljɛr] nf: **en** ~ (slung ou worn) across the shoulder
banlieue [bɑ̃ljø] nf suburbs pl; **lignes/quartiers de** ~ suburban lines/areas; **trains de** ~ commuter trains
bannière [banjɛr] nf banner

bannir [banir] vt to banish
banque [bɑ̃k] nf bank; (activités) banking; ~ **d'affaires** merchant bank; ~**route** [bɑ̃krut] nf bankruptcy
banquet [bɑ̃kɛ] nm dinner; (d'apparat) banquet
banquette [bɑ̃kɛt] nf seat
banquier [bɑ̃kje] nm banker
banquise [bɑ̃kiz] nf ice field
baptême [batɛm] nm christening; baptism; ~ **de l'air** first flight
baquet [bakɛ] nm tub, bucket
bar [bar] nm bar
baraque [barak] nf shed; (fam) house; ~ **foraine** fairground stand
baraqué, e [barake] adj well-built, hefty
baraquements [barakmɑ̃] nmpl (pour réfugiés, ouvriers) huts
baratin [baratɛ̃] (fam) nm smooth talk, patter; **baratiner** vt to chat up
barbare [barbar] adj barbaric
barbe [barb(ə)] nf beard; **quelle** ~! (fam) what a drag ou bore!; **à la** ~ **de qn** under sb's nose; ~ **à papa** candy-floss (BRIT), cotton candy (US)
barbelé [barbəle] nm barbed wire no pl
barboter [barbɔte] vi to paddle, dabble; **barboteuse** [barbɔtøz] nf rompers pl
barbouiller [barbuje] vt to daub; **avoir l'estomac barbouillé** to feel queasy
barbu, e [barby] adj bearded
barda [barda] (fam) nm kit, gear
barder [barde] (fam) vi: **ça va** ~ sparks will fly, things are going to get hot
barème [barɛm] nm scale; table
baril [baril] nm barrel; keg
bariolé, e [barjɔle] adj gaudily-coloured
baromètre [barɔmɛtr(ə)] nm barometer
baron [barɔ̃] nm baron; **baronne** nf baroness
baroque [barɔk] adj (ART) baroque; (fig) weird
barque [bark(ə)] nf small boat
barquette [barkɛt] nf (pour repas) tray; (pour fruits) punnet
barrage [baraʒ] nm dam; (sur route) roadblock, barricade
barre [bar] nf bar; (NAVIG) helm; (écrite) line, stroke
barreau, x [baro] nm bar; (JUR): **le** ~ the Bar
barrer [bare] vt (route etc) to block; (mot) to cross out; (chèque) to cross (BRIT); (NAVIG) to steer; **se** ~ vi (fam) to clear off
barrette [barɛt] nf (pour cheveux) (hair) slide (BRIT) ou clip (US)
barricader [barikade] vt to barricade
barrière [barjɛr] nf fence; (obstacle) barrier; (porte) gate
barrique [barik] nf barrel, cask
bas, basse [bɑ, bɑs] adj low ♦ nm bottom, lower part; (vêtement) stocking ♦ adv low;

(*parler*) softly; **au ~ mot** at the lowest estimate; **en ~** down below; at (*ou* to) the bottom; (*dans une maison*) downstairs; **en ~ de** at the bottom of; **mettre ~** to give birth; **à ~ ...!** down with ...!; **~ morceaux** *nmpl* (*viande*) cheap cuts

basané, e [bazane] *adj* tanned, bronzed

bas-côté [bakote] *nm* (*de route*) verge (*BRIT*), shoulder (*US*)

bascule [baskyl] *nf*: (**jeu de**) **~** seesaw; (**balance à**) **~** scales *pl*; **fauteuil à ~** rocking chair

basculer [baskyle] *vi* to fall over, topple (over); (*benne*) to tip up ♦ *vt* to topple over; to tip out, tip up

base [baz] *nf* base; (*POL*) rank and file; (*fondement, principe*) basis; **de ~** basic; **à ~ de café** *etc* coffee *etc* -based; **~ de données** database; **baser** *vt* to base; **se ~r sur** *vt* (*preuves*) to base one's argument on

bas-fond [baf5] *nm* (*NAVIG*) shallow; **~s** *nmpl* (*fig*) dregs

basilic [bazilik] *nm* (*CULIN*) basil

basket [basket] *nm* trainer (*BRIT*), sneaker (*US*); (*aussi*: **~-ball**) basketball

basque [bask(ə)] *adj, nmlf* Basque

basse [bas] *adj voir* **bas** ♦ *nf* (*MUS*) bass; **~-cour** *nf* farmyard

bassin [basɛ̃] *nm* (*cuvette*) bowl; (*pièce d'eau*) pond, pool; (*de fontaine, GÉO*) basin; (*ANAT*) pelvis; (*portuaire*) dock

bassine [basin] *nf* (*ustensile*) basin; (*contenu*) bowl(ful)

basson [bas5] *nm* bassoon

bas-ventre [bavātʀ(ə)] *nm* (lower part of the) stomach

bat *vb voir* **battre**

bât [ba] *nm* packsaddle

bataille [bataj] *nf* battle; fight

bâtard, e [batar, -ard(ə)] *nmlf* illegitimate child, bastard (*pej*)

bateau, x [bato] *nm* boat, ship; **bateau-mouche** *nm* passenger pleasure boat (*on the Seine*)

batelier, ière [batəlje, -jɛʀ] *nmlf* (*de bac*) ferryman(woman)

bâti, e [bati] *adj*: **bien ~** well-built

batifoler [batifɔle] *vi* to frolic about

bâtiment [batimã] *nm* building; (*NAVIG*) ship, vessel; (*industrie*) building trade

bâtir [batiʀ] *vt* to build

bâtisse [batis] *nf* building

bâton [bat5] *nm* stick; **à ~s rompus** informally

bats *vb voir* **battre**

battage [bataʒ] *nm* (*publicité*) (hard) plugging

battant [batã] *nm* (*de cloche*) clapper; (*de volets*) shutter, flap; (*de porte*) side; (*fig: personne*) fighter; **porte à double ~** double door

battement [batmã] *nm* (*de cœur*) beat; (*in-*

---

tervalle) interval (*between classes, trains*); **10 minutes de ~** 10 minutes to spare; **~ de paupières** blinking *no pl* (*of eyelids*)

batterie [batʀi] *nf* (*MIL, ÉLEC*) battery; (*MUS*) drums *pl*, drum kit; **~ de cuisine** pots and pans *pl*; kitchen utensils *pl*

batteur [batœʀ] *nm* (*MUS*) drummer; (*appareil*) whisk

battre [batʀ(ə)] *vt* to beat; (*suj: pluie, vagues*) to beat *ou* lash against; (*blé*) to thresh; (*passer au peigne fin*) to scour ♦ *vi* (*cœur*) to beat; (*volets etc*) to bang, rattle; **se ~** *vi* to fight; **~ la mesure** to beat time; **~ en brèche** to demolish; **~ son plein** to be at its height, be going full swing; **~ des mains** to clap one's hands

battue [baty] *nf* (*chasse*) beat; (*policière etc*) search, hunt

baume [bom] *nm* balm

baux [bo] *nmpl de* **bail**

bavard, e [bavaʀ, -aʀd(ə)] *adj* (very) talkative; gossipy; **bavarder** *vi* to chatter; (*indiscrètement*) to gossip; to blab

bave [bav] *nf* dribble; (*de chien etc*) slobber; (*d'escargot*) slime; **~r** *vi* to dribble; to slobber; **en ~r** (*fam*) to have a hard time (of it); **~tte** *nf* bib; **baveux, euse** *adj* (*omelette*) runny

bavure [bavyʀ] *nf* smudge; (*fig*) hitch; blunder

bayer [baje] *vi*: **~ aux corneilles** to stand gaping

bazar [bazaʀ] *nm* general store; (*fam*) jumble; **~der** (*fam*) *vt* to chuck out

B.C.B.G. *sigle adj* (= *bon chic bon genre*) preppy, smart and trendy

B.C.G. *sigle m* (= *bacille Calmette-Guérin*) BCG

bd. *abr* = **boulevard**

B.D. *sigle f* = **bande dessinée**

béant, e [beã, -ãt] *adj* gaping

béat, e [bea, -at] *adj* showing open-eyed wonder; blissful; **béatitude** *nf* bliss

beau(bel), belle [bo, bɛl] (*mpl* **~x**) *adj* beautiful, lovely; (*homme*) handsome ♦ *adv*: **il fait ~** the weather's fine; **un ~ jour** one (fine) day; **de plus belle** more than ever, even more; **on a ~ essayer** however hard we try; **bel et bien** well and truly; **faire le ~** (*chien*) to sit up and beg

┌─────────────── **MOT CLÉ**

beaucoup [boku] *adv* **1** a lot; **il boit ~** he drinks a lot; **il ne boit pas ~** he doesn't drink much *ou* a lot

2 (*suivi de plus, trop etc*) much, a lot, far; **il est ~ plus grand** he is much *ou* a lot *ou* far taller

3: **~ de** (*nombre*) many, a lot of; (*quantité*) a lot of; **~ d'étudiants/de touristes** a lot of *ou* many students/tourists; **~ de courage** a lot of courage; **il n'a pas ~ d'argent**

he hasn't got much *ou* at lot of money
4: **de** ~ by far

beau: ~**-fils** *nm* son-in-law; *(remariage)* stepson; ~**-frère** *nm* brother-in-law; ~**-père** *nm* father-in-law; *(remariage)* stepfather
beauté [bote] *nf* beauty; **de toute** ~ beautiful; **en** ~ brilliantly
beaux-arts [bozaʀ] *nmpl* fine arts
beaux-parents [boparɑ̃] *nmpl* wife's *(ou* husband's) family, in-laws
bébé [bebe] *nm* baby
bec [bɛk] *nm* beak, bill; *(de récipient)* spout; lip; *(fam)* mouth; ~ **de gaz** (street) gaslamp; ~ **verseur** pouring lip
bécane [bekan] *(fam) nf* bike
bec-de-lièvre [bɛkdəljɛvʀ(ə)] *nm* harelip
bêche [bɛʃ] *nf* spade; **bêcher** *vt* to dig
bécoter [bekɔte]: **se** ~ *vi* to smooch
becqueter [bɛkte] *(fam) vt* to eat
bedaine [bədɛn] *nf* paunch
bedonnant, e [bədɔnɑ̃, -ɑ̃t] *adj* potbellied
bée [be] *adj*: **bouche** ~ gaping
beffroi [befʀwa] *nm* belfry
bégayer [begeje] *vt, vi* to stammer
bègue [bɛg] *nm/f*: **être** ~ to have a stammer
béguin [begɛ̃] *nm*: **avoir le** ~ **de** *ou* **pour** to have a crush on
beige [bɛʒ] *adj* beige
beignet [bɛɲɛ] *nm* fritter
bel [bɛl] *adj voir* **beau**
bêler [bele] *vi* to bleat
belette [bəlɛt] *nf* weasel
belge [bɛlʒ(ə)] *adj, nm/f* Belgian
Belgique [bɛlʒik] *nf*: **la** ~ Belgium
bélier [belje] *nm* ram; *(signe)*: **le B**~ Aries
belle [bɛl] *adj voir* **beau** ♦ *nf (SPORT)* decider; ~**-fille** *nf* daughter-in-law; *(remariage)* stepdaughter; ~**-mère** *nf* mother-in-law; stepmother; ~**-sœur** *nf* sister-in-law
belliqueux, euse [belikø, -øz] *adj* aggressive, warlike
belvédère [bɛlvedɛʀ] *nm* panoramic viewpoint *(or small building there)*
bémol [bemɔl] *nm (MUS)* flat
bénédiction [benediksjɔ̃] *nf* blessing
bénéfice [benefis] *nm (COMM)* profit; *(avantage)* benefit; **bénéficier de** *vt* to enjoy; to benefit by *ou* from; to get, be given; **bénéfique** *adj* beneficial
benêt [bənɛ] *nm* simpleton
bénévole [benevɔl] *adj* voluntary, unpaid
bénin, igne [benɛ̃, -iɲ] *adj* minor, mild; *(tumeur)* benign
bénir [beniʀ] *vt* to bless; **bénit, e** *adj* consecrated; **eau bénite** holy water
benjamin, e [bɛ̃ʒamɛ̃, -in] *nm/f* youngest child
benne [bɛn] *nf* skip; *(de téléphérique)* (cable) car; ~ **basculante** tipper *(BRIT)*,

dump truck *(US)*
B.E.P.C. *sigle m* = **brevet d'études du premier cycle**
béquille [bekij] *nf* crutch; *(de bicyclette)* stand
berceau, x [bɛʀso] *nm* cradle, crib
bercer [bɛʀse] *vt* to rock, cradle; *(suj: musique etc)* to lull; ~ **qn de** *(promesses etc)* to delude sb with; **berceuse** *nf* lullaby
béret (basque) [beʀe(bask(ə))] *nm* beret
berge [bɛʀʒ(ə)] *nf* bank
berger, ère [bɛʀʒe, -ɛʀ] *nm/f* shepherd(ess)
berlingot [bɛʀlɛ̃go] *nm (emballage)* carton *(pyramid shaped)*
berlue [bɛʀly] *nf*: **j'ai la** ~ I must be seeing things
berner [bɛʀne] *vt* to fool
besogne [bəzɔɲ] *nf* work *no pl*, job
besoin [bəzwɛ̃] *nm* need; *(pauvreté)*: **le** ~ need, want; **faire ses** ~**s** to relieve o.s.; **avoir** ~ **de qch/faire qch** to need sth/to do sth; **au** ~ if need be
bestiaux [bɛstjo] *nmpl* cattle
bestiole [bɛstjɔl] *nf* (tiny) creature
bétail [betaj] *nm* livestock, cattle *pl*
bête [bɛt] *nf* animal; *(bestiole)* insect, creature ♦ *adj* stupid, silly; **il cherche la petite** ~ he's being pernickety *ou* overfussy; ~ **noire** pet hate
bêtise [betiz] *nf* stupidity; stupid thing (to say *ou* do)
béton [betɔ̃] *nm* concrete; **(en)** ~ *(alibi, argument)* cast iron; ~ **armé** reinforced concrete; **bétonnière** *nf* cement mixer
betterave [bɛtʀav] *nf* beetroot *(BRIT)*, beet *(US)*; ~ **sucrière** sugar beet
beugler [bøgle] *vi* to low; *(radio etc)* to blare ♦ *vt (chanson)* to bawl out
Beur [bœʀ] *nm/f person of North African origin living in France*
beurre [bœʀ] *nm* butter; **beurrer** *vt* to butter; **beurrier** [bœʀje] *nm* butter dish
beuverie [bœvʀi] *nf* drinking session
bévue [bevy] *nf* blunder
Beyrouth [beʀut] *n* Beirut
bi... [bi] *préfixe* bi..., two-
biais [bjɛ] *nm (moyen)* device, expedient; *(aspect)* angle; **en** ~, **de** ~ *(obliquement)* at an angle; *(fig)* indirectly; **biaiser** *vi (fig)* to sidestep the issue
bibelot [biblo] *nm* trinket, curio
biberon [bibʀɔ̃] *nm* (feeding) bottle; **nourrir au** ~ to bottle-feed
bible [bibl(ə)] *nf* bible
biblio... *préfixe*: ~**bus** *nm* mobile library van; ~**phile** *nm/f* booklover; ~**thécaire** *nm/f* librarian; ~**thèque** *nf* library; *(meuble)* bookcase
bicarbonate [bikaʀbɔnat] *nm*: ~ **(de soude)** bicarbonate of soda
biceps [bisɛps] *nm* biceps

biche [biʃ] *nf* doe
bichonner [biʃɔne] *vt* to groom
bicolore [bikɔlɔʀ] *adj* two-coloured
bicoque [bikɔk] (*péj*) *nf* shack
bicyclette [bisiklɛt] *nf* bicycle
bide [bid] *nm* (*fam: ventre*) belly; (*THÉÂTRE*) flop
bidet [bidɛ] *nm* bidet
bidon [bidɔ̃] *nm* can ♦ *adj inv* (*fam*) phoney
bidonville [bidɔ̃vil] *nm* shanty town
bidule [bidyl] (*fam*) *nm* thingumajig
bielle [bjɛl] *nf* connecting rod

MOT CLÉ

bien [bjɛ̃] *nm* **1** (*avantage, profit*): **faire du ~ à qn** to do sb good; **dire du ~ de** to speak well of; **c'est pour son ~** it's for his own good

2 (*possession, patrimoine*) possession, property; **son ~ le plus précieux** his most treasured possession; **avoir du ~** to have property; **~s (de consommation** *etc***)** (consumer *etc*) goods

3 (*moral*): **le ~** good; **distinguer le ~ du mal** to tell good from evil

♦ *adv* **1** (*de façon satisfaisante*) well; **elle travaille/mange ~** she works/eats well; **croyant ~ faire, je/il ...** thinking I/he was doing the right thing, I/he ...; **c'est ~ fait!** it serves him (*ou* her *etc*) right!

2 (*valeur intensive*) quite; **~ jeune** quite young; **~ assez** quite enough; **~ mieux** (very) much better; **j'espère ~ y aller** I do hope to go; **je veux ~ le faire** (*concession*) I'm quite willing to do it; **il faut ~ le faire** it has to be done

3: **~ du temps/des gens** quite a time/a number of people

♦ *adj inv* **1** (*en bonne forme, à l'aise*): **je me sens ~** I feel fine; **je ne me sens pas ~** I don't feel well; **on est ~ dans ce fauteuil** this chair is very comfortable

2 (*joli, beau*) good-looking; **tu es ~ dans cette robe** you look good in that dress

3 (*satisfaisant*) good; **elle est ~, cette maison/secrétaire** it's a good house/she's a good secretary

4 (*moralement*) right; (*: personne*) good, nice; (*respectable*) respectable; **ce n'est pas ~ de ...** it's not right to ...; **elle est ~, cette femme** she's a nice woman, she's a good sort; **des gens ~s** respectable people

5 (*en bons termes*): **être ~ avec qn** to be on good terms with sb

♦ *préfixe*: **~-aimé** *adj, nmf* beloved; **~-être** *nm* well-being; **~faisance** *nf* charity; **~faisant, e** *adj* (*chose*) beneficial; **~fait** *nm* act of generosity, benefaction; (*de la science* *etc*) benefit; **~faiteur, trice** *nmf* benefactor/benefactress; **~-fondé** *nm* soundness; **~-fonds** *nm* property; **~heureux, euse** *adj* happy; (*REL*) blessed, blest;

~ que *conj* (al)though; **~ sûr** *adv* certainly

bienséant, e [bjɛ̃seɑ̃, -ɑ̃t] *adj* seemly
bientôt [bjɛ̃to] *adv* soon; **à ~** see you soon
bienveillant, e [bjɛ̃vɛjɑ̃, -ɑ̃t] *adj* kindly
bienvenu, e [bjɛ̃vny] *adj* welcome; **bienvenue** *nf*: **souhaiter la ~e à** to welcome; **~e à** welcome to
bière [bjɛʀ] *nf* (*boisson*) beer; (*cercueil*) bier; **~ (à la) pression** draught beer; **~ blonde** lager; **~ brune** brown ale
biffer [bife] *vt* to cross out
bifteck [biftɛk] *nm* steak
bifurquer [bifyʀke] *vi* (*route*) to fork; (*véhicule*) to turn off
bigarré, e [bigaʀe] *adj* multicoloured; (*disparate*) motley
bigorneau, x [bigɔʀno] *nm* winkle
bigot, e [bigo, -ɔt] (*péj*) *adj* bigoted
bigoudi [bigudi] *nm* curler
bijou, x [biʒu] *nm* jewel; **bijouterie** *nf* jeweller's (shop); jewellery; **bijoutier, ière** *nmf* jeweller
bilan [bilɑ̃] *nm* (*COMM*) balance sheet(s); end of year statement; (*fig*) (net) outcome; (*: de victimes*) toll; **faire le ~ de** to assess; to review; **déposer son ~** to file a bankruptcy statement
bile [bil] *nf* bile; **se faire de la ~** (*fam*) to worry o.s. sick
bilieux, euse [biljø, -jøz] *adj* bilious; (*fig: colérique*) testy
bilingue [bilɛ̃g] *adj* bilingual
billard [bijaʀ] *nm* billiards *sg*; billiard table; **c'est du ~** (*fam*) it's a cinch
bille [bij] *nf* (*gén*) ball; (*du jeu de billes*) marble; (*de bois*) log
billet [bijɛ] *nm* (*aussi*: **~ de banque**) (bank)note; (*de cinéma, de bus* *etc*) ticket; (*courte lettre*) note; **~ circulaire** round-trip ticket
billetterie [bijɛtʀi] *nf* ticket office; (*distributeur*) ticket machine; (*BANQUE*) cash dispenser
billion [biljɔ̃] *nm* billion (*BRIT*), trillion (*US*)
billot [bijo] *nm* block
bimensuel, le [bimɑ̃sɥɛl] *adj* bimonthly
binette [binɛt] *nf* hoe
binocle [binɔkl(ə)] *nm* pince-nez
bio... *préfixe* bio...; **~graphie** *nf* biography; **~logie** *nf* biology; **~logique** *adj* biological
Birmanie [biʀmani] *nf* Burma
bis¹, e [bi, biz] *adj* (*couleur*) greyish brown
bis² [bis] *adv*: **12 bis** 12a *ou* A ♦ *excl, nm* encore
bisannuel, le [bizanɥɛl] *adj* biennial
biscornu, e [biskɔʀny] *adj* twisted
biscotte [biskɔt] *nf* (*breakfast*) rusk
biscuit [biskɥi] *nm* biscuit; sponge cake
bise [biz] *nf* (*baiser*) kiss; (*vent*) North wind
bissextile [bisɛkstil] *adj*: **année ~** leap year

bistouri [bistuʀi] *nm* lancet
bistro(t) [bistʀo] *nm* bistro, café
bitume [bitym] *nm* asphalt
bizarre [bizaʀ] *adj* strange, odd
blafard, e [blafaʀ, -aʀd(ə)] *adj* wan
blague [blag] *nf (propos)* joke; *(farce)* trick; **sans ~l** no kidding!; **~ à tabac** tobacco pouch
blaguer [blage] *vi* to joke ♦ *vt* to tease
blaireau, x [blɛʀo] *nm (ZOOL)* badger; *(brosse)* shaving brush
blairer [blɛʀe] *vt*: **je ne peux pas le ~** I can't bear *ou* stand him
blâme [blɑm] *nm* blame; *(sanction)* reprimand
blâmer [blɑme] *vt* to blame
blanc, blanche [blɑ̃, blɑ̃ʃ] *adj* white; *(non imprimé)* blank; *(innocent)* pure ♦ *nm/f* white, white man(woman) ♦ *nm (couleur)* white; *(espace non écrit)* blank; *(aussi: ~ d'œuf)* (egg-)white; *(: ~ de poulet)* breast, white meat; *(: vin ~)* white wine; **~ cassé** off-white; **chèque en ~** blank cheque; **à ~** *(chauffer)* white-hot; *(tirer, charger)* with blanks; **~-bec** *nm* greenhorn; **blanche** *nf (MUS)* minim *(BRIT)*, half-note *(US)*; **blancheur** *nf* whiteness
blanchir [blɑ̃ʃiʀ] *vt (gén)* to whiten; *(linge)* to launder; *(CULIN)* to blanch; *(fig: disculper)* to clear ♦ *vi* to grow white; *(cheveux)* to go white
blanchisserie *nf* laundry
blason [blazɔ̃] *nm* coat of arms
blazer [blazɛʀ] *nm* blazer
blé [ble] *nm* wheat; **~ noir** *(nm)* buckwheat
bled [blɛd] *(péj) nm* hole
blême [blɛm] *adj* pale
blessé, e [blese] *adj* injured ♦ *nm/f* injured person; casualty
blesser [blese] *vt* to injure; *(délibérément: MIL etc)* to wound; *(suj: souliers etc, offenser)* to hurt; **se ~** to injure o.s.; **se ~ au pied etc** to injure one's foot *etc*
blessure [blesyʀ] *nf* injury; wound
bleu, e [blø] *adj* blue; *(bifteck)* very rare ♦ *nm (couleur)* blue; *(novice)* greenhorn; *(contusion)* bruise; *(vêtement: aussi: ~s)* overalls *pl*; **~ marine** navy blue
bleuet [bløɛ] *nm* cornflower
bleuté, e [bløte] *adj* blue-shaded
blinder [blɛ̃de] *vt* to armour; *(fig)* to harden
bloc [blɔk] *nm (de pierre etc)* block; *(de papier à lettres)* pad; *(ensemble)* group, block; **serré à ~** tightened right down; **en ~** as a whole; wholesale; **~ opératoire** operating *ou* theatre block; **~ sanitaire** toilet block; **~age** [blɔkaʒ] *nm* blocking; jamming; freezing; *(PSYCH)* hang-up
bloc-notes [blɔknɔt] *nm* note pad
blocus [blɔkys] *nm* blockade
blond, e [blɔ̃, -ɔ̃d] *adj* fair; blond; *(sable,*

blés) golden; **~ cendré** ash blond
bloquer [blɔke] *vt (passage)* to block; *(pièce mobile)* to jam; *(crédits, compte)* to freeze
blottir [blɔtiʀ]: **se ~** *vi* to huddle up
blouse [bluz] *nf* overall
blouson [bluzɔ̃] *nm* blouson jacket; **~ noir** *(fig)* ≈ rocker
bluff [blœf] *nm* bluff
bluffer [blœfe] *vi* to bluff
bobard [bɔbaʀ] *(fam) nm* tall story
bobine [bɔbin] *nf* reel; *(ÉLEC)* coil
bocal, aux [bɔkal, -o] *nm* jar
bock [bɔk] *nm* glass of beer
bœuf [bœf, *pl* bø] *nm* ox, steer; *(CULIN)* beef
bof! [bɔf] *(fam) excl* don't care!; *(pas terrible)* nothing special
bohème [bɔɛm] *adj* happy-go-lucky, unconventional; **bohémien, ne** [bɔemjɛ̃, -jɛn] *nm/f* gipsy
boire [bwaʀ] *vt* to drink; *(s'imprégner de)* to soak up; **~ un coup** to have a drink
bois [bwa] *nm* wood; **de ~, en ~** wooden
boisé, e [bwaze] *adj* woody, wooded
boisson [bwasɔ̃] *nf* drink; **pris de ~** drunk, intoxicated
boîte [bwat] *nf* box; *(entreprise)* place, firm; **aliments en ~** canned *ou* tinned *(BRIT)* foods; **~ à gants** glove compartment; **~ aux lettres** letter box; **~ d'allumettes** box of matches; *(vide)* matchbox; **~ (de conserve)** can *ou* tin *(BRIT)* (of food); **~ de nuit** night club; **~ de vitesses** gear box; **~ postale** PO Box
boiter [bwate] *vi* to limp; *(fig)* to wobble; to be shaky
boîtier [bwatje] *nm* case
boive *etc vb voir* **boire**
bol [bɔl] *nm* bowl; **un ~ d'air** a breath of fresh air; **j'en ai ras le ~** *(fam)* I'm fed up with this
bolide [bɔlid] *nm* racing car; **comme un ~** at top speed, like a rocket
bombance [bɔ̃bɑ̃s] *nf*: **faire ~** to have a feast, revel
bombarder [bɔ̃baʀde] *vt* to bomb; **~ qn de** *(cailloux, lettres)* to bombard sb with; **bombardier** *nm* bomber
bombe [bɔ̃b] *nf* bomb; *(atomiseur)* (aerosol) spray
bomber [bɔ̃be] *vi* to bulge; to camber ♦ *vt*: **~ le torse** to swell out one's chest

─────────── MOT CLÉ ───────────

bon, bonne [bɔ̃, bɔn] *adj* **1** *(agréable, satisfaisant)* good; **un ~ repas/restaurant** a good meal/restaurant; **être ~ en maths** to be good at maths
2 *(charitable)*: **être ~ (envers)** to be good (to)
3 *(correct)* right; **le ~ numéro/moment** the

right number/moment
4 (*souhaits*): ~ **anniversaire** happy birthday; ~ **voyage** have a good trip; **bonne chance** good luck; **bonne année** happy New Year; **bonne nuit** good night
5 (*approprié*): ~ **à/pour** fit to/for
6: ~ **enfant** *adj* accommodating, easygoing; **bonne femme** (*péj*) woman; **de bonne heure** early; ~ **marché** *adj inv* cheap; ♦ *adv* cheap; ~ **mot** witticism; ~ **sens** common sense; ~ **vivant** jovial chap; **bonnes œuvres** charitable works, charities
♦ *nm* **1** (*billet*) voucher; (*aussi*: ~ **cadeau**) gift voucher; ~ **d'essence** petrol coupon; ~ **du Trésor** Treasury bond
2: **avoir du** ~ to have its good points; **pour de** ~ for good
♦ *adv*: **il fait** ~ it's *ou* the weather is fine; **sentir** ~ to smell good; **tenir** ~ to stand firm
♦ *excl* good!; **ah** ~**?** really?; *voir aussi* **bonne**

bonbon [bɔ̃bɔ̃] *nm* (boiled) sweet
bonbonne [bɔ̃bɔn] *nf* demijohn
bond [bɔ̃] *nm* leap; **faire un** ~ to leap in the air
bonde [bɔ̃d] *nf* bunghole
bondé, e [bɔ̃de] *adj* packed (full)
bondir [bɔ̃diʀ] *vi* to leap
bonheur [bɔnœʀ] *nm* happiness; **porter** ~ (**à qn**) to bring (sb) luck; **au petit** ~ haphazardly; **par** ~ fortunately
bonhomie [bɔnɔmi] *nf* goodnaturedness
bonhomme [bɔnɔm] (*pl* **bonshommes**) *nm* fellow; ~ **de neige** snowman
bonification [bɔnifikasjɔ̃] *nf* bonus
bonifier [bɔnifje] *vt* to improve
boniment [bɔnimɑ̃] *nm* patter *no pl*
bonjour [bɔ̃ʒuʀ] *excl, nm* hello; good morning (*ou* afternoon)
bonne [bɔn] *adj voir* **bon** ♦ *nf* (*domestique*) maid; **à tout faire** general help; ~ **d'enfant** nanny; ~**ment** *adv*: **tout** ~**ment** quite simply
bonnet [bɔnɛ] *nm* bonnet, hat; (*de soutiengorge*) cup; ~ **d'âne** dunce's cap; ~ **de bain** bathing cap
bonneterie [bɔnɛtʀi] *nf* hosiery
bonshommes [bɔ̃zɔm] *nmpl de* **bonhomme**
bonsoir [bɔ̃swaʀ] *excl* good evening
bonté [bɔ̃te] *nf* kindness *no pl*
bonus [bɔnys] *nm* no-claims bonus
bord [bɔʀ] *nm* (*de table, verre, falaise*) edge; (*de rivière, lac*) bank; (*de route*) side; (**monter**) **à** ~ (to go) on board; **jeter par-dessus** ~ to throw overboard; **le commandant de** ~**/les hommes du** ~ the ship's master/crew; **au** ~ **de la mer** at the seaside; **être au** ~ **des larmes** to be on the verge of tears
bordeaux [bɔʀdo] *nm* Bordeaux (wine) ♦

adj inv maroon
bordel [bɔʀdɛl] *nm* brothel; (*fam!*) bloody mess (*!*)
border [bɔʀde] *vt* (*être le long de*) to border; to line; (*garnir*): ~ **qch de** to line sth with; to trim sth with; (*qn dans son lit*) to tuck up
bordereau, x [bɔʀdəʀo] *nm* slip; statement
bordure [bɔʀdyʀ] *nf* border; **en** ~ **de** on the edge of
borgne [bɔʀɲ(ə)] *adj* one-eyed
borne [bɔʀn(ə)] *nf* boundary stone; (*aussi*: ~ **kilométrique**) kilometre-marker, ≈ milestone; ~**s** *nfpl* (*fig*) limits; **dépasser les** ~**s** to go too far
borné, e [bɔʀne] *adj* narrow; narrow-minded
borner [bɔʀne] *vt* to limit; to confine; **se** ~ **à faire** to content o.s. with doing; to limit o.s. to doing
Bosnie-Herzégovine [bɔzni-ɛʀtzegɔvin] *nf* Bosnia (and) Herzegovina
bosquet [bɔskɛ] *nm* grove
bosse [bɔs] *nf* (*de terrain etc*) bump; (*enflure*) lump; (*du bossu, du chameau*) hump; **avoir la** ~ **des maths** *etc* to have a gift for maths *etc*; **il a roulé sa** ~ he's been around
bosser [bɔse] (*fam*) *vi* to work; to slave (away)
bossu, e [bɔsy] *nm/f* hunchback
bot [bo] *adj m*: **pied** ~ club foot
botanique [bɔtanik] *nf* botany ♦ *adj* botanic(al)
botte [bɔt] *nf* (*soulier*) (high) boot; (*gerbe*): ~ **de paille** bundle of straw; ~ **de radis** bunch of radishes; ~**s de caoutchouc** wellington boots; ~**r** [bɔte] *vt* to put boots on; to kick; (*fam*): **ça me botte** I fancy that
bottin [bɔtɛ̃] *nm* directory
bottine [bɔtin] *nf* ankle boot
bouc [buk] *nm* goat; (*barbe*) goatee; ~ **émissaire** scapegoat
boucan [bukɑ̃] *nm* din, racket
bouche [buʃ] *nf* mouth; **le** ~ **à** ~ the kiss of life; ~ **d'égout** manhole; ~ **d'incendie** fire hydrant; ~ **de métro** metro entrance
bouché, e [buʃe] *adj* (*temps, ciel*) overcast; (*péj: personne*) thick
bouchée [buʃe] *nf* mouthful; ~**s à la reine** chicken vol-au-vents
boucher, ère [buʃe, -ɛʀ] *nm/f* butcher ♦ *vt* (*pour colmater*) to stop up; to fill up; (*obstruer*) to block (up); **se** ~ *vi* (*tuyau etc*) to block up, get blocked up; **se** ~ **le nez** to hold one's nose; ~**rie** [buʃʀi] *nf* butcher's (shop); (*fig*) slaughter
bouche-trou [buʃtʀu] *nm* (*fig*) stop-gap
bouchon [buʃɔ̃] *nm* stopper; (*en liège*) cork; (*fig: embouteillage*) holdup; (*PÊCHE*) float; ~ **doseur** measuring cap
boucle [bukl(ə)] *nf* (*forme, figure*) loop;

(objet) buckle; ~ **(de cheveux)** curl; ~ **d'oreilles** earring

bouclé, e [bukle] *adj* curly

boucler [bukle] *vt (fermer: ceinture etc)* to fasten; *(: magasin)* to shut; *(terminer)* to finish off; *(: budget)* to balance; *(enfermer)* to shut away; *(: quartier)* to seal off ♦ *vi* to curl

bouclier [buklije] *nm* shield

bouddhiste [budist(ə)] *nm/f* Buddhist

bouder [bude] *vi* to sulk ♦ *vt* to turn one's nose up at; to refuse to have anything to do with

boudin [budɛ̃] *nm (CULIN)* black pudding

boue [bu] *nf* mud

bouée [bwe] *nf* buoy; ~ **(de sauvetage)** lifebuoy

boueux, euse [bwø, -øz] *adj* muddy ♦ *nm* refuse collector

bouffe [buf] *(fam) nf* grub *(fam)*, food

bouffée [bufe] *nf* puff; ~ **de fièvre/de honte** flush of fever/shame

bouffer [bufe] *(fam) vi* to eat

bouffi, e [bufi] *adj* swollen

bouge [buʒ] *nm* (low) dive; hovel

bougeoir [buʒwaʀ] *nm* candlestick

bougeotte [buʒɔt] *nf*: **avoir la** ~ to have the fidgets

bouger [buʒe] *vi* to move; *(dent etc)* to be loose; *(changer)* to alter; *(agir)* to stir ♦ *vt* to move

bougie [buʒi] *nf* candle; *(AUTO)* spark(ing) plug

bougon, ne [bugɔ̃, -ɔn] *adj* grumpy

bougonner [bugɔne] *vi, vt* to grumble

bouillabaisse [bujabɛs] *nf* type of fish soup

bouillant, e [bujɑ̃, -ɑ̃t] *adj (qui bout)* boiling; *(très chaud)* boiling (hot)

bouillie [buji] *nf* gruel; *(de bébé)* cereal; **en ~** *(fig)* crushed

bouillir [bujiʀ] *vi, vt* to boil

bouilloire [bujwaʀ] *nf* kettle

bouillon [bujɔ̃] *nm (CULIN)* stock *no pl*; ~**ner** [bujɔne] *vi* to bubble; *(fig)* to bubble up; to foam

bouillotte [bujɔt] *nf* hot-water bottle

boulanger, ère [bulɑ̃ʒe, -ɛʀ] *nm/f* baker

boulangerie [bulɑ̃ʒʀi] *nf* bakery

boule [bul] *nf (gén)* ball; *(pour jouer)* bowl; *(de machine à écrire)* golf-ball; **se mettre en** ~ *(fig: fam)* to fly off the handle, to blow one's top; ~ **de neige** snowball

bouleau, x [bulo] *nm* (silver) birch

boulet [bulɛ] *nm (aussi: ~ de canon)* cannonball

boulette [bulɛt] *nf* ball

boulevard [bulvaʀ] *nm* boulevard

bouleversement [bulvɛʀsəmɑ̃] *nm* upheaval

bouleverser [bulvɛʀse] *vt (émouvoir)* to overwhelm; *(causer du chagrin)* to distress; *(pays, vie)* to disrupt; *(papiers, objets)* to

turn upside down

boulier [bulje] *nm* abacus

boulon [bulɔ̃] *nm* bolt

boulot, te [bulo, -ɔt] *adj* plump, tubby ♦ *nm (fam: travail)* work

boum [bum] *nm* bang ♦ *nf (fam)* party

bouquet [bukɛ] *nm (de fleurs)* bunch (of flowers), bouquet; *(de persil etc)* bunch; *(parfum)* bouquet

bouquin [bukɛ̃] *(fam) nm* book; **bouquiner** *(fam) vi* to read; to browse around (in a bookshop); **bouquiniste** *nm/f* bookseller

bourbeux, euse [buʀbø, -øz] *adj* muddy

bourbier [buʀbje] *nm (quag)mire*

bourde [buʀd(ə)] *nf (erreur)* howler; *(gaffe)* blunder

bourdon [buʀdɔ̃] *nm* bumblebee

bourdonner [buʀdɔne] *vi* to buzz

bourg [buʀ] *nm* small market town

bourgeois, e [buʀʒwa, -waz] *adj (péj)* ≈ (upper) middle class; bourgeois; ~**ie** [buʀʒwazi] *nf* ≈ upper middle classes *pl*; bourgeoisie

bourgeon [buʀʒɔ̃] *nm* bud

Bourgogne [buʀgɔɲ] *nf*: **la** ~ Burgundy ♦ *nm*: **b**~ burgundy (wine)

bourguignon, ne [buʀgiɲɔ̃, -ɔn] *adj of ou* from Burgundy, Burgundian

bourlinguer [buʀlɛ̃ge] *vi* to knock about a lot, get around a lot

bourrade [buʀad] *nf* shove, thump

bourrage [buʀaʒ] *nm*: ~ **de crâne** brainwashing; *(SCOL)* cramming

bourrasque [buʀask(ə)] *nf* squall

bourratif, ive [buʀatif, -iv] *(fam) adj* filling, stodgy *(pej)*

bourré, e [buʀe] *adj (rempli)*: ~ **de** crammed full of; *(fam: ivre)* plastered, tanked up *(BRIT)*

bourreau, x [buʀo] *nm* executioner; *(fig)* torturer; ~ **de travail** workaholic

bourrelet [buʀlɛ] *nm* draught excluder; *(de peau)* fold *ou* roll (of flesh)

bourrer [buʀe] *vt (pipe)* to fill; *(poêle)* to pack; *(valise)* to cram (full)

bourrique [buʀik] *nf (âne)* ass

bourru, e [buʀy] *adj* surly, gruff

bourse [buʀs(ə)] *nf (subvention)* grant; *(porte-monnaie)* purse; **la B**~ the Stock Exchange

boursoufler [buʀsufle] *vt* to puff up, bloat

bous [bu] *vb voir* **bouillir**

bousculade [buskylad] *nf* rush; crush; **bousculer** [buskyle] *vt* to knock over; to knock into; *(fig)* to push, rush

bouse [buz] *nf* dung *no pl*

boussole [busɔl] *nf* compass

bout [bu] *vb voir* **bouillir** ♦ *nm* bit; *(d'un bâton etc)* tip; *(d'une ficelle, table, rue, période)* end; **au** ~ **de** at the end of, after; **pousser qn à** ~ to push sb to the limit; **venir à** ~ **de** to manage to finish; **à** ~ **por-**

tant at point-blank range; ~ **filtre** filter tip
boutade [butad] *nf* quip, sally
boute-en-train [butɑ̃trɛ̃] *nm inv* (*fig*) live wire
bouteille [butɛj] *nf* bottle; (*de gaz butane*) cylinder
boutique [butik] *nf* shop
bouton [butɔ̃] *nm* button; (*BOT*) bud; (*sur la peau*) spot; (*de porte*) knob; ~ **de manchette** cuff-link; ~ **d'or** buttercup; **boutonner** *vt* to button up; **boutonnière** *nf* buttonhole; **bouton-pression** *nm* press stud
bouture [butyʀ] *nf* cutting
bovins [bovɛ̃] *nmpl* cattle *pl*
bowling [boliŋ] *nm* (tenpin) bowling; (*salle*) bowling alley
box [bɔks] *nm* lock-up (garage); (*d'écurie*) loose-box
boxe [bɔks(ə)] *nf* boxing
boyau, x [bwajo] *nm* (*galerie*) passage(way); (narrow) gallery; ~**x** *nmpl* (*viscères*) entrails, guts
B.P. *abr* = **boîte postale**
bracelet [bʀaslɛ] *nm* bracelet; **bracelet-montre** *nm* wristwatch
braconnier [bʀakɔnje] *nm* poacher
brader [bʀade] *vt* to sell off; ~**ie** [bʀadʀi] *nf* cut-price shop *ou* stall
braguette [bʀagɛt] *nf* fly *ou* flies *pl* (*BRIT*), zipper (*US*)
brailler [bʀaje] *vi* to bawl, yell
braire [bʀɛʀ] *vi* to bray
braise [bʀɛz] *nf* embers *pl*
brancard [bʀɑ̃kaʀ] *nm* (*civière*) stretcher; **brancardier** *nm* stretcher-bearer
branchages [bʀɑ̃ʃaʒ] *nmpl* boughs
branche [bʀɑ̃ʃ] *nf* branch
branché, e [bʀɑ̃ʃe] (*fam*) *adj* trendy
brancher [bʀɑ̃ʃe] *vt* to connect (up); (*en mettant la prise*) to plug in
branle [bʀɑ̃l] *nm*: **donner le ~ à, mettre en ~** to set in motion
branle-bas [bʀɑ̃lba] *nm inv* commotion
braquer [bʀake] *vi* (*AUTO*) to turn (the wheel) ♦ *vt* (*revolver etc*): ~ **qch sur** to aim sth at, point sth at; (*mettre en colère*): ~ **qn** to put sb's back up
bras [bʀa] *nm* arm ♦ *nmpl* (*fig: travailleurs*) labour *sg*, hands; **à ~ raccourcis** with fists flying; ~ **droit** (*fig*) right hand man
brasier [bʀazje] *nm* blaze, inferno
bras-le-corps [bʀalkɔʀ] : **à ~** *adv* (a)round the waist
brassard [bʀasaʀ] *nm* armband
brasse [bʀas] *nf* (*nage*) breast-stroke; ~ **papillon** butterfly
brassée [bʀase] *nf* armful
brasser [bʀase] *vt* to mix; ~ **l'argent/les affaires** to handle a lot of money/business
brasserie [bʀasʀi] *nf* (*restaurant*) café-restaurant; (*usine*) brewery

brave [bʀav] *adj* (*courageux*) brave; (*bon, gentil*) good, kind
braver [bʀave] *vt* to defy
bravo [bʀavo] *excl* bravo ♦ *nm* cheer
bravoure [bʀavuʀ] *nf* bravery
break [bʀɛk] *nm* (*AUTO*) estate car
brebis [bʀəbi] *nf* ewe; ~ **galeuse** black sheep
brèche [bʀɛʃ] *nf* breach, gap; **être sur la ~** (*fig*) to be on the go
bredouille [bʀəduj] *adj* empty-handed
bredouiller [bʀəduje] *vi, vt* to mumble, stammer
bref, brève [bʀɛf, bʀɛv] *adj* short, brief ♦ *adv* in short; **d'un ton ~** sharply, curtly; **en ~** in short, in brief
Brésil [bʀezil] *nm* Brazil
Bretagne [bʀətaɲ] *nf* Brittany
bretelle [bʀətɛl] *nf* (*de fusil etc*) sling; (*de vêtement*) strap; (*d'autoroute*) slip road (*BRIT*), entrance/exit ramp (*US*); ~**s** *nfpl* (*pour pantalon*) braces (*BRIT*), suspenders (*US*)
breton, ne [bʀətɔ̃, -ɔn] *adj, nm/f* Breton
breuvage [bʀœvaʒ] *nm* beverage, drink
brève [bʀɛv] *adj voir* **bref**
brevet [bʀəvɛ] *nm* diploma, certificate; ~ **d'études du premier cycle** school certificate (*taken at age 16*); ~ **(d'invention)** patent; **breveté, e** *adj* patented; (*diplômé*) qualified
bribes [bʀib] *nfpl* bits, scraps; snatches; **par ~** piecemeal
bricolage [bʀikɔlaʒ] *nm*: **le ~** do-it-yourself
bricole [bʀikɔl] *nf* trifle; small job
bricoler [bʀikɔle] *vi* to do DIY jobs; to potter about ♦ *vt* to fix up; to tinker with; **bricoleur, euse** *nm/f* handyman(woman), DIY enthusiast
bride [bʀid] *nf* bridle; (*d'un bonnet*) string, tie; **à ~ abattue** flat out, hell for leather; **laisser la ~ sur le cou à** to give free rein to
bridé, e [bʀide] *adj*: **yeux ~s** slit eyes
bridge [bʀidʒ(ə)] *nm* bridge
brièvement [bʀijɛvmɑ̃] *adv* briefly
brigade [bʀigad] *nf* (*POLICE*) squad; (*MIL*) brigade; (*gén*) team
brigadier [bʀigadje] *nm* sergeant
brigandage [bʀigɑ̃daʒ] *nm* robbery
briguer [bʀige] *vt* to aspire to
brillamment [bʀijamɑ̃] *adv* brilliantly
brillant, e [bʀijɑ̃, -ɑ̃t] *adj* brilliant; bright; (*luisant*) shiny, shining ♦ *nm* (*diamant*) brilliant
briller [bʀije] *vi* to shine
brimer [bʀime] *vt* to harass; to bully
brin [bʀɛ̃] *nm* (*de laine, ficelle etc*) strand; (*fig*): **un ~ de** a bit of; ~ **d'herbe** blade of grass; ~ **de muguet** sprig of lily of the valley
brindille [bʀɛ̃dij] *nf* twig

brio [brijo] *nm:* **avec ~** with panache
brioche [brijɔʃ] *nf* brioche (bun); *(fam:
ventre)* paunch
brique [brik] *nf* brick ♦ *adj inv* brick red
briquer [brike] *vt* to polish up
briquet [brike] *nm* (cigarette) lighter
brise [briz] *nf* breeze
briser [brize] *vt* to break; **se ~** *vi* to break
britannique [britanik] *adj* British ♦ *nm/f:*
B~ British person, Briton; **les B~s** the
British
brocante [brɔkɑ̃t] *nf* junk, second-hand
goods *pl*
brocanteur, euse [brɔkɑ̃tœr, -øz] *nm/f*
junkshop owner; junk dealer
broche [brɔʃ] *nf* brooch; *(CULIN)* spit;
(MÉD) pin; **à la ~** spit-roasted
broché, e [brɔʃe] *adj (livre)* paper-backed
brochet [brɔʃe] *nm* pike *inv*
brochette [brɔʃet] *nf* skewer
brochure [brɔʃyr] *nf* pamphlet, brochure,
booklet
broder [brɔde] *vt* to embroider ♦ *vi* to embroider the facts; **broderie** *nf* embroidery
broncher [brɔ̃ʃe] *vi:* **sans ~** without
flinching; without turning a hair
bronches [brɔ̃ʃ] *nfpl* bronchial tubes; **bronchite** *nf* bronchitis
bronze [brɔ̃z] *nm* bronze
bronzer [brɔ̃ze] *vt* to tan ♦ *vi* to get a tan;
se ~ to sunbathe
brosse [brɔs] *nf* brush; **coiffé en ~** with a
crewcut; **~ à cheveux** hairbrush; **~ à
dents** toothbrush; **~ à habits** clothesbrush;
brosser *vt (nettoyer)* to brush; *(fig: tableau
etc)* to paint; to draw; **se brosser les dents**
to brush one's teeth
brouette [bruɛt] *nf* wheelbarrow
brouhaha [bruaa] *nm* hubbub
brouillard [brujar] *nm* fog
brouille [bruj] *nf* quarrel
brouiller [bruje] *vt* to mix up; to confuse;
(rendre trouble) to cloud; *(désunir: amis)* to
set at odds; **se ~** *vi (vue)* to cloud over;
(détails) to become confused; *(gens)* to fall
out
brouillon, ne [brujɔ̃, -ɔn] *adj* disorganised;
unmethodical ♦ *nm* draft
broussailles [brusaj] *nfpl* undergrowth *sg;*
broussailleux, euse *adj* bushy
brousse [brus] *nf:* **la ~** the bush
brouter [brute] *vi* to graze
broutille [brutij] *nf* trifle
broyer [brwaje] *vt* to crush; **~ du noir** to
be down in the dumps
bru [bry] *nf* daughter-in-law
brugnon [bryɲɔ̃] *nm (BOT)* nectarine
bruiner [bruine] *vb impers:* **il bruine** it's
drizzling, there's a drizzle
bruire [bruir] *vi* to murmur; to rustle
bruit [brui] *nm:* **un ~** a noise, a sound;
(fig: rumeur) a rumour; **le ~** noise; **sans ~**

without a sound, noiselessly; **~ de fond**
background noise
bruitage [bruitaʒ] *nm* sound effects *pl*
brûlant, e [brylɑ̃, -ɑ̃t] *adj* burning; *(liquide)*
boiling (hot); *(regard)* fiery
brûlé, e [bryle] *adj (fig: démasqué)* blown
♦ *nm:* **odeur de ~** smell of burning
brûle-pourpoint [brylpurpwɛ̃] : **à ~** *adv*
point-blank
brûler [bryle] *vt* to burn; *(suj: eau bouil-
lante)* to scald; *(consommer: électricité, essence)* to use; *(feu rouge, signal)* to go
through ♦ *vi* to burn; *(jeu)* to be warm; **se
~** to burn o.s.; to scald o.s.; **se ~ la cervelle** to blow one's brains out
brûlure [brylyr] *nf (lésion)* burn; *(sensation)* burning (sensation); **~s d'estomac**
heartburn *sg*
brume [brym] *nf* mist
brun, e [brœ̃, -yn] *adj* brown; *(cheveux,
personne)* dark; **brunir** *vi* to get a tan
brusque [brysk(ə)] *adj* abrupt; **brusquer**
vt to rush
brut, e [bryt] *adj* raw, crude, rough;
(COMM) gross; *(données)* raw; **(pétrole) ~**
crude (oil)
brutal, e, aux [brytal, -o] *adj* brutal; **brutaliser** *vt* to handle roughly, manhandle
Bruxelles [brysɛl] *n* Brussels
bruyamment [bruijamɑ̃] *adv* noisily
bruyant, e [bruijɑ̃, -ɑ̃t] *adj* noisy
bruyère [bruijɛr] *nf* heather
bu, e *pp de* **boire**
buccal, e, aux [bykal, -o] *adj:* **par voie ~e**
orally
bûche [byʃ] *nf* log; **prendre une ~** *(fig)* to
come a cropper; **~ de Noël** Yule log; **~r**
[byʃe] *nm* pyre; bonfire ♦ *vi (fam)* to swot
(BRIT), slave *(away)* ♦ *vt* to swot up *(BRIT)*,
slave away at; **~ron** [byʃrɔ̃] *nm* woodcut-
ter
budget [bydʒe] *nm* budget
buée [bye] *nf (sur une vitre)* mist; *(de
l'haleine)* steam
buffet [byfe] *nm (meuble)* sideboard; *(de réception)* buffet; **~ (de gare)** (station) buffet,
snack bar
buffle [byfl(ə)] *nm* buffalo
buis [bui] *nm* box tree; *(bois)* box(wood)
buisson [buisɔ̃] *nm* bush
buissonnière [buisɔnjɛr] *adj:* **faire l'école
~** to skip school
bulbe [bylb(ə)] *nm (BOT, ANAT)* bulb; *(coupole)* onion-shaped dome
Bulgarie [bylgari] *nf* Bulgaria
bulle [byl] *nf* bubble
bulletin [byltɛ̃] *nm (communiqué, journal)*
bulletin; *(papier)* form; *(SCOL)* report; **~
d'informations** news bulletin; **~ de salaire**
pay-slip; **~ (de vote)** ballot paper; **~ mé-
téorologique** weather report
bureau, x [byro] *nm (meuble)* desk; *(pièce,*

service) office; ~ **de change** (foreign) exchange office *ou* bureau; ~ **de location** box office; ~ **de poste** post office; ~ **de tabac** tobacconist's (shop); ~ **de vote** polling station; **bureaucratie** nf bureaucracy
bureautique [byʀotik] nf office automation
burin [byʀɛ̃] nm cold chisel; (ART) burin
burlesque [byʀlɛsk(ə)] adj ridiculous; (LITTÉRATURE) burlesque
bus¹ [by] vb voir **boire**; **bus²** [bys] nm bus
busqué, e [byske] adj (nez) hook(ed)
buste [byst(ə)] nm (ANAT) chest; bust
but [by] vb voir **boire** ♦ nm (cible) target; (fig) goal; aim; (FOOTBALL etc) goal; **de ~ en blanc** point-blank; **avoir pour ~ de faire** to aim to do; **dans le ~ de** with the intention of
butane [bytan] nm butane; Calor gas (®)
buté, e [byte] adj stubborn, obstinate
buter [byte] vi: ~ **contre/sur** to bump into; to stumble against ♦ vt to antagonize; **se ~** vi to get obstinate; to dig in one's heels
butin [bytɛ̃] nm booty, spoils pl; (d'un vol) loot
butte [byt] nf mound, hillock; **être en ~ à** to be exposed to
buvais etc vb voir **boire**
buvard [byvaʀ] nm blotter
buvette [byvɛt] nf bar
buveur, euse [byvœʀ, -øz] nm/f drinker

C c

c' [s] dét voir **ce**
ça [sa] pron (pour désigner) this; (: plus loin) that; (comme sujet indéfini) it; ~ **va?** how are you?; how are things?; (d'accord?) OK?, all right?; ~ **alors!** well really!; ~ **fait 10 ans (que)** it's 10 years (since); **c'est** ~ that's right
çà [sa] adv: ~ **et là** here and there
cabane [kaban] nf hut, cabin
cabaret [kabaʀɛ] nm night club
cabas [kaba] nm shopping bag
cabillaud [kabijo] nm cod inv
cabine [kabin] nf (de bateau) cabin; (de plage) (beach) hut; (de piscine etc) cubicle; (de camion, train) cab; (d'avion) cockpit; ~ **d'essayage** fitting room; ~ **spatiale** space capsule; ~ **(téléphonique)** call ou (tele)phone box
cabinet [kabinɛ] nm (petite pièce) closet;

(de médecin) surgery (BRIT), office (US); (de notaire etc) office; (: clientèle) practice; (POL) Cabinet; ~**s** nmpl (w.-c.) toilet sg; ~ **d'affaires** business consultants' (bureau), business partnership; ~ **de toilette** toilet; ~ **de travail** study
câble [kabl(ə)] nm cable
cabrer [kabʀe]: **se ~** vi (cheval) to rear up; (avion) to nose up; (fig) to revolt, rebel
cabriole [kabʀijɔl] nf caper; somersault
cacahuète [kakaɥɛt] nf peanut
cacao [kakao] nm cocoa (powder); (boisson) cocoa
cache [kaʃ] nm mask, card (for masking) ♦ nf hiding place
cache-cache [kaʃkaʃ] nm: **jouer à ~** to play hide-and-seek
cachemire [kaʃmiʀ] nm cashmere
cache-nez [kaʃne] nm inv scarf, muffler
cacher [kaʃe] vt to hide, conceal; **se ~** vi to hide; to be hidden ou concealed; ~ **qch à qn** to hide ou conceal sth from sb; **il ne s'en cache pas** he makes no secret of it
cachet [kaʃɛ] nm (comprimé) tablet; (sceau: du roi) seal; (: de la poste) postmark; (rétribution) fee; (fig) style, character; **cacheter** vt to seal
cachette [kaʃɛt] nf hiding place; **en ~** on the sly, secretly
cachot [kaʃo] nm dungeon
cachotterie [kaʃɔtʀi] nf: **faire des ~s** to be secretive
cactus [kaktys] nm cactus
cadavre [kadavʀ(ə)] nm corpse, (dead) body
caddie [kadi] nm (supermarket) trolley
caddy nm = **caddie**
cadeau, x [kado] nm present, gift; **faire un ~ à qn** to give sb a present ou gift; **faire ~ de qch à qn** to make a present of sth to sb, give sb sth as a present
cadenas [kadna] nm padlock
cadence [kadɑ̃s] nf (MUS) cadence; (: tempo) rhythm; (de travail etc) rate; **en ~** rhythmically; in time
cadet, te [kadɛ, -ɛt] adj younger; (le plus jeune) youngest ♦ nm/f youngest child ou one, youngest boy ou son/girl ou daughter
cadran [kadʀɑ̃] nm dial; ~ **solaire** sundial
cadre [kadʀ(ə)] nm frame; (environnement) surroundings pl; (limites) scope ♦ nm/f (ADMIN) managerial employee, executive; **dans le ~ de** (fig) within the framework ou context of; **rayer qn des ~s** to dismiss sb
cadrer [kadʀe] vi: ~ **avec** to tally ou correspond with ♦ vt to centre
caduc, uque [kadyk] adj obsolete; (BOT) deciduous
cafard [kafaʀ] nm cockroach; **avoir le ~** to be down in the dumps
café [kafe] nm coffee; (bistro) café ♦ adj inv coffee(-coloured); ~ **au lait** white coffee; ~

FRANÇAIS–ANGLAIS 30

noir black coffee; ~ tabac *tobacconist's or newsagent's serving coffee and spirits*; **cafetière** nf (*pot*) coffee-pot
cafouillage [kafujaʒ] nm shambles sg
cage [kaʒ] nf cage; ~ **(des buts)** goal; ~ **d'escalier** (stair)well; ~ **thoracique** rib cage
cageot [kaʒo] nm crate
cagibi [kaʒibi] nm shed
cagneux, euse [kaɲø, -øz] adj knock-kneed
cagnotte [kaɲɔt] nf kitty
cagoule [kagul] nf cowl; hood; (*SKI etc*) cagoule
cahier [kaje] nm notebook; ~ **de brouillons** roughbook, jotter; ~ **d'exercices** exercise book
cahot [kao] nm jolt, bump
caïd [kaid] nm big chief, boss
caille [kaj] nf quail
cailler [kaje] vi (*lait*) to curdle; (*sang*) to clot
caillot [kajo] nm (blood) clot
caillou, x [kaju] nm (little) stone; **cailloux, euse** adj stony; pebbly
Caire [kɛʀ] nm: **le** ~ Cairo
caisse [kɛs] nf box; (*où l'on met la recette*) cashbox; till; (*où l'on paye*) cash desk (*BRIT*), check-out; (*de banque*) cashier's desk; (*TECH*) case, casing; ~ **d'épargne** savings bank; ~ **de retraite** pension fund; ~ **enregistreuse** cash register; **caissier, ière** nm/f cashier
cajoler [kaʒɔle] vt to wheedle, coax; to surround with love
cake [kɛk] nm fruit cake
calandre [kalɑ̃dʀ(ə)] nf radiator grill
calanque [kalɑ̃k] nf rocky inlet
calcaire [kalkɛʀ] nm limestone ♦ adj (*eau*) hard; (*GÉO*) limestone cpd
calciné, e [kalsine] adj burnt to ashes
calcul [kalkyl] nm calculation; **le** ~ (*SCOL*) arithmetic; ~ **(biliaire)** (gall)stone; ~ **(rénal)** (kidney) stone; **calculateur** nm calculator; **calculatrice** nf calculator
calculer [kalkyle] vt to calculate, work out; (*combiner*) to calculate
calculette [kalkylɛt] nf pocket calculator
cale [kal] nf (*de bateau*) hold; (*en bois*) wedge; ~ **sèche** dry dock
calé, e [kale] adj (*fam*) clever, bright
caleçon [kalsɔ̃] nm pair of underpants, trunks pl
calembour [kalɑ̃buʀ] nm pun
calendes [kalɑ̃d] nfpl: **renvoyer aux** ~ **grecques** to postpone indefinitely
calendrier [kalɑ̃dʀije] nm calendar; (*fig*) timetable
calepin [kalpɛ̃] nm notebook
caler [kale] vt to wedge; ~ **(son moteur/ véhicule)** to stall (one's engine/vehicle)
calfeutrer [kalføtʀe] vt to (make) draught-proof; **se** ~ vi to make o.s. snug and comfortable
calibre [kalibʀ(ə)] nm (*d'un fruit*) grade; (*d'une arme*) bore, calibre; (*fig*) calibre
califourchon [kalifuʀʃɔ̃]: **à** ~ adv astride
câlin, e [kalɛ̃, -in] adj cuddly, cuddlesome; tender
câliner [kaline] vt to fondle, cuddle
calmant [kalmɑ̃] nm tranquillizer, sedative; (*pour la douleur*) painkiller
calme [kalm(ə)] adj calm, quiet ♦ nm calm(ness), quietness
calmer [kalme] vt to calm (down); (*douleur, inquiétude*) to ease, soothe; **se** ~ vi to calm down
calomnie [kalɔmni] nf slander; (*écrite*) libel; **calomnier** vt to slander; to libel
calorie [kalɔʀi] nf calorie
calorifuge [kalɔʀifyʒ] adj (heat-) insulating, heat-retaining
calotte [kalɔt] nf (*coiffure*) skullcap; (*gifle*) slap; **calotte glaciaire** (*GÉO*) icecap
calquer [kalke] vt to trace; (*fig*) to copy exactly
calvaire [kalvɛʀ] nm (*croix*) wayside cross, calvary; (*souffrances*) suffering
calvitie [kalvisi] nf baldness
camarade [kamaʀad] nm/f friend, pal; (*POL*) comrade; **camaraderie** nf friendship
cambouis [kɑ̃bwi] nm dirty oil ou grease
cambrer [kɑ̃bʀe] vt to arch
cambriolage [kɑ̃bʀijɔlaʒ] nm burglary; **cambrioler** [kɑ̃bʀijɔle] vt to burgle (*BRIT*), burglarize (*US*); **cambrioleur, euse** nm/f burglar
came [kam] nf: **arbre à** ~**s** camshaft
camelote [kamlɔt] nf rubbish, trash, junk
caméra [kameʀa] nf (*CINÉMA, TV*) camera; (*d'amateur*) cine-camera
caméscope nm camcorder
camion [kamjɔ̃] nm lorry (*BRIT*), truck; (*plus petit, fermé*) van; ~ **de dépannage** breakdown (*BRIT*) ou tow (*US*) truck; **camion-citerne** nm tanker; **camionnette** nf (small) van; **camionneur** nm (*entrepreneur*) haulage contractor (*BRIT*), trucker (*US*); (*chauffeur*) lorry (*BRIT*) ou truck driver; van driver
camisole [kamizɔl] nf: ~ **(de force)** straitjacket
camomille [kamɔmij] nf camomile; (*boisson*) camomile tea
camoufler [kamufle] vt to camouflage; (*fig*) to conceal, cover up
camp [kɑ̃] nm camp; (*fig*) side
campagnard, e [kɑ̃paɲaʀ, -aʀd(ə)] adj country cpd
campagne [kɑ̃paɲ] nf country, countryside; (*MIL, POL, COMM*) campaign; **à la** ~ in the country
camper [kɑ̃pe] vi to camp ♦ vt to sketch; **se** ~ **devant** to plant o.s. in front of; **cam-**

peur, euse nm/f camper
camphre [kɑ̃fʀ(ə)] nm camphor
camping [kɑ̃piŋ] nm camping; **(terrain de)** ~ campsite, camping site; **faire du** ~ to go camping
Canada [kanada] nm: **le** ~ Canada; **canadien, ne** adj, nm/f Canadian; **canadienne** nf (veste) fur-lined jacket
canaille [kanɑj] (péj) nf scoundrel
canal, aux [kanal, -o] nm canal; (naturel) channel; **canalisation** [kanalizɑsjɔ̃] nf (tuyau) pipe; **canaliser** [kanalize] vt to canalize; (fig) to channel
canapé [kanape] nm settee, sofa
canard [kanaʀ] nm duck
canari [kanaʀi] nm canary
cancans [kɑ̃kɑ̃] nmpl (malicious) gossip sg
cancer [kɑ̃sɛʀ] nm cancer; (signe): **le C~** Cancer; ~ **de la peau** skin cancer
cancre [kɑ̃kʀ(ə)] nm dunce
candeur [kɑ̃dœʀ] nf ingenuousness, guilelessness
candidat, e [kɑ̃dida, -at] nm/f candidate; (à un poste) applicant, candidate; **candidature** nf candidature; application; **poser sa candidature** to submit an application, apply
candide [kɑ̃did] adj ingenuous, guileless
cane [kan] nf (female) duck
caneton [kantɔ̃] nm duckling
canette [kanɛt] nf (de bière) (flip-top) bottle
canevas [kanva] nm (COUTURE) canvas
caniche [kaniʃ] nm poodle
canicule [kanikyl] nf scorching heat
canif [kanif] nm penknife, pocket knife
canine [kanin] nf canine (tooth)
caniveau, x [kanivo] nm gutter
canne [kan] nf (walking) stick; ~ **à pêche** fishing rod; ~ **à sucre** sugar cane
cannelle [kanɛl] nf cinnamon
canoë [kanɔe] nm canoe; (sport) canoeing
canon [kanɔ̃] nm (arme) gun; (HISTOIRE) cannon; (d'une arme: tube) barrel; (fig) model; (MUS) canon; ~ **rayé** rifled barrel
canot [kano] nm ding(h)y; ~ **de sauvetage** lifeboat; ~ **pneumatique** inflatable ding(h)y; ~**age** nm rowing; ~**ier** [kanɔtje] nm boater
cantatrice [kɑ̃tatʀis] nf (opera) singer
cantine [kɑ̃tin] nf canteen
cantique [kɑ̃tik] nm hymn
canton [kɑ̃tɔ̃] nm district consisting of several communes; (en Suisse) canton
cantonade [kɑ̃tɔnad] : **à la** ~ adv to everyone in general; from the rooftops
cantonner [kɑ̃tɔne] vt (MIL) to quarter, station; **se** ~ **dans** to confine o.s. to
cantonnier [kɑ̃tɔnje] nm roadmender
canular [kanylaʀ] nm hoax
caoutchouc [kautʃu] nm rubber; ~ **mousse** foam rubber

cap [kap] nm (GÉO) cape; headland; (fig) hurdle; watershed; (NAVIG): **changer de** ~ to change course; **mettre le** ~ **sur** to head ou steer for
C.A.P. sigle m (= Certificat d'aptitude professionnelle) vocational training certificate taken at secondary school
capable [kapabl(ə)] adj able, capable; ~ **de qch/faire** capable of sth/doing
capacité [kapasite] nf (compétence) ability; (JUR, contenance) capacity; ~ **(en droit)** basic legal qualification
cape [kap] nf cape, cloak; **rire sous** ~ to laugh up one's sleeve
C.A.P.E.S. [kapɛs] sigle m (= Certificat d'aptitude pédagogique à l'enseignement secondaire) teaching diploma
capillaire [kapilɛʀ] adj (soins, lotion) hair cpd; (vaisseau etc) capillary
capitaine [kapitɛn] nm captain
capital, e, aux [kapital, -o] adj major; of paramount importance; fundamental ♦ nm capital; (fig) stock; asset; voir aussi **capitaux**; ~ **(social)** authorized capital; ~**e** nf (ville) capital; (lettre) capital (letter); ~**iser** vt to amass, build up; ~**isme** nm capitalism; ~**iste** adj, nm/f capitalist; **capitaux** [kapito] nmpl (fonds) capital sg
capitonné, e [kapitɔne] adj padded
caporal, aux [kapɔʀal, -o] nm lance corporal
capot [kapo] nm (AUTO) bonnet (BRIT), hood (US)
capote [kapɔt] nf (de voiture) hood (BRIT), top (US); (fam) condom
capoter [kapɔte] vi to overturn
câpre [kɑpʀ(ə)] nf caper
caprice [kapʀis] nm whim, caprice; passing fancy; **capricieux, euse** adj capricious; whimsical; temperamental
Capricorne [kapʀikɔʀn] nm: **le** ~ Capricorn
capsule [kapsyl] nf (de bouteille) cap; (BOT etc, spatiale) capsule
capter [kapte] vt (ondes radio) to pick up; (eau) to harness; (fig) to win, capture
captivant, e [kaptivɑ̃, ɑ̃t] adj captivating; fascinating
captivité [kaptivite] nf captivity
capturer [kaptyʀe] vt to capture
capuche [kapyʃ] nf hood
capuchon [kapyʃɔ̃] nm hood; (de stylo) cap, top
caquet [kakɛ] nm: **rabattre le** ~ **à qn** to bring sb down a peg or two
caqueter [kakte] vi to cackle
car [kaʀ] nm coach ♦ conj because, for
carabine [kaʀabin] nf carbine, rifle
caractère [kaʀaktɛʀ] nm (gén) character; **avoir bon/mauvais** ~ to be good-/ill-natured; **en** ~**s gras** in bold type; **en petits** ~**s** in small print; ~**s d'imprimerie**

(block) capitals; **caractériel, le** *adj* (of) character ♦ *nm/f* emotionally disturbed child

caractérisé, e [karakterize] *adj:* **c'est une grippe ~e** it is a clear (-cut) case of flu

caractéristique [karakteristik] *adj, nf* characteristic

carafe [karaf] *nf* decanter; carafe

caraïbe [karaib] *adj* Caribbean ♦ *n:* **les C~s** the Caribbean (Islands); **la mer des C~s** the Caribbean Sea

carambolage [karãbɔlaʒ] *nm* multiple crash, pileup

caramel [karamɛl] *nm* (*bonbon*) caramel, toffee; (*substance*) caramel

carapace [karapas] *nf* shell

caravane [karavan] *nf* caravan; **caravaning** *nm* caravanning; (*emplacement*) caravan site

carbone [karbɔn] *nm* carbon; (*feuille*) carbon, sheet of carbon paper; (*double*) carbon (copy); **carbonique** [karbɔnik] *adj:* **neige carbonique** dry ice; **carbonisé, e** [karbɔnize] *adj* charred

carburant [karbyrã] *nm* (motor) fuel

carburateur [karbyratœr] *nm* carburettor

carcan [karkã] *nm* (*fig*) yoke, shackles *pl*

carcasse [karkas] *nf* carcass; (*de véhicule etc*) shell

cardiaque [kardjak] *adj* cardiac, heart *cpd* ♦ *nm/f* heart patient

cardigan [kardigã] *nm* cardigan

cardiologue [kardjɔlɔg] *nm/f* cardiologist, heart specialist

carême [karɛm] *nm:* **le C~** Lent

carence [karãs] *nf* incompetence, inadequacy; (*manque*) deficiency

caresse [karɛs] *nf* caress

caresser [karese] *vt* to caress, fondle; (*fig: projet*) to toy with

cargaison [kargɛzɔ̃] *nf* cargo, freight

cargo [kargo] *nm* cargo boat, freighter

carie [kari] *nf:* **la ~ (dentaire)** tooth decay; **une ~** a bad tooth

carillon [karijɔ̃] *nm* (*d'église*) bells *pl*; (*de pendule*) chimes *pl*; (*de porte*) door chime *ou* bell

carlingue [karlɛ̃g] *nf* cabin

carnassier, ière [karnasje, -jɛr] *adj* carnivorous

carnaval [karnaval] *nm* carnival

carnet [karnɛ] *nm* (*calepin*) notebook; (*de tickets, timbres etc*) book; (*d'école*) school report; (*journal intime*) diary; **~ de chèques** cheque book

carotte [karɔt] *nf* carrot

carpette [karpɛt] *nf* rug

carré, e [kare] *adj* square; (*fig: franc*) straightforward ♦ *nm* (*de terrain, jardin*) patch, plot; (*MATH*) square; **mètre/kilomètre ~** square metre/kilometre

carreau, x [karo] *nm* (*en faïence etc*)

(floor) tile; (wall) tile; (*de fenêtre*) (window) pane; (*motif*) check, square; (*CARTES: couleur*) diamonds *pl*; (*: carte*) diamond; **tissu à ~x** checked fabric

carrefour [karfur] *nm* crossroads *sg*

carrelage [karlaʒ] *nm* tiling; (tiled) floor

carrelet [karlɛ] *nm* (*poisson*) plaice

carrément [karemã] *adv* straight out, bluntly; completely, altogether

carrière [karjɛr] *nf* (*de roches*) quarry; (*métier*) career; **militaire de ~** professional soldier

carriole [karjɔl] *nf* (*péj*) old cart

carrossable [karɔsabl(ə)] *adj* suitable for (motor) vehicles

carrosse [karɔs] *nm* (horse-drawn) coach

carrosserie [karɔsri] *nf* body, coachwork *no pl*; (*activité, commerce*) coachbuilding

carrure [karyr] *nf* build; (*fig*) stature, calibre

cartable [kartabl(ə)] *nm* (*d'écolier*) satchel, (school)bag

carte [kart(ə)] *nf* (*de géographie*) map; (*marine, du ciel*) chart; (*de fichier, d'abonnement etc, à jouer*) card; (*au restaurant*) menu; (*aussi:* **~ postale**) (post)card; (*: ~ de visite*) (visiting) card; **à la ~** (*au restaurant*) à la carte; **~ bancaire** cash card; **~ de crédit** credit card; **~ d'identité** identity card; **~ de séjour** residence permit; **~ grise** (*AUTO*) ≈ (car) registration book, logbook; **~ routière** road map; **~ téléphonique** phonecard

carter [kartɛr] *nm* sump

carton [kartɔ̃] *nm* (*matériau*) cardboard; (*boîte*) (cardboard) box; (*d'invitation*) invitation card; **faire un ~** (*au tir*) to have a go at the rifle range; to score a hit; **~ (à dessin)** portfolio; **cartonné, e** *adj* (*livre*) hardback, cased; **carton-pâte** *nm* pasteboard

cartouche [kartuʃ] *nf* cartridge; (*de cigarettes*) carton

cas [ka] *nm* case; **faire peu de ~/grand ~ de** to attach little/great importance to; **en aucun ~** on no account; **au ~ où** in case; **en ~ de** in case of, in the event of; **en ~ de besoin** if need be; **en tout ~** in any case, at any rate; **~ de conscience** matter of conscience

casanier, ière [kazanje, -jɛr] *adj* stay-at-home

cascade [kaskad] *nf* waterfall, cascade; (*fig*) stream, torrent

cascadeur, euse [kaskadœr, -øz] *nm/f* stuntman(girl)

case [kaz] *nf* (*hutte*) hut; (*compartiment*) compartment; (*pour le courrier*) pigeonhole; (*sur un formulaire, de mots croisés etc*) box

caser [kaze] *vt* (*trouver de la place pour*) to put (away); to put up; (*fig*) to find a job for; to marry off

caserne [kazɛrn(ə)] *nf* barracks *pl*

cash [kaʃ] adv: **payer** ~ to pay cash down

casier [kazje] nm (à journaux etc) rack; (de bureau) filing cabinet; (: à cases) set of pigeonholes; (case) compartment; pigeonhole; (: à clef) locker; ~ **judiciaire** police record

casino [kazino] nm casino

casque [kask(ə)] nm helmet; (chez le coiffeur) (hair-)drier; (pour audition) (head-)phones pl, headset

casquette [kaskɛt] nf cap

cassant, e [kasɑ̃, -ɑ̃t] adj brittle; (fig) brusque, abrupt

cassation [kasasjɔ̃] nf: **cour de** ~ final court of appeal

casse [kas] nf (pour voitures): **mettre à la** ~ to scrap; (dégâts): **il y a eu de la** ~ there were a lot of breakages; ~**-cou** adj inv daredevil, reckless; ~**-croûte** nm inv snack; ~**-noisette(s)** nm inv nutcrackers pl; ~**-noix** nm inv nutcrackers pl; ~**-pieds** (fam) adj inv: **il est** ~**-pieds** he's a pain in the neck

casser [kase] vt to break; (ADMIN: gradé) to demote; (JUR) to quash; **se** ~ vi to break

casserole [kasrɔl] nf saucepan

casse-tête [kastɛt] nm inv (jeu) brain teaser; (difficultés) headache (fig)

cassette [kasɛt] nf (bande magnétique) cassette; (coffret) casket

casseur [kasœʀ] nm hooligan

cassis [kasis] nm blackcurrant

cassoulet [kasulɛ] nm bean and sausage hot-pot

cassure [kasyʀ] nf break, crack

castor [kastɔʀ] nm beaver

castrer [kastʀe] vt (mâle) to castrate; (: cheval) to geld; (femelle) to spay

catalogue [katalɔg] nm catalogue

cataloguer [katalɔge] vt to catalogue, to list; (péj) to put a label on

catalyseur [katalizœʀ] nm catalyst

catalyseur [katalizœʀ] nm catalyst

cataplasme [kataplasm(ə)] nm poultice

cataracte [kataʀakt(ə)] nf cataract

catastrophe [katastʀɔf] nf catastrophe, disaster; **catastrophé, e** [katastʀɔfe] (fam) adj deeply saddened

catch [katʃ] nm (all-in) wrestling; **catcheur, euse** [katʃœʀ] nm/f (all-in) wrestler

catéchisme [kateʃism(ə)] nm catechism

catégorie [kategɔʀi] nf category

catégorique [kategɔʀik] adj categorical

cathédrale [katedʀal] nf cathedral

catholique [katɔlik] adj, nm/f (Roman) Catholic; **pas très** ~ adv a bit shady ou fishy

catimini [katimini] : **en** ~ adv on the sly

cauchemar [koʃmaʀ] nm nightmare

cause [koz] nf cause; (JUR) lawsuit, case; **à** ~ **de** because of, owing to; **pour** ~ **de** on account of; owing to; (**et) pour** ~ and for (a very) good reason; **être en** ~ to be at

stake; to be involved; to be in question; **mettre en** ~ to implicate; to call into question; **remettre en** ~ to challenge; ~**r** [koze] vt to cause ♦ vi to chat, talk; ~**rie** [kozʀi] nf talk

caution [kosjɔ̃] nf guarantee, security; deposit; (JUR) bail (bond); (fig) backing, support; **payer la** ~ **de qn** to stand bail for sb; **libéré sous** ~ released on bail; ~**ner** [kosjɔne] vt to guarantee; (soutenir) to support

cavalcade [kavalkad] nf (fig) stampede

cavalier, ière [kavalje, -jɛʀ] adj (désinvolte) offhand ♦ nm/f rider; (au bal) partner ♦ nm (ÉCHECS) knight; **faire** ~ **seul** to go it alone

cave [kav] nf cellar ♦ adj: **yeux** ~**s** sunken eyes

caveau, x [kavo] nm vault

caverne [kavɛʀn(ə)] nf cave

C.C.P. sigle m = **compte chèques postaux**

CD sigle m (= compact disc) CD

CD-ROM sigle m CD-ROM

CE n abr (= Communauté Européenne) EC

─────────────── MOT CLÉ

ce, cette [sə, sɛt] (devant nm **cet** + voyelle ou h aspiré; pl **ces**) dét (proximité) this; these pl; (non-proximité) that; those pl; **cette maison-ci/là** this/that house; **cette nuit** (qui vient) tonight; (passée) last night ♦ pron **1:** **c'est** it's ou it is; **c'est un peintre** he's ou he is a painter; **ce sont des peintres** they're ou they are painters; **c'est le facteur** etc (à la porte) it's the postman; **qui est-ce?** who is it?; (en désignant) who is he/she?; **qu'est-ce?** what is it?

2: ~ **qui**, ~ **que** what; (chose qui): **il est bête,** ~ **qui me chagrine** he's stupid, which saddens me; **tout** ~ **qui bouge** everything ou that which moves; **tout** ~ **que je sais** all I know; ~ **dont j'ai parlé** what I talked about; ~ **que c'est grand!** it's so big!; voir aussi **-ci; est-ce que; n'est-ce pas; c'est-à-dire**

─────────────────────────

ceci [səsi] pron this

cécité [sesite] nf blindness

céder [sede] vt to give up ♦ vi (pont, barrage) to give way; (personne) to give in; ~ **à** to yield to, give in to

CEDEX [sedɛks] sigle m (= courrier d'entreprise à distribution exceptionnelle) postal service for bulk users

cédille [sedij] nf cedilla

cèdre [sɛdʀ(ə)] nm cedar

CEI abr m (= Communauté des États Indépendants) CIS

ceinture [sɛtyʀ] nf belt; (taille) waist; (fig) ring; belt; circle; ~ **de sécurité** safety ou seat belt; ~**r** vt (saisir) to grasp (round the waist)

cela [səla] *pron* that; (*comme sujet indéfini*) it; **quand/où ~?** when/where (was that)?

célèbre [selɛbʀ(ə)] *adj* famous

célébrer [selebʀe] *vt* to celebrate; (*louer*) to extol

céleri [sɛlʀi] *nm*: **~(-rave)** celeriac; **~ (en branche)** celery

célérité [seleʀite] *nf* speed, swiftness

célibat [seliba] *nm* celibacy; bachelorhood; spinsterhood; **célibataire** [selibatɛʀ] *adj* single, unmarried

celle(s) [sɛl] *pron voir* **celui**

cellier [selje] *nm* storeroom

cellulaire [selylɛʀ] *adj*: **voiture** *ou* **fourgon ~** prison *ou* police van

cellule [selyl] *nf* (*gén*) cell

cellulite [selylit] *nf* excess fat, cellulite

MOT CLÉ

celui, celle [səlɥi, sɛl] (*mpl* **ceux**, *fpl* **celles**) *pron* **1**: **~-ci/là**, **celle-ci/là** this one/that one; **ceux-ci**, **celles-ci** these (ones); **ceux-là**, **celles-là** those (ones); **~ de mon frère** my brother's; **~ du salon/du dessous** the one in (*ou* from) the lounge/below

2: **~ qui bouge** the one which *ou* that moves; (*personne*) the one who moves; **~ que je vois** the one (which *ou* that) I see; the one (whom) I see; **~ dont je parle** the one I'm talking about

3 (*valeur indéfinie*): **~ qui veut** whoever wants

---

cendre [sɑ̃dʀ(ə)] *nf* ash; **~s** *nfpl* (*d'un foyer*) ash(es), cinders; (*volcaniques*) ash *sg*; (*d'un défunt*) ashes; **sous la ~** (*CULIN*) in (the) embers; **cendrier** *nm* ashtray

cène [sɛn] *nf*: **la ~** (*Holy*) Communion

censé, e [sɑ̃se] *adj*: **être ~ faire** to be supposed to do

censeur [sɑ̃sœʀ] *nm* (*SCOL*) deputy-head (*BRIT*), vice-principal (*US*); (*CINÉMA, POL*) censor

censure [sɑ̃syʀ] *nf* censorship; **~r** [sɑ̃syʀe] *vt* (*CINÉMA, PRESSE*) to censor; (*POL*) to censure

cent [sɑ̃] *num* a hundred, one hundred; **centaine** *nf*: **une centaine (de)** about a hundred, a hundred or so; **plusieurs centaines (de)** several hundred; **des centaines (de)** hundreds (of); **centenaire** *adj* hundred-year-old ♦ *nm* (*anniversaire*) centenary; **centième** *num* hundredth; **centigrade** *nm* centigrade; **centilitre** *nm* centilitre; **centime** *nm* centime; **centimètre** *nm* centimetre; (*ruban*) tape measure, measuring tape

central, e, aux [sɑ̃tʀal, -o] *adj* central ♦ *nm*: **~ (téléphonique)** (telephone) exchange; **centrale** *nf* power station

centre [sɑ̃tʀ(ə)] *nm* centre; **~ commercial** shopping centre; **~ d'apprentissage** training college; **centre-ville** *nm* town centre, downtown (area) (*US*)

centuple [sɑ̃typl(ə)] *nm*: **le ~ de qch** a hundred times sth; **au ~** a hundredfold

cep [sɛp] *nm* (vine) stock

cèpe [sɛp] *nm* (edible) boletus

cependant [səpɑ̃dɑ̃] *adv* however

céramique [seʀamik] *nf* ceramics *sg*

cercle [sɛʀkl(ə)] *nm* circle; (*objet*) band, hoop; **~ vicieux** vicious circle

cercueil [sɛʀkœj] *nm* coffin

céréale [seʀeal] *nf* cereal

cérémonie [seʀemɔni] *nf* ceremony; **~s** *nfpl* (*péj*) fuss *sg*, to-do *sg*

cerf [sɛʀ] *nm* stag

cerfeuil [sɛʀfœj] *nm* chervil

cerf-volant [sɛʀvɔlɑ̃] *nm* kite

cerise [sʀiz] *nf* cherry; **cerisier** *nm* cherry (tree)

cerné, e [sɛʀne] *adj*: **les yeux ~s** with dark rings *ou* shadows under the eyes

cerner [sɛʀne] *vt* (*MIL etc*) to surround; (*fig: problème*) to delimit, define

certain, e [sɛʀtɛ̃, -ɛn] *adj* certain ♦ *dét* certain; **d'un ~ âge** past one's prime, not so young; **un ~ temps** (quite) some time; **~s** some; **certainement** *adv* (*probablement*) most probably *ou* likely; (*bien sûr*) certainly, of course

certes [sɛʀt(ə)] *adv* admittedly; of course; indeed (yes)

certificat [sɛʀtifika] *nm* certificate

certitude [sɛʀtityd] *nf* certainty

cerveau, x [sɛʀvo] *nm* brain

cervelas [sɛʀvɔla] *nm* saveloy

cervelle [sɛʀvɛl] *nf* (*ANAT*) brain

ces [se] *dét voir* **ce**

C.E.S. *sigle m* (= *Collège d'enseignement secondaire*) ≈ (junior) secondary school (*BRIT*)

cesse [sɛs]: **sans ~** *adv* continually, constantly; continuously; **il n'avait de ~ que** he would not rest until

cesser [sese] *vt* to stop ♦ *vi* to stop, cease; **~ de faire** to stop doing

cessez-le-feu *nm inv* ceasefire

c'est-à-dire [sɛtadiʀ] *adv* that is (to say)

cet, cette [sɛt] *dét voir* **ce**

ceux [sø] *pron voir* **celui**

CFC *abr* (= *chlorofluorocarbon*) CFC

C.F.D.T. *sigle f* = **Confédération française démocratique du travail**

C.G.T. *sigle f* = **Confédération générale du travail**

chacun, e [ʃakœ̃, -yn] *pron* each; (*indéfini*) everyone, everybody

chagrin [ʃagʀɛ̃] *nm* grief, sorrow; **chagriner** *vt* to grieve; to bother

chahut [ʃay] *nm* uproar; **chahuter** *vt* to rag, bait ♦ *vi* to make an uproar

chaîne [ʃɛn] *nf* chain; (*RADIO, TV: stations*)

channel; **travail à la ~** production line work; **~ (de montage** ou **de fabrication)** production ou assembly line; **~ (de montagnes)** (mountain) range; **~ (haute-fidélité** ou **hi-fi)** hi-fi system; **~ (stéréo)** stereo (system)

chair [ʃɛR] nf flesh ♦ adj: **(couleur) ~** flesh-coloured; **avoir la ~ de poule** to have goosepimples ou gooseflesh; **bien en ~** plump, well-padded; **en ~ et en os** in the flesh

chaire [ʃɛR] nf **(d'église)** pulpit; **(d'université)** chair

chaise [ʃɛz] nf chair; **~ longue** deckchair

châle [ʃal] nm shawl

chaleur [ʃalœR] nf heat; (fig) warmth; fire, fervour; heat

chaleureux, euse [ʃalœRø, -øz] adj warm

chaloupe [ʃalup] nf launch; (de sauvetage) lifeboat

chalumeau, x [ʃalymo] nm blowlamp, blowtorch

chalutier [ʃalytje] nm trawler

chamailler [ʃamaje]: **se ~** vi to squabble, bicker

chambouler [ʃābule] vt to disrupt, turn upside down

chambre [ʃābR(ə)] nf bedroom; (TECH) chamber; (POL) chamber, house; (JUR) court; (COMM) chamber; federation; **faire ~ à part** to sleep in separate rooms; **~ à air** (de pneu) (inner) tube; **~ à coucher** bedroom; **~ à un lit/deux lits** (à l'hôtel) single-/twin-bedded room; **~ d'amis** spare ou guest room; **~ noire** (PHOTO) dark room

chambrer [ʃābRe] vt (vin) to bring to room temperature

chameau, x [ʃamo] nm camel

champ [ʃā] nm field; **prendre du ~** to draw back; **~ de bataille** battlefield; **~ de courses** racecourse; **~ de tir** rifle range

champagne [ʃāpaɲ] nm champagne

champêtre [ʃāpɛtR(ə)] adj country cpd, rural

champignon [ʃāpiɲɔ̃] nm mushroom; (terme générique) fungus; **~ de Paris** button mushroom

champion, ne [ʃāpjɔ̃, -jɔn] adj, nm/f champion; **championnat** nm championship

chance [ʃās] nf: **la ~** luck; **~s** nfpl (probabilités) chances; **une ~** a stroke ou piece of luck ou good fortune; (occasion) a lucky break; **avoir de la ~** to be lucky

chanceler [ʃāsle] vi to totter

chancelier [ʃāsəlje] nm (allemand) chancellor

chanceux, euse [ʃāsø, -øz] adj lucky

chandail [ʃādaj] nm (thick) sweater

chandelier [ʃādəlje] nm candlestick

chandelle [ʃādɛl] nf (tallow) candle; **dîner**

aux ~s candlelight dinner

change [ʃāʒ] nm (COMM) exchange

changement [ʃāʒmā] nm change; **~ de vitesses** gears pl; gear change

changer [ʃāʒe] vt (modifier) to change, alter; (remplacer, COMM, rhabiller) to change ♦ vi to change, alter; **se ~** vi to change (o.s.); **~ de** (remplacer: adresse, nom, voiture etc) to change one's; (échanger, alterner: côté, place, train etc) to change +npl; **~ de couleur/direction** to change colour/direction; **~ d'idée** to change one's mind; **~ de vitesse** to change gear

chanson [ʃāsɔ̃] nf song

chant [ʃā] nm song; (art vocal) singing; (d'église) hymn; **~age** [ʃātaʒ] nm blackmail; **faire du ~** to use blackmail; **~er** [ʃāte] vt, vi to sing; **si cela lui chante** (fam) if he feels like it; **~eur, euse** [ʃātœR, -øz] nm/f singer

chantier [ʃātje] nm (building) site; (sur une route) roadworks pl; **mettre en ~** to put in hand; **~ naval** shipyard

chantilly [ʃātiji] nf voir **crème**

chantonner [ʃātɔne] vi, vt to sing to oneself, hum

chanvre [ʃāvR(ə)] nm hemp

chaparder [ʃapaRde] vt to pinch

chapeau, x [ʃapo] nm hat; **~ mou** trilby

chapelet [ʃaplɛ] nm (REL) rosary

chapelle [ʃapɛl] nf chapel; **~ ardente** chapel of rest

chapelure [ʃaplyR] nf (dried) bread-crumbs pl

chapiteau, x [ʃapito] nm (de cirque) marquee, big top

chapitre [ʃapitR(ə)] nm chapter; (fig) subject, matter

chaque [ʃak] dét each, every; (indéfini) every

char [ʃaR] nm (à foin etc) cart, waggon; (de carnaval) float; **~ (d'assaut)** tank

charabia [ʃaRabja] nm (péj) gibberish

charade [ʃaRad] nf riddle; (mimée) charade

charbon [ʃaRbɔ̃] nm coal; **~ de bois** charcoal

charcuterie [ʃaRkytRi] nf (magasin) pork butcher's shop and delicatessen; (produits) cooked pork meats pl; **charcutier, ière** nm/f pork butcher

chardon [ʃaRdɔ̃] nm thistle

charge [ʃaRʒ(ə)] nf (fardeau) load, burden; (explosif, ÉLEC, MIL, JUR) charge; (rôle, mission) responsibility; **~s** nfpl (du loyer) service charges; **à la ~ de** (dépendant de) dependent upon; (aux frais de) chargeable to; **j'accepte, à ~ de revanche** I accept, provided I can do the same for you one day; **prendre en ~** to take charge of; (suj: véhicule) to take on; (dépenses) to take care of; **~s sociales** social security contributions; **~ment** [ʃaRʒmā] nm (objets) load

charger [ʃaʀʒe] vt (*voiture, fusil, caméra*) to load; (*batterie*) to charge ♦ vi (*MIL etc*) to charge; **se ~ de** vt to see to; **~ qn de (faire) qch** to put sb in charge of (doing) sth

chariot [ʃaʀjo] nm trolley; (*charrette*) waggon; (*de machine à écrire*) carriage

charité [ʃaʀite] nf charity; **faire la ~ à** to give (something) to

charmant, e [ʃaʀmɑ̃, -ɑ̃t] adj charming

charme [ʃaʀm(ə)] nm charm; **charmer** vt to charm

charnel, le [ʃaʀnɛl] adj carnal

charnière [ʃaʀnjɛʀ] nf hinge; (*fig*) turning-point

charnu, e [ʃaʀny] adj fleshy

charpente [ʃaʀpɑ̃t] nf frame(work); **charpentier** nm carpenter

charpie [ʃaʀpi] nf: **en ~** (*fig*) in shreds ou ribbons

charrette [ʃaʀɛt] nf cart

charrier [ʃaʀje] vt to carry (along); to cart, carry

charrue [ʃaʀy] nf plough (*BRIT*), plow (*US*)

chasse [ʃas] nf hunting; (*au fusil*) shooting; (*poursuite*) chase; (*aussi:* **~ d'eau**) flush; **la ~ est ouverte** the hunting season pl is open; **~ gardée** private hunting grounds pl; **prendre en ~** to give chase to; **tirer la ~ (d'eau)** to flush the toilet, pull the chain; **à courre** hunting

chassé-croisé [ʃasekʀwaze] nm (*fig*) mix-up where people miss each other in turn

chasse-neige [ʃasnɛʒ] nm inv snowplough (*BRIT*), snowplow (*US*)

chasser [ʃase] vt to hunt; (*expulser*) to chase away ou out, drive away ou out; **chasseur, euse** nm/f hunter ♦ nm (*avion*) fighter; **chasseur de têtes** nm (*fig*) head-hunter

châssis [ʃasi] nm (*AUTO*) chassis; (*cadre*) frame; (*de jardin*) cold frame

chat [ʃa] nm cat

châtaigne [ʃatɛɲ] nf chestnut; **châtaignier** nm chestnut (tree)

châtain [ʃatɛ̃] adj inv chestnut (brown); chestnut-haired

château, x [ʃato] nm castle; **~ d'eau** water tower; **~ fort** stronghold, fortified castle

châtier [ʃatje] vt to punish; (*fig: style*) to polish; **châtiment** nm punishment

chaton [ʃatɔ̃] nm (*ZOOL*) kitten

chatouiller [ʃatuje] vt to tickle; (*l'odorat, le palais*) to titillate; **chatouilleux, euse** adj ticklish; (*fig*) touchy, over-sensitive

chatoyer [ʃatwaje] vi to shimmer

châtrer [ʃatʀe] vt (*mâle*) to castrate; (: *cheval*) to geld; (*femelle*) to spay

chatte [ʃat] nf (she-)cat

chaud, e [ʃo, -od] adj (*gén*) warm; (*très chaud*) hot; (*fig*) hearty; heated; **il fait ~** it's warm; it's hot; **avoir ~** to be warm; to

be hot; **ça me tient ~** it keeps me warm; **rester au ~** to stay in the warm

chaudière [ʃodjɛʀ] nf boiler

chaudron [ʃodʀɔ̃] nm cauldron

chauffage [ʃofaʒ] nm heating; **~ central** central heating

chauffard [ʃofaʀ] nm (*péj*) reckless driver; hit-and-run driver

chauffe-eau [ʃofo] nm inv water-heater

chauffer [ʃofe] vt to heat ♦ vi to heat up, warm up; (*trop* **~:** *moteur*) to overheat; **se ~** vi (*se mettre en train*) to warm up; (*au soleil*) to warm o.s.

chauffeur [ʃofœʀ] nm driver; (*privé*) chauffeur

chaume [ʃom] nm (*du toit*) thatch

chaumière [ʃomjɛʀ] nf (thatched) cottage

chaussée [ʃose] nf road(way)

chausse-pied [ʃospje] nm shoe-horn

chausser [ʃose] vt (*bottes, skis*) to put on; (*enfant*) to put shoes on; **~ du 38/42** to take size 38/42

chaussette [ʃosɛt] nf sock

chausson [ʃosɔ̃] nm slipper; (*de bébé*) bootee; (**~ aux pommes**) (apple) turnover

chaussure [ʃosyʀ] nf shoe; **~s basses** flat shoes; **~s de ski** ski boots

chauve [ʃov] adj bald

chauve-souris [ʃovsuʀi] nf bat

chauvin, e [ʃovɛ̃, -in] adj chauvinistic

chaux [ʃo] nf lime; **blanchi à la ~** white-washed

chavirer [ʃaviʀe] vi to capsize

chef [ʃɛf] nm head, leader; (*de cuisine*) chef; **en ~** (*MIL etc*) in chief; **~ d'accusation** charge; **~ d'entreprise** company head; **~ d'état** head of state; **~ de file** (*de parti etc*) leader; **~ de gare** station master; **~ d'orchestre** conductor (*BRIT*), director (*US*); **~-d'œuvre** [ʃɛdœvʀ(ə)] nm masterpiece; **~-lieu** [ʃɛfljø] nm county town

chemin [ʃ(ə)mɛ̃] nm path; (*itinéraire, direction, trajet*) way; **en ~** on the way; **~ de fer** railway (*BRIT*), railroad (*US*); **par chemin de fer** by rail

cheminée [ʃ(ə)mine] nf chimney; (*à l'intérieur*) chimney piece, fireplace; (*de bateau*) funnel

cheminement [ʃ(ə)minmɑ̃] nm progress; course

cheminot [ʃ(ə)mino] nm railwayman

chemise [ʃ(ə)miz] nf shirt; (*dossier*) folder; **~ de nuit** nightdress

chemisier [ʃ(ə)mizje] nm blouse

chenal, aux [ʃ(ə)nal, -o] nm channel

chêne [ʃɛn] nm oak (tree); (*bois*) oak

chenil [ʃ(ə)nil] nm kennels pl

chenille [ʃ(ə)nij] nf (*ZOOL*) caterpillar; (*AUTO*) caterpillar track

chèque [ʃɛk] nm cheque (*BRIT*), check (*US*); **~ sans provision** bad cheque; **~ de voyage** traveller's cheque; **chéquier** nm cheque book

cher, ère [ʃɛʀ] adj (aimé) dear; (coûteux) expensive, dear ♦ adv: **cela coûte ~** it's expensive

chercher [ʃɛʀʃe] vt to look for; (gloire etc) to seek; **aller ~** to go for, go and fetch; **à faire** to try to do; **chercheur, euse** [ʃɛʀʃœʀ, -øz] nm/f researcher, research worker

chère [ʃɛʀ] adj voir **cher** ♦ nf: **la bonne ~** good food

chéri, e [ʃeʀi] adj beloved, dear; **(mon) ~** darling

chérir [ʃeʀiʀ] vt to cherish

cherté [ʃɛʀte] nf: **la ~ de la vie** the high cost of living

chétif, ive [ʃetif, -iv] adj puny, stunted

cheval, aux [ʃəval, -o] nm horse; (AUTO): **~ (vapeur)** horsepower no pl; **faire du ~** to ride; **à ~** on horseback; **à ~ sur** astride; (fig) overlapping; **~ de course** racehorse

chevalet [ʃəvalɛ] nm easel

chevalier [ʃəvalje] nm knight

chevalière [ʃəvaljɛʀ] nf signet ring

chevalin, e [ʃəvalɛ̃, -in] adj: **boucherie ~e** horse-meat butcher's

chevaucher [ʃəvoʃe] vi (aussi: **se ~**) to overlap (each other) ♦ vt to be astride, straddle

chevaux [ʃəvo] nmpl de **cheval**

chevelu, e [ʃəvly] adj with a good head of hair, hairy (péj)

chevelure [ʃəvlyʀ] nf hair no pl

chevet [ʃəvɛ] nm: **au ~ de qn** at sb's bedside; **lampe de ~** bedside lamp

cheveu, x [ʃəvø] nm hair; **~x** nmpl (chevelure) hair sg; **avoir les ~x courts** to have short hair

cheville [ʃəvij] nf (ANAT) ankle; (de bois) peg; (pour une vis) plug

chèvre [ʃɛvʀ(ə)] nf (she-)goat

chevreau, x [ʃəvʀo] nm kid

chèvrefeuille [ʃɛvʀəfœj] nm honeysuckle

chevreuil [ʃəvʀœj] nm roe deer inv; (CULIN) venison

chevronné, e [ʃəvʀɔne] adj seasoned

MOT CLÉ
---

chez [ʃe] prép **1** (à la demeure de) at; (: direction) to; **~ qn** at/to sb's house ou place; **~ moi** at home; (direction) home

2 (+profession) at; (: direction) to; **~ le boulanger/dentiste** at or to the baker's/dentist's

3 (dans le caractère, l'œuvre de) in; **~ les renards/Racine** in foxes/Racine

---

chez-soi [ʃeswa] nm inv home

chic [ʃik] adj inv chic, smart; (généreux) nice, decent ♦ nm stylishness; **~!** great!; **avoir le ~ de** to have the knack of

chicane [ʃikan] nf (querelle) squabble

chicaner [ʃikane] vi (ergoter): **~ sur** to quibble about

chiche [ʃiʃ] adj niggardly, mean ♦ excl (à un défi) you're on!

chichi [ʃiʃi] (fam) nm fuss

chicorée [ʃikɔʀe] nf (café) chicory; (salade) endive

chien [ʃjɛ̃] nm dog; **en ~ de fusil** curled up; **~ de garde** guard dog

chiendent [ʃjɛ̃dɑ̃] nm couch grass

chienne [ʃjɛn] nf dog, bitch

chier [ʃje] (fam!) vi to crap (!)

chiffon [ʃifɔ̃] nm (piece of) rag; **~ner** [ʃifɔne] vt to crumple; (tracasser) to concern; **~nier** [ʃifɔnje] nm rag-and-bone man

chiffre [ʃifʀ(ə)] nm (représentant un nombre) figure; numeral; (montant, total) total, sum; **en ~s ronds** in round figures; **~ d'affaires** turnover; **chiffrer** vt (dépense) to put a figure to, assess; (message) to (en)code, cipher

chignon [ʃiɲɔ̃] nm chignon, bun

Chili [ʃili] nm: **le ~** Chile

chimie [ʃimi] nf chemistry; **chimique** adj chemical; **produits chimiques** chemicals

Chine [ʃin] nf: **la ~** China

chinois, e [ʃinwa, -waz] adj, nm/f Chinese ♦ nm (LING) Chinese

chiot [ʃjo] nm pup(py)

chips [ʃips] nfpl crisps (BRIT), (potato) chips (US)

chiquenaude [ʃiknod] nf flick, flip

chirurgical, e, aux [ʃiʀyʀʒikal, -o] adj surgical

chirurgie [ʃiʀyʀʒi] nf surgery; **~ esthétique** plastic surgery; **chirurgien, ne** nm/f surgeon

choc [ʃɔk] nm impact; shock; crash; (moral) shock; (affrontement) clash

chocolat [ʃɔkɔla] nm chocolate; (boisson) (hot) chocolate; **~ au lait** milk chocolate

chœur [kœʀ] nm (chorale) choir; (OPÉRA, THÉÂTRE) chorus; **en ~** in chorus

choisir [ʃwaziʀ] vt to choose, select

choix [ʃwa] nm choice, selection; **avoir le ~** to have the choice; **premier ~** (COMM) class one; **de ~** choice, selected; **au ~** as you wish

chômage [ʃomaʒ] nm unemployment; **mettre au ~** to make redundant, put out of work; **être au ~** to be unemployed ou out of work; **chômeur, euse** nm/f unemployed person

chope [ʃɔp] nf tankard

choquer [ʃɔke] vt (offenser) to shock; (commotionner) to shake (up)

choriste [kɔʀist(ə)] nm/f choir member; (OPÉRA) chorus member

chorus [kɔʀys] nm: **faire ~ (avec)** to voice one's agreement (with)

chose [ʃoz] nf thing; **c'est peu de ~** it's nothing (really); it's not much

chou, x [ʃu] *nm* cabbage; **mon petit ~** (my) sweetheart; **~ à la crème** cream bun *(made of choux pastry)*
chouchou, te [ʃuʃu, -ut] *nm/f (SCOL)* teacher's pet
choucroute [ʃukʀut] *nf* sauerkraut
chouette [ʃwɛt] *nf* owl ♦ *adj (fam)* great, smashing
chou-fleur [ʃuflœʀ] *nm* cauliflower
choyer [ʃwaje] *vt* to cherish; to pamper
chrétien, ne [kʀetjɛ̃, -ɛn] *adj, nm/f* Christian
Christ [kʀist] *nm*: **le ~** Christ; **christianisme** *nm* Christianity
chrome [kʀom] *nm* chromium; **chromé, e** *adj* chromium-plated
chronique [kʀonik] *adj* chronic ♦ *nf (de journal)* column, page; *(historique)* chronicle; *(RADIO, TV)*: **la ~ sportive/théâtrale** the sports/theatre review; **la ~ locale** local news and gossip
chronologique [kʀonoloʒik] *adj* chronological
chronomètre [kʀonometʀ(ə)] *nm* stopwatch; **chronométrer** *vt* to time
chrysanthème [kʀizɑ̃tɛm] *nm* chrysanthemum
C.H.U. *sigle m* (= *centre hospitalier universitaire*) ≈ (teaching) hospital
chuchoter [ʃyʃote] *vt, vi* to whisper
chuinter [ʃɥɛ̃te] *vi* to hiss
chut [ʃyt] *excl* sh!
chute [ʃyt] *nf* fall; *(de bois, papier: déchet)* scrap; **faire une ~ (de 10 m)** to fall (10 m); **~ (d'eau)** waterfall; **la ~ des cheveux** hair loss; **~ libre** free fall; **~s de pluie/neige** rain/snowfalls
Chypre [ʃipʀ] *nm/f* Cyprus
-ci [si] *adv voir* **par** ♦ *dét*: **ce garçon-ci/-là** this/that boy; **ces femmes-ci/-là** these/those women
ci-après [siapʀɛ] *adv* hereafter
cible [sibl(ə)] *nf* target
ciboulette [sibulɛt] *nf* (small) chive
cicatrice [sikatʀis] *nf* scar
cicatriser [sikatʀize] *vt* to heal
ci-contre [sikɔ̃tʀ(ə)] *adv* opposite
ci-dessous [sidəsu] *adv* below
ci-dessus [sidəsy] *adv* above
cidre [sidʀ(ə)] *nm* cider
Cie *abr* (= *compagnie*) Co.
ciel [sjɛl] *nm* sky; *(REL)* heaven; **cieux** *nmpl (littéraire)* sky *sg*, skies; **à ~ ouvert** open-air; *(mine)* opencast
cierge [sjɛʀʒ(ə)] *nm* candle
cieux [sjø] *nmpl de* **ciel**
cigale [sigal] *nf* cicada
cigare [sigaʀ] *nm* cigar
cigarette [sigaʀɛt] *nf* cigarette
ci-gît [siʒi] *adv* +*vb* here lies
cigogne [sigɔɲ] *nf* stork
ci-inclus, e [siɛ̃kly, -yz] *adj, adv* enclosed

ci-joint, e [siʒwɛ̃, -ɛ̃t] *adj, adv* enclosed
cil [sil] *nm* (eye)lash
cime [sim] *nf* top; *(montagne)* peak
ciment [simɑ̃] *nm* cement; **~ armé** reinforced concrete
cimetière [simtjɛʀ] *nm* cemetery; *(d'église)* churchyard
cinéaste [sineast(ə)] *nm/f* film-maker
cinéma [sinema] *nm* cinema; **~tographique** *adj* film *cpd*, cinema *cpd*
cinéphile [sinefil] *nm/f* cinema-goer
cinglant, e [sɛ̃glɑ̃, -ɑ̃t] *adj (échec)* crushing
cinglé, e [sɛ̃gle] *(fam) adj* crazy
cingler [sɛ̃gle] *vt* to lash; *(fig)* to sting
cinq [sɛ̃k] *num* five
cinquantaine [sɛ̃kɑ̃tɛn] *nf*: **une ~ (de)** about fifty; **avoir la ~ (âge)** to be around fifty
cinquante [sɛ̃kɑ̃t] *num* fifty; **cinquantenaire** *adj, nm/f* fifty-year-old
cinquième [sɛ̃kjɛm] *num* fifth
cintre [sɛ̃tʀ(ə)] *nm* coat-hanger
cintré, e [sɛ̃tʀe] *adj (chemise)* fitted
cirage [siʀaʒ] *nm* (shoe) polish
circonflexe [siʀkɔ̃flɛks(ə)] *adj*: **accent ~** circumflex accent
circonscription [siʀkɔ̃skʀipsjɔ̃] *nf* district; **~ électorale** *(d'un député)* constituency
circonscrire [siʀkɔ̃skʀiʀ] *vt* to define, delimit; *(incendie)* to contain
circonstance [siʀkɔ̃stɑ̃s] *nf* circumstance; *(occasion)* occasion
circonvenir [siʀkɔ̃vniʀ] *vt* to circumvent
circuit [siʀkɥi] *nm (trajet)* tour, (round) trip; *(ÉLEC, TECH)* circuit
circulaire [siʀkylɛʀ] *adj, nf* circular
circulation [siʀkylɑsjɔ̃] *nf* circulation; *(AUTO)*: **la ~** (the) traffic
circuler [siʀkyle] *vi* to drive (along); to walk along; *(train etc)* to run; *(sang, devises)* to circulate; **faire ~** *(nouvelle)* to spread (about), circulate; *(badauds)* to move on
cire [siʀ] *nf* wax; **ciré** [siʀe] *nm* oilskin; **cirer** [siʀe] *vt* to wax, polish
cirque [siʀk(ə)] *nm* circus; *(GÉO)* cirque; *(fig)* chaos, bedlam; carry-on
cisaille(s) [sizaj] *nf(pl)* (gardening) shears *pl*
ciseau, x [sizo] *nm*: **~ (à bois)** chisel; **~x** *nmpl (paire de ~x)* (pair of) scissors
ciseler [sizle] *vt* to chisel, carve
citadin, e [sitadɛ̃, -in] *nm/f* city dweller
citation [sitasjɔ̃] *nf (d'auteur)* quotation; *(JUR)* summons *sg*
cité [site] *nf* town; *(plus grande)* city; **~ universitaire** students' residences *pl*
citer [site] *vt (un auteur)* to quote (from); *(nommer)* to name; *(JUR)* to summon
citerne [sitɛʀn(ə)] *nf* tank
citoyen, ne [sitwajɛ̃, -ɛn] *nm/f* citizen
citron [sitʀɔ̃] *nm* lemon; **~ vert** lime; **citronnade** *nf* lemonade; **citronnier** *nm*

lemon tree
citrouille [sitʀuj] *nf* pumpkin
civet [sivɛ] *nm* stew
civière [sivjɛʀ] *nf* stretcher
civil, e [sivil] *adj* (*JUR, ADMIN, poli*) civil; (*non militaire*) civilian; **en ~** in civilian clothes; **dans le ~** in civilian life
civilisation [sivilizasjɔ̃] *nf* civilization
civisme [sivism(ə)] *nm* public-spiritedness
clair, e [klɛʀ] *adj* light; (*chambre*) light, bright; (*eau, son, fig*) clear ♦ *adv*: **voir ~** to see clearly; **tirer qch au ~** to clear sth up, clarify sth; **mettre au ~** (*notes etc*) to tidy up; **le plus ~ de son temps** the better part of his time; **~ de lune** *nm* moonlight; **clairement** *adv* clearly
clairière [klɛʀjɛʀ] *nf* clearing
clairon [klɛʀɔ̃] *nm* bugle
claironner [klɛʀɔne] *vt* (*fig*) to trumpet, shout from the rooftops
clairsemé, e [klɛʀsəme] *adj* sparse
clairvoyant, e [klɛʀvwajɑ̃, -ɑ̃t] *adj* perceptive, clear-sighted
clandestin, e [klɑ̃dɛstɛ̃, -in] *adj* clandestine, covert; **passager ~** stowaway
clapier [klapje] *nm* (*rabbit*) hutch
clapoter [klapɔte] *vi* to lap
claque [klak] *nf* (*gifle*) slap
claquer [klake] *vi* (*drapeau*) to flap; (*porte*) to bang, slam; (*coup de feu*) to ring out ♦ *vt* (*porte*) to slam, bang; (*doigts*) to snap; **se ~ un muscle** to pull *ou* strain a muscle
claquettes [klakɛt] *nfpl* tap-dancing *sg*
clarinette [klaʀinɛt] *nf* clarinet
clarté [klaʀte] *nf* lightness; brightness; (*d'un son, de l'eau*) clearness; (*d'une explication*) clarity
classe [klɑs] *nf* class; (*SCOL: local*) class(room); (: *leçon, élèves*) class; **faire la ~** to be a *ou* the teacher; to teach; **~ment** [klɑsmɑ̃] *nm* (*rang: SCOL*) place; (: *SPORT*) placing; (*liste: SCOL*) class list (in order of merit); (: *SPORT*) placings *pl*; **~r** [klɑse] *vt* (*idées, livres*) to classify; (*papiers*) to file; (*candidat, concurrent*) to grade; (*JUR: affaire*) to close; **se ~r premier/dernier** to come first/last; (*SPORT*) to finish first/last
classeur [klɑsœʀ] *nm* (*cahier*) file; (*meuble*) filing cabinet
classique [klasik] *adj* classical; (*sobre: coupe etc*) classic(al); (*habituel*) standard, classic
clause [kloz] *nf* clause
claustrer [klostʀe] *vt* to confine
clavecin [klavsɛ̃] *nm* harpsichord
clavicule [klavikyl] *nf* collarbone
clavier [klavje] *nm* keyboard
clé [kle] *nf* key; (*MUS*) clef; (*de mécanicien*) spanner (*BRIT*), wrench (*US*); **prix ~s en main** (*d'une voiture*) on-the-road price; **~ anglaise** (monkey) wrench; **~ de contact** ignition key

clef [kle] *nf* = **clé**
clément, e [klemɑ̃, -ɑ̃t] *adj* (*temps*) mild; (*indulgent*) lenient
clerc [klɛʀ] *nm*: **~ de notaire** solicitor's clerk
clergé [klɛʀʒe] *nm* clergy
cliché [kliʃe] *nm* (*PHOTO*) negative; print; (*LING*) cliché
client, e [klijɑ̃, -ɑ̃t] *nm/f* (*acheteur*) customer, client; (*d'hôtel*) guest, patron; (*du docteur*) patient; (*de l'avocat*) client; **clientèle** *nf* (*du magasin*) customers *pl*, clientèle; (*du docteur, de l'avocat*) practice
cligner [kliɲe] *vi*: **~ des yeux** to blink (one's eyes); **~ de l'œil** to wink
clignotant [kliɲɔtɑ̃] *nm* (*AUTO*) indicator
clignoter [kliɲɔte] *vi* (*étoiles etc*) to twinkle; (*lumière*) to flash; (: *vaciller*) to flicker
climat [klima] *nm* climate
climatisation [klimatizasjɔ̃] *nf* air conditioning; **climatisé, e** *adj* air-conditioned
clin d'œil [klɛ̃dœj] *nm* wink; **en un ~** in a flash
clinique [klinik] *nf* nursing home
clinquant, e [klɛ̃kɑ̃, -ɑ̃t] *adj* flashy
cliqueter [klikte] *vi* to clash; to jangle, jingle; to chink
clochard, e [klɔʃaʀ, -aʀd(ə)] *nm/f* tramp
cloche [klɔʃ] *nf* (*d'église*) bell; (*fam*) clot; **~ à fromage** cheese-cover
cloche-pied [klɔʃpje] : **à ~** *adv* on one leg, hopping (along)
clocher [klɔʃe] *nm* church tower; (*en pointe*) steeple ♦ *vi* (*fam*) to be *ou* go wrong; **de ~** (*péj*) parochial
cloison [klwazɔ̃] *nf* partition (wall)
cloître [klwatʀ(ə)] *nm* cloister
cloîtrer [klwatʀe] *vt*: **se ~** to shut o.s. up *ou* away
cloque [klɔk] *nf* blister
clore [klɔʀ] *vt* to close; **clos, e** *adj voir* **maison**; **huis** ♦ *nm* (enclosed) field
clôture [klotyʀ] *nf* closure; (*barrière*) enclosure; **clôturer** *vt* (*terrain*) to enclose; (*débats*) to close
clou [klu] *nm* nail; (*MÉD*) boil; **~s** *nmpl* (*passage clouté*) pedestrian crossing; **pneus à ~s** studded tyres; **le ~ du spectacle** the highlight of the show; **~ de girofle** clove; **clouer** *vt* to nail down *ou* up
clown [klun] *nm* clown
club [klœb] *nm* club
C.N.R.S. *sigle m* = **Centre nationale de la recherche scientifique**
coasser [kɔase] *vi* to croak
cobaye [kɔbaj] *nm* guinea-pig
coca [kɔka] *nm* Coke (®)
cocaïne [kɔkain] *nf* cocaine
cocasse [kɔkas] *adj* comical, funny
coccinelle [kɔksinɛl] *nf* ladybird (*BRIT*), ladybug (*US*)
cocher [kɔʃe] *nm* coachman ♦ *vt* to tick

off; (*entailler*) to notch
cochère [kɔʃɛr] *adj f*: **porte** ~ carriage entrance
cochon, ne [kɔʃɔ̃, -ɔn] *nm* pig ♦ *adj* (*fam*) dirty, smutty; **cochonnerie** (*fam*) *nf* filth; rubbish, trash
cocktail [kɔktɛl] *nm* cocktail; (*réception*) cocktail party
coco [kɔko] *nm voir* **noix**; (*fam*) bloke
cocorico [kɔkɔriko] *excl, nm* cock-a-doodle-do
cocotier [kɔkɔtje] *nm* coconut palm
cocotte [kɔkɔt] *nf* (*en fonte*) casserole; ~ **(minute)** pressure cooker; **ma** ~ (*fam*) sweetie (pie)
cocu [kɔky] *nm* cuckold
code [kɔd] *nm* code ♦ *adj*: **phares** ~**s** dipped lights; **se mettre en** ~**(s)** to dip one's (head)lights; ~ **à barres** bar code; ~ **civil** Common Law; ~ **de la route** highway code; ~ **pénal** penal code; ~ **postal** (*numéro*) post (*BRIT*) ou zip (*US*) code
cœur [kœr] *nm* heart; (*CARTES: couleur*) hearts *pl*; (: *carte*) heart; **avoir bon** ~ to be kind-hearted; **avoir mal au** ~ to feel sick; **en avoir le** ~ **net** to be clear in one's own mind (about it); **par** ~ by heart; **de bon** ~ willingly; **cela lui tient à** ~ that's (very) close to his heart
coffre [kɔfr(ə)] *nm* (*meuble*) chest; (*d'auto*) boot (*BRIT*), trunk (*US*); **coffre(-fort)** *nm* safe
coffret [kɔfrɛ] *nm* casket
cognac [kɔɲak] *nm* brandy, cognac
cogner [kɔɲe] *vi* to knock
cohérent, e [kɔerɑ̃, -ɑ̃t] *adj* coherent, consistent
cohorte [kɔɔrt(ə)] *nf* troop
cohue [kɔy] *nf* crowd
coi, coite [kwa, kwat] *adj*: **rester** ~ to remain silent
coiffe [kwaf] *nf* headdress
coiffé, e [kwafe] *adj*: **bien/mal** ~ with tidy/untidy hair; ~ **en arrière** with one's hair brushed ou combed back
coiffer [kwafe] *vt* (*fig*) to cover, top; **se** ~ *vi* to do one's hair; to put on one's hat; ~ **qn** to do sb's hair
coiffeur, euse [kwafœr, -øz] *nm/f* hairdresser; **coiffeuse** *nf* (*table*) dressing table
coiffure [kwafyr] *nf* (*cheveux*) hairstyle, hairdo; (*chapeau*) hat, headgear *no pl*; (*art*): **la** ~ hairdressing
coin [kwɛ̃] *nm* corner; (*pour coincer*) wedge; **l'épicerie du** ~ the local grocer; **dans le** ~ (*aux alentours*) in the area, around about; locally; **au** ~ **du feu** by the fireside; **regard en** ~ sideways glance
coincé, e [kwɛ̃se] *adj* stuck, jammed; (*fig: inhibé*) inhibited, hung up (*fam*)
coincer [kwɛ̃se] *vt* to jam
coïncidence [kɔɛ̃sidɑ̃s] *nf* coincidence

coïncider [kɔɛ̃side] *vi* to coincide
col [kɔl] *nm* (*de chemise*) collar; (*encolure, cou*) neck; (*de montagne*) pass; ~ **de l'utérus** cervix; ~ **roulé** polo-neck
colère [kɔlɛr] *nf* anger; **une** ~ a fit of anger; (**se mettre) en** ~ (to get) angry; **coléreux, euse** *adj*; **colérique** *adj* quick-tempered, irascible
colifichet [kɔlifiʃɛ] *nm* trinket
colimaçon [kɔlimasɔ̃] *nm*: **escalier en** ~ spiral staircase
colin [kɔlɛ̃] *nm* hake
colique [kɔlik] *nf* diarrhoea, colic (pains)
colis [kɔli] *nm* parcel
collaborateur, trice [kɔlabɔratœr, -tris] *nm/f* (*aussi POL*) collaborator; (*d'une revue*) contributor
collaborer [kɔlabɔre] *vi* to collaborate; ~ **à** to collaborate on; (*revue*) to contribute to
collant, e [kɔlɑ̃, -ɑ̃t] *adj* sticky; (*robe etc*) clinging, skintight; (*péj*) clinging ♦ *nm* (*bas*) tights *pl*
collation [kɔlasjɔ̃] *nf* light meal
colle [kɔl] *nf* glue; (*à papiers peints*) (wallpaper) paste; (*devinette*) teaser, riddle; (*SCOL: fam*) detention
collecte [kɔlɛkt(ə)] *nf* collection
collectif, ive [kɔlɛktif, -iv] *adj* collective; (*visite, billet*) group *cpd*
collection [kɔlɛksjɔ̃] *nf* collection; (*ÉDITION*) series; **collectionner** *vt* (*tableaux, timbres*) to collect; **collectionneur, euse** *nm/f* collector
collectivité [kɔlɛktivite] *nf* group; ~**s locales** *nfpl* (*ADMIN*) local authorities
collège [kɔlɛʒ] *nm* (*école*) (secondary) school; (*assemblée*) body; **collégien** *nm* schoolboy; **collégienne** *nf* schoolgirl
collègue [kɔlɛg] *nm/f* colleague
coller [kɔle] *vt* (*papier, timbre*) to stick (on); (*affiche*) to stick up; (*enveloppe*) to stick down; (*morceaux*) to stick ou glue together; (*fam: mettre, fourrer*) to stick, shove; (*SCOL: fam*) to keep in ♦ *vi* (*être collant*) to be sticky; (*adhérer*) to stick; ~ **à** to stick to
collet [kɔlɛ] *nm* (*piège*) snare, noose; (*cou*): **prendre qn au** ~ to grab sb by the throat; ~ **monté** *adj inv* straight-laced
collier [kɔlje] *nm* (*bijou*) necklace; (*de chien, TECH*) collar; ~ **(de barbe)** narrow beard along the line of the jaw
collimateur [kɔlimatœr] *nm*: **avoir qn/qch dans le** ~ (*fig*) to have sb/sth in one's sights
colline [kɔlin] *nf* hill
collision [kɔlizjɔ̃] *nf* collision, crash; **entrer en** ~ (**avec**) to collide (with)
colmater [kɔlmate] *vt* (*fuite*) to seal off; (*brèche*) to plug, fill in
colombe [kɔlɔ̃b] *nf* dove
colon [kɔlɔ̃] *nm* settler
colonel [kɔlɔnɛl] *nm* colonel

colonie [kɔlɔni] nf colony; ~ **(de vacances)** holiday camp (for children)

colonne [kɔlɔn] nf column; **se mettre en ~ par deux** to get into twos; ~ **(vertébrale)** spine, spinal column

colorant [kɔlɔʀɑ̃] nm colouring

colorer [kɔlɔʀe] vt to colour

colorier [kɔlɔʀje] vt to colour (in)

coloris [kɔlɔʀi] nm colour, shade

colporter [kɔlpɔʀte] vt to hawk, peddle

colza [kɔlza] nm rape (seed)

coma [kɔma] nm coma

combat [kɔ̃ba] nm fight; fighting no pl; ~ **de boxe** boxing match

combattant [kɔ̃batɑ̃] nm: **ancien ~** war veteran

combattre [kɔ̃batʀ(ə)] vt to fight; (épidémie, ignorance) to combat, fight against

combien [kɔ̃bjɛ̃] adv (quantité) how much; (nombre) how many; (exclamatif) how; ~ **de** how much; how many; ~ **de temps** how long; ~ **coûte/pèse ceci?** how much does this cost/weigh?

combinaison [kɔ̃binɛzɔ̃] nf combination; (astuce) device, scheme; (de femme) slip; (d'aviateur) flying suit; (d'homme-grenouille) wetsuit; (bleu de travail) boiler suit (BRIT), coveralls pl (US)

combine [kɔ̃bin] nf trick; (péj) scheme, fiddle (BRIT)

combiné [kɔ̃bine] nm (aussi: ~ **téléphonique**) receiver

combiner [kɔ̃bine] vt to combine; (plan, horaire) to work out, devise

comble [kɔ̃bl(ə)] adj (salle) packed (full) ♦ nm (du bonheur, plaisir) height; ~**s** nmpl (CONSTR) attic sg, loft sg; **c'est le ~!** that beats everything!

combler [kɔ̃ble] vt (trou) to fill in; (besoin, lacune) to fill; (déficit) to make good; (satisfaire) to fulfil

combustible [kɔ̃bystibl(ə)] nm fuel

comédie [kɔmedi] nf comedy; (fig) play-acting no pl; ~ **musicale** musical; **comédien, ne** nm/f actor(tress)

comestible [kɔmestibl(ə)] adj edible

comique [kɔmik] adj (drôle) comical; (THÉÂTRE) comic ♦ nm (artiste) comic, comedian

comité [kɔmite] nm committee; ~ **d'entreprise** works council

commandant [kɔmɑ̃dɑ̃] nm (gén) commander, commandant; (NAVIG, AVIAT) captain

commande [kɔmɑ̃d] nf (COMM) order; ~**s** nfpl (AVIAT etc) controls; **sur ~** to order; ~ **à distance** remote control

commandement [kɔmɑ̃dmɑ̃] nm command; (REL) commandment

commander [kɔmɑ̃de] vt (COMM) to order; (diriger, ordonner) to command; ~ **à qn de faire** to command ou order sb to do

commando [kɔmɑ̃do] nm commando (squad)

MOT CLÉ

comme [kɔm] prép **1** (comparaison) like; **tout ~ son père** just like his father; **fort ~ un boeuf** as strong as an ox; **joli ~ tout** ever so pretty

2 (manière) like; **faites-le ~ ça** do it like this, do it this way; ~ **ci**, ~ **ça** so-so, middling

3 (en tant que) as a; **donner ~ prix** to give as a prize; **travailler ~ secrétaire** to work as a secretary

♦ conj **1** (ainsi que) as; **elle écrit ~ elle parle** she writes as she talks; ~ **si** as if

2 (au moment où, alors que) as; **il est parti ~ j'arrivais** he left as I arrived

3 (parce que, puisque) as; ~ **il était en retard, il** ... as he was late, he ...

♦ adv: ~ **il est fort/c'est bon!** he's so strong/it's so good!

---

commémorer [kɔmemɔʀe] vt to commemorate

commencement [kɔmɑ̃smɑ̃] nm beginning, start, commencement

commencer [kɔmɑ̃se] vt, vi to begin, start, commence; ~ **à** ou **de faire** to begin ou start doing

comment [kɔmɑ̃] adv how ♦ nm: **le ~ et le pourquoi** the whys and wherefores; ~**?** (que dites-vous) pardon?

commentaire [kɔmɑ̃tɛʀ] nm comment; remark

commenter [kɔmɑ̃te] vt (jugement, événement) to comment (up)on; (RADIO, TV: match, manifestation) to cover

commérages [kɔmeʀaʒ] nmpl gossip sg

commerçant, e [kɔmeʀsɑ̃, -ɑ̃t] nm/f shopkeeper, trader

commerce [kɔmeʀs(ə)] nm (activité) trade, commerce; (boutique) business; **vendu dans le ~** sold in the shops; **commercial, e, aux** adj commercial, trading; (péj) commercial; **commercialiser** vt to market

commère [kɔmeʀ] nf gossip

commettre [kɔmetʀ(ə)] vt to commit

commis [kɔmi] nm (de magasin) (shop) assistant; (de banque) clerk; ~ **voyageur** commercial traveller

commissaire [kɔmisɛʀ] nm (de police) ≈ (police) superintendent; ~**-priseur** nm auctioneer

commissariat [kɔmisaʀja] nm police station

commission [kɔmisjɔ̃] nf (comité, pourcentage) commission; (message) message; (course) errand; ~**s** nfpl (achats) shopping sg

commode [kɔmɔd] adj (pratique) convenient, handy; (facile) easy; (air, personne) easy-going; (*personne*): **pas ~** awkward (to deal with) ♦ *nf* chest of drawers; **commodité** *nf* convenience

commotion [kɔmosjɔ̃] *nf*: **~ (cérébrale)** concussion; **commotionné, e** *adj* shocked, shaken

commun, e [kɔmœ̃, -yn] *adj* common; (*pièce*) communal, shared; (*réunion, effort*) joint; **cela sort du ~** it's out of the ordinary; **le ~ des mortels** the common run of people; **en ~** (*faire*) jointly; **mettre en ~** to pool, share; *voir aussi* **communs**

communauté [kɔmynote] *nf* community; (*JUR*): **régime de la ~** communal estate settlement

commune [kɔmyn] *nf* (*ADMIN*) commune, ≈ district; (: *urbaine*) ≈ borough

communication [kɔmynikasjɔ̃] *nf* communication; **~ (téléphonique)** (telephone) call

communier [kɔmynje] *vi* (*REL*) to receive communion; (*fig*) to be united; **communion** [kɔmynjɔ̃] *nf* communion

communiquer [kɔmynike] *vt* (*nouvelle, dossier*) to pass on, convey; (*maladie*) to pass on; (*peur etc*) to communicate; (*chaleur, mouvement*) to transmit ♦ *vi* to communicate; **se ~ à** (*se propager*) to spread to

communisme [kɔmynism(ə)] *nm* communism; **communiste** *adj, nm/f* communist

communs [kɔmœ̃] *nmpl* (*bâtiments*) outbuildings

commutateur [kɔmytatœʀ] *nm* (*ÉLEC*) (change-over) switch, commutator

compact, e [kɔ̃pakt] *adj* dense; compact

compagne [kɔ̃paɲ] *nf* companion

compagnie [kɔ̃paɲi] *nf* (*firme, MIL*) company; (*groupe*) gathering; **tenir ~ à qn** to keep sb company; **fausser ~ à qn** to give sb the slip, slip *ou* sneak away from sb; **~ aérienne** airline (company)

compagnon [kɔ̃paɲɔ̃] *nm* companion

comparable [kɔ̃paʀabl(ə)] *adj*: **~ (à)** comparable (to)

comparaison [kɔ̃paʀɛzɔ̃] *nf* comparison

comparaître [kɔ̃paʀɛtʀ(ə)] *vi*: **~ (devant)** to appear (before)

comparer [kɔ̃paʀe] *vt* to compare; **~ qch/qn à** *ou* **et** (*pour choisir*) to compare sth/sb with *ou* and; (*pour établir une similitude*) to compare sth/sb to

comparse [kɔ̃paʀs(ə)] (*péj*) *nm/f* associate, stooge

compartiment [kɔ̃paʀtimã] *nm* compartment

comparution [kɔ̃paʀysjɔ̃] *nf* appearance

compas [kɔ̃pa] *nm* (*GÉOM*) (pair of) compasses *pl*; (*NAVIG*) compass

compatible [kɔ̃patibl(ə)] *adj* compatible

compatir [kɔ̃patiʀ] *vi*: **~ (à)** to sympathize (with)

compatriote [kɔ̃patʀijɔt] *nm/f* compatriot

compenser [kɔ̃pãse] *vt* to compensate for, make up for

compère [kɔ̃pɛʀ] *nm* accomplice

compétence [kɔ̃petãs] *nf* competence

compétent, e [kɔ̃petã, -ãt] *adj* (*apte*) competent, capable

compétition [kɔ̃petisjɔ̃] *nf* (*gén*) competition; (*SPORT: épreuve*) event; **la ~** competitive sport; **la ~ automobile** motor racing

complainte [kɔ̃plɛ̃t] *nf* lament

complaire [kɔ̃plɛʀ] : **se ~** *vi*: **se ~ dans/parmi** to take pleasure in/in being among

complaisance [kɔ̃plɛzãs] *nf* kindness; **pavillon de ~** flag of convenience; **complaisant, e** [kɔ̃plɛzã, -ãt] *adj* (*aimable*) kind, obliging

complément [kɔ̃plemã] *nm* complement; remainder; **~ d'information** (*ADMIN*) supplementary *ou* further information; **complémentaire** *adj* complementary; (*additionnel*) supplementary

complet, ète [kɔ̃plɛ, -et] *adj* complete; (*plein: hôtel etc*) full ♦ *nm* (*aussi: ~-veston*) suit; **complètement** *adv* completely; **compléter** *vt* (*porter à la quantité voulue*) to complete; (*augmenter*) to complement, supplement; to add to

complexe [kɔ̃plɛks(ə)] *adj, nm* complex; **complexé, e** *adj* mixed-up, hung-up

complication [kɔ̃plikasjɔ̃] *nf* complexity, intricacy; (*difficulté, ennui*) complication

complice [kɔ̃plis] *nm* accomplice

compliment [kɔ̃plimã] *nm* (*louange*) compliment; **~s** *nmpl* (*félicitations*) congratulations

compliqué, e [kɔ̃plike] *adj* complicated, complex; (*personne*) complicated

complot [kɔ̃plo] *nm* plot

comportement [kɔ̃pɔʀtəmã] *nm* behaviour

comporter [kɔ̃pɔʀte] *vt* to consist of, comprise; (*être équipé de*) to have; (*impliquer*) to entail; **se ~** *vi* to behave

composant [kɔ̃pozã] *nm* component

composante [kɔ̃pozãt] *nf* component

composé [kɔ̃poze] *nm* compound

composer [kɔ̃poze] *vt* (*musique, texte*) to compose; (*mélange, équipe*) to make up; (*faire partie de*) to make up, form ♦ *vi* (*transiger*) to come to terms; **se ~ de** to be composed of, be made up of; **~ un numéro** to dial a number

compositeur, trice [kɔ̃pozitœʀ, -tʀis] *nm/f* (*MUS*) composer

composition [kɔ̃pozisjɔ̃] *nf* composition; (*SCOL*) test; **de bonne ~** (*accommodant*) easy to deal with

composter [kɔ̃pɔste] *vt* to date-stamp; to punch

compote [kɔ̃pɔt] *nf* stewed fruit *no pl*; **~ de pommes** stewed apples; **compotier** *nm* fruit dish *ou* bowl

compréhensible [kɔ̃pʀeɑ̃sibl(ə)] *adj* comprehensible; (*attitude*) understandable
compréhensif, ive [kɔ̃pʀeɑ̃sif, -iv] *adj* understanding
comprendre [kɔ̃pʀɑ̃dʀ(ə)] *vt* to understand; (*se composer de*) to comprise, consist of
compresse [kɔ̃pʀɛs] *nf* compress
compression [kɔ̃pʀesjɔ̃] *nf* compression; reduction
comprimé [kɔ̃pʀime] *nm* tablet
comprimer [kɔ̃pʀime] *vt* to compress; (*fig: crédit etc*) to reduce, cut down
compris, e [kɔ̃pʀi, -iz] *pp de* **comprendre** ♦ *adj* (*inclus*) included; ~ **entre** (*situé*) contained between; **la maison** ~**e/non** ~**e, y/ non** ~ **la maison** including/excluding the house; **100 F tout** ~ 100 F all inclusive *ou* all-in
compromettre [kɔ̃pʀɔmɛtʀ(ə)] *vt* to compromise
compromis [kɔ̃pʀɔmi] *nm* compromise
comptabilité [kɔ̃tabilite] *nf* (*activité, technique*) accounting, accountancy; (*d'une société: comptes*) accounts *pl*, books *pl*; (*: service*) accounts office
comptable [kɔ̃tabl(ə)] *nm/f* accountant
comptant [kɔ̃tɑ̃] *adv*: **payer** ~ to pay cash; **acheter** ~ to buy for cash
compte [kɔ̃t] *nm* count, counting; (*total, montant*) count, (right) number; (*bancaire, facture*) account; ~**s** *nmpl* (*FINANCE*) accounts, books; (*fig*) explanation *sg*; **en fin de** ~ all things considered; **à bon** ~ at a favourable price; (*fig*) lightly; **avoir son** ~ (*: fam*) to have had it; **pour le** ~ **de** on behalf of; **pour son propre** ~ for one's own benefit; **tenir** ~ **de** to take account of; **travailler à son** ~ to work for oneself; **rendre** ~ (**à qn**) **de qch** to give (sb) an account of sth; *voir aussi* **rendre**; ~ **à rebours** countdown; ~ **chèques postaux** Post Office account; ~ **courant** current account
compte-gouttes [kɔ̃tgut] *nm inv* dropper
compter [kɔ̃te] *vt* to count; (*facturer*) to charge for; (*avoir à son actif, comporter*) to have; (*prévoir*) to allow, reckon; (*penser, espérer*) ♦ *vi*: ~ **réussir** to expect to succeed ♦ *vi* to count; (*être économe*) to economize; (*figurer*): ~ **parmi** to be *ou* rank among; ~ **sur** to count (up)on; ~ **avec qch/qn** to reckon with *ou* take account of sth/sb; **sans** ~ **que** besides which
compte rendu [kɔ̃tʀɑ̃dy] *nm* account, report; (*de film, livre*) review
compte-tours [kɔ̃ttuʀ] *nm inv* rev(olution) counter
compteur [kɔ̃tœʀ] *nm* meter; ~ **de vitesse** speedometer
comptine [kɔ̃tin] *nf* nursery rhyme
comptoir [kɔ̃twaʀ] *nm* (*de magasin*) counter

compulser [kɔ̃pylse] *vt* to consult
comte [kɔ̃t] *nm* count
comtesse [kɔ̃tɛs] *nf* countess
con, ne [kɔ̃, kɔn] (*fam!*) *adj* damned *ou* bloody (*BRIT*) stupid (*!*)
concéder [kɔ̃sede] *vt* to grant; (*défaite, point*) to concede
concentrer [kɔ̃sɑ̃tʀe] *vt* to concentrate; **se** ~ *vi* to concentrate
concept [kɔ̃sɛpt] *nm* concept
conception [kɔ̃sɛpsjɔ̃] *nf* conception; (*d'une machine etc*) design
concerner [kɔ̃sɛʀne] *vt* to concern; **en ce qui me concerne** as far as I am concerned
concert [kɔ̃sɛʀ] *nm* concert; **de** ~ in unison; together
concerter [kɔ̃sɛʀte] *vt* to devise; **se** ~ *vi* (*collaborateurs etc*) to put our (*ou* their *etc*) heads together
concessionnaire [kɔ̃sesjɔnɛʀ] *nm/f* agent, dealer
concevoir [kɔ̃svwaʀ] *vt* (*idée, projet*) to conceive (of); (*méthode, plan d'appartement, décoration*) to plan, design; (*enfant*) to conceive; **bien/mal conçu** well-/badly-designed
concierge [kɔ̃sjɛʀʒ(ə)] *nm/f* caretaker; (*d'hôtel*) head porter
concile [kɔ̃sil] *nm* council
conciliabules [kɔ̃siljabyl] *nmpl* (private) discussions, confabulations
concilier [kɔ̃silje] *vt* to reconcile; **se** ~ *vt* to win over
concitoyen, ne [kɔ̃sitwajɛ̃, -jɛn] *nm/f* fellow citizen
concluant, e [kɔ̃klyɑ̃, -ɑ̃t] *adj* conclusive
conclure [kɔ̃klyʀ] *vt* to conclude
conclusion [kɔ̃klyzjɔ̃] *nf* conclusion
conçois *etc vb voir* **concevoir**
concombre [kɔ̃kɔ̃bʀ(ə)] *nm* cucumber
concorder [kɔ̃kɔʀde] *vi* to tally, agree
concourir [kɔ̃kuʀiʀ] *vi* (*SPORT*) to compete; ~ **à** (*effet etc*) to work towards
concours [kɔ̃kuʀ] *nm* competition; (*SCOL*) competitive examination; (*assistance*) aid, help; ~ **de circonstances** combination of circumstances; ~ **hippique** horse show
concret, ète [kɔ̃kʀɛ, -ɛt] *adj* concrete
concrétiser [kɔ̃kʀetize] *vt* (*plan, projet*) to put in concrete form; **se** ~ *vi* to materialize
conçu, e [kɔ̃sy] *pp de* **concevoir**
concubinage [kɔ̃kybinaʒ] *nm* (*JUR*) cohabitation
concurrence [kɔ̃kyʀɑ̃s] *nf* competition; **jusqu'à** ~ **de** up to
concurrent, e [kɔ̃kyʀɑ̃, -ɑ̃t] *nm/f* (*SPORT, ÉCON etc*) competitor; (*SCOL*) candidate
condamner [kɔ̃dane] *vt* (*blâmer*) to condemn; (*JUR*) to sentence; (*porte, ouverture*) to fill in, block up; (*malade*) to give up (hope for); ~ **qn à 2 ans de prison** to sentence sb to 2 years' imprisonment
condensation [kɔ̃dɑ̃sɑsjɔ̃] *nf* condensation

condenser [kɔ̃dɑ̃se] vt to condense; **se ~**
vi to condense

condisciple [kɔ̃disipl(ə)] nm/f school fellow, fellow student

condition [kɔ̃disjɔ̃] nf condition; **~s** nfpl
(*tarif, prix*) terms; (*circonstances*) conditions;
sans ~ unconditional ♦ *adv* uncondition-
ally; **à ~ de** *ou* **que** provided that; **condi-
tionnel, le** *adj* conditional ♦ *nm* conditional (tense)

conditionnement [kɑ̃disjɔnmɑ̃] nm (emballage) packaging

conditionner [kɔ̃disjɔne] vt (*déterminer*) to
determine; (*COMM: produit*) to package;
(*fig: personne*) to condition; **air condition-
né** air conditioning

condoléances [kɔ̃dɔleɑ̃s] nfpl condolences

conducteur, trice [kɔ̃dyktœʀ, -tʀis] nm/f
driver ♦ nm (*ÉLEC etc*) conductor

conduire [kɔ̃dɥiʀ] vt to drive; (*délégation,
troupeau*) to lead; **se ~** *vi* to behave; **~
vers/à** to lead towards/to; **~ qn quelque
part** to take sb somewhere; to drive sb
somewhere

conduite [kɔ̃dɥit] nf (*comportement*) behaviour; (*d'eau, de gaz*) pipe; **sous la ~ de**
led by; **~ à gauche** left-hand drive; **~ intérieure** saloon (car)

cône [kon] nm cone

confection [kɔ̃fɛksjɔ̃] nf (*fabrication*) making; (*COUTURE*): **la ~** the clothing industry;
vêtement de ~ ready-to-wear *ou* off-the-
peg garment

confectionner [kɔ̃fɛksjɔne] vt to make

conférence [kɔ̃feʀɑ̃s] nf (*exposé*) lecture;
(*pourparlers*) conference; **~ de presse** press
conference

confesser [kɔ̃fese] vt to confess; **se ~** *vi*
(*REL*) to go to confession

confession [kɔ̃fesjɔ̃] nf confession; (*culte:
catholique etc*) denomination

confiance [kɔ̃fjɑ̃s] nf confidence, trust;
faith; **avoir ~ en** to have confidence *ou*
faith in, trust; **mettre qn en ~** to win sb's
trust; **~ en soi** self-confidence

confiant, e [kɔ̃fjɑ̃, -ɑ̃t] adj confident; trust-
ing

confidence [kɔ̃fidɑ̃s] nf confidence

confidentiel, le [kɔ̃fidɑ̃sjɛl] adj confidential

confier [kɔ̃fje] vt: **~ à qn** (*objet en dépôt,
travail etc*) to entrust to sb; (*secret, pensée*)
to confide to sb; **se ~ à qn** to confide in
sb

confiné, e [kɔ̃fine] adj enclosed; stale

confins [kɔ̃fɛ̃] nmpl: **aux ~ de** on the bor-
ders of

confirmation [kɔ̃fiʀmasjɔ̃] nf confirmation

confirmer [kɔ̃fiʀme] vt to confirm

confiserie [kɔ̃fizʀi] nf (*magasin*) confectioner's *ou* sweet shop; **~s** nfpl (*bonbons*)
confectionery *sg*; **confiseur, euse** nm/f

confectioner

confisquer [kɔ̃fiske] vt to confiscate

confit, e [kɔ̃fi, -it] adj: **fruits ~s** crystallized fruits ♦ nm: **~ d'oie** conserve of
goose

confiture [kɔ̃fityʀ] nf jam; **~ d'oranges**
(orange) marmalade

conflit [kɔ̃fli] nm conflict

confondre [kɔ̃fɔ̃dʀ(ə)] vt (*jumeaux, faits*) to
confuse, mix up; (*témoin, menteur*) to confound; **se ~** *vi* to merge; **se ~ en excuses**
to apologize profusely; **confondu, e**
[kɔ̃fɔ̃dy] adj (*stupéfait*) speechless, overcome

conforme [kɔ̃fɔʀm(ə)] adj: **~ à** in accordance with; in keeping with; true to

conformément [kɔ̃fɔʀmemɑ̃] adv: **~ à** in
accordance with

conformer [kɔ̃fɔʀme] vt: **se ~ à** to conform to

conformité [kɔ̃fɔʀmite] nf: **en ~ avec** in
accordance with, in keeping with

confort [kɔ̃fɔʀ] nm comfort; **tout ~**
(*COMM*) with all modern conveniences;
confortable adj comfortable

confrère [kɔ̃fʀɛʀ] nm colleague; fellow
member; **confrérie** nf brotherhood

confronter [kɔ̃fʀɔ̃te] vt to confront; (*textes*)
to compare, collate

confus, e [kɔ̃fy, -yz] adj (*vague*) confused;
(*embarrassé*) embarrassed

confusion [kɔ̃fyzjɔ̃] nf (*voir confus*) confusion; embarrassment; (*voir confondre*) confusion, mixing up

congé [kɔ̃ʒe] nm (*vacances*) holiday; **en ~**
on holiday; **~ (of work)**; **semaine de ~**
week off; **prendre ~ de qn** to take one's
leave of sb; **donner son ~ à** to give in
one's notice to; **~ de maladie** sick leave;
~s payés paid holiday

congédier [kɔ̃ʒedje] vt to dismiss

congélateur [kɔ̃ʒelatœʀ] nm freezer, deep
freeze

congeler [kɔ̃ʒle] vt to freeze

congestion [kɔ̃ʒɛstjɔ̃] nf congestion; **~ cérébrale** stroke

congestionner [kɔ̃ʒɛstjɔne] vt to congest;
(*MÉD*) to flush

congrès [kɔ̃gʀɛ] nm congress

congru, e [kɔ̃gʀy] adj: **la portion ~e** the
smallest *ou* meanest share

conifère [kɔnifɛʀ] nm conifer

conjecture [kɔ̃ʒɛktyʀ] nf conjecture

conjoint, e [kɔ̃ʒwɛ̃, -wɛ̃t] adj joint ♦ nm/f
spouse

conjonction [kɔ̃ʒɔ̃ksjɔ̃] nf (*LING*) conjunction

conjonctivite [kɔ̃ʒɔ̃ktivit] nf conjunctivitis

conjoncture [kɔ̃ʒɔ̃ktyʀ] nf circumstances
pl; climate

conjugaison [kɔ̃ʒygɛzɔ̃] nf (*LING*) conjugation

conjuguer [kɔ̃ʒyge] vt (*LING*) to conjugate;

(efforts etc) to combine
conjuration [kɔ̃ʒyʀasjɔ̃] *nf* conspiracy
conjurer [kɔ̃ʒyʀe] *vt* (*sort, maladie*) to avert; (*implorer*) to beseech, entreat
connaissance [kɔnɛsɑ̃s] *nf* (*savoir*) knowledge *no pl*; (*personne connue*) acquaintance; **être sans ~** to be unconscious; **perdre/reprendre ~** to lose/regain consciousness; **à ma/sa ~** to (the best of) my/his knowledge; **avoir ~ de** to be aware of; **prendre ~ de** (*document etc*) to peruse; **en ~ de cause** with full knowledge of the facts
connaître [kɔnɛtʀ(ə)] *vt* to know; (*éprouver*) to experience; (*avoir*) to have; to enjoy; **~ de nom/vue** to know by name/sight; **ils se sont connus à Genève** they (first) met in Geneva
connecté, e [kɔnɛkte] *adj* on line
connecter [kɔnɛkte] *vt* to connect
connerie [kɔnʀi] (*fam!*) *nf* stupid thing (to do *ou* say)
connu, e [kɔny] *adj* (*célèbre*) well-known
conquérir [kɔ̃keʀiʀ] *vt* to conquer, win; **conquête** *nf* conquest
consacrer [kɔ̃sakʀe] *vt* (*REL*) to consecrate; (*fig: usage etc*) to sanction, establish; (*employer*) to devote, dedicate
conscience [kɔ̃sjɑ̃s] *nf* conscience; **avoir/prendre ~ de** to be/become aware of; **perdre ~** to lose consciousness; **avoir bonne/mauvaise ~** to have a clear/guilty conscience; **consciencieux, euse** *adj* conscientious; **conscient, e** *adj* conscious
conscrit [kɔ̃skʀi] *nm* conscript
consécutif, ive [kɔ̃sekytif, -iv] *adj* consecutive; **~ à** following upon
conseil [kɔ̃sɛj] *nm* (*avis*) piece of advice, advice *no pl*; (*assemblée*) council; **prendre ~ (auprès de qn)** to take advice (from sb); **~ d'administration** board (of directors); **le ~ des ministres** ≈ the Cabinet
conseiller, ère [kɔ̃seje, kɔ̃sejɛʀ] *nm/f* adviser ♦ *vt* (*personne*) to advise; (*méthode, action*) to recommend, advise; **~ à qn de** to advise sb to
consentement [kɔ̃sɑ̃tmɑ̃] *nm* consent
consentir [kɔ̃sɑ̃tiʀ] *vt* to agree, consent
conséquence [kɔ̃sekɑ̃s] *nf* consequence; **en ~** (*donc*) consequently; (*de façon appropriée*) accordingly; **ne pas tirer à ~** to be unlikely to have any repercussions
conséquent, e [kɔ̃sekɑ̃, -ɑ̃t] *adj* logical, rational; (*fam: important*) substantial; **par ~** consequently
conservateur, trice [kɔ̃sɛʀvatœʀ, -tʀis] *nm/f* (*POL*) conservative; (*de musée*) curator
conservatoire [kɔ̃sɛʀvatwaʀ] *nm* academy; (*ÉCOLOGIE*) conservation area
conserve [kɔ̃sɛʀv(ə)] *nf* (*gén pl*) canned *ou* tinned (*BRIT*) food; **en ~** canned, tinned (*BRIT*)

conserver [kɔ̃sɛʀve] *vt* (*faculté*) to retain, keep; (*amis, livres*) to keep; (*préserver, aussi CULIN*) to preserve
considérable [kɔ̃sideʀabl(ə)] *adj* considerable, significant, extensive
considération [kɔ̃sideʀasjɔ̃] *nf* consideration; (*estime*) esteem
considérer [kɔ̃sideʀe] *vt* to consider; **~ qch comme** to regard sth as
consigne [kɔ̃siɲ] *nf* (*de gare*) left luggage (office) (*BRIT*), checkroom (*US*); (*ordre, instruction*) instructions *pl*; **~ (automatique)** left-luggage locker; **~r** [kɔ̃siɲe] *vt* (*note, pensée*) to record; (*punir*) to confine to barracks; to put in detention; (*COMM*) to put a deposit on
consistant, e [kɔ̃sistɑ̃, -ɑ̃t] *adj* thick; solid
consister [kɔ̃siste] *vi*: **~ en/dans/à faire** to consist of/in/in doing
consœur [kɔ̃sœʀ] *nf* (lady) colleague; fellow member
consoler [kɔ̃sɔle] *vt* to console
consolider [kɔ̃sɔlide] *vt* to strengthen; (*fig*) to consolidate
consommateur, trice [kɔ̃sɔmatœʀ, -tʀis] *nm/f* (*ÉCON*) consumer; (*dans un café*) customer
consommation [kɔ̃sɔmasjɔ̃] *nf* (*boisson*) drink; **~ aux 100 km** (*AUTO*) (fuel) consumption per 100 km
consommer [kɔ̃sɔme] *vt* (*suj: personne*) to eat *ou* drink, consume; (: *voiture, usine, poêle*) to use, consume ♦ *vi* (*dans un café*) to (have a) drink
consonne [kɔ̃sɔn] *nf* consonant
conspirer [kɔ̃spiʀe] *vi* to conspire
constamment [kɔ̃stamɑ̃] *adv* constantly
constant, e [kɔ̃stɑ̃, -ɑ̃t] *adj* constant; (*personne*) steadfast
constat [kɔ̃sta] *nm* (*d'huissier*) certified report; (*de police*) report; (*affirmation*) statement
constatation [kɔ̃statasjɔ̃] *nf* (*observation*) (observed) fact, observation; (*affirmation*) statement
constater [kɔ̃state] *vt* (*remarquer*) to note; (*ADMIN, JUR: attester*) to certify; (*dire*) to state
consterner [kɔ̃stɛʀne] *vt* to dismay
constipé, e [kɔ̃stipe] *adj* constipated
constitué, e [kɔ̃stitɥe] *adj*: **~ de** made up *ou* composed of
constituer [kɔ̃stitɥe] *vt* (*comité, équipe*) to set up; (*dossier, collection*) to put together; (*suj: éléments: composer*) to make up, constitute; (*représenter, être*) to constitute; **se ~ prisonnier** to give o.s. up
constitution [kɔ̃stitysjɔ̃] *nf* (*composition*) composition, make-up; (*santé, POL*) constitution
constructeur [kɔ̃stʀyktœʀ] *nm* manufacturer, builder

construction [kɔ̃stʀyksjɔ̃] *nf* construction, building

construire [kɔ̃stʀɥiʀ] *vt* to build, construct

consul [kɔ̃syl] *nm* consul; **consulat** *nm* consulate

consultation [kɔ̃syltɑsjɔ̃] *nf* consultation; **~s** *nfpl* (POL) talks; **heures de ~** (MÉD) surgery (BRIT) *ou* office (US) hours

consulter [kɔ̃sylte] *vt* to consult ♦ *vi* (médecin) to hold surgery (BRIT), be in (the office) (US)

consumer [kɔ̃syme] *vt* to consume; **se ~** *vi* to burn

contact [kɔ̃takt] *nm* contact; **au ~ de** (air, peau) on contact with; (gens) through contact with; **mettre/couper le ~** (AUTO) to switch on/off the ignition; **entrer en** *ou* **prendre ~ avec** to get in touch *ou* contact with; **contacter** *vt* to contact, get in touch with

contagieux, euse [kɔ̃taʒjø, -øz] *adj* contagious; infectious

contaminer [kɔ̃tamine] *vt* to contaminate

conte [kɔ̃t] *nm* tale; **~ de fées** fairy tale

contempler [kɔ̃tɑ̃ple] *vt* to contemplate, gaze at

contemporain, e [kɔ̃tɑ̃pɔʀɛ̃, -ɛn] *adj, nm/f* contemporary

contenance [kɔ̃tnɑ̃s] *nf* (d'un récipient) capacity; (attitude) bearing, attitude; **perdre ~** to lose one's composure

conteneur [kɔ̃tnœʀ] *nm* container

contenir [kɔ̃tniʀ] *vt* to contain; (avoir une capacité de) to hold

content, e [kɔ̃tɑ̃, -ɑ̃t] *adj* pleased, glad; **~ de** pleased with; **contenter** *vt* to satisfy, please; **se ~er de** to content o.s. with

contentieux [kɔ̃tɑ̃sjø] *nm* (COMM) litigation; litigation department

contenu [kɔ̃tny] *nm* (d'un bol) contents *pl*; (d'un texte) content

conter [kɔ̃te] *vt* to recount, relate

contestable [kɔ̃tɛstabl(ə)] *adj* questionable

contestation [kɔ̃tɛstɑsjɔ̃] *nf* (POL) protest

conteste [kɔ̃tɛst(ə)] : **sans ~** *adv* unquestionably, indisputably

contester [kɔ̃tɛste] *vt* to question, contest ♦ *vi* (POL, gén) to protest, rebel (against established authority)

contexte [kɔ̃tɛkst(ə)] *nm* context

contigu, ë [kɔ̃tigy] *adj*: **~ (à)** adjacent (to)

continent [kɔ̃tinɑ̃] *nm* continent

continu, e [kɔ̃tiny] *adj* continuous; **(courant) ~** direct current, DC

continuel, le [kɔ̃tinɥɛl] *adj* (qui se répète) constant, continual; (continu) continuous

continuer [kɔ̃tinɥe] *vt* (travail, voyage etc) to continue (with), carry on (with), go on (with); (prolonger: alignement, rue) to continue ♦ *vi* (pluie, vie, bruit) to continue, go on; (voyageur) to go on; **~ à** *ou* **de faire** to go on *ou* continue doing

contorsionner [kɔ̃tɔʀsjɔne]: **se ~** *vi* to contort o.s., writhe about

contour [kɔ̃tuʀ] *nm* outline, contour

contourner [kɔ̃tuʀne] *vt* to go round

contraceptif, ive [kɔ̃tʀasɛptif, -iv] *adj, nm* contraceptive; **contraception** [kɔ̃tʀasɛpsjɔ̃] *nf* contraception

contracté, e [kɔ̃tʀakte] *adj* tense

contracter [kɔ̃tʀakte] *vt* (muscle etc) to tense, contract; (maladie, dette, obligation) to contract; (assurance) to take out; **se ~** *vi* (métal, muscles) to contract

contractuel, le [kɔ̃tʀaktɥɛl] *nm/f* (agent) traffic warden

contradiction [kɔ̃tʀadiksjɔ̃] *nf* contradiction; **contradictoire** *adj* contradictory, conflicting

contraignant, e [kɔ̃tʀɛɲɑ̃, -ɑ̃t] *adj* restricting

contraindre *vt*: **~ qn à faire** to compel sb to do; **contraint, e** [kɔ̃tʀɛ̃, -ɛ̃t] *adj* (mine, air) constrained, forced; **contrainte** *nf* constraint

contraire [kɔ̃tʀɛʀ] *adj, nm* opposite; **~ à** contrary to; **au ~** on the contrary

contrarier [kɔ̃tʀaʀje] *vt* (personne) to annoy, bother; (fig) to impede; to thwart, frustrate; **contrariété** [kɔ̃tʀaʀjete] *nf* annoyance

contraste [kɔ̃tʀast(ə)] *nm* contrast

contrat [kɔ̃tʀa] *nm* contract; **~ de travail** employment contract

contravention [kɔ̃tʀavɑ̃sjɔ̃] *nf* (amende) fine; (P.V. pour stationnement interdit) parking ticket

contre [kɔ̃tʀ(ə)] *prép* against; (en échange) (in exchange) for; **par ~** on the other hand

contrebande [kɔ̃tʀəbɑ̃d] *nf* (trafic) contraband, smuggling; (marchandise) contraband, smuggled goods *pl*; **faire la ~ de** to smuggle

contrebas [kɔ̃tʀəba] : **en ~** *adv* (down) below

contrebasse [kɔ̃tʀəbas] *nf* (double) bass

contre: ~carrer *vt* to thwart; **~cœur: à ~cœur** *adv* (be)grudgingly, reluctantly; **~coup** *nm* repercussions *pl*; **par ~coup** as an indirect consequence; **~dire** *vt* (personne) to contradict; (témoignage, assertion, faits) to refute

contrée [kɔ̃tʀe] *nf* region; land

contrefaçon [kɔ̃tʀəfasɔ̃] *nf* forgery

contrefaire [kɔ̃tʀəfɛʀ] *vt* (document, signature) to forge, counterfeit; (personne, démarche) to mimic; (dénaturer: sa voix etc) to disguise

contre-indication (*pl* **contre-indications**) *nf* (MÉD) contra-indication

contre-jour [kɔ̃tʀəʒuʀ] : **à ~** *adv* against the sunlight

contremaître [kɔ̃tʀəmɛtʀ(ə)] *nm* foreman

contrepartie [kɔ̃tʀəpaʀti] *nf* compensation;

en ~ in return

contre-pied [kɔ̃tʀəpje] nm: **prendre le ~ de** to take the opposing view of; to take the opposite course to

contre-plaqué [kɔ̃tʀəplake] nm plywood

contrepoids [kɔ̃tʀəpwa] nm counterweight, counterbalance

contrer [kɔ̃tʀe] vt to counter

contresens [kɔ̃tʀəsɑ̃s] nm misinterpretation; mistranslation; nonsense no pl; **à ~** the wrong way

contretemps [kɔ̃tʀətɑ̃] nm hitch; **à ~** (MUS) out of time; (fig) at an inopportune moment

contrevenir [kɔ̃tʀəvniʀ]: **~ à** vt to contravene

contribuable [kɔ̃tʀibɥabl(ə)] nm/f taxpayer

contribuer [kɔ̃tʀibɥe]: **~ à** vt to contribute towards; **contribution** nf contribution; **contributions directes/indirectes** direct/indirect taxation; **mettre à contribution** to call upon

contrôle [kɔ̃tʀol] nm checking no pl, check; supervision; monitoring; (test) test, examination; **perdre le ~ de** (véhicule) to lose control of; **~ continu** (SCOL) continuous assessment; **~ d'identité** identity check; **~ des naissances** birth control

contrôler [kɔ̃tʀole] vt to check; (surveiller) to supervise; to monitor, control; (maîtriser, COMM: firme) to control; **contrôleur, euse** nm/f (de train) (ticket) inspector; (de bus) (bus) conductor(tress)

contrordre [kɔ̃tʀɔʀdʀ(ə)] nm: **sauf ~** unless otherwise directed

controversé, e [kɔ̃tʀɔvɛʀse] adj (personnage, question) controversial

contusion [kɔ̃tyzjɔ̃] nf bruise, contusion

convaincre [kɔ̃vɛ̃kʀ(ə)] vt: **~ qn (de qch)** to convince sb (of sth); **~ qn (de faire)** to persuade sb (to do); **~ qn de** (JUR: délit) to convict sb of

convalescence [kɔ̃valesɑ̃s] nf convalescence

convenable [kɔ̃vnabl(ə)] adj suitable; (assez bon, respectable) decent

convenance [kɔ̃vnɑ̃s] nf: **à ma/votre ~** to my/your liking; **~s** nfpl (normes sociales) proprieties

convenir [kɔ̃vniʀ] vi to be suitable; **~ à** to suit; **il convient de** it is advisable to; (bienséant) it is right ou proper to; **~ de** (bienfondé de qch) to admit (to), acknowledge; (date, somme etc) to agree upon; **~ que** (admettre) to admit that; **~ de faire** to agree to do

convention [kɔ̃vɑ̃sjɔ̃] nf convention; **~s** nfpl (convenances) convention sg; **~ collective** (ÉCON) collective agreement; **conventionné, e** adj (ADMIN) applying charges laid down by the state

convenu, e [kɔ̃vny] pp de **convenir** ♦ adj agreed

conversation [kɔ̃vɛʀsasjɔ̃] nf conversation

convertir [kɔ̃vɛʀtiʀ] vt: **~ qn (à)** to convert sb (to); **se ~ (à)** to be converted (to); **~ qch en** to convert sth into

conviction [kɔ̃viksjɔ̃] nf conviction

convienne etc vb voir **convenir**

convier [kɔ̃vje] vt: **~ qn à** (dîner etc) to (cordially) invite sb to

convive [kɔ̃viv] nm/f guest (at table)

convivial, e [kɔ̃vivjal] adj (INFORM) userfriendly

convocation [kɔ̃vɔkasjɔ̃] nf (document) notification to attend; summons sg

convoi [kɔ̃vwa] nm (de voitures, prisonniers) convoy; (train) train

convoiter [kɔ̃vwate] vt to covet

convoquer [kɔ̃vɔke] vt (assemblée) to convene; (subordonné) to summon; (candidat) to ask to attend; **~ qn (à)** (réunion) to invite sb (to attend)

convoyeur [kɔ̃vwajœʀ] nm (NAVIG) escort ship; **~ de fonds** security guard

coopération [kɔɔpeʀasjɔ̃] nf co-operation; (ADMIN): **la C~** ≈ Voluntary Service Overseas (BRIT), ≈ Peace Corps (US)

coopérer [kɔɔpeʀe] vi: **~ (à)** to co-operate (in)

coordonner [kɔɔʀdɔne] vt to coordinate

copain [kɔpɛ̃] nm mate, pal

copeau, x [kɔpo] nm shaving

copie [kɔpi] nf copy; (SCOL) script, paper; exercise

copier [kɔpje] vt, vi to copy; **~ sur** to copy from

copieur [kɔpjœʀ] nm (photo)copier

copieux, euse [kɔpjø, -øz] adj copious

copine [kɔpin] nf = **copain**

copropriété [kɔpʀɔpʀijete] nf coownership, joint ownership

coq [kɔk] nm cock, rooster; **~-à-l'âne** [kɔkalan] nm inv abrupt change of subject

coque [kɔk] nf (de noix, mollusque) shell; (de bateau) hull; **à la ~** (CULIN) (soft-)boiled

coquelicot [kɔkliko] nm poppy

coqueluche [kɔklyʃ] nf whooping-cough

coquet, te [kɔkɛ, -ɛt] adj flirtatious; appearance-conscious; pretty

coquetier [kɔktje] nm egg-cup

coquillage [kɔkijaʒ] nm (mollusque) shellfish inv; (coquille) shell

coquille [kɔkij] nf shell; (TYPO) misprint; **~ St Jacques** scallop

coquin, e [kɔkɛ̃, -in] adj mischievous, roguish; (polisson) naughty

cor [kɔʀ] nm (MUS) horn; (MÉD): **~ (au pied)** corn; **réclamer à ~ et à cri** to clamour for

corail, aux [kɔʀaj, -o] nm coral no pl

Coran [kɔʀɑ̃] nm: **le ~** the Koran

corbeau, x [kɔʀbo] nm crow

corbeille [kɔʀbɛj] *nf* basket; ~ **à papier** waste paper basket *ou* bin

corbillard [kɔʀbijaʀ] *nm* hearse

corde [kɔʀd(ə)] *nf* rope; (*de violon, raquette, d'arc*) string; (*ATHLÉTISME, AUTO*): **la ~** the rails *pl*; **usé jusqu'à la ~** threadbare; ~ **à linge** washing *ou* clothes line; ~ **à sauter** skipping rope; ~**s vocales** vocal cords; **cordée** [kɔʀde] *nf* (*d'alpinistes*) rope, roped party

cordialement [kɔʀdjalmã] *adv* (*formule épistolaire*) (kind) regards

cordon [kɔʀdõ] *nm* cord, string; ~ **ombilical** umbilical cord; ~ **sanitaire/de police** sanitary/police cordon

cordonnerie [kɔʀdɔnʀi] *nf* shoe repairer's (shop); **cordonnier** [kɔʀdɔnje] *nm* shoe repairer

Corée [kɔʀe] *nf*: **la ~ du Sud/du Nord** South/North Korea

coriace [kɔʀjas] *adj* tough

corne [kɔʀn(ə)] *nf* horn; (*de cerf*) antler

corneille [kɔʀnɛj] *nf* crow

cornemuse [kɔʀnəmyz] *nf* bagpipes *pl*

cornet [kɔʀnɛ] *nm* (paper) cone; (*de glace*) cornet, cone

corniche [kɔʀniʃ] *nf* (*de meuble, neigeuse*) cornice; (*route*) coast road

cornichon [kɔʀniʃõ] *nm* gherkin

Cornouailles [kɔʀnwaj] *nf* Cornwall

corporation [kɔʀpɔʀasjõ] *nf* corporate body

corporel, le [kɔʀpɔʀɛl] *adj* bodily; (*punition*) corporal

corps [kɔʀ] *nm* body; **à son ~ défendant** against one's will; **à ~ perdu** headlong; **perdu ~ et biens** lost with all hands; **prendre ~** to take shape; **à ~** *adv* hand-to-hand ♦ *nm* clinch; ~ **de garde** guardroom; **le ~ électoral** the electorate; **le ~ enseignant** the teaching profession

corpulent, e [kɔʀpylã, -ãt] *adj* stout

correct, e [kɔʀɛkt] *adj* correct; (*passable*) adequate

correction [kɔʀɛksjõ] *nf* (*voir corriger*) correction; (*voir correct*) correctness; (*rature, surcharge*) correction, emendation; (*coups*) thrashing

correctionnel, le [kɔʀɛksjɔnɛl] *adj* (*JUR*): **tribunal ~** ≈ criminal court

correspondance [kɔʀɛspõdãs] *nf* correspondence; (*de train, d'avion*) connection; **cours par ~** correspondence course; **vente par ~** mail-order business

correspondant, e [kɔʀɛspõdã, -ãt] *nm/f* correspondent; (*TÉL*) person phoning (*ou* being phoned)

correspondre [kɔʀɛspõdʀ(ə)] *vi* to correspond; ~ **à** to correspond to; ~ **avec qn** to correspond with sb

corrida [kɔʀida] *nf* bullfight

corridor [kɔʀidɔʀ] *nm* corridor

corriger [kɔʀiʒe] *vt* (*devoir*) to correct; (*punir*) to thrash; ~ **qn de** (*défaut*) to cure sb of

corrompre [kɔʀõpʀ(ə)] *vt* to corrupt; (*acheter: témoin etc*) to bribe

corruption [kɔʀypsjõ] *nf* corruption; bribery

corsage [kɔʀsaʒ] *nm* bodice; blouse

corse [kɔʀs(ə)] *adj, nm/f* Corsican ♦ *nf*: **la C~** Corsica

corsé, e [kɔʀse] *adj* vigorous; (*vin, goût*) full-flavoured; (*fig*) spicy; tricky

corset [kɔʀsɛ] *nm* corset; bodice

cortège [kɔʀtɛʒ] *nm* procession

corvée [kɔʀve] *nf* chore, drudgery *no pl*

cosmétique [kɔsmetik] *nm* beauty care product

cossu, e [kɔsy] *adj* well-to-do

costaud, e [kɔsto, -od] *adj* strong, sturdy

costume [kɔstym] *nm* (*d'homme*) suit; (*de théâtre*) costume; **costumé, e** *adj* dressed up

cote [kɔt] *nf* (*en Bourse etc*) quotation; quoted value; (*d'un cheval*): **la ~ de** the odds *pl* on; (*d'un candidat etc*) rating; (*un croquis*) dimension; ~ **d'alerte** danger *ou* flood level

côte [kot] *nf* (*rivage*) coast(line); (*pente*) slope; (: *sur une route*) hill; (*ANAT*) rib; (*d'un tricot, tissu*) rib, ribbing *no pl*; ~ **à ~** side by side; **la C~ (d'Azur)** the (French) Riviera

côté [kote] *nm* (*gén*) side; (*direction*) way, direction; **de chaque ~ (de)** on each side (of); **de tous les ~s** from all directions; **de quel ~ est-il parti?** which way did he go?; **de ce/de l'autre ~** this/the other way; **du ~ de** (*provenance*) from; (*direction*) towards; (*proximité*) near; **de ~** sideways; on one side; to one side; aside; **laisser/mettre de ~** to leave/put to one side; **à ~** (right) nearby; beside; next door; (*d'autre part*) besides; **à ~ de** beside; next to; **être aux ~s de** to be by the side of

coteau, x [kɔto] *nm* hill

côtelette [kotlɛt] *nf* chop

coter [kɔte] *vt* (*en Bourse*) to quote

côtier, ière [kotje, -jɛʀ] *adj* coastal

cotisation [kɔtizasjõ] *nf* subscription, dues *pl*; (*pour une pension*) contributions *pl*

cotiser [kɔtize] *vi*: ~ **(à)** to pay contributions (to); **se ~** *vi* to club together

coton [kɔtõ] *nm* cotton; ~ **hydrophile** cotton wool (*BRIT*), absorbent cotton (*US*)

côtoyer [kotwaje] *vt* to be close to; to rub shoulders with; to run alongside

cou [ku] *nm* neck

couchant [kuʃã] *adj*: **soleil ~** setting sun

couche [kuʃ] *nf* (*strate: gén, GÉO*) layer; (*de peinture, vernis*) coat; (*de bébé*) nappy (*BRIT*), diaper (*US*); ~**s** *nfpl* (*MÉD*) confinement *sg*; ~ **d'ozone** ozone layer; ~**s socia-**

les social levels *ou* strata

couché, e [kuʃe] *adj* lying down; *(au lit)* in bed

couche-culotte [kuʃkylɔt] *nf* disposable nappy *(BRIT)* *ou* diaper *(US)* and waterproof pants in one

coucher [kuʃe] *nm (du soleil)* setting ♦ *vt (personne)* to put to bed; (: *loger)* to put up; *(objet)* to lay on its side ♦ *vi* to sleep; **se ~** *vi (pour dormir)* to go to bed; *(pour se reposer)* to lie down; *(soleil)* to set; **~ de soleil** sunset

couchette [kuʃɛt] *nf* couchette; *(de marin)* bunk

coucou [kuku] *nm* cuckoo

coude [kud] *nm (ANAT)* elbow; *(de tuyau, de la route)* bend; **~ à ~** shoulder to shoulder, side by side

coudre [kudʀ(ə)] *vt (bouton)* to sew on; *(robe)* to sew (up) ♦ *vi* to sew

couenne [kwan] *nf (de lard)* rind

couette [kwɛt] *nf* duvet, quilt; **~s** *nfpl (cheveux)* bunches

couffin [kufɛ̃] *nm* Moses basket

couler [kule] *vi* to flow, run; *(fuir: stylo, récipient)* to leak; *(sombrer: bateau)* to sink ♦ *vt (cloche, sculpture)* to cast; *(bateau)* to sink; *(fig)* to ruin, bring down

couleur [kulœʀ] *nf* colour *(BRIT)*, color *(US)*; *(CARTES)* suit; **film/télévision en ~s** colo(u)r film/television

couleuvre [kulœvʀ(ə)] *nf* grass snake

coulisse [kulis] *nf:* **~s** *nfpl (THÉÂTRE)* wings; *(fig):* **dans les ~s** behind the scenes; **coulisser** *vi* to slide, run

couloir [kulwaʀ] *nm* corridor, passage; *(de bus)* gangway; *(d'avion)* aisle; *(sur la route)* bus lane; *(SPORT: de piste)* lane; *(GÉO)* gully; **~ aérien/de navigation** air/shipping lane

coup [ku] *nm (heurt, choc)* knock; *(affectif)* blow, shock; *(agressif)* blow; *(avec arme à feu)* shot; *(de l'horloge)* chime; stroke; *(SPORT)* stroke; shot; blow; *(fam: fois)* time; **~ de coude** nudge (with the elbow); **~ de tonnerre** clap of thunder; **~ de sonnette** ring of the bell; **~ de crayon** stroke of the pencil; **donner un ~ de balai** to give the floor a sweep; **avoir le ~** *(fig)* to have the knack; **boire un ~** to have a drink; **être dans le ~** to be in on it; **du ~ ...** so (you see) ...; **d'un seul ~** *(subitement)* suddenly; *(à la fois)* at one go; in one blow; **du premier ~** first time; **du même ~** at the same time; **à ~ sûr** definitely, without fail; **~ sur ~** in quick succession; **sur le ~** outright; **sous le ~ de** *(surprise etc)* under the influence of; **~ de chance** stroke of luck; **~ de couteau** stab (of a knife); **~ d'envoi** kick-off; **~ d'essai** first attempt; **~ de feu** shot; **~ de filet** *(POLICE)* haul; **~ de frein** (sharp) braking *no pl*; **~ de main:**

donner un ~ de main à qn to give sb a (helping) hand; **~ d'œil** glance; **~ de pied** kick; **~ de poing** punch; **~ de soleil** sunburn *no pl*; **~ de téléphone** phone call; **~ de tête** *(fig)* (sudden) impulse; **~ de théâtre** *(fig)* dramatic turn of events; **~ de vent** gust of wind; **en coup de vent** in a tearing hurry; **~ franc** free kick

coupable [kupabl(ə)] *adj* guilty ♦ *nm/f (gén)* culprit; *(JUR)* guilty party

coupe [kup] *nf (verre)* goblet; *(à fruits)* dish; *(SPORT)* cup; *(de cheveux, de vêtement)* cut; *(graphique, plan)* (cross) section; **être sous la ~ de** to be under the control of

coupe-papier [kuppapje] *nm inv* paper knife

couper [kupe] *vt* to cut; *(retrancher)* to cut (out); *(route, courant)* to cut off; *(appétit)* to take away; *(vin, cidre)* to blend; (: *à table)* to dilute ♦ *vi* to cut; *(prendre un raccourci)* to take a short-cut; **se ~** *vi (se blesser)* to cut o.s.; **~ la parole à qn** to cut sb short

couple [kupl(ə)] *nm* couple

couplet [kuplɛ] *nm* verse

coupole [kupɔl] *nf* dome; cupola

coupon [kupɔ̃] *nm (ticket)* coupon; *(de tissu)* remnant; roll; **~-réponse** *nm* reply coupon

coupure [kupyʀ] *nf* cut; *(billet de banque)* note; *(de journal)* cutting; **~ de courant** power cut

cour [kuʀ] *nf (de ferme, jardin)* (court)yard; *(d'immeuble)* back yard; *(JUR, royale)* court; **faire la ~ à qn** to court sb; **~ d'assises** court of assizes; **~ martiale** court-martial

courage [kuʀaʒ] *nm* courage, bravery; **courageux, euse** *adj* brave, courageous

couramment [kuʀamɑ̃] *adv* commonly; *(parler)* fluently

courant, e [kuʀɑ̃, -ɑ̃t] *adj (fréquent)* common; *(COMM: gén: normal)* standard; *(en cours)* current ♦ *nm* current; *(fig)* movement; trend; **être au ~ (de)** *(fait, nouvelle)* to know (about); **mettre qn au ~ (de)** to tell sb (about); *(nouveau travail etc)* to teach sb the basics (of); **se tenir au ~ (de)** *(techniques etc)* to keep o.s. up-to-date (on); **dans le ~ de** *(pendant)* in the course of; **le 10 ~** *(COMM)* the 10th inst.; **~ d'air** draught; **~ électrique** (electric) current, power

courbature [kuʀbatyʀ] *nf* ache

courbe [kuʀb(ə)] *adj* curved ♦ *nf* curve; **~r** [kuʀbe] *vt* to bend

coureur, euse [kuʀœʀ, -øz] *nm/f (SPORT)* runner *(ou* driver); *(péj)* womanizer; manhunter; **~ automobile** racing driver

courge [kuʀʒ(ə)] *nf (CULIN)* marrow; **courgette** [kuʀʒɛt] *nf* courgette *(BRIT)*, zucchini *(US)*

courir [kuʀiʀ] *vi* to run ♦ *vt (SPORT: épreuve)* to compete in; *(risque)* to run;

(*danger*) to face; ~ **les magasins** to go round the shops; **le bruit court que** the rumour is going round that

couronne [kuʀɔn] *nf* crown; (*de fleurs*) wreath, circlet

courons *etc vb voir* **courir**

courrier [kuʀje] *nm* mail, post; (*lettres à écrire*) letters *pl*; **avion long/moyen ~** long-/medium-haul plane

courroie [kuʀwa] *nf* strap; (*TECH*) belt

courrons *etc vb voir* **courir**

cours [kuʀ] *nm* (*leçon*) lesson; class; (*série de leçons, cheminement*) course; (*écoulement*) flow; (*COMM*) rate; price; **donner libre ~ à** to give free expression to; **avoir ~** (*monnaie*) to be legal tender; (*fig*) to be current; (*SCOL*) to have a class *ou* lecture; **en ~** (*année*) current; (*travaux*) in progress; **en ~ de route** on the way; **au ~ de** in the course of, during; **~ d'eau** waterway; **~ du soir** night school

course [kuʀs(ə)] *nf* running; (*SPORT: épreuve*) race; (*d'un taxi, autocar*) journey, trip; (*petite mission*) errand; **~s** *nfpl* (*achats*) shopping *sg*; **faire des ~s** to do some shopping

court, e [kuʀ, kuʀt(ə)] *adj* short ♦ *adv* short ♦ *nm*: ~ (**de tennis**) (tennis) court; **tourner ~** to come to a sudden end; **ça fait ~** that's not very long; **à ~ de** short of; **prendre qn de ~** to catch sb unawares; **tirer à la ~e paille** to draw lots; **~-circuit** *nm* short-circuit

courtier, ère [kuʀtje, -jɛʀ] *nm/f* broker

courtiser [kuʀtize] *vt* to court, woo

courtois, e [kuʀtwa, -waz] *adj* courteous

couru, e [kuʀy] *pp de* **courir** ♦ *adj*: **c'est ~** it's a safe bet

cousais *etc vb voir* **coudre**

couscous [kuskus] *nm* couscous

cousin, e [kuzɛ̃, -in] *nm/f* cousin

coussin [kusɛ̃] *nm* cushion

cousu, e [kuzy] *pp de* **coudre**

coût [ku] *nm* cost; **le ~ de la vie** the cost of living

coûtant [kutɑ̃] *adj m*: **au prix ~** at cost price

couteau, x [kuto] *nm* knife; **~ à cran d'arrêt** flick-knife

coûter [kute] *vt, vi* to cost; **combien ça coûte?** how much is it?, what does it cost?; **coûte que coûte** at all costs; **coûteux, euse** *adj* costly, expensive

coutume [kutym] *nf* custom

couture [kutyʀ] *nf* sewing; dress-making; (*points*) seam; **couturier** [kutyʀje] *nm* fashion designer; **couturière** [kutyʀjɛʀ] *nf* dressmaker

couvée [kuve] *nf* brood, clutch

couvent [kuvɑ̃] *nm* (*de sœurs*) convent; (*de frères*) monastery

couver [kuve] *vt* to hatch; (*maladie*) to be

sickening for ♦ *vi* (*feu*) to smoulder; (*révolte*) to be brewing

couvercle [kuvɛʀkl(ə)] *nm* lid; (*de bombe aérosol etc, qui se visse*) cap, top

couvert, e [kuvɛʀ, -ɛʀt(ə)] *pp de* **couvrir** ♦ *adj* (*ciel*) overcast ♦ *nm* place setting; (*place à table*) place; (*au restaurant*) cover charge; **~s** *nmpl* (*ustensiles*) cutlery *sg*; **~ de** covered with *ou* in; **mettre le ~** to lay the table

couverture [kuvɛʀtyʀ] *nf* blanket; (*de bâtiment*) roofing; (*de livre, assurance, fig*) cover; (*presse*) coverage; **~ chauffante** electric blanket

couveuse [kuvøz] *nf* (*de maternité*) incubator

couvre-feu *nm* curfew

couvre-lit *nm* bedspread

couvrir [kuvʀiʀ] *vt* to cover; **se ~** *vi* (*ciel*) to cloud over; (*s'habiller*) to cover up; (*se coiffer*) to put on one's hat

crabe [kʀab] *nm* crab

cracher [kʀaʃe] *vi, vt* to spit

crachin [kʀaʃɛ̃] *nm* drizzle

craie [kʀɛ] *nf* chalk

craindre [kʀɛ̃dʀ(ə)] *vt* to fear, be afraid of; (*être sensible à: chaleur, froid*) to be easily damaged by

crainte [kʀɛ̃t] *nf* fear; **de ~ de/que** for fear of/that; **craintif, ive** *adj* timid

cramoisi, e [kʀamwazi] *adj* crimson

crampe [kʀɑ̃p] *nf* cramp

cramponner [kʀɑ̃pɔne]: **se ~** *vi*: **se ~ (à)** to hang *ou* cling on (to)

cran [kʀɑ̃] *nm* (*entaille*) notch; (*de courroie*) hole; (*courage*) guts *pl*; **~ d'arrêt** safety catch

crâne [kʀɑn] *nm* skull

crâner [kʀane] (*fam*) *vi* to show off

crapaud [kʀapo] *nm* toad

crapule [kʀapyl] *nf* villain

craquement [kʀakmɑ̃] *nm* crack, snap; (*du plancher*) creak, creaking *no pl*

craquer [kʀake] *vi* (*bois, plancher*) to creak; (*fil, branche*) to snap; (*couture*) to come apart; (*fig*) to break down ♦ *vt* (*allumette*) to strike

crasse [kʀas] *nf* grime, filth

cravache [kʀavaʃ] *nf* (riding) crop

cravate [kʀavat] *nf* tie

crawl [kʀol] *nm* crawl; **dos ~é** backstroke

crayeux, euse [kʀɛjø, -øz] *adj* chalky

crayon [kʀɛjɔ̃] *nm* pencil; **~ à bille** ball-point pen; **~ de couleur** crayon, colouring pencil; **~ optique** light pen; **crayon-feutre** [kʀɛjɑ̃føtʀ(ə)] (*pl* **crayons-feutres**) *nm* felt(-tip) pen

créancier, ière [kʀeɑ̃sje, -jɛʀ] *nm/f* creditor

création [kʀeasjɔ̃] *nf* creation

créature [kʀeatyʀ] *nf* creature

crèche [kʀɛʃ] *nf* (*de Noël*) crib; (*garderie*)

crèche, day nursery

crédit [kʀedi] nm (gén) credit; **~s** nmpl (fonds) funds; **payer/acheter à ~** to pay/buy on credit ou on easy terms; **faire ~ à qn** to give sb credit; **créditer** vt: **créditer un compte (de)** to credit an account (with)

crédule [kʀedyl] adj credulous, gullible

créer [kʀee] vt to create; (THÉÂTRE) to produce ou for the first time)

crémaillère [kʀemajeʀ] nf (RAIL) rack; **pendre la ~** to have a house-warming party

crématoire [kʀematwaʀ] adj: **four ~** crematorium

crème [kʀɛm] nf cream; (entremets) cream dessert ♦ adj inv cream (-coloured); **un (café) ~** ≈ a white coffee; **~ à raser** shaving cream; **~ chantilly** whipped cream; **~ fouettée = crème chantilly; crémerie** nf dairy; **crémeux, euse** adj creamy

créneau, x [kʀeno] nm (de fortification) crenel(le); (fig) gap, slot; (AUTO): **faire un ~** to reverse into a parking space (alongside the kerb)

crêpe [kʀɛp] nf (galette) pancake ♦ nm (tissu) crêpe; **crêpé, e** adj (cheveux) backcombed; **crêperie** nf pancake shop ou restaurant

crépir [kʀepiʀ] vt to roughcast

crépiter [kʀepite] vi to sputter, splutter; to crackle

crépu, e [kʀepy] adj frizzy, fuzzy

crépuscule [kʀepyskyl] nm twilight, dusk

cresson [kʀesɔ̃] nm watercress

crête [kʀɛt] nf (de coq) comb; (de vague, montagne) crest

creuser [kʀøze] vt (trou, tunnel) to dig; (sol) to dig a hole in; (bois) to hollow out; (fig) to go (deeply) into; **ça creuse** that gives you a real appetite; **se ~ (la cervelle)** to rack one's brains

creux, euse [kʀø, -øz] adj hollow ♦ nm hollow; (fig: sur graphique etc) trough; **heures creuses** slack periods; off-peak periods

crevaison [kʀəvɛzɔ̃] nf puncture

crevasse [kʀəvas] nf (dans le sol) crack, fissure; (de glacier) crevasse

crevé, e [kʀəve] adj (fatigué) all in, exhausted

crever [kʀəve] vt (papier) to tear, break; (tambour, ballon) to burst ♦ vi (pneu) to burst; (automobiliste) to have a puncture (BRIT) ou a flat (tire) (US); (fam) to die; **cela lui a crevé un œil** it blinded him in one eye

crevette [kʀəvɛt] nf: **~ (rose)** prawn; **~ grise** shrimp

cri [kʀi] nm cry, shout; (d'animal: spécifique) cry, call; **c'est le dernier ~** (fig) it's the latest fashion

criant, e [kʀijɑ̃, -ɑ̃t] adj (injustice) glaring

criard, e [kʀijaʀ, -aʀd(ə)] adj (couleur) garish, loud; (voix) yelling

crible [kʀibl(ə)] nm riddle; **passer qch au ~** (fig) to go over sth with a fine-tooth comb

criblé, e [kʀible] adj: **~ de** riddled with; (de dettes) crippled with

cric [kʀik] nm (AUTO) jack

crier [kʀije] vi (pour appeler) to shout, cry (out); (de peur, de douleur etc) to scream, yell ♦ vt (ordre, injure) to shout (out), yell (out)

crime [kʀim] nm crime; (meurtre) murder; **criminel, le** nm/f criminal; murderer

crin [kʀɛ̃] nm hair no pl; (fibre) horsehair; **~ière** [kʀinjɛʀ] nf mane

crique [kʀik] nf creek, inlet

criquet [kʀike] nm locust; grasshopper

crise [kʀiz] nf crisis; (MÉD) attack; fit; **~ cardiaque** heart attack; **~ de foie** bilious attack; **~ de nerfs** attack of nerves

crisper [kʀispe] vt to tense; (poings) to clench; **se ~** vi to tense; to clench; (personne) to get tense

crisser [kʀise] vi (neige) to crunch; (pneu) to screech

cristal, aux [kʀistal, -o] nm crystal; **~lin, e** adj crystal-clear

critère [kʀitɛʀ] nm criterion

critiquable [kʀitikabl(ə)] adj open to criticism

critique [kʀitik] adj critical ♦ nm/f (de théâtre, musique) critic ♦ nf criticism; (THÉÂTRE etc: article) review; **~r** [kʀitike] vt (dénigrer) to criticize; (évaluer, juger) to assess, examine (critically)

croasser [kʀoase] vi to caw

Croatie [kʀɔasi] nf Croatia

croc [kʀo] nm (dent) fang; (de boucher) hook

croc-en-jambe [kʀɔkɑ̃ʒɑ̃b] nm: **faire un ~ à qn** to trip sb up

croche [kʀɔʃ] nf (MUS) quaver (BRIT), eighth note (US); **~-pied** [kʀɔʃpje] nm = **croc-en-jambe**

crochet [kʀɔʃɛ] nm hook; (détour) detour; (TRICOT: aiguille) crochet hook; (: technique) crochet; **vivre aux ~s de qn** to live ou sponge off sb; **crocheter** vt (serrure) to pick

crochu, e [kʀɔʃy] adj hooked; claw-like

crocodile [kʀɔkɔdil] nm crocodile

crocus [kʀɔkys] nm crocus

croire [kʀwaʀ] vt to believe; **se ~ fort** to think one is strong; **~ que** to believe ou think that; **~ à, ~ en** to believe in

croîs vb voir **croître**

croisade [kʀwazad] nf crusade

croisé, e [kʀwaze] adj (veston) double-breasted

croisement [kʀwazmɑ̃] nm (carrefour) crossroads sg; (BIO) crossing; crossbreed

croiser [kʀwaze] vt (personne, voiture) to

pass; (*route*) to cross, cut across; (*BIO*) to cross ♦ *vi* (*NAVIG*) to cruise; **se ~** *vi* (*personnes, véhicules*) to pass each other; (*routes, lettres*) to cross; (*regards*) to meet; **~ les jambes/bras** to cross one's legs/fold one's arms

croiseur [kʀwazœʀ] *nm* cruiser (*warship*)

croisière [kʀwazjɛʀ] *nf* cruise; **vitesse de ~** (*AUTO etc*) cruising speed

croissance [kʀwasɑ̃s] *nf* growth

croissant [kʀwasɑ̃] *nm* (*à manger*) croissant; (*motif*) crescent

croître [kʀwatʀ(ə)] *vi* to grow

croix [kʀwa] *nf* cross; **en ~** in the form of a cross; **la C~ Rouge** the Red Cross

croque-monsieur [kʀɔkməsjø] *nm inv* toasted ham and cheese sandwich

croquer [kʀɔke] *vt* (*manger*) to crunch; to munch; (*dessiner*) to sketch ♦ *vi* to be crisp *ou* crunchy; **chocolat à ~** plain dessert chocolate

croquis [kʀɔki] *nm* sketch

crosse [kʀɔs] *nf* (*de fusil*) butt; (*de revolver*) grip

crotte [kʀɔt] *nf* droppings *pl*

crotté, e [kʀɔte] *adj* muddy, mucky

crottin [kʀɔtɛ̃] *nm* dung, manure

crouler [kʀule] *vi* (*s'effondrer*) to collapse; (*être délabré*) to be crumbling

croupe [kʀup] *nf* rump; **en ~** pillion

croupir [kʀupiʀ] *vi* to stagnate

croustillant, e [kʀustijɑ̃, -ɑ̃t] *adj* crisp; (*fig*) spicy

croûte [kʀut] *nf* crust; (*du fromage*) rind; (*MÉD*) scab; **en ~** (*CULIN*) in pastry

croûton [kʀutɔ̃] *nm* (*CULIN*) crouton; (*bout du pain*) crust, heel

croyable [kʀwajabl(ə)] *adj* credible

croyant, e [kʀwajɑ̃, -ɑ̃t] *nm/f* believer

C.R.S. *sigle fpl* (= Compagnies républicaines de sécurité) state security police force ♦ *sigle m* member of the C.R.S.

cru, e [kʀy] *pp de* **croire** ♦ *adj* (*non cuit*) raw; (*lumière, couleur*) harsh; (*paroles, description*) crude ♦ *nm* (*vignoble*) vineyard; (*vin*) wine

crû *pp de* **croître**

cruauté [kʀyote] *nf* cruelty

cruche [kʀyʃ] *nf* pitcher, jug

crucifix [kʀysifi] *nm* crucifix

crucifixion [kʀysifiksjɔ̃] *nf* crucifixion

crudités [kʀydite] *nfpl* (*CULIN*) salads

cruel, le [kʀyɛl] *adj* cruel

crus *etc vb voir* **croire**; **croître**

crûs *etc vb voir* **croître**

crustacés [kʀystase] *nmpl* shellfish

Cuba [kyba] *nf* Cuba

cube [kyb] *nm* cube; (*jouet*) brick; **mètre ~** cubic metre; **2 au ~** 2 cubed

cueillette [kœjɛt] *nf* picking; (*quantité*) crop, harvest

cueillir [kœjiʀ] *vt* (*fruits, fleurs*) to pick, gather; (*fig*) to catch

cuiller [kɥijɛʀ] *nf* spoon; **~ à café** coffee spoon; (*poterie*) teaspoonful; **~ à soupe** soup-spoon; (*CULIN*) ≈ tablespoonful

cuillère [kɥijɛʀ] *nf* = **cuiller**

cuillerée [kɥijɛʀ] *nf* spoonful

cuir [kɥiʀ] *nm* leather; **~ chevelu** scalp

cuire [kɥiʀ] *vt* (*aliments*) to cook; (*au four*) to bake; (*poterie*) to fire ♦ *vi* to cook; **bien cuit** (*viande*) well done; **trop cuit** overdone

cuisant, e [kɥizɑ̃, -ɑ̃t] *adj* (*douleur*) stinging; (*fig: souvenir, échec*) bitter

cuisine [kɥizin] *nf* (*pièce*) kitchen; (*art culinaire*) cookery, cooking; (*nourriture*) cooking, food; **faire la ~** to cook

cuisiné, e [kɥizine] *adj*: **plat ~** ready-made meal *or* dish; **cuisiner** *vt* to cook; (*fam*) to grill ♦ *vi* to cook; **cuisinier, ière** *nm/f* cook; **cuisinière** *nf* (*poêle*) cooker

cuisse [kɥis] *nf* thigh; (*CULIN*) leg

cuisson [kɥisɔ̃] *nf* cooking; firing

cuit, e *pp de* **cuire**

cuivre [kɥivʀ(ə)] *nm* copper; **les ~s** (*MUS*) the brass

cul [ky] (*fam!*) *nm* arse (*!*)

culasse [kylas] *nf* (*AUTO*) cylinder-head; (*de fusil*) breech

culbute [kylbyt] *nf* somersault; (*accidentelle*) tumble, fall

culminant, e [kylminɑ̃, -ɑ̃t] *adj*: **point ~** highest point

culminer [kylmine] *vi* to reach its highest point; to tower

culot [kylo] *nm* (*effronterie*) cheek

culotte [kylɔt] *nf* (*de femme*) knickers *pl* (*BRIT*), panties *pl*; **~ de cheval** riding breeches *pl*

culpabilité [kylpabilite] *nf* guilt

culte [kylt(ə)] *nm* (*religion*) religion; (*hommage, vénération*) worship; (*protestant*) service

cultivateur, trice [kyltivatœʀ, -tʀis] *nm/f* farmer

cultivé, e [kyltive] *adj* (*personne*) cultured, cultivated

cultiver [kyltive] *vt* to cultivate; (*légumes*) to grow, cultivate

culture [kyltyʀ] *nf* cultivation; growing; (*connaissances etc*) culture; **~ physique** physical training; **culturisme** *nm* body-building

cumin [kymɛ̃] *nm* cumin; (*carvi*) caraway seeds *pl*

cumuler [kymyle] *vt* (*emplois, honneurs*) to hold concurrently; (*salaires*) to draw concurrently; (*JUR: droits*) to accumulate

cupide [kypid] *adj* greedy, grasping

cure [kyʀ] *nf* (*MÉD*) course of treatment; **n'avoir ~ de** to pay no attention to

curé [kyʀe] *nm* parish priest

cure-dent [kyʀdɑ̃] *nm* toothpick

cure-pipe [kyʀpip] *nm* pipe cleaner

curer [kyʀe] *vt* to clean out

curieux, euse [kyʀjø, -øz] *adj* (*étrange*) strange, curious; (*indiscret*) curious, inquisitive ♦ *nmpl* (*badauds*) onlookers; **curiosité** *nf* curiosity; (*site*) unusual feature

curriculum vitae [kyʀikylɔmvite] *nm inv* curriculum vitae

curseur [kyʀsœʀ] *nm* (*INFORM*) cursor

cuti-réaction [kytiʀeaksjɔ̃] *nf* (*MÉD*) skin-test

cuve [kyv] *nf* vat; (*à mazout etc*) tank; **cuvée** *nf* vintage

cuvette [kyvɛt] *nf* (*récipient*) bowl, basin; (*GÉO*) basin

C.V. *sigle m* (*AUTO*) = **cheval vapeur**; (*COMM*) = **curriculum vitae**

cyanure [sjanyʀ] *nm* cyanide

cyclable [siklabl(ə)] *adj*: **piste** ~ cycle track

cycle [sikl] *nm* cycle

cyclisme [siklism(ə)] *nm* cycling

cycliste [siklist(ə)] *nmf* cyclist ♦ *adj* cycle *cpd*; **coureur** ~ racing cyclist

cyclomoteur [siklɔmɔtœʀ] *nm* moped

cyclone [siklon] *nm* hurricane

cygne [siɲ] *nm* swan

cylindre [silɛ̃dʀ(ə)] *nm* cylinder; **cylindrée** *nf* (*AUTO*) (cubic) capacity

cymbale [sɛ̃bal] *nf* cymbal

cynique [sinik] *adj* cynical

cystite [sistit] *nf* cystitis

D d

d' [d] *prép voir* de

dactylo [daktilo] *nf* (*aussi:* ~*graphe*) typist; (: ~*graphie*) typing; ~**graphier** *vt* to type (out)

dada [dada] *nm* hobby-horse

daigner [deɲe] *vt* to deign

daim [dɛ̃] *nm* (*fallow*) deer *inv*; (*peau*) buckskin; (*imitation*) suede

dalle [dal] *nf* paving stone; slab

daltonien, ne [daltɔnjɛ̃, -jɛn] *adj* colour-blind

dam [dam] *nm*: **au grand** ~ **de** much to the detriment (*ou* annoyance) of

dame [dam] *nf* lady; (*CARTES, ÉCHECS*) queen; ~**s** *nfpl* (*jeu*) draughts *sg* (*BRIT*), checkers *sg* (*US*)

damner [dɑne] *vt* to damn

dancing [dɑ̃siŋ] *nm* dance hall

Danemark [danmaʀk] *nm* Denmark

danger [dɑ̃ʒe] *nm* danger; **dangereux, euse** [dɑ̃ʒʀø, -øz] *adj* dangerous

danois, e [danwa, -waz] *adj* Danish ♦ *nmf*: **D~, e** Dane ♦ *nm* (*LING*) Danish

---
— MOT CLÉ

dans [dɑ̃] *prép* **1** (*position*) in; (*à l'intérieur de*) inside; **c'est** ~ **le tiroir/le salon** it's in the drawer/lounge; ~ **la boîte** in *ou* inside the box; **marcher** ~ **la ville** to walk about the town

2 (*direction*) into; **elle a couru** ~ **le salon** she ran into the lounge

3 (*provenance*) out of, from; **je l'ai pris** ~ **le tiroir/salon** I took it out of *ou* from the drawer/lounge; **boire** ~ **un verre** to drink out of *ou* from a glass

4 (*temps*) in; ~ **2 mois** in 2 months, in 2 months' time

5 (*approximation*) about; ~ **les 20F** about 20F

---

danse [dɑ̃s] *nf*: **la** ~ dancing; **une** ~ a dance; **danser** *vi, vt* to dance; **danseur, euse** *nm/f* ballet dancer; (*au bal etc*) dancer; partner

dard [daʀ] *nm* sting (*organ*)

date [dat] *nf* date; **de longue** ~ longstanding; ~ **de naissance** date of birth; ~ **limite** deadline; **dater** *vt, vi* to date; **dater de** to date from; **à dater de** (as) from

datte [dat] *nf* date; **dattier** *nm* date palm

dauphin [dofɛ̃] *nm* (*ZOOL*) dolphin

davantage [davɑ̃taʒ] *adv* more; (*plus longtemps*) longer; ~ **de** more

---
— MOT CLÉ

de(d') (*de* +*le* = **du**, *de* +*les* = **des**) *prép* **1** (*appartenance*) of; **le toit** ~ **la maison** the roof of the house; **la voiture d'Elisabeth/**~ **mes parents** Elizabeth's/my parents' car

2 (*provenance*) from; **il vient** ~ **Londres** he comes from London; **elle est sortie du cinéma** she came out of the cinema

3 (*caractérisation, mesure*): **un mur** ~ **brique/bureau d'acajou** a brick wall/mahogany desk; **un billet** ~ **50F** a 50F note; **une pièce** ~ **2m** ~ **large** *ou* **large** ~ **2m** a room 2m wide, a 2m-wide room; **un bébé** ~ **10 mois** a 10-month-old baby; **12 mois** ~ **crédit/travail** 12 months' credit/work; **augmenter** ~ **10F** to increase by 10F; ~ **14 à 18** from 14 to 18

♦ *dét* **1** (*phrases affirmatives*) some (*souvent omis*); **du vin**, ~ **l'eau, des pommes** (some) wine, (some) water, (some) apples; **des enfants sont venus** some children came; **pendant des mois** for months

2 (*phrases interrogatives et négatives*) any; **a-t-il du vin?** has he got any wine?; **il n'a pas** ~ **pommes/d'enfants** he hasn't (got) any apples/children, he has no apples/

children

dé [de] *nm* (*à jouer*) die *ou* dice; (*aussi:* ~ *à coudre*) thimble

déambuler [deãbyle] *vi* to stroll about

débâcle [debɑkl(ə)] *nf* rout

déballer [debale] *vt* to unpack

débandade [debãdad] *nf* rout; scattering

débarbouiller [debaʀbuje] *vt* to wash; **se ~** *vi* to wash (one's face)

débarcadère [debaʀkadɛʀ] *nm* wharf

débardeur [debaʀdœʀ] *nm* (*maillot*) tank top

débarquer [debaʀke] *vt* to unload, land ♦ *vi* to disembark; (*fig*) to turn up

débarras [debaʀa] *nm* lumber room; junk cupboard; **bon ~!** good riddance!

débarrasser [debaʀase] *vt* to clear; **se ~ de** *vt* to get rid of; **~ qn de** (*vêtements, paquets*) to relieve sb of

débat [deba] *nm* discussion, debate

débattre [debatʀ(ə)] *vt* to discuss, debate; **se ~** *vi* to struggle

débaucher [deboʃe] *vt* (*licencier*) to lay off, dismiss; (*entraîner*) to lead astray, debauch

débile [debil] *adj* weak, feeble; (*fam: idiot*) dim-witted

débit [debi] *nm* (*d'un liquide, fleuve*) flow; (*d'un magasin*) turnover (of goods); (*élocution*) delivery; (*bancaire*) debit; **~ de boissons** drinking establishment; **~ de tabac** tobacconist's; **~er** *vt* (*compte*) to debit; (*liquide, gaz*) to give out; (*couper: bois, viande*) to cut up; (*péj: paroles etc*) to churn out; **~eur, trice** *nm/f* debtor ♦ *adj* in debit; (*compte*) debit *cpd*

déblayer [debleje] *vt* to clear

débloquer [debloke] *vt* (*frein*) to release; (*prix, crédits*) to free

déboires [debwaʀ] *nmpl* setbacks

déboiser [debwaze] *vt* to deforest

déboîter [debwate] *vt* (*AUTO*) to pull out; **se ~ le genou** *etc* to dislocate one's knee *etc*

débonnaire [debonɛʀ] *adj* easy-going, good-natured

débordé, e [debɔʀde] *adj*: **être ~ (de)** (*travail, demandes*) to be snowed under (with)

déborder [debɔʀde] *vi* to overflow; (*lait etc*) to boil over; **~ (de) qch** (*dépasser*) to extend beyond sth

débouché [debuʃe] *nm* (*pour vendre*) outlet; (*perspective d'emploi*) opening

déboucher [debuʃe] *vt* (*évier, tuyau etc*) to unblock; (*bouteille*) to uncork ♦ *vi:* **~ de** to emerge from; **~ sur** to come out onto; to open out onto

débourser [debuʀse] *vt* to pay out

debout [dəbu] *adv:* **être ~** (*personne*) to be standing, stand; (: *levé, éveillé*) to be up; (*chose*) to be upright; **être encore ~** (*fig: en état*) to be still going; **se mettre ~** to stand up; **se tenir ~** to stand; **~!** stand up!; (*du lit*) get up!; **cette histoire ne tient pas ~** this story doesn't hold water

déboutonner [debutɔne] *vt* to undo, unbutton

débraillé, e [debʀaje] *adj* slovenly, untidy

débrancher [debʀɑ̃ʃe] *vt* to disconnect; (*appareil électrique*) to unplug

débrayage [debʀɛjaʒ] *nm* (*AUTO*) clutch; **débrayer** [debʀɛje] *vi* (*AUTO*) to declutch; (*cesser le travail*) to stop work

débris [debʀi] *nm* (*fragment*) fragment ♦ *nmpl* rubbish *sg*; debris *sg*

débrouillard, e [debʀujaʀ, -aʀd(ə)] *adj* smart, resourceful

débrouiller [debʀuje] *vt* to disentangle, untangle; **se ~** *vi* to manage

débusquer [debyske] *vt* to drive out (from cover)

début [deby] *nm* beginning, start; **~s** *nmpl* (*dans la vie*) beginnings; (*de carrière*) début *sg*

débutant, e [debytã, -ãt] *nm/f* beginner, novice

débuter [debyte] *vi* to begin, start; (*faire ses débuts*) to start out

deçà [dəsa] : **en ~ de** *prép* this side of

décacheter [dekaʃte] *vt* to unseal

décadence [dekadãs] *nf* decadence; decline

décaféiné, e [dekafeine] *adj* decaffeinated

décalage [dekalaʒ] *nm* gap; discrepancy; **~ horaire** time difference (*between time zones*); time-lag

décaler [dekale] *vt* (*dans le temps: avancer*) to bring forward; (: *retarder*) to put back; (*changer de position*) to shift forward *ou* back

décalquer [dekalke] *vt* to trace; (*par pression*) to transfer

décamper [dekãpe] *vi* to clear out *ou* off

décaper [dekape] *vt* to strip; (*avec abrasif*) to scour; (*avec papier de verre*) to sand

décapiter [dekapite] *vt* to behead; (*par accident*) to decapitate

décapotable [dekapɔtabl(ə)] *adj* convertible

décapsuler [dekapsyle] *vt* to take the cap *ou* top off; **décapsuleur** *nm* bottle-opener

décédé, e [desede] *adj* deceased

décéder [desede] *vi* to die

déceler [desle] *vt* to discover, detect; to indicate, reveal

décembre [desɑ̃bʀ(ə)] *nm* December

décemment [desamã] *adv* decently

décennie [deseni] *nf* decade

décent, e [desã, -ãt] *adj* decent

déception [desɛpsjɔ̃] *nf* disappointment

décerner [desɛʀne] *vt* to award

décès [desɛ] *nm* death, decease

décevoir [desvwaʀ] *vt* to disappoint

déchaîner [deʃene] *vt* to unleash, arouse; **se ~** to be unleashed

déchanter [deʃɑ̃te] *vi* to become disillusioned

décharge [deʃaʀʒ(ə)] *nf* (*dépôt d'ordures*) rubbish tip *ou* dump; (*électrique*) electrical discharge; **à la ~ de** in defence of

décharger [deʃaʀʒe] *vt* (*marchandise, véhicule*) to unload; (*ÉLEC, faire feu*) to discharge; **~ qn de** (*responsabilité*) to release sb from

décharné, e [deʃaʀne] *adj* emaciated

déchausser [deʃose] *vt* (*skis*) to take off; **se ~** *vi* to take off one's shoes; (*dent*) to come *ou* work loose

déchéance [deʃeɑ̃s] *nf* degeneration; decay, decline; fall

déchet [deʃɛ] *nm* (*de bois, tissu etc*) scrap; (*perte: gén COMM*) wastage, waste; **~s** *nmpl* (*ordures*) refuse *sg*, rubbish *sg*

déchiffrer [deʃifʀe] *vt* to decipher

déchiqueter [deʃikte] *vt* to tear *ou* pull to pieces

déchirant, e [deʃiʀɑ̃, -ɑ̃t] *adj* heart-rending

déchirement [deʃiʀmɑ̃] *nm* (*chagrin*) wrench, heartbreak; (*gén pl: conflit*) rift, split

déchirer [deʃiʀe] *vt* to tear; (*en morceaux*) to tear up; (*pour ouvrir*) to tear off; (*arracher*) to tear out; (*fig*) to rack; (*tear (apart*)) to tear, rip; **se ~** *vi* to tear, rip; **se ~ un muscle** to tear a muscle

déchirure [deʃiʀyʀ] *nf* (*accroc*) tear, rip; **~ musculaire** torn muscle

déchoir [deʃwaʀ] *vi* (*personne*) to lower o.s., demean o.s.

déchu, e [deʃy] *adj* fallen; deposed

décidé, e [deside] *adj* (*personne, air*) determined; **c'est ~** it's decided

décidément [desidemɑ̃] *adv* undoubtedly; really

décider [deside] *vt*: **~ qch** to decide on sth; **se ~ (à faire)** to decide (to do), make up one's mind (to do); **se ~ pour** to decide on *ou* in favour of; **~ de faire/que** to decide to do/that; **~ qn (à faire qch)** to persuade sb (to do sth); **~ de qch** to decide upon sth; (*suj: chose*) to determine sth

décilitre [desilitʀ(ə)] *nm* decilitre

décimal, e, aux [desimal, -o] *adj* decimal; **décimale** *nf* decimal

décimètre [desimɛtʀ(ə)] *nm* decimetre; **double ~** (20 cm) ruler

décisif, ive [desizif, -iv] *adj* decisive

décision [desizjɔ̃] *nf* decision; (*fermeté*) decisiveness, decision

déclaration [deklaʀasjɔ̃] *nf* declaration; registration; (*discours: POL etc*) statement; **~ (d'impôts)** ≈ tax return; **~ (de sinistre)** (insurance) claim

déclarer [deklaʀe] *vt* to declare; (*décès, naissance*) to register; **se ~** *vi* (*feu, maladie*) to break out

déclasser [deklase] *vt* to relegate; to down-

grade; to lower in status

déclencher [deklɑ̃ʃe] *vt* (*mécanisme etc*) to release; (*sonnerie*) to set off, activate; (*attaque, grève*) to launch; (*provoquer*) to trigger off; **se ~** *vi* to release itself; to go off

déclic [deklik] *nm* trigger mechanism; (*bruit*) click

décliner [dekline] *vi* to decline ♦ *vt* (*invitation*) to decline; (*responsabilité*) to refuse to accept; (*nom, adresse*) to state

déclivité [deklivite] *nf* slope, incline

décocher [dekɔʃe] *vt* to throw; to shoot

décoiffer [dekwafe] *vt*: **se ~** to take off one's hat

déçois *etc vb voir* **décevoir**

décollage [dekɔlaʒ] *nm* (*AVIAT*) takeoff

décoller [dekɔle] *vt* to unstick ♦ *vi* (*avion*) to take off; **se ~** *vi* to come unstuck

décolleté, e [dekɔlte] *adj* low-cut; wearing a low-cut dress ♦ *nm* low neck(line); (*bare*) neck and shoulders; (*plongeant*) cleavage

décolorer [dekɔlɔʀe] *vt* (*tissu*) to fade; (*cheveux*) to bleach, lighten; **se ~** *vi* to fade

décombres [dekɔ̃bʀ(ə)] *nmpl* rubble *sg*, debris *sg*

décommander [dekɔmɑ̃de] *vt* to cancel; (*invités*) to put off; **se ~** *vi* to cancel one's appointment *etc*, cry off

décomposé, e [dekɔ̃poze] *adj* (*pourri*) decomposed; (*visage*) haggard, distorted

décompte [dekɔ̃t] *nm* deduction; (*facture*) detailed account

déconcerter [dekɔ̃sɛʀte] *vt* to disconcert, confound

déconfit, e [dekɔ̃fi, -it] *adj* crestfallen; **~ure** [dekɔ̃fityʀ] *nf* failure, defeat; collapse, ruin

décongeler [dekɔ̃ʒle] *vt* to thaw

déconner [dekɔne] (*fam*) *vi* to talk rubbish

déconseiller [dekɔ̃seje] *vt*: **~ qch (à qn)** to advise (sb) against sth

déconsidérer [dekɔ̃sideʀe] *vt* to discredit

décontracté, e [dekɔ̃tʀakte] *adj* relaxed, laid-back (*fam*)

décontracter [dekɔ̃tʀakte] *vt* to relax; **se ~** *vi* to relax

déconvenue [dekɔ̃vny] *nf* disappointment

décor [dekɔʀ] *nm* décor; (*paysage*) scenery; **~s** *nmpl* (*THÉÂTRE*) scenery *sg*, décor *sg*; (*CINÉMA*) set *sg*; **~ateur** [dekɔʀatœʀ] *nm* (interior) decorator; (*CINÉMA*) set designer; **~ation** [dekɔʀasjɔ̃] *nf* decoration; **~er** [dekɔʀe] *vt* to decorate

décortiquer [dekɔʀtike] *vt* to shell; (*riz*) to hull; (*fig*) to dissect

découcher [dekuʃe] *vi* to spend the night away from home

découdre [dekudʀ(ə)] *vt* to unpick; **se ~** *vi* to come unstitched; **en ~** (*fig*) to fight, do battle

découler [dekule] *vi*: **~ de** to ensue *ou* follow from

découper [dekupe] *vt* (*papier, tissu etc*) to cut up; (*volaille, viande*) to carve; (*détacher*: *manche, article*) to cut out; **se ~ sur** (*ciel, fond*) to stand out against

décourager [dekuraʒe] *vt* to discourage; **se ~** *vi* to lose heart, become discouraged

décousu, e [dekuzy] *adj* unstitched; (*fig*) disjointed, disconnected

découvert, e [dekuvɛr, -ɛrt(ə)] *adj* (*tête*) bare, uncovered; (*lieu*) open, exposed ♦ *nm* (*bancaire*) overdraft; **découverte** *nf* discovery

découvrir [dekuvrir] *vt* to discover; (*apercevoir*) to see; (*enlever ce qui couvre ou protège*) to uncover; (*montrer, dévoiler*) to reveal; **se ~** *vi* to take off one's hat; to take something off; (*au lit*) to uncover o.s.; (*ciel*) to clear

décret [dekrɛ] *nm* decree; **décréter** *vt* to decree; to order; to declare

décrié, e [dekrije] *adj* disparaged

décrire [dekrir] *vt* to describe

décrocher [dekrɔʃe] *vt* (*dépendre*) to take down; (*téléphone*) to take off the hook; (: *pour répondre*): **~ (le téléphone)** to lift the receiver; (*fig*: *contrat etc*) to get, land ♦ *vi* to drop out; to switch off

décroître [dekrwatr(ə)] *vi* to decrease, decline

décrypter [dekripte] *vt* to decipher

déçu, e [desy] *pp de* **décevoir**

décupler [dekyple] *vt, vi* to increase tenfold

dédaigner [dedeɲe] *vt* to despise, scorn; (*négliger*) to disregard, spurn

dédaigneux, euse [dedɛɲø, -øz] *adj* scornful, disdainful

dédain [dedɛ̃] *nm* scorn, disdain

dédale [dedal] *nm* maze

dedans [dədɑ̃] *adv* inside; (*pas en plein air*) indoors, inside ♦ *nm* inside; **au ~** on the inside; inside; **en ~** (*vers l'intérieur*) inwards; *voir aussi* **là**

dédicacer [dedikase] *vt*: **~ (à qn)** to sign (for sb), autograph (for sb)

dédier [dedje] *vt* to dedicate

dédire [dedir] : **se ~** *vi* to go back on one's word; to retract, recant

dédommager [dedɔmaʒe] *vt*: **~ qn (de)** to compensate sb (for); (*fig*) to repay sb (for)

dédouaner [dedwane] *vt* to clear through customs

dédoubler [deduble] *vt* (*classe, effectifs*) to split (into two); **~ les trains** to run additional trains

déduire [dedɥir] *vt*: **~ qch (de)** (*ôter*) to deduct sth (from); (*conclure*) to deduce ou infer sth (from)

déesse [deɛs] *nf* goddess

défaillance [defajɑ̃s] *nf* (*syncope*) blackout; (*fatigue*) (sudden) weakness *no pl*; (*technique*) fault, failing; (*morale etc*) weak-

ness; **~ cardiaque** heart failure

défaillir [defajir] *vi* to faint; to feel faint; (*mémoire etc*) to fail

défaire [defɛr] *vt* (*installation*) to take down, dismantle; (*paquet etc, nœud, vêtement*) to undo; **se ~** *vi* to come undone; **se ~ de** (*se débarrasser de*) to get rid of; (*se séparer de*) to part with

défait, e [defɛ, -ɛt] *adj* (*visage*) haggard, ravaged; **défaite** *nf* defeat

défalquer [defalke] *vt* to deduct

défaut [defo] *nm* (*moral*) fault, failing, defect; (*d'étoffe, métal*) fault, flaw, defect; (*manque, carence*): **~ de** lack of; shortage of; **en ~** at fault; in the wrong; **faire ~** (*manquer*) to be lacking; **à ~** failing that; **à ~ de** for lack ou want of; **par ~** (*JUR*) in his (*ou her etc*) absence

défavorable [defavɔrabl(ə)] *adj* (*avis, conditions, jury*) unfavourable (*BRIT*), unfavorable (*US*)

défavoriser [defavɔrize] *vt* to put at a disadvantage

défection [defɛksjɔ̃] *nf* defection, failure to give support ou assistance; failure to appear; **faire ~** (*d'un parti etc*) to withdraw one's support, leave

défectueux, euse [defɛktɥø, -øz] *adj* faulty, defective

défendre [defɑ̃dr(ə)] *vt* to defend; (*interdire*) to forbid; **se ~** *vi* to defend o.s.; **~ à qn qch/de faire** to forbid sb sth/to do; **il se défend** (*fig*) he can hold his own; **se ~ de/contre** (*se protéger*) to protect o.s. from/against; **se ~ de** (*se garder de*) to refrain from; (*nier*): **se ~ de vouloir** to deny wanting

défense [defɑ̃s] *nf* defence; (*d'éléphant etc*) tusk; **"~ de fumer/cracher"** "no smoking/spitting"

déférer [defere] *vt* (*JUR*) to refer; **~ à** (*requête, décision*) to defer to

déferler [defɛrle] *vi* (*vagues*) to break; (*fig*) to surge

défi [defi] *nm* (*provocation*) challenge; (*bravade*) defiance

défiance [defjɑ̃s] *nf* mistrust, distrust

déficit [defisit] *nm* (*COMM*) deficit

défier [defje] *vt* (*provoquer*) to challenge; (*fig*) to defy, brave; **se ~ de** (*se méfier de*) to distrust

défigurer [defigyre] *vt* to disfigure

défilé [defile] *nm* (*GÉO*) (narrow) gorge ou pass; (*soldats*) parade; (*manifestants*) procession, march

défiler [defile] *vi* (*troupes*) to march past; (*sportifs*) to parade; (*manifestants*) to march; (*visiteurs*) to pour, stream; **se ~** *vi* (*se dérober*) to slip away, sneak off

définir [definir] *vt* to define

définitif, ive [definitif, -iv] *adj* (*final*) final, definitive; (*pour longtemps*) permanent, definitive; (*sans appel*) final, definite; **définitive** nf: **en définitive** eventually; (*somme toute*) when all is said and done

définitivement [definitivmɑ̃] adv definitively; permanently; definitely

déflagration [deflagʀɑsjɔ̃] nf explosion

défoncer [defɔ̃se] vt (*caisse*) to stave in; (*porte*) to smash in *ou* down; (*lit, fauteuil*) to burst (the springs of); (*terrain, route*) to rip *ou* plough up

déformation [defɔʀmɑsjɔ̃] nf: ~ **professionnelle** conditioning by one's job

déformer [defɔʀme] vt to put out of shape; (*corps*) to deform; (*pensée, fait*) to distort; **se ~** vi to lose its shape

défouler [defule]: **se ~** vi to unwind, let off steam

défraîchir [defʀeʃiʀ]: **se ~** vi to fade; to become worn

défrayer [defʀeje] vt: ~ **qn** to pay sb's expenses; ~ **la chronique** to be in the news

défricher [defʀiʃe] vt to clear (for cultivation)

défroquer [defʀɔke] vi (*aussi*: **se ~**) to give up the cloth

défunt, e [defœ̃, -œ̃t] adj: **son ~ père** his late father ♦ nm/f deceased

dégagé, e [degaʒe] adj clear; (*ton, air*) casual, jaunty

dégagement [degaʒmɑ̃] nm: **voie de ~** slip road; **itinéraire de ~** alternative route (*to relieve congestion*)

dégager [degaʒe] vt (*exhaler*) to give off; (*délivrer*) to free, extricate; (*désencombrer*) to clear; (*isoler: idée, aspect*) to bring out; **se ~** vi (*odeur*) to be given off; (*passage, ciel*) to clear

dégarnir [degaʀniʀ] vt (*vider*) to empty, clear; **se ~** vi (*tempes, crâne*) to go bald

dégâts [dega] nmpl damage *sg*

dégel [deʒɛl] nm thaw

dégeler [deʒle] vt to thaw (out); (*fig*) to unfreeze ♦ vi to thaw (out)

dégénérer [deʒenere] vi to degenerate; (*empirer*) to go from bad to worse

dégingandé, e [deʒɛ̃gɑ̃de] adj gangling

dégivrer [deʒivʀe] vt (*frigo*) to defrost; (*vitres*) to de-ice

déglutir [deglytiʀ] vt, vi to swallow

dégonflé, e [degɔ̃fle] adj (*pneu*) flat

dégonfler [degɔ̃fle] vt (*pneu, ballon*) to let down, deflate; **se ~** vi (*fam*) to chicken out

dégouliner [deguline] vi to trickle, drip

dégourdi, e [deguʀdi] adj smart, resourceful

dégourdir [deguʀdiʀ] vt: **se ~ (les jambes)** to stretch one's legs (*fig*)

dégoût [degu] nm disgust, distaste

dégoûtant, e [degutɑ̃, -ɑ̃t] adj disgusting

dégoûté, e [degute] adj disgusted; ~ **de** sick of

dégoûter [degute] vt to disgust; ~ **qn de**

qch to put sb off sth

dégoutter [degute] vi to drip

dégradé [degʀade] nm (*PEINTURE*) gradation

dégrader [degʀade] vt (*MIL: officier*) to degrade; (*abîmer*) to damage, deface; **se ~** vi (*relations, situation*) to deteriorate

dégrafer [degʀafe] vt to unclip, unhook

degré [dəgʀe] nm degree; (*d'escalier*) step; **alcool à 90 ~s** surgical spirit

dégressif, ive [degʀesif, -iv] adj on a decreasing scale

dégrèvement [degʀɛvmɑ̃] nm tax relief

dégringoler [degʀɛ̃gɔle] vi to tumble (down)

dégrossir [degʀosiʀ] vt (*fig*) to work out roughly; to knock the rough edges off

déguenillé, e [degnije] adj ragged, tattered

déguerpir [degɛʀpiʀ] vi to clear off

dégueulasse [degølas] (*fam*) adj disgusting

déguisement [degizmɑ̃] nm disguise

déguiser [degize] vt to disguise; **se ~** vi (*se costumer*) to dress up; (*pour tromper*) to disguise o.s.

déguster [degyste] vt (*vins*) to taste; (*fromages etc*) to sample; (*savourer*) to enjoy, savour

dehors [dəɔʀ] adv outside; (*en plein air*) outdoors ♦ nm outside ♦ nmpl (*apparences*) appearances; **mettre** *ou* **jeter** ~ (*expulser*) to throw out; **au ~** outside; outwardly; **au ~ de** outside; **en ~** (*vers l'extérieur*) outside; outwards; **en ~ de** (*hormis*) apart from

déjà [deʒa] adv already; (*auparavant*) before, already

déjeuner [deʒœne] vi to (have) lunch; (*le matin*) to have breakfast ♦ nm lunch; breakfast

déjouer [deʒwe] vt to elude; to foil

delà [dəla] adv: **par ~, en ~ (de), au ~ (de)** beyond

délabrer [delabʀe]: **se ~** vi to fall into decay, become dilapidated

délacer [delase] vt to unlace

délai [dele] nm (*attente*) waiting period; (*sursis*) extension of (time); (*temps accordé*) time limit; **à bref ~** shortly, very soon; at short notice; **dans les ~s** within the time limit

délaisser [delese] vt to abandon, desert

délasser [delase] vt (*reposer*) to relax; (*divertir*) to divert, entertain; **se ~** vi to relax

délateur, trice [delatœʀ, -tʀis] nm/f informer

délavé, e [delave] adj faded

délayer [deleje] vt (*CULIN*) to mix (with water *etc*); (*peinture*) to thin down

delco [dɛlko] nm (*AUTO*) distributor

délecter [delɛkte]: **se ~** vi to revel *ou* delight in

délégué, e [delege] nm/f delegate; representative

déléguer [delege] *vt* to delegate

délibéré, e [delibeʀe] *adj (conscient)* deliberate; *(déterminé)* determined

délibérer [delibeʀe] *vi* to deliberate

délicat, e [delika, -at] *adj* delicate; *(plein de tact)* tactful; *(attentionné)* thoughtful; *(exigeant)* fussy, particular; **procédés peu ~s** unscrupulous methods; **délicatement** *adv* delicately; *(avec douceur)* gently

délice [delis] *nm* delight

délicieux, euse [delisjø, -jøz] *adj (au goût)* delicious; *(sensation, impression)* delightful

délimiter [delimite] *vt* to delimit, demarcate; to determine; to define

délinquance [delēkɑ̃s] *nf* criminality; **délinquant, e** [delēkɑ̃, -ɑ̃t] *adj, nm/f* delinquent

délirer [deliʀe] *vi* to be delirious; *(fig)* to be raving, be going wild

délit [deli] *nm (criminal)* offence; **~ d'initié** *(BOURSE)* insider dealing *ou* trading

délivrer [delivʀe] *vt (prisonnier)* to (set) free, release; *(passeport, certificat)* to issue; **~ qn (ennemis)** to deliver *ou* free sb from; *(fig)* to relieve sb of; to rid sb of

déloger [delɔʒe] *vt (locataire)* to turn out; *(objet coincé, ennemi)* to dislodge

deltaplane [dɛltaplan] *nm* hang-glider

déluge [delyʒ] *nm (biblique)* Flood

déluré, e [delyʀe] *adj* smart, resourceful; *(péj)* forward, pert

demain [dəmɛ̃] *adv* tomorrow

demande [dəmɑ̃d] *nf (requête)* request; *(revendication)* demand; *(ADMIN, formulaire)* application; *(ÉCON)* **la ~** demand; **"~s d'emploi"** "situations wanted"; **~ de poste** job application

demandé, e [dəmɑ̃de] *adj (article etc)*: **très ~** (very) much in demand

demander [dəmɑ̃de] *vt* to ask for; *(date, heure etc)* to ask; *(nécessiter)* to require, demand; **se ~** to wonder; *(sens purement réfléchi)* to ask o.s.; **~ qch à qn** to ask sb for sth; to ask sb sth; **~ à qn de faire** to ask sb to do; **on vous demande au téléphone** you're wanted on the phone

demandeur, euse [dəmɑ̃dœʀ, -øz] *nm/f*: **~ d'emploi** job-seeker; (job) applicant

démangeaison [demɑ̃ʒɛzɔ̃] *nf* itching

démanger [demɑ̃ʒe] *vi* to itch

démanteler [demɑ̃tle] *vt* to break up; to demolish

démaquillant [demakijɑ̃] *nm* make-up remover

démaquiller [demakije] *vt*: **se ~** to remove one's make-up

démarche [demaʀʃ(ə)] *nf (allure)* gait, walk; *(intervention)* step; approach; *(fig: intellectuelle)* thought processes *pl*; approach; **faire des ~s auprès de qn** to approach sb

démarcheur, euse [demaʀʃœʀ, -øz] *nm/f*

(COMM) door-to-door salesman(woman)

démarquer [demaʀke] *vt (prix)* to mark down; *(joueur)* to stop marking

démarrage [demaʀaʒ] *nm* start

démarrer [demaʀe] *vi (conducteur)* to start (up); *(véhicule)* to move off; *(travaux)* to get moving; **démarreur** *nm (AUTO)* starter

démêler [demele] *vt* to untangle

démêlés [demele] *nmpl* problems

déménagement [demenaʒmɑ̃] *nm* move, removal; **camion de ~** removal van

déménager [demenaʒe] *vt (meubles)* to (re)move ♦ *vi* to move (house); **déménageur** *nm* removal man; *(entrepreneur)* furniture remover

démener [demne]: **se ~** *vi* to thrash about; *(fig)* to exert o.s.

dément, e [demɑ̃, -ɑ̃t] *adj (fou)* mad, crazy; *(fam)* brilliant, fantastic

démentiel, le [demɑ̃sjɛl] *adj* insane

démentir [demɑ̃tiʀ] *vt* to refute; **~ que** to deny that

démerder [demɛʀde] *(fam)*: **se ~** *vi* to sort things out for o.s.

démesuré, e [deməzyʀe] *adj* immoderate

démettre [demɛtʀ(ə)] *vt*: **~ qn de *(fonction, poste)*** to dismiss sb from; **se ~ (de ses fonctions)** to resign (from) one's duties; **se ~ l'épaule** *etc* to dislocate one's shoulder *etc*

demeurant [dəmœʀɑ̃]: **au ~** *adv* for all that

demeure [dəmœʀ] *nf* residence; **mettre qn en ~ de faire** to enjoin *ou* order sb to do; **à ~** permanently

demeurer [dəmœʀe] *vi (habiter)* to live; *(séjourner)* to stay; *(rester)* to remain

demi, e [dəmi] *adj* half ♦ *nm (bière)* ≈ half-pint *(0,25 litres)* ♦ *préfixe*: **~...** half-, semi..., demi-; **trois heures/bouteilles et ~es** three and a half hours/bottles, three hours/bottles and a half; **il est 2 heures/midi et ~e** it's half past 2/12; **à ~** half-; **à la ~e** *(heure)* on the half-hour; **~-cercle** *nm* semicircle; **en ~-cercle** *adj* semicircular ♦ *adv* in a half circle; **~-douzaine** *nf* half-dozen, half a dozen; **~-finale** *nf* semifinal; **~-frère** *nm* half-brother; **~-heure** *nf* half-hour, half an hour; **~-journée** *nf* half-day, half a day; **~-litre** *nm* half-litre, half a litre; **~-livre** *nf* half-pound, half a pound; **~-mot** *adv*: **à ~-mot** without having to spell things out; **~-pension** *nf (à l'hôtel)* half-board; **~-place** *nf* half-fare

démis, e [demi, -iz] *adj (épaule etc)* dislocated

demi: **~-saison** *nf*: **vêtements de ~saison** spring *ou* autumn clothing; **~-sel** *adj inv (beurre, fromage)* slightly salted; **~-sœur** *nf* half-sister

démission [demisjɔ̃] *nf* resignation; **donner sa ~** to give *ou* hand in one's notice; **dé-**

missionner vi (de son poste) to resign
demi-tarif [dəmitaRif] nm half-price; (TRANSPORTS) half-fare
demi-tour [dəmituR] nm about-turn; **faire ~** to turn (and go) back; (AUTO) to do a U-turn
démocratie [demɔkRasi] nf democracy; **démocratique** [demɔkRatik] adj democratic
démodé, e [demɔde] adj old-fashioned
démographique [demɔgRafik] adj demographic, population cpd
demoiselle [dəmwazɛl] nf (jeune fille) young lady; (célibataire) single lady, maiden lady; **~ d'honneur** bridesmaid
démolir [demɔliR] vt to demolish
démon [demɔ̃] nm (enfant turbulent) devil, demon; **le D~** the Devil
démonstration [demɔ̃stRasjɔ̃] nf demonstration; (aérienne, navale) display
démonté, e [demɔ̃te] adj (fig) raging, wild
démonter [demɔ̃te] vt (machine etc) to take down, dismantle; **se ~** vi (personne) to lose countenance
démontrer [demɔ̃tRe] vt to demonstrate
démordre [demɔRdR(ə)] vi: **ne pas ~ de** to refuse to give up
démouler [demule] vt (gâteau) to turn out
démuni, e [demyni] adj (sans argent) impoverished
démunir [demyniR] vt: **~ qn de** to deprive sb of; **se ~ de** to part with, give up
dénatalité [denatalite] nf fall in the birth rate
dénaturer [denatyRe] vt (goût) to alter; (pensée, fait) to distort
déniaiser [denjeze] vt: **~ qn** to teach sb about life
dénicher [deniʃe] vt to unearth; to track ou hunt down
dénier [denje] vt to deny
dénigrer [denigRe] vt to denigrate, run down
dénivellation [denivɛlɑsjɔ̃] nf = **dénivellement**
dénivellement [denivɛlmɑ̃] nm ramp; dip; difference in level
dénombrer [denɔ̃bRe] vt (compter) to count; (énumérer) to enumerate, list
dénomination [denɔminɑsjɔ̃] nf designation, appellation
dénommer [denɔme] vt to name
dénoncer [denɔ̃se] vt to denounce; **se ~** vi to give o.s. up, come forward
dénouement [denumɑ̃] nm outcome
dénouer [denwe] vt to unknot, undo
dénoyauter [denwajote] vt to stone
denrée [dɑ̃Re] nf: **~s (alimentaires)** foodstuffs
dense [dɑ̃s] adj dense
densité [dɑ̃site] nf density
dent [dɑ̃] nf tooth; **en ~s de scie** serrated; jagged; **~ de lait/sagesse** milk/wisdom

tooth; **~aire** adj dental
dentelé, e [dɑ̃tle] adj jagged, indented
dentelle [dɑ̃tɛl] nf lace no pl
dentier [dɑ̃tje] nm denture
dentifrice [dɑ̃tifRis] nm toothpaste
dentiste [dɑ̃tist(ə)] nm/f dentist
dénuder [denyde] vt to bare
dénué, e [denye] adj: **~ de** devoid of; lacking in; **dénuement** [denymɑ̃] nm destitution
déodorant [deɔdɔRɑ̃] nm deodorant
dépannage [depanaʒ] nm: **service de ~** (AUTO) breakdown service
dépanner [depane] vt (voiture, télévision) to fix, repair; (fig) to bail out, help out; **dépanneuse** nf breakdown lorry (BRIT), tow truck (US)
dépareillé, e [depaReje] adj (collection, service) incomplete; (objet) odd
déparer [depaRe] vt to spoil, mar
départ [depaR] nm leaving no pl, departure; (SPORT) start; (sur un horaire) departure; **au ~** at the start; **à son ~** when he left
départager [depaRtaʒe] vt to decide between
département [depaRtəmɑ̃] nm department
départir [depaRtiR] : **se ~ de** vt to abandon, depart from
dépassé, e [depase] adj superseded, outmoded; (affolé) panic-stricken
dépasser [depase] vt (véhicule, concurrent) to overtake; (endroit) to pass, go past; (somme, limite) to exceed; (fig: en beauté etc) to surpass, outshine; (être en saillie sur) to jut out above (ou in front of) ♦ vi (jupon) to show
dépaysé, e [depeize] adj disoriented
dépecer [depəse] vt to joint, cut up
dépêche [depɛʃ] nf dispatch
dépêcher [depeʃe] vt to dispatch; **se ~** vi to hurry
dépeindre [depɛ̃dR(ə)] vt to depict
dépendre [depɑ̃dR(ə)]: **~ de** vt to depend on; (financièrement) to be dependent on
dépens [depɑ̃] nmpl: **aux ~ de** at the expense of
dépense [depɑ̃s] nf spending no pl, expense, expenditure no pl; (fig) consumption; expenditure
dépenser [depɑ̃se] vt to spend; (gaz, eau) to use; (fig) to expend, use up; **se ~** vi (se fatiguer) to exert o.s.
dépensier, ère [depɑ̃sje, -jɛR] adj: **il est ~** he's a spendthrift
déperdition [depɛRdisjɔ̃] nf loss
dépérir [depeRiR] vi to waste away; to wither
dépêtrer [depetRe] vt: **se ~ de** to extricate o.s. from
dépeupler [depœple] vt to depopulate; **se ~** vi to be depopulated
dépilatoire [depilatwaR] adj depilatory,

hair-removing

dépister [depiste] *vt* to detect; (*voleur*) to track down; (*poursuivants*) to throw off the scent

dépit [depi] *nm* vexation, frustration; **en ~ de** in spite of; **en ~ du bon sens** contrary to all good sense; **dépité, e** *adj* vexed, frustrated

déplacé, e [deplase] *adj* (*propos*) out of place, uncalled-for

déplacement [deplasmɑ̃] *nm* (*voyage*) trip, travelling *no pl*

déplacer [deplase] *vt* (*table, voiture*) to move, shift; (*employé*) to transfer, move; (*os, vertèbre etc*) to displace; **se ~** *vi* to move; (*voyager*) to travel

déplaire [deplɛʀ] *vt*: **ceci me déplaît** I don't like this, I dislike this; **se ~** *vr*: **se ~ quelque part** to be unhappy somewhere; **déplaisant, e** *adj* disagreeable

dépliant [deplijɑ̃] *nm* leaflet

déplier [deplije] *vt* to unfold

déplorer [deplɔʀe] *vt* (*regretter*) to deplore

déployer [deplwaje] *vt* to open out, spread; to deploy; to display, exhibit

déporter [depɔʀte] *vt* (*POL*) to deport; (*dévier*) to carry off course

déposer [depoze] *vt* (*gén: mettre, poser*) to lay *ou* put down; (*à la banque, à la consigne*) to deposit; (*passager*) to drop (off), set down; (*roi*) to depose; (*ADMIN: faire enregistrer*) to file; to register; (*JUR*): **~ (contre)** to testify *ou* give evidence (against); **se ~** *vi* to settle; **dépositaire** *nm/f* (*COMM*) agent

dépôt [depo] *nm* (*à la banque, sédiment*) deposit; (*entrepôt, réserve*) warehouse, store; (*gare*) depot; (*prison*) cells *pl*

dépotoir [depotwaʀ] *nm* dumping ground, rubbish dump

dépouille [depuj] *nf* (*d'animal*) skin, hide; (*humaine*): **~ (mortelle)** mortal remains *pl*

dépouillé, e [depuje] *adj* (*fig*) bare, bald

dépouiller [depuje] *vt* (*animal*) to skin; (*spolier*) to deprive of one's possessions; (*documents*) to go through, peruse; **~ qn/ qch de** to strip sb/sth of; **~ le scrutin** to count the votes

dépourvu, e [depuʀvy] *adj*: **~ de** lacking in, without; **au ~** unprepared

déprécier [depʀesje] *vt* to depreciate; **se ~** *vi* to depreciate

dépression [depʀesjɔ̃] *nf* depression; **~ (nerveuse)** (nervous) breakdown

déprimer [depʀime] *vt* to depress

MOT CLÉ
---

depuis [dəpɥi] *prép* **1** (*point de départ dans le temps*) since; **il habite Paris ~ 1983/l'an dernier** he has been living in Paris since 1983/last year; **~ quand le connaissez-vous?** how long have you known him?

2 (*temps écoulé*) for; **il habite Paris ~ 5 ans** he has been living in Paris for 5 years; **je le connais ~ 3 ans** I've known him for 3 years

3 (*lieu*): **il a plu ~ Metz** it's been raining since Metz; **elle a téléphoné ~ Valence** she rang from Valence

4 (*quantité, rang*) from; **~ les plus petits jusqu'aux plus grands** from the youngest to the oldest

♦ *adv* (*temps*) since (then); **je ne lui ai pas parlé ~** I haven't spoken to him since (then); **~ que** *conj* (ever) since; **~ qu'il m'a dit ça** (ever) since he said that to me

---

député, e [depyte] *nm/f* (*POL*) ≈ Member of Parliament (*BRIT*), ≈ Member of Congress (*US*)

députer [depyte] *vt* to delegate

déraciner [deʀasine] *vt* to uproot

dérailler [deʀaje] *vi* (*train*) to be derailed; **faire ~** to derail

déraisonner [deʀɛzɔne] *vi* to talk nonsense, rave

dérangement [deʀɑ̃ʒmɑ̃] *nm* (*gêne*) trouble; (*gastrique etc*) disorder; (*mécanique*) breakdown; **en ~** (*téléphone*) out of order

déranger [deʀɑ̃ʒe] *vt* (*personne*) to trouble, bother; to disturb; (*projets*) to disrupt, upset; (*objets, vêtements*) to disarrange; **se ~** *vi* to put o.s. out; to (take the trouble to) come *ou* go out; **est-ce que cela vous dérange si ...?** do you mind if ...?

déraper [deʀape] *vi* (*voiture*) to skid; (*personne, semelles, couteau*) to slip

déréglé, e [deʀegle] *adj* (*mœurs*) dissolute

dérégler [deʀegle] *vt* (*mécanisme*) to put out of order; (*estomac*) to upset

dérider [deʀide] *vt* to brighten up; **se ~** *vi* to brighten up

dérision [deʀizjɔ̃] *nf*: **tourner en ~** to deride

dérivatif [deʀivatif] *nm* distraction

dérive [deʀiv] *nf* (*de dériveur*) centre-board; **aller à la ~** (*NAVIG, fig*) to drift

dérivé, e [deʀive] *nm* (*TECH*) by-product; **~e** *nf* (*MATH*) derivative

dériver [deʀive] *vt* (*MATH*) to derive; (*cours d'eau etc*) to divert ♦ *vi* (*bateau*) to drift; **~ de** to derive from

dermatologue [dɛʀmatɔlɔg] *nm/f* dermatologist

dernier, ière [dɛʀnje, -jɛʀ] *adj* last; (*le plus récent*) latest, last; **lundi/le mois ~** last Monday/month; **du ~ chic** extremely smart; **les ~s honneurs** last tribute; **en ~** last; **ce ~** the latter; **dernièrement** *adv* recently

dérobé, e [deʀobe] *adj* (*porte*) secret, hidden; **à la ~e** surreptitiously

dérober [deʀobe] *vt* to steal; **se ~** *vi* (*s'esquiver*) to slip away; to shy away; **se ~**

sous (*s'effondrer*) to give way beneath; **se ~ à** (*justice, regards*) to hide from; (*obligation*) to shirk; **~ qch à (la vue de) qn** to conceal *ou* hide sth from sb('s view)

dérogation [derɔgasjɔ̃] *nf* (special) dispensation

déroger [derɔʒe] : **~ à** *vt* to go against, depart from

dérouiller [deruje] *vt*: **se ~ les jambes** to stretch one's legs (*fig*)

déroulement [derulmɑ̃] *nm* (*d'une opération etc*) progress

dérouler [derule] *vt* (*ficelle*) to unwind; (*papier*) to unroll; **se ~** *vi* (*avoir lieu*) to take place; (*se passer*) to go on; to go (off); to unfold

déroute [derut] *nf* rout; total collapse; **~r** [derute] *vt* (*avion, train*) to reroute, divert; (*étonner*) to disconcert, throw (out)

derrière [dɛrjɛr] *adv, prép* behind **♦** *nm* (*d'une maison*) back; (*postérieur*) behind, bottom; **les pattes de ~** the back *ou* hind legs; **par ~** from behind; (*fig*) behind one's back

des [de] *dét voir de* **♦** *prép* +*dét* = **de** +**les**

dès [de] *prép* from; **~ que** as soon as; **~ son retour** as soon as he was (*ou* is) back; **~ lors** from then on; **~ lors que** from the moment (that)

désabusé, e [dezabyze] *adj* disillusioned

désaccord [dezakɔr] *nm* disagreement; **~é, e** [dezakɔrde] *adj* (*MUS*) out of tune

désaffecté, e [dezafɛkte] *adj* disused

désagréable [dezagreable(ə)] *adj* unpleasant

désagréger [dezagreʒe] : **se ~** *vi* to disintegrate, break up

désagrément [dezagremɑ̃] *nm* annoyance, trouble *no pl*

désaltérer [dezaltere] *vt*: **se ~** to quench one's thirst

désamorcer [dezamɔrse] *vt* to defuse; to forestall

désapprobateur, trice [dezaprɔbatœr, -tris] *adj* disapproving

désapprouver [dezapruve] *vt* to disapprove of

désarçonner [dezarsɔne] *vt* to unseat, throw; (*fig*) to throw, puzzle

désarmant, e [dezarmɑ̃, -ɑ̃t] *adj* disarming

désarroi [dezarwa] *nm* disarray

désarticulé, e [dezartikyle] *adj* (*pantin, corps*) dislocated

désastre [dezastr(ə)] *nm* disaster

désavantage [dezavɑ̃taʒ] *nm* disadvantage; (*inconvénient*) drawback, disadvantage; **désavantager** *vt* to put at a disadvantage

désavouer [dezavwe] *vt* to disown

désaxé, e [dezakse] *adj* (*fig*) unbalanced

descendre [desɑ̃dr(ə)] *vt* (*escalier, montagne*) to go (*ou* come) down; (*valise, paquet*) to take *ou* get down; (*étagère etc*) to

lower; (*fam: abattre*) to shoot down **♦** *vi* to go (*ou* come) down; (*passager: s'arrêter*) to get out, alight; **~ à pied/en voiture** to walk/drive down; **~ de** (*famille*) to be descended from; **~ du train** to get out of *ou* get off the train; **~ d'un arbre** to climb down from a tree; **~ de cheval** to dismount; **~ à l'hôtel** to stay at a hotel

descente [desɑ̃t] *nf* descent, going down; (*chemin*) way down; (*SKI*) downhill (race); **au milieu de la ~** halfway down; **~ de lit** bedside rug; **~ (de police)** (police) raid

description [dɛskripsjɔ̃] *nf* description

désemparé, e [dezɑ̃pare] *adj* bewildered, distraught

désemparer [dezɑ̃pare] *vi*: **sans ~** without stopping

désemplir [dezɑ̃plir] *vi*: **ne pas ~** to be always full

déséquilibre [dezekilibr(ə)] *nm* (*position*): **en ~** unsteady; (*fig: des forces, du budget*) imbalance; **déséquilibré, e** [dezekilibre] *nm/f* (*PSYCH*) unbalanced person; **déséquilibrer** [dezekilibre] *vt* to throw off balance

désert, e [dezɛr, -ɛrt(ə)] *adj* deserted **♦** *nm* desert

déserter [dezɛrte] *vi, vt* to desert

désertique [dezɛrtik] *adj* desert *cpd*; barren, empty

désespéré, e [dezɛspere] *adj* desperate

désespérer [dezɛspere] *vt* to drive to despair **♦** *vi*: **~ de** to despair of

désespoir [dezɛspwar] *nm* despair; **en ~ de cause** in desperation

déshabillé [dezabije] *nm* négligée

déshabiller [dezabije] *vt* to undress; **se ~** *vi* to undress (o.s.)

désherbant [dezɛrbɑ̃] *nm* weed-killer

déshériter [dezerite] *vt* to disinherit

déshérités [dezerite] *nmpl*: **les ~** the underprivileged

déshonneur [dezɔnœr] *nm* dishonour

déshydraté, e [dezidrate] *adj* dehydrated

desiderata [deziderata] *nmpl* requirements

désigner [dezine] *vt* (*montrer*) to point out, indicate; (*dénommer*) to denote; (*candidat etc*) to name

désinfectant, e [dezɛ̃fɛkta, -ɑ̃t] *adj, nm* disinfectant; **désinfecter** [dezɛ̃fɛkte] *vt* to disinfect

désintégrer [dezɛ̃tegre] *vt* to disintegrate; **se ~** *vi* to disintegrate

désintéressé, e [dezɛ̃terese] *adj* disinterested, unselfish

désintéresser [dezɛ̃terese] *vt*: **se ~ (de)** to lose interest (in)

désintoxication [dezɛ̃tɔksikasjɔ̃] *nf*: **faire une cure de ~** to undergo treatment for alcoholism (*ou* drug addiction)

désinvolte [dezɛ̃vɔlt(ə)] *adj* casual, off-hand; **désinvolture** *nf* casualness

désir [dezir] *nm* wish; *(fort, sensuel)* desire

désirer [dezire] *vt* to want, wish for; *(sexuellement)* to desire; **je désire ...** *(formule de politesse)* I would like ...

désister [deziste]: **se ~** *vi* to stand down, withdraw

désobéir [dezɔbeir] *vi*: **~ (à qn/qch)** to disobey (sb/sth); **désobéissant, e** *adj* disobedient

désobligeant, e [dezɔbliʒã, -ãt] *adj* disagreeable

désodorisant [dezɔdɔrizã] *nm* air freshener, deodorizer

désœuvré, e [dezœvre] *adj* idle

désolé, e [dezɔle] *adj (paysage)* desolate; **je suis ~** I'm sorry

désoler [dezɔle] *vt* to distress, grieve

désolidariser [desɔlidarize] *vt*: **se ~ de** *ou* **d'avec** to dissociate o.s. from

désopilant, e [dezɔpilã, -ãt] *adj* hilarious

désordonné, e [dezɔrdɔne] *adj* untidy

désordre [dezɔrdr(ə)] *nm* disorder(liness), untidiness; *(anarchie)* disorder; **~s** *nmpl (POL)* disturbances, disorder *sg*; **en ~** in a mess, untidy

désorienté, e [dezɔrjãte] *adj* disorientated

désormais [dezɔrmɛ] *adv* from now on

désosser [dezɔse] *vt* to bone

desquelles [dekɛl] *prép +pron* = **de +lesquelles**

desquels [dekɛl] *prép +pron* = **de +lesquels**

dessaisir [desezir]: **se ~ de** *vt* to give up, part with

dessaler [desale] *vt (eau de mer)* to desalinate; *(CULIN)* to soak

desséché, e [deseʃe] *adj* dried up

dessécher [deseʃe] *vt* to dry out, parch; **se ~** *vi* to dry out

dessein [desɛ̃] *nm* design; **à ~** intentionally, deliberately

desserrer [desere] *vt* to loosen; *(frein)* to release

dessert [desɛr] *nm* dessert, pudding

desserte [desɛrt(ə)] *nf (table)* side table; *(transport)*: **la ~ du village est assurée par autocar** there is a coach service to the village

desservir [desɛrvir] *vt (ville, quartier)* to serve; *(nuire à)* to go against, put at a disadvantage; *(débarrasser)*: **~ (la table)** to clear the table

dessin [desɛ̃] *nm (œuvre, art)* drawing; *(motif)* pattern, design; *(contour)* (out)line; **~ animé** cartoon (film); **~ humoristique** cartoon

dessinateur, trice [desinatœr, -tris] *nm/f* drawer; *(de bandes dessinées)* cartoonist; *(industriel)* draughtsman(woman) *(BRIT)*, draftsman(woman) *(US)*

dessiner [desine] *vt* to draw; *(concevoir)* to design

dessous [dəsu] *adv* underneath, beneath ♦ *nm* underside ♦ *nmpl (sous-vêtements)* underwear *sg*; **en ~, par ~** underneath; below; **au-dessous (de)** below; *(peu digne de)* beneath; **avoir le ~** to get the worst of it; **dessous-de-plat** *nm inv* tablemat

dessus [dəsy] *adv* on top; *(collé, écrit)* on it ♦ *nm* top; **en ~** above; **par ~** *adv* over it ♦ *prép* over; **au-dessus (de)** above; **avoir le ~** to get the upper hand; **dessus-de-lit** *nm inv* bedspread

destin [destɛ̃] *nm* fate; *(avenir)* destiny

destinataire [destinatɛr] *nm/f (POSTES)* addressee; *(d'un colis)* consignee

destination [destinasjɔ̃] *nf (lieu)* destination; *(usage)* purpose; **à ~ de** bound for, travelling to

destinée [destine] *nf* fate; *(existence, avenir)* destiny

destiner [destine] *vt*: **~ qn à** *(poste, sort)* to destine sb for; **~ qn/qch à** *(prédestiner)* to destine sb/sth to +*verbe*; **~ qch à qn** *(envisager de donner)* to intend sb to have sth; *(adresser)* to intend sth for sb; to aim sth at sb; **être destiné à** *(sort)* to be destined to +*verbe*; *(usage)* to be meant for; *(suj: sort)* to be in store for

destituer [destitɥe] *vt* to depose

désuet, ète [desɥɛ, -ɛt] *adj* outdated, outmoded; *(ADMIN)*: **désuétude** *nf*: **tomber en désuétude** to fall into disuse

détachant [detaʃã] *nm* stain remover

détachement [detaʃmã] *nm* detachment

détacher [detaʃe] *vt (enlever)* to detach, remove; *(délier)* to untie; *(ADMIN)*: **~ qn (auprès de** *ou* **à)** to post sb (to); **se ~** *vi (tomber)* to come off; to come out; *(se défaire)* to come undone; **se ~ sur** to stand out against; **se ~ de** *(se désintéresser)* to grow away from

détail [detaj] *nm* detail; *(COMM)*: **le ~** retail; **en ~** in detail; **au ~** *(COMM)* retail; separately

détaillant [detajã] *nm* retailer

détailler [detaje] *vt (expliquer)* to explain in detail; to detail; *(examiner)* to look over, examine

détartrant [detartrã] *nm* scale remover

détecter [detɛkte] *vt* to detect

détective [detɛktiv] *nm* detective; **~ (privé)** private detective

déteindre [detɛ̃dr(ə)] *vi (tissu)* to fade; *(fig)*: **~ sur** to rub off on

dételer [detle] *vt* to unharness

détendre [detãdr(ə)] *vt*: **se ~** to lose its tension; to relax

détenir [detnir] *vt (fortune, objet, secret)* to be in possession of; *(prisonnier)* to detain, hold; *(record, pouvoir)* to hold

détente [detãt] *nf* relaxation; *(d'une arme)* trigger

détention [detãsjɔ̃] *nf* possession; detention; holding; ~ **préventive** (pre-trial) custody

détenu, e [detny] *nm/f* prisoner

détergent [detɛrʒɑ̃] *nm* detergent

détériorer [deterjɔre] *vt* to damage; **se ~** *vi* to deteriorate

déterminé, e [detɛrmine] *adj* (*résolu*) determined; (*précis*) specific, definite

déterminer [detɛrmine] *vt* (*fixer*) to determine; (*décider*): ~ **qn à faire qch** to decide sb to do

déterrer [detere] *vt* to dig up

détestable [detɛstabl(ə)] *adj* foul, ghastly; detestable, odious

détester [detɛste] *vt* to hate, detest

détonation [detɔnasjɔ̃] *nf* detonation, bang, report (of a gun)

détonner [detɔne] *vi* (*MUS*) to go out of tune; (*fig*) to clash

détour [detur] *nm* detour; (*tournant*) bend, curve; **sans ~** (*fig*) plainly

détourné, e [deturne] *adj* (*moyen*) roundabout

détournement [deturnəmɑ̃] *nm*: ~ **d'avion** hijacking; ~ **de mineur** corruption of a minor

détourner [deturne] *vt* to divert; (*par la force*) to hijack; (*yeux, tête*) to turn away; (*de l'argent*) to embezzle; **se ~** *vi* to turn away

détracteur, trice [detraktœr, -tris] *nm/f* disparager, critic

détraquer [detrake] *vt* to put out of order; (*estomac*) to upset; **se ~** *vi* to go wrong

détrempé, e [detrɑ̃pe] *adj* (*sol*) sodden, waterlogged

détresse [detrɛs] *nf* distress

détriment [detrimɑ̃] *nm*: **au ~ de** to the detriment of

détritus [detritys] *nmpl* rubbish *sg*, refuse *sg*

détroit [detrwa] *nm* strait

détromper [detrɔ̃pe] *vt* to disabuse

détrôner [detrone] *vt* to dethrone

détrousser [detruse] *vt* to rob

détruire [detrɥir] *vt* to destroy

dette [dɛt] *nf* debt

D.E.U.G. [dœg] *sigle m* = **diplôme d'études universitaires générales**

deuil [dœj] *nm* (*perte*) bereavement; (*période*) mourning; (*chagrin*) grief; **être en ~** to be in mourning

deux [dø] *num* two; **les ~** both; **ses ~ mains** both his hands, his two hands; **deuxième** *num* second; **deuxièmement** *adv* secondly, in the second place; **deux-pièces** *nm inv* (*tailleur*) two-piece suit; (*de bain*) two-piece (swimsuit); (*appartement*) two-roomed flat (*BRIT*) *ou* apartment (*US*); **deux-roues** *nm inv* two-wheeled vehicle

deux points *nm inv* colon *sg*

devais *etc vb voir* **devoir**

dévaler [devale] *vt* to hurtle down

dévaliser [devalize] *vt* to rob, burgle

dévaloriser [devalɔrize] *vt* to depreciate; **se ~** *vi* to depreciate

dévaluation [devalɥasjɔ̃] *nf* depreciation; (*ÉCON: mesure*) devaluation

devancer [dəvɑ̃se] *vt* to be ahead of; to get ahead of; to arrive before; (*prévenir*) to anticipate

devant [dəvɑ̃] *adv* in front; (*à distance: en avant*) ahead ♦ *prép* in front of; ahead of; (*avec mouvement: passer*) past; (*fig*) before, in front of; faced with; in view of ♦ *nm* front; **prendre les ~s** to make the first move; **les pattes de ~** the front legs, the forelegs; **par ~** (*boutonner*) at the front; (*entrer*) the front way; **aller au-devant de qn** to go out to meet sb; **aller au-devant de** (*désirs de qn*) to anticipate

devanture [dəvɑ̃tyr] *nf* (*façade*) (shop) front; (*étalage*) display; (shop) window

déveine [devɛn] *nf* rotten luck *no pl*

développement [devlɔpmɑ̃] *nm* development

développer [devlɔpe] *vt* to develop; **se ~** *vi* to develop

devenir [dəvnir] *vb +attrib* to become; ~ **instituteur** to become a teacher; **que sont-ils devenus?** what has become of them?

dévergondé, e [devɛrgɔ̃de] *adj* wild, shameless

déverser [devɛrse] *vt* (*liquide*) to pour (out); (*ordures*) to tip (out); **se ~ dans** (*fleuve, mer*) to flow into

dévêtir [devetir] *vt* to undress; **se ~** *vi* to undress

devez *etc vb voir* **devoir**

déviation [devjasjɔ̃] *nf* deviation; (*AUTO*) diversion (*BRIT*), detour (*US*)

dévider [devide] *vt* to unwind

devienne *etc vb voir* **devenir**

dévier [devje] *vt* (*fleuve, circulation*) to divert; (*coup*) to deflect ♦ *vi* to veer (off course)

devin [dəvɛ̃] *nm* soothsayer, seer

deviner [dəvine] *vt* to guess; (*prévoir*) to foresee; (*apercevoir*) to distinguish; **devinette** [dəvinɛt] *nf* riddle

devins *etc vb voir* **devenir**

devis [dəvi] *nm* estimate, quotation

dévisager [devizaʒe] *vt* to stare at

devise [dəviz] *nf* (*formule*) motto, watchword; (*ÉCON: monnaie*) currency; **~s** *nfpl* (*argent*) currency *sg*

deviser [dəvize] *vi* to converse

dévisser [devise] *vt* to unscrew, undo; **se ~** *vi* to come unscrewed

dévoiler [devwale] *vt* to unveil

devoir [dəvwar] *nm* duty; (*SCOL*) homework *no pl*; (: en classe) exercise ♦ *vt* (*argent, respect*): ~ **qch (à qn)** to owe (sb) sth; (*suivi de l'infinitif: obligation*): **il doit le faire** he has to do it, he must do it; (: in-

tention): **il doit partir demain** he is (due) to leave tomorrow; (: *probabilité*): **il doit être tard** it must be late

dévolu, e [devɔly] *adj*: ~ **à** allotted to ♦ *nm*: **jeter son** ~ **sur** to fix one's choice on

dévorer [devɔʀe] *vt* to devour; (*suj: feu, soucis*) to consume

dévot, e [devo, -ɔt] *adj* devout, pious

dévotion [devɔsjɔ̃] *nf* devoutness; **être à la** ~ **de qn** to be totally devoted to sb

dévoué, e [devwe] *adj* devoted

dévouer [devwe] : **se** ~ *vi* (*se sacrifier*): **se** ~ **(pour)** to sacrifice o.s. (for); (*se consacrer*): **se** ~ **à** to devote *ou* dedicate o.s. to

dévoyé, e [devwaje] *adj* delinquent

devrai *etc vb voir* **devoir**

diabète [djabɛt] *nm* diabetes *sg*; **diabétique** *nm/f* diabetic

diable [djɑbl(ə)] *nm* devil

diabolo [djabɔlo] *nm* (*boisson*) lemonade with fruit cordial

diacre [djakʀ(ə)] *nm* deacon

diagnostic [djagnɔstik] *nm* diagnosis *sg*

diagonal, e, aux [djagɔnal, -o] *adj* diagonal; ~**e** *nf* diagonal; **en** ~**e** diagonally; **lire en** ~**e** to skim through

diagramme [djagʀam] *nm* chart, graph

dialecte [djalɛkt(ə)] *nm* dialect

dialogue [djalɔg] *nm* dialogue

diamant [djamɑ̃] *nm* diamond; **diamantaire** *nm* diamond dealer

diamètre [djamɛtʀ(ə)] *nm* diameter

diapason [djapazɔ̃] *nm* tuning fork

diaphragme [djafʀagm(ə)] *nm* diaphragm

diaporama [djapɔrama] *nm* slide show

diapositive [djapozitiv] *nf* transparency, slide

diarrhée [djaʀe] *nf* diarrhoea

dictateur [diktatœʀ] *nm* dictator; **dictature** *nf* dictatorship

dictée [dikte] *nf* dictation

dicter [dikte] *vt* to dictate

dictionnaire [diksjɔnɛʀ] *nm* dictionary

dicton [diktɔ̃] *nm* saying, dictum

dièse [djɛz] *nm* sharp

diesel [djezɛl] *nm* diesel ♦ *adj inv* diesel

diète [djɛt] *nf* (*jeûne*) starvation diet; (*régime*) diet

diététique [djetetik] *adj*: **magasin** ~ health food shop

dieu, x [djø] *nm* god; **D~** God; **mon D~!** good heavens!

diffamation [difamɑsjɔ̃] *nf* slander; (*écrite*) libel

différé [difeʀe] *nm* (*TV*): **en** ~ (pre-)recorded

différence [difeʀɑ̃s] *nf* difference; **à la** ~ **de** unlike; **différencier** [difeʀɑ̃sje] *vt* to differentiate; **différend** [difeʀɑ̃] *nm* difference (of opinion), disagreement

différent, e [difeʀɑ̃, -ɑ̃t] *adj*: ~ **(de)** different (from); ~**s objets** different *ou* various objects

différer [difeʀe] *vt* to postpone, put off ♦ *vi*: ~ **(de)** to differ (from)

difficile [difisil] *adj* difficult; (*exigeant*) hard to please; **difficilement** *adv* with difficulty

difficulté [difikylte] *nf* difficulty; **en** ~ (*bateau, alpiniste*) in difficulties

difforme [difɔʀm(ə)] *adj* deformed, misshapen

diffuser [difyze] *vt* (*chaleur, bruit*) to diffuse; (*émission, musique*) to broadcast; (*nouvelle, idée*) to circulate; (*COMM*) to distribute

digérer [diʒeʀe] *vt* to digest; (*fig: accepter*) to stomach, put up with; **digestif** *nm* (after-dinner) liqueur

digne [diɲ] *adj* dignified; ~ **de** worthy of; ~ **de foi** trustworthy

dignité [diɲite] *nf* dignity

digression [digʀesjɔ̃] *nf* digression

digue [dig] *nf* dike, dyke

dilapider [dilapide] *vt* to squander

dilemme [dilɛm] *nm* dilemma

diligence [diliʒɑ̃s] *nf* stagecoach; (*empressement*) despatch

diluer [dilɥe] *vt* to dilute

diluvien, ne [dilyvjɛ̃, -jɛn] *adj*: **pluie** ~**ne** torrential rain

dimanche [dimɑ̃ʃ] *nm* Sunday

dimension [dimɑ̃sjɔ̃] *nf* (*grandeur*) size; (*cote, de l'espace*) dimension

diminuer [diminɥe] *vt* to reduce, decrease; (*ardeur etc*) to lessen; (*personne: physiquement*) to undermine; (*dénigrer*) to belittle ♦ *vi* to decrease, diminish; **diminutif** *nm* (*surnom*) pet name; **diminution** *nf* decreasing, diminishing

dinde [dɛ̃d] *nf* turkey

dindon [dɛ̃dɔ̃] *nm* turkey

dîner [dine] *nm* dinner ♦ *vi* to have dinner

dingue [dɛ̃g] (*fam*) *adj* crazy

diplomate [diplɔmat] *adj* diplomatic ♦ *nm* diplomat; (*fig*) diplomatist

diplomatie [diplɔmasi] *nf* diplomacy

diplôme [diplom] *nm* diploma; **diplômé, e** *adj* qualified

dire [diʀ] *nm*: **au** ~ **de** according to ♦ *vt* to say; (*secret, mensonge*) to tell; **leurs** ~**s** what they say; ~ **l'heure/la vérité** to tell the time/the truth; ~ **qch à qn** to tell sb sth; ~ **à qn qu'il fasse** *ou* **de faire** to tell sb to do; **on dit que** they say that; **ceci dit** that being said; (*à ces mots*) whereupon; **si cela lui dit** (*plaire*) if he fancies it; **que dites-vous de** (*penser*) what do you think of; **on dirait que** it looks (*ou* sounds *etc*) as if; **dis/dites (donc)** I say; (*à propos*) by the way

direct, e [diʀɛkt] *adj* direct ♦ *nm* (*TV*): **en** ~ live; **directement** *adv* directly

directeur, trice [diʀɛktœʀ, -tʀis] *nm/f* (*d'entreprise*) director; (*de service*) manager(eress); (d'école) head (teacher) (BRIT), principal (US)

direction [diʀɛksjɔ̃] nf management; conducting; supervision; (AUTO) steering; (sens) direction; **"toutes ~s"** "all routes"

dirent vb voir **dire**

dirigeant, e [diʀiʒɑ̃, -ɑ̃t] adj managerial; ruling ♦ nm/f (d'un parti etc) leader; (d'entreprise) manager

diriger [diʀiʒe] vt (entreprise) to manage, run; (véhicule) to steer; (orchestre) to conduct; (recherches, travaux) to supervise; (braquer: regard, arme): ~ **sur** to point ou level at; **se** ~ vi (s'orienter) to find one's way; **se** ~ **vers** ou **sur** to make ou head for

dirigisme [diʀiʒism(ə)] nm (ÉCON) state intervention, interventionism

dis etc vb voir **dire**

discernement [disɛʀnəmɑ̃] nm (bon sens) discernment, judgement

discerner [disɛʀne] vt to discern, make out

discipline [disiplin] nf discipline; **discipliner** vt to discipline; to control

discontinu, e [diskɔ̃tiny] adj intermittent

discontinuer [diskɔ̃tinɥe] vi: **sans** ~ without stopping, without a break

disconvenir [diskɔ̃vniʀ] vi: **ne pas** ~ **de** qch/que not to deny sth/that

discordant, e [diskɔʀdɑ̃, -ɑ̃t] adj discordant; conflicting

discothèque [diskɔtɛk] nf (disques) record collection; (: dans une bibliothèque) record library; (boîte de nuit) disco(thèque)

discourir [diskuʀiʀ] vi to discourse, hold forth

discours [diskuʀ] nm speech

discret, ète [diskʀɛ, -ɛt] adj discreet; (fig) unobtrusive; quiet

discrétion [diskʀesjɔ̃] nf discretion; **être à la** ~ **de** qn to be in sb's hands; **à** ~ unlimited; as much as one wants

discrimination [diskʀiminasjɔ̃] nf discrimination; **sans** ~ indiscriminately

disculper [diskylpe] vt to exonerate

discussion [diskysjɔ̃] nf discussion

discutable [diskytabl(ə)] adj debatable

discuté, e [diskyte] adj controversial

discuter [diskyte] vt (contester) to question, dispute; (débattre: prix) to discuss ♦ vi to talk; (ergoter) to argue; ~ **de** to discuss

dise etc vb voir **dire**

disette [dizɛt] nf food shortage

diseuse [dizøz] nf: ~ **de bonne aventure** fortuneteller

disgracieux, euse [disgʀasjø, -jøz] adj ungainly, awkward

disjoindre [disʒwɛ̃dʀ(ə)] vt to take apart; **se** ~ vi to come apart

disjoncteur [disʒɔ̃ktœʀ] nm (ÉLEC) circuit breaker

disloquer [dislɔke] vt (chaise) to dismantle;

se ~ vi (parti, empire) to break up; **se** ~ **l'épaule** to dislocate one's shoulder

disons vb voir **dire**

disparaître [dispaʀɛtʀ(ə)] vi to disappear; (à la vue) to vanish, disappear; to be hidden ou concealed; (se perdre: traditions etc) to die out; **faire** ~ to remove; to get rid of

disparition [dispaʀisjɔ̃] nf disappearance

disparu, e [dispaʀy] nm/f missing person; (défunt) dead person, departed (littér)

dispensaire [dispɑ̃sɛʀ] nm community clinic

dispenser [dispɑ̃se] vt (donner) to lavish, bestow; (exempter): ~ **qn de** to exempt sb from; **se** ~ **de** vt to avoid; to get out of

disperser [dispɛʀse] vt to scatter; (fig: son attention) to dissipate

disponibilité [dispɔnibilite] nf (ADMIN): **être en** ~ to be on leave of absence

disponible [dispɔnibl(ə)] adj available

dispos [dispo] adj m: (frais et) ~ fresh (as a daisy)

disposé, e [dispoze] adj: **bien/mal** ~ (humeur) in a good/bad mood; ~ **à** (prêt à) willing ou prepared to

disposer [dispoze] vt (arranger, placer) to arrange ♦ vi: **vous pouvez** ~ you may leave; ~ **de** to have (at one's disposal); to use; **se** ~ **à faire** to prepare to, be about to do

dispositif [dispozitif] nm device; (fig) system, plan of action; set-up

disposition [dispozisjɔ̃] nf (arrangement) arrangement, layout; (humeur) mood; (tendance) tendency; ~s nfpl (mesures) steps, measures; (préparatifs) arrangements; (loi, testament) provisions; (aptitudes) bent sg, aptitude sg; **à la** ~ **de** qn at sb's disposal

disproportionné, e [dispʀopɔʀsjɔne] adj disproportionate, out of all proportion

dispute [dispyt] nf quarrel, argument

disputer [dispyte] vt (match) to play; (combat) to fight; (course) to run, fight; **se** ~ vi to quarrel; ~ **qch à** qn to fight with sb over sth

disquaire [diskɛʀ] nm/f record dealer

disqualifier [diskalifje] vt to disqualify

disque [disk(ə)] nm (MUS) record; (forme, pièce) disc; (SPORT) discus; ~ **compact** compact disc; ~ **d'embrayage** (AUTO) clutch plate

disquette [diskɛt] nf floppy disk, diskette

disséminer [disemine] vt to scatter

disséquer [diseke] vt to dissect

dissertation [disɛʀtasjɔ̃] nf (SCOL) essay

disserter [disɛʀte] vi: ~ **sur** to discourse upon

dissimuler [disimyle] vt to conceal

dissiper [disipe] vt to dissipate; (fortune) to squander; **se** ~ vi (brouillard) to clear, disperse; (doutes) to melt away; (élève) to become unruly

dissolu, e [disɔly] *adj* dissolute
dissolvant [disɔlvɑ̃] *nm* solvent; ~ **(gras)** nail polish remover
dissonant, e [disɔnɑ̃, -ɑ̃t] *adj* discordant
dissoudre [disudʀ(ə)] *vt* to dissolve; **se ~** *vi* to dissolve
dissuader [disɥade] *vt*: ~ **qn de faire/de qch** to dissuade sb from doing/from sth
dissuasion [disɥazjɔ̃] *nf*: **force de ~** deterrent power
distance [distɑ̃s] *nf* distance; *(fig: écart)* gap; **à ~** at *ou* from a distance; **distancer** *vt* to outdistance
distant, e [distɑ̃, -ɑ̃t] *adj* *(réservé)* distant; ~ **de** *(lieu)* far away from
distendre [distɑ̃dʀ(ə)] *vt* to distend; **se ~** *vi* to distend
distiller [distile] *vt* to distil; **distillerie** *nf* distillery
distinct, e [distɛ̃(kt), distɛ̃kt(ə)] *adj* distinct; **distinctif, ive** *adj* distinctive
distingué, e [distɛ̃ge] *adj* distinguished
distinguer [distɛ̃ge] *vt* to distinguish
distraction [distʀaksjɔ̃] *nf* *(manque d'attention)* absent-mindedness; *(oubli)* lapse (in concentration); *(détente)* diversion, recreation; *(passe-temps)* distraction, entertainment
distraire [distʀɛʀ] *vt* *(déranger)* to distract; *(divertir)* to entertain, divert; **se ~** *vi* to amuse *ou* enjoy o.s.
distrait, e [distʀɛ, -ɛt] *adj* absent-minded
distribuer [distʀibɥe] *vt* to distribute; to hand out; *(CARTES)* to deal (out); *(courrier)* to deliver; **distributeur** *nm* *(COMM)* distributor; *(automatique)* (vending) machine; (: *de billets)* (cash) dispenser; **distribution** *nf* distribution; *(postale)* delivery; *(choix d'acteurs)* casting, cast
dit, e [di, dit] *pp de* **dire** ♦ *adj* *(fixé)*: **le jour ~** the arranged day; *(surnommé)*: **X, ~ Pierrot** X, known as Pierrot
dites *vb voir* **dire**
divaguer [divage] *vi* to ramble; to rave
divan [divɑ̃] *nm* divan
divers, es [divɛʀ, -ɛʀs(ə)] *adj* *(varié)* diverse, varied; *(différent)* different, various ♦ *dét* *(plusieurs)* various, several; **(frais)** ~ sundries, miscellaneous (expenses)
divertir [divɛʀtiʀ] *vt* to amuse, entertain; **se ~** *vi* to amuse *ou* enjoy o.s.
divin, e [divɛ̃, -in] *adj* divine
diviser [divize] *vt* *(gén, MATH)* to divide; *(morceler, subdiviser)* to divide (up), split (up); **division** *nf* division
divorce [divɔʀs(ə)] *nm* divorce; **divorcé, e** *nm/f* divorcee; **divorcer** *vi* to get a divorce, get divorced; **divorcer de** *ou* **d'avec qn** to divorce sb
divulguer [divylge] *vt* to divulge, disclose
dix [dis] *num* ten; **dixième** *num* tenth
dizaine [dizɛn] *nf* *(10)* ten; *(environ 10)*:

une ~ (de) about ten, ten or so
do [do] *nm* *(note)* C; *(en chantant la gamme)* do(h)
dock [dɔk] *nm* dock
docker [dɔkɛʀ] *nm* docker
docte [dɔkt(ə)] *adj* learned
docteur [dɔktœʀ] *nm* doctor
doctorat [dɔktɔʀa] *nm*: ~ **(d'Université)** doctorate; ~ **d'État** ≈ Ph.D.
doctrine [dɔktʀin] *nf* doctrine
document [dɔkymɑ̃] *nm* document
documentaire [dɔkymɑ̃tɛʀ] *adj, nm* documentary
documentaliste [dɔkymɑ̃talist(ə)] *nm/f* archivist; researcher
documentation [dɔkymɑ̃tasjɔ̃] *nf* documentation, literature; *(PRESSE, TV: service)* research
documenter [dɔkymɑ̃te] *vt*: **se ~ (sur)** to gather information (on)
dodeliner [dɔdline] *vi*: ~ **de la tête** to nod one's head gently
dodo [dɔdo] *nm*: **aller faire ~** to go to beddy-byes
dodu, e [dɔdy] *adj* plump
dogue [dɔg] *nm* mastiff
doigt [dwa] *nm* finger; **à deux ~s de** within an inch of; **un ~ de lait** a drop of milk; ~ **de pied** toe
doigté [dwate] *nm* *(MUS)* fingering; *(fig: habileté)* diplomacy, tact
doit *etc vb voir* **devoir**
doléances [dɔleɑ̃s] *nfpl* complaints; grievances
dollar [dɔlaʀ] *nm* dollar
D.O.M. [deɔm, dɔm] *sigle m* = **département d'outre-mer**
domaine [dɔmɛn] *nm* estate, property; *(fig)* domain, field
domestique [dɔmɛstik] *adj* domestic ♦ *nm/f* servant, domestic
domicile [dɔmisil] *nm* home, place of residence; **à ~** at home; **domicilié, e** *adj*: **être domicilié à** to have one's home in *ou* at
dominant, e [dɔminɑ̃, -ɑ̃t] *adj* dominant; predominant
dominateur, trice [dɔminatœʀ, -tʀis] *adj* dominating; domineering
dominer [dɔmine] *vt* to dominate; *(passions etc)* to control, master; *(surpasser)* to outclass, surpass ♦ *vi* to be in the dominant position; **se ~** *vi* to control o.s.
domino [dɔmino] *nm* domino
dommage [dɔmaʒ] *nm* *(préjudice)* harm, injury; *(dégâts, pertes)* damage *no pl*; **c'est ~ de faire/que** it's a shame *ou* pity to do/ that; **dommages-intérêts** *nmpl* damages
dompter [dɔ̃te] *vt* to tame; **dompteur, euse** *nm/f* trainer; liontamer
don [dɔ̃] *nm* *(cadeau)* gift; *(charité)* donation; *(aptitude)* gift, talent; **avoir des ~s pour** to have a gift *ou* talent for

donc [dɔ̃k] *conj* therefore, so; *(après une digression)* so, then

donjon [dɔ̃ʒɔ̃] *nm* keep

donné, e [dɔne] *adj (convenu)* given; *(pas cher)*: **c'est** ~ it's a gift; **étant** ~ ... given ...; **donnée** *nf (MATH, gén)* datum

donner [dɔne] *vt* to give; *(vieux habits etc)* to give away; *(spectacle)* to put on; *(film)* to show; ~ **qch à qn** to give sb sth, give sth to sb; ~ **sur** *(suj: fenêtre, chambre)* to look (out) onto; ~ **dans** *(piège etc)* to fall into; **se** ~ **à fond** to give one's all; **s'en** ~ **à cœur joie** *(fam)* to have a great time

───────────── MOT CLÉ ─────────────

dont [dɔ̃] *pron relatif* **1** *(appartenance: objets)* whose, of which; *(appartenance: êtres animés)* whose; **la maison** ~ **le toit est rouge** the house the roof of which is red; the house whose roof is red; **l'homme** ~ **je connais la sœur** the man whose sister I know

2 *(parmi lesquel(le)s)*: **2 livres,** ~ **l'un est ...** 2 books, one of which is ...; **il y avait plusieurs personnes,** ~ **Gabrielle** there were several people, among them Gabrielle; **10 blessés,** ~ **2 grièvement** 10 injured, 2 of them seriously

3 *(complément d'adjectif, de verbe)*: **le fils** ~ **il est si fier** the son he's so proud of; **ce** ~ **je parle** what I'm talking about

──────────────────────────────────

doré, e [dɔre] *adj* golden; *(avec dorure)* gilt, gilded

dorénavant [dɔrenavɑ̃] *adv* henceforth

dorer [dɔre] *vt (cadre)* to gild; **(faire)** ~ *(CULIN)* to brown

dorloter [dɔrlɔte] *vt* to pamper

dormir [dɔrmir] *vi* to sleep; *(être endormi)* to be asleep

dortoir [dɔrtwar] *nm* dormitory

dorure [dɔryr] *nf* gilding

dos [do] *nm* back; *(de livre)* spine; **"voir au** ~**"** "see over"; **de** ~ from the back

dosage [dozaʒ] *nm* mixture

dose [doz] *nf* dose; ~**r** [doze] *vt* to measure out; to mix in the correct proportions; *(fig)* to expend in the right amounts; to strike a balance between

dossard [dosar] *nm* number *(worn by competitor)*

dossier [dosje] *nm (renseignements, fichier)* file; *(de chaise)* back; *(PRESSE)* feature

dot [dɔt] *nf* dowry

doter [dɔte] *vt* to equip

douane [dwan] *nf (poste, bureau)* customs *pl*; *(taxes)* (customs) duty; **douanier, ière** *adj* customs *cpd* ♦ *nm* customs officer

double [dubl(ə)] *adj, adv* double ♦ *nm* (2 *fois plus)*: **le** ~ **(de)** twice as much (ou many) (as); *(autre exemplaire)* duplicate, copy; *(sosie)* double; *(TENNIS)* doubles *sg*;

en ~ **(exemplaire)** in duplicate; **faire** ~ **emploi** to be redundant

doubler [duble] *vt (multiplier par 2)* to double; *(vêtement)* to line; *(dépasser)* to overtake, pass; *(film)* to dub; *(acteur)* to stand in for ♦ *vi* to double

doublure [dublyr] *nf* lining; *(CINÉMA)* stand-in

douce [dus] *adj voir* **doux**; **douceâtre** *adj* sickly sweet; **doucement** *adv* gently; slowly; **doucereux, euse** *(péj) adj* sugary; **douceur** *nf* softness; sweetness; mildness; gentleness; **douceurs** *nfpl (friandises)* sweets

douche [duʃ] *nf* shower; ~**s** *nfpl (salle)* shower room *sg*; **doucher: se doucher** *vi* to have *ou* take a shower

doudoune [dudun] *nf* padded jacket; boob *(fam)*

doué, e [dwe] *adj* gifted, talented; ~ **de** endowed with

douille [duj] *nf (ÉLEC)* socket; *(de projectile)* case

douillet, te [dujɛ, -ɛt] *adj* cosy; *(péj)* soft

douleur [dulœr] *nf* pain; *(chagrin)* grief, distress; **douloureux, euse** *adj* painful

doute [dut] *nm* doubt; **sans** ~ no doubt; *(probablement)* probably

douter [dute] *vt* to doubt; ~ **de** *(allié)* to doubt, have (one's) doubts about; *(résultat)* to be doubtful of; **se** ~ **de qch/que** to suspect sth/that; **je m'en doutais** I suspected as much

douteux, euse [dutø, -øz] *adj (incertain)* doubtful; *(discutable)* dubious, questionable; *(péj)* dubious-looking

Douvres [duvr(ə)] *n* Dover

doux, douce [du, dus] *adj (gén)* soft; *(sucré, agréable)* sweet; *(peu fort: moutarde, clément: climat)* mild; *(pas brusque)* gentle

douzaine [duzɛn] *nf (12)* dozen; *(environ 12)*: **une** ~ **(de)** a dozen or so, twelve or so

douze [duz] *num* twelve; **douzième** *num* twelfth

doyen, ne [dwajɛ̃, -ɛn] *nm/f (en âge, ancienneté)* most senior member; *(de faculté)* dean

dragée [draʒe] *nf* sugared almond; *(MÉD)* (sugar-coated) pill

dragon [dragɔ̃] *nm* dragon

draguer [drage] *vt (rivière)* to dredge; to drag; *(fam)* to try to pick up

dramatique [dramatik] *adj* dramatic; *(tragique)* tragic ♦ *nf (TV)* (television) drama

dramaturge [dramatyrʒ(ə)] *nm* dramatist, playwright

drame [dram] *nm (THÉÂTRE)* drama

drap [dra] *nm (de lit)* sheet; *(tissu)* woollen fabric

drapeau, x [drapo] *nm* flag; **sous les** ~**x** with the colours, in the army

dresser [drese] *vt (mettre vertical, monter)*

to put up, erect; (*fig: liste, bilan, contrat*) to draw up; (*animal*) to train; **se** ~ *vi* (*falaise, obstacle*) to stand; to tower (up); (*personne*) to draw o.s. up; ~ **l'oreille** to prick up one's ears

drogue [dʀɔg] *nf* drug; **la** ~ drugs *pl*; **drogué, e** [dʀɔge] *nm/f* drug addict

droguer [dʀɔge] *vt* (*victime*) to drug; (*malade*) to give drugs to; **se** ~ *vi* (*aux stupéfiants*) to take drugs; (*péj: de médicaments*) to dose o.s. up

droguerie [dʀɔgʀi] *nf* hardware shop

droguiste [dʀɔgist(ə)] *nm* keeper (*ou* owner) of a hardware shop

droit, e [dʀwa, dʀwat] *adj* (*non courbe*) straight; (*vertical*) upright, straight; (*fig: loyal*) upright, straight(forward); (*opposé à gauche*) right, right-hand ♦ *adv* straight ♦ *nm* (*prérogative*) right; (*taxe*) duty, tax; (: *d'inscription*) fee; (*JUR*): **le** ~ law; **avoir le** ~ **de** to be allowed to; **avoir** ~ **à** to be entitled to; **être en** ~ **de** to have a *ou* the right to; **être dans son** ~ to be within one's rights; **à** ~**e** on the right; (*direction*) (to the) right; ~**s d'auteur** royalties; ~**s d'inscription** *nmpl* enrolment fee; (*competition*) entry fee; **droite** *nf* (*POL*): **la droite** the right (wing)

droitier, ière [dʀwatje, -jɛʀ] *nm/f* right-handed person

droits *nmpl voir* **droit**

droiture [dʀwatyʀ] *nf* uprightness, straightness

drôle [dʀol] *adj* funny; **une** ~ **d'idée** a funny idea; **drôlement** *adv* (*très*) terribly, awfully

dromadaire [dʀɔmadɛʀ] *nm* dromedary

dru, e [dʀy] *adj* (*cheveux*) thick, bushy; (*pluie*) heavy

du [dy] *dét voir* **de** ♦ *prép* +*dét* = **de** +**le**

dû, due [dy] *vb voir* **devoir** ♦ *adj* (*somme*) owing, owed; (: *venant à échéance*) due; (*causé par*): ~ **à** due to ♦ *nm* due; (*somme*) dues *pl*

dubitatif, ive [dybitatif, -iv] *adj* doubtful, dubious

duc [dyk] *nm* duke; **duchesse** *nf* duchess

dûment [dymɑ̃] *adv* duly

Dunkerque [dœkɛʀk] *n* Dunkirk

duo [dɥo] *nm* (*MUS*) duet

dupe [dyp] *nf* dupe ♦ *adj*: (**ne pas**) **être** ~ **de** (not) to be taken in by

duplex [dyplɛks] *nm* (*appartement*) split-level apartment, duplex

duplicata [dyplikata] *nm* duplicate

duquel [dykɛl] *prép* +*pron* = **de** +**lequel**

dur, e [dyʀ] *adj* (*pierre, siège, travail, problème*) hard; (*lumière, voix, climat*) harsh; (*sévère*) hard, harsh; (*cruel*) hard(-hearted); (*porte, col*) stiff; (*viande*) tough ♦ *adv* hard; ~ **d'oreille** hard of hearing

durant [dyʀɑ̃] *prép* (*au cours de*) during; (*pendant*) for; **des mois** ~ for months

durcir [dyʀsiʀ] *vt, vi* to harden; **se** ~ *vi* to harden

durée [dyʀe] *nf* length; (*d'une pile etc*) life; (*déroulement: des opérations etc*) duration

durement [dyʀmɑ̃] *adv* harshly

durer [dyʀe] *vi* to last

dureté [dyʀte] *nf* hardness; harshness; stiffness; toughness

durit [dyʀit] ® *nf* (*car radiator*) hose

dus *etc vb voir* **devoir**

duvet [dyvɛ] *nm* down; (*sac de couchage*) down-filled sleeping bag

dynamique [dinamik] *adj* dynamic

dynamite [dinamit] *nf* dynamite

dynamiter [dinamite] *vt* to (blow up with) dynamite

dynamo [dinamo] *nf* dynamo

dysenterie [disɑ̃tʀi] *nf* dysentery

dyslexie [dislɛksi] *nf* dyslexia, word-blindness

E e

eau, x [o] *nf* water; ~**x** *nfpl* (*MED*) waters; **prendre l'**~ to leak, let in water; **tomber à l'**~ (*fig*) to fall through; ~ **courante** running water; ~ **de Cologne** Eau de Cologne; ~ **de Javel** bleach; ~ **de toilette** toilet water; ~ **douce** fresh water; ~ **minérale** mineral water; ~ **plate** still water; ~ **salée** salt water; **eau-de-vie** *nf* brandy; **eau-forte** *nf* etching

ébahi, e [ebai] *adj* dumbfounded

ébattre [ebatʀ(ə)] : **s'**~ *vi* to frolic

ébaucher [ebɔʃe] *vt* to sketch out, outline; **s'**~ *vi* to take shape

ébène [ebɛn] *nf* ebony

ébéniste [ebenist(ə)] *nm* cabinetmaker

éberlué, e [ebɛʀlɥe] *adj* astounded

éblouir [ebluiʀ] *vt* to dazzle

éblouissement [ebluismɑ̃] *nm* (*faiblesse*) dizzy turn

éborgner [ebɔʀɲe] *vt*: ~ **qn** to blind sb in one eye

éboueur [ebwœʀ] *nm* dustman (*BRIT*), garbageman (*US*)

ébouillanter [ebujɑ̃te] *vt* to scald; (*CULIN*) to blanch

éboulement [ebulmɑ̃] *nm* rock fall

ébouler [ebule] : **s'**~ *vi* to crumble, collapse

éboulis [ebuli] *nmpl* fallen rocks
ébouriffé, e [eburife] *adj* tousled
ébranler [ebrɑ̃le] *vt* to shake; *(rendre instable: mur)* to weaken; **s'~** *vi (partir)* to move off
ébrécher [ebreʃe] *vt* to chip
ébriété [ebrijete] *nf*: **en état d'~** in a state of intoxication
ébrouer [ebrue]: **s'~** *vi* to shake o.s.; *(souffler)* to snort
ébruiter [ebrɥite] *vt* to spread, disclose
ébullition [ebylisjɔ̃] *nf* boiling point; **en ~** boiling; *(fig)* in an uproar
écaille [ekɑj] *nf (de poisson)* scale; *(de coquillage)* shell; *(matière)* tortoiseshell; **~r** [ekɑje] *vt (poisson)* to scale; *(huître)* to open; **s'~r** *vi* to flake *ou* peel (off)
écarlate [ekarlat] *adj* scarlet
écarquiller [ekarkije] *vt*: **~ les yeux** to stare wide-eyed
écart [ekar] *nm* gap; *(embardée)* swerve; sideways leap; *(fig)* departure, deviation; **à l'~** out of the way; **à l'~ de** away from
écarté, e [ekarte] *adj (lieu)* out-of-the-way, remote; *(ouvert)*: **les jambes ~es** legs apart; **les bras ~s** arms outstretched
écarteler [ekartəle] *vt* to quarter; *(fig)* to tear
écarter [ekarte] *vt (séparer)* to move apart, separate; *(éloigner)* to push back, move away; *(ouvrir: rideau)* to draw (back); *(éliminer: candidat, possibilité)* to dismiss; **s'~** *vi* to part; to move away; **s'~ de** to wander from
écervelé, e [esɛrvəle] *adj* scatterbrained, featherbrained
échafaud [eʃafo] *nm* scaffold
échafaudage [eʃafodaʒ] *nm* scaffolding
échafauder [eʃafode] *vt (plan)* to construct
échalote [eʃalɔt] *nf* shallot
échancrure [eʃɑ̃kryr] *nf (de robe)* scoop neckline; *(de côte, arête rocheuse)* indentation
échange [eʃɑ̃ʒ] *nm* exchange; **en ~ de** in exchange *ou* return for
échanger [eʃɑ̃ʒe] *vt*: **~ qch (contre)** to exchange sth (for); **échangeur** *nm (AUTO)* interchange
échantillon [eʃɑ̃tijɔ̃] *nm* sample
échappement [eʃapmɑ̃] *nm (AUTO)* exhaust
échapper [eʃape]: **~ à** *vt (gardien)* to escape (from); *(punition, péril)* to escape; **s'~** *vi* to escape; **~ à qn** *(détail, sens)* to escape sb; *(objet qu'on tient)* to slip out of sb's hands; **laisser ~** *(cri etc)* to let out; **l'~ belle** to have a narrow escape
écharde [eʃard(ə)] *nf* splinter (of wood)
écharpe [eʃarp(ə)] *nf* scarf; *(de maire)* sash; *(MÉD)* sling
échasse [eʃas] *nf* stilt

échauffer [eʃofe] *vt (métal, moteur)* to overheat; *(fig: exciter)* to fire, excite; **s'~** *vi (SPORT)* to warm up; *(dans la discussion)* to become heated
échéance [eʃeɑ̃s] *nf (d'un paiement: date)* settlement date; *(: somme due)* financial commitment(s); *(fig)* deadline; **à brève/longue ~** *adj* short-/long-term ♦ *adv* in the short/long run
échéant [eʃeɑ̃]: **le cas ~** *adv* if the case arises
échec [eʃɛk] *nm* failure; *(ÉCHECS)*: **~ et mat/au roi** checkmate/check; **~s** *nmpl (jeu)* chess *sg*; **tenir en ~** to hold in check; **faire ~ à** to foil *ou* thwart
échelle [eʃɛl] *nf* ladder; *(fig, d'une carte)* scale
échelon [eʃlɔ̃] *nm (d'échelle)* rung; *(ADMIN)* grade
échelonner [eʃlɔne] *vt* to space out
échevelé, e [eʃəvle] *adj* tousled, dishevelled; wild, frenzied
échine [eʃin] *nf* backbone, spine
échiquier [eʃikje] *nm* chessboard
écho [eko] *nm* echo; **~s** *nmpl (potins)* gossip *sg*, rumours
échoir [eʃwar] *vi (dette)* to fall due; *(délais)* to expire; **~ à** to fall to
échouer [eʃwe] *vi* to fail; **s'~** *vi* to run aground
échu, e [eʃy] *pp de* **échoir**
éclabousser [eklabuse] *vt* to splash
éclair [eklɛr] *nm (d'orage)* flash of lightning, lightning *no pl*; *(gâteau)* éclair
éclairage [eklɛraʒ] *nm* lighting
éclaircie [eklɛrsi] *nf* bright interval
éclaircir [eklɛrsir] *vt* to lighten; *(fig)* to clear up; to clarify; *(CULIN)* to thin (down); **s'~** *vi (ciel)* to clear; **s'~ la voix** to clear one's throat; **éclaircissement** *nm* clearing up; clarification
éclairer [eklɛre] *vt (lieu)* to light (up); *(personne: avec une lampe etc)* to light the way for; *(fig)* to enlighten; to shed light on ♦ *vi*: **~ mal/bien** to give a poor/good light; **s'~ à l'électricité** to have electric lighting
éclaireur, euse [eklɛrœr, -øz] *nm/f (scout)* (boy) scout/(girl) guide ♦ *nm (MIL)* scout
éclat [ekla] *nm (de bombe, de verre)* fragment; *(du soleil, d'une couleur etc)* brightness, brilliance; *(d'une cérémonie)* splendour; *(scandale)*: **faire un ~** to cause a commotion; **~s de voix** shouts; **~ de rire** *nm* roar of laughter
éclatant, e [eklatɑ̃, -ɑ̃t] *adj* brilliant
éclater [eklate] *vi (pneu)* to burst; *(bombe)* to explode; *(guerre, épidémie)* to break out; *(groupe, parti)* to break up; **~ en sanglots/de rire** to burst out sobbing/laughing
éclipser [eklipse]: **s'~** *vi* to slip away
éclopé, e [eklɔpe] *adj* lame

éclore [eklɔʀ] *vi* (*œuf*) to hatch; (*fleur*) to open (out)

écluse [eklyz] *nf* lock

écœurant, e [ekœʀɑ̃, -ɑ̃t] *adj* (*gâteau etc*) sickly

écœurer [ekœʀe] *vt*: ~ **qn** to make sb feel sick

école [ekɔl] *nf* school; **aller à l'**~ to go to school; ~ **normale** teachers' training college; ~ **publique** state school; **écolier, ière** *nm/f* schoolboy/girl

écologie [ekɔlɔʒi] *nf* ecology; environmental studies *pl*

écologique [ekɔlɔʒik] *adj* environment-friendly

éconduire [ekɔ̃dɥiʀ] *vt* to dismiss

économe [ekɔnɔm] *adj* thrifty ♦ *nm/f* (*de lycée etc*) bursar (BRIT), treasurer (US)

économie [ekɔnɔmi] *nf* economy; (*gain: d'argent, de temps etc*) saving; (*science*) economics *sg*; ~**s** *nfpl* (*pécule*) savings; **économique** *adj* (*avantageux*) economical; (*ÉCON*) economic; **économiser** [ekɔnɔmize] *vt*, *vi* to save

écoper [ekɔpe] *vi* to bale out; (*fig*) to cop it; ~ (**de**) to get

écorce [ekɔʀs(ə)] *nf* bark; (*de fruit*) peel

écorcher [ekɔʀʃe] *vt* (*animal*) to skin; (*égratigner*) to graze; **écorchure** *nf* graze

écossais, e [ekɔsɛ, -ɛz] *adj* Scottish ♦ *nm/ f*: **É**~**, e** Scot

Écosse [ekɔs] *nf*: **l'**~ Scotland

écosser [ekɔse] *vt* to shell

écouler [ekule] *vt* to sell; to dispose of; **s'**~ *vi* (*eau*) to flow (out); (*jours, temps*) to pass (by)

écourter [ekuʀte] *vt* to curtail, cut short

écoute [ekut] *nf* (*RADIO, TV*): **temps/heure d'**~ listening (*ou* viewing) time/hour; **prendre l'**~ to tune in; **rester à l'**~ (**de**) to stay tuned in (to)

écouter [ekute] *vt* to listen to; **écoutes téléphoniques** phone tapping *sg*; **écouteur** *nm* (*TÉL*) receiver; (*RADIO*) headphones *pl*, headset

écran [ekʀɑ̃] *nm* screen

écrasant, e [ekʀazɑ̃, -ɑ̃t] *adj* overwhelming

écraser [ekʀɑze] *vt* to crush; (*piéton*) to run over; **s'**~ (**au sol**) to crash; **s'**~ **contre** to crash into

écrémer [ekʀeme] *vt* to skim

écrevisse [ekʀəvis] *nf* crayfish *inv*

écrier [ekʀije]: **s'**~ *vi* to exclaim

écrin [ekʀɛ̃] *nm* case, box

écrire [ekʀiʀ] *vt* to write; **s'**~ to write to each other; **ça s'écrit comment?** how is it spelt?; **écrit** *nm* document; (*examen*) written paper; **par écrit** in writing

écriteau, x [ekʀito] *nm* notice, sign

écriture [ekʀityʀ] *nf* writing; (*COMM*) entry; ~**s** *nfpl* accounts, books; **l'É**~, **les É**~**s** the Scriptures

écrivain [ekʀivɛ̃] *nm* writer

écrou [ekʀu] *nm* nut

écrouer [ekʀue] *vt* to imprison; to remand in custody

écrouler [ekʀule]: **s'**~ *vi* to collapse

écru, e [ekʀy] *adj* (*toile*) raw, unbleached; (*couleur*) off-white, écru

ECU *sigle m* ECU

écueil [ekœj] *nm* reef; (*fig*) pitfall; stumbling block

écuelle [ekɥɛl] *nf* bowl

éculé, e [ekyle] *adj* (*chaussure*) down-at-heel; (*fig: péj*) hackneyed

écume [ekym] *nf* foam; (*CULIN*) scum; **écumer** *vt* (*CULIN*) to skim; (*fig*) to plunder

écureuil [ekyʀœj] *nm* squirrel

écurie [ekyʀi] *nf* stable

écusson [ekysɔ̃] *nm* badge

écuyer, ère [ekɥije, -ɛʀ] *nm/f* rider

eczéma [ɛgzema] *nm* eczema

édenté, e [edɑ̃te] *adj* toothless

E.D.F. *sigle f* (= *Électricité de France*) national electricity company

édifice [edifis] *nm* edifice, building

édifier [edifje] *vt* to build, erect; (*fig*) to edify

édit [edi] *nm* edict

éditer [edite] *vt* (*publier*) to publish; (: *disque*) to produce; **éditeur, trice** *nm/f* editor; publisher; **édition** *nf* editing *no pl*; edition; (*industrie du livre*) publishing

édredon [edʀədɔ̃] *nm* eiderdown, comforter (US)

éducateur, trice [edykatœʀ, -tʀis] *nm/f* teacher; (*in special school*) instructor

éducatif, ive [edykatif, -iv] *adj* educational

éducation [edykasjɔ̃] *nf* education; (*familiale*) upbringing; (*manières*) (good) manners *pl*; ~ **physique** physical education

édulcorer [edylkɔʀe] *vt* to sweeten; (*fig*) to tone down

éduquer [edyke] *vt* to educate; (*élever*) to bring up; (*faculté*) to train

effacé, e [efase] *adj* unassuming

effacer [efase] *vt* to erase, rub out; **s'**~ *vi* (*inscription etc*) to wear off; (*pour laisser passer*) to step aside

effarant, e [efaʀɑ̃, -ɑ̃t] *adj* alarming

effarer [efaʀe] *vt* to alarm

effaroucher [efaʀuʃe] *vt* to frighten *ou* scare away; to alarm

effectif, ive [efɛktif, -iv] *adj* real; effective ♦ *nm* (*MIL*) strength; (*SCOL*) (pupil) numbers *pl*; **effectivement** *adv* effectively; (*réellement*) actually, really; (*en effet*) indeed

effectuer [efɛktɥe] *vt* (*opération*) to carry out; (*déplacement, trajet*) to make; (*mouvement*) to execute

efféminé, e [efemine] *adj* effeminate

effervescent, e [efɛʀvesɑ̃, -ɑ̃t] *adj* efferves-

cent; (fig) agitated
effet [efɛ] nm (résultat, artifice) effect; (impression) impression; ~**s** nmpl (vêtements etc) things; **faire de l'**~ (médicament, menace) to have an effect; **en** ~ indeed; ~ **de serre** greenhouse effect; **gaz à** ~ **de serre** greenhouse gas
efficace [efikas] adj (personne) efficient; (action, médicament) effective
effilé, e [efile] adj slender; sharp; streamlined
effiler [efile] vt (tissu) to fray
effilocher [efiloʃe]: **s'**~ vi to fray
efflanqué, e [eflɑ̃ke] adj emaciated
effleurer [eflœʀe] vt to brush (against); (sujet) to touch upon; (suj: idée, pensée): ~ **qn** to cross sb's mind
effluves [eflyv] nmpl exhalation(s)
effondrer [efɔ̃dʀe]: **s'**~ vi to collapse
efforcer [efɔʀse]: **s'**~ **de** vt: **s'**~ **de faire** to try hard to do, hard to
effort [efɔʀ] nm effort
effraction [efʀaksjɔ̃] nf: **s'introduire par** ~ **dans** to break into
effrayant, e [efʀɛjɑ̃, -ɑ̃t] adj frightening
effrayer [efʀeje] vt to frighten, scare
effréné, e [efʀene] adj wild
effriter [efʀite]: **s'**~ vi to crumble
effroi [efʀwa] nm terror, dread no pl
effronté, e [efʀɔ̃te] adj insolent, brazen
effroyable [efʀwajabl(ə)] adj horrifying, appalling
effusion [efyzjɔ̃] nf effusion; **sans** ~ **de sang** without bloodshed
égal, e, aux [egal, -o] adj equal; (plan: surface) even, level; (constant: vitesse) steady; (équitable) even ♦ nm/f equal; **être** ~ **à** (prix, nombre) to be equal to; **ça lui est** ~ it's all the same to him; he doesn't mind; **sans** ~ matchless, unequalled; **à l'**~ **de** (comme) just like; **d'**~ **à** ~ as equals; ~**ement** adv equally; evenly; steadily; (aussi) too, as well; ~**er** vt to equal; ~**iser** vt (sol, salaires) to level (out); (chances) to equalize ♦ vi (SPORT) to equalize; ~**ité** nf equality; evenness; steadiness; (MATH) identity; **être à** ~**ité (de points)** to be level
égard [egaʀ] nm: ~**s** nmpl consideration sg; **à cet** ~ in this respect; **eu** ~ **à** in view of; **par** ~ **pour** out of consideration for; **sans** ~ **pour** without regard for; **à l'**~ **de** towards; concerning
égarement [egaʀmɑ̃] nm distraction; aberration
égarer [egaʀe] vt to mislay; (moralement) to lead astray; **s'**~ vi to get lost, lose one's way; (objet) to go astray; (dans une discussion) to wander
égayer [egeje] vt (personne) to amuse; to cheer up; (récit, endroit) to brighten up, liven up
églantine [eglɑ̃tin] nf wild ou dog rose

église [egliz] nf church; **aller à l'**~ to go to church
égoïsme [egɔism(ə)] nm selfishness; **égoïste** adj selfish
égorger [egɔʀʒe] vt to cut the throat of
égosiller [egozije]: **s'**~ vi to shout o.s. hoarse
égout [egu] nm sewer
égoutter [egute] vt (linge) to wring out; (vaisselle) to drain ♦ vi to drip; **s'**~ vi to drip; **égouttoir** nm draining board; (mobile) draining rack
égratigner [egʀatiɲe] vt to scratch; **égratignure** nf scratch
égrillard, e [egʀijaʀ, -aʀd(ə)] adj ribald
Égypte [eʒipt(ə)] nf: **l'**~ Egypt; **égyptien, ne** adj, nm/f Egyptian
eh [e] excl hey!; ~ **bien** well
éhonté, e [eɔ̃te] adj shameless, brazen
éjecter [eʒɛkte] vt (TECH) to eject; (fam) to kick ou chuck out
élaborer [elabɔʀe] vt to elaborate; (projet, stratégie) to work out; (rapport) to draft
élaguer [elage] vt to prune
élan [elɑ̃] nm (ZOOL) elk, moose; (SPORT: avant le saut) run up; (d'objet en mouvement) momentum; (fig: de tendresse etc) surge; **prendre de l'**~ to gather speed
élancé, e [elɑ̃se] adj slender
élancement [elɑ̃smɑ̃] nm shooting pain
élancer [elɑ̃se]: **s'**~ vi to dash, hurl o.s.; (fig: arbre, clocher) to soar (upwards)
élargir [elaʀʒiʀ] vt to widen; (vêtement) to let out; (JUR) to release; **s'**~ vi to widen; (vêtement) to stretch
élastique [elastik] adj elastic ♦ nm (de bureau) rubber band; (pour la couture) elastic no pl
électeur, trice [elɛktœʀ, -tʀis] nm/f elector, voter
élection [elɛksjɔ̃] nf election
électorat [elɛktɔʀa] nm electorate
électricien, ne [elɛktʀisjɛ̃, -jɛn] nm/f electrician
électricité [elɛktʀisite] nf electricity; **allumer/éteindre l'**~ to put on/off the light
électrique [elɛktʀik] adj electric(al)
électrochoc [elɛktʀoʃɔk] nm electric shock treatment
électroménager [elɛktʀomenaʒe] adj, nm: **appareils** ~**s**, **l'**~ domestic (electrical) appliances
électronique [elɛktʀonik] adj electronic ♦ nf electronics sg
électrophone [elɛktʀofɔn] nm record player
élégant, e [elegɑ̃, -ɑ̃t] adj elegant; (solution) neat, elegant; (attitude, procédé) courteous, civilized
élément [elemɑ̃] nm element; (pièce) component, part; **élémentaire** adj elementary

éléphant [elefɑ̃] nm elephant

élevage [ɛlvaʒ] nm breeding; (de bovins) cattle rearing

élévation [elevasjɔ̃] nf (gén) elevation; (voir élever) raising; (voir s'élever) rise

élevé, e [ɛlve] adj (prix, sommet) high; (fig: noble) elevated; **bien/mal** ~ well-/ill-mannered

élève [elɛv] nm/f pupil

élever [ɛlve] vt (enfant) to bring up, raise; (bétail, volaille) to breed; (abeilles) to keep; (hausser: taux, niveau) to raise; (fig: âme, esprit) to elevate; (édifier: monument) to put up, erect; **s'**~ vi (avion, alpiniste) to go up; (niveau, température, aussi: cri etc) to rise; (survenir: difficultés) to arise; **s'**~ à (suj: frais, dégâts) to amount to, add up to; **s'**~ **contre qch** to rise up against sth; ~ **la voix** to raise one's voice; **éleveur, euse** nm/f breeder

élimé, e [elime] adj threadbare

éliminatoire [eliminatwaʀ] nf (SPORT) heat

éliminer [elimine] vt to eliminate

élire [eliʀ] vt to elect

elle [ɛl] pron (sujet) she; (: chose) it; (complément) her; it; ~**s** they; them; ~**-même** herself; itself; ~**s-mêmes** themselves; voir aussi **il**

élocution [elɔkysjɔ̃] nf delivery; **défaut d'**~ speech impediment

éloge [elɔʒ] nm (gén no pl) praise; **élogieux, euse** adj laudatory, full of praise

éloigné, e [elwaɲe] adj distant, far-off; **éloignement** [elwaɲmɑ̃] nm removal; putting off; estrangement; (fig) distance

éloigner [elwaɲe] vt (objet): ~ **qch (de)** to move ou take sth away (from); (personne): ~ **qn (de)** to take sb away ou remove sb (from); (échéance) to put off, postpone; (soupçons, danger) to ward off; **s'**~ **(de)** (personne) to go away (from); (véhicule) to move away (from); (affectivement) to become estranged (from)

élongation [elɔ̃gasjɔ̃] nf strained muscle

élu, e [ely] pp de **élire** ♦ nm/f (POL) elected representative

élucubrations [elykybʀasjɔ̃] nfpl wild imaginings

éluder [elyde] vt to evade

Élysée nm: **(le palais de) l'**~ the Élysée Palace (the French president's residence)

émacié, e [emasje] adj emaciated

émail, aux [emaj, -o] nm enamel

émaillé, e [emaje] adj (fig): ~ **de** dotted with

émanciper [emɑ̃sipe] vt to emancipate; **s'**~ vi (fig) to become emancipated ou liberated

émaner [emane]: ~ **de** vt to come from; (ADMIN) to proceed from

emballage [ɑ̃balaʒ] nm wrapping; packaging

emballer [ɑ̃bale] vt to wrap (up); (dans un carton) to pack (up); (fig: fam) to thrill (to bits); **s'**~ vi (moteur) to race; (cheval) to bolt; (fig: personne) to get carried away

embarcadère [ɑ̃baʀkadɛʀ] nm wharf, pier

embarcation [ɑ̃baʀkasjɔ̃] nf (small) boat, (small) craft inv

embardée [ɑ̃baʀde] nf: **faire une** ~ to swerve

embarquement [ɑ̃baʀkəmɑ̃] nm embarkation; loading; boarding

embarquer [ɑ̃baʀke] vt (personne) to embark; (marchandise) to load; (fam) to cart off; to nick ♦ vi (passager) to board; **s'**~ vi to board; **s'**~ **dans** (affaire, aventure) to embark upon

embarras [ɑ̃baʀa] nm (obstacle) hindrance; (confusion) embarrassment

embarrassant, e [ɑ̃baʀasɑ̃, -ɑ̃t] adj embarrassing

embarrasser [ɑ̃baʀase] vt (encombrer) to clutter (up); (gêner) to hinder, hamper; (fig) to cause embarrassment to; to put in an awkward position

embauche [ɑ̃boʃ] nf hiring; **bureau d'**~ labour office; ~**r** [ɑ̃boʃe] vt to take on, hire

embaumer [ɑ̃bome] vt to embalm; to fill with its fragrance; ~ **la lavande** to be fragrant with (the scent of) lavender

embellie [ɑ̃beli] nf brighter period

embellir [ɑ̃beliʀ] vt to make more attractive; (une histoire) to embellish ♦ vi to grow lovelier ou more attractive

embêtements [ɑ̃bɛtmɑ̃] nmpl trouble sg

embêter [ɑ̃bete] vt to bother; **s'**~ vi (s'ennuyer) to be bored

emblée [ɑ̃ble]: **d'**~ adv straightaway

emboîter [ɑ̃bwate] vt to fit together; **s'**~ **(dans)** to fit (into); ~ **le pas à qn** to follow in sb's footsteps

embonpoint [ɑ̃bɔ̃pwɛ̃] nm stoutness

embouchure [ɑ̃buʃyʀ] nf (GÉO) mouth

embourber [ɑ̃buʀbe]: **s'**~ vi to get stuck in the mud

embourgeoiser [ɑ̃buʀʒwaze]: **s'**~ vi to adopt a middle-class outlook

embouteillage [ɑ̃butejaʒ] nm traffic jam

emboutir [ɑ̃butiʀ] vt (heurter) to crash into, ram

embranchement [ɑ̃bʀɑ̃ʃmɑ̃] nm (routier) junction; (classification) branch

embraser [ɑ̃bʀaze]: **s'**~ vi to flare up

embrasser [ɑ̃bʀase] vt to kiss; (sujet, période) to embrace, encompass; (carrière, métier) to enter upon

embrasure [ɑ̃bʀazyʀ] nf: **dans l'**~ **de la porte** in the door(way)

embrayage [ɑ̃bʀɛjaʒ] nm clutch

embrayer [ɑ̃bʀeje] vi (AUTO) to let in the clutch

embrigader [ɑ̃bʀigade] vt to recruit

embrocher [ɑ̃bʀɔʃe] vt to put on a spit

embrouiller [ɑ̃bʀuje] vt (fils) to tangle

(up); (fiches, idées, personne) to muddle up; **s'~** vi (personne) to get in a muddle

embruns [ɑ̃bʀœ̃] nmpl sea spray sg

embûches [ɑ̃byʃ] nfpl pitfalls, traps

embué, e [ɑ̃bɥe] adj misted up

embuscade [ɑ̃byskad] nf ambush

éméché, e [emeʃe] adj tipsy, merry

émeraude [ɛmʀod] nf emerald

émerger [emɛʀʒe] vi to emerge; (faire saillie, aussi fig) to stand out

émeri [emʀi] nm: **toile** ou **papier ~** emery paper

émérite [emeʀit] adj highly skilled

émerveiller [emɛʀveje] vt to fill with wonder; **s'~ de** to marvel at

émetteur, trice [emetœʀ, -tʀis] adj transmitting; **(poste) ~** transmitter

émettre [emɛtʀ(ə)] vt (son, lumière) to give out, emit; (message etc: RADIO) to transmit; (billet, timbre, emprunt) to issue; (hypothèse, avis) to voice, put forward ♦ vi to broadcast

émeus etc vb voir **émouvoir**

émeute [emøt] nf riot

émietter [emjete] vt to crumble

émigrer [emigʀe] vi to emigrate

éminence [eminɑ̃s] nf distinction; (colline) knoll, hill; **Son É~** His Eminence; **éminent, e** [eminɑ̃, -ɑ̃t] adj distinguished

émission [emisjɔ̃] nf emission; transmission; issue; (RADIO, TV) programme, broadcast; **~s** fpl emissions

emmagasiner [ɑ̃magazine] vt to (put into) store; (fig) to store up

emmanchure [ɑ̃mɑ̃ʃyʀ] nf armhole

emmêler [ɑ̃mele] vt to tangle (up); (fig) to muddle up; **s'~** vi to get into a tangle

emménager [ɑ̃menaʒe] vi to move in; **~ dans** to move into

emmener [ɑ̃mne] vt to take (with one); (comme otage, capture) to take away; **~ qn au cinéma** to take sb to the cinema

emmerder [ɑ̃mɛʀde] (fam!) vt to bug, bother; **s'~** vi to be bored stiff

emmitoufler [ɑ̃mitufle] vt to wrap up (warmly)

émoi [emwa] nm commotion; (trouble) agitation

émonder [emɔ̃de] vt to prune

émotif, ive [emɔtif, -iv] adj emotional

émotion [emosjɔ̃] nf emotion

émousser [emuse] vt to blunt; (fig) to dull

émouvoir [emuvwaʀ] vt (troubler) to stir, affect; (toucher, attendrir) to move; (indigner) to rouse; **s'~** vi to be affected; to be moved; to be roused

empailler [ɑ̃paje] vt to stuff

empaler [ɑ̃pale] vt to impale

emparer [ɑ̃paʀe]: **s'~ de** vt (objet) to seize, grab; (comme otage, MIL) to seize; (suj: peur etc) to take hold of

empâter [ɑ̃pɑte]: **s'~** vi to thicken out

empêchement [ɑ̃pɛʃmɑ̃] nm (unexpected) obstacle, hitch

empêcher [ɑ̃peʃe] vt to prevent; **~ qn de faire** to prevent ou stop sb (from) doing; **il n'empêche que** nevertheless; **il n'a pas pu s'~ de rire** he couldn't help laughing

empereur [ɑ̃pʀœʀ] nm emperor

empeser [ɑ̃pəze] vt to starch

empester [ɑ̃pɛste] vt to stink, reek

empêtrer [ɑ̃petʀe] vt: **s'~ dans** (fils etc) to get tangled up in

emphase [ɑ̃faz] nf pomposity, bombast

empiéter [ɑ̃pjete] vi: **~ sur** to encroach upon

empiffrer [ɑ̃pifʀe]: **s'~** (péj) vi to stuff o.s.

empiler [ɑ̃pile] vt to pile (up)

empire [ɑ̃piʀ] nm empire; (fig) influence

empirer [ɑ̃piʀe] vi to worsen, deteriorate

emplacement [ɑ̃plasmɑ̃] nm site

emplettes [ɑ̃plɛt] nfpl shopping sg

emplir [ɑ̃pliʀ] vt to fill; **s'~ (de)** to fill (with)

emploi [ɑ̃plwa] nm use; (COMM, ÉCON) employment; (poste) job, situation; **~ du temps** timetable, schedule

employé, e [ɑ̃plwaje] nm/f employee; **~ de bureau** office employee ou clerk

employer [ɑ̃plwaje] vt (outil, moyen, méthode, mot) to use; (ouvrier, maind'œuvre) to employ; **s'~ à faire** to apply ou devote o.s. to doing; **employeur, euse** nm/f employer

empocher [ɑ̃pɔʃe] vt to pocket

empoigner [ɑ̃pwaɲe] vt to grab

empoisonner [ɑ̃pwazɔne] vt to poison; (empester: air, pièce) to stink out; (fam): **~ qn** to drive sb mad

emporté, e [ɑ̃pɔʀte] adj quick-tempered

emporter [ɑ̃pɔʀte] vt to take (with one); (en dérobant ou enlevant, emmener: blessés, voyageurs) to take away; (entraîner) to carry away; (arracher) to tear off; (avantage, approbation) to win; **s'~** vi (de colère) to lose one's temper; **l'~ (sur)** to get the upper hand (of); (méthode etc) to prevail (over); **boissons à ~** take-away drinks

empreint, e [ɑ̃pʀɛ̃, -ɛ̃t] adj: **~ de** marked with; tinged with; **empreinte** nf (de pied, main) print; (fig) stamp, mark; **~e (digitale)** fingerprint

empressé, e [ɑ̃pʀese] adj attentive

empressement [ɑ̃pʀɛsmɑ̃] nm (hâte) eagerness

empresser [ɑ̃pʀese]: **s'~** vi: **s'~ auprès de qn** to surround sb with attentions; **s'~ de faire** (se hâter) to hasten to do

emprise [ɑ̃pʀiz] nf hold, ascendancy

emprisonner [ɑ̃pʀizɔne] vt to imprison

emprunt [ɑ̃pʀœ̃] nm borrowing no pl, loan

emprunté, e [ɑ̃pʀɑ̃te] adj (fig) ill-at-ease, awkward

emprunter [ɑ̃pʀɑ̃te] vt to borrow; (itiné-

raire) to take, follow; *(style, manière)* to adopt, assume

ému, e [emy] *pp de* **émouvoir** ♦ *adj* excited; touched; moved

émulsion [emylsjɔ̃] *nf (cosmétique)* (water-based) lotion

MOT CLÉ
---

en [ã] *prép* **1** *(endroit, pays)* in; *(direction)* to; **habiter** ~ **France/ville** to live in France/town; **aller** ~ **France/ville** to go to France/town
2 *(moment, temps)* in; ~ **été/juin** in summer/June
3 *(moyen)* by; ~ **avion/taxi** by plane/taxi
4 *(composition)* made of; **c'est** ~ **verre** it's (made of) glass; **un collier** ~ **argent** a silver necklace
5 *(description, état)*: **une femme (habillée)** ~ **rouge** a woman (dressed) in red; **peindre qch** ~ **rouge** to paint sth red; ~ **T/ étoile** T/star-shaped; ~ **chemise/ chaussettes** in one's shirt sleeves/socks: ~ **soldat** as a soldier; **cassé** ~ **plusieurs morceaux** broken into several pieces; ~ **réparation** being repaired, under repair; ~ **vacances** on holiday; ~ **deuil** in mourning; **le même** ~ **plus grand** the same but *ou* only bigger
6 *(avec gérondif)* while; on; by; ~ **dormant** while sleeping, as one sleeps; ~ **sortant** on going out, as he *etc* went out; **sortir** ~ **courant** to run out
♦ *pron* **1** *(indéfini)*: **j'**~ **ai/veux** I have/want some; ~ **as-tu?** have you got any?; **je n'**~ **veux pas** I don't want any; **j'**~ **ai 2** I've got 2; **combien y** ~ **a-t-il?** how many (of them) are there?; **j'**~ **ai assez** I've got enough (of it *ou* them); *(j'en ai marre)* I've had enough
2 *(provenance)* from there; **j'**~ **viens** I've come from there
3 *(cause)*: **il** ~ **est malade/perd le sommeil** he is ill/can't sleep because of it
4 *(complément de nom, d'adjectif, de verbe)*: **j'**~ **connais les dangers** I know its *ou* the dangers; **j'**~ **suis fier/ai besoin** I am proud of it/need it

---

E.N.A. [ena] *sigle f* (= *École Nationale d'Administration)* one of the *Grandes Écoles*

encadrer [ãkadʀe] *vt (tableau, image)* to frame; *(fig: entourer)* to surround; *(personnel, soldats etc)* to train

encaissé, e [ãkese] *adj* steep-sided; with steep banks

encaisser [ãkese] *vt (chèque)* to cash; *(argent)* to collect; *(fig: coup, défaite)* to take

encart [ãkaʀ] *nm* insert

encastrer [ãkastʀe] *vt*: ~ **qch dans** *(mur)* to embed sth in(to); *(boîtier)* to fit sth into

encaustique [ãkostik] *nf* polish, wax

enceinte [ãsɛ̃t] *adj f*: ~ **(de 6 mois)** (6 months) pregnant ♦ *nf (mur)* wall; *(espace)* enclosure

encens [ãsã] *nm* incense

encercler [ãsɛʀkle] *vt* to surround

enchaîner [ãʃene] *vt* to chain up; *(mouvements, séquences)* to link (together) ♦ *vi* to carry on

enchanté, e [ãʃãte] *adj* delighted; enchanted; ~ **(de faire votre connaissance)** pleased to meet you

enchantement [ãʃãtmã] *nm* delight; *(magie)* enchantment

enchâsser [ãʃase] *vt* to set

enchère [ãʃɛʀ] *nf* bid; **mettre/vendre aux** ~**s** to put up for (sale by)/sell by auction

enchevêtrer [ãʃvetʀe] *vt* to tangle (up)

enclencher [ãklãʃe] *vt (mécanisme)* to engage; **s'**~ *vi* to engage

enclin, e [ãklɛ̃, -in] *adj*: ~ **à** inclined *ou* prone to

enclos [ãklo] *nm* enclosure

enclume [ãklym] *nf* anvil

encoche [ãkɔʃ] *nf* notch

encoignure [ãkɔɲyʀ] *nf* corner

encolure [ãkɔlyʀ] *nf (tour de cou)* collar size; *(col, cou)* neck

encombrant, e [ãkɔ̃bʀã, -ãt] *adj* cumbersome, bulky

encombre [ãkɔ̃bʀ(ə)]: **sans** ~ *adv* without mishap *ou* incident

encombrer [ãkɔ̃bʀe] *vt* to clutter (up); *(gêner)* to hamper; **s'**~ **de** *(bagages etc)* to load *ou* burden o.s. with

encontre [ãkɔ̃tʀ(ə)]: **à l'**~ **de** *prép* against, counter to

---
MOT CLÉ
---

encore [ãkɔʀ] *adv* **1** *(continuation)* still; **il y travaille** ~ he's still working on it; **pas** ~ not yet
2 *(de nouveau)* again; **j'irai** ~ **demain** I'll go again tomorrow; ~ **une fois** (once) again; ~ **deux jours** two more days
3 *(intensif)* even, still; ~ **plus fort/mieux** even louder/better, louder/better still
4 *(restriction)* even then, only; ~ **pourrais-je le faire si ...** even so, I might be able to do it if ...; **si** ~ if only
encore que *conj* although

---

encourager [ãkuʀaʒe] *vt* to encourage

encourir [ãkuʀiʀ] *vt* to incur

encrasser [ãkʀase] *vt* to clog up; *(AUTO: bougies)* to soot up

encre [ãkʀ(ə)] *nf* ink; ~ **de Chine** Indian ink; **encrier** *nm* inkwell

encroûter [ãkʀute]: **s'**~ *vi (fig)* to get into a rut, get set in one's ways

encyclopédie [ãsiklɔpedi] *nf* encyclopaedia

endetter [ãdete] *vt* to get into debt; **s'**~ *vi* to get into debt

endiablé, e [ɑ̃djable] adj furious; boisterous

endiguer [ɑ̃dige] vt to dyke (up); (fig) to check, hold back

endimancher [ɑ̃dimɑ̃ʃe] vt: **s'~** to put on one's Sunday best

endive [ɑ̃div] nf chicory no pl

endoctriner [ɑ̃dɔktrine] vt to indoctrinate

endommager [ɑ̃dɔmaʒe] vt to damage

endormi, e [ɑ̃dɔrmi] adj asleep

endormir [ɑ̃dɔrmir] vt to put to sleep; (suj: chaleur etc) to send to sleep; (MÉD: dent, nerf) to anaesthetize; (fig: soupçons) to allay; **s'~** vi to fall asleep, go to sleep

endosser [ɑ̃dose] vt (responsabilité) to take, shoulder; (chèque) to endorse; (uniforme, tenue) to put on, don

endroit [ɑ̃drwa] nm place; (opposé à l'envers) right side; **à l'~** the right way out; the right way up; **à l'~ de** regarding

enduire [ɑ̃dɥir] vt to coat

enduit [ɑ̃dɥi] nm coating

endurant, e [ɑ̃dyrɑ̃, -ɑ̃t] adj tough, hardy

endurcir [ɑ̃dyrsir] vt (physiquement) to toughen; (moralement) to harden; **s'~** vi to become tougher; to become hardened

endurer [ɑ̃dyre] vt to endure, bear

énergie [enɛrʒi] nf (PHYSIQUE) energy; (TECH) power; (morale) vigour, spirit; **énergique** adj energetic; vigorous; (mesures) drastic, stringent

énergumène [enɛrgymɛn] nm rowdy character ou customer

énerver [enɛrve] vt to irritate, annoy; **s'~** vi to get excited, get worked up

enfance [ɑ̃fɑ̃s] nf (âge) childhood; (fig) infancy; (enfants) children pl

enfant [ɑ̃fɑ̃] nm/f child; **~ de chœur** nm (REL) altar boy; **~er** vi to give birth ♦ vt to give birth to; **~illage** (péj) nm childish behaviour no pl; **~in, e** adj childlike; child cpd

enfer [ɑ̃fɛr] nm hell

enfermer [ɑ̃fɛrme] vt to shut up; (à clef, interner) to lock up

enfiévré, e [ɑ̃fjevre] adj (fig) feverish

enfiler [ɑ̃file] vt (vêtement) to slip on, slip into; (insérer): **~ qch dans** to stick sth into; (rue, couloir) to take; (perles) to string; (aiguille) to thread

enfin [ɑ̃fɛ̃] adv at last; (en énumérant) lastly; (de restriction, résignation) still; well; (pour conclure) in a word

enflammer [ɑ̃flame] vt to set fire to; (MÉD) to inflame; **s'~** vi to catch fire; to become inflamed

enflé, e [ɑ̃fle] adj swollen

enfler [ɑ̃fle] vi to swell (up)

enfoncer [ɑ̃fɔ̃se] vt (clou) to drive in; (faire pénétrer): **~ qch dans** to push (ou drive) sth into; (forcer: porte) to break open; (: plancher) to cause to cave in ♦ vi (dans la

vase etc) to sink in; (sol, surface) to give way; **s'~** vi to sink; **s'~ dans** to sink into; (forêt, ville) to disappear into

enfouir [ɑ̃fwir] vt (dans le sol) to bury; (dans un tiroir etc) to tuck away

enfourcher [ɑ̃furʃe] vt to mount

enfourner [ɑ̃furne] vt to put in the oven

enfreindre [ɑ̃frɛdr(ə)] vt to infringe, break

enfuir [ɑ̃fɥir]: **s'~** vi to run away ou off

enfumer [ɑ̃fyme] vt to smoke out

engageant, e [ɑ̃gaʒɑ̃, -ɑ̃t] adj attractive, appealing

engagement [ɑ̃gaʒmɑ̃] nm (promesse, contrat, POL) commitment; (MIL: combat) engagement

engager [ɑ̃gaʒe] vt (embaucher) to take on, engage; (commencer) to start; (lier) to bind, commit; (impliquer, entraîner) to involve; (investir) to invest, lay out; (faire intervenir) to engage; (inciter) to urge; (faire pénétrer) to insert; **s'~** vi to hire o.s., get taken on; (MIL) to enlist; (promettre, politiquement) to commit o.s.; (débuter) to start (up); **s'~ à faire** to undertake to do; **s'~ dans** (rue, passage) to turn into; (s'emboîter) to engage into; (fig: affaire, discussion) to enter into, embark on

engelures [ɑ̃ʒlyr] nfpl chilblains

engendrer [ɑ̃ʒɑ̃dre] vt to father

engin [ɑ̃ʒɛ̃] nm machine; instrument; vehicle; (AVIAT) aircraft inv; missile

englober [ɑ̃glɔbe] vt to include

engloutir [ɑ̃glutir] vt to swallow up

engoncé, e [ɑ̃gɔ̃se] adj: **~ dans** cramped in

engorger [ɑ̃gɔrʒe] vt to obstruct, block

engouement [ɑ̃gumɑ̃] nm (sudden) passion

engouffrer [ɑ̃gufre] vt to swallow up, devour; **s'~ dans** to rush into

engourdir [ɑ̃gurdir] vt to numb; (fig) to dull, blunt; **s'~** vi to go numb

engrais [ɑ̃grɛ] nm manure; **~ (chimique)** (chemical) fertilizer

engraisser [ɑ̃grese] vt to fatten (up)

engrenage [ɑ̃grənaʒ] nm gears pl, gearing; (fig) chain

engueuler [ɑ̃gœle] vt (fam) to bawl at

enhardir [ɑ̃ardir]: **s'~** vi to grow bolder

énigme [enigm(ə)] nf riddle

enivrer [ɑ̃nivre] vt: **s'~** to get drunk; **s'~ de** (fig) to become intoxicated with

enjambée [ɑ̃ʒɑ̃be] nf stride

enjamber [ɑ̃ʒɑ̃be] vt to stride over; (suj: pont etc) to span, straddle

enjeu, x [ɑ̃ʒø] nm stakes pl

enjoindre [ɑ̃ʒwɛdr(ə)] vt to enjoin, order

enjôler [ɑ̃ʒole] vt to coax, wheedle

enjoliver [ɑ̃ʒɔlive] vt to embellish; **enjoliveur** nm (AUTO) hub cap

enjoué, e [ɑ̃ʒwe] adj playful

enlacer [ɑ̃lɑse] vt (étreindre) to embrace,

hug

enlaidir [ɑ̃lediʀ] *vt* to make ugly ♦ *vi* to become ugly

enlèvement [ɑ̃lɛvmɑ̃] *nm* (*rapt*) abduction, kidnapping

enlever [ɑ̃lve] *vt* (*ôter: gén*) to remove; (: *vêtement, lunettes*) to take off; (*emporter: ordures etc*) to take away; (*prendre*): ~ **qch à qn** to take sth (away) from sb; (*kidnapper*) to abduct, kidnap; (*obtenir: prix, contrat*) to win

enliser [ɑ̃lize]: **s'~** *vi* to sink, get stuck

enluminure [ɑ̃lyminyʀ] *nf* illumination

enneigé, e [ɑ̃neʒe] *adj* snowy; snowed-up

ennemi, e [ɛnmi] *adj* hostile; (*MIL*) enemy *cpd* ♦ *nm/f* enemy

ennui [ɑ̃nɥi] *nm* (*lassitude*) boredom; (*difficulté*) trouble *no pl*; **avoir des** ~**s** to have problems; **ennuyer** *vt* to bother; (*lasser*) to bore; **s'ennuyer** *vi* to be bored; **s'ennuyer de** (*regretter*) to miss; **ennuyeux, euse** *adj* boring, tedious; annoying

énoncé [enɔ̃se] *nm* terms *pl*; wording

énoncer [enɔ̃se] *vt* to say, express; (*conditions*) to set out, state

enorgueillir [ɑ̃nɔʀɡœjiʀ]: **s'~ de** *vt* to pride o.s. on; to boast

énorme [enɔʀm(ə)] *adj* enormous, huge; **énormément** *adv* enormously; **énormément de neige/gens** an enormous amount of snow/number of people

enquérir [ɑ̃keʀiʀ]: **s'~ de** *vt* to inquire about

enquête [ɑ̃kɛt] *nf* (*de journaliste, de police*) investigation; (*judiciaire, administrative*) inquiry; (*sondage d'opinion*) survey; **enquêter** *vi* to investigate; to hold an inquiry; to conduct a survey

enquiers *etc vb voir* **enquérir**

enraciné, e [ɑ̃rasine] *adj* deep-rooted

enragé, e [ɑ̃raʒe] *adj* (*MÉD*) rabid, with rabies; (*fig*) fanatical

enrageant, e [ɑ̃raʒɑ̃, -ɑ̃t] *adj* infuriating

enrager [ɑ̃raʒe] *vi* to be in a rage

enrayer [ɑ̃reje] *vt* to check, stop; **s'~** *vi* (*arme à feu*) to jam

enregistrement [ɑ̃ʀʒistʀəmɑ̃] *nm* recording; (*ADMIN*) registration; ~ **des bagages** (*à l'aéroport*) baggage check-in; **enregistrer** [ɑ̃ʀʒistʀe] *vt* (*MUS etc, remarquer, noter*) to record; (*fig: mémoriser*) to make a mental note of; (*ADMIN*) to register; (*bagages: par train*) to register; (: *à l'aéroport*) to check in

enrhumer [ɑ̃ryme]: **s'~** *vi* to catch a cold

enrichir [ɑ̃riʃiʀ] *vt* to make rich(er); (*fig*) to enrich; **s'~** *vi* to get rich(er)

enrober [ɑ̃rɔbe] *vt*: ~ **qch de** to coat sth with; (*fig*) to wrap sth up in

enrôler [ɑ̃role] *vt* to enlist; **s'~ (dans)** to enlist (in)

enrouer [ɑ̃rwe]: **s'~** *vi* to go hoarse

enrouler [ɑ̃rule] *vt* (*fil, corde*) to wind (up); **s'~** *vi* to coil up; to wind; ~ **qch autour de** to wind sth (a)round

ensanglanté, e [ɑ̃sɑ̃glɑ̃te] *adj* covered with blood

enseignant, e [ɑ̃sɛɲɑ̃, -ɑ̃t] *nm/f* teacher

enseigne [ɑ̃sɛɲ] *nf* sign; **à telle ~ que** so much so that; ~ **lumineuse** neon sign

enseignement [ɑ̃sɛɲmɑ̃] *nm* teaching; (*ADMIN*) education

enseigner [ɑ̃seɲe] *vt, vi* to teach; ~ **qch à qn/à qn que** to teach sb sth/sb that

ensemble [ɑ̃sɑ̃bl(ə)] *adv* together ♦ *nm* (*assemblage, MATH*) set; (*totalité*): **l'~ du/de la** the whole *ou* entire; (*unité, harmonie*) unity; **impression/idée d'~** overall *ou* general impression/idea; **dans l'~** (*en gros*) on the whole

ensemencer [ɑ̃smɑ̃se] *vt* to sow

ensevelir [ɑ̃səvliʀ] *vt* to bury

ensoleillé, e [ɑ̃sɔleje] *adj* sunny

ensommeillé, e [ɑ̃sɔmeje] *adj* drowsy

ensorceler [ɑ̃sɔʀsəle] *vt* to enchant, bewitch

ensuite [ɑ̃sɥit] *adv* then, next; (*plus tard*) afterwards, later; ~ **de quoi** after which

ensuivre [ɑ̃sɥivʀ(ə)]: **s'~** *vi* to follow, ensue

entailler [ɑ̃taje] *vt* to notch; to cut

entamer [ɑ̃tame] *vt* (*pain, bouteille*) to start; (*hostilités, pourparlers*) to open; (*fig: altérer*) to make a dent in; to shake; to damage

entasser [ɑ̃tase] *vt* (*empiler*) to pile up, heap up; (*tenir à l'étroit*) to cram together; **s'~** *vi* to pile up; to cram

entendre [ɑ̃tɑ̃dʀ(ə)] *vt* to hear; (*comprendre*) to understand; (*vouloir dire*) to mean; (*vouloir*): ~ **être obéi/que** to mean to be obeyed/that; **s'~** *vi* (*sympathiser*) to get on; (*se mettre d'accord*) to agree; **s'~ à qch/à faire** (*être compétent*) to be good at sth/doing; **j'ai entendu dire que** I've heard (it said) that

entendu, e [ɑ̃tɑ̃dy] *adj* (*réglé*) agreed; (*au courant: air*) knowing; (**c'est**) ~ all right, agreed; **c'est** ~ (*concession*) all right, granted; **bien** ~ of course

entente [ɑ̃tɑ̃t] *nf* understanding; (*accord, traité*) agreement; **à double** ~ (*sens*) with a double meaning

entériner [ɑ̃teʀine] *vt* to ratify, confirm

enterrement [ɑ̃tɛʀmɑ̃] *nm* (*cérémonie*) funeral, burial

enterrer [ɑ̃teʀe] *vt* to bury

entêtant, e [ɑ̃tɛtɑ̃, -ɑ̃t] *adj* heady

entêté, e [ɑ̃tete] *adj* stubborn

en-tête [ɑ̃tɛt] *nm* heading; **papier à** ~ headed notepaper

entêter [ɑ̃tete]: **s'~** *vi*: **s'~ (à faire)** to persist (in doing)

enthousiasme [ɑ̃tuzjasm(ə)] *nm* enthusiasm; ~r vt to fill with enthusiasm; s'~r (pour qch) to get enthusiastic (about sth)

enticher [ɑ̃tiʃe]: **s'~ de** vt to become infatuated with

entier, ère [ɑ̃tje, -jɛʀ] adj (non entamé, en totalité) whole; (total, complet) complete; (fig: caractère) unbending ♦ nm (MATH) whole; **en ~** totally; in its entirety; **lait ~** full-cream milk; **entièrement** adv entirely, wholly

entonner [ɑ̃tɔne] vt (chanson) to strike up

entonnoir [ɑ̃tɔnwaʀ] nm funnel

entorse [ɑ̃tɔʀs(ə)] nf (MÉD) sprain; (fig): ~ au règlement infringement of the rule

entortiller [ɑ̃tɔʀtije] vt (envelopper) to wrap; (enrouler) to twist, wind; (duper) to deceive

entourage [ɑ̃tuʀaʒ] nm circle; family (circle); entourage; (ce qui enclôt) surround

entourer [ɑ̃tuʀe] vt to surround; (apporter son soutien à) to rally round; ~ **de** to surround with; (trait) to encircle with

entourloupettes [ɑ̃tuʀlupɛt] nfpl mean tricks

entracte [ɑ̃tʀakt(ə)] nm interval

entraide [ɑ̃tʀɛd] nf mutual aid; **s'~r** vi to help each other

entrain [ɑ̃tʀɛ̃] nm spirit; **avec/sans ~** spiritedly/half-heartedly

entraînement [ɑ̃tʀɛnmɑ̃] nm training; (TECH) drive

entraîner [ɑ̃tʀene] vt (tirer: wagons) to pull; (charrier) to carry ou drag along; (TECH) to drive; (emmener: personne) to take (off); (mener à l'assaut, influencer) to lead; (SPORT) to train; (impliquer) to entail; (causer) to lead to, bring about; **s'~** vi (SPORT) to train; **s'~ à qch/à faire** to train o.s. for sth/to do; ~ **qn à faire** (inciter) to lead sb to do; **entraîneur, euse** nm/f (SPORT) coach, trainer ♦ nm (HIPPISME) trainer; **entraîneuse** nf (de bar) hostess

entraver [ɑ̃tʀave] vt (circulation) to hold up; (action, progrès) to hinder

entre [ɑ̃tʀ(ə)] prép between; (parmi) among(st); **l'un d'~ eux/nous** one of them/us; ~ **eux** among(st) themselves

entre-: ~bâillé, e adj half-open, ajar; **~choquer: s'~choquer** vi to knock ou bang together; **~côte** nf entrecôte ou rib steak; **~couper** vt: **~couper qch de** to intersperse sth with; **~croiser: s'~croiser** vi to intertwine

entrée [ɑ̃tʀe] nf entrance; (accès: au cinéma etc) admission; (billet) (admission) ticket; (CULIN) first course; **d'~** from the outset; ~ **en matière** introduction

entrefaites [ɑ̃tʀəfɛt]: **sur ces ~** adv at this juncture

entrefilet [ɑ̃tʀəfilɛ] nm paragraph (short article)

entrejambes [ɑ̃tʀəʒɑ̃b] nm crotch

entrelacer [ɑ̃tʀəlase] vt to intertwine

entrelarder [ɑ̃tʀəlaʀde] vt to lard

entremêler [ɑ̃tʀəmele] vt: ~ **qch de** to (inter)mingle sth with

entremets [ɑ̃tʀəmɛ] nm (cream) dessert

entremetteur, euse [ɑ̃tʀəmɛtœʀ, -øz] nm/f go-between

entremise [ɑ̃tʀəmiz] nf intervention; **par l'~ de** through

entreposer [ɑ̃tʀəpoze] vt to store, put into storage

entrepôt [ɑ̃tʀəpo] nm warehouse

entreprenant, e [ɑ̃tʀəpʀənɑ̃, -ɑ̃t] adj (actif) enterprising; (trop galant) forward

entreprendre [ɑ̃tʀəpʀɑ̃dʀ(ə)] vt (se lancer dans) to undertake; (commencer) to begin ou start (upon); (personne) to buttonhole; to tackle

entrepreneur [ɑ̃tʀəpʀənœʀ] nm: ~ **(en bâtiment)** (building) contractor

entreprise [ɑ̃tʀəpʀiz] nf (société) firm, concern; (action) undertaking, venture

entrer [ɑ̃tʀe] vi to go (ou come) in, enter ♦ vt (INFORM) to enter, input; **(faire) ~ qch dans** to get sth into; ~ **dans** (gén) to enter; (pièce) to go (ou come) into, enter; (club) to join; (heurter) to run into; (être une composante de) to go into; to form part of; ~ **à l'hôpital** to go into hospital; **faire ~** (visiteur) to show in

entresol [ɑ̃tʀəsɔl] nm mezzanine

entre-temps [ɑ̃tʀətɑ̃] adv meanwhile

entretenir [ɑ̃tʀətniʀ] vt to maintain; (famille, maîtresse) to support, keep; **s'~ (de)** to converse (about); ~ **qn (de)** to speak to sb (about)

entretien [ɑ̃tʀətjɛ̃] nm maintenance; (discussion) discussion, talk; (audience) interview

entrevoir [ɑ̃tʀəvwaʀ] vt (à peine) to make out; (brièvement) to catch a glimpse of

entrevue [ɑ̃tʀəvy] nf meeting; (audience) interview

entrouvert, e [ɑ̃tʀuvɛʀ, -ɛʀt(ə)] adj half-open

énumérer [enymeʀe] vt to list, enumerate

envahir [ɑ̃vaiʀ] vt to invade; (suj: inquiétude, peur) to come over; **envahissant, e** (péj) adj (personne) interfering, intrusive

enveloppe [ɑ̃vlɔp] nf (de lettre) envelope; (TECH) casing; outer layer

envelopper [ɑ̃vlɔpe] vt to wrap; (fig) to envelop, shroud

envenimer [ɑ̃vnime] vt to aggravate

envergure [ɑ̃vɛʀgyʀ] nf (fig) scope; calibre

enverrai etc vb voir **envoyer**

envers [ɑ̃vɛʀ] prép towards, to ♦ nm other side; (d'une étoffe) wrong side; **à l'~** upside down; back to front; (vêtement) inside out

envie [ɑ̃vi] nf (sentiment) envy; (souhait) desire, wish; **avoir ~ de (faire)** to feel like (doing); (plus fort) to want (to do); **avoir ~**

que to wish that; **ça lui fait ~** he would like that; **envier** vt to envy; **envieux, euse** adj envious

environ [ãviʀɔ̃] adv: **~ 3 h/2 km** (around) about 3 o'clock/2 km; voir aussi **environs**

environnement [ãviʀɔnmã] nm environment

environner [ãviʀɔne] vt to surround

environs [ãviʀɔ̃] nmpl surroundings

envisager [ãvizaʒe] vt (examiner, considérer) to view, contemplate; (avoir en vue) to envisage

envoi [ãvwa] nm (paquet) parcel, consignment

envoler [ãvɔle]: **s'~** vi (oiseau) to fly away ou off; (avion) to take off; (papier, feuille) to blow away; (fig) to vanish (into thin air)

envoûter [ãvute] vt to bewitch

envoyé, e [ãvwaje] nm/f (POL) envoy; (PRESSE) correspondent

envoyer [ãvwaje] vt to send; (lancer) to hurl, throw; **~ chercher** to send for

épagneul, e [epaɲœl] nm/f spaniel

épais, se [epɛ, -ɛs] adj thick; **épaisseur** nf thickness

épancher [epãʃe]: **s'~** vi to open one's heart

épanouir [epanwiʀ]: **s'~** vi (fleur) to bloom, open out; (visage) to light up; (fig) to blossom; to open up

épargne [epaʀɲ(ə)] nf saving

épargner [epaʀɲe] vt to save; (ne pas tuer ou endommager) to spare ♦ vi to save; **~ qch à qn** to spare sb sth

éparpiller [epaʀpije] vt to scatter; (pour répartir) to disperse; **s'~** vi to scatter; (fig) to dissipate one's efforts

épars, e [epaʀ, -aʀs(ə)] adj scattered

épatant, e [epatã, -ãt] (fam) adj super

épater [epate] vt to amaze; to impress

épaule [epol] nf shoulder

épauler [epole] vt (aider) to back up, support; (arme) to raise (to one's shoulder) ♦ vi to (take) aim

épaulette [epolɛt] nf epaulette; (rembourrage) shoulder pad

épave [epav] nf wreck

épée [epe] nf sword

épeler [eple] vt to spell

éperdu, e [epɛʀdy] adj distraught, overcome; passionate; frantic

éperon [epʀɔ̃] nm spur

épi [epi] nm (de blé, d'orge) ear

épice [epis] nf spice

épicer [epise] vt to spice

épicerie [episʀi] nf grocer's shop; (denrées) groceries pl; **~ fine** delicatessen; **épicier, ière** nm/f grocer

épidémie [epidemi] nf epidemic

épier [epje] vt to spy on, watch closely; (occasion) to look out for

épilepsie [epilɛpsi] nf epilepsy

épiler [epile] vt (jambes) to remove the hair from; (sourcils) to pluck

épilogue [epilɔg] nm (fig) conclusion, dénouement; **~r** [epilɔge] vi: **~r sur** to hold forth on

épinards [epinaʀ] nmpl spinach sg

épine [epin] nf thorn, prickle; (d'oursin etc) spine; **~ dorsale** backbone

épingle [epɛ̃gl(ə)] nf pin; **~ de nourrice** safety pin; **~ de sûreté** ou **double** safety pin

épingler [epɛ̃gle] vt (badge, décoration): **~ qch sur** to pin sth on(to); (fam) to catch, nick

épique [epik] adj epic

épisode [epizɔd] nm episode; **film/roman à ~s** serial; **épisodique** adj occasional

éploré, e [eplɔʀe] adj tearful

épluche-légumes [eplyʃlegym] nm inv (potato) peeler

éplucher [eplyʃe] vt (fruit, légumes) to peel; (fig) to go over with a fine-tooth comb; **épluchures** nfpl peelings

éponge [epɔ̃ʒ] nf sponge; **~r** vt (liquide) to mop up; (surface) to sponge; (fig: déficit) to soak up; **s'~r le front** to mop one's brow

épopée [epɔpe] nf epic

époque [epɔk] nf (de l'histoire) age, era; (de l'année, la vie) time; **d'~** (meuble) period cpd

époumoner [epumɔne]: **s'~** vi to shout o.s. hoarse

épouse [epuz] nf wife

épouser [epuze] vt to marry; (fig: idées) to espouse; (: forme) to fit

épousseter [epuste] vt to dust

époustouflant, e [epustuflã, -ãt] adj staggering, mind-boggling

épouvantable [epuvãtabl(ə)] adj appalling, dreadful

épouvantail [epuvãtaj] nm (à oiseaux) scarecrow

épouvante [epuvãt] nf terror; **film d'~** horror film; **épouvanter** vt to terrify

époux [epu] nm husband ♦ nmpl (married) couple

éprendre [epʀãdʀ(ə)]: **s'~ de** vt to fall in love with

épreuve [epʀœv] nf (d'examen) test; (malheur, difficulté) trial, ordeal; (PHOTO) print; (TYPO) proof; (SPORT) event; **à l'~ des balles** bulletproof; **à toute ~** unfailing; **mettre à l'~** to put to the test

épris, e [epʀi, -iz] pp de **éprendre**

éprouver [epʀuve] vt (tester) to test; (marquer, faire souffrir) to afflict, distress; (ressentir) to experience

éprouvette [epʀuvɛt] nf test tube

épuisé, e [epɥize] adj exhausted; (livre) out of print; **épuisement** [epɥizmã] nm exhaustion

épuiser [epɥize] vt (fatiguer) to exhaust,

wear *ou* tire out; *(stock, sujet)* to exhaust; **s'~** *vi* to wear *ou* tire o.s. out, exhaust o.s.; *(stock)* to run out

épurer [epyʀe] *vt (liquide)* to purify; *(parti etc)* to purge; *(langue, texte)* to refine

équateur [ekwatœʀ] *nm* equator; **(la république de) l'É~** Ecuador

équation [ekwɑsjɔ̃] *nf* equation

équerre [ekɛʀ] *nf (à dessin)* (set) square; *(pour fixer)* brace; **en ~** at right angles; **à l'~, d'~** straight

équilibre [ekilibʀ(ə)] *nm* balance; *(d'une balance)* equilibrium; **garder/perdre l'~** to keep/lose one's balance; **être en ~** to be balanced; **équilibré, e** *adj (fig)* well-balanced, stable; **équilibrer** *vt* to balance; **s'~r** *vi (poids)* to balance; *(fig: défauts etc)* to balance each other out

équipage [ekipaʒ] *nm* crew

équipe [ekip] *nf* team; *(bande: parfois péj)* bunch

équipé, e [ekipe] *adj:* **bien/mal ~** well-/poorly-equipped

équipée [ekipe] *nf* escapade

équipement [ekipmɑ̃] *nm* equipment; **~s** *nmpl (installations)* amenities, facilities

équiper [ekipe] *vt* to equip; *(voiture, cuisine)* to equip, fit out; **~ qn/qch de** to equip sb/sth with

équipier, ière [ekipje, -jɛʀ] *nm/f* team member

équitable [ekitabl(ə)] *adj* fair

équitation [ekitɑsjɔ̃] *nf* (horse-) riding

équivalent, e [ekivalɑ̃, -ɑ̃t] *adj, nm* equivalent

équivaloir [ekivalwaʀ]: **~ à** *vt* to be equivalent to

équivoque [ekivɔk] *adj* equivocal, ambiguous; *(louche)* dubious

érable [eʀabl(ə)] *nm* maple

érafler [eʀafle] *vt* to scratch; **éraflure** *nf* scratch

éraillé, e [eʀaje] *adj (voix)* rasping

ère [ɛʀ] *nf* era; **en l'an 1050 de notre ~** in the year 1050 A.D.

érection [eʀɛksjɔ̃] *nf* erection

éreinter [eʀɛ̃te] *vt* to exhaust, wear out

ériger [eʀiʒe] *vt (monument)* to erect

ermite [ɛʀmit] *nm* hermit

éroder [eʀɔde] *vt* to erode

érotique [eʀɔtik] *adj* erotic

errer [eʀe] *vi* to wander

erreur [eʀœʀ] *nf* mistake, error; *(morale)* error; **faire ~** to be mistaken; **par ~** by mistake; **~ judiciaire** miscarriage of justice

érudit, e [eʀydi, -it] *nm/f* scholar

éruption [eʀypsjɔ̃] *nf* eruption; *(MÉD)* rash

es *vb voir* **être**

ès [ɛs] *prép:* **licencié ~ lettres/sciences** ≈ Bachelor of Arts/Science

escabeau, x [ɛskabo] *nm (tabouret)* stool; *(échelle)* stepladder

escadre [ɛskadʀ(ə)] *nf (NAVIG)* squadron; *(AVIAT)* wing

escadron [ɛskadʀɔ̃] *nm* squadron

escalade [ɛskalad] *nf* climbing *no pl*; *(POL etc)* escalation

escalader [ɛskalade] *vt* to climb

escale [ɛskal] *nf (NAVIG)* call; port of call; *(AVIAT)* stop(over); **faire ~ à** to put in at; to stop over at

escalier [ɛskalje] *nm* stairs *pl*; **dans l'~** *ou* **les ~s** on the stairs; **~ roulant** escalator

escamoter [ɛskamɔte] *vt (esquiver)* to get round, evade; *(faire disparaître)* to conjure away

escapade [ɛskapad] *nf:* **faire une ~** to go on a jaunt; to run away *ou* off

escargot [ɛskaʀgo] *nm* snail

escarmouche [ɛskaʀmuʃ] *nf* skirmish

escarpé, e [ɛskaʀpe] *adj* steep

escient [esjɑ̃]*nm:* **à bon ~** advisedly

esclaffer [ɛsklafe] : **s'~** *vi* to guffaw

esclandre [ɛsklɑ̃dʀ(ə)] *nm* scene, fracas

esclavage [ɛsklavaʒ] *nm* slavery

esclave [ɛsklav] *nm/f* slave

escompter [ɛskɔ̃te] *vt (COMM)* to discount; *(espérer)* to expect, reckon upon

escorte [ɛskɔʀt(ə)] *nf* escort

escrime [ɛskʀim] *nf* fencing

escrimer [ɛskʀime]: **s'~** *vi:* **s'~ à faire** to wear o.s. out doing

escroc [ɛskʀo] *nm* swindler, conman

escroquer [ɛskʀɔke] *vt:* **~ qn (de qch)/qch (à qn)** to swindle sb (out of sth)/sth (out of sb); **escroquerie** *nf* swindle

espace [ɛspas] *nm* space

espacer [ɛspase] *vt* to space out; **s'~** *vi (visites etc)* to become less frequent

espadon [ɛspadɔ̃] *nm* swordfish *inv*

espadrille [ɛspadʀij] *nf* rope-soled sandal

Espagne [ɛspaɲ(ə)] *nf:* **l'~** Spain; **espagnol, e** *adj* Spanish ♦ *nm/f:* **Espagnol, e** Spaniard ♦ *nm (LING)* Spanish

espèce [ɛspɛs] *nf (BIO, BOT, ZOOL)* species *inv*; *(gén: sorte)* sort, kind, type; *(péj):* **~ de maladroit!** you clumsy oaf!; **~s** *nfpl (COMM)* cash *sg*; **en ~** in cash; **en l'~** in the case in point

espérance [ɛspeʀɑ̃s] *nf* hope; **~ de vie** life expectancy

espérer [ɛspeʀe] *vt* to hope for; **j'espère (bien)** I hope so; **~ que/faire** to hope that/to do; **~ en** to trust in

espiègle [ɛspjɛgl(ə)] *adj* mischievous

espion, ne [ɛspjɔ̃, -ɔn] *nm/f* spy

espionnage [ɛspjɔnaʒ] *nm* espionage, spying

espionner [ɛspjɔne] *vt* to spy (up)on

esplanade [ɛsplanad] *nf* esplanade

espoir [ɛspwaʀ] *nm* hope

esprit [ɛspʀi] *nm (pensée, intellect)* mind; *(humour, ironie)* wit; *(mentalité, d'une loi etc, fantôme etc)* spirit; **faire de l'~** to try to be witty; **reprendre ses ~s** to come to; **perdre l'~** to lose one's mind

esquimau, de, x [ɛskimo, -od] *adj, nm/f* Eskimo ♦ *nm* ice lolly (*BRIT*), popsicle (*US*)

esquinter [ɛskɛ̃te] (*fam*) *vt* to mess up

esquisse [ɛskis] *nf* sketch

esquisser [ɛskise] *vt* to sketch; **s'~** *vi* (*amélioration*) to begin to be detectable; **~ un sourire** to give a vague smile

esquiver [ɛskive] *vt* to dodge; **s'~** *vi* to slip away

essai [esɛ] *nm* trying; testing; (*tentative*) attempt, try; (*RUGBY*) try; (*LITTÉRATURE*) essay; **~s** *nmpl* (*AUTO*) trials; **~ gratuit** (*COMM*) free trial; **à l'~** on a trial basis

essaim [esɛ̃] *nm* swarm

essayer [eseje] *vt* (*gén*) to try; (*vêtement, chaussures*) to try (on); (*restaurant, méthode, voiture*) to try (out) ♦ *vi* to try; **~ de faire** to try ou attempt to do

essence [esɑ̃s] *nf* (*de voiture*) petrol (*BRIT*), gas(oline) (*US*); (*extrait de plante, PHILOSOPHIE*) essence; (*espèce d'arbre*) species

essentiel, le [esɑ̃sjɛl] *adj* essential; **c'est l'~** (*ce qui importe*) that's the main thing; **l'~ de** the main part of

essieu, x [esjø] *nm* axle

essor [esɔʀ] *nm* (*de l'économie etc*) rapid expansion

essorer [esɔʀe] *vt* (*en tordant*) to wring (out); (*par la force centrifuge*) to spin-dry; **essoreuse** *nf* mangle, wringer; spin-dryer

essouffler [esufle] *vt* to make breathless; **s'~** *vi* to get out of breath; (*fig*) to run out of steam

essuie-glace [esɥiglas] *nm inv* windscreen (*BRIT*) ou windshield (*US*) wiper

essuie-main [esɥimɛ̃] *nm* hand towel

essuyer [esɥije] *vt* to wipe; (*fig: subir*) to suffer; **s'~** *vi* (*après le bain*) to dry o.s.; **~ la vaisselle** to dry up

est¹ [ɛ] *vb voir* **être**

est² [ɛst] *nm* east ♦ *adj inv* east; (*région*) east(ern); **à l'est in** the east; (*direction*) to the east, east(wards); **à l'est de** (to the) east of

estampe [ɛstɑ̃p] *nf* print, engraving

est-ce que [ɛskə] *adv*: **~ c'est cher/c'était bon?** is it expensive/was it good?; **quand est-ce qu'il part?** when does he leave?, when is he leaving?; *voir aussi* **que**

esthéticienne [ɛstetisjɛn] *nf* beautician

esthétique [ɛstetik] *adj* attractive; aesthetically pleasing

estimation [ɛstimasjɔ̃] *nf* valuation; assessment

estime [ɛstim] *nf* esteem, regard

estimer [ɛstime] *vt* (*respecter*) to esteem; (*expertiser*) to value; (*évaluer*) to assess, estimate; (*penser*): **~ que/être** to consider that/o.s. to be

estival, e, aux [ɛstival, -o] *adj* summer *cpd*

estivant, e [ɛstivɑ̃, -ɑ̃t] *nm/f* (summer) holiday-maker

estomac [ɛstɔma] *nm* stomach

estomaqué, e [ɛstɔmake] *adj* flabbergasted

estomper [ɛstɔ̃pe] *vt* (*fig*) to blur, dim; **s'~** *vi* to soften; to become blurred

estrade [ɛstʀad] *nf* platform, rostrum

estragon [ɛstʀagɔ̃] *nm* tarragon

estropier [ɛstʀɔpje] *vt* to cripple, maim; (*fig*) to twist, distort

et [e] *conj* and; **~ lui?** what about him?; **~ alors!** so what!

étable [etabl(ə)] *nf* cowshed

établi [etabli] *nm* (work)bench

établir [etabliʀ] *vt* (*papiers d'identité, facture*) to make out; (*liste, programme*) to draw up; (*entreprise, camp, gouvernement, artisan*) to set up; (*réputation, usage, fait, culpabilité*) to establish; **s'~** *vi* (*se faire: entente etc*) to be established; **s'~** (*à son compte*) to set up in business; **s'~** **à/près de** to settle in/near

établissement [etablismɑ̃] *nm* making out; drawing up; setting up, establishing; (*entreprise, institution*) establishment; **~ scolaire** school, educational establishment

étage [etaʒ] *nm* (*d'immeuble*) storey, floor; (*de fusée*) stage; (*GÉO: de culture, végétation*) level; **à l'~** upstairs; **au 2ème ~** on the 2nd (*BRIT*) ou 3rd (*US*) floor; **de bas ~** low-born

étagère [etaʒɛʀ] *nf* (*rayon*) shelf; (*meuble*) shelves *pl*

étai [etɛ] *nm* stay, prop

étain [etɛ̃] *nm* tin; (*ORFÈVRERIE*) pewter *no pl*

étais *etc vb voir* **être**

étal [etal] *nm* stall

étalage [etalaʒ] *nm* display; display window; **faire ~ de** to show off, parade

étaler [etale] *vt* (*carte, nappe*) to spread (out); (*peinture, liquide*) to spread; (*échelonner: paiements, vacances*) to spread, stagger; (*marchandises*) to display; (*richesses, connaissances*) to parade; **s'~** *vi* (*liquide*) to spread out; (*fam*) to fall flat on one's face; **s'~ sur** (*suj: paiements etc*) to be spread out over

étalon [etalɔ̃] *nm* (*mesure*) standard; (*cheval*) stallion

étamer [etame] *vt* (*casserole*) to tin(plate); (*glace*) to silver

étanche [etɑ̃ʃ] *adj* (*récipient*) watertight; (*montre, vêtement*) waterproof

étancher [etɑ̃ʃe] *vt*: **~ sa soif** to quench one's thirst

étang [etɑ̃] *nm* pond

étant [etɑ̃] *vb voir* **être; donné**

étape [etap] *nf* stage; (*lieu d'arrivée*) stopping place; (: *CYCLISME*) staging point; **faire ~ à** to stop off at

état [eta] *nm* (*POL, condition*) state; (*liste*)

inventory, statement; **en mauvais** ~ in poor condition; **en** ~ **(de marche)** in (working) order; **remettre en** ~ to repair; **hors d'**~ out of order; **être en** ~/**hors d'**~ **de faire** to be in a/in no fit state to do; **en tout** ~ **de cause** in any event; **être dans tous ses** ~**s** to be in a state; **faire** ~ **de** *(alléguer)* to put forward; **en** ~ **d'arrestation** under arrest; ~ **civil** civil status; ~ **des lieux** inventory of fixtures; **étatiser** *vt* to bring under state control

état-major [etamaʒɔʀ] *nm* (MIL) staff

États-Unis [etazyni] *nmpl:* **les** ~ the United States

étau, x [eto] *nm* vice *(BRIT)*, vise *(US)*

étayer [eteje] *vt* to prop *ou* shore up

etc. *adv* etc

et c(a)etera [ɛtsetera] *adv* et cetera, and so on

été [ete] *pp de* être ♦ *nm* summer

éteindre [etɛ̃dʀ(ə)] *vt (lampe, lumière, radio)* to turn *ou* switch off; *(cigarette, incendie, bougie)* to put out, extinguish; *(JUR: dette)* to extinguish; **s'**~ *vi* to go out; to go off; *(mourir)* to pass away; **éteint, e** *adj (fig)* lacklustre, dull; *(volcan)* extinct

étendard [etɑ̃daʀ] *nm* standard

étendre [etɑ̃dʀ(ə)] *vt (pâte, liquide)* to spread; *(carte etc)* to spread out; *(linge)* to hang up; *(bras, jambes, par terre: blessé)* to stretch out; *(diluer)* to dilute, thin; *(fig: agrandir)* to extend; **s'**~ *vi (augmenter, se propager)* to spread; *(terrain, forêt etc)* to stretch; *(s'allonger)* to stretch out; *(se coucher)* to lie down; *(fig: expliquer)* to elaborate

étendu, e [etɑ̃dy] *adj* extensive; **étendue** *nf (d'eau, de sable)* stretch, expanse; *(importance)* extent

éternel, le [etɛʀnɛl] *adj* eternal

éterniser [etɛʀnize]: **s'**~ *vi* to last for ages; to stay for ages

éternité [etɛʀnite] *nf* eternity

éternuer [etɛʀnɥe] *vi* to sneeze

êtes *vb voir* être

éthique [etik] *adj* ethical

ethnie [ɛtni] *nf* ethnic group

éthylisme [etilism(ə)] *nm* alcoholism

étiez *vb voir* être

étinceler [etɛ̃sle] *vi* to sparkle

étincelle [etɛ̃sɛl] *nf* spark

étioler [etjɔle]: **s'**~ *vi* to wilt

étiqueter [etikte] *vt* to label

étiquette [etikɛt] *nf* label; *(protocole):* **l'**~ etiquette

étirer [etiʀe] *vt* to stretch; **s'**~ *vi (personne)* to stretch; *(convoi, route):* **s'**~ **sur** to stretch out over

étoffe [etɔf] *nf* material, fabric

étoffer [etɔfe] *vt* to fill out; **s'**~ *vi* to fill out

étoile [etwal] *nf* star; **à la belle** ~ in the open; ~ **de mer** starfish; ~ **filante** shooting star; **étoilé, e** *adj* starry

étole [etɔl] *nf* stole

étonnant, e [etɔnɑ̃, -ɑ̃t] *adj* amazing

étonner [etɔne] *vt* to surprise, amaze; **s'**~ **que/de** to be amazed that/at; **cela m'**~**ait (que)** *(j'en doute)* I'd be very surprised (if)

étouffée [etufe]: **à l'**~ *adv (CULIN)* steamed; braised

étouffer [etufe] *vt* to suffocate; *(bruit)* to muffle; *(scandale)* to hush up ♦ *vi* to suffocate; **s'**~ *vi (en mangeant etc)* to choke

étourderie [etuʀdəʀi] *nf* heedlessness *no pl*; thoughtless blunder

étourdi, e [etuʀdi] *adj (distrait)* scatterbrained, heedless

étourdir [etuʀdiʀ] *vt (assommer)* to stun, daze; *(griser)* to make dizzy *ou* giddy; **étourdissement** *nm* dizzy spell

étourneau, x [etuʀno] *nm* starling

étrange [etʀɑ̃ʒ] *adj* strange

étranger, ère [etʀɑ̃ʒe, -ɛʀ] *adj* foreign; *(pas de la famille, non familier)* strange ♦ *nm/f* foreigner; stranger ♦ *nm:* **à l'**~ abroad; **de l'**~ from abroad; ~ **à** *(fig)* unfamiliar to; irrelevant to

étranglement [etʀɑ̃gləmɑ̃] *nm (d'une vallée etc)* constriction

étrangler [etʀɑ̃gle] *vt* to strangle; **s'**~ *vi (en mangeant etc)* to choke

étrave [etʀav] *nf* stem

────────────── *MOT CLÉ*

être [ɛtʀ(ə)] *nm* being; ~ **humain** human being

♦ *vb +attrib* **1** *(état, description)* to be; **il est instituteur** he is *ou* he's a teacher; **vous êtes grand/intelligent/fatigué** you are *ou* you're tall/clever/tired

2 *(+à: appartenir)* to be; **le livre est à Paul** the book is Paul's *ou* belongs to Paul; **c'est à moi/eux** it is *ou* it's mine/theirs

3 *(+de: provenance):* **il est de Paris** he is from Paris; *(: appartenance):* **il est des nôtres** he is one of us

4 *(date):* **nous sommes le 10 janvier** it's the 10th of January (today)

♦ *vi* to be; **je ne serai pas ici demain** I won't be here tomorrow

♦ *vb aux* **1** to have; to be; ~ **arrivé/allé** to have arrived/gone; **il est parti** he has left, he has gone

2 *(forme passive)* to be; ~ **fait par** to be made by; **il a été promu** he has been promoted

3 *(+à: obligation):* **c'est à réparer** it needs repairing; **c'est à essayer** it should be tried

♦ *vb impers* **1**: **il est** +*adjectif* it is +*adjective*; **il est impossible de le faire** it's impossible to do it

2 *(heure, date):* **il est 10 heures** it is *ou* it's 10 o'clock

3 (*emphatique*): **c'est moi** it's me; **c'est à lui de le faire** it's up to him to do it

étreindre [etʀɛ̃dʀ(ə)] *vt* to clutch, grip; (*amoureusement, amicalement*) to embrace; **s'~** *vi* to embrace

étrenner [etʀene] *vt* to use (*ou* wear) for the first time

étrennes [etʀen] *nfpl* Christmas box *sg*

étrier [etʀije] *nm* stirrup

étriller [etʀije] *vt* (*cheval*) to curry; (*fam: battre*) to slaughter (*fig*)

étriqué, e [etʀike] *adj* skimpy

étroit, e [etʀwa, -wat] *adj* narrow; (*vêtement*) tight; (*fig: serré*) close, tight; **à l'~** cramped; **~ d'esprit** narrow-minded

étude [etyd] *nf* studying; (*ouvrage, rapport*) study; (*de notaire: bureau*) office; (: *charge*) practice; (*SCOL: salle de travail*) study room; **~s** *nfpl* (*SCOL*) studies; **être à l'~** (*projet etc*) to be under consideration; **faire des ~s** (**de droit/médecine**) to study (law/medicine)

étudiant, e [etydjɑ̃, -ɑ̃t] *nm/f* student

étudié, e [etydje] *adj* (*démarche*) studied; (*système*) carefully designed; (*prix*) keen

étudier [etydje] *vt, vi* to study

étui [etɥi] *nm* case

étuve [etyv] *nf* steamroom

étuvée [etyve]: **à l'~** *adv* braised

eu, eue [y] *pp de* **avoir**

euh [ø] *excl* er

Europe [øʀɔp] *nf*: **l'~** Europe; **européen, ne** *adj, nm/f* European

eus *etc vb voir* **avoir**

eux [ø] *pron* (*sujet*) they; (*objet*) them

évacuer [evakɥe] *vt* to evacuate

évader [evade]: **s'~** *vi* to escape

évangile [evɑ̃ʒil] *nm* gospel

évanouir [evanwiʀ]: **s'~** *vi* to faint; (*disparaître*) to vanish, disappear

évanouissement [evanwismɑ̃] *nm* (*syncope*) fainting fit; (*dans un accident*) loss of consciousness

évaporer [evapɔʀe]: **s'~** *vi* to evaporate

évaser [evaze] *vt* (*tuyau*) to widen, open out; (*jupe, pantalon*) to flare

évasif, ive [evazif, -iv] *adj* evasive

évasion [evazjɔ̃] *nf* escape

évêché [eveʃe] *nm* bishopric; bishop's palace

éveil [evɛj] *nm* awakening; **être en ~** to be alert

éveillé, e [eveje] *adj* awake; (*vif*) alert, sharp

éveiller [eveje] *vt* to (a)waken; **s'~** *vi* to (a)waken; (*fig*) to be aroused

événement [evenmɑ̃] *nm* event

éventail [evɑ̃taj] *nm* fan; (*choix*) range

éventaire [evɑ̃tɛʀ] *nm* stall, stand

éventer [evɑ̃te] *vt* (*secret*) to uncover; **s'~** *vi* (*parfum*) to go stale

éventrer [evɑ̃tʀe] *vt* to disembowel; (*fig*) to tear *ou* rip open

éventualité [evɑ̃tɥalite] *nf* eventuality; possibility; **dans l'~ de** in the event of

éventuel, le [evɑ̃tɥel] *adj* possible; **éventuellement** *adv* possibly

évêque [evɛk] *nm* bishop

évertuer [evɛʀtɥe]: **s'~** *vi*: **s'~ à faire** to try very hard to do

éviction [eviksjɔ̃] *nf* ousting; (*de locataire*) eviction

évidemment [evidamɑ̃] *adv* obviously

évidence [evidɑ̃s] *nf* obviousness; obvious fact; **de toute ~** quite obviously *ou* evidently; **en ~** conspicuous; **mettre en ~** to highlight; to bring to the fore; **évident, e** [evidɑ̃, -ɑ̃t] *adj* obvious, evident

évider [evide] *vt* to scoop out

évier [evje] *nm* (kitchen) sink

évincer [evɛ̃se] *vt* to oust

éviter [evite] *vt* to avoid; **~ de faire/que qch ne se passe** to avoid doing/sth happening; **~ qch à qn** to spare sb sth

évolué, e [evɔlɥe] *adj* advanced

évoluer [evɔlɥe] *vi* (*enfant, maladie*) to develop; (*situation, moralement*) to evolve, develop; (*aller et venir: danseur etc*) to move about, circle; **évolution** *nf* development; evolution

évoquer [evɔke] *vt* to call to mind, evoke; (*mentionner*) to mention

ex... [ɛks] *préfixe* ex-

exact, e [ɛgzakt] *adj* (*précis*) exact, accurate, precise; (*correct*) correct; (*ponctuel*) punctual; **l'heure ~e** the right *ou* exact time; **exactement** *adv* exactly, accurately, precisely; correctly; (*c'est cela même*) exactly

ex aequo [ɛgzeko] *adj* equally placed

exagéré, e [ɛgzaʒeʀe] *adj* (*prix etc*) excessive

exagérer [ɛgzaʒeʀe] *vt* to exaggerate ♦ *vi* (*abuser*) to go too far; to overstep the mark; (*déformer les faits*) to exaggerate

exalter [ɛgzalte] *vt* (*enthousiasmer*) to excite, elate; (*glorifier*) to exalt

examen [ɛgzamɛ̃] *nm* examination; (*SCOL*) exam, examination; **à l'~** under consideration; (*COMM*) on approval

examiner [ɛgzamine] *vt* to examine

exaspérant, e [ɛgzaspeʀɑ̃, -ɑ̃t] *adj* exasperating

exaspérer [ɛgzaspeʀe] *vt* to exasperate; to exacerbate

exaucer [ɛgzose] *vt* (*vœu*) to grant

excédent [ɛksedɑ̃] *nm* surplus; **en ~** surplus; **~ de bagages** excess luggage

excéder [ɛksede] *vt* (*dépasser*) to exceed; (*agacer*) to exasperate

excellence [ɛkselɑ̃s] *nf* (*titre*) Excellency

excellent, e [ɛkselɑ̃, -ɑ̃t] *adj* excellent

excentrique [ɛksɑ̃tʀik] *adj* eccentric;

(quartier) outlying

excepté, e [ɛksɛpte] *adj, prép*: **les élèves ~s, ~ les élèves** except for the pupils; **~ si** except if

exception [ɛksɛpsjɔ̃] *nf* exception; **à l'~ de** except for, with the exception of; **d'~** *(mesure, loi)* special, exceptional; **exceptionnel, le** *adj* exceptional

excès [ɛksɛ] *nm* surplus ♦ *nmpl* excesses; **à l'~** to excess; **~ de vitesse** speeding *no pl*; **excessif, ive** *adj* excessive

excitant, e [ɛksitɑ̃, -ɑ̃t] *adj* exciting ♦ *nm* stimulant; **excitation** [ɛksitasjɔ̃] *nf (état)* excitement

exciter [ɛksite] *vt* to excite; *(suj: café etc)* to stimulate; **s'~** *vi* to get excited

exclamation [ɛksklamasjɔ̃] *nf* exclamation

exclamer [ɛksklame]: **s'~** *vi* to exclaim

exclure [ɛksklyʀ] *vt (faire sortir)* to expel; *(ne pas compter)* to exclude, leave out; *(rendre impossible)* to exclude, rule out; **il est exclu que** it's out of the question that ...; **il n'est pas exclu que ...**, it's not impossible that ...; **exclusif, ive** *adj* exclusive; **exclusion** *nf* expulsion; **à l'exclusion de** with the exclusion *ou* exception of; **exclusivité** *nf (COMM)* exclusive rights *pl*; **film passant en exclusivité** à film showing only at

excursion [ɛkskyʀsjɔ̃] *nf (en autocar)* excursion, trip; *(à pied)* walk, hike

excuse [ɛkskyz] *nf* excuse; **~s** *nfpl (regret)* apology *sg*, apologies

excuser [ɛkskyze] *vt* to excuse; **s'~ (de)** to apologize (for); **"excusez-moi"** "I'm sorry"; *(pour attirer l'attention)* "excuse me"

exécrable [ɛgzekʀabl(ə)] *adj* atrocious

exécrer [ɛgzekʀe] *vt* to loathe, abhor

exécuter [ɛgzekyte] *vt (prisonnier)* to execute; *(tâche etc)* to execute, carry out; *(MUS: jouer)* to perform, execute; *(INFORM)* to run; **s'~** *vi* to comply; **exécutif, ive** *adj, nm (POL)* executive; **exécution** *nf* execution; carrying out; **mettre à exécution** to carry out

exemplaire [ɛgzɑ̃plɛʀ] *nm* copy

exemple [ɛgzɑ̃pl(ə)] *nm* example; **par ~** for instance, for example; **donner l'~** to set an example; **prendre ~ sur** to take as a model; **à l'~ de** just like

exempt, e [ɛgzɑ̃, -ɑ̃t] *adj*: **~ de** *(dispensé de)* exempt from; *(sans)* free from

exercer [ɛgzɛʀse] *vt (pratiquer)* to exercise, practise; *(prérogative)* to exercise; *(influence, contrôle)* to exert; *(former)* to exercise, train; **s'~** *vi (sportif, musicien)* to practise; *(se faire sentir: pression etc)* to be exerted

exercice [ɛgzɛʀsis] *nm (tâche, travail)* exercise; **l'~** exercise; *(MIL)* drill; **en ~** *(juge)* in office; *(médecin)* practising

exhaustif, ive [ɛgzostif, -iv] *adj* exhaustive

exhiber [ɛgzibe] *vt (montrer: papiers, certifi-*cat) to present, produce; *(péj)* to display, flaunt; **s'~** *vi* to parade; *(suj: exhibitionniste)* to expose o.s.

exhorter [ɛgzɔʀte] *vt* to urge

exigeant, e [ɛgziʒɑ̃, -ɑ̃t] *adj* demanding; *(péj)* hard to please

exigence [ɛgziʒɑ̃s] *nf* demand, requirement

exiger [ɛgziʒe] *vt* to demand, require

exigu, ë [ɛgzigy] *adj (lieu)* cramped, tiny

exil [ɛgzil] *nm* exile; **exiler** *vt* to exile; **s'~er** *vi* to go into exile

existence [ɛgzistɑ̃s] *nf* existence

exister [ɛgziste] *vi* to exist; **il existe un/des** there is a/are (some)

exonérer [ɛgzɔneʀe] *vt*: **~ de** to exempt from

exorbitant, e [ɛgzɔʀbitɑ̃, -ɑ̃t] *adj (somme, nombre)* exorbitant

exorbité, e [ɛgzɔʀbite] *adj*: **yeux ~s** bulging eyes

exotique [ɛgzɔtik] *adj* exotic

expatrier [ɛkspatʀije] *vt*: **s'~** to leave one's country

expectative [ɛkspɛktativ] *nf*: **être dans l'~** to be still waiting

expédient [ɛkspedjɑ̃] *(péj) nm* expedient; **vivre d'~s** to live by one's wits

expédier [ɛkspedje] *vt (lettre, paquet)* to send; *(troupes)* to dispatch; *(péj: travail etc)* to dispose of, dispatch; **expéditeur, trice** *nm/f* sender

expédition [ɛkspedisjɔ̃] *nf* sending; *(scientifique, sportive, MIL)* expedition

expérience [ɛkspeʀjɑ̃s] *nf (de la vie)* experience; *(scientifique)* experiment

expérimenté, e [ɛkspeʀimɑ̃te] *adj* experienced

expérimenter [ɛkspeʀimɑ̃te] *vt* to test out, experiment with

expert, e [ɛkspɛʀ, -ɛʀt(ə)] *adj, nm* expert; **~ en assurances** insurance valuer; **expert-comptable** *nm* ≈ chartered accountant *(BRIT)*, ≈ certified public accountant *(US)*

expertise [ɛkspɛʀtiz] *nf* valuation; assessment; valuer's *(ou* assessor's) report; *(JUR)* (forensic) examination

expertiser [ɛkspɛʀtize] *vt (objet de valeur)* to value; *(voiture accidentée etc)* to assess damage to

expier [ɛkspje] *vt* to expiate, atone for

expirer [ɛkspiʀe] *vi (prendre fin, mourir)* to expire; *(respirer)* to breathe out

explicatif, ive [ɛksplikatif, -iv] *adj* explanatory

explication [ɛksplikasjɔ̃] *nf* explanation; *(discussion)* discussion; argument; **~ de texte** *(SCOL)* critical analysis

explicite [ɛksplisit] *adj* explicit

expliquer [ɛksplike] *vt* to explain; **s'~** to explain (o.s.); *(discuter)* to discuss things; to have it out; **son erreur s'explique** one can understand his mistake

exploit [ɛksplwa] nm exploit, feat

exploitation [ɛksplwatasjɔ̃] nf exploitation; running; ~ **agricole** farming concern; **exploiter** [ɛksplwate] vt (mine) to exploit, work; (entreprise, ferme) to run, operate; (clients, ouvriers, erreur, don) to exploit

explorer [ɛksplɔre] vt to explore

exploser [ɛksploze] vi to explode, blow up; (engin explosif) to go off; (fig: joie, colère) to burst out, explode; **explosif, ive** adj, nm explosive; **explosion** nf explosion

exportateur, trice [ɛkspɔrtatœr, -tris] adj export cpd, exporting ♦ nm exporter

exportation [ɛkspɔrtasjɔ̃] nf exportation; export

exporter [ɛkspɔrte] vt to export

exposant [ɛkspozɑ̃] nm exhibitor

exposé, e [ɛkspoze] nm talk ♦ adj: ~ **au sud** facing south; **bien ~** well situated

exposer [ɛkspoze] vt (marchandise) to display; (peinture) to exhibit, show; (parler de) to explain, set out; (mettre en danger, orienter, PHOTO) to expose; **exposition** nf (manifestation) exhibition; (PHOTO) exposure

exprès¹ [ɛksprɛ] adv (délibérément) on purpose; (spécialement) specially

exprès², esse [ɛksprɛs] adj (ordre, défense) express, formal ♦ adj inv (PTT) express ♦ adv express

express [ɛksprɛs] adj, nm: **(café)** ~ espresso (coffee); **(train)** ~ fast train

expressément [ɛksprɛsemɑ̃] adv expressly; specifically

expression [ɛksprɛsjɔ̃] nf expression

exprimer [ɛksprime] vt (sentiment, idée) to express; (jus, liquide) to press out; **s'~** vi (personne) to express o.s.

exproprier [ɛksprɔprije] vt to buy up by compulsory purchase, expropriate

expulser [ɛkspylse] vt to expel; (locataire) to evict; (SPORT) to send off

exquis, e [ɛkski, -iz] adj exquisite; delightful

exsangue [ɛksɑ̃g] adj bloodless, drained of blood

extase [ɛkstaz] nf ecstasy; **extasier: s'extasier** vi to go into raptures over

extension [ɛkstɑ̃sjɔ̃] nf (d'un muscle, ressort) stretching; (fig) extension; expansion

exténuer [ɛkstenɥe] vt to exhaust

extérieur, e [ɛksterjœr] adj (porte, mur etc) outer, outside; (au dehors: escalier, w.-c.) outside; (commerce) foreign; (influences) external; (apparent: calme, gaieté etc) surface cpd ♦ nm (d'une maison, d'un récipient etc) outside, exterior; (apparence) exterior; (d'un groupe social): l'~ the outside world; à l'~ outside; (à l'étranger) abroad; **extérieurement** adv on the outside; (en apparence) on the surface

exterminer [ɛkstɛrmine] vt to exterminate, wipe out

externat [ɛkstɛrna] nm day school

externe [ɛkstɛrn(ə)] adj external, outer ♦ nm/f (MÉD) non-resident medical student (BRIT), extern (US); (SCOL) day pupil

extincteur [ɛkstɛ̃ktœr] nm (fire) extinguisher

extinction [ɛkstɛ̃ksjɔ̃] nf: ~ **de voix** loss of voice

extorquer [ɛkstɔrke] vt to extort

extra [ɛkstra] adj inv first-rate; top-quality ♦ nm inv extra help

extrader [ɛkstrade] vt to extradite

extraire [ɛkstrɛr] vt to extract; **extrait** nm extract

extraordinaire [ɛkstraɔrdinɛr] adj extraordinary; (POL: mesures etc) special

extravagant, e [ɛkstravagɑ̃, -ɑ̃t] adj extravagant; wild

extraverti, e [ɛkstraverti] adj extrovert

extrême [ɛkstrɛm] adj, nm extreme; **extrêmement** adv extremely; **extrême-onction** nf last rites pl; **Extrême-Orient** nm Far East

extrémité [ɛkstremite] nf end; (situation) straits pl, plight; (geste désespéré) extreme action; ~**s** nfpl (pieds et mains) extremities; à **la dernière** ~ on the point of death

exutoire [ɛgzytwar] nm outlet, release

_F f_

F abr = **franc**

fa [fa] nm inv (MUS) F; (en chantant la gamme) fa

fable [fabl(ə)] nf fable

fabricant [fabrikɑ̃] nm manufacturer

fabrication [fabrikasjɔ̃] nf manufacture

fabrique [fabrik] nf factory

fabriquer [fabrike] vt to make; (industriellement) to manufacture; (fig): **qu'est-ce qu'il fabrique?** what is he doing?

fabulation [fabylasjɔ̃] nf fantasizing

fac [fak] (fam) abr f (SCOL) = **faculté**

façade [fasad] nf front, façade

face [fas] nf face; (fig: aspect) side ♦ adj: **le côté** ~ heads; **perdre la** ~ to lose face; **en** ~ **de** opposite; (fig) in front of; **de** ~ from the front; face on; ~ **à** facing; (fig) faced with, in the face of; **faire** ~ **à** to face; ~ **à** ~ adv facing each other ♦ nm inv encounter

facétieux, euse [fasesjø, -øz] *adj* mischievous

fâché, e [fɑʃe] *adj* angry; (*désolé*) sorry

fâcher [fɑʃe] *vt* to anger; **se ~** *vi* to get angry; **se ~ avec** (*se brouiller*) to fall out with

fâcheux, euse [fɑʃø, -øz] *adj* unfortunate, regrettable

facile [fasil] *adj* easy; (*accommodant*) easygoing; **~ment** *adv* easily; **facilité** *nf* easiness; (*disposition, don*) aptitude; **facilités** *nfpl* (*possibilités*) facilities; **facilités de paiement** easy terms; **faciliter** *vt* to make easier

façon [fasɔ̃] *nf* (*manière*) way; (*d'une robe etc*) making-up; cut; **~s** *nfpl* (*péj*) fuss *sg*; **de quelle ~?** (in) what way?; **de ~ à/à ce que** so as to/that; **de toute ~** anyway, in any case; **~ner** [fasɔne] *vt* (*fabriquer*) to manufacture; (*travailler: matière*) to shape, fashion; (*fig*) to mould, shape

facteur, trice [faktœr, -tris] *nm/f* postman(woman) (*BRIT*), mailman(woman) (*US*) ♦ *nm* (*MATH, fig: élément*) factor; **~ de pianos** piano maker

factice [faktis] *adj* artificial

faction [faksjɔ̃] *nf* faction; (*MIL*) guard *ou* sentry (duty); watch

facture [faktyr] *nf* (*à payer: gén*) bill; (: *COMM*) invoice; (*d'un artisan, artiste*) technique, workmanship; **facturer** *vt* to invoice

facultatif, ive [fakyltatif, -iv] *adj* optional; (*arrêt de bus*) request *cpd*

faculté [fakylte] *nf* (*intellectuelle, d'université*) faculty; (*pouvoir, possibilité*) power

fade [fad] *adj* insipid

faible [fɛbl(ə)] *adj* weak; (*voix, lumière, vent*) faint; (*rendement, intensité, revenu etc*) low ♦ *nm* weak point; (*pour quelqu'un*) weakness, soft spot; **~ d'esprit** feebleminded; **faiblesse** *nf* weakness; **faiblir** *vi* to weaken; (*lumière*) to dim; (*vent*) to drop

faïence [fajɑ̃s] *nf* earthenware *no pl*; piece of earthenware

faignant, e [fɛɲɑ̃, -ɑ̃t] *nm/f* = **fainéant, e**

faille [faj] *vb voir* **falloir** ♦ *nf* (*GÉO*) fault; (*fig*) flaw, weakness

faillir [fajir] *vi*: **j'ai failli tomber** I almost *ou* very nearly fell

faillite [fajit] *nf* bankruptcy

faim [fɛ̃] *nf* hunger; **avoir ~** to be hungry; **rester sur sa ~** (*aussi fig*) to be left wanting more

fainéant, e [fɛneɑ̃, -ɑ̃t] *nm/f* idler, loafer

─────────── MOT CLÉ ───────────

faire [fɛr] *vt* **1** (*fabriquer, être l'auteur de*) to make; **~ du vin/une offre/un film** to make wine/an offer/a film; **~ du bruit** to make a noise

2 (*effectuer: travail, opération*) to do; **que faites-vous?** (*quel métier etc*) what do you do?; (*quelle activité: au moment de la question*) what are you doing?; **~ la lessive** to do the washing

3 (*études*) to do; (*sport, musique*) to play; **~ du droit/du français** to do law/French; **~ du rugby/piano** to play rugby/the piano

4 (*simuler*): **~ le malade/l'ignorant** to act the invalid/the fool

5 (*transformer, avoir un effet sur*): **~ de qn un frustré/avocat** to make sb frustrated/a lawyer; **ça ne me fait rien** (*m'est égal*) I don't care *ou* mind; (*me laisse froid*) it has no effect on me; **ça ne fait rien** it doesn't matter; **~ que** (*impliquer*) to mean that

6 (*calculs, prix, mesures*): **2 et 2 font 4** 2 and 2 are *ou* make 4; **ça fait 10 m/15F** it's 10 m/15F; **je vous le fais 10F** I'll let you have it for 10F

7: **qu'a-t-il fait de sa valise?** what has he done with his case?

8: **ne ~ que**: **il ne fait que critiquer** (*sans cesse*) all he (ever) does is criticize; (*seulement*) he's only criticizing

9 (*dire*) to say; **vraiment? fit-il** really? he said

10 (*maladie*) to have; **~ du diabète** to have diabetes *sg*

♦ *vi* **1** (*agir, s'y prendre*) to act, do; **il faut ~ vite** we (*ou* you *etc*) must act quickly; **comment a-t-il fait pour?** how did he manage to?; **faites comme chez vous** make yourself at home

2 (*paraître*) to look; **~ vieux/démodé** to look old/old-fashioned; **ça fait bien** it looks good

♦ *vb substitut* to do; **ne le casse pas comme je l'ai fait** don't break it as I did; **je peux le voir? - faites!** can I see it? - please do!

♦ *vb impers* **1**: **il fait beau** *etc* the weather is fine *etc*; *voir aussi* **jour froid** *etc*

2 (*temps écoulé, durée*): **ça fait 2 ans qu'il est parti** it's 2 years since he left; **ça fait 2 ans qu'il y est** he's been there for 2 years

♦ *vb semi-aux* **1**: **~ +infinitif** (*action directe*) to make; **~ tomber/bouger qch** to make sth fall/move; **~ démarrer un moteur/chauffer de l'eau** to start up an engine/heat some water; **cela fait dormir** it makes you sleep; **~ travailler les enfants** to make the children work *ou* get the children to work

2 (*indirectement, par un intermédiaire*): **~ réparer qch** to get *ou* have sth repaired; **~ punir les enfants** to have the children punished **se ~** *vi* **1** (*vin, fromage*) to mature

2: **cela se fait beaucoup/ne se fait pas** it's done a lot/not done

3: **se ~ +nom ou pron**: **se faire une jupe** to make o.s. a skirt; **se ~ des amis** to make friends; **se ~ du souci** to worry; **il**

ne s'en fait pas he doesn't worry
4: se ~ +*adj* (*devenir*): se faire vieux to be getting old; (*délibérément*): se ~ beau to do o.s. up
5: se ~ à (*s'habituer*) to get used to; je n'arrive pas à me ~ à la nourriture/au climat I can't get used to the food/climate
6: se ~ +*infinitif*: se ~ examiner la vue/opérer to have one's eyes tested/have an operation; se ~ couper les cheveux to get one's hair cut; il va se ~ tuer/punir he's going to get himself killed/get (himself) punished; il s'est fait aider he got somebody to help him; il s'est fait aider par Simon he got Simon to help him; se ~ ~ un vêtement to get a garment made for o.s.
7 (*impersonnel*): comment se fait-il/faisait-il que? how is it/was it that?

faire-part [fɛrpar] nm inv announcement (*of birth, marriage etc*)
faisable [fəzabl(ə)] adj feasible
faisan, e [fəzã, -an] nm/f pheasant
faisandé, e [fəzãde] adj high (*bad*)
faisceau, x [fɛso] nm (*de lumière etc*) beam; (*de branches etc*) bundle
faisons vb voir faire
fait, e [fɛ, fɛt] adj (*mûr: fromage, melon*) ripe ♦ nm (*événement*) event, occurrence; (*réalité, donnée*) fact; c'en est ~ de that's the end of; être le ~ de (*causé par*) to be the work of; être au ~ (de) to be informed (of); au ~ (*à propos*) by the way; en venir au ~ to get to the point; de ~ adj (*opposé à: de droit*) de facto ♦ adv in fact; du ~ de ceci/qu'il a menti because of ou on account of this/his having lied; de ce ~ for this reason; en ~ in fact; en ~ de repas by way of a meal; prendre ~ et cause pour qn to support sb, side with sb; prendre qn sur le ~ to catch sb in the act; ~ divers news item; ~s et gestes: les ~s et gestes de qn sb's actions ou doings
faîte [fɛt] nm top; (*fig*) pinnacle, height
faites vb voir faire
faitout [fetu] nm = fait-tout
fait-tout [fetu] nm inv stewpot
falaise [falɛz] nf cliff
fallacieux, euse [falasjø, -øz] adj fallacious; deceptive; illusory
falloir [falwar] vb impers: il va ~ 100 F we'll ou (*ou*) I'll) need 100 F; s'en ~: il s'en est fallu de 100 F/5 minutes que (ou they) were 100 F short/5 minutes late (ou early); il s'en faut de beaucoup qu'il soit he is far from being; il s'en est fallu de peu que cela n'arrive it very nearly happened; ou peu s'en faut or as good as; il doit ~ du temps that must take time; il me faudrait 100 F I would need 100 F; il vous faut tourner à gauche après l'église you have

to turn left past the church; nous avons ce qu'il (nous) faut we have what we need; il faut qu'il parte/a fallu qu'il parte (*obligation*) he has to ou must leave/had to leave; il a fallu le faire it had to be done
falsifier [falsifje] vt to falsify; to doctor
famé, e [fame] adj: mal ~ disreputable, of ill repute
famélique [famelik] adj half-starved
fameux, euse [famø, -øz] adj (*illustre*) famous; (*bon: repas, plat etc*) first-rate, first-class; (*valeur intensive*) real, downright
familial, e, aux [familjal, -o] adj family cpd; familiale nf (*AUTO*) estate car (*BRIT*), station wagon (*US*)
familiarité [familjarite] nf informality; familiarity; ~s nfpl (*privautés*) familiarities
familier, ère [familje, -ɛr] adj (*connu, impertinent*) familiar; (*dénotant une certaine intimité*) informal, friendly; (*LING*) informal, colloquial ♦ nm regular (*visitor*)
famille [famij] nf family; il a de la ~ à Paris he has relatives in Paris
famine [famin] nf famine
fanatique [fanatik] adj fanatical ♦ nm/f fanatic; fanatisme nm fanaticism
faner [fane]: se ~ vi to fade
fanfare [fãfar] nf (*orchestre*) brass band; (*musique*) fanfare
fanfaron, ne [fãfarõ, -ɔn] nm/f braggart
fanion [fanjõ] nm pennant
fantaisie [fãtezi] nf (*spontanéité*) fancy, imagination; (*caprice*) whim; extravagance ♦ adj: bijou/pain (de) ~ costume jewellery/fancy bread; fantaisiste adj (*péj*) unorthodox, eccentric ♦ nm/f (*de music-hall*) variety artist ou entertainer
fantasme [fãtasm(ə)] nm fantasy
fantasque [fãtask(ə)] adj whimsical, capricious; fantastic
fantastique [fãtastik] adj fantastic
fantôme [fãtom] nm ghost, phantom
faon [fã] nm fawn
farce [fars(ə)] nf (*viande*) stuffing; (*blague*) (practical) joke; (*THÉÂTRE*) farce; farcir vt (*viande*) to stuff
fard [far] nm make-up
fardeau, x [fardo] nm burden
farder [farde] vt to make up
farfelu, e [farfəly] adj hare-brained
farine [farin] nf flour; farineux, euse adj (*sauce, pomme*) floury ♦ nmpl (*aliments*) starchy foods
farouche [faruʃ] adj shy, timid; savage; wild; fierce
fart [far(t)] nm (ski) wax
fascicule [fasikyl] nm volume
fasciner [fasine] vt to fascinate
fascisme [fasism(ə)] nm fascism
fasse etc vb voir faire
faste [fast(ə)] nm splendour ♦ adj: c'est un jour ~ it's his (ou our etc) lucky day

fastidieux, euse [fastidjø, -øz] *adj* tedious, tiresome

fastueux, euse [fastɥø, -øz] *adj* sumptuous, luxurious

fatal, e [fatal] *adj* fatal; (*inévitable*) inevitable; **fatalité** *nf* fate; fateful coincidence; inevitability

fatidique [fatidik] *adj* fateful

fatigant, e [fatigɑ̃, -ɑ̃t] *adj* tiring; (*agaçant*) tiresome

fatigue [fatig] *nf* tiredness, fatigue

fatigué, e [fatige] *adj* tired

fatiguer [fatige] *vt* to tire, make tired; (*TECH*) to put a strain on, strain; (*fig: importuner*) to wear out ♦ *vi* (*moteur*) to labour, strain; **se ~** to get tired; to tire o.s. (out)

fatras [fatʀa] *nm* jumble, hotchpotch

fatuité [fatɥite] *nf* conceitedness, smugness

faubourg [fobuʀ] *nm* suburb

fauché, e [foʃe] (*fam*) *adj* broke

faucher [foʃe] *vt* (*herbe*) to cut; (*champs, blés*) to reap; (*fig*) to cut down; to mow down

faucille [fosij] *nf* sickle

faucon [fokɔ̃] *nm* falcon, hawk

faudra *vb voir* **falloir**

faufiler [fofile] *vt* to tack, baste; **se ~** *vi*: **se ~ dans** to edge one's way into; **se ~ parmi/entre** to thread one's way among/between

faune [fon] *nf* (*ZOOL*) wildlife, fauna

faussaire [fosɛʀ] *nm* forger

fausse [fos] *adj voir* **faux**

faussement [fosmɑ̃] *adv* (*accuser*) wrongly, wrongfully; (*croire*) falsely

fausser [fose] *vt* (*objet*) to bend, buckle; (*fig*) to distort

fausseté [foste] *nf* wrongness; falseness

faut *vb voir* **falloir**

faute [fot] *nf* (*erreur*) mistake, error; (*péché, manquement*) misdemeanour; (*FOOTBALL etc*) offence; (*TENNIS*) fault; **c'est de sa/ma ~** it's his/my fault; **être en ~** to be in the wrong; **~ de** (*temps, argent*) for ou through lack of; **sans ~** without fail; **~ de frappe** typing error; **~ professionnelle** professional misconduct *no pl*

fauteuil [fotœj] *nm* armchair; **~ d'orchestre** seat in the front stalls; **~ roulant** wheelchair

fauteur [fotœʀ] *nm*: **~ de troubles** trouble-maker

fautif, ive [fotif, -iv] *adj* (*incorrect*) incorrect, inaccurate; (*responsable*) at fault, in the wrong; guilty

fauve [fov] *nm* wildcat ♦ *adj* (*couleur*) fawn

faux¹ [fo] *nf* scythe

faux², fausse [fo, fos] *adj* (*inexact*) wrong; (*piano, voix*) out of tune; (*falsifié*) fake; forged; (*sournois, postiche*) false ♦ *adv* (*MUS*) out of tune ♦ *nm* (*copie*) fake, forgery; (*opposé au vrai*): **le faux** falsehood; **faire faux bond à qn** to stand sb up; **fausse alerte** false alarm; **fausse couche** miscarriage; **faux frais** *nmpl* extras, incidental expenses; **faux pas** tripping *no pl*; (*fig*) faux pas; **faux témoignage** (*délit*) perjury; **faux-filet** *nm* sirloin; **faux-fuyant** *nm* equivocation; **faux-monnayeur** *nm* counterfeiter, forger

faveur [favœʀ] *nf* favour; **traitement de ~** preferential treatment; **à la ~ de** under cover of; thanks to; **en ~ de** in favour of

favorable [favɔʀabl(ə)] *adj* favourable

favori, te [favɔʀi, -it] *adj, nm/f* favourite; **~s** *nmpl* (*barbe*) sideboards (*BRIT*), sideburns

favoriser [favɔʀize] *vt* to favour

fax [faks] *nm* fax

fébrile [febʀil] *adj* feverish, febrile

fécond, e [fekɔ̃, -ɔ̃d] *adj* fertile; **~er** *vt* to fertilize; **~ité** *nf* fertility

fécule [fekyl] *nf* potato flour

féculent [fekylɑ̃] *nm* starchy food

fédéral, e, aux [federal, -o] *adj* federal

fée [fe] *nf* fairy; **~rie** *nf* enchantment; **~rique** *adj* magical, fairytale *cpd*

feignant, e [fɛɲɑ̃, -ɑ̃t] *nm/f* = **fainéant, e**

feindre [fɛ̃dʀ(ə)] *vt* to feign ♦ *vi* to dissemble; **~ de faire** to pretend to do

feinte [fɛ̃t] *nf* (*SPORT*) dummy

fêler [fele] *vt* to crack

félicitations [felisitasjɔ̃] *nfpl* congratulations

féliciter [felisite] *vt*: **~ qn (de)** to congratulate sb (on); **se ~ (de)** to congratulate o.s. (on)

félin, e [felɛ̃, -in] *adj* feline ♦ *nm* (big) cat

fêlure [felyʀ] *nf* crack

femelle [fəmɛl] *adj, nf* female

féminin, e [feminɛ̃, -in] *adj* feminine; (*sexe*) female; (*équipe, vêtements etc*) women's ♦ *nm* (*LING*) feminine; **féministe** *adj* feminist

femme [fam] *nf* woman; (*épouse*) wife; **~ au foyer** *nf* housewife; **~ de chambre** cleaning lady; **~ de ménage** = **femme de chambre**

fémur [femyʀ] *nm* femur, thighbone

fendre [fɑ̃dʀ(ə)] *vt* (*couper en deux*) to split; (*fissurer*) to crack; (*fig: traverser*) to cut through; to cleave through; **se ~** *vi* to crack

fenêtre [fənɛtʀ(ə)] *nf* window

fenouil [fənuj] *nm* fennel

fente [fɑ̃t] *nf* (*fissure*) crack; (*de boîte à lettres etc*) slit

féodal, e, aux [feɔdal, -o] *adj* feudal

fer [fɛʀ] *nm* iron; (*de cheval*) shoe; **~ à cheval** horseshoe; **~ (à repasser)** iron; **~ forgé** wrought iron

ferai *etc vb voir* **faire**

fer-blanc [fɛʀblɑ̃] *nm* tin(plate)

férié, e [feʀje] *adj*: **jour ~** public holiday

ferions *etc vb voir* **faire**

ferme [fɛʀm] *adj* firm ♦ *adv* (*travailler etc*) hard ♦ *nf* (*exploitation*) farm; (*maison*) farmhouse

fermé, e [fɛʀme] *adj* closed, shut; (*gaz, eau etc*) off; (*fig: personne*) uncommunicative; (: *milieu*) exclusive

fermenter [fɛʀmɑ̃te] *vi* to ferment

fermer [fɛʀme] *vt* to close, shut; (*cesser l'exploitation de*) to close down, shut down; (*eau, lumière, électricité, robinet*) to put off, turn off; (*aéroport, route*) to close ♦ *vi* to close, shut; to close down, shut down; **se ~** *vi* (*yeux*) to close, shut; (*fleur, blessure*) to close up

fermeté [fɛʀməte] *nf* firmness

fermeture [fɛʀmətyʀ] *nf* closing; shutting; closing *ou* shutting down; putting *ou* turning off; (*dispositif*) catch; fastening, fastener; **~ à glissière = fermeture éclair**; **~ éclair**® zip (fastener) (*BRIT*), zipper (*US*)

fermier [fɛʀmje] *nm* farmer; **fermière** *nf* woman farmer; farmer's wife

fermoir [fɛʀmwaʀ] *nm* clasp

féroce [feʀɔs] *adj* ferocious, fierce

ferons *vb voir* **faire**

ferraille [feʀɑj] *nf* scrap iron; **mettre à la ~** to scrap

ferré, e [feʀe] *adj* hobnailed; steel-tipped; (*fam*): **~ en** well up on, hot at; **ferrer** [feʀe] *vt* (*cheval*) to shoe

ferronnerie [feʀɔnʀi] *nf* ironwork

ferroviaire [feʀɔvjɛʀ] *adj* rail(way) *cpd* (*BRIT*), rail(road) *cpd* (*US*)

ferry(boat) [feʀe(bot)] *nm* ferry

fertile [fɛʀtil] *adj* fertile; **~ en incidents** eventful, packed with incidents

féru, e [feʀy] *adj*: **~ de** with a keen interest in

férule [feʀyl] *nf*: **être sous la ~ de qn** to be under sb's (iron) rule

fervent, e [fɛʀvɑ̃, -ɑ̃t] *adj* fervent

fesse [fɛs] *nf* buttock; **fessée** *nf* spanking

festin [fɛstɛ̃] *nm* feast

festival [fɛstival] *nm* festival

festoyer [fɛstwaje] *vi* to feast

fêtard [fɛtaʀ] *nm* (*péj*) high liver, merrymaker

fête [fɛt] *nf* (*religieuse*) feast; (*publique*) holiday; (*en famille etc*) celebration; (*kermesse*) fête, fair, festival; (*du nom*) feast day, name day; **faire la ~** to live it up; **faire ~ à qn** to give sb a warm welcome; **les ~s (de fin d'année)** the festive season; **la salle/le comité des ~s** the village hall/festival committee; **~ foraine** (fun)fair; **la F~ Nationale** the national holiday; **fêter** *vt* to celebrate; (*personne*) to have a celebration for

fétu [fety] *nm*: **~ de paille** wisp of straw

feu, x [fø] *nm* (*gén*) fire; (*signal lumineux*)

light; (*de cuisinière*) ring; (*sensation de brûlure*) burning (sensation) ♦ *adj inv*: **~ son père** his late father; **~x** *nmpl* (*éclat, lumière*) fire *sg*; (*AUTO*) (traffic) lights; **au ~!** (*incendie*) fire!; **à ~ doux/vif** over a slow/brisk heat; **à petit ~** (*CULIN*) over a gentle heat; (*fig*) slowly; **faire ~** to fire; **prendre ~** to catch fire; **mettre le ~ à** to set fire to; **faire du ~** to make a fire; **avez-vous du ~?** (*pour cigarette*) have you (got) a light?; **~ arrière** rear light; **~ d'artifice** firework; (*spectacle*) fireworks *pl*; **~ de joie** bonfire; **~ rouge/vert/orange** red/green/amber (*BRIT*) *ou* yellow (*US*) light; **~x de brouillard** fog-lamps; **~x de croisement** dipped (*BRIT*) *ou* dimmed (*US*) headlights; **~x de position** sidelights; **~x de route** headlights

feuillage [fœjaʒ] *nm* foliage, leaves *pl*

feuille [fœj] *nf* (*d'arbre*) leaf; (*de papier*) sheet; **~ d'impôts** tax form; **~ de maladie** medical expenses claim form; **~ de paie** pay slip; **~ de vigne** (*BOT*) vine leaf; (*sur statue*) fig leaf; **~ volante** loose sheet

feuillet [fœjɛ] *nm* leaf

feuilleté, e [fœjte] *adj* (*CULIN*) flaky; (*verre*) laminated

feuilleter [fœjte] *vt* (*livre*) to leaf through

feuilleton [fœjtɔ̃] *nm* serial

feuillu, e [fœjy] *adj* leafy ♦ *nm* broadleaved tree

feutre [føtʀ(ə)] *nm* felt; (*chapeau*) felt hat; (*aussi: stylo~*) felt-tip pen; **feutré, e** *adj* feltlike; (*pas, voix*) muffled

fève [fɛv] *nf* broad bean

février [fevʀije] *nm* February

fi [fi] *excl*: **faire ~ de** to snap one's fingers at

fiable [fjabl(ə)] *adj* reliable

fiacre [fjakʀ(ə)] *nm* (hackney) cab *ou* carriage

fiançailles [fjɑ̃sɑj] *nfpl* engagement *sg*

fiancé, e [fjɑ̃se] *nm/f* fiancé(fiancée) ♦ *adj*: **être ~ (à)** to be engaged (to)

fiancer [fjɑ̃se]: **se ~** *vi* to become engaged

fibre [fibʀ(ə)] *nf* fibre; **~ de verre** fibreglass, glass fibre

ficeler [fisle] *vt* to tie up

ficelle [fisɛl] *nf* string *no pl*; piece *ou* length of string

fiche [fiʃ] *nf* (*pour fichier*) (index) card; (*formulaire*) form; (*ÉLEC*) plug

ficher [fiʃe] *vt* (*dans un fichier*) to file; (*POLICE*) to put on file; (*planter*) to stick, drive; (*fam*) to do; to give; to stick *ou* shove; **se ~ de** (*fam*) to make fun of; not to care about; **fiche(-moi) le camp** (*fam*) clear off; **fiche-moi la paix** leave me alone

fichier [fiʃje] *nm* file; card index

fichu, e [fiʃy] *pp de* **ficher** (*fam*) ♦ *adj* (*fam*: *fini, inutilisable*) bust, done for; (: *intensif*) wretched, darned ♦ *nm* (*foulard*) (head)scarf; **mal** ~ (fam) feeling lousy; useless

fictif, ive [fiktif, -iv] adj fictitious

fiction [fiksjɔ̃] nf fiction; (fait imaginé) invention

fidèle [fidɛl] adj faithful ♦ nm/f (REL): **les** ~**s** the faithful pl; (à l'église) the congregation sg

fief [fjɛf] nm fief; (fig) preserve; stronghold

fier[1] [fje]: **se fier à** vt to trust

fier[2], **fière** [fjɛr] adj proud; **fierté** nf pride

fièvre [fjɛvr(ə)] nf fever; **avoir de la** ~**/39 de** ~ to have a high temperature/a temperature of 39°C; **fiévreux, euse** adj feverish

figer [fiʒe] vt to congeal; (fig: personne) to freeze, root to the spot; **se** ~ vi to congeal; to freeze; (institutions etc) to become set, stop evolving

figue [fig] nf fig; **figuier** nm fig tree

figurant, e [figyrɑ̃, -ɑ̃t] nm/f (THÉÂTRE) walk-on; (CINÉMA) extra

figure [figyr] nf (visage) face; (image, tracé, forme, personnage) figure; (illustration) picture, diagram; **faire** ~ **de** to look like

figuré, e [figyre] adj (sens) figurative

figurer [figyre] vi to appear ♦ vt to represent; **se** ~ **que** to imagine that

fil [fil] nm (brin, fig: d'une histoire) thread; (du téléphone) cable, wire; (textile de lin) linen; (d'un couteau) edge; **au** ~ **des années** with the passing of the years; **au** ~ **de l'eau** with the stream ou current; **coup de** ~ phone call; ~ **à coudre** (sewing) thread; ~ **à pêche** fishing line; ~ **à plomb** plumbline; ~ **de fer** wire; ~ **de fer barbelé** barbed wire; ~ **électrique** electric wire

filament [filamɑ̃] nm (ÉLEC) filament; (de liquide) trickle, thread

filandreux, euse [filɑ̃drø, -øz] adj stringy

filasse [filas] adj inv white blond

filature [filatyr] nf (fabrique) mill; (policière) shadowing no pl, tailing no pl

file [fil] nf line; (AUTO) lane; **en** ~ **indienne** in single file; **à la** ~ (d'affilée) in succession; ~ **(d'attente)** queue (BRIT), line (US)

filer [file] vt (tissu, toile) to spin; (prendre en filature) to shadow, tail; (fam: donner): ~ **qch à qn** to slip sb sth ♦ vi (bas, liquide, pâte) to run; (aller vite) to fly past; (fam: partir) to make off; ~ **doux** to toe the line

filet [filɛ] nm net; (CULIN) fillet; (d'eau, de sang) trickle; ~ **(à provisions)** string bag

filiale [filjal] nf (COMM) subsidiary

filière [filjɛr] nf: **passer par la** ~ to go through the (administrative) channels; **suivre la** ~ (dans sa carrière) to work one's way up (through the hierarchy)

filiforme [filifɔrm(ə)] adj spindly; threadlike

filigrane [filigran] nm (d'un billet, timbre) watermark; **en** ~ (fig) showing just beneath the surface

fille [fij] nf girl; (opposé à fils) daughter; **vieille** ~ old maid; **fillette** nf (little) girl

filleul, e [fijœl] nm/f godchild, godson/daughter

film [film] nm (pour photo) (roll of) film; (œuvre) film, picture, movie; (couche) film; ~ **d'animation** animated film; ~ **policier** thriller

filon [filɔ̃] nm vein, lode; (fig) lucrative line, money spinner

fils [fis] nm son; ~ **à papa** daddy's boy

filtre [filtr(ə)] nm filter; ~ **à air** (AUTO) air filter; **filtrer** vt to filter; (fig: candidats, visiteurs) to screen ♦ vi to filter (through)

fin[1] [fɛ̃] nf end; **fins** nfpl (but) ends; **prendre fin** to come to an end; **mettre fin à** to put an end to; **à la fin** in the end, eventually; **sans fin** adj endless ♦ adv endlessly

fin[2], **e** [fɛ̃, fin] adj (papier, couche, fil) thin; (cheveux, poudre, pointe, visage) fine; (taille) neat, slim; (esprit, remarque) subtle; shrewd ♦ adv (moudre, couper) finely; **un fin tireur** a crack shot; **avoir la vue/l'ouïe fine** to have sharp ou keen eyes/ears; **vin fin** fine wine; **fin gourmet** gourmet; **fin prêt** quite ready; **fines herbes** mixed herbs

final, e [final] adj final ♦ nm (MUS) finale; **finale** nf final; **quarts de finale** quarter finals; **8èmes/16èmes de finale** 2nd/1st round (in knock-out competition); **finalement** adv finally, in the end; (après tout) after all

finance [finɑ̃s] nf finance; ~**s** nfpl (situation) finances; (activités) finance sg; **moyennant** ~ for a fee; **financer** vt to finance; **financier, ière** adj financial

finaud, e [fino, -od] adj wily

fine [fin] nf (alcool) liqueur brandy

finesse [finɛs] nf thinness, fineness; neatness, slimness; subtlety; shrewdness

fini, e [fini] adj finished; (MATH) finite; (intensif): **un menteur** ~ a liar through and through ♦ nm (d'un objet manufacturé) finish

finir [finir] vt to finish ♦ vi to finish, end; ~ **quelque part/par faire** to end up ou finish up somewhere/doing; ~ **de faire** to finish doing; (cesser) to stop doing; **il finit par m'agacer** he's beginning to get on my nerves; ~ **en pointe/tragédie** to end in a point/in tragedy; **en** ~ **avec** to be ou have done with; **il va mal** ~ he will come to a bad end

finition [finisjɔ̃] nf finishing; finish

finlandais, e [fɛ̃lɑ̃dɛ, -ɛz] adj Finnish ♦ nm/f: **F**~, **e** Finn

Finlande [fɛ̃lɑ̃d] nf: **la** ~ Finland

fiole [fjɔl] nf phial

fioriture [fjɔrityr] nf embellishment, flourish

firme [firm(ə)] nf firm

fis vb voir **faire**

fisc [fisk] nm tax authorities pl; ~**al, e, aux** adj tax cpd, fiscal; ~**alité** nf tax system; (charges) taxation

fissure [fisyR] nf crack; ~**r** [fisyRe] vt to crack; **se ~r** vi to crack

fiston [fistɔ̃] (fam) nm son, lad

fit vb voir **faire**

fixation [fiksɑsjɔ̃] nf fixing; fastening; setting; (de ski) binding; (PSYCH) fixation

fixe [fiks(ə)] adj fixed; (emploi) steady, regular ♦ nm (salaire) basic salary; **à heure** ~ at a set time; **menu à prix** ~ set menu

fixé, e [fikse] adj: **être** ~ **(sur)** (savoir à quoi s'en tenir) to have made up one's mind (about); to know for certain (about)

fixer [fikse] vt (attacher): ~ **qch (à/sur)** to fix ou fasten sth (to/onto); (déterminer) to fix, set; (CHIMIE, PHOTO) to fix; (regarder) to stare at; **se** ~ vi (s'établir) to settle down; **se** ~ **sur** (suj: attention) to focus on

flacon [flakɔ̃] nm bottle

flageller [flaʒele] vt to flog, scourge

flageoler [flaʒɔle] vi (jambes) to sag

flageolet [flaʒɔle] nm (MUS) flageolet; (CULIN) dwarf kidney bean

flagrant, e [flagRɑ̃, -ɑ̃t] adj flagrant, blatant; **en** ~ **délit** in the act

flair [flɛR] nm sense of smell; (fig) intuition; **flairer** vt (humer) to sniff (at); (détecter) to scent

flamand, e [flamɑ̃, -ɑ̃d] adj Flemish ♦ nm (LING) Flemish ♦ nm/f: F~, e Fleming; **les F~s** the Flemish

flamant [flamɑ̃] nm flamingo

flambant [flɑ̃bɑ̃] adv: ~ **neuf** brand new

flambé, e [flɑ̃be] adj (CULIN) flambé

flambeau, x [flɑ̃bo] nm (flaming) torch

flambée [flɑ̃be] nf blaze; (fig) flaring-up, explosion

flamber [flɑ̃be] vi to blaze (up)

flamboyer [flɑ̃bwaje] vi to blaze (up); to flame

flamme [flam] nf flame; (fig) fire, fervour; **en ~s** on fire, ablaze

flan [flɑ̃] nm (CULIN) custard tart ou pie

flanc [flɑ̃] nm side; (MIL) flank; **prêter le** ~ **à** (fig) to lay o.s. open to

flancher [flɑ̃ʃe] vi to fail, pack up; to quit

flanelle [flanɛl] nf flannel

flâner [flɑne] vi to stroll; **flânerie** nf stroll

flanquer [flɑ̃ke] vt to flank; (fam: mettre) to chuck, shove; (: jeter): ~ **par terre/à la porte** to fling to the ground/chuck out

flaque [flak] nf (d'eau) puddle; (d'huile, de sang etc) pool

flash [flaʃ] (pl **flashes**) nm (PHOTO) flash; ~ **(d'information)** newsflash

flasque [flask(ə)] adj flabby

flatter [flate] vt to flatter; **se** ~ **de qch** to pride o.s. on sth; **flatterie** nf flattery no pl; **flatteur, euse** adj flattering ♦ nm/f flatterer

fléau, x [fleo] nm scourge

flèche [flɛʃ] nf arrow; (de clocher) spire; (de grue) jib; **monter en** ~ (fig) to soar, rocket; **partir en** ~ to be off like a shot; **fléchette** nf dart; **fléchettes** nfpl (jeu) darts sg

fléchir [fleʃiR] vt (corps, genou) to bend; (fig) to sway, weaken ♦ vi (poutre) to sag, bend; (fig) to weaken, flag; to yield

flemmard, e [flemaR, -aRd(ə)] nm/f lazybones sg, loafer

flétrir [fletRiR] vt to wither; **se** ~ vi to wither

fleur [flœR] nf flower; (d'un arbre) blossom; **en** ~ (arbre) in blossom; **à** ~ **de terre** just above the ground

fleurer [flœRe] vt: ~ **la lavande** to have the scent of lavender

fleuri, e [flœRi] adj in flower ou bloom; surrounded by flowers; (fig) flowery; florid

fleurir [flœRiR] vi (rose) to flower; (arbre) to blossom; (fig) to flourish ♦ vt (tombe) to put flowers on; (chambre) to decorate with flowers

fleuriste [flœRist(ə)] nm/f florist

fleuron [flœRɔ̃] nm (fig) jewel

fleuve [flœv] nm river

flexible [flɛksibl(ə)] adj flexible

flexion [flɛksjɔ̃] nf flexing, bending

flic [flik] (fam: péj) nm cop

flipper [flipœR] nm pinball (machine)

flirter [flœRte] vi to flirt

flocon [flɔkɔ̃] nm flake

floraison [flɔRezɔ̃] nf flowering; blossoming; flourishing

flore [flɔR] nf flora

florissant [flɔRisɑ̃] vb voir **fleurir**

flot [flo] nm flood, stream; ~**s** nmpl (de la mer) waves; **être à** ~ (NAVIG) to be afloat; (fig) to be on an even keel; **entrer à** ~**s** to stream ou pour in

flotte [flɔt] nf (NAVIG) fleet; (fam) water; rain

flottement [flɔtmɑ̃] nm (fig) wavering, hesitation

flotter [flɔte] vi to float; (nuage, odeur) to drift; (drapeau) to fly; (vêtements) to hang loose; (monnaie) to float ♦ vt to float; **faire** ~ to float; **flotteur** nm float

flou, e [flu] adj fuzzy, blurred; (fig) woolly, vague

flouer [flue] vt to swindle

fluctuation [flyktɥɑsjɔ̃] nf fluctuation

fluet, te [flyɛ, -ɛt] adj thin, slight

fluide [flɥid] adj fluid; (circulation etc) flowing freely ♦ nm fluid; (force) (mysterious) power

fluor [flyɔR] nm fluorine

fluorescent, e [flyɔResɑ̃, -ɑ̃t] adj fluorescent

flûte [flyt] nf flute; (verre) flute glass; (pain) long loaf; ~! drat it!; ~ **à bec** recorder

flux [fly] nm incoming tide; (écoulement) flow; **le ~ et le reflux** the ebb and flow

FM sigle f (= fréquence modulée) FM

foc [fɔk] nm jib

foi [fwa] nf faith; **sous la ~ du serment** under ou on oath; **ajouter ~ à** to lend credence to; **digne de ~** reliable; **sur la ~ de** on the word ou strength of; **être de bonne/mauvaise ~** to be sincere/insincere; **ma ~ ...** well ...

foie [fwa] nm liver

foin [fwɛ̃] nm hay; **faire du ~** (fig: fam) to kick up a row

foire [fwaʀ] nf fair; (fête foraine) (fun) fair; **faire la ~** (fig: fam) to whoop it up; **~ (exposition)** trade fair

fois [fwa] nf time; **une/deux ~** once/twice; **2 ~ 2** 2 times 2; **quatre ~ plus grand (que)** four times as big (as); **une ~** (passé) once; (futur) sometime; **une ~ pour toutes** once and for all; **une ~ que** once; **des ~** (parfois) sometimes; **à la ~** (ensemble) at once

foison [fwazɔ̃] nf: **une ~ de** an abundance of; **à ~** in plenty

foisonner [fwazɔne] vi to abound

fol [fɔl] adj voir **fou**

folâtrer [fɔlɑtʀe] vi to frolic (about)

folie [fɔli] nf (d'une décision, d'un acte) madness, folly; (état) madness, insanity; (acte) folly; **la ~ des grandeurs** delusions of grandeur; **faire des ~s** (en dépenses) to be extravagant

folklorique [fɔlklɔʀik] adj folk cpd; (fam) weird

folle [fɔl] adj, nf voir **fou**; **follement** adv (très) madly, wildly

foncé, e [fɔ̃se] adj dark

foncer [fɔ̃se] vi to go darker; (fam: aller vite) to tear ou belt along; **~ sur** to charge at

foncier, ère [fɔ̃sje, -ɛʀ] adj (honnêteté etc) basic, fundamental; (malhonnêteté) deep-rooted; (COMM) real estate cpd

fonction [fɔ̃ksjɔ̃] nf (rôle, MATH, LING) function; (emploi, poste) post, position; **~s** nfpl (professionnelles) duties; **entrer en ~s** to take up one's post ou duties; to take up office; **voiture de ~** company car; **être ~ de** (dépendre de) to depend on; **en ~ de** (par rapport à) according to; **faire ~ de** to serve as; **la ~ publique** the state ou civil (BRIT) service; **fonctionnaire** [fɔ̃ksjɔnɛʀ] nm/f state employee, local authority employee; (dans l'administration) ≈ civil servant; **fonctionner** [fɔ̃ksjɔne] vi to work, function; (entreprise) to operate, function

fond [fɔ̃] nm (d'un récipient, trou) bottom; (d'une salle, scène) back; (d'un tableau, décor) background; (opposé à la forme) content; (SPORT): **le ~** long distance (running); **sans ~** bottomless; **au ~ de** at the

bottom of; at the back of; **à ~** (connaître, soutenir) thoroughly; (appuyer, visser) right down ou home; **à ~ (de train)** (fam) full tilt; **dans le ~, au ~** (en somme) basically, really; **de ~ en comble** from top to bottom; voir aussi **fonds**; **~ de teint** (make-up) foundation; **~ sonore** background noise; background music

fondamental, e, aux [fɔ̃damɑ̃tal, -o] adj fundamental

fondant, e [fɔ̃dɑ̃, -ɑ̃t] adj (neige) melting; (fruit) that melts in the mouth

fondateur, trice [fɔ̃datœʀ, -tʀis] nm/f founder

fondation [fɔ̃dasjɔ̃] nf founding; (établissement) foundation; **~s** nfpl (d'une maison) foundations

fondé, e [fɔ̃de] adj (accusation etc) well-founded ♦ nm: **~ de pouvoir** authorized representative; **être ~ à** to have grounds for ou good reason to

fondement [fɔ̃dmɑ̃] nm (derrière) behind; **~s** nmpl (base) foundations; **sans ~** (rumeur etc) groundless, unfounded

fonder [fɔ̃de] vt to found; (fig) to base; **se ~ sur** (suj: personne) to base o.s. on

fonderie [fɔ̃dʀi] nf smelting works sg

fondre [fɔ̃dʀ(ə)] vt (aussi: **faire ~**) to melt; (dans l'eau) to dissolve; (fig: mélanger) to merge, blend ♦ vi to melt; to dissolve; (fig) to melt away; (se précipiter): **~ sur** to swoop down on; **~ en larmes** to burst into tears

fonds [fɔ̃] nm (de bibliothèque) collection; (COMM): **~ (de commerce)** business ♦ nmpl (argent) funds; **à ~ perdus** with little or no hope of getting the money back

fondu, e [fɔ̃dy] adj (beurre, neige) melted; (métal) molten; **fondue** f (CULIN) fondue

font vb voir **faire**

fontaine [fɔ̃tɛn] nf fountain; (source) spring

fonte [fɔ̃t] nf melting; (métal) cast iron; **la ~ des neiges** the (spring) thaw

foot [fut] (fam) nm football

football [futbol] nm football, soccer; **footballeur** nm footballer

footing [futiŋ] nm jogging; **faire du ~** to go jogging

for [fɔʀ] nm: **dans son ~ intérieur** in one's heart of hearts

forain, e [fɔʀɛ̃, -ɛn] adj fairground cpd ♦ nm stallholder; fairground entertainer

forçat [fɔʀsa] nm convict

force [fɔʀs(ə)] nf strength; (puissance: surnaturelle etc) power; (PHYSIQUE, MÉCANIQUE) force; **~s** nfpl (physiques) strength sg; (MIL) forces; **à ~ d'insister** by dint of insisting; as he (ou l etc) kept on insisting; **de ~** forcibly, by force; **être de ~ à faire** to be up to doing; **de première ~** first class; **les ~s de l'ordre** the police

forcé, e [fɔʀse] adj forced; unintended; inevitable

forcément [fɔʀsemɑ̃] *adv* necessarily; inevitably; (*bien sûr*) of course

forcené, e [fɔʀsəne] *nm/f* maniac

forcer [fɔʀse] *vt* (*porte, serrure, plante*) to force; (*moteur, voix*) to strain ♦ *vi* (SPORT) to overtax o.s.; ~ **la dose** to overdo it; ~ **l'allure** to increase the pace; **se ~ (pour faire)** to force o.s. (to do)

forcir [fɔʀsiʀ] *vi* (*grossir*) to broaden out; (*vent*) to freshen

forer [fɔʀe] *vt* to drill, bore

forestier, ère [fɔʀɛstje, -ɛʀ] *adj* forest *cpd*

forêt [fɔʀɛ] *nf* forest

forfait [fɔʀfɛ] *nm* (COMM) fixed *ou* set price; all-in deal *ou* price; (*crime*) infamy; **déclarer** ~ to withdraw; **travailler à** ~ to work for a lump sum; **~aire** *adj* inclusive; set

forge [fɔʀʒ(ə)] *nf* forge, smithy

forger [fɔʀʒe] *vt* to forge; (*fig: personnalité*) to form; (: *prétexte*) to contrive, make up

forgeron [fɔʀʒəʀɔ̃] *nm* (black)smith

formaliser [fɔʀmalize]: **se ~** *vi*: **se ~ (de)** to take offence (at)

formalité [fɔʀmalite] *nf* (ADMIN, JUR) formality; (*acte sans importance*): **simple ~** mere formality

format [fɔʀma] *nm* size

formater [fɔʀmate] *vt* (*disque*) to format

formation [fɔʀmɑsjɔ̃] *nf* forming; training; (MUS) group; (MIL, AVIAT, GÉO) formation; ~ **permanente** continuing education; ~ **professionnelle** vocational training

forme [fɔʀm(ə)] *nf* (*gén*) form; (*d'un objet*) shape, form; ~**s** *nfpl* (*bonnes manières*) proprieties; (*d'une femme*) figure *sg*; **en ~ de poire** pear-shaped; **être en ~** (SPORT *etc*) to be on form; **en bonne et due** ~ in due form

formel, le [fɔʀmɛl] *adj* (*preuve, décision*) definite, positive; (*logique*) formal; **formellement** *adv* (*absolument*) positively

former [fɔʀme] *vt* to form; (*éduquer*) to train; **se ~** *vi* to form

formidable [fɔʀmidabl(ə)] *adj* tremendous

formulaire [fɔʀmylɛʀ] *nm* form

formule [fɔʀmyl] *nf* (*gén*) formula; (*formulaire*) form; ~ **de politesse** polite phrase; letter ending

formuler [fɔʀmyle] *vt* (*émettre: réponse, vœux*) to formulate; (*expliciter: sa pensée*) to express

fort, e [fɔʀ, fɔʀt(ə)] *adj* strong; (*intensité, rendement*) high, great; (*corpulent*) stout; (*doué*) good, able ♦ *adv* (*serrer, frapper*) hard; (*sonner*) loud(ly); (*beaucoup*) greatly, very much; (*très*) very ♦ *nm* (*édifice*) fort; (*point fort*) strong point, forte; **se faire** ~ **de** ... to claim one can ...; **au plus** ~ **de** (*au milieu de*) in the thick of; at the height of; ~**e tête** rebel

fortifiant [fɔʀtifjɑ̃] *nm* tonic

fortifier [fɔʀtifje] *vt* to strengthen, fortify; (MIL) to fortify

fortiori [fɔʀtjɔʀi] : **à** ~ *adv* all the more so

fortuit, e [fɔʀtɥi, -it] *adj* fortuitous, chance *cpd*

fortune [fɔʀtyn] *nf* fortune; **faire** ~ to make one's fortune; **de** ~ makeshift; chance *cpd*

fortuné, e [fɔʀtyne] *adj* wealthy

fosse [fos] *nf* (*grand trou*) pit; (*tombe*) grave; ~ **(d'orchestre)** (orchestra) pit

fossé [fose] *nm* ditch; (*fig*) gulf, gap

fossette [fosɛt] *nf* dimple

fossile [fosil] *nm* fossil

fossoyeur [foswajœʀ] *nm* gravedigger

fou(fol), folle [fu, fɔl] *adj* mad; (*déréglé etc*) wild, erratic; (*fam: extrême, très grand*) terrific, tremendous ♦ *nm/f* madman(woman) ♦ *nm* (*du roi*) jester; **être fou de** to be mad *ou* crazy about; **avoir le fou rire** to have the giggles; **faire le fou** to act the fool

foudre [fudʀ(ə)] *nf*: **la** ~ lightning

foudroyant, e [fudʀwajɑ̃, -ɑ̃t] *adj* lightning *cpd*, stunning; (*maladie, poison*) violent

foudroyer [fudʀwaje] *vt* to strike down; **être foudroyé** to be struck by lightning; ~ **qn du regard** to glare at sb

fouet [fwɛ] *nm* whip; (CULIN) whisk; **de plein** ~ (*se heurter*) head on; **fouetter** *vt* to whip; to whisk

fougère [fuʒɛʀ] *nf* fern

fougue [fug] *nf* ardour, spirit

fouille [fuj] *nf* search; ~**s** *nfpl* (*archéologiques*) excavations

fouiller [fuje] *vt* to search; (*creuser*) to dig ♦ *vi* to rummage

fouillis [fuji] *nm* jumble, muddle

fouiner [fwine] (*péj*) *vi*: ~ **dans** to nose around *ou* about in

foulard [fulaʀ] *nm* scarf

foule [ful] *nf* crowd; **les** ~**s** the masses; **la** ~ crowds *pl*; **une** ~ **de** masses of

foulée [fule] *nf* stride

fouler [fule] *vt* to press; (*sol*) to tread upon; **se** ~ *vi* (*fam*) to overexert o.s.; **se** ~ **la cheville** to sprain one's ankle; ~ **aux pieds** to trample underfoot; **foulure** [fulyʀ] *nf* sprain

four [fuʀ] *nm* oven; (*de potier*) kiln; (THÉÂTRE: *échec*) flop

fourbe [fuʀb(ə)] *adj* deceitful

fourbu, e [fuʀby] *adj* exhausted

fourche [fuʀʃ(ə)] *nf* pitchfork; (*de bicyclette*) fork

fourchette [fuʀʃɛt] *nf* fork; (STATISTIQUE) bracket, margin

fourgon [fuʀgɔ̃] *nm* van; (RAIL) wag(g)on

fourmi [fuʀmi] *nf* ant; ~**s** *nfpl* (*fig*) pins and needles; **fourmilière** *nf* ant-hill

fourmiller [fuʀmije] *vi* to swarm

fournaise [furnɛz] *nf* blaze; *(fig)* furnace, oven

fourneau, x [furno] *nm* stove

fournée [furne] *nf* batch

fourni, e [furni] *adj (barbe, cheveux)* thick; *(magasin)*: **bien ~ (en)** well stocked (with)

fournir [furnir] *vt* to supply; *(preuve, exemple)* to provide, supply; *(effort)* to put in; **fournisseur, euse** *nm/f* supplier

fourniture [furnityr] *nf* supply(ing); **~s** *nfpl (provisions)* supplies

fourrage [furaʒ] *nm* fodder

fourrager¹, ère [furaʒe, -ɛr] *adj* fodder *cpd*

fourrager² *vi*: **fourrager dans/parmi** *(fouiller)* to rummage through /among

fourré, e [fure] *adj (bonbon etc)* filled; *(manteau etc)* fur-lined ♦ *nm* thicket

fourreau, x [furo] *nm* sheath

fourrer [fure] *(fam) vt* to stick, shove; **se ~ dans/sous** to get into/under

fourre-tout [furtu] *nm inv (sac)* holdall; *(péj)* junk room *(ou* cupboard); *(fig)* rag-bag

fourrière [furjɛr] *nf* pound

fourrure [furyr] *nf* fur; *(sur l'animal)* coat

fourvoyer [furvwaje]: **se ~** *vi* to go astray, stray

foutre [futr(ə)] *(fam!) vt* = **ficher; foutu, e** *(fam!) adj* = **fichu, e**

foyer [fwaje] *nm (de cheminée)* hearth; *(famille)* family; *(maison)* home; *(de jeunes etc)* (social) club; hostel; *(salon)* foyer; *(OPTIQUE, PHOTO)* focus *sg*; **lunettes à double ~** bi-focal glasses

fracas [fraka] *nm* din; crash; roar

fracasser [frakase] *vt* to smash

fraction [fraksjɔ̃] *nf* fraction; **fractionner** *vt* to divide (up), split (up)

fracture [fraktyr] *nf* fracture; **~ du crâne** fractured skull; **~r** [fraktyre] *vt (coffre, serrure)* to break open; *(os, membre)* to fracture

fragile [fraʒil] *adj* fragile, delicate; *(fig)* frail; **fragilité** *nf* fragility

fragment [fragmɑ̃] *nm (d'un objet)* fragment, piece; *(d'un texte)* passage, extract

fraîche [frɛʃ] *adj voir* **frais; fraîcheur** *nf* coolness; freshness; **fraîchir** *vi* to get cooler; *(vent)* to freshen

frais, fraîche [frɛ, frɛʃ] *adj* fresh; *(froid)* cool ♦ *adv (récemment)* newly, fresh(ly) ♦ *nm*: **mettre au ~** to put in a cool place ♦ *nmpl (débours)* expenses; *(COMM)* costs; *(factures)* charges; **il fait ~** it's cool; **servir ~** serve chilled; **prendre le ~** to take a breath of cool air; **faire des ~** to spend; to go to a lot of expense; **faire les ~ de** to bear the brunt of; **~ de scolarité** school fees *(BRIT)*, tuition *(US)*; **~ généraux** overheads

fraise [frɛz] *nf* strawberry; *(TECH)* countersink (bit); *(de dentiste)* drill; **~ des bois** wild strawberry

framboise [frɑ̃bwaz] *nf* raspberry

franc, franche [frɑ̃, frɑ̃ʃ] *adj (personne)* frank, straightforward; *(visage)* open; *(net: refus, couleur)* clear; *(: coupure)* clean; *(intensif)* downright; *(exempt)*: **~ de port** postage paid ♦ *adv*: **parler ~** to be frank ♦ *ou candid ♦ nm* franc

français, e [frɑ̃sɛ, -ɛz] *adj* French ♦ *nm/f*: **F~, e** Frenchman(woman) ♦ *nm (LING)* French; **les F~** the French

France [frɑ̃s] *nf*: **la ~** France

franche [frɑ̃ʃ] *adj voir* **franc; franchement** *adv* frankly; clearly; *(tout à fait)* down-right

franchir [frɑ̃ʃir] *vt (obstacle)* to clear, get over; *(seuil, ligne, rivière)* to cross; *(distance)* to cover

franchise [frɑ̃ʃiz] *nf* frankness; *(douanière, d'impôt)* exemption; *(ASSURANCES)* excess

franciser [frɑ̃size] *vt* to gallicize, Frenchify

franc-maçon [frɑ̃masɔ̃] *nm* freemason

franco [frɑ̃ko] *adv (COMM)*: **~ (de port)** postage paid

francophone [frɑ̃kɔfɔn] *adj* French-speaking; **francophonie** *nf* French-speaking communities

franc-parler [frɑ̃parle] *nm inv* outspokenness

franc-tireur [frɑ̃tirœr] *nm (MIL)* irregular; *(fig)* freelance

frange [frɑ̃ʒ] *nf* fringe

frangipane [frɑ̃ʒipan] *nf* almond paste

franquette [frɑ̃kɛt]: **à la bonne ~** *adv* without any fuss

frappe [frap] *nf (de pianiste, machine à écrire)* touch; *(BOXE)* punch

frappé, e [frape] *adj* iced

frapper [frape] *vt* to hit, strike; *(étonner)* to strike; *(monnaie)* to strike, stamp; **se ~** *vi* *(s'inquiéter)* to get worked up; **~ dans ses mains** to clap one's hands; **~ du poing sur** to bang one's fist on; **frappé de stupeur** dumbfounded

frasques [frask(ə)] *nfpl* escapades

fraternel, le [fratɛrnɛl] *adj* brotherly, fraternal

fraternité [fratɛrnite] *nf* brotherhood

fraude [frod] *nf* fraud; *(SCOL)* cheating; **passer qch en ~** to smuggle sth in *(ou* out); **~ fiscale** tax evasion; **frauder** *vi, vt* to cheat; **frauduleux, euse** *adj* fraudulent

frayer [freje] *vt* to open up, clear ♦ *vi* to spawn; *(fréquenter)*: **~ avec** to mix with

frayeur [frejœr] *nf* fright

fredonner [frədɔne] *vt* to hum

freezer [frizœr] *nm* freezing compartment

frein [frɛ̃] *nm* brake; **~ à main** handbrake; **~s à disques/tambour** disc/drum brakes

freiner [frene] *vi* to brake ♦ *vt (progrès etc)* to check

frelaté, e [frəlate] *adj* adulterated; *(fig)*

tainted

frêle [fʀɛl] *adj* frail, fragile

frelon [fʀɔlɔ̃] *nm* hornet

frémir [fʀemiʀ] *vi* to tremble, shudder; to shiver; to quiver

frêne [fʀɛn] *nm* ash

frénétique [fʀenetik] *adj* frenzied, frenetic

fréquemment [fʀekamɑ̃] *adv* frequently

fréquent, e [fʀekɑ̃, -ɑ̃t] *adj* frequent

fréquentation [fʀekɑ̃tɑsjɔ̃] *nf* frequenting; seeing; ~**s** *nfpl* (*relations*) company *sg*

fréquenté, e [fʀekɑ̃te] *adj*: **très ~** (very) busy; **mal ~** patronized by disreputable elements

fréquenter [fʀekɑ̃te] *vt* (*lieu*) to frequent; (*personne*) to see; **se ~** to see each other

frère [fʀɛʀ] *nm* brother

fresque [fʀɛsk(ə)] *nf* (*ART*) fresco

fret [fʀɛ] *nm* freight

frétiller [fʀetije] *vi* to wriggle; to quiver; (*chien*) to wag its tail

fretin [fʀɔtɛ̃] *nm*: **menu ~** small fry

friable [fʀijabl(ə)] *adj* crumbly

friand, e [fʀijɑ̃, -ɑ̃d] *adj*: ~ **de** very fond of

friandise [fʀijɑ̃diz] *nf* sweet

fric [fʀik] (*fam*) *nm* cash, bread

friche [fʀiʃ] : **en ~** *adj, adv* (lying) fallow

friction [fʀiksjɔ̃] *nf* (*massage*) rub, rub-down; (*TECH, fig*) friction; **frictionner** *vt* to rub (down); to massage

frigidaire [fʀiʒidɛʀ] ® *nm* refrigerator

frigide [fʀiʒid] *adj* frigid

frigo [fʀigo] *nm* fridge

frigorifier [fʀigɔʀifje] *vt* to refrigerate; **frigorifique** *adj* refrigerating

frileux, euse [fʀilø, -øz] *adj* sensitive to (the) cold

frimer [fʀime] *vi* to put on an act

frimousse [fʀimus] *nf* (sweet) little face

fringale [fʀɛ̃gal] *nf*: **avoir la ~** to be ravenous

fringant, e [fʀɛ̃gɑ̃, -ɑ̃t] *adj* dashing

fringues [fʀɛ̃g] (*fam*) *nfpl* clothes

fripé, e [fʀipe] *adj* crumpled

fripon, ne [fʀipɔ̃, -ɔn] *adj* roguish, mischievous ♦ *nm/f* rascal, rogue

fripouille [fʀipuj] *nf* scoundrel

frire [fʀiʀ] *vt, vi*: **faire ~** to fry

frisé, e [fʀize] *adj* curly; curly-haired

frisson [fʀisɔ̃] *nm* shudder, shiver; quiver; **frissonner** *vi* to shudder, shiver; to quiver

frit, e [fʀi, fʀit] *pp de* **frire**; **frite** *nf*: (pommes) **frites** chips (*BRIT*), French fries; **friteuse** *nf* chip pan; **friture** *nf* (*huile*) (deep) fat; (*plat*): **friture (de poissons)** fried fish; (*RADIO*) crackle

frivole [fʀivɔl] *adj* frivolous

froid, e [fʀwa, fʀwad] *adj, nm* cold; **il fait ~** it's cold; **avoir/prendre ~** to be/catch cold; **être en ~ avec** to be on bad terms with; ~**ement** *adv* (*accueillir*) coldly; (*décider*) coolly

froisser [fʀwase] *vt* to crumple (up), crease; (*fig*) to hurt, offend; **se ~** *vi* to crumple, crease; to take offence; **se ~ un muscle** to strain a muscle

frôler [fʀole] *vt* to brush against; (*suj: projectile*) to skim past; (*fig*) to come very close to

fromage [fʀɔmaʒ] *nm* cheese; ~ **blanc** soft white cheese; **fromager, ère** *nm/f* cheese merchant

froment [fʀɔmɑ̃] *nm* wheat

froncer [fʀɔ̃se] *vt* to gather; ~ **les sourcils** to frown

frondaisons [fʀɔ̃dɛzɔ̃] *nfpl* foliage *sg*

fronde [fʀɔ̃d] *nf* sling; (*fig*) rebellion, rebelliousness

front [fʀɔ̃] *nm* forehead, brow; (*MIL*) front; **de ~** (*se heurter*) head-on; (*rouler*) together (*i.e.* 2 *or* 3 *abreast*); (*simultanément*) at once; **faire ~ à** to face up to; ~ **de mer** (sea) front

frontalier, ère [fʀɔ̃talje, -ɛʀ] *adj* border *cpd*, frontier *cpd* ♦ *nm/f*: (**travailleurs**) ~**s** commuters from across the border

frontière [fʀɔ̃tjɛʀ] *nf* frontier, border; (*fig*) frontier, boundary

fronton [fʀɔ̃tɔ̃] *nm* pediment

frotter [fʀote] *vi* to rub, scrape ♦ *vt* to rub; (*pour nettoyer*) to rub (up); to scrub; ~ **une allumette** to strike a match

fructifier [fʀyktifje] *vi* to yield a profit; **faire ~** to turn to good account

fructueux, euse [fʀyktɥø, -øz] *adj* fruitful; profitable

fruit [fʀɥi] *nm* fruit *gen no pl*; ~**s de mer** seafood(s); ~**s secs** dried fruit *sg*; ~**é, e** *adj* fruity; ~**ier, ère** *adj*: **arbre** ~**ier** fruit tree ♦ *nm/f* fruiterer (*BRIT*), fruit merchant (*US*)

fruste [fʀyst(ə)] *adj* unpolished, uncultivated

frustrer [fʀystʀe] *vt* to frustrate

fuel(-oil) [fjul(ɔjl)] *nm* fuel oil; heating oil

fugace [fygas] *adj* fleeting

fugitif, ive [fyʒitif, -iv] *adj* (*lueur, amour*) fleeting; (*prisonnier etc*) fugitive, runaway ♦ *nm/f* fugitive

fugue [fyg] *nf*: **faire une ~** to run away, abscond

fuir [fɥiʀ] *vt* to flee from; (*éviter*) to shun ♦ *vi* to run away; (*gaz, robinet*) to leak

fuite [fɥit] *nf* flight; (*écoulement, divulgation*) leak; **être en ~** to be on the run; **mettre en ~** to put to flight

fulgurant, e [fylgyʀɑ̃, -ɑ̃t] *adj* lightning *cpd*, dazzling

fulminer [fylmine] *vi* to thunder forth

fumé, e [fyme] *adj* (*CULIN*) smoked; (*verre*) tinted

fume-cigarette [fymsigaʀɛt] *nm inv* cigarette holder

fumée [fyme] *nf* smoke

fumer [fyme] *vi* to smoke; *(soupe)* to steam ♦ *vt* to smoke; *(terre, champ)* to manure
fûmes *etc vb voir* **être**
fumet [fymɛ] *nm* aroma
fumeur, euse [fymœʀ, -øz] *nm/f* smoker
fumeux, euse [fymø, -øz] *(péj) adj* woolly, hazy
fumier [fymje] *nm* manure
fumiste [fymist(ə)] *nm/f (péj: paresseux)* shirker; *(charlatan)* phoney
fumisterie [fymistəʀi] *(péj) nf* fraud, con
funambule [fynãbyl] *nm* tightrope walker
funèbre [fynɛbʀ(ə)] *adj* funeral *cpd*; *(fig)* doleful; funereal
funérailles [fyneʀɑj] *nfpl* funeral *sg*
funeste [fynɛst(ə)] *adj* disastrous; deathly
fur [fyʀ] : **au ~ et à mesure** *adv* as one goes along; **au ~ et à mesure que** as
furet [fyʀɛ] *nm* ferret
fureter [fyʀte] *(péj) vi* to nose about
fureur [fyʀœʀ] *nf* fury; *(passion):* **~ de** passion for; **faire ~** to be all the rage
furibond, e [fyʀibɔ̃, -ɔ̃d] *adj* furious
furie [fyʀi] *nf* fury; *(femme)* shrew, vixen; **en ~** *(mer)* raging; **furieux, euse** *adj* furious
furoncle [fyʀɔ̃kl(ə)] *nm* boil
furtif, ive [fyʀtif, -iv] *adj* furtive
fus *vb voir* **être**
fusain [fyzɛ̃] *nm (ART)* charcoal
fuseau, x [fyzo] *nm (pour filer)* spindle; *(pantalon)* (ski) pants; **~ horaire** time zone
fusée [fyze] *nf* rocket; **~ éclairante** flare
fuselé, e [fyzle] *adj* slender; tapering
fuser [fyze] *vi (rires etc)* to burst forth
fusible [fyzibl(ə)] *nm (ÉLEC: fil)* fuse wire; *(: fiche)* fuse
fusil [fyzi] *nm (de guerre, à canon rayé)* rifle, gun; *(de chasse, à canon lisse)* shotgun, gun; **fusillade** *nf* gunfire *no pl*, shooting *no pl*; shooting battle; **fusiller** *vt* to shoot; **fusil-mitrailleur** *nm* machine gun
fusionner [fyzjɔne] *vi* to merge
fustiger [fystiʒe] *vt* to denounce
fut *vb voir* **être**
fût [fy] *vb voir* **être** ♦ *nm (tonneau)* barrel, cask
futaie [fytɛ] *nf* forest, plantation
futé, e [fyte] *adj* crafty
futile [fytil] *adj* futile; frivolous
futur, e [fytyʀ] *adj, nm* future
fuyant, e [fɥijã, -ãt] *vb voir* **fuir** ♦ *adj (regard etc)* evasive; *(lignes etc)* receding; *(perspective)* vanishing
fuyard, e [fɥijaʀ, -aʀd(ə)] *nm/f* runaway

G g

gabarit [gabaʀi] *nm (fig)* size; calibre
gâcher [gɑʃe] *vt (gâter)* to spoil, ruin; *(gaspiller)* to waste
gâchette [gɑʃɛt] *nf* trigger
gâchis [gɑʃi] *nm* waste *no pl*
gadoue [gadu] *nf* sludge
gaffe [gaf] *nf (instrument)* boat hook; *(erreur)* blunder; **faire ~** *(fam)* to be careful
gage [gaʒ] *nm (dans un jeu)* forfeit; *(fig: de fidélité)* token; **~s** *nmpl (salaire)* wages; *(garantie)* guarantee *sg*; **mettre en ~** to pawn
gager [gaʒe] *vt* to bet, wager
gageure [gaʒyʀ] *nf*: **c'est une ~** it's attempting the impossible
gagnant, e [gaɲã, -ãt] *nm/f* winner
gagne-pain [gaɲpɛ̃] *nm inv* job
gagner [gaɲe] *vt* to win; *(somme d'argent, revenu)* to earn; *(aller vers, atteindre)* to reach; *(envahir)* to overcome; to spread to ♦ *vi* to win; *(fig)* to gain; **~ du temps/de la place** to gain time/save space; **~ sa vie** to earn one's living
gai, e [ge] *adj* gay, cheerful; *(un peu ivre)* merry
gaieté [gete] *nf* cheerfulness; **de ~ de cœur** with a light heart
gaillard, e [gajaʀ, -aʀd(ə)] *adj (grivois)* bawdy, ribald ♦ *nm (strapping)* fellow
gain [gɛ̃] *nm (revenu)* earnings *pl*; *(bénéfice: gén pl)* profits *pl*; *(au jeu)* winnings *pl*; *(fig: de temps, place)* saving; **avoir ~ de cause** to win the case; *(fig)* to be proved right
gaine [gɛn] *nf (corset)* girdle; *(fourreau)* sheath
galant, e [galã, -ãt] *adj (courtois)* courteous, gentlemanly; *(entreprenant)* flirtatious, gallant; *(aventure, poésie)* amorous
galère [galɛʀ] *nf* galley
galérer [galeʀe] *(fam) vi* to slog away, work hard
galerie [galʀi] *nf* gallery; *(THÉÂTRE)* circle; *(de voiture)* roof rack; *(fig: spectateurs)* audience; **~ de peinture** *(private)* art gallery; **~ marchande** shopping arcade
galet [galɛ] *nm* pebble; *(TECH)* wheel
galette [galɛt] *nf* flat cake
Galles [gal] *nfpl*: **le pays de ~** Wales
gallois, e [galwa, -waz] *adj* Welsh ♦ *nm (LING)* Welsh ♦ *nm/f*: **G~, e** Welsh-

man(woman)

galon [galɔ̃] nm (MIL) stripe; (décoratif) piece of braid

galop [galo] nm gallop

galoper [galɔpe] vi to gallop

galopin [galɔpɛ̃] nm urchin, ragamuffin

galvauder [galvode] vt to debase

gambader [gɑ̃bade] vi (animal, enfant) to leap about

gamelle [gamɛl] nf mess tin; billy can

gamin, e [gamɛ̃, -in] nm/f kid ♦ adj mischievous, playful

gamme [gam] nf (MUS) scale; (fig) range

gammé, e [game] adj: **croix** ~**e** swastika

gant [gɑ̃] nm glove; ~ **de toilette** face flannel (BRIT), face cloth

garage [gaʀaʒ] nm garage; **garagiste** nm/f garage owner; garage mechanic

garant, e [gaʀɑ̃, -ɑ̃t] nm/f guarantor ♦ nm guarantee; **se porter** ~ **de** to vouch for; to be answerable for

garantie [gaʀɑ̃ti] nf guarantee; (gage) security, surety; **(bon de)** ~ guarantee ou warranty slip

garantir [gaʀɑ̃tiʀ] vt to guarantee; (protéger): ~ **de** to protect from

garçon [gaʀsɔ̃] nm boy; (célibataire) bachelor; (serveur): ~ **(de café)** waiter; ~ **de courses** messenger; **garçonnet** nm small boy; **garçonnière** nf bachelor flat

garde [gaʀd(ə)] nm (de prisonnier) guard; (de domaine etc) warden; (soldat, sentinelle) guardsman ♦ nf guarding; looking after; (soldats, BOXE, ESCRIME) guard; (faction) watch; (TYPO): **(page de)** ~ endpaper; flyleaf; **de** ~ on duty; **monter la** ~ to stand guard; **mettre en** ~ to warn; **prendre** ~ **(à)** to be careful (of); ~ **champêtre** nm rural policeman; ~ **du corps** nm bodyguard; ~ **des enfants** (après divorce) custody of the children; ~ **des Sceaux** nm ≈ Lord Chancellor (BRIT), ≈ Attorney General (US); ~ **à vue** nf (JUR) ≈ police custody; ~**-à-vous** nm: **être/se mettre au** ~**-à-vous** to be at/stand to attention; ~**-barrière** nm/f level-crossing keeper; ~**-boue** nm inv mudguard; ~**-chasse** nm gamekeeper; ~**-fou** nm railing, parapet; ~**-malade** nf home nurse; ~**-manger** nm inv meat safe; pantry, larder

garder [gaʀde] vt (conserver) to keep; (surveiller: enfants) to look after; (: immeuble, lieu, prisonnier) to guard; **se** ~ vi (aliment: se conserver) to keep; **se** ~ **de faire** to be careful not to do; ~ **le lit/la chambre** to stay in bed/indoors; **pêche/chasse gardée** private fishing/hunting (ground)

garderie [gaʀdəʀi] nf day nursery, crèche

garde-robe [gaʀdəʀɔb] nf wardrobe

gardien, ne [gaʀdjɛ̃, -jɛn] nm/f (garde) guard; (de prison) warder; (de domaine, réserve) warden; (de musée etc) attendant;

(de phare, cimetière) keeper; (d'immeuble) caretaker; (fig) guardian; ~ **de but** goalkeeper; ~ **de la paix** policeman; ~ **de nuit** night watchman

gare [gaʀ] nf (railway) station, train station (US) ♦ excl watch out!; ~ **routière** bus station

garer [gaʀe] vt to park; **se** ~ vi to park; (pour laisser passer) to draw into the side

gargariser [gaʀgaʀize]: **se** ~ vi to gargle; **gargarisme** nm gargling no pl; gargle

gargote [gaʀgɔt] nf cheap restaurant

gargouille [gaʀguj] nf gargoyle

gargouiller [gaʀguje] vi to gurgle

garnement [gaʀnəmɑ̃] nm rascal, scallywag

garni, e [gaʀni] adj (plat) served with vegetables (and chips or rice etc) ♦ nm furnished accommodation no pl

garnir [gaʀniʀ] vt (orner) to decorate; to trim; (approvisionner) to fill, stock; (protéger) to fit

garnison [gaʀnizɔ̃] nf garrison

garniture [gaʀnityʀ] nf (CULIN) vegetables pl; filling; (décoration) trimming; (protection) fittings pl; ~ **de frein** brake lining

garrot [gaʀo] nm (MÉD) tourniquet

gars [gɑ] nm lad; guy

Gascogne [gaskɔɲ] nf Gascony; **le golfe de** ~ the Bay of Biscay

gas-oil [gazɔjl] nm diesel (oil)

gaspiller [gaspije] vt to waste

gastronomique [gastʀɔnɔmik] adj gastronomic

gâteau, x [gɑto] nm cake; ~ **sec** biscuit

gâter [gɑte] vt to spoil; **se** ~ vi (dent, fruit) to go bad; (temps, situation) to change for the worse

gâterie [gɑtʀi] nf little treat

gâteux, euse [gɑtø, -øz] adj senile

gauche [goʃ] adj left, left-hand; (maladroit) awkward, clumsy ♦ nf (POL) left (wing); **à** ~ on the left; (direction) (to the) left; **gaucher, ère** adj left-handed; **gauchiste** nm/f leftist

gaufre [gofʀ(ə)] nf waffle

gaufrette [gofʀɛt] nf wafer

gaulois, e [golwa, -waz] adj Gallic; (grivois) bawdy ♦ nm/f: **G**~, **e** Gaul

gausser [gose]: **se** ~ **de** vt to deride

gaver [gave] vt to force-feed; (fig): ~ **de** to cram with, fill up with

gaz [gaz] nm inv gas

gaze [gɑz] nf gauze

gazéifié, e [gazeifje] adj aerated

gazette [gazɛt] nf news sheet

gazeux, euse [gazø, -øz] adj gaseous; (boisson) fizzy; (eau) sparkling

gazoduc [gazɔdyk] nm gas pipeline

gazon [gazɔ̃] nm (herbe) turf; grass; (pelouse) lawn

gazouiller [gazuje] vi to chirp; (enfant) to

babble

geai [ʒɛ] *nm* jay

géant, e [ʒeɑ̃, -ɑ̃t] *adj* gigantic, giant; (*COMM*) giant-size ♦ *nm/f* giant

geindre [ʒɛ̃dʀ(ə)] *vi* to groan, moan

gel [ʒɛl] *nm* frost; freezing

gélatine [ʒelatin] *nf* gelatine

gelée [ʒɔle] *nf* jelly; (*gel*) frost

geler [ʒɔle] *vt, vi* to freeze; **il gèle** it's freezing

gélule [ʒelyl] *nf* (*MÉD*) capsule

gelures [ʒɔlyʀ] *nfpl* frostbite *sg*

Gémeaux [ʒemo] *nmpl*: **les** ~ Gemini

gémir [ʒemiʀ] *vi* to groan, moan

gemme [ʒɛm] *nf* gem(stone)

gênant, e [ʒɛnɑ̃, -ɑ̃t] *adj* annoying; embarrassing

gencive [ʒɑ̃siv] *nf* gum

gendarme [ʒɑ̃daʀm(ə)] *nm* gendarme; ~**rie** *nf* military police force in countryside and small towns; their police station or barracks

gendre [ʒɑ̃dʀ(ə)] *nm* son-in-law

gène [ʒɛn] *nf* (*à respirer, bouger*) discomfort, difficulty; (*dérangement*) bother, trouble; (*manque d'argent*) financial difficulties *pl ou* straits *pl*; (*confusion*) embarrassment

gêné, e [ʒene] *adj* embarrassed

gêner [ʒene] *vt* (*incommoder*) to bother; (*encombrer*) to hamper; to be in the way; (*embarrasser*): ~ **qn** to make sb feel ill-at-ease; **se** ~ *vi* to put o.s. out

général, e, aux [ʒeneʀal, -o] *adj, nm* general; **en** ~ usually, in general; ~**e** *nf*: (*répétition*) ~**e** final dress rehearsal; ~**ement** *adv* generally

généraliser [ʒeneʀalize] *vt, vi* to generalize; **se** ~ *vi* to become widespread

généraliste [ʒeneʀalist(ə)] *nm/f* general practitioner, G.P.

générateur, trice [ʒeneʀatœʀ, -tʀis] *adj*: ~ **de** which causes

génération [ʒeneʀasjɔ̃] *nf* generation

généreux, euse [ʒeneʀø, -øz] *adj* generous

générique [ʒeneʀik] *nm* (*CINÉMA*) credits *pl*, credit titles *pl*

générosité [ʒeneʀozite] *nf* generosity

genêt [ʒɔnɛ] *nm* broom *no pl* (*shrub*)

génétique [ʒenetik] *adj* genetic

Genève [ʒɔnɛv] *n* Geneva

génial, e, aux [ʒenjal, -o] *adj* of genius; (*fam: formidable*) fantastic, brilliant

génie [ʒeni] *nm* genius; (*MIL*): **le** ~ the Engineers *pl*; ~ **civil** civil engineering

genièvre [ʒɔnjɛvʀ(ə)] *nm* juniper

génisse [ʒenis] *nf* heifer

genou, x [ʒnu] *nm* knee; **à** ~**x** on one's knees; **se mettre à** ~**x** to kneel down

genre [ʒɑ̃ʀ] *nm* kind, type, sort; (*allure*) manner; (*LING*) gender

gens [ʒɑ̃] *nmpl* (*f in some phrases*) people *pl*

gentil, le [ʒɑ̃ti, -ij] *adj* kind; (*enfant: sage*) good; (*endroit etc*) nice; **gentillesse** *nf* kindness; **gentiment** *adv* kindly

géographie [ʒeɔgʀafi] *nf* geography

geôlier [ʒolje] *nm* jailer

géologie [ʒeɔlɔʒi] *nf* geology

géomètre [ʒeɔmɛtʀ(ə)] *nm*: (**arpenteur-**)~ (land) surveyor

géométrie [ʒeɔmetʀi] *nf* geometry; **géométrique** *adj* geometric

gérance [ʒeʀɑ̃s] *nf* management; **mettre en** ~ to appoint a manager for

géranium [ʒeʀanjɔm] *nm* geranium

gérant, e [ʒeʀɑ̃, -ɑ̃t] *nm/f* manager(eress)

gerbe [ʒɛʀb(ə)] *nf* (*de fleurs*) spray; (*de blé*) sheaf; (*fig*) shower, burst

gercé, e [ʒɛʀse] *adj* chapped

gerçure [ʒɛʀsyʀ] *nf* crack

gérer [ʒeʀe] *vt* to manage

germain, e [ʒɛʀmɛ̃, -ɛn] *adj*: **cousin** ~ first cousin

germe [ʒɛʀm(ə)] *nm* germ; ~**r** [ʒɛʀme] *vi* to sprout; to germinate

geste [ʒɛst(ə)] *nm* gesture; move; motion

gestion [ʒɛstjɔ̃] *nf* management

gibecière [ʒibsjɛʀ] *nf* gamebag

gibet [ʒibɛ] *nm* gallows *pl*

gibier [ʒibje] *nm* (*animaux*) game; (*fig*) prey

giboulée [ʒibule] *nf* sudden shower

gicler [ʒikle] *vi* to spurt, squirt

gifle [ʒifl(ə)] *nf* slap (in the face); **gifler** *vt* to slap (in the face)

gigantesque [ʒigɑ̃tɛsk(ə)] *adj* gigantic

gigogne [ʒigɔɲ] *adj*: **lits** ~**s** truckle (*BRIT*) *ou* trundle beds

gigot [ʒigo] *nm* leg (of mutton *ou* lamb)

gigoter [ʒigɔte] *vi* to wriggle (about)

gilet [ʒilɛ] *nm* waistcoat; (*pull*) cardigan; (*de corps*) vest; ~ **de sauvetage** life jacket

gingembre [ʒɛ̃ʒɑ̃bʀ(ə)] *nm* ginger

girafe [ʒiʀaf] *nf* giraffe

giratoire [ʒiʀatwaʀ] *adj*: **sens** ~ roundabout

girofle [ʒiʀɔfl(ə)] *nf*: **clou de** ~ clove

girouette [ʒiʀwɛt] *nf* weather vane *ou* cock

gisait *etc vb voir* **gésir**

gisement [ʒizmɑ̃] *nm* deposit

gît *vb voir* **gésir**

gitan, e [ʒitɑ̃, -an] *nm/f* gipsy

gîte [ʒit] *nm* home; shelter; ~ (**rural**) holiday cottage *ou* apartment

givre [ʒivʀ(ə)] *nm* (hoar) frost

glabre [glabʀ(ə)] *adj* hairless; clean-shaven

glace [glas] *nf* ice; (*crème glacée*) ice cream; (*verre*) sheet of glass; (*miroir*) mirror; (*de voiture*) window

glacé, e [glase] *adj* icy; (*boisson*) iced

glacer [glase] *vt* to freeze; (*boisson*) to chill, ice; (*gâteau*) to ice; (*papier, tissu*) to glaze; (*fig*): ~ **qn** to chill sb; to make sb's blood run cold

glacial, e [glasjal] *adj* icy
glacier [glasje] *nm* (*GÉO*) glacier; (*marchand*) ice-cream maker
glacière [glasjɛʀ] *nf* icebox
glaçon [glasɔ̃] *nm* icicle; (*pour boisson*) ice cube
glaise [glɛz] *nf* clay
gland [glɑ̃] *nm* acorn; (*décoration*) tassel
glande [glɑ̃d] *nf* gland
glaner [glane] *vt, vi* to glean
glapir [glapiʀ] *vi* to yelp
glas [glɑ] *nm* knell, toll
glauque [glok] *adj* dull blue-green
glissant, e [glisɑ̃, -ɑ̃t] *adj* slippery
glissement [glismɑ̃] *nm*: ~ **de terrain** landslide
glisser [glise] *vi* (*avancer*) to glide *ou* slide along; (*coulisser, tomber*) to slide; (*déraper*) to slip; (*être glissant*) to be slippery ♦ *vt* to slip; **se ~ dans** to slip into
global, e, aux [glɔbal, -o] *adj* overall
globe [glɔb] *nm* globe
globule [glɔbyl] *nm* (*du sang*) corpuscle
globuleux, euse [glɔbylø, -øz] *adj*: **yeux ~** protruding eyes
gloire [glwaʀ] *nf* glory; (*mérite*) distinction, credit; (*personne*) celebrity; **glorieux, euse** *adj* glorious
glousser [gluse] *vi* to cluck; (*rire*) to chuckle
glouton, ne [glutɔ̃, -ɔn] *adj* gluttonous
gluant, e [glyɑ̃, -ɑ̃t] *adj* sticky, gummy
glycine [glisin] *nf* wisteria
go [go] : **tout de ~** *adv* straight out
G.O. *sigle* = **grandes ondes**
gobelet [gɔblɛ] *nm* tumbler; beaker; (*à dés*) cup
gober [gɔbe] *vt* to swallow
godasse [gɔdas] (*fam*) *nf* shoe
godet [gɔdɛ] *nm* pot
goéland [gɔelɑ̃] *nm* (sea)gull
goélette [gɔelɛt] *nf* schooner
goémon [gɔemɔ̃] *nm* wrack
gogo [gɔgo] : **à ~** *adv* galore
goguenard, e [gɔgnaʀ, -aʀd(ə)] *adj* mocking
goinfre [gwɛ̃fʀ(ə)] *nm* glutton
golf [gɔlf] *nm* golf; golf course
golfe [gɔlf(ə)] *nm* gulf; bay
gomme [gɔm] *nf* (*à effacer*) rubber (*BRIT*), eraser; **gommer** *vt* to rub out (*BRIT*), erase
gond [gɔ̃] *nm* hinge; **sortir de ses ~s** (*fig*) to fly off the handle
gondoler [gɔ̃dɔle] : **se ~** *vi* to warp; to buckle
gonflé, e [gɔ̃fle] *adj* swollen; bloated
gonfler [gɔ̃fle] *vt* (*pneu, ballon*) to inflate, blow up; (*nombre, importance*) to inflate ♦ *vi* to swell (up); (*CULIN: pâte*) to rise
gonzesse [gɔ̃zɛs] (*fam*) *nf* chick, bird (*BRIT*)
goret [gɔʀɛ] *nm* piglet

gorge [gɔʀʒ(ə)] *nf* (*ANAT*) throat; (*poitrine*) breast
gorgé, e [gɔʀʒe] *adj*: ~ **de** filled with; (*eau*) saturated with; **gorgée** *nf* mouthful; sip; gulp
gorille [gɔʀij] *nm* gorilla; (*fam*) bodyguard
gosier [gozje] *nm* throat
gosse [gɔs] *nm/f* kid
goudron [gudʀɔ̃] *nm* tar; **goudronner** *vt* to tar(mac) (*BRIT*), asphalt (*US*)
gouffre [gufʀ(ə)] *nm* abyss, gulf
goujat [guʒa] *nm* boor
goulot [gulo] *nm* neck; **boire au ~** to drink from the bottle
goulu, e [guly] *adj* greedy
gourd, e [guʀ, guʀd(ə)] *adj* numb (with cold)
gourde [guʀd(ə)] *nf* (*récipient*) flask; (*fam*) (clumsy) clot *ou* oaf ♦ *adj* oafish
gourdin [guʀdɛ̃] *nm* club, bludgeon
gourmand, e [guʀmɑ̃, -ɑ̃d] *adj* greedy; **gourmandise** *nf* greed; (*bonbon*) sweet
gousse [gus] *nf*: ~ **d'ail** clove of garlic
goût [gu] *nm* taste; **de bon ~** tasteful; **de mauvais ~** tasteless; **prendre ~ à** to develop a taste *ou* a liking for
goûter [gute] *vt* (*essayer*) to taste; (*apprécier*) to enjoy ♦ *vi* to have (afternoon) tea ♦ *nm* (afternoon) tea
goutte [gut] *nf* drop; (*MÉD*) gout; (*alcool*) brandy
goutte-à-goutte [gutagut] *nm* (*MÉD*) drip; **tomber ~** to drip
gouttière [gutjɛʀ] *nf* gutter
gouvernail [guvɛʀnaj] *nm* rudder; (*barre*) helm, tiller
gouvernante [guvɛʀnɑ̃t] *nf* governess
gouverne [guvɛʀn(ə)] *nf*: **pour sa ~** for his guidance
gouvernement [guvɛʀnəmɑ̃] *nm* government; **gouvernemental, e, aux** *adj* government *cpd*; pro-government
gouverner [guvɛʀne] *vt* to govern
grabuge [gʀabyʒ] *nm* mayhem
grâce [gʀɑs] *nf* grace; favour; (*JUR*) pardon; **~s** *nfpl* (*REL*) grace *sg*; **faire ~ à qn de qch** to spare sb sth; **rendre ~(s) à** to give thanks to; **demander ~** to beg for mercy; **~ à** thanks to; **gracier** *vt* to pardon; **gracieux, euse** *adj* graceful
grade [gʀad] *nm* rank; **monter en ~** to be promoted
gradé [gʀade] *nm* officer
gradin [gʀadɛ̃] *nm* tier; step; **~s** *nmpl* (*de stade*) terracing *sg*
graduel, le [gʀadɥɛl] *adj* gradual; progressive
graduer [gʀadɥe] *vt* (*effort etc*) to increase gradually; (*règle, verre*) to graduate
grain [gʀɛ̃] *nm* (*gén*) grain; (*NAVIG*) squall; ~ **de beauté** beauty spot; ~ **de café** coffee bean; ~ **de poivre** peppercorn; ~ **de pous-**

sière speck of dust; **~ de raisin** grape

graine [gʀɛn] *nf* seed

graissage [gʀɛsaʒ] *nm* lubrication, greasing

graisse [gʀɛs] *nf* fat; *(lubrifiant)* grease; **graisser** *vt* to lubricate, grease; *(tacher)* to make greasy

grammaire [gʀamɛʀ] *nf* grammar; **grammatical, e, aux** *adj* grammatical

gramme [gʀam] *nm* gramme

grand, e [gʀɑ̃, gʀɑ̃d] *adj (haut)* tall; *(gros, vaste, large)* big, large; *(long)* long; *(sens abstraits)* great ♦ *adv*: **~ ouvert** wide open; **au ~ air** in the open (air); **les ~s blessés** the severely injured; **~ ensemble** housing scheme; **~ magasin** department store; **~e personne** grown-up; **~e surface** hypermarket; **~es écoles** *prestige schools of university level*; **~es lignes** *(RAIL)* main lines; **~es vacances** summer holidays; **grand-chose** *nm/f inv*: **pas grand-chose** not much; **Grande-Bretagne** *nf* (Great) Britain; **grandeur** *nf (dimension)* size; magnitude; *(fig)* greatness; **~eur nature** life-size; **grandir** *vi* to grow ♦ *vt*: **grandir qn** *(suj: vêtement, chaussure)* to make sb look taller; **~-mère** *nf* grandmother; **~-messe** *nf* high mass; **~-peine** *adv*: **à ~-peine** with difficulty; **~-père** *nm* grandfather; **~-route** *nf* main road; **~-parents** *nmpl* grandparents

grange [gʀɑ̃ʒ] *nf* barn

granit(e) [gʀanit] *nm* granite

graphique [gʀafik] *adj* graphic ♦ *nm* graph

grappe [gʀap] *nf* cluster; **~ de raisin** bunch of grapes

grappiller [gʀapije] *vt* to glean

grappin [gʀapɛ̃] *nm* grapnel; **mettre le ~ sur** *(fig)* to get one's claws on

gras, se [gʀɑ, gʀɑs] *adj (viande, soupe)* fatty; *(personne)* fat; *(surface, main)* greasy; *(plaisanterie)* coarse; *(TYPO)* bold ♦ *nm (CULIN)* fat; **faire la ~se matinée** to have a lie-in *(BRIT)*, sleep late *(US)*; **grassement** *adv*: **grassement payé** handsomely paid; **grassouillet, te** *adj* podgy, plump

gratifiant, e [gʀatifjɑ̃, -ɑ̃t] *adj* gratifying, rewarding

gratifier [gʀatifje] *vt*: **~ qn de** to favour sb with; to reward sb with

gratiné, e [gʀatine] *adj (CULIN)* au gratin

gratis [gʀatis] *adv* free

gratitude [gʀatityd] *nf* gratitude

gratte-ciel [gʀatsjɛl] *nm inv* skyscraper

gratte-papier [gʀatpapje] *(péj) nm inv* pen-pusher

gratter [gʀate] *vt (frotter)* to scrape; *(enlever)* to scrape off; *(bras, bouton)* to scratch

gratuit, e [gʀatɥi, -ɥit] *adj (entrée, billet)* free; *(fig)* gratuitous

gravats [gʀava] *nmpl* rubble *sg*

grave [gʀav] *adj (maladie, accident)* serious, bad; *(sujet, problème)* serious, grave; *(air)*

grave, solemn; *(voix, son)* deep, low-pitched; **gravement** *adv* seriously; gravely

graver [gʀave] *vt* to engrave

gravier [gʀavje] *nm* gravel *no pl*; **gravillons** *nmpl* loose gravel *sg*

gravir [gʀaviʀ] *vt* to climb (up)

gravité [gʀavite] *nf* seriousness; gravity

graviter [gʀavite] *vi* to revolve

gravure [gʀavyʀ] *nf* engraving; *(reproduction)* print; plate

gré [gʀe] *nm*: **à son ~** to his liking; as he pleases; **au ~ de** according to, following; **contre le ~ de qn** against sb's will; **de son (plein) ~** of one's own free will; **bon ~ mal ~** like it or not; **de ~ ou de force** whether one likes it or not; **savoir ~ à qn de qch** to be grateful to sb for sth

grec, grecque [gʀɛk] *adj* Greek; *(classique: vase etc)* Grecian ♦ *nm/f* Greek

Grèce [gʀɛs] *nf*: **la ~** Greece

gréement [gʀemɑ̃] *nm* rigging

greffer [gʀefe] *vt (BOT, MÉD: tissu)* to graft; *(MÉD: organe)* to transplant

greffier [gʀefje] *nm* clerk of the court

grêle [gʀɛl] *adj (very)* thin ♦ *nf* hail

grêlé, e [gʀele] *adj* pockmarked

grêler [gʀele] *vb impers*: **il grêle** it's hailing; **grêlon** [gʀelɔ̃] *nm* hailstone

grelot [gʀəlo] *nm* little bell

grelotter [gʀəlɔte] *vi* to shiver

grenade [gʀənad] *nf (explosive)* grenade; *(BOT)* pomegranate

grenat [gʀəna] *adj inv* dark red

grenier [gʀənje] *nm* attic; *(de ferme)* loft

grenouille [gʀənuj] *nf* frog

grès [gʀɛ] *nm* sandstone; *(poterie)* stoneware

grésiller [gʀezije] *vi* to sizzle; *(RADIO)* to crackle

grève [gʀɛv] *nf (d'ouvriers)* strike; *(plage)* shore; **se mettre en/faire ~** to go on/be on strike; **~ de la faim** hunger strike; **~ du zèle** work-to-rule *(BRIT)*, slowdown *(US)*

grever [gʀəve] *vt* to put a strain on

gréviste [gʀevist(ə)] *nm/f* striker

gribouiller [gʀibuje] *vt* to scribble, scrawl

grief [gʀijɛf] *nm* grievance; **faire ~ à qn de** to reproach sb for

grièvement [gʀijɛvmɑ̃] *adv* seriously

griffe [gʀif] *nf* claw; *(fig)* signature

griffer [gʀife] *vt* to scratch

griffonner [gʀifɔne] *vt* to scribble

grignoter [gʀiɲɔte] *vt* to nibble *ou* gnaw at

gril [gʀil] *nm* steak *ou* grill pan

grillade [gʀijad] *nf* grill

grillage [gʀijaʒ] *nm (treillis)* wire netting; wire fencing

grille [gʀij] *nf (clôture)* railings *pl*; *(portail)* (metal) gate; *(d'égout)* (metal) grate; *(fig)* grid

grille-pain [gʀijpɛ̃] *nm inv* toaster

griller [gʀije] vt (aussi: faire ~: pain) to toast; (: viande) to grill; (fig: ampoule etc) to burn out, blow

grillon [gʀijɔ̃] nm cricket

grimace [gʀimas] nf grimace; (pour faire rire): faire des ~s to pull ou make faces

grimer [gʀime] vt to make up

grimper [gʀɛ̃pe] vi, vt to climb

grincer [gʀɛ̃se] vi (porte, roue) to grate; (plancher) to creak; ~ des dents to grind one's teeth

grincheux, euse [gʀɛ̃ʃø, -øz] adj grumpy

grippe [gʀip] nf flu, influenza; **grippé, e** adj: **etre grippé** to have flu

gris, e [gʀi, gʀiz] adj grey; (ivre) tipsy; **faire ~e mine** to pull a miserable ou wry face

grisaille [gʀizaj] nf greyness, dullness

griser [gʀize] vt to intoxicate

grisonner [gʀizɔne] vi to be going grey

grisou [gʀizu] nm firedamp

grive [gʀiv] nf thrush

grivois, e [gʀivwa, -waz] adj saucy

Groenland [gʀɔɛnlɑ̃d] nm Greenland

grogner [gʀɔɲe] vi to growl; (fig) to grumble

groin [gʀwɛ̃] nm snout

grommeler [gʀɔmle] vi to mutter to o.s.

gronder [gʀɔ̃de] vi to rumble; (fig: révolte) to be brewing ♦ vt to scold

gros, se [gʀo, gʀos] adj big, large; (obèse) fat; (travaux, dégâts) extensive; (large: trait, fil) thick, heavy ♦ adv: **risquer/gagner ~** to risk/win a lot ♦ nm (COMM): **le ~** the wholesale business; **prix de ~** wholesale price; **par ~ temps/grosse mer** in rough weather/heavy seas; **le ~ de** the main body of; the bulk of; **en ~** roughly; (COMM) wholesale; **~ lot** jackpot; **~ mot** coarse word; **~ œuvre** nm (CONSTR) shell (of building); **~ plan** (PHOTO) close-up; **~ sel** cooking salt; **~se caisse** big drum

groseille [gʀozɛj] nf: **~ (rouge)/(blanche)** red/white currant; **~ à maquereau** gooseberry

grosse [gʀos] adj voir **gros**

grossesse [gʀosɛs] nf pregnancy

grosseur [gʀosœʀ] nf size; fatness; (tumeur) lump

grossier, ière [gʀosje, -ɛʀ] adj coarse; (travail) rough, crude; (évident: erreur) gross

grossir [gʀosiʀ] vi (personne) to put on weight; (fig) to grow, get bigger; (rivière) to swell ♦ vt to increase; to exaggerate; (au microscope) to magnify; (suj: vêtement): **~ qn** to make sb look fatter

grossiste [gʀosist(ə)] nm/f wholesaler

grosso modo [gʀosomodo] adv roughly

grotte [gʀɔt] nf cave

grouiller [gʀuje] vi to mill about; to swarm about; **~ de** to be swarming with

groupe [gʀup] nm group; **le ~ des 7** Group of 7; **~ sanguin** nm blood group; **~ment** [gʀupmɑ̃] nm grouping; group

grouper [gʀupe] vt to group; **se ~** vi to get together

grue [gʀy] nf crane

grumeaux [gʀymo] nmpl lumps

gué [ge] nm ford; **passer à ~** to ford

guenilles [gənij] nfpl rags

guenon [gənɔ̃] nf female monkey

guépard [gepaʀ] nm cheetah

guêpe [gɛp] nf wasp

guêpier [gepje] nm (fig) trap

guère [gɛʀ] adv (avec adjectif, adverbe): **ne ... ~** hardly; (avec verbe): **ne ... ~ tournure négative** +much; hardly ever; tournure négative +(very) long; **il n'y a ~ que/de** there's hardly anybody (ou anything) but/ hardly any

guéridon [geʀidɔ̃] nm pedestal table

guérilla [geʀija] nf guerrilla warfare

guérir [geʀiʀ] vt (personne, maladie) to cure; (membre, plaie) to heal ♦ vi to recover, be cured; to heal; **guérison** nf curing; healing; recovery

guérite [geʀit] nf sentry box

guerre [gɛʀ] nf war; (méthode): **~ atomique** atomic warfare no pl; **en ~** at war; **faire la ~ à** to wage war against; **de ~ lasse** finally; **~ d'usure** war of attrition; **guerrier, ière** adj warlike ♦ nm/f warrior

guet [gɛ] nm: **faire le ~** to be on the watch ou look-out

guet-apens [gɛtapɑ̃] nm ambush

guetter [gete] vt (épier) to watch (intently); (attendre) to watch (out) for; to be lying in wait for

gueule [gœl] nf mouth; (fam) face; mouth; **ta ~!** (fam) shut up!; **~ de bois** (fam) hangover

gueuler [gœle] (fam) vi to bawl

gui [gi] nm mistletoe

guichet [giʃɛ] nm (de bureau, banque) counter, window; (d'une porte) wicket, hatch; **les ~s** (à la gare, au théâtre) the ticket office sg

guide [gid] nm guide

guider [gide] vt to guide

guidon [gidɔ̃] nm handlebars pl

guignol [giɲɔl] nm ≈ Punch and Judy show; (fig) clown

guillemets [gijmɛ] nmpl: **entre ~** in inverted commas

guillotiner [gijɔtine] vt to guillotine

guindé, e [gɛ̃de] adj stiff, starchy

guirlande [giʀlɑ̃d] nf garland; (de papier) paper chain

guise [giz] nf: **à votre ~** as you wish ou please; **en ~ de** by way of

guitare [gitaʀ] nf guitar

gymnase [ʒimnɑz] nm gym(nasium)

gymnastique [ʒimnastik] nf gymnastics sg; (au réveil etc) keep-fit exercises pl

gynécologie [ʒinekɔlɔʒi] nf gynaecology; **gynécologue** nm/f gynaecologist

H h

habile [abil] *adj* skilful; *(malin)* clever; **habileté** *nf* skill, skilfulness; cleverness

habilité, e [abilite] *adj*: ~ **à faire** entitled to do, empowered to do

habillé, e [abije] *adj* dressed; *(chic)* dressy; *(TECH)*: ~ **de** covered with; encased in

habillement [abijmɑ̃] *nm* clothes *pl*

habiller [abije] *vt* to dress; *(fournir en vêtements)* to clothe; **s'~** *vi* to dress (o.s.); *(se déguiser, mettre des vêtements chic)* to dress up

habit [abi] *nm* outfit; ~**s** *nmpl (vêtements)* clothes; ~ **(de soirée)** tails *pl*; evening dress

habitant, e [abitɑ̃, -ɑ̃t] *nm/f* inhabitant; *(d'une maison)* occupant

habitation [abitɑsjɔ̃] *nf* living; residence, home; house; ~**s à loyer modéré** low-rent housing *sg*

habiter [abite] *vt* to live in; *(suj: sentiment)* to dwell in ♦ *vi*: ~ **à/dans** to live in *ou* at/in

habitude [abityd] *nf* habit; **avoir l'~ de faire** to be in the habit of doing; *(expérience)* to be used to doing; **d'~** usually; **comme d'~** as usual

habitué, e [abitɥe] *nm/f* regular visitor; regular (customer)

habituel, le [abitɥɛl] *adj* usual

habituer [abitɥe] *vt*: ~ **qn à** to get sb used to; **s'~ à** to get used to

hache [aʃ] *nf* axe

hacher [aʃe] *vt (viande)* to mince; *(persil)* to chop

hachis [aʃi] *nm* mince *no pl*

hachoir [aʃwaʀ] *nm* chopper; (meat) mincer; chopping board

hagard, e [agaʀ, -aʀd(ə)] *adj* wild, distraught

haie [ɛ] *nf* hedge; *(SPORT)* hurdle; *(fig: rang)* line, row

haillons [ajɔ̃] *nmpl* rags

haine [ɛn] *nf* hatred

haïr [aiʀ] *vt* to detest, hate

hâlé, e [ɑle] *adj* (sun)tanned, sunburnt

haleine [alɛn] *nf* breath; **hors d'~** out of breath; **tenir en ~** to hold spellbound; to keep in suspense; **de longue ~** long-term

haler [ale] *vt* to haul in; to tow

haleter [alte] *vt* to pant

hall [ol] *nm* hall

halle [al] *nf* (covered) market; ~**s** *nfpl (d'une grande ville)* central food market *sg*

hallucinant, e [alysinɑ̃, -ɑ̃t] *adj* staggering

hallucination [alysinɑsjɔ̃] *nf* hallucination

halte [alt(ə)] *nf* stop, break; stopping place; *(RAIL)* halt ♦ *excl* stop!; **faire ~** to stop

haltère [altɛʀ] *nm* dumbbell, barbell; ~**s** *nmpl*: **(poids et) ~s** *(activité)* weight lifting *sg*

hamac [amak] *nm* hammock

hameau, x [amo] *nm* hamlet

hameçon [amsɔ̃] *nm* (fish) hook

hanche [ɑ̃ʃ] *nf* hip

handicapé, e [ɑ̃dikape] *nm/f* physically *(ou* mentally) handicapped person; ~ **moteur** spastic

hangar [ɑ̃gaʀ] *nm* shed; *(AVIAT)* hangar

hanneton [antɔ̃] *nm* cockchafer

hanter [ɑ̃te] *vt* to haunt

hantise [ɑ̃tiz] *nf* obsessive fear

happer [ape] *vt* to snatch; *(suj: train etc)* to hit

haras [aʀɑ] *nm* stud farm

harassant, e [aʀasɑ̃, -ɑ̃t] *adj* exhausting

harceler [aʀsəle] *vt (MIL, CHASSE)* to harass, harry; *(importuner)* to plague

hardi, e [aʀdi] *adj* bold, daring

hareng [aʀɑ̃] *nm* herring

hargne [aʀɲ(ə)] *nf* aggressiveness

haricot [aʀiko] *nm* bean; **haricot blanc** haricot bean; **haricot vert** green bean

harmonica [aʀmɔnika] *nm* mouth organ

harmonie [aʀmɔni] *nf* harmony

harnacher [aʀnaʃe] *vt* to harness

harnais [aʀnɛ] *nm* harness

harpe [aʀp(ə)] *nf* harp

harponner [aʀpɔne] *vt* to harpoon; *(fam)* to collar

hasard [azaʀ] *nm*: **le ~** chance, fate; **un ~** a coincidence; a stroke of luck; **au ~** aimlessly; at random; haphazardly; **par ~** by chance; **à tout ~** just in case; on the off chance *(BRIT)*; **hasarder** [azaʀde] *vt (mot)* to venture; *(fortune)* to risk

hâte [ɑt] *nf* haste; **à la ~** hurriedly, hastily; **en ~** posthaste, with all possible speed; **avoir ~ de** to be eager *ou* anxious to; ~**r** *vt* to hasten; **se ~r** *vi* to hurry

hâtif, ive [ɑtif, -iv] *adj* hurried; hasty; *(légume)* early

hausse [os] *nf* rise, increase

hausser [ose] *vt* to raise; ~ **les épaules** to shrug (one's shoulders)

haut, e [o, ot] *adj* high; *(grand)* tall; *(son, voix)* high(-pitched) ♦ *adv* high ♦ *nm* top (part); **de 3 m de ~** 3 m high, 3 m in height; **des ~s et des bas** ups and downs; **en ~ lieu** in high places; **à ~e voix, (tout) ~** aloud, out loud; **du ~ de** from the top of; **de ~ en bas** from top to bottom;

downwards; **plus ~** higher up, further up; (*dans un texte*) above; (*parler*) louder; **en ~** up above; at (*ou* to) the top; (*dans une maison*) upstairs; **en ~ de** at the top of

'hautain, e ['otɛ̃, -ɛn] *adj* haughty

'hautbois ['obwa] *nm* oboe

'haut-de-forme ['odfɔʀm(ə)] *nm* top hat

'hauteur ['otœʀ] *nf* height; (*fig*) loftiness; haughtiness; **à la ~ de** (*sur la même ligne*) level with; by; (*fig*) equal to; **à la ~ up to** it

'haut-fond ['ofɔ̃] *nm* shallow, shoal

'haut-fourneau ['ofuʀno] *nm* blast *ou* smelting furnace

'haut-le-cœur ['olkœʀ] *nm inv* retch, heave

'haut-parleur ['opaʀlœʀ] *nm* (loud) speaker

'havre ['avʀ(ə)] *nm* haven

'Haye ['ɛ] *n*: **la Haye** the Hague

hebdo [ɛbdo] (*fam*) *nm* weekly

hebdomadaire [ɛbdɔmadɛʀ] *adj, nm* weekly

héberger [ebɛʀʒe] *vt* to accommodate, lodge; (*réfugiés*) to take in

hébété, e [ebete] *adj* dazed

hébreu, x [ebʀø] *adj m, nm* Hebrew

hécatombe [ekatɔ̃b] *nf* slaughter

hectare [ɛktaʀ] *nm* hectare

'hein ['ɛ̃] *excl* eh?

'hélas ['elas] *excl* alas! ♦ *adv* unfortunately

'héler ['ele] *vt* to hail

hélice [elis] *nf* propeller

hélicoptère [elikɔptɛʀ] *nm* helicopter

helvétique [elvetik] *adj* Swiss

hémicycle [emisikl(ə)] *nm* semicircle; (*POL*): **l'~** ≈ the benches (of the Commons) (*BRIT*), ≈ the floor (of the House of Representatives) (*US*)

hémorragie [emɔʀaʒi] *nf* bleeding *no pl*, haemorrhage

hémorroïdes [emɔʀɔid] *nfpl* piles, haemorrhoids

'hennir ['enir] *vi* to neigh, whinny

herbe [ɛʀb(ə)] *nf* grass; (*CULIN, MÉD*) herb; **en ~** unripe; (*fig*) budding; **herbicide** *nm* weed-killer; **herboriste** *nm/f* herbalist

'hère ['ɛʀ] *nm*: **pauvre hère** poor wretch

héréditaire [eʀeditɛʀ] *adj* hereditary

'hérisser ['eʀise] *vt*: **~ qn** (*fig*) to ruffle sb; **se ~** *vi* to bristle, bristle up

'hérisson ['eʀisɔ̃] *nm* hedgehog

héritage [eʀitaʒ] *nm* inheritance; (*fig*) heritage; legacy

hériter [eʀite] *vi*: **~ de qch (de qn)** to inherit sth (from sb); **héritier, ière** *nm/f* heir(ess)

hermétique [ɛʀmetik] *adj* airtight; watertight; (*fig*) abstruse; impenetrable

hermine [ɛʀmin] *nf* ermine

'hernie ['ɛʀni] *nf* hernia

héroïne [eʀɔin] *nf* heroine; (*drogue*) heroin

'héron ['eʀɔ̃] *nm* heron

'héros ['eʀo] *nm* hero

hésitation [ezitasjɔ̃] *nf* hesitation

hésiter [ezite] *vi*: **~ (à faire)** to hesitate (to do)

hétéroclite [eteʀɔklit] *adj* heterogeneous; (*objets*) sundry

'hêtre ['ɛtʀ(ə)] *nm* beech

heure [œʀ] *nf* hour; (*SCOL*) period; (*moment*) time; **c'est l'~** it's time; **quelle ~ est-il?** what time is it?; **2 ~s (du matin)** 2 o'clock (in the morning); **être à l'~** to be on time; (*montre*) to be right; **mettre à l'~** to set right; **à toute ~** at any time; **24 ~s sur 24** round the clock, 24 hours a day; **à l'~ qu'il est** at this time (of day); by now; **sur l'~** at once; **~ de pointe** *nf* rush hour; **~s supplémentaires** overtime *sg*

heureusement [œʀøzmɑ̃] *adv* (*par bonheur*) fortunately, luckily

heureux, euse [œʀø, -øz] *adj* happy; (*chanceux*) lucky, fortunate; (*judicieux*) felicitous, fortunate

'heurt ['œʀ] *nm* (*choc*) collision; **~s** *nmpl* (*fig*) clashes

'heurter ['œʀte] *vt* (*mur*) to strike, hit; (*personne*) to collide with; (*fig*) to go against, upset; **se ~ à** *vt* to come up against; **'heurtoir** *nm* door knocker

hexagone [ɛgzagɔn] *nm* hexagon; (*la France*) France (*because of its shape*)

hiberner [ibɛʀne] *vi* to hibernate

'hibou, x ['ibu] *nm* owl

'hideux, euse ['idø, -øz] *adj* hideous

hier [jɛʀ] *adv* yesterday; **toute la journée d'~** all day yesterday; **toute la matinée d'~** all yesterday morning

'hiérarchie ['jeʀaʀʃi] *nf* hierarchy

hilare [ilaʀ] *adj* mirthful

hippique [ipik] *adj* equestrian, horse *cpd*

hippodrome [ipɔdʀom] *nm* racecourse

hippopotame [ipɔpɔtam] *nm* hippopotamus

hirondelle [iʀɔ̃dɛl] *nf* swallow

'hirsute [iʀsyt] *adj* hairy; shaggy; tousled

'hisser ['ise] *vt* to hoist, haul up

histoire [istwaʀ] *nf* (*science, événements*) history; (*anecdote, récit, mensonge*) story; (*affaire*) business *no pl*; **~s** *nfpl* (*chichis*) fuss *no pl*; (*ennuis*) trouble *sg*; **historique** *adj* historical; (*important*) historic

hiver [ivɛʀ] *nm* winter; **hivernal, e, aux** *adj* winter *cpd*; wintry; **hiverner** *vi* to winter

HLM *sigle m/f* = **habitation(s) à loyer modéré**

'hobby ['ɔbi] *nm* hobby

'hocher ['ɔʃe] *vt*: **~ la tête** to nod; (*signe négatif ou dubitatif*) to shake one's head

'hochet ['ɔʃɛ] *nm* rattle

'hockey ['ɔkɛ] *nm*: **~ (sur glace/gazon)** (ice/field) hockey

'hold-up ['ɔldœp] nm inv hold-up

'hollandais, e ['ɔlɑ̃dɛ, -ɛz] adj Dutch ♦ nm (LING) Dutch ♦ nm/f: **Hollandais, e** Dutchman(woman); **les Hollandais** the Dutch

'Hollande ['ɔlɑ̃d] nf: **la ~** Holland

'homard ['ɔmaʀ] nm lobster

homéopathique [ɔmeɔpatik] adj homoeopathic

homicide [ɔmisid] nm murder; **~ involontaire** manslaughter

hommage [ɔmaʒ] nm tribute; **~s** nmpl: **présenter ses ~s** to pay one's respects; **rendre ~ à** to pay tribute ou homage to

homme [ɔm] nm man; **~ d'affaires** businessman; **~ d'État** statesman; **~ de main** hired man; **~ de paille** stooge; **~-grenouille** nm frogman

homo: **~gène** adj homogeneous; **~logue** nm/f counterpart, opposite number; **~logué, e** adj (SPORT) officially recognized, ratified; (tarif) authorized; **~nyme** nm (LING) homonym; (d'une personne) namesake; **~sexuel, le** adj homosexual

'Hongrie ['ɔ̃gʀi] nf: **la Hongrie** Hungary; **'hongrois, e** adj, nm/f Hungarian

honnête [ɔnɛt] adj (intègre) honest; (juste, satisfaisant) fair; **~ment** adv honestly; **~té** nf honesty

honneur [ɔnœʀ] nm honour; (mérite) credit; **en l'~ de** in honour of; (événement) on the occasion of; **faire ~ à** (engagements) to honour; (famille) to be a credit to; (fig: repas etc) to do justice to

honorable [ɔnɔʀabl(ə)] adj worthy, honourable; (suffisant) decent

honoraire [ɔnɔʀɛʀ] adj honorary; **professeur ~** professor emeritus; **honoraires** nmpl fees pl

honorer [ɔnɔʀe] vt to honour; (estimer) to hold in high regard; (faire honneur à) to do credit to; **s'~ de** vt to pride o.s. upon; **honorifique** adj honorary

'honte ['ɔ̃t] nf shame; **avoir ~ de** to be ashamed of; **faire ~ à qn** to make sb (feel) ashamed; **'honteux, euse** adj ashamed; (conduite, acte) shameful, disgraceful

hôpital, aux [ɔpital, -o] nm hospital

'hoquet ['ɔkɛ] nm: **avoir le hoquet** to have (the) hiccoughs; **'hoqueter** vi to hiccough

horaire [ɔʀɛʀ] adj hourly ♦ nm timetable, schedule; **~s** nmpl (d'employé) hours; **~ souple** flexitime

horizon [ɔʀizɔ̃] nm horizon; (paysage) landscape, view

horizontal, e, aux [ɔʀizɔ̃tal, -o] adj horizontal

horloge [ɔʀlɔʒ] nf clock; **horloger, ère** nm/f watchmaker; clockmaker; **horlogerie** nf watch-making; watchmaker's (shop); clockmaker's (shop)

'hormis ['ɔʀmi] prép save

horoscope [ɔʀɔskɔp] nm horoscope

horreur [ɔʀœʀ] nf horror; **avoir ~ de** to loathe ou detest; **horrible** adj horrible

horripiler [ɔʀipile] vt to exasperate

'hors ['ɔʀ] prép except (for); **~ de** out of; **~ pair** outstanding; **~ de propos** inopportune; **être ~ de soi** to be beside o.s.; **~ d'usage** out of service; **~-bord** nm inv speedboat (with outboard motor); **~-concours** adj ineligible to compete; **~-d'œuvre** nm inv hors d'œuvre; **~-jeu** nm inv offside; **~-la-loi** nm inv outlaw; **~-taxe** adj (boutique, articles) duty-free

hospice [ɔspis] nm (de vieillards) home

hospitalier, ière [ɔspitalje, -jɛʀ] adj (accueillant) hospitable; (MÉD: service, centre) hospital cpd

hospitalité [ɔspitalite] nf hospitality

hostie [ɔsti] nf host (REL)

hostile [ɔstil] adj hostile; **hostilité** nf hostility

hôte [ot] nm (maître de maison) host; (invité) guest

hôtel [otɛl] nm hotel; **aller à l'~** to stay in a hotel; **~ de ville** town hall; **~ (particulier)** (private) mansion; **hôtelier, ière** adj hotel cpd ♦ nm/f hotelier; **hôtellerie** nf hotel business; (auberge) inn

hôtesse [otɛs] nf hostess; **~ de l'air** air stewardess

'hotte ['ɔt] nf (panier) basket (carried on the back); (de cheminée) hood; **hotte aspirante** cooker hood

'houblon ['ublɔ̃] nm (BOT) hop; (pour la bière) hops pl

'houille ['uj] nf coal; **houille blanche** hydroelectric power

'houle ['ul] nf swell

'houlette ['ulɛt] nf: **sous la ~ de** under the guidance of

'houleux, euse ['ulø, -øz] adj heavy, swelling; (fig) stormy, turbulent

'houspiller ['uspije] vt to scold

'housse ['us] nf cover; dust cover; loose ou stretch cover

'houx ['u] nm holly

'hublot ['yblo] nm porthole

'huche ['yʃ] nf: **~ à pain** bread bin

'huer ['ɥe] vt to boo

huile [ɥil] nf oil; **huiler** vt to oil; **huileux, euse** adj oily

huis [ɥi] nm: **à ~ clos** in camera

huissier [ɥisje] nm usher; (JUR) ≈ bailiff

'huit ['ɥit] num eight; **samedi en huit** a week on Saturday; **'huitaine** nf: **une huitaine (de jours)** a week or so; **'huitième** num eighth

huître [ɥitʀ(ə)] nf oyster

humain, e [ymɛ̃, -ɛn] adj human; (compatissant) humane ♦ nm human (being); **humanité** nf humanity

humble [œ̃bl(ə)] adj humble

humecter [ymɛkte] vt to dampen

'humer ['yme] *vt* to smell; to inhale

humeur [ymœʀ] *nf* mood; (*tempérament*) temper; (*irritation*) bad temper; **de bonne/ mauvaise ~** in a good/bad mood

humide [ymid] *adj* damp; (*main, yeux*) moist; (*climat, chaleur*) humid; (*saison, route*) wet

humilier [ymilje] *vt* to humiliate

humilité [ymilite] *nf* humility, humbleness

humoristique [ymɔʀistik] *adj* humorous; humoristic

humour [ymuʀ] *nm* humour; **avoir de l'~** to have a sense of humour; **~ noir** sick humour

'hurlement ['yʀləmɑ̃] *nm* howling *no pl*, howl, yelling *no pl*, yell

'hurler ['yʀle] *vi* to howl, yell

hurluberlu [yʀlybɛʀly] (*péj*) *nm* crank

'hutte ['yt] *nf* hut

hydratant, e [idʀatɑ̃, -ɑ̃t] *adj* (*crème*) moisturizing

hydrate [idʀat] *nm*: **~s de carbone** carbohydrates

hydraulique [idʀolik] *adj* hydraulic

hydravion [idʀavjɔ̃] *nm* seaplane

hydrogène [idʀɔʒɛn] *nm* hydrogen

hydroglisseur [idʀɔglisœʀ] *nm* hydroplane

hygiénique [iʒjenik] *adj* hygienic

hymne [imn(ə)] *nm* hymn; **~ national** national anthem

hypermarché [ipɛʀmaʀʃe] *nm* hypermarket

hypermétrope [ipɛʀmetʀɔp] *adj* longsighted

hypnotiser [ipnɔtize] *vt* to hypnotize

hypocrite [ipɔkʀit] *adj* hypocritical

hypothèque [ipɔtɛk] *nf* mortgage

hypothèse [ipɔtɛz] *nf* hypothesis

hystérique [isteʀik] *adj* hysterical

_____ **/ i**

iceberg [isbɛʀg] *nm* iceberg

ici [isi] *adv* here; **jusqu'~** as far as this; **until now; d'~ là** by then; in the meantime; **d'~ peu** before long

idéal, e, aux [ideal, -o] *adj* ideal ♦ *nm* ideal; ideals *pl*

idée [ide] *nf* idea; **avoir dans l'~ que** to have an idea that; **~s noires** black *ou* dark thoughts

identifier [idɑ̃tifje] *vt* to identify; **s'~ à** (*héros etc*) to identify with

identique [idɑ̃tik] *adj*: **~ (à)** identical (to)

identité [idɑ̃tite] *nf* identity

idiot, e [idjo, idjɔt] *adj* idiotic ♦ *nm/f* idiot

idole [idɔl] *nf* idol

if [if] *nm* yew

ignare [iɲaʀ] *adj* ignorant

ignoble [iɲɔbl(ə)] *adj* vile

ignorant, e [iɲɔʀɑ̃, -ɑ̃t] *adj* ignorant

ignorer [iɲɔʀe] *vt* (*ne pas connaître*) not to know, be unaware *ou* ignorant of; (*être sans expérience de: plaisir, guerre etc*) not to know about, have no experience of; (*bouder: personne*) to ignore

il [il] *pron* he; (*animal, chose, en tournure impersonnelle*) it; **~s** they; *voir aussi* **avoir**

île [il] *nf* island; **les ~s anglo-normandes** the Channel Islands; **les ~s Britanniques** the British Isles

illégal, e, aux [ilegal, -o] *adj* illegal

illégitime [ileʒitim] *adj* illegitimate

illettré, e [iletʀe] *adj, nm/f* illiterate

illimité, e [ilimite] *adj* unlimited

illisible [ilizibl(ə)] *adj* illegible; (*roman*) unreadable

illumination [ilyminasjɔ̃] *nf* illumination, floodlighting; (*idée*) flash of inspiration

illuminer [ilymine] *vt* to light up; (*monument, rue: pour une fête*) to illuminate, floodlight

illusion [ilyzjɔ̃] *nf* illusion; **se faire des ~s** to delude o.s.; **faire ~** to delude *ou* fool people; **illusionniste** *nm/f* conjuror

illustration [ilystʀasjɔ̃] *nf* illustration

illustre [ilystʀ(ə)] *adj* illustrious

illustré, e [ilystʀe] *adj* illustrated ♦ *nm* illustrated magazine; comic

illustrer [ilystʀe] *vt* to illustrate; **s'~** to become famous, win fame

îlot [ilo] *nm* small island, islet; (*de maisons*) block

ils [il] *pron voir* **il**

image [imaʒ] *nf* (*gén*) picture; (*comparaison, ressemblance, OPTIQUE*) image; **~ de marque** brand image; (*fig*) public image

imagination [imaʒinasjɔ̃] *nf* imagination; (*chimère*) fancy; **avoir de l'~** to be imaginative

imaginer [imaʒine] *vt* to imagine; (*inventer: expédient*) to devise, think up; **s'~** *vt* (*se figurer: scène etc*) to imagine, picture; **s'~ que** to imagine that

imbécile [ɛ̃besil] *adj* idiotic ♦ *nm/f* idiot

imberbe [ɛ̃bɛʀb(ə)] *adj* beardless

imbiber [ɛ̃bibe] *vt* to moisten, wet; **s'~ de** to become saturated with

imbu, e [ɛ̃by] *adj*: **~ de** full of

imitateur, trice [imitatœʀ, -tʀis] *nm/f* (*gén*) imitator; (*MUSIC-HALL*) impersonator

imitation [imitasjɔ̃] *nf* imitation; (*sketch*) imitation, impression; impersonation

imiter [imite] *vt* to imitate; (*contrefaire*) to forge; (*ressembler à*) to look like

immaculé, e [imakyle] *adj* spotless; immaculate

immatriculation [imatʀikylɑsjɔ̃] *nf* registration

immatriculer [imatʀikyle] *vt* to register; **faire/se faire ~** to register

immédiat, e [imedja, -at] *adj* immediate ♦ *nm*: **dans l'~** for the time being; **~ement** *adv* immediately

immense [imɑ̃s] *adj* immense

immerger [imɛʀʒe] *vt* to immerse, submerge

immeuble [imœbl(ə)] *nm* building; **~ locatif** block of rented flats (*BRIT*), rental building (*US*)

immigration [imigʀɑsjɔ̃] *nf* immigration

immigré, e [imigʀe] *nm/f* immigrant

imminent, e [iminɑ̃, -ɑ̃t] *adj* imminent

immiscer [imise]: **s'~** *vi* to interfere in *ou* with

immobile [imɔbil] *adj* still, motionless; (*fig*) unchanging

immobilier, ière [imɔbilje, -jɛʀ] *adj* property *cpd* ♦ *nm*: **l'~** the property business

immobiliser [imɔbilize] *vt* (*gén*) to immobilize; (*circulation, véhicule, affaires*) to bring to a standstill; **s'~** (*personne*) to stand still; (*machine, véhicule*) to come to a halt

immonde [imɔ̃d] *adj* foul

immondices [imɔ̃dis] *nmpl* refuse *sg*; filth *sg*

immoral, e, aux [imɔʀal, -o] *adj* immoral

immuable [imɥabl(ə)] *adj* immutable; unchanging

immunisé, e [imynize] *adj*: **~ contre** immune to

immunité [imynite] *nf* immunity

impact [ɛ̃pakt] *nm* impact

impair, e [ɛ̃pɛʀ] *adj* odd ♦ *nm* faux pas, blunder

impardonnable [ɛ̃paʀdɔnabl(ə)] *adj* unpardonable, unforgivable

imparfait, e [ɛ̃paʀfɛ, -ɛt] *adj* imperfect

impartial, e, aux [ɛ̃paʀsjal, -o] *adj* impartial, unbiased

impartir [ɛ̃paʀtiʀ] *vt* to assign; to bestow

impasse [ɛ̃pɑs] *nf* dead-end, cul-de-sac; (*fig*) deadlock

impassible [ɛ̃pasibl(ə)] *adj* impassive

impatience [ɛ̃pasjɑ̃s] *nf* impatience

impatient, e [ɛ̃pasjɑ̃, -ɑ̃t] *adj* impatient

impayable [ɛ̃pɛjabl(ə)] *adj* (*drôle*) priceless

impeccable [ɛ̃pekabl(ə)] *adj* faultless, impeccable; spotlessly clean; impeccably dressed; (*fam*) smashing

impensable [ɛ̃pɑ̃sabl(ə)] *adj* unthinkable; unbelievable

impératif, ive [ɛ̃peʀatif, -iv] *adj* imperative ♦ *nm* (*LING*) imperative; **~s** *nmpl* (*exigences*) requirements; demands

impératrice [ɛ̃peʀatʀis] *nf* empress

impérial, e, aux [ɛ̃peʀjal, -o] *adj* imperial; **impériale** *nf* top deck

impérieux, euse [ɛ̃peʀjø, -øz] *adj* (*caractère, ton*) imperious; (*obligation, besoin*) pressing, urgent

impérissable [ɛ̃peʀisabl(ə)] *adj* undying; imperishable

imperméable [ɛ̃pɛʀmeabl(ə)] *adj* waterproof; (*GÉO*) impermeable; (*fig*): **~ à** impervious to ♦ *nm* raincoat

impertinent, e [ɛ̃pɛʀtinɑ̃, -ɑ̃t] *adj* impertinent

impétueux, euse [ɛ̃petɥø, -øz] *adj* fiery

impie [ɛ̃pi] *adj* impious, ungodly

impitoyable [ɛ̃pitwajabl(ə)] *adj* pitiless, merciless

implanter [ɛ̃plɑ̃te] *vt* (*usine, industrie, usage*) to establish; (*colons etc*) to settle; (*idée, préjugé*) to implant

impliquer [ɛ̃plike] *vt* to imply; **~ qn (dans)** to implicate sb (in)

impoli, e [ɛ̃pɔli] *adj* impolite, rude

importance [ɛ̃pɔʀtɑ̃s] *nf* importance; **sans ~** unimportant

important, e [ɛ̃pɔʀtɑ̃, -ɑ̃t] *adj* important; (*en quantité*) considerable, sizeable; extensive; (*péj: airs, ton*) self-important ♦ *nm*: **l'~** the important thing

importateur, trice [ɛ̃pɔʀtatœʀ, -tʀis] *nm/f* importer

importation [ɛ̃pɔʀtɑsjɔ̃] *nf* importation; introduction; (*produit*) import

importer [ɛ̃pɔʀte] *vt* (*COMM*) to import; (*maladies, plantes*) to introduce ♦ *vi* (*être important*) to matter; **il importe qu'il fasse** it is important that he should do; **peu m'importe** I don't mind; I don't care; **peu importe (que)** it doesn't matter (if); *voir aussi* **n'importe**

importun, e [ɛ̃pɔʀtœ̃, -yn] *adj* irksome, importunate; (*arrivée, visite*) inopportune, illtimed ♦ *nm* intruder; **importuner** *vt* to bother

imposable [ɛ̃pozabl(e)] *adj* taxable

imposant, e [ɛ̃pozɑ̃, -ɑ̃t] *adj* imposing

imposer [ɛ̃poze] *vt* (*taxer*) to tax; **s'~** (*être nécessaire*) to be imperative; (*montrer sa proéminence*) to stand out, emerge; (*artiste: se faire connaître*) to win recognition; **~ qch à qn** to impose sth on sb; **en ~ à** to impress; **imposition** [ɛ̃pozisjɔ̃] *nf* (*ADMIN*) taxation

impossible [ɛ̃pɔsibl(ə)] *adj* impossible; **il m'est ~ de le faire** it is impossible for me to do it, I can't possibly do it; **faire l'~** to do one's utmost

impôt [ɛ̃po] *nm* tax; (*taxes*) taxation; taxes *pl*; **~s** *nmpl* (*contributions*) (income) tax *sg*; **payer 1000 F d'~s** to pay 1,000 F in tax; **~ foncier** land tax; **~ sur le chiffre d'affaires** corporation (*BRIT*) *ou* corporate (*US*) tax; **~ sur le revenu** income tax

impotent, e [ɛ̃pɔtɑ̃, -ɑ̃t] *adj* disabled
impraticable [ɛ̃pʀatikabl(ə)] *adj* (*projet*) impracticable, unworkable; (*piste*) impassable
imprécis, e [ɛ̃pʀesi, -iz] *adj* imprecise
imprégner [ɛ̃pʀeɲe] *vt* (*tissu, tampon*) to soak, impregnate; (*lieu, air*) to fill; **s'~ de** (*fig*) to absorb
imprenable [ɛ̃pʀənabl(ə)] *adj* (*forteresse*) impregnable; **vue ~** unrestricted view
impression [ɛ̃pʀesjɔ̃] *nf* impression; (*d'un ouvrage, tissu*) printing; **faire bonne ~** to make a good impression
impressionnant, e [ɛ̃pʀesjɔnɑ̃, -ɑ̃t] *adj* impressive; upsetting
impressionner [ɛ̃pʀesjɔne] *vt* (*frapper*) to impress; (*troubler*) to upset
imprévisible [ɛ̃pʀevizibl(ə)] *adj* unforeseeable
imprévoyant, e [ɛ̃pʀevwajɑ̃, -ɑ̃t] *adj* lacking in foresight; (*en matière d'argent*) improvident
imprévu, e [ɛ̃pʀevy] *adj* unforeseen, unexpected ♦ *nm* unexpected incident; **en cas d'~** if anything unexpected happens
imprimante [ɛ̃pʀimɑ̃t] *nf* printer; **~ matricielle** dot-matrix printer
imprimé [ɛ̃pʀime] *nm* (*formulaire*) printed form; (*POSTES*) printed matter *no pl*
imprimer [ɛ̃pʀime] *vt* to print; (*empreinte etc*) to imprint; (*publier*) to publish; (*communiquer: mouvement, impulsion*) to impart, transmit; **imprimerie** *nf* printing; (*établissement*) printing works *sg*; **imprimeur** *nm* printer
impromptu, e [ɛ̃pʀɔ̃pty] *adj* impromptu; sudden
impropre [ɛ̃pʀɔpʀ(ə)] *adj* inappropriate; **~ à** unsuitable for
improviser [ɛ̃pʀɔvize] *vt, vi* to improvise
improviste [ɛ̃pʀɔvist(ə)]: **à l'~** *adv* unexpectedly, without warning
imprudence [ɛ̃pʀydɑ̃s] *nf* carelessness *no pl*; imprudence *no pl*
imprudent, e [ɛ̃pʀydɑ̃, -ɑ̃t] *adj* (*conducteur, geste, action*) careless; (*remarque*) unwise, imprudent; (*projet*) foolhardy
impudent, e [ɛ̃pydɑ̃, -ɑ̃t] *adj* impudent; brazen
impudique [ɛ̃pydik] *adj* shameless
impuissant, e [ɛ̃pɥisɑ̃, -ɑ̃t] *adj* helpless; (*sans effet*) ineffectual; (*sexuellement*) impotent; **~ à faire** powerless to do
impulsif, ive [ɛ̃pylsif, -iv] *adj* impulsive
impulsion [ɛ̃pylsjɔ̃] *nf* (*ÉLEC, instinct*) impulse; (*élan, influence*) impetus
impunément [ɛ̃pynemɑ̃] *adv* with impunity
imputer [ɛ̃pyte] *vt* (*attribuer*) to ascribe, impute; (*COMM*): **~ à ou sur** to charge to
inabordable [inabɔʀdabl(ə)] *adj* (*cher*) prohibitive

inaccessible [inaksesibl(ə)] *adj* inaccessible; unattainable; (*insensible*): **~ à** impervious to
inachevé, e [inaʃve] *adj* unfinished
inadapté, e [inadapte] *adj* (*gén*): **~ à** not adapted to, unsuited to; (*PSYCH*) maladjusted
inadmissible [inadmisibl(ə)] *adj* inadmissible
inadvertance [inadvɛʀtɑ̃s]: **par ~** *adv* inadvertently
inaltérable [inalteʀabl(ə)] *adj* (*matière*) stable; (*fig*) unchanging; **~ à** unaffected by
inamovible [inamɔvibl(ə)] *adj* fixed; (*JUR*) irremovable
inanimé, e [inanime] *adj* (*matière*) inanimate; (*évanoui*) unconscious; (*sans vie*) lifeless
inanition [inanisjɔ̃] *nf*: **tomber d'~** to faint with hunger (and exhaustion)
inaperçu, e [inapɛʀsy] *adj*: **passer ~** to go unnoticed
inappréciable [inapʀesjabl(ə)] *adj* (*service*) invaluable
inapte [inapt(ə)] *adj*: **~ à** incapable of; (*MIL*) unfit for
inattaquable [inatakabl(ə)] *adj* (*texte, preuve*) irrefutable
inattendu, e [inatɑ̃dy] *adj* unexpected
inattentif, ive [inatɑ̃tif, -iv] *adj* inattentive; **~ à** (*dangers, détails*) heedless of; **inattention** *nf*: **faute d'inattention** careless mistake
inaugurer [inɔgyʀe] *vt* (*monument*) to unveil; (*exposition, usine*) to open; (*fig*) to inaugurate
inavouable [inavwabl(ə)] *adj* shameful; undisclosable
inavoué, e [inavwe] *adj* unavowed
incandescence [ɛ̃kɑ̃desɑ̃s] *nf*: **porter à ~** to heat white-hot
incapable [ɛ̃kapabl(ə)] *adj* incapable; **~ de faire** incapable of doing; (*empêché*) unable to do
incapacité [ɛ̃kapasite] *nf* incapability; (*JUR*) incapacity
incarcérer [ɛ̃kaʀseʀe] *vt* to incarcerate, imprison
incarner [ɛ̃kaʀne] *vt* to embody, personify; (*THÉÂTRE*) to play
incartade [ɛ̃kaʀtad] *nf* prank
incassable [ɛ̃kɑsabl(ə)] *adj* unbreakable
incendiaire [ɛ̃sɑ̃djɛʀ] *adj* incendiary; (*fig: discours*) inflammatory ♦ *nm/f* fire-raiser, arsonist
incendie [ɛ̃sɑ̃di] *nm* fire; **~ criminel** arson *no pl*; **~ de forêt** forest fire; **~r** [ɛ̃sɑ̃dje] *vt* (*mettre le feu à*) to set fire to, set alight; (*brûler complètement*) to burn down
incertain, e [ɛ̃sɛʀtɛ̃, -ɛn] *adj* uncertain; (*temps*) uncertain, unsettled; (*imprécis: contours*) indistinct, blurred; **incertitude** *nf*

uncertainty

incessamment [ɛ̃sɛsamɑ̃] *adv* very shortly

incidemment [ɛ̃sidamɑ̃] *adv* in passing

incident [ɛ̃sidɑ̃] *nm* incident; ~ **de parcours** minor hitch *ou* setback; ~ **technique** technical difficulties *pl*

incinérer [ɛ̃sinere] *vt* (*ordures*) to incinerate; (*mort*) to cremate

incisive [ɛ̃siziv] *nf* incisor

inciter [ɛ̃site] *vt*: ~ **qn à (faire) qch** to encourage sb to do sth; (*à la révolte etc*) to incite sb to do sth

inclinable [ɛ̃klinabl(ə)] *adj*: **siège à dossier ~** reclining seat

inclinaison [ɛ̃klinɛzɔ̃] *nf* (*déclivité: d'une route etc*) incline; (: *d'un toit*) slope; (*état penché*) tilt

inclination [ɛ̃klinasjɔ̃] *nf*: ~ **de (la) tête** nod (of the head); ~ (**de buste**) bow

incliner [ɛ̃kline] *vt* (*tête, bouteille*) to tilt ♦ *vi*: ~ **à qch/à faire** to incline towards sth/doing; **s'~ (devant)** to bow (before); (*céder*) to give in *ou* yield (to); ~ **la tête** *ou* **le front** to give a slight bow

inclure [ɛ̃klyʀ] *vt* to include; (*joindre à un envoi*) to enclose; **jusqu'au 10 mars inclus** until 10th March inclusive

incoercible [ɛ̃kɔɛʀsibl(ə)] *adj* uncontrollable

incohérent, e [ɛ̃kɔeʀɑ̃, -ɑ̃t] *adj* inconsistent; incoherent

incollable [ɛ̃kɔlabl(ə)] *adj*: **il est ~** he's got all the answers

incolore [ɛ̃kɔlɔʀ] *adj* colourless

incomber [ɛ̃kɔ̃be] : ~ **à** *vt* (*suj: devoirs, responsabilité*) to rest upon; (: *frais, travail*) to be the responsibility of

incommensurable [ɛ̃kɔmɑ̃syʀabl(ə)] *adj* immeasurable

incommode [ɛ̃kɔmɔd] *adj* inconvenient; (*posture, siège*) uncomfortable

incommoder [ɛ̃kɔmɔde] *vt*: ~ **qn** to inconvenience sb; (*embarrasser*) to make sb feel uncomfortable

incompétent, e [ɛ̃kɔ̃petɑ̃, -ɑ̃t] *adj* incompetent

incompris, e [ɛ̃kɔ̃pʀi, -iz] *adj* misunderstood

inconcevable [ɛ̃kɔ̃svabl(ə)] *adj* incredible

inconciliable [ɛ̃kɔ̃siljabl(ə)] *adj* irreconcilable

inconditionnel, le [ɛ̃kɔ̃disjɔnɛl] *adj* unconditional; (*partisan*) unquestioning

incongru, e [ɛ̃kɔ̃gʀy] *adj* unseemly

inconnu, e [ɛ̃kɔny] *adj* unknown; new, strange ♦ *nm/f* stranger; unknown person (*ou artist etc*) ♦ *nm*: **l'~** the unknown; **~e** *nf* unknown

inconsciemment [ɛ̃kɔ̃sjamɑ̃] *adv* unconsciously

inconscient, e [ɛ̃kɔ̃sjɑ̃, -ɑ̃t] *adj* unconscious; (*irréfléchi*) thoughtless, reckless ♦

nm (*PSYCH*): **l'~** the unconscious; ~ **de** unaware of

inconsidéré, e [ɛ̃kɔ̃sidere] *adj* ill-considered

inconsistant, e [ɛ̃kɔ̃sistɑ̃, -ɑ̃t] *adj* flimsy, weak; runny

incontestable [ɛ̃kɔ̃tɛstabl(ə)] *adj* indisputable

incontournable [ɛ̃kɔ̃tuʀnabl(ə)] *adj* unavoidable

inconvenant, e [ɛ̃kɔ̃vnɑ̃, -ɑ̃t] *adj* unseemly, improper

inconvénient [ɛ̃kɔ̃venjɑ̃] *nm* (*d'une situation, d'un projet*) disadvantage, drawback; (*d'un remède, changement etc*) inconvenience; **si vous n'y voyez pas d'~** if you have no objections

incorporer [ɛ̃kɔʀpɔʀe] *vt*: ~ (**à**) to mix in (with); (*paragraphe etc*): ~ (**dans**) to incorporate (in); (*MIL: appeler*) to recruit, call up

incorrect, e [ɛ̃kɔʀɛkt] *adj* (*impropre, inconvenant*) improper; (*défectueux*) faulty; (*inexact*) incorrect; (*impoli*) impolite; (*déloyal*) underhand

incrédule [ɛ̃kʀedyl] *adj* incredulous; (*REL*) unbelieving

increvable [ɛ̃kʀəvabl(ə)] (*fam*) *adj* tireless

incriminer [ɛ̃kʀimine] *vt* (*personne*) to incriminate; (*action, conduite*) to bring under attack; (*bonne foi, honnêteté*) to call into question

incroyable [ɛ̃kʀwajabl(ə)] *adj* incredible; unbelievable

incruster [ɛ̃kʀyste] *vt* (*ART*) to inlay; **s'~** *vi* (*invité*) to take root; (*radiateur etc*) to become coated with fur *ou* scale

inculpé, e [ɛ̃kylpe] *nm/f* accused

inculper [ɛ̃kylpe] *vt*: ~ (**de**) to charge (with)

inculquer [ɛ̃kylke] *vt*: ~ **qch à** to inculcate sth in *ou* instil sth into

inculte [ɛ̃kylt(ə)] *adj* uncultivated; (*esprit, peuple*) uncultured; (*barbe*) unkempt

Inde [ɛ̃d] *nf*: **l'~** India

indécis, e [ɛ̃desi, -iz] *adj* indecisive; (*perplexe*) undecided

indéfendable [ɛ̃defɑ̃dabl(ə)] *adj* indefensible

indéfini, e [ɛ̃defini] *adj* (*imprécis, incertain*) undefined; (*illimité, LING*) indefinite; **indéfiniment** *adv* indefinitely; **indéfinissable** *adj* indefinable

indélébile [ɛ̃delebil] *adj* indelible

indélicat, e [ɛ̃delika, -at] *adj* tactless; dishonest

indemne [ɛ̃dɛmn(ə)] *adj* unharmed

indemniser [ɛ̃dɛmnize] *vt*: ~ **qn (de)** to compensate sb (for)

indemnité [ɛ̃dɛmnite] *nf* (*dédommagement*) compensation *no pl*; (*allocation*) allowance; ~ **de licenciement** redundancy payment

indépendamment [ɛ̃depɑ̃damɑ̃] *adv* independently; ~ **de** (*abstraction faite de*) irrespective of; (*en plus de*) over and above

indépendance [ɛ̃depɑ̃dɑ̃s] *nf* independence

indépendant, e [ɛ̃depɑ̃dɑ̃, -ɑ̃t] *adj* independent; ~ **de** independent of

indescriptible [ɛ̃dɛskriptibl(ə)] *adj* indescribable

indétermination [ɛ̃detɛrminasjɔ̃] *nf* indecision; indecisiveness

indéterminé, e [ɛ̃detɛrmine] *adj* unspecified; indeterminate

index [ɛ̃dɛks] *nm* (*doigt*) index finger; (*d'un livre etc*) index; **mettre à l'~** to blacklist

indexé, e [ɛ̃dɛkse] *adj* (*ÉCON*): ~ **(sur)** index-linked (to)

indicateur [ɛ̃dikatœr] *nm* (*POLICE*) informer; (*livre*) guide; directory; (*TECH*) gauge; indicator; ~ **des chemins de fer** railway timetable

indicatif, ive [ɛ̃dikatif, -iv] *adj*: **à titre ~** for (your) information ♦ *nm* (*LING*) indicative; (*RADIO*) theme *ou* signature tune; (*TÉL*) dialling code

indication [ɛ̃dikasjɔ̃] *nf* indication; (*renseignement*) information *no pl*; ~**s** *nfpl* (*directives*) instructions

indice [ɛ̃dis] *nm* (*marque, signe*) indication, sign; (*POLICE: lors d'une enquête*) clue; (*JUR: présomption*) piece of evidence; (*SCIENCE, ÉCON, TECH*) index

indicible [ɛ̃disibl(ə)] *adj* inexpressible

indien, ne [ɛ̃djɛ̃, -jɛn] *adj, nm/f* Indian

indifféremment [ɛ̃diferamɑ̃] *adv* (*sans distinction*) equally (well); indiscriminately

indifférence [ɛ̃diferɑ̃s] *nf* indifference; **indifférent, e** [ɛ̃diferɑ̃, -ɑ̃t] *adj* (*peu intéressé*) indifferent

indigence [ɛ̃diʒɑ̃s] *nf* poverty

indigène [ɛ̃diʒɛn] *adj* native, indigenous; local ♦ *nm/f* native

indigeste [ɛ̃diʒɛst(ə)] *adj* indigestible

indigestion [ɛ̃diʒɛstjɔ̃] *nf* indigestion *no pl*

indigne [ɛ̃diɲ] *adj* unworthy

indigner [ɛ̃diɲe] *vt*: **s'~ (de** *ou* **contre)** to be indignant (at)

indiqué, e [ɛ̃dike] *adj* (*date, lieu*) given; (*adéquat, conseillé*) suitable

indiquer [ɛ̃dike] *vt* (*désigner*): ~ **qch/qn à qn** to point sth/sb out to sb; (*suj: pendule, aiguille*) to show; (: *étiquette, plan*) to show, indicate; (*faire connaître: médecin, restaurant*): ~ **qch/qn à qn** to tell sb of sth/sb; (*renseigner sur*) to point out, tell; (*déterminer: date, lieu*) to give, state; (*dénoter*) to indicate, point to

indirect, e [ɛ̃dirɛkt] *adj* indirect

indiscipline [ɛ̃disiplin] *nf* lack of discipline; **indiscipliné, e** *adj* undisciplined; (*fig*) unmanageable

indiscret, ète [ɛ̃diskrɛ, -ɛt] *adj* indiscreet

indiscutable [ɛ̃diskytabl(ə)] *adj* indisputable

indispensable [ɛ̃dispɑ̃sabl(ə)] *adj* indispensable; essential

indisposé, e [ɛ̃dispoze] *adj* indisposed

indisposer [ɛ̃dispoze] *vt* (*incommoder*) to upset; (*déplaire à*) to antagonize

indistinct, e [ɛ̃distɛ̃, -ɛkt(ə)] *adj* indistinct; **indistinctement** *adv* (*voir, prononcer*) indistinctly; (*sans distinction*) indiscriminately

individu [ɛ̃dividy] *nm* individual

individuel, le [ɛ̃dividɥɛl] *adj* (*gén*) individual; (*opinion, livret, contrôle, avantages*) personal; **chambre ~le** single room; **maison ~le** detached house

indolore [ɛ̃dɔlɔr] *adj* painless

indomptable [ɛ̃dɔ̃tabl(ə)] *adj* untameable; (*fig*) invincible, indomitable

Indonésie [ɛ̃donezi] *nf* Indonesia

indu, e [ɛ̃dy] *adj*: **à des heures ~es** at some ungodly hour

induire [ɛ̃dɥir] *vt*: ~ **qn en erreur** to lead sb astray, mislead sb

indulgent, e [ɛ̃dylʒɑ̃, -ɑ̃t] *adj* (*parent, regard*) indulgent; (*juge, examinateur*) lenient

indûment [ɛ̃dymɑ̃] *adv* wrongfully; without due cause

industrie [ɛ̃dystri] *nf* industry; **industriel, le** *adj* industrial ♦ *nm* industrialist; manufacturer

inébranlable [inebrɑ̃labl(ə)] *adj* (*masse, colonne*) solid; (*personne, certitude, foi*) steadfast, unwavering

inédit, e [inedi, -it] *adj* (*correspondance etc*) hitherto unpublished; (*spectacle, moyen*) novel, original

ineffaçable [inefasabl(ə)] *adj* indelible

inefficace [inefikas] *adj* (*remède, moyen*) ineffective; (*machine, employé*) inefficient

inégal, e, aux [inegal, -o] *adj* unequal; uneven; **inégalable** [inegalabl(e)] *adj* matchless; **inégalé, e** [inegale] *adj* unmatched, unequalled

inerte [inɛrt(ə)] *adj* lifeless; inert

inestimable [inɛstimabl(e)] *adj* priceless; (*fig: bienfait*) invaluable

inévitable [inevitabl(ə)] *adj* unavoidable; (*fatal, habituel*) inevitable

inexact, e [inɛgzakt] *adj* inaccurate, inexact; unpunctual

in extremis [inɛkstremis] *adv* at the last minute ♦ *adj* last-minute

infaillible [ɛ̃fajibl(ə)] *adj* infallible

infâme [ɛ̃fɑm] *adj* vile

infanticide [ɛ̃fɑ̃tisid] *nm/f* childmurderer(eress) ♦ *nm* (*meurtre*) infanticide

infarctus [ɛ̃farktys] *nm*: ~ **(du myocarde)** coronary (thrombosis)

infatigable [ɛ̃fatigabl(ə)] *adj* tireless

infect, e [ɛ̃fɛkt] *adj* vile; foul; (*repas, vin*) revolting

infecter [ɛ̃fɛkte] *vt* (*atmosphère, eau*) to contaminate; (*MÉD*) to infect; **s'~** to become infected *ou* septic; **infection** *nf* infection

inférieur, e [ɛ̃feʀjœʀ] *adj* lower; (*en qualité, intelligence*) inferior; ~ **à** (*somme, quantité*) less *ou* smaller than; (*moins bon que*) inferior to

infernal, e, aux [ɛ̃feʀnal, -o] *adj* (*chaleur, rythme*) infernal; (*méchanceté, complot*) diabolical

infidèle [ɛ̃fidɛl] *adj* unfaithful

infiltrer [ɛ̃filtʀe] : **s'~** *vi* to penetrate into; (*liquide*) to seep into; (*fig: noyauter*) to infiltrate

infime [ɛ̃fim] *adj* minute, tiny; (*inférieur*) lowly

infini, e [ɛ̃fini] *adj* infinite ♦ *nm* infinity; **à l'~** (*MATH*) to infinity; (*agrandir, varier*) infinitely; (*interminablement*) endlessly; **infinité** *nf*: **une infinité de** an infinite number of

infinitif [ɛ̃finitif] *nm* infinitive

infirme [ɛ̃fiʀm(ə)] *adj* disabled ♦ *nm/f* disabled person; ~ **de guerre** war cripple

infirmerie [ɛ̃fiʀməʀi] *nf* sick bay

infirmier, ière [ɛ̃fiʀmje, -jɛʀ] *nm/f* nurse; **infirmière chef** sister; **infirmière visiteuse** ≈ district nurse

infirmité [ɛ̃fiʀmite] *nf* disability

inflammable [ɛ̃flamabl(ə)] *adj* (in)flammable

inflation [ɛ̃flasjɔ̃] *nf* inflation

inflexion [ɛ̃flɛksjɔ̃] *nf* inflexion; ~ **de la tête** slight nod (of the head)

infliger [ɛ̃fliʒe] *vt*: ~ **qch (à qn)** to inflict sth (on sb); (*amende, sanction*) to impose sth (on sb)

influence [ɛ̃flyɑ̃s] *nf* influence; (*d'un médicament*) effect; **influencer** *vt* to influence; **influent, e** *adj* influential

influer [ɛ̃flye] : ~ **sur** *vt* to have an influence upon

informaticien, ne [ɛ̃fɔʀmatisjɛ̃, -jɛn] *nm/f* computer scientist

information [ɛ̃fɔʀmasjɔ̃] *nf* (*renseignement*) piece of information; (*PRESSE, TV: nouvelle*) item of news; (*diffusion de renseignements, INFORM*) information; (*JUR*) inquiry, investigation; **~s** *nfpl* (*TV*) news *sg*; **voyage d'~** fact-finding trip

informatique [ɛ̃fɔʀmatik] *nf* (*technique*) data processing; (*science*) computer science ♦ *adj* computer *cpd*; **informatiser** *vt* to computerize

informe [ɛ̃fɔʀm(ə)] *adj* shapeless

informer [ɛ̃fɔʀme] *vt*: ~ **qn (de)** to inform sb (of); **s'~ (de/si)** to inquire *ou* find out (about/whether *ou* if)

infortune [ɛ̃fɔʀtyn] *nf* misfortune

infraction [ɛ̃fʀaksjɔ̃] *nf* offence; ~ **à** violation *ou* breach of; **être en** ~ to be in breach of the law

infranchissable [ɛ̃fʀɑ̃ʃisabl(ə)] *adj* impassable; (*fig*) insuperable

infrastructure [ɛ̃fʀastʀyktyʀ] *nf* (*AVIAT, MIL*) ground installations *pl*; (*ÉCON: touristique etc*) infrastructure

infuser [ɛ̃fyze] *vt, vi* (*thé*) to brew; (*tisane*) to infuse; **infusion** *nf* (*tisane*) herb tea

ingénier [ɛ̃ʒenje] : **s'~** *vi* to strive to do

ingénierie [ɛ̃ʒenjəʀi] *nf* engineering; ~ **génétique** genetic engineering

ingénieur [ɛ̃ʒenjœʀ] *nm* engineer; ~ **du son** sound engineer

ingénieux, euse [ɛ̃ʒenjø, -øz] *adj* ingenious, clever

ingénu, e [ɛ̃ʒeny] *adj* ingenuous, artless

ingérer [ɛ̃ʒeʀe] : **s'~** *vi* to interfere in

ingrat, e [ɛ̃gʀa, -at] *adj* (*personne*) ungrateful; (*sol*) poor; (*travail, sujet*) thankless; (*visage*) unprepossessing

ingrédient [ɛ̃gʀedjɑ̃] *nm* ingredient

ingurgiter [ɛ̃gyʀʒite] *vt* to swallow

inhabitable [inabitabl(ə)] *adj* uninhabitable

inhabituel, le [inabitɥɛl] *adj* unusual

inhérent, e [ineʀɑ̃, -ɑ̃t] *adj*: ~ **à** inherent in

inhibition [inibisjɔ̃] *nf* inhibition

inhumain, e [inymɛ̃, -ɛn] *adj* inhuman

inhumer [inyme] *vt* to inter, bury

inimitié [inimitje] *nf* enmity

initial, e, aux [inisjal, -o] *adj* initial; **initiale** *nf* initial

initiateur, trice [inisjatœʀ, -tʀis] *nm/f* initiator; (*d'une mode, technique*) innovator, pioneer

initiative [inisjativ] *nf* initiative

initier [inisje] *vt*: ~ **qn à** to initiate sb into; (*faire découvrir: art, jeu*) to introduce sb to

injecté, e [ɛ̃ʒɛkte] *adj*: **yeux ~s de sang** bloodshot eyes

injecter [ɛ̃ʒɛkte] *vt* to inject; **injection** *nf* injection; **à injection** (*AUTO*) fuel injection *cpd*

injure [ɛ̃ʒyʀ] *nf* insult, abuse *no pl*

injurier [ɛ̃ʒyʀje] *vt* to insult, abuse; **injurieux, euse** *adj* abusive, insulting

injuste [ɛ̃ʒyst(ə)] *adj* unjust, unfair; **injustice** *nf* injustice

inlassable [ɛ̃lasabl(ə)] *adj* tireless

inné, e [ine] *adj* innate, inborn

innocent, e [inɔsɑ̃, -ɑ̃t] *adj* innocent; **innocenter** *vt* to clear, prove innocent

innombrable [inɔ̃bʀabl(ə)] *adj* innumerable

innommable [inɔmabl(ə)] *adj* unspeakable

innover [inɔve] *vi* to break new ground

inoccupé, e [inɔkype] *adj* unoccupied

inoculer [inɔkyle] *vt* (*volontairement*) to inoculate; (*accidentellement*) to infect

inodore [inɔdɔʀ] *adj* (*gaz*) odourless; (*fleur*) scentless

inoffensif, ive [inɔfɑ̃sif, -iv] *adj* harmless, innocuous

inondation [inɔ̃dasjɔ̃] *nf* flooding *no pl*;

flood; **inonder** [inɔ̃de] *vt* to flood; *(fig)* to inundate, overrun

inopérant, e [inɔperɑ̃, -ɑ̃t] *adj* inoperative, ineffective

inopiné, e [inɔpine] *adj* unexpected, sudden

inopportun, e [inɔpɔʀtœ̃, -yn] *adj* ill-timed, untimely; inappropriate

inoubliable [inublijabl(ə)] *adj* unforgettable

inouï, e [inwi] *adj* unheard-of, extraordinary

inox(ydable) [inɔks(idabl(ə))] *adj* stainless

inqualifiable [ɛ̃kalifjabl(ə)] *adj* unspeakable

inquiet, ète [ɛ̃kjɛ, -ɛt] *adj* anxious

inquiétant, e [ɛ̃kjetɑ̃, -ɑ̃t] *adj* worrying, disturbing

inquiéter [ɛ̃kjete] *vt* to worry; *(harceler)* to harass; **s'~** to worry; **s'~ de** to worry about; *(s'enquérir de)* to inquire about

inquiétude [ɛ̃kjetyd] *nf* anxiety

insaisissable [ɛ̃sezisabl(ə)] *adj* elusive

insatisfait, e [ɛ̃satisfɛ, -ɛt] *adj (non comblé)* unsatisfied; unfulfilled; *(mécontent)* dissatisfied

inscription [ɛ̃skʀipsjɔ̃] *nf* inscription; *(voir s'inscrire)* enrolment; registration

inscrire [ɛ̃skʀiʀ] *vt (marquer: sur son calepin etc)* to note *ou* write down; (: *sur un mur, une affiche etc)* to write; (: *dans la pierre, le métal)* to inscribe; *(mettre: sur une liste, un budget etc)* to put down; **s'~** *(pour une excursion etc)* to put one's name down; **s'~ (à)** *(club, parti)* to join; *(université)* to register *ou* enrol (at); *(examen, concours)* to register (for); **s'~ en faux contre** to challenge; **~ qn à** *(club, parti)* to enrol sb at

insecte [ɛ̃sɛkt(ə)] *nm* insect; **insecticide** *nm* insecticide

insensé, e [ɛ̃sɑ̃se] *adj* mad

insensibiliser [ɛ̃sɑ̃sibilize] *vt* to anaesthetize

insensible [ɛ̃sɑ̃sibl(ə)] *adj (nerf, membre)* numb; *(dur, indifférent)* insensitive; *(imperceptible)* imperceptible

insérer [ɛ̃seʀe] *vt* to insert; **s'~ dans** to fit into; to come within

insigne [ɛ̃siɲ] *nm (d'un parti, club)* badge ♦ *adj* distinguished

insignifiant, e [ɛ̃siɲifjɑ̃, -ɑ̃t] *adj* insignificant; trivial

insinuer [ɛ̃sinɥe] *vt* to insinuate, imply; **s'~ dans** *(fig)* to creep into

insister [ɛ̃siste] *vi* to insist; *(s'obstiner)* to keep on; **~ sur** *(détail, note)* to stress

insolation [ɛ̃sɔlasjɔ̃] *nf (MÉD)* sunstroke *no pl*

insolent, e [ɛ̃sɔlɑ̃, -ɑ̃t] *adj* insolent

insolite [ɛ̃sɔlit] *adj* strange, unusual

insomnie [ɛ̃sɔmni] *nf* insomnia *no pl*, sleeplessness *no pl*

insondable [ɛ̃sɔ̃dabl(ə)] *adj* unfathomable

insonoriser [ɛ̃sɔnɔʀize] *vt* to soundproof

insouciant, e [ɛ̃susjɑ̃, -ɑ̃t] *adj* carefree; *(imprévoyant)* heedless

insoumis, e [ɛ̃sumi, -iz] *adj (caractère, enfant)* rebellious, refractory; *(contrée, tribu)* unsubdued

insoupçonnable [ɛ̃supsɔnabl(ə)] *adj* unsuspected; *(personne)* above suspicion

insoupçonné, e [ɛ̃supsɔne] *adj* unsuspected

insoutenable [ɛ̃sutnabl(ə)] *adj (argument)* untenable; *(chaleur)* unbearable

inspecter [ɛ̃spɛkte] *vt* to inspect

inspecteur, trice [ɛ̃spɛktœʀ, -tʀis] *nm/f* inspector; **~ d'Académie** (regional) director of education; **~ des finances** ≈ tax inspector *(BRIT)*, ≈ Internal Revenue Service agent *(US)*

inspection [ɛ̃spɛksjɔ̃] *nf* inspection

inspirer [ɛ̃spiʀe] *vt (gén)* to inspire ♦ *vi (aspirer)* to breathe in; **s'~ de** *(suj: artiste)* to draw one's inspiration from

instable [ɛ̃stabl(ə)] *adj (meuble, équilibre)* unsteady; *(population, temps)* unsettled; *(régime, caractère)* unstable

installation [ɛ̃stalasjɔ̃] *nf* putting in *ou* up; fitting out; settling in; *(appareils etc)* fittings *pl*, installations *pl*; **~s** *nfpl (appareils)* equipment; *(équipements)* facilities

installer [ɛ̃stale] *vt (loger)*: **~ qn** to get sb settled; *(placer)* to put, place; *(meuble, gaz, électricité)* to put in; *(rideau, étagère, tente)* to put up; *(appartement)* to fit out; **s'~** *(s'établir: artisan, dentiste etc)* to set o.s. up; *(se loger)* to settle (o.s.); *(emménager)* to settle in; *(sur un siège, à un emplacement)* to settle (down); *(fig: maladie, grève)* to take a firm hold

instamment [ɛ̃stamɑ̃] *adv* urgently

instance [ɛ̃stɑ̃s] *nf (ADMIN: autorité)* authority; **~s** *nfpl (prières)* entreaties; **affaire en ~** matter pending; **être en ~ de divorce** to be awaiting a divorce

instant [ɛ̃stɑ̃] *nm* moment, instant; **dans un ~** in a moment; **à l'~** this instant; **à tout** *ou* **chaque ~** at any moment; constantly; **pour l'~** for the moment, for the time being; **par ~s** at times; **de tous les ~s** perpetual

instantané, e [ɛ̃stɑ̃tane] *adj (lait, café)* instant; *(explosion, mort)* instantaneous ♦ *nm* snapshot

instar [ɛ̃staʀ] : **à l'~ de** *prép* following the example of, like

instaurer [ɛ̃stɔʀe] *vt* to institute

instinct [ɛ̃stɛ̃] *nm* instinct

instituer [ɛ̃stitɥe] *vt* to set up

institut [ɛ̃stity] *nm* institute; **~ de beauté** beauty salon; **I~ Universitaire de Technologie** ≈ polytechnic

instituteur, trice [ɛ̃stitytœʀ, -tʀis] *nm/f* (primary school) teacher

institution [ɛ̃stitysjɔ̃] nf institution; (collège) private school

instruction [ɛ̃stryksjɔ̃] nf (enseignement, savoir) education; (JUR) (preliminary) investigation and hearing; ~s nfpl (ordres, mode d'emploi) directions, instructions; ~ **civique** civics sg

instruire [ɛ̃struir] vt (élèves) to teach; (recrues) to train; (JUR: affaire) to conduct the investigation for; **s'~** to educate o.s.; **instruit, e** adj educated

instrument [ɛ̃strymɑ̃] nm instrument; ~ **à cordes/vent** stringed/wind instrument; ~ **de mesure** measuring instrument; ~ **de musique** musical instrument; ~ **de travail** (working) tool

insu [ɛ̃sy] nm: **à l'~ de qn** without sb knowing (it)

insubmersible [ɛ̃sybmɛrsibl(ə)] adj unsinkable

insubordination [ɛ̃sybɔrdinasjɔ̃] nf rebelliousness; (MIL) insubordination

insuccès [ɛ̃syksɛ] nm failure

insuffisant, e [ɛ̃syfizɑ̃, -ɑ̃t] adj insufficient; (élève, travail) inadequate

insuffler [ɛ̃syfle] vt to blow; to inspire

insulaire [ɛ̃sylɛr] adj island cpd; (attitude) insular

insuline [ɛ̃sylin] nf insulin

insulte [ɛ̃sylt(ə)] nf insult; **insulter** vt to insult

insupportable [ɛ̃sypɔrtabl(ə)] adj unbearable

insurger [ɛ̃syrʒe]: **s'~ (contre)** vi to rise up ou rebel (against)

insurmontable [ɛ̃syrmɔ̃tabl(ə)] adj (difficulté) insuperable; (aversion) unconquerable

intact, e [ɛ̃takt] adj intact

intangible [ɛ̃tɑ̃ʒibl(ə)] adj intangible; (principe) inviolable

intarissable [ɛ̃tarisabl(ə)] adj inexhaustible

intégral, e, aux [ɛ̃tegral, -o] adj complete

intégrant, e [ɛ̃tegrɑ̃, -ɑ̃t] adj: **faire partie ~e de** to be an integral part of

intègre [ɛ̃tɛgr(ə)] adj upright

intégrer [ɛ̃tegre] vt to integrate; **s'~ à** ou **dans** to become integrated into

intégrisme [ɛ̃tegrism(ə)] nm fundamentalism

intellectuel, le [ɛ̃telɛktyɛl] adj intellectual ♦ nm/f intellectual; (péj) highbrow

intelligence [ɛ̃teliʒɑ̃s] nf intelligence; (compréhension): **l'~ de** the understanding of; (complicité): **regard d'~** glance of complicity; (accord): **vivre en bonne ~ avec qn** to be on good terms with sb

intelligent, e [ɛ̃teliʒɑ̃, -ɑ̃t] adj intelligent

intempéries [ɛ̃tɑ̃peri] nfpl bad weather sg

intempestif, ive [ɛ̃tɑ̃pɛstif, -iv] adj untimely

intenable [ɛ̃tnabl(ə)] adj (chaleur) unbearable

intendant, e [ɛ̃tɑ̃dɑ̃, -ɑ̃t] nm/f (MIL) quartermaster; (SCOL) bursar; (d'une propriété) steward

intense [ɛ̃tɑ̃s] adj intense; **intensif, ive** adj intensive

intenter [ɛ̃tɑ̃te] vt: ~ **un procès contre** ou **à** to start proceedings against

intention [ɛ̃tɑ̃sjɔ̃] nf intention; (JUR) intent; **avoir l'~ de faire** to intend to do; **à l'~ de** for; (renseignement) for the benefit of; (film, ouvrage) aimed at; **à cette ~ with** this aim in view; **intentionné, e** adj: **bien intentionné** well-meaning ou -intentioned; **mal intentionné** ill-intentioned

interactif, ive [ɛ̃tɛraktif, -iv] adj (COMPUT) interactive

intercaler [ɛ̃tɛrkale] vt to insert

intercepter [ɛ̃tɛrsɛpte] vt to intercept; (lumière, chaleur) to cut off

interchangeable [ɛ̃tɛrʃɑ̃ʒabl(ə)] adj interchangeable

interclasse [ɛ̃tɛrklɑs] nm (SCOL) break (between classes)

interdiction [ɛ̃tɛrdiksjɔ̃] nf ban

interdire [ɛ̃tɛrdir] vt to forbid; (ADMIN) to ban, prohibit; (: journal, livre) to ban; ~ **à qn de faire** to forbid sb to do, prohibit sb from doing; (suj: empêchement) to prevent sb from doing

interdit, e [ɛ̃tɛrdi, -it] adj (stupéfait) taken aback ♦ nm prohibition

intéressant, e [ɛ̃terɛsɑ̃, -ɑ̃t] adj interesting

intéressé, e [ɛ̃terese] adj (parties) involved, concerned; (amitié, motifs) self-interested

intéresser [ɛ̃terese] vt (captiver) to interest; (toucher) to be of interest to; (ADMIN: concerner) to affect, concern; **s'~ à** to be interested in

intérêt [ɛ̃terɛ] nm (aussi COMM) interest; (égoïsme) self-interest; **avoir ~ à faire** to do well to do

intérieur, e [ɛ̃terjœr] adj (mur, escalier, poche) inside; (commerce, politique) domestic; (cour, calme, vie) inner; (navigation) inland ♦ nm (d'une maison, d'un récipient etc) inside; (d'un pays, aussi: décor, mobilier) interior; (POL): **l'I~** the Interior; **à l'~ (de)** inside; (fig) within

intérim [ɛ̃terim] nm interim period; **assurer l'~ (de)** to deputize (for); **par ~** interim

intérimaire [ɛ̃terimɛr] nm/f (secrétaire) temporary secretary, temp (BRIT); (suppléant) temporary replacement

intérioriser [ɛ̃terjɔrize] vt to internalize

interlocuteur, trice [ɛ̃tɛrlɔkytœr, -tris] nm/f speaker; **son ~** the person he was speaking to

interloquer [ɛ̃tɛrlɔke] vt to take aback

intermède [ɛ̃tɛrmɛd] nm interlude

intermédiaire [ɛ̃tɛrmedjɛr] adj intermediate; middle; half-way ♦ *nm/f* intermediary; (COMM) middleman; **sans** ~ directly; **par l'**~ **de** through

intermittence [ɛ̃tɛʀmitɑ̃s] *nf*: **par** ~ sporadically, intermittently

internat [ɛ̃tɛʀna] *nm* (SCOL) boarding school

international, e, aux [ɛ̃tɛʀnasjɔnal, -o] *adj, nm/f* international

interne [ɛ̃tɛʀn(ə)] *adj* internal ♦ *nm/f* (SCOL) boarder; (MÉD) houseman; ~**r** [ɛ̃tɛʀne] *vt* (POL) to intern; (MÉD) to confine to a mental institution

interpeller [ɛ̃tɛʀpele] *vt* (*appeler*) to call out to; (*apostropher*) to shout at; (POLICE) to take in for questioning; (POL) to question

interphone [ɛ̃tɛʀfɔn] *nm* intercom

interposer [ɛ̃tɛʀpoze] *vt* to interpose; **s'**~ *vi* to intervene; **par personnes interposées** through a third party

interprète [ɛ̃tɛʀpʀɛt] *nm/f* interpreter; (*porte-parole*) spokesperson

interpréter [ɛ̃tɛʀpʀete] *vt* to interpret

interrogateur, trice [ɛ̃teʀɔgatœʀ, -tʀis] *adj* questioning, inquiring

interrogatif, ive [ɛ̃teʀɔgatif, -iv] *adj* (LING) interrogative

interrogation [ɛ̃teʀɔgasjɔ̃] *nf* question; (SCOL) (written *ou* oral) test

interrogatoire [ɛ̃teʀɔgatwaʀ] *nm* (POLICE) questioning *no pl*; (JUR) cross-examination

interroger [ɛ̃teʀɔʒe] *vt* to question; (IN-FORM) to consult; (SCOL) to test

interrompre [ɛ̃teʀɔ̃pʀ(ə)] *vt* (*gén*) to interrupt; (*travail, voyage*) to break off, interrupt; **s'**~ to break off

interrupteur [ɛ̃teʀyptœʀ] *nm* switch

interruption [ɛ̃teʀypsjɔ̃] *nf* interruption; (*pause*) break

interstice [ɛ̃tɛʀstis] *nm* crack; slit

interurbain [ɛ̃tɛʀyʀbɛ̃] *nm* (TÉL) long-distance call service ♦ *adj* long-distance

intervalle [ɛ̃tɛʀval] *nm* (*espace*) space; (*de temps*) interval; **dans l'**~ in the meantime

intervenir [ɛ̃tɛʀvəniʀ] *vi* (*gén*) to intervene; (*survenir*) to take place; ~ **auprès de qn** to intervene with sb

intervention [ɛ̃tɛʀvɑ̃sjɔ̃] *nf* intervention; (*discours*) paper; ~ **chirurgicale** (surgical) operation

intervertir [ɛ̃tɛʀvɛʀtiʀ] *vt* to invert (the order of), reverse

interview [ɛ̃tɛʀvju] *nf* interview

intestin, e [ɛ̃tɛstɛ̃, -in] *adj* internal ♦ *nm* intestine

intime [ɛ̃tim] *adj* intimate; (*vie, journal*) private; (*conviction*) inmost; (*dîner, cérémonie*) quiet ♦ *nm/f* close friend

intimer [ɛ̃time] *vt* (JUR) to notify; ~ **à qn l'ordre de faire** to order sb to do

intimider [ɛ̃timide] *vt* to intimidate

intimité [ɛ̃timite] *nf*: **dans l'**~ in private; (*sans formalités*) with only a few friends, quietly

intitulé, e [ɛ̃tityle] *adj* entitled

intolérable [ɛ̃tɔleʀabl(ə)] *adj* intolerable

intoxication [ɛ̃tɔksikasjɔ̃] *nf*: ~ **alimentaire** food poisoning

intoxiquer [ɛ̃tɔksike] *vt* to poison; (*fig*) to brainwash

intraduisible [ɛ̃tʀadyizibl(ə)] *adj* untranslatable; (*fig*) inexpressible

intraitable [ɛ̃tʀetabl(ə)] *adj* inflexible, uncompromising

intransigeant, e [ɛ̃tʀɑ̃ziʒɑ̃, -ɑ̃t] *adj* intransigent; (*morale*) uncompromising

intransitif, ive [ɛ̃tʀɑ̃zitif, -iv] *adj* (LING) intransitive

intrépide [ɛ̃tʀepid] *adj* dauntless

intrigue [ɛ̃tʀig] *nf* (*scénario*) plot

intriguer [ɛ̃tʀige] *vi* to scheme ♦ *vt* to puzzle, intrigue

intrinsèque [ɛ̃tʀɛ̃sɛk] *adj* intrinsic

introduction [ɛ̃tʀɔdyksjɔ̃] *nf* introduction

introduire [ɛ̃tʀɔdɥiʀ] *vt* to introduce; (*visiteur*) to show in; (*aiguille, clef*): ~ **qch dans** to insert *ou* introduce sth into; **s'**~ **dans** to gain entry into; to get o.s. accepted into; (*eau, fumée*) to get into

introuvable [ɛ̃tʀuvabl(ə)] *adj* which cannot be found; (COMM) unobtainable

introverti, e [ɛ̃tʀɔvɛʀti] *nm/f* introvert

intrus, e [ɛ̃tʀy, -yz] *nm/f* intruder

intrusion [ɛ̃tʀyzjɔ̃] *nf* intrusion; interference

intuition [ɛ̃tɥisjɔ̃] *nf* intuition

inusable [inyzabl(ə)] *adj* hard-wearing

inusité, e [inyzite] *adj* rarely used

inutile [inytil] *adj* useless; (*superflu*) unnecessary; **inutilisable** *adj* unusable

invalide [ɛ̃valid] *adj* disabled ♦ *nm*: ~ **de guerre** disabled ex-serviceman

invasion [ɛ̃vazjɔ̃] *nf* invasion

invectiver [ɛ̃vɛktive] *vt* to hurl abuse at

invendable [ɛ̃vɑ̃dabl(ə)] *adj* unsaleable; unmarketable; **invendus** *nmpl* unsold goods

inventaire [ɛ̃vɑ̃tɛʀ] *nm* inventory; (COMM: *liste*) stocklist; (: *opération*) stocktaking *no pl*; (*fig*) survey

inventer [ɛ̃vɑ̃te] *vt* to invent; (*subterfuge*) to devise, invent; (*histoire, excuse*) to make up, invent; **inventeur** *nm* inventor; **inventif, ive** *adj* inventive; **invention** *nf* invention

inverse [ɛ̃vɛʀs(ə)] *adj* reverse; opposite; inverse ♦ *nm* inverse, reverse; **dans l'ordre** ~ in the reverse order; **en sens** ~ in (*ou* from) the opposite direction; **inversement** *adv* conversely; **inverser** *vt* to invert, reverse; (ÉLEC) to reverse

investir [ɛ̃vɛstiʀ] *vt* to invest; **investissement** *nm* investment; **investiture** *nf* investiture; (*à une élection*) nomination

invétéré, e [ɛ̃vetere] *adj* (*habitude*) ingrained; (*bavard, buveur*) inveterate

invisible [ɛ̃vizibl(ə)] *adj* invisible

invitation [ɛ̃vitɑsjɔ̃] *nf* invitation

invité, e [ɛ̃vite] *nm/f* guest

inviter [ɛ̃vite] *vt* to invite; ~ **qn à faire** (*suj: chose*) to induce *ou* tempt sb to do

involontaire [ɛ̃vɔlɔ̃tɛʀ] *adj* (*mouvement*) involuntary; (*insulte*) unintentional; (*complice*) unwitting

invoquer [ɛ̃vɔke] *vt* (*Dieu, muse*) to call upon, invoke; (*prétexte*) to put forward (as an excuse); (*loi, texte*) to refer to

invraisemblable [ɛ̃vʀɛsɑ̃blabl(ə)] *adj* unlikely, improbable; incredible

iode [jɔd] *nm* iodine

irai *etc vb voir* **aller**

Irak [iʀak] *nm* Iraq

Iran [iʀɑ̃] *nm* Iran

irions *etc vb voir* **aller**

irlandais, e [iʀlɑ̃dɛ, -ɛz] *adj* Irish ♦ *nm/f*: **I~**, **e** Irishman/woman; **les I~** the Irish

Irlande [iʀlɑ̃d] *nf* Ireland; ~ **du Nord** Northern Ireland

ironie [iʀɔni] *nf* irony; **ironique** *adj* ironical; **ironiser** *vi* to be ironical

irons *etc vb voir* **aller**

irradier [iʀadje] *vi* to radiate ♦ *vt* (*aliment*) to irradiate

irraisonné, e [iʀezɔne] *adj* irrational, unreasoned

irrationnel, le [iʀasjɔnɛl] *adj* irrational

irréalisable [iʀealizabl(ə)] *adj* unrealizable; impracticable

irrécupérable [iʀekypeʀabl(ə)] *adj* unreclaimable, beyond repair; (*personne*) beyond redemption

irrécusable [iʀekyzabl(ə)] *adj* unimpeachable; incontestable

irréductible [iʀedyktibl(ə)] *adj* indomitable, implacable

irréel, le [iʀeɛl] *adj* unreal

irréfléchi, e [iʀefleʃi] *adj* thoughtless

irrégularité [iʀegylaʀite] *nf* irregularity; unevenness *no pl*

irrégulier, ière [iʀegylje, -jɛʀ] *adj* irregular; uneven; (*élève, athlète*) erratic

irrémédiable [iʀemedjabl(ə)] *adj* irreparable

irréprochable [iʀepʀɔʃabl(ə)] *adj* irreproachable, beyond reproach; (*tenue*) impeccable

irrésistible [iʀezistibl(ə)] *adj* irresistible; (*preuve, logique*) compelling

irrespectueux, euse [iʀɛspɛktɥø, -øz] *adj* disrespectful

irriguer [iʀige] *vt* to irrigate

irritable [iʀitabl(ə)] *adj* irritable

irriter [iʀite] *vt* to irritate

irruption [iʀypsjɔ̃] *nf* irruption *no pl*; **faire** ~ **dans** to burst into

islamique [islamik] *adj* Islamic

Islande [islɑ̃d] *nf* Iceland

isolant, e [izɔlɑ̃, -ɑ̃t] *adj* insulating; (*insonorisant*) soundproofing

isolation [izɔlɑsjɔ̃] *nf* insulation

isolé, e [izɔle] *adj* isolated; insulated

isoler [izɔle] *vt* to isolate; (*prisonnier*) to put in solitary confinement; (*ville*) to cut off, isolate; (*ÉLEC*) to insulate

isoloir *nm* polling booth

Israël [isʀaɛl] *nm* Israel; **israélien, ne** *adj, nm/f* Israeli; **israélite** *adj* Jewish ♦ *nm/f* Jew(Jewess)

issu, e [isy] *adj*: ~ **de** descended from; (*fig*) stemming from; ~**e** *nf* (*ouverture, sortie*) exit; (*solution*) way out, solution; (*dénouement*) outcome; **à l'**~**e de** at the conclusion *ou* close of; **rue sans** ~**e** dead end

Italie [itali] *nf* Italy; **italien, ne** *adj, nm/f* Italian ♦ *nm* (*LING*) Italian

italique [italik] *nm*: **en** ~ in italics

itinéraire [itineʀɛʀ] *nm* itinerary, route

IUT *sigle m* = **Institut universitaire de technologie**

IVG *sigle f* (= *interruption volontaire de grossesse*) abortion

ivoire [ivwaʀ] *nm* ivory

ivre [ivʀ(ə)] *adj* drunk; ~ **de** (*colère, bonheur*) wild with; **ivresse** *nf* drunkenness; **ivrogne** *nm/f* drunkard

J j

j' [ʒ] *pron* I

jachère [ʒaʃɛʀ] *nf*: (**être**) **en** ~ (to lie) fallow

jacinthe [ʒasɛ̃t] *nf* hyacinth

jack [ʒak] *nm* jack plug

jadis [ʒadis] *adv* in times past, formerly

jaillir [ʒajiʀ] *vi* (*liquide*) to spurt out; (*fig*) to burst out; to flood out

jais [ʒɛ] *nm* jet; (**d'un noir**) **de** ~ jet-black

jalon [ʒalɔ̃] *nm* range pole; (*fig*) milestone; **jalonner** *vt* to mark out; (*fig*) to mark, punctuate

jalousie [ʒaluzi] *nf* jealousy; (*store*) (Venetian) blind

jaloux, ouse [ʒalu, -uz] *adj* jealous

jamais [ʒamɛ] *adv* never; (*sans négation*) ever; **ne ...** ~ never; **à** ~ for ever

jambe [ʒɑ̃b] *nf* leg

jambon [ʒɑ̃bɔ̃] *nm* ham

jambonneau, x [ʒɑ̃bɔno] *nm* knuckle of

ham
jante [ʒɑ̃t] *nf* (wheel) rim
janvier [ʒɑ̃vje] *nm* January
Japon [ʒapɔ̃] *nm* Japan; **japonais, e** *adj, nm/f* Japanese ♦ *nm* (LING) Japanese
japper [ʒape] *vi* to yap, yelp
jaquette [ʒakɛt] *nf* (de cérémonie) morning coat; (de dame) jacket
jardin [ʒaRdɛ̃] *nm* garden; ~ **d'enfants** nursery school; **jardinage** *nm* gardening; **jardinier, ière** *nm/f* gardener; **jardinière** *nf* (de fenêtre) window box
jarre [ʒaR] *nf* (earthenware) jar
jarret [ʒaRɛ] *nm* back of knee, ham; (CULIN) knuckle, shin
jarretelle [ʒaRtɛl] *nf* suspender (BRIT), garter (US)
jarretière [ʒaRtjɛR] *nf* garter
jaser [ʒaze] *vi* to chatter, prattle; (indiscrètement) to gossip
jatte [ʒat] *nf* basin, bowl
jauge [ʒoʒ] *nf* (instrument) gauge; **jauger** *vt* (fig) to size up
jaune [ʒon] *adj, nm* yellow ♦ *adv* (fam): **rire** ~ to laugh on the other side of one's face; ~ **d'œuf** (egg) yolk; **jaunir** *vi, vt* to turn yellow
jaunisse [ʒonis] *nf* jaundice
Javel [ʒavɛl] *nf voir* **eau**
javelot [ʒavlo] *nm* javelin
J.-C. *sigle* = Jésus-Christ
je(j') [ʒ(ə)] *pron* I
jean [dʒin] *nm* jeans *pl*
Jésus-Christ [ʒezykRi(st)] *n* Jesus Christ; **600 avant/après** ~ *ou* **J.-C.** 600 B.C./A.D.
jet¹ [ʒɛ] *nm* (lancer) throwing *no pl*, throw; (jaillissement) jet; spurt; (de tuyau) nozzle; **du premier jet** at the first attempt *or* shot; **jet d'eau** fountain; spray
jet² [dʒɛt] *nm* (avion) jet
jetable [ʒətabl(ə)] *adj* disposable
jetée [ʒəte] *nf* jetty; pier
jeter [ʒəte] *vt* (gén) to throw; (se défaire de) to throw away *ou* out; (son, lueur etc) to give out; **se** ~ **dans** to flow into; ~ **qch à qn** to throw sth to sb; (de façon agressive) to throw sth at sb; ~ **un coup d'œil (à)** to take a look (at); ~ **un sort à qn** to cast a spell on sb
jeton [ʒətɔ̃] *nm* (au jeu) counter; (de téléphone) token
jette *etc vb voir* **jeter**
jeu, x [ʒø] *nm* (divertissement, TECH: d'une pièce) play; (TENNIS: partie, FOOTBALL etc: façon de jouer) game; (THÉÂTRE etc) acting; (au casino): **le** ~ gambling; (fonctionnement) working, interplay; (série d'objets, jouet) set; (CARTES) hand; **en** ~ at stake; at work; **remettre en** ~ to throw in; **entrer/mettre en** ~ to come/bring into play; ~ **de cartes** pack of cards; ~ **d'échecs** chess set; ~ **de hasard** game of

chance; ~ **de mots** pun
jeudi [ʒødi] *nm* Thursday
jeun [ʒœ̃]: **à** ~ *adv* on an empty stomach
jeune [ʒœn] *adj* young; ~ **fille** girl; ~ **homme** young man
jeûne [ʒøn] *nm* fast
jeunesse [ʒœnɛs] *nf* youth; (aspect) youthfulness; youngness
joaillerie [ʒoajRi] *nf* jewel trade; jewellery; **joaillier, ière** *nm/f* jeweller
joie [ʒwa] *nf* joy
joindre [ʒwɛ̃dR(ə)] *vt* to join; (à une lettre): ~ **qch à** to enclose sth with; (contacter) to contact, get in touch with; **se** ~ **à** to join; ~ **les mains** to put one's hands together
joint, e [ʒwɛ̃, ʒwɛ̃t] *adj*: **pièce** ~e enclosure ♦ *nm* joint; (ligne) join; ~ **de culasse** cylinder head gasket; ~ **de robinet** washer
joli, e [ʒɔli] *adj* pretty, attractive; **c'est du** ~! (ironique) that's very nice!; **c'est bien** ~, **mais ...** that's all very well but ...
jonc [ʒɔ̃] *nm* (bul)rush
joncher [ʒɔ̃ʃe] *vt* (suj: choses) to be strewed on
jonction [ʒɔ̃ksjɔ̃] *nf* joining; (point de) ~ junction
jongleur, euse [ʒɔ̃glœR, -øz] *nm/f* juggler
jonquille [ʒɔ̃kij] *nf* daffodil
Jordanie [ʒɔRdani] *nf*: **la** ~ Jordan
joue [ʒu] *nf* cheek; **mettre en** ~ to take aim at
jouer [ʒwe] *vt* to play; (somme d'argent, réputation) to stake, wager; (pièce, rôle) to perform; (film) to show; (simuler: sentiment) to affect, feign ♦ *vi* to play; (THÉÂTRE, CINÉMA) to act, perform; (bois, porte: se voiler) to warp; (clef, pièce: avoir du jeu) to be loose; **se** ~ **de** (difficultés) to make light of; to deceive; ~ **sur** (miser) to gamble on; ~ **de** (MUS) to play; ~ **des coudes** to use one's elbows; ~ **à** (jeu, sport, roulette) to play; ~ **avec** (risquer) to gamble with; ~ **un tour à qn** to play a trick on sb; ~ **serré** to play a close game; ~ **de malchance** to be dogged with ill-luck
jouet [ʒwɛ] *nm* toy; **être le** ~ **de** (illusion etc) to be the victim of
joueur, euse [ʒwœR, -øz] *nm/f* player; **être beau** ~ to be a good loser
joufflu, e [ʒufly] *adj* chubby-cheeked
joug [ʒu] *nm* yoke
jouir [ʒwiR] : ~ **de** *vt* to enjoy; **jouissance** *nf* pleasure; (JUR) use
joujou [ʒuʒu] (fam) *nm* toy
jour [ʒuR] *nm* day; (opposé à la nuit) day, daytime; (clarté) daylight; (fig: aspect) light; (ouverture) opening; **au** ~ **le** ~ from day to day; **de nos** ~s these days; **il fait** ~ it's daylight; **au grand** ~ (fig) in the open; **mettre au** ~ to disclose; **mettre à** ~ to update; **donner le** ~ **à** to give birth to; **voir le** ~ to be born; ~ **férié** *nm* public holiday

journal, aux [ʒuʀnal, -o] *nm* (news)paper; (*personnel*) journal, diary; ~ **de bord** log; ~ **parlé/télévisé** radio/television news *sg*

journalier, ière [ʒuʀnalje, -jɛʀ] *adj* daily; (*banal*) everyday

journalisme [ʒuʀnalism(ə)] *nm* journalism; **journaliste** *nm/f* journalist

journée [ʒuʀne] *nf* day; **la ~ continue** the 9 to 5 working day

journellement [ʒuʀnɛlmɑ̃] *adv* daily

joyau, x [ʒwajo] *nm* gem, jewel

joyeux, euse [ʒwajø, -øz] *adj* joyful, merry; ~ **Noël!** merry Christmas!; ~ **anniversaire!** happy birthday!

jubiler [ʒybile] *vi* to be jubilant, exult

jucher [ʒyʃe] *vt, vi* to perch

judas [ʒyda] *nm* (*trou*) spy-hole

judiciaire [ʒydisjɛʀ] *adj* judicial

judicieux, euse [ʒydisjø, -øz] *adj* judicious

judo [ʒydo] *nm* judo

juge [ʒyʒ] *nm* judge; ~ **d'instruction** examining (*BRIT*) *ou* committing (*US*) magistrate; ~ **de paix** justice of the peace

jugé [ʒyʒe] : **au ~** *adv* by guesswork

jugement [ʒyʒmɑ̃] *nm* judgment; (*JUR: au pénal*) sentence; (: *au civil*) decision

juger [ʒyʒe] *vt* to judge; ~ **qn/qch satisfaisant** to consider sb/sth (to be) satisfactory; ~ **bon de faire** to see fit to do; ~ **de** to appreciate

juif, ive [ʒɥif, -iv] *adj* Jewish ♦ *nm/f* Jew(Jewess)

juillet [ʒɥijɛ] *nm* July

juin [ʒɥɛ̃] *nm* June

jumeau, elle, x [ʒymo, -ɛl] *adj, nm/f* twin; *voir aussi* **jumelle**

jumeler [ʒymle] *vt* to twin

jumelle [ʒymɛl] *adj, nf voir* **jumeau**; (*appareil*) binoculars

jument [ʒymɑ̃] *nf* mare

jungle [ʒɔ̃gl(ə)] *nf* jungle

jupe [ʒyp] *nf* skirt

jupon [ʒypɔ̃] *nm* waist slip

juré, e [ʒyʀe] *nm/f* juror

jurer [ʒyʀe] *vt* (*obéissance etc*) to swear, vow ♦ *vi* (*dire des jurons*) to swear, curse; (*dissoner*): ~ (**avec**) to clash (with); (*s'engager*): ~ **de faire/que** to swear *ou* vow to do/that; (*affirmer*): ~ **que** to swear *ou* vouch that; ~ **de qch** (*s'en porter garant*) to swear to sth

juridique [ʒyʀidik] *adj* legal

juron [ʒyʀɔ̃] *nm* curse, swearword

jury [ʒyʀi] *nm* jury; board

jus [ʒy] *nm* juice; (*de viande*) gravy, (meat) juice; ~ **de fruit** fruit juice

jusque [ʒysk(ə)] : **jusqu'à** *prép* (*endroit*) as far as, (up) to; (*moment*) until, till; (*limite*) up to; ~ **sur/dans** up to; (*y compris*) even on/in; **jusqu'à ce que** until; **jusqu'à présent** until now

juste [ʒyst(ə)] *adj* (*équitable*) just, fair; (*légitime*) just, justified; (*exact, vrai*) right; (*étroit, insuffisant*) tight ♦ *adv* right; tight; (*chanter*) in tune; (*seulement*) just; ~ **assez/au-dessus** just enough/above; **au ~** exactly; **le ~ milieu** the happy medium; **justement** *adv* rightly, justly; (*précisément*) just, precisely; **justesse** *nf* (*précision*) accuracy; (*d'une remarque*) aptness; (*d'une opinion*) soundness; **de justesse** just

justice [ʒystis] *nf* (*équité*) fairness, justice; (*ADMIN*) justice; **rendre la ~** to dispense justice; **rendre ~ à qn** to do sb justice; **justicier, ière** [ʒystisje, -jɛʀ] *nm/f* judge, righter of wrongs

justificatif, ive [ʒystifikatif, -iv] *adj* (*document*) supporting; **pièce justificative** written proof

justifier [ʒystifje] *vt* to justify; ~ **de** to prove

juteux, euse [ʒytø, -øz] *adj* juicy

juvénile [ʒyvenil] *adj* young, youthful

K k

K [ka] *nm* (*INFORM*) K

kaki [kaki] *adj inv* khaki

kangourou [kɑ̃guʀu] *nm* kangaroo

karaté [kaʀate] *nm* karate

karting [kaʀtiŋ] *nm* go-carting, karting

kermesse [kɛʀmɛs] *nf* bazaar, (charity) fête; village fair

kidnapper [kidnape] *vt* to kidnap

kilo [kilo] *nm* = **kilogramme**

kilo [kilo] : ~**gramme** *nm* kilogramme; ~**métrage** *nm* number of kilometres travelled, ≈ mileage; ~**mètre** *nm* kilometre; ~**métrique** *adj* (*distance*) in kilometres

kinésithérapeute [kineziteʀapøt] *nm/f* physiotherapist

kiosque [kjɔsk(ə)] *nm* kiosk, stall

klaxon [klaksɔn] *nm* horn; **klaxonner** *vi, vt* to hoot (*BRIT*), honk (*US*)

km. *abr* = **kilomètre**; **km/h** (= *kilomètres/heure*) ≈ m.p.h.

Ko [kao] *abr* (*INFORM*: *kilooctet*) K

K.-O. [kao] *adj inv* (knocked) out

kyste [kist(ə)] *nm* cyst

L l

l' [l] *dét voir* **le**

la [la] *dét voir* **le** ♦ *nm* (MUS) A; (*en chantant la gamme*) la

là [la] *adv* there; (*ici*) here; (*dans le temps*) then; **elle n'est pas ~** she isn't here; **c'est ~ que** this is where; **~ où** where; **de ~** (*fig*) hence; **par ~** by that; **tout est ~** that's what it's all about; *voir aussi* **-ci; celui; là-bas** *adv* there

label [label] *nm* stamp, seal

labeur [labœʀ] *nm* toil *no pl*, toiling *no pl*

labo [labo] *abr m* (= *laboratoire*) lab

laboratoire [labɔʀatwaʀ] *nm* laboratory; **~ de langues** language laboratory

laborieux, euse [labɔʀjø, -øz] *adj* (*tâche*) laborious; **classes laborieuses** working classes

labour [labuʀ] *nm* ploughing *no pl*; **~s** *nmpl* (*champs*) ploughed fields; **cheval de ~** plough- *ou* cart-horse; **bœuf de ~** ox

labourer [labuʀe] *vt* to plough; (*fig*) to make deep gashes *ou* furrows in

labyrinthe [labiʀɛ̃t] *nm* labyrinth, maze

lac [lak] *nm* lake

lacer [lase] *vt* to lace *ou* do up

lacérer [laseʀe] *vt* to tear to shreds

lacet [lasɛ] *nm* (*de chaussure*) lace; (*de route*) sharp bend; (*piège*) snare

lâche [lɑʃ] *adj* (*poltron*) cowardly; (*desserré*) loose, slack ♦ *nm/f* coward

lâcher [lɑʃe] *nm* (*de ballons, oiseaux*) release ♦ *vt* to let go of; (*ce qui tombe, abandonner*) to drop; (*oiseau, animal: libérer*) to release, set free; (*fig: mot, remarque*) to let slip, come out with; (SPORT: *distancer*) to leave behind ♦ *vi* (*fil, amarres*) to break, give way; (*freins*) to fail; **~ les amarres** (NAVIG) to cast off (the moorings); **~ les chiens** to unleash the dogs; **~ prise** to let go

lâcheté [lɑʃte] *nf* cowardice; lowness

lacrymogène [lakʀimɔʒɛn] *adj*: **gaz ~** teargas

lacté, e [lakte] *adj* (*produit, régime*) milk *cpd*

lacune [lakyn] *nf* gap

là-dedans [ladədɑ̃] *adv* inside (there), in it; (*fig*) in that

là-dessous [ladsu] *adv* underneath, under there; (*fig*) behind that

là-dessus [ladsy] *adv* on there; (*fig*) at that point; about that

ladite [ladit] *dét voir* **ledit**

lagune [lagyn] *nf* lagoon

là-haut [la'o] *adv* up there

laïc [laik] *adj*, *nm/f* = **laïque**

laid, e [lɛ, lɛd] *adj* ugly; **laideur** *nf* ugliness *no pl*

lainage [lɛnaʒ] *nm* woollen garment; woollen material

laine [lɛn] *nf* wool

laïque [laik] *adj* lay, civil; (SCOL) state *cpd* ♦ *nm/f* layman(woman)

laisse [lɛs] *nf* (*de chien*) lead, leash; **tenir en ~** to keep on a lead *ou* leash

laisser [lɛse] *vt* to leave ♦ *vb aux*: **~ qn faire** to let sb do; **se ~ aller** to let o.s. go; **laisse-toi faire** let me (*ou* him *etc*) do it; **laisser-aller** *nm* carelessness, slovenliness; **laissez-passer** *nm inv* pass

lait [lɛ] *nm* milk; **frère/sœur de ~** foster brother/sister; **~ condensé/concentré** evaporated/condensed milk; **laiterie** *nf* dairy; **laitier, ière** *adj* dairy *cpd* ♦ *nm/f* milkman(dairywoman)

laiton [lɛtɔ̃] *nm* brass

laitue [lety] *nf* lettuce

laïus [lajys] (*péj*) *nm* spiel

lambeau, x [lɑ̃bo] *nm* scrap; **en ~x** in tatters, tattered

lambris [lɑ̃bʀi] *nm* panelling *no pl*

lame [lam] *nf* blade; (*vague*) wave; (*lamelle*) strip; **~ de fond** ground swell *no pl*; **~ de rasoir** razor blade

lamelle [lamɛl] *nf* thin strip *ou* blade

lamentable [lamɑ̃tabl(ə)] *adj* appalling; pitiful

lamenter [lamɑ̃te]: **se ~** *vi* to moan (over)

lampadaire [lɑ̃padɛʀ] *nm* (*de salon*) standard lamp; (*dans la rue*) street lamp

lampe [lɑ̃p(ə)] *nf* lamp; (TECH) valve; **~ à souder** blowlamp; **~ de poche** torch (BRIT), flashlight (US)

lampion [lɑ̃pjɔ̃] *nm* Chinese lantern

lance [lɑ̃s] *nf* spear; **~ d'incendie** fire hose

lancée [lɑ̃se] *nf*: **être/continuer sur sa ~** to be under way/keep going

lancement [lɑ̃smɑ̃] *nm* launching

lance-pierres [lɑ̃spjɛʀ] *nm inv* catapult

lancer [lɑ̃se] *nm* (SPORT) throwing *no pl*, throw ♦ *vt* to throw; (*émettre, projeter*) to throw out, send out; (*produit, fusée, bateau, artiste*) to launch; (*injure*) to hurl, fling; (*proclamation, mandat d'arrêt*) to issue; **se ~** *vi* (*prendre de l'élan*) to build up speed; (*se précipiter*): **se ~ sur** *ou* **contre** to rush at; **se ~ dans** (*discussion*) to launch into; (*aventure*) to embark on; **~ qch à qn** to throw sth to sb; (*de façon agressive*) to throw sth at sb; **~ du poids** *nm* putting the shot

lancinant, e [lɑ̃sinɑ̃, -ɑ̃t] *adj* (*regrets etc*)

haunting; (*douleur*) shooting
landau [lɑ̃do] *nm* pram (*BRIT*), baby carriage (*US*)
lande [lɑ̃d] *nf* moor
langage [lɑ̃gaʒ] *nm* language
langer [lɑ̃ʒe] *vt* to change (the nappy (*BRIT*) ou diaper (*US*) of)
langouste [lɑ̃gust(ə)] *nf* crayfish *inv*; **langoustine** *nf* Dublin Bay prawn
langue [lɑ̃g] *nf* (*ANAT*, *CULIN*) tongue; (*LING*) language; **tirer la ~** (à) to stick out one's tongue (at); **de ~ française** French-speaking; **~ maternelle** native language, mother tongue; **~ verte** slang; **~ vivante** modern language
langueur [lɑ̃gœʀ] *nf* languidness
languir [lɑ̃giʀ] *vi* to languish; (*conversation*) to flag; **faire ~ qn** to keep sb waiting
lanière [lanjɛʀ] *nf* (*de fouet*) lash; (*de valise, bretelle*) strap
lanterne [lɑ̃tɛʀn(ə)] *nf* (*portable*) lantern; (*électrique*) light, lamp; (*de voiture*) (side)light
laper [lape] *vt* to lap up
lapidaire [lapidɛʀ] *adj* stone *cpd*; (*fig*) terse
lapin [lapɛ̃] *nm* rabbit; (*peau*) rabbitskin; (*fourrure*) cony
Laponie [laponi] *nf* Lapland
laps [laps] *nm:* **~ de temps** space of time, time *no pl*
laque [lak] *nf* lacquer; (*brute*) shellac; (*pour cheveux*) hair spray
laquelle [lakɛl] *pron voir* **lequel**
larcin [laʀsɛ̃] *nm* theft
lard [laʀ] *nm* (*graisse*) fat; (*bacon*) (streaky) bacon
lardon [laʀdɔ̃] *nm:* **~s** chopped bacon
large [laʀʒ(ə)] *adj* wide; broad; (*fig*) generous ♦ *adv:* **calculer/voir ~** to allow extra/think big ♦ *nm* (*largeur*): **5 m de ~** 5 m wide *ou* in width; (*mer*): **le ~** the open sea; **au ~ de** off; **~ d'esprit** broad-minded; **largement** *adv* widely; greatly; easily; generously; **largesse** *nf* generosity; **largesses** *nfpl* (*dons*) liberalities; **largeur** *nf* (*qu'on mesure*) width; (*impression visuelle*) wideness, width; breadth; broadness
larguer [laʀge] *vt* to drop; **~ les amarres** to cast off (the moorings)
larme [laʀm(ə)] *nf* tear; (*fig*) drop; **en ~s** in tears; **larmoyer** *vi* (*yeux*) to water; (*se plaindre*) to whimper
larvé, e [laʀve] *adj* (*fig*) latent
laryngite [laʀɛ̃ʒit] *nf* laryngitis
las, lasse [la, las] *adj* weary
laser [lazɛʀ] *nm:* (*rayon*) **~** laser (beam); **chaîne ~** compact disc (player); **disque ~** compact disc
lasse [las] *adj voir* **las**
lasser [lase] *vt* to weary, tire; **se ~ de** *vt* to grow weary *ou* tired of
latéral, e, aux [lateʀal, -o] *adj* side *cpd*, lateral

latin, e [latɛ̃, -in] *adj*, *nm/f* Latin ♦ *nm* (*LING*) Latin
latitude [latityd] *nf* latitude
latte [lat] *nf* lath, slat; (*de plancher*) board
lauréat, e [lɔʀea, -at] *nm/f* winner
laurier [lɔʀje] *nm* (*BOT*) laurel; (*CULIN*) bay leaves *pl*; **~s** *nmpl* (*fig*) laurels
lavable [lavabl(ə)] *adj* washable
lavabo [lavabo] *nm* washbasin; **~s** *nmpl* (*toilettes*) toilet *sg*
lavage [lavaʒ] *nm* washing *no pl*, wash; **~ de cerveau** brainwashing *no pl*
lavande [lavɑ̃d] *nf* lavender
lave [lav] *nf* lava *no pl*
lave-glace [lavglas] *nm* windscreen (*BRIT*) *ou* windshield (*US*) washer
lave-linge [lavlɛ̃ʒ] *nm inv* washing machine
laver [lave] *vt* to wash; (*tache*) to wash off; **se ~** *vi* to have a wash, wash; **se ~ les mains/dents** to wash one's hands/clean one's teeth; **~ qn de** (*accusation*) to clear sb of; **laverie** *nf:* **laverie** (**automatique**) launderette; **lavette** *nf* dish cloth; (*fam*) drip; **laveur, euse** *nm/f* cleaner; **~-vaisselle** *nm inv* dishwasher; *lavoir nm* wash house
laxatif, ive [laksatif, -iv] *adj*, *nm* laxative

─────────── *MOT CLÉ*

le(l'), la [l(ə)] (*pl* **les**) *art déf* **1** the; **~ livre/la pomme/l'arbre** the book/the apple/the tree; **les étudiants** the students
2 (*noms abstraits*): **~ courage/l'amour/la jeunesse** courage/love/youth
3 (*indiquant la possession*): **se casser la jambe** *etc* to break one's leg *etc*; **levez la main** put your hand up; **avoir les yeux gris/~ nez rouge** to have grey eyes/a red nose
4 (*temps*): **~ matin/soir** in the morning/evening; mornings/evenings; **~ jeudi** *etc* (*d'habitude*) on Thursdays *etc*; (*ce jeudi-là etc*) on (the) Thursday
5 (*distribution, évaluation*) a, an; **10F ~ mètre/kilo** 10F a *ou* per metre/kilo; **~ tiers/quart de** a third/quarter of
♦ *pron* **1** (*personne: mâle*) him; (: *femelle*) her; (: *pluriel*) them; **je ~/la/les vois** I can see him/her/them
2 (*animal, chose: singulier*) it; (: *pluriel*) them; **je ~** (*ou* **la**) **vois** I can see it; **je les vois** I can see them
3 (*remplaçant une phrase*): **je ne ~ savais pas** I didn't know (about it); **il était riche et ne l'est plus** he was once rich but no longer is

─────────

lécher [leʃe] *vt* to lick; (*laper: lait, eau*) to lick *ou* lap up; **~ les vitrines** to go window-shopping
leçon [ləsɔ̃] *nf* lesson; **faire la ~ à** (*fig*) to

give a lecture to; **~s de conduite** driving lessons

lecteur, trice [lɛktœʀ, -tʀis] *nm/f* reader; (*d'université*) foreign language assistant ♦ *nm* (*TECH*): **~ de cassettes** cassette player; **~ de disque compact** compact disc player; **~ de disquette** disk drive

lecture [lɛktyʀ] *nf* reading

ledit, ladite [lədi] (*mpl* **lesdits**, *fpl* **lesdites**) *dét* the aforesaid

légal, e, aux [legal, -o] *adj* legal

légende [leʒãd] *nf* (*mythe*) legend; (*de carte, plan*) key; (*de dessin*) caption

léger, ère [leʒe, -ɛʀ] *adj* light; (*bruit, retard*) slight; (*superficiel*) thoughtless; (*volage*) free and easy; flighty; **à la légère** (*parler, agir*) rashly, thoughtlessly; **légèrement** *adv* lightly; thoughtlessly; slightly

législatif, ive [leʒislatif, -iv] *adj* legislative; **législatives** *nfpl* general election *sg*; **législature** [leʒislatyʀ] *nf* legislature; term (of office)

légitime [leʒitim] *adj* (*JUR*) lawful, legitimate; (*fig*) rightful, legitimate; **en état de ~ défense** in self-defence

legs [lɛg] *nm* legacy

léguer [lege] *vt*: **~ qch à qn** (*JUR*) to bequeath sth to sb; (*fig*) to hand sth down *ou* pass sth on to sb

légume [legym] *nm* vegetable

lendemain [lɑ̃dmɛ̃] *nm*: **le ~** the next *ou* following day; **le ~ matin/soir** the next *ou* following morning/evening; **le ~ de** the day after; **sans ~** short-lived

lent, e [lɑ̃, lɑ̃t] *adj* slow; **lentement** *adv* slowly; **lenteur** *nf* slowness no *pl*

lentille [lɑ̃tij] *nf* (*OPTIQUE*) lens *sg*; (*CULIN*) lentil

léopard [leopaʀ] *nm* leopard

lèpre [lɛpʀ(ə)] *nf* leprosy

──────── **MOT CLÉ** ────────

lequel, laquelle [ləkɛl, lakɛl] (*mpl* **lesquels**, *fpl* **lesquelles**; *à + lequel* = **auquel**, *de + lequel* = **duquel**) *pron* **1** (*interrogatif*) which, which one

2 (*relatif: personne: sujet*) who; (: *objet, après préposition*) whom; (: *chose*) which ♦ *adj*: **auquel cas** in which case

les [le] *dét voir* **le**

lesbienne [lɛsbjɛn] *nf* lesbian

lesdites [ledit] *dét pl voir* **ledit**

lesdits [ledi] *dét pl voir* **ledit**

léser [leze] *vt* to wrong

lésiner [lezine] *vi*: **~ (sur)** to skimp (on)

lésion [lezjɔ̃] *nf* lesion, damage no *pl*

lesquelles [lekɛl] *pron pl voir* **lequel**

lesquels [lekɛl] *pron pl voir* **lequel**

lessive [lesiv] *nf* (*poudre*) washing powder; (*linge*) washing no *pl*, wash

lessiver [lesive] *vt* to wash

lest [lɛst] *nm* ballast

leste [lɛst(ə)] *adj* sprightly, nimble

lettre [lɛtʀ(ə)] *nf* letter; **~s** *nfpl* (*littérature*) literature *sg*; (*SCOL*) arts (subjects); **à la ~** literally; **en toutes ~s** in full

lettré, e [letʀe] *adj* well-read

leucémie [løsemi] *nf* leukaemia

──────── **MOT CLÉ** ────────

leur [lœʀ] *adj possessif* their; **~ maison** their house; **~s amis** their friends ♦ *pron* **1** (*objet indirect*) (to) them; **je ~ ai dit la vérité** I told them the truth; **je le ~ ai donné** I gave it to them, I gave it to them **2** (*possessif*): **le(la) ~, les ~s** theirs

leurre [lœʀ] *nm* (*appât*) lure; (*fig*) delusion; snare

leurrer [lœʀe] *vt* to delude, deceive

leurs [lœʀ] *dét voir* **leur**

levain [ləvɛ̃] *nm* leaven

levé, e [ləve] *adj*: **être ~** to be up

levée [ləve] *nf* (*POSTES*) collection; (*CARTES*) trick; **~ de boucliers** general outcry

lever [ləve] *vt* (*vitre, bras etc*) to raise; (*soulever de terre, supprimer: interdiction, siège*) to lift; (*séance*) to close; (*impôts, armée*) to levy ♦ *vi* to rise ♦ *nm*: **au ~** on getting up; **se ~** *vi* to get up; (*soleil*) to rise; (*jour*) to break; (*brouillard*) to lift; **~ de soleil** sunrise; **~ du jour** daybreak

levier [ləvje] *nm* lever

lèvre [lɛvʀ(ə)] *nf* lip

lévrier [levʀije] *nm* greyhound

levure [ləvyʀ] *nf* yeast; **~ chimique** baking powder

lexique [lɛksik] *nm* vocabulary; lexicon

lézard [lezaʀ] *nm* lizard

lézarde [lezaʀd(ə)] *nf* crack

liaison [ljɛzɔ̃] *nf* link; (*amoureuse*) affair; (*PHONÉTIQUE*) liaison; **entrer/être en ~ avec** to get/be in contact with

liane [ljan] *nf* creeper

liant, e [ljɑ̃, -ɑ̃t] *adj* sociable

liasse [ljas] *nf* wad, bundle

Liban [libɑ̃] *nm*: **le ~** (the) Lebanon; **libanais, e** *adj, nm/f* Lebanese

libeller [libele] *vt* (*chèque, mandat*): **~ (au nom de)** to make out (to); (*lettre*) to word

libellule [libelyl] *nf* dragonfly

libéral, e, aux [liberal, -o] *adj, nm/f* liberal

libérer [libeʀe] *vt* (*délivrer*) to free, liberate; (: *moralement, PSYCH*) to liberate; (*relâcher, dégager: gaz*) to release; to discharge; **se ~** *vi* (*de rendez-vous*) to get out of previous engagements

liberté [libɛʀte] *nf* freedom; (*loisir*) free time; **~s** *nfpl* (*privautés*) liberties; **mettre/être en ~** to set/be free; **en ~ provisoire/surveillée/conditionnelle** on bail/

probation/parole; **~s individuelles** personal freedom *sg*

libraire [libʀɛʀ] *nm/f* bookseller

librairie [libʀɛʀi] *nf* bookshop

libre [libʀ(ə)] *adj* free; (*route*) clear; (*place etc*) vacant; empty; not engaged; not taken; (*SCOL*) non-state; **de ~** (*place*) free; **~ de qch/de faire** free from sth/to do; **~ arbitre** free will; **~-échange** *nm* free trade; **~-service** *nm* self-service store

Libye [libi] *nf*: **la ~** Libya

licence [lisɑ̃s] *nf* (*permis*) permit; (*diplôme*) degree; (*liberté*) liberty; licence (*BRIT*), license (*US*); licentiousness; **licencié, e** *nm/f* (*SCOL*): **licencié ès lettres/en droit** ≈ Bachelor of Arts/Law; (*SPORT*) member of a sports federation

licencier [lisɑ̃sje] *vt* (*renvoyer*) to dismiss; (*débaucher*) to make redundant; to lay off

licite [lisit] *adj* lawful

lie [li] *nf* dregs *pl*, sediment

lié, e [lje] *adj*: **très ~ avec** very friendly with *ou* close to; **~ par** (*serment*) bound by

liège [ljɛʒ] *nm* cork

lien [ljɛ̃] *nm* (*corde, fig: affectif*) bond; (*rapport*) link, connection; **~ de parenté** family tie

lier [lje] *vt* (*attacher*) to tie up; (*joindre*) to link up; (*fig: unir, engager*) to bind; (*CULIN*) to thicken; **se ~ avec** to make friends with; **~ qch à** to tie *ou* link sth to; **~ conversation avec** to strike up a conversation with

lierre [ljɛʀ] *nm* ivy

liesse [ljɛs] *nf*: **être en ~** to be celebrating *ou* jubilant

lieu, x [ljø] *nm* place; **~x** *nmpl* (*habitation*) premises; (*endroit: d'un accident etc*) scene *sg*; **en ~ sûr** in a safe place; **en premier ~** in the first place; **en dernier ~** lastly; **avoir ~** to take place; **avoir ~ de faire** to have grounds for doing; **tenir ~ de** to take the place of; to serve as; **donner ~ à** to give rise to; **au ~ de** instead of

lieu-dit [ljødi] (*pl* lieux-dits) *nm* locality

lieutenant [ljøtnɑ̃] *nm* lieutenant

lièvre [ljɛvʀ(ə)] *nm* hare

ligament [ligamɑ̃] *nm* ligament

ligne [liɲ] *nf* (*gén*) line; (*TRANSPORTS: liaison*) service; (: *trajet*) route; (*silhouette*) figure; **entrer en ~ de compte** to come into it

lignée [liɲe] *nf* line; lineage; descendants *pl*

ligoter [ligɔte] *vt* to tie up

ligue [lig] *nf* league; **liguer** *vt*: **se liguer contre** (*fig*) to combine against

lilas [lila] *nm* lilac

limace [limas] *nf* slug

limaille [limɑj] *nf*: **~ de fer** iron filings *pl*

limande [limɑ̃d] *nf* dab

lime [lim] *nf* file; **~ à ongles** nail file; **limer** *vt* to file

limier [limje] *nm* bloodhound; (*détective*) sleuth

limitation [limitasjɔ̃] *nf*: **~ de vitesse** speed limit

limite [limit] *nf* (*de terrain*) boundary; (*partie ou point extrême*) limit; **vitesse/charge ~** maximum speed/load; **cas ~** borderline case; **date ~** deadline

limiter [limite] *vt* (*restreindre*) to limit, restrict; (*délimiter*) to border

limitrophe [limitʀɔf] *adj* border *cpd*

limoger [limɔʒe] *vt* to dismiss

limon [limɔ̃] *nm* silt

limonade [limɔnad] *nf* lemonade (*BRIT*), (lemon) soda (*US*)

lin [lɛ̃] *nm* flax

linceul [lɛ̃sœl] *nm* shroud

linge [lɛ̃ʒ] *nm* (*serviettes etc*) linen; (*pièce de tissu*) cloth; (*aussi:* **~ de corps**) underwear; (: **~ de toilette**) towels *pl*; (*lessive*) washing

lingerie [lɛ̃ʒʀi] *nf* lingerie, underwear

lingot [lɛ̃go] *nm* ingot

linguistique [lɛ̃gɥistik] *adj* linguistic ♦ *nf* linguistics *sg*

lion, ne [ljɔ̃, ljɔn] *nm/f* lion(lioness); (*signe*): **le L~** Leo; **lionceau, x** *nm* lion cub

liqueur [likœʀ] *nf* liqueur

liquide [likid] *adj* liquid ♦ *nm* liquid; (*COMM*): **en ~** in ready money *ou* cash; **liquider** [likide] *vt* (*société, biens, témoin gênant*) to liquidate; (*compte, problème*) to settle; (*COMM: articles*) to clear, sell off; **liquidités** [likidite] *nfpl* (*COMM*) liquid assets

lire [liʀ] *nf* (*monnaie*) lira ♦ *vt, vi* to read

lis [lis] *nm* = **lys**

lisible [lizibl(ə)] *adj* legible

lisière [lizjɛʀ] *nf* (*de forêt*) edge; (*de tissu*) selvage

lisons *vb voir* **lire**

lisse [lis] *adj* smooth

liste [list(ə)] *nf* list; **faire la ~ de** to list; **~ électorale** electoral roll

listing [listiŋ] *nm* (*INFORM*) printout

lit [li] *nm* (*gén*) bed; **faire son ~** to make one's bed; **aller/se mettre au ~** to go to/ get into bed; **~ de camp** campbed; **~ d'enfant** cot (*BRIT*), crib (*US*)

literie [litʀi] *nf* bedding, bedclothes *pl*

litière [litjɛʀ] *nf* litter

litige [litiʒ] *nm* dispute

litre [litʀ(ə)] *nm* litre; (*récipient*) litre measure

littéraire [liteʀɛʀ] *adj* literary

littéral, e, aux [liteʀal, -o] *adj* literal

littérature [liteʀatyʀ] *nf* literature

littoral, aux [litɔʀal, -o] *nm* coast

liturgie [lityʀʒi] *nf* liturgy

livide [livid] *adj* livid, pallid

livraison [livʀɛzɔ̃] *nf* delivery
livre [livʀ(ə)] *nm* book ♦ *nf* (*poids, monnaie*) pound; ~ **de bord** logbook; ~ **de poche** paperback (*pocket size*)
livré, e [livʀe] *adj*: ~ **à soi-même** left to o.s. *ou* one's own devices; **livrée** *nf* livery
livrer [livʀe] *vt* (*COMM*) to deliver; (*otage, coupable*) to hand over; (*secret, information*) to give away; **se** ~ **à** (*se confier*) to confide in; (*se rendre, s'abandonner*) to give o.s. up to; (*faire: pratiques, actes*) to indulge in; (*: travail*) to engage in; (*: sport*) to practise; (*travail: enquête*) to carry out
livret [livʀɛ] *nm* booklet; (*d'opéra*) libretto; ~ **de caisse d'épargne** (savings) bankbook; ~ **de famille** (official) family record book; ~ **scolaire** (school) report book
livreur, euse [livʀœʀ, -øz] *nm/f* delivery boy *ou* man/girl *ou* woman
local, e, aux [lɔkal, -o] *adj* local ♦ *nm* (*salle*) premises *pl*; *voir aussi* **locaux**
localiser [lɔkalize] *vt* (*repérer*) to locate, place; (*limiter*) to confine
localité [lɔkalite] *nf* locality
locataire [lɔkatɛʀ] *nm/f* tenant; (*de chambre*) lodger
location [lɔkasjɔ̃] *nf* (*par le locataire, le loueur*) renting; (*par le propriétaire*) renting out, letting; (*THÉÂTRE*) booking office; "~ **de voitures**" "car rental"
location-vente [lɔkasjɔ̃vɑ̃t] (*pl* ~**s**-~**s**) *nf* hire purchase (*BRIT*), instalment plan (*US*)
locaux [lɔko] *nmpl* premises
locomotive [lɔkɔmɔtiv] *nf* locomotive, engine; (*fig*) pacesetter, pacemaker
locution [lɔkysjɔ̃] *nf* phrase
loge [lɔʒ] *nf* (*THÉÂTRE: d'artiste*) dressing room; (*: de spectateurs*) box; (*de concierge, franc-maçon*) lodge
logement [lɔʒmɑ̃] *nm* accommodation *no pl* (*BRIT*), accommodations *pl* (*US*); flat (*BRIT*), apartment (*US*); housing *no pl*
loger [lɔʒe] *vt* to accommodate ♦ *vi* to live; **se** ~ **dans** (*suj: balle, flèche*) to lodge itself in; **trouver à se** ~ to find accommodation; **logeur, euse** *nm/f* landlord(lady)
logiciel [lɔʒisjɛl] *nm* software
logique [lɔʒik] *adj* logical ♦ *nf* logic
logis [lɔʒi] *nm* home; abode, dwelling
loi [lwa] *nf* law; **faire la** ~ to lay down the law
loin [lwɛ̃] *adv* far; (*dans le temps*) a long way off; a long time ago; **plus** ~ further; ~ **de** far from; **au** ~ far off; **de** ~ from a distance; (*fig: de beaucoup*) by far; **il vient de** ~ he's come a long way
lointain, e [lwɛ̃tɛ̃, -ɛn] *adj* faraway, distant; (*dans le futur, passé*) distant, far-off; (*cause, parent*) remote, distant ♦ *nm*: **dans le** ~ in the distance
loir [lwaʀ] *nm* dormouse
loisir [lwaziʀ] *nm*: **heures de** ~ spare time;

~**s** *nmpl* leisure *sg*; leisure activities; **avoir le** ~ **de faire** to have the time *ou* opportunity to do; **à** ~ at leisure; at one's pleasure
londonien, ne [lɔ̃dɔnjɛ̃, -jɛn] *adj* London *cpd*, of London ♦ *nm/f*: **L~, ne** Londoner
Londres [lɔ̃dʀ(ə)] *n* London
long, longue [lɔ̃, lɔ̃ɡ] *adj* long ♦ *adv*: **en savoir** ~ to know a great deal ♦ *nm*: **de 3 m de** ~ 3 m long, 3 m in length; **ne pas faire** ~ **feu** not to last long; **(tout) le** ~ **de** (all) along; **tout au** ~ **de** (*année, vie*) throughout; **de** ~ **en large** (*marcher*) to and fro, up and down; *voir aussi* **longue**
longer [lɔ̃ʒe] *vt* to go (*ou* walk *ou* drive) along(side); (*suj: mur, route*) to border
longiligne [lɔ̃ʒiliɲ] *adj* long-limbed
longitude [lɔ̃ʒityd] *nf* longitude
longitudinal, e, aux [lɔ̃ʒitydinal, -o] *adj* (*running*) lengthways
longtemps [lɔ̃tɑ̃] *adv* (for) a long time, (for) long; **avant** ~ before long; **pour** *ou* **pendant** ~ for a long time; **mettre** ~ **à faire** to take a long time to do
longue [lɔ̃ɡ] *adj voir* **long** ♦ *nf*: **à la** ~ in the end; **longuement** *adv* for a long time
longueur [lɔ̃ɡœʀ] *nf* length; ~**s** *nfpl* (*fig: d'un film etc*) tedious parts; **en** ~ lengthwise; **tirer en** ~ to drag on; **à** ~ **de journée** all day long; ~ **d'onde** wavelength
longue-vue [lɔ̃ɡvy] *nf* telescope
lopin [lɔpɛ̃] *nm*: ~ **de terre** patch of land
loque [lɔk] *nf* (*personne*) wreck; ~**s** *nfpl* (*habits*) rags
loquet [lɔkɛ] *nm* latch
lorgner [lɔʀɲe] *vt* to eye; (*fig*) to have one's eye on
lors [lɔʀ] *nm*: ~ **de** *prép* at the time of; during; ~ **même que** even though
lorsque [lɔʀsk(ə)] *conj* when, as
losange [lɔzɑ̃ʒ] *nm* diamond; (*GÉOM*) lozenge
lot [lo] *nm* (*part*) share; (*de loterie*) prize; (*fig: destin*) fate, lot; (*COMM, INFORM*) batch
loterie [lɔtʀi] *nf* lottery; raffle
loti, e [lɔti] *adj*: **bien/mal** ~ well-/badly off
lotion [lɔsjɔ̃] *nf* lotion
lotir [lɔtiʀ] *vt* (*terrain*) to divide into plots; to sell by lots; **lotissement** *nm* housing development; plot, lot
loto [lɔto] *nm* lotto; numerical lottery
louable [lwabl(ə)] *adj* commendable
louanges [lwɑ̃ʒ] *nfpl* praise *sg*
loubard [lubaʀ] (*fam*) *nm* lout
louche [luʃ] *adj* shady, fishy, dubious ♦ *nf* ladle
loucher [luʃe] *vi* to squint
louer [lwe] *vt* (*maison: suj: propriétaire*) to let, rent (out); (*: locataire*) to rent; (*voiture etc: entreprise*) to hire out (*BRIT*), rent (out); (*: locataire*) to hire, rent; (*réserver*) to

book; (faire l'éloge de) to praise; **"à ~"** "to
let" (BRIT), "for rent" (US)
loup [lu] nm wolf
loupe [lup] nf magnifying glass
louper [lupe] vt (manquer) to miss
lourd, e [luʀ, luʀd] adj, adv heavy; ~ **de**
(conséquences, menaces) charged with;
lourdaud, e (péj) adj clumsy
loutre [lutʀ(ə)] nf otter
louveteau, x [luvto] nm wolf-cub; (scout)
cub (scout)
louvoyer [luvwaje] vi (NAVIG) to tack; (fig)
to hedge, evade the issue
lover [lɔve] : **se ~** vi to coil up
loyal, e, aux [lwajal, -o] adj (fidèle) loyal,
faithful; (fair-play) fair; **loyauté** nf loyalty,
faithfulness; fairness
loyer [lwaje] nm rent
lu, e [ly] pp de lire
lubie [lybi] nf whim, craze
lubrifiant [lybʀifjɑ̃] nm lubricant
lubrifier [lybʀifje] vt to lubricate
lubrique [lybʀik] adj lecherous
lucarne [lykaʀn(ə)] nf skylight
lucratif, ive [lykʀatif, -iv] adj lucrative;
profitable; **à but non** ~ non profit-making
lueur [lɥœʀ] nf (chatoyante) glimmer no pl;
(métallique, mouillée) gleam no pl; (rou-
geoyante, chaude) glow no pl; (pâle) (faint)
light; (fig) glimmer; gleam
luge [lyʒ] nf sledge (BRIT), sled (US)
lugubre [lygybʀ(ə)] adj gloomy; dismal

────────── MOT CLÉ ──────────

lui [lɥi] pron **1** (objet indirect: mâle) (to)
him; (: femelle) (to) her; (: chose, animal)
(to) it; **je ~ ai parlé** I have spoken to him
(ou to her); **il ~ a offert un cadeau** he
gave him (ou her) a present
2 (après préposition, comparatif: personne)
him; (: chose, animal) it; **elle est contente
de ~** she is pleased with him; **je le
connais mieux que ~** I know her better
than he does; I know her better than him
3 (sujet, forme emphatique) he; ~, **il est à
Paris** HE is in Paris
4: ~-**même** himself; itself

luire [lɥiʀ] vi to shine; to glow
lumière [lymjɛʀ] nf light; ~**s** nfpl (d'une
personne) wisdom sg; **mettre en ~** (fig) to
highlight; ~ **du jour** daylight
luminaire [lyminɛʀ] nm lamp, light
lumineux, euse [lyminø, -øz] adj (émet-
tant de la lumière) luminous; (éclairé) illu-
minated; (ciel, couleur) bright; (relatif à la
lumière: rayon etc) of light, light cpd; (fig:
regard) radiant
lunaire [lynɛʀ] adj lunar, moon cpd
lunatique [lynatik] adj whimsical, temperamental
lundi [lœdi] nm Monday; ~ **de Pâques**

Easter Monday
lune [lyn] nf moon; ~ **de miel** honeymoon
lunette [lynɛt] nf: ~**s** nfpl glasses, spectacles; (protectrices) goggles; ~ **arrière**
(AUTO) rear window; ~**s de soleil** sun
glasses; ~**s noires** dark glasses
lus etc vb voir lire
lustre [lystʀ(ə)] nm (de plafond) chandelier;
(fig: éclat) lustre
lustrer [lystʀe] vt to shine
lut vb voir lire
luth [lyt] nm lute
lutin [lytɛ̃] nm imp, goblin
lutte [lyt] nf (conflit) struggle; (sport) wrestling; **lutter** vi to fight, struggle
luxe [lyks(ə)] nm luxury; **de ~** luxury cpd
Luxembourg [lyksɑ̃buʀ] nm: **le ~** Luxembourg
luxer [lykse] vt: **se ~ l'épaule** to dislocate
one's shoulder
luxueux, euse [lyksɥø, -øz] adj luxurious
luxure [lyksyʀ] nf lust
lycée [lise] nm secondary school; **lycéen,
ne** nm/f secondary school pupil
lyrique [liʀik] adj lyrical; (OPÉRA) lyric; **artiste ~** opera singer
lys [lis] nm lily

M m

M abr = Monsieur
m' [m] pron voir me
ma [ma] dét voir mon
macaron [makaʀɔ̃] nm (gâteau) macaroon;
(insigne) (round) badge
macaronis [makaʀɔni] nmpl macaroni sg
macédoine [masedwan] nf: ~ **de fruits**
fruit salad; ~ **de légumes** nf mixed vegetables
macérer [maseʀe] vi, vt to macerate; (dans
du vinaigre) to pickle
mâcher [mɑʃe] vt to chew; **ne pas ~ ses
mots** not to mince one's words
machin [maʃɛ̃] (fam) nm thing(umajig)
machinal, e, aux [maʃinal, -o] adj mechanical, automatic
machination [maʃinasjɔ̃] nf scheming,
frame-up
machine [maʃin] nf machine; (locomotive)
engine; (fig: rouages) engine; ~ **à écrire**
typewriter; ~ **à laver/coudre** washing/
sewing machine; ~ **à sous** fruit machine; ~
~ **à vapeur** steam engine; **machinerie** nf

machinery, plant; *(d'un navire)* engine room; **machiniste** *nm (de bus, métro)* driver

mâchoire [mɑʃwaʀ] *nf* jaw; ~ **de frein** brake shoe

mâchonner [mɑʃɔne] *vt* to chew (at)

maçon [masɔ̃] *nm* bricklayer; builder; **~nerie** [masɔnʀi] *nf (murs)* brickwork; masonry, stonework; *(activité)* bricklaying; building

maculer [makyle] *vt* to stain

Madame [madam] *(pl* **Mesdames)** *nf:* ~ **X** Mrs X; **occupez-vous de** ~/**Monsieur/Mademoiselle** please serve this lady/gentleman/(young) lady; **bonjour** ~/**Monsieur/Mademoiselle** good morning; *(ton déférent)* good morning Madam/Sir/Madam; *(le nom est connu)* good morning Mrs/Mr/Miss X; ~/**Monsieur/Mademoiselle!** *(pour appeler)* Madam/Sir/Miss!; ~/**Monsieur/Mademoiselle** *(sur lettre)* Dear Madam/Sir/Madam; **chère** ~/**cher Monsieur/chère Mademoiselle** Dear Mrs/Mr/Miss X; **Mesdames** Ladies

Mademoiselle [madmwazɛl] *(pl* **Mesdemoiselles)** *nf* Miss; *voir aussi* **Madame**

madère [madɛʀ] *nm* Madeira (wine)

magasin [magazɛ̃] *nm (boutique)* shop; *(entrepôt)* warehouse; *(d'une arme)* magazine; **en** ~ *(COMM)* in stock

magazine [magazin] *nm* magazine

magicien, ne [maʒisjɛ̃, -jɛn] *nm/f* magician

magie [maʒi] *nf* magic; **magique** *adj* magic; *(enchanteur)* magical

magistral, e, aux [maʒistʀal, -o] *adj (œuvre, adresse)* masterly; *(ton)* authoritative; *(ex cathedra)*: **enseignement** ~ lecturing, lectures *pl*

magistrat [maʒistʀa] *nm* magistrate

magnétique [maɲetik] *adj* magnetic

magnétiser [maɲetize] *vt* to magnetize; *(fig)* to mesmerize, hypnotize

magnétophone [maɲetɔfɔn] *nm* tape recorder; ~ **à cassettes** cassette recorder

magnétoscope [maɲetɔskɔp] *nm* videotape recorder

magnifique [maɲifik] *adj* magnificent

magot [mago] *nm (argent)* pile (of money); nest egg

magouille [maguj] *nf* scheming

mai [mɛ] *nm* May

maigre [mɛgʀ(ə)] *adj (very)* thin, skinny; *(viande)* lean; *(fromage)* low-fat; *(végétation)* thin, sparse; *(fig)* poor, meagre, skimpy ♦ *adv:* **faire** ~ not to eat meat; **jours** ~**s** days of abstinence, fish days; **maigreur** *nf* thinness; **maigrir** *vi* to get thinner, lose weight

maille [mɑj] *nf* stitch; **avoir** ~ **à partir avec qn** to have a brush with sb; ~ **à l'endroit/à l'envers** plain/purl stitch

maillet [majɛ] *nm* mallet

maillon [majɔ̃] *nm* link

maillot [majo] *nm (aussi:* ~ **de corps)** vest; *(de danseur)* leotard; *(de sportif)* jersey; ~ **de bain** swimsuit; *(d'homme)* bathing trunks *pl*

main [mɛ̃] *nf* hand; **à la** ~ in one's hand; **se donner la** ~ to hold hands; **donner** *ou* **tendre la** ~ **à qn** to hold out one's hand to sb; **se serrer la** ~ to shake hands; **serrer la** ~ **à qn** to shake hands with sb; **sous la** ~ to *ou* at hand; **attaque à** ~ **armée** armed attack; **à** ~ **droite/gauche** to the right/left; **à remettre en** ~**s propres** to be delivered personally; **de première** ~ *(COMM: voiture etc)* second-hand with only one previous owner; **mettre la dernière** ~ **à** to put the finishing touches to; **se faire/perdre la** ~ to get one's hand in/lose one's touch; **avoir qch bien en** ~ to have (got) the hang of sth

main-d'œuvre [mɛ̃dœvʀ(ə)] *nf* manpower, labour

main-forte [mɛ̃fɔʀt(ə)] *nf:* **prêter** ~ **à qn** to come to sb's assistance

mainmise [mɛ̃miz] *nf* seizure; *(fig):* ~ **sur** complete hold on

maint, e [mɛ̃, mɛ̃t] *adj* many a; ~**s** many; **à** ~**es reprises** time and (time) again

maintenant [mɛ̃tnɑ̃] *adv* now; *(actuellement)* nowadays

maintenir [mɛ̃tniʀ] *vt (retenir, soutenir)* to support; *(contenir: foule etc)* to hold back; *(conserver, affirmer)* to maintain; **se** ~ *vi* to hold; to keep steady; to persist

maintien [mɛ̃tjɛ̃] *nm* maintaining; *(attitude)* bearing

maire [mɛʀ] *nm* mayor

mairie [meʀi] *nf (bâtiment)* town hall; *(administration)* town council

mais [mɛ] *conj* but; ~ **non!** of course not!; ~ **enfin** but after all; *(indignation)* look here!; ~ **encore?** is that all?

maïs [mais] *nm* maize *(BRIT)*, corn *(US)*

maison [mɛzɔ̃] *nf* house; *(chez-soi)* home; *(COMM)* firm ♦ *adj inv (CULIN)* home-made; made by the chef; *(fig)* in-house, own; **à la** ~ at home; *(direction)* home; ~ **close** *ou* **de passe** brothel; ~ **de correction** reformatory; ~ **de repos** convalescent home; ~ **de santé** mental home; ~ **des jeunes** ≈ youth club; ~ **mère** parent company; **maisonnée** *nf* household, family; **maisonnette** *nf* small house, cottage

maître, esse [mɛtʀ(ə), mɛtʀɛs] *nm/f* master(mistress); *(SCOL)* teacher, schoolmaster(mistress) ♦ *nm (peintre etc)* master; *(titre):* **M**~ Maître, *term of address seen for a barrister* ♦ *adj (principal, essentiel)* main; **être** ~ **de** *(soi-même, situation)* to be in control of; **une** ~**sse femme** a managing woman; ~ **chanteur** blackmailer; ~/**maîtresse d'école** schoolmaster(mistress);

~ **d'hôtel** (*domestique*) butler; (*d'hôtel*) head waiter; ~ **nageur** lifeguard; **maîtresse** *nf* (*amante*) mistress; **maîtresse de maison** hostess; housewife

maîtrise [metʀiz] *nf* (*aussi*: ~ **de soi**) self-control, self-possession; (*habileté*) skill, mastery; (*suprématie*) mastery, command; (*diplôme*) ≈ master's degree

maîtriser [metʀize] *vt* (*cheval, incendie*) to (bring under) control; (*sujet*) to master; (*émotion*) to control, master; **se** ~ to control o.s.

majestueux, euse [maʒɛstɥø, -øz] *adj* majestic

majeur, e [maʒœʀ] *adj* (*important*) major; (*JUR*) of age; (*fig*) adult ♦ *nm* (*doigt*) middle finger; **en** ~**e partie** for the most part

majorer [maʒɔʀe] *vt* to increase

majoritaire [maʒɔʀitɛʀ] *adj* majority *cpd*

majorité [maʒɔʀite] *nf* (*gén*) majority; (*parti*) party in power; **en** ~ mainly

majuscule [maʒyskyl] *adj, nf*: (**lettre**) ~ capital (letter)

mal [mal, mo] (*pl* **maux**) *nm* (*opposé au bien*) evil; (*tort, dommage*) harm; (*douleur physique*) pain, ache; (*maladie*) illness, sickness *no pl* ♦ *adv* badly ♦ *adj* bad, wrong; **être** ~ to be uncomfortable; **être** ~ **avec qn** to be on bad terms with sb; **être au plus** ~ (*malade*) to be at death's door; (*brouillé*) to be at daggers drawn; **il a** ~ **compris** he misunderstood; **dire/penser du** ~ **de** to speak/think ill of; **ne voir aucun** ~ **à** to see no harm in, see nothing wrong in; **craignant** ~ **faire** fearing he was doing the wrong thing; **faire du** ~ **à qn** to hurt sb; to harm sb; **se faire** ~ to hurt o.s.; **se donner du** ~ **pour faire qch** to go to a lot of trouble to do sth; **ça fait** ~ it hurts; **j'ai** ~ **au dos** my back hurts; **avoir** ~ **à la tête/à la gorge/aux dents** to have a headache/a sore throat/toothache; **avoir le** ~ **du pays** to be homesick; **prendre** ~ to be taken ill, feel unwell; *voir aussi* **cœur**; **maux;** ~ **de mer** seasickness; ~ **en point** *adj inv* in a bad state

malade [malad] *adj* ill, sick; (*poitrine, jambe*) bad; (*plante*) diseased ♦ *nm/f* invalid, sick person; (*à l'hôpital etc*) patient; **tomber** ~ to fall ill; **être** ~ **du cœur** to have heart trouble *ou* a bad heart; ~ **mental** mentally sick *ou* ill person

maladie [maladi] *nf* (*spécifique*) disease, illness; (*mauvaise santé*) illness, sickness; ~ **d'Alzheimer** *nf* Alzheimer's (disease); **maladif, ive** *adj* sickly; (*curiosité, besoin*) pathological

maladresse [maladʀɛs] *nf* clumsiness *no pl*; (*gaffe*) blunder

maladroit, e [maladʀwa, -wat] *adj* clumsy

malaise [malɛz] *nm* (*MÉD*) feeling of faintness; feeling of discomfort; (*fig*) uneasiness, malaise

malaisé, e [maleze] *adj* difficult

malaria [malaʀja] *nf* malaria

malaxer [malakse] *vt* to knead; to mix

malchance [malʃɑ̃s] *nf* misfortune, ill luck *no pl*; **par** ~ unfortunately

mâle [mɑl] *adj* (*aussi ÉLEC, TECH*) male; (*viril: voix, traits*) manly ♦ *nm* male

malédiction [malediksjɔ̃] *nf* curse

mal: ~**encontreux, euse** *adj* unfortunate, untoward; ~**-en-point** *adj inv* in a sorry state; ~**entendu** *nm* misunderstanding; ~**façon** *nf* fault; ~**faisant, e** *adj* evil, harmful; ~**faiteur** *nm* lawbreaker, criminal; burglar, thief; ~**famé, e** *adj* disreputable

malgache [malgaʃ] *adj, nm/f* Madagascan, Malagasy ♦ *nm* (*LING*) Malagasy

malgré [malgʀe] *prép* in spite of, despite; ~ **tout** all the same

malheur [malœʀ] *nm* (*situation*) adversity, misfortune; (*événement*) misfortune; disaster, tragedy; **faire un** ~ to be a smash hit; **malheureusement** *adv* unfortunately; **malheureux, euse** *adj* (*triste*) unhappy, miserable; (*infortuné, regrettable*) unfortunate; (*malchanceux*) unlucky; (*insignifiant*) wretched ♦ *nm/f* poor soul; unfortunate creature; **les** ~**eux** the destitute

malhonnête [malɔnɛt] *adj* dishonest

malice [malis] *nf* mischievousness; (*méchanceté*): **par** ~ out of malice *ou* spite; **sans** ~ guileless; **malicieux, euse** *adj* mischievous

malin, igne [malɛ̃, -iɲ] *adj* (*futé: f gén: maline*) smart, shrewd; (*MÉD*) malignant

malingre [malɛ̃gʀ(ə)] *adj* puny

malle [mal] *nf* trunk

mallette [malɛt] *nf* (small) suitcase; overnight case; attaché case

malmener [malməne] *vt* to manhandle; (*fig*) to give a rough handling to

malodorant, e [malɔdɔʀɑ̃, -ɑ̃t] *adj* foul- *ou* ill-smelling

malotru [malɔtʀy] *nm* lout, boor

malpropre [malpʀɔpʀ(ə)] *adj* dirty

malsain, e [malsɛ̃, -ɛn] *adj* unhealthy

malt [malt] *nm* malt

Malte [malt(ə)] *nf* Malta

maltraiter [maltʀete] *vt* (*brutaliser*) to manhandle, ill-treat

malveillance [malvɛjɑ̃s] *nf* (*animosité*) ill will; (*intention de nuire*) malevolence; (*JUR*) malicious intent *no pl*

malversation [malvɛʀsɑsjɔ̃] *nf* embezzlement

maman [mamɑ̃] *nf* mum(my), mother

mamelle [mamɛl] *nf* teat

mamelon [mamlɔ̃] *nm* (*ANAT*) nipple; (*colline*) knoll, hillock

mamie [mami] (*fam*) *nf* granny

mammifère [mamifɛʀ] *nm* mammal

manche [mɑ̃ʃ] *nf* (*de vêtement*) sleeve; (*d'un jeu, tournoi*) round; (*GÉO*): **la M~** the Channel ♦ *nm* (*d'outil, casserole*) handle; (*de pelle, pioche etc*) shaft; ~ **à balai** *nm* broomstick; (*AVIAT, INFORM*) joystick

manchette [mɑ̃ʃɛt] *nf* (*de chemise*) cuff; (*coup*) forearm blow; (*titre*) headline

manchon [mɑ̃ʃɔ̃] *nm* (*de fourrure*) muff

manchot [mɑ̃ʃo] *nm* one-armed man; armless man; (*ZOOL*) penguin

mandarine [mɑ̃daʀin] *nf* mandarin (orange), tangerine

mandat [mɑ̃da] *nm* (*postal*) postal *ou* money order; (*d'un député etc*) mandate; (*procuration*) power of attorney, proxy; (*POLICE*) warrant; ~ **d'amener** summons *sg*; ~ **d'arrêt** warrant for arrest; **mandataire** *nm/f* representative; proxy

manège [manɛʒ] *nm* riding school; (*à la foire*) roundabout, merry-go-round; (*fig*) game, ploy

manette [manɛt] *nf* lever, tap; ~ **de jeu** joystick

mangeable [mɑ̃ʒabl(ə)] *adj* edible, eatable

mangeoire [mɑ̃ʒwaʀ] *nf* trough, manger

manger [mɑ̃ʒe] *vt* to eat; (*ronger: suj: rouille etc*) to eat into *ou* away ♦ *vi* to eat

mangue [mɑ̃g] *nf* mango

maniable [manjabl(ə)] *adj* (*outil*) handy; (*voiture, voilier*) easy to handle

maniaque [manjak] *adj* finicky, fussy; suffering from a mania ♦ *nm/f* maniac

manie [mani] *nf* mania; (*tic*) odd habit

manier [manje] *vt* to handle

manière [manjɛʀ] *nf* (*façon*) way, manner; ~**s** *nfpl* (*attitude*) manners; (*chichis*) fuss *sg*; **de** ~ **à** so as to; **de telle** ~ **que** in such a way that; **de cette** ~ in this way *ou* manner; **d'une certaine** ~ in a way; **d'une** ~ **générale** generally speaking, as a general rule; **de toute** ~ in any case

maniéré, e [manjeʀe] *adj* affected

manifestant, e [manifɛstɑ̃, -ɑ̃t] *nm/f* demonstrator

manifestation [manifɛstasjɔ̃] *nf* (*de joie, mécontentement*) expression, demonstration; (*symptôme*) outward sign; (*fête etc*) event; (*POL*) demonstration

manifeste [manifɛst(ə)] *adj* obvious, evident ♦ *nm* manifesto

manifester [manifɛste] *vt* (*volonté, intentions*) to show, indicate; (*joie, peur*) to express, show ♦ *vi* to demonstrate; **se** ~ *vi* (*émotion*) to show *ou* express itself; (*difficultés*) to arise; (*symptômes*) to appear; (*témoin etc*) to come forward

manigance [manigɑ̃s] *nf* scheme

manigancer [manigɑ̃se] *vt* to plot

manipuler [manipyle] *vt* to handle; (*fig*) to manipulate

manivelle [manivɛl] *nf* crank

mannequin [mankɛ̃] *nm* (*COUTURE*) dummy; (*MODE*) model

manœuvre [manœvʀ(ə)] *nf* (*gén*) manœuvre (*BRIT*), maneuver (*US*) ♦ *nm* labourer; ~**r** [manœvʀe] *vt* to manœuvre (*BRIT*), maneuver (*US*); (*levier, machine*) to operate ♦ *vi* to manœuvre

manoir [manwaʀ] *nm* manor *ou* country house

manque [mɑ̃k] *nm* (*insuffisance*): ~ **de** lack of; (*vide*) emptiness, gap; (*MÉD*) withdrawal; ~**s** *nmpl* (*lacunes*) faults, defects

manqué, e [mɑ̃ke] *adj* failed; **garçon** ~ tomboy

manquer [mɑ̃ke] *vi* (*faire défaut*) to be lacking; (*être absent*) to be missing; (*échouer*) to fail ♦ *vt* to miss ♦ *vb impers*: **il (nous) manque encore 100 F** we are still 100 F short; **il manque des pages (au livre)** there are some pages missing (from the book); **il/cela me manque** I miss him/this; ~ **à** (*règles etc*) to be in breach of, fail to observe; ~ **de** to lack; **il a manqué (de) se tuer** he very nearly got killed

mansarde [mɑ̃saʀd(ə)] *nf* attic

mansuétude [mɑ̃sɥetyd] *nf* leniency

manteau, x [mɑ̃to] *nm* coat

manucure [manykyʀ] *nf* manicurist

manuel, le [manɥɛl] *adj* manual ♦ *nm* (*ouvrage*) manual, handbook

manufacture [manyfaktyʀ] *nf* factory; **manufacturé, e** [manyfaktyʀe] *adj* manufactured

manuscrit, e [manyskʀi, -it] *adj* handwritten ♦ *nm* manuscript

manutention [manytɑ̃sjɔ̃] *nf* (*COMM*) handling; (*local*) storehouse

mappemonde [mapmɔ̃d] *nf* (*plane*) map of the world; (*sphère*) globe

maquereau, x [makʀo] *nm* (*ZOOL*) mackerel *inv*; (*fam*) pimp

maquette [makɛt] *nf* (*d'un décor, bâtiment, véhicule*) (scale) model; (*d'une page illustrée*) paste-up

maquillage [makijaʒ] *nm* making up; faking; (*crème etc*) make-up

maquiller [makije] *vt* (*personne, visage*) to make up; (*truquer: passeport, statistique*) to fake; (: *voiture volée*) to do over (*respray etc*); **se** ~ *vi* to make up (one's face)

maquis [maki] *nm* (*GÉO*) scrub; (*MIL*) maquis, underground fighting *no pl*

maraîcher, ère [maʀeʃe, maʀeʃɛʀ] *adj*: **cultures maraîchères** market gardening *sg* ♦ *nm/f* market gardener; **jardin** ~ market garden (*BRIT*), truck farm (*US*)

marais [maʀɛ] *nm* marsh, swamp

marasme [maʀasm(ə)] *nm* stagnation, slump

marathon [maʀatɔ̃] *nm* marathon

marâtre [maʀɑtʀ(ə)] *nf* cruel mother

maraudeur [maʀodœʀ] *nm* prowler

marbre [maʀbʀ(ə)] *nm* (*pierre, statue*) mar-

ble; (*d'une table, commode*) marble top;
marbrer *vt* to mottle, blotch
marc [maʀ] *nm* (*de raisin, pommes*) marc;
~ **de café** coffee grounds *pl ou* dregs *pl*
marchand, e [maʀʃɑ̃, -ɑ̃d] *nm/f* shopkeeper, tradesman(woman); (*au marché*)
stallholder ♦ *adj:* **prix/valeur** ~(**e**) market
price/value; ~/**e de fruits** fruiterer (*BRIT*),
fruit seller (*US*); ~/**e de journaux** newsagent (*BRIT*), newsdealer (*US*); ~/**e de légumes** greengrocer (*BRIT*), produce dealer
(*US*); ~/**e de quatre saisons** costermonger
(*BRIT*), street vendor (selling fresh fruit and
vegetables) (*US*)
marchander [maʀʃɑ̃de] *vi* to bargain, haggle
marchandise [maʀʃɑ̃diz] *nf* goods *pl*,
merchandise *no pl*
marche [maʀʃ(ə)] *nf* (*d'escalier*) step; (*activité*) walking; (*promenade, trajet, allure*)
walk; (*démarche*) walk, gait; (*MIL etc, MUS*)
march; (*fonctionnement*) running; (*progres-
sion*) progress; course; **ouvrir/fermer la** ~
to lead the way/bring up the rear; **dans le
sens de la** ~ (*RAIL*) facing the engine; **en**
~ (*monter etc*) while the vehicle is moving
ou in motion; **mettre en** ~ to start; **se
mettre en** ~ (*personne*) to get moving;
(*machine*) to start; ~ **à suivre** (correct)
procedure; (*sur notice*) (step by step) instructions *pl*; ~ **arrière** reverse (gear); **faire**
~ **arrière** to reverse; (*fig*) to backtrack,
back-pedal
marché [maʀʃe] *nm* (*lieu, COMM, ÉCON*)
market; (*ville*) trading centre; (*transaction*)
bargain, deal; **faire du** ~ **noir** to buy and
sell on the black market; ~ **aux puces** flea
market; **M~ commun** Common Market
marchepied [maʀʃəpje] *nm* (*RAIL*) step;
(*fig*) stepping stone
marcher [maʀʃe] *vi* to walk; (*MIL*) to
march; (*aller: voiture, train, affaires*) to go;
(*prospérer*) to go well; (*fonctionner*) to
work, run; (*fam*) to go along, agree; to be
taken in; ~ **sur** to walk on; (*mettre le pied
sur*) to step on *ou* in; (*MIL*) to march upon;
~ **dans** (*herbe etc*) to walk in *ou* on; (*flaque*) to step in; **faire** ~ **qn** to pull sb's leg;
to lead sb up the garden path; **marcheur,
euse** *nm/f* walker
mardi [maʀdi] *nm* Tuesday; **M~ gras**
Shrove Tuesday
mare [maʀ] *nf* pond
marécage [maʀekaʒ] *nm* marsh, swamp
maréchal, aux [maʀeʃal, -o] *nm* marshal
marée [maʀe] *nf* tide; (*poissons*) fresh (sea)
fish; ~ **haute/basse** high/low tide; ~
montante/descendante rising/ebb tide
marémotrice [maʀemɔtʀis] *adj f* tidal
margarine [maʀgaʀin] *nf* margarine
marge [maʀʒ(ə)] *nf* margin; **en** ~ **de** (*fig*)
on the fringe of; cut off from; ~ **bénéficiai-**

re profit margin
marguerite [maʀgəʀit] *nf* marguerite, (ox-
eye) daisy; (*d'imprimante*) daisy-wheel
mari [maʀi] *nm* husband
mariage [maʀjaʒ] *nm* (*union, état, fig*) marriage; (*noce*) wedding; ~ **civil/religieux** registry office (*BRIT*) *ou* civil/church wedding
marié, e [maʀje] *adj* married ♦ *nm*
(bride)groom; **les** ~**s** the bride and groom;
les (jeunes) ~**s** the newly-weds; **mariée** *nf*
bride
marier [maʀje] *vt* to marry; (*fig*) to blend;
se ~ (**avec**) to marry
marin, e [maʀɛ̃, -in] *adj* sea *cpd*, marine ♦
nm sailor
marine [maʀin] *adj voir* **marin** ♦ *adj inv*
navy (blue) ♦ *nm* (*MIL*) marine ♦ *nf* navy;
~ **de guerre** navy; ~ **marchande** merchant
navy
marionnette [maʀjɔnɛt] *nf* puppet
maritime [maʀitim] *adj* sea *cpd*, maritime
mark [maʀk] *nm* mark
marmelade [maʀməlad] *nf* stewed fruit,
compote; ~ **d'oranges** marmalade
marmite [maʀmit] *nf* (cooking-)pot
marmonner [maʀmɔne] *vt, vi* to mumble,
mutter
marmotter [maʀmɔte] *vt* to mumble
Maroc [maʀɔk] *nm:* **le** ~ Morocco; **maro-
cain, e** *adj, nm/f* Moroccan
maroquinerie [maʀɔkinʀi] *nf* leather craft;
fine leather goods *pl*
marquant, e [maʀkɑ̃, -ɑ̃t] *adj* outstanding
marque [maʀk(ə)] *nf* mark; (*SPORT, JEU:
décompte des points*) score; (*COMM: de produits*) brand; make; (*de disques*) label; **de**
~ (*COMM*) brand-name *cpd*; proprietary;
(*fig*) high-class; distinguished; ~ **de fabrique** trademark; ~ **déposée** registered
trademark
marquer [maʀke] *vt* to mark; (*inscrire*) to
write down; (*bétail*) to brand; (*SPORT: but
etc*) to score; (: *joueur*) to mark; (*accentuer:
taille etc*) to emphasize; (*manifester: refus,
intérêt*) to show ♦ *vi* (*événement, personnalité*) to stand out, be outstanding; (*SPORT*)
to score; ~ **les points** (*tenir la marque*) to
keep the score
marqueterie [maʀkɛtʀi] *nf* inlaid work,
marquetry
marquis [maʀki] *nm* marquis *ou* marquess
marquise [maʀkiz] *nf* marchioness;
(*auvent*) glass canopy *ou* awning
marraine [maʀɛn] *nf* godmother
marrant, e [maʀɑ̃, -ɑ̃t] (*fam*) *adj* funny
marre [maʀ] (*fam*) *adv:* **en avoir** ~ **de** to
be fed up with
marrer [maʀe] : **se** ~ (*fam*) *vi* to have a
(good) laugh
marron [maʀɔ̃] *nm* (*fruit*) chestnut ♦ *adj inv*
brown; **marronnier** *nm* chestnut (tree)
mars [maʀs] *nm* March

marsouin [marswɛ̃] nm porpoise
marteau, x [marto] nm hammer; *(de porte)* knocker; **marteau-piqueur** nm pneumatic drill
marteler [martəle] vt to hammer
martien, ne [marsjɛ̃, -jɛn] adj Martian, of *ou* from Mars
martinet [martinɛ] nm *(fouet)* small whip; *(ZOOL)* swift
martyr, e [martir] nm/f martyr
martyre [martir] nm martyrdom; *(fig: sens affaibli)* agony, torture
martyriser [martirize] vt *(REL)* to martyr; *(fig)* to bully; *(enfant)* to batter, beat
marxiste [marksist(ə)] adj, nm/f Marxist
masculin, e [maskylɛ̃, -in] adj masculine; *(sexe, population)* male; *(équipe, vêtements)* men's; *(viril)* manly ♦ nm masculine
masque [mask(ə)] nm mask; **~r** [maske] vt *(cacher: paysage, porte)* to hide, conceal; *(dissimuler: vérité, projet)* to mask, obscure
massacre [masakʀ(ə)] nm massacre, slaughter; **~r** [masakʀe] vt to massacre, slaughter; *(fig: texte etc)* to murder
massage [masaʒ] nm massage
masse [mas] nf mass; *(péj)*: **la ~** the masses pl; *(ÉLEC)* earth; *(maillet)* sledgehammer; **une ~ de** *(fam)* masses *ou* loads of; **en ~** *(en bloc)* in bulk; *(en foule)* en masse ♦ adj *(exécutions, production)* mass cpd
masser [mase] vt *(assembler)* to gather; *(pétrir)* to massage; **se ~** vi to gather; **masseur, euse** [masœʀ, øz] nm/f masseur(euse)
massif, ive [masif, -iv] adj *(porte)* solid, massive; *(visage)* heavy, large; *(bois, or)* solid; *(dose)* massive; *(déportations etc)* mass cpd ♦ nm *(montagneux)* massif; *(de fleurs)* clump, bank
massue [masy] nf club, bludgeon
mastic [mastik] nm *(pour vitres)* putty; *(pour fentes)* filler
mastiquer [mastike] vt *(aliment)* to chew, masticate; *(fente)* to fill; *(vitre)* to putty
mat, e [mat] adj *(couleur, métal)* mat(t); *(bruit, son)* dull ♦ adj inv *(ÉCHECS)*: **être ~** to be checkmate
mât [mɑ] nm *(NAVIG)* mast; *(poteau)* pole, post
match [matʃ] nm match; **faire ~ nul** to draw; **~ aller** first leg; **~ retour** second leg, return match
matelas [matla] nm mattress; **~ pneumatique** air bed *ou* mattress
matelassé, e [matlase] adj padded; quilted
matelot [matlo] nm sailor, seaman
mater [mate] vt *(personne)* to bring to heel, subdue; *(révolte)* to put down
matérialiste [materjalist(ə)] adj materialistic
matériaux [materjo] nmpl material(s)
matériel, le [materjɛl] adj material ♦ nm equipment no pl; *(de camping etc)* gear no pl

maternel, le [matɛrnɛl] adj *(amour, geste)* motherly, maternal; *(grand-père, oncle)* maternal; **maternelle** nf *(aussi: école maternelle)* (state) nursery school
maternité [matɛrnite] nf *(établissement)* maternity hospital; *(état de mère)* motherhood, maternity; *(grossesse)* pregnancy
mathématique [matematik] adj mathematical; **mathématiques** nfpl *(science)* mathematics sg
matière [matjɛr] nf *(PHYSIQUE)* matter; *(COMM, TECH)* material, matter no pl; *(fig: d'un livre etc)* subject matter, material; *(SCOL)* subject; **en ~ de** as regards; **~s grasses** fat content sg; **~s premières** raw materials
matin [matɛ̃] nm, adv morning; **du ~ au soir** from morning till night; **de bon** *ou* **grand ~** early in the morning; **matinal, e, aux** adj *(toilette, gymnastique)* morning cpd; *(de bonne heure)* early; **être matinal** *(personne)* to be up early; to be an early riser
matinée [matine] nf morning; *(spectacle)* matinée
matou [matu] nm tom(cat)
matraque [matrak] nf club; *(de policier)* truncheon *(BRIT)*, billy *(US)*
matricule [matrikyl] nf *(aussi: registre ~)* roll, register ♦ nm *(: numéro ~: MIL)* regimental number; *(: ADMIN)* reference number
matrimonial, e, aux [matrimɔnjal, -o] adj marital, marriage cpd
maudire [modir] vt to curse
maudit, e [modi, -it] *(fam)* adj *(satané)* blasted, confounded
maugréer [mogree] vi to grumble
maussade [mosad] adj sullen
mauvais, e [mɔvɛ, -ɛz] adj bad; *(faux)*: **le ~ numéro/moment** the wrong number/moment; *(méchant, malveillant)* malicious, spiteful; **il fait ~** the weather is bad; **la mer est ~e** the sea is rough; **~ plaisant** hoaxer; **~e herbe** weed; **~e langue** gossip, scandalmonger *(BRIT)*; **~e passe** difficult situation; bad patch; **~e tête** rebellious *ou* headstrong customer
maux [mo] nmpl de **mal**; **~ de ventre** stomachache sg
maximum [maksimɔm] adj, nm maximum; **au ~** *(le plus possible)* to the full; as much as one can; *(tout au plus)* at the (very) most *ou* maximum
mayonnaise [majɔnɛz] nf mayonnaise
mazout [mazut] nm *(fuel)* oil
Me abr = **Maître**
me(m') [m(ə)] pron me; *(réfléchi)* myself
mec [mɛk] *(fam)* nm bloke, guy
mécanicien, ne [mekanisjɛ̃, -jɛn] nm/f mechanic; *(RAIL)* (train *ou* engine) driver
mécanique [mekanik] adj mechanical ♦ nf

(*science*) mechanics *sg*; (*technologie*) mechanical engineering; (*mécanisme*) mechanism; engineering; works *pl*; **ennui** ~ engine trouble *no pl*

mécanisme [mekanism(ə)] *nm* mechanism

méchamment [meʃamɑ̃] *adv* nastily, maliciously, spitefully

méchanceté [meʃɑ̃ste] *nf* nastiness, maliciousness; nasty *ou* spiteful *ou* malicious remark (*ou* action)

méchant, e [meʃɑ̃, -ɑ̃t] *adj* nasty, malicious, spiteful; (*enfant: pas sage*) naughty; (*animal*) vicious; (*avant le nom: valeur péjorative*) nasty; miserable; (: *intensive*) terrific

mèche [mɛʃ] *nf* (*de lampe, bougie*) wick; (*d'un explosif*) fuse; (*de vilebrequin, perceuse*) bit; (*de cheveux*) lock; **de ~ avec** in league with

mécompte [mekɔ̃t] *nm* miscalculation; (*déception*) disappointment

méconnaissable [mekɔnɛsabl(ə)] *adj* unrecognizable

méconnaître [mekɔnɛtr(ə)] *vt* (*ignorer*) to be unaware of; (*mésestimer*) to misjudge

mécontent, e [mekɔ̃tɑ̃, -ɑ̃t] *adj*: ~ **(de)** discontented *ou* dissatisfied *ou* displeased (with); (*contrarié*) annoyed (at); **mécontentement** *nm* dissatisfaction, discontent, displeasure; annoyance

médaille [medaj] *nf* medal

médaillon [medajɔ̃] *nm* (*portrait*) medallion; (*bijou*) locket

médecin [medsɛ̃] *nm* doctor; ~ **légiste** forensic surgeon

médecine [medsin] *nf* medicine; ~ **légale** forensic medicine

média [medja] *nmpl*: **les** ~ the media

médiatique [medjatik] *adj* media *cpd*

médical, e, aux [medikal, -o] *adj* medical

médicament [medikamɑ̃] *nm* medicine, drug

médiéval, e, aux [medjeval, -o] *adj* medieval

médiocre [medjɔkr(ə)] *adj* mediocre, poor

médire [medir] *vi*: ~ **de** to speak ill of; **médisance** *nf* scandalmongering (*BRIT*); piece of scandal *ou* of malicious gossip

méditer [medite] *vt* (*approfondir*) to meditate on, ponder (over); (*combiner*) to meditate ♦ *vi* to meditate

Méditerranée [mediterane] *nf*: **la (mer)** ~ the Mediterranean (Sea); **méditerranéen, ne** *adj, nm/f* Mediterranean

méduse [medyz] *nf* jellyfish

meeting [mitiŋ] *nm* (*POL, SPORT*) rally

méfait [mefɛ] *nm* (*faute*) misdemeanour, wrongdoing; ~**s** *nmpl* (*ravages*) ravages, damage *sg*

méfiance [mefjɑ̃s] *nf* mistrust, distrust; **méfiant, e** [mefjɑ̃, -ɑ̃t] *adj* mistrustful, distrustful

méfier [mefje]: **se** ~ *vi* to be wary; to be careful; **se** ~ **de** to mistrust, distrust, be wary of; (*faire attention*) to be careful about

mégarde [megard(ə)] *nf*: **par** ~ accidentally; by mistake

mégère [meʒɛr] *nf* shrew

mégot [mego] *nm* cigarette end

meilleur, e [mɛjœr] *adj, adv* better; (*valeur superlative*) best ♦ *nm*: **le** ~ (*celui qui ...*) the best (one); (*ce qui ...*) the best; **le** ~ **des deux** the better of the two; **de** ~**e heure** earlier; ~ **marché** cheaper; **meilleure** *nf*: **la meilleure** the best (one)

mélancolie [melɑ̃kɔli] *nf* melancholy, gloom; **mélancolique** *adj* melancholic, melancholy

mélange [melɑ̃ʒ] *nm* mixture

mélanger [melɑ̃ʒe] *vt* (*substances*) to mix; (*vins, couleurs*) to blend; (*mettre en désordre*) to mix up, muddle (up)

mélasse [melas] *nf* treacle, molasses *sg*

mêlée [mele] *nf* mêlée, scramble; (*RUGBY*) scrum(mage)

mêler [mele] *vt* (*substances, odeurs, races*) to mix; (*embrouiller*) to muddle (up), mix up; **se** ~ *vi* to mix; to mingle; **se** ~ **à** (*suj: personne*) to join; to mix with; (*suj: odeurs etc*) to mingle with; **se** ~ **de** (: *personne*) to meddle with, interfere in; ~ **qn à** (*affaire*) to get sb mixed up *ou* involved in

mélodie [melɔdi] *nf* melody

melon [məlɔ̃] *nm* (*BOT*) (honeydew) melon; (*aussi: chapeau* ~) bowler (hat)

membre [mɑ̃br(ə)] *nm* (*ANAT*) limb; (*personne, pays, élément*) member ♦ *adj* member *cpd*

mémé [meme] (*fam*) *nf* granny

─────── MOT CLÉ ───────

même [mɛm] *adj* **1** (*avant le nom*) same; **en** ~ **temps** at the same time

2 (*après le nom: renforcement*): **il est la loyauté** ~ he is loyalty itself; **ce sont ses paroles/celles-là** ~ they are his very words/the very ones

♦ *pron*: **le(la)** ~ the same one

♦ *adv* **1** (*renforcement*): **il n'a** ~ **pas pleuré** he didn't even cry; ~ **lui l'a dit** even HE said it; **ici** ~ at this very place

2: ~ **si** even if; **à** ~ **la bouteille** straight from the bottle; **à** ~ **la peau** next to the skin; **être à** ~ **de faire** to be in a position to do, be able to do

3: **de** ~ to do likewise; **lui de** ~ so does (*ou* did *ou* is) he; **de** ~ **que** just as; **il en va de** ~ **pour** the same goes for

───────────────────────

mémento [memɛ̃to] *nm* (*agenda*) appointments diary; (*résumé*) summary

mémoire [memwar] *nf* memory ♦ *nm* (*ADMIN, JUR*) memorandum; (*SCOL*) dissertation, paper; ~**s** *nmpl* (*souvenirs*) memoirs;

à la ~ de to the ou in memory of; **pour** ~ for the record; **de** ~ from memory; ~ **morte/vive** (*INFORM*) ROM/RAM

menace [mənas] *nf* threat

menacer [mənase] *vt* to threaten

ménage [menaʒ] *nm* (*travail*) housekeeping, housework; (*couple*) (married) couple; (*famille, ADMIN*) household; **faire le** ~ to do the housework

ménagement [menaʒmã] *nm* care and attention; ~**s** *nmpl* (*égards*) consideration *sg*, attention *sg*

ménager, ère [menaʒe, -ɛʀ] *adj* household *cpd*, domestic ♦ *vt* (*traiter*) to handle with tact; to treat considerately; (*utiliser*) to use sparingly; to use with care; (*prendre soin de*) to take (great) care of, look after; (*organiser*) to arrange; (*installer*) to put in; to make; ~ **qch à qn** (*réserver*) to have sth in store for sb; **ménagère** *nf* housewife

mendiant, e [mãdjã, -ãt] *nm/f* beggar; **mendier** [mãdje] *vi* to beg ♦ *vt* to beg (for)

mener [məne] *vt* to lead; (*enquête*) to conduct; (*affaires*) to manage ♦ *vi*: ~ **(à la marque)** to lead, be in the lead; ~ **à/dans** (*emmener*) to take to/into; ~ **qch à terme** ou **à bien** to see sth through (to a successful conclusion), complete sth successfully

meneur, euse [mənœʀ, -øz] *nm/f* leader; (*péj*) agitator; ~ **de jeu** host, quizmaster

méningite [menẽʒit] *nf* meningitis *no pl*

ménopause [menopoz] *nf* menopause

menottes [mənɔt] *nfpl* handcuffs

mensonge [mãsɔ̃ʒ] *nm* lie; lying *no pl*; **mensonger, ère** *adj* false

mensualité [mãsyalite] *nf* monthly payment; monthly salary

mensuel, le [mãsyɛl] *adj* monthly

mensurations [mãsyʀɑsjɔ̃] *nfpl* measurements

mentalité [mãtalite] *nf* mentality

menteur, euse [mãtœʀ, -øz] *nm/f* liar

menthe [mãt] *nf* mint

mention [mãsjɔ̃] *nf* (*note*) note, comment; (*SCOL*): ~ **bien** *etc* ≈ grade B *etc* (*ou* upper 2nd class *etc*) pass (*BRIT*), ≈ pass with (high) honors (*US*); **mentionner** *vt* to mention

mentir [mãtiʀ] *vi* to lie; to be lying

menton [mãtɔ̃] *nm* chin

menu, e [məny] *adj* slim, slight; tiny; (*frais, difficulté*) minor ♦ *adv* (*couper, hacher*) very fine ♦ *nm* menu; **par le** ~ (*raconter*) in minute detail; ~**e monnaie** small change

menuiserie [mənɥizʀi] *nf* (*travail*) joinery, carpentry; woodwork; (*local*) joiner's workshop; (*ouvrage*) woodwork *no pl*; **menuisier** [mənɥizje] *nm* joiner, carpenter

méprendre [mepʀɑ̃dʀ(ə)] : **se** ~ *vi* to be mistaken (about)

mépris [mepʀi] *nm* (*dédain*) contempt, scorn; (*indifférence*): **le** ~ **de** contempt ou

disregard for; **au** ~ **de** regardless of, in defiance of

méprisable [mepʀizabl(ə)] *adj* contemptible, despicable

méprise [mepʀiz] *nf* mistake, error; misunderstanding

mépriser [mepʀize] *vt* to scorn, despise; (*gloire, danger*) to scorn, spurn

mer [mɛʀ] *nf* sea; (*marée*) tide; **en** ~ at sea; **prendre la** ~ to put out to sea; **en haute** ou **pleine** ~ off shore, on the open sea; **la** ~ **du Nord/Rouge** the North/Red Sea

mercantile [mɛʀkãtil] (*péj*) *adj* mercenary

mercenaire [mɛʀsənɛʀ] *nm* mercenary, hired soldier

mercerie [mɛʀsəʀi] *nf* haberdashery (*BRIT*), notions (*US*); haberdasher's shop (*BRIT*), notions store (*US*)

merci [mɛʀsi] *excl* thank you ♦ *nf*: **à la** ~ **de qn/qch** at sb's mercy/the mercy of sth; ~ **de** thank you for; **sans** ~ merciless(ly)

mercredi [mɛʀkʀədi] *nm* Wednesday

mercure [mɛʀkyʀ] *nm* mercury

merde [mɛʀd(ə)] (*fam!*) *nf* shit (*!*) ♦ *excl* (bloody) hell (*!*)

mère [mɛʀ] *nf* mother; ~ **célibataire** unmarried mother

méridional, e, aux [meʀidjɔnal, -o] *adj* southern ♦ *nm/f* Southerner

meringue [məʀɛ̃g] *nf* meringue

mérite [meʀit] *nm* merit; **le** ~ **(de ceci) lui revient** the credit (for this) is his

mériter [meʀite] *vt* to deserve

merlan [mɛʀlã] *nm* whiting

merle [mɛʀl(ə)] *nm* blackbird

merveille [mɛʀvɛj] *nf* marvel, wonder; **faire** ~ to work wonders; **à** ~ perfectly, wonderfully

merveilleux, euse [mɛʀvɛjø, -øz] *adj* marvellous, wonderful

mes [me] *dét voir* **mon**

mésange [mezãʒ] *nf* tit(mouse)

mésaventure [mezavãtyʀ] *nf* misadventure, misfortune

Mesdames [medam] *nfpl de* **Madame**

Mesdemoiselles [medmwazɛl] *nfpl de* **Mademoiselle**

mésentente [mezãtãt] *nf* dissension, disagreement

mesquin, e [mɛskẽ, -in] *adj* mean, petty

message [mesaʒ] *nm* message; **messager, ère** *nm/f* messenger

messe [mɛs] *nf* mass; **aller à la** ~ to go to mass; ~ **de minuit** midnight mass

Messieurs [mesjø] *nmpl de* **Monsieur**

mesure [məzyʀ] *nf* (*évaluation, dimension*) measurement; (*étalon, récipient, contenu*) measure; (*MUS*: *cadence*) time, tempo; (: *division*) bar; (*retenue*) moderation; (*disposition*) measure, step; **sur** ~ (*costume*) made-to-measure; **à la** ~ **de** (*fig*) worthy of; on the same scale as; **dans la** ~ **où** insofar as, inasmuch as; **à ~ que** as; **être en ~ de** to be in a position to

mesurer [məzyʀe] *vt* to measure; (*juger*) to weigh up, assess; (*limiter*) to limit, ration; (*modérer*) to moderate; **se ~ avec** to have a confrontation with; to tackle; **il mesure 1 m 80** he's 1 m 80 tall

met *vb voir* **mettre**

métal, aux [metal, -o] *nm* metal; **métallique** *adj* metallic

météo [meteo] *nf* weather report; ≈ Met Office (*BRIT*), ≈ National Weather Service (*US*)

météorologie [meteɔʀɔlɔʒi] *nf* meteorology

méthode [metɔd] *nf* method; (*livre, ouvrage*) manual, tutor

métier [metje] *nm* (*profession: gén*) job; (: *manuel*) trade; (*artisanal*) craft; (*technique, expérience*) (acquired) skill *ou* technique; (*aussi: ~ à tisser*) (weaving) loom

métis, se [metis] *adj, nm/f* half-caste, half-breed

métisser [metise] *vt* to cross

métrage [metʀaʒ] *nm* (*de tissu*) length, ≈ yardage; (*CINÉMA*) footage, length; **long/moyen/court ~** full-length/medium-length/short film

mètre [mɛtʀ(ə)] *nm* metre; (*règle*) (metre) rule; (*ruban*) tape measure; **métrique** *adj* metric

métro [metʀo] *nm* underground (*BRIT*), subway

métropole [metʀɔpɔl] *nf* (*capitale*) metropolis; (*pays*) home country

mets [mɛ] *nm* dish

metteur [metœʀ] *nm:* **~ en scène** (*THÉÂTRE*) producer; (*CINÉMA*) director; **~ en ondes** producer

──────────── MOT CLÉ ────────────

mettre [mɛtʀ(ə)] *vt* **1** (*placer*) to put; **~ en bouteille/en sac** to bottle/put in bags *ou* sacks

2 (*vêtements: revêtir*) to put on; (: *porter*) to wear; **mets ton gilet** put your cardigan on; **je ne mets plus mon manteau** I no longer wear my coat

3 (*faire fonctionner: chauffage, électricité*) to put on; (: *reveil, minuteur*) to set; (*installer: gaz, eau*) to lay on; **~ en marche** to start up

4 (*consacrer*): **~ du temps à faire qch** to take time to do sth *ou* over sth

5 (*noter, écrire*) to say, put (down); **qu'est-ce qu'il a mis sur la carte?** what did he say *ou* write on the card?; **mettez au pluriel ...** put ... into the plural

6 (*supposer*): **mettons que ...** let's suppose *ou* say that ...

7: y ~ du sien to pull one's weight

se ~ *vi* **1** (*se placer*): **vous pouvez vous ~** **là** you can sit (*ou* stand) there; **où ça se met?** where does it go?; **se ~ au lit** to get into bed; **se ~ au piano** to sit down at the piano; **se ~ de l'encre sur les doigts** to get ink on one's fingers

2 (*s'habiller*): **se ~ en maillot de bain** to get into *ou* put on a swimsuit; **n'avoir rien à se ~** to have nothing to wear

3: se ~ à to begin, start; **se ~ à faire** to begin *ou* start doing *ou* to do; **se ~ au piano** to start learning the piano; **se ~ au travail/à l'étude** to get down to work/one's studies

────────────────────

meuble [mœbl(ə)] *nm* piece of furniture; furniture *no pl* ♦ *adj* (*terre*) loose, friable; **meublé** *nm* furnished flatlet (*BRIT*) *ou* room; **meubler** *vt* to furnish; (*fig*): **meubler qch (de)** to fill sth (with)

meugler [møgle] *vi* to low, moo

meule [møl] *nf* (*à broyer*) millstone; (*à aiguiser*) grindstone; (*de foin, blé*) stack; (*de fromage*) round

meunier [mønje] *nm* miller; **meunière** *nf* miller's wife

meure *etc vb voir* **mourir**

meurtre [mœʀtʀ(ə)] *nm* murder; **meurtrier, ière** *adj* (*arme etc*) deadly; (*fureur, instincts*) murderous ♦ *nm/f* murderer (eress); **meurtrière** *nf* (*ouverture*) loophole

meurtrir [mœʀtʀiʀ] *vt* to bruise; (*fig*) to wound; **meurtrissure** *nf* bruise; (*fig*) scar

meus *etc vb voir* **mouvoir**

meute [møt] *nf* pack

Mexico [mɛksiko] *n* Mexico City

Mexique [mɛksik] *nm:* **le ~** Mexico

Mgr *abr* = **Monseigneur**

mi [mi] *nm* (*MUS*) E; (*en chantant la gamme*) mi ♦ *préfixe:* **~...** half(-); mid-; **à la ~-janvier** in mid-January; **à ~-jambes/-corps** (up *ou* down) to the knees/waist; **à ~-hauteur/-pente** halfway up *ou* down/up *ou* down the hill

miauler [mjole] *vi* to mew

miche [miʃ] *nf* round *ou* cob loaf

mi-chemin [miʃmɛ̃] : **à ~** *adv* halfway, midway

mi-clos, e [miklo, -kloz] *adj* half-closed

micro [mikʀo] *nm* mike, microphone; (*IN-FORM*) micro

microbe [mikʀɔb] *nm* germ, microbe

micro: **~-onde** *nf:* **four à ~s** microwave oven; **~-ordinateur** *nm* microcomputer; **~scope** *nm* microscope

midi [midi] *nm* midday, noon; (*moment du déjeuner*) lunchtime; (*sud*) south; **à ~** at 12 (o'clock) *ou* midday *ou* noon; **en plein ~** (right) in the middle of the day; facing south; **le M~** the South (of France), the Midi

mie [mi] *nf* crumb (of the loaf)

miel [mjɛl] *nm* honey

mien, ne [mjɛ̃, mjɛn] *pron*: **le(la) ~(ne), les ~(ne)s** mine; **les ~s** my family

miette [mjɛt] *nf* (*de pain, gâteau*) crumb; (*fig: de la conversation etc*) scrap; **en ~s** in pieces *ou* bits

───────── *MOT CLÉ* ─────────

mieux [mjø] *adv* **1** (*d'une meilleure façon*): **~ (que)** better (than); **elle travaille/mange ~** she works/eats better; **elle va ~** she is better

2 (*de la meilleure façon*) best; **ce que je sais le ~** what I know best; **les livres les ~ faits** the best made books

3: de ~ en ~ better and better

♦ *adj* **1** (*plus à l'aise, en meilleure forme*) better; **se sentir ~** to feel better

2 (*plus satisfaisant*) better; **c'est ~ ainsi** it's better like this; **c'est le ~ des deux** it's the better of the two; **le(la) ~, les ~** the best; **demandez-lui, c'est le ~** ask him, it's the best thing

3 (*plus joli*) better-looking

4: au ~ at best; **au ~ avec** on the best of terms with; **pour le ~** for the best

♦ *nm* **1** (*progrès*) improvement

2: de mon/ton ~ as best I/you can (*ou* could); **faire de son ~** to do one's best

─────────────────────────

mièvre [mjɛvʀ(ə)] *adj* mawkish (*BRIT*), sickly sentimental

mignon, ne [miɲɔ̃, -ɔn] *adj* sweet, cute

migraine [migʀɛn] *nf* headache; migraine

mijoter [miʒɔte] *vt* to simmer; (*préparer avec soin*) to cook lovingly; (*affaire, projet*) to plot, cook up ♦ *vi* to simmer

mil [mil] *num* = **mille**

milieu, x [miljø] *nm* (*centre*) middle; (*fig*) middle course *ou* way; happy medium; (*BIO, GÉO*) environment; (*entourage social*) milieu; background; circle; (*pègre*): **le ~** the underworld; **au ~ de** in the middle of; **au beau** *ou* **en plein ~ (de)** right in the middle (of)

militaire [militɛʀ] *adj* military, army *cpd* ♦ *nm* serviceman

militant, e [militɑ̃, -ɑ̃t] *adj, nm/f* militant

militer [milite] *vi* to be a militant; **~ pour/contre** (*suj: faits, raisons etc*) to militate in favour of/against

mille [mil] *num* a *ou* one thousand ♦ *nm* (*mesure*): **~ (marin)** nautical mile; **mettre dans le ~** to hit the bull's-eye; to be bang on target; **millefeuille** *nm* cream *ou* vanilla slice; **millénaire** *nm* millennium ♦ *adj* thousand-year-old; (*fig*) ancient; **mille-pattes** *nm inv* centipede

millésime [milezim] *nm* year; **millésimé, e** *adj* vintage *cpd*

millet [mijɛ] *nm* millet

milliard [miljaʀ] *nm* milliard, thousand million (*BRIT*), billion (*US*); **milliardaire** *nm/f*

multimillionaire (*BRIT*), billionaire (*US*)

millier [milje] *nm* thousand; **un ~ (de)** a thousand *ou* so, about a thousand; **par ~s** in (their) thousands, by the thousand

milligramme [miligʀam] *nm* milligramme

millimètre [milimɛtʀ(ə)] *nm* millimetre

million [miljɔ̃] *nm* million; **deux ~s de** two million; **millionnaire** *nm/f* millionaire

mime [mim] *nm/f* (*acteur*) mime(r) ♦ *nm* (*art*) mime, miming

mimer [mime] *vt* to mime; (*singer*) to mimic, take off

mimique [mimik] *nf* (*funny*) face; (*signes*) gesticulations *pl*, sign language *no pl*

minable [minabl(ə)] *adj* shabby(-looking); pathetic

mince [mɛ̃s] *adj* thin; (*personne, taille*) slim, slender; (*fig: profit, connaissances*) slight, small, weak ♦ *excl*: **~ alors!** drat it!, darn it! (*US*); **minceur** *nf* thinness; slimness, slenderness

mine [min] *nf* (*physionomie*) expression, look; (*extérieur*) exterior, appearance; (*de crayon*) lead; (*gisement, exploitation, explosif, fig*) mine; **avoir bonne ~** (*personne*) to look well; (*ironique*) to look an utter idiot; **avoir mauvaise ~** to look unwell *ou* poorly; **faire ~ de faire** to make a pretence of doing; to make as if to do; **~ de rien** with a casual air; although you wouldn't think so

miner [mine] *vt* (*saper*) to undermine, erode; (*MIL*) to mine

minerai [minʀɛ] *nm* ore

minéral, e, aux [mineʀal, -o] *adj, nm* mineral

minéralogique [mineʀalɔʒik] *adj*: **numéro ~** registration number

minet, te [minɛ, -ɛt] *nm/f* (*chat*) pussy-cat; (*péj*) young trendy

mineur, e [minœʀ] *adj* minor ♦ *nm/f* (*JUR*) minor, person under age ♦ *nm* (*travailleur*) miner

miniature [minjatyʀ] *adj, nf* miniature

minibus [minibys] *nm* minibus

mini-cassette [minikasɛt] *nf* cassette (recorder)

minier, ière [minje, -jɛʀ] *adj* mining

mini-jupe [miniʒyp] *nf* mini-skirt

minime [minim] *adj* minor, minimal

minimiser [minimize] *vt* to minimize; (*fig*) to play down

minimum [minimɔm] *adj, nm* minimum; **au ~** (*au moins*) at the very least

ministère [ministɛʀ] *nm* (*aussi REL*) ministry; (*cabinet*) government; **~ public** (*JUR*) Prosecution, public prosecutor

ministre [ministʀ(ə)] *nm* (*aussi REL*) minister; **~ d'État** senior minister

Minitel [minitɛl] (®) *nm* videotext terminal and service

minorité [minɔʀite] *nf* minority; **être en ~**

to be in the *ou* a minority; **mettre en ~** (*POL*) to defeat

minoterie [minɔtʀi] *nf* flour-mill

minuit [minɥi] *nm* midnight

minuscule [minyskyl] *adj* minute, tiny ♦ *nf*: **(lettre) ~** small letter

minute [minyt] *nf* minute; (*JUR*: *original*) minute, draft; **à la ~** (just) this instant; there and then; **minuter** *vt* to time; **minuterie** *nf* time switch

minutieux, euse [minysjø, -øz] *adj* meticulous; minutely detailed

mirabelle [miʀabɛl] *nf* (cherry) plum

miracle [miʀakl(ə)] *nm* miracle

mirage [miʀaʒ] *nm* mirage

mire [miʀ] *nf*: **point de ~** target; (*fig*) focal point; **ligne de ~** line of sight

miroir [miʀwaʀ] *nm* mirror

miroiter [miʀwate] *vi* to sparkle, shimmer; **faire ~ qch à qn** to paint sth in glowing colours for sb, dangle sth in front of sb's eyes

mis, e [mi, miz] *pp de* **mettre** ♦ *adj*: **bien ~** well-dressed

mise [miz] *nf* (*argent: au jeu*) stake; (*tenue*) clothing; attire; **être de ~** to be acceptable *ou* in season; **~ à feu** blast-off; **~ au point** (*fig*) clarification; **~ de fonds** capital outlay; **~ en plis** set; **~ en scène** production

miser [mize] *vt* (*enjeu*) to stake, bet; **~ sur** (*cheval, numéro*) to bet on; (*fig*) to bank *ou* count on

misérable [mizeʀabl(ə)] *adj* (*lamentable, malheureux*) pitiful, wretched; (*pauvre*) poverty-stricken; (*insignifiant, mesquin*) miserable ♦ *nm/f* wretch; (*miséreux*) poor wretch

misère [mizɛʀ] *nf* (extreme) poverty, destitution; **~s** *nfpl* (*malheurs*) woes, miseries; (*ennuis*) little troubles; **salaire de ~** starvation wage

miséricorde [mizeʀikɔʀd(ə)] *nf* mercy, forgiveness

missile [misil] *nm* missile

mission [misjɔ̃] *nf* mission; **partir en ~** (*ADMIN, POL*) to go on an assignment; **missionnaire** *nm/f* missionary

mit *vb voir* **mettre**

mité, e [mite] *adj* moth-eaten

mi-temps [mitɑ̃] *nf inv* (*SPORT: période*) half; (: *pause*) half-time; **à ~** part-time

mitigé, e [mitiʒe] *adj* lukewarm; mixed

mitonner [mitɔne] *vt* to cook with loving care; (*fig*) to cook up quietly

mitoyen, ne [mitwajɛ̃, -ɛn] *adj* common, party *cpd*

mitrailler [mitʀaje] *vt* to machine-gun; (*fig*) to pelt, bombard; (: *photographier*) to take shot after shot of; **mitraillette** *nf* submachine gun; **mitrailleuse** *nf* machine gun

mi-voix [mivwa]: **à ~** *adv* in a low *ou* hushed voice

mixage [miksaʒ] *nm* (*CINÉMA*) (sound) mixing

mixer [miksœʀ] *nm* (food) mixer

mixte [mikst(ə)] *adj* (*gén*) mixed; (*SCOL*) mixed, coeducational; **à usage ~** dual-purpose

mixture [mikstyʀ] *nf* mixture; (*fig*) concoction

MLF *sigle m* = Mouvement de Libération de la femme

Mlle (*pl* **Mlles**) *abr* = **Mademoiselle**

MM *abr* = **Messieurs**

Mme (*pl* **Mmes**) *abr* = **Madame**

Mo *abr* = **métro**

mobile [mɔbil] *adj* mobile; (*pièce de machine*) moving; (*élément de meuble etc*) movable ♦ *nm* (*motif*) motive; (*œuvre d'art*) mobile

mobilier, ière [mɔbilje, -jɛʀ] *adj* (*JUR*) personal ♦ *nm* furniture

mobiliser [mɔbilize] *vt* (*MIL, gén*) to mobilize

moche [mɔʃ] (*fam*) *adj* ugly; rotten

modalité [mɔdalite] *nf* form, mode; **~s** *nfpl* (*d'un accord etc*) clauses, terms

mode [mɔd] *nf* fashion ♦ *nm* (*manière*) form, mode; **à la ~** fashionable, in fashion; **~ d'emploi** directions *pl* (for use)

modèle [mɔdɛl] *adj, nm* model; (*qui pose: de peintre*) sitter; **~ déposé** registered design; **~ réduit** small-scale model; **modeler** [mɔdle] *vt* (*ART*) to model, mould; (*suj: vêtement, érosion*) to mould, shape

modem [mɔdɛm] *nm* modem

modéré, e [mɔdeʀe] *adj, nm/f* moderate

modérer [mɔdeʀe] *vt* to moderate; **se ~** *vi* to restrain o.s.

moderne [mɔdɛʀn(ə)] *adj* modern ♦ *nm* modern style; modern furniture; **moderniser** *vt* to modernize

modeste [mɔdɛst(ə)] *adj* modest; **modestie** *nf* modesty

modifier [mɔdifje] *vt* to modify, alter; **se ~** *vi* to alter

modique [mɔdik] *adj* modest

modiste [mɔdist(ə)] *nf* milliner

modulation [mɔdylɑsjɔ̃] *nf*: **~ de fréquence** frequency modulation

module [mɔdyl] *nm* module

moelle [mwal] *nf* marrow

moelleux, euse [mwalø, -øz] *adj* soft; (*au goût, à l'ouïe*) mellow

moellon [mwalɔ̃] *nm* rubble stone

mœurs [mœʀ] *nfpl* (*conduite*) morals; (*manières*) manners; (*pratiques sociales, mode de vie*) habits

mohair [mɔɛʀ] *nm* mohair

moi [mwa] *pron* me; (*emphatique*): **~, je ...** for my part, I ... myself ...

moignon [mwaɲɔ̃] *nm* stump

moi-même [mwamɛm] *pron* myself; (*emphatique*) I myself

moindre [mwɛ̃dʀ(ə)] *adj* lesser; lower; **le(la) ~, les ~s** the least, the slightest
moine [mwan] *nm* monk, friar
moineau, x [mwano] *nm* sparrow

─────────── MOT CLÉ ───────────

moins [mwɛ̃] *adv* **1** (*comparatif*): **~ (que)** less (than); **~ grand que** less tall than, not as tall as; **~ je travaille, mieux je me porte** the less I work, the better I feel
2 (*superlatif*): **le ~** (the) least; **c'est ce que j'aime le ~** it's what I like (the) least; **le(la) ~ doué(e)** the least gifted; **au ~, du ~** at least; **pour le ~** at the very least
3: **~ de** (*quantité*) less (than); (*nombre*) fewer (than); **~ de sable/d'eau** less sand/water; **~ de livres/gens** fewer books/people; **~ de 2 ans** less than 2 years; **~ de midi** not yet midday
4: **de ~, en ~: 100F/3 jours de ~** 100F/3 days less; **3 livres en ~** 3 books fewer; **3 books too few; de l'argent en ~** less money; **le soleil en ~** but for the sun, minus the sun; **de ~ en ~** less and less
5: **à ~ de, à ~ que** unless; **à ~ de faire** unless we do (*ou* he does *etc*); **à ~ que tu ne fasses** unless you do; **à ~ d'un accident** barring any accident
♦ *prép*: **4 ~ 2** 4 minus 2; **il est ~ 5** it's 5 to; **il fait ~ 5** it's 5 (degrees) below (freezing), it's minus 5

──────────────────────────

mois [mwa] *nm* month; **~ double** (COMM) extra month's salary
moisi [mwazi] *nm* mould, mildew; **odeur de ~** musty smell
moisir [mwaziʀ] *vi* to go mouldy; (*fig*) to rot; to hang about
moisissure [mwazisyʀ] *nf* mould *nopl*
moisson [mwasɔ̃] *nf* harvest; **moissonner** *vt* to harvest, reap; **moissonneuse** *nf* (*machine*) harvester
moite [mwat] *adj* sweaty, sticky
moitié [mwatje] *nf* half; **la ~** half; **la ~ de** half (of); **la ~ du temps/des gens** half the time/the people; **à la ~ de** halfway through; **à ~** (*avant le verbe*) half; (*avant l'adjectif*) half-; **de ~** by half; **~ ~** half-and-half
mol [mɔl] *adj voir* **mou**
molaire [mɔlɛʀ] *nf* molar
molester [mɔlɛste] *vt* to manhandle, maul (about)
molle [mɔl] *adj voir* **mou; mollement** *adv* softly; (*péj*) sluggishly; (*protester*) feebly
mollet [mɔlɛ] *nm* calf ♦ *adj m*: **œuf ~** soft-boiled egg
molletonné, e [mɔltɔne] *adj* fleece-lined
mollir [mɔliʀ] *vi* to give way; to relent; to go soft
môme [mom] (*fam*) *nm/f* (*enfant*) brat ♦ *nf* (*fille*) chick

moment [mɔmɑ̃] *nm* moment; **ce n'est pas le ~** this is not the (right) time; **à un certain ~** at some point; **à un ~ donné** at a certain point; **pour un bon ~** for a good while; **pour le ~** for the moment, for the time being; **au ~ de** at the time of; **au ~ où** as; at a time when; **à tout ~** at any time *ou* moment; constantly, continually; **en ce ~** at the moment; at present; **sur le ~** at the time; **par ~s** now and then, at times; **du ~ où** *ou* **que** seeing that, since; **momentané, e** *adj* temporary, momentary
momie [mɔmi] *nf* mummy
mon, ma [mɔ̃, ma] (*pl* **mes**) *dét* my
Monaco [mɔnako] *nm*: **le ~** Monaco
monarchie [mɔnaʀʃi] *nf* monarchy
monastère [mɔnastɛʀ] *nm* monastery
monceau, x [mɔ̃so] *nm* heap
mondain, e [mɔ̃dɛ̃, -ɛn] *adj* society *cpd*; social; fashionable; **~e** *nf*: **la M~e, la police ~e** ≈ the vice squad
monde [mɔ̃d] *nm* world; (*haute société*): **le ~** (high) society; (*milieu*): **être du même ~** to move in the same circles; (*gens*): **il y a du ~** (*beaucoup de gens*) there are a lot of people; (*quelques personnes*) there are some people; **beaucoup/peu de ~** many/few people; **le meilleur** *etc* **du ~** the best *etc* in the world *ou* on earth; **mettre au ~** to bring into the world; **pas le moins du ~** not in the least; **se faire un ~ de qch** to make a great fuss about sth; **mondial, e, aux** *adj* (*population*) world *cpd*; (*influence*) world-wide; **mondialement** *adv* throughout the world
monégasque [mɔnegask(ə)] *adj* Monegasque, of *ou* from Monaco
monétaire [mɔnetɛʀ] *adj* monetary
moniteur, trice [mɔnitœʀ, -tʀis] *nm/f* (SPORT) instructor(tress); (*de colonie de vacances*) supervisor ♦ *nm* (*écran*) monitor
monnaie [mɔnɛ] *nf* (*pièce*) coin; (ÉCON, *gén*: *moyen d'échange*) currency; (*petites pièces*): **avoir de la ~** to have (some) change; **faire de la ~** to get (some) change; **avoir/faire la ~ de 20 F** to have change of/get change for 20 F; **rendre à qn la ~ (sur 20 F)** to give sb the change (out of *ou* from 20 F); **monnayer** *vt* to convert into cash; (*talent*) to capitalize on
monologue [mɔnɔlɔg] *nm* monologue, soliloquy; **monologuer** *vi* to soliloquize
monopole [mɔnɔpɔl] *nm* monopoly
monotone [mɔnɔtɔn] *adj* monotonous
monseigneur [mɔ̃sɛɲœʀ] *nm* (*archevêque, évêque*) Your (*ou* His) Grace; (*cardinal*) Your (*ou* His) Eminence
Monsieur [məsjø] (*pl* **Messieurs**) *titre* Mr ♦ *nm* (*homme quelconque*): **un/le m~** a/the gentleman; *voir aussi* **Madame**
monstre [mɔ̃stʀ(ə)] *nm* monster ♦ *adj*: **un travail ~** a fantastic amount of work; **an**

enormous job

mont [mɔ̃] *nm:* **par ~s et par vaux** up hill and down dale; **le M~ Blanc** Mont Blanc

montage [mɔ̃taʒ] *nm* putting up; mounting, setting; assembly; (*PHOTO*) photomontage; (*CINÉMA*) editing

montagnard, e [mɔ̃taɲaʀ, -aʀd(ə)] *adj* mountain *cpd* ♦ *nm/f* mountain-dweller

montagne [mɔ̃taɲ] *nf* (*cime*) mountain; (*région*): **la ~** the mountains *pl;* **~s russes** big dipper *sg,* switchback *sg;* **montagneux, euse** [mɔ̃taɲø, -øz] *adj* mountainous; hilly

montant, e [mɔ̃tɑ̃, -ɑ̃t] *adj* rising; (*robe, corsage*) high-necked ♦ *nm* (*somme, total*) (sum) total, (total) amount; (*de fenêtre*) upright; (*de lit*) post

monte-charge [mɔ̃tʃaʀʒ(ə)] *nm inv* goods lift, hoist

montée [mɔ̃te] *nf* rising, rise; ascent, climb; (*chemin*) way up; (*côte*) hill; **au milieu de la ~** halfway up

monter [mɔ̃te] *vt* (*escalier, côte*) to go (*ou* come) up; (*valise, paquet*) to take (*ou* bring) up; (*cheval*) to mount; (*étagère*) to raise; (*tente, échafaudage*) to put up; (*machine*) to assemble; (*bijou*) to mount, set; (*COUTURE*) to set in; to sew on; (*CINÉMA*) to edit; (*THÉÂTRE*) to put on, stage; (*société etc*) to set up ♦ *vi* to go (*ou* come) up; (*avion etc*) to climb, go up; (*chemin, niveau, température*) to go up, rise; (*passager*) to get on; (*à cheval*): **~ bien/mal** to ride well/badly; **se ~ à** (*frais etc*) to add up to, come to; **~ à pied** to walk up, go up on foot; **~ à bicyclette/en voiture** to cycle/drive up, go up by bicycle/by car; **~ dans le train/l'avion** to get into the train/plane, board the train/plane; **~ sur** to climb up onto; **~ à cheval** to get on *ou* mount a horse

monticule [mɔ̃tikyl] *nm* mound

montre [mɔ̃tʀ(ə)] *nf* watch; **faire ~ de** to show, display; **contre la ~** (*SPORT*) against the clock; **montre-bracelet** *nf* wristwatch

montrer [mɔ̃tʀe] *vt* to show; **~ qch à qn** to show sb sth

monture [mɔ̃tyʀ] *nf* (*bête*) mount; (*d'une bague*) setting; (*de lunettes*) frame

monument [mɔnymɑ̃] *nm* monument; **~ aux morts** war memorial

moquer [mɔke] : **se ~ de** *vt* to make fun of, laugh at; (*fam:* **se désintéresser de**) not to care about; (*tromper*): **se ~ de qn** to take sb for a ride

moquette [mɔkɛt] *nf* fitted carpet

moqueur, euse [mɔkœʀ, -øz] *adj* mocking

moral, e, aux [mɔʀal, -o] *adj* moral ♦ *nm* morale; **avoir le ~ à zéro** to be really down; **morale** *nf* (*conduite*) morals *pl;* (*règles*) moral code, ethic; (*valeurs*) moral standards *pl,* morality; (*science*) ethics *sg,* moral philosophy; (*conclusion: d'une fable etc*) moral; **faire la morale à** to lecture, preach at; **moralité** *nf* morality; (*conduite*) morals *pl;* (*conclusion, enseignement*) moral

morceau, x [mɔʀso] *nm* piece, bit; (*d'une œuvre*) passage, extract; (*MUS*) piece; (*CULIN: de viande*) cut; **mettre en ~x** to pull to pieces *ou* bits

morceler [mɔʀsəle] *vt* to break up, divide up

mordant, e [mɔʀdɑ̃, -ɑ̃t] *adj* scathing, cutting; biting

mordiller [mɔʀdije] *vt* to nibble at, chew at

mordre [mɔʀdʀ(ə)] *vt* to bite; (*suj: lime, vis*) to bite into ♦ *vi* (*poisson*) to bite; **~ sur** (*fig*) to go over into, overlap into; **~ à l'hameçon** to bite, rise to the bait

mordu, e [mɔʀdy] *nm/f:* **un ~ du jazz** a jazz fanatic

morfondre [mɔʀfɔ̃dʀ(ə)] : **se ~** *vi* to mope

morgue [mɔʀg(ə)] *nf* (*arrogance*) haughtiness; (*lieu: de la police*) morgue; (: *à l'hôpital*) mortuary

morne [mɔʀn(ə)] *adj* dismal, dreary

mors [mɔʀ] *nm* bit

morse [mɔʀs(ə)] *nm* (*ZOOL*) walrus; (*TÉL*) Morse (code)

morsure [mɔʀsyʀ] *nf* bite

mort[1] [mɔʀ] *nf* death

mort[2]**, e** [mɔʀ, mɔʀt(ə)] *pp de* **mourir** ♦ *adj* dead ♦ *nm/f* (*défunt*) dead man(woman); (*victime*): **il y a eu plusieurs ~s** several people were killed, there were several killed ♦ *nm* (*CARTES*) dummy; **~ ou vif** dead or alive; **~ de peur/fatigue** frightened to death/dead tired

mortalité [mɔʀtalite] *nf* mortality, death rate

mortel, le [mɔʀtɛl] *adj* (*poison etc*) deadly, lethal; (*accident, blessure*) fatal; (*REL*) mortal; (*fig*) deathly; deadly boring

mortier [mɔʀtje] *nm* (*gén*) mortar

mort-né, e [mɔʀne] *adj* (*enfant*) stillborn

mortuaire [mɔʀtɥeʀ] *adj* funeral *cpd*

morue [mɔʀy] *nf* (*ZOOL*) cod *inv*

mosaïque [mɔzaik] *nf* (*ART*) mosaic; (*fig*) patchwork

Moscou [mɔsku] *n* Moscow

mosquée [mɔske] *nf* mosque

mot [mo] *nm* word; (*message*) line, note; (*bon mot etc*) saying; sally; **~ à ~** word for word; **~ d'ordre** watchword; **~ de passe** password; **~s croisés** crossword (puzzle) *sg*

motard [mɔtaʀ] *nm* biker; (*policier*) motorcycle cop

motel [mɔtɛl] *nm* motel

moteur, trice [mɔtœʀ, -tʀis] *adj* (*ANAT, PHYSIOL*) motor; (*TECH*) driving; (*AUTO*): **à 4 roues motrices** 4-wheel drive ♦ *nm* engine, motor; **à ~** power-driven, motor *cpd*

motif [mɔtif] *nm* (*cause*) motive; (*décoratif*)

design, pattern, motif; (*d'un tableau*) subject, motif; ~**s** *nmpl* (*JUR*) grounds *pl*; **sans ~** groundless

motiver [mɔtive] *vt* (*justifier*) to justify, account for; (*ADMIN, JUR, PSYCH*) to motivate

moto [mɔto] *nf* (motor)bike; **motocycliste** *nm/f* motorcyclist

motorisé, e [mɔtɔʀize] *adj* (*troupe*) motorized; (*personne*) having transport *ou* a car

motrice [mɔtʀis] *adj voir* **moteur**

motte [mɔt] *nf*: ~ **de terre** lump of earth, clod (of earth); ~ **de beurre** lump of butter; ~ **de gazon** turf, sod

mou(mol), molle [mu, mɔl] *adj* soft; (*péj*) flabby; sluggish ♦ *nm* (*abats*) lights *pl*, lungs *pl*; (*de la corde*) **avoir du ~** to be slack

mouche [muʃ] *nf* fly

moucher [muʃe] *vt* (*enfant*) to blow the nose of; (*chandelle*) to snuff (out); **se ~** *vi* to blow one's nose

moucheron [muʃʀɔ̃] *nm* midge

moucheté, e [muʃte] *adj* dappled; flecked

mouchoir [muʃwaʀ] *nm* handkerchief, hanky; ~ **en papier** tissue, paper hanky

moudre [mudʀ(ə)] *vt* to grind

moue [mu] *nf* pout; **faire la ~** to pout; (*fig*) to pull a face

mouette [mwɛt] *nf* (sea)gull

moufle [mufl(ə)] *nf* (*gant*) mitt(en)

mouillé, e [muje] *adj* wet

mouiller [muje] *vt* (*humecter*) to wet, moisten; (*tremper*): ~ **qn/qch** to make sb/sth wet; (*couper, diluer*) to water down; (*mine etc*) to lay (*NAVIG*) to lie *ou* be at anchor; **se ~** to get wet; (*fam*) to commit o.s.; to get o.s. involved

moule [mul] *nf* mussel ♦ *nm* (*creux, CULIN*) mould; (*modèle plein*) cast; ~ **à gâteaux** *nm* cake tin (*BRIT*) *ou* pan (*US*)

moulent *vb voir* **moudre; mouler**

mouler [mule] *vt* (*suj: vêtement*) to hug, fit closely round; ~ **qch sur** (*fig*) to model sth on

moulin [mulɛ̃] *nm* mill; ~ **à café/à poivre** coffee/pepper mill; ~ **à légumes** (vegetable) shredder; ~ **à paroles** (*fig*) chatterbox; ~ **à vent** windmill

moulinet [mulinɛ] *nm* (*de treuil*) winch; (*de canne à pêche*) reel; (*mouvement*): **faire des ~s avec qch** to whirl sth around

moulinette [mulinɛt] *nf* (vegetable) shredder

moulu, e [muly] *pp de* **moudre**

moulure [mulyʀ] *nf* (*ornement*) moulding

mourant, e [muʀɑ̃, -ɑ̃t] *adj* dying

mourir [muʀiʀ] *vi* to die; (*civilisation*) to die out; ~ **de froid/faim** to die of exposure/hunger; ~ **de faim/d'ennui** (*fig*) to be starving/be bored to death; ~ **d'envie de faire** to be dying to do

mousse [mus] *nf* (*BOT*) moss; (*écume: sur eau, bière*) froth, foam; (: *shampooing*) lather; (*CULIN*) mousse ♦ *nm* (*NAVIG*) ship's boy; **bas ~** stretch stockings; ~ **à raser** shaving foam; ~ **carbonique** (firefighting) foam

mousseline [muslin] *nf* muslin; chiffon

mousser [muse] *vi* to foam; to lather

mousseux, euse [musø, -øz] *adj* frothy ♦ *nm*: (*vin*) ~ sparkling wine

mousson [musɔ̃] *nf* monsoon

moustache [mustaʃ] *nf* moustache; ~**s** *nfpl* (*du chat*) whiskers *pl*

moustiquaire [mustikɛʀ] *nf* mosquito net (*ou* screen)

moustique [mustik] *nm* mosquito

moutarde [mutaʀd(ə)] *nf* mustard

mouton [mutɔ̃] *nm* (*ZOOL, péj*) sheep *inv*; (*peau*) sheepskin; (*CULIN*) mutton

mouvant, e [muvɑ̃, -ɑ̃t] *adj* unsettled; changing; shifting

mouvement [muvmɑ̃] *nm* (*gén, aussi: mécanisme*) movement; (*fig*) activity; impulse; gesture; (*MUS: rythme*) tempo; **en ~** in motion; on the move; **mouvementé, e** *adj* (*vie, poursuite*) eventful; (*réunion*) turbulent

mouvoir [muvwaʀ] *vt* (*levier, membre*) to move; **se ~** *vi* to move

moyen, ne [mwajɛ̃, -ɛn] *adj* average; medium; (*tailles, prix*) medium; (*de grandeur moyenne*) medium-sized ♦ *nm* (*façon*) means *sg*, way; ~**s** *nmpl* (*capacités*) means; **au ~ de** by means of; **par tous les ~s** by every possible means, every possible way; **par ses propres ~s** all by oneself; ~ **âge** Middle Ages; ~ **de transport** means of transport

moyennant [mwajɛnɑ̃] *prép* (*somme*) for; (*service, conditions*) in return for; (*travail, effort*) with

moyenne [mwajɛn] *nf* average; (*MATH*) mean; (*SCOL: à l'examen*) pass mark; (*AUTO*) average speed; **en ~** on (an) average; ~ **d'âge** average age

Moyen-Orient [mwajɛnɔʀjɑ̃] *nm*: **le ~** the Middle East

moyeu, x [mwajø] *nm* hub

MST *sigle f* (= *maladie sexuellement transmissible*) STD

mû, mue [my] *pp de* **mouvoir**

muer [mɥe] *vi* (*oiseau, mammifère*) to moult; (*serpent*) to slough; (*jeune garçon*): **il mue** his voice is breaking; **se ~ en** to transform into

muet, te [mɥɛ, -ɛt] *adj* dumb; (*fig*): ~ **d'admiration** *etc* speechless with admiration *etc*; (*joie, douleur, CINÉMA*) silent; (*carte*) blank mute

mufle [myfl(ə)] *nm* muzzle; (*goujat*) boor

mugir [myʒiʀ] *vi* (*taureau*) to bellow; (*vache*) to low; (*fig*) to howl

muguet [mygɛ] *nm* lily of the valley

mule [myl] *nf* (*ZOOL*) (she-)mule

mulet [mylɛ] nm (ZOOL) (he-)mule
multiple [myltipl(ə)] adj multiple, numerous; (varié) many, manifold ♦ nm (MATH) multiple
multiplication [myltiplikasjɔ̃] nf multiplication
multiplier [myltiplije] vt to multiply; **se ~** vi to multiply; to increase in number
municipal, e, aux [mynisipal, -o] adj municipal; town cpd, ≈ borough cpd
municipalité [mynisipalite] nf (corps municipal) town council, corporation
munir [mynir] vt: **~ qn/qch de** to equip sb/sth with
munitions [mynisjɔ̃] nfpl ammunition sg
mur [myr] nm wall; **~ du son** sound barrier
mûr, e [myr] adj ripe; (personne) mature
muraille [myraj] nf (high) wall
mural, e, aux [myral, -o] adj wall cpd; mural
mûre [myr] nf blackberry; mulberry
murer [myre] vt (enclos) to wall (in); (porte, issue) to wall up; (personne) to wall up ou in
muret [myrɛ] nm low wall
mûrir [myrir] vi (fruit, blé) to ripen; (abcès, furoncle) to come to a head; (fig: idée, personne) to mature ♦ vt to ripen; to (make) mature
murmure [myrmyr] nm murmur; **~s** nmpl (plaintes) murmurings, mutterings; **murmurer** vi to murmur; (se plaindre) to mutter, grumble
muscade [myskad] nf (aussi: noix ~) nutmeg
muscat [myska] nm muscat grape; muscatel (wine)
muscle [myskl(ə)] nm muscle; **musclé, e** adj muscular; (fig) strong-arm
museau, x [myzo] nm muzzle
musée [myze] nm museum; art gallery
museler [myzle] vt to muzzle; **muselière** nf muzzle
musette [myzɛt] nf (sac) lunchbag ♦ adj inv (orchestre etc) accordion cpd
musical, e, aux [myzikal, -o] adj musical
music-hall [myzikol] nm variety theatre; (genre) variety
musicien, ne [myzisjɛ̃, -jɛn] adj musical ♦ nm/f musician
musique [myzik] nf music; (fanfare) band; **~ de chambre** chamber music
musulman, e [myzylmɑ̃, -an] adj, nm/f Moslem, Muslim
mutation [mytasjɔ̃] nf (ADMIN) transfer
mutilé, e [mytile] nm/f disabled person (through loss of limbs)
mutiler [mytile] vt to mutilate, maim
mutin, e [mytɛ̃, -in] adj (air, ton) mischievous, impish ♦ nm/f (MIL, NAVIG) mutineer
mutinerie [mytinri] nf mutiny

mutisme [mytism(ə)] nm silence
mutuel, le [mytɥɛl] adj mutual; **mutuelle** nf mutual benefit society
myope [mjɔp] adj short-sighted
myosotis [mjozɔtis] nm forget-me-not
myrtille [mirtij] nf bilberry
mystère [mistɛr] nm mystery; **mystérieux, euse** adj mysterious
mystifier [mistifje] vt to fool; to mystify
mythe [mit] nm myth
mythologie [mitɔlɔʒi] nf mythology

N n

n' [n] adv voir **ne**
nacre [nakr(ə)] nf mother-of-pearl
nage [naʒ] nf swimming; style of swimming, stroke; **traverser/s'éloigner à la ~** to swim across/away; **en ~** bathed in perspiration
nageoire [naʒwar] nf fin
nager [naʒe] vi to swim; **nageur, euse** nm/f swimmer
naguère [nagɛr] adv formerly
naïf, ïve [naif, naiv] adj naïve
nain, e [nɛ̃, nɛn] nm/f dwarf
naissance [nɛsɑ̃s] nf birth; **donner ~ à** to give birth to; (fig) to give rise to
naître [nɛtr(ə)] vi to be born; (fig): **~ de** to arise from, be born out of; **il est né en 1960** he was born in 1960; **faire ~** (fig) to give rise to, arouse
naïve [naiv] adj voir **naïf**
nana [nana] (fam) nf (fille) chick, bird (BRIT)
nantir [nɑ̃tir] vt: **~ qn de** to provide sb with; **les nantis** (péj) the well-to-do
nappe [nap] nf tablecloth; (fig) sheet; layer; **napperon** nm table-mat
naquit etc vb voir **naître**
narguer [narge] vt to taunt
narine [narin] nf nostril
narquois, e [narkwa, -waz] adj derisive, mocking
naseau, x [nazo] nm nostril
natal, e [natal] adj native
natalité [natalite] nf birth rate
natation [natasjɔ̃] nf swimming
natif, ive [natif, -iv] adj native
nation [nasjɔ̃] nf nation
national, e, aux [nasjonal, -o] adj national; **nationale** nf: **(route) nationale** ≈ A road (BRIT), ≈ state highway (US); **nationaliser** vt to nationalize; **nationalité** nf

nationality

natte [nat] *nf (tapis)* mat; *(cheveux)* plait

naturaliser [natyralize] *vt* to naturalize

nature [natyr] *nf* nature ♦ *adj, adv (CULIN)* plain, without seasoning or sweetening; *(café, thé)* black, without sugar; **payer en ~** to pay in kind; **~ morte** still-life; **naturel, le** *adj (gén, aussi: enfant)* natural ♦ *nm* naturalness; disposition, nature; *(autochtone)* native; **naturellement** *adv* naturally; *(bien sûr)* of course

naufrage [nofraʒ] *nm* (ship)wreck; *(fig)* wreck; **faire ~** to be shipwrecked

nauséabond, e [nozeabɔ̃, -ɔ̃d] *adj* foul, nauseous

nausée [noze] *nf* nausea

nautique [notik] *adj* nautical, water *cpd*

nautisme [notism(ə)] *nm* water sports

navet [navɛ] *nm* turnip

navette [navɛt] *nf* shuttle; **faire la ~ (entre)** to go to and fro *ou* shuttle (between)

navigateur [navigatœr] *nm (NAVIG)* seafarer, sailor; *(AVIAT)* navigator

navigation [navigasjɔ̃] *nf* navigation, sailing; shipping

naviguer [navige] *vi* to navigate, sail

navire [navir] *nm* ship

navrer [navre] *vt* to upset, distress; **je suis navré** I'm so sorry

ne(n') [n(ə)] *adv voir* **pas; plus; jamais** *etc*; *(explétif)* non traduit

né, e [ne] *pp (voir naître)*: **~ en 1960** born in 1960; **~e Scott** née Scott

néanmoins [neɑ̃mwɛ̃] *adv* nevertheless

néant [neɑ̃] *nm* nothingness; **réduire à ~** to bring to nought; *(espoir)* to dash

nécessaire [nesesɛr] *adj* necessary ♦ *nm* necessary; *(sac)* kit; **~ de couture** sewing kit; **~ de toilette** toilet bag; **nécessité** *nf* necessity; **nécessiter** *vt* to require; **nécessiteux, euse** *adj* needy

nécrologique [nekrɔlɔʒik] *adj*: **article ~** obituary; **rubrique ~** obituary column

nectar [nɛktar] *nm (sucré)* nectar; *(boisson)* sweetened, diluted fruit juice

néerlandais, e [neɛrlɑ̃dɛ, -ɛz] *adj* Dutch

nef [nɛf] *nf (d'église)* nave

néfaste [nefast(ə)] *adj* baneful; ill-fated

négatif, ive [negatif, -iv] *adj* negative ♦ *nm (PHOTO)* negative

négligé, e [negliʒe] *adj (en désordre)* slovenly ♦ *nm (tenue)* negligee

négligent, e [negliʒɑ̃, -ɑ̃t] *adj* careless; negligent

négliger [negliʒe] *vt (épouse, jardin)* to neglect; *(tenue)* to be careless about; *(avis, précautions)* to disregard; **~ de faire** to fail to do, not bother to do

négoce [negɔs] *nm* trade

négociant [negɔsjɑ̃] *nm* merchant

négociation [negɔsjasjɔ̃] *nf* negotiation

négocier [negɔsje] *vi, vt* to negotiate

nègre [nɛgr(ə)] *nm* Negro; ghost (writer)

négresse [negrɛs] *nf* Negro woman

neige [nɛʒ] *nf* snow; **neiger** *vi* to snow

nénuphar [nenyfar] *nm* water-lily

néon [neɔ̃] *nm* neon

néophyte [neɔfit] *nm/f* novice

néo-zélandais, e [neozelɑ̃dɛ, -ɛz] *adj* New Zealand *cpd* ♦ *nm/f*: **N~, e** New Zealander

nerf [nɛr] *nm* nerve; *(fig)* spirit; stamina; **nerveux, euse** *adj* nervous; *(voiture)* nippy, responsive; *(tendineux)* sinewy; **nervosité** *nf* excitability; state of agitation; nervousness

nervure [nɛrvyr] *nf* vein

n'est-ce pas [nɛspɑ] *adv* isn't it?, won't you? *etc, selon le verbe qui précède*

net, nette [nɛt] *adj (sans équivoque, distinct)* clear; *(évident)* definite; *(propre)* neat, clean; *(COMM: prix, salaire)* net ♦ *adv (refuser)* flatly ♦ *nm*: **mettre au ~** to copy out; **s'arrêter ~** to stop dead; **nettement** *adv* clearly, distinctly; **netteté** *nf* clearness

nettoyage [nɛtwajaʒ] *nm* cleaning; **~ à sec** dry cleaning

nettoyer [nɛtwaje] *vt* to clean; *(fig)* to clean out

neuf¹ [nœf] *num* nine

neuf², neuve [nœf, nœv] *adj* new ♦ *nm*: **repeindre à ~** to redecorate; **remettre à ~** to do up (as good as new), refurbish

neutre [nøtr(ə)] *adj* neutral; *(LING)* neuter ♦ *nm* neuter

neuve [nœv] *adj voir* **neuf²**

neuvième [nœvjɛm] *num* ninth

neveu, x [nəvø] *nm* nephew

névrosé, e [nevroze] *adj, nm/f* neurotic

nez [ne] *nm* nose; **~ à ~ avec** face to face with; **avoir du ~** to have flair

ni [ni] *conj*: **~ l'un ~ l'autre ne sont** neither one nor the other are; **il n'a rien dit ~ fait** he hasn't said or done anything

niais, e [njɛ, -ɛz] *adj* silly, thick

niche [niʃ] *nf (du chien)* kennel; *(de mur)* recess, niche

nicher [niʃe] *vi* to nest

nid [ni] *nm* nest; **~ de poule** pothole

nièce [njɛs] *nf* niece

nier [nje] *vt* to deny

nigaud, e [nigo, -od] *nm/f* booby, fool

Nil [nil] *nm*: **le ~** the Nile

n'importe [nɛ̃pɔrt(ə)] *adv*: **~ qui/quoi/où** anybody/anything/anywhere; **~ quand** any time; **~ quel/quelle** any; **~ lequel/laquelle** any (one); **~ comment** *(sans soin)* carelessly

niveau, x [nivo] *nm* level; *(des élèves, études)* standard; **de ~ (avec)** level (with); **le ~ de la mer** sea level; **~ de vie** standard of living

niveler [nivle] *vt* to level

NN *abr (= nouvelle norme)* revised standard of hotel classification

noble [nɔbl(ə)] *adj* noble; **noblesse** *nf* no-

bility; (d'une action etc) nobleness
noce [nɔs] nf wedding; (gens) wedding party (ou guests pl); **faire la ~** (fam) to go on a binge; **~s d'or/d'argent** golden/silver wedding

nocif, ive [nɔsif, -iv] adj harmful, noxious

noctambule [nɔktɑ̃byl] nm night-bird

nocturne [nɔktyʁn(ə)] adj nocturnal ♦ nf late-night opening

Noël [nɔɛl] nm Christmas

nœud [nø] nm (de corde, du bois, NAVIG) knot; (ruban) bow; (fig: liens) bond, tie; **~ papillon** bow tie

noir, e [nwaʁ] adj black; (obscur, sombre) dark ♦ nm/f black man(woman), Negro ♦ nm: **dans le ~** in the dark; **travail au ~** moonlighting; **noirceur** nf blackness; darkness; **noircir** vt, vi to blacken; **noire** nf (MUS) crotchet (BRIT), quarter note (US)

noisette [nwazɛt] nf hazelnut

noix [nwa] nf walnut; (CULIN): **une ~ de beurre** a knob of butter; **~ de cajou** cashew nut; **~ de coco** coconut

nom [nɔ̃] nm name; (LING) noun; **~ d'emprunt** assumed name; **~ de famille** surname; **~ de jeune fille** maiden name; **~ déposé** nm trade name; **~ propre** nm proper noun

nombre [nɔ̃bʁ(ə)] nm number; **venir en ~** to come in large numbers; **depuis ~ d'années** for many years; **ils sont au ~ de 3** there are 3 of them; **au ~ de mes amis** among my friends

nombreux, euse [nɔ̃bʁø, -øz] adj many, numerous; (avec nom sg: foule etc) large; **peu ~** few; small

nombril [nɔ̃bʁi] nm navel

nommer [nɔme] vt (baptiser, mentionner) to name; (qualifier) to call; (élire) to appoint, nominate; **se ~: il se nomme Pascal** his name's Pascal, he's called Pascal

non [nɔ̃] adv (réponse) no; (avec loin, sans, seulement) not; **~ pas que = non que**; **~ que** not that; **moi ~ plus** neither do I, I don't either

non: **~-alcoolisé, e** adj non-alcoholic; **~-fumeur** nm non-smoker; **~-lieu** nm: **il y a eu ~-lieu** the case was dismissed; **~-sens** nm absurdity

nord [nɔʁ] nm North ♦ adj northern; north; **au ~** (situation) in the north; (direction) to the north; **au ~ de** (to the) north of; **nord-est** nm North-East; **nord-ouest** nm North-West

normal, e, aux [nɔʁmal, -o] adj normal; **normale** nf: **la normale** the norm, the average; **normalement** adv (en général) normally; **normaliser** vt (COMM, TECH) to standardize

normand, e [nɔʁmɑ̃, -ɑ̃d] adj of Normandy

Normandie [nɔʁmɑ̃di] nf Normandy

norme [nɔʁm(ə)] nf norm; (TECH) standard

Norvège [nɔʁvɛʒ] nf Norway; **norvégien, ne** adj, nm/f Norwegian ♦ nm (LING) Norwegian

nos [no] dét voir **notre**

nostalgie [nɔstalʒi] nf nostalgia

notable [nɔtabl(ə)] adj notable, noteworthy; (marqué) noticeable, marked ♦ nm prominent citizen

notaire [nɔtɛʁ] nm notary; solicitor

notamment [nɔtamɑ̃] adv in particular, among others

note [nɔt] nf (écrite, MUS) note; (SCOL) mark (BRIT), grade; (facture) bill; **~ de service** memorandum

noté, e [nɔte] adj: **être bien/mal ~** (employé etc) to have a good/bad record

noter [nɔte] vt (écrire) to write down; (remarquer) to note, notice

notice [nɔtis] nf summary, short article; (brochure) leaflet, instruction book

notifier [nɔtifje] vt: **~ qch à qn** to notify sb of sth, notify sth to sb

notion [nɔsjɔ̃] nf notion, idea

notoire [nɔtwaʁ] adj widely known; (en mal) notorious

notre [nɔtʁ(ə), no] (pl nos) dét our

nôtre [notʁ(ə)] pron: **le ~, la ~, les ~s** ours ♦ adj ours; **les ~s** ours; (alliés etc) our own people; **soyez des ~s** join us

nouer [nwe] vt to tie, knot; (fig: alliance etc) to strike up

noueux, euse [nwø, -øz] adj gnarled

nouilles [nuj] nfpl noodles; pasta sg

nourrice [nuʁis] nf wet-nurse

nourrir [nuʁiʁ] vt to feed; (fig: espoir) to harbour, nurse; **logé nourri** with board and lodging; **nourrissant, e** adj nourishing, nutritious

nourrisson [nuʁisɔ̃] nm (unweaned) infant

nourriture [nuʁityʁ] nf food

nous [nu] pron (sujet) we; (objet) us; **nous-mêmes** pron ourselves

nouveau(nouvel), elle, x [nuvo, -ɛl] adj new ♦ nm/f new pupil (ou employee); **de ~, à ~** again; **~ venu, nouvelle venue** newcomer; **~-né, e** nm/f newborn baby; **~té** nf novelty; (COMM) new film (ou book ou creation etc)

nouvel [nuvɛl] adj voir **nouveau**; **N~ An** New Year

nouvelle [nuvɛl] adj voir **nouveau** ♦ nf (piece of) news sg; (LITTÉRATURE) short story; **je suis sans ~s de lui** I haven't heard from him; **N~-Calédonie** nf New Caledonia; **N~-Zélande** nf New Zealand

novembre [nɔvɑ̃bʁ(ə)] nm November

novice [nɔvis] adj inexperienced

noyade [nwajad] nf drowning no pl

noyau, x [nwajo] nm (de fruit) stone; (BIO, PHYSIQUE) nucleus; (ÉLEC, GÉO, fig: centre) core; **noyauter** vt (POL) to infiltrate

noyer [nwaje] *nm* walnut (tree); (*bois*) walnut ♦ *vt* to drown; (*fig*) to flood; to submerge; **se ~** *vi* to be drowned, drown; (*suicide*) to drown o.s.

nu, e [ny] *adj* naked; (*membres*) naked, bare; (*chambre, fil, plaine*) bare ♦ *nm* (ART) nude; **se mettre ~** to strip; **mettre à ~** to bare

nuage [nɥaʒ] *nm* cloud; **nuageux, euse** *adj* cloudy

nuance [nɥãs] *nf* (*de couleur, sens*) shade; **il y a une ~ (entre)** there's a slight difference (between); **nuancer** *vt* (*opinion*) to bring some reservations *ou* qualifications to

nucléaire [nykleɛʀ] *adj* nuclear

nudiste [nydist(ə)] *nm/f* nudist

nuée [nɥe] *nf*: **une ~ de** a cloud *ou* host *ou* swarm of

nues [ny] *nfpl*: **tomber des ~** to be taken aback; **porter qn aux ~** to praise sb to the skies

nuire [nɥiʀ] *vi* to be harmful; **~ à** to harm, do damage to; **nuisible** *adj* harmful; **animal nuisible** pest

nuit [nɥi] *nf* night; **il fait ~** it's dark; **cette ~** last night; tonight; **~ blanche** sleepless night; **~ de noces** wedding night

nul, nulle [nyl] *adj* (*aucun*) no; (*minime*) nil, non-existent; (*non valable*) null; (*péj*) useless, hopeless ♦ *pron* none, no one; **match ~** draw; **résultat : = match nul**; **~le part** nowhere; **nullement** *adv* by no means

numérique [nymeʀik] *adj* numerical

numéro [nymeʀo] *nm* number; (*spectacle*) act, turn; **~ de téléphone** (tele)phone number; **~ vert** *nm* ≈ freefone (®) number (*BRIT*), ≈ toll-free number (*US*); **numéroter** *vt* to number

nu-pieds [nypje] *adj inv* barefoot

nuque [nyk] *nf* nape of the neck

nu-tête [nytɛt] *adj inv* bareheaded

nutritif, ive [nytʀitif, -iv] *adj* nutritional; (*aliment*) nutritious

nylon [nilɔ̃] *nm* nylon

O o

oasis [ɔazis] *nf* oasis

obéir [ɔbeiʀ] *vi* to obey; **~ à** to obey; (*suj: moteur, véhicule*) to respond to; **obéissant, e** *adj* obedient

objecter [ɔbʒɛkte] *vt* (*prétexter*) to plead, put forward as an excuse; **~ (à qn) que** to object (to sb) that

objecteur [ɔbʒɛktœʀ] *nm*: **~ de conscience** conscientious objector

objectif, ive [ɔbʒɛktif, -iv] *adj* objective ♦ *nm* (OPTIQUE, PHOTO) lens *sg*, objective; (MIL, *fig*) objective; **~ à focale variable** zoom lens

objection [ɔbʒɛksjɔ̃] *nf* objection

objet [ɔbʒɛ] *nm* object; (*d'une discussion, recherche*) subject; **être** *ou* **faire l'~ de** (*discussion*) to be the subject of; (*soins*) to be given *ou* shown; **sans ~** purposeless; groundless; **~ d'art** objet d'art; **~s personnels** personal items; **~s trouvés** lost property *sg* (BRIT), lost-and-found *sg* (US)

obligation [ɔbligasjɔ̃] *nf* obligation; (COMM) bond, debenture; **obligatoire** *adj* compulsory, obligatory

obligé, e [ɔbliʒe] *adj* (*redevable*): **être très ~ à qn** to be most obliged to sb

obligeance [ɔbliʒãs] *nf*: **avoir l'~ de ... to** be kind *ou* good enough to ...; **obligeant, e** *adj* obliging; kind

obliger [ɔbliʒe] *vt* (*contraindre*): **~ qn à faire** to force *ou* oblige sb to do; (JUR: *engager*) to bind; (*rendre service à*) to oblige; **je suis bien obligé** I have to

oblique [ɔblik] *adj* oblique; **regard ~** sidelong glance; **en ~** diagonally; **obliquer** *vi*: **obliquer vers** to turn off towards

oblitérer [ɔblitere] *vt* (*timbre-poste*) to cancel

obscène [ɔpsɛn] *adj* obscene

obscur, e [ɔpskyʀ] *adj* dark; (*fig*) obscure; lowly; **~cir** *vt* to darken; (*fig*) to obscure; **s'~cir** *vi* to grow dark; **~ité** *nf* darkness; **dans l'~ité** in the dark, in darkness

obséder [ɔpsede] *vt* to obsess, haunt

obsèques [ɔpsɛk] *nfpl* funeral *sg*

observateur, trice [ɔpsɛʀvatœʀ, -tʀis] *adj* observant, perceptive ♦ *nm/f* observer

observation [ɔpsɛʀvasjɔ̃] *nf* observation; (*d'un règlement etc*) observance; (*reproche*) reproof

observatoire [ɔpsɛʀvatwaʀ] *nm* observatory; (*lieu élevé*) observation post, vantage point

observer [ɔpsɛʀve] *vt* (*regarder*) to observe, watch; (*examiner*) to examine; (*scientifiquement, aussi: règlement, jeûne etc*) to observe; (*surveiller*) to watch; (*remarquer*) to observe, notice; **faire ~ qch à qn** (*dire*) to point out sth to sb

obstacle [ɔpstakl(ə)] *nm* obstacle; (ÉQUITATION) jump, hurdle; **faire ~ à** (*lumière*) to block out; (*projet*) to hinder, put obstacles in the path of

obstiné, e [ɔpstine] *adj* obstinate

obstiner [ɔpstine]: **s'~** *vi* to insist, dig one's heels in; **s'~ à faire** to persist (obstinately) in doing; **s'~ sur qch** to keep working at sth, labour away at sth

obstruer [ɔpstʀye] vt to block, obstruct

obtempérer [ɔptɑ̃peʀe] vi to obey

obtenir [ɔptəniʀ] vt to obtain, get; (total, résultat) to arrive at, reach; to achieve, obtain; ~ **de pouvoir faire** to obtain permission to do; ~ **de qn qu'il fasse** to get sb to agree to do; **obtention** nf obtaining

obturateur [ɔptyʀatœʀ] nm (PHOTO) shutter

obturer [ɔptyʀe] vt to close (up); (dent) to fill

obus [ɔby] nm shell

occasion [ɔkɑzjɔ̃] nf (aubaine, possibilité) opportunity; (circonstance) occasion; (COMM: article non neuf) secondhand buy; (: acquisition avantageuse) bargain; **à plusieurs ~s** on several occasions; **être l'~ de** to occasion, give rise to; **à l'~** sometimes, on occasions; some time; **d'~** secondhand; **occasionnel, le** adj (fortuit) chance cpd; (non régulier) occasional; casual

occasionner [ɔkazjɔne] vt to cause, bring about; ~ **qch à qn** to cause sb sth

occident [ɔksidɑ̃] nm: **l'O~** the West; **occidental, e, aux** adj western; (POL) Western

occupation [ɔkypasjɔ̃] nf occupation

occupé, e [ɔkype] adj (MIL, POL) occupied; (personne: affairé, pris) busy; (place, sièges) taken; (toilettes) engaged; (ligne) engaged (BRIT), busy (US)

occuper [ɔkype] vt to occupy; (main-d'œuvre) to employ; **s'~ de** (être responsable de) to be in charge of; (se charger de: affaire) to take charge of, deal with; (: clients etc) to attend to; (s'intéresser à, pratiquer) to be involved in; **s'~ (à qch)** to occupy o.s. ou keep o.s. busy (with sth); **ça occupe trop de place** it takes up too much room

occurrence [ɔkyʀɑ̃s] nf: **en l'~** in this case

océan [ɔseɑ̃] nm ocean; **l'~ Indien** the Indian Ocean

octet [ɔktɛt] nm byte

octobre [ɔktɔbʀ(ə)] nm October

octroyer [ɔktʀwaje] vt: ~ **qch à qn** to grant sth to sb, grant sb sth

oculiste [ɔkylist(ə)] nm/f eye specialist

odeur [ɔdœʀ] nf smell

odieux, euse [ɔdjø, -øz] adj hateful

odorant, e [ɔdɔʀɑ̃, -ɑ̃t] adj sweet-smelling, fragrant

odorat [ɔdɔʀa] nm (sense of) smell

œil [œj] (pl yeux) nm eye; **à l'~** (fam) for free; **à l'~ nu** with the naked eye; **tenir qn à l'~** to keep an eye ou a watch on sb; **avoir l'~ à** to keep an eye on; **fermer les yeux (sur)** (fig) to turn a blind eye (to)

œillade [œjad] nf: **lancer une ~ à qn** to wink at sb, give sb a wink; **faire des ~s à** to make eyes at

œillères [œjɛʀ] nfpl blinkers (BRIT), blin-

ders (US)

œillet [œjɛ] nm (BOT) carnation

œuf [œf, pl ø] nm egg; ~ **à la coque** nm boiled egg; ~ **au plat** fried egg; ~ **de Pâques** Easter egg; ~ **dur** hard-boiled egg; ~**s brouillés** scrambled eggs

œuvre [œvʀ(ə)] nf (tâche) task, undertaking; (ouvrage achevé, livre, tableau etc) work; (ensemble de la production artistique) works pl; (organisation charitable) charity ♦ nm (d'un artiste) works pl; (CONSTR): **le gros ~** the shell; **être à l'~** to be at work; **mettre en ~** (moyens) to make use of; ~ **d'art** work of art

offense [ɔfɑ̃s] nf insult

offenser [ɔfɑ̃se] vt to offend, hurt; (principes, Dieu) to offend against; **s'~ de** to take offence at

offert, e [ɔfɛʀ, -ɛʀt(ə)] pp de **offrir**

office [ɔfis] nm (charge) office; (agence) bureau, agency; (REL) service ♦ nm ou nf (pièce) pantry; **faire ~ de** to act as; to do duty as; **d'~** automatically; ~ **du tourisme** tourist bureau

officiel, le [ɔfisjɛl] adj, nm/f official

officier [ɔfisje] nm officer ♦ vi to officiate; ~ **de l'état-civil** registrar

officieux, euse [ɔfisjø, -øz] adj unofficial

officinal, e, aux [ɔfisinal, -o] adj: **plantes ~es** medicinal plants

officine [ɔfisin] nf (de pharmacie) dispensary; (bureau) agency, office

offrande [ɔfʀɑ̃d] nf offering

offre [ɔfʀ(ə)] nf offer; (aux enchères) bid; (ADMIN: soumission) tender; (ÉCON): **l'~** supply; "~**s d'emploi**" "situations vacant"; ~ **d'emploi** job advertised; ~ **publique d'achat** takeover bid

offrir [ɔfʀiʀ] vt: ~ **(à qn)** to offer (to sb); (faire cadeau de) to give (to sb); **s'~** vi (occasion, paysage) to present itself ♦ vt (vacances, voiture) to treat o.s. to; ~ **(à qn) de faire qch** to offer to do sth (for sb); ~ **à boire à qn** to offer sb a drink; **s'~ comme guide/en otage** to offer one's services as (a) guide/offer o.s. as hostage

offusquer [ɔfyske] vt to offend

ogive [ɔʒiv] nf: ~ **nucléaire** nuclear warhead

oie [wa] nf (ZOOL) goose

oignon [ɔɲɔ̃] nm (BOT, CULIN) onion; (de tulipe etc: bulbe) bulb; (MÉD) bunion

oiseau, x [wazo] nm bird; ~ **de proie** bird of prey

oiseux, euse [wazø, -øz] adj pointless; trivial

oisif, ive [wazif, -iv] adj idle ♦ nm/f (péj) man(woman) of leisure

oléoduc [ɔleɔdyk] nm (oil) pipeline

olive [ɔliv] nf (BOT) olive; **olivier** nm olive (tree)

OLP sigle f = **Organisation de libération**

de la Palestine

olympique [ɔlɛ̃pik] *adj* Olympic

ombrage [ɔ̃braʒ] *nm* (*ombre*) (leafy) shade; **ombragé, e** *adj* shaded, shady; **ombrageux, euse** *adj* (*cheval*) skittish, nervous; (*personne*) touchy, easily offended

ombre [ɔ̃br(ə)] *nf* (*espace non ensoleillé*) shade; (~ *portée, tache*) shadow; **à l'~** in the shade; **tu me fais de l'~** you're in my light; **ça nous donne de l'~** it gives us (some) shade; **dans l'~** (*fig*) in obscurity; in the dark; **~ à paupières** eyeshadow; **ombrelle** [ɔ̃brɛl] *nf* parasol, sunshade

omelette [ɔmlɛt] *nf* omelette

omettre [ɔmɛtr(ə)] *vt* to omit, leave out

omnibus [ɔmnibys] *nm* slow *ou* stopping train

omoplate [ɔmɔplat] *nf* shoulder blade

─────── MOT CLÉ ───────

on [ɔ̃] *pron* **1** (*indéterminé*) you, one; ~ **peut le faire ainsi** you *ou* one can do it like this, it can be done like this

2 (*quelqu'un*): ~ **les a attaqués** they were attacked; ~ **vous demande au téléphone** there's a phone call for you, you're wanted on the phone

3 (*nous*) we; ~ **va y aller demain** we're going tomorrow

4 (*les gens*) they; **autrefois,** ~ **croyait ...** they used to believe ...

5: ~ **ne peut plus** *adv*: ~ **ne peut plus stupide** as stupid as can be

─────────────────────────

oncle [ɔ̃kl(ə)] *nm* uncle

onctueux, euse [ɔ̃ktɥø, -øz] *adj* creamy, smooth; (*fig*) smooth, unctuous

onde [ɔ̃d] *nf* (*PHYSIQUE*) wave; **sur les ~s** on the radio; **mettre en ~s** to produce for the radio; **sur ~s courtes** on short wave *sg*; **moyennes/longues ~s** medium/long wave *sg*

ondée [ɔ̃de] *nf* shower

on-dit [ɔ̃di] *nm inv* rumour

ondoyer [ɔ̃dwaje] *vi* to ripple, wave

onduler [ɔ̃dyle] *vi* to undulate; (*cheveux*) to wave

onéreux, euse [ɔnerø, -øz] *adj* costly; **à titre ~** in return for payment

ongle [ɔ̃gl(ə)] *nm* (*ANAT*) nail; **se faire les ~s** to do one's nails

onguent [ɔ̃gɑ̃] *nm* ointment

ont *vb voir* avoir

O.N.U. [ɔny] *sigle f* = **Organisation des Nations Unies**

onze [ɔ̃z] *num* eleven; **onzième** *num* eleventh

O.P.A. *sigle f* = **offre publique d'achat**

opaque [ɔpak] *adj* opaque

opéra [ɔpera] *nm* opera; (*édifice*) opera house

opérateur, trice [ɔperatœr, -tris] *nm/f* operator; ~ **(de prise de vues)** cameraman

opération [ɔperasjɔ̃] *nf* operation; (*COMM*) dealing

opératoire [ɔperatwar] *adj* operating; (*choc etc*) post-operative

opérer [ɔpere] *vt* (*MÉD*) to operate on; (*faire, exécuter*) to carry out, make ♦ *vi* (*remède: faire effet*) to act, work; (*procéder*) to proceed; (*MÉD*) to operate; **s'~** *vi* (*avoir lieu*) to occur, take place; **se faire ~** to have an operation

opiner [ɔpine] *vi*: ~ **de la tête** to nod assent

opinion [ɔpinjɔ̃] *nf* opinion; **l'~ (publique)** public opinion

opportun, e [ɔpɔrtœ̃, -yn] *adj* timely, opportune; **en temps ~** at the appropriate time; **~iste** [ɔpɔrtynist(ə)] *nm/f* opportunist

opposant, e [ɔpozɑ̃, -ɑ̃t] *adj* opposing; **opposants** *nmpl* opponents

opposé, e [ɔpoze] *adj* (*direction, rive*) opposite; (*faction*) opposing; (*couleurs*) contrasting; (*opinions, intérêts*) conflicting; (*contre*): ~ **à** opposed to, against ♦ *nm*: **l'~** the other *ou* opposite side (*ou* direction); (*contraire*) the opposite; **à l'~** (*fig*) on the other hand; **à l'~ de** on the other *ou* opposite side from; (*fig*) contrary to, unlike

opposer [ɔpoze] *vt* (*personnes, armées, équipes*) to oppose; (*couleurs, termes, tons*) to contrast; **s'~** (*sens réciproque*) to conflict; to clash; to contrast; **s'~ à** (*interdire, empêcher*) to oppose; (*tenir tête à*) to rebel against; ~ **qch à** (*comme obstacle, défense*) to set sth against; (*comme objection*) to put sth forward against

opposition [ɔpozisjɔ̃] *nf* opposition; **par ~ à** as opposed to, in contrast with; **entrer en ~ avec** to come into conflict with; **être en ~ avec** (*idées, conduite*) to be at variance with; **faire ~ à un chèque** to stop a cheque

oppresser [ɔprese] *vt* to oppress; **oppression** *nf* oppression; (*malaise*) feeling of suffocation

opprimer [ɔprime] *vt* to oppress; (*liberté, opinion*) to suppress, stifle; (*suj: chaleur etc*) to suffocate, oppress

opter [ɔpte] *vi*: ~ **pour** to opt for; ~ **entre** to choose between

opticien, ne [ɔptisjɛ̃, -ɛn] *nm/f* optician

optimiste [ɔptimist(ə)] *nm/f* optimist ♦ *adj* optimistic

option [ɔpsjɔ̃] *nf* option; **matière à ~** (*SCOL*) optional subject

optique [ɔptik] *adj* (*nerf*) optic; (*verres*) optical ♦ *nf* (*PHOTO: lentilles etc*) optics *pl*; (*science, industrie*) optics *sg*; (*fig: manière de voir*) perspective

opulent, e [ɔpylɑ̃, -ɑ̃t] *adj* wealthy, opulent; (*formes, poitrine*) ample, generous

or [ɔr] *nm* gold ♦ *conj* now, but; **en ~ ~** gold

cpd; (fig) golden, marvellous
orage [ɔʀaʒ] nm (thunder)storm; **orageux, euse** adj stormy
oraison [ɔʀezɔ̃] nf orison, prayer; ~ **funèbre** funeral oration
oral, e, aux [ɔʀal, -o] adj, nm oral
orange [ɔʀãʒ] nf orange ♦ adj inv orange; **oranger** nm orange tree
orateur [ɔʀatœʀ] nm speaker; orator
orbite [ɔʀbit] nf (ANAT) (eye-) socket; (PHYSIQUE) orbit
orchestre [ɔʀkɛstʀ(ə)] nm orchestra; (de jazz, danse) band; (places) stalls pl (BRIT), orchestra (US); **orchestrer** vt (MUS) to orchestrate; (fig) to mount, stage-manage
orchidée [ɔʀkide] nf orchid
ordinaire [ɔʀdinɛʀ] adj ordinary; everyday; standard ♦ nm ordinary; (menus) everyday fare ♦ nf (essence) ≈ two-star (petrol) (BRIT), ≈ regular gas (US); **d'~** usually, normally; **à l'~** usually, ordinarily
ordinateur [ɔʀdinatœʀ] nm computer; ~ **domestique** home computer; ~ **individuel** personal computer
ordonnance [ɔʀdɔnɑ̃s] nf organization; layout; (MÉD) prescription; (JUR) order; (MIL) orderly, batman (BRIT)
ordonné, e [ɔʀdɔne] adj tidy, orderly; (MATH) ordered
ordonner [ɔʀdɔne] vt (agencer) to organize, arrange; (donner un ordre): ~ **à qn de faire** to order sb to do; (REL) to ordain; (MÉD) to prescribe
ordre [ɔʀdʀ(ə)] nm (gén) order; (propreté et soin) orderliness, tidiness; (nature): **d'~ pratique** of a practical nature; ~**s** nmpl (REL) holy orders; **mettre en** ~ to tidy (up), put in order; **à l'~ de qn** payable to sb; **être aux ~s de qn/sous les ~s de qn** to be at sb's disposal/under sb's command; **jusqu'à nouvel** ~ until further notice; **dans le même** ~ **d'idées** in this connection; **donnez-nous un** ~ **de grandeur** give us some idea as regards size (ou the amount); **de premier** ~ first-rate; ~ **du jour** (d'une réunion) agenda; (MIL) order of the day; **à l'~ du jour** topical
ordure [ɔʀdyʀ] nf filth no pl; ~**s** nfpl (balayures, déchets) rubbish sg, refuse sg; ~**s ménagères** household refuse
oreille [ɔʀɛj] nf (ANAT) ear; (de marmite, tasse) handle; **avoir de l'~** to have a good ear (for music)
oreiller [ɔʀeje] nm pillow
oreillons [ɔʀejɔ̃] nmpl mumps sg
ores [ɔʀ] : **d'~ et déjà** adv already
orfèvrerie [ɔʀfɛvʀəʀi] nf goldsmith's (ou silversmith's) trade; (ouvrage) gold (ou silver) plate
organe [ɔʀgan] nm organ; (porte-parole) representative, mouthpiece
organigramme [ɔʀganigʀam] nm organi-

zation chart; flow chart
organique [ɔʀganik] adj organic
organisateur, trice [ɔʀganizatœʀ, -tʀis] nm/f organizer
organisation [ɔʀganizɑsjɔ̃] nf organization; **O~ des Nations Unies** United Nations (Organization); **O~ du traité de l'Atlantique Nord** North Atlantic Treaty Organization
organiser [ɔʀganize] vt to organize; (mettre sur pied: service etc) to set up; **s'~** to get organized
organisme [ɔʀganism(ə)] nm (BIO) organism; (corps, ADMIN) body
organiste [ɔʀganist(ə)] nm/f organist
orgasme [ɔʀgasm(ə)] nm orgasm, climax
orge [ɔʀʒ(ə)] nf barley
orgie [ɔʀʒi] nf orgy
orgue [ɔʀg(ə)] nm organ; ~**s** nfpl (MUS) organ sg
orgueil [ɔʀgœj] nm pride; **orgueilleux, euse** adj proud
Orient [ɔʀjɑ̃] nm: **l'~** the East, the Orient
oriental, e, aux [ɔʀjɑ̃tal, -o] adj oriental, eastern; (frontière) eastern
orientation [ɔʀjɑ̃tɑsjɔ̃] nf positioning; orientation; (d'une maison etc) aspect; (d'un journal) leanings pl; **avoir le sens de l'~** to have a (good) sense of direction; ~ **professionnelle** careers advising; careers advisory service
orienté, e [ɔʀjɑ̃te] adj (fig: article, journal) slanted; **bien/mal** ~ (appartement) well/badly positioned; ~ **au sud** facing south, with a southern aspect
orienter [ɔʀjɑ̃te] vt (placer, disposer: pièce mobile) to adjust, position; (tourner) to direct, turn; (voyageur, touriste, recherches) to direct; (fig: élève) to orientate; **s'~** (se repérer) to find one's bearings; **s'~ vers** (fig) to turn towards
origan [ɔʀigɑ̃] nm (BOT) oregano
originaire [ɔʀiʒinɛʀ] adj: **être** ~ **de** to be a native of
original, e, aux [ɔʀiʒinal, -o] adj original; (bizarre) eccentric ♦ nm/f eccentric ♦ nm (document etc, ART) original; (dactylographie) top copy
origine [ɔʀiʒin] nf origin; **dès l'~** at ou from the outset; **à l'~** originally; **originel, le** adj original
O.R.L. sigle nm/f = **oto-rhinolaryngologiste**
orme [ɔʀm(ə)] nm elm
ornement [ɔʀnəmɑ̃] nm ornament; (fig) embellishment, adornment
orner [ɔʀne] vt to decorate, adorn
ornière [ɔʀnjɛʀ] nf rut
orphelin, e [ɔʀfəlɛ̃, -in] adj orphan(ed) ♦ nm/f orphan; ~ **de père/mère** fatherless/motherless; **orphelinat** nm orphanage
orteil [ɔʀtɛj] nm toe; **gros** ~ big toe

orthographe [ɔʀtɔgʀaf] *nf* spelling; **orthographier** *vt* to spell

orthopédiste [ɔʀtɔpedist(ə)] *nm/f* orthopaedic specialist

ortie [ɔʀti] *nf* (stinging) nettle

os [ɔs, *pl* o] *nm* bone

osciller [ɔsile] *vi* (*pendule*) to swing; (*au vent etc*) to rock; (*TECH*) to oscillate; (*fig*): ~ **entre** ou **waver** ou fluctuate between

osé, e [oze] *adj* daring, bold

oseille [ozɛj] *nf* sorrel

oser [oze] *vi, vt* to dare; ~ **faire** to dare (to) do

osier [ozje] *nm* willow; **d'~** wicker(work); **en ~ = d'osier**

ossature [ɔsatyʀ] *nf* (*ANAT*) frame, skeletal structure; (*fig*) framework

osseux, euse [ɔsø, -øz] *adj* bony; (*tissu, maladie, greffe*) bone *cpd*

ostensible [ɔstɑ̃sibl(ə)] *adj* conspicuous

otage [ɔtaʒ] *nm* hostage; **prendre qn comme ~** to take sb hostage

O.T.A.N. [ɔtɑ̃] *sigle f* = **Organisation du traité de l'Atlantique Nord**

otarie [ɔtaʀi] *nf* sea-lion

ôter [ote] *vt* to remove; (*soustraire*) to take away; ~ **qch à qn** to take sth (away) from sb; ~ **qch de** to remove sth from

otite [ɔtit] *nf* ear infection

oto-rhino(-laryngologiste) [ɔtɔʀino(laʀɛ̃gɔlɔʒist(ə))] *nm/f* ear nose and throat specialist

ou [u] *conj* or; ~ ... ~ either ... or; ~ **bien** or (else)

─────── MOT CLÉ ───────

où [u] *pron relatif* **1** (*position, situation*) where, that (*souvent omis*); **la chambre ~ il était** the room (that) he was in, the room where he was; **la ville ~ je l'ai rencontré** the town where I met him; **la pièce d'~ il est sorti** the room he came out of; **le village d'~ je viens** the village I come from; **les villes par ~ il est passé** the towns he went through

2 (*temps, état*) that (*souvent omis*); **le jour ~ il est parti** the day (that) he left; **au prix ~ c'est** at the price it is

♦ *adv* **1** (*interrogation*) where; ~ **est-il/va-t-il?** where is he/is he going?; **par ~?** which way?; **d'~ vient que ...?** how come ...?

2 (*position*) where; **je sais ~ il est** I know where he is; ~ **que l'on aille** wherever you go

ouate [wat] *nf* cotton wool (*BRIT*), cotton (*US*); (*bourre*) padding, wadding

oubli [ubli] *nm* (*acte*): **l'~** de forgetting; (*étourderie*) forgetfulness *no pl*; (*négligence*) omission, oversight; (*absence de souvenirs*) oblivion

oublier [ublije] *vt* (*gén*) to forget; (*ne pas voir: erreurs etc*) to miss; (*ne pas mettre: virgule, nom*) to leave out; (*laisser quelque part: chapeau etc*) to leave behind; **s'~** to forget o.s.

oubliettes [ublijɛt] *nfpl* dungeon *sg*

ouest [wɛst] *nm* west ♦ *adj inv* west; (*région*) western; **à l'~** in the west; (*to the*) west, westwards; **à l'~ de** (to the) west of

ouf [uf] *excl* phew!

oui [wi] *adv* yes

ouï-dire [widiʀ]: **par ~** *adv* by hearsay

ouïe [wi] *nf* hearing; ~**s** *nfpl* (*de poisson*) gills

ouïr [wiʀ] *vt* to hear; **avoir ouï dire que** to have heard it said that

ouragan [uʀagɑ̃] *nm* hurricane

ourlet [uʀlɛ] *nm* hem

ours [uʀs] *nm* bear; ~ **brun/blanc** brown/polar bear; ~ (**en peluche**) teddy (bear)

oursin [uʀsɛ̃] *nm* sea urchin

ourson [uʀsɔ̃] *nm* (bear-)cub

ouste [ust(ə)] *excl* hop it!

outil [uti] *nm* tool

outiller [utije] *vt* (*ouvrier, usine*) to equip

outrage [utʀaʒ] *nm* insult; **faire subir les derniers ~s à** (*femme*) to ravish; ~ **à la pudeur** indecent conduct *no pl*; ~**r** [utʀaʒe] *vt* to offend gravely

outrance [utʀɑ̃s]: **à ~** *adv* excessively, to excess

outre [utʀ(ə)] *nf* goatskin, water skin ♦ *prép* besides ♦ *adv*: **passer ~ à** to disregard, take no notice of; **en ~** besides, moreover; ~ **que** apart from the fact that; ~ **mesure** immoderately; unduly; ~**-Atlantique** *adv* across the Atlantic; ~**-Manche** *adv* across the Channel; ~**mer** *adj inv* ultramarine; ~**-mer** *adv* overseas; ~**passer** *vt* to go beyond, exceed

ouvert, e [uvɛʀ, -ɛʀt(ə)] *pp de* **ouvrir** ♦ *adj* open; (*robinet, gaz etc*) on; **ouvertement** *adv* openly

ouverture [uvɛʀtyʀ] *nf* opening; (*MUS*) overture; (*PHOTO*): ~ (**du diaphragme**) aperture; ~**s** *nfpl* (*propositions*) overtures; ~ **d'esprit** open-mindedness

ouvrable [uvʀabl(ə)] *adj*: **jour ~** working day, weekday

ouvrage [uvʀaʒ] *nm* (*tâche, de tricot etc, MIL*) work *no pl*; (*texte, livre*) work

ouvragé, e [uvʀaʒe] *adj* finely embroidered (*ou* worked *ou* carved)

ouvre-boîte(s) [uvʀəbwat] *nm inv* tin (*BRIT*) *ou* can opener

ouvre-bouteille(s) [uvʀəbutɛj] *nm inv* bottle-opener

ouvreuse [uvʀøz] *nf* usherette

ouvrier, ière [uvʀje, -jɛʀ] *nm/f* worker ♦ *adj* working-class; industrial, labour *cpd*; **classe ouvrière** working class

ouvrir [uvʀiʀ] *vt* (*gén*) to open; (*brèche,*

passage, MÉD: abcès) to open up; (commencer l'exploitation de, créer) to open (up); (eau, électricité, chauffage, robinet) to turn on ♦ vi to open; to open up; **s'~** vi to open; **s'~ à qn** to open one's heart to sb; **~ l'appétit à qn** to whet sb's appetite

ovaire [ɔvɛʀ] nm ovary
ovale [ɔval] adj oval
ovni [ɔvni] sigle m (= objet volant non identifié) UFO
oxyder [ɔkside]: **s'~** vi to become oxidized
oxygène [ɔksiʒɛn] nm oxygen; (fig): **cure d'~** fresh air cure
oxygéné, e [ɔksiʒene] adj: **eau ~e** hydrogen peroxide

P p

pacifique [pasifik] adj peaceful ♦ nm: **le P~, l'océan P~** the Pacific (Ocean)
pacte [pakt(ə)] nm pact, treaty
pactiser [paktize] vi: **~ avec** to come to terms with
pagaie [pagɛ] nf paddle
pagaille [pagaj] nf mess, shambles sg
page [paʒ] nf page ♦ nm page (boy); **à la ~** (fig) up-to-date
paiement [pɛmɑ̃] nm payment
païen, ne [pajɛ̃, -jɛn] adj, nm/f pagan, heathen
paillard, e [pajaʀ, -aʀd(ə)] adj bawdy
paillasson [pajasɔ̃] nm doormat
paille [paj] nf straw; (défaut) flaw
paillettes [pajɛt] nfpl (décoratives) sequins, spangles; **lessive en ~** soapflakes pl
pain [pɛ̃] nm (substance) bread; (unité) loaf (of bread); (morceau): **~ de cire etc** bar of wax etc; **~ bis/complet** brown/wholemeal (BRIT) ou wholewheat (US) bread; **~ d'épice** gingerbread; **~ de mie** sandwich loaf; **~ de sucre** sugar loaf; **~ grillé** toast
pair, e [pɛʀ] adj (nombre) even ♦ nm peer; **aller de ~** to go hand in hand ou together; **jeune fille au ~** au pair
paire [pɛʀ] nf pair
paisible [pezibl(ə)] adj peaceful, quiet
paître [pɛtʀ(ə)] vi to graze
paix [pɛ] nf peace; (fig) peacefulness, peace; **faire/avoir la ~** to make/have peace
Pakistan [pakistɑ̃] nm: **le ~** Pakistan
palace [palas] nm luxury hotel
palais [palɛ] nm palace; (ANAT) palate
pale [pal] nf (d'hélice, de rame) blade

pâle [pɑl] adj pale; **bleu ~** pale blue
Palestine [palɛstin] nf: **la ~** Palestine
palet [palɛ] nm disc, (HOCKEY) puck
palette [palɛt] nf (de peintre) palette; (produits) range
pâleur [pɑlœʀ] nf paleness
palier [palje] nm (d'escalier) landing; (fig) level, plateau; (TECH) bearing; **par ~s** in stages
pâlir [pɑliʀ] vi to turn ou go pale; (couleur) to fade
palissade [palisad] nf fence
palliatif [paljatif] nm palliative; (expédient) stopgap measure
pallier [palje]: **~ à** vt to offset, make up for
palmarès [palmaʀɛs] nm record (of achievements); (SCOL) prize list; (SPORT) list of winners
palme [palm(ə)] nf (symbole) palm; (de plongeur) flipper; **palmé, e** adj (pattes) webbed
palmier [palmje] nm palm tree
palombe [palɔ̃b] nf woodpigeon
pâlot, te [pɑlo, -ɔt] adj pale, peaky
palourde [paluʀd(ə)] nf clam
palper [palpe] vt to feel, finger
palpitant, e [palpitɑ̃, -ɑ̃t] adj thrilling
palpiter [palpite] vi (cœur, pouls) to beat; (: plus fort) to pound, throb
paludisme [palydism(ə)] nm malaria
pamphlet [pɑ̃flɛ] nm lampoon, satirical tract
pamplemousse [pɑ̃pləmus] nm grapefruit
pan [pɑ̃] nm section, piece ♦ excl bang!
panachage [panaʃaʒ] nm blend, mix
panache [panaʃ] nm plume; (fig) spirit, panache
panaché, e [panaʃe] adj: **glace ~e** mixed-flavour ice cream; **bière ~e** shandy
pancarte [pɑ̃kaʀt(ə)] nf sign, notice; (dans un défilé) placard
pancréas [pɑ̃kʀeas] nm pancreas
pané, e [pane] adj fried in breadcrumbs
panier [panje] nm basket; **mettre au ~** to chuck away; **~ à provisions** shopping basket
panique [panik] nf, adj panic; **paniquer** vi to panic
panne [pan] nf (d'un mécanisme, moteur) breakdown; **être/tomber en ~** to have broken down/break down; **être en ~ d'essence** ou **sèche** to have run out of petrol (BRIT) ou gas (US); **~ d'électricité** ou **de courant** power ou electrical failure
panneau, x [pano] nm (écriteau) sign, notice; (de boiserie, de tapisserie etc) panel; **~ d'affichage** notice board; **~ de signalisation** roadsign
panonceau, x [panɔ̃so] nm sign
panoplie [panɔpli] nf (jouet) outfit; (d'armes) display; (fig) array

panorama [panɔʀama] *nm* panorama

panse [pɑ̃s] *nf* paunch

pansement [pɑ̃smɑ̃] *nm* dressing, bandage;
~ **adhésif** sticking plaster

panser [pɑ̃se] *vt* (*plaie*) to dress, bandage;
(*bras*) to put a dressing on, bandage; (*cheval*) to groom

pantalon [pɑ̃talɔ̃] *nm* (*aussi:* ~s, **paire de**
~s) trousers *pl*, pair of trousers; ~ **de ski**
ski pants *pl*

pantelant, e [pɑ̃tlɑ̃, -ɑ̃t] *adj* gasping for
breath, panting

panthère [pɑ̃tɛʀ] *nf* panther

pantin [pɑ̃tɛ̃] *nm* jumping jack; (*péj*) puppet

pantois [pɑ̃twa] *adj m:* **rester** ~ to be flabbergasted

pantomime [pɑ̃tɔmim] *nf* mime; (*pièce*)
mime show

pantoufle [pɑ̃tufl(ə)] *nf* slipper

paon [pɑ̃] *nm* peacock

papa [papa] *nm* dad(dy)

pape [pap] *nm* pope

paperasse [papʀas] (*péj*) *nf* bumf *no pl*, papers *pl*; **paperasserie** (*péj*) *nf* red tape *no
pl*; paperwork *no pl*

papeterie [papetʀi] *nf* (*usine*) paper mill;
(*magasin*) stationer's (shop)

papier [papje] *nm* paper; (*article*) article;
~s *nmpl* (*aussi:* ~s **d'identité**) (identity) papers; ~ **à lettres** writing paper, notepaper;
~ **buvard** blotting paper; ~ **carbone** carbon paper; ~ **(d')aluminium** aluminium
(*BRIT*) *ou* aluminum (*US*) foil, tinfoil; ~ **de
verre** sandpaper; ~ **hygiénique** toilet paper; ~ **journal** newsprint; (*pour emballer*)
newspaper; ~ **peint** wallpaper

papillon [papijɔ̃] *nm* butterfly; (*fam: contravention*) (parking) ticket; (*TECH: écrou*)
wing nut; ~ **de nuit** moth

papilloter [papijɔte] *vi* to blink, flicker

paquebot [pakbo] *nm* liner

pâquerette [pɑkʀɛt] *nf* daisy

Pâques [pɑk] *nm, nfpl* Easter

paquet [pakɛ] *nm* packet; (*colis*) parcel;
(*fig: tas*): ~ **de pile** *ou* heap of; **paquet-cadeau** *nm* gift-wrapped parcel

par [paʀ] *prép* by; **finir** *etc* ~ to end *etc*
with; ~ **amour** out of love; **passer** ~
Lyon/la côte to go via *ou* through Lyons/
along by the coast; ~ **la fenêtre** (*jeter, regarder*) out of the window; **3** ~ **jour/
personne** 3 a *ou* per day/head; **2** ~ **2** two
at a time; in twos; ~ **ici** this way; (*dans le
coin*) round here; ~**-ci,** ~**-là** here and there

parabole [paʀabɔl] *nf* (*REL*) parable

parachever [paʀaʃ(ə)ve] *vt* to perfect

parachute [paʀaʃyt] *nm* parachute

parachutiste [paʀaʃytist(ə)] *nm/f* parachutist; (*MIL*) paratrooper

parade [paʀad] *nf* (*spectacle, défilé*) parade;
(*ESCRIME, BOXE*) parry

paradis [paʀadi] *nm* heaven, paradise

paradoxe [paʀadɔks(ə)] *nm* paradox

paraffine [paʀafin] *nf* paraffin

parages [paʀaʒ] *nmpl:* **dans les** ~ **(de)** in
the area *ou* vicinity (of)

paragraphe [paʀagʀaf] *nm* paragraph

paraître [paʀɛtʀ(ə)] *vb* +*attrib* to seem,
look, appear ♦ *vi* to appear; (*être visible*) to
show; (*PRESSE, ÉDITION*) to be published,
come out, appear; (*briller*) to show off ♦ *vb
impers:* **il paraît que ...** it seems *ou* appears that ...; **they say that ...; il me paraît
que ...** it seems to me that ...

parallèle [paʀalɛl] *adj* parallel; (*police,
marché*) unofficial ♦ *nm* (*comparaison*): **faire un** ~ **entre** to draw a parallel between;
(*GÉO*) parallel ♦ *nf* parallel (line)

paralyser [paʀalize] *vt* to paralyse

paramédical, e, aux [paʀamedikal] *adj:*
personnel ~ paramedics *pl*, paramedical
workers *pl*

parapet [paʀapɛ] *nm* parapet

parapher [paʀafe] *vt* to initial; to sign

paraphrase [paʀafʀɑz] *nf* paraphrase

parapluie [paʀaplɥi] *nm* umbrella

parasite [paʀazit] *nm* parasite; ~s *nmpl*
(*TÉL*) interference *sg*

parasol [paʀasɔl] *nm* parasol, sunshade

paratonnerre [paʀatɔnɛʀ] *nm* lightning
conductor

paravent [paʀavɑ̃] *nm* folding screen

parc [paʀk] *nm* (*public*) park, gardens *pl*;
(*de château etc*) grounds *pl*; (*pour le bétail*)
pen, enclosure; (*d'enfant*) playpen; (*MIL: entrepôt*) depot; (*ensemble d'unités*) stock; (*de
voitures etc*) fleet; ~ **automobile** (*d'un
pays*) number of cars on the roads; ~
(d'attractions) à thème theme park; ~ **de
stationnement** car park

parcelle [paʀsɛl] *nf* fragment, scrap; (*de terrain*) plot, parcel

parce que [paʀsk(ə)] *conj* because

parchemin [paʀʃəmɛ̃] *nm* parchment

parc(o)mètre [paʀk(ɔ)mɛtʀ(ə)] *nm* parking
meter

parcourir [paʀkuʀiʀ] *vt* (*trajet, distance*) to
cover; (*article, livre*) to skim *ou* glance
through; (*lieu*) to go all over, travel up and
down; (*suj: frisson, vibration*) to run
through

parcours [paʀkuʀ] *nm* (*trajet*) journey; (*itinéraire*) route; (*SPORT: terrain*) course; (*:
tour*) round; run; lap

par-dessous [paʀdəsu] *prép, adv* under(neath)

pardessus [paʀdəsy] *nm* overcoat

par-dessus [paʀdəsy] *prép* over (the top
of) ♦ *adv* over (the top); ~ **le marché** on
top of all that

par-devant [paʀdəvɑ̃] *prép* in the presence
of, before ♦ *adv* at the front; round the
front

pardon [paʀdɔ̃] nm forgiveness no pl ♦ excl sorry!; (pour interpeller etc) excuse me!; **demander** ~ **à qn (de)** to apologize to sb (for); **je vous demande** ~ I'm sorry; excuse me

pardonner [paʀdɔne] vt to forgive; ~ **qch à qn** to forgive sb for sth

pare: ~**-balles** adj inv bulletproof; ~**-boue** nm inv mudguard; ~**-brise** nm inv windscreen (BRIT), windshield (US); ~**-chocs** nm inv bumper

pareil, le [paʀɛj] adj (identique) the same, alike; (similaire) similar; (tel): **un courage/ livre** ~ such courage/a book, courage/a book like this; **de** ~**s livres** such books; **ses** ~**s** one's fellow men; one's peers; **ne pas avoir son(sa)** ~**(le)** to be second to none; ~ **à** the same as; similar to; **sans** ~ unparalleled, unequalled

parent, e [paʀɑ̃, -ɑ̃t] nm/f: **un/une** ~**/e** a relative ou relation ♦ adj: **être** ~ **de** to be related to; ~**s** nmpl (père et mère) parents; **parenté** nf (lien) relationship

parenthèse [paʀɑ̃tɛz] nf (ponctuation) bracket, parenthesis; (MATH) bracket; (digression) parenthesis, digression; **ouvrir/ fermer la** ~ to open/close the brackets; **entre** ~**s** in brackets; (fig) incidentally

parer [paʀe] vt to adorn; (CULIN) to dress, trim; (éviter) to ward off

paresse [paʀɛs] nf laziness; **paresseux, euse** adj lazy; (fig) slow, sluggish

parfaire [paʀfɛʀ] vt to perfect

parfait, e [paʀfɛ, -ɛt] adj perfect ♦ nm (LING) perfect (tense); **parfaitement** adv perfectly ♦ excl (most) certainly

parfois [paʀfwa] adv sometimes

parfum [paʀfœ̃] nm (produit) perfume, scent; (odeur: de fleur) scent, fragrance; (: de tabac, vin) aroma; (goût) flavour; **parfumé, e** adj (fleur, fruit) fragrant; (femme) perfumed; **parfumé au café** coffee-flavoured; **parfumer** vt (suj: odeur, bouquet) to perfume; (mouchoir) to put scent ou perfume on; (crème, gâteau) to flavour; **parfumerie** nf (commerce) perfumery; (produits) perfumes pl; (boutique) perfume shop

pari [paʀi] nm bet, wager; (SPORT) bet

paria [paʀja] nm outcast

parier [paʀje] vt to bet

Paris [paʀi] n Paris; **parisien, ne** adj Parisian; (GÉO, ADMIN) Paris cpd ♦ nm/f: **Parisien, ne** Parisian

paritaire [paʀitɛʀ] adj joint

parjure [paʀʒyʀ] nm perjury

parking [paʀkiŋ] nm (lieu) car park

parlant, e [paʀlɑ̃, -ɑ̃t] adj (fig) graphic, vivid; eloquent; (CINÉMA) talking

parlement [paʀləmɑ̃] nm parliament; **parlementaire** adj parliamentary ♦ nm/f member of parliament

parlementer [paʀləmɑ̃te] vi to negotiate, parley

parler [paʀle] vi to speak, talk; (avouer) to talk; ~ **(à qn) de** to talk ou speak (to sb) about; ~ **le/en français** to speak French/in French; ~ **affaires** to talk business; ~ **en dormant** to talk in one's sleep; **sans** ~ **de** (fig) not to mention, to say nothing of; **tu parles!** you must be joking!

parloir [paʀlwaʀ] nm (de prison, d'hôpital) visiting room; (REL) parlour

parmi [paʀmi] prép among(st)

paroi [paʀwa] nf wall; (cloison) partition; ~ **rocheuse** rock face

paroisse [paʀwas] nf parish

parole [paʀɔl] nf (faculté): **la** ~ speech; (mot, promesse) word; ~**s** nfpl (MUS) words, lyrics; **tenir** ~ to keep one's word; **prendre la** ~ to speak; **demander la** ~ to ask for permission to speak; **je le crois sur** ~ I'll take his word for it

parquer [paʀke] vt (voiture, matériel) to park; (bestiaux) to pen (in ou up)

parquet [paʀkɛ] nm (parquet) floor; (JUR): **le** ~ the Public Prosecutor's department

parrain [paʀɛ̃] nm godfather; (d'un nouvel adhérent) sponsor, proposer

parrainer [paʀene] vt (suj: entreprise) to sponsor

pars vb voir **partir**

parsemer [paʀsəme] vt (suj: feuilles, papiers) to be scattered over; ~ **qch de** to scatter sth with

part [paʀ] nf (qui revient à qn) share; (fraction, partie) part; (FINANCE) (non-voting) share; **prendre** ~ **à** (débat etc) to take part in; (soucis, douleur de qn) to share in; **faire** ~ **de qch à qn** to announce sth to sb, inform sb of sth; **pour ma** ~ as for me, as far as I'm concerned; **à** ~ **entière** full; **de la** ~ **de** (au nom de) on behalf of; (donné par) from; **de toute(s)** ~**(s)** from all sides ou quarters; **de** ~ **et d'autre** on both sides, on either side; **de** ~ **en** ~ right through; **d'une** ~ ... **d'autre** ~ on the one hand ... on the other hand; **à** ~ adv separately; (de côté) aside ♦ prép apart from, except for ♦ adj exceptional, special; **faire la** ~ **des choses** to make allowances

partage [paʀtaʒ] nm dividing up; sharing (out) no pl, share-out; sharing; **recevoir qch en** ~ to receive sth as one's share (ou lot)

partager [paʀtaʒe] vt to share; (distribuer, répartir) to share (out); (morceler, diviser) to divide (up); **se** ~ vt (héritage etc) to share between themselves (ou ourselves)

partance [paʀtɑ̃s]: **en** ~ adv outbound, due to leave; **en** ~ **pour** (bound) for

partant, e [paʀtɑ̃] vb voir **partir** ♦ nm (SPORT) starter; (HIPPISME) runner

partenaire [paʀtənɛʀ] nm/f partner

parterre [partɛr] nm (de fleurs) (flower) bed; (THÉÂTRE) stalls pl

parti [parti] nm (POL) party; (décision) course of action; (personne à marier) match; **tirer ~ de** to take advantage of, turn to good account; **prendre le ~ de qn** to stand up for sb, side with sb; **prendre ~ (pour/contre)** to take sides ou a stand (for/against); **prendre son ~ de** to come to terms with; **~ pris** bias

partial, e, aux [parsjal, -o] adj biased, partial

participant, e [partisipã, -ãt] nm/f participant; (à un concours) entrant

participation [partisipasjɔ̃] nf participation; sharing; (COMM) interest; **la ~ aux bénéfices** profit-sharing

participe [partisip] nm participle

participer [partisipe]: **~ à** vt (course, réunion) to take part in; (profits etc) to share in; (frais etc) to contribute to; (chagrin, succès de qn) to share (in)

particularité [partikylarite] nf particularity; (distinctive) characteristic

particule [partikyl] nf particle

particulier, ière [partikylje, -jɛr] adj (personnel, privé) private; (spécial) special, particular; (caractéristique) characteristic, distinctive; (spécifique) particular ♦ nm (individu: ADMIN) private individual; **~ à** peculiar to; **en ~** (surtout) in particular, particularly; (en privé) in private; **particulièrement** adv particularly

partie [parti] nf (gén) part; (profession, spécialité) field, subject; (JUR etc: protagonistes) party; (de cartes, tennis etc) game; **une ~ de campagne/de pêche** an outing in the country/a fishing party ou trip; **en ~** partly, in part; **faire ~ de** to belong to; (suj: chose) to be part of; **prendre qn à ~** to take sb to task; (malmener) to set on sb; **en grande ~** largely, in the main; **~ civile** (JUR) party claiming damages in a criminal case

partiel, le [parsjɛl] adj partial ♦ nm (SCOL) class exam

partir [partir] vi (gén) to go; (quitter) to go, leave; (s'éloigner) to go (ou drive etc) away ou off; (moteur) to start; **~ de** (lieu: quitter) to leave; (: commencer à) to start from; (date) to run ou start from; **à ~ de** from

partisan, e [partizã, -an] nm/f partisan ♦ adj: **être ~ de qch/de faire** to be in favour of sth/doing

partition [partisjɔ̃] nf (MUS) score

partout [partu] adv everywhere; **~ où il allait** everywhere ou wherever he went; **trente ~** (TENNIS) thirty all

paru pp de **paraître**

parure [paryr] nf (bijoux etc) finery no pl; jewellery no pl; (assortiment) set

parution [parysjɔ̃] nf publication, appearance

parvenir [parvənir]: **~ à** vt (atteindre) to reach; (réussir): **~ à** faire to manage to do, succeed in doing; **faire ~ qch à qn** to have sth sent to sb

parvis [parvi] nm square (in front of a church)

pas¹ [pɑ] nm (allure, mesure) pace; (démarche) tread; (enjambée, DANSE) step; (bruit) (foot)step; (trace) footprint; (TECH: de vis, d'écrou) thread; **~ à ~** step by step; **au ~** at walking pace; **à ~ de loup** stealthily; **faire les cent ~** to pace up and down; **faire les premiers ~** to make the first move; **sur le ~ de la porte** on the doorstep

───────── *MOT CLÉ* ─────────

pas² [pɑ] adv **1** (en corrélation avec ne, non etc) not; **il ne pleure ~** he does not ou doesn't cry; he's not ou isn't crying; **il n'a ~ pleuré/ne pleurera ~** he did not ou didn't/will not ou won't cry; **ils n'ont ~ de voiture/d'enfants** they haven't got a car/any children, they have no car/children; **il m'a dit de ne ~ le faire** he told me not to do it; **non ~ que ... not** that ...

2 (employé sans ne etc): **~ moi** not me; not I, I don't (ou can't etc); **une pomme ~ mûre** an apple which isn't ripe; **~ plus tard qu'hier** only yesterday; **~ du tout** not at all

3: **~ mal** not bad; not badly; **~ mal de** quite a lot of

─────────────────────────────

passage [pɑsaʒ] nm (fait de passer) voir **passer**; (lieu, prix de la traversée, extrait) passage; (chemin) way; **de ~** (touristes) passing through; (amants etc) casual; **~ à niveau** level crossing; **~ clouté** pedestrian crossing; **"~ interdit"** "no entry"; **"~ protégé"** right of way over secondary road(s) on your right; **~ souterrain** subway (BRIT), underpass

passager, ère [pɑsaʒe, -ɛr] adj passing ♦ nm/f passenger; **~ clandestin** stowaway

passant, e [pɑsã, -ãt] adj (rue, endroit) busy ♦ nm/f passer-by; **en ~** in passing

passe [pɑs] nf (SPORT, magnétique, NAVIG) pass ♦ nm (passe-partout) master ou skeleton key; **être en ~ de faire** to be on the way to doing

passé, e [pɑse] adj (événement, temps) past; (couleur, tapisserie) faded ♦ prép after ♦ nm past; (LING) past (tense); **~ de mode** out of fashion; **~ composé** perfect (tense); **~ simple** past historic

passe: **~-droit** nm special privilege; **~-montagne** nm balaclava; **~-partout** nm inv master ou skeleton key ♦ adj inv all-purpose; **~-~** nm: **tour de ~-~** trick, sleight of hand no pl

passeport [paspɔʀ] nm passport

passer [pase] vi (se rendre, aller) to go; (voiture, piétons: défiler) to pass (by), go by; (faire une halte rapide: facteur, laitier etc) to come, call; (: pour rendre visite) to call ou drop in; (air, lumière: franchir un obstacle etc) to get through; (accusé, projet de loi): ~ **devant** to come before; (film, émission) to be on; (temps, jours) to go by, pass; (couleur, papier) to fade; (mode) to die out; (douleur) to pass, go away; (CARTES) to pass; (SCOL) to go up (to the next class) ♦ vt (frontière, rivière etc) to cross; (douane) to go through; (examen) to sit, take; (visite médicale etc) to have; (journée, temps) to spend; (donner): ~ **qch à qn** to pass sth to sb; to give sb sth; (transmettre): ~ **qch à qn** to pass sth on to sb; (enfiler: vêtement) to slip on; (faire entrer, mettre): (faire) ~ **qch dans/par** to get sth into/through; (café) to pour the water on; (thé, soupe) to strain; (film, pièce) to show, put on; (disque) to play, put on; (marché, accord) to agree on; (tolérer): ~ **qch à qn** to let sb get away with sth; **se ~** vi (avoir lieu: scène, action) to take place; (se dérouler: entretien etc) to go; (s'écouler: semaine etc) to pass, go by; (arriver): **que s'est-il passé?** what happened?; ~ **de** to go ou do without; **se ~ les mains sous l'eau/de l'eau sur le visage** to put one's hands under the tap/run water over one's face; ~ **par** to go through; ~ **sur** (faute, détail inutile) to pass over; ~ **avant qch/qn** (fig) to come before sth/sb; **laisser** ~ (air, lumière, personne) to let through; (occasion) to let slip, miss; (erreur) to overlook; ~ **à la radio/télévision** to be on the radio/on television; ~ **pour riche** to be taken for a rich man; ~ **en seconde**, ~ **la seconde** (AUTO) to change into second; ~ **le balai/l'aspirateur** to sweep up/hoover; **je vous passe M. X** (je vous mets en communication avec lui) I'm putting you through to Mr X; (je lui passe l'appareil) here is Mr X, I'll hand you over to Mr X

passerelle [pasʀɛl] nf footbridge; (de navire, avion) gangway

passe-temps [pɑstɑ̃] nm inv pastime

passeur, euse [pasœʀ, -øz] nm/f smuggler

passible [pasibl(ə)] adj: ~ **de** liable to

passif, ive [pasif, -iv] adj passive ♦ nm (LING) passive; (COMM) liabilities pl

passion [pasjɔ̃] nf passion; **passionnant, e** adj fascinating; **passionné, e** adj passionate; impassioned; **passionner** vt (personne) to fascinate, grip; **se passionner pour** to take an avid interest in; to have a passion for

passoire [paswaʀ] nf sieve; (à légumes) colander; (à thé) strainer

pastèque [pastɛk] nf watermelon

pasteur [pastœʀ] nm (protestant) minister, pastor

pastille [pastij] nf (à sucer) lozenge, pastille; (de papier etc) (small) disc

patate [patat] nf: ~ **douce** sweet potato

patauger [patoʒe] vi (pour s'amuser) to splash about; (avec effort) to wade about

pâte [pɑt] nf (à tarte) pastry; (à pain) dough; (à frire) batter; (substance molle) paste; cream; ~**s** nfpl (macaroni etc) pasta sg; ~ **à modeler** modelling clay, Plasticine (®: BRIT); ~ **brisée** shortcrust pastry; ~ **d'amandes** almond paste; ~ **de fruits** crystallized fruit no pl

pâté [pɑte] nm (charcuterie) pâté; (tache) ink blot; (de sable) sandpie; ~ **de maisons** block (of houses); ~ **en croûte** ≈ pork pie

pâtée [pɑte] nf mash, feed

patente [patɑ̃t] nf (COMM) trading licence

paternel, le [patɛʀnɛl] adj (amour, soins) fatherly; (ligne, autorité) paternal

pâteux, euse [pɑtø, -øz] adj thick; pasty

pathétique [patetik] adj moving

patience [pasjɑ̃s] nf patience

patient, e [pasjɑ̃, -ɑ̃t] adj, nm/f patient

patienter [pasjɑ̃te] vi to wait

patin [patɛ̃] nm skate; (sport) skating; ~**s (à glace)** (ice) skates; ~**s à roulettes** roller skates

patinage [patinaʒ] nm skating

patiner [patine] vi to skate; (embrayage) to slip; (roue, voiture) to spin; **se ~** vi (meuble, cuir) to acquire a sheen; **patineur, euse** nm/f skater; **patinoire** nf skating rink, (ice) rink

pâtir [pɑtiʀ]: ~ **de** vt to suffer because of

pâtisserie [pɑtisʀi] nf (boutique) cake shop; (métier) confectionery; (à la maison) pastry- ou cake-making, baking; ~**s** nfpl (gâteaux) pastries, cakes; **pâtissier, ière** nm/f pastrycook; confectioner

patois [patwa] nm dialect, patois

patrie [patʀi] nf homeland

patrimoine [patʀimwan] nm inheritance, patrimony; (culture) heritage

patriotique [patʀijɔtik] adj patriotic

patron, ne [patʀɔ̃, -ɔn] nm/f boss; (REL) patron saint ♦ nm (COUTURE) pattern

patronat [patʀona] nm employers pl

patronner [patʀone] vt to sponsor, support

patrouille [patʀuj] nf patrol

patte [pat] nf (jambe) leg; (pied: de chien, chat) paw; (: d'oiseau) foot; (languette) strap

pâturage [pɑtyʀaʒ] nm pasture

pâture [pɑtyʀ] nf food

paume [pom] nf palm

paumé, e [pome] (fam) nm/f drop-out

paumer [pome] (fam) vt to lose

paupière [popjɛʀ] nf eyelid

pause [poz] nf (arrêt) break; (en parlant, MUS) pause

pauvre [povʀ(ə)] *adj* poor; **pauvreté** *nf* (*état*) poverty

pavaner [pavane]: **se ~** *vi* to strut about

pavé, e [pave] *adj* paved; cobbled ♦ *nm* (*bloc*) paving stone; cobblestone; (*pavage*) paving

pavillon [pavijɔ̃] *nm* (*de banlieue*) small (detached) house; (*kiosque*) lodge; pavilion; (*drapeau*) flag

pavoiser [pavwaze] *vi* to put out flags; (*fig*) to rejoice, exult

pavot [pavo] *nm* poppy

payant, e [pɛjɑ̃, -ɑ̃t] *adj* (*spectateurs etc*) paying; (*fig: entreprise*) profitable; **c'est ~** you have to pay, there is a charge

paye [pɛj] *nf* pay, wages *pl*

payer [peje] *vt* (*créancier, employé, loyer*) to pay; (*achat, réparations, fig: faute*) to pay for ♦ *vi* to pay; (*métier*) to be well-paid; (*tactique etc*) to pay off; **il me l'a fait ~ 10 F** he charged me 10 F for it; **~ qch à qn** to buy sth for sb, buy sb sth; **cela ne paie pas de mine** it doesn't look much

pays [pei] *nm* country; land; region; village; **du ~** local

paysage [peizaʒ] *nm* landscape

paysan, ne [peizɑ̃, -an] *nm/f* countryman(woman); farmer; (*péj*) peasant ♦ *adj* country *cpd*, farming; farmers'

Pays-Bas [peiba] *nmpl*: **les ~** the Netherlands

PC *nm* (*INFORM*) PC

PDG *sigle m* = **président directeur général**

péage [peaʒ] *nm* toll; (*endroit*) tollgate; **pont à ~** toll bridge

peau, x [po] *nf* skin; **gants de ~** fine leather gloves; **~ de chamois** (*chiffon*) chamois leather, shammy; **Peau-Rouge** *nm/f* Red Indian, redskin

péché [peʃe] *nm* sin

pêche [pɛʃ] *nf* (*sport, activité*) fishing; (*poissons pêchés*) catch; (*fruit*) peach; **~ à la ligne** (*en rivière*) angling

pécher [peʃe] *vi* (*REL*) to sin; (*fig: personne*) to err; (: *chose*) to be flawed

pêcher [peʃe] *nm* peach tree ♦ *vi* to go fishing ♦ *vt* to catch; to fish for

pêcheur, eresse [peʃœʀ, peʃʀɛs] *nm/f* sinner

pêcheur [peʃœʀ] *nm* fisherman; angler

pécule [pekyl] *nm* savings *pl*, nest egg

pécuniaire [pekynjɛʀ] *adj* financial

pédagogie [pedagɔʒi] *nf* educational methods *pl*, pedagogy; **pédagogique** *adj* educational

pédale [pedal] *nf* pedal

pédalo [pedalo] *nm* pedal-boat

pédant, e [pedɑ̃, -ɑ̃t] (*péj*) *adj* pedantic

pédestre [pedɛstʀ(ə)] *adj*: **tourisme ~** hiking

pédiatre [pedjatʀ(ə)] *nm/f* paediatrician, child specialist

pédicure [pedikyʀ] *nm/f* chiropodist

pègre [pɛgʀ(ə)] *nf* underworld

peignais *etc vb voir* **peindre; peigner**

peigne [pɛɲ] *nm* comb

peigner [peɲe] *vt* to comb (the hair of); **se ~** *vi* to comb one's hair

peignoir [pɛɲwaʀ] *nm* dressing gown; **~ de bain** bathrobe

peindre [pɛ̃dʀ(ə)] *vt* to paint; (*fig*) to portray, depict

peine [pɛn] *nf* (*affliction*) sorrow, sadness *no pl*; (*mal, effort*) trouble *no pl*, effort; (*difficulté*) difficulty; (*punition, châtiment*) punishment; (*JUR*) sentence; **faire de la ~ à qn** to distress *ou* upset sb; **prendre la ~ de faire** to go to the trouble of doing; **se donner de la ~** to make an effort; **ce n'est pas la ~ de faire** there's no point in doing, it's not worth doing; **à ~** scarcely, hardly, barely; **à ~ ... que** hardly ... than; **défense d'afficher sous ~ d'amende** billposters will be fined; **~ capitale** *ou* **de mort** capital punishment, death sentence; **peiner** *vi* to work hard; to struggle; (*moteur, voiture*) to labour ♦ *vt* to grieve, sadden

peintre [pɛ̃tʀ(ə)] *nm* painter; **~ en bâtiment** house painter

peinture [pɛ̃tyʀ] *nf* painting; (*couche de couleur, couleur*) paint; (*surfaces peintes: aussi: ~s*) paintwork; **"~ fraîche"** "wet paint"; **~ mate/brillante** matt/gloss paint

péjoratif, ive [peʒɔʀatif, -iv] *adj* pejorative, derogatory

pelage [pəlaʒ] *nm* coat, fur

pêle-mêle [pɛlmɛl] *adv* higgledy-piggledy

peler [pəle] *vt, vi* to peel

pèlerin [pɛlʀɛ̃] *nm* pilgrim

pelle [pɛl] *nf* shovel; (*d'enfant, de terrassier*) spade; **~ mécanique** mechanical digger

pellicule [pelikyl] *nf* film; **~s** *nfpl* (*MÉD*) dandruff *sg*

pelote [pəlɔt] *nf* (*de fil, laine*) ball; (*d'épingles*) pin cushion; **~ basque** pelota

peloton [pəlɔtɔ̃] *nm* group, squad; (*CYCLISME*) pack; **~ d'exécution** firing squad

pelotonner [pəlɔtɔne]: **se ~** *vi* to curl (o.s.) up

pelouse [pəluz] *nf* lawn

peluche [pəlyʃ] *nf*: **animal en ~** fluffy animal, soft toy

pelure [pəlyʀ] *nf* peeling, peel *no pl*

pénal, e, aux [penal, -o] *adj* penal

pénalité [penalite] *nf* penalty

penaud, e [pəno, -od] *adj* sheepish, contrite

penchant [pɑ̃ʃɑ̃] *nm* tendency, propensity; liking, fondness

pencher [pɑ̃ʃe] *vi* to tilt, lean over ♦ *vt* to tilt; **se ~** *vi* to lean over; (*se baisser*) to bend down; **se ~ sur** to bend over; (*fig: problème*) to look into; **se ~ au dehors** to lean out; **~ pour** to be inclined to favour

pendaison [pɑ̃dɛzɔ̃] nf hanging
pendant [pɑ̃dɑ̃] nm: **faire ~ à** to match; to be the counterpart of ♦ prép during; ~ **que** while
pendentif [pɑ̃dɑ̃tif] nm pendant
penderie [pɑ̃dʀi] nf wardrobe
pendre [pɑ̃dʀ(ə)] vt, vi to hang; **se ~ (à)** (se suicider) to hang o.s. (on); ~ **à** to hang (down) from; ~ **qch à** to hang sth (up) on
pendule [pɑ̃dyl] nf clock ♦ nm pendulum
pénétrer [penetʀe] vi, vt to penetrate; ~ **dans** to enter; (suj: projectile) to penetrate; (: air, eau) to come into, get into
pénible [penibl(ə)] adj (astreignant) hard; (affligeant) painful; (personne, caractère) tiresome; **~ment** adv with difficulty
péniche [peniʃ] nf barge
pénicilline [penisilin] nf penicillin
péninsule [penɛ̃syl] nf peninsula
pénis [penis] nm penis
pénitence [penitɑ̃s] nf (repentir) penitence; (peine) penance
pénitencier [penitɑ̃sje] nm penitentiary
pénombre [penɔ̃bʀ(ə)] nf half-light; darkness
pensée [pɑ̃se] nf thought; (démarche, doctrine) thinking no pl; (BOT) pansy; **en ~** in one's mind
penser [pɑ̃se] vi to think ♦ vt to think; (concevoir: problème, machine) to think out; ~ **à** to think of (songer à: ami, vacances) to think of ou about; (réfléchir à: problème, offre): ~ **à qch** to think about sth ou think sth over; **faire ~ à** to remind one of; ~ **faire qch** to be thinking of doing sth, intend to do sth
pensif, ive [pɑ̃sif, -iv] adj pensive, thoughtful
pension [pɑ̃sjɔ̃] nf (allocation) pension; (prix du logement) board and lodgings, bed and board; (maison particulière) boarding house; (hôtel) guesthouse, hotel; (école) boarding school; **prendre qn en ~** to take sb (in) as a lodger; **mettre en ~** to send to boarding school; ~ **alimentaire** (d'étudiant) living allowance; (de divorcée) maintenance allowance; alimony; ~ **complète** full board; ~ **de famille** boarding house, guesthouse; **pensionnaire** nm/f boarder; guest; **pensionnat** nm boarding school
pente [pɑ̃t] nf slope; **en ~** sloping
Pentecôte [pɑ̃tkot] nf: **la ~** Whitsun (BRIT), Pentecost
pénurie [penyʀi] nf shortage
pépé [pepe] (fam) nm grandad
pépin [pepɛ̃] nm (BOT: graine) pip; (ennui) snag, hitch
pépinière [pepinjɛʀ] nf nursery
perçant, e [pɛʀsɑ̃, -ɑ̃t] adj sharp, keen; piercing, shrill
percée [pɛʀse] nf (trouée) opening; (MIL, technologique) breakthrough; (SPORT) break

perce-neige [pɛʀsənɛʒ] nf inv snowdrop
percepteur [pɛʀsɛptœʀ] nm tax collector
perception [pɛʀsɛpsjɔ̃] nf perception; (d'impôts etc) collection; (bureau) tax office
percer [pɛʀse] vt to pierce; (ouverture etc) to make; (mystère, énigme) to penetrate ♦ vi to come through; to break through; ~ **une dent** to cut a tooth; **perceuse** nf drill
percevoir [pɛʀsəvwaʀ] vt (distinguer) to perceive, detect; (taxe, impôt) to collect; (revenu, indemnité) to receive
perche [pɛʀʃ] nf (bâton) pole
percher [pɛʀʃe] vt, vi to perch; **se ~** vi to perch; **perchoir** nm perch
perçois etc vb voir **percevoir**
percolateur [pɛʀkɔlatœʀ] nm percolator
perçu, e pp de **percevoir**
percussion [pɛʀkysjɔ̃] nf percussion
percuter [pɛʀkyte] vt to strike; (suj: véhicule) to crash into
perdant, e [pɛʀdɑ̃, -ɑ̃t] nm/f loser
perdition [pɛʀdisjɔ̃] nf: **en ~** (NAVIG) in distress; **lieu de ~** den of vice
perdre [pɛʀdʀ(ə)] vt to lose; (gaspiller: temps, argent) to waste; (personne: moralement etc) to ruin ♦ vi to lose; (sur une vente etc) to lose out; **se ~** vi (s'égarer) to get lost, lose one's way; (fig) to go to waste; to disappear, vanish
perdrix [pɛʀdʀi] nf partridge
perdu, e [pɛʀdy] pp de **perdre** ♦ adj (isolé) out-of-the-way; (COMM: emballage) nonreturnable; (malade): **il est ~** there's no hope left for him; **à vos moments ~s** in your spare time
père [pɛʀ] nm father; **~s** nmpl (ancêtres) forefathers; ~ **de famille** father; family man; **le ~ Noël** Father Christmas
perfectionné, e [pɛʀfɛksjɔne] adj sophisticated
perfectionner [pɛʀfɛksjɔne] vt to improve, perfect
perforatrice [pɛʀfɔʀatʀis] nf (pour cartes) card-punch; (de bureau) punch
perforer [pɛʀfɔʀe] vt to perforate; to punch a hole (ou holes) in; (ticket, bande, carte) to punch
performant, e [pɛʀfɔʀmɑ̃, -ɑ̃t] adj: **très ~** high-performance cpd
perfusion [pɛʀfyzjɔ̃] nf: **faire une ~ à qn** to put sb on a drip
péril [peʀil] nm peril
périmé, e [peʀime] adj (out)dated; (ADMIN) out-of-date, expired
périmètre [peʀimɛtʀ(ə)] nm perimeter
période [peʀjɔd] nf period; **périodique** adj (phases) periodic; (publication) periodical ♦ nm periodical
péripéties [peʀipesi] nfpl events, episodes
périphérique [peʀifeʀik] adj (quartiers) outlying; (ANAT, TECH) peripheral; (station

de radio) operating from outside France ♦
nm (AUTO) ring road; (INFORM) peripheral
périple [peʀipl(ə)] *nm* journey
périr [peʀiʀ] *vi* to die, perish
périssable [peʀisabl(ə)] *adj* perishable
perle [pɛʀl(ə)] *nf* pearl; (*de plastique, métal, sueur*) bead
perlé, e [pɛʀle] *adj*: **grève** ~**e** go-slow
perler [pɛʀle] *vi* to form in droplets
permanence [pɛʀmanɑ̃s] *nf* permanence; (*local*) (duty) office; emergency service; **assurer une** ~ (*service public, bureaux*) to operate *ou* maintain a basic service; **être de** ~ to be on call *ou* duty; **en** ~ permanently; continuously
permanent, e [pɛʀmanɑ̃, -ɑ̃t] *adj* permanent; (*spectacle*) continuous; **permanente** *nf* perm
perméable [pɛʀmeabl(ə)] *adj* (*terrain*) permeable; ~ **à** (*fig*) receptive *ou* open to
permettre [pɛʀmɛtʀ(ə)] *vt* to allow, permit; ~ **à qn de faire/qch** to allow sb to do/sth; **se** ~ **de faire** to take the liberty of doing; **permettez!** excuse me!
permis [pɛʀmi] *nm* permit, licence; ~ **de chasse** hunting permit; ~ **(de conduire)** (driving) licence (BRIT), (driver's) license (US); ~ **de construire** planning permission (BRIT), building permit (US); ~ **de séjour** residence permit; ~ **de travail** work permit
permission [pɛʀmisjɔ̃] *nf* permission; (MIL) leave; **avoir la** ~ **de faire** to have permission to do; **en** ~ on leave
permuter [pɛʀmyte] *vt* to change around, permutate ♦ *vi* to change, swap
Pérou [peʀu] *nm* Peru
perpétuel, le [pɛʀpetɥɛl] *adj* perpetual; (ADMIN etc) permanent; for life
perpétuité [pɛʀpetɥite] *nf*: **à** ~ *adj, adv* for life; **être condamné à** ~ to receive a life sentence
perplexe [pɛʀplɛks(ə)] *adj* perplexed, puzzled
perquisitionner [pɛʀkizisjɔne] *vi* to carry out a search
perron [pɛʀɔ̃] *nm* steps *pl* (*in front of mansion etc*)
perroquet [pɛʀɔkɛ] *nm* parrot
perruche [pɛʀyʃ] *nf* budgerigar (BRIT), budgie (BRIT), parakeet (US)
perruque [pɛʀyk] *nf* wig
persan, e [pɛʀsɑ̃, -an] *adj* Persian
persécuter [pɛʀsekyte] *vt* to persecute
persévérer [pɛʀsevere] *vi* to persevere
persiennes [pɛʀsjɛn] *nfpl* (metal) shutters
persiflage [pɛʀsiflaʒ] *nm* mockery *no pl*
persil [pɛʀsi] *nm* parsley
Persique [pɛʀsik] *adj*: **le golfe** ~ the (Persian) Gulf
persistant, e [pɛʀsistɑ̃, -ɑ̃t] *adj* persistent; (*feuilles*) evergreen
persister [pɛʀsiste] *vi* to persist; ~ **à faire**

qch to persist in doing sth
personnage [pɛʀsɔnaʒ] *nm* (*notable*) personality; figure; (*individu*) character, individual; (THÉÂTRE) character; (PEINTURE) figure
personnalité [pɛʀsɔnalite] *nf* personality; (*personnage*) prominent figure
personne [pɛʀsɔn] *nf* person ♦ *pron* nobody, no one; (*quelqu'un*) anybody, anyone; ~**s** *nfpl* (*gens*) people *pl*; **il n'y a** ~ there's nobody there, there isn't anybody there; ~ **âgée** elderly person; **personnel, le** *adj* personal ♦ *nm* staff, personnel; **personnellement** *adv* personally
perspective [pɛʀspɛktiv] *nf* (ART) perspective; (*vue, coup d'œil*) view; (*point de vue*) viewpoint, angle; (*chose escomptée, envisagée*) prospect; **en** ~ in prospect
perspicace [pɛʀspikas] *adj* clear-sighted, gifted with (*ou* showing) insight
persuader [pɛʀsɥade] *vt*: ~ **qn (de/de faire)** to persuade sb (of/to do)
perte [pɛʀt(ə)] *nf* loss; (*de temps*) waste; (*fig: morale*) ruin; **à** ~ (COMM) at a loss; **à** ~ **de vue** as far as the eye can (*ou* could) see; ~ **sèche** dead loss; ~**s blanches** (vaginal) discharge *sg*
pertinemment [pɛʀtinamɑ̃] *adv* to the point; full well
pertinent, e [pɛʀtinɑ̃, -ɑ̃t] *adj* apt, relevant
perturbation [pɛʀtyʀbasjɔ̃] *nf* disruption; perturbation; ~ **(atmosphérique)** atmospheric disturbance
perturber [pɛʀtyʀbe] *vt* to disrupt; (PSYCH) to perturb, disturb
pervers, e [pɛʀvɛʀ, -ɛʀs(ə)] *adj* perverted, depraved; perverse
pervertir [pɛʀvɛʀtiʀ] *vt* to pervert
pesant, e [pəzɑ̃, -ɑ̃t] *adj* heavy; (*fig*) burdensome
pesanteur [pəzɑ̃tœʀ] *nf* gravity
pèse-personne [pɛzpɛʀsɔn] *nm* (bathroom) scales *pl*
peser [pəze] *vt* to weigh ♦ *vi* to be heavy; (*fig*) to carry weight; ~ **sur** (*fig*) to lie heavy on; to influence
pessimiste [pesimist(ə)] *adj* pessimistic ♦ *nm/f* pessimist
peste [pɛst(ə)] *nf* plague
pester [pɛste] *vi*: ~ **contre** to curse
pétale [petal] *nm* petal
pétanque [petɑ̃k] *nf* type of bowls
pétarader [petaʀade] *vi* to backfire
pétard [petaʀ] *nm* banger (BRIT), firecracker
péter [pete] *vi* (*fam: casser, sauter*) to burst; to bust; (*fam!*) to fart (*!*)
pétillant, e [petijɑ̃, -ɑ̃t] *adj* (*eau etc*) sparkling
pétiller [petije] *vi* (*flamme, bois*) to crackle; (*mousse, champagne*) to bubble; (*yeux*) to sparkle

petit, e [pəti, -it] *adj* (*gén*) small; (*main, objet, colline, en âge: enfant*) small, little; (*voyage*) short, little; (*bruit etc*) faint, slight; (*mesquin*) mean; **~s** *nmpl* (*d'un animal*) young *pl*; **faire des ~s** to have kittens (*ou* puppies *etc*); **les tout-petits** the little ones, the tiny tots; **~ à ~** bit by bit, gradually; **~(e) ami(e)** boyfriend/girlfriend; **~ déjeuner** breakfast; **~ pain** (bread) roll; **les ~es annonces** the small ads; **~s pois** garden peas; **~-bourgeois** (*f* **~-bourgeoise**: *péj*) *adj* middle-class; **~-fille** *nf* granddaughter; **~-fils** *nm* grandson

pétition [petisjɔ̃] *nf* petition

petits-enfants [pətizɑ̃fɑ̃] *nmpl* grandchildren

petit-suisse [pətisɥis] (*pl* **petits-suisses**) *nm small individual pot of cream cheese*

pétrin [petrɛ̃] *nm* kneading-trough; (*fig*): **dans le ~** in a jam *ou* fix

pétrir [petrir] *vt* to knead

pétrole [petrɔl] *nm* oil; (*pour lampe, réchaud etc*) paraffin (oil); **pétrolier, ière** *adj* oil *cpd* ♦ *nm* oil tanker

─────── MOT CLÉ ───────

peu [pø] *adv* **1** (*modifiant verbe, adjectif, adverbe*): **il boit ~** he doesn't drink (very) much; **il est ~ bavard** he's not very talkative; **~ avant/après** shortly before/afterwards

2 (*modifiant nom*): **~ de:** **~ de gens/d'arbres** few *ou* not (very) many people/trees; **il a ~ d'espoir** he hasn't (got) much hope, he has little hope; **pour ~ de temps** for (only) a short while

3: **~ à ~** little by little; **à ~ près** just about, more or less; **à ~ près 10 kg/10F** approximately 10 kg/10F

♦ *nm* **1**: **le ~ de gens qui** the few people who; **le ~ de sable qui** what little sand, the little sand which

2: **un ~** a little; **un petit ~** a little bit; **un ~ d'espoir** a little hope

♦ *pron*: **~ le savent** few know (it); **avant** *ou* **sous ~** shortly, before long; **de ~** (only) just

─────────────────────────

peuple [pœpl(ə)] *nm* people

peupler [pœple] *vt* (*pays, région*) to populate; (*étang*) to stock; (*suj: hommes, poissons*) to inhabit; (*fig: imagination, rêves*) to fill

peuplier [pøplije] *nm* poplar (tree)

peur [pœr] *nf* fear; **avoir ~** to be frightened *ou* afraid (of/of doing/that); **faire ~ à** to frighten; **de ~ de/que** for fear of/that; **peureux, euse** *adj* fearful, timorous

peut *vb voir* **pouvoir**

peut-être [pøtɛtr(ə)] *adv* perhaps, maybe; **~ que** perhaps, maybe; **~ bien qu'il fera/**

est he may well do/be

peux *etc vb voir* **pouvoir**

phare [far] *nm* (*en mer*) lighthouse; (*de véhicule*) headlight; **mettre ses ~s** to put on one's headlights; **~s de recul** reversing lights

pharmacie [farmasi] *nf* (*magasin*) chemist's (*BRIT*), pharmacy; (*officine*) pharmacy; (*de salle de bain*) medicine cabinet; **pharmacien, ne** *nm/f* pharmacist, chemist (*BRIT*)

phénomène [fenɔmɛn] *nm* phenomenon; (*monstre*) freak

philanthrope [filɑ̃trɔp] *nm/f* philanthropist

philatélie [filateli] *nf* philately, stamp collecting

philosophe [filɔzɔf] *nm/f* philosopher ♦ *adj* philosophical

philosophie [filɔzɔfi] *nf* philosophy

phobie [fɔbi] *nf* phobia

phonétique [fɔnetik] *nf* phonetics *sg*

phoque [fɔk] *nm* seal; (*fourrure*) sealskin

phosphorescent, e [fɔsfɔresɑ̃, -ɑ̃t] *adj* luminous

photo [fɔto] *nf* photo(graph); **en ~** in *ou* on a photograph; **prendre en ~** to take a photo of; **aimer la/faire de la ~** to like taking/take photos; **~ d'identité** passport photograph; **~copie** *nf* photocopying; **~copier** *vt* to photocopy; **~copieuse** [fɔtɔkɔpjøz] *nf* photocopier; **~graphe** *nm/f* photographer; **~graphie** *nf* (*procédé, technique*) photography; (*cliché*) photograph; **~graphier** *vt* to photograph

phrase [fraz] *nf* (*LING*) sentence; (*propos, MUS*) phrase

physicien, ne [fizisjɛ̃, -ɛn] *nm/f* physicist

physionomie [fizjɔnɔmi] *nf* face

physique [fizik] *adj* physical ♦ *nm* physique ♦ *nf* physics *sg*; **au ~** physically; **~ment** *adv* physically

piaffer [pjafe] *vi* to stamp

piailler [pjɑje] *vi* to squawk

pianiste [pjanist(ə)] *nm/f* pianist

piano [pjano] *nm* piano

pianoter [pjanɔte] *vi* to tinkle away (at the piano); (*tapoter*): **~ sur** to drum one's fingers on

pic [pik] *nm* (*instrument*) pick(axe); (*montagne*) peak; (*ZOOL*) woodpecker; **à ~** vertically; (*fig*) just at the right time

pichet [piʃɛ] *nm* jug

picorer [pikɔre] *vt* to peck

picoter [pikɔte] *vt* (*suj: oiseau*) to peck ♦ *vi* (*irriter*) to smart, prickle

pie [pi] *nf* magpie; (*fig*) chatterbox

pièce [pjɛs] *nf* (*d'un logement*) room; (*THÉÂTRE*) play; (*de mécanisme, machine*) part; (*de monnaie*) coin; (*COUTURE*) patch; (*document*) document; (*de drap, fragment, de collection*) piece; **dix francs ~** ten francs each; **vendre à la ~** to sell separately; **travailler/payer à la ~** to do piecework/

pay piece rate; **un maillot une ~** a one-piece swimsuit; **un deux-pièces cuisine** a two-room(ed) flat (*BRIT*) ou apartment (*US*) with kitchen; **~ à conviction** exhibit; **~ d'eau** ornamental lake ou pond; **~ d'identité: avez-vous un ~ d'identité?** have you got any (means of) identification?; **~ montée** tiered cake; **~s détachées** spares, (spare) parts; **~s justificatives** supporting documents

pied [pje] *nm* foot; (*de verre*) stem; (*de table*) leg; (*de lampe*) base; (*plante*) plant; **à ~ on** foot; **à ~ sec** without getting one's feet wet; **au ~ de la lettre** literally; **de ~ en cap** from head to foot; **en ~** (*portrait*) full-length; **avoir ~** to be able to touch the bottom, not to be out of one's depth; **avoir le ~ marin** to be a good sailor; **sur ~** (*debout, rétabli*) up and about; **mettre sur ~** (*entreprise*) to set up; **mettre à ~** to dismiss, to lay off; **~ de vigne** vine

piédestal, aux [pjedestal, -o] *nm* pedestal

pied-noir [pjenwaʀ] *nm* Algerian-born Frenchman

piège [pjɛʒ] *nm* trap; **prendre au ~** to trap; **piéger** (*avec une bombe*) to booby-trap; **lettre/voiture piégée** letter-/car-bomb

pierraille [pjeʀɑj] *nf* loose stones *pl*

pierre [pjɛʀ] *nf* stone; **~ à briquet** flint; **~ fine** semiprecious stone; **~ tombale** tombstone; **pierreries** [pjeʀʀi] *nfpl* gems, precious stones

piétiner [pjetine] *vi* (*trépigner*) to stamp (one's foot); (*marquer le pas*) to stand about; (*fig*) to be at a standstill ♦ *vt* to trample on

piéton, ne [pjetɔ̃, -ɔn] *nm/f* pedestrian; **piétonnier, ière** *adj:* **rue** ou **zone piétonnière** pedestrian precinct

pieu, x [pjø] *nm* post; (*pointu*) stake

pieuvre [pjœvʀ(ə)] *nf* octopus

pieux, euse [pjø, -øz] *adj* pious

piffer [pife] (*fam*) *vt:* **je ne peux pas le ~** I can't stand him

pigeon [piʒɔ̃] *nm* pigeon

piger [piʒe] (*fam*) *vi, vt* to understand

pigiste [piʒist(ə)] *nm/f* freelance(r)

pignon [piɲɔ̃] *nm* (*de mur*) gable; (*d'engrenage*) cog(wheel), gearwheel

pile [pil] *nf* (*tas*) pile; (*ÉLEC*) battery ♦ *adv* (*s'arrêter etc*) dead; **à deux heures ~** at two on the dot; **jouer à ~** ou **face** to toss up (for it); **~ ou face?** heads or tails?

piler [pile] *vt* to crush, pound

pileux, euse [pilø, -øz] *adj:* **système ~** (body) hair

pilier [pilje] *nm* pillar

piller [pije] *vt* to pillage, plunder, loot

pilon [pilɔ̃] *nm* pestle

pilote [pilɔt] *nm* pilot; (*de char, voiture*) driver ♦ *adj* pilot *cpd;* **~ de course** racing driver; **~ de ligne/d'essai/de chasse** air-

line/test/fighter pilot; **~r** [pilɔte] *vt* to pilot, fly; to drive

pilule [pilyl] *nf* pill; **prendre la ~** to be on the pill

piment [pimɑ̃] *nm* (*BOT*) pepper, capsicum; (*fig*) spice, piquancy

pimpant, e [pɛ̃pɑ̃, -ɑ̃t] *adj* spruce

pin [pɛ̃] *nm* pine (tree); (*bois*) pine(wood)

pinard [pinaʀ] (*fam*) *nm* (cheap) wine, plonk (*BRIT*)

pince [pɛ̃s] *nf* (*outil*) pliers *pl;* (*de homard, crabe*) pincer, claw; (*COUTURE: pli*) dart; **~ à épiler** tweezers *pl;* **~ à linge** clothes peg (*BRIT*) ou pin (*US*); **~ à sucre** sugar tongs *pl*

pincé, e [pɛ̃se] *adj* (*air*) stiff

pinceau, x [pɛ̃so] *nm* (paint)brush

pincée [pɛ̃se] *nf:* **une ~ de** a pinch of

pincer [pɛ̃se] *vt* to pinch; (*MUS: cordes*) to pluck; (*fam*) to nab

pincettes [pɛ̃sɛt] *nfpl* (*pour le feu*) (fire) tongs

pinède [pinɛd] *nf* pinewood, pine forest

pingouin [pɛ̃gwɛ̃] *nm* penguin

ping-pong [piŋpɔ̃g] ® *nm* table tennis

pingre [pɛ̃gʀ(ə)] *adj* niggardly

pinson [pɛ̃sɔ̃] *nm* chaffinch

pintade [pɛ̃tad] *nf* guinea-fowl

pioche [pjɔʃ] *nf* pickaxe; **piocher** *vt* to dig up (with a pickaxe)

piolet [pjɔlɛ] *nm* ice axe

pion [pjɔ̃] *nm* (*ÉCHECS*) pawn; (*DAMES*) piece

pionnier [pjɔnje] *nm* pioneer

pipe [pip] *nf* pipe

pipeau, x [pipo] *nm* (reed-)pipe

piquant, e [pikɑ̃, -ɑ̃t] *adj* (*barbe, rosier etc*) prickly; (*saveur, sauce*) hot, pungent; (*fig*) racy; biting ♦ *nm* (*épine*) thorn, prickle; (*fig*) spiciness, spice

pique [pik] *nf* pike; (*fig*) cutting remark ♦ *nm* (*CARTES: couleur*) spades *pl;* (*: carte*) spade

pique-nique [piknik] *nm* picnic

piquer [pike] *vt* (*percer*) to prick; (*planter*): **~ qch dans** to stick sth into; (*MÉD*) to give a jab to; (*: animal blessé etc*) to put to sleep; (*suj: insecte, fumée, ortie*) to sting; (*: poivre*) to burn; (*: froid*) to bite; (*COUTURE*) to machine (stitch); (*intérêt etc*) to arouse; (*fam*) to pick up; (*: voler*) to pinch; (*: arrêter*) to nab ♦ *vi* (*avion*) to go into a dive; **se ~ de faire** to pride o.s. on doing; **~ un galop/un cent mètres** to break into a gallop/put on a sprint

piquet [pikɛ] *nm* (*pieu*) post, stake; (*de tente*) peg; **~ de grève** (strike-) picket; **~ d'incendie** fire-fighting squad

piqûre [pikyʀ] *nf* (*d'épingle*) prick; (*d'ortie*) sting; (*de moustique*) bite; (*MÉD*) injection, shot (*US*); (*COUTURE*) (straight) stitch; straight stitching; **faire une ~ à qn** to give sb an injection

pirate [piʀat] *nm, adj* pirate; ~ **de l'air** hijacker

pire [piʀ] *adj* worse; (*superlatif*): **le(la)** ~ ... the worst ... ♦ *nm*: **le** ~ **(de)** the worst (of)

pis [pi] *nm* (*de vache*) udder; (*pire*): **le** ~ the worst ♦ *adj, adv* worse; **~-aller** *nm inv* stopgap

piscine [pisin] *nf* (swimming) pool; ~ **couverte** indoor (swimming) pool

pissenlit [pisãli] *nm* dandelion

pistache [pistaʃ] *nf* pistachio (nut)

piste [pist(ə)] *nf* (*d'un animal, sentier*) track, trail; (*indice*) lead; (*de stade, de magnétophone*) track; (*de cirque*) ring; (*de danse*) floor; (*de patinage*) rink; (*de ski*) run; (*AVIAT*) runway; ~ **cyclable** cycle track

pistolet [pistɔlɛ] *nm* (*arme*) pistol, gun; (*à peinture*) spray gun; ~ **à air comprimé** airgun; **~-mitrailleur** *nm* submachine gun

piston [pistɔ̃] *nm* (*TECH*) piston; **pistonner** *vt* (*candidat*) to pull strings for

piteux, euse [pitø, -øz] *adj* pitiful (*avant le nom*), sorry (*avant le nom*)

pitié [pitje] *nf* pity; **faire** ~ to inspire pity; **avoir** ~ **de** (*compassion*) to pity, feel sorry for; (*merci*) to have pity *ou* mercy on

piton [pitɔ̃] *nm* (*clou*) peg; ~ **rocheux** rocky outcrop

pitoyable [pitwajabl(ə)] *adj* pitiful

pitre [pitʀ(ə)] *nm* clown; **pitrerie** *nf* tomfoolery *no pl*

pittoresque [pitɔʀɛsk(ə)] *adj* picturesque

pivot [pivo] *nm* pivot; **pivoter** *vi* to swivel; to revolve

P.J. *sigle f* (= *police judiciaire*) ≈ CID (*BRIT*), ≈ FBI (*US*)

placard [plakaʀ] *nm* (*armoire*) cupboard; (*affiche*) poster, notice; **~er** *vt* (*affiche*) to put up

place [plas] *nf* (*emplacement, situation, classement*) place; (*de ville, village*) square; (*espace libre*) room, space; (*de parking*) space; (*siège: de train, cinéma, voiture*) seat; (*emploi*) job; **en** ~ (*mettre*) in its place; **sur** ~ on the spot; **faire** ~ **à** to give way to; **faire de la** ~ **à** to make room for; **ça prend de la** ~ it takes up a lot of room *ou* space; **à la** ~ **de** in place of, instead of; **il y a 20 ~s assises/debout** there are 20 seats/there is standing room for 20

placement [plasmã] *nm* placing; (*FINANCE*) investment; **bureau de** ~ employment agency

placer [plase] *vt* to place; (*convive, spectateur*) to seat; (*capital, argent*) to place, invest; (*dans la conversation*) to put *ou* get in; **se** ~ **au premier rang** to go and stand (*ou* sit) in the first row

plafond [plafɔ̃] *nm* ceiling

plafonner [plafɔne] *vi* to reach one's (*ou* a) ceiling

plage [plaʒ] *nf* beach; (*fig*) band, bracket; (*de disque*) track, band; ~ **arrière** (*AUTO*) parcel *ou* back shelf

plagiat [plaʒja] *nm* plagiarism

plaider [plede] *vi* (*avocat*) to plead; (*plaignant*) to go to court, litigate ♦ *vt* to plead; ~ **pour** (*fig*) to speak for; **plaidoyer** *nm* (*JUR*) speech for the defence; (*fig*) plea

plaie [plɛ] *nf* wound

plaignant, e [plɛɲã, -ãt] *nm/f* plaintiff

plaindre [plɛ̃dʀ(ə)] *vt* to pity, feel sorry for; **se** ~ *vi* (*gémir*) to moan; (*protester, rouspéter*): **se** ~ **(à qn) (de)** to complain (to sb) (about); (*souffrir*): **se** ~ **de** to complain of

plaine [plɛn] *nf* plain

plain-pied [plɛ̃pje] *adv*: **de** ~ **(avec)** on the same level (as)

plainte [plɛ̃t] *nf* (*gémissement*) moan, groan; (*doléance*) complaint; **porter** ~ to lodge a complaint

plaire [plɛʀ] *vi* to be a success, be successful; to please; ~ **à**: **cela me plaît** I like it; **se** ~ **quelque part** to like being somewhere *ou* like it somewhere; **s'il vous plaît** please

plaisance [plɛzãs] *nf* (*aussi*: *navigation de* ~) (pleasure) sailing, yachting

plaisant, e [plɛzã, -ãt] *adj* pleasant; (*histoire, anecdote*) amusing

plaisanter [plɛzãte] *vi* to joke; **plaisanterie** *nf* joke; joking *no pl*

plaise *etc vb voir* **plaire**

plaisir [plɛziʀ] *nm* pleasure; **faire** ~ **à qn** (*délibérément*) to be nice to sb, please sb; (*suj: cadeau, nouvelle etc*): **ceci me fait** ~ I'm delighted *ou* very pleased with this; **pour le** *ou* **par** ~ for pleasure

plaît *vb voir* **plaire**

plan, e [plã, -an] *adj* flat ♦ *nm* plan; (*GÉOM*) plane; (*fig*) level, plane; (*CINÉMA*) shot; **au premier/second** ~ in the foreground/middle distance; **à l'arrière** ~ in the background; ~ **d'eau** lake; pond

planche [plãʃ] *nf* (*pièce de bois*) plank, (wooden) board; (*illustration*) plate; **les ~s** *nfpl* (*THÉÂTRE*) the stage *sg*, the boards; ~ **à repasser** ironing board; ~ **à roulettes** skateboard; ~ **de salut** (*fig*) sheet anchor

plancher [plãʃe] *nm* floor; floorboards *pl*; (*fig*) minimum level ♦ *vi* to work hard

planer [plane] *vi* to glide; ~ **sur** (*fig*) to hang over; to hover above

planète [planɛt] *nf* planet

planeur [planœʀ] *nm* glider

planification [planifikɑsjɔ̃] *nf* (economic) planning

planifier [planifje] *vt* to plan

planning [planiŋ] *nm* programme, schedule; ~ **familial** family planning

planque [plãk] (*fam*) *nf* (*emploi peu fatigant*) cushy (*BRIT*) *ou* easy number; (*cachette*) hiding place

plant [plɑ̃] nm seedling, young plant

plante [plɑ̃t] nf plant; ~ **d'appartement** house ou pot plant; ~ **du pied** sole (of the foot)

planter [plɑ̃te] vt (plante) to plant; (enfoncer) to hammer ou drive in; (tente) to put up, pitch; (fam) to dump; to ditch; **se** ~ (fam: se tromper) to get it wrong

plantureux, euse [plɑ̃tyʀø, -øz] adj copious, lavish; (femme) buxom

plaque [plak] nf plate; (de verglas, d'eczéma) patch; (avec inscription) plaque; ~ **chauffante** hotplate; ~ **de chocolat** bar of chocolate; ~ (**minéralogique** ou **d'immatriculation**) number (BRIT) ou license (US) plate; ~ **tournante** (fig) centre

plaqué, e [plake] adj: ~ **or/argent** gold-/silver-plated; ~ **acajou** veneered in mahogany

plaquer [plake] vt (aplatir): ~ **qch sur** ou **contre** to make sth stick ou cling to; (RUG-BY) to bring down; (fam: laisser tomber) to drop

plaquette [plakɛt] nf (de chocolat) bar; (beurre) pack(et)

plastic [plastik] nm plastic explosive

plastique [plastik] adj, nm plastic

plastiquer [plastike] vt to blow up (with a plastic bomb)

plat, e [pla, -at] adj flat; (cheveux) straight; (personne, livre) dull ♦ nm (récipient, CU-LIN) dish; (d'un repas): **le premier** ~ the first course; **à** ~ **ventre** face down; **à** ~ (pneu, batterie) flat; (personne) dead beat; ~ **cuisiné** pre-cooked meal; ~ **de résistance** main course; ~ **du jour** dish of the day

platane [platan] nm plane tree

plateau, x [plato] nm (support) tray; (GÉO) plateau; (de tourne-disques) turntable; (CI-NÉMA) set; ~ **à fromages** cheeseboard

plate-bande [platbɑ̃d] nf flower bed

plate-forme [platfɔʀm(ə)] nf platform; ~ **de forage/pétrolière** drilling/oil rig

platine [platin] nm platinum ♦ nf (d'un tourne-disque) turntable

plâtras [plɑtʀa] nm rubble no pl

plâtre [plɑtʀ(ə)] nm (matériau) plaster; (statue) plaster statue; (MÉD) (plaster) cast; **avoir un bras dans le** ~ to have an arm in plaster

plein, e [plɛ̃, -ɛn] adj full; (porte, roue) solid; (chienne, jument) big (with young) ♦ nm: **faire le** ~ (**d'essence**) to fill up (with petrol); **à** ~**es mains** (ramasser) in handfuls; (empoigner) firmly; **à** ~ **régime** at maximum revs; (fig) full steam; **à** ~ **temps** full-time; **en** ~ **air** in the open air; **en** ~ **soleil** in direct sunlight; **en** ~e **nuit/rue** in the middle of the night/street; **en** ~ **jour** in broad daylight; **en** ~ **sur** right on; **plein-emploi** nm full employment

plénitude [plenityd] nf fullness

pleurer [plœʀe] vi to cry; (yeux) to water ♦ vt to mourn (for); ~ **sur** to lament (over), to bemoan

pleurnicher [plœʀniʃe] vi to snivel, whine

pleurs [plœʀ] nmpl: **en** ~ in tears

pleut vb voir **pleuvoir**

pleuvoir [pløvwaʀ] vb impers to rain ♦ vi (fig): ~ (**sur**) to shower down (upon); to be showered upon; **il pleut** it's raining

pli [pli] nm fold; (de jupe) pleat; (de pantalon) crease; (aussi: faux ~) crease; (enveloppe) envelope; (lettre) letter; (CARTES) trick

pliant, e [plijɑ̃, -ɑ̃t] adj folding ♦ nm folding stool, campstool

plier [plije] vt to fold; (pour ranger) to fold up; (table pliante) to fold down; (genou, bras) to bend ♦ vi to bend; (fig) to yield; **se** ~ **à** to submit to

plinthe [plɛ̃t] nf skirting board

plisser [plise] vt (rider, chiffonner) to crease; (jupe) to put pleats in

plomb [plɔ̃] nm (métal) lead; (d'une cartouche) (lead) shot; (PÊCHE) sinker; (sceau) (lead) seal; (ÉLEC) fuse; **sans** ~ (essence etc) unleaded

plombage [plɔ̃baʒ] nm (de dent) filling

plomber [plɔ̃be] vt (canne, ligne) to weight (with lead); (dent) to fill

plomberie [plɔ̃bʀi] nf plumbing

plombier [plɔ̃bje] nm plumber

plongeant, e [plɔ̃ʒɑ̃, -ɑ̃t] adj (vue) from above; (tir, décolleté) plunging

plongée [plɔ̃ʒe] nf (SPORT) diving no pl; (: sans scaphandre) skin diving

plongeoir [plɔ̃ʒwaʀ] nm diving board

plongeon [plɔ̃ʒɔ̃] nm dive

plonger [plɔ̃ʒe] vi to dive ♦ vt: ~ **qch dans** to plunge sth into

ployer [plwaje] vt to bend ♦ vi to sag; to bend

plu pp de **plaire; pleuvoir**

pluie [plɥi] nf rain; (fig): ~ **de** shower of

plume [plym] nf feather; (pour écrire) (pen) nib; (fig) pen; ~**r** [plyme] vt to pluck; **plumier** [plymje] nm pencil box

plupart [plypaʀ]: **la** ~ pron the majority, most (of them); **la** ~ **des** most, the majority of; **la** ~ **du temps/d'entre nous** most of the time/of us; **pour la** ~ for the most part, mostly

pluriel [plyʀjɛl] nm plural

plus[1] [ply] vb voir **plaire**

─────────── MOT CLÉ

plus[2] [ply] adv 1 (forme négative): **ne ... ~** no more, no longer; **je n'ai ~ d'argent** I've got no more money ou no money left; **il ne travaille ~** he's no longer working, he doesn't work any more

2 [ply, plyz, + voyelle] (comparatif) more, ...+er; (superlatif): **le** ~ the most, the

...+est; ~ **grand/intelligent (que)** bigger/more intelligent (than); **le** ~ **grand/intelligent** the biggest/most intelligent; **tout au** ~ at the very most

3 [plys] (*davantage*) more; **il travaille** ~ **(que)** he works more (than); ~ **il travaille,** ~ **il est heureux** the more he works, the happier he is; ~ **de pain** more bread; ~ **de 10 personnes** more than 10 people, over 10 people; **3 heures de** ~ **que** 3 hours more than; **de** ~ what's more, moreover; **3 kilos en** ~ 3 kilos more; **en** ~ **de** in addition to; **de** ~ **en** ~ more and more; ~ **ou moins** more or less; **ni** ~ **ni moins** no more, no less

♦ *prép* [plys]: **4** ~ **2** 4 plus 2

plusieurs [plyzjœR] *dét, pron* several; **ils sont** ~ there are several of them
plus-que-parfait [plyskǝpaRfɛ] *nm* pluperfect, past perfect
plus-value [plyvaly] *nf* appreciation; capital gain; surplus
plut *vb voir* **plaire**
plutôt [plyto] *adv* rather; **je ferais** ~ **ceci** I'd rather *ou* sooner do this; **fais** ~ **comme ça** try this way instead, you'd better try this way; ~ **que (de) faire** rather than *ou* instead of doing
pluvieux, euse [plyvjø, -øz] *adj* rainy, wet
PMU *sigle m* (= *pari mutuel urbain*) system of betting on horses; (*café*) betting agency
pneu [pnø] *nm* tyre (*BRIT*), tire (*US*)
pneumatique [pnømatik] *nm* tyre (*BRIT*), tire (*US*)
pneumonie [pnømɔni] *nf* pneumonia
poche [pɔʃ] *nf* pocket; (*déformation*): **faire une** *ou* **des** ~**(s)** to bag; (*sous les yeux*) bag, pouch; **de** ~ pocket *cpd*
pocher [pɔʃe] *vt* (*CULIN*) to poach
pochette [pɔʃɛt] *nf* (*de timbres*) wallet, envelope; (*d'aiguilles etc*) case; (*mouchoir*) breast pocket handkerchief; ~ **de disque** record sleeve
poêle [pwal] *nm* stove ♦ *nf*: ~ (**à frire**) frying pan
poêlon [pwalɔ̃] *nm* casserole
poème [pɔɛm] *nm* poem
poésie [pɔezi] *nf* (*poème*) poem; (*art*): **la** ~ poetry
poète [pɔɛt] *nm* poet
poids [pwa] *nm* weight; (*SPORT*) shot; **vendre au** ~ to sell by weight; **prendre du** ~ to put on weight; ~ **lourd** (*camion*) lorry (*BRIT*), truck (*US*)
poignard [pwaɲaR] *nm* dagger; ~**er** *vt* to stab, knife
poigne [pwaɲ] *nf* grip; (*fig*): **à** ~ firmhanded
poignée [pwaɲe] *nf* (*de sel etc, fig*) handful; (*de couvercle, porte*) handle; ~ **de main** handshake

poignet [pwaɲɛ] *nm* (*ANAT*) wrist; (*de chemise*) cuff
poil [pwal] *nm* (*ANAT*) hair; (*de pinceau, brosse*) bristle; (*de tapis*) strand; (*pelage*) coat; **à** ~ (*fam*) starkers; **au** ~ (*fam*) hunky-dory; **poilu, e** *adj* hairy
poinçon [pwɛ̃sɔ̃] *nm* awl; bodkin; (*marque*) hallmark; **poinçonner** *vt* to stamp; to hallmark; (*billet*) to punch
poing [pwɛ̃] *nm* fist
point [pwɛ̃] *nm* (*marque, signe*) dot; (: de ponctuation*) full stop, period (*US*); (*moment, de score etc, fig*: *question*) point; (*endroit*) spot; (*COUTURE, TRICOT*) stitch ♦ *adv* = **pas**; **faire le** ~ (*NAVIG*) to take a bearing; (*fig*) to take stock (of the situation); **en tout** ~ in every respect; **sur le** ~ **de faire** (just) about to do; **à tel** ~ **que** so much so that; **mettre au** ~ (*mécanisme, procédé*) to develop; (*appareil-photo*) to focus; (*affaire*) to settle; **à** ~ (*CULIN*) medium; just right; **à** ~ (*nommé*) just at the right time; ~ (**de côté**) stitch (*pain*); ~ **d'eau** spring; water point; ~ **d'exclamation** exclamation mark; ~ **d'interrogation** question mark; ~ **de repère** landmark; (*dans le temps*) point of reference; ~ **de vente** retail outlet; ~ **de vue** viewpoint; (*fig*: *opinion*) point of view; ~ **faible** weak point; ~ **final** full stop, period; ~ **mort** (*AUTO*): **au** ~ **mort** in neutral; ~**s de suspension** suspension points
pointe [pwɛ̃t] *nf* point; (*fig*): **une** ~ **de** a hint of; **être à la** ~ **de** (*fig*) to be in the forefront of; **sur la** ~ **des pieds** on tiptoe; **en** ~ *adv* (*tailler*) into a point ♦ *adj* pointed, tapered; **de** ~ (*technique etc*) leading; **heures/jours de** ~ peak hours/days; ~ **de vitesse** burst of speed
pointer [pwɛ̃te] *vt* (*cocher*) to tick off; (*employés etc*) to check in; (*diriger: canon, doigt*): ~ **vers qch** to point at sth ♦ *vi* (*employé*) to clock in
pointillé [pwɛ̃tije] *nm* (*trait*) dotted line
pointilleux, euse [pwɛ̃tijø, -øz] *adj* particular, pernickety
pointu, e [pwɛ̃ty] *adj* pointed; (*clou*) sharp; (*voix*) shrill; (*analyse*) precise
pointure [pwɛ̃tyR] *nf* size
point-virgule [pwɛ̃viRgyl] *nm* semi-colon
poire [pwaR] *nf* pear; (*fam: péj*) mug
poireau, x [pwaRo] *nm* leek
poirier [pwaRje] *nm* pear tree
pois [pwa] *nm* (*BOT*) pea; (*sur une étoffe*) dot, spot; **à** ~ (*cravate etc*) spotted, polka-dot *cpd*
poison [pwazɔ̃] *nm* poison
poisse [pwas] *nf* rotten luck
poisseux, euse [pwasø, -øz] *adj* sticky
poisson [pwasɔ̃] *nm* fish *gén inv*; **les P~s** (*signe*) Pisces; ~ **d'avril!** April fool!; ~ **rouge** goldfish; **poissonnerie** *nf* fish-shop;

poissonnier, ière *nm/f* fishmonger (*BRIT*), fish merchant (*US*)

poitrine [pwatʀin] *nf* chest; (*seins*) bust, bosom; (*CULIN*) breast; ~ **de bœuf** brisket

poivre [pwavʀ(ə)] *nm* pepper; **poivrier** *nm* (*ustensile*) pepperpot

poivron [pwavʀõ] *nm* pepper, capsicum

polar [pɔlaʀ] *nm* (*fam*) detective novel

pôle [pol] *nm* (*GÉO, ÉLEC*) pole

poli, e [pɔli] *adj* polite; (*lisse*) smooth; polished

police [pɔlis] *nf* police; **peine de simple ~** sentence given by magistrates' or police court; ~ **d'assurance** insurance policy; ~ **des mœurs** vice squad; ~ **judiciaire** ≈ Criminal Investigation Department (*BRIT*), ≈ Federal Bureau of Investigation (*US*); ~ **secours** ≈ emergency services *pl* (*BRIT*), ≈ paramedics *pl* (*US*)

policier, ière [pɔlisje, -jɛʀ] *adj* police *cpd* ♦ *nm* policeman; (*aussi: roman ~*) detective novel

polio [pɔljo] *nf* polio

polir [pɔliʀ] *vt* to polish

polisson, ne [pɔlisõ, -ɔn] *adj* naughty

politesse [pɔlites] *nf* politeness

politicien, ne [pɔlitisjɛ̃, -ɛn] *nm/f* politician

politique [pɔlitik] *adj* political ♦ *nf* (*science, pratique, activité*) politics *sg*; (*mesures, méthode*) policies *pl*; **politiser** *vt* to politicize

pollen [pɔlɛn] *nm* pollen

pollution [pɔlysjõ] *nf* pollution

polo [pɔlo] *nm* polo shirt

Pologne [pɔlɔɲ] *nf*: **la ~** Poland; **polonais, e** *adj, nm* (*LING*) Polish; **Polonais, e** *nm/f* Pole

poltron, ne [pɔltʀõ, -ɔn] *adj* cowardly

polycopier [pɔlikɔpje] *vt* to duplicate

Polynésie [pɔlinezi] *nf*: **la ~** Polynesia

polyvalent, e [pɔlivalɑ̃, -ɑ̃t] *adj* versatile; multi-purpose

pommade [pɔmad] *nf* ointment, cream

pomme [pɔm] *nf* (*BOT*) apple; **tomber dans les ~s** (*fam*) to pass out; ~ **d'Adam** Adam's apple; ~ **d'arrosoir** (sprinkler) rose; ~ **de pin** pine *ou* fir cone; ~ **de terre** potato

pommeau, x [pɔmo] *nm* (*boule*) knob; (*de selle*) pommel

pommette [pɔmɛt] *nf* cheekbone

pommier [pɔmje] *nm* apple tree

pompe [põp] *nf* pump; (*faste*) pomp (and ceremony); ~ **à essence** petrol (*BRIT*) *ou* gas (*US*) pump; ~**s funèbres** funeral parlour *sg*, undertaker's *sg*

pomper [põpe] *vt* to pump; (*évacuer*) to pump out; (*aspirer*) to pump up; (*absorber*) to soak up

pompeux, euse [põpø, -øz] *adj* pompous

pompier [põpje] *nm* fireman

pompiste [põpist(ə)] *nm/f* petrol (*BRIT*) *ou* gas (*US*) pump attendant

poncer [põse] *vt* to sand (down)

ponctuation [põktɥasjõ] *nf* punctuation

ponctuel, le [põktɥɛl] *adj* (*à l'heure, aussi TECH*) punctual; (*fig: opération etc*) one-off, single; (*scrupuleux*) punctilious, meticulous

ponctuer [põktɥe] *vt* to punctuate

pondéré, e [põdeʀe] *adj* level-headed, composed

pondre [põdʀ(ə)] *vt* to lay; (*fig*) to produce

poney [pɔnɛ] *nm* pony

pont [põ] *nm* bridge; (*AUTO*) axle; (*NAVIG*) deck; **faire le ~** to take the extra day off; ~ **de graissage** ramp (*in garage*); ~ **suspendu** suspension bridge; **P~s et Chaussées** highways department

pont-levis [põlvi] *nm* drawbridge

pop [pɔp] *adj inv* pop

populace [pɔpylas] (*péj*) *nf* rabble

populaire [pɔpylɛʀ] *adj* popular; (*manifestation*) mass *cpd*; (*milieux, clientèle*) working-class

population [pɔpylɑsjõ] *nf* population; ~ **active** *nf* working population

populeux, euse [pɔpylø, -øz] *adj* densely populated

porc [pɔʀ] *nm* (*ZOOL*) pig; (*CULIN*) pork; (*peau*) pigskin

porcelaine [pɔʀsəlɛn] *nf* porcelain, china; piece of china(ware)

porc-épic [pɔʀkepik] *nm* porcupine

porche [pɔʀʃ(ə)] *nm* porch

porcherie [pɔʀʃəʀi] *nf* pigsty

pore [pɔʀ] *nm* pore

porno [pɔʀno] *adj abr* pornographic, porno

port [pɔʀ] *nm* (*NAVIG*) harbour, port; (*ville*) port; (*de l'uniforme etc*) wearing; (*pour lettre*) postage; (*pour colis, aussi: posture*) carriage; ~ **d'arme** (*JUR*) carrying of a firearm

portable [pɔʀtabl(ə)] *nm* (*COMPUT*) laptop (computer)

portail [pɔʀtaj] *nm* gate; (*de cathédrale*) portal

portant, e [pɔʀtɑ̃, -ɑ̃t] *adj*: **bien/mal ~** in good/poor health

portatif, ive [pɔʀtatif, -iv] *adj* portable

porte [pɔʀt(ə)] *nf* (*d'une arme*) range; (*fig*) door; (*de ville, forteresse, SKI*) gate; **mettre à la ~** to throw out; ~ **à ~** *nm* door-to-door selling; ~ **d'entrée** front door; ~**-à-faux** *nm*: **en ~-à-faux** cantilevered; (*fig*) in an awkward position; ~**-avions** *nm inv* aircraft carrier; ~**-bagages** *nm inv* luggage rack; ~**-clefs** *nm inv* key ring; ~**-documents** *nm inv* attaché *ou* document case

portée [pɔʀte] *nf* (*d'une arme*) range; (*fig*) impact, import; scope, capability; (*de chatte etc*) litter; (*MUS*) stave, staff; **à/hors de ~ (de)** within/out of reach (of); **à ~ de (la) main** within (arm's) reach; **à ~ de voix**

within earshot; **à la ~ de qn** *(fig)* at sb's level, within sb's capabilities

porte: **~-fenêtre** *nf* French window; **~feuille** *nm* wallet; *(POL, BOURSE)* portfolio; **~-manteau, x** *nm* coat hanger; coat rack; **~-mine** *nm* propelling *(BRIT)* ou mechanical *(US)* pencil; **~-monnaie** *nm inv* purse; **~-parole** *nm inv* spokesman

porter [pɔʀte] *vt* to carry; *(sur soi: vêtement, barbe, bague)* to wear; *(fig: responsabilité etc)* to bear, carry; *(inscription, marque, titre, patronyme: suj: arbre, fruits, fleurs)* to bear; *(apporter)*: ~ **qch quelque part/à** **qn** to take sth somewhere/to sb ♦ *vi (voix, regard, canon)* to carry; *(coup, argument)* to hit home; **se ~** *vi (se sentir)*: **se ~ bien/mal** to be well/unwell; ~ **sur** *(peser)* to rest on; *(accent)* to fall on; *(conférence etc)* to concern; *(heurter)* to strike; **être porté à faire** to be apt ou inclined to do; **se faire ~ malade** to report sick; ~ **la main à son chapeau** to raise one's hand to one's hat; ~ **son effort sur** to direct one's efforts towards; ~ **à croire** to lead one to believe

porte-serviettes [pɔʀtsɛʀvjɛt] *nm inv* towel rail

porteur [pɔʀtœʀ] *nm (de bagages)* porter; *(de chèque)* bearer

porte-voix [pɔʀtəvwa] *nm inv* megaphone

portier [pɔʀtje] *nm* doorman

portière [pɔʀtjɛʀ] *nf* door

portillon [pɔʀtijɔ̃] *nm* gate

portion [pɔʀsjɔ̃] *nf (part)* portion, share; *(partie)* portion, section

portique [pɔʀtik] *nm (RAIL)* gantry

porto [pɔʀto] *nm* port (wine)

portrait [pɔʀtʀɛ] *nm* portrait; photograph; **portrait-robot** *nm* Identikit ® ou photofit ® picture

portuaire [pɔʀtɥɛʀ] *adj* port *cpd*, harbour *cpd*

portugais, e [pɔʀtygɛ, -ɛz] *adj, nm/f* Portuguese

Portugal [pɔʀtygal] *nm*: **le ~** Portugal

pose [poz] *nf* laying; hanging; *(attitude, d'un modèle)* pose; *(PHOTO)* exposure

posé, e [poze] *adj* serious

poser [poze] *vt (déposer)*: ~ **qch (sur)/qn à** to put sth down (on)/drop sb at; *(placer)*: ~ **qch sur/quelque part** to put sth on/somewhere; *(installer: moquette, carrelage)* to lay; *(rideaux, papier peint)* to hang; *(question)* to ask; *(principe, conditions)* to lay ou set down; *(problème)* to formulate; *(difficulté)* to pose ♦ *vi (modèle)* to pose; **se ~** *vi (oiseau, avion)* to land; *(question)* to arise

positif, ive [pozitif, -iv] *adj* positive

position [pozisjɔ̃] *nf* position; **prendre ~** *(fig)* to take a stand

posologie [pozɔlɔʒi] *nf* directions for use, dosage

posséder [pɔsede] *vt* to own, possess; *(qualité, talent)* to have, possess; *(bien connaître: métier, langue)* to have mastered, have a thorough knowledge of; *(sexuellement, aussi: suj: colère etc)* to possess; **possession** *nf* ownership *no pl*; possession

possibilité [pɔsibilite] *nf* possibility; **~s** *nfpl (moyens)* means; *(potentiel)* potential *sg*

possible [pɔsibl(ə)] *adj* possible; *(projet, entreprise)* feasible ♦ *nm*: **faire son ~** to do all one can, do one's utmost; **le plus/moins de livres ~** as many/few books as possible; **le plus/moins d'eau ~** as much/little water as possible; **dès que ~** as soon as possible

postal, e, aux [pɔstal, -o] *adj* postal

poste [pɔst(ə)] *nf (service)* post, postal service; *(administration, bureau)* post office ♦ *nm (fonction, MIL)* post; *(TÉL)* extension; *(de radio etc)* set; **mettre à la ~** to post; **P~s, Télécommunications et Télédiffusion** postal and telecommunications service; ~ **d'essence** *nm* petrol ou filling station; ~ **d'incendie** *nm* fire point; ~ **de pilotage** *nm* cockpit; ~ **(de police)** *nm* police station; ~ **de secours** *nm* first-aid post; ~ **de travail** *nm* work station; **poste restante** *nf* poste restante *(BRIT)*, general delivery *(US)*

poster¹ [pɔste] *vt* to post

poster² [pɔstɛʀ] *nm* poster

postérieur, e [pɔsteʀjœʀ] *adj (date)* later; *(partie)* back ♦ *nm (fam)* behind

posthume [pɔstym] *adj* posthumous

postiche [pɔstiʃ] *nm* hairpiece

postuler [pɔstyle] *vt (emploi)* to apply for, put in for

posture [pɔstyʀ] *nf* posture; position

pot [po] *nm* jar, pot; *(en plastique, carton)* carton; *(en métal)* tin; **boire** ou **prendre un ~** *(fam)* to have a drink; ~ **(de chambre)** *(chamber)pot; ~ **d'échappement** exhaust pipe; ~ **de fleurs** plant pot, flowerpot; *(plante)* pot plant

potable [pɔtabl(ə)] *adj*: **eau (non) ~** (non-)drinking water

potage [pɔtaʒ] *nm* soup; soup course

potager, ère [pɔtaʒe, -ɛʀ] *adj (plante)* edible, vegetable *cpd*; **(jardin)** ~ kitchen ou vegetable garden

pot-au-feu [pɔtofø] *nm inv* (beef) stew

pot-de-vin [pɔdvɛ̃] *nm* bribe

pote [pɔt] *(fam) nm* pal

poteau, x [pɔto] *nm* post; ~ **indicateur** signpost

potelé, e [pɔtle] *adj* plump, chubby

potence [pɔtɑ̃s] *nf* gallows *sg*

potentiel, le [pɔtɑ̃sjɛl] *adj, nm* potential

poterie [pɔtʀi] *nf* pottery; piece of pottery

potier [pɔtje] *nm* potter
potins [pɔtɛ̃] *nmpl* gossip *sg*
potiron [pɔtirɔ̃] *nm* pumpkin
pou, x [pu] *nm* louse
poubelle [pubɛl] *nf* (dust)bin
pouce [pus] *nm* thumb
poudre [pudʀ(ə)] *nf* powder; (*fard*) (face) powder; (*explosif*) gunpowder; **en ~: café en ~** instant coffee; **lait en ~** dried *ou* powdered milk; **poudrier** *nm* (powder) compact
pouffer [pufe] *vi:* **~ (de rire)** to snigger; to giggle
pouilleux, euse [pujø, -øz] *adj* flea-ridden; (*fig*) grubby; seedy
poulailler [pulaje] *nm* henhouse
poulain [pulɛ̃] *nm* foal; (*fig*) protégé
poule [pul] *nf* (ZOOL) hen; (CULIN) (boiling) fowl
poulet [pulɛ] *nm* chicken; (*fam*) cop
poulie [puli] *nf* pulley; block
pouls [pu] *nm* pulse; **prendre le ~ de qn** to feel sb's pulse
poumon [pumɔ̃] *nm* lung
poupe [pup] *nf* stern; **en ~** astern
poupée [pupe] *nf* doll
poupon [pupɔ̃] *nm* babe-in-arms; **pouponnière** *nf* crèche, day nursery
pour [puʀ] *prép* for ♦ *nm*: **le ~ et le contre** the pros and cons; **~ faire** (so as) to do, in order to do; **~ avoir fait** for having done; **~ que** so that, in order that; **~ 100 francs d'essence** 100 francs' worth of petrol; **~ cent** per cent; **~ ce qui est de** as for
pourboire [puʀbwaʀ] *nm* tip
pourcentage [puʀsɑ̃taʒ] *nm* percentage
pourchasser [puʀʃase] *vt* to pursue
pourparlers [puʀpaʀle] *nmpl* talks, negotiations
pourpre [puʀpʀ(ə)] *adj* crimson
pourquoi [puʀkwa] *adv, conj* why ♦ *nm inv:* **le ~ (de)** the reason (for)
pourrai *etc vb voir* **pouvoir**
pourri, e [puʀi] *adj* rotten
pourrir [puʀiʀ] *vi* to rot; (*fruit*) to go rotten *ou* bad ♦ *vt* to rot; (*fig*) to spoil thoroughly; **pourriture** *nf* rot
pourrons *etc vb voir* **pouvoir**
poursuite [puʀsɥit] *nf* pursuit, chase; **~s** *nfpl* (JUR) legal proceedings
poursuivre [puʀsɥivʀ(ə)] *vt* to pursue, chase (after); (*relancer*) to hound, harry; (*obséder*) to haunt; (JUR) to bring proceedings against, prosecute; (: *au civil*) to sue; (*but*) to strive towards; (*voyage, études*) to carry on with, continue ♦ *vi* to carry on, go on; **se ~** *vi* to go on, continue
pourtant [puʀtɑ̃] *adv* yet; **c'est ~ facile** (and) yet it's easy
pourtour [puʀtuʀ] *nm* perimeter
pourvoir [puʀvwaʀ] *vt:* **~ qch/qn de** to equip sth/sb with ♦ *vi:* **~ à** to provide for;

(*emploi*) to fill; **se ~** *vi* (JUR): **se ~ en cassation** to take one's case to the Court of Appeal
pourvoyeur [puʀvwajœʀ] *nm* supplier
pourvu, e [puʀvy] *adj:* **~ de** equipped with; **~ que** (*si*) provided that, so long as; (*espérons que*) let's hope (that)
pousse [pus] *nf* growth; (*bourgeon*) shoot
poussé, e [puse] *adj* exhaustive
poussée [puse] *nf* thrust; (*coup*) push; (MÉD) eruption; (*fig*) upsurge
pousser [puse] *vt* to push; (*inciter*): **~ qn à** to urge *ou* press sb to +*infin*; (*acculer*): **~ qn à** to drive sb to; (*émettre: cri etc*) to give; (*stimuler*) to urge on; to drive hard; (*poursuivre*) to carry on (further) ♦ *vi* to push; (*croître*) to grow; **se ~** *vi* to move over; **faire ~** (*plante*) to grow
poussette [pusɛt] *nf* (*voiture d'enfant*) push chair (BRIT), stroller (US)
poussière [pusjɛʀ] *nf* dust; (*grain*) speck of dust; **poussiéreux, euse** *adj* dusty
poussin [pusɛ̃] *nm* chick
poutre [putʀ(ə)] *nf* beam; (*en fer, ciment armé*) girder

─────────── MOT CLÉ ───────────

pouvoir [puvwaʀ] *nm* power; (POL: *dirigeants*): **le ~** those in power; **les ~s publics** the authorities; **~ d'achat** purchasing power

♦ *vb semi-aux* **1** (*être en état de*) can, be able to; **je ne peux pas le réparer** I can't *ou* I am not able to repair it; **déçu de ne pas ~ le faire** disappointed not to be able to do it

2 (*avoir la permission*) can, may, be allowed to; **vous pouvez aller au cinéma** you can *ou* may go to the pictures

3 (*probabilité, hypothèse*) may, might, could; **il a pu avoir un accident** he may *ou* might *ou* could have had an accident; **il aurait pu le dire!** he might *ou* could have said (so)!

♦ *vb impers* may, might, could; **il peut arriver que** it may *ou* might *ou* could happen that

♦ *vt* can, be able to; **j'ai fait tout ce que j'ai pu** I did all I could; **je n'en peux plus** (*épuisé*) I'm exhausted; (*à bout*) I can't take any more

se ~ *vi:* **il se peut que** it may *ou* might be that; **cela se pourrait** that's quite possible

───────────────────────────────

prairie [pʀeʀi] *nf* meadow
praline [pʀalin] *nf* sugared almond
praticable [pʀatikabl(ə)] *adj* passable, practicable
praticien, ne [pʀatisjɛ̃, -jɛn] *nm/f* practitioner
pratique [pʀatik] *nf* practice ♦ *adj* practical
pratiquement [pʀatikmɑ̃] *adv* (*pour ainsi*

dire) practically, virtually

pratiquer [pʀatike] *vt* to practise; (*SPORT etc*) to go in for; to play; (*intervention, opération*) to carry out; (*ouverture, abri*) to make

pré [pʀe] *nm* meadow

préalable [pʀealabl(ə)] *adj* preliminary; **condition ~ (de)** precondition (for), prerequisite (for); **au ~** beforehand

préambule [pʀeɑ̃byl] *nm* preamble; (*fig*) prelude; **sans ~** straight away

préavis [pʀeavi] *nm* notice; **communication avec ~** (*TÉL*) personal *ou* person to person call

précaution [pʀekosjɔ̃] *nf* precaution; **avec ~** cautiously; **par ~** as a precaution

précédemment [pʀesedamɑ̃] *adv* before, previously

précédent, e [pʀesedɑ̃, -ɑ̃t] *adj* previous ♦ *nm* precedent; **le jour ~** the day before, the previous day; **sans ~** unprecedented

précéder [pʀesede] *vt* to precede; (*marcher ou rouler devant*) to be in front of

précepteur, trice [pʀesɛptœʀ, -tʀis] *nm/f* (private) tutor

prêcher [pʀeʃe] *vt* to preach

précieux, euse [pʀesjø, -øz] *adj* precious, invaluable; (*style, écrivain*) précieux, precious

précipice [pʀesipis] *nm* drop, chasm; (*fig*) abyss

précipitamment [pʀesipitamɑ̃] *adv* hurriedly, hastily

précipitation [pʀesipitɑsjɔ̃] *nf* (*hâte*) haste; **~s** *nfpl* (*pluie*) rain *sg*

précipité, e [pʀesipite] *adj* hurried, hasty

précipiter [pʀesipite] *vt* (*faire tomber*): **~ qn/qch du haut de** to throw *ou* hurl sb/sth off *ou* from; (*hâter: marche*) to quicken; (: *départ*) to hasten; **se ~** *vi* to speed up; **se ~ sur/vers** to rush at/towards

précis, e [pʀesi, -iz] *adj* precise; (*tir, mesures*) accurate, precise ♦ *nm* handbook; **précisément** *adv* precisely; **préciser** *vt* (*expliquer*) to be more specific about, clarify; (*spécifier*) to state, specify; **se ~er** *vi* to become clear(er); **précision** *nf* precision; accuracy; point *ou* detail (*being or to be clarified*)

précoce [pʀekɔs] *adj* early; (*enfant*) precocious; (*calvitie*) premature

préconiser [pʀekɔnize] *vt* to advocate

prédécesseur [pʀedesesœʀ] *nm* predecessor

prédilection [pʀedilɛksjɔ̃] *nf*: **avoir une ~ pour** to be partial to; **de ~** favourite

prédire [pʀediʀ] *vt* to predict

prédominer [pʀedɔmine] *vi* to predominate; (*avis*) to prevail

préface [pʀefas] *nf* preface

préfecture [pʀefɛktyʀ] *nf* prefecture; **~ de police** police headquarters *pl*

préférable [pʀefeʀabl(ə)] *adj* preferable

préféré, e [pʀefeʀe] *adj, nm/f* favourite

préférence [pʀefeʀɑ̃s] *nf* preference; **de ~** preferably

préférer [pʀefeʀe] *vt*: **~ qn/qch (à)** to prefer sb/sth (to), like sb/sth better (than); **~ faire** to prefer to do; **je ~ais du thé** I would rather have tea, I'd prefer tea

préfet [pʀefɛ] *nm* prefect

préfixe [pʀefiks(ə)] *nm* prefix

préhistorique [pʀeistɔʀik] *adj* prehistoric

préjudice [pʀeʒydis] *nm* (*matériel*) loss; (*moral*) harm *no pl*; **porter ~ à** to harm, be detrimental to; **au ~ de** at the expense of

préjugé [pʀeʒyʒe] *nm* prejudice; **avoir un ~ contre** to be prejudiced *ou* biased against

préjuger [pʀeʒyʒe]: **~ de** *vt* to prejudge

prélasser [pʀelɑse]: **se ~** *vi* to lounge

prélèvement [pʀelɛvmɑ̃] *nm*: **faire un ~ de sang** to take a blood sample

prélever [pʀelve] *vt* (*échantillon*) to take; (*argent*): **~ (sur)** to deduct (from); (: *sur son compte*) to withdraw (from)

prématuré, e [pʀematyʀe] *adj* premature; (*retraite*) early ♦ *nm* premature baby

premier, ière [pʀəmje, -jɛʀ] *adj* first; (*branche, marche*) bottom; (*fig*) basic; prime; initial; **le ~ venu** the first person to come along; **P~ Ministre** Prime Minister; **première** *nf* (*THÉÂTRE*) first night; (*AUTO*) first (gear); (*AVIAT, RAIL etc*) first class; (*CINÉMA*) première; (*exploit*) first; **premièrement** *adv* firstly

prémonition [pʀemɔnisjɔ̃] *nf* premonition

prémunir [pʀemyniʀ]: **se ~** *vi*: **se ~ contre** to guard against

prenant, e [pʀənɑ̃, -ɑ̃t] *adj* absorbing, engrossing

prénatal, e [pʀenatal] *adj* (*MÉD*) antenatal

prendre [pʀɑ̃dʀ(ə)] *vt* to take; (*ôter*): **~ qch à** to take sth from; (*aller chercher*) to get, fetch; (*se procurer*) to get; (*malfaiteur, poisson*) to catch; (*passager*) to pick up; (*personnel, aussi: couleur, goût*) to take on; (*locataire*) to take in; (*élève etc: traiter*) to handle; (*voix, ton*) to put on; (*coincer*): **se ~ les doigts dans** to get one's fingers caught in ♦ *vi* (*liquide, ciment*) to set; (*greffe, vaccin*) to take; (*feu: foyer*) to go; (: *incendie*) to start; (*allumette*) to light; (*se diriger*): **~ à gauche** to turn (to the) left; **à tout ~** on the whole, all in all; **se ~ pour** to think one is; **s'en ~ à** to attack; **se ~ d'amitié/d'affection pour** to befriend/ become fond of; **s'y ~** (*procéder*) to set about it

preneur [pʀənœʀ] *nm*: **être/trouver ~** to be willing to buy/find a buyer

preniez *vb voir* **prendre**

prenne *etc vb voir* **prendre**

prénom [pʀenɔ̃] *nm* first *ou* Christian

name
prénuptial, e, aux [pʀenypsjal, -o] *adj* premarital

préoccupation [pʀeɔkypasjɔ̃] *nf* (*souci*) concern; (*idée fixe*) preoccupation

préoccuper [pʀeɔkype] *vt* to concern; to preoccupy

préparatifs [pʀepaʀatif] *nmpl* preparations

préparation [pʀepaʀasjɔ̃] *nf* preparation; (SCOL) piece of homework

préparer [pʀepaʀe] *vt* to prepare; (*café*) to make; (*examen*) to prepare for; (*voyage, entreprise*) to plan; **se** ~ *vi* (*orage, tragédie*) to brew, be in the air; **se** ~ **(à qch/faire)** to prepare (o.s.) ou get ready (for sth/to do); ~ **qch à qn** (*surprise etc*) to have sth in store for sb

prépondérant, e [pʀepɔ̃deʀɑ̃, -ɑ̃t] *adj* major, dominating

préposé, e [pʀepoze] *adj*: ~ **à** in charge of ♦ *nm/f* employee; official; attendant

préposition [pʀepozisjɔ̃] *nf* preposition

près [pʀɛ] *adv* near, close; ~ **de** near (to), close to; (*environ*) nearly, almost; **de** ~ closely; **à 5 kg** ~ to within about 5 kg; **à cela** ~ **que** apart from the fact that

présage [pʀezaʒ] *nm* omen

présager [pʀezaʒe] *vt* to foresee

presbyte [pʀɛsbit] *adj* long-sighted

presbytère [pʀɛsbitɛʀ] *nm* presbytery

prescription [pʀɛskʀipsjɔ̃] *nf* (*instruction*) order, instruction; (MÉD, JUR) prescription

prescrire [pʀɛskʀiʀ] *vt* to prescribe

préséance [pʀeseɑ̃s] *nf* precedence *no pl*

présence [pʀezɑ̃s] *nf* presence; (*au bureau etc*) attendance; ~ **d'esprit** presence of mind

présent, e [pʀezɑ̃, -ɑ̃t] *adj, nm* present; **à** ~ **(que)** now (that)

présentation [pʀezɑ̃tasjɔ̃] *nf* introduction; presentation; (*allure*) appearance

présenter [pʀezɑ̃te] *vt* to present; (*sympathie, condoléances*) to offer; (*soumettre*) to submit; (*invité, conférencier*): ~ **qn (à)** to introduce sth (to) ♦ *vi*: ~ **mal/bien** to have an unattractive/a pleasing appearance; **se** ~ *vi* (*sur convocation*) to report, come; (*à une élection*) to stand; (*occasion*) to arise; **se** ~ **bien/mal** to look good/not too good; **se** ~ **à** (*examen*) to sit

préservatif [pʀezɛʀvatif] *nm* sheath, condom

préserver [pʀezɛʀve] *vt*: ~ **de** to protect from; to save from

président [pʀezidɑ̃] *nm* (POL) president; (*d'une assemblée, COMM*) chairman; ~ **directeur général** chairman and managing director

présider [pʀezide] *vt* to preside over; (*dîner*) to be the guest of honour at; ~ **à** to direct; to govern

présomptueux, euse [pʀezɔ̃ptɥø, -øz] *adj*

presumptuous

presque [pʀɛsk(ə)] *adv* almost, nearly; ~ **rien** hardly anything; ~ **pas** hardly (at all); ~ **pas de** hardly any

presqu'île [pʀɛskil] *nf* peninsula

pressant, e [pʀesɑ̃, -ɑ̃t] *adj* urgent; **se faire** ~ to become insistent

presse [pʀɛs] *nf* press; (*affluence*): **heures de** ~ busy times

pressé, e [pʀese] *adj* in a hurry; (*air*) hurried; (*besogne*) urgent; **orange** ~**e** fresh orange juice

pressentiment [pʀesɑ̃timɑ̃] *nm* foreboding, premonition

pressentir [pʀesɑ̃tiʀ] *vt* to sense; (*prendre contact avec*) to approach

presse-papiers [pʀɛspapje] *nm inv* paperweight

presser [pʀese] *vt* (*fruit, éponge*) to squeeze; (*bouton*) to press; (*allure, affaire*) to speed up; (*inciter*): ~ **qn de faire** to urge ou press sb to do ♦ *vi* to be urgent; **se** ~ *vi* (*se hâter*) to hurry (up); **se** ~ **contre qn** to squeeze up against sb; **rien ne presse** there's no hurry

pressing [pʀesiŋ] *nm* steam-pressing; (*magasin*) dry-cleaner's

pression [pʀesjɔ̃] *nf* pressure; **faire** ~ **sur** to put pressure on; ~ **artérielle** blood pressure

pressoir [pʀeswaʀ] *nm* (*wine ou oil etc*) press

prestance [pʀestɑ̃s] *nf* presence, imposing bearing

prestataire [pʀestatɛʀ] *nm/f* supplier

prestation [pʀestasjɔ̃] *nf* (*allocation*) benefit; (*d'une entreprise*) service provided; (*d'un artiste*) performance

prestidigitateur, trice [pʀestidiʒitatœʀ, -tʀis] *nm/f* conjurer

prestigieux, euse [pʀestiʒjø, -øz] *adj* prestigious

présumer [pʀezyme] *vt*: ~ **que** to presume ou assume that; ~ **de** to overrate

présupposer [pʀesypoze] *vt* to presuppose

prêt, e [pʀɛ, pʀɛt] *adj* ready ♦ *nm* lending *no pl*; loan; **prêt-à-porter** *nm* ready-to-wear ou off-the-peg (BRIT) clothes *pl*

prétendant [pʀetɑ̃dɑ̃] *nm* pretender; (*d'une femme*) suitor

prétendre [pʀetɑ̃dʀ(ə)] *vt* (*affirmer*): ~ **que** to claim that; (*avoir l'intention de*): ~ **faire qch** to mean ou intend to do sth; ~ **à** (*droit, titre*) to lay claim to; **prétendu, e** *adj* (*supposé*) so-called

prête-nom [pʀɛtnɔ̃] (*péj*) *nm* figurehead

prétentieux, euse [pʀetɑ̃sjø, -øz] *adj* pretentious

prétention [pʀetɑ̃sjɔ̃] *nf* claim; pretentiousness

prêter [pʀete] *vt* (*livres, argent*): ~ **qch (à)** to lend sth (to); (*supposer*): ~ **à qn** (*carac-*

tère, propos) to attribute to sb ♦ _vi (aussi: se ~: tissu, cuir_) to give; **se ~ à** to lend o.s. (_ou_ itself) to; (_manigances etc_) to go along with; **~ à** (_commentaires etc_) to be open to, give rise to; **~ assistance à** to give help to; **~ attention à** to pay attention to; **~ serment** to take the oath; **~ l'oreille** to listen

prétexte [pretɛkst(ə)] _nm_ pretext, excuse; **sous aucun ~** on no account; **prétexter** _vt_ to give as a pretext _ou_ an excuse

prêtre [prɛtr(ə)] _nm_ priest

preuve [prœv] _nf_ proof; (_indice_) proof, evidence _no pl_; **faire ~ de** to show; **faire ses ~s** to prove o.s. (_ou_ itself)

prévaloir [prevalwar] _vi_ to prevail; **se ~ de** _vt_ to take advantage of; to pride o.s. on

prévenant, e [prevnɑ̃, -ɑ̃t] _adj_ thoughtful, kind

prévenir [prevnir] _vt_ (_avertir_): **~ qn (de)** to warn sb (about); (_informer_): **~ qn (de)** to tell _ou_ inform sb (about); (_éviter_) to avoid, prevent; (_anticiper_) to forestall; to anticipate

prévention [prevɑ̃sjɔ̃] _nf_ prevention; **~ routière** road safety

prévenu, e [prevny] _nm/f_ (_JUR_) defendant, accused

prévision [previzjɔ̃] _nf_: **~s** predictions; forecast _sg_; **en ~ de** in anticipation of; **~s météorologiques** weather forecast _sg_

prévoir [prevwar] _vt_ (_deviner_) to foresee; (_s'attendre à_) to expect, reckon on; (_prévenir_) to anticipate; (_organiser_) to plan; (_préparer, réserver_) to allow; **prévu pour 10h** scheduled for 10 o'clock

prévoyance [prevwajɑ̃s] _nf_: **caisse de ~** contingency fund

prévoyant, e [prevwajɑ̃, -ɑ̃t] _adj_ gifted with (_ou_ showing) foresight

prévu, e [prevy] _pp de_ **prévoir**

prier [prije] _vi_ to pray ♦ _vt_ (_Dieu_) to pray to; (_implorer_) to beg; (_demander_): **~ qn de faire** to ask sb to do; **se faire ~** to need coaxing _ou_ persuading; **je vous en prie** (_allez-y_) please do; (_de rien_) don't mention it

prière [prijɛr] _nf_ prayer; "**~ de faire ...**" "please do ..."

primaire [primɛr] _adj_ primary; (_péj_) simple-minded; simplistic ♦ _nm_ (_SCOL_) primary education

prime [prim] _nf_ (_bonification_) bonus; (_subside_) premium; allowance; (_COMM: cadeau_) free gift; (_ASSURANCES, BOURSE_) premium ♦ _adj_: **de ~ abord** at first glance

primer [prime] _vt_ (_l'emporter sur_) to prevail over; (_récompenser_) to award a prize to ♦ _vi_ to dominate; to prevail

primeurs [primœr] _nfpl_ early fruits and vegetables

primevère [primvɛr] _nf_ primrose

primitif, ive [primitif, -iv] _adj_ primitive; (_originel_) original

prince [prɛ̃s] _nm_ prince; **princesse** _nf_ princess

principal, e, aux [prɛ̃sipal, -o] _adj_ principal, main ♦ _nm_ (_SCOL_) principal, head(master); (_essentiel_) main thing

principe [prɛ̃sip] _nm_ principle; **pour le ~** on principle; **de ~** (_accord, hostilité_) automatic; **par ~** on principle; **en ~** (_habituellement_) as a rule; (_théoriquement_) in principle

printemps [prɛ̃tɑ̃] _nm_ spring

priorité [prijɔrite] _nf_ (_AUTO_): **avoir la ~ (sur)** to have right of way (over); **~ à droite** right of way to vehicles coming from the right

pris, e [pri, priz] _pp de_ **prendre** ♦ _adj_ (_place_) taken; (_journée, mains_) full; (_billets_) sold; (_personne_) busy; **avoir le nez/la gorge ~(e)** to have a stuffy nose/a hoarse throat; **être ~ de panique** to be panic-stricken

prise [priz] _nf_ (_d'une ville_) capture; (_PÊCHE, CHASSE_) catch; (_point d'appui ou pour empoigner_) hold; (_ÉLEC: fiche_) plug; (: _femelle_) socket; **être aux ~s avec** to be grappling with; **~ de contact** (_rencontre_) initial meeting, first contact; **~ de courant** power point; **~ de sang** blood test; **~ de terre** earth; **~ de vue** (_photo_) shot; **~ multiple** adaptor

priser [prize] _vt_ (_tabac, héroïne_) to take; (_estimer_) to prize, value ♦ _vi_ to take snuff

prison [prizɔ̃] _nf_ prison; **aller/être en ~** to go to/be in prison _ou_ jail; **faire de la ~** to serve time; **prisonnier, ière** _nm/f_ prisoner ♦ _adj_ captive

prit _vb voir_ **prendre**

privé, e [prive] _adj_ private; **en ~** in private

priver [prive] _vt_: **~ qn de** to deprive sb of; **se ~ de** to go _ou_ do without

privilège [privilɛʒ] _nm_ privilege

prix [pri] _nm_ (_valeur_) price; (_récompense, SCOL_) prize; **hors de ~** exorbitantly priced; **à aucun ~** not at any price; **à tout ~** at all costs; **~ d'achat/de vente/de revient** purchasing/selling/cost price

probable [prɔbabl(ə)] _adj_ likely, probable; **~ment** _adv_ probably

probant, e [prɔbɑ̃, -ɑ̃t] _adj_ convincing

problème [prɔblɛm] _nm_ problem

procédé [prɔsede] _nm_ (_méthode_) process; (_comportement_) behaviour _no pl_

procéder [prɔsede] _vi_ to proceed; to behave; **~ à** to carry out

procès [prɔsɛ] _nm_ trial; (_poursuites_) proceedings _pl_; **être en ~ avec** to be involved in a lawsuit with

processus [prɔsesys] _nm_ process

procès-verbal, aux [prɔsɛvɛrbal, -o] _nm_ (_constat_) statement; (_aussi: P.V._): **avoir un ~** to get a parking ticket; to be booked; (_de réunion_) minutes _pl_

prochain, e [prɔʃɛ̃, -ɛn] *adj* next; *(proche)* impending; near ♦ *nm* fellow man; **la ~e fois/semaine** ~e next time/week; **prochainement** *adv* soon, shortly

proche [prɔʃ] *adj* nearby; *(dans le temps)* imminent; *(parent, ami)* close; **~s** *nmpl (parents)* close relatives; **être ~ (de)** to be near, be close (to); **de ~ en ~** gradually; **le P~ Orient** the Middle East

proclamer [prɔklame] *vt* to proclaim

procuration [prɔkyrasjɔ̃] *nf* proxy; power of attorney

procurer [prɔkyre] *vt*: **~ qch à qn** *(fournir)* to obtain sth for sb; *(causer: plaisir etc)* to bring sb sth; **se ~** *vt* to get

procureur [prɔkyrœr] *nm* public prosecutor

prodige [prɔdiʒ] *nm* marvel, wonder; *(personne)* prodigy

prodigue [prɔdig] *adj* generous; extravagant; **fils ~** prodigal son

prodiguer [prɔdige] *vt (argent, biens)* to be lavish with; *(soins, attentions)*: **~ qch à qn** to give sb sth

producteur, trice [prɔdyktœr, -tris] *nm/f* producer

production [prɔdyksjɔ̃] *nf (gén)* production; *(rendement)* output

produire [prɔdɥir] *vt* to produce; **se ~** *vi (acteur)* to perform, appear; *(événement)* to happen, occur

produit [prɔdɥi] *nm (gén)* product; **~ d'entretien** cleaning product; **~ national brut** gross national product; **~s agricoles** farm produce *sg*; **~s alimentaires** *nmpl* foodstuffs

prof [prɔf] *(fam) nm* teacher

profane [prɔfan] *adj (REL)* secular ♦ *nm/f* layman(woman)

proférer [prɔfere] *vt* to utter

professeur [prɔfesœr] *nm* teacher; *(titulaire d'une chaire)* professor; **~ (de faculté)** (university) lecturer

profession [prɔfesjɔ̃] *nf* profession; **sans ~** unemployed; **professionnel, le** *adj, nm/f* professional

profil [prɔfil] *nm* profile; *(d'une voiture)* line, contour; **de ~** in profile; **profiler** *vt* to streamline

profit [prɔfi] *nm (avantage)* benefit, advantage; *(COMM, FINANCE)* profit; **au ~ de** in aid of; **tirer ~ de** to profit from

profitable [prɔfitabl(ə)] *adj* beneficial; profitable

profiter [prɔfite] *vi*: **~ de** to take advantage of; to make the most of; **~ à** to benefit; to be profitable to

profond, e [prɔfɔ̃, -ɔ̃d] *adj* deep; *(méditation, mépris)* profound; **profondeur** *nf* depth

progéniture [prɔʒenityr] *nf* offspring *inv*

programme [prɔgram] *nm* programme;

(TV, RADIO) programmes *pl*; *(SCOL)* syllabus, curriculum; *(INFORM)* program; **programmer** *vt (TV, RADIO)* to put on, show; *(INFORM)* to program; **programmeur, euse** *nm/f* programmer

progrès [prɔgrɛ] *nm* progress *no pl*; **faire des ~** to make progress

progresser [prɔgrese] *vi* to progress; *(troupes etc)* to make headway *ou* progress; **progressif, ive** *adj* progressive

prohiber [prɔibe] *vt* to prohibit, ban

proie [prwa] *nf* prey *no pl*

projecteur [prɔʒɛktœr] *nm* projector; *(de théâtre, cirque)* spotlight

projectile [prɔʒɛktil] *nm* missile

projection [prɔʒɛksjɔ̃] *nf* projection; showing; **conférence avec ~s** lecture with slides *(ou a film)*

projet [prɔʒɛ] *nm* plan; *(ébauche)* draft; **~ de loi** bill

projeter [prɔʒte] *vt (envisager)* to plan; *(film, photos)* to project; *(passer)* to show; *(ombre, lueur)* to throw, cast; *(jeter)* to throw up *(ou* off *ou* out)

prolixe [prɔliks(ə)] *adj* verbose

prolongement [prɔlɔ̃ʒmɑ̃] *nm* extension; **~s** *nmpl (fig)* repercussions, effects; **dans le ~ de** running on from

prolonger [prɔlɔ̃ʒe] *vt (débat, séjour)* to prolong; *(délai, billet, rue)* to extend; *(suj: chose)* to be a continuation *ou* an extension of; **se ~** *vi* to go on

promenade [prɔmnad] *nf* walk *(ou* drive *ou* ride); **faire une ~** to go for a walk; **une ~ en voiture/à vélo** a drive/(bicycle) ride

promener [prɔmne] *vt (chien)* to take out for a walk; *(doigts, regard)*: **~ qch sur** to run sth over; **se ~** *vi* to go for *(ou* be out for) a walk

promesse [prɔmɛs] *nf* promise

promettre [prɔmɛtr(ə)] *vt* to promise ♦ *vi* to be *ou* look promising; **~ à qn de faire** to promise sb that one will do

promiscuité [prɔmiskɥite] *nf* crowding; lack of privacy

promontoire [prɔmɔ̃twar] *nm* headland

promoteur, trice [prɔmɔtœr, -tris] *nm/f (instigateur)* instigator, promoter; **~ (immobilier)** property developer *(BRIT)*, real estate promoter *(US)*

promotion [prɔmosjɔ̃] *nf* promotion

promouvoir [prɔmuvwar] *vt* to promote

prompt, e [prɔ̃, prɔ̃t] *adj* swift, rapid

prôner [prone] *vt* to advocate

pronom [prɔnɔ̃] *nm* pronoun

prononcer [prɔnɔ̃se] *vt (son, mot, jugement)* to pronounce; *(dire)* to utter; *(allocution)* to deliver; **se ~** *vi* to reach a decision, give a verdict; **se ~ sur** to give an opinion on; **se ~ contre** to come down against; **prononciation** *nf* pronunciation

pronostic [prɔnɔstik] *nm (MÉD)* prognosis;

(fig: aussi: ~s) forecast

propagande [pʀɔpagɑ̃d] *nf* propaganda

propager [pʀɔpaʒe] *vt* to spread; **se ~** *vi* to spread

prophète [pʀɔfɛt] *nm* prophet

prophétie [pʀɔfesi] *nf* prophecy

propice [pʀɔpis] *adj* favourable

proportion [pʀɔpɔʀsjɔ̃] *nf* proportion; **toute(s) ~(s) gardée(s)** making due allowance(s)

propos [pʀɔpo] *nm (paroles)* talk *no pl*, remark; *(intention)* intention, aim; *(sujet)*: **à quel ~?** what about?; **à ~ de** about, regarding; **à tout ~** for no reason at all; **à ~** by the way; *(opportunément)* at the right moment

proposer [pʀɔpoze] *vt (suggérer)*: **~ qch (à qn)/de faire** to suggest sth (to sb)/doing, propose sth (to sb)/to do; *(offrir)*: **~ qch à qn/de faire** to offer sb sth/to do; *(candidat)* to put forward; *(loi, motion)* to propose; **se ~ to** offer one's services; **se ~ de faire** to intend *ou* propose to do; **proposition** *nf* suggestion; proposal; offer; *(LING)* clause

propre [pʀɔpʀ(ə)] *adj* clean; *(net)* neat, tidy; *(possessif)* own; *(sens)* literal; *(particulier)*: **~** à peculiar to; *(approprié)*: **à ~** suitable for; *(de nature à)*: **~ à faire** likely to do ♦ *nm*: **recopier au ~** to make a fair copy of; **proprement** *adv* cleanly, neatly, tidily; **le village proprement dit** the village itself; **à proprement parler** strictly speaking; **propreté** *nf* cleanliness; neatness; tidiness

propriétaire [pʀɔpʀijetɛʀ] *nm/f* owner; *(pour le locataire)* landlord(lady)

propriété [pʀɔpʀijete] *nf (gén)* property; *(droit)* ownership; *(objet, immeuble, terres)* property *gén no pl*

propulser [pʀɔpylse] *vt (missile)* to propel; *(projeter)* to hurl, fling

proroger [pʀɔʀɔʒe] *vt* to put back, defer; *(prolonger)* to extend

proscrire [pʀɔskʀiʀ] *vt (bannir)* to banish; *(interdire)* to ban, prohibit

prose [pʀoz] *nf (style)* prose

prospecter [pʀɔspɛkte] *vt* to prospect; *(COMM)* to canvass

prospectus [pʀɔspɛktys] *nm* leaflet

prospère [pʀɔspɛʀ] *adj* prosperous

prosterner [pʀɔstɛʀne] : **se ~** *vi* to bow low, prostrate o.s.

prostituée [pʀɔstitɥe] *nf* prostitute

protecteur, trice [pʀɔtɛktœʀ, -tʀis] *adj* protective; *(air, ton: péj)* patronizing ♦ *nm/f* protector

protection [pʀɔtɛksjɔ̃] *nf* protection; *(d'un personnage influent: aide)* patronage

protéger [pʀɔteʒe] *vt* to protect; **se ~ de ou contre** to protect o.s. from

protéine [pʀɔtein] *nf* protein

protestant, e [pʀɔtɛstɑ̃, -ɑ̃t] *adj, nm/f* Protestant

protestation [pʀɔtɛstɑsjɔ̃] *nf (plainte)* protest

protester [pʀɔtɛste] *vi*: **~ (contre)** to protest (against *ou* about); **~ de** *(son innocence, sa loyauté)* to protest

prothèse [pʀɔtɛz] *nf* artificial limb, prosthesis; **~ dentaire** denture

protocole [pʀɔtɔkɔl] *nm (fig)* etiquette

proue [pʀu] *nf* bow(s *pl*), prow

prouesse [pʀuɛs] *nf* feat

prouver [pʀuve] *vt* to prove

provenance [pʀɔvnɑ̃s] *nf* origin; *(de mot, coutume)* source; **avion en ~ de** plane (arriving) from

provenir [pʀɔvniʀ] : **~ de** *vt* to come from; *(résulter de)* to be the result of

proverbe [pʀɔvɛʀb(ə)] *nm* proverb

province [pʀɔvɛ̃s] *nf* province

proviseur [pʀɔvizœʀ] *nm* ≈ head(teacher) *(BRIT)*, ≈ principal *(US)*

provision [pʀɔvizjɔ̃] *nf (réserve)* stock, supply; *(avance: à un avocat, avoué)* retainer, retaining fee; *(COMM)* funds *pl* (in account); reserve; **~s** *nfpl (vivres)* provisions, food *no pl*

provisoire [pʀɔvizwaʀ] *adj* temporary; *(JUR)* provisional

provoquer [pʀɔvɔke] *vt (inciter)*: **~ qn à** to incite sb to; *(défier)* to provoke; *(causer)* to cause, bring about

proxénète [pʀɔksenɛt] *nm* procurer

proximité [pʀɔksimite] *nf* nearness, closeness; *(dans le temps)* imminence, closeness; **à ~** near *ou* close by; **à ~ de** near (to), close to

prude [pʀyd] *adj* prudish

prudemment [pʀydamɑ̃] *adv* carefully, cautiously; wisely, sensibly

prudence [pʀydɑ̃s] *nf* carefulness; caution; **avec ~** carefully; cautiously; **par (mesure de) ~** as a precaution

prudent, e [pʀydɑ̃, -ɑ̃t] *adj (pas téméraire)* careful, cautious; *(en général)* safety-conscious; *(sage, conseillé)* wise, sensible; *(réservé)* cautious

prune [pʀyn] *nf* plum

pruneau, x [pʀyno] *nm* prune

prunelle [pʀynɛl] *nf* pupil; eye

prunier [pʀynje] *nm* plum tree

psaume [psom] *nm* psalm

pseudonyme [psødɔnim] *nm (gén)* fictitious name; *(d'écrivain)* pseudonym, pen name; *(de comédien)* stage name

psychiatre [psikjatʀ(ə)] *nm/f* psychiatrist

psychiatrique [psikjatʀik] *adj* psychiatric

psychique [psifik] *adj* psychological

psychologie [psikɔlɔʒi] *nf* psychology; **psychologique** *adj* psychological; **psychologue** *nm/f* psychologist

P.T.T. *sigle fpl* = **Postes, Télécommunications et Télédiffusion**

pu *pp de* **pouvoir**
puanteur [pɥɑ̃tœʀ] *nf* stink, stench
pub [pyb] *(fam) abr f* (= *publicité*): **la** ~ advertising
public, ique [pyblik] *adj* public; *(école, instruction)* state *cpd* ♦ *nm* public; *(assistance)* audience; **en** ~ in public
publicitaire [pyblisitɛʀ] *adj* advertising *cpd*; *(film, voiture)* publicity *cpd*
publicité [pyblisite] *nf* (*méthode, profession*) advertising; *(annonce)* advertisement; *(révélations)* publicity
publier [pyblije] *vt* to publish
publique [pyblik] *adj voir* **public**
puce [pys] *nf* flea; *(INFORM)* chip; ~**s** *nfpl* *(marché)* flea market *sg*
pudeur [pydœʀ] *nf* modesty
pudique [pydik] *adj* (*chaste*) modest; *(discret)* discreet
puer [pɥe] *(péj) vi* to stink
puéricultrice [pɥeʀikyltʀis] *nf* p(a)ediatric nurse
puériculture [pɥeʀikyltyʀ] *nf* p(a)ediatric nursing; infant care
puéril, e [pɥeʀil] *adj* childish
puis [pɥi] *vb voir* **pouvoir** ♦ *adv* then
puiser [pɥize] *vt*: ~ **(dans)** to draw (from)
puisque [pɥisk(ə)] *conj* since
puissance [pɥisɑ̃s] *nf* power; **en** ~ *adj* potential
puissant, e [pɥisɑ̃, -ɑ̃t] *adj* powerful
puisse *etc vb voir* **pouvoir**
puits [pɥi] *nm* well; ~ **de mine** mine shaft
pull(-over) [pul(ɔvœʀ)] *nm* sweater
pulluler [pylyle] *vi* to swarm
pulpe [pylp(ə)] *nf* pulp
pulvérisateur [pylveʀizatœʀ] *nm* spray
pulvériser [pylveʀize] *vt* to pulverize; *(liquide)* to spray
punaise [pynɛz] *nf* (*ZOOL*) bug; *(clou)* drawing pin *(BRIT)*, thumbtack *(US)*
punch[1] [pɔ̃ʃ] *nm* (*boisson*) punch
punch[2] [pœnʃ] *nm* (*BOXE, fig*) punch
punir [pyniʀ] *vt* to punish; **punition** *nf* punishment
pupille [pypij] *nf* (*ANAT*) pupil ♦ *nm/f* (*enfant*) ward; ~ **de l'État** child in care
pupitre [pypitʀ(ə)] *nm* (*SCOL*) desk; *(REL)* lectern; *(de chef d'orchestre)* rostrum
pur, e [pyʀ] *adj* pure; *(vin)* undiluted; *(whisky)* neat; **en** ~**e perte** to no avail
purée [pyʀe] *nf*: ~ **(de pommes de terre)** mashed potatoes *pl*; ~ **de marrons** chestnut purée
purger [pyʀʒe] *vt* (*radiateur*) to drain; *(circuit hydraulique)* to bleed; *(MÉD, POL)* to purge; *(JUR: peine)* to serve
purin [pyʀɛ̃] *nm* liquid manure
pur-sang [pyʀsɑ̃] *nm inv* thoroughbred
pusillanime [pyzilanim] *adj* fainthearted
putain [pytɛ̃] *(fam!) nf* whore (!)
puzzle [pœzl(ə)] *nm* jigsaw (puzzle)

P.V. *sigle m* = **procès-verbal**
pyjama [piʒama] *nm* pyjamas *pl* (*BRIT*), pajamas *pl* (*US*)
pyramide [piʀamid] *nf* pyramid
Pyrénées [piʀene] *nfpl*: **les** ~ the Pyrenees

Q q

QG [kyʒe] *sigle m* (= *quartier général*) HQ
QI [kyi] *sigle m* (= *quotient intellectuel*) IQ
quadragénaire [kadʀaʒenɛʀ] *nm/f* man/woman in his/her forties
quadriller [kadʀije] *vt* (*papier*) to mark out in squares; *(POLICE)* to keep under tight control
quadruple [k(w)adʀypl(ə)] *nm*: **le** ~ **de** four times as much as; **quadruplés, ées** *nm/fpl* quadruplets, quads
quai [ke] *nm* (*de port*) quay; *(de gare)* platform; **être à** ~ (*navire*) to be alongside; *(train)* to be in the station
qualifier [kalifje] *vt* to qualify; **se** ~ *vi* to qualify; ~ **qch/qn de** to describe sth/sb as
qualité [kalite] *nf* quality; *(titre, fonction)* position
quand [kɑ̃] *conj, adv* when; ~ **je serai riche** when I'm rich; ~ **même** all the same; really; ~ **bien même** even though
quant [kɑ̃] : ~ **à** *prép* as for, as to; regarding
quant-à-soi [kɑ̃taswa] *nm*: **rester sur son** ~ to remain aloof
quantité [kɑ̃tite] *nf* quantity, amount; *(SCIENCE)* quantity; *(grand nombre)*: **une** *ou* **des** ~**(s) de** a great deal of
quarantaine [kaʀɑ̃tɛn] *nf* (*MÉD*) quarantine; **avoir la** ~ *(âge)* to be around forty; **une** ~ **(de)** forty or so, about forty
quarante [kaʀɑ̃t] *num* forty
quart [kaʀ] *nm* (*fraction, partie*) quarter; *(surveillance)* watch; **un** ~ **de beurre** a quarter kilo of butter; **un** ~ **de vin** a quarter litre of wine; **une livre un** ~ *ou* **et** ~ one and a quarter pounds; **le** ~ **de** of; ~ **d'heure** quarter of an hour
quartier [kaʀtje] *nm* (*de ville*) district, area; *(de bœuf)* quarter; *(de fruit, fromage)* piece; ~**s** *nmpl* (*MIL, BLASON*) quarters; **cinéma de** ~ local cinema; **avoir** ~ **libre** *(fig)* to be free; ~ **général** headquarters *pl*
quartz [kwaʀts] *nm* quartz
quasi [kazi] *adv* almost, nearly; **quasiment** *adv* almost, nearly

quatorze [katɔʀz(ə)] *num* fourteen
quatre [katʀ(ə)] *num* four; **à ~ pattes** on
all fours; **tiré à ~ épingles** dressed up to
the nines; **faire les ~ cent coups** to get a
bit wild; **se mettre en ~ pour qn** to go
out of one's way for sb; **~ à ~** (*monter,
descendre*) four at a time; **quatre-vingt-
dix** *num* ninety; **quatre-vingts** *num*
eighty; **quatrième** *num* fourth
quatuor [kwatyɔʀ] *nm* quartet(te)

─────────── MOT CLÉ ───────────

que [kə] *conj* **1** (*introduisant complétive*)
that; **il sait ~ tu es là** he knows (that)
you're here; **je veux ~ tu acceptes** I want
you to accept; **il a dit ~ oui** he said he
would (*ou* it was *etc*)
2 (*reprise d'autres conjonctions*): **quand il
rentrera et qu'il aura mangé** when he gets
back and (when) he has eaten; **si vous y
allez ou ~ vous ...** if you go there or if
you ...
3 (*en tête de phrase: hypothèse, souhait etc*):
qu'il le veuille ou non whether he likes it
or not; **qu'il fasse ce qu'il voudra!** let him
do as he pleases!
4 (*après comparatif*) than; as; *voir aussi*
plus; **aussi**; **autant** *etc*
5 (*seulement*): **ne ... ~** only; **il ne boit ~
de l'eau** he only drinks water
♦ *adv* (*exclamation*): **qu'il ou qu'est-ce qu'il
est bête/court vite!** he's so silly!/he runs
so fast!; **~ de livres!** what a lot of books!
♦ *pron* **1** (*relatif: personne*) whom; (*: chose*)
that, which; **l'homme ~ je vois** the man
(whom) I see; **le livre ~ tu vois** the book
(that *ou* which) you see; **un jour ~ j'étais
...** a day when I was ...
2 (*interrogatif*) what; **~ fais-tu?, qu'est-ce
~ tu fais?** what are you doing?; **qu'est-ce
~ c'est?** what is it?, what's that?; **~ faire?**
what can one do?

─────────── MOT CLÉ ───────────

quel, quelle [kɛl] *adj* **1** (*interrogatif: personne*) who; (*: chose*) what; which; **~ est
cet homme?** who is this man?; **~ est ce
livre?** what is this book?; **~ livre/homme?**
what book/man?; (*parmi un certain choix*)
which book/man?; **~s acteurs préférez-
vous?** which actors do you prefer?; **dans
~s pays êtes-vous allé?** which *ou* what
countries did you go to?
2 (*exclamatif*): **quelle surprise!** what a surprise!
3: **quel(le) que soit le coupable** whoever
is guilty; **~ que soit votre avis** whatever
your opinion

quelconque [kɛlkɔ̃k] *adj* (*médiocre*) indifferent, poor; (*sans attrait*) ordinary, plain;

(*indéfini*): **un ami ~** some friend or other

─────────── MOT CLÉ ───────────

quelque [kɛlk] *adj* **1** some; a few; (*tournure interrogative*) any; **~ espoir** some
hope; **il a ~s amis** he has a few *ou* some
friends; **a-t-il ~s amis?** has he any
friends?; **les ~s livres qui** the few books
which; **20 kg et ~(s)** a bit over 20 kg
2: **~ ... que**: **quelque livre qu'il choisisse**
whatever (*ou* whichever) book he chooses
3: **~ chose** something; (*tournure interrogative*) anything; **~ chose d'autre** something
else; anything else; **~ part** somewhere;
anywhere; **en ~ sorte** as it were
♦ *adv* **1** (*environ*): **~ 100 mètres** some 100
metres
2: **~ peu** rather, somewhat

quelquefois [kɛlkəfwa] *adv* sometimes
quelques-uns, -unes [kɛlkəzœ̃, -yn] *pron*
a few, some
quelqu'un [kɛlkœ̃] *pron* someone, somebody; (*+tournure interrogative*) anyone *ou*
anybody; **~ d'autre** someone *ou* somebody
else; anybody else
quémander [kemɑ̃de] *vt* to beg for
qu'en dira-t-on [kɑ̃diʀatɔ̃] *nm inv*: **le ~**
gossip, what people say
querelle [kəʀɛl] *nf* quarrel
quereller: **se ~** *vi* to quarrel
qu'est-ce que [kɛskə] *voir* **que**
qu'est-ce qui [kɛski] *voir* **qui**
question [kɛstjɔ̃] *nf* (*gén*) question; (*fig*)
matter; issue; **il a été ~ de** we (*ou* they)
spoke about; **de quoi est-il ~?** what is it
about?; **il n'en est pas ~** there's no question of it; **hors de ~** out of the question;
remettre en ~ to question; **~naire**
[kɛstjɔnɛʀ] *nm* questionnaire; **~ner**
[kɛstjɔne] *vt* to question
quête [kɛt] *nf* collection; (*recherche*) quest,
search; **faire la ~** (*à l'église*) to take the
collection; (*artiste*) to pass the hat round;
quêter *vi* (*à l'église*) to take the collection
quetsche [kwɛtʃ(ə)] *nf* damson
queue [kø] *nf* tail; (*fig: du classement*) bottom; (*: de poêle*) handle; (*: de fruit, feuille*)
stalk; (*: de train, colonne, file*) rear; **faire la
~** to queue (*BRIT*), line up (*US*); **~ de
cheval** ponytail; **queue-de-pie** *nf* (*habit*)
tails *pl*, tail coat
qui [ki] *pron* (*personne*) who; (*+prép*)
whom; (*chose, animal*) which, that; **qu'est-
ce ~ est sur la table?** what is on the table?; **~ est-ce ~?** who?; **~ est-ce que?**
who?; whom?; **à ~ est ce sac?** whose bag
is this?; **à ~ parlais-tu?** who were you
talking to?, to whom were you talking?;
amenez ~ vous voulez bring who you
like; **~ que ce soit** whoever it may be
quiconque [kikɔ̃k] *pron* (*celui qui*) who-

ever, anyone who; *(personne)* anyone, anybody

quiétude [kjetyd] *nf (d'un lieu)* quiet, tranquillity; **en toute ~** in complete peace

quille [kij] *nf:* **(jeu de) ~s** skittles *sg* *(BRIT)*, bowling *(US)*

quincaillerie [kɛ̃kɑjʀi] *nf (ustensiles)* hardware; *(magasin)* hardware shop; **quincaillier, ière** *nm/f* hardware dealer

quinquagénaire [kɛ̃kaʒenɛʀ] *nm/f* man/ woman in his/her fifties

quintal, aux [kɛ̃tal, -o] *nm* quintal *(100 kg)*

quinte [kɛ̃t] *nf:* **~ (de toux)** coughing fit

quintuple [kɛ̃typl(ə)] *nm:* **le ~ de** five times as much as; **quintuplés, ées** *nm/fpl* quintuplets, quins

quinzaine [kɛ̃zɛn] *nf:* **une ~ (de)** about fifteen, fifteen or so; **une ~ (de jours)** a fortnight *(BRIT)*, two weeks

quinze [kɛ̃z] *num* fifteen; **demain en ~** a fortnight *ou* two weeks tomorrow; **dans ~ jours** in a fortnight('s time), in two weeks (' time)

quiproquo [kipʀɔko] *nm* misunderstanding

quittance [kitɑ̃s] *nf (reçu)* receipt; *(facture)* bill

quitte [kit] *adj:* **être ~ envers qn** to be no longer in sb's debt; *(fig)* to be quits with sb; **être ~ de** *(obligation)* to be clear of; **en être ~ à bon compte** to have got off lightly; **~ à faire** even if it means doing

quitter [kite] *vt* to leave; *(espoir, illusion)* to give up; *(vêtement)* to take off; **se ~** *vi* *(couples, interlocuteurs)* to part; **ne quittez pas** *(au téléphone)* hold the line

qui-vive [kiviv] *nm:* **être sur le ~** to be on the alert

quoi [kwa] *pron (interrogatif)* what; **~ de neuf?** what's the news?; **as-tu de ~ écrire?** have you anything to write with?; **il n'a pas de ~ se l'acheter** he can't afford it; **~ qu'il arrive** whatever happens; **~ qu'il en soit** be that as it may; **que ce soit** anything at all; **"il n'y a pas de ~"** "(please) don't mention it"; **à ~ bon?** what's the use?; **en ~ puis-je vous aider?** how can I help you?

quoique [kwak(ə)] *conj* (al)though

quolibet [kɔlibɛ] *nm* gibe, jeer

quote-part [kɔtpaʀ] *nf* share

quotidien, ne [kɔtidjɛ̃, -ɛn] *adj* daily; *(banal)* everyday ♦ *nm (journal)* daily (paper)

R r

r. *abr* = **route; rue**

rab [ʀab] *(fam) abr m* = **rabiot**

rabâcher [ʀabɑʃe] *vt* to keep on repeating

rabais [ʀabɛ] *nm* reduction, discount

rabaisser [ʀabese] *vt (rabattre)* to reduce; *(dénigrer)* to belittle

rabattre [ʀabatʀ(ə)] *vt (couvercle, siège)* to pull down; *(gibier)* to drive; **se ~** *vi (bords, couvercle)* to fall shut; *(véhicule, coureur)* to cut in; **se ~ sur** to fall back on

rabbin [ʀabɛ̃] *nm* rabbi

rabiot [ʀabjo] *(fam) nm* extra, more

râblé, e [ʀɑble] *adj* stocky

rabot [ʀabo] *nm* plane

rabougri, e [ʀabugʀi] *adj* stunted

rabrouer [ʀabʀue] *vt* to snub

racaille [ʀakɑj] *(péj) nf* rabble, riffraff

raccommoder [ʀakɔmɔde] *vt* to mend, repair; *(chaussette etc)* to darn

raccompagner [ʀakɔ̃paɲe] *vt* to take *ou* see back

raccord [ʀakɔʀ] *nm* link

raccorder [ʀakɔʀde] *vt* to join (up), link up; *(suj: pont etc)* to connect, link

raccourci [ʀakuʀsi] *nm* short cut

raccourcir [ʀakuʀsiʀ] *vt* to shorten

raccrocher [ʀakʀɔʃe] *vt (tableau)* to hang back up; *(récepteur)* to put down ♦ *vi (TÉL)* to hang up, ring off; **se ~ à** *vt* to cling to, hang on to

race [ʀas] *nf* race; *(d'animaux, fig)* breed; *(ascendance)* stock, race; **de ~** purebred, pedigree

rachat [ʀaʃa] *nm* buying; buying back

racheter [ʀaʃte] *vt (article perdu)* to buy another; *(davantage):* **~ du lait/3 œufs** to buy more milk/another 3 eggs *ou* 3 more eggs; *(après avoir vendu)* to buy back; *(d'occasion)* to buy; *(COMM: part, firme)* to buy up; *(: pension, rente)* to redeem; **se ~** *vi (fig)* to make amends

racial, e, aux [ʀasjal, -o] *adj* racial

racine [ʀasin] *nf* root; **~ carrée/cubique** square/cube root

raciste [ʀasist(ə)] *adj, nm/f* raci(al)ist

racket [ʀakɛt] *nm* racketeering *no pl*

racler [ʀɑkle] *vt (surface)* to scrape; *(tache, boue)* to scrape off

racoler [ʀakɔle] *vt (attirer: suj: prostituée)* to solicit; *(: parti, marchand)* to tout for

racontars [Rakɔ̃taR] *nmpl* gossip *sg*

raconter [Rakɔ̃te] *vt*: ~ **(à qn)** (*décrire*) to relate (to sb), tell (sb) about; (*dire*) to tell (sb)

racorni, e [Rakɔrni] *adj* hard(ened)

radar [RadaR] *nm* radar

rade [Rad] *nf* (natural) harbour; **rester en** ~ (*fig*) to be left stranded

radeau, x [Rado] *nm* raft

radiateur [RadjatœR] *nm* radiator, heater; (*AUTO*) radiator; ~ **électrique/à gaz** electric/gas heater *ou* fire

radiation [Radjasjɔ̃] *nf* (*voir radier*) striking off *no pl*; (*PHYSIQUE*) radiation

radical, e, aux [Radikal, -o] *adj* radical

radier [Radje] *vt* to strike off

radieux, euse [Radjø, -øz] *adj* radiant; brilliant, glorious

radin, e [Radɛ̃, -in] (*fam*) *adj* stingy

radio [Radjo] *nf* radio; (*MÉD*) X-ray ♦ *nm* radio operator; **à la** ~ on the radio; **ra-dioactif, ive** *adj* radioactive; **radiodiffuser** *vt* to broadcast; **radiographie** *nf* radiography; (*photo*) X-ray photograph; **radio-phonique** *adj* radio *cpd*; **radio-réveil** (*pl* **radios-réveils**) *nm* radio alarm clock; **ra-diotélévisé, e** *adj* broadcast on radio and television

radis [Radi] *nm* radish

radoter [Radɔte] *vi* to ramble on

radoucir [RadusiR]: **se** ~ *vi* (*se réchauffer*) to become milder; (*se calmer*) to calm down; to soften

rafale [Rafal] *nf* (*vent*) gust (of wind); (*tir*) burst of gunfire

raffermir [RafɛRmiR] *vt* to firm up; (*fig*) to strengthen

raffiner [Rafine] *vt* to refine; **raffinerie** *nf* refinery

raffoler [Rafɔle]: ~ **de** *vt* to be very keen on

rafle [Rafl(ə)] *nf* (*de police*) raid

rafler [Rafle] (*fam*) *vt* to swipe, nick

rafraîchir [RafʀeʃiR] *vt* (*atmosphère, tem-pérature*) to cool (down); (*aussi: mettre à* ~) to chill; (*fig: rénover*) to brighten up; **se** ~ *vi* to grow cooler; to freshen up; to re-fresh o.s.; **rafraîchissant, e** *adj* refreshing; **rafraîchissement** *nm* cooling; (*boisson*) cool drink; **rafraîchissements** *nmpl* (*bois-sons, fruits etc*) refreshments

rage [Raʒ] *nf* (*MÉD*): **la** ~ rabies; (*fureur*) rage, fury; **faire** ~ to rage; ~ **de dents** (raging) toothache

ragot [Rago] (*fam*) *nm* malicious gossip *no pl*

ragoût [Ragu] *nm* (*plat*) stew

raide [Rɛd] *adj* (*tendu*) taut, tight; (*escarpé*) steep; (*droit: cheveux*) straight; (*ankylosé, dur, guindé*) stiff; (*fam*) steep, stiff; flat broke ♦ *adv* (*en pente*) steeply; ~ **mort** stone dead; **raidir** *vt* (*muscles*) to stiffen;

(*câble*) to pull taut; **se raidir** *vi* to stiffen; to become taut; (*personne*) to tense up; to brace o.s.

raie [Rɛ] *nf* (*ZOOL*) skate, ray; (*rayure*) stripe; (*des cheveux*) parting

raifort [RefɔR] *nm* horseradish

rail [Raj] *nm* rail; (*chemins de fer*) railways *pl*; **par** ~ by rail

railler [Raje] *vt* to scoff at, jeer at

rainure [RenyR] *nf* groove; slot

raisin [Rezɛ̃] *nm* (*aussi*: ~**s**) grapes *pl*; ~**s secs** raisins

raison [Rezɔ̃] *nf* reason; **avoir** ~ to be right; **donner** ~ **à qn** to agree with sb; to prove sb right; **se faire une** ~ to learn to live with it; **perdre la** ~ to become insane; to take leave of one's senses; ~ **de plus** all the more reason; **à plus forte** ~ all the more so; **en** ~ **de** because of; according to; in proportion to; **à** ~ **de** at the rate of; ~ **sociale** corporate name; **raisonnable** *adj* reasonable, sensible

raisonnement [Rezɔnmɑ̃] *nm* reasoning; arguing; argument

raisonner [Rezɔne] *vi* (*penser*) to reason; (*argumenter, discuter*) to argue ♦ *vt* (*per-sonne*) to reason with

rajeunir [RaʒœniR] *vt* (*suj: coiffure, robe*): ~ **qn** to make sb look younger; (: *cure etc*) to rejuvenate; (*fig*) to give a new look to; to inject new blood into ♦ *vi* to become (*ou* look) younger

rajouter [Raʒute] *vt*: ~ **du sel/un œuf** to add some more salt/another egg

rajuster [Raʒyste] *vt* (*vêtement*) to straight-en, tidy; (*salaires*) to adjust; (*machine*) to readjust

ralenti [Ralɑ̃ti] *nm*: **au** ~ (*AUTO*): **tourner au** ~ to tick over (*AUTO*), idle; **au** ~ (*CINÉMA*) in slow motion; (*fig*) at a slower pace

ralentir [Ralɑ̃tiR] *vt* to slow down

râler [Rɑle] *vi* to groan; (*fam*) to grouse, moan (and groan)

rallier [Ralje] *vt* (*rassembler*) to rally; (*re-joindre*) to rejoin; (*gagner à sa cause*) to win over; **se** ~ **à** (*avis*) to come over *ou* round to

rallonge [Ralɔ̃ʒ] *nf* (*de table*) (extra) leaf; (*argent etc*) extra *no pl*

rallonger [Ralɔ̃ʒe] *vt* to lengthen

rallye [Rali] *nm* rally; (*POL*) march

ramassage [Ramasaʒ] *nm*: ~ **scolaire** school bus service

ramassé, e [Ramase] *adj* (*trapu*) squat

ramasser [Ramase] *vt* (*objet tombé ou par terre, fam*) to pick up; (*recueillir*) to collect; (*récolter*) to gather; **se** ~ *vi* (*sur soi-même*) to huddle up; to crouch; **ramassis** (*péj*) *nm* bunch; jumble

rambarde [Rɑ̃baRd(ə)] *nf* guardrail

rame [Ram] *nf* (*aviron*) oar; (*de métro*)

train; (*de papier*) ream

rameau, x [ʀamo] *nm* (small) branch; **les R~x** (*REL*) Palm Sunday *sg*

ramener [ʀamne] *vt* to bring back; (*reconduire*) to take back; (*rabattre: couverture, visière*): ~ **qch sur** to pull sth back over; ~ **qch à** (*réduire à, aussi MATH*) to reduce sth to

ramer [ʀame] *vi* to row

ramollir [ʀamɔliʀ] *vt* to soften; **se ~** *vi* to go soft

ramoner [ʀamɔne] *vt* to sweep

rampe [ʀɑ̃p] *nf* (*d'escalier*) banister(s *pl*); (*dans un garage, d'un terrain*) ramp; (*THÉÂTRE*): **la ~** the footlights *pl*; ~ **de lancement** launching pad

ramper [ʀɑ̃pe] *vi* to crawl

rancard [ʀɑ̃kaʀ] (*fam*) *nm* date; tip

rancart [ʀɑ̃kaʀ] *nm*: **mettre au ~** to scrap

rance [ʀɑ̃s] *adj* rancid

rancœur [ʀɑ̃kœʀ] *nf* rancour

rançon [ʀɑ̃sɔ̃] *nf* ransom; (*fig*) price

rancune [ʀɑ̃kyn] *nf* grudge, rancour; **garder ~ à qn (de qch)** to bear sb a grudge (for sth); **sans ~!** no hard feelings!; **rancunier, ière** *adj* vindictive, spiteful

randonnée [ʀɑ̃dɔne] *nf* ride; (*à pied*) walk, ramble; hike, hiking *no pl*

rang [ʀɑ̃] *nm* (*rangée*) row; (*grade, classement*) rank; ~**s** *nmpl* (*MIL*) ranks; **se mettre en ~s/sur un ~** to get into *ou* form rows/a line; **au premier ~** in the first row; (*fig*) ranking first

rangé, e [ʀɑ̃ʒe] *adj* (*sérieux*) orderly, steady

rangée [ʀɑ̃ʒe] *nf* row

ranger [ʀɑ̃ʒe] *vt* (*classer, grouper*) to order, arrange; (*mettre à sa place*) to put away; (*voiture dans la rue*) to park; (*mettre de l'ordre dans*) to tidy up; (*arranger*) to arrange; (*fig: classer*): ~ **qn/qch parmi** to rank sb/sth among; **se ~** *vi* (*véhicule, conducteur*) to pull over *ou* in; (*piéton*) to step aside; (*s'assagir*) to settle down; **se ~ à** (*avis*) to come round to

ranimer [ʀanime] *vt* (*personne*) to bring round; (*forces, courage*) to restore; (*troupes etc*) to kindle new life in; (*douleur, souvenir*) to revive; (*feu*) to rekindle

rap [ʀap] *nm* rap (music)

rapace [ʀapas] *nm* bird of prey

râpe [ʀɑp] *nf* (*CULIN*) grater

râpé, e [ʀɑpe] *adj* (*tissu*) threadbare

râper [ʀɑpe] *vt* (*CULIN*) to grate

rapetisser [ʀaptise] *vt* to shorten

rapide [ʀapid] *adj* fast; (*prompt*) quick ♦ *nm* express (train); (*de cours d'eau*) rapid; **rapidement** *adv* fast; quickly

rapiécer [ʀapjese] *vt* to patch

rappel [ʀapɛl] *nm* (*THÉÂTRE*) curtain call; (*MÉD: vaccination*) booster; (*ADMIN: de salaire*) back pay *no pl*; (*d'une aventure, d'un nom*) reminder

rappeler [ʀaple] *vt* to call back; (*ambassadeur, MIL*) to recall; (*faire se souvenir*): ~ **qch à qn** to remind sb of sth; **se ~** *vt* (*se souvenir de*) to remember, recall

rapport [ʀapɔʀ] *nm* (*compte rendu*) report; (*profit*) yield, return; revenue; (*lien, analogie*) relationship; (*MATH, TECH*) ratio; ~**s** *nmpl* (*entre personnes, pays*) relations; **avoir ~ à** to have something to do with; **être en ~ avec** (*idée de corrélation*) to be related to; **être/se mettre en ~ avec qn** to be/get in touch with sb; **par ~ à** in relation to; ~ **qualité-prix** *nm* value (for money); ~**s (sexuels)** (sexual) intercourse *sg*

rapporter [ʀapɔʀte] *vt* (*rendre, ramener*) to bring back; (*apporter davantage*) to bring more; (*suj: investissement*) to yield; (: *activité*) to bring in; (*relater*) to report ♦ *vi* (*investissement*) to give a good return *ou* yield; (: *activité*) to be very profitable; **se ~ à** (*correspondre à*) to relate to; **s'en ~ à** to rely on; ~ **qch à** (*fig: rattacher*) to relate sth to; **rapporteur, euse** *nm/f* (*de procès, commission*) reporter; (*péj*) telltale ♦ *nm* (*GÉOM*) protractor

rapprochement [ʀapʀɔʃmɑ̃] *nm* (*de nations, familles*) reconciliation; (*analogie, rapport*) parallel

rapprocher [ʀapʀɔʃe] *vt* (*chaise d'une table*): ~ **qch (de)** to bring sth closer (to); (*deux objets*) to bring closer together; (*réunir*) to bring together; (*comparer*) to establish a parallel between; **se ~** *vi* to draw closer *ou* nearer; **se ~ de** to come closer to; (*présenter une analogie avec*) to be close to

rapt [ʀapt] *nm* abduction

raquette [ʀakɛt] *nf* (*de tennis*) racket; (*de ping-pong*) bat; (*à neige*) snowshoe

rare [ʀaʀ] *adj* rare; (*main-d'œuvre, denrées*) scarce; (*cheveux, herbe*) sparse

rarement [ʀaʀmɑ̃] *adv* rarely, seldom

ras, e [ʀɑ, ʀɑz] *adj* (*tête, cheveux*) close-cropped; (*poil, herbe*) short ♦ *adv* short; **en ~e campagne** in open country; **à ~ bords** to the brim; **au ~ de** level with; **en avoir ~ le bol** (*fam*) to be fed up; ~ **du cou** *adj* (*pull, robe*) crew-neck

rasade [ʀazad] *nf* glassful

raser [ʀaze] *vt* (*barbe, cheveux*) to shave off; (*menton, personne*) to shave; (*fam: ennuyer*) to bore; (*démolir*) to raze (to the ground); (*frôler*) to graze, skim; **se ~** *vi* to shave; (*fam*) to be bored (to tears); **rasoir** *nm* razor

rassasier [ʀasazje] *vt* to satisfy

rassemblement [ʀasɑ̃bləmɑ̃] *nm* (*groupe*) gathering; (*POL*) union

rassembler [ʀasɑ̃ble] *vt* (*réunir*) to assemble, gather; (*regrouper, amasser*) to gather together, collect; **se ~** *vi* to gather

rassis, e [Rasi, -iz] *adj* (*pain*) stale
rassurer [RasyRe] *vt* to reassure; **se ~** *vi* to be reassured; **rassure-toi** don't worry
rat [Ra] *nm* rat
rate [Rat] *nf* spleen
raté, e [Rate] *adj* (*tentative*) unsuccessful, failed ♦ *nm/f* failure ♦ *nm* misfiring *no pl*
râteau, x [Rɑto] *nm* rake
râtelier [Rɑtəlje] *nm* rack; (*fam*) false teeth *pl*
rater [Rate] *vi* (*affaire, projet etc*) to go wrong, fail ♦ *vt* (*cible, train, occasion*) to miss; (*démonstration, plat*) to spoil; (*examen*) to fail
ration [Rɑsjɔ̃] *nf* ration; (*fig*) share
ratisser [Ratise] *vt* (*allée*) to rake; (*feuilles*) to rake up; (*suj: armée, police*) to comb
R.A.T.P. *sigle f* (= *Régie autonome des transports parisiens*) Paris transport authority
rattacher [Rataʃe] *vt* (*animal, cheveux*) to tie up again; (*incorporer: ADMIN etc*): **~ qch à** to join sth to; (*fig: relier*): **~ qch à** to link sth with; (*: lier*): **~ qn à** to bind *ou* tie sb to
rattraper [RatRape] *vt* (*fugitif*) to recapture; (*empêcher de tomber*) to catch (hold of); (*atteindre, rejoindre*) to catch up with; (*réparer: imprudence, erreur*) to make up for; **se ~** *vi* to make good one's losses; to make up for it; **se ~ (à)** (*se raccrocher*) to stop o.s. falling (by catching hold of)
rature [RatyR] *nf* deletion, erasure
rauque [Rok] *adj* raucous; hoarse
ravages [Rava3] *nmpl*: **faire des ~** to wreak havoc
ravaler [Ravale] *vt* (*mur, façade*) to restore; (*déprécier*) to lower
ravi, e [Ravi] *adj*: **être ~ de/que** to be delighted with/that
ravin [Ravɛ̃] *nm* gully, ravine
ravir [RaviR] *vt* (*enchanter*) to delight; (*enlever*): **~ qch à qn** to rob sb of sth; **à ~** beautifully
raviser [Ravize] : **se ~** *vi* to change one's mind
ravissant, e [Ravisɑ̃, -ɑ̃t] *adj* delightful
ravisseur, euse [RavisœR, -øz] *nm/f* abductor, kidnapper
ravitailler [Ravitaje] *vt* to resupply; (*véhicule*) to refuel; **se ~** *vi* to get fresh supplies
raviver [Ravive] *vt* (*feu, douleur*) to revive; (*couleurs*) to brighten up
rayé, e [Reje] *adj* (*à rayures*) striped
rayer [Reje] *vt* (*érafler*) to scratch; (*barrer*) to cross out; (*d'une liste*) to cross off
rayon [Rejɔ̃] *nm* (*de soleil etc*) ray; (*GÉOM*) radius; (*de roue*) spoke; (*étagère*) shelf; (*de grand magasin*) department; **dans un ~ de** within a radius of; **~ d'action** range; **~ de soleil** sunbeam; **~s X** X-rays
rayonnement [Rejɔnmɑ̃] *nm* radiation; (*fig*) radiance; influence

rayonner [Rejone] *vi* (*chaleur, énergie*) to radiate; (*fig*) to shine forth; to be radiant; (*touriste*) to go touring (*from one base*)
rayure [RejyR] *nf* (*motif*) stripe; (*éraflure*) scratch; (*rainure, d'un fusil*) groove
raz-de-marée [Radmare] *nm inv* tidal wave
ré [Re] *nm* (*MUS*) D; (*en chantant la gamme*) re
réacteur [ReaktœR] *nm* jet engine
réaction [Reaksjɔ̃] *nf* reaction; **moteur à ~** jet engine
réadapter [Readapte] *vt* to readjust; (*MÉD*) to rehabilitate; **se ~ (à)** to readjust (to)
réagir [Rea3iR] *vi* to react
réalisateur, trice [RealizatœR, -tRis] *nm/f* (*TV, CINÉMA*) director
réalisation [Realizasjɔ̃] *nf* carrying out; realization; fulfilment; achievement; production; (*œuvre*) production; creation; work
réaliser [Realize] *vt* (*projet, opération*) to carry out, realize; (*rêve, souhait*) to realize, fulfil; (*exploit*) to achieve; (*achat, vente*) to make; (*film*) to produce; (*se rendre compte de, COMM: bien, capital*) to realize; **se ~** *vi* to be realized
réaliste [Realist(ə)] *adj* realistic
réalité [Realite] *nf* reality; **en ~** in (actual) fact; **dans la ~** in reality; **~ virtuelle** (*COMPUT*) virtual reality
réanimation [Reanimasjɔ̃] *nf* resuscitation; **service de ~** intensive care unit
réarmer [ReaRme] *vt* (*arme*) to reload ♦ *vi* (*état*) to rearm
rébarbatif, ive [RebaRbatif, -iv] *adj* forbidding
rebattu, e [Rəbaty] *adj* hackneyed
rebelle [Rəbɛl] *nm/f* rebel ♦ *adj* (*troupes*) rebel; (*enfant*) rebellious; (*mèche etc*) unruly; **~ à** unamenable to
rebeller [Rəbele]: **se ~** *vi* to rebel
rebondi, e [Rəbɔ̃di] *adj* rounded; chubby
rebondir [Rəbɔ̃diR] *vi* (*ballon: au sol*) to bounce; (*: contre un mur*) to rebound; (*fig*) to get moving again; **rebondissement** *nm* new development
rebord [RəbɔR] *nm* edge
rebours [RəbuR]: **à ~** *adv* the wrong way
rebrousse-poil [Rəbruspwal] : **à ~** *adv* the wrong way
rebrousser [Rəbruse] *vt*: **~ chemin** to turn back
rebut [Rəby] *nm*: **mettre au ~** to scrap; **~er** [Rəbyte] *vt* to put off
récalcitrant, e [Rekalsitrɑ̃, -ɑ̃t] *adj* refractory
recaler [Rəkale] *vt* (*SCOL*) to fail
récapituler [Rekapityle] *vt* to recapitulate; to sum up
receler [Rəsəle] *vt* (*produit d'un vol*) to receive; (*malfaiteur*) to harbour; (*fig*) to con-

ceal; **receleur, euse** *nm/f* receiver
récemment [ʀesamɑ̃] *adv* recently
recenser [ʀəsɑ̃se] *vt* (*population*) to take a census of; (*inventorier*) to list
récent, e [ʀesɑ̃, -ɑ̃t] *adj* recent
récépissé [ʀesepise] *nm* receipt
récepteur [ʀeseptœʀ] *nm* receiver; ~ **(de radio)** radio set *ou* receiver
réception [ʀesepsjɔ̃] *nf* receiving *no pl*; (*accueil*) reception, welcome; (*bureau*) reception desk; (*réunion mondaine*) reception, party; **réceptionniste** *nm/f* receptionist
recette [ʀəsɛt] *nf* (CULIN) recipe; (*fig*) formula, recipe; (COMM) takings *pl*; ~**s** *nfpl* (*rentrées*) receipts
receveur, euse [ʀəsvœʀ, -øz] *nm/f* (*des contributions*) tax collector; (*des postes*) postmaster(mistress); (*d'autobus*) conductor(tress)
recevoir [ʀəsvwaʀ] *vt* to receive; (*client, patient*) to see ♦ *vi* to receive visitors; to give parties; to see patients *etc*; **se ~** *vi* (*athlète*) to land; **être reçu** (*à un examen*) to pass
rechange [ʀəʃɑ̃ʒ]: **de ~** *adj* (*pièces, roue*) spare; (*fig: solution*) alternative; **des vêtements de ~** a change of clothes
rechaper [ʀəʃape] *vt* to remould, retread
réchapper [ʀeʃape]: ~ **de** *ou* **à** *vt* (*accident, maladie*) to come through
recharge [ʀəʃaʀʒ] *nf* refill
recharger [ʀəʃaʀʒe] *vt* (*camion, fusil, appareil-photo*) to reload; (*briquet, stylo*) to refill; (*batterie*) to recharge
réchaud [ʀeʃo] *nm* (*portable*) stove; plate-warmer
réchauffer [ʀeʃofe] *vt* (*plat*) to reheat; (*mains, personne*) to warm; **se ~** *vi* (*température*) to get warmer
rêche [ʀɛʃ] *adj* rough
recherche [ʀəʃɛʀʃ(ə)] *nf* (*action*): **la ~ de** the search for; (*raffinement*) affectedness, studied elegance; (*scientifique etc*): **la ~** research; ~**s** *nfpl* (*de la police*) investigations; (*scientifiques*) research *sg*; **se mettre à la ~ de** to go in search of
recherché, e [ʀəʃɛʀʃe] *adj* (*rare, demandé*) much sought-after; (*raffiné*) studied, affected
rechercher [ʀəʃɛʀʃe] *vt* (*objet égaré, personne*) to look for; (*causes, nouveau procédé*) to try to find; (*bonheur, amitié*) to seek
rechute [ʀəʃyt] *nf* (MÉD) relapse
récidiver [ʀesidive] *vi* to commit a subsequent offence; (*fig*) to do it again
récif [ʀesif] *nm* reef
récipient [ʀesipjɑ̃] *nm* container
réciproque [ʀesipʀɔk] *adj* reciprocal
récit [ʀesi] *nm* story
récital [ʀesital] *nm* recital
réciter [ʀesite] *vt* to recite
réclamation [ʀeklamasjɔ̃] *nf* complaint; ~**s**

nfpl (*bureau*) complaints department *sg*
réclame [ʀeklam] *nf* ad, advert(isement); **article en ~** special offer
réclamer [ʀeklame] *vt* (*aide, nourriture etc*) to ask for; (*revendiquer*) to claim, demand; (*nécessiter*) to demand, require ♦ *vi* to complain
réclusion [ʀeklyzjɔ̃] *nf* imprisonment
recoin [ʀəkwɛ̃] *nm* nook, corner; (*fig*) hidden recess
reçois *etc vb voir* **recevoir**
récolte [ʀekɔlt(ə)] *nf* harvesting; gathering; (*produits*) harvest, crop; (*fig*) crop, collection
récolter [ʀekɔlte] *vt* to harvest, gather (in); (*fig*) to collect; to get
recommandé [ʀəkɔmɑ̃de] *nm* (POSTES): **en ~** by registered mail
recommander [ʀəkɔmɑ̃de] *vt* to recommend; (*suj: qualités etc*) to commend; (POSTES) to register; **se ~ de qn** to give sb's name as a reference
recommencer [ʀəkɔmɑ̃se] *vt* (*reprendre: lutte, séance*) to resume, start again; (*refaire: travail, explications*) to start afresh, start (over) again; (*récidiver: erreur*) to make again ♦ *vi* to start again; (*récidiver*) to do it again
récompense [ʀekɔ̃pɑ̃s] *nf* reward; (*prix*) award; **récompenser** *vt*: **récompenser qn (de** *ou* **pour)** to reward sb (for)
réconcilier [ʀekɔ̃silje] *vt* to reconcile; **se ~ (avec)** to be reconciled (with)
reconduire [ʀəkɔ̃dɥiʀ] *vt* (*raccompagner*) to take *ou* see back; (JUR, POL: *renouveler*) to renew
réconfort [ʀekɔ̃fɔʀ] *nm* comfort
réconforter [ʀekɔ̃fɔʀte] *vt* (*consoler*) to comfort; (*revigorer*) to fortify
reconnaissance [ʀəkɔnɛsɑ̃s] *nf* recognition; acknowledgement; (*gratitude*) gratitude, gratefulness; (MIL) reconnaissance, recce; **reconnaissant, e** [ʀəkɔnɛsɑ̃, -ɑ̃t] *adj* grateful
reconnaître [ʀəkɔnɛtʀ(ə)] *vt* to recognize; (MIL: *lieu*) to reconnoitre; (JUR: *enfant, dette, droit*) to acknowledge; ~ **que** to admit *ou* acknowledge that; ~ **qn/qch à** to recognize sb/sth by
reconnu, e [ʀ(ə)kɔny] *adj* (*indiscuté, connu*) recognized
reconstituant, e [ʀəkɔ̃stitɥɑ̃, -ɑ̃t] *adj* (*aliment, régime*) strength-building
reconstituer [ʀəkɔ̃stitɥe] *vt* (*monument ancien*) to recreate; (*fresque, vase brisé*) to piece together, reconstitute; (*événement, accident*) to reconstruct; (*fortune, patrimoine*) to rebuild
reconstruire [ʀəkɔ̃stʀɥiʀ] *vt* to rebuild
reconvertir [ʀəkɔ̃vɛʀtiʀ]: **se ~** *vr* (*un métier, une branche*) to go into
record [ʀəkɔʀ] *nm, adj* record

recoupement [ʀəkupmɑ̃] *nm*: par ~ by cross-checking

recouper [ʀəkupe]: **se** ~ *vi (témoignages)* to tie *ou* match up

recourbé, e [ʀəkuʀbe] *adj* curved; hooked; bent

recourir [ʀəkuʀiʀ]: ~ **à** *vt (ami, agence)* to turn *ou* appeal to; *(force, ruse, emprunt)* to resort to

recours [ʀəkuʀ] *nm (JUR)* appeal; **avoir** ~ **à** = **recourir à**; **en dernier** ~ as a last resort; ~ **en grâce** plea for clemency

recouvrer [ʀəkuvʀe] *vt (vue, santé etc)* to recover, regain; *(impôts)* to collect; *(créance)* to recover

recouvrir [ʀəkuvʀiʀ] *vt (couvrir à nouveau)* to re-cover; *(couvrir entièrement, aussi fig)* to cover; *(cacher, masquer)* to conceal, hide; **se** ~ *vi (se superposer)* to overlap

récréation [ʀekʀeɑsjɔ̃] *nf* recreation, entertainment; *(SCOL)* break

récrier [ʀekʀije]: **se** ~ *vi* to exclaim

récriminations [ʀekʀiminɑsjɔ̃] *nfpl* remonstrations, complaints

recroqueviller [ʀəkʀɔkvije]: **se** ~ *vi (feuilles)* to curl *ou* shrivel up; *(personne)* to huddle up

recrudescence [ʀəkʀydesɑ̃s] *nf* fresh outbreak

recrue [ʀəkʀy] *nf* recruit

recruter [ʀəkʀyte] *vt* to recruit

rectangle [ʀɛktɑ̃gl(ə)] *nm* rectangle; **rectangulaire** *adj* rectangular

recteur [ʀɛktœʀ] *nm* ≈ (regional) director of education *(BRIT)*, ≈ state superintendent of education *(US)*

rectificatif [ʀɛktifikatif, -iv] *nm* correction

rectifier [ʀɛktifje] *vt (tracé, virage)* to straighten; *(calcul, adresse)* to correct; *(erreur, faute)* to rectify

rectiligne [ʀɛktiliɲ] *adj* straight; *(GÉOM)* rectilinear

reçu, e [ʀəsy] *pp de* **recevoir** ♦ *adj (admis, consacré)* accepted ♦ *nm (COMM)* receipt

recueil [ʀəkœj] *nm* collection

recueillir [ʀəkœjiʀ] *vt* to collect; *(voix, suffrages)* to win; *(accueillir: réfugiés, chat)* to take in; **se** ~ *vi* to gather one's thoughts; to meditate

recul [ʀəkyl] *nm* retreat; recession; decline; *(d'arme à feu)* recoil, kick; **avoir un mouvement de** ~ to recoil; **prendre du** ~ to stand back

reculé, e [ʀəkyle] *adj* remote

reculer [ʀəkyle] *vi* to move back, back away; *(AUTO)* to reverse, back (up); *(fig)* to (be on the) decline; to be losing ground; *(: se dérober)* to shrink back ♦ *vt* to move back; to reverse, back (up); *(fig: possibilités, limites)* to extend; *(: date, décision)* to postpone

reculons [ʀəkylɔ̃]: **à** ~ *adv* backwards

récupérer [ʀekypeʀe] *vt* to recover, get back; *(heures de travail)* to make up; *(déchets)* to salvage; *(délinquant etc)* to rehabilitate ♦ *vi* to recover

récurer [ʀekyʀe] *vt* to scour

récuser [ʀekyze] *vt* to challenge; **se** ~ *vi* to decline to give an opinion

reçut *vb voir* **recevoir**

recycler [ʀəsikle] *vt (SCOL)* to reorientate; *(employés)* to retrain; *(TECH)* to recycle

rédacteur, trice [ʀedaktœʀ, -tʀis] *nm/f (journaliste)* writer; subeditor; *(d'ouvrage de référence)* editor, compiler; ~ **en chef** chief editor; ~ **publicitaire** copywriter

rédaction [ʀedaksjɔ̃] *nf* writing; *(rédacteurs)* editorial staff; *(bureau)* editorial office(s); *(SCOL: devoir)* essay, composition

reddition [ʀedisjɔ̃] *nf* surrender

redemander [ʀədmɑ̃de] *vt* to ask again for; to ask for more of

redescendre [ʀədesɑ̃dʀ(ə)] *vi* to go back down ♦ *vt (pente etc)* to go down

redevable [ʀədvabl(ə)] *adj*: **être** ~ **de qch à qn** *(somme)* to owe sb sth; *(fig)* to be indebted to sb for sth

redevance [ʀədvɑ̃s] *nf (TÉL)* rental charge; *(TV)* licence fee

rédiger [ʀedige] *vt* to write; *(contrat)* to draw up

redire [ʀədiʀ] *vt* to repeat; **trouver à** ~ **à** to find fault with

redoublé, e [ʀəduble] *adj*: **à coups** ~s even harder, twice as hard

redoubler [ʀəduble] *vi (tempête, violence)* to intensify; *(SCOL)* to repeat a year; ~ **de** to be twice as +*adjectif*

redoutable [ʀədutabl(ə)] *adj* formidable, fearsome

redouter [ʀədute] *vt* to fear; *(appréhender)* to dread

redresser [ʀədʀese] *vt (arbre, mât)* to set upright; *(pièce tordue)* to straighten out; *(situation, économie)* to put right; **se** ~ *vi (objet penché)* to right itself; *(personne)* to sit *(ou* stand) up (straight)

réduction [ʀedyksjɔ̃] *nf* reduction

réduire [ʀeduiʀ] *vt* to reduce; *(prix, dépenses)* to cut, reduce; *(MÉD: fracture)* to set; **se** ~ **à** *(revenir à)* to boil down to; **se** ~ **en** *(se transformer en)* to be reduced to

réduit [ʀedui] *nm* tiny room; recess

rééducation [ʀeedykɑsjɔ̃] *nf (d'un membre)* re-education; *(de délinquants, d'un blessé)* rehabilitation

réel, le [ʀeɛl] *adj* real

réellement [ʀeɛlmɑ̃] *adv* really

réévaluer [ʀeevalɥe] *vt* to revalue

réexpédier [ʀeɛkspedje] *vt (à l'envoyeur)* to return, send back; *(au destinataire)* to send on, forward

refaire [ʀəfɛʀ] *vt (faire de nouveau, recommencer)* to do again; *(réparer, restaurer)* to do up

réfection [ʀefɛksjɔ̃] *nf* repair

réfectoire [ʀefɛktwaʀ] *nm* refectory

référence [ʀefeʀɑ̃s] *nf* reference; ~s *nfpl* (*recommandations*) reference *sg*

référer [ʀefeʀe] : se ~ **à** *vt* to refer to; **en ~ à qn** to refer the matter to sb

réfléchi, e [ʀefleʃi] *adj* (*caractère*) thoughtful; (*action*) well-thought-out; (*LING*) reflexive

réfléchir [ʀefleʃiʀ] *vt* to reflect ♦ *vi* to think; ~ **à** *ou* **sur** to think about

reflet [ʀəflɛ] *nm* reflection; (*sur l'eau etc*) sheen *no pl*, glint

refléter [ʀəflete] *vt* to reflect; **se** ~ *vi* to be reflected

réflexe [ʀeflɛks(ə)] *nm, adj* reflex

réflexion [ʀeflɛksjɔ̃] *nf* (*de la lumière etc, pensée*) reflection; (*fait de penser*) thought; (*remarque*) remark; ~ **faite, à la** ~ on reflection

refluer [ʀəflye] *vi* to flow back; (*foule*) to surge back

reflux [ʀəfly] *nm* (*de la mer*) ebb

réforme [ʀefɔʀm(ə)] *nf* reform; (*REL*): **la R~** the Reformation

réformer [ʀefɔʀme] *vt* to reform; (*MIL*) to declare unfit for service

refouler [ʀəfule] *vt* (*envahisseurs*) to drive back; (*liquide*) to force back; (*fig*) to suppress; (*PSYCH*) to repress

réfractaire [ʀefʀaktɛʀ] *adj*: **être** ~ **à** to resist

refrain [ʀəfʀɛ̃] *nm* (*MUS*) refrain, chorus; (*air, fig*) tune

refréner [ʀəfʀene] *vt* to curb, check

réfréner [ʀefʀene] *vt* = **refréner**

réfrigérateur [ʀefʀiʒeʀatœʀ] *nm* refrigerator, fridge

refroidir [ʀəfʀwadiʀ] *vt* to cool ♦ *vi* to cool (down); **se** ~ *vi* (*prendre froid*) to catch a chill; (*temps*) to get cooler *ou* colder; (*fig*) to cool (off); **refroidissement** *nm* (*grippe etc*) chill

refuge [ʀəfyʒ] *nm* refuge; (*pour piétons*) (traffic) island

réfugié, e [ʀefyʒje] *adj, nm/f* refugee

réfugier [ʀefyʒje]: **se** ~ *vi* to take refuge

refus [ʀəfy] *nm* refusal; **ce n'est pas de** ~ I won't say no, it's welcome

refuser [ʀəfyze] *vt* to refuse; (*SCOL: candidat*) to fail; ~ **qch à qn** to refuse sb sth; ~ **du monde** to have to turn people away; **se** ~ **à faire** to refuse to do

réfuter [ʀefyte] *vt* to refute

regagner [ʀəgaɲe] *vt* (*argent, faveur*) to win back; (*lieu*) to get back to; ~ **le temps perdu** to make up (for) lost time

regain [ʀəgɛ̃] *nm* (*renouveau*): **un** ~ **de** renewed +*nom*

régal [ʀegal] *nm* treat

régaler [ʀegale]: **se** ~ *vi* to have a deli-

cious meal; (*fig*) to enjoy o.s.

regard [ʀəgaʀ] *nm* (*coup d'œil*) look, glance; (*expression*) look (in one's eye); **au** ~ **de** (*loi, morale*) from the point of view of; **en** ~ (*vis à vis*) opposite; **en** ~ **de** in comparison with

regardant, e [ʀəgaʀdɑ̃, -ɑ̃t] *adj*: **très/peu** ~ **(sur)** quite fussy/very free (about); (*économe*) very tight-fisted/quite generous (with)

regarder [ʀəgaʀde] *vt* (*examiner, observer, lire*) to look at; (*film, télévision, match*) to watch; (*envisager: situation, avenir*) to view; (*considérer: son intérêt etc*) to be concerned with; (*être orienté vers*): ~ **(vers)** to face; (*concerner*) to concern ♦ *vi* to look; ~ **à** (*dépense*) to be fussy with *ou* over; ~ **qn/ qch comme** to regard sb/sth as

régie [ʀeʒi] *nf* (*COMM, INDUSTRIE*) state-owned company; (*THÉÂTRE, CINÉMA*) production; (*RADIO, TV*) control room

regimber [ʀəʒɛ̃be] *vi* to balk, jib

régime [ʀeʒim] *nm* (*POL*) régime; (*ADMIN: carcéral, fiscal etc*) system; (*MÉD*) diet; (*TECH*) (*engine*) speed; (*fig*) rate, pace; (*de bananes, dattes*) bunch; **se mettre au/ suivre un** ~ to go on/be on a diet

régiment [ʀeʒimɑ̃] *nm* regiment; (*fig: fam*): **un** ~ **de** an army of

région [ʀeʒjɔ̃] *nf* region; **régional, e, aux** *adj* regional

régir [ʀeʒiʀ] *vt* to govern

régisseur [ʀeʒisœʀ] *nm* (*d'un domaine*) steward; (*CINÉMA, TV*) assistant director; (*THÉÂTRE*) stage manager

registre [ʀeʒistʀ(ə)] *nm* (*livre*) register; logbook; ledger; (*MUS, LING*) register

réglage [ʀeglaʒ] *nm* adjustment; tuning

règle [ʀɛgl(ə)] *nf* (*instrument*) ruler; (*loi, prescription*) rule; ~s *nfpl* (*PHYSIOL*) period *sg*; **en** ~ (*papiers d'identité*) in order; **en** ~ **générale** as a (general) rule

réglé, e [ʀegle] *adj* well-ordered; steady; (*papier*) ruled; (*arrangé*) settled

règlement [ʀɛgləmɑ̃] *nm* (*paiement*) settlement; (*arrêté*) regulation; (*règles, statuts*) regulations *pl*, rules *pl*; ~ **de compte(s)** *nm* settling of old scores; **réglementaire** *adj* conforming to the regulations; (*tenue*) regulation *cpd*; **réglementer** [ʀɛgləmɑ̃te] *vt* to regulate

régler [ʀegle] *vt* (*mécanisme, machine*) to regulate, adjust; (*moteur*) to tune; (*thermostat etc*) to set, adjust; (*conflit, facture*) to settle; (*fournisseur*) to settle up with

réglisse [ʀeglis] *nf* liquorice

règne [ʀɛɲ] *nm* (*d'un roi etc, fig*) reign; (*BIO*): **le** ~ **végétal/animal** the vegetable/ animal kingdom

régner [ʀeɲe] *vi* (*roi*) to rule, reign; (*fig*) to reign

regorger [ʀəgɔʀʒe] *vi*: ~ **de** to overflow

with, be bursting with

regret [ʀəgʀɛ] *nm* regret; **à ~** with regret; **avec ~** regretfully; **être au ~ de devoir faire** to regret having to do

regrettable [ʀəgʀɛtabl(ə)] *adj* regrettable

regretter [ʀəgʀete] *vt* to regret; (*personne*) to miss; **je regrette** I'm sorry

regrouper [ʀəgʀupe] *vt* (*grouper*) to group together; (*contenir*) to include, comprise; **se ~** *vi* to gather (together)

régulier, ière [ʀegylje, -jɛʀ] *adj* (*gén*) regular; (*vitesse, qualité*) steady; (*répartition, pression, paysage*) even; (*TRANSPORTS: ligne, service*) scheduled, regular; (*légal, réglementaire*) lawful, in order; (*fam: correct*) straight, on the level; **régulièrement** *adv* regularly; steadily; evenly; normally

rehausser [ʀəose] *vt* to heighten, raise

rein [ʀɛ̃] *nm* kidney; **~s** *nmpl* (*dos*) back *sg*

reine [ʀɛn] *nf* queen

reine-claude [ʀɛnklod] *nf* greengage

réintégrer [ʀeɛ̃tegʀe] *vt* (*lieu*) to return to; (*fonctionnaire*) to reinstate

rejaillir [ʀəʒajiʀ] *vi* to splash up; **~ sur** to splash up onto; (*fig*) to rebound on; to fall upon

rejet [ʀəʒɛ] *nm* (*action, aussi MÉD*) rejection

rejeter [ʀəʒte] *vt* (*relancer*) to throw back; (*vomir*) to bring ou throw up; (*écarter*) to reject; (*déverser*) to throw out, discharge; **~ la responsabilité de qch sur qn** to lay the responsibility for sth at sb's door

rejoindre [ʀəʒwɛ̃dʀ(ə)] *vt* (*famille, régiment*) to rejoin, return to; (*lieu*) to get (back) to; (*suj: route etc*) to meet, join; (*rattraper*) to catch up (with); **se ~** *vi* to meet; **je te rejoins au café** I'll see *ou* meet you at the café

réjouir [ʀeʒwiʀ] *vt* to delight; **se ~** *vi* to be delighted; to rejoice; **réjouissances** *nfpl* (*joie*) rejoicing *sg*; (*fête*) festivities

relâche [ʀəlɑʃ]: **sans ~** without respite *ou* a break

relâché, e [ʀəlɑʃe] *adj* loose, lax

relâcher [ʀəlɑʃe] *vt* to release; (*étreinte*) to loosen; **se ~** *vi* to loosen; (*discipline*) to become slack *ou* lax; (*élève etc*) to slacken off

relais [ʀəlɛ] *nm* (*SPORT*): **(course de) ~** relay (race); **équipe de ~** shift team; (*SPORT*) relay team; **prendre le ~ (de)** to take over (from); **~ routier** ≈ transport café (*BRIT*), ≈ truck stop (*US*)

relancer [ʀəlɑ̃se] *vt* (*balle*) to throw back; (*moteur*) to restart; (*fig*) to boost, revive; (*personne*): **~ qn** to pester sb

relater [ʀəlate] *vt* to relate, recount

relatif, ive [ʀəlatif, -iv] *adj* relative

relation [ʀəlasjɔ̃] *nf* (*récit*) account, report; (*rapport*) relation(ship); **~s** *nfpl* (*rapports*) relations; relationship *sg*; (*connaissances*) connections; **être/entrer en ~(s) avec** to be/get in contact with

relaxer [ʀəlakse] *vt* to relax; (*JUR*) to discharge; **se ~** *vi* to relax

relayer [ʀəleje] *vt* (*collaborateur, coureur etc*) to relieve; **se ~** *vi* (*dans une activité*) to take it in turns

reléguer [ʀəlege] *vt* to relegate

relent(s) [ʀəlɑ̃] *nm(pl)* (foul) smell

relevé, e [ʀəlve] *adj* (*manches*) rolled-up; (*sauce*) highly-seasoned ♦ *nm* (*lecture*) reading; (*liste*) statement; list; (*facture*) account; **~ de compte** bank statement

relève [ʀəlɛv] *nf* relief; relief team (*ou* troops *pl*); **prendre la ~** to take over

relever [ʀəlve] *vt* (*statue, meuble*) to stand up again; (*personne tombée*) to help up; (*vitre, niveau de vie*) to raise; (*col*) to turn up; (*style, conversation*) to elevate; (*plat, sauce*) to season; (*sentinelle, équipe*) to relieve; (*fautes, points*) to pick out; (*constater: traces etc*) to find, pick up; (*répliquer à: remarque*) to react to, reply to; (*: défi*) to accept, take up; (*noter: adresse etc*) to take down, note; (*: plan*) to sketch; (*: cotes etc*) to plot; (*compteur*) to read; (*ramasser: cahiers*) to collect, take in; **se ~** *vi* (*se remettre debout*) to get up; **~ de** (*maladie*) to be recovering from; (*être du ressort de*) to be a matter for; (*ADMIN: dépendre de*) to come under; (*fig*) to pertain to; **~ qn de** (*fonctions*) to relieve sb of; **~ la tête** to look up; to hold up one's head

relief [ʀəljɛf] *nm* relief; **~s** *nmpl* (*restes*) remains; **mettre en ~** (*fig*) to bring out, highlight

relier [ʀəlje] *vt* to link (up); (*livre*) to bind; **~ qch à** to link sth to

religieuse [ʀəliʒjøz] *nf* nun; (*gâteau*) cream bun

religieux, euse [ʀəliʒjø, -øz] *adj* religious ♦ *nm* monk

religion [ʀəliʒjɔ̃] *nf* religion; (*piété, dévotion*) faith

relire [ʀəliʀ] *vt* (*à nouveau*) to reread, read again; (*vérifier*) to read over

reliure [ʀəljyʀ] *nf* binding

reluire [ʀəlɥiʀ] *vi* to gleam

remanier [ʀəmanje] *vt* to reshape, recast; (*POL*) to reshuffle

remarquable [ʀəmaʀkabl(ə)] *adj* remarkable

remarque [ʀəmaʀk(ə)] *nf* remark; (*écrite*) note

remarquer [ʀəmaʀke] *vt* (*voir*) to notice; **se ~** *vi* to be noticeable; **faire ~ (à qn) que** to point out (to sb) that; **faire ~ qch (à qn)** to point sth out (to sb); **remarquez, ... mind you ...**

remblai [ʀɑ̃blɛ] *nm* embankment

rembourrer [ʀɑ̃buʀe] *vt* to stuff; (*dossier, vêtement, souliers*) to pad

remboursement [ʀɑ̃buʀsəmɑ̃] *nm* repayment; **envoi contre ~** cash on delivery;

rembourser [ʀɑ̃buʀse] vt to pay back, repay

remède [ʀəmɛd] nm (*médicament*) medicine; (*traitement, fig*) remedy, cure

remémorer: [ʀəmemɔʀe] **se** ~ vt to recall, recollect

remerciements [ʀəmɛʀsimɑ̃] nmpl thanks

remercier [ʀəmɛʀsje] vt to thank; (*congédier*) to dismiss; ~ **qn de/d'avoir fait** to thank sb for/for having done

remettre [ʀəmɛtʀ(ə)] vt (*vêtement*): ~ **qch** to put sth back on; (*replacer*): ~ **qch quelque part** to put sth back somewhere; (*ajouter*): ~ **du sel/un sucre** to add more salt/another lump of sugar; (*ajourner*): ~ **qch (à)** to postpone sth (until); **se** ~ vi to get better, recover; **se** ~ **de** to recover from, get over; **s'en** ~ **à** to leave it (up) to; ~ **qch à qn** (*rendre, restituer*) to give sth back to sb; (*donner, confier: paquet, argent*) to hand over sth to sb, deliver sth to sb; (: *prix, décoration*) to present sb with sth

remise [ʀəmiz] nf delivery; presentation; (*rabais*) discount; (*local*) shed; ~ **de peine** reduction of sentence; ~ **en jeu** (FOOTBALL) throw-in

remontant [ʀəmɔ̃tɑ̃] nm tonic, pick-me-up

remonte-pente [ʀəmɔ̃tpɑ̃t] nm ski-lift

remonter [ʀəmɔ̃te] vi to go back up; (*jupe*) to ride up ♦ vt (*pente*) to go up; (*fleuve*) to sail (*ou* swim etc) up; (*manches, pantalon*) to roll up; (*col*) to turn up; (*niveau, limite*) to raise; (*fig: personne*) to buck up; (*moteur, meuble*) to put back together, reassemble; (*montre, mécanisme*) to wind up; ~ **le moral à qn** to raise sb's spirits; ~ **à** (*dater de*) to date ou go back to

remontrance [ʀəmɔ̃tʀɑ̃s] nf reproof, reprimand

remontrer [ʀəmɔ̃tʀe] vt (*fig*): **en** ~ **à** to prove one's superiority over

remords [ʀəmɔʀ] nm remorse no pl; **avoir des** ~ to feel remorse

remorque [ʀəmɔʀk(ə)] nf trailer; **être en** ~ to be on tow; **remorquer** vt to tow; **remorqueur** nm tug(boat)

remous [ʀəmu] nm (*d'un navire*) (back)wash no pl; (*de rivière*) swirl, eddy ♦ nmpl (*fig*) stir sg

remparts [ʀɑ̃paʀ] nmpl walls, ramparts

remplaçant, e [ʀɑ̃plasɑ̃, -ɑ̃t] nm/f replacement, stand-in; (THÉÂTRE) understudy; (SCOL) supply teacher

remplacement [ʀɑ̃plasmɑ̃] nm replacement; (*job*) replacement work no pl

remplacer [ʀɑ̃plase] vt to replace; (*tenir lieu de*) to take the place of; ~ **qch/qn par** to replace sth/sb with

rempli, e [ʀɑ̃pli] adj (*emploi du temps*) full, busy; ~ **de** full of, filled with

remplir [ʀɑ̃pliʀ] vt to fill (up); (*questionnaire*) to fill out ou up; (*obligations, fonc-*

tion, condition) to fulfil; **se** ~ vi to fill up

remporter [ʀɑ̃pɔʀte] vt (*marchandise*) to take away; (*fig*) to win, achieve

remuant, e [ʀəmɥɑ̃, -ɑ̃t] adj restless

remue-ménage [ʀəmymenaʒ] nm inv commotion

remuer [ʀəmɥe] vt to move; (*café, sauce*) to stir ♦ vi to move; **se** ~ vi to move

rémunérer [ʀemyneʀe] vt to remunerate

renard [ʀənaʀ] nm fox

renchérir [ʀɑ̃ʃeʀiʀ] vi (*fig*): ~ **(sur)** to add something (to)

rencontre [ʀɑ̃kɔ̃tʀ(ə)] nf meeting; (*imprévue*) encounter; **aller à la** ~ **de qn** to go and meet sb

rencontrer [ʀɑ̃kɔ̃tʀe] vt to meet; (*mot, expression*) to come across; (*difficultés*) to meet with; **se** ~ vi to meet; (*véhicules*) to collide

rendement [ʀɑ̃dmɑ̃] nm (*d'un travailleur, d'une machine*) output; (*d'une culture*) yield; (*d'un investissement*) return; **à plein** ~ at full capacity

rendez-vous [ʀɑ̃devu] nm (*rencontre*) appointment; (: *d'amoureux*) date; (*lieu*) meeting place; **donner** ~ **à qn** to arrange to meet sb; **avoir/prendre** ~ **(avec)** to have/make an appointment (with)

rendre [ʀɑ̃dʀ(ə)] vt (*livre, argent etc*) to give back, return; (*otages, visite etc*) to return; (*sang, aliments*) to bring up; (*exprimer, traduire*) to render; (*faire devenir*): ~ **qn célèbre/qch possible** to make sb famous/sth possible; **se** ~ vi (*capituler*) to surrender, give o.s. up; (*aller*): **se** ~ **quelque part** to go somewhere; **se** ~ **compte de qch** to realize sth

rênes [ʀɛn] nfpl reins

renfermé, e [ʀɑ̃fɛʀme] adj (*fig*) withdrawn ♦ nm: **sentir le** ~ to smell stuffy

renfermer [ʀɑ̃fɛʀme] vt to contain

renflement [ʀɑ̃fləmɑ̃] nm bulge

renflouer [ʀɑ̃flue] vt to refloat; (*fig*) to set back on its (*ou* his/her etc) feet

renfoncement [ʀɑ̃fɔ̃smɑ̃] nm recess

renforcer [ʀɑ̃fɔʀse] vt to reinforce

renfort [ʀɑ̃fɔʀ] : ~**s** nmpl reinforcements; **à grand** ~ **de** with a great deal of

renfrogné, e [ʀɑ̃fʀɔɲe] adj sullen

rengaine [ʀɑ̃gɛn] (*péj*) nf old tune

renier [ʀənje] vt (*parents*) to disown, repudiate; (*foi*) to renounce

renifler [ʀənifle] vi, vt to sniff

renne [ʀɛn] nm reindeer inv

renom [ʀənɔ̃] nm reputation; (*célébrité*) renown; **renommé, e** adj celebrated, renowned; **renommée** nf fame

renoncer [ʀənɔ̃se]: ~ **à** vt to give up; ~ **à faire** to give up the idea of doing

renouer [ʀənwe] vt: ~ **avec** (*tradition*) to revive; (*habitude*) to take up again; ~ **avec qn** to take up with sb again

renouvelable [R(ə)nuvlabl(ə)] *adj* (*énergie etc*) renewable

renouveler [Rənuvle] *vt* to renew; (*exploit, méfait*) to repeat; **se ~** *vi* (*incident*) to recur, happen again; **renouvellement** *nm* renewal; recurrence

rénover [Renɔve] *vt* (*immeuble*) to renovate, do up; (*enseignement*) to reform; (*quartier*) to redevelop

renseignement [Rãsɛɲmã] *nm* information *no pl*, piece of information; (**guichet des**) **~s** information desk

renseigner [Rãsɛɲe] *vt*: **~ qn (sur)** to give information to sb (about); **se ~** *vi* to ask for information, make inquiries

rentabilité [Rãtabilite] *nf* profitablity

rentable [Rãtabl(ə)] *adj* profitable

rente [Rãt] *nf* income; pension; government stock *ou* bond; **rentier, ière** *nm/f* person of private means

rentrée [Rãtre] *nf*: **~ (d'argent)** cash *no pl* coming in; **la ~ (des classes)** the start of the new school year

rentrer [Rãtre] *vi* (*entrer de nouveau*) to go (*ou* come) back in; (*entrer*) to go (*ou* come) in; (*revenir chez soi*) to go (*ou* come) (back) home; (*air, clou: pénétrer*) to go in; (*revenu, argent*) to come in ♦ *vt* (*foins*) to bring in; (*véhicule*) to put away; (*chemise dans pantalon etc*) to tuck in; (*griffes*) to draw in; (*fig: larmes, colère etc*) to hold back; **~ le ventre** to pull in one's stomach; **~ dans** (*heurter*) to crash into; **~ dans l'ordre** to be back to normal; **~ dans ses frais** to recover one's expenses

renversant, e [Rãvɛrsã, -ãt] *adj* astounding

renverse [Rãvɛrs(ə)]: **à la ~** *adv* backwards

renverser [Rãvɛrse] *vt* (*faire tomber: chaise, verre*) to knock over, overturn; (*piéton*) to knock down; (*liquide, contenu*) to spill, upset; (*retourner*) to turn upside down; (: *ordre des mots etc*) to reverse; (*fig: gouvernement etc*) to overthrow; (*stupéfier*) to bowl over; **se ~** *vi* to fall over; to overturn; to spill

renvoi [Rãvwa] *nm* (*référence*) cross-reference; (*éructation*) belch

renvoyer [Rãvwaje] *vt* to send back; (*congédier*) to dismiss; (*lumière*) to reflect; (*son*) to echo; (*ajourner*): **~ qch (à)** to put sth off *ou* postpone sth (until); **~ qn à** (*fig*) to refer sb to

repaire [Rəpɛr] *nm* den

répandre [Repãdr(ə)] *vt* (*renverser*) to spill; (*étaler, diffuser*) to spread; (*lumière*) to shed; (*chaleur, odeur*) to give off; **se ~** *vi* to spill; to spread; **répandu, e** *adj* (*opinion, usage*) widespread

réparation [Reparasjɔ̃] *nf* repair

réparer [Repare] *vt* to repair; (*fig: offense*) to make up for, atone for; (: *oubli, erreur*) to put right

repartie [Rəparti] *nf* retort; **avoir de la ~** to be quick at repartee

repartir [Rəpartir] *vi* to set off again; to leave again; (*fig*) to get going again; **~ à zéro** to start from scratch (again)

répartir [Repartir] *vt* (*pour attribuer*) to share out; (*pour disperser, disposer*) to divide up; (*poids, chaleur*) to distribute; **se ~** *vt* (*travail, rôles*) to share out between themselves; **répartition** *nf* sharing out; dividing up; distribution

repas [Rəpɑ] *nm* meal

repasser [Rəpase] *vi* to come (*ou* go) back ♦ *vt* (*vêtement, tissu*) to iron; (*examen*) to retake, resit; (*film*) to show again; (*leçon, rôle: revoir*) to go over (again)

repêcher [Rəpeʃe] *vt* (*noyé*) to recover the body of; (*candidat*) to pass (*by inflating marks*)

repentir [Rəpãtir] *nm* repentance; **se ~** *vi* to repent; **se ~ de** to repent of

répercussions [Reperkysjɔ̃] *nfpl* (*fig*) repercussions

répercuter [Reperkyte] *vt* (*information, hausse des prix*) to pass on; **se ~** *vi* (*bruit*) to reverberate; (*fig*): **se ~ sur** to have repercussions on

repère [Rəpɛr] *nm* mark; (*monument etc*) landmark

repérer [Rəpere] *vt* (*erreur, connaissance*) to spot; (*abri, ennemi*) to locate; **se ~** *vi* to find one's way about

répertoire [Repertwar] *nm* (*liste*) (alphabetical) list; (*carnet*) index notebook; (*d'un artiste*) repertoire

répéter [Repete] *vt* to repeat; (*préparer: leçon; aussi vi*) to learn, go over; (*THÉÂTRE*) to rehearse; **se ~** *vi* (*redire*) to repeat o.s.; (*se reproduire*) to be repeated, recur

répétition [Repetisjɔ̃] *nf* repetition; (*THÉÂTRE*) rehearsal; **~ générale** final dress rehearsal

répit [Repi] *nm* respite

replet, ète [Rəplɛ, -ɛt] *adj* chubby

replier [Rəplije] *vt* (*rabattre*) to fold down *ou* over; **se ~** *vi* (*troupes, armée*) to withdraw, fall back

réplique [Replik] *nf* (*repartie, fig*) reply; (*THÉÂTRE*) line; (*copie*) replica; **~r** [Replike] *vi* to reply; (*riposter*) to retaliate

répondeur *nm*: **~ automatique** (*TÉL*) answering machine

répondre [Repɔ̃dr(ə)] *vi* to answer, reply; (*freins, mécanisme*) to respond; **~ à** to reply to, answer; (*affection, salut*) to return; (*provocation, suj: mécanisme etc*) to respond to; (*correspondre à: besoin*) to answer; (: *conditions*) to meet; (: *description*) to match; (*avec impertinence*): **~ à qn** to answer sb back; **~ de** to answer for

réponse [ʀepɔ̃s] *nf* answer, reply; **en ~ à** in reply to

reportage [ʀəpɔʀtaʒ] *nm* (*bref*) report; (*écrit: documentaire*) story; article; (*en direct*) commentary; (*genre, activité*): **le ~** reporting

reporter¹ [ʀəpɔʀtɛʀ] *nm* reporter

reporter² [ʀəpɔʀte] *vt* (*total*): **~ qch sur** to carry sth forward *ou* over to; (*ajourner*): **~ qch (à)** to postpone sth (until); (*transférer*): **~ qch sur** to transfer sth to; **se ~ à** (*époque*) to think back to; (*document*) to refer to

repos [ʀəpo] *nm* rest; (*fig*) peace (and quiet); peace of mind; (*MIL*): **~!** stand at ease!; **en ~** at rest; **de tout ~** safe

reposant, e [ʀəpozɑ̃, -ɑ̃t] *adj* restful

reposer [ʀəpoze] *vt* (*verre, livre*) to put down; (*délasser*) to rest; (*problème*) to reformulate ♦ *vi* (*liquide, pâte*) to settle, rest; **se ~** *vi* to rest; **se ~ sur qn** to rely on sb; **~ sur** to be built on; (*fig*) to rest on

repoussant, e [ʀəpusɑ̃, -ɑ̃t] *adj* repulsive

repousser [ʀəpuse] *vi* to grow again ♦ *vt* to repel, repulse; (*offre*) to turn down, reject; (*tiroir, personne*) to push back; (*différer*) to put back

reprendre [ʀəpʀɑ̃dʀ(ə)] *vt* (*prisonnier, ville*) to recapture; (*objet prêté, donné*) to take back; (*chercher*): **je viendrai te ~ à 4h** I'll come and fetch you at 4; (*se resservir de*): **~ du pain/un œuf** to take (*ou* eat) more bread/another egg; (*firme, entreprise*) to take over; (*travail, promenade*) to resume; (*emprunter: argument, idée*) to take up, use; (*refaire: article etc*) to go over again; (*jupe etc*) to alter; (*émission, pièce*) to put on again; (*réprimander*) to tell off; (*corriger*) to correct ♦ *vi* (*classes, pluie*) to start (up) again; (*activités, travaux, combats*) to resume, start (up) again; (*affaires, industrie*) to pick up; (*dire*): **reprit-il** he went on; **se ~** *vi* (*se ressaisir*) to recover; **s'y ~** to make another attempt; **~ des forces** to recover one's strength; **~ courage** to take new heart; **~ la route** to set off again; **~ haleine** *ou* **son souffle** to get one's breath back

représailles [ʀəpʀezaj] *nfpl* reprisals

représentant, e [ʀəpʀezɑ̃tɑ̃, -ɑ̃t] *nm/f* representative

représentation [ʀəpʀezɑ̃tasjɔ̃] *nf* (*symbole, image*) representation; (*spectacle*) performance

représenter [ʀəpʀezɑ̃te] *vt* to represent; (*donner: pièce, opéra*) to perform; **se ~** *vt* (*se figurer*) to imagine; to visualize

répression [ʀepʀesjɔ̃] *nf* (*voir réprimer*) suppression; repression

réprimer [ʀepʀime] *vt* (*émotions*) to suppress; (*peuple etc*) to repress

repris [ʀəpʀi] *nm*: **~ de justice** ex-prisoner, ex-convict

reprise [ʀəpʀiz] *nf* (*recommencement*) resumption; recovery; (*TV*) repeat; (*CINÉMA*) rerun; (*AUTO*) acceleration *no pl*; (*COMM*) trade-in, part exchange; **à plusieurs ~s** on several occasions

repriser [ʀəpʀize] *vt* to darn; to mend

reproche [ʀəpʀɔʃ] *nm* (*remontrance*) reproach; **faire des ~s à qn** to reproach sb; **sans ~(s)** beyond reproach

reprocher [ʀəpʀɔʃe] *vt*: **~ qch à qn** to reproach *ou* blame sb for sth; **~ qch à** (*machine, théorie*) to have sth against

reproduction [ʀəpʀɔdyksjɔ̃] *nf* reproduction

reproduire [ʀəpʀɔdɥiʀ] *vt* to reproduce; **se ~** *vi* (*BIO*) to reproduce; (*recommencer*) to recur, re-occur

reptile [ʀɛptil] *nm* reptile

repu, e [ʀəpy] *adj* satisfied, sated

républicain, e [ʀepyblikɛ̃, -ɛn] *adj, nm/f* republican

république [ʀepyblik] *nf* republic

répugnant, e [ʀepyɲɑ̃, -ɑ̃t] *adj* repulsive; loathsome

répugner [ʀepyɲe]: **~ à** *vt* to repel *ou* disgust sb; **~ à faire** to be loath *ou* reluctant to do

réputation [ʀepytasjɔ̃] *nf* reputation; **réputé, e** *adj* renowned

requérir [ʀəkeʀiʀ] *vt* (*nécessiter*) to require, call for; (*JUR: peine*) to call for, demand

requête [ʀəkɛt] *nf* request; (*JUR*) petition

requin [ʀəkɛ̃] *nm* shark

requis, e [ʀəki, -iz] *adj* required

R.E.R. *sigle m* (= *réseau express régional*) Greater Paris high-speed train service

rescapé, e [ʀɛskape] *nm/f* survivor

rescousse [ʀɛskus] *nf*: **aller à la ~ de qn** to go to sb's aid *ou* rescue

réseau, x [ʀezo] *nm* network

réservation [ʀezɛʀvasjɔ̃] *nf* booking, reservation

réserve [ʀezɛʀv(ə)] *nf* (*retenue*) reserve; (*entrepôt*) storeroom; (*restriction, d'Indiens*) reservation; (*de pêche, chasse*) preserve; **sous ~ de** subject to; **sans ~** unreservedly; **de ~** (*provisions etc*) in reserve

réservé, e [ʀezɛʀve] *adj* (*discret*) reserved; (*chasse, pêche*) private

réserver [ʀezɛʀve] *vt* (*gén*) to reserve; (*chambre, billet etc*) to book, reserve; (*garder*): **~ qch pour/à** to keep *ou* save sth for; **~ qch à qn** to reserve (*ou* book) sth for sb

réservoir [ʀezɛʀvwaʀ] *nm* tank

résidence [ʀezidɑ̃s] *nf* residence; **(en) ~ surveillée** (under) house arrest; **~ secondaire** second home

résidentiel, le [ʀezidɑ̃sjɛl] *adj* residential

résider [ʀezide] *vi*: **~ à/dans/en** to reside in; **~ dans** (*fig*) to lie in

résidu [ʀezidy] *nm* residue *no pl*

résigner [rezine]: **se ~** *vi*: **se ~ (à qch/à faire)** to resign o.s. (to sth/to doing)

résilier [rezilje] *vt* to terminate

résistance [rezistɑ̃s] *nf* resistance; (*de réchaud, bouilloire: fil*) element

résistant, e [rezistɑ̃, -ɑ̃t] *adj* (*personne*) robust, tough; (*matériau*) strong, hard-wearing

résister [reziste] *vi* to resist; **~ à** (*assaut, tentation*) to resist; (*effort, souffrance*) to withstand; (*désobéir à*) to stand up to, oppose

résolu, e [rezɔly] *pp de* **résoudre** ♦ *adj*: **être ~ à qch/faire** to be set upon sth/doing

résolution [rezɔlysjɔ̃] *nf* solving; (*fermeté, décision*) resolution

résolve *etc vb voir* **résoudre**

résonner [rezɔne] *vi* (*cloche, pas*) to reverberate, resound; (*salle*) to be resonant; **~ de** to resound with

résorber [rezɔrbe]: **se ~** *vi* (*fig*) to be reduced; to be absorbed

résoudre [rezudr(ə)] *vt* to solve; **se ~ à faire** to bring o.s. to do

respect [rɛspɛ] *nm* respect; **tenir en ~** to keep at bay

respecter [rɛspɛkte] *vt* to respect

respectueux, euse [rɛspɛktɥø, -øz] *adj* respectful; **~ de** respectful of

respiration [rɛspirasjɔ̃] *nf* breathing *no pl*; **~ artificielle** artificial respiration

respirer [rɛspire] *vi* to breathe; (*fig*) to get one's breath; to breathe again ♦ *vt* to breathe (in), inhale; (*manifester: santé, calme etc*) to exude

resplendir [rɛsplɑ̃dir] *vi* to shine; (*fig*): **~ (de)** to be radiant (with)

responsabilité [rɛspɔ̃sabilite] *nf* responsibility; (*légale*) liability

responsable [rɛspɔ̃sabl(ə)] *adj* responsible ♦ *nm/f* (*du ravitaillement etc*) person in charge; (*de parti, syndicat*) official; **~ de** responsible for; (*chargé de*) in charge of, responsible for

ressaisir [rəsezir]: **se ~** *vi* to regain one's self-control

ressasser [rəsase] *vt* to keep going over

ressemblance [rəsɑ̃blɑ̃s] *nf* resemblance, similarity, likeness

ressemblant, e [rəsɑ̃blɑ̃, -ɑ̃t] *adj* (*portrait*) lifelike, true to life

ressembler [rəsɑ̃ble]: **~ à** *vt* to be like; to resemble; (*visuellement*) to look like; **se ~** *vi* to be (*ou* look) alike

ressemeler [rəsəmle] *vt* to (re)sole

ressentiment [rəsɑ̃timɑ̃] *nm* resentment

ressentir [rəsɑ̃tir] *vt* to feel; **se ~ de** to feel (*ou* show) the effects of

resserrer [rəsere] *vt* (*nœud, boulon*) to tighten (up); (*fig: liens*) to strengthen; **se ~** *vi* (*vallée*) to narrow

resservir [rəsɛrvir] *vi* to do *ou* serve again

♦ *vt*: **~ qn (d'un plat)** to give sb a second helping (of a dish)

ressort [rəsɔr] *nm* (*pièce*) spring; (*force morale*) spirit; (*recours*): **en dernier ~** as a last resort; (*compétence*): **être du ~ de** to fall within the competence of

ressortir [rəsɔrtir] *vi* to go (*ou* come) out (again); (*contraster*) to stand out; **~ de** to emerge from; **faire ~** (*fig: souligner*) to bring out

ressortissant, e [rəsɔrtisɑ̃, -ɑ̃t] *nm/f* national

ressource [rəsurs(ə)] *nf*: **avoir la ~ de** to have the possibility of; **~s** *nfpl* (*moyens*) resources; **leur seule ~ était de** the only course open to them was to

ressusciter [resysite] *vt* (*fig*) to revive, bring back ♦ *vi* to rise (from the dead)

restant, e [rɛstɑ̃, -ɑ̃t] *adj* remaining ♦ *nm*: **le ~ (de)** the remainder (of); **un ~ de** (*de trop*) some left-over

restaurant [rɛstɔrɑ̃] *nm* restaurant

restauration [rɛstɔrasjɔ̃] *nf* restoration; (*hôtellerie*) catering; **~ rapide** fast food

restaurer [rɛstɔre] *vt* to restore; **se ~** *vi* to have something to eat

reste [rɛst(ə)] *nm* (*restant*): **le ~ (de)** the rest (of); (*de trop*): **un ~ (de)** some left-over; (*vestige*): **un ~ de** a remnant *ou* last trace of; (*MATH*) remainder; **~s** *nmpl* (*nourriture*) left-overs; (*d'une cité etc, dépouille mortelle*) remains; **du ~, au ~** besides, moreover

rester [rɛste] *vi* to stay, remain; (*subsister*) to remain, be left; (*durer*) to last, live on ♦ *vb impers*: **il reste du pain/2 œufs** there's some bread/there are 2 eggs left (over); **il me reste assez de temps** I have enough time left; **ce qui reste à faire** what remains to be done; **restons-en là** let's leave it at that

restituer [rɛstitɥe] *vt* (*objet, somme*): **~ qch (à qn)** to return sth (to sb); (*TECH*) to release; (: *son*) to reproduce

restoroute [rɛstɔrut] *nm* motorway (*BRIT*) *ou* highway (*US*) restaurant

restreindre [rɛstrɛ̃dr(ə)] *vt* to restrict, limit

restriction [rɛstriksjɔ̃] *nf* restriction

résultat [rezylta] *nm* result; (*d'élection etc*) results *pl*

résulter [rezylte]: **~ de** *vt* to result from, be the result of

résumé [rezyme] *nm* summary, résumé

résumer [rezyme] *vt* (*texte*) to summarize; (*récapituler*) to sum up; **se ~ à** to come down to

résurrection [rezyrɛksjɔ̃] *nf* resurrection; (*fig*) revival

rétablir [retablir] *vt* to restore, re-establish; **se ~** *vi* (*guérir*) to recover; (*silence, calme*) to return, be restored; **rétablissement** *nm* restoring; recovery; (*SPORT*) pull-up

retaper [ʀətape] *vt* (*maison, voiture etc*) to do up; (*fam: revigorer*) to buck up; (*redactylographier*) to retype

retard [ʀətaʀ] *nm* (*d'une personne attendue*) lateness *no pl*; (*sur l'horaire, un programme*) delay; (*fig: scolaire, mental etc*) backwardness; **en ~ (de 2 heures)** (2 hours) late; **avoir du ~** to be late; (*sur un programme*) to be behind (schedule); **prendre du ~** (*train, avion*) to be delayed; (*montre*) to lose (time); **sans ~** without delay

retardement [ʀətaʀdəmɑ̃] : **à ~** *adj* delayed action *cpd*; **bombe à ~** time bomb

retarder [ʀətaʀde] *vt* (*sur un horaire*): **~ qn (d'une heure)** to delay sb (an hour); (*départ, date*): **~ qch (de 2 jours)** to put sth back (2 days), delay sth (for *ou* by 2 days); (*horloge*) to put back ♦ *vi* (*montre*) to be slow; to lose (time)

retenir [ʀətniʀ] *vt* (*garder, retarder*) to keep, detain; (*maintenir: objet qui glisse, fig: colère, larmes*) to hold back; (: *objet suspendu*) to hold; (*fig: empêcher d'agir*): **~ qn (de faire)** to hold sb back (from doing); (*se rappeler*) to retain; (*réserver*) to reserve; (*accepter*) to accept; (*prélever*): **~ qch (sur)** to deduct sth (from); **se ~** *vi* (*se raccrocher*): **se ~ à** to hold onto; (*se contenir*): **se ~ de faire** to restrain o.s. from doing; **~ son souffle** to hold one's breath

retentir [ʀətɑ̃tiʀ] *vi* to ring out; (*salle*): **~ de** to ring *ou* resound with

retentissant, e [ʀətɑ̃tisɑ̃, -ɑ̃t] *adj* resounding; (*fig*) impact-making

retentissement [ʀətɑ̃tismɑ̃] *nm* repercussion; effect, impact; stir

retenu, e [ʀətny] *adj* (*place*) reserved; (*personne: empêché*) held up

retenue [ʀətny] *nf* (*prélèvement*) deduction; (*SCOL*) detention; (*modération*) (self-)restraint; (*réserve*) reserve, reticence

réticence [ʀetisɑ̃s] *nf* hesitation, reluctance *no pl*

rétine [ʀetin] *nf* retina

retiré, e [ʀətiʀe] *adj* secluded; remote

retirer [ʀətiʀe] *vt* to withdraw; (*vêtement, lunettes*) to take off, remove; (*extraire*): **~ qch de** to take sth out of, remove sth from; (*reprendre: bagages, billets*) to collect, pick up

retombées [ʀətɔ̃be] *nfpl* (*radioactives*) fallout *sg*; (*fig*) fallout; spin-offs

retomber [ʀətɔ̃be] *vi* (*à nouveau*) to fall again; (*atterrir: après un saut etc*) to land; (*tomber, redescendre*) to fall back; (*pendre*) to fall, hang (down); (*échoir*): **~ sur qn** to fall on sb

rétorquer [ʀetɔʀke] *vt*: **~ (à qn) que** to retort (to sb) that

retors, e [ʀətɔʀ, -ɔʀs(ə)] *adj* wily

retoucher [ʀətuʃe] *vt* (*photographie*) to touch up; (*texte, vêtement*) to alter

retour [ʀətuʀ] *nm* return; **au ~** when we (*ou* they *etc*) get (*ou* got) back; (*en route*) on the way back; **être de ~ (de)** to be back (from); **par ~ du courrier** by return of post

retourner [ʀətuʀne] *vt* (*dans l'autre sens: matelas, crêpe, foin, terre*) to turn (over); (: *caisse*) to turn upside down; (: *sac, vêtement*) to turn inside out; (*émouvoir: personne*) to shake; (*renvoyer, restituer*): **~ qch à qn** to return sth to sb ♦ *vi* (*aller, revenir*): **~ quelque part/à** to go back *ou* return somewhere/to; **se ~** *vi* to turn over; (*tourner la tête*) to turn round; **~ à** (*état, activité*) to return to, go back to; **se ~ contre** (*fig*) to turn against; **savoir de quoi il retourne** to know what it is all about

retracer [ʀətʀase] *vt* to relate, recount

retrait [ʀətʀɛ] *nm* (*voir retirer*) withdrawal; collection; **en ~** set back; **~ du permis (de conduire)** disqualification from driving (*BRIT*), revocation of driver's license (*US*)

retraite [ʀətʀɛt] *nf* (*d'une armée, REL, refuge*) retreat; (*d'un employé*) retirement; (*revenu*) pension; **prendre sa ~** to retire; **~ anticipée** early retirement; **retraité, e** *adj* retired ♦ *nm/f* pensioner

retrancher [ʀətʀɑ̃ʃe] *vt* (*passage, détails*) to take out, remove; (*nombre, somme*): **~ qch de** to take *ou* deduct sth from; (*couper*) to cut off; **se ~ derrière/dans** to take refuge behind/in

retransmettre [ʀətʀɑ̃smɛtʀ(ə)] *vt* (*RADIO*) to broadcast; (*TV*) to show

rétrécir [ʀetʀesiʀ] *vt* (*vêtement*) to take in ♦ *vi* to shrink; **se ~** *vi* to narrow

rétribution [ʀetʀibysjɔ̃] *nf* payment

rétro [ʀetʀo] *adj inv*: **la mode ~** the nostalgia vogue

rétrograde [ʀetʀɔgʀad] *adj* reactionary, backward-looking

rétrograder [ʀetʀɔgʀade] *vi* (*économie*) to regress; (*AUTO*) to change down

rétroprojecteur [ʀetʀɔpʀɔʒɛktœʀ] *nm* overhead projector

rétrospective [ʀetʀɔspɛktiv] *nf* retrospective exhibition/season; **rétrospectivement** *adv* in retrospect

retrousser [ʀətʀuse] *vt* to roll up

retrouvailles [ʀətʀuvaj] *nfpl* reunion *sg*

retrouver [ʀətʀuve] *vt* (*fugitif, objet perdu*) to find; (*occasion*) to find again; (*calme, santé*) to regain; (*revoir*) to see again; (*rejoindre*) to meet (again), join; **se ~** *vi* to meet; (*s'orienter*) to find one's way; **se ~ quelque part** to find o.s. somewhere; **s'y ~** (*rentrer dans ses frais*) to break even

rétroviseur [ʀetʀɔvizœʀ] *nm* (rear-view) mirror

réunion [ʀeynjɔ̃] *nf* bringing together; join-

ing; (*séance*) meeting
réunir [ʀeyniʀ] vt (*convoquer*) to call together; (*rassembler*) to gather together; (*cumuler*) to combine; (*rapprocher*) to bring together (again), reunite; (*rattacher*) to join (together); **se** ~ vi (*se rencontrer*) to meet
réussi, e [ʀeysi] adj successful
réussir [ʀeysiʀ] vi to succeed, be successful; (*à un examen*) to pass; (*plante, culture*) to thrive, do well ♦ vt to make a success of; ~ **à faire** to succeed in doing; ~ **à qn** to go right for sb; (*aliment*) to agree with sb
réussite [ʀeysit] nf success; (*CARTES*) patience
revaloir [ʀəvalwaʀ] vt: **je vous revaudrai cela** I'll repay you some day; (*en mal*) I'll pay you back for this
revaloriser [ʀəvalɔʀize] vt (*monnaie*) to revalue; (*salaires*) to raise the level of
revanche [ʀəvɑ̃ʃ] nf revenge; **en** ~ on the other hand
rêve [ʀɛv] nm dream; (*activité psychique*): **le** ~ dreaming
revêche [ʀəvɛʃ] adj surly, sour-tempered
réveil [ʀevɛj] nm (*d'un dormeur*) waking up no pl; (*fig*) awakening; (*pendule*) alarm (clock); (*MIL*) reveille; **au** ~ on waking (up)
réveille-matin [ʀevɛjmatɛ̃] nm inv alarm clock
réveiller [ʀeveje] vt (*personne*) to wake up; (*fig*) to awaken, revive; **se** ~ vi to wake up; (*fig*) to reawaken
réveillon [ʀevejɔ̃] nm Christmas Eve; (*de la Saint-Sylvestre*) New Year's Eve; **réveillonner** vi to celebrate Christmas Eve (ou New Year's Eve)
révélateur, trice [ʀevelatœʀ, -tʀis] adj: ~ **(de qch)** revealing (sth) ♦ nm (*PHOTO*) developer
révéler [ʀevele] vt (*gén*) to reveal; (*faire connaître au public*): ~ **qn/qch** to make sb/sth widely known, bring sb/sth to the public's notice; **se** ~ vi to be revealed, reveal itself ♦ vb +attrib to prove (to be), to be revealed, reveal itself
revenant, e [ʀəvnɑ̃, -ɑ̃t] nm/f ghost
revendeur, euse [ʀəvɑ̃dœʀ, -øz] nm/f (*détaillant*) retailer; (*d'occasions*) secondhand dealer
revendication [ʀəvɑ̃dikasjɔ̃] nf claim, demand; **journée de** ~ day of action
revendiquer [ʀəvɑ̃dike] vt to claim, demand; (*responsabilité*) to claim
revendre [ʀəvɑ̃dʀ(ə)] vt (*d'occasion*) to resell; (*détailler*) to sell; **à** ~ (*en abondance*) to spare
revenir [ʀəvniʀ] vi to come back; (*CULIN*): **faire** ~ to brown; (*coûter*): ~ **cher/à 100 F (à qn)** to cost (sb) a lot/100 F; ~ **à** (*études, projet*) to return to, go back to; (*équivaloir à*) to amount to; ~ **à qn** (*part,*

honneur) to go to sb, be sb's; (*souvenir, nom*) to come back to sb; ~ **de** (*fig: maladie, étonnement*) to recover from; ~ **sur** (*question, sujet*) to go back over; (*engagement*) to go back on; ~ **à la charge** to return to the attack; ~ **à soi** to come round; **n'en pas** ~: **je n'en reviens pas** I can't get over it; ~ **sur ses pas** to retrace one's steps; **cela revient à dire que/au même** it amounts to saying that/the same thing
revenu [ʀəvny] nm income; (*de l'État*) revenue; (*d'un capital*) yield; ~**s** nmpl income sg
rêver [ʀeve] vi, vt to dream; ~ **de/à** to dream of
réverbère [ʀeveʀbɛʀ] nm street lamp ou light
réverbérer [ʀeveʀbeʀe] vt to reflect
révérence [ʀeveʀɑ̃s] nf (*salut*) bow; (: *de femme*) curtsey
rêverie [ʀɛvʀi] nf daydreaming no pl, daydream
revers [ʀəvɛʀ] nm (*de feuille, main*) back; (*d'étoffe*) wrong side; (*de pièce, médaille*) back, reverse; (*TENNIS, PING-PONG*) backhand; (*de veston*) lapel; (*de pantalon*) turnup; (*fig: échec*) setback
revêtement [ʀəvɛtmɑ̃] nm (*de paroi*) facing; (*des sols*) flooring; (*de chaussée*) surface; (*de tuyau etc: enduit*) coating
revêtir [ʀəvetiʀ] vt (*habit*) to don, put on; (*fig*) to take on; ~ **qn de** to endow ou invest sb with; ~ **qch de** to cover sth with; (*fig*) to cloak sth in
rêveur, euse [ʀɛvœʀ, -øz] adj dreamy ♦ nm/f dreamer
revient [ʀəvjɛ̃] vb voir **revenir**
revigorer [ʀəvigɔʀe] vt to invigorate, brace up; to revive, buck up
revirement [ʀəviʀmɑ̃] nm change of mind; (*d'une situation*) reversal
réviser [ʀevize] vt (*texte, SCOL: matière*) to revise; (*machine, installation, moteur*) to overhaul, service; (*JUR: procès*) to review
révision [ʀevizjɔ̃] nf revision; auditing no pl; overhaul; servicing no pl; review; **la** ~ **des 10000 km** (*AUTO*) the 10,000 km service
revivre [ʀəvivʀ(ə)] vi (*reprendre des forces*) to come alive again; (*traditions*) to be revived ♦ vt (*épreuve, moment*) to relive
revoir [ʀəvwaʀ] vt to see again; (*réviser*) to revise ♦ nm: **au** ~ goodbye
révoltant, e [ʀevɔltɑ̃, -ɑ̃t] adj revolting; appalling
révolte [ʀevɔlt(ə)] nf rebellion, revolt
révolter [ʀevɔlte] vt to revolt; to outrage, appal; **se** ~ (**contre**) to rebel (against)
révolu, e [ʀevɔly] adj past; (*ADMIN*): **âgé de 18 ans** ~**s** over 18 years of age; **après 3 ans** ~**s** when 3 full years have passed
révolution [ʀevɔlysjɔ̃] nf revolution; **révo-**

lutionnaire adj, nm/f revolutionary

revolver [ʀevɔlvɛʀ] nm gun; (à barillet) revolver

révoquer [ʀevɔke] vt (fonctionnaire) to dismiss; (arrêt, contrat) to revoke

revue [ʀəvy] nf (inventaire, examen, MIL) review; (périodique) review, magazine; (de music-hall) variety show; **passer en ~** to review; to go through

rez-de-chaussée [ʀedʃose] nm inv ground floor

RF sigle = République Française

Rhin [ʀɛ̃] nm: **le ~** the Rhine

rhinocéros [ʀinɔseʀɔs] nm rhinoceros

Rhône [ʀon] nm: **le ~** the Rhone

rhubarbe [ʀybaʀb(ə)] nf rhubarb

rhum [ʀɔm] nm rum

rhumatisme [ʀymatism(ə)] nm rheumatism no pl

rhume [ʀym] nm cold; **~ de cerveau** head cold; **le ~ des foins** hay fever

ri [ʀi] pp de **rire**

riant, e [ʀjɑ̃, -ɑ̃t] adj smiling, cheerful

ricaner [ʀikane] vi (avec méchanceté) to snigger; (bêtement) to giggle

riche [ʀiʃ] adj (gén) rich; (personne, pays) rich, wealthy; **~ en** rich in; **~ de** full of; rich in; **richesse** nf wealth; (fig) richness; **richesses** nfpl (ressources, argent) wealth sg; (fig: trésors) treasures

ricin [ʀisɛ̃] nm: **huile de ~** castor oil

ricocher [ʀikɔʃe] vi: **~ (sur)** to rebound (off); (sur l'eau) to bounce (on ou off)

ricochet [ʀikɔʃe] nm: **faire des ~s** to skip stones; **par ~** on the rebound; (fig) as an indirect result

rictus [ʀiktys] nm grin; (snarling) grimace

ride [ʀid] nf wrinkle; (fig) ripple

rideau, x [ʀido] nm curtain; (POL): **le ~ de fer** the Iron Curtain

rider [ʀide] vt to wrinkle; (eau) to ripple; **se ~** vi to become wrinkled

ridicule [ʀidikyl] adj ridiculous ♦ nm: **le ~** ridicule: **se ridiculiser** vi to make a fool of o.s.

──────── MOT CLÉ ────────

rien [ʀjɛ̃] pron 1: **(ne)** ... **~** nothing; tournure negative + anything; **qu'est-ce que vous avez?** - **~** what have you got? - nothing; **il n'a ~ dit/fait** he said/did nothing; he hasn't said/done anything; **il n'a ~** (n'est pas blessé) he's all right; **de ~!** not at all!

2 (quelque chose): **a-t-il jamais ~ fait pour nous?** has he ever done anything for us?

3: **~ de**: **~ d'intéressant** nothing interesting; **~ d'autre** nothing else; **~ du tout** nothing at all

4: **~ que** just, only; nothing but; **~ que pour lui faire plaisir** only ou just to please him; **~ que la vérité** nothing but the truth;

~ que cela that alone

♦ nm: **un petit ~** (cadeau) a little something; **des ~s** trivia pl; **un ~ de** a hint of; **en un ~ de temps** in no time at all

rieur, euse [ʀjœʀ, -øz] adj cheerful

rigide [ʀiʒid] adj stiff; (fig) rigid; strict

rigole [ʀigɔl] nf (conduit) channel; (filet d'eau) rivulet

rigoler [ʀigɔle] vi (rire) to laugh; (s'amuser) to have (some) fun; (plaisanter) to be joking ou kidding

rigolo, ote [ʀigɔlo, -ɔt] (fam) adj funny ♦ nm/f comic; (péj) fraud, phoney

rigoureux, euse [ʀiguʀø, -øz] adj (morale) rigorous, strict; (personne) stern, strict; (climat, châtiment) rigorous, harsh; (interdiction, neutralité) strict

rigueur [ʀigœʀ] nf rigour; strictness; harshness; **être de ~** to be the rule; **à la ~** at a pinch; possibly; **tenir ~ à qn de qch** to hold sth against sb

rime [ʀim] nf rhyme

rinçage [ʀɛ̃saʒ] nm rinsing (out); (opération) rinse

rincer [ʀɛ̃se] vt to rinse; (récipient) to rinse out

ring [ʀiŋ] nm (boxing) ring

ringard, e [ʀɛ̃gaʀ, -aʀd(ə)] adj old-fashioned

rions vb voir **rire**

riposter [ʀipɔste] vi to retaliate ♦ vt: **~ que** to retort that; **~ à** to counter; to reply to

rire [ʀiʀ] vi to laugh; (se divertir) to have fun ♦ nm laugh; **le ~** laughter; **~ de** to laugh at; **pour ~** (pas sérieusement) for a joke ou a laugh

risée [ʀize] nf: **être la ~ de** to be the laughing stock of

risible [ʀizibl(ə)] adj laughable

risque [ʀisk(ə)] nm risk; **le ~** danger; **à ses ~s et périls** at his own risk

risqué, e [ʀiske] adj risky; (plaisanterie) risqué, daring

risquer [ʀiske] vt to risk; (allusion, question) to venture, hazard; **ça ne risque rien** it's quite safe; **~ de**: **il risque de se tuer** he could get himself killed; **ce qui risque de se produire** what might ou could well happen; **il ne risque pas de recommencer** there's no chance of him doing that again; **se ~ à faire** (tenter) to venture ou dare to do

rissoler [ʀisɔle] vi, vt: **(faire) ~** to brown

ristourne [ʀistuʀn(ə)] nf rebate

rite [ʀit] nm rite; (fig) ritual

rivage [ʀivaʒ] nm shore

rival, e, aux [ʀival, -o] adj, nm/f rival

rivaliser [ʀivalize] vi: **~ avec** to rival, vie with; (être comparable) to hold its own against, compare with

rivalité [ʀivalite] nf rivalry

rive [ʀiv] nf shore; (*de fleuve*) bank
river [ʀive] vt (*clou, pointe*) to clinch; (*plaques*) to rivet together
riverain, e [ʀivʀɛ̃, -ɛn] nm/f riverside (*ou* lakeside) resident; local resident
rivet [ʀive] nm rivet
rivière [ʀivjɛʀ] nf river
rixe [ʀiks(ə)] nf brawl, scuffle
riz [ʀi] nm rice
R.N. sigle f = **route nationale**
robe [ʀɔb] nf dress; (*de juge, d'ecclésiastique*) robe; (*de professeur*) gown; (*pelage*) coat; ~ **de chambre** dressing gown; ~ **de grossesse** maternity dress; ~ **de soirée/de mariée** evening/wedding dress
robinet [ʀɔbinɛ] nm tap
robot [ʀɔbo] nm robot
robuste [ʀɔbyst(ə)] adj robust, sturdy
roc [ʀɔk] nm rock
rocaille [ʀɔkaj] nf loose stones pl; rocky *ou* stony ground; (*jardin*) rockery, rock garden
roche [ʀɔʃ] nf rock
rocher [ʀɔʃe] nm rock
rocheux, euse [ʀɔʃø, -øz] adj rocky
rodage [ʀɔdaʒ] nm: **en** ~ running in
roder [ʀɔde] vt (*AUTO*) to run in
rôder [ʀode] vi to roam about; (*de façon suspecte*) to lurk (about *ou* around); **rôdeur, euse** nm/f prowler
rogne [ʀɔɲ] nf: **être en** ~ to be in a temper
rogner [ʀɔɲe] vt to clip; ~ **sur** (*fig*) to cut down *ou* back on
rognons [ʀɔɲɔ̃] nmpl kidneys
roi [ʀwa] nm king; **le jour** *ou* **la fête des R~s, les R~s** Twelfth Night
roitelet [ʀwatlɛ] nm wren
rôle [ʀol] nm role; (*contribution*) part
romain, e [ʀɔmɛ̃, -ɛn] adj, nm/f Roman
roman, e [ʀɔmɑ̃, -an] adj (*ARCHIT*) Romanesque ♦ nm novel; ~ **d'espionnage** spy novel *ou* story; ~ **photo** romantic picture story
romance [ʀɔmɑ̃s] nf ballad
romancer [ʀɔmɑ̃se] vt to make into a novel; to romanticize
romancier, ière [ʀɔmɑ̃sje, -jɛʀ] nm/f novelist
romanesque [ʀɔmanɛsk(ə)] adj (*fantastique*) fantastic; storybook cpd; (*sentimental*) romantic
roman-feuilleton [ʀɔmɑ̃fœjtɔ̃] nm serialized novel
romanichel, le [ʀɔmaniʃɛl] nm/f gipsy
romantique [ʀɔmɑ̃tik] adj romantic
romarin [ʀɔmaʀɛ̃] nm rosemary
rompre [ʀɔ̃pʀ(ə)] vt to break; (*entretien, fiançailles*) to break off ♦ vi (*fiancés*) to break it off; **se** ~ vi to break; (*MÉD*) to burst, rupture
rompu, e [ʀɔ̃py] adj: ~ **à** with wide ex-

perience of; inured to
ronces [ʀɔ̃s] nfpl brambles
ronchonner [ʀɔ̃ʃɔne] (*fam*) vi to grouse, grouch
rond, e [ʀɔ̃, ʀɔ̃d] adj round; (*joues, mollets*) well-rounded; (*fam: ivre*) tight ♦ nm (*cercle*) ring; (*fam: sou*): **je n'ai plus un** ~ I haven't a penny left; **en** ~ (*s'asseoir, danser*) in a ring; **ronde** nf (*gén: de surveillance*) rounds pl, patrol; (*danse*) round (dance); (*MUS*) semibreve (*BRIT*), whole note (*US*); **à la ronde** (*alentour*): **à 10 km à la ronde** for 10 km round; **rondelet, te** adj plump
rondelle [ʀɔ̃dɛl] nf (*TECH*) washer; (*tranche*) slice, round
rondement [ʀɔ̃dmɑ̃] adv briskly; frankly
rondin [ʀɔ̃dɛ̃] nm log
rond-point [ʀɔ̃pwɛ̃] nm roundabout
ronflant, e [ʀɑ̃flɑ̃, -ɑ̃t] (*péj*) adj high-flown, grand
ronfler [ʀɑ̃fle] vi to snore; (*moteur, poêle*) to hum; to roar
ronger [ʀɔ̃ʒe] vt to gnaw (at); (*suj: vers, rouille*) to eat into; **se** ~ **les sangs** to worry o.s. sick; **se** ~ **les ongles** to bite one's nails; **rongeur** nm rodent
ronronner [ʀɔ̃ʀɔne] vi to purr
roquet [ʀɔkɛ] nm nasty little lap-dog
rosace [ʀozas] nf (*vitrail*) rose window
rosbif [ʀɔsbif] nm: **du** ~ roasting beef; (*cuit*) roast beef; **un** ~ a joint of beef
rose [ʀoz] nf rose ♦ adj pink
rosé, e [ʀoze] adj pinkish; (*vin*) ~ rosé
roseau, x [ʀozo] nm reed
rosée [ʀoze] nf dew
roseraie [ʀozʀɛ] nf rose garden
rosier [ʀozje] nm rosebush, rose tree
rosse [ʀɔs] nf (*péj: cheval*) nag ♦ adj nasty, vicious
rossignol [ʀɔsiɲɔl] nm (*ZOOL*) nightingale
rot [ʀo] nm belch; (*de bébé*) burp
rotatif, ive [ʀɔtatif, -iv] adj rotary
rotation [ʀɔtɑsjɔ̃] nf rotation; (*fig*) rotation, swap-around; turnover
roter [ʀɔte] (*fam*) vi to burp, belch
rôti [ʀoti] nm: **du** ~ roasting meat; (*cuit*) roast meat; ~ **de bœuf/porc** joint of beef/pork
rotin [ʀɔtɛ̃] nm rattan (cane); **fauteuil en** ~ cane (arm)chair
rôtir [ʀotiʀ] vi, vt (*aussi: faire* ~) to roast; **rôtisserie** nf steakhouse; roast meat counter (*ou* shop); **rôtissoire** nf (roasting) spit
rotule [ʀɔtyl] nf kneecap, patella
roturier, ière [ʀɔtyʀje, -jɛʀ] nm/f commoner
rouage [ʀwaʒ] nm cog(wheel), gearwheel; (*de montre*) part; (*fig*) cog
roucouler [ʀukule] vi to coo
roue [ʀu] nf wheel; ~ **dentée** cogwheel; ~ **de secours** spare wheel
roué, e [ʀwe] adj wily

rouer [ʀwe] *vt*: ~ **qn de coups** to give sb a thrashing

rouet [ʀwe] *nm* spinning wheel

rouge [ʀuʒ] *adj, nm/f* ♦ *nm* red; (*fard*) rouge; (**vin**) ~ red wine; **sur la liste** ~ ex-directory (*BRIT*), unlisted (*US*); **passer au** ~ (*signal*) to go red; (*automobiliste*) to go through a red light; ~ (**à lèvres**) lipstick; **rouge-gorge** *nm* robin (redbreast)

rougeole [ʀuʒɔl] *nf* measles *sg*

rougeoyer [ʀuʒwaje] *vi* to glow red

rouget [ʀuʒɛ] *nm* mullet

rougeur [ʀuʒœʀ] *nf* redness

rougir [ʀuʒiʀ] *vi* (*de honte, timidité*) to blush, flush; (*de plaisir, colère*) to flush; (*fraise, tomate*) to go ou turn red; (*ciel*) to redden

rouille [ʀuj] *nf* rust

rouillé, e [ʀuje] *adj* rusty

rouiller [ʀuje] *vt* to rust ♦ *vi* to rust, go rusty; **se** ~ *vi* to rust

roulant, e [ʀulɑ̃, -ɑ̃t] *adj* (*meuble*) on wheels; (*surface, trottoir*) moving

rouleau, x [ʀulo] *nm* (*de papier, tissu, SPORT*) roll; (*de machine à écrire*) roller, platen; (*à mise en plis, à peinture, vague*) roller; ~ **compresseur** steamroller; ~ **à pâtisserie** rolling pin

roulement [ʀulmɑ̃] *nm* (*bruit*) rumbling *no pl*, rumble; (*rotation*) rotation; turnover; **par** ~ on a rota (*BRIT*) ou rotation (*US*) basis; ~ (**à billes**) ball bearings *pl*; ~ **de tambour** drum roll

rouler [ʀule] *vt* to roll; (*papier, tapis*) to roll up; (*CULIN: pâte*) to roll out; (*fam*) to do, con ♦ *vi* (*bille, boule*) to roll; (*voiture, train*) to go, run; (*automobiliste*) to drive; (*cycliste*) to ride; (*bateau*) to roll; (*tonnerre*) to rumble, roll; **se** ~ **dans** (*boue*) to roll in; (*couverture*) to roll o.s. (up) in

roulette [ʀulɛt] *nf* (*de table, fauteuil*) castor; (*de pâtissier*) pastry wheel; (*jeu*): **la** ~ roulette; **à ~s** on castors

roulis [ʀuli] *nm* roll(ing)

roulotte [ʀulɔt] *nf* caravan

Roumanie [ʀumani] *nf* Rumania

rouquin, e [ʀukɛ̃, -in] (*péj*) *nm/f* redhead

rouspéter [ʀuspete] (*fam*) *vi* to moan

rousse [ʀus] *adj voir* **roux**

roussi [ʀusi] *nm*: **ça sent le** ~ there's a smell of burning; (*fig*) I can smell trouble

roussir [ʀusiʀ] *vt* to scorch ♦ *vi* (*feuilles*) to go ou turn brown; (*CULIN*): **faire** ~ to brown

route [ʀut] *nf* road; (*fig: chemin*) way; (*itinéraire, parcours*) route; (*fig: voie*) road, path; **par (la)** ~ by road; **il y a 3h de** ~ it's a 3-hour ride ou journey; **en** ~ on the way; **mettre en** ~ to start up; **se mettre en** ~ to set off; **faire** ~ **vers** to head towards; ~ **nationale** ≈ A road (*BRIT*), ≈ state highway (*US*); **routier, ière** *adj* road *cpd* ♦ *nm* (*camionneur*) (long-distance) lorry (*BRIT*) ou truck (*US*) driver; (*restaurant*) ≈ transport café (*BRIT*), ≈ truck stop (*US*); **routière** *nf* (*voiture*) touring car

routine [ʀutin] *nf* routine; **routinier, ière** (*péj*) *adj* humdrum; addicted to routine

rouvrir [ʀuvʀiʀ] *vt, vi* to reopen, open again; **se** ~ *vi* to reopen, open again

roux, rousse [ʀu, ʀus] *adj* red; (*personne*) red-haired ♦ *nm/f* redhead

royal, e, aux [ʀwajal, -o] *adj* royal; (*fig*) princely

royaume [ʀwajom] *nm* kingdom; (*fig*) realm; **le R~-Uni** the United Kingdom

royauté [ʀwajote] *nf* (*dignité*) kingship; (*régime*) monarchy

ruban [ʀybɑ̃] *nm* (*gén*) ribbon; (*d'acier*) strip; ~ **adhésif** adhesive tape

rubéole [ʀybeɔl] *nf* German measles *sg*, rubella

rubis [ʀybi] *nm* ruby

rubrique [ʀybʀik] *nf* (*titre, catégorie*) heading; (*PRESSE: article*) column

ruche [ʀyʃ] *nf* hive

rude [ʀyd] *adj* (*barbe, toile*) rough; (*métier, tâche*) hard, tough; (*climat*) severe, harsh; (*bourru*) harsh, rough; (*fruste*) rugged, tough; (*fam*) jolly good

rudement [ʀydmɑ̃] (*fam*) *adv* (*très*) terribly; (*beaucoup*) terribly hard

rudimentaire [ʀydimɑ̃tɛʀ] *adj* rudimentary, basic

rudoyer [ʀydwaje] *vt* to treat harshly

rue [ʀy] *nf* street

ruée [ʀɥe] *nf* rush

ruelle [ʀɥɛl] *nf* alley(-way)

ruer [ʀɥe] *vi* (*cheval*) to kick out; **se** ~ *vi*: **se** ~ **sur** to pounce on; **se** ~ **vers/dans/hors de** to rush ou dash towards/into/out of

rugby [ʀygbi] *nm* rugby (football)

rugir [ʀyʒiʀ] *vi* to roar

rugueux, euse [ʀygø, -øz] *adj* rough

ruine [ʀɥin] *nf* ruin; ~**s** *nfpl* (*de château etc*) ruins

ruiner [ʀɥine] *vt* to ruin

ruineux, euse [ʀɥinø, øz] *adj* ruinous

ruisseau, x [ʀɥiso] *nm* stream, brook

ruisseler [ʀɥisle] *vi* to stream

rumeur [ʀymœʀ] *nf* (*bruit confus*) rumbling; hubbub *no pl*; murmur(ing); (*nouvelle*) rumour

ruminer [ʀymine] *vt* (*herbe*) to ruminate; (*fig*) to ruminate on ou over, chew over

rupture [ʀyptyʀ] *nf* (*de câble, digue*) breaking; (*de tendon*) rupture, tearing; (*de négociations etc*) breakdown; (*de contrat*) breach; (*séparation, désunion*) break-up, split

rural, e, aux [ʀyʀal, -o] *adj* rural, country *cpd*

ruse [ʀyz] *nf*: **la** ~ cunning, craftiness;

trickery; **une ~** a trick, a ruse; **rusé, e** *adj* cunning, crafty

russe [ʀys] *adj, nm/f* Russian ♦ *nm* (*LING*) Russian

Russie [ʀysi] *nf*: **la ~** Russia

rustique [ʀystik] *adj* rustic

rustre [ʀystʀ(ə)] *nm* boor

rutilant, e [ʀytilã, -ãt] *adj* gleaming

rythme [ʀitm(ə)] *nm* rhythm; (*vitesse*) rate; (: *de la vie*) pace, tempo

---

S s

---

s' [s] *pron voir* **se**

sa [sa] *dét voir* **son¹**

S.A. *sigle* (= *société anonyme*) ≈ Ltd (*BRIT*), ≈ Inc. (*US*)

sable [sabl(ə)] *nm* sand; **~s mouvants** quicksand(s)

sablé [sable] *nm* shortbread biscuit

sabler [sable] *vt* to sand; (*contre le verglas*) to grit; **~ le champagne** to drink champagne

sablier [sablije] *nm* hourglass; (*de cuisine*) egg timer

sablonneux, euse [sablɔnø, -øz] *adj* sandy

saborder [sabɔʀde] *vt* (*navire*) to scuttle; (*fig*) to wind up, shut down

sabot [sabo] *nm* clog; (*de cheval, bœuf*) hoof; **~ de frein** brake shoe

saboter [sabɔte] *vt* to sabotage

sac [sak] *nm* bag; (*à charbon etc*) sack; **mettre à ~** to sack; **~ à dos** rucksack; **~ à main** handbag; **~ à provisions/de voyage** shopping/travelling bag; **~ de couchage** sleeping bag

saccade [sakad] *nf* jerk

saccager [sakaʒe] *vt* (*piller*) to sack; (*dévaster*) to create havoc in

saccharine [sakaʀin] *nf* saccharin

sacerdoce [sasɛʀdɔs] *nm* priesthood; (*fig*) calling, vocation

sache *etc vb voir* **savoir**

sachet [saʃɛ] *nm* (small) bag; (*de lavande, poudre, shampooing*) sachet; **~ de thé** tea bag

sacoche [sakɔʃ] *nf* (*gén*) bag; (*de bicyclette*) saddlebag

sacre [sakʀ(ə)] *nm* coronation; consecration

sacré, e [sakʀe] *adj* sacred; (*fam: satané*) blasted; (: *fameux*): **un ~ ...** a heck of a ...

sacrement [sakʀəmã] *nm* sacrament

sacrifice [sakʀifis] *nm* sacrifice

sacrifier [sakʀifje] *vt* to sacrifice; **~ à** to conform to

sacristie [sakʀisti] *nf* sacristy; (*culte protestant*) vestry

sadique [sadik] *adj* sadistic

sage [saʒ] *adj* wise; (*enfant*) good ♦ *nm* wise man; sage

sage-femme [saʒfam] *nf* midwife

sagesse [saʒɛs] *nf* wisdom

Sagittaire [saʒitɛʀ] *nm*: **le ~** Sagittarius

Sahara [saaʀa] *nm*: **le ~** the Sahara (desert)

saignant, e [sɛɲã, -ãt] *adj* (*viande*) rare

saignée [sɛɲe] *nf* (*fig*) heavy losses *pl*

saigner [sɛɲe] *vi* to bleed ♦ *vt* to bleed; (*animal*) to kill (by bleeding); **~ du nez** to have a nosebleed

saillie [saji] *nf* (*sur un mur etc*) projection; (*trait d'esprit*) witticism

saillir [sajiʀ] *vi* to project, stick out; (*veine, muscle*) to bulge

sain, e [sɛ̃, sɛn] *adj* healthy; (*lectures*) wholesome; **~ d'esprit** sound in mind, sane; **~ et sauf** safe and sound, unharmed

saindoux [sɛ̃du] *nm* lard

saint, e [sɛ̃, sɛ̃t] *adj* holy; (*fig*) saintly ♦ *nm/f* saint; **le S~-Esprit** the Holy Spirit *ou* Ghost; **la S~e Vierge** the Blessed Virgin; **la S~-Sylvestre** New Year's Eve; **sainteté** *nf* holiness

sais *etc vb voir* **savoir**

saisie [sezi] *nf* seizure; **~ (de données)** (data) capture

saisir [seziʀ] *vt* to take hold of, grab; (*fig: occasion*) to seize; (*comprendre*) to grasp; (*entendre*) to get, catch; (*données*) to capture; (*suj: émotions*) to take hold of, come over; (*CULIN*) to fry quickly; (*JUR: biens, publication*) to seize; (: *juridiction*): **~ un tribunal d'une affaire** to submit *ou* refer a case to a court; **se ~ de** *vt* to seize; **saisissant, e** *adj* startling, striking

saison [sezɔ̃] *nf* season; **morte ~** slack season; **saisonnier, ière** *adj* seasonal

sait *vb voir* **savoir**

salade [salad] *nf* (*BOT*) lettuce *etc*; (*CULIN*) (green) salad; (*fam*) tangle, muddle; **~ de fruits** fruit salad; **saladier** *nm* (salad) bowl

salaire [salɛʀ] *nm* (*annuel, mensuel*) salary; (*hebdomadaire, journalier*) pay, wages *pl*; (*fig*) reward; **~ de base** basic salary (*ou* wage); **~ minimum interprofessionnel de croissance** index-linked guaranteed minimum wage

salarié, e [salaʀje] *nm/f* salaried employee; wage-earner

salaud [salo] (*fam!*) *nm* sod (*!*), bastard (*!*)

sale [sal] *adj* dirty, filthy

salé, e [sale] *adj* (*liquide, saveur*) salty; (*CULIN*) salted; (*fig*) spicy; steep

saler [sale] *vt* to salt
saleté [salte] *nf* (*état*) dirtiness; (*crasse*) dirt, filth; (*tache etc*) dirt *no pl*; (*fig*) dirty trick; rubbish *no pl*; filth *no pl*
salière [saljɛʀ] *nf* saltcellar
salin, e [salɛ̃, -in] *adj* saline; **saline** *nf* salt-works *sg*; salt marsh
salir [saliʀ] *vt* to (make) dirty; (*fig*) to soil the reputation of; **se** ~ *vi* to get dirty; **salissant, e** *adj* (*tissu*) which shows the dirt; (*métier*) dirty, messy
salle [sal] *nf* room; (*d'hôpital*) ward; (*de restaurant*) dining room; (*d'un cinéma*) auditorium; (: *public*) audience; **faire ~ comble** to have a full house; ~ **à manger** dining room; ~ **commune** (*d'hôpital*) ward; ~ **d'attente** waiting room; ~ **de bain(s)** bathroom; ~ **de classe** classroom; ~ **de concert** concert hall; ~ **de consultation** consulting room; ~ **d'eau** shower-room; ~ **d'embarquement** (*à l'aéroport*) departure lounge; ~ **de jeux** games room; playroom; ~ **d'opération** (*d'hôpital*) operating theatre; ~ **de séjour** living room; ~ **de spectacle** theatre; cinema; ~ **des ventes** saleroom
salon [salɔ̃] *nm* lounge, sitting room; (*mobilier*) lounge suite; (*exposition*) exhibition, show; ~ **de thé** tearoom
salopard [salopaʀ] (*fam!*) *nm* bastard (*!*)
salope [salɔp] (*fam!*) *nf* bitch (*!*)
saloperie [salɔpʀi] (*fam!*) *nf* filth *no pl*; dirty trick; rubbish *no pl*
salopette [salɔpɛt] *nf* dungarees *pl*; (*d'ouvrier*) overall(s)
salsifis [salsifi] *nm* salsify
salubre [salybʀ(ə)] *adj* healthy, salubrious
saluer [salɥe] *vt* (*pour dire bonjour, fig*) to greet; (*pour dire au revoir*) to take one's leave; (*MIL*) to salute
salut [saly] *nm* (*sauvegarde*) safety; (*REL*) salvation; (*geste*) wave; (*parole*) greeting; (*MIL*) salute ♦ *excl* (*fam*) hi (there)
salutations [salytasjɔ̃] *nfpl* greetings; **recevez mes** ~ **distinguées** *ou* **respectueuses** yours faithfully
samedi [samdi] *nm* Saturday
SAMU [samy] *sigle m* (= *service d'assistance médicale d'urgence*) ≈ ambulance (service) (*BRIT*), ≈ paramedics *pl* (*US*)
sanction [sɑ̃ksjɔ̃] *nf* sanction; (*fig*) penalty; **sanctionner** *vt* (*loi, usage*) to sanction; (*punir*) to punish
sandale [sɑ̃dal] *nf* sandal
sandwich [sɑ̃dwitʃ] *nm* sandwich
sang [sɑ̃] *nm* blood; **en** ~ covered in blood; **se faire du mauvais** ~ to fret, get in a state
sang-froid [sɑ̃fʀwa] *nm* calm, sangfroid; **de** ~ in cold blood
sanglant, e [sɑ̃glɑ̃, -ɑ̃t] *adj* bloody, covered in blood; (*combat*) bloody

sangle [sɑ̃gl(ə)] *nf* strap
sanglier [sɑ̃glije] *nm* (wild) boar
sanglot [sɑ̃glo] *nm* sob
sangsue [sɑ̃sy] *nf* leech
sanguin, e [sɑ̃gɛ̃, -in] *adj* blood *cpd*; (*fig*) fiery; **sanguinaire** [sɑ̃ginɛʀ] *adj* bloodthirsty; bloody
sanisette [sanizɛt] *nf* (automatic) public toilet
sanitaire [sanitɛʀ] *adj* health *cpd*; ~**s** *nmpl* (*lieu*) bathroom *sg*
sans [sɑ̃] *prép* without; ~ **qu'il s'en aperçoive** without him *ou* his noticing; ~**-abri** *nmpl* homeless; ~**-emploi** [sɑ̃zɑ̃plwa] *n inv* unemployed person; **les** ~**-emploi** the unemployed; ~**-façon** *adj inv* fuss-free; free and easy; ~**-gêne** *adj inv* inconsiderate; ~**-logis** *nmpl* homeless
santé [sɑ̃te] *nf* health; **en bonne** ~ in good health; **boire à la** ~ **de qn** to drink (to) sb's health; **"à la** ~ **de"** "here's to"; **à ta/ votre** ~! cheers!
saoudien, ne [saudjɛ̃, -jɛn] *adj* Saudi Arabian ♦ *nm/f*: **S~(ne)** Saudi Arabian
saoul, e [su, sul] *adj* = **soûl**
saper [sape] *vt* to undermine, sap
sapeur-pompier [sapœʀpɔ̃pje] *nm* fireman
saphir [safiʀ] *nm* sapphire
sapin [sapɛ̃] *nm* fir (tree); (*bois*) fir; ~ **de Noël** Christmas tree
sarcastique [saʀkastik] *adj* sarcastic
sarcler [saʀkle] *vt* to weed
Sardaigne [saʀdɛɲ] *nf*: **la** ~ Sardinia
sardine [saʀdin] *nf* sardine
SARL *sigle* (= *société à responsabilité limitée*) ≈ plc (*BRIT*), ≈ Inc. (*US*)
sas [sas] *nm* (*de sous-marin, d'engin spatial*) airlock; (*d'écluse*) lock
satané, e [satane] *adj* confounded
satellite [satelit] *nm* satellite
satin [satɛ̃] *nm* satin
satire [satiʀ] *nf* satire; **satirique** *adj* satirical
satisfaction [satisfaksjɔ̃] *nf* satisfaction
satisfaire [satisfɛʀ] *vt* to satisfy; ~ **à** (*engagement*) to fulfil; (*revendications, conditions*) to satisfy, meet; to comply with; **satisfaisant, e** *adj* satisfactory; (*qui fait plaisir*) satisfying; **satisfait, e** *adj* satisfied; **satisfait de** happy *ou* satisfied with
saturer [satyʀe] *vt* to saturate
sauce [sos] *nf* sauce; (*avec un rôti*) gravy; **saucière** *nf* sauceboat
saucisse [sosis] *nf* sausage
saucisson [sosisɔ̃] *nm* (slicing) sausage
sauf, sauve [sof, sov] *adj* unharmed, unhurt; (*fig: honneur*) intact, saved ♦ *prép* except; **laisser la vie sauve à qn** to spare sb's life; ~ **si** (*à moins que*) unless; ~ **erreur** if I'm not mistaken; ~ **avis contraire** unless you hear to the contrary

sauge [soʒ] *nf* sage
saugrenu, e [sogʀəny] *adj* preposterous
saule [sol] *nm* willow (tree)
saumon [somɔ̃] *nm* salmon *inv*
saumure [somyʀ] *nf* brine
saupoudrer [sopudʀe] *vt*: ~ qch de to sprinkle sth with
saur [sɔʀ] *adj m*: **hareng** ~ smoked *ou* red herring, kipper
saurai *etc vb voir* **savoir**
saut [so] *nm* jump; (*discipline sportive*) jumping; **faire un** ~ **chez qn** to pop over to sb's (place); **au** ~ **du lit** on getting out of bed; ~ **à la corde** skipping; ~ **à la perche** pole vaulting; ~ **en hauteur/longueur** high/long jump; ~ **périlleux** somersault
saute [sot] *nf* sudden change
saute-mouton [sotmutɔ̃] *nm*: **jouer à** ~ to play leapfrog
sauter [sote] *vi* to jump, leap; (*exploser*) to blow up, explode; (: *fusibles*) to blow; (*se rompre*) to snap, burst; (*se détacher*) to pop out (*ou* off) ♦ *vt* to jump (over), leap (over); (*fig: omettre*) to skip, miss (out); **faire** ~ to blow up; to burst open; (*CULIN*) to sauté; ~ **au cou de qn** to fly into sb's arms
sauterelle [sotʀɛl] *nf* grasshopper
sautiller [sotije] *vi* to hop; to skip
sautoir [sotwaʀ] *nm*: ~ **(de perles)** string of pearls
sauvage [sovaʒ] *adj* (*gén*) wild; (*peuplade*) savage; (*farouche*) unsociable; (*barbare*) wild, savage; (*non officiel*) unauthorized, unofficial ♦ *nm/f* savage; (*timide*) unsociable type
sauve [sov] *adj f voir* **sauf**
sauvegarde [sovgaʀd(ə)] *nf* safeguard;
sauvegarder *vt* to safeguard; (*INFORM: enregistrer*) to save; (: *copier*) to back up
sauve-qui-peut [sovkipø] *excl* run for your life!
sauver [sove] *vt* to save; (*porter secours à*) to rescue; (*récupérer*) to salvage, rescue; **se** ~ *vi* (*s'enfuir*) to run away; (*fam: partir*) to be off; **sauvetage** *nm* rescue; **sauveteur** *nm* rescuer; **sauvette: à la sauvette** *adv* (*vendre*) without authorization; (*se marier etc*) hastily, hurriedly; **sauveur** *nm* saviour (*BRIT*), savior (*US*)
savais *etc vb voir* **savoir**
savamment [savamɑ̃] *adv* (*avec érudition*) learnedly; (*habilement*) skilfully, cleverly
savant, e [savɑ̃, -ɑ̃t] *adj* scholarly, learned; (*calé*) clever ♦ *nm* scientist
saveur [savœʀ] *nf* flavour; (*fig*) savour
savoir [savwaʀ] *vt* to know; (*être capable de*): **il sait nager** he can swim ♦ *nm* knowledge; **se** ~ *vi* (*être connu*) to be known; **à** ~ that is; namely; **faire** ~ **qch à qn** to let sb know sth; **pas que je sache** not as far as I know
savon [savɔ̃] *nm* (*produit*) soap; (*morceau*)

bar of soap; (*fam*): **passer un** ~ **à qn** to give sb a good dressing-down; **savonnette** *nf* bar of soap; **savonneux, euse** *adj* soapy
savons *vb voir* **savoir**
savourer [savuʀe] *vt* to savour
savoureux, euse [savuʀø, -øz] *adj* tasty; (*fig*) spicy, juicy
saxo(phone) [saksɔ(fɔn)] *nm* sax(ophone)
scabreux, euse [skabʀø, -øz] *adj* risky; (*indécent*) improper, shocking
scandale [skɑ̃dal] *nm* scandal; (*tapage*): **faire du** ~ to make a scene, create a disturbance; **faire** ~ to scandalize people; **scandaleux, euse** *adj* scandalous, outrageous
scandinave [skɑ̃dinav] *adj, nm/f* Scandinavian
Scandinavie [skɑ̃dinavi] *nf* Scandinavia
scaphandre [skafɑ̃dʀ(ə)] *nm* (*de plongeur*) diving suit; (*de cosmonaute*) space-suit
scarabée [skaʀabe] *nm* beetle
sceau, x [so] *nm* seal; (*fig*) stamp, mark
scélérat, e [seleʀa, -at] *nm/f* villain
sceller [sele] *vt* to seal
scénario [senaʀjo] *nm* (*CINÉMA*) scenario; script; (*fig*) scenario
scène [sɛn] *nf* (*gén*) scene; (*estrade, fig: théâtre*) stage; **entrer en** ~ to come on stage; **mettre en** ~ (*THÉÂTRE*) to stage; (*CINÉMA*) to direct; (*fig*) to present, introduce; ~ **de ménage** *nf* domestic scene
sceptique [sɛptik] *adj* sceptical
schéma [ʃema] *nm* (*diagramme*) diagram, sketch; (*fig*) outline; pattern; ~**tique** *adj* diagrammatic(al), schematic; (*fig*) oversimplified
sciatique [sjatik] *nf* sciatica
scie [si] *nf* saw; ~ **à découper** fretsaw; ~ **à métaux** hacksaw
sciemment [sjamɑ̃] *adv* knowingly
science [sjɑ̃s] *nf* science; (*savoir*) knowledge; (*savoir-faire*) art, skill; ~**s naturelles** (*SCOL*) natural science *sg*, biology *sg*; ~**s po** *nfpl* political science *ou* studies *pl*; **scientifique** *adj* scientific ♦ *nm/f* scientist; science student
scier [sje] *vt* to saw; (*retrancher*) to saw off; **scierie** *nf* sawmill
scinder [sɛ̃de] *vt* to split up; **se** ~ *vi* to split up
scintiller [sɛ̃tije] *vi* to sparkle
scission [sisjɔ̃] *nf* split
sciure [sjyʀ] *nf*: ~ **(de bois)** sawdust
sclérose [skleʀoz] *nf*: ~ **en plaques** multiple sclerosis
scolaire [skɔlɛʀ] *adj* school *cpd*; (*péj*) schoolish; **scolariser** *vt* to provide with schooling (*ou* schools); **scolarité** *nf* schooling
scooter [skutœʀ] *nm* (motor) scooter
score [skɔʀ] *nm* score
scorpion [skɔʀpjɔ̃] *nm* (*signe*): **le S**~ Scor-

pio
Scotch [skɔtʃ] (®) nm adhesive tape
scout, e [skut] adj, nm scout
script [skript] nm printing; (CINÉMA)
(shooting) script
script-girl [skriptgœrl] nf continuity girl
scrupule [skrypyl] nm scruple
scruter [skryte] vt to scrutinize;
(l'obscurité) to peer into
scrutin [skrytɛ̃] nm (vote) ballot; (ensemble
des opérations) poll
sculpter [skylte] vt to sculpt; (suj: érosion)
to carve; **sculpteur** nm sculptor
sculpture [skyltyr] nf sculpture; ~ **sur bois**
wood carving

─────────── MOT CLÉ ───────────

se(s') [s(ə)] pron 1 (emploi réfléchi) oneself;
(: masc) himself; (: fém) herself; (: sujet non
humain) itself; (: pl) themselves; **se voir
comme l'on est** to see o.s. as one is
2 (réciproque) one another, each other; **ils
s'aiment** they love one another ou each
other
3 (passif): **cela se répare facilement** it is
easily repaired
4 (possessif): **se casser la jambe/laver les
mains** to break one's leg/wash one's hands

─────────────────────────────

séance [seɑ̃s] nf (d'assemblée, récréative)
meeting, session; (de tribunal) sitting, session; (musicale, CINÉMA, THÉÂTRE) performance; ~ **tenante** forthwith
seau, x [so] nm bucket, pail
sec, sèche [sɛk, sɛʃ] adj dry; (raisins,
figues) dried; (cœur, personne: insensible)
hard, cold ♦ nm: **tenir au** ~ to keep in a
dry place ♦ adv hard; **je le bois** ~ I drink
it straight ou neat; **à** ~ dried up
sécateur [sekatœr] nm secateurs pl (BRIT),
shears pl
sèche [sɛʃ] adj f voir sec
sèche-cheveux [sɛʃʃəvø] nm inv hair-drier
sèche-linge [sɛʃlɛ̃ʒ] nm inv tumble dryer
sécher [seʃe] vt to dry; (dessécher: peau,
blé) to dry (out); (: étang) to dry up ♦ vi to
dry; to dry out; to dry up; (fam: candidat)
to be stumped ♦ **se** ~ (après le bain) to dry
o.s.
sécheresse [sɛʃrɛs] nf dryness; (absence
de pluie) drought
séchoir [seʃwar] nm drier
second, e [s(ə)gɔ̃, -ɔ̃d] adj second ♦ nm (assistant) second in command; (NAVIG) first
mate; **voyager en** ~e to travel second-
class; **de** ~e **main** second-hand; **secondaire** adj secondary; **seconde** nf second; **se-
conder** vt to assist
secouer [s(ə)kwe] vt to shake; (passagers) to
rock; (traumatiser) to shake (up)
secourir [s(ə)kurir] vt (aller sauver) to (go
and) rescue; (prodiguer des soins à) to help,

assist; (venir en aide à) to assist, aid; **se-
courisme** nm first aid; life saving
secours [s(ə)kur] nm help, aid, assistance ♦
nmpl aid sg; **au** ~! help!; **appeler au** ~ to
shout ou call for help; **porter** ~ **à qn** to
give sb assistance, help sb; **les premiers** ~
first aid sg
secousse [s(ə)kus] nf jolt, bump; (électrique)
shock; (fig: psychologique) jolt, shock; ~
sismique ou **tellurique** earth tremor
secret, ète [s(ə)krɛ, -ɛt] adj secret; (fig: renfermé) reticent, reserved ♦ nm secret; (discrétion absolue): **le** ~ secrecy; **au** ~ in solitary confinement
secrétaire [s(ə)kretɛr] nm/f secretary ♦ nm
(meuble) writing desk; ~ **de direction** private ou personal secretary; ~ **d'État** junior
minister; ~ **général** nm (COMM) company
secretary; **secrétariat** nm (profession) se-
cretarial work; (bureau) office; (:
d'organisation internationale) secretariat
secteur [sɛktœr] nm sector; (ADMIN) district; (ÉLEC): **branché sur le** ~ plugged
into the mains (supply)
section [sɛksjɔ̃] nf section; (de parcours
d'autobus) fare stage; (MIL: unité) platoon;
sectionner vt to sever
Sécu [seky] abr f = sécurité sociale
séculaire [sekylɛr] adj secular; (très vieux)
age-old
sécuriser [sekyrize] vt to give (a feeling of)
security to
sécurité [sekyrite] nf safety; security; **système de** ~ safety system; **être en** ~ to be
safe; **la** ~ **routière** road safety; **la** ~ **sociale**
≈ (the) Social Security (BRIT), ≈ Welfare
(US)
sédition [sedisjɔ̃] nf insurrection; sedition
séduction [sedyksjɔ̃] nf seduction; (charme,
attrait) appeal, charm
séduire [sedɥir] vt to charm; (femme: abuser de) to seduce; **séduisant, e** adj
(femme) seductive; (homme, offre) very attractive
ségrégation [segregasjɔ̃] nf segregation
seigle [sɛgl(ə)] nm rye
seigneur [sɛɲœr] nm lord
sein [sɛ̃] nm breast; (entrailles) womb; **au** ~
de (équipe, institution) within; (flots, bonheur) in the midst of
séisme [seism(ə)] nm earthquake
seize [sɛz] num sixteen; **seizième** num six-
teenth
séjour [seʒur] nm stay; (pièce) living room;
séjourner vi to stay
sel [sɛl] nm salt; (fig) wit; spice; ~ **de
cuisine/de table** cooking/table salt
sélection [selɛksjɔ̃] nf selection; **sélectionner** vt to select
self-service [sɛlfsɛrvis] adj, nm self-service
selle [sɛl] nf saddle; ~**s** nfpl (MÉD) stools;
seller vt to saddle

sellette [sɛlɛt] *nf*: **être sur la ~** to be on the carpet

selon [səlɔ̃] *prép* according to; (*en se conformant à*) in accordance with; **~ que** according to whether; **~ moi** as I see it

semaine [səmɛn] *nf* week; **en ~** during the week, on weekdays

semblable [sɑ̃blabl(ə)] *adj* similar; (*de ce genre*): **de ~s mésaventures** such mishaps ♦ *nm* fellow creature *ou* man; **~ à** similar to, like

semblant [sɑ̃blɑ̃] *nm*: **un ~ de vérité** a semblance of truth; **faire ~ (de faire)** to pretend (to do)

sembler [sɑ̃ble] *vb +attrib* to seem ♦ *vb impers*: **il semble (bien) que/inutile de it** (really) seems *ou* appears that/useless to me; **il me semble que** it seems to me that; I think (that); **comme bon lui semble** as he sees fit

semelle [səmɛl] *nf* sole; (*intérieure*) insole, inner sole

semence [səmɑ̃s] *nf* (*graine*) seed

semer [səme] *vt* to sow; (*fig: éparpiller*) to scatter; (*: confusion*) to spread; (*: poursuivants*) to lose, shake off; **semé de** (*difficultés*) riddled with

semestre [səmɛstʀ(ə)] *nm* half-year; (*SCOL*) semester

séminaire [seminɛʀ] *nm* seminar

semi-remorque [səmiʀəmɔʀk(ə)] *nm* articulated lorry (*BRIT*), semi(trailer) (*US*)

semonce [səmɔ̃s] *nf*: **un coup de ~** a shot across the bows

semoule [səmul] *nf* semolina

sempiternel, le [sɛ̃pitɛʀnɛl] *adj* eternal, never-ending

sénat [sena] *nm* Senate; **sénateur** *nm* Senator

sens [sɑ̃s] *nm* (*PHYSIOL, instinct*) sense; (*signification*) meaning, sense; (*direction*) direction; **à mon ~** to my mind; **reprendre ses ~** to regain consciousness; **dans le ~ des aiguilles d'une montre** clockwise; **~ commun** common sense; **~ dessus dessous** upside down; **~ interdit** one-way street; **~ unique** one-way street

sensass [sɑ̃sas] (*fam*) *adj* fantastic

sensation [sɑ̃sɑsjɔ̃] *nf* sensation; **à ~** (*péj*) sensational

sensé, e [sɑ̃se] *adj* sensible

sensibiliser [sɑ̃sibilize] *vt*: **~ qn à** to make sb sensitive to

sensibilité [sɑ̃sibilite] *nf* sensitivity

sensible [sɑ̃sibl(ə)] *adj* sensitive; (*aux sens*) perceptible; (*appréciable: différence, progrès*) appreciable, noticeable; **sensiblement** *adv* (*notablement*) appreciably, noticeably; (*à peu près*): **ils ont sensiblement le même poids** they weigh approximately the same; **sensiblerie** *nf* sentimentality; squeamishness

sensuel, le [sɑ̃sɥɛl] *adj* sensual; sensuous

sentence [sɑ̃tɑ̃s] *nf* (*jugement*) sentence; (*adage*) maxim

sentier [sɑ̃tje] *nm* path

sentiment [sɑ̃timɑ̃] *nm* feeling; **recevez mes ~s respectueux** yours faithfully; **sentimental, e, aux** *adj* sentimental; (*vie, aventure*) love *cpd*

sentinelle [sɑ̃tinɛl] *nf* sentry

sentir [sɑ̃tiʀ] *vt* (*par l'odorat*) to smell; (*par le goût*) to taste; (*au toucher, fig*) to feel; (*répandre une odeur de*) to smell of; (*: ressemblance*) to smell like; (*avoir la saveur de*) to taste of; to taste like ♦ *vi* to smell; **~ mauvais** to smell bad; **se ~ bien** to feel good; **se ~ mal** (*être indisposé*) to feel unwell *ou* ill; **se ~ le courage/la force de faire** to feel brave/strong enough to do; **il ne peut pas le ~** (*fam*) he can't stand him

séparation [separɑsjɔ̃] *nf* separation; (*cloison*) division, partition; **~ de corps** legal separation

séparé, e [separe] *adj* (*appartements, pouvoirs*) separate; (*époux*) separated; **~ment** *adv* separately

séparer [separe] *vt* (*gén*) to separate; (*suj: divergences etc*) to divide; to drive apart; (*suj: différences, obstacles*) to stand between; (*détacher*): **~ qch de** to pull sth (off) from; (*diviser*) to divide; **se ~** *vi* (*époux, amis, adversaires*) to separate, part; (*se diviser: route, tige etc*) to divide; (*se détacher*): **se ~ (de)** to split off (from); to come off; **se ~ de** (*époux*) to separate *ou* part from; (*employé, objet personnel*) to part with; **~ une pièce en deux** to divide a room into two

sept [sɛt] *num* seven

septembre [sɛptɑ̃bʀ(ə)] *nm* September

septennat [sɛptena] *nm* seven year term of office (of French President)

septentrional, e, aux [sɛptɑ̃tʀijɔnal, -o] *adj* northern

septicémie [sɛptisemi] *nf* blood poisoning, septicaemia

septième [sɛtjɛm] *num* seventh

septique [sɛptik] *adj*: **fosse ~** septic tank

sépulture [sepyltyʀ] *nf* burial; burial place, grave

séquelles [sekɛl] *nfpl* after-effects; (*fig*) aftermath *sg*; consequences

séquestrer [sekɛstʀe] *vt* (*personne*) to confine illegally; (*biens*) to impound

serai *etc vb voir* **être**

serein, e [səʀɛ̃, -ɛn] *adj* serene; (*jugement*) dispassionate

serez *vb voir* **être**

sergent [sɛʀʒɑ̃] *nm* sergeant

série [seʀi] *nf* (*de questions, d'accidents*) series *inv*; (*de clés, casseroles, outils*) set; (*catégorie: SPORT*) rank; class; **en ~** in quick succession; (*COMM*) mass *cpd*; **de ~**

standard; **hors ~** (*COMM*) custom-built; (*fig*) outstanding

sérieusement [seʀjøzmɑ̃] *adv* seriously; reliably; responsibly

sérieux, euse [seʀjø, -øz] *adj* serious; (*élève, employé*) reliable, responsible; (*client, maison*) reliable, dependable ♦ *nm* seriousness; reliability; **garder son ~** to keep a straight face; **prendre qch/qn au ~** to take sth/sb seriously

serin [s(ə)ʀɛ̃] *nm* canary

seringue [s(ə)ʀɛ̃g] *nf* syringe

serions *vb voir* **être**

serment [seʀmɑ̃] *nm* (*juré*) oath; (*promesse*) pledge, vow

sermon [seʀmɔ̃] *nm* sermon

séro-positif, ive [seʀo-] *adj* (*MED*) HIV-positive

serpent [seʀpɑ̃] *nm* snake

serpenter [seʀpɑ̃te] *vi* to wind

serpentin [seʀpɑ̃tɛ̃] *nm* (*tube*) coil; (*ruban*) streamer

serpillière [seʀpijɛʀ] *nf* floorcloth

serre [seʀ] *nf* (*AGR*) greenhouse; **~s** *nfpl* (*griffes*) claws, talons

serré, e [seʀe] *adj* (*réseau*) dense; (*écriture*) close; (*habits*) tight; (*fig: lutte, match*) tight, close-fought; (*passagers etc*) (tightly) packed

serrer [seʀe] *vt* (*tenir*) to grip *ou* hold tight; (*comprimer, coincer*) to squeeze; (*poings, mâchoires*) to clench; (*suj: vêtement*) to be too tight for; to fit tightly; (*rapprocher*) to close up, move closer together; (*ceinture, nœud, frein, vis*) to tighten ♦ *vi*: **~ à droite** to keep *ou* get over to the right; **se ~** *vi* (*se rapprocher*) to squeeze up; **se ~ contre qn** to huddle up to sb; **~ la main à qn** to shake sb's hand; **~ qn dans ses bras** to hug sb, clasp sb in one's arms

serrure [seʀyʀ] *nf* lock

serrurier [seʀyʀje] *nm* locksmith

sert *etc vb voir* **servir**

sertir [seʀtiʀ] *vt* (*pierre*) to set

servante [seʀvɑ̃t] *nf* (maid)servant

serveur, euse [seʀvœʀ, -øz] *nm/f* waiter(waitress)

serviable [seʀvjabl(ə)] *adj* obliging, willing to help

service [seʀvis] *nm* (*gén*) service; (*série de repas*): **premier ~** first sitting; (*assortiment de vaisselle*) set, service; (*bureau: de la vente etc*) department, section; (*travail*): **pendant le ~** on duty; **~s** *nmpl* (*travail, ÉCON*) services; **faire le ~** to serve; **rendre ~ à qn** to help *ou* do sb a favour; **mettre en ~** to put into service *ou* operation; **hors ~** out of order; **~ après-vente** after-sales service; **~ d'ordre** police (*ou* stewards) in charge of maintaining order; **~ militaire** military service; **~s secrets** secret service *sg*

serviette [seʀvjɛt] *nf* (*de table*) (table) napkin, serviette; (*de toilette*) towel; (*porte-documents*) briefcase; **~ hygiénique** sanitary towel

servir [seʀviʀ] *vt* (*gén*) to serve; (*au restaurant*) to wait on; (*au magasin*) to serve, attend to; (*fig: aider*): **~ qn** to aid sb; to serve sb's interests; (*COMM: rente*) to pay ♦ *vi* (*TENNIS*) to serve; (*CARTES*) to deal; **se ~** *vi* (*prendre d'un plat*) to help o.s.; **se ~ de** (*plat*) to help o.s. to; (*voiture, outil, relations*) to use; **vous êtes servi?** are you being served?; **~ à qn** (*diplôme, livre*) to be of use to sb; **~ à qch/faire** (*outil etc*) to be used for sth/doing; **à quoi cela sert-il (de faire)?** what's the use (of doing)?; **cela ne sert à rien** it's no use; **~ (à qn) de** to serve as (for sb); **~ à dîner (à qn)** to serve dinner (to sb)

serviteur [seʀvitœʀ] *nm* servant

servitude [seʀvityd] *nf* servitude; (*fig*) constraint

ses [se] *dét voir* **son**[1]

seuil [sœj] *nm* doorstep; (*fig*) threshold

seul, e [sœl] *adj* (*sans compagnie*) alone; (*avec nuance affective: isolé*) lonely; (*unique*): **un ~ livre** only one book, a single book ♦ *adv* (*vivre*) alone, on one's own ♦ *nm, nf*: **il en reste un(e) ~(e)** there's only one left; **le ~ livre** the only book; **ce livre, ce livre ~** this book alone, only this book; **parler tout ~** to talk to oneself; **faire qch (tout) ~** to do sth (all) on one's own *ou* (all) by oneself; **à lui (tout) ~** single-handed, on his own

seulement [sœlmɑ̃] *adv* only; **non ~ ... mais aussi *ou* encore** not only ... but also

sève [sɛv] *nf* sap

sévère [sevɛʀ] *adj* severe

sévices [sevis] *nmpl* (physical) cruelty *sg*, ill treatment *sg*

sévir [seviʀ] *vi* (*punir*) to use harsh measures, crack down; (*suj: fléau*) to rage, be rampant

sevrer [səvʀe] *vt* (*enfant etc*) to wean

sexe [sɛks(ə)] *nm* sex; (*organe mâle*) member

sexuel, le [sɛksɥɛl] *adj* sexual

seyant, e [sɛjɑ̃, -ɑ̃t] *adj* becoming

shampooing [ʃɑ̃pwɛ̃] *nm* shampoo; **se faire un ~** to shampoo one's hair

short [ʃɔʀt] *nm* (pair of) shorts *pl*

――――――――― MOT CLÉ

si [si] *nm* (*MUS*) B; (*en chantant la gamme*) ti

♦ *adv* **1** (*oui*) yes

2 (*tellement*) so; **~ gentil/rapidement** so kind/fast; (*tant et*) **~ bien que** so much so that; **~ rapide qu'il soit** however fast he may be

♦ *conj* if; **~ tu veux** if you want; **je me de-**

mande ~ I wonder if *ou* whether; ~ **seulement** if only

Sicile [sisil] *nf*: **la ~** Sicily
SIDA [sida] *sigle m* (= *syndrome immunodéficitaire acquis*) AIDS *sg*
sidéré, e [sidere] *adj* staggered
sidérurgie [sideryrʒi] *nf* steel industry
siècle [sjɛkl(ə)] *nm* century; (*époque*) age
siège [sjɛʒ] *nm* seat; (*d'entreprise*) head office; (*d'organisation*) headquarters *pl*; (*MIL*) siege; ~ **social** registered office
siéger [sjeʒe] *vi* to sit
sien, ne [sjɛ̃, sjɛn] *pron*: **le(la) ~(ne)**, **les ~(ne)s** his; hers; its; **les ~s** (*sa famille*) one's family; **faire des ~nes** (*fam*) to be up to one's (usual) tricks
sieste [sjɛst(ə)] *nf* (afternoon) snooze *ou* nap, siesta; **faire la ~** to have a snooze *ou* nap
sifflement [sifləmɑ̃] *nm* whistle, whistling *no pl*; wheezing *no pl*; hissing *no pl*
siffler [sifle] *vi* (*gén*) to whistle; (*en respirant*) to wheeze; (*serpent, vapeur*) to hiss ♦ *vt* (*chanson*) to whistle; (*chien etc*) to whistle for; (*fille*) to whistle at; (*pièce, orateur*) to hiss, boo; (*faute*) to blow one's whistle at; (*fin du match, départ*) to blow one's whistle for; (*fam: verre*) to guzzle
sifflet [siflɛ] *nm* whistle; **coup de ~** whistle
siffloter [siflɔte] *vi*, *vt* to whistle
sigle [sigl(ə)] *nm* acronym
signal, aux [siɲal, -o] *nm* (*signe convenu, appareil*) signal; (*indice, écriteau*) sign; **donner le ~ de** to give the signal for; ~ **d'alarme** alarm signal; **signaux (lumineux)** (*AUTO*) traffic signals
signalement [siɲalmɑ̃] *nm* description, particulars *pl*
signaler [siɲale] *vt* to indicate; to announce; to report; (*faire remarquer*): ~ **qch à qn/(à qn) que** to point out sth to sb/(to sb) that; **se ~ (par)** to distinguish o.s. (by)
signature [siɲatyʀ] *nf* signature (*action*), signing
signe [siɲ] *nm* sign; (*TYPO*) mark; **faire un ~ de la main** to give a sign with one's hand; **faire ~ à qn** (*fig*) to get in touch with sb; **faire ~ à qn d'entrer** to motion (to) sb to come in; ~**s particuliers** *nmpl* distinguishing marks
signer [siɲe] *vt* to sign; **se ~** *vi* to cross o.s.
signet [siɲɛ] *nm* bookmark
significatif, ive [siɲifikatif, -iv] *adj* significant
signification [siɲifikasjɔ̃] *nf* meaning
signifier [siɲifje] *vt* (*vouloir dire*) to mean; (*faire connaître*): ~ **qch (à qn)** to make sth known (to sb); (*JUR*): ~ **qch à qn** to serve notice of sth on sb
silence [silɑ̃s] *nm* silence; (*MUS*) rest; **gar-**

der le ~ to keep silent, say nothing; **passer sous ~** to pass over (in silence); **silencieux, euse** *adj* quiet, silent ♦ *nm* silencer
silex [silɛks] *nm* flint
silhouette [silwɛt] *nf* outline, silhouette; (*lignes, contour*) outline; (*figure*) figure
silicium [silisjɔm] *nm* silicon; **plaquette de ~** silicon chip
sillage [sijaʒ] *nm* wake; (*fig*) trail
sillon [sijɔ̃] *nm* furrow; (*de disque*) groove; **sillonner** *vt* to criss-cross
simagrées [simagre] *nfpl* fuss *sg*; airs and graces
similaire [similɛʀ] *adj* similar; **similicuir** *nm* imitation leather; **similitude** *nf* similarity
simple [sɛ̃pl(ə)] *adj* (*gén*) simple; (*non multiple*) single; ~**s** *nmpl* (*MÉD*) medicinal plants; ~ **d'esprit** *nm/f* simpleton; ~ **messieurs** *nm* (*TENNIS*) men's singles *sg*; **un ~ particulier** an ordinary citizen; ~ **soldat** private
simulacre [simylakʀ(ə)] *nm* (*péj*): **un ~ de** a pretence of
simuler [simyle] *vt* to sham, simulate
simultané, e [simyltane] *adj* simultaneous
sincère [sɛ̃sɛʀ] *adj* sincere; genuine; **sincérité** *nf* sincerity
sine qua non [sinekwanɔn] *adj*: **condition ~** indispensable condition
singe [sɛ̃ʒ] *nm* monkey; (*de grande taille*) ape; ~**r** [sɛ̃ʒe] *vt* to ape, mimic
singeries [sɛ̃ʒʀi] *nfpl* antics; (*simagrées*) airs and graces
singulariser [sɛ̃gylarize] *vt* to mark out; **se ~** *vi* to call attention to o.s.
singularité [sɛ̃gylarite] *nf* peculiarity
singulier, ière [sɛ̃gylje, -jɛʀ] *adj* remarkable, singular ♦ *nm* singular
sinistre [sinistʀ(ə)] *adj* sinister ♦ *nm* (*incendie*) blaze; (*catastrophe*) disaster; (*ASSURANCES*) damage (*giving rise to a claim*); **sinistré, e** *adj* disaster-stricken ♦ *nm/f* disaster victim
sinon [sinɔ̃] *conj* (*autrement, sans quoi*) otherwise, or else; (*sauf*) except, other than; (*si ce n'est*) if not
sinueux, euse [sinɥø, -øz] *adj* winding; (*fig*) tortuous
sinus [sinys] *nm* (*ANAT*) sinus; (*GÉOM*) sine; **sinusite** *nf* sinusitis
siphon [sifɔ̃] *nm* (*tube, d'eau gazeuse*) siphon; (*d'évier etc*) U-bend
sirène [siʀɛn] *nf* siren; ~ **d'alarme** air-raid siren; fire alarm
sirop [siʀo] *nm* (*à diluer: de fruit etc*) syrup; (*boisson*) fruit drink; (*pharmaceutique*) syrup, mixture
siroter [siʀɔte] *vt* to sip
sismique [sismik] *adj* seismic
site [sit] *nm* (*paysage, environnement*) setting; (*d'une ville etc: emplacement*) site; ~

(pittoresque) beauty spot; **~s touristiques** places of interest

sitôt [sito] *adv:* **~ parti** as soon as he *etc* had left; **~ après** straight after; **pas de ~** not for a long time

situation [situasjɔ̃] *nf* (*gén*) situation; (*d'un édifice, d'une ville*) situation, position; location; **~ de famille** marital status

situé, e [situe] *adj:* **bien ~** well situated; **~ à** situated at

situer [situe] *vt* to site, situate; (*en pensée*) to set, place; **se ~** *vi:* **se ~ à/près de** to be situated at/near

six [sis] *num* six; **sixième** *num* sixth

ski [ski] *nm* (*objet*) ski; (*sport*) skiing; **faire du ~** to ski; **~ de fond** cross-country skiing; **~ nautique** water-skiing; **~ de piste** downhill skiing; **~ de randonnée** cross-country skiing; **skier** *vi* to ski; **skieur, euse** *nm/f* skier

slip [slip] *nm* (*sous-vêtement*) pants *pl*, briefs *pl*; (*de bain: d'homme*) trunks *pl*; (: *du bikini*) (bikini) briefs *pl*

slogan [slɔgɑ̃] *nm* slogan

S.M.I.C. [smik] *sigle m* = **salaire minimum interprofessionnel de croissance**

smicard, e [smikaʀ, -aʀd(ə)] (*fam*) *nm/f* minimum wage earner

smoking [smɔkiŋ] *nm* dinner *ou* evening suit

S.N.C.F. *sigle f* (= *société nationale des chemins de fer français*) French railways

snob [snɔb] *adj* snobbish ♦ *nm/f* snob

sobre [sɔbʀ(ə)] *adj* temperate, abstemious; (*élégance, style*) sober; **~ de** (*gestes, compliments*) sparing of

sobriquet [sɔbʀikɛ] *nm* nickname

social, e, aux [sɔsjal, -o] *adj* social

socialisme [sɔsjalism(ə)] *nm* socialism; **socialiste** *nm/f* socialist

société [sɔsjete] *nf* society; (*sportive*) club; (*COMM*) company; **la ~ d'abondance/de consommation** the affluent/consumer society; **~ à responsabilité limitée** *type of limited liability company*; **~ anonyme** ≈ limited (*BRIT*) *ou* incorporated (*US*) company

sociologie [sɔsjɔlɔʒi] *nf* sociology

socle [sɔkl(ə)] *nm* (*de colonne, statue*) plinth, pedestal; (*de lampe*) base

socquette [sɔkɛt] *nf* ankle sock

sœur [sœʀ] *nf* sister; (*religieuse*) nun, sister

soi [swa] *pron* oneself; **cela va de ~** that *ou* it goes without saying; **soi-disant** *adj inv* so-called ♦ *adv* supposedly

soie [swa] *nf* silk; (*de porc, sanglier: poil*) bristle; **soierie** *nf* (*tissu*) silk

soif [swaf] *nf* thirst; **avoir ~** to be thirsty; **donner ~ à qn** to make sb thirsty

soigné, e [swaɲe] *adj* (*tenue*) well-groomed, neat; (*travail*) careful, meticulous; (*fam*) whopping; stiff

soigner [swaɲe] *vt* (*malade, maladie: suj:*

docteur) to treat; (*suj: infirmière, mère*) to nurse, look after; (*blessé*) to tend; (*travail, détails*) to take care over; (*jardin, chevelure, invités*) to look after

soigneux, euse [swaɲø, -øz] *adj* (*propre*) tidy, neat; (*méticuleux*) painstaking, careful; **~ de** careful with

soi-même [swamɛm] *pron* oneself

soin [swɛ̃] *nm* (*application*) care; (*propreté, ordre*) tidiness, neatness; **~s** *nmpl* (*à un malade, blessé*) treatment *sg*, medical attention *sg*; (*attentions, prévenance*) care and attention *sg*; (*hygiène*) care *sg*; **prendre ~ de** to take care of, look after; **prendre ~ de faire** to take care to do; **les premiers ~s** first aid *sg*; **aux bons ~s de** c/o, care of

soir [swaʀ] *nm* evening; **ce ~** this evening, tonight; **demain ~** tomorrow evening, tomorrow night

soirée [swaʀe] *nf* evening; (*réception*) party

soit [swa] *vb voir* **être** ♦ *conj* (*à savoir*) namely; (*ou*): **~ ... ~** either ... or ♦ *adv* so be it, very well; **~ que ... ~ que** *ou* **ou que** whether ... or whether

soixantaine [swasɑ̃tɛn] *nf:* **une ~ (de)** sixty or so, about sixty; **avoir la ~** (*âge*) to be around sixty

soixante [swasɑ̃t] *num* sixty; **soixante-dix** *num* seventy

soja [sɔʒa] *nm* soya; (*graines*) soya beans *pl*

sol [sɔl] *nm* ground; (*de logement*) floor; (*revêtement*) flooring *no pl*; (*territoire, AGR, GÉO*) soil; (*MUS*) G; (: *en chantant la gamme*) so(h)

solaire [sɔlɛʀ] *adj* solar, sun *cpd*

soldat [sɔlda] *nm* soldier

solde [sɔld(ə)] *nf* pay ♦ *nm* (*COMM*) balance; **~s** *nm ou f pl* sale goods; sales; **en ~** at sale price

solder [sɔlde] *vt* (*compte*) to settle; (*marchandise*) to sell at sale price, sell off; **se ~ par** (*fig*) to end in; **article soldé (à) 10 F** item reduced to 10 F

sole [sɔl] *nf* sole *inv* (*fish*)

soleil [sɔlɛj] *nm* sun; (*lumière*) sun(light); (*temps ensoleillé*) sun(shine); (*BOT*) sunflower; **il fait du ~** it's sunny; **au ~** in the sun

solennel, le [sɔlanɛl] *adj* solemn; ceremonial; **solennité** *nf* (*d'une fête*) solemnity

solfège [sɔlfɛʒ] *nm* rudiments *pl* of music; (*exercices*) ear training *no pl*

solidaire [sɔlidɛʀ] *adj* (*personnes*) who stand together, who show solidarity; (*pièces mécaniques*) interdependent; **être ~ de** (*collègues*) to stand by; **solidarité** *nf* solidarity; interdependence; **par solidarité (avec)** in sympathy (with)

solide [sɔlid] *adj* solid; (*mur, maison, meuble*) solid, sturdy; (*connaissances, argument*) sound; (*personne, estomac*) robust, sturdy ♦

nm solid

soliste [sɔlist(ə)] *nm/f* soloist

solitaire [sɔlitɛʀ] *adj (sans compagnie)* solitary, lonely; *(lieu)* lonely ♦ *nm/f* recluse; loner

solitude [sɔlityd] *nf* loneliness; *(paix)* solitude

solive [sɔliv] *nf* joist

sollicitations [sɔlisitɑsjɔ̃] *nfpl* entreaties, appeals; enticements; *(TECH)* stress *sg*

solliciter [sɔlisite] *vt (personne)* to appeal to; *(emploi, faveur)* to seek; *(suj: occupations, attractions etc)*: ~ **qn** to appeal to sb's curiosity *etc*; to entice sb; to make demands on sb's time

sollicitude [sɔlisityd] *nf* concern

soluble [sɔlybl(ə)] *adj* soluble

solution [sɔlysjɔ̃] *nf* solution; ~ **de facilité** easy way out

solvable [sɔlvabl(ə)] *adj* solvent

sombre [sɔ̃bʀ(ə)] *adj* dark; *(fig)* gloomy

sombrer [sɔ̃bʀe] *vi (bateau)* to sink; ~ **dans** *(misère, désespoir)* to sink into

sommaire [sɔmɛʀ] *adj (simple)* basic; *(expéditif)* summary ♦ *nm* summary

sommation [sɔmasjɔ̃] *nf (JUR)* summons *sg*; *(avant de faire feu)* warning

somme [sɔm] *nf (MATH)* sum; *(fig)* amount; *(argent)* sum, amount ♦ *nm*: **faire un** ~ to have a (short) nap; **en** ~ all in all; ~ **toute** all in all

sommeil [sɔmɛj] *nm* sleep; **avoir** ~ to be sleepy; **sommeiller** *vi* to doze; *(fig)* to lie dormant

sommelier [sɔməlje] *nm* wine waiter

sommer [sɔme] *vt*: ~ **qn de faire** to command *ou* order sb to do; *(JUR)* to summon sb to do

sommes *vb voir* **être**

sommet [sɔmɛ] *nm* top; *(d'une montagne)* summit, top; *(fig: de la perfection, gloire)* height

sommier [sɔmje] *nm* (bed) base

sommité [sɔmite] *nf* prominent person, leading light

somnambule [sɔmnɑ̃byl] *nm/f* sleepwalker

somnifère [sɔmnifɛʀ] *nm* sleeping drug *no pl (ou* pill)

somnoler [sɔmnɔle] *vi* to doze

somptueux, euse [sɔ̃ptɥø, -øz] *adj* sumptuous; lavish

son¹, sa [sɔ̃, sa] *(pl* **ses)** *dét (antécédent humain: mâle)* his; *(: femelle)* her; *(: valeur indéfinie)* one's, his/her; *(antécédent non humain)* its

son² [sɔ̃] *nm* sound; *(de blé)* bran

sondage [sɔ̃daʒ] *nm*: ~ **(d'opinion)** (opinion) poll

sonde [sɔ̃d] *nf (NAVIG)* lead *ou* sounding line; *(MÉD)* probe; catheter; feeding tube; *(TECH)* borer, driller; *(pour fouiller etc)* probe

sonder [sɔ̃de] *vt (NAVIG)* to sound; *(atmosphère, plaie, bagages etc)* to probe; *(TECH)* to bore, drill; *(fig)* to sound out; to probe

songe [sɔ̃ʒ] *nm* dream

songer [sɔ̃ʒe] *vi*: ~ **à** *(penser à)* to think of; ~ **que** to consider that; to think that; **songeur, euse** *adj* pensive

sonnant, e [sɔnɑ̃, -ɑ̃t] *adj*: **à 8 heures** ~**es** on the stroke of 8

sonné, e [sɔne] *adj (fam)* cracked; **il est midi** ~ it's gone twelve

sonner [sɔne] *vi* to ring ♦ *vt (cloche)* to ring; *(glas, tocsin)* to sound; *(portier, infirmière)* to ring for; *(messe)* to sound the bell for; ~ **faux** *(instrument)* to sound out of tune; *(rire)* to ring false; ~ **les heures** to strike the hours

sonnerie [sɔnʀi] *nf (son)* ringing; *(sonnette)* bell; *(mécanisme d'horloge)* striking mechanism; ~ **d'alarme** alarm bell

sonnette [sɔnɛt] *nf* bell; ~ **d'alarme** alarm bell

sono [sɔno] *abr f* = **sonorisation**

sonore [sɔnɔʀ] *adj (voix)* sonorous, ringing; *(salle, métal)* resonant; *(ondes, film, signal)* sound *cpd*

sonorisation [sɔnɔʀizasjɔ̃] *nf (installations)* public address system, P.A. system

sonorité [sɔnɔʀite] *nf (de piano, violon)* tone; *(de voix, mot)* sonority; *(d'une salle)* resonance; acoustics *pl*

sont *vb voir* **être**

sophistiqué, e [sɔfistike] *adj* sophisticated

sorbet [sɔʀbɛ] *nm* water ice, sorbet

sorcellerie [sɔʀsɛlʀi] *nf* witchcraft *no pl*

sorcier [sɔʀsje] *nm* sorcerer; **sorcière** *nf* witch *ou* sorceress

sordide [sɔʀdid] *adj* sordid; squalid

sornettes [sɔʀnɛt] *nfpl* twaddle *sg*

sort [sɔʀ] *nm (fortune, destinée)* fate; *(condition, situation)* lot; *(magique)* curse, spell; **tirer au** ~ to draw lots

sorte [sɔʀt(ə)] *nf* sort, kind; **de la** ~ in that way; **de (telle)** ~ **que, en** ~ **que** so that; so much so that; **faire en** ~ **que** to see to it that

sortie [sɔʀti] *nf (issue)* way out, exit; *(MIL)* sortie; *(fig: verbale)* outburst; sally; *(promenade)* outing; *(le soir: au restaurant etc)* night out; *(COMM: somme)*: ~**s** items of expenditure; outgoings *sans sg*; ~ **de bain** *(vêtement)* bathrobe; ~ **de secours** emergency exit

sortilège [sɔʀtilɛʒ] *nm* (magic) spell

sortir [sɔʀtiʀ] *vi (gén)* to come out; *(partir, se promener, aller au spectacle)* to go out; *(numéro gagnant)* to come up ♦ *vt (gén)* to take out; *(produit, ouvrage, modèle)* to bring out; *(INFORM)* to output; *(: sur papier)* to print out; *(fam: expulser)* to throw out; **se** ~ **de** *(affaire, situation)* to get out of; **s'en** ~ *(malade)* to pull through; *(d'une* *difficulté etc*) to get through; ~ **de** (*gén*) to leave; (*endroit*) to go (*ou* come) out of, leave; (*rainure etc*) to come out of; (*cadre, compétence*) to be outside

sosie [sozi] *nm* double

sot, sotte [so, sɔt] *adj* silly, foolish ♦ *nm/f* fool; **sottise** *nf* silliness; silly *ou* foolish thing

sou [su] *nm*: **près de ses ~s** tight-fisted; **sans le ~** penniless

soubresaut [subʀəso] *nm* start; jolt

souche [suʃ] *nf* (*d'arbre*) stump; (*de carnet*) counterfoil (*BRIT*), stub; **de vieille ~** of old stock

souci [susi] *nm* (*inquiétude*) worry; (*préoccupation*) concern; (*BOT*) marigold; **se faire du ~** to worry

soucier [susje] : **se ~ de** *vt* to care about :

soucieux, euse [susjø, -øz] *adj* concerned, worried

soucoupe [sukup] *nf* saucer; ~ **volante** flying saucer

soudain, e [sudɛ̃, -ɛn] *adj* (*douleur, mort*) sudden ♦ *adv* suddenly, all of a sudden

soude [sud] *nf* soda

souder [sude] *vt* (*avec fil à souder*) to solder; (*par soudure autogène*) to weld; (*fig*) to bind together

soudoyer [sudwaje] (*péj*) *vt* to bribe

soudure [sudyʀ] *nf* soldering; welding; (*joint*) soldered joint; weld

souffert, e [sufɛʀ, -ɛʀt(ə)] *pp de* **souffrir**

souffle [sufl(ə)] *nm* (*en expirant*) breath; (*en soufflant*) puff, blow; (*respiration*) breathing; (*d'explosion, de ventilateur*) blast; (*du vent*) blowing; **être à bout de ~** to be out of breath; **un ~ d'air** *ou* **de vent** a breath of air, a puff of wind

soufflé, e [sufle] *adj* (*fam: stupéfié*) staggered ♦ *nm* (*CULIN*) soufflé

souffler [sufle] *vi* (*gén*) to blow; (*haleter*) to puff (and blow) ♦ *vt* (*feu, bougie*) to blow out; (*chasser: poussière etc*) to blow away; (*TECH: verre*) to blow; (*suj: explosion*) to destroy (with its blast); (*dire*): ~ **qch à qn** to whisper sth to sb; (*fam: voler*): ~ **qch à qn** to pinch sth from sb

soufflet [sufle] *nm* (*instrument*) bellows *pl*; (*gifle*) slap (in the face)

souffleur [suflœʀ] *nm* (*THÉÂTRE*) prompter

souffrance [sufʀɑ̃s] *nf* suffering; **en ~** (*marchandise*) awaiting delivery; (*affaire*) pending

souffrant, e [sufʀɑ̃, -ɑ̃t] *adj* unwell

souffre-douleur [sufʀədulœʀ] *nm inv* butt, underdog

souffrir [sufʀiʀ] *vi* to suffer; to be in pain ♦ *vt* to suffer, endure; (*supporter*) to bear, stand; (*admettre: exception etc*) to allow *ou* admit of; ~ **de** (*maladie, froid*) to suffer from

soufre [sufʀ(ə)] *nm* sulphur

souhait [swɛ] *nm* wish; **tous nos ~s de** good wishes *ou* our best wishes for; **riche etc à ~** as rich *etc* as one could wish; **à vos ~s!** bless you!; ~**able** [swɛtabl(ə)] *adj* desirable

souhaiter [swete] *vt* to wish for; ~ **la bonne année à qn** to wish sb a happy New Year

souiller [suje] *vt* to dirty, soil; (*fig*) to sully, tarnish

soûl, e [su, sul] *adj* drunk ♦ *nm*: **tout son ~** to one's heart's content

soulagement [sulaʒmɑ̃] *nm* relief

soulager [sulaʒe] *vt* to relieve

soûler [sule] *vt*: ~ **qn** to get sb drunk; (*suj: boisson*) to make sb drunk; (*fig*) to make sb's head spin *ou* reel; **se ~** *vi* to get drunk

soulever [sulve] *vt* to lift; (*vagues, poussière*) to send up; (*peuple*) to stir up (to revolt); (*enthousiasme*) to arouse; (*question, débat*) to raise; **se ~** *vi* (*peuple*) to rise up; (*personne couchée*) to lift o.s. up; **cela me soulève le cœur** it makes me feel sick

soulier [sulje] *nm* shoe

souligner [suliɲe] *vt* to underline; (*fig*) to emphasize, to stress

soumettre [sumɛtʀ(ə)] *vt* (*pays*) to subject, subjugate; (*rebelle*) to put down, subdue; **se ~ (à)** to submit (to); ~ **qn/qch à** to subject sb/sth to; ~ **qch à qn** (*projet etc*) to submit sth to sb

soumis, e [sumi, -iz] *adj* submissive; **revenus ~ à l'impôt** taxable income; **soumission** [sumisjɔ̃] *nf* submission; (*docilité*) submissiveness; (*COMM*) tender

soupape [supap] *nf* valve

soupçon [supsɔ̃] *nm* suspicion; (*petite quantité*): **un ~ de** a hint *ou* touch of; **soupçonner** *vt* to suspect; **soupçonneux, euse** *adj* suspicious

soupe [sup] *nf* soup; ~ **au lait** *adj inv* quick-tempered

souper [supe] *vi* to have supper ♦ *nm* supper

soupeser [supəze] *vt* to weigh in one's hand(s); (*fig*) to weigh up

soupière [supjɛʀ] *nf* (*soup*) tureen

soupir [supiʀ] *nm* sigh; (*MUS*) crotchet rest

soupirail, aux [supiʀaj, -o] *nm* (small) basement window

soupirer [supiʀe] *vi* to sigh; ~ **après qch** to yearn for sth

souple [supl(ə)] *adj* supple; (*fig: règlement, caractère*) flexible; (: *démarche, taille*) lithe, supple

source [suʀs(ə)] *nf* (*point d'eau*) spring; (*d'un cours d'eau, fig*) source; **de bonne ~** on good authority

sourcil [suʀsij] *nm* (eye)brow

sourciller [suʀsije] *vi*: **sans ~** without turning a hair *ou* batting an eyelid

sourcilleux, euse [suʀsijø, -øz] *adj* pernickety

sourd, e [suʀ, suʀd(ə)] *adj* deaf; *(bruit, voix)* muffled; *(douleur)* dull; *(lutte)* silent, hidden ♦ *nm/f* deaf person

sourdine [suʀdin] *nf (MUS)* mute; **en ~** softly, quietly

sourd-muet, sourde-muette [suʀmɥɛ, suʀdmɥɛt] *adj* deaf-and-dumb ♦ *nm/f* deaf-mute

souriant, e [suʀjã, -ãt] *adj* cheerful

souricière [suʀisjɛʀ] *nf* mousetrap; *(fig)* trap

sourire [suʀiʀ] *nm* smile ♦ *vi* to smile; **~ à qn** to smile at sb; *(fig)* to appeal to sb; to smile on sb; **garder le ~** to keep smiling

souris [suʀi] *nf* mouse

sournois, e [suʀnwa, -waz] *adj* deceitful, underhand

sous [su] *prép (gén)* under; **~ la pluie/le soleil** in the rain/sunshine; **~ terre** underground; **~ peu** shortly, before long

sous-bois [subwa] *nm inv* undergrowth

souscrire [suskʀiʀ]: **~ à** *vt* to subscribe to

sous: ~-directeur, trice *nm/f* assistant manager(manageress); **~-entendre** *vt* to imply, infer; **~-entendu, e** *adj* implied; *(LING)* understood ♦ *nm* innuendo, insinuation; **~-estimer** *vt* to under-estimate; **~-jacent, e** *adj* underlying; **~-louer** *vt* to sublet; **~-main** *nm inv* desk blotter; **en ~-main** secretly; **~-marin, e** *adj (flore, volcan)* submarine; *(navigation, pêche, explosif)* underwater ♦ *nm* submarine; **~-officier** *nm* ≈ non-commissioned officer (N.C.O.); **~-produit** *nm* by-product; *(fig: péj)* pale imitation; **~-signé, e** *adj*: **je ~-signé** I the undersigned; **~-sol** *nm* basement; **~-titre** *nm* subtitle

soustraction [sustʀaksjɔ̃] *nf* subtraction

soustraire [sustʀɛʀ] *vt* to subtract, take away; *(dérober)*: **~ qch à qn** to remove sth from sb; **se ~ à** *(autorité etc)* to elude, escape from; **~ qn à** *(danger)* to shield sb from

sous-traitant [sutʀɛtɑ̃] *nm* sub-contractor

sous-vêtements [suvɛtmɑ̃] *nmpl* underwear *sg*

soutane [sutan] *nf* cassock, soutane

soute [sut] *nf* hold

soutènement [sutɛnmɑ̃] *nm*: **mur de ~** retaining wall

souteneur [sutnœʀ] *nm* procurer

soutenir [sutniʀ] *vt* to support; *(assaut, choc)* to stand up to, withstand; *(intérêt, effort)* to keep up; *(assurer)*: **~ que** to maintain that; **~ la comparaison avec** to bear *ou* stand comparison with; **soutenu, e** *adj (efforts)* sustained, unflagging; *(style)* elevated

souterrain, e [sutɛʀɛ̃, -ɛn] *adj* underground ♦ *nm* underground passage

soutien [sutjɛ̃] *nm* support; **~ de famille** breadwinner; **~-gorge** [sutjɛ̃gɔʀʒ(ə)] *nm* bra

soutirer [sutiʀe] *vt*: **~ qch à qn** to squeeze *ou* get sth out of sb

souvenir [suvniʀ] *nm (réminiscence)* memory; *(objet)* souvenir ♦ *vb*: **se ~ de** *vt* to remember; **se ~ que** to remember that; **en ~ de** in memory *ou* remembrance of

souvent [suvɑ̃] *adv* often; **peu ~** seldom, infrequently

souverain, e [suvʀɛ̃, -ɛn] *adj* sovereign; *(fig: mépris)* supreme ♦ *nm/f* sovereign, monarch

soviétique [sɔvjetik] *nm/f*: **Soviétique** Soviet citizen

soyeux, euse [swajø, øz] *adj* silky

soyons *etc vb voir* **être**

spacieux, euse [spasjø, -øz] *adj* spacious; roomy

spaghettis [spageti] *nmpl* spaghetti *sg*

sparadrap [spaʀadʀa] *nm* sticking plaster *(BRIT)*, Bandaid (®: *US*)

spatial, e, aux [spasjal, -o] *adj (AVIAT)* space *cpd*

speaker, ine [spikœʀ, -kʀin] *nm/f* announcer

spécial, e, aux [spesjal, -o] *adj* special; *(bizarre)* peculiar; **spécialement** *adv* especially, particularly; *(tout exprès)* specially

spécialiser [spesjalize]: **se ~** *vi* to specialize

spécialiste [spesjalist(ə)] *nm/f* specialist

spécialité [spesjalite] *nf* speciality; *(SCOL)* special field

spécifier [spesifje] *vt* to specify, state

spécimen [spesimɛn] *nm* specimen; *(revue etc)* specimen *ou* sample copy

spectacle [spɛktakl(ə)] *nm (tableau, scène)* sight; *(représentation)* show; *(industrie)* show business; **spectaculaire** *adj* spectacular

spectateur, trice [spɛktatœʀ, -tʀis] *nm/f (CINÉMA etc)* member of the audience; *(SPORT)* spectator; *(d'un événement)* onlooker, witness

spéculer [spekyle] *vi* to speculate; **~ sur** *(COMM)* to speculate in; *(réfléchir)* to speculate on

spéléologie [speleɔlɔʒi] *nf* potholing

sperme [spɛʀm(ə)] *nm* semen, sperm

sphère [sfɛʀ] *nf* sphere

spirale [spiʀal] *nf* spiral

spirituel, le [spiʀitɥɛl] *adj* spiritual; *(fin, piquant)* witty

spiritueux [spiʀitɥø] *nm* spirit

splendide [splɑ̃did] *adj* splendid; magnificent

spontané, e [spɔ̃tane] *adj* spontaneous

sport [spɔʀ] *nm* sport ♦ *adj inv (vêtement)* casual; **faire du ~** to do sport; **sportif, ive** *adj (journal, association, épreuve)* sports *cpd*; *(allure, démarche)* athletic; *(attitude, esprit)* sporting; **~s d'hiver** winter sports

spot [spɔt] *nm* (*lampe*) spot(light); (*annonce*): **~ (publicitaire)** commercial (break)

square [skwaʀ] *nm* public garden(s)

squelette [skəlɛt] *nm* skeleton; **squeletti-que** *adj* scrawny; (*fig*) skimpy

stabiliser [stabilize] *vt* to stabilize; (*terrain*) to consolidate

stable [stabl(ə)] *adj* stable, steady

stade [stad] *nm* (*SPORT*) stadium; (*phase, niveau*) stage

stage [staʒ] *nm* training period; training course; **stagiaire** *nm/f*, *adj* trainee

stalle [stal] *nf* stall, box

stand [stɑ̃d] *nm* (*d'exposition*) stand; (*de foire*) stall; **~ de tir** (*à la foire, SPORT*) shooting range

standard [stɑ̃daʀ] *adj inv* standard ♦ *nm* switchboard; **standardiste** *nm/f* switch-board operator

standing [stɑ̃diŋ] *nm* standing; **immeuble de grand ~** block of luxury flats (*BRIT*), condo(minium) (*US*)

starter [staʀtɛʀ] *nm* (*AUTO*) choke

station [stasjɔ̃] *nf* station; (*de bus*) stop; (*de villégiature*) resort; (*posture*): **la ~ debout** standing, an upright posture; **~ de ski** ski resort; **~ de taxis** taxi rank (*BRIT*) ou stand (*US*)

stationnement [stasjɔnmɑ̃] *nm* parking; **stationner** [stasjɔne] *vi* to park

station-service [stasjɔsɛʀvis] *nf* service station

statistique [statistik] *nf* (*science*) statistics *sg*; (*rapport, étude*) statistic ♦ *adj* statistical

statue [staty] *nf* statue

statuer [statye] *vi*: **~ sur** to rule on, give a ruling on

statut [staty] *nm* status; **~s** *nmpl* (*JUR, AD-MIN*) statutes; **statutaire** *adj* statutory

Sté *abr* = **société**

steak [stɛk] *nm* steak

sténo(dactylo) [steno(daktilo)] *nf* short-hand typist (*BRIT*), stenographer (*US*)

sténo(graphie) [steno(grafi)] *nf* shorthand

stéréo(phonique) [stereo(fɔnik)] *adj* stereo(phonic)

stérile [steʀil] *adj* sterile; (*terre*) barren; (*fig*) fruitless, futile

stérilet [steʀilɛ] *nm* coil, loop

stériliser [steʀilize] *vt* to sterilize

stigmates [stigmat] *nmpl* scars, marks

stimulant [stimylɑ̃] *nm* (*fig*) stimulus, incentive

stimuler [stimyle] *vt* to stimulate

stipuler [stipyle] *vt* to stipulate

stock [stɔk] *nm* stock; **~ d'or** (*FINANCE*) gold reserves *pl*; **stocker** *vt* to stock

stop [stɔp] *nm* (*AUTO*: *écriteau*) stop sign; (: *signal*) brake-light; **~per** [stɔpe] *vt* to stop, halt; (*COUTURE*) to mend ♦ *vi* to stop, halt

store [stɔʀ] *nm* blind; (*de magasin*) shade, awning

strabisme [stʀabism(ə)] *nm* squinting

strapontin [stʀapɔ̃tɛ̃] *nm* jump ou fold-away seat

stratégie [stʀateʒi] *nf* strategy; **stratégi-que** *adj* strategic

stressant, e [stʀesɑ̃, -ɑ̃t] *adj* stressful

strict, e [stʀikt(ə)] *adj* strict; (*tenue, décor*) severe, plain; **son droit le plus ~** his most basic right; **le ~ nécessaire/minimum** the bare essentials/minimum

strie [stʀi] *nf* streak

strophe [stʀɔf] *nf* verse, stanza

structure [stʀyktyʀ] *nf* structure; **~s d'ac-cueil** reception facilities

studieux, euse [stydjø, -øz] *adj* studious; devoted to study

studio [stydjo] *nm* (*logement*) (one-roomed) flatlet (*BRIT*) ou apartment (*US*); (*d'artiste, TV etc*) studio

stupéfait, e [stypefɛ, -ɛt] *adj* astonished

stupéfiant [stypefjɑ̃] *nm* (*MÉD*) drug, nar-cotic

stupéfier [stypefje] *vt* to stupefy; (*étonner*) to stun, astonish

stupeur [stypœʀ] *nf* astonishment

stupide [stypid] *adj* stupid; **stupidité** *nf* stupidity; stupid thing (to do ou say)

style [stil] *nm* style; **meuble de ~** piece of period furniture

stylé, e [stile] *adj* well-trained

styliste [stilist(ə)] *nm/f* designer

stylo [stilo] *nm*: **~ (à encre)** (fountain) pen; **~ (à) bille** ball-point pen

su, e [sy] *pp de* **savoir** ♦ *nm*: **au ~ de** with the knowledge of

suave [sɥav] *adj* sweet; (*goût*) mellow

subalterne [sybaltɛʀn(ə)] *adj* (*employé, officier*) junior; (*rôle*) subordinate, subsidi-ary ♦ *nm/f* subordinate

subconscient [sybkɔ̃sjɑ̃] *nm* subconscious

subir [sybiʀ] *vt* (*affront, dégâts*) to suffer; (*influence, charme*) to be under; (*opération, châtiment*) to undergo

subit, e [sybi, -it] *adj* sudden; **subitement** *adv* suddenly, all of a sudden

subjectif, ive [sybʒɛktif, -iv] *adj* subjective

subjonctif [sybʒɔ̃ktif] *nm* subjunctive

submerger [sybmɛʀʒe] *vt* to submerge; (*fig*) to overwhelm

subordonné, e [sybɔʀdɔne] *adj*, *nm/f* sub-ordinate; **~ à** subordinate to; subject to, depending on

subornation [sybɔʀnasjɔ̃] *nf* bribing

subrepticement [sybʀɛptismɑ̃] *adv* surrep-titiously

subside [sypsid] *nm* grant

subsidiaire [sypsidjɛʀ] *adj*: **question ~** deciding question

subsister [sybziste] *vi* (*rester*) to remain, subsist; (*vivre*) to live; (*survivre*) to live on

substance [sypstɑ̃s] *nf* substance

substituer [sypstitɥe] *vt*: ~ **qn/qch à** to substitute sb/sth for; **se** ~ **à qn** (*évincer*) to substitute o.s. for sb

substitut [sypstity] *nm* (*JUR*) deputy public prosecutor; (*succédané*) substitute

subterfuge [syptɛʀfyʒ] *nm* subterfuge

subtil, e [syptil] *adj* subtle

subtiliser [syptilize] *vt*: ~ **qch (à qn)** to spirit sth away (from sb)

subvenir [sybvəniʀ]: ~ **à** *vt* to meet

subvention [sybvɑ̃sjɔ̃] *nf* subsidy, grant; **subventionner** *vt* to subsidize

suc [syk] *nm* (*BOT*) sap; (*de viande, fruit*) juice

succédané [syksedane] *nm* substitute

succéder [syksede]: ~ **à** *vt* (*directeur, roi etc*) to succeed; (*venir après: dans une série*) to follow, succeed; **se** ~ *vi* (*accidents, années*) to follow one another

succès [syksɛ] *nm* success; **avoir du** ~ to be a success, be successful; **à** ~ successful; ~ **de librairie** bestseller; ~ **(féminins)** conquests

succession [syksesjɔ̃] *nf* (*série, POL*) succession; (*JUR: patrimoine*) estate, inheritance

succomber [sykɔ̃be] *vi* to die, succumb; (*fig*): ~ **à** to give way to, succumb to

succursale [sykyʀsal] *nf* branch

sucer [syse] *vt* to suck

sucette [sysɛt] *nf* (*bonbon*) lollipop; (*de bébé*) dummy (*BRIT*), pacifier (*US*)

sucre [sykʀ(ə)] *nm* (*substance*) sugar; (*morceau*) lump of sugar, sugar lump *ou* cube; ~ **d'orge** barley sugar; ~ **en morceaux/cristallisé/en poudre** lump/granulated/caster sugar; **sucré, e** *adj* (*produit alimentaire*) sweetened; (*au goût*) sweet; (*péj*) sugary, honeyed; **sucrer** *vt* (*thé, café*) to sweeten, put sugar in; **sucreries** *nfpl* (*bonbons*) sweets, sweet things; **sucrier** *nm* (*récipient*) sugar bowl

sud [syd] *nm*: **le** ~ the south ♦ *adj inv* south; (*côte*) south, southern; **au** ~ (*situation*) in the south; (*direction*) to the south; **au** ~ **de** to the south of; **sud-africain, e** *adj, nm/f* South African; **sud-américain, e** *adj, nm/f* South American; **sud-est** [sydɛst] *nm* south-east ♦ *adj inv* south-east; **sud-ouest** [sydwɛst] *nm* south-west ♦ *adj inv* south-west

Suède [sɥɛd] *nf*: **la** ~ Sweden; **suédois, e** *adj* Swedish ♦ *nm/f*: **Suédois, e** Swede ♦ *nm* (*LING*) Swedish

suer [sɥe] *vi* to sweat; (*suinter*) to ooze

sueur [sɥœʀ] *nf* sweat; **en** ~ sweating, in a sweat

suffire [syfiʀ] *vi* (*être assez*): ~ **(à qn/pour qch/pour faire)** to be enough *ou* sufficient (for sb/for sth/to do); **cela suffit pour les irriter/qu'ils se fâchent** it's enough to annoy them/for them to get angry; **il suffit d'une négligence ...** it only takes one act of carelessness ...; **il suffit qu'on oublie pour que ...** one only needs to forget for ...

suffisamment [syfizamɑ̃] *adv* sufficiently, enough; ~ **de** sufficient, enough

suffisant, e [syfizɑ̃, -ɑ̃t] *adj* (*temps, ressources*) sufficient; (*résultats*) satisfactory; (*vaniteux*) self-important, bumptious

suffixe [syfiks(ə)] *nm* suffix

suffoquer [syfɔke] *vt* to choke, suffocate; (*stupéfier*) to stagger, astound ♦ *vi* to choke, suffocate

suffrage [syfʀaʒ] *nm* (*POL: voix*) vote; (*du public etc*) approval *no pl*

suggérer [syɡʒeʀe] *vt* to suggest; **suggestion** *nf* suggestion

suicide [sɥisid] *nm* suicide

suicider [sɥiside]: **se** ~ *vi* to commit suicide

suie [sɥi] *nf* soot

suinter [sɥɛ̃te] *vi* to ooze

suis *vb voir* **être; suivre**

suisse [sɥis] *adj* Swiss ♦ *nm*: **S~** Swiss *pl inv* ♦ *nf*: **la S~** Switzerland; **la S~ romande/allemande** French-speaking/German-speaking Switzerland; **Suissesse** *nf* Swiss (woman *ou* girl)

suite [sɥit] *nf* (*continuation: d'énumération etc*) rest, remainder; (: *de feuilleton*) continuation; (: *film etc sur le même thème*) sequel; (*série: de maisons, succès*): **une** ~ **de** a series *ou* succession of; (*conséquence*) result; (*ordre, liaison logique*) coherence; (*appartement, MUS*) suite; (*escorte*) retinue, suite; ~**s** *nfpl* (*d'une maladie etc*) effects; **prendre la** ~ **de** (*directeur etc*) to succeed, take over from; **donner** ~ **à** (*requête, projet*) to follow up; **faire** ~ **à** to follow; (*faisant*) ~ **à votre lettre du ...** further to your letter of the ...; **de** ~ (*d'affilée*) in succession; (*immédiatement*) at once; **par la** ~ afterwards, subsequently; **à la** ~ one after the other; **à la** ~ **de** (*derrière*) behind; (*en conséquence de*) following; **par** ~ **de** owing to, as a result of

suivant, e [sɥivɑ̃, -ɑ̃t] *adj* next, following; (*ci-après*): **l'exercice** ~ the following exercise ♦ *prép* (*selon*) according to; **au** ~! next!

suivi, e [sɥivi] *adj* (*régulier*) regular, (*cohérent*) consistent; coherent; **très/peu** ~ (*cours*) well-/poorly-attended

suivre [sɥivʀ(ə)] *vt* (*gén*) to follow; (*SCOL: cours*) to attend; (: *programme*) to keep up with; (*COMM: article*) to continue to stock ♦ *vi* to follow; (*élève*) to attend; to keep up; **se** ~ *vi* (*accidents etc*) to follow one after the other; (*raisonnement*) to be coherent; **faire** ~ (*lettre*) to forward; **son cours** (*suj: enquête etc*) to run *ou* take its course; **"à** ~**"** "to be continued"

sujet, te [syʒɛ, -ɛt] *adj*: **être** ~ **à** (*vertige* *etc*) to be liable *ou* subject to ♦ *nm/f* (*d'un souverain*) subject ♦ *nm* subject; **au ~ de** about; **~ à caution** questionable; **~ de conversation** topic *ou* subject of conversation; **~ d'examen** (*SCOL*) examination question; examination paper

summum [sɔmɔm] *nm*: **le ~ de** the height of

superbe [sypɛʀb(ə)] *adj* magnificent, superb

super(carburant) [sypɛʀ(kaʀbyʀɑ̃)] *nm* ≈ 4-star petrol (*BRIT*), ≈ high-octane gasoline (*US*)

supercherie [sypɛʀʃəʀi] *nf* trick

supérette [sypeʀɛt] *nf* (*COMM*) minimarket, superette (*US*)

superficie [sypɛʀfisi] *nf* (surface) area; (*fig*) surface

superficiel, le [sypɛʀfisjɛl] *adj* superficial

superflu, e [sypɛʀfly] *adj* superfluous

supérieur, e [sypeʀjœʀ] *adj* (*lèvre, étages, classes*) upper; (*plus élevé: température, niveau*): **~ (à)** higher (than); (*meilleur: qualité, produit*): **~ (à)** superior (to); (*excellent, hautain*) superior ♦ *nm, nf* superior; **à l'étage ~** on the next floor up; **supériorité** *nf* superiority

superlatif [sypɛʀlatif] *nm* superlative

supermarché [sypɛʀmaʀʃe] *nm* supermarket

superposer [sypɛʀpoze] *vt* (*faire chevaucher*) to superimpose; **lits superposés** bunk beds

superproduction [sypɛʀpʀɔdyksjɔ̃] *nf* (*film*) spectacular

superpuissance [sypɛʀpɥisɑ̃s] *nf* superpower

superstitieux, euse [sypɛʀstisjø, -øz] *adj* superstitious

superviser [sypɛʀvize] *vt* to supervise

suppléant, e [sypleɑ̃, -ɑ̃t] *adj* (*juge, fonctionnaire*) deputy *cpd*; (*professeur*) supply *cpd* ♦ *nm/f* deputy; supply teacher

suppléer [syplee] *vt* (*ajouter: mot manquant etc*) to supply, provide; (*compenser: lacune*) to fill in; (: *défaut*) to make up for; (*remplacer*) to stand in for; **~ à** to make up for; to substitute for

supplément [syplemɑ̃] *nm* supplement; (*de frites etc*) extra portion; **un ~ de travail** extra *ou* additional work; **ceci est en ~** (*au menu etc*) this is extra, there is an extra charge for this; **~aire** *adj* additional, further; (*train, bus*) relief *cpd*, extra

supplications [syplikasjɔ̃] *nfpl* pleas, entreaties

supplice [syplis] *nm* (*peine corporelle*) torture *no pl*; form of torture; (*douleur physique, morale*) torture, agony

supplier [syplije] *vt* to implore, beseech

supplique [syplik] *nf* petition

support [sypɔʀ] *nm* support; (*pour livre, outils*) stand

supportable [sypɔʀtabl(ə)] *adj* (*douleur*) bearable

supporter¹ [sypɔʀtɛʀ] *nm* supporter, fan

supporter² [sypɔʀte] *vt* (*poids, poussée*) to support; (*conséquences, épreuve*) to bear, endure; (*défauts, personne*) to put up with; (*suj: chose: chaleur etc*) to withstand; (: *personne: chaleur, vin*) to be able to take

supposé, e [sypoze] *adj* (*nombre*) estimated; (*auteur*) supposed

supposer [sypoze] *vt* to suppose; (*impliquer*) to presuppose; **à ~ que** supposing (that)

suppositoire [sypozitwaʀ] *nm* suppository

suppression [sypʀesjɔ̃] *nf* (*voir supprimer*) removal; deletion; cancellation; suppression

supprimer [sypʀime] *vt* (*cloison, cause, anxiété*) to remove; (*clause, mot*) to delete; (*congés, service d'autobus etc*) to cancel; (*emplois, privilèges, témoin gênant*) to do away with

supputer [sypyte] *vt* to calculate

suprême [sypʀɛm] *adj* supreme

MOT CLÉ

sur *prép* **1** (*position*) on; (*par-dessus*) over; (*au-dessus*) above; **pose-le ~ la table** put it on the table; **je n'ai pas d'argent ~ moi** I haven't any money on me
2 (*direction*) towards; **en allant ~ Paris** going towards Paris; **~ votre droite** on *ou* to your right
3 (*à propos de*) on, about; **un livre/une conférence ~ Balzac** a book/lecture on *ou* about Balzac
4 (*proportion, mesures*) out of; by; **un ~ 10** one in 10; (*SCOL*) one out of 10; **4 m ~ 2** 4 m by 2
sur ce *adv* hereupon

---

sûr, e [syʀ] *adj* sure, certain; (*digne de confiance*) reliable; (*sans danger*) safe; **le plus ~ est de** the safest thing is to; **~ de soi** self-confident; **~ et certain** absolutely certain

suranné, e [syʀane] *adj* outdated, outmoded

surcharge [syʀʃaʀʒ(ə)] *nf* (*de passagers, marchandises*) excess load; (*correction*) alteration

surcharger [syʀʃaʀʒe] *vt* to overload

surchoix [syʀʃwa] *adj inv* top-quality

surclasser [syʀklase] *vt* to outclass

surcroît [syʀkʀwa] *nm*: **un ~ de** additional +*nom*; **par** *ou* **de ~** moreover; **en ~** in addition

surdité [syʀdite] *nf* deafness

surélever [syʀelve] *vt* to raise, heighten

sûrement [syʀmɑ̃] *adv* reliably; safely, securely; (*certainement*) certainly

surenchère [syʀɑ̃ʃɛʀ] *nf* (*aux enchères*)

higher bid; (*sur prix fixe*) overbid; (*fig*) overstatement; outbidding tactics *pl*; **surenchérir** *vi* to bid higher; (*fig*) to try and outbid each other

surent *vb voir* **savoir**

surestimer [syʀɛstime] *vt* to overestimate

sûreté [syʀte] *nf* (*voir* **sûr**) reliability; safety; (*JUR*) guaranty, surety; **mettre en ~** to put in a safe place; **pour plus de ~** as an extra precaution; **to be on the safe side**

surf [syʀf] *nm* surfing

surface [syʀfas] *nf* surface; (*superficie*) surface area; **faire ~** to surface; **en ~** near the surface; (*fig*) superficially

surfait, e [syʀfɛ, -ɛt] *adj* overrated

surfin, e [syʀfɛ̃, -in] *adj* superfine

surgelé, e [syʀʒəle] *adj* (deep-) frozen

surgir [syʀʒiʀ] *vi* to appear suddenly; (*jaillir*) to shoot up; (*fig: problème, conflit*) to arise

sur: ~**humain, e** *adj* superhuman; ~**impression** *nf* (*PHOTO*) double exposure; **en ~impression** superimposed; ~**-le-champ** *adv* immediately; ~**lendemain** *nm:* **le ~lendemain (soir)** two days later (in the evening); **le ~lendemain de** two days after; ~**mener** *vt* to overwork; **se ~mener** *vi* to overwork

surmonter [syʀmɔ̃te] *vt* (*suj: coupole etc*) to top; (*vaincre*) to overcome

surnager [syʀnaʒe] *vi* to float

surnaturel, le [syʀnatyʀɛl] *adj, nm* supernatural

surnom [syʀnɔ̃] *nm* nickname

surnombre [syʀnɔ̃bʀ(ə)] *nm:* **être en ~** to be too many (*ou* one too many)

surpeuplé, e [syʀpœple] *adj* overpopulated

sur-place [syʀplas] *nm:* **faire du ~** to mark time

surplomber [syʀplɔ̃be] *vi* to be overhanging ♦ *vt* to overhang; to tower above

surplus [syʀply] *nm* (*COMM*) surplus; (*reste*): ~ **de bois** wood left over

surprenant, e [syʀpʀənã, -ãt] *adj* amazing

surprendre [syʀpʀãdʀ(ə)] *vt* (*étonner, prendre à l'improviste*) to surprise; (*tomber sur: intrus etc*) to catch; (*fig*) to detect; to chance upon; to overhear

surpris, e [syʀpʀi, -iz] *adj:* ~ **(de/que)** surprised (at/that)

surprise [syʀpʀiz] *nf* surprise; **faire une ~ à qn** to give sb a surprise; ~**-partie** [syʀpʀizpaʀti] *nf* party

sursaut [syʀso] *nm* start, jump; ~ **de** (*énergie, indignation*) sudden fit *ou* burst of; **en ~** with a start; **sursauter** *vi* to (give a) start, jump

surseoir [syʀswaʀ] : ~ **à** *vt* to defer

sursis [syʀsi] *nm* (*JUR: gén*) suspended sentence; (*à l'exécution capitale, aussi fig*) reprieve; (*MIL*) deferment

surtaxe [syʀtaks(ə)] *nf* surcharge

surtout [syʀtu] *adv* (*avant tout, d'abord*) above all; (*spécialement, particulièrement*) especially; ~, **ne dites rien!** whatever you do don't say anything!; ~ **pas!** certainly not!; ~ **que ...** especially as ...

surveillance [syʀvɛjãs] *nf* watch; (*POLICE, MIL*) surveillance; **sous ~ médicale** under medical supervision

surveillant, e [syʀvɛjã, -ãt] *nm/f* (*de prison*) warder; (*SCOL*) monitor; (*de travaux*) supervisor, overseer

surveiller [syʀveje] *vt* (*enfant, élèves, bagages*) to watch, keep an eye on; (*malade*) to watch over; (*prisonnier, suspect*) to keep (a) watch on; (*territoire, bâtiment*) to (keep) watch over; (*travaux, cuisson*) to supervise; (*SCOL: examen*) to invigilate; **se ~** *vi* to keep a check *ou* watch on o.s.; ~ **son langage/sa ligne** to watch one's language/figure

survenir [syʀvəniʀ] *vi* (*incident, retards*) to occur, arise; (*événement*) to take place; (*personne*) to appear, arrive

survêt(ement) [syʀvɛt(mã)] *nm* tracksuit

survie [syʀvi] *nf* survival; (*REL*) afterlife

survivant, e [syʀvivã, -ãt] *nm/f* survivor

survivre [syʀvivʀ(ə)] *vi* to survive; ~ **à** (*accident etc*) to survive; (*personne*) to outlive

survoler [syʀvɔle] *vt* to fly over; (*fig: livre*) to skim through

survolté, e [syʀvɔlte] *adj* (*fig*) worked up

sus [sy(s)]: **en ~ de** *prép* in addition to, over and above; **en ~** in addition; ~ **à:** ~ **au tyran!** at the tyrant!

susceptible [sysɛptibl(ə)] *adj* touchy, sensitive; ~ **d'amélioration** that can be improved, open to improvement; ~ **de faire** able to do; liable to do

susciter [sysite] *vt* (*admiration*) to arouse; (*obstacles, ennuis*): ~ **(à qn)** to create (for sb)

suspect, e [syspɛ(kt), -ɛkt(ə)] *adj* suspicious; (*témoignage, opinions*) suspect ♦ *nm/f* suspect

suspecter [syspɛkte] *vt* to suspect; (*honnêteté de qn*) to question, have one's suspicions about

suspendre [syspãdʀ(ə)] *vt* (*accrocher: vêtement*): ~ **qch (à)** to hang sth up (on); (*fixer: lustre etc*): ~ **qch à** to hang sth from; (*interrompre, démettre*) to suspend; (*remettre*) to defer; **se ~ à** to hang from

suspendu, e [syspãdy] *adj* (*accroché*): ~ **à** hanging on (*ou* from); (*perché*): ~ **au-dessus de** suspended over

suspens [syspã]: **en ~** *adv* (*affaire*) in abeyance; **tenir en ~** to keep in suspense

suspense [syspãs] *nm* suspense

suspension [syspãsjɔ̃] *nf* suspension; ~ **d'audience** adjournment

sut *vb voir* **savoir**

suture [sytyʀ] *nf* (*MÉD*): **point de ~** stitch

svelte [svɛlt(ə)] *adj* slender, svelte
S.V.P. *sigle* (= *s'il vous plaît*) please
syllabe [silab] *nf* syllable
sylviculture [silvikyltyʀ] *nf* forestry
symbole [sɛ̃bɔl] *nm* symbol; **symbolique** *adj* symbolic(al); (*geste, offrande*) token *cpd*; (*salaire, dommage-intérêts*) nominal; **symboliser** *vt* to symbolize
symétrique [simetʀik] *adj* symmetrical
sympa [sɛ̃pa] *adj abr* = **sympathique**
sympathie [sɛ̃pati] *nf* (*inclination*) liking; (*affinité*) fellow feeling; (*condoléances*) sympathy; **accueillir avec ~** (*projet*) to receive favourably; **croyez à toute ma ~** you have my deepest sympathy
sympathique [sɛ̃patik] *adj* nice, friendly; likeable; pleasant
sympathisant, e [sɛ̃patizɑ̃, -ɑ̃t] *nm/f* sympathizer
sympathiser [sɛ̃patize] *vi* (*voisins etc: s'entendre*) to get on (*BRIT*) *ou* along (*US*) (well)
symphonie [sɛ̃fɔni] *nf* symphony
symptôme [sɛ̃ptom] *nm* symptom
synagogue [sinagɔg] *nf* synagogue
syncope [sɛ̃kɔp] *nf* (*MÉD*) blackout; **tomber en ~** to faint, pass out
syndic [sɛ̃dik] *nm* managing agent
syndical, e, aux [sɛ̃dikal, -o] *adj* (trade) union *cpd*; **syndicaliste** *nm/f* trade unionist
syndicat [sɛ̃dika] *nm* (*d'ouvriers, employés*) (trade) union; (*autre association d'intérêts*) union, association; **~ d'initiative** tourist office
syndiqué, e [sɛ̃dike] *adj* belonging to a (trade) union; **non ~** non-union
syndiquer [sɛ̃dike]: **se ~** *vi* to form a trade union; (*adhérer*) to join a trade union
synonyme [sinɔnim] *adj* synonymous ♦ *nm* synonym; **~ de** synonymous with
syntaxe [sɛ̃taks(ə)] *nf* syntax
synthèse [sɛ̃tɛz] *nf* synthesis
synthétique [sɛ̃tetik] *adj* synthetic
Syrie [siʀi] *nf*: **la ~** Syria
systématique [sistematik] *adj* systematic
système [sistɛm] *nm* system; **~ D** (*fam*) resourcefulness

T t

t' [t(ə)] *pron voir* **te**
ta [ta] *dét voir* **ton**[1]
tabac [taba] *nm* tobacco; tobacconist's (shop); **~ blond/brun** light/dark tobacco
tabagisme [tabaʒism] *nm*: **~ passif** passive smoking
table [tabl(ə)] *nf* table; **à ~!** dinner *etc* is ready!; **se mettre à ~** to sit down to eat; (*fig: fam*) to come clean; **mettre la ~** to lay the table; **faire ~ rase de** to make a clean sweep of; **~ de cuisson** *nf* (*à l'électricité*) hotplate; (*au gaz*) gas ring; **~ de nuit** *ou* **de chevet** bedside table; **~ des matières** (table of) contents *pl*
tableau, x [tablo] *nm* painting; (*reproduction, fig*) picture; (*panneau*) board; (*schéma*) table, chart; **~ d'affichage** notice board; **~ de bord** dashboard; (*AVIAT*) instrument panel; **~ noir** blackboard
tabler [table] *vi*: **~ sur** to bank on
tablette [tablɛt] *nf* (*planche*) shelf; **~ de chocolat** bar of chocolate
tableur [tablœʀ] *nm* spreadsheet
tablier [tablije] *nm* apron
tabouret [tabuʀɛ] *nm* stool
tac [tak] *nm*: **du ~ au ~** tit for tat
tache [taʃ] *nf* (*saleté*) stain, mark; (*ART, de couleur, lumière*) spot; splash, patch; **~ de rousseur** *nf* freckle
tâche [tɑʃ] *nf* task; **travailler à la ~** to do piecework
tacher [taʃe] *vt* to stain, mark; (*fig*) to sully, stain
tâcher [tɑʃe] *vi*: **~ de faire** to try *ou* endeavour to do
tacot [tako] (*péj*) *nm* banger (*BRIT*), (old) heap
tact [takt] *nm* tact; **avoir du ~** to be tactful
tactique [taktik] *adj* tactical ♦ *nf* (*technique*) tactics *sg*; (*plan*) tactic
taie [tɛ] *nf*: **~ (d'oreiller)** pillowslip, pillowcase
taille [tɑj] *nf* cutting; pruning; (*milieu du corps*) waist; (*hauteur*) height; (*grandeur*) size; **de ~ à faire** capable of doing; **de ~** sizeable
taille-crayon(s) [tɑjkʀɛjɔ̃] *nm* pencil sharpener
tailler [tɑje] *vt* (*pierre, diamant*) to cut; (*arbre, plante*) to prune; (*vêtement*) to cut

out; (*crayon*) to sharpen

tailleur [tɑjœʀ] *nm* (*couturier*) tailor; (*vêtement*) suit; **en ~** (*assis*) cross-legged

taillis [tɑji] *nm* copse

taire [tɛʀ] *vt* to keep to o.s., conceal ♦ *vi*: **faire ~ qn** to make sb be quiet; (*fig*) to silence sb; **se ~** *vi* to be silent *ou* quiet

talc [talk] *nm* talc, talcum powder

talent [talɑ̃] *nm* talent

talon [talɔ̃] *nm* heel; (*de chèque, billet*) stub, counterfoil (*BRIT*); **~s plats/aiguilles** flat/stiletto heels

talonner [talɔne] *vt* to follow hard behind; (*fig*) to hound

talus [taly] *nm* embankment

tambour [tɑ̃buʀ] *nm* (*MUS, aussi TECH*) drum; (*musicien*) drummer; (*porte*) revolving door(s *pl*)

tamis [tami] *nm* sieve

Tamise [tamiz] *nf*: **la ~** the Thames

tamisé, e [tamize] *adj* (*fig*) subdued, soft

tamiser [tamize] *vt* to sieve, sift

tampon [tɑ̃pɔ̃] *nm* (*de coton, d'ouate*) wad, pad; (*amortisseur*) buffer; (*bouchon*) plug, stopper; (*cachet, timbre*) stamp; (**mémoire**) **~** (*INFORM*) buffer; **~ hygiénique** tampon; **tamponner** *vt* (*timbres*) to stamp; (*heurter*) to crash *ou* ram into; **tamponneuse** *adj*: **autos tamponneuses** dodgems

tandis [tɑ̃di] : **~ que** *conj* while

tanguer [tɑ̃ge] *vi* to pitch (and toss)

tanière [tanjɛʀ] *nf* lair, den

tanné, e [tane] *adj* weather-beaten

tanner [tane] *vt* to tan

tant [tɑ̃] *adv* so much; **~ de** (*sable, eau*) so much; (*gens, livres*) so many; **~ que** as long as; (*comparatif*) as much as; **~ mieux** that's great; so much the better; **~ pis** never mind; too bad

tante [tɑ̃t] *nf* aunt

tantôt [tɑ̃to] *adv* (*parfois*): **~ ... ~** now ... now; (*cet après-midi*) this afternoon

tapage [tapaʒ] *nm* uproar, din

tapageur, euse [tapaʒœʀ, -øz] *adj* loud, flashy; noisy

tape [tap] *nf* slap

tape-à-l'œil [tapalœj] *adj inv* flashy, showy

taper [tape] *vt* (*porte*) to bang, slam; (*dactylographier*) to type (out); (*fam: emprunter*): **~ qn de 10 F** to touch sb for 10 F ♦ *vi* (*soleil*) to beat down; **~ sur qn** to thump sb; (*fig*) to run sb down; **~ sur qch** to hit sth; to bang on sth; **~ à** (*porte etc*) to knock on; **~ dans** (*se servir*) to dig into; **~ des mains/pieds** to clap one's hands/stamp one's feet; **~ (à la machine)** to type; **se ~ un travail** (*fam*) to land o.s. a job

tapi, e [tapi] *adj* crouching, cowering; hidden away

tapis [tapi] *nm* carpet; (*de table*) cloth; **mettre sur le ~** (*fig*) to bring up for discussion; **~ de sol** (*de tente*) groundsheet;

~ roulant conveyor belt

tapisser [tapise] *vt* (*avec du papier peint*) to paper; (*recouvrir*): **~ qch (de)** to cover sth (with)

tapisserie [tapisʀi] *nf* (*tenture, broderie*) tapestry; (*papier peint*) wallpaper

tapissier, ière [tapisje, -jɛʀ] *nm/f*: **~(-décorateur)** upholsterer (and decorator)

tapoter [tapɔte] *vt* to pat, tap

taquiner [takine] *vt* to tease

tarabiscoté, e [taʀabiskɔte] *adj* overornate, fussy

tard [taʀ] *adv* late; **plus ~** later (on); **au plus ~** at the latest; **sur le ~** late in life

tarder [taʀde] *vi* (*chose*) to be a long time coming; (*personne*): **~ à faire** to delay doing; **il me tarde d'être** I am longing to be; **sans (plus) ~** without (further) delay

tardif, ive [taʀdif, -iv] *adj* late

targuer [taʀge] : **se ~ de** *vt* to boast about

tarif [taʀif] *nm* (*liste*) price list; tariff; (*barème*) rates *pl*; fares *pl*; tariff; (*prix*) rate; fare

tarir [taʀiʀ] *vi* to dry up, run dry

tarte [taʀt(ə)] *nf* tart

tartine [taʀtin] *nf* slice of bread; **~ de miel** slice of bread and honey; **tartiner** *vt* to spread; **fromage à tartiner** cheese spread

tartre [taʀtʀ(ə)] *nm* (*des dents*) tartar; (*de chaudière*) fur, scale

tas [tɑ] *nm* heap, pile; (*fig*): **un ~ de** heaps of, lots of; **en ~** in a heap *ou* pile; **formé sur le ~** trained on the job

tasse [tɑs] *nf* cup; **~ à café** coffee cup

tassé, e [tɑse] *adj*: **bien ~** (*café etc*) strong

tasser [tɑse] *vt* (*terre, neige*) to pack down; (*entasser*): **~ qch dans** to cram sth into; **se ~** *vi* (*terrain*) to settle; (*fig*) to sort itself out, settle down

tâter [tɑte] *vt* to feel; (*fig*) to try out; **se ~** (*hésiter*) to be in two minds; **~ de** (*prison etc*) to have a taste of

tatillon, ne [tatijɔ̃, -ɔn] *adj* pernickety

tâtonnement [tɑtɔnmɑ̃] *nm*: **par ~s** (*fig*) by trial and error

tâtonner [tɑtɔne] *vi* to grope one's way along

tâtons [tɑtɔ̃] : **à ~**: **chercher/avancer à tâtons** *adv* to grope around for/grope one's way forward

tatouer [tatwe] *vt* to tattoo

taudis [todi] *nm* hovel, slum

taule [tol] (*fam*) *nf* nick (*fam*), prison

taupe [top] *nf* mole

taureau, x [tɔʀo] *nm* bull; (*signe*): **le T~** Taurus

tauromachie [tɔʀɔmaʃi] *nf* bullfighting

taux [to] *nm* rate; (*d'alcool*) level; **~ d'intérêt** interest rate

taxe [taks] *nf* tax; (*douanière*) duty; **~ à la valeur ajoutée** value added tax (*BRIT*); **~ de séjour** tourist tax

taxer [takse] *vt* (*personne*) to tax; (*produit*) to put a tax on, tax; (*fig*): ~ **qn de** to call sb +*attrib*; to accuse sb of, tax sb with

taxi [taksi] *nm* taxi

Tchécoslovaquie [tʃekɔslɔvaki] *nf* Czechoslovakia; **tchèque** *adj*, *nm/f* Czech ♦ *nm* (*LING*) Czech

te(t') [t(ə)] *pron* you; (*réfléchi*) yourself

technicien, ne [tɛknisjɛ̃, -jɛn] *nm/f* technician

technique [tɛknik] *adj* technical ♦ *nf* technique; **techniquement** *adv* technically

technologie [tɛknɔlɔʒi] *nf* technology; **technologique** *adj* technological

teck [tɛk] *nm* teak

teignais *etc vb voir* **teindre**

teindre [tɛ̃dʀ(ə)] *vt* to dye

teint, e [tɛ̃, tɛ̃t] *adj* dyed ♦ *nm* (*du visage*) complexion; colour ♦ *nf* shade; **grand** ~ colourfast

teinté, e [tɛ̃te] *adj*: ~ **de** (*fig*) tinged with

teinter [tɛ̃te] *vt* to tint; (*bois*) to stain; **teinture** *nf* dyeing; (*substance*) dye; (*MÉD*) tincture

teinturerie [tɛ̃tyʀʀi] *nf* dry cleaner's

teinturier [tɛ̃tyʀje] *nm* dry cleaner

tel, telle [tɛl] *adj* (*pareil*) such; (*comme*): ~ **un/des** ... like a/like ...; (*indéfini*) such-and-such a, a given; (*intensif*): **un** ~/**de** ~**s** ... such (a)/such ...; **rien de** ~ nothing like it, no such thing; ~ **que** like, such as; ~ **quel** as it is *ou* stands (*ou* was *etc*)

télé [tele] *abr f* (= *télévision*) TV, telly (*BRIT*); (*poste*) TV (set), telly; **à la** ~ on TV, on telly

télécabine [telekabin] *nf* (*benne*) cable car

télécarte [telekaʀt(ə)] *nf* phonecard

télé-: ~**commande** *nf* remote control; ~**copie** *nf* fax; **envoyer qch par** ~**copie** to fax sth; ~**distribution** *nf* cable TV; ~**férique** *nm* = **téléphérique**; ~**gramme** *nm* telegram; ~**graphier** *vt* to telegraph, cable; ~**guider** *vt* to operate by remote control, radio-control; ~**journal** *nm* TV news magazine programme; ~**matique** *nf* telematics *sg*; ~**objectif** *nm* telephoto lens *sg*

téléphérique [teleferik] *nm* cable car

téléphone [telefɔn] *nm* telephone; **avoir le** ~ to be on the (tele)phone; **au** ~ on the phone; ~ **de voiture** car phone; **téléphoner** *vi* to telephone, ring; to make a phone call; **téléphoner à** to phone, call up; **téléphonique** *adj* (tele)phone *cpd*

télescope [teleskɔp] *nm* telescope

télescoper [teleskɔpe] *vt* to smash up; **se** ~ (*véhicules*) to concertina

télé-: ~**scripteur** *nm* teleprinter; ~**siège** *nm* chairlift; ~**ski** *nm* ski-tow; ~**spectateur, trice** *nm/f* (television) viewer; ~**viseur** *nm* television set; ~**vision** *nf* television; **à la** ~**vision** on television

télex [telɛks] *nm* telex

telle [tɛl] *adj voir* **tel**

tellement [tɛlmɑ̃] *adv* (*tant*) so much; (*si*) so; ~ **de** (*sable, eau*) so much; (*gens, livres*) so many; **il s'est endormi** ~ **il était fatigué** he was so tired (that) he fell asleep; **pas** ~ not (all) that much; not (all) that +*adjectif*

téméraire [temeʀɛʀ] *adj* reckless, rash; **témérité** *nf* recklessness, rashness

témoignage [temwaɲaʒ] *nm* (*JUR: déclaration*) testimony *no pl*, evidence *no pl*; (: *faits*) evidence *no pl*; (*rapport, récit*) account; (*fig: d'affection etc*) token, mark; expression

témoigner [temwaɲe] *vt* (*intérêt, gratitude*) to show ♦ *vi* (*JUR*) to testify, give evidence; ~ **de** to bear witness to, testify to

témoin [temwɛ̃] *nm* witness; (*fig*) testimony ♦ *adj* control *cpd*, test *cpd*; **appartement** ~ show flat (*BRIT*); **être** ~ **de** to witness; ~ **oculaire** eyewitness

tempe [tɑ̃p] *nf* temple

tempérament [tɑ̃peʀamɑ̃] *nm* temperament, disposition; **à** ~ (*vente*) on deferred (payment) terms; (*achat*) by instalments, hire purchase *cpd*

température [tɑ̃peʀatyʀ] *nf* temperature; **avoir** *ou* **faire de la** ~ to be running *ou* have a temperature

tempéré, e [tɑ̃peʀe] *adj* temperate

tempête [tɑ̃pɛt] *nf* storm; ~ **de sable/ neige** sand/snowstorm

temple [tɑ̃pl(ə)] *nm* temple; (*protestant*) church

temporaire [tɑ̃pɔʀɛʀ] *adj* temporary

temps [tɑ̃] *nm* (*atmosphérique*) weather; (*durée*) time; (*époque*) time, times *pl*; (*LING*) tense; (*MUS*) beat; (*TECH*) stroke; **il fait beau/mauvais** ~ the weather is fine/ bad; **avoir le** ~/**tout le** ~ to have time/ plenty of time; **en** ~ **de paix/guerre** in peacetime/wartime; **en** ~ **utile** *ou* **voulu** in due time *ou* course; **de** ~ **en** ~, **de** ~ **à autre** from time to time; **à** ~ (*partir, arriver*) in time; **à** ~ **partiel** part-time; **dans le** ~ at one time; **de tout** ~ always; ~ **d'arrêt** pause, halt; ~ **mort** (*COMM*) slack period

tenable [tənabl(ə)] *adj* bearable

tenace [tənas] *adj* tenacious, persistent

tenailler [tənaje] *vt* (*fig*) to torment

tenailles [tənaj] *nfpl* pincers

tenais *etc vb voir* **tenir**

tenancier, ière [tənɑ̃sje, -jɛʀ] *nm/f* manager/manageress

tenant, e [tənɑ̃, -ɑ̃t] *nm/f* (*SPORT*): ~ **du titre** title-holder

tendance [tɑ̃dɑ̃s] *nf* (*opinions*) leanings *pl*, sympathies *pl*; (*inclination*) tendency; (*évolution*) trend; **avoir** ~ **à** to have a tendency to, tend to

tendeur [tɑ̃dœʀ] *nm* (*attache*) elastic strap

tendre [tɑ̃dʀ(ə)] *adj* tender; (*bois, roche,*

couleur) soft ♦ *vt* (*élastique, peau*) to stretch, draw tight; (*muscle*) to tense; (*donner*): ~ **qch à qn** to hold sth out to sb; to offer sb sth; (*fig: piège*) to set, lay; **se** ~ *vi* (*corde*) to tighten; (*relations*) to become strained; ~ **à qch/à faire** to tend towards sth/to do; ~ **l'oreille** to prick up one's ears; ~ **la main/le bras** to hold out one's hand/stretch out one's arm; **tendrement** *adv* tenderly; **tendresse** *nf* tenderness

tendu, e [tɑ̃dy] *pp de* **tendre** ♦ *adj* tight; tensed; strained

ténèbres [tenɛbʀ(ə)] *nfpl* darkness *sg*

teneur [tənœʀ] *nf* content; (*d'une lettre*) terms *pl*, content

tenir [təniʀ] *vt* to hold; (*magasin, hôtel*) to run; (*promesse*) to keep ♦ *vi* to hold; (*neige, gel*) to last; **se** ~ *vi* (*avoir lieu*) to be held, take place; (*être: personne*) to stand; **se** ~ **droit** to stand (*ou* sit) up straight; **bien se** ~ to behave well; **se** ~ **à qch** to hold on to sth; **s'en** ~ **à qch** to confine o.s. to sth; to stick to sth; ~ **à** to be attached to; to care about; to depend on; to stem from; ~ **à faire** to want to do; ~ **de** to partake of; to take after; **ça ne tient qu'à lui** it is entirely up to him; ~ **qn pour** to take sb for; ~ **qch de qn** (*histoire*) to have heard *ou* learnt sth from sb; (*qualité, défaut*) to have inherited *ou* got sth from sb; ~ **les comptes** to keep the books; ~ **le coup** to hold out; ~ **au chaud** to keep hot; **tiens/tenez, voilà le stylo** there's the pen!; **tiens, Alain!** look, here's Alain!; **tiens?** (*surprise*) really?

tennis [tenis] *nm* tennis; (*court*) tennis court ♦ *nm ou f pl* (*aussi: chaussures de* ~) tennis *ou* gym shoes; ~ **de table** table tennis; **tennisman** *nm* tennis player

tension [tɑ̃sjɔ̃] *nf* tension; (*fig*) tension; strain; (*MÉD*) blood pressure; **faire** *ou* **avoir de la** ~ to have high blood pressure

tentation [tɑ̃tasjɔ̃] *nf* temptation

tentative [tɑ̃tativ] *nf* attempt, bid

tente [tɑ̃t] *nf* tent

tenter [tɑ̃te] *vt* (*éprouver, attirer*) to tempt; (*essayer*): ~ **qch/de faire** to attempt *ou* try sth/to do; ~ **sa chance** to try one's luck

tenture [tɑ̃tyʀ] *nf* hanging

tenu, e [təny] *pp de* **tenir** ♦ *adj* (*maison, comptes*): **bien** ~ well-kept; (*obligé*): ~ **de faire** under an obligation to do ♦ *nf* (*action de tenir*) running; keeping; holding; (*vêtements*) clothes *pl*, gear; (*allure*) dress *no pl*, appearance; (*comportement*) manners *pl*, behaviour; **en petite tenue** scantily dressed *ou* clad; ~**e de route** (*AUTO*) road-holding; ~**e de soirée** evening dress

ter [tɛʀ] *adj*: **16** ~ **16b** *ou* **B**

térébenthine [teʀebɑ̃tin] *nf*: (**essence de**) ~ (oil of) turpentine

terme [tɛʀm(ə)] *nm* term; (*fin*) end; à

court/long ~ short-/long-term *ou* -range ♦ *adv* in the short/long term; **avant** ~ (*MÉD*) prematurely; **mettre un** ~ **à** to put an end *ou* a stop to

terminaison [tɛʀminɛzɔ̃] *nf* (*LING*) ending

terminal, e, aux [tɛʀminal, -o] *adj* final ♦ *nm* terminal; **terminale** *nf* (*SCOL*) ≈ sixth form *ou* year (*BRIT*), ≈ twelfth grade (*US*)

terminer [tɛʀmine] *vt* to end; (*travail, repas*) to finish; **se** ~ *vi* to end

terne [tɛʀn(ə)] *adj* dull

ternir [tɛʀniʀ] *vt* to dull; (*fig*) to sully, tarnish; **se** ~ *vi* to become dull

terrain [tɛʀɛ̃] *nm* (*sol, fig*) ground; (*COMM*) land *no pl*, plot (of land); site; **sur le** ~ (*fig*) on the field; ~ **d'aviation** airfield; ~ **de camping** campsite; ~ **de football/rugby** football/rugby pitch (*BRIT*) *ou* field (*US*); ~ **de golf** golf course; ~ **de jeu** games field; playground; ~ **de sport** sports ground; ~ **vague** waste ground *no pl*

terrasse [tɛʀas] *nf* terrace; **à la** ~ (*café*) outside; ~**ment** [tɛʀasmɑ̃] *nm* earthmoving, earthworks *pl*; embankment; ~**r** [tɛʀase] *vt* (*adversaire*) to floor; (*suj: maladie etc*) to lay low

terre [tɛʀ] *nf* (*gén, aussi* ÉLEC) earth; (*substance*) soil, earth; (*opposé à mer*) land *no pl*; (*contrée*) land; ~**s** *nfpl* (*terrains*) lands, land *sg*; **en** ~ (*pipe, poterie*) clay *cpd*; **à** ~ *ou* **par** ~ (*mettre, être*) on the ground (*ou* floor); (*jeter, tomber*) to the ground, down; ~ **à** ~ *adj inv* down-to-earth; ~ **cuite** earthenware; terracotta; **la** ~ **ferme** dry land; ~ **glaise** clay

terreau [tɛʀo] *nm* compost

terre-plein [tɛʀplɛ̃] *nm* platform

terrer [tɛʀe]: **se** ~ *vi* to hide away; to go to ground

terrestre [tɛʀɛstʀ(ə)] *adj* (*surface*) earth's, of the earth; (*BOT, ZOOL, MIL*) land *cpd*; (*REL*) earthly, worldly

terreur [tɛʀœʀ] *nf* terror *no pl*

terrible [tɛʀibl(ə)] *adj* terrible, dreadful; (*fam*) terrific

terrien, ne [tɛʀjɛ̃, -jɛn] *adj*: **propriétaire** ~ landowner ♦ *nm/f* (*non martien etc*) earthling

terrier [tɛʀje] *nm* burrow, hole; (*chien*) terrier

terril [tɛʀil] *nm* slag heap

terrine [tɛʀin] *nf* (*récipient*) terrine; (*CULIN*) pâté

territoire [tɛʀitwaʀ] *nm* territory

terroir [tɛʀwaʀ] *nm* (*AGR*) soil; region

terrorisme [tɛʀɔʀism(ə)] *nm* terrorism; **terroriste** *nm/f* terrorist

tertiaire [tɛʀsjɛʀ] *adj* tertiary ♦ *nm* (*ÉCON*) service industries *pl*

tertre [tɛʀtʀ(ə)] *nm* hillock, mound

tes [te] *dét voir* **ton**[1]

tesson [tesɔ̃] *nm*: ~ **de bouteille** piece of

broken bottle

test [tɛst] *nm* test

testament [tɛstamɑ̃] *nm* (*JUR*) will; (*REL*) Testament; (*fig*) legacy

tester [tɛste] *vt* to test

testicule [tɛstikyl] *nm* testicle

tétanos [tetanos] *nm* tetanus

têtard [tɛtaʀ] *nm* tadpole

tête [tɛt] *nf* head; (*cheveux*) hair *no pl*; (*visage*) face; **de** ~ (*wagon etc*) front *cpd* ♦ *adv* (*calculer*) in one's head, mentally; **tenir** ~ **à qn** to stand up to sb; **la** ~ **en bas** with one's head down; **la** ~ **la première** (*tomber*) headfirst; **faire une** ~ (*FOOTBALL*) to head the ball; **faire la** ~ (*fig*) to sulk; **en** ~ (*SPORT*) in the lead; at the front; **en** ~ **à** ~ in private, alone together; **de la** ~ **aux pieds** from head to toe; ~ **de lecture** (playback) head; ~ **de liste** (*POL*) chief candidate; ~ **de série** (*TENNIS*) seeded player, seed

tête-à-queue [tɛtakø] *nm inv*: **faire un** ~ to spin round

téter [tete] *vt*: ~ (**sa mère**) to suck at one's mother's breast, feed

tétine [tetin] *nf* teat; (*sucette*) dummy (*BRIT*), pacifier (*US*)

têtu, e [tety] *adj* stubborn, pigheaded

texte [tɛkst(ə)] *nm* text

textile [tɛkstil] *adj* textile *cpd* ♦ *nm* textile; textile industry

texture [tɛkstyʀ] *nf* texture

TGV *sigle m* (= *train à grande vitesse*) high-speed train

thé [te] *nm* tea; **prendre le** ~ to have tea; **faire le** ~ to make the tea

théâtral, e, aux [teɑtʀal, -o] *adj* theatrical

théâtre [teɑtʀ(ə)] *nm* theatre; (*œuvres*) plays *pl*, dramatic works *pl*; (*fig: lieu*): **le** ~ **de** the scene of; (*péj*) histrionics *pl*, playacting; **faire du** ~ to be on the stage; to do some acting

théière [tejɛʀ] *nf* teapot

thème [tɛm] *nm* theme; (*SCOL: traduction*) prose (composition)

théologie [teɔlɔʒi] *nf* theology

théorie [teɔʀi] *nf* theory; **théorique** *adj* theoretical

thérapie [teʀapi] *nf* therapy

thermal, e, aux [tɛʀmal, -o] *adj*: **station** ~**e** spa; **cure** ~**e** water cure

thermes [tɛʀm(ə)] *nmpl* thermal baths

thermomètre [tɛʀmɔmɛtʀ(ə)] *nm* thermometer

thermos [tɛʀmos] ® *nm ou nf*: (**bouteille**) ~ vacuum ou Thermos ® flask

thermostat [tɛʀmɔsta] *nm* thermostat

thèse [tɛz] *nf* thesis

thon [tɔ̃] *nm* tuna (fish)

thym [tɛ̃] *nm* thyme

tibia [tibja] *nm* shinbone, tibia; shin

tic [tik] *nm* tic, (nervous) twitch; (*de langage etc*) mannerism

ticket [tikɛ] *nm* ticket; ~ **de caisse** *nm* receipt; ~ **de quai** platform ticket

tiède [tjɛd] *adj* lukewarm; tepid; (*vent, air*) mild, warm; **tiédir** *vi* to cool; to grow warmer

tien, ne [tjɛ̃, tjɛn] *pron*: **le(la)** ~(**ne**), **les** ~(**ne**)**s** yours; **à la** ~**ne!** cheers!

tiens [tjɛ̃] *vb, excl voir* **tenir**

tierce [tjɛʀs(ə)] *adj voir* **tiers**

tiercé [tjɛʀse] *nm* system of forecast betting giving first 3 horses

tiers, tierce [tjɛʀ, tjɛʀs(ə)] *adj* third ♦ *nm* (*JUR*) third party; (*fraction*) third; **le** ~ **monde** the Third World

tige [tiʒ] *nf* stem; (*baguette*) rod

tignasse [tiɲas] (*péj*) *nf* mop of hair

tigre [tigʀ(ə)] *nm* tiger

tigré, e [tigʀe] *adj* striped; spotted

tilleul [tijœl] *nm* lime (tree), linden (tree); (*boisson*) lime(-blossom) tea

timbale [tɛ̃bal] *nf* (metal) tumbler; ~**s** *nfpl* (*MUS*) timpani, kettledrums

timbre [tɛ̃bʀ(ə)] *nm* (*tampon*) stamp; (*aussi*: ~**-poste**) (postage) stamp; (*MUS: de voix, instrument*) timbre, tone

timbré, e [tɛ̃bʀe] (*fam*) *adj* daft

timide [timid] *adj* shy; timid; (*timoré*) timid, timorous; **timidement** *adv* shyly; timidly; **timidité** *nf* shyness; timidity

tins *etc vb voir* **tenir**

tintamarre [tɛ̃tamaʀ] *nm* din, uproar

tinter [tɛ̃te] *vi* to ring, chime; (*argent, clefs*) to jingle

tir [tiʀ] *nm* (*sport*) shooting; (*fait ou manière de tirer*) firing *no pl*; (*stand*) shooting gallery; ~ **à l'arc** archery; ~ **au pigeon** clay pigeon shooting

tirage [tiʀaʒ] *nm* (*action*) printing; (*PHOTO*) print; (*de journal*) circulation; (*de livre*) (print-)run; edition; (*de loterie*) draw; ~ **au sort** drawing lots

tirailler [tiʀaje] *vt* to pull at, tug at ♦ *vi* to fire at random

tirant [tiʀɑ̃] *nm*: ~ **d'eau** draught

tire [tiʀ] *nf*: **vol à la** ~ pickpocketing

tiré, e [tiʀe] *adj* (*traits*) drawn ♦ *nm* (*COMM*) drawee; ~ **par les cheveux** far-fetched

tire-au-flanc [tiʀoflɑ̃] (*péj*) *nm inv* skiver

tire-bouchon [tiʀbuʃɔ̃] *nm* corkscrew

tirelire [tiʀliʀ] *nf* moneybox

tirer [tiʀe] *vt* (*gén*) to pull; (*extraire*): ~ **qch de** to take ou pull sth out of; to get sth out of; to extract sth from; (*tracer: ligne, trait*) to draw, trace; (*fermer: rideau*) to draw, close; (*choisir: carte, conclusion, aussi COMM: chèque*) to draw; (*en faisant feu: balle, coup*) to fire; (: *animal*) to shoot; (*journal, livre, photo*) to print; (*FOOTBALL: corner etc*) to take ♦ *vi* (*faire feu*) to fire; (*faire du tir, FOOTBALL*) to shoot; (*chemi-*

tiret → torse

née) to draw; **se ~** *vi* (*fam*) to push off; **s'en ~** to pull through, get off; **~ sur** to pull on *ou* at; to shoot *ou* fire at; (*pipe*) to draw on; (*fig*: *avoisiner*) to verge *ou* border on; **~ qn de** (*embarras etc*) to help *ou* get sb out of; **~ à l'arc/la carabine** to shoot with a bow and arrow/with a rifle

tiret [tiʀɛ] *nm* dash

tireur, euse [tiʀœʀ, -øz] *nm/f* (*COMM*) drawer ♦ *nm* gunman; **~ d'élite** marksman

tiroir [tiʀwaʀ] *nm* drawer; **tiroir-caisse** *nm* till

tisane [tizan] *nf* herb tea

tisonnier [tizɔnje] *nm* poker

tisser [tise] *vt* to weave; **tisserand** *nm* weaver

tissu [tisy] *nm* fabric, material, cloth *no pl*; (*ANAT*, *BIO*) tissue

tissu-éponge [tisyepɔ̃ʒ] *nm* (terry) towelling *no pl*

titre [titʀ(ə)] *nm* (*gén*) title; (*de journal*) headline; (*diplôme*) qualification; (*COMM*) security; **en ~** (*champion*) official; **à juste ~** with just cause, rightly; **à quel ~?** on what grounds?; **à aucun ~** on no account; **au même ~ (que)** in the same way (as); **à ~ d'information** for (your) information; **à ~ gracieux** free of charge; **à ~ d'essai** on a trial basis; **à ~ privé** in a private capacity; **~ de propriété** title deed; **~ de transport** ticket

tituber [titybe] *vi* to stagger (along)

titulaire [titylɛʀ] *adj* (*ADMIN*) appointed, with tenure ♦ *nm/f* incumbent; **être ~ de** (*poste*) to hold; (*permis*) to be the holder of

toast [tost] *nm* slice *ou* piece of toast; (*de bienvenue*) (welcoming) toast; **porter un ~ à qn** to propose *ou* drink a toast to sb

toboggan [tɔbɔgɑ̃] *nm* toboggan; (*jeu*) slide

tocsin [tɔksɛ̃] *nm* alarm (bell)

toge [tɔʒ] *nf* toga; (*de juge*) gown

toi [twa] *pron* you

toile [twal] *nf* (*matériau*) cloth *no pl*; (*bâche*) piece of canvas; (*tableau*) canvas; **~ cirée** oilcloth; **~ d'araignée** cobweb; **~ de fond** (*fig*) backdrop

toilette [twalɛt] *nf* wash; (*habits*) outfit; dress *no pl*; **~s** *nfpl* (*w.-c.*) toilet *sg*; **faire sa ~** to have a wash, get washed; **articles de ~** toiletries

toi-même [twamɛm] *pron* yourself

toiser [twaze] *vt* to eye up and down

toison [twazɔ̃] *nf* (*de mouton*) fleece; (*cheveux*) mane

toit [twa] *nm* roof; **~ ouvrant** sunroof

toiture [twatyʀ] *nf* roof

tôle [tol] *nf* (*plaque*) steel *ou* iron sheet; **~ ondulée** corrugated iron

tolérable [tɔleʀabl(ə)] *adj* tolerable, bearable

tolérant, e [tɔleʀɑ̃, -ɑ̃t] *adj* tolerant

tolérer [tɔleʀe] *vt* to tolerate; (*ADMIN*: *hors taxe etc*) to allow

tollé [tɔle] *nm* outcry

tomate [tɔmat] *nf* tomato

tombe [tɔ̃b] *nf* (*sépulture*) grave; (*avec monument*) tomb

tombeau, x [tɔ̃bo] *nm* tomb

tombée [tɔ̃be] *nf*: **à la ~ de la nuit** at the close of day, at nightfall

tomber [tɔ̃be] *vi* to fall; **laisser ~** to drop; **~ sur** (*rencontrer*) to come across; (*attaquer*) to set about; **~ de fatigue/sommeil** to drop from exhaustion/be falling asleep on one's feet; **ça tombe bien** that's come at the right time; **il est bien tombé** he's been lucky

tome [tɔm] *nm* volume

ton¹, ta [tɔ̃, ta] (*pl* **tes**) *dét* your

ton² [tɔ̃] *nm* (*gén*) tone; (*MUS*) key; (*couleur*) shade, tone; **de bon ton** in good taste

tonalité [tɔnalite] *nf* (*au téléphone*) dialling tone; (*MUS*) key; (*fig*) tone

tondeuse [tɔ̃døz] *nf* (*à gazon*) (lawn)mower; (*du coiffeur*) clippers *pl*; (*pour la tonte*) shears *pl*

tondre [tɔ̃dʀ(ə)] *vt* (*pelouse*, *herbe*) to mow; (*haie*) to cut, clip; (*mouton*, *toison*) to shear; (*cheveux*) to crop

tonifier [tɔnifje] *vt* (*peau*, *organisme*) to tone up

tonique [tɔnik] *adj* fortifying ♦ *nm* tonic

tonne [tɔn] *nf* metric ton, tonne

tonneau, x [tɔno] *nm* (*à vin*, *cidre*) barrel; (*NAVIG*) ton; **faire des ~x** (*voiture*, *avion*) to roll over

tonnelle [tɔnɛl] *nf* bower, arbour

tonner [tɔne] *vi* to thunder; **il tonne** it is thundering, there's some thunder

tonnerre [tɔnɛʀ] *nm* thunder

tonus [tɔnys] *nm* dynamism

top [tɔp] *nm*: **au 3ème ~** at the 3rd stroke

topinambour [tɔpinɑ̃buʀ] *nm* Jerusalem artichoke

toque [tɔk] *nf* (*de fourrure*) fur hat; **~ de cuisinier** chef's hat; **~ de jockey/juge** jockey's/judge's cap

toqué, e [tɔke] (*fam*) *adj* cracked

torche [tɔʀʃ(ə)] *nf* torch

torchon [tɔʀʃɔ̃] *nm* cloth, duster; (*à vaisselle*) tea towel *ou* cloth

tordre [tɔʀdʀ(ə)] *vt* (*chiffon*) to wring; (*barre*, *fig*: *visage*) to twist; **se ~** *vi* (*barre*) to bend; (*roue*) to twist, buckle; (*ver*, *serpent*) to writhe; **se ~ le pied/bras** to twist one's foot/arm; **tordu, e** [tɔʀdy] *adj* (*fig*) warped, twisted

tornade [tɔʀnad] *nf* tornado

torpille [tɔʀpij] *nf* torpedo

torréfier [tɔʀefje] *vt* to roast

torrent [tɔʀɑ̃] *nm* torrent

torse [tɔʀs(ə)] *nm* (*ANAT*) torso; chest

torsion [tɔRsjɔ̃] *nf* twisting; torsion

tort [tɔR] *nm* (*défaut*) fault; (*préjudice*) wrong *no pl*; **~s** *nmpl* (*JUR*) fault *sg*; **avoir ~** to be wrong; **être dans son ~** to be in the wrong; **donner ~ à qn** to lay the blame on sb; (*fig*) to prove sb wrong; **causer du ~ à** to harm; to be harmful *ou* detrimental to; **à ~** wrongly; **à ~ et à travers** wildly

torticolis [tɔRtikɔli] *nm* stiff neck

tortiller [tɔRtije] *vt* to twist; to twiddle; **se ~** *vi* to wriggle, squirm

tortionnaire [tɔRsjɔnɛR] *nm* torturer

tortue [tɔRty] *nf* tortoise

tortueux, euse [tɔRtɥø, -øz] *adj* (*rue*) twisting; (*fig*) tortuous

torture [tɔRtyR] *nf* torture; **torturer** *vt* to torture; (*fig*) to torment

tôt [to] *adv* early; **~ ou tard** sooner or later; **si ~** so early; (*déjà*) so soon; **au plus ~** at the earliest; **il eut ~ fait de faire** he soon did

total, e, aux [tɔtal, -o] *adj, nm* total; **au ~** in total *ou* all; **faire le ~** to work out the total, add up; **totalement** *adv* totally, completely; **totaliser** *vt* to total (up)

totalité [tɔtalite] *nf*: **la ~ de** all of, the total amount (*ou* number) of; the whole **+***sg*; **en ~** entirely

toubib [tubib] (*fam*) *nm* doctor

touchant, e [tuʃɑ̃, -ɑ̃t] *adj* touching

touche [tuʃ] *nf* (*de piano, de machine à écrire*) key; (*PEINTURE etc*) stroke, touch; (*fig: de nostalgie*) touch, hint; (*FOOTBALL: aussi: remise en ~*) throw-in; (*aussi: ligne de ~*) touch-line

toucher [tuʃe] *nm* touch ♦ *vt* to touch; (*palper*) to feel; (*atteindre: d'un coup de feu etc*) to hit; (*concerner*) to concern, affect; (*contacter*) to reach, contact; (*recevoir: récompense*) to receive, get; (: *salaire*) to draw, get; (: *chèque*) to cash; **se ~** (*être en contact*) to touch; **au ~** to the touch; **~ à** to touch; (*concerner*) to have to do with, concern; **je vais lui en ~ un mot** I'll have a word with him about it; **~ à sa fin** to be drawing to a close

touffe [tuf] *nf* tuft

touffu, e [tufy] *adj* thick, dense

toujours [tuʒuR] *adv* always; (*encore*) still; (*constamment*) forever; **~ plus** more and more; **pour ~** forever; **~ est-il que** the fact remains that; **essaie ~** (you can) try anyway

toupet [tupɛ] (*fam*) *nm* cheek

toupie [tupi] *nf* (spinning) top

tour [tuR] *nf* tower; (*immeuble*) high-rise block (*BRIT*) *ou* building (*US*); (*ÉCHECS*) castle, rook ♦ *nm* (*excursion*) stroll, walk; run, ride; trip; (*SPORT: aussi: ~ de piste*) lap; (*d'être servi ou de jouer etc*) turn; (*de roue etc*) revolution; (*circonférence*): **de 3 m**

de **~** 3 m round, with a circumference *ou* girth of 3 m; (*POL: aussi: ~ de scrutin*) ballot; (*ruse, de prestidigitation*) trick; (*de potier*) wheel; (*à bois, métaux*) lathe; **faire le ~ de** to go round; (*à pied*) to walk round; **c'est au ~ de Renée** it's Renée's turn; **à ~ de rôle, ~ à ~** in turn; **~ de chant** song recital; **~ de contrôle** nf control tower; **~ de garde** spell of duty; **~ d'horizon** (*fig*) general survey; **~ de taille/tête** waist/head measurement

tourbe [tuRb(ə)] *nf* peat

tourbillon [tuRbijɔ̃] *nm* whirlwind; (*d'eau*) whirlpool; (*fig*) whirl, swirl; **tourbillonner** *vi* to whirl (round)

tourelle [tuRɛl] *nf* turret

tourisme [tuRism(ə)] *nm* tourism; **agence de ~** tourist agency; **faire du ~** to go sightseeing; to go touring; **touriste** *nm/f* tourist; **touristique** *adj* tourist *cpd*; (*région*) touristic

tourment [tuRmɑ̃] *nm* torment

tourmenter [tuRmɑ̃te] *vt* to torment; **se ~** *vi* to fret, worry o.s.

tournant [tuRnɑ̃] *nm* (*de route*) bend; (*fig*) turning point

tournebroche [tuRnəbRɔʃ] *nm* roasting spit

tourne-disque [tuRnədisk(ə)] *nm* record player

tournée [tuRne] *nf* (*du facteur etc*) round; (*d'artiste, politicien*) tour; (*au café*) round (of drinks)

tournemain [tuRnəmɛ̃] : **en un ~** *adv* (as) quick as a flash

tourner [tuRne] *vt* to turn; (*sauce, mélange*) to stir; (*contourner*) to get round; (*CINÉMA*) to shoot; to make ♦ *vt* to turn; (*moteur*) to run; (*compteur*) to tick away; (*lait etc*) to turn (sour); **se ~** *vi* to turn round; **se ~ vers** to turn to; to turn towards; **bien ~** to turn out well; **~ autour de** to go round; (*péj*) to hang round; **~ à/en** to turn into; **~ le dos à** to turn one's back on; to have one's back to; **~ de l'œil** to pass out

tournesol [tuRnəsɔl] *nm* sunflower

tournevis [tuRnəvis] *nm* screwdriver

tourniquet [tuRnikɛ] *nm* (*pour arroser*) sprinkler; (*portillon*) turnstile; (*présentoir*) revolving stand, spinner

tournoi [tuRnwa] *nm* tournament

tournoyer [tuRnwaje] *vi* to whirl round; to swirl round

tournure [tuRnyR] *nf* (*LING*) turn of phrase; form; phrasing; (*évolution*): **la ~ de qch** the way sth is developing; (*aspect*): **la ~ de** the look of; **~ d'esprit** turn *ou* cast of mind; **la ~ des événements** the turn of events

tourte [tuRt(ə)] *nf* pie

tous [*adj* tu, *pron* tus] *adj, pron voir* **tout**

Toussaint [tusɛ̃] *nf*: **la ~** All Saints' Day

tousser [tuse] *vi* to cough

─────────── MOT CLÉ ───────────

tout, e [tu, tut] (*mpl* **tous**, *fpl* **toutes**) *adj* **1**
(*avec article singulier*) all; **~ le lait** all the
milk; **~e la nuit** all night, the whole night;
~ le livre the whole book; **~ un pain** a
whole loaf; **~ le temps** all the time; the
whole time; **c'est ~ le contraire** it's quite
the opposite
2 (*avec article pluriel*) every; all; **tous les li-**
vres all the books; **~es les nuits** every
night; **~es les fois** every time; **~es les**
trois/deux semaines every third/other *ou*
second week, every three/two weeks; **tous**
les deux both *ou* each of us (*ou* them *ou*
you); **~es les trois** all three of us (*ou* them
ou you)
3 (*sans article*): **à ~ âge** at any age; **pour**
~e nourriture, il avait ... his only food
was ...
♦ *pron* everything, all; **il a ~ fait** he's done
everything; **je les vois tous** I can see them
all *ou* all of them; **nous y sommes tous**
allés all of us went, we all went; **en ~** in
all; **~ ce qu'il sait** all he knows
♦ *nm* whole; **le ~ all of it** (*ou* them); **le ~**
est de ... the main thing is to ...; **pas du ~**
not at all
♦ *adv* **1** (*très, complètement*) very; **~ près**
very near; **le ~ premier** the very first; **~**
seul all alone; **le livre ~ entier** the whole
book; **~ en haut** right at the top; **~ droit**
straight ahead
2: **~ en** while; **~ en travaillant** while
working, as he *etc* works
3 ~ d'abord first of all; **~ à coup** suddenly; **~ à fait** absolutely; **~ à l'heure** a
short while ago; (*futur*) in a short while,
shortly; **à ~ à l'heure!** see you later!; **~ de**
même all the same; **~ le monde** everybody; **~ de suite** immediately, straight
away; **~ terrain** *ou* **tous terrains** all-terrain

toutefois [tutfwa] *adv* however
toutes [tut] *adj, pron voir* **tout**
toux [tu] *nf* cough
toxicomane [tɔksikɔman] *nm/f* drug addict
trac [tʁak] *nm* nerves *pl*
tracasser [tʁakase] *vt* to worry, bother; to
harass; **tracasseries** [tʁakasʁi] *nfpl* (*chi-*
canes) annoyances
trace [tʁas] *nf* (*empreintes*) tracks *pl*; (*mar-*
ques, aussi fig) mark; (*restes, vestige*) trace;
(*indice*) sign; **~s de pas** footprints
tracé [tʁase] *nm* line; layout
tracer [tʁase] *vt* to draw; (*mot*) to trace;
(*piste*) to open up
tract [tʁakt] *nm* tract, pamphlet
tractations [tʁaktɑsjɔ̃] *nfpl* dealings, bar-
gaining *sg*
tracteur [tʁaktœʁ] *nm* tractor
traction [tʁaksjɔ̃] *nf*: **~ avant/arrière**

front-wheel/rear-wheel drive
tradition [tʁadisjɔ̃] *nf* tradition; **tradition-**
nel, le *adj* traditional
traducteur, trice [tʁadyktœʁ, -tʁis] *nm/f*
translator
traduction [tʁadyksjɔ̃] *nf* translation
traduire [tʁadɥiʁ] *vt* to translate; (*exprimer*)
to render, convey
trafic [tʁafik] *nm* traffic; **~ d'armes** arms
dealing; **trafiquant, e** *nm/f* trafficker; dealer; **trafiquer** (*péj*) *vt* to doctor, tamper
with
tragédie [tʁaʒedi] *nf* tragedy
tragique [tʁaʒik] *adj* tragic
trahir [tʁaiʁ] *vt* to betray; (*fig*) to give
away, reveal; **trahison** *nf* betrayal; (*JUR*)
treason
train [tʁɛ̃] *nm* (*RAIL*) train; (*allure*) pace;
(*fig: ensemble*) set; **mettre qch en ~** to get
sth under way; **mettre qn en ~** to put sb
in good spirits; **se mettre en ~** to get
started; to warm up; **se sentir en ~** to feel
in good form; **~ d'atterrissage** undercarriage; **~ de vie** style of living; **~ électrique**
(*jouet*) (electric) train set; **~-autos-**
couchettes car-sleeper train
traîne [tʁɛn] *nf* (*de robe*) train; **être à la ~**
to be in tow; to lag behind
traîneau, x [tʁɛno] *nm* sleigh, sledge
traînée [tʁene] *nf* streak, trail; (*péj*) slut
traîner [tʁene] *vt* (*remorque*) to pull; (*en-*
fant, chien) to drag *ou* trail along ♦ *vi* (*être*
en désordre) to lie around; (*marcher*) to
dawdle (along); (*vagabonder*) to hang
about; (*agir lentement*) to idle about; (*du-*
rer) to drag on; **se ~** *vi* to drag o.s. along;
~ les pieds to drag one's feet
train-train [tʁɛ̃tʁɛ̃] *nm* humdrum routine
traire [tʁɛʁ] *vt* to milk
trait [tʁɛ] *nm* (*ligne*) line; (*de dessin*)
stroke; (*caractéristique*) feature, trait; **~s**
nmpl (*du visage*) features; **d'un ~** (*boire*)
in one gulp; **de ~** (*animal*) draught; **avoir ~**
à to concern; **~ d'union** hyphen; (*fig*) link
traitant, e [tʁetɑ̃, -ɑ̃t] *adj*: **votre médecin**
~ your usual *ou* family doctor; **crème ~e**
conditioning cream
traite [tʁet] *nf* (*COMM*) draft; (*AGR*) milk-
ing; **d'une ~** without stopping; **la ~ des**
noirs the slave trade
traité [tʁete] *nm* treaty
traitement [tʁetmɑ̃] *nm* treatment; processing; (*salaire*) salary; **~ de données/**
texte data/word processing
traiter [tʁete] *vt* (*gén*) to treat; (*TECH, IN-*
FORM) to process; (*affaire*) to deal with,
handle; (*qualifier*): **~ qn d'idiot** to call sb a
fool ♦ *vi* to deal; **~ de** to deal with
traiteur [tʁetœʁ] *nm* caterer
traître, esse [tʁetʁ(ə), -tʁɛs] *adj* (*dange-*
reux) treacherous ♦ *nm* traitor
trajectoire [tʁaʒɛktwaʁ] *nf* path

trajet [tʀaʒɛ] nm journey; (itinéraire) route; (fig) path, course

trame [tʀam] nf (de tissu) weft; (fig) framework; texture

tramer [tʀame] vt to plot, hatch

tramway [tʀamwɛ] nm tram(way); tram(car) (BRIT), streetcar (US)

tranchant, e [tʀɑ̃ʃɑ̃, -ɑ̃t] adj sharp; (fig) peremptory ♦ nm (d'un couteau) cutting edge; (de la main) edge

tranche [tʀɑ̃ʃ] nf (morceau) slice; (arête) edge; (partie) section; (série) block; issue; bracket

tranché, e [tʀɑ̃ʃe] adj (couleurs) distinct, sharply contrasted; (opinions) clear-cut, definite; **tranchée** nf trench

trancher [tʀɑ̃ʃe] vt to cut, sever; (fig: résoudre) to settle ♦ vi to take a decision; ~ **avec** to contrast sharply with

tranquille [tʀɑ̃kil] adj calm, quiet; (enfant, élève) quiet; (rassuré) easy in one's mind, with one's mind at rest; **se tenir** ~ (enfant) to be quiet; **laisse-moi/laisse-ça** ~ leave me/it alone; **tranquillité** nf quietness; peace (and quiet)

transat [tʀɑ̃zat] nm deckchair

transborder [tʀɑ̃sbɔʀde] vt to tran(s)ship

trans: ~**férer** vt to transfer; ~**fert** nm transfer; ~**figurer** vt to transform; ~**formation** nf transformation; (RUGBY) conversion

transformer [tʀɑ̃sfɔʀme] vt to transform, alter; (matière première, appartement, RUGBY) to convert; ~ **en** to transform into; to turn into; to convert into

transfusion [tʀɑ̃sfyzjɔ̃] nf: ~ **sanguine** blood transfusion

transgresser [tʀɑ̃sgʀese] vt to contravene, disobey

transi, e [tʀɑ̃zi] adj numb (with cold), chilled to the bone

transiger [tʀɑ̃ziʒe] vi to compromise

transit [tʀɑ̃zit] nm transit; **transiter** vi to pass in transit

transitif, ive [tʀɑ̃zitif, -iv] adj transitive

transition [tʀɑ̃zisjɔ̃] nf transition; **transitoire** adj transitional; transient

translucide [tʀɑ̃slysid] adj translucent

transmetteur [tʀɑ̃smetœʀ] nm transmitter

transmettre [tʀɑ̃smetʀ(ə)] vt (passer): ~ **qch à qn** to pass sth on to sb; (TECH, TÉL, MÉD) to transmit; (TV, RADIO: re~) to broadcast

trans: ~**mission** nf transmission; ~**paraître** vi to show (through); ~**parence** nf transparence; **par** ~**parence** (regarder) against the light; (voir) showing through; ~**parent, e** adj transparent; ~**percer** vt to go through, pierce; ~**piration** nf perspiration; ~**pirer** vi to perspire; ~**planter** vt (MÉD, BOT) to transplant; (personne) to uproot; ~**port** nm transport; ~**ports en commun** public transport sg

transporter [tʀɑ̃spɔʀte] vt to carry, move; (COMM) to transport, convey; **transporteur** nm haulage contractor (BRIT), trucker (US)

transversal, e, aux [tʀɑ̃sveʀsal, -o] adj transverse, cross-(-); cross-country; running at right angles

trapèze [tʀapɛz] nm (au cirque) trapeze

trappe [tʀap] nf trap door

trapu, e [tʀapy] adj squat, stocky

traquenard [tʀaknaʀ] nm trap

traquer [tʀake] vt to track down; (harceler) to hound

traumatiser [tʀomatize] vt to traumatize

travail, aux [tʀavaj, -o] nm (gén) work; (tâche, métier) work no pl, job; (ÉCON, MÉD) labour; **être sans** ~ (employé) to be out of work ou unemployed; voir aussi **travaux**; ~ **(au) noir** moonlighting

travailler [tʀavaje] vi to work; (bois) to warp ♦ vt (bois, métal) to work; (objet d'art, discipline, fig: influencer) to work on; **cela le travaille** it is on his mind; ~ **à** to work on; (fig: contribuer à) to work towards; **travailleur, euse** adj hard-working ♦ nm/f worker; **travailliste** adj ≈ Labour (BRIT) cpd

travaux [tʀavo] nmpl (de réparation, agricoles etc) work sg; (sur route) roadworks pl; (de construction) building (work); ~ **des champs** farmwork sg; ~ **dirigés** (SCOL) supervised practical work sg; ~ **forcés** hard labour sg; ~ **manuels** (SCOL) handicrafts; ~ **ménagers** housework sg

travée [tʀave] nf row; (ARCHIT) bay; span

travers [tʀavɛʀ] nm fault, failing; **en** ~ **(de)** across; **au** ~ **(de)** through; **de** ~ askew ♦ adv sideways; (fig) the wrong way; **à** ~ through; **regarder de** ~ (fig) to look askance at

traverse [tʀavɛʀs(ə)] nf (de voie ferrée) sleeper; **chemin de** ~ shortcut

traversée [tʀavɛʀse] nf crossing

traverser [tʀavɛʀse] vt (gén) to cross; (ville, tunnel, aussi: percer, fig) to go through; (suj: ligne, trait) to run across

traversin [tʀavɛʀsɛ̃] nm bolster

travestir [tʀavɛstiʀ] vt (vérité) to misrepresent; **se** ~ vi to dress up; to dress as a woman

trébucher [tʀebyʃe] vi: ~ **(sur)** to stumble (over), trip (against)

trèfle [tʀefl(ə)] nm (BOT) clover; (CARTES: couleur) clubs pl; (: carte) club

treille [tʀɛj] nf vine arbour; climbing vine

treillis [tʀeji] nm (métallique) wire-mesh

treize [tʀɛz] num thirteen; **treizième** num thirteenth

tréma [tʀema] nm diaeresis

tremblement [tʀɑ̃bləmɑ̃] nm: ~ **de terre** earthquake

trembler [tʀɑ̃ble] vi to tremble, shake; ~ **de** (froid, fièvre) to shiver ou tremble with; (peur) to shake ou tremble with; ~ **pour qn** to fear for sb

trémousser [tʀemuse] : **se ~** vi to jig about, wriggle about

trempe [tʀɑ̃p] nf (fig): **de cette/sa ~** of this/his calibre

trempé, e [tʀɑ̃pe] adj soaking (wet), drenched; (TECH) tempered

tremper [tʀɑ̃pe] vt to soak, drench; (aussi: faire ~, mettre à ~) to soak; (plonger): ~ **qch dans** to dip sth in(to) ♦ vi to soak; (fig): ~ **dans** to be involved ou have a hand in; **se ~** vi to have a quick dip; **trempette** nf: **faire trempette** to go paddling

tremplin [tʀɑ̃plɛ̃] nm springboard; (SKI) ski-jump

trentaine [tʀɑ̃tɛn] nf: **une ~ (de)** thirty or so, about thirty; **avoir la ~** (âge) to be around thirty

trente [tʀɑ̃t] num thirty; **trentième** num thirtieth

trépidant, e [tʀepidɑ̃, -ɑ̃t] adj (fig: rythme) pulsating; (: vie) hectic

trépied [tʀepje] nm tripod

trépigner [tʀepiɲe] vi to stamp (one's feet)

très [tʀɛ] adv very; much +pp, highly +pp

trésor [tʀezɔʀ] nm treasure; (ADMIN) finances pl; funds pl; **T~ (public)** public revenue

trésorerie [tʀezɔʀʀi] nf (gestion) accounts pl; (bureaux) accounts department; **difficultés de ~** cash problems, shortage of cash ou funds

trésorier, ière [tʀezɔʀje, -jɛʀ] nm/f treasurer

tressaillir [tʀesajiʀ] vi to shiver, shudder; to quiver

tressauter [tʀesote] vi to start, jump

tresse [tʀɛs] nf braid, plait

tresser [tʀese] vt (cheveux) to braid, plait; (fil, jonc) to plait; (corbeille) to weave; (corde) to twist

tréteau, x [tʀeto] nm trestle

treuil [tʀœj] nm winch

trêve [tʀɛv] nf (MIL, POL) truce; (fig) respite; ~ **de ...** enough of this ...

tri [tʀi] nm sorting out no pl; selection; (POSTES) sorting; sorting office

triangle [tʀijɑ̃gl(ə)] nm triangle

tribord [tʀibɔʀ] nm: **à ~** to starboard, on the starboard side

tribu [tʀiby] nf tribe

tribunal, aux [tʀibynal, -o] nm (JUR) court; (MIL) tribunal

tribune [tʀibyn] nf (estrade) platform, rostrum; (débat) forum; (d'église, de tribunal) gallery; (de stade) stand

tribut [tʀiby] nm tribute

tributaire [tʀibytɛʀ] adj: **être ~ de** to be

dependent on

tricher [tʀiʃe] vi to cheat

tricolore [tʀikɔlɔʀ] adj three-coloured; (français) red, white and blue

tricot [tʀiko] nm (technique, ouvrage) knitting no pl; (tissu) knitted fabric; (vêtement) jersey, sweater

tricoter [tʀikɔte] vt to knit

trictrac [tʀiktʀak] nm backgammon

tricycle [tʀisikl(ə)] nm tricycle

triennal, e, aux [tʀienal, -o] adj three-yearly; three-year

trier [tʀije] vt to sort out; (POSTES, fruits) to sort

trimestre [tʀimɛstʀ(ə)] nm (SCOL) term; (COMM) quarter; **trimestriel, le** adj quarterly; (SCOL) end-of-term

tringle [tʀɛ̃gl(ə)] nf rod

trinquer [tʀɛ̃ke] vi to clink glasses

triomphe [tʀijɔ̃f] nm triumph

triompher [tʀijɔ̃fe] vi to triumph, win; ~ **de** to triumph over, overcome

tripes [tʀip] nfpl (CULIN) tripe sg

triple [tʀipl(ə)] adj triple; treble ♦ nm: **le ~ (de)** (comparaison) three times as much (as); **en ~ exemplaire** in triplicate; **tripler** vi, vt to triple, treble

triplés, ées [tʀiple] nm/fpl triplets

tripoter [tʀipɔte] vt to fiddle with

trique [tʀik] nf cudgel

triste [tʀist(ə)] adj sad; (péj): ~ **personnage/affaire** sorry individual/affair; **tristesse** nf sadness

trivial, e, aux [tʀivjal, -o] adj coarse, crude; (commun) mundane

troc [tʀɔk] nm barter

trognon [tʀɔɲɔ̃] nm (de fruit) core; (de légume) stalk

trois [tʀwa] num three; **troisième** num third; **trois quarts** nmpl: **les trois quarts de** three-quarters of

trombe [tʀɔ̃b] nf: **des ~s d'eau** a downpour; **en ~** like a whirlwind

trombone [tʀɔ̃bɔn] nm (MUS) trombone; (de bureau) paper clip

trompe [tʀɔ̃p] nf (d'éléphant) trunk; (MUS) trumpet, horn

tromper [tʀɔ̃pe] vt to deceive; (vigilance, poursuivants) to elude; **se ~** vi to make a mistake, be mistaken; **se ~ de voiture/jour** to take the wrong car/get the day wrong; **se ~ de 3 cm/20 F** to be out by 3 cm/20 F; **~ie** nf deception, trickery no pl

trompette [tʀɔ̃pɛt] nf trumpet; **en ~** (nez) turned-up

tronc [tʀɔ̃] nm (BOT, ANAT) trunk; (d'église) collection box

tronçon [tʀɔ̃sɔ̃] nm section

tronçonner [tʀɔ̃sɔne] vt to saw up

trône [tʀon] nm throne

trop [tʀo] adv (+vb) too much; (+adjectif, adverbe) too; ~ **(nombreux)** too many; ~

peu (nombreux) too few; ~ **(souvent)** too often; ~ **(longtemps)** (for) too long; ~ **de** (nombre) too many; (quantité) too much; **de** ~, **en** ~: **des livres en** ~ a few books too many; **du lait en** ~ too much milk; **3 livres/3 F de** ~ 3 books too many/3 F too much

tropical, e, aux [trɔpikal, -o] adj tropical

tropique [trɔpik] nm tropic

trop-plein [trɔplɛ̃] nm (tuyau) overflow ou outlet (pipe); (liquide) overflow

troquer [trɔke] vt: ~ **qch contre** to barter ou trade sth for; (fig) to swap sth for

trot [trɔ] nm trot; ~**ter** [trɔte] vi to trot; (fig) to scamper along (ou about)

trottiner [trɔtine] vi (fig) to scamper along (ou about); **trottinette** [trɔtinet] nf (child's) scooter

trottoir [trɔtwar] nm pavement; **faire le** ~ (péj) to walk the streets; ~ **roulant** moving walkway, travellator

trou [tru] nm hole; (fig) gap; (COMM) deficit; ~ **d'air** air pocket; (AVIAT) air hole; **le** ~ **de la serrure** the keyhole; ~ **de mémoire** blank, lapse of memory

trouble [trubl(ə)] adj (liquide) cloudy; (image, mémoire) indistinct, hazy; (affaire) shady, murky ♦ nm (désarroi) agitation; (embarras) confusion; (zizanie) unrest, discord; ~**s** nmpl (POL) disturbances, troubles, unrest sg; (MÉD) trouble sg, disorders

troubler [truble] vt (embarrasser) to confuse, disconcert; (émouvoir) to agitate; to disturb; (perturber: ordre etc) to disrupt; (liquide) to make cloudy; **se** ~ vi (personne) to become flustered ou confused

trouée [true] nf gap; (MIL) breach

trouer [true] vt to make a hole (ou holes) in; (fig) to pierce

trouille [truj] (fam) nf: **avoir la** ~ to be scared to death

troupe [trup] nf troop; ~ **(de théâtre)** (theatrical) company

troupeau, x [trupo] nm (de moutons) flock; (de vaches) herd

trousse [trus] nf case, kit; (d'écolier) pencil case; (de docteur) instrument case; **aux** ~**s de** (fig) on the heels ou tail of; ~ **à outils** toolkit; ~ **de toilette** toilet bag

trousseau, x [truso] nm (de mariée) trousseau; ~ **de clefs** bunch of keys

trouvaille [truvaj] nf find

trouver [truve] vt to find; (rendre visite): **aller/venir** ~ **qn** to go/come and see sb; **se** ~ vi (être) to be; (être soudain) to find o.s.; **il se trouve que** it happens that, it turns out that; **se** ~ **bien** to feel well; **se** ~ **mal** to pass out; **je trouve que** I find ou think that; ~ **à boire/critiquer** to find something to drink/criticize

truand [tryɑ̃] nm villain, crook

truander [tryɑ̃de] vt to cheat

truc [tryk] nm (astuce) way, device; (de cinéma, prestidigitateur) trick effect; (chose) thing, thingumajig; **avoir le** ~ to have the knack

truchement [tryʃmɑ̃] nm: **par le** ~ **de qn** through (the intervention of) sb

truelle [tryɛl] nf trowel

truffe [tryf] nf truffle; (nez) nose

truffé, e [tryfe] adj: ~ **de** (fig) peppered with; bristling with

truie [trɥi] nf sow

truite [trɥit] nf trout inv

truquer [tryke] vt (élections, serrure, dés) to fix; (CINÉMA) to use special effects in

T.S.V.P. sigle (= tournez s.v.p.) P.T.O.

T.T.C. sigle = **toutes taxes comprises**

tu[1] [ty] pron you

tu[2], **e** [ty] pp de **taire**

tuba [tyba] nm (MUS) tuba; (SPORT) snorkel

tube [tyb] nm tube; pipe; (chanson, disque) hit song ou record

tuer [tɥe] vt to kill; **se** ~ vi to be killed; (suicide) to kill o.s.; **tuerie** nf slaughter no pl

tue-tête [tytɛt] : **à** ~ adv at the top of one's voice

tueur [tɥœr] nm killer; ~ **à gages** hired killer

tuile [tɥil] nf tile; (fam) spot of bad luck, blow

tulipe [tylip] nf tulip

tuméfié, e [tymefje] adj puffy, swollen

tumeur [tymœr] nf growth, tumour

tumulte [tymylt(ə)] nm commotion

tumultueux, euse [tymyltɥø, -øz] adj stormy, turbulent

tunique [tynik] nf tunic

Tunisie [tynizi] nf: **la** ~ Tunisia; **tunisien, ne** adj, nm/f Tunisian

tunnel [tynɛl] nm tunnel

turbulences [tyrbylɑ̃s] nfpl (AVIAT) turbulence sg

turbulent, e [tyrbylɑ̃, -ɑ̃t] adj boisterous, unruly

turc, turque [tyrk(ə)] adj Turkish ♦ nm/f: **T~, Turque** Turk/Turkish woman ♦ nm (LING) Turkish

turf [tyrf] nm racing; **turfiste** nm/f racegoer

Turquie [tyrki] nf: **la** ~ Turkey

turquoise [tyrkwaz] nf turquoise ♦ adj inv turquoise

tus etc vb voir **taire**

tutelle [tytɛl] nf (JUR) guardianship; (POL) trusteeship; **sous la** ~ **de** (fig) under the supervision of

tuteur [tytœr] nm (JUR) guardian; (de plante) stake, support

tutoyer [tytwaje] vt: ~ **qn** to address sb as "tu"

tuyau, x [tɥijo] nm pipe; (flexible) tube; (fam) tip; gen no pl; ~ **d'arrosage** hosepipe; ~ **d'échappement** exhaust pipe; **~te-rie** nf piping no pl

T.V.A. sigle f (= taxe à la valeur ajoutée) VAT

tympan [tɛ̃pɑ̃] nm (ANAT) eardrum

type [tip] nm type; (fam) chap, guy ♦ adj typical, standard

typé, e [tipe] adj ethnic

typhoïde [tifɔid] nf typhoid

typique [tipik] adj typical

tyran [tiʀɑ̃] nm tyrant

tzigane [dzigan] adj gypsy ♦ nm/f gypsy

U u

ulcère [ylsɛʀ] nm ulcer; **ulcérer** [ylseʀe] vt (fig) to sicken, appal

ultérieur, e [ylteʀjœʀ] adj later, subsequent; **remis à une date ~e** postponed to a later date

ultime [yltim] adj final

ultra... [yltʀa] préfixe: **ultramoderne/-rapide** ultra-modern/-fast

─────── MOT CLÉ ───────

un, une [œ̃, yn] art indéf a; (devant voyelle) an; ~ **garçon/vieillard** a boy/an old man; **une fille** a girl

♦ pron one; **l'~ des meilleurs** one of the best; **l'~ ..., l'autre** (the) one ..., the other; **les ~s ..., les autres** some ..., others; **l'~ et l'autre** both (of them); **l'~ ou l'autre** either (of them); **l'~ l'autre, les ~s les autres** each other, one another; **pas ~ seul** not a single one; ~ **par** ~ one by one

♦ num one; **une pomme seulement** one apple only

─────────────────────────

unanime [ynanim] adj unanimous; **unanimité** nf: **à l'unanimité** unanimously

uni, e [yni] adj (ton, tissu) plain; (surface) smooth, even; (famille) close-(knit); (pays) united

unifier [ynifje] vt to unite, unify

uniforme [ynifɔʀm(ə)] adj (mouvement) regular, uniform; (surface, ton) even; (objets, maisons) uniform ♦ nm uniform; **uniformiser** vt to make uniform; (systèmes) to standardize

union [ynjɔ̃] nf union; ~ **de consommateurs** consumers' association; **l'U~ soviétique** the Soviet Union

unique [ynik] adj (seul) only; (le même): **un**

prix/système ~ a single price/system; (exceptionnel) unique; **fils/fille** ~ only son/daughter, only child; **uniquement** adv only, solely; (juste) only, merely

unir [yniʀ] vt (nations) to unite; (éléments, couleurs) to combine; (en mariage) to unite, join together; **s'~** to unite; (en mariage) to be joined together; ~ **qch à** to unite sth with; to combine sth with

unité [ynite] nf (harmonie, cohésion) unity; (COMM, MIL, de mesure, MATH) unit

univers [ynivɛʀ] nm universe

universel, le [ynivɛʀsɛl] adj universal; (esprit) all-embracing

universitaire [ynivɛʀsitɛʀ] adj university cpd; (diplôme, études) academic, university cpd ♦ nm/f academic

université [ynivɛʀsite] nf university

urbain, e [yʀbɛ̃, -ɛn] adj urban, city cpd, town cpd; (poli) urbane; **urbanisme** nm town planning

urgence [yʀʒɑ̃s] nf urgency; (MÉD etc) emergency; **d'~** emergency cpd ♦ adv as a matter of urgency

urgent, e [yʀʒɑ̃, -ɑ̃t] adj urgent

urine [yʀin] nf urine; **urinoir** nm (public) urinal

urne [yʀn(ə)] nf (électorale) ballot box; (vase) urn

urticaire [yʀtikɛʀ] nf nettle rash

us [ys] nmpl: ~ **et coutumes** (habits and) customs

USA sigle mpl: **les** ~ **the** USA

usage [yzaʒ] nm (emploi, utilisation) use; (coutume) custom; (LING): **l'**~ usage; **à l'**~ **de** (pour) for (use of); **en** ~ in use; **hors d'**~ out of service; wrecked; **à** ~ **interne** to be taken; **à** ~ **externe** for external use only; **usagé, e** [yzaʒe] adj (usé) worn; (d'occasion) used; **usager, ère** [yzaʒe, -ɛʀ] nm/f user

usé, e [yze] adj worn; (banal) hackneyed

user [yze] vt (outil) to wear down; (vêtement) to wear out; (matière) to wear away; (consommer: charbon etc) to use; **s'~** vi to wear; to wear out; (fig) to decline; ~ **de** (moyen, procédé) to use, employ; (droit) to exercise

usine [yzin] nf factory; ~ **marémotrice** tidal power station

usité, e [yzite] adj common

ustensile [ystɑ̃sil] nm implement; ~ **de cuisine** kitchen utensil

usuel, le [yzɥɛl] adj everyday, common

usure [yzyʀ] nf wear; worn state

ut [yt] nm (MUS) C

utérus [yteʀys] nm uterus, womb

utile [ytil] adj useful

utilisation [ytilizɑsjɔ̃] nf use

utiliser [ytilize] vt to use

utilitaire [ytilitɛʀ] adj utilitarian; (objets) practical

utilité [ytilite] *nf* usefulness *no pl*; use; **reconnu d'~ publique** state-approved

V v

va *vb voir* **aller**
vacance [vakɑ̃s] *nf* (ADMIN) vacancy; **~s** *nfpl* holiday(s *pl*), vacation *sg*; **prendre des/ses ~s** to take a holiday/one's holiday(s); **aller en ~s** to go on holiday; **vacancier, ière** *nm/f* holiday-maker
vacant, e [vakɑ̃, -ɑ̃t] *adj* vacant
vacarme [vakaʀm(ə)] *nm* row, din
vaccin [vaksɛ̃] *nm* vaccine; (*opération*) vaccination; **vaccination** *nf* vaccination; **vacciner** *vt* to vaccinate; (*fig*) to make immune
vache [vaʃ] *nf* (ZOOL) cow; (*cuir*) cowhide ♦ *adj* (*fam*) rotten, mean; **~ment** (*fam*) *adv* damned, hellish
vaciller [vasije] *vi* to sway, wobble; (*bougie, lumière*) to flicker; (*fig*) to be failing, falter
va-et-vient [vaevjɛ̃] *nm inv* (*de personnes, véhicules*) comings and goings *pl*, to-ings and fro-ings *pl*
vagabond [vagabɔ̃] *nm* (*rôdeur*) tramp, vagrant; (*voyageur*) wanderer; **~er** [vagabɔ̃de] *vi* to roam, wander
vagin [vaʒɛ̃] *nm* vagina
vague [vag] *nf* wave ♦ *adj* vague; (*regard*) faraway; (*manteau, robe*) loose(-fitting); (*quelconque*): **un ~ bureau/cousin** some office/cousin or other; **~ de fond** ground swell
vaillant, e [vajɑ̃, -ɑ̃t] *adj* (*courageux*) gallant; (*robuste*) hale and hearty
vaille *vb voir* **valoir**
vain, e [vɛ̃, vɛn] *adj* vain; **en ~** in vain
vaincre [vɛ̃kʀ(ə)] *vt* to defeat; (*fig*) to conquer, overcome; **vaincu, e** *nm/f* defeated party; **vainqueur** *nm* victor; (SPORT) winner
vais *vb voir* **aller**
vaisseau, x [veso] *nm* (ANAT) vessel; (NAVIG) ship, vessel; **~ spatial** spaceship
vaisselier [vesəlje] *nm* dresser
vaisselle [vesɛl] *nf* (*service*) crockery; (*plats etc à laver*) (dirty) dishes *pl*; (*lavage*) washing-up (BRIT), dishes *pl*
val [val] (*pl* **vaux** *ou* **~s**) *nm* valley
valable [valabl(ə)] *adj* valid; (*acceptable*) decent, worthwhile
valent *etc vb voir* **valoir**

valet [valɛ] *nm* valet; (CARTES) jack
valeur [valœʀ] *nf* (*gén*) value; (*mérite*) worth, merit; (COMM: *titre*) security; **mettre en ~** (*terrain, région*) to develop; (*fig*) to highlight; to show off to advantage; **avoir de la ~** to be valuable; **sans ~** worthless; **prendre de la ~** to go up *ou* gain in value
valide [valid] *adj* (*en bonne santé*) fit; (*valable*) valid; **valider** *vt* to validate
valions *vb voir* **valoir**
valise [valiz] *nf* (suit)case
vallée [vale] *nf* valley
vallon [valɔ̃] *nm* small valley
valoir [valwaʀ] *vi* (*être valable*) to hold, apply ♦ *vt* (*prix, valeur, effort*) to be worth; (*causer*): **~ qch à qn** to earn sb sth; **se ~** *vi* to be of equal merit; (*péj*) to be two of a kind; **faire ~** (*droits, prérogatives*) to assert; **faire ~ que** to point out that; **à ~ sur** to be deducted from; **vaille que vaille** somehow or other; **cela ne me dit rien qui vaille** I don't like the look of it at all; **ce climat ne me vaut rien** this climate doesn't suit me; **~ la peine** to be worth the trouble *ou* worth it; **~ mieux: il vaut mieux se taire** it's better to say nothing; **ça ne vaut rien** it's worthless; **que vaut ce candidat?** how good is this applicant?
valoriser [valɔʀize] *vt* (ÉCON) to develop (the economy of); (PSYCH) to increase the standing of
valse [vals(ə)] *nf* waltz
valu, e [valy] *pp de* **valoir**
vandalisme [vɑ̃dalism(ə)] *nm* vandalism
vanille [vanij] *nf* vanilla
vanité [vanite] *nf* vanity; **vaniteux, euse** *adj* vain, conceited
vanne [van] *nf* gate; (*fig*) joke
vannerie [vanʀi] *nf* basketwork
vantard, e [vɑ̃tar, -aʀd(ə)] *adj* boastful
vanter [vɑ̃te] *vt* to speak highly of, vaunt; **se ~** *vi* to boast, brag; **se ~ de** to pride o.s. on; (*péj*) to boast of
vapeur [vapœʀ] *nf* steam; (*émanation*) vapour, fumes *pl*; **~s** *nfpl* (*bouffées*) vapours; **à ~** steam-powered, steam *cpd*; **cuit à la ~** steamed
vaporeux, euse [vapɔʀø, -øz] *adj* (*flou*) hazy, misty; (*léger*) filmy
vaporisateur [vapɔʀizatœʀ] *nm* spray; **vaporiser** [vapɔʀize] *vt* (*parfum etc*) to spray
varappe [vaʀap] *nf* rock climbing
vareuse [vaʀøz] *nf* (*blouson*) pea jacket; (*d'uniforme*) tunic
variable [vaʀjabl(ə)] *adj* variable; (*temps, humeur*) changeable; (*divers: résultats*) varied, various
varice [vaʀis] *nf* varicose vein
varicelle [vaʀisɛl] *nf* chickenpox
varié, e [vaʀje] *adj* varied; (*divers*) various
varier [vaʀje] *vi* to vary; (*temps, humeur*) to change ♦ *vt* to vary

variété [vaʀjete] *nf* variety; **~s** *nfpl*: **spectacle/émission de ~s** variety show

variole [vaʀjɔl] *nf* smallpox

vas *vb voir* **aller**

vase [vɑz] *nm* vase ♦ *nf* silt, mud

vaseux, euse [vɑzø, -øz] *adj* silty, muddy; *(fig: confus)* woolly, hazy; *(: fatigué)* peaky; woozy

vasistas [vazistas] *nm* fanlight

vaste [vast(ə)] *adj* vast, immense

vaudrai *etc vb voir* **valoir**

vaurien, ne [voʀjɛ̃, -ɛn] *nm/f* good-for-nothing, guttersnipe

vaut *vb voir* **valoir**

vautour [votuʀ] *nm* vulture

vautrer [votʀe]: **se ~** *vi*: **se ~ dans/sur** to wallow in/sprawl on

vaux [vo] *nmpl de* **val** ♦ *vb voir* **valoir**

va-vite [vavit]: **à la ~** *adv* in a rush *ou* hurry

veau, x [vo] *nm (ZOOL)* calf; *(CULIN)* veal; *(peau)* calfskin

vécu, e [veky] *pp de* **vivre**

vedette [vədet] *nf (artiste etc)* star; *(canot)* patrol boat; launch

végétal, e, aux [veʒetal, -o] *adj* vegetable ♦ *nm* vegetable, plant

végétarien, ne [veʒetaʀjɛ̃, -ɛn] *adj, nm/f* vegetarian

végétation [veʒetɑsjɔ̃] *nf* vegetation; **~s** *nfpl (MÉD)* adenoids

véhicule [veikyl] *nm* vehicle; **~ utilitaire** commercial vehicle

veille [vɛj] *nf (garde)* watch; *(PSYCH)* wakefulness; *(jour)*: **la ~ (de)** the day before; **la ~ au soir** the previous evening; **à la ~ de** on the eve of

veillée [veje] *nf (soirée)* evening; *(réunion)* evening gathering; **~ (mortuaire)** watch

veiller [veje] *vi* to stay up; to be awake; to be on watch ♦ *vt (malade, mort)* to watch over, sit up with; **~ à** to attend to, see to; **~ à ce que** to make sure that; **~ sur** to keep a watch on

veilleur [vɛjœʀ] *nm*: **~de nuit** night watchman

veilleuse [vɛjøz] *nf (lampe)* night light; *(AUTO)* sidelight; *(flamme)* pilot light; **en ~** *(lampe)* dimmed

veine [vɛn] *nf (ANAT, du bois etc)* vein; *(filon)* vein, seam; *(fam: chance)*: **avoir de la ~** to be lucky

véliplanchiste [veliplɑ̃ʃist(ə)] *nm/f* windsurfer

velléités [veleite] *nfpl* vague impulses

vélo [velo] *nm* bike, cycle; **faire du ~** to go cycling; **~ tout-terrain** mountain bike

vélomoteur [velɔmɔtœʀ] *nm* moped

velours [vəluʀ] *nm* velvet; **~ côtelé** corduroy

velouté, e [vəlute] *adj (au toucher)* velvety; *(à la vue)* soft, mellow; *(au goût)* smooth, mellow

velu, e [vəly] *adj* hairy

venais *etc vb voir* **venir**

venaison [vənɛzɔ̃] *nf* venison

vendange [vɑ̃dɑ̃ʒ] *nf (opération, période: aussi: ~s)* grape harvest; *(raisins)* grape crop, grapes *pl*; **~r** [vɑ̃dɑ̃ʒe] *vi* to harvest the grapes

vendeur, euse [vɑ̃dœʀ, -øz] *nm/f (de magasin)* shop assistant; *(COMM)* salesman(woman) ♦ *nm (JUR)* vendor, seller; **~ de journaux** newspaper seller

vendre [vɑ̃dʀ(ə)] *vt* to sell; **~ qch à qn** to sell sb sth; **"à ~"** "for sale"

vendredi [vɑ̃dʀədi] *nm* Friday; **V~ saint** Good Friday

vendu, e [vɑ̃dy] *adj (péj: corrompu)* corrupt

vénéneux, euse [venenø, -øz] *adj* poisonous

vénérien, ne [veneʀjɛ̃, -ɛn] *adj* venereal

vengeance [vɑ̃ʒɑ̃s] *nf* vengeance *no pl*, revenge *no pl*

venger [vɑ̃ʒe] *vt* to avenge; **se ~** *vi* to avenge o.s.; **se ~ de qch** to avenge o.s. for sth; to take one's revenge for sth; **se ~ de qn** to take revenge on sb; **se ~ sur** to take revenge on; to take it out on

venimeux, euse [vənimø, -øz] *adj* poisonous, venomous; *(fig: haineux)* venomous, vicious

venin [vənɛ̃] *nm* venom, poison

venir [vəniʀ] *vi* to come; **~ de** to come from; **~ de faire: je viens d'y aller/de le voir** I've just been there/seen him; **s'il vient à pleuvoir** if it should rain; **j'en viens à croire que** I have come to believe that; **faire ~** *(docteur, plombier)* to call (out)

vent [vɑ̃] *nm* wind; **il y a du ~** it's windy; **c'est du ~** it's all hot air; **au ~** to windward; **sous le ~** to leeward; **avoir le ~ debout/arrière** to head into the wind/have the wind astern; **dans le ~** *(fam)* trendy

vente [vɑ̃t] *nf* sale; **la ~** *(activité)* selling; *(secteur)* sales *pl*; **mettre en ~** to put on sale; *(objets personnels)* to put up for sale; **~ aux enchères** auction sale; **~ de charité** jumble sale

venteux, euse [vɑ̃tø, -øz] *adj* windy

ventilateur [vɑ̃tilatœʀ] *nm* fan

ventiler [vɑ̃tile] *vt* to ventilate; *(total, statistiques)* to break down

ventouse [vɑ̃tuz] *nf (de caoutchouc)* suction pad; *(ZOOL)* sucker

ventre [vɑ̃tʀ(ə)] *nm (ANAT)* stomach; *(fig)* belly; **avoir mal au ~** to have stomach ache *(BRIT)* ou a stomach ache *(US)*

ventriloque [vɑ̃tʀilɔk] *nm/f* ventriloquist

venu, e [vəny] *pp de* **venir** ♦ *adj*: **être mal ~ à** ou **de faire** to have no grounds for doing, be in no position to do

ver [vɛʀ] *nm* worm; *(des fruits etc)* maggot; *(du bois)* woodworm *no pl*; *voir aussi* **vers**;

~ **à soie** silkworm; ~ **de terre** earthworm; ~ **luisant** glow-worm; ~ **solitaire** tapeworm

verbaliser [vɛʀbalize] vi (POLICE) to book ou report an offender

verbe [vɛʀb(ə)] nm verb

verdeur [vɛʀdœʀ] nf (vigueur) vigour, vitality; (crudité) forthrightness

verdict [vɛʀdik(t)] nm verdict

verdir [vɛʀdiʀ] vi, vt to turn green

verdure [vɛʀdyʀ] nf greenery

véreux, euse [veʀø, -øz] adj worm-eaten; (malhonnête) shady, corrupt

verge [vɛʀʒ(ə)] nf (ANAT) penis; (baguette) stick, cane

verger [vɛʀʒe] nm orchard

verglacé, e [vɛʀglase] adj icy, iced-over

verglas [vɛʀgla] nm (black) ice

vergogne [vɛʀgɔɲ]: **sans** ~ adv shamelessly

véridique [veʀidik] adj truthful

vérification [veʀifikasjɔ̃] nf checking no pl, check

vérifier [veʀifje] vt to check; (corroborer) to confirm, bear out

véritable [veʀitabl(ə)] adj real; (ami, amour) true

vérité [veʀite] nf truth; (d'un portrait romanesque) lifelikeness; (sincérité) truthfulness, sincerity

vermeil, le [vɛʀmɛj] adj ruby red

vermine [vɛʀmin] nf vermin pl

vermoulu, e [vɛʀmuly] adj worm-eaten, with woodworm

verni, e [vɛʀni] adj (fam) lucky; **cuir** ~ patent leather

vernir [vɛʀniʀ] vt (bois, tableau, ongles) to varnish; (poterie) to glaze

vernis [vɛʀni] nm (enduit) varnish; glaze; (fig) veneer; ~ **à ongles** nail polish ou varnish; ~**sage** [vɛʀnisaʒ] nm varnishing; glazing; (d'une exposition) preview

vérole [veʀɔl] nf (variole) smallpox

verrai etc vb voir **voir**

verre [vɛʀ] nm glass; (de lunettes) lens sg; **boire** ou **prendre un** ~ to have a drink; ~**s de contact** contact lenses; **verrerie** [vɛʀʀi] nf (fabrique) glassworks sg; (activité) glass-making; (objets) glassware; **verrière** [vɛʀjɛʀ] nf (grand vitrage) window; (toit vitré) glass roof

verrons etc vb voir **voir**

verrou [vɛʀu] nm (targette) bolt; (fig) constriction; **mettre qn sous les** ~**s** to put sb behind bars; **verrouillage** nm locking; **verrouiller** vt to bolt; to lock

verrue [vɛʀy] nf wart

vers [vɛʀ] nm line ♦ nmpl (poésie) verse sg ♦ prép (en direction de) toward(s); (près de) around (about); (temporel) about, around

versant [vɛʀsɑ̃] nm slopes pl, side

versatile [vɛʀsatil] adj fickle, changeable

verse [vɛʀs(ə)]: **à** ~ adv: **il pleut à** ~ it's pouring (with rain)

Verseau [vɛʀso] nm: **le** ~ Aquarius

versement [vɛʀsəmɑ̃] nm payment; **en 3** ~**s** in 3 instalments

verser [vɛʀse] vt (liquide, grains) to pour; (larmes, sang) to shed; (argent) to pay ♦ vi (véhicule) to overturn; (fig): ~ **dans** to lapse into

verset [vɛʀsɛ] nm verse

version [vɛʀsjɔ̃] nf version; (SCOL) translation (into the mother tongue)

verso [vɛʀso] nm back; **voir au** ~ see over(leaf)

vert, e [vɛʀ, vɛʀt(ə)] adj green; (vin) young; (vigoureux) sprightly; (cru) forthright ♦ nm green

vertèbre [vɛʀtɛbʀ(ə)] nf vertebra

vertement [vɛʀtəmɑ̃] adv (réprimander) sharply

vertical, e, aux [vɛʀtikal, -o] adj vertical; ~**e** nf vertical; **à la** ~**e** vertically; ~**ement** adv vertically

vertige [vɛʀtiʒ] nm (peur du vide) vertigo; (étourdissement) dizzy spell; (fig) fever; **vertigineux, euse** adj breathtaking

vertu [vɛʀty] nf virtue; **en** ~ **de** in accordance with; **vertueux, euse** adj virtuous

verve [vɛʀv(ə)] nf witty eloquence; **être en** ~ to be in brilliant form

verveine [vɛʀvɛn] nf (BOT) verbena, vervain; (infusion) verbena tea

vésicule [vezikyl] nf vesicle; ~ **biliaire** gall-bladder

vessie [vesi] nf bladder

veste [vɛst(ə)] nf jacket; ~ **droite/croisée** single-/double-breasted jacket

vestiaire [vɛstjɛʀ] nm (au théâtre etc) cloakroom; (de stade etc) changing-room (BRIT), locker-room (US)

vestibule [vɛstibyl] nm hall

vestige [vɛstiʒ] nm relic; (fig) vestige; ~**s** nmpl remains

vestimentaire [vɛstimɑ̃tɛʀ] adj (détail) of dress; (élégance) sartorial; **dépenses** ~**s** spending on clothes

veston [vɛstɔ̃] nm jacket

vêtement [vɛtmɑ̃] nm garment, item of clothing; ~**s** nmpl clothes

vétérinaire [veteʀinɛʀ] nm/f vet, veterinary surgeon

vêtir [vetiʀ] vt to clothe, dress

veto [veto] nm veto; **opposer un** ~ **à** to veto

vêtu, e [vety] pp de **vêtir**

vétuste [vetyst(ə)] adj ancient, timeworn

veuf, veuve [vœf, vœv] adj widowed ♦ nm widower

veuille etc vb voir **vouloir**

veuillez vb voir **vouloir**

veule [vøl] adj spineless

veuve [vœv] nf widow

veux *vb voir* **vouloir**
vexations [vɛksasjɔ̃] *nfpl* humiliations
vexer [vɛkse] *vt* to hurt, upset; **se ~** *vi* to be hurt, get upset
viabiliser [vjabilize] *vt* to provide with services (*water etc*)
viable [vjabl(ə)] *adj* viable; (*économie, industrie etc*) sustainable
viager, ère [vjaʒe, -ɛʀ] *adj*: **rente viagère** life annuity
viande [vjɑ̃d] *nf* meat
vibrer [vibʀe] *vi* to vibrate; (*son, voix*) to be vibrant; (*fig*) to be stirred; **faire ~** to (cause to) vibrate; to stir, thrill
vice [vis] *nm* vice; (*défaut*) fault ♦ *préfixe*: **~ ... vice-**; **~ de forme** legal flaw *ou* irregularity
vichy [viʃi] *nm* (*toile*) gingham
vicié, e [visje] *adj* (*air*) polluted, tainted; (*JUR*) invalidated
vicieux, euse [visjø, -øz] *adj* (*pervers*) dirty(-minded); nasty; (*fautif*) incorrect, wrong
vicinal, e, aux [visinal, -o] *adj*: **chemin ~** by-road, byway
victime [viktim] *nf* victim; (*d'accident*) casualty
victoire [viktwaʀ] *nf* victory
victuailles [viktɥaj] *nfpl* provisions
vidange [vidɑ̃ʒ] *nf* (*d'un fossé, réservoir*) emptying; (*AUTO*) oil change; (*de lavabo: bonde*) waste outlet; **~s** *nfpl* (*matières*) sewage *sg*; **vidanger** *vt* to empty
vide [vid] *adj* empty ♦ *nm* (*PHYSIQUE*) vacuum; (*espace*) (empty) space, gap; (*futilité, néant*) void; **avoir peur du ~** to be afraid of heights; **emballé sous ~** vacuum packed; **à ~** (*sans occupants*) empty; (*sans charge*) unladen
vidéo [video] *nf* video ♦ *adj*: **cassette ~** video cassette
vide-ordures [vidɔʀdyʀ] *nm inv* (rubbish) chute
vide-poches [vidpɔʃ] *nm inv* tidy; (*AUTO*) glove compartment
vider [vide] *vt* to empty; (*CULIN: volaille, poisson*) to gut, clean out; **se ~** *vi* to empty; **~ les lieux** to quit *ou* vacate the premises; **videur** *nm* (*de boîte de nuit*) bouncer
vie [vi] *nf* life; **être en ~** to be alive; **sans ~** lifeless; **à ~** for life
vieil [vjɛj] *adj m voir* **vieux**
vieillard [vjɛjaʀ] *nm* old man; **les ~s** old people, the elderly
vieille [vjɛj] *adj, nf voir* **vieux**
vieilleries [vjɛjʀi] *nfpl* old things
vieillesse [vjɛjɛs] *nf* old age
vieillir [vjejiʀ] *vi* (*prendre de l'âge*) to grow old; (*population, vin*) to age; (*doctrine, auteur*) to become dated ♦ *vt* to age; **vieillissement** *nm* growing old; ageing

Vienne [vjɛn] *nf* Vienna
viens *vb voir* **venir**
vierge [vjɛʀʒ(ə)] *adj* virgin; (*page*) clean, blank ♦ *nf* virgin; (*signe*): **la V~** Virgo; **~ de** (*sans*) free from, unsullied by
Vietnam [vjɛtnam] *nm* = **Viêt-nam**
Viêt-nam [vjɛtnam] *nm* Vietnam
vietnamien, ne [vjɛtnamjɛ̃, -jɛn] *adj, nm/f* Vietnamese
vieux(vieil), vieille [vjø, vjɛj] *adj* old ♦ *nm/f* old man(woman) ♦ *nmpl* old people; **mon vieux/ma vieille** (*fam*) old man/girl; **prendre un coup de vieux** to put years on; **vieux garçon** bachelor; **vieux jeu** *adj inv* old-fashioned
vif, vive [vif, viv] *adj* (*animé*) lively; (*alerte, brusque, aigu*) sharp; (*lumière, couleur*) brilliant; (*air*) crisp; (*vent, émotion*) keen; (*fort: regret, déception*) great, deep; (*vivant*): **brûlé ~** burnt alive; **de vive voix** personally; **piquer qn au ~** to cut sb to the quick; **à ~** (*plaie*) open; **avoir les nerfs à ~** to be on edge
vigie [viʒi] *nf* look-out; look-out post
vigne [viɲ] *nf* (*plante*) vine; (*plantation*) vineyard
vigneron [viɲʀɔ̃] *nm* wine grower
vignette [viɲɛt] *nf* (*motif*) vignette; (*de marque*) manufacturer's label *ou* seal; (*ADMIN*) ≈ (road) tax disc (*BRIT*), ≈ license plate sticker (*US*); price label (*used for reimbursement*)
vignoble [viɲɔbl(ə)] *nm* (*plantation*) vineyard; (*vignes d'une région*) vineyards *pl*
vigoureux, euse [viguʀø, -øz] *adj* vigorous, robust
vigueur [vigœʀ] *nf* vigour; **entrer en ~** to come into force; **en ~** current
vil, e [vil] *adj* vile, base; **à ~ prix** at a very low price
vilain, e [vilɛ̃, -ɛn] *adj* (*laid*) ugly; (*affaire, blessure*) nasty; (*pas sage: enfant*) naughty
villa [vila] *nf* (*detached*) house; **~ en multipropriété** time-share villa
village [vilaʒ] *nm* village; **villageois, e** *adj* village *cpd* ♦ *nm/f* villager
ville [vil] *nf* town; (*importante*) city; (*administration*): **la ~** ≈ the Corporation; ≈ the (town) council
villégiature [vileʒjatyʀ] *nf* holiday; (*holiday*) resort
vin [vɛ̃] *nm* wine; **avoir le ~ gai** to get happy after a few drinks; **~ d'honneur** reception (*with wine and snacks*); **~ de pays** local wine; **~ ordinaire** table wine
vinaigre [vinɛgʀ(ə)] *nm* vinegar; **vinaigrette** *nf* vinaigrette, French dressing
vindicatif, ive [vɛ̃dikatif, -iv] *adj* vindictive
vineux, euse [vinø, -øz] *adj* win(e)y
vingt [vɛ̃, vɛ̃t] *num* twenty; **~aine** *nf*: **une ~aine (de)** about twenty, twenty or so; **~ième** *num* twentieth

vinicole [vinikɔl] *adj* wine *cpd*, wine-growing

vins *etc vb voir* **venir**

vinyle [vinil] *nm* vinyl

viol [vjɔl] *nm* (*d'une femme*) rape; (*d'un lieu sacré*) violation

violacé, e [vjɔlase] *adj* purplish, mauvish

violemment [vjɔlamɑ̃] *adv* violently

violence [vjɔlɑ̃s] *nf* violence

violent, e [vjɔlɑ̃, -ɑ̃t] *adj* violent; (*remède*) drastic

violer [vjɔle] *vt* (*femme*) to rape; (*sépulture, loi, traité*) to violate

violet, te [vjɔlɛ, -ɛt] *adj, nm* purple, mauve; **violette** *nf* (*fleur*) violet

violon [vjɔlɔ̃] *nm* violin; (*fam: prison*) lock-up

violoncelle [vjɔlɔ̃sɛl] *nm* cello

violoniste [vjɔlɔnist(ə)] *nm/f* violinist

vipère [vipɛʀ] *nf* viper, adder

virage [viʀaʒ] *nm* (*d'un véhicule*) turn; (*d'une route, piste*) bend; (*fig: POL*) about-turn

virée [viʀe] *nf* (*courte*) run; (: *à pied*) walk; (*longue*) trip; hike, walking tour

virement [viʀmɑ̃] *nm* (*COMM*) transfer

virent *vb voir* **voir**

virer [viʀe] *vt* (*COMM*): ~ **qch (sur)** to transfer sth (into) ♦ *vi* to turn; (*CHIMIE*) to change colour; ~ **de bord** to tack

virevolter [viʀvɔlte] *vi* to twirl around

virgule [viʀgyl] *nf* comma; (*MATH*) point

viril, e [viʀil] *adj* (*propre à l'homme*) masculine; (*énergique, courageux*) manly, virile

virtuel, le [viʀtɥɛl] *adj* potential; (*théorique*) virtual

virtuose [viʀtɥoz] *nm/f* (*MUS*) virtuoso; (*gén*) master

virus [viʀys] *nm* (*aussi: COMPUT*) virus

vis¹ [vi] *vb voir* **voir; vivre**

vis² [vis] *nf* screw

visa [viza] *nm* (*sceau*) stamp; (*validation de passeport*) visa

visage [vizaʒ] *nm* face

vis-à-vis [vizavi] *adv* face to face ♦ *nm* person opposite; house *etc* opposite; ~ **de** opposite; (*fig*) vis-à-vis; **en** ~ facing each other

viscéral, e, aux [viseʀal, -o] *adj* (*fig*) deep-seated, deep-rooted

visée [vize] *nf*: ~**s** *nfpl* (*intentions*) designs

viser [vize] *vi* to aim ♦ *vt* to aim at; (*concerner*) to be aimed *ou* directed at; (*apposer un visa sur*) to stamp, visa; ~ **à qch/faire** to aim at sth/at doing *ou* to do; **viseur** [vizœʀ] *nm* (*d'arme*) sights *pl*; (*PHOTO*) viewfinder

visibilité [vizibilite] *nf* visibility

visible [vizibl(ə)] *adj* visible; (*disponible*): **est-il** ~? can he see me?, will he see visitors?

visière [vizjɛʀ] *nf* (*de casquette*) peak; (*qui s'attache*) eyeshade

vision [vizjɔ̃] *nf* vision; (*sens*) (eye)sight, vision; (*fait de voir*): **la** ~ **de** the sight of

visionneuse [vizjɔnøz] *nf* viewer

visite [vizit] *nf* visit; (*visiteur*) visitor; (*médicale, à domicile*) visit, call; **la** ~ (*MÉD*) medical examination; **faire une** ~ **à qn** to call on sb, pay sb a visit; **rendre** ~ **à qn** to visit sb, pay sb a visit; **être en** ~ (**chez qn**) to be visiting (sb); **heures de** ~ (*hôpital, prison*) visiting hours

visiter [vizite] *vt* to visit; (*musée, ville*) to visit, go round; **visiteur, euse** *nm/f* visitor

vison [vizɔ̃] *nm* mink

visser [vise] *vt*: ~ **qch** (*fixer, serrer*) to screw sth on

visuel, le [vizɥɛl] *adj* visual

vit *vb voir* **voir; vivre**

vital, e, aux [vital, -o] *adj* vital

vitamine [vitamin] *nf* vitamin

vite [vit] *adv* (*rapidement*) quickly, fast; (*sans délai*) quickly; soon; **faire** ~ to act quickly; to be quick

vitesse [vites] *nf* speed; (*AUTO: dispositif*) gear; **prendre qn de** ~ to outstrip sb; get ahead of sb; **rendre de la** ~ to pick up *ou* gather speed; **à toute** ~ at full *ou* top speed

viticole [vitikɔl] *adj* wine *cpd*, wine-growing

viticulteur [vitikyltœʀ] *nm* wine grower

vitrage [vitʀaʒ] *nm* glass *no pl*; (*rideau*) net curtain

vitrail, aux [vitʀaj, -o] *nm* stained-glass window

vitre [vitʀ(ə)] *nf* (window) pane; (*de portière, voiture*) window

vitré, e [vitʀe] *adj* glass *cpd*

vitrer [vitʀe] *vt* to glaze

vitreux, euse [vitʀø, -øz] *adj* (*terne*) glassy

vitrine [vitʀin] *nf* (*devanture*) (shop) window; (*étalage*) display; (*petite armoire*) display cabinet; ~ **publicitaire** display case, showcase

vitupérer [vitypeʀe] *vi* to rant and rave

vivace [vivas] *adj* (*arbre, plante*) hardy; (*fig*) indestructible, inveterate

vivacité [vivasite] *nf* liveliness, vivacity; sharpness; brilliance

vivant, e [vivɑ̃, -ɑ̃t] *adj* (*qui vit*) living, alive; (*animé*) lively; (*preuve, exemple*) living ♦ *nm*: **du** ~ **de qn** in sb's lifetime

vivats [viva] *nmpl* cheers

vive [viv] *adj f voir* **vif** ♦ *vb voir* **vivre** ♦ *excl*: ~ **le roi!** long live the king!; **vivement** *adv* vivaciously; sharply ♦ *excl*: **vivement les vacances!** roll on the holidays!

viveur [vivœʀ] *nm* (*péj*) high liver, pleasure-seeker

vivier [vivje] *nm* fish tank; fishpond

vivifiant, e [vivifjɑ̃, -ɑ̃t] *adj* invigorating

vivions *vb voir* **vivre**

vivoter [vivɔte] *vi* (*personne*) to scrape a

living, get by; (*fig: affaire etc*) to struggle along

vivre [vivʀ(ə)] *vi, vt* to live; **il vit encore** he is still alive; **se laisser** ~ to take life as it comes; **ne plus** ~ (*être anxieux*) to live on one's nerves; **il a vécu** (*eu une vie aventureuse*) he has seen life; **être facile à** ~ to be easy to get on with; **faire** ~ **qn** (*pourvoir à sa subsistance*) to provide (a living) for sb; **vivres** *nmpl* provisions, food supplies

vlan [vlɑ̃] *excl* wham!, bang!

vocable [vɔkabl(ə)] *nm* term

vocabulaire [vɔkabylɛʀ] *nm* vocabulary

vocation [vɔkasjɔ̃] *nf* vocation, calling

vociférer [vɔsifeʀe] *vi, vt* to scream

vœu, x [vø] *nm* wish; (*à Dieu*) vow; **faire** ~ **de** to take a vow of; **~x de bonne année** best wishes for the New Year

vogue [vɔg] *nf* fashion, vogue

voguer [vɔge] *vi* to sail

voici [vwasi] *prép* (*pour introduire, désigner*) here is +*sg*, here are +*pl*; **et** ~ **que ...** and now it (*ou* he) ...; *voir aussi* **voilà**

voie [vwa] *nf* way; (*RAIL*) track, line; (*AUTO*) lane; **être en bonne** ~ to be going well; **mettre qn sur la** ~ to put sb on the right track; **être en** ~ **d'achèvement/de rénovation** to be nearing completion/in the process of renovation; **par** ~ **buccale** *ou* **orale** orally; **à** ~ **étroite** narrow-gauge; ~ **d'eau** (*NAVIG*) leak; ~ **de garage** (*RAIL*) siding; ~ **ferrée** track; railway line

voilà [vwala] *prép* (*en désignant*) there is +*sg*, there are +*pl*; **les** ~ *ou* **voici** here *ou* there they are; **en** ~ *ou* **voici un** here's one, there's one; ~ *ou* **voici deux ans** two years ago; ~ *ou* **voici deux ans que** it's two years since; **et** ~**!** there we are!; ~ **tout** that's all; "~ *ou* **voici**" (*en offrant etc*) "there *ou* here you are"

voile [vwal] *nm* veil; (*tissu léger*) net ♦ *nf* sail; (*sport*) sailing

voiler [vwale] *vt* to veil; (*fausser: roue*) to buckle; (: *bois*) to warp; **se** ~ *vi* (*lune, regard*) to mist over; (*voix*) to become husky; (*roue, disque*) to buckle; (*planche*) to warp

voilier [vwalje] *nm* sailing ship; (*de plaisance*) sailing boat

voilure [vwalyʀ] *nf* (*de voilier*) sails *pl*

voir [vwaʀ] *vi, vt* to see; **se** ~ *vt*: **se** ~ **critiquer/transformer** to be criticized/transformed; **cela se voit** (*cela arrive*) it happens; (*c'est visible*) that's obvious, it shows; ~ **venir** (*fig*) to wait and see; **faire** ~ **qch à qn** to show sb sth; **en faire** ~ **à qn** (*fig*) to give sb a hard time; **ne pas pouvoir** ~ **qn** not to be able to stand sb; **voyons!** let's see now; (*indignation etc*) come (along) now!; **avoir quelque chose à** ~ **avec** to have something to do with

voire [vwaʀ] *adv* indeed; nay; or even

voisin, e [vwazɛ̃, -in] *adj* (*proche*) neighbouring; (*contigu*) next; (*ressemblant*) connected ♦ *nm/f* neighbour; **voisinage** *nm* (*proximité*) proximity; (*environs*) vicinity; (*quartier, voisins*) neighbourhood

voiture [vwatyʀ] *nf* car; (*wagon*) coach, carriage; ~ **d'enfant** pram (*BRIT*), baby carriage (*US*); ~ **de sport** sports car; ~**-lit** *nf* sleeper

voix [vwa] *nf* voice; (*POL*) vote; **à haute** ~ aloud; **à** ~ **basse** in a low voice; **à 2/4** ~ (*MUS*) in 2/4 parts; **avoir** ~ **au chapitre** to have a say in the matter

vol [vɔl] *nm* (*mode de locomotion*) flying; (*trajet, voyage, groupe d'oiseaux*) flight; (*larcin*) theft; **à** ~ **d'oiseau** as the crow flies; **au** ~: **attraper qch au** ~ to catch sth as it flies past; **en** ~ in flight; ~ **à main armée** armed robbery; ~ **à voile** gliding; ~ **libre** hang-gliding

volage [vɔlaʒ] *adj* fickle

volaille [vɔlaj] *nf* (*oiseaux*) poultry *pl*; (*viande*) poultry *no pl*; (*oiseau*) fowl

volant, e [vɔlɑ̃, -ɑ̃t] *adj voir* **feuille** *etc* ♦ *nm* (*d'automobile*) (steering) wheel; (*de commande*) wheel; (*objet lancé*) shuttlecock; (*bande de tissu*) flounce

volcan [vɔlkɑ̃] *nm* volcano

volée [vɔle] *nf* (*TENNIS*) volley; **à la** ~: **rattraper à la** ~ to catch in mid-air; **à toute** ~ (*sonner les cloches*) vigorously; (*lancer un projectile*) with full force; ~ **de coups/de flèches** volley of blows/arrows

voler [vɔle] *vi* (*avion, oiseau, fig*) to fly; (*voleur*) to steal ♦ *vt* (*objet*) to steal; (*personne*) to rob; ~ **qch à qn** to steal sth from sb

volet [vɔlɛ] *nm* (*de fenêtre*) shutter; (*de feuillet, document*) section

voleur, euse [vɔlœʀ, -øz] *nm/f* thief ♦ *adj* thieving

volontaire [vɔlɔ̃tɛʀ] *adj* voluntary; (*caractère, personne*) *décidé* self-willed ♦ *nm/f* volunteer

volonté [vɔlɔ̃te] *nf* (*faculté de vouloir*) will; (*énergie, fermeté*) will(power); (*souhait, désir*) wish; **à** ~ as much as one likes; **bonne** ~ goodwill, willingness; **mauvaise** ~ lack of goodwill, unwillingness

volontiers [vɔlɔ̃tje] *adv* (*de bonne grâce*) willingly; (*avec plaisir*) willingly, gladly; (*habituellement, souvent*) readily, willingly

volt [vɔlt] *nm* volt

volte-face [vɔltəfas] *nf inv* about-turn

voltige [vɔltiʒ] *nf* (*ÉQUITATION*) trick riding; (*au cirque*) acrobatics *sg*; ~**r** [vɔltiʒe] *vi* to flutter (about)

volume [vɔlym] *nm* volume; (*GÉOM: solide*) solid; **volumineux, euse** *adj* voluminous, bulky

volupté [vɔlypte] *nf* sensual delight *ou* pleasure

vomir [vɔmiʀ] vi to vomit, be sick ♦ vt to vomit, bring up; (fig) to belch out, spew out; (exécrer) to loathe, abhor

vont [vɔ̃] vb voir **aller**

vos [vo] dét voir **votre**

vote [vɔt] nm vote; ~ **par correspondance/procuration** postal/proxy vote

voter [vɔte] vi to vote ♦ vt (loi, décision) to vote for

votre [vɔtʀ(ə)] (pl **vos**) dét your

vôtre [votʀ(ə)] pron: **le ~, la ~, les ~s** yours; **les ~s** (fig) your family ou folks; **à la ~** (toast) your (good) health!

voudrai etc vb voir **vouloir**

voué, e [vwe] adj: ~ **à** doomed to

vouer [vwe] vt: ~ **qch à** (Dieu/un saint) to dedicate sth to; ~ **sa vie à** (étude, cause etc) to devote one's life to; ~ **une amitié éternelle à qn** to vow undying friendship to sb

─────────── MOT CLÉ ───────────

vouloir [vulwaʀ] nm: **le bon ~ de qn** sb's goodwill; sb's pleasure

♦ vt **1** (exiger, désirer) to want; ~ **faire/que qn fasse** to want to do/sb to do; **voulez-vous du thé?** would you like ou do you want some tea?; **que me veut-il?** what does he want with me?; **sans le ~** (involontairement) without meaning to, unintentionally; **je voudrais ceci/faire** I would ou I'd like this/to do

2 (consentir): **je veux bien** (bonne volonté) I'll be happy to; (concession) fair enough, that's fine; **oui, si on veut** (en quelque sorte) yes, if you like; **veuillez attendre** please wait; **veuillez agréer ...** (formule épistolaire) yours faithfully

3: **en ~ à qn** to bear sb a grudge; **s'en ~ (de)** to be annoyed with o.s. (for); **il en veut à mon argent** he's after my money

4: ~ **de**: **l'entreprise ne veut plus de lui** the firm doesn't want him any more; **elle ne veut pas de son aide** she doesn't want his help

5: ~ **dire** to mean

──────────────────────────────

voulu, e [vuly] adj (requis) required, requisite; (délibéré) deliberate, intentional; voir aussi **vouloir**

vous [vu] pron you; (objet indirect) (to) you; (réfléchi: sg) yourself; (: pl) yourselves; (réciproque) each other; ~-**même** yourself; ~-**mêmes** yourselves

voûte [vut] nf vault

voûter [vute] vt: **se ~** vi (dos, personne) to become stooped

vouvoyer [vuvwaje] vt: ~ **qn** to address sb as "vous"

voyage [vwajaʒ] nm journey, trip; (fait de voyager): **le ~** travel(ling); **partir/être en ~**

to go off/be away on a journey ou trip; **faire bon ~** to have a good journey; ~ **d'agrément/d'affaires** pleasure/business trip; ~ **de noces** honeymoon; ~ **organisé** package tour

voyager [vwajaʒe] vi to travel; **voyageur, euse** nm/f traveller; (passager) passenger

voyant, e [vwajã, -ãt] adj (couleur) loud, gaudy ♦ nm (signal) (warning) light.

voyante nf clairvoyant

voyelle [vwajɛl] nf vowel

voyons etc vb voir **voir**

voyou [vwaju] nm lout, hoodlum; (enfant) guttersnipe

vrac [vʀak] : **en ~** adv higgledy-piggledy; (COMM) in bulk

vrai, e [vʀɛ] adj (véridique: récit, faits) true; (non factice, authentique) real; **à ~ dire** to tell the truth

vraiment [vʀɛmã] adv really

vraisemblable [vʀɛsɑ̃blabl(ə)] adj likely, probable

vraisemblance [vʀɛsɑ̃blɑ̃s] nf likelihood; (romanesque) verisimilitude

vrille [vʀij] nf (de plante) tendril; (outil) gimlet; (spirale) spiral; (AVIAT) spin

vrombir [vʀɔ̃biʀ] vi to hum

vu, e [vy] pp de voir ♦ adj: **bien/mal ~** (fig) well/poorly thought of; good/bad form ♦ prép (en raison de) in view of; ~ **que** in view of the fact that

vue [vy] nf (fait de voir): **la ~ de** the sight of; (sens, faculté) (eye)sight; (panorama, image, photo) view; ~**s** nfpl (idées) views; (dessein) designs; **hors de ~** out of sight; **tirer à ~** to shoot on sight; **à ~ d'œil** visibly; at a quick glance; **en ~** (visible) in sight; (COMM) in the public eye; **en ~ de faire** with a view to doing

vulgaire [vylgɛʀ] adj (grossier) vulgar, coarse; (trivial) commonplace, mundane; (péj: quelconque): **de ~s touristes** common tourists; (BOT, ZOOL: non latin) common; **vulgariser** vt to popularize

vulnérable [vylneʀabl(ə)] adj vulnerable

W w

wagon [vagɔ̃] nm (de voyageurs) carriage; (de marchandises) truck, wagon; **wagon-lit** nm sleeper, sleeping car; **wagon-restaurant** nm restaurant ou dining car

wallon, ne [valɔ̃, -ɔn] adj Walloon

waters [watɛʀ] *nmpl* toilet *sg*
watt [wat] *nm* watt
w.-c. [vese] *nmpl* toilet *sg*, lavatory *sg*
week-end [wikɛnd] *nm* weekend
western [wɛstɛʀn] *nm* western
whisky [wiski] (*pl* **whiskies**) *nm* whisky

yoghourt [jɔɡuʀt] *nm* = yaourt
yougoslave [juɡɔslav] *nm/f* Yugo-slav(ian)
Yougoslavie [juɡɔslavi] *nf* Yugoslavia

xérès [ɡzeʀɛs] *nm* sherry
xylophone [ksilɔfɔn] *nm* xylophone

zèbre [zɛbʀ(ə)] *nm* (*ZOOL*) zebra
zébré, e [zebʀe] *adj* striped, streaked
zèle [zɛl] *nm* zeal; **faire du ~** (*péj*) to be over-zealous
zéro [zeʀo] *nm* zero, nought (*BRIT*); **au-dessous de ~** below zero (Centigrade) *ou* freezing; **partir de ~** to start from scratch; **trois (buts) à ~** 3 (goals to) nil
zeste [zɛst(ə)] *nm* peel, zest
zézayer [zezeje] *vi* to have a lisp
zigzag [ziɡzaɡ] *nm* zigzag
zinc [zɛ̃ɡ] *nm* (*CHIMIE*) zinc; (*comptoir*) bar, counter
zizanie [zizani] *nf*: **semer la ~** to stir up ill-feeling
zodiaque [zɔdjak] *nm* zodiac
zona [zona] *nm* shingles *sg*
zone [zon] *nf* zone, area; (*quartiers*): **la ~** the slum belt; **~ bleue** ≈ restricted parking area; **~ industrielle** *nf* industrial estate
zoo [zoo] *nm* zoo
zoologie [zɔɔlɔʒi] *nf* zoology; **zoologique** *adj* zoological
zut [zyt] *excl* dash (it)! (*BRIT*), nuts! (*US*)

y [i] *adv* (*à cet endroit*) there; (*dessus*) on it (*ou* them); (*dedans*) in it (*ou* them) ♦ *pron* (about *ou* on *ou* of) it (*d'après le verbe employé*); **j'~ pense** I'm thinking about it; *voir aussi* **aller; avoir**
yacht [jɔt] *nm* yacht
yaourt [jauʀt] *nm* yoghurt
yeux [jø] *nmpl de* œil

ENGLISH - FRENCH
ANGLAIS - FRANÇAIS

A a

A [eɪ] n (MUS) la m

KEYWORD
---

a [eɪ, ə] (before vowel or silent h: an) indef art **1** un(e); ~ **book** un livre; **an apple** une pomme; **she's** ~ **doctor** elle est médecin
2 (instead of the number 'one') un(e); ~ **year ago** il y a un an; ~ **hundred/thousand etc pounds** cent/mille etc livres
3 (in expressing ratios, prices etc): **3** ~ **day/week** 3 par jour/semaine; **10 km** ~**n hour** 10 km à l'heure; **30p** ~ **kilo** 30p le kilo

---

A.A. n abbr = **Alcoholics Anonymous**; (BRIT: = Automobile Association) ≈ TCF m
A.A.A. (US) n abbr (= American Automobile Association) ≈ TCF m
aback [ə'bæk] adv: **to be taken** ~ être stupéfait(e), être décontenancé(e)
abandon [ə'bændən] vt abandonner ♦ n: **with** ~ avec désinvolture
abate [ə'beɪt] vi s'apaiser, se calmer
abbey ['æbɪ] n abbaye f
abbot ['æbət] n père supérieur
abbreviation [əbri:vɪ'eɪʃən] n abréviation f
abdicate ['æbdɪkeɪt] vt, vi abdiquer
abdomen ['æbdəmən] n abdomen m
abduct [æb'dʌkt] vt enlever
aberration [æbə'reɪʃən] n anomalie f
abet [ə'bet] vt see aid
abeyance [ə'beɪəns] n: **in** ~ (law) tombé(e) en désuétude; (matter) en suspens
abide [ə'baɪd] vt: **I can't** ~ **it/him** je ne peux pas le souffrir or supporter; ~ **by** vt fus observer, respecter
ability [ə'bɪlɪtɪ] n compétence f; capacité f; (skill) talent m
abject ['æbdʒekt] adj (poverty) sordide; (apology) plat(e)
ablaze [ə'bleɪz] adj en feu, en flammes
able ['eɪbl] adj capable, compétent(e); **to be**

~ **to do sth** être capable de faire qch, pouvoir faire qch; ~**-bodied** adj robuste; **ably** ['eɪblɪ] adv avec compétence or talent, habilement
abnormal [æb'nɔ:məl] adj anormal(e)
aboard [ə'bɔ:d] adv à bord ♦ prep à bord de
abode [ə'bəud] n (LAW): **of no fixed** ~ sans domicile fixe
abolish [ə'bɒlɪʃ] vt abolir
aborigine [æbə'rɪdʒɪni:] n aborigène m/f
abort [ə'bɔ:t] vt faire avorter; ~**ion** [ə'bɔ:ʃən] n avortement m; **to have an** ~**ion** se faire avorter; ~**ive** adj manqué(e)
abound [ə'baund] vi abonder; **to** ~ **in** or **with** abonder en, regorger de

---
KEYWORD
---

about [ə'baut] adv **1** (approximately) environ, à peu près; ~ **a hundred/thousand etc** environ cent/mille etc, une centaine (de)/un millier (de) etc; **it takes** ~ **10 hours** ça prend environ or à peu près 10 heures; **at** ~ **2 o'clock** vers 2 heures; **I've just** ~ **finished** j'ai presque fini
2 (referring to place) çà et là, deci delà; **to run** ~ courir çà et là; **to walk** ~ se promener, aller et venir
3: **to be** ~ **to do sth** être sur le point de faire qch
♦ prep **1** (relating to) au sujet de, à propos de; **a book** ~ **London** un livre sur Londres; **what is it** ~? de quoi s'agit-il?; **we talked** ~ **it** nous en avons parlé; **what** or **how** ~ **doing this?** et si nous faisions ceci?
2 (referring to place) dans; **to walk** ~ **the town** se promener dans la ville

---

about-face [ə'baut'feɪs] n demi-tour m
about-turn [ə'baut'tɜ:n] n (MIL) demi-tour m; (fig) volte-face f

above [ə'bʌv] *adv* au-dessus ♦ *prep* au-dessus de; (*more*) plus de; **mentioned** ~ mentionné ci-dessus; ~ **all** par-dessus tout, surtout; ~**board** *adj* franc(franche); honnête

abrasive [ə'breızıv] *adj* abrasif(ive); (*fig*) caustique, agressif(ive)

abreast [ə'brest] *adv* de front; **to keep** ~ **of** se tenir au courant de

abridge [ə'brıdʒ] *vt* abréger

abroad [ə'brɔːd] *adv* à l'étranger

abrupt [ə'brʌpt] *adj* (*steep, blunt*) abrupt(e); (*sudden, gruff*) brusque; ~**ly** *adv* (*speak, end*) brusquement

abscess ['æbsıs] *n* abcès *m*

abscond [əb'skɒnd] *vi* disparaître, s'enfuir

absence ['æbsəns] *n* absence *f*

absent ['æbsənt] *adj* absent(e); ~**ee** [æbsən'tiː] *n* absent(e); (*habitual*) absentéiste *m/f*; ~**-minded** *adj* distrait(e)

absolute ['æbsəluːt] *adj* absolu(e); ~**ly** [æbsə'luːtlı] *adv* absolument

absolve [əb'zɒlv] *vt*: **to** ~ **sb (from)** (*blame, responsibility, sin*) absoudre qn (de)

absorb [əb'zɔːb] *vt* absorber; **to be** ~**ed in a book** être plongé(e) dans un livre; ~**ent cotton** (*US*) *n* coton *m* hydrophile; **absorption** [əb'zɔːpʃən] *n* absorption *f*; (*fig*) concentration *f*

abstain [əb'steın] *vi*: **to** ~ (**from**) s'abstenir (de)

abstract ['æbstrækt] *adj* abstrait(e)

absurd [əb'sɜːd] *adj* absurde

abuse [*n* ə'bjuːs, *vb* ə'bjuːz] *n* abus *m*; (*insults*) insultes *fpl*, injures *fpl* ♦ *vt* abuser de; (*insult*) insulter; **abusive** [ə'bjuːsıv] *adj* grossier(ère), injurieux(euse)

abysmal [ə'bızməl] *adj* exécrable; (*ignorance etc*) sans bornes

abyss [ə'bıs] *n* abîme *m*, gouffre *m*

AC *abbr* (= *alternating current*) courant alternatif

academic [ækə'demık] *adj* universitaire; (*person: scholarly*) intellectuel(le); (*pej: issue*) oiseux(euse), purement théorique ♦ *n* universitaire *m/f*; ~ **year** *n* année *f* universitaire

academy [ə'kædəmı] *n* (*learned body*) académie *f*; (*school*) collège *m*; ~ **of music** conservatoire *m*

accelerate [æk'seləreıt] *vt, vi* accélérer; **accelerator** [æk'seləreıtə*] *n* accélérateur *m*

accent ['æksənt] *n* accent *m*

accept [ək'sept] *vt* accepter; ~**able** *adj* acceptable; ~**ance** *n* acceptation *f*

access ['ækses] *n* accès *m*; (*JUR: in divorce*) droit *m* de visite; ~**ible** [æk'sesıbl] *adj* accessible

accessory [æk'sesərı] *n* accessoire *m*; (*LAW*): ~ **to** complice de

accident ['æksıdənt] *n* accident *m*; (*chance*) hasard *m*; **by** ~ accidentellement; par ha-

sard; ~**al** [æksı'dentl] *adj* accidentel(le); ~**ally** [æksı'dentəlı] *adv* accidentellement; ~**-prone** *adj* sujet(te) aux accidents

acclaim [ə'kleım] *n* acclamations *fpl* ♦ *vt* acclamer

accommodate [ə'kɒmədeıt] *vt* loger, recevoir; (*oblige, help*) obliger; (*car etc*) contenir; **accommodating** [ə'kɒmədeıtıŋ] *adj* obligeant(e), arrangeant(e); **accommodation** [əkɒmə'deıʃən] (*US* ~**s**) *n* logement *m*

accompany [ə'kʌmpənı] *vt* accompagner

accomplice [ə'kʌmplıs] *n* complice *m/f*

accomplish [ə'kʌmplıʃ] *vt* accomplir; ~**ment** *n* accomplissement *m*; réussite *f*; (*skill: gen pl*) talent *m*

accord [ə'kɔːd] *n* accord *m* ♦ *vt* accorder; **of his own** ~ de son plein gré; ~**ance** *n*: **in** ~**ance with** conformément à; ~**ing**: ~**ing to** *prep* selon; ~**ingly** *adv* en conséquence

accordion [ə'kɔːdıən] *n* accordéon *m*

accost [ə'kɒst] *vt* aborder

account [ə'kaunt] *n* (*COMM*) compte *m*; (*report*) compte rendu *m*; récit *m*; ~**s** *npl* (*COMM*) comptabilité *f*, comptes; **of no** ~ sans importance; **on** ~ en acompte; **on no** ~ en aucun cas; **on** ~ **of** à cause de; **to take into** ~, **take** ~ **of** tenir compte de; ~ **for** *vt fus* expliquer, rendre compte de; ~**able** *adj*: ~**able (to)** responsable (devant); ~**ancy** [ə'kauntənsı] *n* comptabilité *f*; ~**ant** [ə'kauntənt] *n* comptable *m/f*; ~ **number** *n* (*at bank etc*) numéro *m* de compte

accrued interest [əkruːd] *n* intérêt *m* cumulé

accumulate [ə'kjuːmjuleıt] *vt* accumuler, amasser ♦ *vi* s'accumuler, s'amasser

accuracy ['ækjurəsı] *n* exactitude *f*, précision *f*

accurate ['ækjurıt] *adj* exact(e), précis(e); ~**ly** *adv* avec précision

accusation [ækjuː'zeıʃən] *n* accusation *f*

accuse [ə'kjuːz] *vt*: **to** ~ **sb (of sth)** accuser qn (de qch); ~**d** *n*: **the** ~**d** l'accusé(e)

accustom [ə'kʌstəm] *vt* accoutumer, habituer; ~**ed** *adj* (*usual*) habituel(le); (*in the habit*): ~**ed to** habitué(e) *or* accoutumé(e) à

ace [eıs] *n* as *m*

ache [eık] *n* mal *m*, douleur *f* ♦ *vi* (*yearn*): **to** ~ **to do sth** mourir d'envie de faire qch; **my head** ~**s** j'ai mal à la tête

achieve [ə'tʃiːv] *vt* (*aim*) atteindre; (*victory, success*) remporter, obtenir; ~**ment** *n* exploit *m*, réussite *f*

acid ['æsıd] *adj* acide ♦ *n* acide *m*; ~ **rain** *n* pluies *fpl* acides

acknowledge [ək'nɒlıdʒ] *vt* (*letter: also*: ~ **receipt of**) accuser réception de; (*fact*) reconnaître; ~**ment** *n* (*of letter*) accusé *m* de réception

acne ['æknɪ] n acné m

acorn ['eɪkɔːn] n gland m

acoustic [ə'kuːstɪk] adj acoustique; ~**s** n, npl acoustique f

acquaint [ə'kweɪnt] vt: **to ~ sb with sth** mettre qn au courant de qch; **to be ~ed with** connaître; ~**ance** n connaissance f

acquiesce [ækwɪ'es] vi: **to ~ to** acquiescer or consentir à

acquire [ə'kwaɪə*] vt acquérir

acquit [ə'kwɪt] vt acquitter; **to ~ o.s. well** bien se comporter, s'en tirer très honorablement

acre ['eɪkə*] n acre f (= 4047 m²)

acrid ['ækrɪd] adj âcre

acrobat ['ækrəbæt] n acrobate m/f

across [ə'krɒs] prep (on the other side) de l'autre côté de; (crosswise) en travers de ♦ adv de l'autre côté; en travers; **to run/swim ~** traverser en courant/à la nage; ~ **from** en face de

acrylic [ə'krɪlɪk] adj acrylique

act [ækt] n acte m, action f; (of play) acte; (in music-hall etc) numéro m; (LAW) loi f ♦ vi agir; (THEATRE) jouer; (pretend) jouer la comédie ♦ vt (part) jouer, tenir; **in the ~ of** en train de; **to ~ as** servir de; ~**ing** adj suppléant(e), par intérim ♦ n (activity): **to do some ~ing** faire du théâtre (or du cinéma)

action ['ækʃən] n action f; (MIL) combat(s) m(pl); (LAW) procès m, action en justice; **out of ~** hors de combat; (machine) hors d'usage; **to take ~** agir, prendre des mesures; ~ **replay** n (TV) ralenti m

activate ['æktɪveɪt] vt (mechanism) actionner, faire fonctionner

active ['æktɪv] adj actif(ive); (volcano) en activité; ~**ly** adv activement

activity [æk'tɪvɪtɪ] n activité f

actor ['æktə*] n acteur m

actress ['æktrɪs] n actrice f

actual ['æktjʊəl] adj réel(le), véritable; ~**ly** adv (really) réellement, véritablement; (in fact) en fait

acumen ['ækjʊmen] n perspicacité f

acute [ə'kjuːt] adj aigu(ë); (mind, observer) pénétrant(e), perspicace

ad [æd] n abbr = **advertisement**

A.D. adv abbr (= anno Domini) ap. J.-C.

adamant ['ædəmənt] adj inflexible

adapt [ə'dæpt] vt adapter ♦ vi: **to ~ (to)** s'adapter (à); ~**able** adj (device) adaptable; (person) qui s'adapte facilement; ~**er**, ~**or** n (ELEC) adapteur m, adaptateur m

add [æd] vt ajouter; (figures: also: **to ~ up**) additionner ♦ vi: **to ~ to** (increase) ajouter à, accroître

adder ['ædə*] n vipère f

addict ['ædɪkt] n intoxiqué(e); (fig) fanatique m/f; ~**ed** [ə'dɪktɪd] adj: **to be ~ed to**

(drugs, drink etc) être adonné(e) à; (fig: football etc) être un(e) fanatique de; ~**ion** [ə'dɪkʃən] n (MED) dépendance f; ~**ive** adj qui crée une dépendance

addition [ə'dɪʃən] n addition f; (thing added) ajout m; **in ~** de plus; de surcroît; **in ~ to** en plus de; ~**al** adj supplémentaire

additive ['ædɪtɪv] n additif m

address [ə'dres] n adresse f; (talk) discours m, allocution f ♦ vt adresser; (speak to) s'adresser à; **to ~ (o.s. to) a problem** s'attaquer à un problème

adept ['ædept] adj: ~ **at** expert(e) à or en

adequate ['ædɪkwɪt] adj adéquat(e); suffisant(e)

adhere [əd'hɪə*] vi: **to ~ to** adhérer à; (fig: rule, decision) se tenir à

adhesive [əd'hiːzɪv] n adhésif m; ~ **tape** n (BRIT) ruban adhésif; (US: MED) sparadrap m

ad hoc [æd'hɒk] adj improvisé(e), ad hoc

adjective ['ædʒəktɪv] n adjectif m

adjoining [ə'dʒɔɪnɪŋ] adj voisin(e), adjacent(e), attenant(e)

adjourn [ə'dʒɜːn] vt ajourner ♦ vi suspendre la séance; lever la séance; clore la session

adjust [ə'dʒʌst] vt ajuster, régler; rajuster ♦ vi: **to ~ (to)** s'adapter (à); ~**able** adj réglable; ~**ment** n (PSYCH) adaptation f; (to machine) ajustage m, réglage m; (of prices, wages) rajustement m

ad-lib [æd'lɪb] vt, vi improviser; **ad lib** adv à volonté, à loisir

administer [æd'mɪnɪstə*] vt administrer; (justice) rendre

administration [ədmɪnɪs'treɪʃən] n administration f

administrative [əd'mɪnɪstrətɪv] adj administratif(ive)

admiral ['ædmərəl] n amiral m; **A~ty** ['ædmərəltɪ] (BRIT) n (also: **A~ty Board**): **the A~ty** ministère m de la Marine

admire [əd'maɪə*] vt admirer

admission [əd'mɪʃən] n admission f; (to exhibition, night club etc) entrée f; (confession) aveu m

admit [əd'mɪt] vt laisser entrer; admettre; (agree) reconnaître, admettre; ~ **to** vt fus reconnaître, avouer; ~**tance** n admission f, (droit m d')entrée f; ~**tedly** adv il faut en convenir

admonish [əd'mɒnɪʃ] vt donner un avertissement à; réprimander

ad nauseam [æd'nɔːsɪæm] adv (repeat, talk) à n'en plus finir

ado [ə'duː] n: **without (any) more ~** sans plus de cérémonies

adolescence [ædə'lesns] n adolescence f;
adolescent [ædə'lesnt] adj, n adolescent(e)

adopt [ə'dɒpt] vt adopter; ~**ed** adj adoptif(ive), adopté(e); ~**ion** [ə'dɒpʃən] n adop-

tion f
adore [ə'dɔː*] vt adorer
adorn [ə'dɔːn] vt orner
Adriatic (Sea) [eɪdrɪ'ætɪk-] n Adriatique f
adrift [ə'drɪft] adv à la dérive
adult ['ædʌlt] n adulte m/f ♦ adj adulte; (*literature, education*) pour adultes
adultery [ə'dʌltərɪ] n adultère m
advance [əd'vɑːns] n avance f ♦ adj: ~ **booking** réservation f ♦ vt avancer ♦ vi avancer, s'avancer; ~ **notice** avertissement m; **to make** ~**s** (**to sb**) faire des propositions (à qn); (*amorously*) faire des avances (à qn); **in** ~ à l'avance, d'avance; ~**d** adj avancé(e); (*SCOL: studies*) supérieur(e)
advantage [əd'vɑːntɪdʒ] n (*also TENNIS*) avantage m; **to take** ~ **of** (*person*) exploiter
advent ['ædvənt] n avènement m, venue f; **A**~ Avent m
adventure [əd'ventʃə*] n aventure f
adverb ['ædvɜːb] n adverbe m
adverse ['ædvɜːs] adj défavorable, contraire
advert ['ædvɜːt] (*BRIT*) n abbr = **advertisement**
advertise ['ædvətaɪz] vi(vt) faire de la publicité (pour); mettre une annonce (pour vendre); **to** ~ **for** (*staff, accommodation*) faire paraître une annonce pour trouver; ~**ment** [əd'vɜːtɪsmənt] n (*COMM*) réclame f, publicité f; (*in classified ads*) annonce f; ~**r** ['ædvətaɪzə*] n (*in newspaper etc*) annonceur m; **advertising** ['ædvətaɪzɪŋ] n publicité f
advice [əd'vaɪs] n conseils mpl; (*notification*) avis m; **piece of** ~ conseil; **to take legal** ~ consulter un avocat
advisable [əd'vaɪzəbl] adj conseillé(e), indiqué(e)
advise [əd'vaɪz] vt conseiller; **to** ~ **sb of sth** aviser or informer qn de qch; **to** ~ **against sth/doing sth** déconseiller qch/ conseiller de ne pas faire qch; ~**dly** [əd'vaɪzədlɪ] adv (*deliberately*) délibérément; ~**r** n conseiller(ère); **advisory** [əd'vaɪzərɪ] adj consultatif(ive)
advocate [vb 'ædvəkeɪt, n 'ædvəkət] n (*upholder*) défenseur m, avocat(e), partisan(e); (*LAW*) avocat(e) ♦ vt recommander, prôner
aerial ['ɛərɪəl] n antenne f ♦ adj aérien(ne)
aerobics [ɛər'əubɪks] n aérobic f
aeroplane ['ɛərəpleɪn] (*BRIT*) n avion m
aerosol ['ɛərəsɒl] n aérosol m
aesthetic [ɪs'θetɪk] adj esthétique
afar [ə'fɑː*] adv: **from** ~ de loin
affair [ə'fɛə*] n affaire f; (*also: love* ~) liaison f, aventure f
affect [ə'fekt] vt affecter; (*disease*) atteindre; ~**ed** adj affecté(e)
affection [ə'fekʃən] n affection f, ~**ate** [ə'fekʃənɪt] adj affectueux(euse)
affinity [ə'fɪnɪtɪ] n (*bond, rapport*): **to have**

an ~ **with/for** avoir une affinité avec/pour; (*resemblance*): **to have an** ~ **with** avoir une ressemblance avec
afflict [ə'flɪkt] vt affliger
affluence ['æfluəns] n abondance f, opulence f
affluent ['æfluənt] adj (*person, family, surroundings*) aisé(e), riche; **the** ~ **society** la société d'abondance
afford [ə'fɔːd] vt se permettre; avoir les moyens d'acheter or d'entretenir; (*provide*) fournir, procurer
afield [ə'fiːld] adv: (**from**) **far** ~ (de) loin
afloat [ə'fləut] adj, adv à flot; **to stay** ~ surnager
afoot [ə'fut] adv: **there is something** ~ il se prépare quelque chose
afraid [ə'freɪd] adj effrayé(e); **to be** ~ **of** or **to** avoir peur de; **I am** ~ **that ...** je suis désolé(e), mais ...; **I am** ~ **so/not** hélas oui/non
afresh [ə'freʃ] adv de nouveau
Africa ['æfrɪkə] n Afrique f, ~**n** adj africain(e) ♦ n Africain(e)
aft [ɑːft] adv à l'arrière, vers l'arrière
after ['ɑːftə*] prep, adv après ♦ conj après que, après avoir or être +pp; **what/who are you** ~? que/qui cherchez-vous?; ~ **he left/having done** après qu'il fut parti/après avoir fait; **ask** ~ **him** demandez de ses nouvelles; **to name sb** ~ **sb** donner à qn le nom de qn; **twenty** ~ **eight** (*US*) huit heures vingt; ~ **all** après tout; ~ **you!** après vous, Monsieur (or Madame etc); ~-**effects** npl (*of disaster, radiation, drink etc*) répercussions fpl; (*of illness*) séquelles fpl, suites fpl; ~**math** n conséquences fpl, suites fpl; ~**noon** n après-midi m or f; ~**s** (*inf*) n (*dessert*) dessert m; ~-**sales service** (*BRIT*) n (*for car, washing machine etc*) service m après-vente; ~-**shave (lotion)** n after-shave m; ~**thought** n: **I had an** ~**thought** il m'est venu une idée après coup; ~**wards** (*US* ~**ward**) adv après
again [ə'gen] adv de nouveau; encore (une fois); **to do sth** ~ refaire qch; **not ...** ~ ne ... plus; ~ **and** ~ à plusieurs reprises
against [ə'genst] prep contre; (*compared to*) par rapport à
age [eɪdʒ] n âge m ♦ vt, vi vieillir; **it's been** ~**s since** ça fait une éternité que ... ne; **he is 20 years of** ~ il a 20 ans; **to come of** ~ atteindre sa majorité; ~**d¹** adj: ~**d 10** âgé(e) de 10 ans; ~**d²** ['eɪdʒɪd] npl: **the** ~**d** les personnes âgées; ~ **group** n tranche f d'âge; ~ **limit** n limite f d'âge
agency ['eɪdʒənsɪ] n agence f; (*government body*) organisme m, office m
agenda [ə'dʒendə] n ordre m du jour
agent ['eɪdʒənt] n agent m, représentant m; (*firm*) concessionnaire m
aggravate ['ægrəveɪt] vt aggraver; (*annoy*)

exaspérer

aggregate ['ægrɪgɪt] *n* ensemble *m*, total *m*

aggressive [ə'gresɪv] *adj* agressif(ive)

aggrieved [ə'griːvd] *adj* chagriné(e), affligé(e)

aghast [ə'gɑːst] *adj* consterné(e), atterré(e)

agitate ['ædʒɪteɪt] *vt* (*person*) agiter, émouvoir, troubler ♦ *vi*: **to ~ for/against** faire campagne pour/contre

AGM *n abbr* (= *annual general meeting*) AG *f*, assemblée générale

ago [ə'gəʊ] *adv*: **2 days ~** il y a deux jours; **not long ~** il n'y a pas longtemps; **how long ~?** il y a combien de temps (de cela)?

agog [ə'gɒg] *adj* en émoi

agonizing ['ægənaɪzɪŋ] *adj* angoissant(e); déchirant(e)

agony ['ægənɪ] *n* (*pain*) douleur *f* atroce; **to be in ~** souffrir le martyre

agree [ə'griː] *vt* (*price*) convenir de ♦ *vi*: **to ~ with** (*person*) être d'accord avec; (*statements etc*) concorder avec; (*LING*) s'accorder avec; **to ~ to do** accepter le *or* consentir à faire; **to ~ to sth** consentir à qch; **to ~ that** (*admit*) convenir *or* reconnaître que; **garlic doesn't ~ with me** je ne supporte pas l'ail; **~able** *adj* agréable; (*willing*) consentant(e), d'accord; **~d** *adj* (*time, place*) convenu(e); **~ment** *n* accord *m*; **in ~ment** d'accord

agricultural [ægrɪ'kʌltʃərəl] *adj* agricole

agriculture ['ægrɪkʌltʃə*] *n* agriculture *f*

aground [ə'graʊnd] *adv*: **to run ~** échouer, s'échouer

ahead [ə'hed] *adv* (*in front: of position, place*) devant; (: *at the head*) en avant; (*look, plan, think*) en avant; **~ of** devant; (*fig: schedule etc*) en avance sur; **~ of time** en avance; **go right** *or* **straight ~** allez tout droit; **go ~!** (*fig: permission*) allez-y!

aid [eɪd] *n* aide *f*; (*device*) appareil *m* ♦ *vt* aider; **in ~ of** en faveur de; **to ~ and abet** (*LAW*) se faire le complice de; *see also* **hearing**

aide [eɪd] *n* (*person*) aide *mf*, assistant(e)

AIDS [eɪdz] *n abbr* (= *acquired immune deficiency syndrome*) SIDA *m*

ailing ['eɪlɪŋ] *adj* malade

ailment ['eɪlmənt] *n* affection *f*

aim [eɪm] *vt*: **to ~ sth (at)** (*gun, camera*) braquer *or* pointer qch (sur); (*missile*) lancer qch (à *or* contre *or* en direction de); (*blow*) allonger qch (à); (*remark*) destiner *or* adresser qch (à) ♦ *vi* (*also: to take ~*) viser ♦ *n* but *m*; (*skill*): **his ~ is bad** il vise mal; **to ~ at** viser; (*fig*) viser (à); **to ~ to do** avoir l'intention de faire; **~less** *adj* sans but

ain't [eɪnt] (*inf*) = **am not; aren't; isn't**

air [ɛə*] *n* air *m* ♦ *vt* (*room, bed, clothes*) aérer; (*grievances, views, ideas*) exposer, faire connaître ♦ *cpd* (*currents, attack etc*) aérien(ne); **to throw sth into the ~** jeter qch en l'air; **by ~** (*travel*) par avion; **to be on the ~** (*RADIO, TV: programme*) être diffusé(e); (: *station*) diffuser; **~bed** *n* matelas *m* pneumatique; **~borne** *adj* en vol; **~-conditioned** *adj* climatisé(e); **~ conditioning** *n* climatisation *f*; **~craft** *n inv* avion *m*; **~craft carrier** *n* porte-avions *m inv*; **~field** *n* terrain *m* d'aviation; **A~ Force** *n* armée *f* de l'air; **~ freshener** *n* désodorisant *m*; **~gun** *n* fusil *m* à air comprimé; **~ hostess** *n* (*BRIT*) hôtesse *f* de l'air; **~letter** *n* (*BRIT*) aérogramme *m*; **~lift** *n* pont aérien; **~line** *n* ligne aérienne, compagnie *f* d'aviation; **~liner** *n* avion *m* de ligne; **~mail** *n*: **by ~mail** par avion; **~plane** *n* (*US*) avion *m*; **~port** *n* aéroport *m*; **~ raid** *n* attaque *or* raid aérien(ne); **~sick** *adj*: **to be ~sick** avoir le mal de l'air; **air space** espace aérien; **~ terminal** *n* aérogare *f*; **~tight** *adj* hermétique; **~-traffic controller** *n* aiguilleur *m* du ciel; **~y** *adj* bien aéré(e); (*manners*) dégagé(e)

aisle [aɪl] *n* (*of church*) allée centrale; nef latérale; (*of theatre etc*) couloir *m*, passage *m*, allée

ajar [ə'dʒɑː*] *adj* entrouvert(e)

akin [ə'kɪn] *adj*: **~ to** (*similar*) qui tient de *or* ressemble à

alarm [ə'lɑːm] *n* alarme *f* ♦ *vt* alarmer; **~ call** *n* coup de fil *m* pour réveiller; **~ clock** *n* réveille-matin *m inv*, réveil *m*

alas [ə'læs] *excl* hélas!

albeit [ɔːl'biːɪt] *conj* (*although*) bien que +*sub*, encore que +*sub*

album ['ælbəm] *n* album *m*

alcohol ['ælkəhɒl] *n* alcool *m*; **~ic** [ælkə'hɒlɪk] *adj* alcoolique ♦ *n* alcoolique *m/f*; **A~ics Anonymous** Alcooliques anonymes

ale [eɪl] *n* bière *f*

alert [ə'lɜːt] *adj* alerte, vif(vive); vigilant(e) ♦ *n* alerte *f* ♦ *vt* alerter; **on the ~** sur le qui-vive; (*MIL*) en état d'alerte

algebra ['ældʒɪbrə] *n* algèbre *f*

Algeria [æl'dʒɪərɪə] *n* Algérie *f*

alias ['eɪlɪəs] *adv* alias ♦ *n* faux nom, nom d'emprunt; (*writer*) pseudonyme *m*

alibi ['ælɪbaɪ] *n* alibi *m*

alien ['eɪlɪən] *n* étranger(ère); (*from outer space*) extraterrestre *mf* ♦ *adj*: **~ (to)** étranger(ère) (à); **~ate** *vt* aliéner; s'aliéner

alight [ə'laɪt] *adj, adv* en feu ♦ *vi* mettre pied à terre; (*passenger*) descendre; (*bird*) se poser

alike [ə'laɪk] *adj* semblable, pareil(le) ♦ *adv* de même; **to look ~** se ressembler

alimony ['ælɪmənɪ] *n* (*payment*) pension *f* alimentaire

alive [ə'laɪv] *adj* vivant(e); (*lively*) plein(e) de vie

─────── *KEYWORD* ───────

all [ɔːl] *adj* (*singular*) tout(e); (*plural*) tous(toutes); ~ **day** toute la journée; ~ **night** toute la nuit; ~ **men** tous les hommes; ~ **five** tous les cinq; ~ **the food** toute la nourriture; ~ **the books** tous les livres; ~ **the time** tout le temps; ~ **his life** toute sa vie
♦ *pron 1* tout; **I ate it ~, I ate ~ of it** j'ai tout mangé; ~ **of us went** nous y sommes tous allés; ~ **of the boys went** tous les garçons y sont allés
2 (*in phrases*): **above ~** surtout, par-dessus tout; **after ~** après tout; **at ~: not at ~** (*in answer to question*) pas du tout; (*in answer to thanks*) je vous en prie!; **I'm not at ~ tired** je ne suis pas du tout fatigué(e); **anything at ~ will do** n'importe quoi fera l'affaire; ~ **in** tout bien considéré, en fin de compte
♦ *adv*: ~ **alone** tout(e) seul(e); **it's not as hard as** ~ **that** ce n'est pas si difficile que ça; ~ **the more/the better** d'autant plus/mieux; ~ **but** presque, pratiquement; **the score is 2** ~ le score est de 2 partout

allay [əˈleɪ] *vt* (*fears*) apaiser, calmer
allege [əˈledʒ] *vt* alléguer, prétendre; ~**dly** [əˈledʒɪdlɪ] *adv* à ce que l'on prétend, paraît-il
allegiance [əˈliːdʒəns] *n* allégeance *f*, fidélité *f*, obéissance *f*
allergic [əˈlɜːdʒɪk] *adj*: ~ **to** allergique à; **allergy** [ˈælədʒɪ] *n* allergie *f*
alleviate [əˈliːvɪeɪt] *vt* soulager, adoucir
alley [ˈælɪ] *n* ruelle *f*
alliance [əˈlaɪəns] *n* alliance *f*
allied [ˈælaɪd] *adj* allié(e)
all-in [ˈɔːlɪn] (*BRIT*) *adj* (*also adv*: *charge*) tout compris; ~ **wrestling** *n* lutte *f* libre
all-night [ɔːlˈnaɪt] *adj* ouvert(e) *or* qui dure toute la nuit
allocate [ˈæləkeɪt] *vt* (*share out*) répartir, distribuer; (*duties*) **to** ~ **sth to** assigner *or* attribuer qch à; (*sum, time*) **to** ~ **sth to** allouer qch à
allot [əˈlɒt] *vt*: **to** ~ (**to**) (*money*) répartir (entre), distribuer (à); (*time*) allouer (à); ~**ment** *n* (*share*) part *f*; (*garden*) lopin *m* de terre (*loué à la municipalité*)
all-out [ˈɔːlˈaʊt] *adj* (*effort etc*) total(e) ♦ *adv*: **all out** à fond
allow [əˈlaʊ] *vt* (*practice, behaviour*) permettre, autoriser; (*sum to spend etc*) accorder; allouer; (*sum, time estimated*) compter, prévoir; (*claim, goal*) admettre; (*concede*): **to** ~ **that** convenir que; **to** ~ **sb to do** permettre à qn de faire, autoriser qn à faire; **he is** ~**ed to ...** on lui permet de ...; ~ **for** *vt fus* tenir compte de; ~**ance** *n* (*money received*) allocation *f*; subside *m*; indemnité *f*;

(*TAX*) somme *f* déductible du revenu imposable, abattement *m*; **to make** ~**ances for** tenir compte de
alloy [ˈælɔɪ] *n* alliage *m*
all: ~ **right** *adv* (*feel, work*) bien; (*as answer*) d'accord; ~**-rounder** *n*: **to be a good** ~**-rounder** être doué(e) en tout; ~**-time** *adj* (*record*) sans précédent, absolu(e)
allude [əˈluːd] *vi*: **to** ~ **to** faire allusion à
alluring [əˈljʊərɪŋ] *adj* séduisant(e)
ally [*n* ˈælaɪ, *vb* əˈlaɪ] *n* allié *m* ♦ *vt*: **to** ~ **o.s. with** s'allier avec
almighty [ɔːlˈmaɪtɪ] *adj* tout-puissant; (*tremendous*) énorme
almond [ˈɑːmənd] *n* amande *f*
almost [ˈɔːlməʊst] *adv* presque
alms [ɑːmz] *npl* aumône *f*
aloft [əˈlɒft] *adv* en l'air
alone [əˈləʊn] *adj, adv* seul(e); **to leave sb** ~ laisser qn tranquille; **to leave sth** ~ ne pas toucher à qch; **let** ~ ... sans parler de ...; encore moins ...
along [əˈlɒŋ] *prep* le long de ♦ *adv*: **is he coming** ~ **with us?** vient-il avec nous?; **he was hopping/limping** ~ il avançait en sautillant/boitant; ~ **with** (*together with*: *person*) en compagnie de; (: *thing*) avec, en plus de; **all** ~ (*all the time*) depuis le début; ~**side** *prep* le long de; à côté de ♦ *adv* bord à bord
aloof [əˈluːf] *adj* distant(e) ♦ *adv*: **to stand** ~ se tenir à distance *or* à l'écart
aloud [əˈlaʊd] *adv* à haute voix
alphabet [ˈælfəbet] *n* alphabet *m*; ~**ical** [ælfəˈbetɪkl] *adj* alphabétique
alpine [ˈælpaɪn] *adj* alpin(e), alpestre
Alps [ælps] *npl*: **the** ~ les Alpes *fpl*
already [ɔːlˈredɪ] *adv* déjà
alright [ˈɔːlˈraɪt] (*BRIT*) *adv* = **all right**
Alsatian [ælˈseɪʃən] (*BRIT*) *n* (*dog*) berger allemand
also [ˈɔːlsəʊ] *adv* aussi
altar [ˈɔːltə*] *n* autel *m*
alter [ˈɔːltə*] *vt, vi* changer
alternate [*adj* ɒlˈtɜːnɪt, *vb* ɒltɜːneɪt] *adj* alterné(e), alternant(e), alternatif(ive) ♦ *vi* alterner; **on** ~ **days** un jour sur deux, tous les deux jours; **alternating current** *n* courant alternatif
alternative [ɒlˈtɜːnətɪv] *adj* (*solutions*) possible, au choix; (*plan*) autre, de rechange; (*lifestyle, medicine*) parallèle ♦ *n* (*choice*) alternative *f*; (*other possibility*) solution *f* de remplacement *or* de rechange, autre possibilité *f*; **an** ~ **comedian** un nouveau comique; ~**ly** *adv*: ~**ly one could** une autre *or* l'autre solution serait de, on pourrait aussi
alternator [ˈɒltɜːneɪtə*] *n* (*AUT*) alternateur *m*
although [ɔːlˈðəʊ] *conj* bien que +*sub*
altitude [ˈæltɪtjuːd] *n* altitude *f*
alto [ˈæltəʊ] *n* (*female*) contralto *m*; (*male*)

haute-contre f
altogether [ɔːltəˈgeðə*] *adv* entièrement,
tout à fait; *(on the whole)* tout compte fait;
(in all) en tout
aluminium [æljuˈmɪnɪəm] *(BRIT)*, **aluminum** [əˈluːmɪnəm] *(US)* n aluminium m
always [ˈɔːlweɪz] *adv* toujours
Alzheimer's (disease) [ælts'haɪməz] *n*
maladie f d'Alzheimer
am [æm] *vb see* be
a.m. *adv abbr* (= *ante meridiem*) du matin
amalgamate [əˈmælgəmeɪt] *vt, vi* fusionner
amateur [ˈæmətə:*] *n* amateur *m*; ~**ish**
(pej) adj d'amateur
amaze [əˈmeɪz] *vt* stupéfier; **to be** ~**d (at)**
être stupéfait(e) (de); ~**ment** *n* stupéfac-
tion f, stupeur f; **amazing** [əˈmeɪzɪŋ] *adj*
étonnant(e); exceptionnel(le)
ambassador [æmˈbæsədə*] *n* ambassadeur
m
amber [ˈæmbə*] *n* ambre *m*; **at** ~ *(BRIT:
AUT)* à l'orange
ambiguous [æmˈbɪgjuəs] *adj* ambigu(ë)
ambition [æmˈbɪʃən] *n* ambition f
ambitious [æmˈbɪʃəs] *adj* ambitieux(euse)
amble [ˈæmbl] *vi (also:* to ~ **along)** aller
d'un pas tranquille
ambulance [ˈæmbjuləns] *n* ambulance f
ambush [ˈæmbuʃ] *n* embuscade f ♦ *vt* tendre une embuscade à
amenable [əˈmiːnəbl] *adj:* ~ **to** *(advice etc)*
disposé(e) à écouter
amend [əˈmend] *vt (law)* amender; *(text)*
corriger; **to make** ~**s** réparer ses torts, faire
amende honorable
amenities [əˈmiːnɪtɪz] *npl* aménagements
mpl, équipements *mpl*
America [əˈmerɪkə] *n* Amérique f; ~**n** *adj*
américain(e) ♦ *n* Américain(e)
amiable [ˈeɪmɪəbl] *adj* aimable, affable
amicable [ˈæmɪkəbl] *adj* amical(e); *(JUR)* à
l'amiable
amid(st) [əˈmɪd(st)] *prep* parmi, au milieu
de
amiss [əˈmɪs] *adj, adv:* **there's something**
~ il y a quelque chose qui ne va pas *or*
qui cloche; **to take sth** ~ prendre qch mal
or de travers
ammonia [əˈməunɪə] *n (gas)* ammoniac *m*;
(liquid) ammoniaque f
ammunition [æmjuˈnɪʃən] *n* munitions *fpl*
amok [əˈmɔk] *adv:* **to run** ~ être pris(e)
d'un accès de folie furieuse
among(st) [əˈmʌŋ(st)] *prep* parmi, entre
amorous [ˈæmərəs] *adj* amoureux(euse)
amount [əˈmaunt] *n (sum)* somme f, montant *m*; *(quantity)* quantité f, nombre *m* ♦
vi: **to** ~ **to** *(total)* s'élever à; *(be same as)*
équivaloir à, revenir à
amp(ere) [ˈæmp(εə*)] *n* ampère *m*
ample [ˈæmpl] *adj* ample; spacieux(euse);
(enough): **this is** ~ c'est largement suffi-

sant; **to have** ~ **time/room** avoir bien assez de temps/place
amplifier [ˈæmplɪfaɪə*] *n* amplificateur *m*
amuse [əˈmjuːz] *vt* amuser, divertir;
~**ment** *n* amusement *m*; ~**ment arcade**
n salle f de jeu
an [æn] *indef art see* a
anaemic [əˈniːmɪk] *(US* **anemic)** *adj* anémique
anaesthetic [ænɪs'θetɪk] *n* anesthésique *m*
analog(ue) [ˈænəlɔg] *adj (watch, computer)*
analogique
analyse [ˈænəlaɪz] *(US* **analyze)** *vt* analyser;
analysis [əˈnælɪsɪs] *(pl* **analyses)** *n* analyse
f; **analyst** [ˈænəlɪst] *n (POL etc)* spécialiste
m/f; *(US)* psychanalyste *m/f*
analyze [ˈænəlaɪz] *(US) vt* = **analyse**
anarchist [ˈænəkɪst] *n* anarchiste *m/f*
anarchy [ˈænəkɪ] *n* anarchie f
anatomy [əˈnætəmɪ] *n* anatomie f
ancestor [ˈænsestə*] *n* ancêtre *m*, aïeul *m*
anchor [ˈæŋkə*] *n* ancre f ♦ *vi (also:* to
drop ~) jeter l'ancre, mouiller ♦ *vt* mettre à
l'ancre; *(fig):* **to** ~ **sth to** fixer qch à; **to
weigh** ~ lever l'ancre
anchovy [ˈæntʃəvɪ] *n* anchois *m*
ancient [ˈeɪnʃənt] *adj* ancien(ne), antique;
(person) d'un âge vénérable; *(car)* antédilu-
vien(ne)
ancillary [ænˈsɪlərɪ] *adj* auxiliaire
and [ænd] *conj* et; ~ **so on** et ainsi de suite; **try** ~ **come** tâchez de venir; **he talked**
~ **talked** il n'a pas arrêté de parler; **better**
~ **better** de mieux en mieux
anew [əˈnjuː] *adv* à nouveau
angel [ˈeɪndʒəl] *n* ange *m*
anger [ˈæŋgə*] *n* colère f
angina [ænˈdʒaɪnə] *n* angine f de poitrine
angle [ˈæŋgl] *n* angle *m*; **from their** ~ de
leur point de vue
angler [ˈæŋglə*] *n* pêcheur(euse) à la ligne
Anglican [ˈæŋglɪkən] *adj, n* anglican(e)
angling [ˈæŋglɪŋ] *n* pêche f à la ligne
angrily [ˈæŋgrɪlɪ] *adv* avec colère
angry [ˈæŋgrɪ] *adj* en colère, furieux(euse);
(wound) enflammé(e); **to be** ~ **with sb/at**
sth être furieux contre qn/de qch; **to get**
~ se fâcher, se mettre en colère
anguish [ˈæŋgwɪʃ] *n (physical)* supplice *m*;
(mental) angoisse f
angular [ˈæŋgjulə*] *adj* anguleux(euse)
animal [ˈænɪməl] *n* animal *m* ♦ *adj* ani-
mal(e)
animate [*vb* 'ænɪmeɪt, *adj* 'ænɪmət] *vt* animer ♦ *adj* animé(e), vivant(e); ~**d** *adj* ani-
mé(e)
aniseed [ˈænɪsiːd] *n* anis *m*
ankle [ˈæŋkl] *n* cheville f; ~ **sock** *n* socquette f
annex [*n* 'æneks, *vb* ə'neks] *n (also: BRIT:*
~**e)** annexe f ♦ *vt* annexer
anniversary [ænɪ'vɜːsərɪ] *n* anniversaire *m*

announce [ə'naʊns] vt annoncer; (birth, death) faire part de; ~**ment** n annonce f; (for births etc: in newspaper) avis m de faire-part; (: letter, card) faire-part m; ~**r** n (RADIO, TV: between programmes) speaker(ine)

annoy [ə'nɔɪ] vt agacer, ennuyer, contrarier; **don't get** ~**ed!** ne vous fâchez pas!; ~**ance** n mécontentement m, contrariété f; ~**ing** adj agaçant(e), contrariant(e)

annual ['ænjuəl] adj annuel(le) ♦ n (BOT) plante annuelle; (children's book) album m

annul [ə'nʌl] vt annuler

annum ['ænəm] n see per

anonymous [ə'nɒnɪməs] adj anonyme

anorak ['ænəræk] n anorak m

another [ə'nʌðə*] adj: ~ **book** (one more) un autre livre, encore un livre, un livre de plus; (a different one) un autre livre ♦ pron un(e) autre, encore un(e), un(e) de plus; see also **one**

answer ['ɑːnsə*] n réponse f; (to problem) solution f ♦ vi répondre ♦ vt (reply to) répondre à; (problem) résoudre; (prayer) exaucer; **in** ~ **to your letter** en réponse à votre lettre; **to** ~ **the phone** répondre (au téléphone); **to** ~ **the bell** or **the door** aller or venir ouvrir (la porte); ~ **back** vi répondre, répliquer; ~ **for** vt fus (person) répondre de, se porter garant de; (crime, one's actions) être responsable de; ~ **to** vt fus (description) répondre or correspondre à; ~**able** adj: ~**able** (**to sb/for sth**) responsable (devant qn/de qch); ~**ing machine** n répondeur m automatique

ant [ænt] n fourmi f

antagonism [æn'tægənɪzəm] n antagonisme m

antagonize [æn'tægənaɪz] vt éveiller l'hostilité de, contrarier

Antarctic [ænt'ɑːktɪk] n: **the** ~ l'Antarctique m

antenatal [æntɪ'neɪtl] adj prénatal(e); ~ **clinic** n service m de consultation prénatale

anthem ['ænθəm] n: **national** ~ hymne national

anti: ~-**aircraft** [æntɪ'ɛəkrɑːft] adj (missile) anti-aérien(ne); ~**biotic** ['æntɪbaɪ'ɒtɪk] n antibiotique m; ~**body** ['æntɪbɒdɪ] n anticorps m

anticipate [æn'tɪsɪpeɪt] vt s'attendre à; prévoir; (wishes, request) aller au devant de, devancer

anticipation [æntɪsɪ'peɪʃən] n attente f; **with** ~ impatiemment

anticlimax ['æntɪ'klaɪmæks] n déception f, douche froide (col)

anticlockwise ['æntɪ'klɒkwaɪz] adj, adv dans le sens inverse des aiguilles d'une montre

antics ['æntɪks] npl singeries fpl

antifreeze ['æntɪfriːz] n antigel m

antihistamine [æntɪ'hɪstəmiːn] n antihistaminique m

antiquated ['æntɪkweɪtɪd] adj vieilli(e), suranné(e), vieillot(te)

antique [æn'tiːk] n objet m d'art ancien, meuble ancien or d'époque, antiquité f ♦ adj ancien(ne); ~ **dealer** n antiquaire m; ~ **shop** n magasin m d'antiquités

anti: ~**Semitism** [æntɪ'semɪtɪzəm] n antisémitisme m; ~**septic** [æntɪ'septɪk] n antiseptique m; ~**social** [æntɪ'səʊʃl] adj peu liant(e), sauvage, insociable; (against society) antisocial(e)

antlers ['æntləz] npl bois mpl, ramure f

anvil ['ænvɪl] n enclume f

anxiety [æŋ'zaɪətɪ] n anxiété f; (keenness): ~ **to do** grand désir or impatience f de faire

anxious ['æŋkʃəs] adj anxieux(euse), angoissé(e); (worrying: time, situation) inquiétant(e); (keen): ~ **to do/that** qui tient beaucoup à faire/à ce que; impatient(e) de faire/que

---

KEYWORD

any ['enɪ] adj **1** (in questions etc: singular) du, de l', de la; (in questions etc: plural) des; **have you** ~ **butter/children/ink?** avez-vous du beurre/des enfants/de l'encre?

2 (with negative) de, d'; **I haven't** ~ **money/books** je n'ai pas d'argent/de livres

3 (no matter which) n'importe quel(le); **choose** ~ **book you like** vous pouvez choisir n'importe quel livre

4 (in phrases): **in** ~ **case** de toute façon; ~ **day now** d'un jour à l'autre; **at** ~ **moment** à tout moment, d'un instant à l'autre; **at** ~ **rate** en tout cas

♦ pron **1** (in questions etc) en; **have you got** ~? est-ce que vous en avez?; **can** ~ **of you sing?** est-ce que parmi vous il y en a qui chantent?

2 (with negative) en; **I haven't** ~ (**of them**) je n'en ai pas, je n'en ai aucun

3 (no matter which one(s)) n'importe lequel (or laquelle); **take** ~ **of those books** (**you like**) vous pouvez prendre n'importe lequel de ces livres

♦ adv **1** (in questions etc): **do you want** ~ **more soup/sandwiches?** voulez-vous encore de la soupe/des sandwichs?; **are you feeling** ~ **better?** est-ce que vous vous sentez mieux?

2 (with negative): **I can't hear him** ~ **more** je ne l'entends plus; **don't wait** ~ **longer** n'attendez pas plus longtemps

---

any: ~**body** ['enɪbɒdɪ] pron n'importe qui; (in interrogative sentences) quelqu'un; (in negative sentences): **I don't see** ~ je ne vois personne; **~how** adv (at any rate) de toute façon, quand même; (haphazard) n'importe comment; **~one** [-wʌn] pron = anybody; **~thing** pron n'importe quoi, quelque chose, ne ... rien; **~way** adv de toute façon; **~where** adv n'importe où, quelque part; **I don't see him ~** je ne le vois nulle part

apart [ə'pɑːt] adv (to one side) à part; de côté; à l'écart; (separately) séparément; **10 miles ~** à 10 miles l'un de l'autre; **to take ~** démonter; **~ from** à part, excepté

apartheid [ə'pɑːtheɪt] n apartheid m

apartment [ə'pɑːtmənt] n (US) appartement m, logement m; (room) chambre f; **~ building** (US) n immeuble m; maison divisée en appartements

ape [eɪp] n (grand) singe ♦ vt singer

apéritif [ə'perɪtiːf] n apéritif m

aperture ['æpətjuə*] n orifice m, ouverture f; (PHOT) ouverture (du diaphragme)

apex ['eɪpeks] n sommet m

apiece [ə'piːs] adv chacun(e)

apologetic [əpɒlə'dʒetɪk] adj (tone, letter) d'excuse; (person): **to be ~** s'excuser

apologize [ə'pɒlədʒaɪz] vi: **to ~ (for sth to sb)** s'excuser (de qch auprès de qn), présenter des excuses (à qn pour qch)

apology [ə'pɒlədʒɪ] n excuses fpl

apostrophe [ə'pɒstrəfɪ] n apostrophe f

appal [ə'pɔːl] vt consterner; **~ling** [ə'pɔːlɪŋ] adj épouvantable; (stupidity) consternant(e)

apparatus [æpə'reɪtəs] n appareil m, dispositif m; (in gymnasium) agrès mpl; (of government) dispositif m

apparel [ə'pærəl] (US) n habillement m

apparent [ə'pærənt] adj apparent(e); **~ly** adv apparemment

appeal [ə'piːl] vi (LAW) faire or interjeter appel ♦ n (request) prière f; appel m; (charm) attrait m, charme m; **to ~** for lancer un appel pour; **to ~ to** (beg) faire appel à; (be attractive) plaire à; **it doesn't ~ to me** cela ne m'attire pas; **~ing** adj (attractive) attrayant(e)

appear [ə'pɪə*] vi apparaître, se montrer; (LAW) comparaître; (publication) paraître, sortir, être publié(e); (seem) paraître, sembler; **it would ~ that** il semble que; **to ~ in Hamlet** jouer dans Hamlet; **to ~ on TV** passer à la télé; **~ance** n apparition f; parution f; (look, aspect) apparence f, aspect m

appease [ə'piːz] vt apaiser, calmer

appendicitis [əpendɪ'saɪtɪs] n appendicite f; **appendix** [ə'pendɪks] (pl **appendices**) n appendice m

appetite ['æpɪtaɪt] n appétit m

appetizer ['æpɪtaɪzə*] n amuse-gueule m; (drink) apéritif m

applaud [ə'plɔːd] vt, vi applaudir

applause [ə'plɔːz] n applaudissements mpl

apple ['æpl] n pomme f; **~ tree** n pommier m

appliance [ə'plaɪəns] n appareil m

applicable [ə'plɪkəbl] adj (relevant): **to be ~ to** valoir pour

applicant ['æplɪkənt] n: **~ (for)** candidat(e) (à)

application [æplɪ'keɪʃən] n application f; (for a job, a grant etc) demande f; candidature f; **~ form** n formulaire m de demande

applied [ə'plaɪd] adj appliqué(e)

apply [ə'plaɪ] vt (paint, ointment): **to ~ (to)** appliquer (sur); (law etc): **to ~ (to)** appliquer (à) ♦ vi: **to ~ to** (be suitable for, relevant to) s'appliquer à; (ask) s'adresser à; **to ~ (for)** (permit, grant) faire une demande (en vue d'obtenir); (job) poser sa candidature (pour), faire une demande d'emploi (concernant); **to ~ o.s. to** s'appliquer à

appoint [ə'pɔɪnt] vt nommer, engager; **~ed** adj: **at the ~ed time** à l'heure dite; **~ment** n nomination f; (meeting) rendezvous m; **to make an ~ment (with)** prendre rendez-vous (avec)

appraisal [ə'preɪzl] n évaluation f

appreciate [ə'priːʃɪeɪt] vt (like) apprécier; (be grateful for) être reconnaissant(e) de; (understand) comprendre; se rendre compte de ♦ vi (FINANCE) prendre de la valeur

appreciation [əpriːʃɪ'eɪʃən] n appréciation f; (gratitude) reconnaissance f; (COMM) hausse f, valorisation f

appreciative [ə'priːʃɪətɪv] adj (person) sensible; (comment) élogieux(euse)

apprehensive [æprɪ'hensɪv] adj inquiet(ète), appréhensif(ive)

apprentice [ə'prentɪs] n apprenti m; **~ship** n apprentissage m

approach [ə'prəʊtʃ] vi approcher ♦ vt (come near) approcher de; (ask, apply to) s'adresser à; (situation, problem) aborder ♦ n approche f; (access) accès m; **~able** adj accessible

appropriate [adj ə'prəʊprɪət, vb ə'prəʊprɪeɪt] adj (moment, remark) opportun(e); (tool etc) approprié(e) ♦ vt (take) s'approprier

approval [ə'pruːvəl] n approbation f; **on ~** à l'examen

approve [ə'pruːv] vt approuver; **~ of** vt fus approuver

approximate [adj ə'prɒksɪmɪt, vb ə'prɒksɪmeɪt] adj approximatif(ive) ♦ vt se rapprocher de, être proche de; **~ly** adv approximativement

apricot ['eɪprɪkɒt] n abricot m

April ['eɪprəl] n avril m; **~ Fool's Day** le premier avril

apron ['eɪprən] n tablier m

apt [æpt] adj (suitable) approprié(e); (likely): **~ to do** susceptible de faire; qui a tendance à faire

Aquarius [əˈkwɛərɪəs] *n* le Verseau
Arab [ˈærəb] *adj* arabe ♦ *n* Arabe *m/f*; **~ian** [əˈreɪbɪən] *adj* arabe; **~ic** [ˈærəbɪk] *adj* arabe ♦ *n* arabe *m*
arbitrary [ˈɑːbɪtrərɪ] *adj* arbitraire
arbitration [ɑːbɪˈtreɪʃən] *n* arbitrage *m*
arcade [ɑːˈkeɪd] *n* arcade *f*; (*passage with shops*) passage *m*, galerie marchande
arch [ɑːtʃ] *n* arc *m*; (*of foot*) cambrure *f*, voûte *f* plantaire ♦ *vt* arquer, cambrer
archaeologist [ɑːkɪˈɒlədʒɪst] *n* archéologue *m/f*; **archaeology** [ɑːkɪˈɒlədʒɪ] *n* archéologie *f*
archbishop [ˈɑːtʃˈbɪʃəp] *n* archevêque *m*
archenemy [ˈɑːtʃˈenɪmɪ] *n* ennemi *m* de toujours *or* juré
archeology *etc* (*US*) = **archaeology** *etc*
archery [ˈɑːtʃərɪ] *n* tir *m* à l'arc
architect [ˈɑːkɪtekt] *n* architecte *m*; **~ure** *n* architecture *f*
archives [ˈɑːkaɪvz] *npl* archives *fpl*
Arctic [ˈɑːktɪk] *adj* arctique ♦ *n*: **the ~** l'Arctique *m*
ardent [ˈɑːdənt] *adj* fervent(e)
are [ɑː*] *vb see* **be**
area [ˈɛərɪə] *n* (*GEOM*) superficie *f*; (*zone*) région *f*; (: *smaller*) secteur *m*, partie *f*; (*in room*) coin *m*; (*knowledge, research*) domaine *m*
aren't [ɑːnt] = **are not**
Argentina [ɑːdʒənˈtiːnə] *n* Argentine *f*; **Argentinian** [ɑːdʒənˈtɪnɪən] *adj* argentin(e) ♦ *n* Argentin(e)
arguably [ˈɑːgjʊəblɪ] *adv*: **it is ~** ... on peut soutenir que c'est ...
argue [ˈɑːgjuː] *vt* (*quarrel*) se disputer; (*reason*) argumenter; **to ~ that** objecter *or* alléguer que
argument [ˈɑːgjʊmənt] *n* (*reasons*) argument *m*; (*quarrel*) dispute *f*; **~ative** [ɑːgjʊˈmentətɪv] *adj* ergoteur(euse), raisonneur(euse)
Aries [ˈɛəriːz] *n* le Bélier
arise [əˈraɪz] (*pt* **arose**, *pp* **arisen**) *vi* survenir, se présenter
aristocrat [ˈærɪstəkræt] *n* aristocrate *m/f*
arithmetic [əˈrɪθmətɪk] *n* arithmétique *f*
ark [ɑːk] *n*: **Noah's A~** l'Arche *f* de Noé
arm [ɑːm] *n* bras *m* ♦ *vt* armer; **~s** *npl* (*weapons, HERALDRY*) armes *fpl*; **~ in ~** bras dessus bras dessous
armaments [ˈɑːməmənts] *npl* armement *m*
arm: **~chair** *n* fauteuil *m*; **~ed** *adj* armé(e); **~ed robbery** *n* vol *m* à main armée
armour [ˈɑːmə*] (*US* **armor**) *n* armure *f*; (*MIL: tanks*) blindés *mpl*; **~ed car** *n* véhicule blindé
armpit [ˈɑːmpɪt] *n* aisselle *f*
armrest [ˈɑːmrest] *n* accoudoir *m*
army [ˈɑːmɪ] *n* armée *f*
aroma [əˈrəumə] *n* arôme *m*

arose [əˈrəuz] *pt of* **arise**
around [əˈraund] *adv* autour; (*nearby*) dans les parages ♦ *prep* autour de; (*near*) près de; (*fig: about*) environ; (: *date, time*) vers
arouse [əˈrauz] *vt* (*sleeper*) éveiller; (*curiosity, passions*) éveiller, susciter; (*anger*) exciter
arrange [əˈreɪndʒ] *vt* arranger; **to ~ to do sth** prévoir de faire qch; **~ment** *n* arrangement *m*; **~ments** *npl* (*plans etc*) arrangements *mpl*, dispositions *fpl*
array [əˈreɪ] *n*: **~ of** déploiement *m or* étalage *m* de
arrears [əˈrɪəz] *npl* arriéré *m*; **to be in ~ with one's rent** devoir un arriéré de loyer
arrest [əˈrest] *vt* arrêter; (*sb's attention*) retenir, attirer ♦ *n* arrestation *f*; **under ~** en état d'arrestation
arrival [əˈraɪvəl] *n* arrivée *f*; **new ~** nouveau venu, nouvelle venue; (*baby*) nouveau-né(e)
arrive [əˈraɪv] *vi* arriver
arrogant [ˈærəgənt] *adj* arrogant(e)
arrow [ˈærəu] *n* flèche *f*
arse [ɑːs] *n* (*BRIT: inf!*) cul *m* (!)
arson [ˈɑːsn] *n* incendie criminel
art [ɑːt] *n* art *m*; **A~s** *npl* (*SCOL*) les lettres *fpl*
artery [ˈɑːtərɪ] *n* artère *f*
artful [ˈɑːtful] *adj* astucieux(euse), rusé(e)
art gallery *n* musée *m* d'art; (*small and private*) galerie *f* de peinture
arthritis [ɑːˈθraɪtɪs] *n* arthrite *f*
artichoke [ˈɑːtɪtʃəuk] *n* (*also:* **globe ~**) artichaut *m*; (: *Jerusalem ~*) topinambour *m*
article [ˈɑːtɪkl] *n* article *m*; **~s** *npl* (*BRIT: LAW: training*) ≈ stage *m*; **~ of clothing** vêtement *m*
articulate [*adj* ɑːˈtɪkjʊlɪt, *vb* ɑːˈtɪkjʊleɪt] *adj* (*person*) qui s'exprime bien; (*speech*) bien articulé(e), prononcé(e) clairement ♦ *vt* exprimer; **~d lorry** (*BRIT*) *n* (camion *m*) semi-remorque *m*
artificial [ɑːtɪˈfɪʃəl] *adj* artificiel(le)
artist [ˈɑːtɪst] *n* artiste *m/f*; **~ic** [ɑːˈtɪstɪk] *adj* artistique; **~ry** *n* art *m*, talent *m*
art school *n* ≈ école *f* des beaux-arts

──────────────── *KEYWORD*

as [æz] *conj* **1** (*referring to time*) comme, alors que; à mesure que; **he came in ~ I was leaving** il est arrivé comme je partais; **~ the years went by** à mesure que les années passaient; **~ from tomorrow** à partir de demain
2 (*in comparisons*): **~ big ~** aussi grand que; **twice ~ big ~** deux fois plus grand que; **~ much** *or* **many ~** autant que; **~ much money/many books ~** autant d'argent/de livres que; **~ soon ~** dès que
3 (*since, because*) comme, puisque; **~ he had to be home by 10** ... comme il or

puisqu'il devait être de retour avant 10h ...
4 (*referring to manner, way*) comme; **do ~ you wish** faites comme vous voudrez
5 (*concerning*): ~ **for** *or* **to that** quant à cela, pour ce qui est de cela
6: ~ **if** *or* **though** comme si; **he looked ~ if he was ill** il avait l'air d'être malade; *see also* **long**; **such**; **well**
♦ *prep*: **he works ~ a driver** il travaille comme chauffeur; ~ **chairman of the company, he ...** en tant que président de la compagnie, il ...; **dressed up ~ a cowboy** déguisé en cowboy; **he gave me it ~ a present** il me l'a offert, il m'en a fait cadeau

a.s.a.p. *abbr* (= *as soon as possible*) dès que possible
asbestos [æz'bɛstəs] *n* amiante *f*
ascend [ə'sɛnd] *vt* gravir; (*throne*) monter sur
ascent [ə'sɛnt] *n* ascension *f*
ascertain [æsə'teɪn] *vt* vérifier
ascribe [ə'skraɪb] *vt*: **to ~ sth to** attribuer qch à
ash [æʃ] *n* (*dust*) cendre *f*; (*also*: ~ *tree*) frêne *m*
ashamed [ə'ʃeɪmd] *adj* honteux(euse), confus(e); **to be ~ of** avoir honte de
ashen [æʃən] *adj* (*pale*) cendreux(euse), blême
ashore [ə'ʃɔː*] *adv* à terre
ashtray ['æʃtreɪ] *n* cendrier *m*
Ash Wednesday *n* mercredi *m* des cendres
Asia ['eɪʃə] *n* Asie *f*; ~**n** *n* Asiatique *m/f* ♦ *adj* asiatique
aside [ə'saɪd] *adv* de côté; à l'écart ♦ *n* aparté *m*
ask [ɑːsk] *vt* demander; (*invite*) inviter; **to ~ sb sth/to do sth** demander qch à qn/à qn de faire qch; **to ~ sb about sth** questionner qn sur qch; **se renseigner auprès de qn sur qch; to ~ (sb) a question** poser une question (à qn); **to ~ sb out to dinner** inviter qn au restaurant; ~ **after** *vt fus* demander des nouvelles de; ~ **for** *vt fus* demander; (*trouble*) chercher
askance [ə'kɑːns] *adv*: **to look ~ at sb** regarder qn de travers *or* d'un œil désapprobateur
asking price ['ɑːskɪŋ] *n*: **the ~** le prix de départ
asleep [ə'sliːp] *adj* endormi(e); **to fall ~** s'endormir
asparagus [əs'pærəgəs] *n* asperges *fpl*
aspect ['æspɛkt] *n* aspect *m*; (*direction in which a building etc faces*) orientation *f*, exposition *f*
aspersions [əs'pɜːʃənz] *npl*: **to cast ~ on** dénigrer
aspire [əs'paɪə*] *vi*: **to ~ to** aspirer à

aspirin ['æsprɪn] *n* aspirine *f*
ass [æs] *n* âne *m*; (*inf*) imbécile *m/f*; (*US: inf!*) cul *m* (!)
assailant [ə'seɪlənt] *n* agresseur *m*; assaillant *m*
assassinate [ə'sæsɪneɪt] *vt* assassiner; **assassination** [əsæsɪ'neɪʃən] *n* assassinat *m*
assault [ə'sɔːlt] *n* (*MIL*) assaut *m*; (*gen: attack*) agression *f* ♦ *vt* attaquer; (*sexually*) violenter
assemble [ə'sɛmbl] *vt* assembler ♦ *vi* s'assembler, se rassembler
assembly [ə'sɛmblɪ] *n* assemblée *f*, réunion *f*; (*institution*) assemblée; (*construction*) assemblage *m*; ~ **line** *n* chaîne *f* de montage
assent [ə'sɛnt] *n* assentiment *m*, consentement *m*
assert [ə'sɜːt] *vt* affirmer, déclarer; (*one's authority*) faire valoir; (*one's innocence*) protester de
assess [ə'sɛs] *vt* évaluer; (*tax, payment*) établir *or* fixer le montant de; (*property etc: for tax*) calculer la valeur imposable de; (*person*) juger la valeur de; ~**ment** *n* évaluation *f*, fixation *f*, calcul *m* de la valeur imposable de, jugement *m*; ~**or** *n* expert *m* (*impôt et assurance*)
asset ['æsɛt] *n* avantage *m*, atout *m*; ~**s** *npl* (*FINANCE*) capital *m*; avoir(s) *m(pl)*; actif *m*
assign [ə'saɪn] *vt* (*date*) fixer; (*task*) assigner à; (*resources*) affecter à; ~**ment** [ə'saɪnmənt] *n* tâche *f*, mission *f*
assist [ə'sɪst] *vt* aider, assister; ~**ance** *n* aide *f*, assistance *f*; ~**ant** *n* assistant(e), adjoint(e); (*BRIT: also: shop* ~**ant**) vendeur(euse)
associate [*adj*, *n* ə'səʊʃɪɪt, *vb* ə'səʊʃɪeɪt] *adj*, *n* associé(e) ♦ *vt* associer ♦ *vi*: **to ~ with sb** fréquenter qn; **association** [əsəʊsɪ'eɪʃən] *n* association *f*
assorted [ə'sɔːtɪd] *adj* assorti(e)
assortment [ə'sɔːtmənt] *n* assortiment *m*
assume [ə'sjuːm] *vt* supposer; (*responsibilities etc*) assumer; (*attitude, name*) prendre, adopter; ~**d name** *n* nom *m* d'emprunt
assumption [ə'sʌmpʃən] *n* supposition *f*, hypothèse *f*; (*of power*) assomption *f*, prise *f*
assurance [ə'ʃʊərəns] *n* assurance *f*
assure [ə'ʃʊə*] *vt* assurer
asthma ['æsmə] *n* asthme *m*
astonish [əs'tɒnɪʃ] *vt* étonner, stupéfier; ~**ment** *n* étonnement *m*
astound [əs'taʊnd] *vt* stupéfier, sidérer
astray [əs'treɪ] *adv*: **to go ~** s'égarer; (*fig*) quitter le droit chemin; **to lead ~** détourner du droit chemin
astride [əs'traɪd] *prep* à cheval sur
astrology [əs'trɒlədʒɪ] *n* astrologie *f*
astronaut ['æstrənɔːt] *n* astronaute *m/f*
astronomy [əs'trɒnəmɪ] *n* astronomie *f*
astute [əs'tjuːt] *adj* astucieux(euse)

asylum [ə'saɪləm] *n* asile *m*

KEYWORD

at [æt] *prep* **1** (*referring to position, direction*) à; ~ **the top** au sommet; ~ **home/school** à la maison *or* chez soi/à l'école; ~ **the baker's** à la boulangerie, chez le boulanger; **to look** ~ **sth** regarder qch
2 (*referring to time*): ~ **4 o'clock** à 4 heures; ~ **Christmas** à Noël; ~ **night** la nuit; ~ **times** par moments, parfois
3 (*referring to rates, speed etc*) à; ~ **£1 a kilo** une livre le kilo; **two** ~ **a time** deux à la fois; ~ **50 km/h** à 50 km/h
4 (*referring to manner*): ~ **a stroke** d'un seul coup; ~ **peace** en paix
5 (*referring to activity*): **to be** ~ **work** être à l'œuvre, travailler; **to play** ~ **cowboys** jouer aux cowboys; **to be good** ~ **sth** être bon en qch
6 (*referring to cause*): **shocked/surprised/annoyed** ~ **sth** choqué par/étonné de/agacé par qch; **I went** ~ **his suggestion** j'y suis allé sur son conseil

---

ate [et, eɪt] *pt of* **eat**
atheist ['eɪθɪɪst] *n* athée *m/f*
Athens ['æθɪnz] *n* Athènes
athlete ['æθliːt] *n* athlète *m/f*
athletic [æθ'letɪk] *adj* athlétique; ~**s** *n* athlétisme *m*
Atlantic [ət'læntɪk] *adj* atlantique ♦ *n*: **the** ~ **(Ocean)** l'Atlantique *m*, l'océan *m* Atlantique
atlas ['ætləs] *n* atlas *m*
atmosphere ['ætməsfɪə*] *n* atmosphère *f*
atom ['ætəm] *n* atome *m*; ~**ic** [ə'tɒmɪk] *adj* atomique; ~**(ic) bomb** *n* bombe *f* atomique; ~**izer** ['ætəmaɪzə*] *n* atomiseur *m*
atone [ə'təʊn] *vi*: **to** ~ **for** expier, racheter
atrocious [ə'trəʊʃəs] *adj* (*very bad*) atroce, exécrable
attach [ə'tætʃ] *vt* attacher; (*document, letter*) joindre; **to be** ~**ed to sb/sth** être attaché à qn/qch
attaché case [ə'tæʃeɪ-] *n* mallette *f*, attaché-case *m*
attachment [ə'tætʃmənt] *n* (*tool*) accessoire *m*; (*love*): ~ **(to)** affection *f* (pour), attachement *m* (à)
attack [ə'tæk] *vt* attaquer; (*task etc*) s'attaquer à ♦ *n* attaque *f*; (*also: heart* ~) crise *f* cardiaque
attain [ə'teɪn] *vt* (*also: to* ~ *to*) parvenir à, atteindre; (*: knowledge*) acquérir; ~**ments** *npl* connaissances *fpl*, résultats *mpl*
attempt [ə'tempt] *n* tentative *f* ♦ *vt* essayer, tenter; **to make an** ~ **on sb's life** attenter à la vie de qn; ~**ed** *adj*: ~**ed murder/suicide** tentative *f* de meurtre/suicide
attend [ə'tend] *vt* (*course*) suivre; (*meeting, talk*) assister à; (*school, church*) aller à, fréquenter; (*patient*) soigner, s'occuper de; ~ **to** *vt fus* (*needs, affairs etc*) s'occuper de; (*customer, patient*) s'occuper de; ~**ance** *n* (*being present*) présence *f*; (*people present*) assistance *f*; ~**ant** *n* employé(e) ♦ *adj* (*dangers*) inhérent(e), concomitant(e)
attention [ə'tenʃən] *n* attention *f*; ~! (*MIL*) garde-à-vous!; **for the** ~ **of** (*ADMIN*) à l'attention de
attentive [ə'tentɪv] *adj* attentif(ive); (*kind*) prévenant(e)
attest [ə'test] *vi*: **to** ~ **to** (*demonstrate*) démontrer; (*confirm*) témoigner
attic ['ætɪk] *n* grenier *m*
attitude ['ætɪtjuːd] *n* attitude *f*; pose *f*, maintien *m*
attorney [ə'tɜːnɪ] *n* (*US: lawyer*) avoué *m*; **A~ General** *n* (*BRIT*) ≈ procureur général; (*US*) ≈ garde *m* des Sceaux, ministre *m* de la Justice
attract [ə'trækt] *vt* attirer; ~**ion** [ə'trækʃən] *n* (*gen pl: pleasant things*) attraction *f*, attrait *m*; (*PHYSICS*) attraction *f*; (*fig: towards sb or sth*) attirance *f*; ~**ive** *adj* attrayant(e); (*person*) séduisant(e)
attribute [*n* 'ætrɪbjuːt, *vb* ə'trɪbjuːt] *n* attribut *m* ♦ *vt*: **to** ~ **sth to** attribuer qch à
attrition [ə'trɪʃən] *n*: **war of** ~ guerre *f* d'usure
aubergine ['əʊbəʒiːn] *n* aubergine *f*
auction ['ɔːkʃən] *n* (*also: sale by* ~) vente *f* aux enchères ♦ *vt* (*: to sell by* ~) vendre aux enchères; (*: to put up for* ~) mettre aux enchères; ~**eer** [ɔːkʃə'nɪə*] *n* commissaire-priseur *m*
audience ['ɔːdɪəns] *n* (*people*) assistance *f*; public *m*; spectateurs *mpl*; (*interview*) audience *f*
audiovisual ['ɔːdɪəʊ'vɪzjʊəl] *adj* audiovisuel(le); ~ **aids** *npl* supports *or* moyens audiovisuels
audit ['ɔːdɪt] *vt* vérifier
audition [ɔː'dɪʃən] *n* audition *f*
auditor ['ɔːdɪtə*] *n* vérificateur *m* des comptes
augur ['ɔːgə*] *vi*: **it** ~**s well** c'est bon signe *or* de bon augure
August ['ɔːgəst] *n* août *m*
aunt [ɑːnt] *n* tante *f*; ~**ie** *n dimin of* **aunt**; ~**y** *n dimin of* **aunt**
au pair ['əʊ'pɛə*] *n* (*also:* ~ *girl*) jeune fille *f* au pair
auspicious [ɔːs'pɪʃəs] *adj* de bon augure, propice
Australia [ɒs'treɪlɪə] *n* Australie *f*; ~**n** *adj* australien(ne) ♦ *n* Australien(ne)
Austria ['ɒstrɪə] *n* Autriche *f*; ~**n** *adj* autrichien(ne) ♦ *n* Autrichien(ne)
authentic [ɔː'θentɪk] *adj* authentique
author ['ɔːθə*] *n* auteur *m*
authoritarian [ɔːθɒrɪ'tɛərɪən] *adj* autoritaire

authoritative [ɔːˈθɒrɪtətɪv] *adj* (*account*) digne de foi; (*study, treatise*) qui fait autorité; (*person, manner*) autoritaire

authority [ɔːˈθɒrɪtɪ] *n* autorité *f*; (*permission*) autorisation (formelle); **the authorities** *npl* (*ruling body*) les autorités *fpl*, l'administration *f*

authorize [ˈɔːθəraɪz] *vt* autoriser

auto [ˈɔːtəʊ] (*US*) *n* auto *f*, voiture *f*

auto: ~**biography** [ɔːtəʊbaɪˈɒɡrəfɪ] *n* autobiographie *f*, ~**graph** [ˈɔːtəɡrɑːf] *n* autographe *m* ♦ *vt* signer, dédicacer; ~**mated** [ˈɔːtəmeɪtɪd] *adj* automatisé(e), automatique; ~**matic** [ɔːtəˈmætɪk] *adj* automatique ♦ *n* (*gun*) automatique *m*; (*washing machine*) machine *f* à laver automatique; (*BRIT: AUT*) voiture *f* à transmission automatique; ~**matically** *adv* automatiquement; ~**mation** [ɔːtəˈmeɪʃən] *n* automatisation *f* (électronique); ~**mobile** [ˈɔːtəməbiːl] (*US*) *n* automobile *f*, ~**nomy** [ɔːˈtɒnəmɪ] *n* autonomie *f*

autumn [ˈɔːtəm] *n* automne *m*; **in** ~ en automne

auxiliary [ɔːɡˈzɪlɪərɪ] *adj* auxiliaire ♦ *n* auxiliaire *m/f*

avail [əˈveɪl] *vt*: **to** ~ **o.s. of** profiter de ♦ *n*: **to no** ~ sans résultat, en vain, en pure perte

availability [əveɪləˈbɪlɪtɪ] *n* disponibilité *f*

available [əˈveɪləbl] *adj* disponible

avalanche [ˈævəlɑːnʃ] *n* avalanche *f*

Ave *abbr* = **avenue**

avenge [əˈvendʒ] *vt* venger

avenue [ˈævənjuː] *n* avenue *f*; (*fig*) moyen *m*

average [ˈævərɪdʒ] *n* moyenne *f*; (*fig*) moyen *m* ♦ *adj* moyen(ne) ♦ *vt* (*a certain figure*) atteindre *or* faire *etc* en moyenne; **on** ~ en moyenne; ~ **out** *vi*: **to** ~ **out at** représenter en moyenne, donner une moyenne de

averse [əˈvɜːs] *adj*: **to be** ~ **to sth/doing sth** éprouver une forte répugnance envers qch/à faire qch

avert [əˈvɜːt] *vt* prévenir, écarter; (*one's eyes*) détourner

aviary [ˈeɪvɪərɪ] *n* volière *f*

avocado [ævəˈkɑːdəʊ] *n* (*also: BRIT:* ~ **pear**) avocat *m*

avoid [əˈvɔɪd] *vt* éviter

await [əˈweɪt] *vt* attendre

awake [əˈweɪk] (*pt* **awoke**, *pp* **awoken**) *adj* éveillé(e) ♦ *vt* éveiller ♦ *vi* s'éveiller; ~ **to** (*dangers, possibilities*) conscient(e) de; **to be** ~ être réveillé(e); **he was still** ~ il ne dormait pas encore; ~**ning** *n* réveil *m*

award [əˈwɔːd] *n* récompense *f*, prix *m*; (*LAW: damages*) dommages-intérêts *mpl* ♦ *vt* (*prize*) décerner; (*LAW: damages*) accorder

aware [əˈwɛə*] *adj*: ~ (**of**) (*conscious*)

conscient(e) (de); (*informed*) au courant (de); **to become** ~ **of/that** prendre conscience de/que; se rendre compte de/ que; ~**ness** *n* conscience *f*, connaissance *f*

awash [əˈwɒʃ] *adj*: ~ (**with**) inondé(e) (de)

away [əˈweɪ] *adj, adv* (au) loin; absent(e); **two kilometres** ~ à (une distance de) deux kilomètres, à deux kilomètres de distance; **two hours** ~ **by car** à deux heures de voiture *or* de route; **the holiday was two weeks** ~ il restait deux semaines jusqu'aux vacances; ~ **from** loin de; **he's for a week** il est parti (pour) une semaine; **to pedal/work/laugh** ~ être en train de pédaler/travailler/rire; **to fade** ~ (*sound*) s'affaiblir; (*colour*) s'estomper; **to wither** ~ (*plant*) se dessécher; **to take** ~ emporter; (*subtract*) enlever; ~ **game** *n* (*SPORT*) match *m* à l'extérieur

awe [ɔː] *n* respect mêlé de crainte; ~**inspiring** *adj* impressionnant(e); ~**some** *adj* impressionnant(e)

awful [ˈɔːful] *adj* affreux(euse); **an** ~ **lot (of)** un nombre incroyable (de); ~**ly** *adv* (*very*) terriblement, vraiment

awhile [əˈwaɪl] *adv* un moment, quelque temps

awkward [ˈɔːkwəd] *adj* (*clumsy*) gauche, maladroit(e); (*inconvenient*) peu pratique; (*embarrassing*) gênant(e), délicat(e)

awning [ˈɔːnɪŋ] *n* (*of tent*) auvent *m*; (*of shop*) store *m*; (*of hotel etc*) marquise *f*

awoke [əˈwəʊk] *pt of* **awake**; ~**n** [əˈwəʊkən] *pp of* **awake**

awry [əˈraɪ] *adj, adv* de travers; **to go** ~ mal tourner

axe [æks] (*US* **ax**) *n* hache *f* ♦ *vt* (*project etc*) abandonner; (*jobs*) supprimer; **axes** [ˈæksɪz] *npl of* **axe**

axis [ˈæksɪs, *pl* -siːz] (*pl* **axes**) *n* axe *m*

axle [ˈæksl] *n* (*also:* ~**-tree**: *AUT*) essieu *m*

ay(e) [aɪ] *excl* (*yes*) oui

B b

B [biː] *n* (*MUS*) si *m*

B.A. *abbr* = **Bachelor of Arts**

babble [ˈbæbl] *vi* bredouiller; (*baby, stream*) gazouiller

baby [ˈbeɪbɪ] *n* bébé *m*; (*US: inf: darling*): **come on,** ~! viens ma belle/mon gars!; ~ **carriage** (*US*) *n* voiture *f* d'enfant; ~**sit** *vi* garder les enfants; ~**-sitter** *n* babysitter *m/f*

bachelor ['bætʃələ*] *n* célibataire *m*; **B~ of Arts/Science** ≈ licencié(e) ès *or* en lettres/sciences

back [bæk] *n* (of person, horse, book) dos *m*; (of hand) dos, revers *m*; (of house) derrière *m*; (of car, train) arrière *m*; (of chair) dossier *m*; (of page) verso *m*; (of room, audience) fond *m*; (SPORT) arrière *m* ♦ *vt* (candidate: also: ~ **up**) soutenir, appuyer; (horse: at races) parier *or* miser sur; (car) (faire) reculer ♦ *vi* (also: ~ **up**) reculer; (: car etc) faire marche arrière ♦ *adj* (in compounds) de derrière, à l'arrière ♦ *adv* (not forward) en arrière; (returned): **he's** ~ il est rentré, il est de retour; (restitution): **throw the ball** ~ renvoie la balle; (again): **he called** ~ il a rappelé; ~ **seat/wheels** (AUT) sièges *mpl*/roues *fpl* arrières; ~ **payments/rent** arriéré *m* de paiements/loyer; **he ran** ~ il est revenu en courant; ~ **down** *vi* rabattre de ses prétentions; ~ **out** *vi* (of promise) se dédire; ~ **up** *vt* (candidate etc) soutenir, appuyer; (COMPUT) sauvegarder; ~**bencher** (BRIT) *n* membre du parlement sans portefeuille; ~**bone** *n* colonne vertébrale, épine dorsale; ~**cloth** (BRIT) *n* toile *f* de fond; ~**date** *vt* (letter) antidater; ~**dated pay rise** augmentation *f* avec effet rétroactif; ~**drop** *n* = **backcloth**; ~**fire** *vi* (AUT) pétarader; (plans) mal tourner; ~**ground** *n* arrière-plan *m*; (of events) situation *f*, conjoncture *f*; (basic knowledge) éléments *mpl* de base; (experience) formation *f*; **family** ~**ground** milieu familial; ~**hand** *n* (TENNIS: also: ~**hand stroke**) revers *m*; ~**hander** (BRIT) *n* (bribe) pot-de-vin *m*; ~**ing** *n* (fig) soutien *m*, appui *m*; ~**lash** *n* contre-coup *m*, répercussion *f*; ~**log** *n*: ~**log of work** travail *m* en retard; ~ **number** *n* (of magazine etc) vieux numéro; ~**pack** *n* sac *m* à dos; ~ **pay** *n* rappel *m* de salaire; ~**side** (inf) *n* derrière *m*, postérieur *m*; ~**stage** *adv* derrière la scène, dans la coulisse; ~**stroke** ~ dos crawlé; ~**up** *adj* (train, plane) supplémentaire, de réserve; (COMPUT) de sauvegarde ♦ *n* (support) appui *m*, soutien *m*; (also: ~**up disk/file**) sauvegarde *f*; ~**ward** *adj* (movement) en arrière; (person, country) arriéré(e); attardé(e); ~**wards** *adv* (move, go) en arrière; (read a list) à l'envers, à rebours; (fall) à la renverse; (walk) à reculons; ~**water** *n* (fig) coin reculé; bled perdu (péj); ~**yard** *n* arrière-cour *f*

bacon ['beɪkən] *n* bacon *m*, lard *m*

bacteria [bæk'tɪərɪə] *npl* bactéries *fpl*

bad [bæd] *adj* mauvais(e); (child) vilain(e); (mistake, accident etc) grave; (meat, food) gâté(e), avarié(e); **his** ~ **leg** sa jambe malade; **to go** ~ (meat, food) se gâter

bade [bæd] *pt of* **bid**

badge [bædʒ] *n* insigne *m*; (of policeman) plaque *f*

badger ['bædʒə*] *n* blaireau *m*

badly ['bædlɪ] *adv* (work, dress etc) mal; ~ **wounded** grièvement blessé; **he needs it** ~ il en a absolument besoin; ~ **off** *adj, adv* dans la gêne

badminton ['bædmɪntən] *n* badminton *m*

bad-tempered ['bæd'tempəd] *adj* (person: by nature) ayant mauvais caractère; (: on one occasion) de mauvaise humeur

baffle ['bæfl] *vt* (puzzle) déconcerter

bag [bæg] *n* sac *m* ♦ *vt* (inf: take) empocher; s'approprier; ~**s of** (inf: lots of) des masses de; ~**gage** *n* bagages *mpl*; ~**gy** *adj* avachi(e), qui fait des poches; ~**pipes** *npl* cornemuse *f*

bail [beɪl] *n* (payment) caution *f*; (release) mise *f* en liberté sous caution ♦ *vt* (prisoner: also: grant ~ **to**) mettre en liberté sous caution; (boat: also: ~ **out**) écoper; **on** ~ (prisoner) sous caution; see also **bale**; ~ **out** *vt* (prisoner) payer la caution de

bailiff ['beɪlɪf] *n* (BRIT) ≈ huissier *m*; (US) ≈ huissier-audiencier *m*

bait [beɪt] *n* appât *m* ♦ *vt* appâter; (fig: tease) tourmenter

bake [beɪk] *vt* (faire) cuire au four ♦ *vi* (bread etc) cuire (au four); (make cakes etc) faire de la pâtisserie; ~**d beans** *npl* haricots blancs à la sauce tomate; ~**r** *n* boulanger *m*; ~**ry** *n* boulangerie *f*; boulangerie industrielle; **baking** *n* cuisson *f*; **baking powder** *n* levure *f* (chimique)

balance ['bæləns] *n* équilibre *m*; (COMM: sum) solde *m*; (remainder) reste *m*; (scales) balance *f* ♦ *vt* mettre *or* faire tenir en équilibre; (pros and cons) peser; (budget) équilibrer; (account) balancer; ~ **of trade/payments** balance commerciale/des comptes *or* paiements; ~**d** *adj* (personality, diet) équilibré(e); (report) objectif(ive); ~ **sheet** *n* bilan *m*

balcony ['bælkənɪ] *n* balcon *m*; (in theatre) deuxième balcon

bald [bɔːld] *adj* chauve; (tyre) lisse

bale [beɪl] *n* balle *f*, ballot *m*; ~ **out** *vi* (of a plane) sauter en parachute

ball [bɔːl] *n* boule *f*; (football) ballon *m*; (for tennis, golf) balle *f*; (of wool) pelote *f* (of string) bobine *f*; (dance) bal *m*; **to play** ~ (**with sb**) (fig) coopérer (avec qn)

ballast ['bæləst] *n* lest *m*

ball bearings *npl* roulement *m* à billes

ballerina [bælə'riːnə] *n* ballerine *f*

ballet ['bæleɪ] *n* ballet *m*; (art) danse *f* (classique); ~ **dancer** *n* danceur(euse) *m/f* de ballet

balloon [bə'luːn] *n* ballon *m*; (in comic strip) bulle *f*

ballot ['bælət] *n* scrutin *m*; ~ **paper** *n* bulletin *m* de vote

ballpoint (pen) ['bɔːlpɔɪnt-] *n* stylo *m* à bille

ballroom ['bɔːlrʊm] *n* salle *f* de bal

balm [bɑːm] *n* baume *m*

ban [bæn] *n* interdiction *f* ♦ *vt* interdire

banana [bə'nɑːnə] *n* banane *f*

band [bænd] *n* bande *f*; (*at a dance*) orchestre *m*; (*MIL*) musique *f*, fanfare *f*; ~ **together** *vi* se liguer

bandage ['bændɪdʒ] *n* bandage *m*, pansement *m* ♦ *vt* bander

Bandaid ['bændeɪd] (*US* ®) *n* pansement adhésif

bandwagon ['bændwægən] *n*: **to jump on the** ~ (*fig*) monter dans *or* prendre le train en marche

bandy ['bændɪ] *vt* (*jokes, insults, ideas*) échanger

bandy-legged ['bændɪ'legɪd] *adj* aux jambes arquées

bang [bæŋ] *n* détonation *f*; (*of door*) claquement *m*; (*blow*) coup (violent) ♦ *vt* frapper (violemment); (*door*) claquer ♦ *vi* détoner; claquer ♦ *excl* pan!

bangs [bæŋz] (*US*) *npl* (*fringe*) frange *f*

banish ['bænɪʃ] *vt* bannir

banister(s) ['bænɪstə(z)] *n(pl)* rampe *f* (d'escalier)

bank [bæŋk] *n* banque *f*; (*of river, lake*) bord *m*, rive *f*; (*of earth*) talus *m*, remblai *m* ♦ *vi* (*AVIAT*) virer sur l'aile; ~ **on** *vt fus* miser *or* tabler sur; ~ **account** *n* compte *m* en banque; ~ **card** *n* carte *f* d'identité bancaire; ~**er** *n* banquier *m*; ~**er's card** (*BRIT*) = **bank card**; ~ **holiday** (*BRIT*) *n* jour férié (*les banques sont fermées*); ~**ing** *n* opérations *fpl* bancaires; profession *f* de banquier; ~**note** *n* billet *m* de banque; ~ **rate** *n* taux *m* de l'escompte

bankrupt ['bæŋkrʌpt] *adj* en faillite; **to go** ~ faire faillite; ~**cy** *n* faillite *f*

bank statement *n* relevé *m* de compte

banner ['bænə*] *n* bannière *f*

bannister(s) ['bænɪstə(z)] *n(pl)* = **banister(s)**

banns [bænz] *npl* bans *mpl*

baptism ['bæptɪzəm] *n* baptême *m*

bar [bɑː*] *n* (*pub*) bar *m*; (*counter: in pub*) comptoir *m*, bar; (*rod: of metal etc*) barre *f*; (*on window etc*) barreau *m*; (*of chocolate*) tablette *f*, plaque *f*; (*fig*) obstacle *m*; (*prohibition*) mesure *f* d'exclusion; (*MUS*) mesure *f* ♦ *vt* (*road*) barrer; (*window*) munir de barreaux; (*person*) exclure; (*activity*) interdire; ~ **of soap** savonnette *f*; **the B~** (*LAW*) le barreau; **behind** ~**s** (*prisoner*) sous les verrous; ~ **none** sans exception

barbaric [bɑː'bærɪk] *adj* barbare

barbecue ['bɑːbɪkjuː] *n* barbecue *m*

barbed wire ['bɑːbd-] *n* fil *m* de fer barbelé

barber ['bɑːbə*] *n* coiffeur *m* (pour hommes)

bar code *n* (*on goods*) code *m* à barres

bare [bɛə*] *adj* nu(e) ♦ *vt* mettre à nu, dénuder; (*teeth*) montrer; **the** ~ **necessities** le strict nécessaire; ~**back** *adv* à cru, sans selle; ~**faced** *adj* impudent(e), effronté(e); ~**foot** *adj, adv* nu-pieds, (les) pieds nus; ~**ly** *adv* à peine

bargain ['bɑːgɪn] *n* (*transaction*) marché *m*; (*good buy*) affaire *f*, occasion *f* ♦ *vi* (*haggle*) marchander; (*negotiate*): **to** ~ (**with sb**) négocier (avec qn), traiter (avec qn); **into the** ~ par-dessus le marché; ~ **for** *vt fus*: **he got more than he** ~**ed for** il ne s'attendait pas à un coup pareil

barge [bɑːdʒ] *n* péniche *f*; ~ **in** *vi* (*walk in*) faire irruption; (*interrupt talk*) intervenir mal à propos

bark [bɑːk] *n* (*of tree*) écorce *f*; (*of dog*) aboiement *m* ♦ *vi* aboyer

barley ['bɑːlɪ] *n* orge *f*; ~ **sugar** *n* sucre *m* d'orge

barmaid ['bɑːmeɪd] *n* serveuse *f* (de bar), barmaid *f*

barman ['bɑːmən] (*irreg*) *n* serveur *m* (de bar), barman *m*

barn [bɑːn] *n* grange *f*

barometer [bə'rɒmɪtə*] *n* baromètre *m*

baron ['bærən] *n* baron *m*; ~**ess** *n* baronne *f*

barracks ['bærəks] *npl* caserne *f*

barrage ['bærɑːʒ] *n* (*MIL*) tir *m* de barrage; (*dam*) barrage *m*; (*fig*) pluie *f*

barrel ['bærəl] *n* tonneau *m*; (*of oil*) baril *m*; (*of gun*) canon *m*

barren ['bærən] *adj* stérile

barricade [bærɪ'keɪd] *n* barricade *f*

barrier ['bærɪə*] *n* barrière *f*; (*fig: to progress etc*) obstacle *m*

barring ['bɑːrɪŋ] *prep* sauf

barrister ['bærɪstə*] (*BRIT*) *n* avocat (plaidant)

barrow ['bærəʊ] *n* (*wheel~*) charrette *f* à bras

bartender ['bɑːtendə*] (*US*) *n* barman *m*

barter ['bɑːtə*] *vt*: **to** ~ **sth for** échanger qch contre

base [beɪs] *n* base *f*; (*of tree, post*) pied *m* ♦ *vt*: **to** ~ **sth on** baser *or* fonder qch sur ♦ *adj* vil(e), bas(se)

baseball ['beɪsbɔːl] *n* base-ball *m*

basement ['beɪsmənt] *n* sous-sol *m*

bases[1] ['beɪsɪz] *npl* of **base**

bases[2] ['beɪsiːz] *npl* of **basis**

bash [bæʃ] (*inf*) *vt* frapper, cogner

bashful ['bæʃfʊl] *adj* timide; modeste

basic ['beɪsɪk] *adj* fondamental(e), de base; (*minimal*) rudimentaire; ~**ally** *adv* fondamentalement, à la base; (*in fact*) en fait, au fond; ~**s** *npl*: **the** ~**s** l'essentiel *m*

basil ['bæzl] *n* basilic *m*

basin ['beɪsn] *n* (*vessel, also GEO*) cuvette *f*,

bassin *m*; (*also: wash~*) lavabo *m*

basis ['beɪsɪs] (*pl* **bases**) *n* base *f*; **on a trial ~** à titre d'essai; **on a part-time ~** à temps partiel

bask [bɑːsk] *vi*: **to ~ in the sun** se chauffer au soleil

basket ['bɑːskɪt] *n* corbeille *f*; (*with handle*) panier *m*; **~ball** *n* basket-ball *m*

bass [beɪs] *n* (MUS) basse *f*

bassoon [bə'suːn] *n* (MUS) basson *m*

bastard ['bɑːstəd] *n* enfant naturel(le), bâtard(e); (*inf!*) salaud *m* (!)

bat [bæt] *n* chauve-souris *f*; (*for baseball etc*) batte *f*; (BRIT: *for table tennis*) raquette *f* ♦ *vt*: **he didn't ~ an eyelid** il n'a pas sourcillé *or* bronché

batch [bætʃ] *n* (*of bread*) fournée *f*; (*of papers*) liasse *f*

bated ['beɪtɪd] *adj*: **with ~ breath** en retenant son souffle

bath [bɑːθ, *pl* bɑːðz] *n* bain *m*; (*~tub*) baignoire *f* ♦ *vt* baigner, donner un bain à; **to have a ~** prendre un bain; *see also* **baths**

bathe [beɪð] *vi* se baigner ♦ *vt* (*wound*) laver

bathing ['beɪðɪŋ] *n* baignade *f*; **~ cap** *n* bonnet *m* de bain; **~ costume** (US **~ suit**) *n* maillot *m* (de bain)

bath: **~robe** *n* peignoir *m* de bain; **~room** *n* salle *f* de bains; **~s** [bɑːðz] *npl* (*also: swimming ~*) piscine *f*; **~ towel** *n* serviette *f* de bain

baton ['bætən] *n* bâton *m*; (MUS) baguette *f*; (*club*) matraque *f*

batter ['bætə*] *vt* battre ♦ *n* pâte *f* à frire; **~ed** *adj* (*hat, pan*) cabossé(e)

battery ['bætəri] *n* batterie *f*; (*of torch*) pile *f*

battle ['bætl] *n* bataille *f*, combat *m* ♦ *vi* se battre, lutter; **~field** *n* champ *m* de bataille; **~ship** *n* cuirassé *m*

bawdy ['bɔːdɪ] *adj* paillard(e)

bawl [bɔːl] *vi* hurler; (*child*) brailler

bay [beɪ] *n* (*of sea*) baie *f*; **to hold sb at ~** tenir qn à distance or en échec; **~ leaf** *n* laurier *m*; **~ window** *n* baie vitrée

bazaar [bə'zɑː*] *n* bazar *m*; vente *f* de charité

B & B *n abbr* = **bed and breakfast**

BBC *n abbr* (= *British Broadcasting Corporation*) office de la radiodiffusion et télévision britannique

B.C. *adv abbr* (= *before Christ*) av. J.-C.

─────── *KEYWORD*

be [biː] (*pt* **was, were**, *pp* **been**) *aux vb* **1** (*with present participle: forming continuous tenses*): **what are you doing?** que faites-vous?; **they're coming tomorrow** ils viennent demain; **I've been waiting for you for 2 hours** je t'attends depuis 2 heures

2 (*with pp: forming passives*) être; **to ~**

killed être tué(e); **he was nowhere to ~ seen** on ne le voyait nulle part

3 (*in tag questions*): **it was fun, wasn't it?** c'était drôle, n'est-ce pas?; **she's back, is she?** elle est rentrée, n'est-ce pas *or* alors?

4 (*+to +infinitive*): **the house is to ~ sold** la maison doit être vendue; **he's not to open it** il ne doit pas l'ouvrir

♦ *vb + complement* **1** (*gen*) être; **I'm English** je suis anglais(e); **I'm tired** je suis fatigué(e); **I'm hot/cold** j'ai chaud/froid; **he's a doctor** il est médecin; **2 and 2 are 4** 2 et 2 font 4

2 (*of health*) aller; **how are you?** comment allez-vous?; **he's fine now** il va bien maintenant; **he's very ill** il est très malade

3 (*of age*) avoir; **how old are you?** quel âge avez-vous?; **I'm sixteen (years old)** j'ai seize ans

4 (*cost*) coûter; **how much was the meal?** combien a coûté le repas?; **that'll ~ £5, please** ça fera 5 livres, s'il vous plaît

♦ *vi* **1** (*exist, occur etc*) être, exister; **the prettiest girl that ever was** la fille la plus jolie qui ait jamais existé; **~ that as it may** quoi qu'il en soit; **so ~ it** soit

2 (*referring to place*) être, se trouver; **I won't ~ here tomorrow** je ne serai pas là demain; **Edinburgh is in Scotland** Édimbourg est *or* se trouve en Écosse

3 (*referring to movement*) aller; **where have you been?** où êtes-vous allé(s)?

♦ *impers vb* **1** (*referring to time, distance*) être; **it's 5 o'clock** il est 5 heures; **it's the 28th of April** c'est le 28 avril; **it's 10 km to the village** le village est à 10 km

2 (*referring to the weather*) faire; **it's too hot/cold** il fait trop chaud/froid; **it's windy** il y a du vent

3 (*emphatic*): **it's me/the postman** c'est moi/le facteur

beach [biːtʃ] *n* plage *f* ♦ *vt* échouer

beacon ['biːkən] *n* (*lighthouse*) fanal *m*; (*marker*) balise *f*

bead [biːd] *n* perle *f*

beak [biːk] *n* bec *m*

beaker ['biːkə*] *n* gobelet *m*

beam [biːm] *n* poutre *f*; (*of light*) rayon *m* ♦ *vi* rayonner

bean [biːn] *n* haricot *m*; (*of coffee*) grain *m*; **runner ~** haricot *m* (à rames); **broad ~** fève *f*; **~sprouts** *npl* germes *mpl* de soja

bear [bɛə*] (*pt* **bore**, *pp* **borne**) *n* ours *m* ♦ *vt* porter; (*endure*) supporter ♦ *vi*: **to ~ right/left** obliquer à droite/gauche, se diriger vers la droite/gauche; **~ out** *vt* corroborer, confirmer; **~ up** *vi* (*person*) tenir le coup

beard [bɪəd] *n* barbe *f*; **~ed** *adj* barbu(e)

bearer ['bɛərə*] *n* porteur *m*; (*of passport*) titulaire *m/f*

bearing ['bɛərɪŋ] n maintien m, allure f; (connection) rapport m; ~**s** npl (also: ball ~s) roulement m (à billes); **to take a** ~ faire le point

beast [biːst] n bête f; (inf: person) brute f; ~**ly** adj infect(e)

beat [biːt] (pt **beat**, pp **beaten**) n battement m; (MUS) temps m, mesure f; (of policeman) ronde f ♦ vt, vi battre; **off the** ~**en track** hors des chemins or sentiers battus; ~ **it!** (inf) fiche(-moi) le camp!; ~ **off** vt repousser; ~ **up** vt (inf: person) tabasser; (eggs) battre; ~**ing** n raclée f

beautiful ['bjuːtɪful] adj beau(belle); ~**ly** adv admirablement

beauty ['bjuːtɪ] n beauté f; ~ **salon** n institut m de beauté; ~ **spot** n (BRIT) (TOURISM) site naturel (d'une grande beauté)

beaver ['biːvə*] n castor m

became [bɪ'keɪm] pt of **become**

because [bɪ'kɒz] conj parce que; ~ **of** prep à cause de

beck [bek] n: **to be at sb's** ~ **and call** être à l'entière disposition de qn

beckon ['bekən] vt (also: ~ **to**) faire signe (de venir) à

become [bɪ'kʌm] (irreg: like **come**) vi devenir; **to** ~ **fat/thin** grossir/maigrir

becoming [bɪ'kʌmɪŋ] adj (behaviour) convenable, bienséant(e); (clothes) seyant(e)

bed [bed] n lit m; (of flowers) parterre m; (of coal, clay) couche f; (of sea) fond m; **to go to** ~ aller se coucher; ~ **and breakfast** n (terms) chambre et petit déjeuner; (place) ≈ chambre d'hôte; ~**clothes** npl couvertures fpl et draps mpl; ~**ding** n literie f

bedraggled [bɪ'drægld] adj (person, clothes) débraillé(e); (hair: wet) trempé(e)

bed: ~**ridden** adj cloué(e) au lit; ~**room** n chambre f (à coucher); ~**side** n: **at sb's** ~**side** au chevet de qn; ~**sit(ter)** n (BRIT) chambre meublée, studio m; ~**spread** n couvre-lit m, dessus-de-lit m inv; ~**time** n heure f du coucher

bee [biː] n abeille f

beech [biːtʃ] n hêtre m

beef [biːf] n boeuf m; **roast** ~ rosbif m; ~**burger** n hamburger m; ~**eater** n hallebardier de la Tour de Londres

beehive ['biːhaɪv] n ruche f

beeline ['biːlaɪn] n: **to make a** ~ **for** se diriger tout droit vers

been [biːn] pp of **be**

beer [bɪə*] n bière f

beet [biːt] n (vegetable) betterave f; (US: also: **red** ~) betterave (potagère)

beetle ['biːtl] n scarabée m

beetroot ['biːtruːt] n (BRIT) betterave f

before [bɪ'fɔː*] prep (in time) avant; (in space) devant ♦ conj avant que +sub; avant de ♦ adv avant; devant; ~ **going** avant de partir; ~ **she goes** avant qu'elle ne parte; **the week** ~ la semaine précédente or d'avant; **I've seen it** ~ je l'ai déjà vu; ~**hand** adv au préalable, à l'avance

beg [beg] vi mendier ♦ vt mendier; (forgiveness, mercy etc) demander; (entreat) supplier; see also **pardon**

began [bɪ'gæn] pt of **begin**

beggar ['begə*] n mendiant(e)

begin [bɪ'gɪn] (pt **began**, pp **begun**) vt, vi commencer; **to** ~ **doing** or **to do sth** commencer à or de faire qch; ~**ner** n débutant(e); ~**ning** n commencement m, début m

behalf [bɪ'hɑːf] n: **on** ~ **of**, (US) **in** ~ **of** (representing) de la part de; (for benefit of) pour le compte de; **on my/his** ~ pour moi/lui

behave [bɪ'heɪv] vi se conduire, se comporter; (well: also: ~ **o.s.**) se conduire bien or comme il faut

behaviour [bɪ'heɪvjə*] (US **behavior**) n comportement m, conduite f

behead [bɪ'hed] vt décapiter

beheld [bɪ'held] pt, pp of **behold**

behind [bɪ'haɪnd] prep derrière; (time, progress) en retard sur; (work, studies) en retard dans ♦ adv derrière ♦ n derrière m; **to be** ~ (schedule) avoir du retard; ~ **the scenes** dans les coulisses

behold [bɪ'həʊld] (irreg: like **hold**) vt apercevoir, voir

beige [beɪʒ] adj beige

Beijing ['beɪ'dʒɪŋ] n Bei-jing, Pékin

being ['biːɪŋ] n être m

Beirut [beɪ'ruːt] n Beyrouth

belated [bɪ'leɪtɪd] adj tardif(ive)

belch [beltʃ] vi avoir un renvoi, roter ♦ vt (also: ~ **out**: smoke etc) vomir, cracher

belfry ['belfrɪ] n beffroi m

Belgian ['beldʒən] adj belge, de Belgique ♦ n Belge m/f

Belgium ['beldʒəm] n Belgique f

belie [bɪ'laɪ] vt démentir

belief [bɪ'liːf] n (opinion) conviction f; (trust, faith) foi f

believe [bɪ'liːv] vt, vi croire; **to** ~ **in** (God) croire en; (method, ghosts) croire à; ~**r** n (in idea, activity): ~**r in** partisan(e) de; (REL) croyant(e)

belittle [bɪ'lɪtl] vt déprécier, rabaisser

bell [bel] n cloche f; (small) clochette f, grelot m; (on door) sonnette f; (electric) sonnerie f

belligerent [bɪ'lɪdʒərənt] adj (person, attitude) agressif(ive)

bellow ['beləʊ] vi (bull) meugler; (person) brailler

belly ['belɪ] n ventre m

belong [bɪ'lɒŋ] vi: **to** ~ **to** appartenir à; (club etc) faire partie de; **this book** ~**s**

here ce livre va ici; **~ings** *npl* affaires *fpl*, possessions *fpl*

beloved [bɪ'lʌvɪd] *adj* (bien-)aimé(e)

below [bɪ'ləʊ] *prep* sous, au-dessous de ♦ *adv* en dessous; **see ~** voir plus bas *or* plus loin *or* ci-dessous

belt [belt] *n* ceinture *f*; (*of land*) région *f*; (*TECH*) courroie *f* ♦ *vt* (*thrash*) donner une raclée à; **~way** (*US*) *n* (*AUT*) route *f* de ceinture; (: *motorway*) périphérique *m*

bemused [bɪ'mjuːzd] *adj* stupéfié(e)

bench [bentʃ] *n* (*gen, also BRIT: POL*) banc *m*; (*in workshop*) établi *m*; **the B~** (*LAW: judge*) le juge; (: *judges collectively*) la magistrature, la Cour

bend [bend] (*pt, pp* **bent**) *vt* courber; (*leg, arm*) plier ♦ *vi* se courber ♦ *n* (*BRIT: in road*) virage *m*, tournant *m*; (*in pipe, river*) coude *m*; **~ down** *vi* se baisser; **~ over** *vi* se pencher

beneath [bɪ'niːθ] *prep* sous, au-dessous de; (*unworthy of*) indigne de ♦ *adv* dessous, au-dessous, en bas

benefactor ['benɪfæktə*] *n* bienfaiteur *m*

beneficial [benɪ'fɪʃl] *adj* salutaire; avantageux(euse); **~ to the health** bon(ne) pour la santé

benefit ['benɪfɪt] *n* avantage *m*, profit *m*; (*allowance of money*) allocation *f* ♦ *vt* faire du bien à, profiter à ♦ *vi*: **he'll ~ from** it cela lui fera du bien, il y gagnera *or* s'en trouvera bien

Benelux ['benɪlʌks] *n* Bénélux *m*

benevolent [bɪ'nevələnt] *adj* bienveillant(e); (*organization*) bénévole

benign [bɪ'naɪn] *adj* (*person, smile*) bienveillant(e), affable; (*MED*) bénin(igne)

bent [bent] *pt, pp of* **bend** ♦ *n* inclination *f*, penchant *m*; **to be ~ on** être résolu(e) à

bequest [bɪ'kwest] *n* legs *m*

bereaved [bɪ'riːvd] *n*: **the ~** la famille du disparu

beret ['bereɪ] *n* béret *m*

Berlin [bɜː'lɪn] *n* Berlin

berm [bɜːm] (*US*) *n* (*AUT*) accotement *m*

berry ['berɪ] *n* baie *f*

berserk [bə'sɜːk] *adj*: **to go ~** (*madman, crowd*) se déchaîner

berth [bɜːθ] *n* (*bed*) couchette *f*; (*for ship*) poste *m* d'amarrage, mouillage *m* ♦ *vi* (*in harbour*) venir à quai; (*at anchor*) mouiller

beseech [bɪ'siːtʃ] (*pt, pp* **besought**) *vt* implorer, supplier

beset [bɪ'set] (*pt, pp* **beset**) *vt* assaillir

beside [bɪ'saɪd] *prep* à côté de; **to be ~ o.s. (with anger)** être hors de soi; **that's ~ the point** cela n'a rien à voir; **~s** [-z] *adv* en outre, de plus; (*in any case*) d'ailleurs ♦ *prep* (*as well as*) en plus de

besiege [bɪ'siːdʒ] *vt* (*town*) assiéger; (*fig*) assaillir

besought [bɪ'sɔːt] *pt, pp of* **beseech**

best [best] *adj* meilleur(e) ♦ *adv* le mieux; **the ~ part of** (*quantity*) le plus clair de, la plus grande partie de; **at ~** au mieux; **to make the ~ of sth** s'accommoder de qch (du mieux que l'on peut); **to do one's ~** faire de son mieux; **to the ~ of my knowledge** pour autant que je sache; **to the ~ of my ability** du mieux que je pourrai; **~ man** *n* garçon *m* d'honneur

bestow [bɪ'stəʊ] *vt*: **to ~ sth on sb** accorder qch à qn; (*title*) conférer qch à qn

bet [bet] *n* pari *m* ♦ *vt, vi* parier

betray [bɪ'treɪ] *vt* trahir; **~al** *n* trahison *f*

better ['betə*] *adj* meilleur(e) ♦ *adv* mieux ♦ *vt* améliorer ♦ *n*: **to get the ~ of** triompher de, l'emporter sur; **you had ~ do it** vous feriez mieux de le faire; **he thought ~ of it** il s'est ravisé; **to get ~** aller mieux; s'améliorer; **~ off** *adj* plus à l'aise financièrement; (*fig*): **you'd be ~ off this way** vous vous en trouveriez mieux ainsi

betting ['betɪŋ] *n* paris *mpl*; **~ shop** (*BRIT*) *n* bureau *m* de paris

between [bɪ'twiːn] *prep* entre ♦ *adv*: **(in) ~** au milieu; dans l'intervalle; (*in time*) dans l'intervalle

beverage ['bevərɪdʒ] *n* boisson *f* (*gén sans alcool*)

beware [bɪ'wɛə*] *vi*: **to ~ (of)** prendre garde (à); **"~ of the dog"** "(attention) chien méchant"

bewildered [bɪ'wɪldəd] *adj* dérouté(e), ahuri(e)

beyond [bɪ'jɒnd] *prep* (*in space, time*) au-delà de; (*exceeding*) au-dessus de ♦ *adv* au-delà; **~ doubt** hors de doute; **~ repair** irréparable

bias ['baɪəs] *n* (*prejudice*) préjugé *m*, parti pris; **~(s)ed** *adj* partial(e), montrant un parti pris

bib [bɪb] *n* bavoir *m*, bavette *f*

Bible ['baɪbl] *n* Bible *f*

bicarbonate of soda [baɪ'kɑːbənɪt-] *n* bicarbonate *m* de soude

bicker ['bɪkə*] *vi* se chamailler

bicycle ['baɪsɪkl] *n* bicyclette *f*

bid [bɪd] (*pt* **bid** *or* **bade**, *pp* **bid(den)**) *n* offre *f*; (*at auction*) enchère *f*; (*attempt*) tentative *f* ♦ *vi* faire une enchère *or* offre ♦ *vt* faire une enchère *or* offre de; **to ~ sb good day** souhaiter le bonjour à qn; **~der** *n*: **the highest ~der** le plus offrant; **~ding** *n* enchères *fpl*

bide [baɪd] *vt*: **to ~ one's time** attendre son heure

bifocals [baɪ'fəʊkəlz] *npl* verres *mpl* à double foyer, lunettes bifocales

big [bɪg] *adj* grand(e); gros(se)

bigheaded ['bɪg'hedɪd] *adj* prétentieux(euse)

bigot ['bɪgət] *n* fanatique *m/f*, sectaire *m/f*;

~ed adj fanatique, sectaire; **~ry** n fanatisme m, sectarisme m

big top n grand chapiteau

bike [baɪk] n vélo m, bécane f

bikini [bɪˈkiːnɪ] n bikini m

bilingual [baɪˈlɪŋgwəl] adj bilingue

bill [bɪl] n note f, facture f; (POL) projet m de loi; (US: banknote) billet m (de banque); (of bird) bec m; (THEATRE): **on the ~** à l'affiche; **"post no ~s"** "défense d'afficher"; **to fit** or **fill the ~** (fig) faire l'affaire; **~board** n panneau m d'affichage

billet [ˈbɪlɪt] n cantonnement m (chez l'habitant)

billfold [ˈbɪlfəʊld] (US) n portefeuille m

billiards [ˈbɪljədz] n (jeu m de) billard m

billion [ˈbɪljən] n (BRIT) billion m (million de millions); (US) milliard m

bin [bɪn] n boîte f; (also: dust~) poubelle f; (for coal) coffre m

bind [baɪnd] (pt, pp **bound**) vt attacher; (book) relier; (oblige) obliger, contraindre ♦ n (inf: nuisance) scie f; **~ing** adj (contract) constituant une obligation

binge [bɪndʒ] (inf) n: **to go on a/the ~** (inf) aller faire la bringue

bingo [ˈbɪŋgəʊ] n jeu de loto pratiqué dans des établissements publics

binoculars [bɪˈnɒkjʊləz] npl jumelles fpl

bio... prefix: **~chemistry** n biochimie f; **~graphy** n biographie f; **~logical** adj biologique; **~logy** n biologie f

birch [bɜːtʃ] n bouleau m

bird [bɜːd] n oiseau m; (BRIT: inf: girl) nana f; **~'s-eye view** n vue f à vol d'oiseau; (fig) vue d'ensemble or générale; **~-watcher** n ornithologue m/f amateur

Biro [ˈbaɪrəʊ] ® n stylo m à bille

birth [bɜːθ] n naissance f; **to give ~ to** (subj: woman) donner naissance à; (: animal) mettre bas; **~ certificate** n acte m de naissance; **~ control** n (policy) limitation f des naissances; (method) méthode(s) contraceptive(s); **~day** n anniversaire m ♦ cpd d'anniversaire; **~place** n lieu m de naissance; (fig) berceau m; **~ rate** n (taux m de) natalité f

biscuit [ˈbɪskɪt] n (BRIT) biscuit m; (US) petit pain au lait

bisect [baɪˈsekt] vt couper or diviser en deux

bishop [ˈbɪʃəp] n évêque m; (CHESS) fou m

bit [bɪt] n pt of **bite** ♦ n morceau m; (of tool) mèche f; (of horse) mors m; (COMPUT) élément m binaire; **a ~ of** un peu de; **a ~ mad** un peu fou; **~ by ~** petit à petit

bitch [bɪtʃ] n (dog) chienne f; (inf!) salope f (!), garce f

bite [baɪt] (pt **bit**, pp **bitten**) vt, vi mordre; (insect) piquer ♦ n (insect ~) piqûre f; (mouthful) bouchée f; **let's have a ~ (to eat)** (inf) mangeons un morceau; **to ~**

one's nails se ronger les ongles

bitter [ˈbɪtə*] adj amer(ère); (weather, wind) glacial(e); (criticism) cinglant(e); (struggle) acharné(e) ♦ n (BRIT: beer) bière f (forte); **~ness** n amertume f; (taste) goût amer

blab [blæb] vi jaser, trop parler

black [blæk] adj noir(e) ♦ n (colour) noir m; (person): **B~** noir(e) ♦ vt (BRIT: INDUSTRY) boycotter; **to give sb a ~ eye** pocher l'œil à qn, faire un œil au beurre noir à qn; **~ and blue** couvert(e) de bleus; **to be in the ~** (in credit) être créditeur(trice); **~berry** n mûre f; **~bird** n merle m; **~board** n tableau noir; **~ coffee** n café noir; **~currant** n cassis m; **~en** vt noircir; **~ ice** n verglas m; **~leg** n (BRIT) briseur m de grève, jaune m; **~list** n liste noire; **~mail** n chantage m ♦ vt faire chanter, soumettre au chantage; **~ market** n marché noir; **~out** n panne f d'électricité; (TV etc) interruption f d'émission; (fainting) syncope f; **B~ Sea** n: **the B~ Sea** la mer Noire; **~ sheep** n brebis galeuse; **~smith** n forgeron m; **~ spot** n (AUT) point noir

bladder [ˈblædə*] n vessie f

blade [bleɪd] n lame f; (of propeller) pale f; **~ of grass** brin m d'herbe

blame [bleɪm] n faute f, blâme m ♦ vt: **to ~ sb/sth for sth** attribuer à qn/qch la responsabilité de qch; reprocher qch à qn/ qch; **who's to ~?** qui est le fautif or coupable or responsable?; **~less** adj irréprochable

bland [blænd] adj (taste, food) doux(douce), fade

blank [blæŋk] adj blanc(blanche); (look) sans expression, dénué(e) d'expression ♦ n espace m vide, blanc m; (cartridge) cartouche f à blanc; **his mind was a ~** il avait la tête vide; **~ cheque** n chèque m en blanc

blanket [ˈblæŋkɪt] n couverture f; (of snow, cloud) couche f

blare [blɛə*] vi beugler

blast [blɑːst] n souffle m; (of explosive) explosion f ♦ vt faire sauter or exploser; **~-off** n (SPACE) lancement m

blatant [ˈbleɪtənt] adj flagrant(e), criant(e)

blaze [bleɪz] n (fire) incendie m; (fig) flamboiement m ♦ vi (fire) flamber; (fig: eyes) flamboyer; (: guns) crépiter ♦ vt: **to ~ a trail** (fig) montrer la voie

blazer [ˈbleɪzə*] n blazer m

bleach [bliːtʃ] n (also: household ~) eau f de Javel ♦ vt (linen etc) blanchir; **~ed** adj (hair) oxygéné(e), décoloré(e); **~ers** [ˈbliːtʃəz] (US) npl (SPORT) gradins mpl (en plein soleil)

bleak [bliːk] adj morne; (countryside) désolé(e)

bleary-eyed [ˈblɪərɪˈaɪd] adj aux yeux pleins de sommeil

bleat [bliːt] vi bêler

bleed [bliːd] (*pt, pp* **bled**) *vt, vi* saigner; **my nose is** ~**ing** je saigne du nez

bleeper ['bliːpə*] *n* (*device*) bip *m*

blemish ['blemɪʃ] *n* défaut *m*; (*on fruit, reputation*) tache *f*

blend [blend] *n* mélange *m* ♦ *vt* mélanger ♦ *vi* (*colours etc: also:* ~ **in**) se mélanger, se fondre

bless [bles] (*pt, pp* **blessed** *or* **blest**) *vt* bénir; ~ **you!** (*after sneeze*) à vos souhaits!; ~**ing** *n* bénédiction *f*; (*godsend*) bienfait *m*

blew [bluː] *pt of* **blow**

blight [blaɪt] *vt* (*hopes etc*) anéantir; (*life*) briser

blimey ['blaɪmɪ] (*BRIT: inf*) *excl* mince alors!

blind [blaɪnd] *adj* aveugle ♦ *n* (*for window*) store *m* ♦ *vt* aveugler; ~ **alley** *n* impasse *f*; ~ **corner** (*BRIT*) *n* virage *m* sans visibilité; ~**fold** *n* bandeau *m* ♦ *adj, adv* les yeux bandés ♦ *vt* bander les yeux à; ~**ly** *adv* aveuglément; ~**ness** *n* cécité *f*; ~ **spot** *n* (*AUT etc*) angle mort; **that is her** ~ (*fig*) elle refuse d'y voir clair sur ce point

blink [blɪŋk] *vi* cligner des yeux; (*light*) clignoter; ~**ers** *npl* œillères *fpl*

bliss [blɪs] *n* félicité *f*, bonheur *m* sans mélange

blister ['blɪstə*] *n* (*on skin*) ampoule *f*, cloque *f*; (*on paintwork, rubber*) boursouflure *f* ♦ *vi* (*paint*) se boursoufler, se cloquer

blithely ['blaɪðlɪ] *adv* (*unconcernedly*) tranquillement

blizzard ['blɪzəd] *n* blizzard *m*, tempête *f* de neige

bloated ['bləʊtɪd] *adj* (*face*) bouffi(e); (*stomach, person*) gonflé(e)

blob [blɒb] *n* (*drop*) goutte *f*; (*stain, spot*) tache *f*

block [blɒk] *n* bloc *m*; (*in pipes*) obstruction *f*; (*toy*) cube *m*; (*of buildings*) pâté *m* (de maisons) ♦ *vt* bloquer; (*fig*) faire obstacle à; ~ **of flats** (*BRIT*) *n* immeuble (locatif); ~ **mental** ~ trou *m* de mémoire; ~**ade** *n* blocus *m*; ~**age** *n* obstruction *f*; ~**buster** *n* (*film, book*) grand succès *m*; ~ **letters** *npl* majuscules *fpl*

bloke [bləʊk] (*BRIT: inf*) *n* type *m*

blond(e) [blɒnd] *adj, n* blond(e)

blood [blʌd] *n* sang *m*; ~ **donor** *n* donneur(euse) de sang; ~ **group** *n* groupe sanguin; ~**hound** *n* limier *m*; ~ **poisoning** *n* empoisonnement *m* du sang; ~ **pressure** *n* tension *f* (artérielle); ~**shed** *n* effusion *f* de sang, carnage *m*; ~**shot** *adj*: ~**shot eyes** yeux injectés de sang; ~**stream** *n* sang *m*, système sanguin; ~ **test** *n* prise *f* de sang; ~**thirsty** *adj* sanguinaire; ~ **vessel** *n* vaisseau sanguin; ~**y** *adj* sanglant(e); (*nose*) en sang; (*BRIT: inf!*): **this** ~**y ...** ce foutu ... (*!*), ce putain de ... (*!*); ~**y strong/good** vachement *or* sacré-

ment fort/bon; ~**y-minded** (*BRIT: inf*) *adj* contrariant(e), obstiné(e)

bloom [bluːm] *n* fleur *f* ♦ *vi* être en fleur

blossom ['blɒsəm] *n* fleur(s) *f(pl)* ♦ *vi* être en fleurs; (*fig*) s'épanouir; **to** ~ **into** devenir

blot [blɒt] *n* tache *f* ♦ *vt* tacher; ~ **out** *vt* (*memories*) effacer; (*view*) cacher, masquer

blotchy ['blɒtʃɪ] *adj* (*complexion*) couvert(e) de marbrures

blotting paper ['blɒtɪŋ-] *n* buvard *m*

blouse [blauz] *n* chemisier *m*, corsage *m*

blow [bləʊ] (*pt* **blew**, *pp* **blown**) *n* coup *m* ♦ *vi* souffler ♦ *vt* souffler; (*fuse*) faire sauter; (*instrument*) jouer de; **to** ~ **one's nose** se moucher; **to** ~ **a whistle** siffler; ~ **away** *vt* chasser, faire s'envoler; ~ **down** *vt* faire tomber, renverser; ~ **off** *vt* emporter; ~ **out** *vi* (*fire, flame*) s'éteindre; ~ **over** *vi* s'apaiser; ~ **up** *vt* faire sauter; (*tyre*) gonfler; (*PHOT*) agrandir ♦ *vi* exploser, sauter; ~**-dry** *n* brushing *m*; ~**lamp** (*BRIT*) *n* chalumeau *m*; ~**-out** *n* (*of tyre*) éclatement *m*; ~**-torch** *n* = **blowlamp**

blue [bluː] *adj* bleu(e); (*fig*) triste; ~**s** *n* (*MUS*): **the** ~**s** le blues; ~ **film/joke** film *m*/histoire *f* pornographique; **to come out of the** ~ (*fig*) être complètement inattendu; ~**bell** *n* jacinthe *f* des bois; ~**bottle** *n* mouche *f* à viande; ~**print** *n* (*fig*) projet *m*, plan directeur

bluff [blʌf] *vi* bluffer ♦ *n* bluff *m*; **to call sb's** ~ mettre qn au défi d'exécuter ses menaces

blunder ['blʌndə*] *n* gaffe *f*, bévue *f* ♦ *vi* faire une gaffe *or* une bévue

blunt [blʌnt] *adj* (*person*) brusque, ne mâchant pas ses mots; (*knife*) émoussé(e), peu tranchant(e); (*pencil*) mal taillé

blur [blɜː*] *n* tache *or* masse floue *or* confuse ♦ *vt* brouiller

blurb [blɜːb] *n* notice *f* publicitaire; (*for book*) texte *m* de présentation

blurt out [blɜːt-] *vt* (*reveal*) lâcher

blush [blʌʃ] *vi* rougir ♦ *n* rougeur *f*

blustery ['blʌstərɪ] *adj* (*weather*) à bourrasques

boar [bɔː*] *n* sanglier *m*

board [bɔːd] *n* planche *f*; (*on wall*) panneau *m*; (*for chess*) échiquier *m*; (*cardboard*) carton *m*; (*committee*) conseil *m*, comité *m*; (*in firm*) conseil d'administration; (*NAUT, AVIAT*): **on** ~ à bord ♦ *vt* (*ship*) monter à bord de; (*train*) monter dans; **full** ~ (*BRIT*) pension complète; **half** ~ demi-pension *f*; ~ **and lodging** chambre *f* avec pension; **which goes by the** ~ (*fig*) qu'on laisse tomber, qu'on abandonne; ~ **up** *vt* (*door, window*) boucher; ~**er** *n* (*SCOL*) interne *m/f*, pensionnaire; ~**ing card** *n* = **boarding pass**; ~**ing house** *n* pension *f*; ~**ing pass** *n* (*AVIAT, NAUT*) carte *f* d'embarquement; ~**ing school** n internat m, pensionnat m; ~ **room** n salle f du conseil d'administration

boast [bəʊst] vi: **to ~ (about** or **of)** se vanter (de)

boat [bəʊt] n bateau m; (small) canot m; barque f; ~**er** n (hat) canotier m

bob [bɒb] vi (boat, cork on water: also: ~ **up and down**) danser, se balancer

bobby ['bɒbɪ] (BRIT: inf) n ≈ agent m (de police)

bobsleigh ['bɒbsleɪ] n bob m

bode [bəʊd] vi: **to ~ well/ill (for)** être de bon/mauvais augure (pour)

bodily ['bɒdɪlɪ] adj corporel(le) ♦ adv dans ses bras

body ['bɒdɪ] n corps m; (of car) carrosserie f; (of plane) fuselage m; (fig: society) organe m, organisme m; (: quantity) ensemble m, masse f; (of wine) corps; ~**-building** n culturisme m; ~**guard** n garde m du corps; ~**work** n carrosserie f

bog [bɒg] n tourbière f ♦ vt: **to get ~ged down** (fig) s'enliser

boggle ['bɒgl] vi: **the mind ~s** c'est incroyable, on en reste sidéré

bogus ['bəʊgəs] adj bidon inv; fantôme

boil [bɔɪl] vt (faire) bouillir ♦ vi bouillir ♦ n (MED) furoncle m; **to come to the** (BRIT) ~ or **a** (US) ~ bouillir; ~ **down to** vt fus (fig) se réduire or ramener à; ~ **over** vi déborder; ~**ed egg** n œuf m à la coque; ~**ed potatoes** npl pommes fpl à l'anglaise or à l'eau; ~**er** n chaudière f; ~**ing point** n point m d'ébullition

boisterous ['bɔɪstərəs] adj bruyant(e), tapageur(euse)

bold [bəʊld] adj hardi(e), audacieux(euse); (pej) effronté(e); (outline, colour) franc(franche), tranché(e), marqué(e); (pattern) grand(e)

bollard ['bɒləd] (BRIT) n (AUT) borne lumineuse or de signalisation

bolster ['bəʊlstə*]: ~ **up** vt soutenir

bolt [bəʊlt] n (lock) verrou m; (with nut) boulon m ♦ adv: ~ **upright** droit(e) comme un piquet ♦ vt verrouiller; (TECH: also: ~ **on, ~ together**) boulonner; (food) engloutir ♦ vi (horse) s'emballer

bomb [bɒm] n bombe f ♦ vt bombarder

bombastic [bɒm'bæstɪk] adj pompeux(euse)

bomb: ~ **disposal unit** n section f de déminage; ~**er** n (AVIAT) bombardier m; ~**shell** n (fig) bombe f

bona fide ['bəʊnə'faɪdɪ] adj (traveller) véritable

bond [bɒnd] n lien m; (binding promise) engagement m, obligation f; (COMM) obligation; **in ~** (of goods) en douane

bondage ['bɒndɪdʒ] n esclavage m

bone [bəʊn] n os m; (of fish) arête f ♦ vt désosser; ôter les arêtes de; ~ **idle** adj fainéant(e)

bonfire ['bɒnfaɪə*] n feu m (de joie); (for rubbish) feu

bonnet ['bɒnɪt] n bonnet m; (BRIT: of car) capot m

bonus ['bəʊnəs] n prime f, gratification f

bony ['bəʊnɪ] adj (arm, face, MED: tissue) osseux(euse); (meat) plein(e) d'os; (fish) plein d'arêtes

boo [buː] excl hou!, peuh! ♦ vt huer

booby trap ['buːbɪ-] n engin piégé

book [bʊk] n livre m; (of stamps, tickets) carnet m ♦ vt (ticket) prendre; (seat, room) réserver; (driver) dresser un procès-verbal à; (football player) prendre le nom de; ~**s** npl (accounts) comptes mpl, comptabilité f; ~**case** n bibliothèque f (meuble); ~**ing office** (BRIT) n bureau m de location; ~**-keeping** n comptabilité f; ~**let** n brochure f; ~**maker** n bookmaker m; ~**seller** n libraire m/f; ~**shop** n librairie f; ~**store** n librairie f

boom [buːm] n (noise) grondement m; (in prices, population) forte augmentation ♦ vi gronder; prospérer

boon [buːn] n bénédiction f, grand avantage

boost [buːst] n stimulant m, remontant m ♦ vt stimuler; ~**er** n (MED) rappel m

boot [buːt] n botte f; (for hiking) chaussure f (de marche); (for football etc) soulier m; (BRIT: of car) coffre m ♦ vt (COMPUT) amorcer, initialiser; **to ~** (in addition) par-dessus le marché

booth [buːð] n (at fair) baraque (foraine); (telephone etc) cabine f; (also: voting ~) isoloir m

booty ['buːtɪ] n butin m

booze [buːz] (inf) n boissons fpl alcooliques, alcool m

border ['bɔːdə*] n bordure f; bord m; (of a country) frontière f ♦ vt border; (also: ~ **on:** country) être limitrophe de; **B~s** n (GEO): **the B~s** la région frontière entre l'Écosse et l'Angleterre; ~ **on** vt fus être voisin(e) de, toucher à; ~**line** n (fig) ligne f de démarcation; ~**line case** n cas m limite

bore [bɔː*] pt of bear ♦ vt (hole) percer; (oil well, tunnel) creuser; (person) ennuyer, raser ♦ n (person) raseur(euse); (of gun) calibre m; **to be ~d** s'ennuyer; ~**dom** n ennui m; **boring** adj ennuyeux(euse)

born [bɔːn] adj: **to be ~** naître; **I was ~ in 1960** je suis né en 1960

borne [bɔːn] pp of bear

borough ['bʌrə] n municipalité f

borrow ['bɒrəʊ] vt: **to ~ sth (from sb)** emprunter qch (à qn)

Bosnia (and) Herzegovina [bɒsnɪə (ənd) hɜːzəgəʊviːnə] n Bosnie-Herzégovine f

bosom ['bʊzəm] n poitrine f; (fig) sein m; ~ **friend** n ami(e) intime

boss [bɒs] *n* patron(ne) ♦ *vt* (*also*: ~ *around/about*) commander; ~**y** *adj* autoritaire

bosun [ˈbəʊsn] *n* maître *m* d'équipage

botany [ˈbɒtənɪ] *n* botanique *f*

botch [bɒtʃ] *vt* (*also*: ~ *up*) saboter, bâcler

both [bəʊθ] *adj* les deux, l'un(e) et l'autre ♦ *pron*: ~ (*of them*) les deux, tous(toutes) (les) deux, l'un(e) et l'autre: **they sell ~ the fabric and the finished curtains** ils vendent (et) le tissu et les rideaux (finis), ils vendent à la fois le tissu et les rideaux (finis); ~ **of us went, we ~ went** nous y sommes allés (tous) les deux

bother [ˈbɒðə*] *vt* (*worry*) tracasser; (*disturb*) déranger ♦ *vi* (*also*: ~ *o.s.*) se tracasser, se faire du souci ♦ *n*: **it is a ~ to have to do** c'est vraiment ennuyeux d'avoir à faire; **it's no ~** aucun problème; **to ~ doing** prendre la peine de faire

bottle [ˈbɒtl] *n* bouteille *f*; (*baby's*) biberon *m* ♦ *vt* mettre en bouteille(s); ~ **up** *vt* refouler, contenir; ~ **bank** *n* conteneur *m* à verre; ~**neck** *n* étranglement *m*; ~**-opener** *n* ouvre-bouteille *m*

bottom [ˈbɒtəm] *n* (*of container, sea etc*) fond *m*; (*buttocks*) derrière *m*; (*of page, list*) bas *m* ♦ *adj* du fond; du bas; **the ~ of the class** le dernier de la classe; ~**less** *adj* (*funds*) inépuisable

bough [baʊ] *n* branche *f*, rameau *m*

bought [bɔːt] *pt, pp of* **buy**

boulder [ˈbəʊldə*] *n* gros rocher

bounce [baʊns] *vi* (*ball*) rebondir; (*cheque*) être refusé(e) (*étant sans provision*) ♦ *vt* faire rebondir ♦ *n* (*rebound*) rebond *m*; ~**r** (*inf*) *n* (*at dance, club*) videur *m*

bound [baʊnd] *pt, pp of* **bind** ♦ *n* (*gen pl*) limite *f*; (*leap*) bond *m* ♦ *vi* (*leap*) bondir ♦ *vt* (*limit*) borner ♦ *adj*: **to be ~ to do sth** (*obliged*) être obligé(e) *or* avoir obligation de faire qch; **he's ~ to fail** (*likely*) il est sûr d'échouer, son échec est inévitable *or* assuré; ~ **by** (*law, regulation*) engagé(e) par; ~ **for** à destination de; **out of ~s** dont l'accès est interdit

boundary [ˈbaʊndərɪ] *n* frontière *f*

boundless [ˈbaʊndlɪs] *adj* sans bornes

bout [baʊt] *n* période *f*; (*of malaria etc*) accès *m*, crise *f*, attaque *f*; (*BOXING etc*) combat *m*, match *m*

bow[1] [bəʊ] *n* nœud *m*; (*weapon*) arc *m*; (*MUS*) archet *m*

bow[2] [baʊ] *n* (*with body*) révérence *f*, inclination *f* (*du buste or corps*); (*NAUT: also*: ~**s**) proue *f* ♦ *vi* faire une révérence, s'incliner; (*yield*): **to ~ to** *or* **before** s'incliner devant, se soumettre à

bowels [ˈbaʊəlz] *npl* intestins *mpl*; (*fig*) entrailles *fpl*

bowl [bəʊl] *n* (*for eating*) bol *m*; (*ball*) boule *f* ♦ *vi* (*CRICKET, BASEBALL*) lancer (la balle)

bow-legged [ˈbəʊˈlegɪd] *adj* aux jambes arquées

bowler [ˈbəʊlə*] *n* (*CRICKET, BASEBALL*) lanceur *m* (*de la balle*); (*BRIT: also*: ~ *hat*) (chapeau *m*) melon *m*

bowling [ˈbəʊlɪŋ] *n* (*game*) jeu *m* de boules; jeu *m* de quilles; ~ **alley** *n* bowling *m*; ~ **green** *n* terrain *m* de boules (*gazonné et carré*)

bowls [bəʊlz] *n* (*game*) (jeu *m* de) boules *fpl*

bow tie [bəʊ-] *n* nœud *m* papillon

box [bɒks] *n* boîte *f*; (*also*: *cardboard* ~) carton *m*; (*THEATRE*) loge *f* ♦ *vt* mettre en boîte; (*SPORT*) boxer avec ♦ *vi* boxer, faire de la boxe; ~**er** *n* (*person*) boxeur *m*; ~**ing** *n* (*SPORT*) boxe *f*; **B~ing Day** (*BRIT*) *n* le lendemain de Noël; ~**ing gloves** *npl* gants *mpl* de boxe; ~**ing ring** *n* ring *m*; ~ **office** *n* bureau *m* de location; ~**room** *n* débarras *m*; chambrette *f*

boy [bɔɪ] *n* garçon *m*

boycott [ˈbɔɪkɒt] *n* boycottage *m* ♦ *vt* boycotter

boyfriend [ˈbɔɪfrend] *n* (petit) ami

boyish [ˈbɔɪɪʃ] *adj* (*behaviour*) de garçon; (*girl*) garçonnier(ière)

BR *abbr* = **British Rail**

bra [brɑː] *n* soutien-gorge *m*

brace [breɪs] *n* (*on teeth*) appareil *m* (dentaire); (*tool*) vilbrequin *m* ♦ *vt* (*knees, shoulders*) appuyer; ~**s** *npl* (*BRIT: for trousers*) bretelles *fpl*; **to ~ o.s.** (*lit*) s'arc-bouter; (*fig*) se préparer mentalement

bracelet [ˈbreɪslɪt] *n* bracelet *m*

bracing [ˈbreɪsɪŋ] *adj* tonifiant(e), tonique

bracket [ˈbrækɪt] *n* (*TECH*) tasseau *m*, support *m*; (*group*) classe *f*, tranche *f*; (*also*: *brace* ~) accolade *f*; (: *round* ~) parenthèse *f*; (: *square* ~) crochet *m* ♦ *vt* mettre entre parenthèse(s); (*fig: also*: ~ *together*) regrouper

brag [bræg] *vi* se vanter

braid [breɪd] *n* (*trimming*) galon *m*; (*of hair*) tresse *f*

brain [breɪn] *n* cerveau *m*; ~**s** *npl* (*intellect, CULIN*) cervelle *f*; **he's got ~s** il est intelligent; ~**child** *n* invention personnelle; ~**wash** *vt* faire subir un lavage de cerveau à; ~**wave** *n* idée géniale; ~**y** *adj* intelligent(e), doué(e)

braise [breɪz] *vt* braiser

brake [breɪk] *n* (*on vehicle, also fig*) frein *m* ♦ *vi* freiner; ~ **fluid** *n* liquide *m* de freins; ~ **light** *n* feu *m* de stop

bran [bræn] *n* son *m*

branch [brɑːntʃ] *n* branche *f*; (*COMM*) succursale *f* ♦ *vi* bifurquer; ~ **out** *vi* (*fig*): **to ~ out into** étendre ses activités à

brand [brænd] *n* marque (commerciale) ♦ *vt* (*cattle*) marquer (au fer rouge); ~**-new** *adj* tout(e) neuf(neuve), flambant neuf(neuve)

brandy ['brændɪ] *n* cognac *m*, fine *f*

brash [bræʃ] *adj* effronté(e)

brass [brɑːs] *n* cuivre *m* (jaune), laiton *m*; **the ~** (*MUS*) les cuivres; **~ band** *n* fanfare *f*

brassière ['bræsɪə*] *n* soutien-gorge *m*

brat [bræt] (*pej*) *n* mioche *m/f*, môme *m/f*

brave [breɪv] *adj* courageux(euse), brave ♦ *n* guerrier indien ♦ *vt* braver, affronter; **~ry** *n* bravoure *f*, courage *m*

brawl [brɔːl] *n* rixe *f*, bagarre *f*

bray [breɪ] *vi* braire

brazen ['breɪzn] *adj* impudent(e), effronté(e) ♦ *vt*: **to ~ it out** payer d'effronterie, crâner

brazier ['breɪzɪə*] *n* brasero *m*

Brazil [brə'zɪl] *n* Brésil *m*

breach [briːtʃ] *vt* ouvrir une brèche dans ♦ *n* (*gap*) brèche *f*; (*breaking*): **~ of contract** rupture de contrat; **~ of the peace** attentat *m* à l'ordre public

bread [bred] *n* pain *m*; **~ and butter** *n* tartines (beurrées) *fpl*, (*fig*) subsistance *f*; **~bin** *n* (*BRIT*) boîte *f* à pain; (*bigger*) huche *f* à pain; **~box** *n* (*US*) = **~bin**; **~crumbs** *npl* miettes *fpl* de pain; (*CULIN*) chapelure *f*, panure *f*; **~line** *n*: **to be on the ~line** être sans le sou or dans l'indigence

breadth [bretθ] *n* largeur *f*; (*fig*) ampleur *f*

breadwinner ['bredwɪnə*] *n* soutien *m* de famille

break [breɪk] (*pt* **broke**, *pp* **broken**) *vt* casser, briser; (*promise*) rompre; (*law*) violer ♦ *vi* (*se*) casser, se briser; (*weather*) tourner; (*story, news*) se répandre; (*day*) se lever ♦ *n* (*gap*) brèche *f*; (*fracture*) cassure *f*; (*pause, interval*) interruption *f*, arrêt *m*; (*: short*) pause *f*; (*: at school*) récréation *f*; (*chance*) chance *f*, occasion *f* favorable; **to ~ one's leg** *etc* se casser la jambe *etc*; **to ~ a record** battre un record; **to ~ the news to sb** annoncer la nouvelle à qn; **~ even** rentrer dans ses frais; **~ free** *or* **loose** se dégager, s'échapper; **~ open** (*door etc*) forcer, fracturer; **~ down** *vt* (*figures, data*) décomposer, analyser ♦ *vi* s'effondrer; (*MED*) faire une dépression (nerveuse); (*AUT*) tomber en panne; **~ in** *vt* (*horse etc*) dresser ♦ *vi* (*burglar*) entrer par effraction; (*interrupt*) interrompre; **~ into** *vt fus* (*house*) s'introduire *or* pénétrer par effraction dans; **~ off** *vi* (*speaker*) s'interrompre; (*branch*) se rompre; **~ out** *vi* éclater, se déclarer; (*prisoner*) s'évader; **to ~ out in spots** *or* **a rash** avoir une éruption de boutons; **~ up** *vi* (*ship*) se disloquer; (*crowd, meeting*) se disperser, se séparer; (*marriage*) se briser; (*SCOL*) entrer en vacances ♦ *vt* casser; (*fight etc*) interrompre, faire cesser; **~age** *n* casse *f*; **~down** *n* (*AUT*) panne *f*; (*in communications, marriage*) rupture *f*; (*MED: also:* nervous ~) dépression (nerveuse); (*of statistics*) ventilation *f*; **~down van** (*BRIT*) *n* dépanneuse *f*; **~er** *n* brisant *m*

breakfast ['brekfəst] *n* petit déjeuner

break: **~-in** *n* cambriolage *m*; **~ing and entering** *n* (*LAW*) effraction *f*; **~through** *n* percée *f*; **~water** *n* brise-lames *m inv*, digue *f*

breast [brest] *n* (*of woman*) sein *m*; (*chest, of meat*) poitrine *f*; **~-feed** (*irreg: like* **feed**) *vt, vi* allaiter; **~stroke** *n* brasse *f*

breath [breθ] *n* haleine *f*; **out of ~** à bout de souffle, essoufflé(e)

Breathalyser ['breθəlaɪzə*] ® *n* Alcootest *m* (®)

breathe [briːð] *vt, vi* respirer; **~ in** *vt, vi* aspirer, inspirer; **~ out** *vt, vi* expirer; **~r** *n* moment *m* de repos *or* de répit; **breathing** ['briːðɪŋ] *n* respiration *f*; **breathing space** *n* (*fig*) (moment *m* de) répit *m*

breathless ['breθlɪs] *adj* essoufflé(e), haletant(e); oppressé(e)

breathtaking ['breθteɪkɪŋ] *adj* stupéfiant(e), à vous couper le souffle

breed [briːd] (*pt, pp* **bred**) *vt* élever, faire l'élevage de ♦ *vi* se reproduire ♦ *n* race *f*, variété *f*; **~ing** *n* (*upbringing*) éducation *f*

breeze [briːz] *n* brise *f*; **breezy** ['briːzɪ] *adj* frais(fraîche); aéré(e); (*manner etc*) désinvolte, jovial(e)

brevity ['brevɪtɪ] *n* brièveté *f*

brew [bruː] *vt* (*tea*) faire infuser; (*beer*) brasser ♦ *vi* (*fig*) se préparer, couver; **~ery** *n* brasserie *f* (fabrique)

bribe ['braɪb] *n* pot-de-vin *m* ♦ *vt* acheter, soudoyer; **~ry** *n* corruption *f*

brick [brɪk] *n* brique *f*; **~layer** *n* maçon *m*

bridal ['braɪdl] *adj* nuptial(e)

bride [braɪd] *n* mariée *f*, épouse *f*; **~groom** *n* marié *m*, époux *m*; **~smaid** *n* demoiselle *f* d'honneur

bridge [brɪdʒ] *n* pont *m*; (*NAUT*) passerelle *f* (de commandement); (*of nose*) arête *f*; (*CARDS, DENTISTRY*) bridge *m* ♦ *vt* (*fig: gap, gulf*) combler

bridle ['braɪdl] *n* bride *f*; **~ path** *n* piste *or* allée cavalière

brief [briːf] *adj* bref(brève) ♦ *n* (*LAW*) dossier *m*, cause *f*; (*gen*) tâche *f* ♦ *vt* mettre au courant; **~s** *npl* (*undergarment*) slip *m*; **~case** *n* serviette *f*; porte-documents *m inv*; **~ly** *adv* brièvement

bright [braɪt] *adj* brillant(e); (*room, weather*) clair(e); (*clever: person, idea*) intelligent(e); (*cheerful: colour, person*) vif(vive)

brighten (*also:* ~ **up**) *vt* (*room*) éclaircir, égayer; (*event*) égayer ♦ *vi* s'éclaircir; (*person*) retrouver un peu de sa gaieté; (*face*) s'éclairer; (*prospects*) s'améliorer

brilliance ['brɪljəns] *n* éclat *m*

brilliant ['brɪljənt] *adj* brillant(e); (*sunshine, light*) éclatant(e); (*inf: holiday etc*) super

brim [brɪm] n bord m
brine [braɪn] n (CULIN) saumure f
bring [brɪŋ] (pt, pp **brought**) vt apporter; (person) amener; ~ **about** vt provoquer, entraîner; ~ **back** vt rapporter; ramener; (restore: hanging) réinstaurer; (price) faire baisser; (enemy plane) descendre; (government) faire tomber; ~ **forward** vt avancer; ~ **off** vt (task, plan) réussir, mener à bien; ~ **out** vt (meaning) faire ressortir; (book) publier; (object) sortir; ~ **round** vt (unconscious person) ranimer; ~ **to** vt = ~ **round**; ~ **up** vt (child) élever; (carry up) monter; (question) soulever; (food: vomit) vomir, rendre
brink [brɪŋk] n bord m
brisk [brɪsk] adj vif(vive)
bristle ['brɪsl] n poil m ♦ vi se hérisser
Britain ['brɪtən] n (also: Great ~) Grande-Bretagne f
British ['brɪtɪʃ] adj britannique ♦ npl: **the ~** les Britanniques mpl; ~ **Isles** npl: **the ~ Isles** les Iles fpl Britanniques; ~ **Rail** n compagnie ferroviaire britannique
Briton ['brɪtən] n Britannique m/f
Brittany ['brɪtənɪ] n Bretagne f
brittle ['brɪtl] adj cassant(e), fragile
broach [brəʊtʃ] vt (subject) aborder
broad [brɔːd] adj large; (general: outlines) grand(e); (: distinction) général(e); (accent) prononcé(e); **in ~ daylight** en plein jour; **~cast** (pt, pp **~cast**) n émission f ♦ vt radiodiffuser; téléviser ♦ vi émettre; **~en** vt élargir ♦ vi s'élargir; **to ~en one's mind** élargir ses horizons; **~ly** adv en gros, généralement; **~-minded** adj large d'esprit
broccoli ['brɒkəlɪ] n brocoli m
brochure ['brəʊʃʊə*] n prospectus m, dépliant m
broil [brɔɪl] vt griller
broke [brəʊk] pt of **break** ♦ adj (inf) fauché(e)
broken ['brəʊkən] pp of **break** ♦ adj cassé(e); (machine: also: ~ **down**) fichu(e); **in ~ English/French** dans un anglais/français approximatif or hésitant; ~ **leg** etc jambe etc cassée; **~-hearted** adj (ayant) le cœur brisé
broker ['brəʊkə*] n courtier m
brolly ['brɒlɪ] n (BRIT: inf) pépin m, parapluie m
bronchitis [brɒŋ'kaɪtɪs] n bronchite f
bronze [brɒnz] n bronze m
brooch [brəʊtʃ] n broche f
brood [bruːd] n couvée f ♦ vi (person) méditer (sombrement), ruminer
broom [bruːm] n balai m; (BOT) genêt m; **~stick** n manche m à balai
Bros. abbr = **Brothers**
broth [brɒθ] n bouillon m de viande et de légumes
brothel ['brɒθl] n maison close, bordel m

brother ['brʌðə*] n frère m; **~-in-law** n beau-frère m
brought [brɔːt] pt, pp of **bring**
brow [braʊ] n front m; (eye~) sourcil m; (of hill) sommet m
brown [braʊn] adj brun(e), marron inv; (hair) châtain inv; brun; (eyes) marron inv; (tanned) bronzé(e) ♦ n (colour) brun m ♦ vt (CULIN) faire dorer; ~ **bread** n pain m bis; **B~ie** ['braʊnɪ] n (also: ~ **Guide**) jeannette f, éclaireuse (cadette); **~ie** ['braʊnɪ] (US) n (cake) gâteau m au chocolat et aux noix; ~ **paper** n papier m d'emballage; ~ **sugar** n cassonade f
browse [braʊz] vi (among books) bouquiner, feuilleter les livres; **to ~ through a book** feuilleter un livre
bruise [bruːz] n bleu m, contusion f ♦ vt contusionner, meurtrir
brunette [bruː'net] n (femme) brune
brunt [brʌnt] n: **the ~ of** (attack, criticism etc) le plus gros de
brush [brʌʃ] n brosse f; (painting) pinceau m; (shaving) blaireau m; (quarrel) accrochage m, prise f de bec ♦ vt brosser; (also: ~ **against**) effleurer, frôler; ~ **aside** vt écarter, balayer; ~ **up** vt (knowledge) rafraîchir, réviser; **~wood** n broussailles fpl, taillis m
Brussels ['brʌslz] n Bruxelles; ~ **sprout** n chou m de Bruxelles
brutal ['bruːtl] adj brutal(e)
brute [bruːt] n brute f ♦ adj: **by ~ force** par la force
BSc abbr = **Bachelor of Science**
bubble ['bʌbl] n bulle f ♦ vi bouillonner, faire des bulles; (sparkle) pétiller; ~ **bath** n bain moussant; ~ **gum** n bubblegum m
buck [bʌk] n mâle m (d'un lapin, daim etc); (US: inf) dollar m ♦ vi ruer, lancer une ruade; **to pass the ~** (**to sb**) se décharger de la responsabilité (sur qn); ~ **up** vi (cheer up) reprendre du poil de la bête, se remonter
bucket ['bʌkɪt] n seau m
buckle ['bʌkl] n boucle f ♦ vt (belt etc) boucler, attacher ♦ vi (warp) tordre, gauchir; (: wheel) se voiler; se déformer
bud [bʌd] n bourgeon m; (of flower) bouton m ♦ vi bourgeonner; (flower) éclore
Buddhism ['bʊdɪzəm] n bouddhisme m
budding ['bʌdɪŋ] adj (poet etc) en herbe; (passion etc) naissant(e)
buddy ['bʌdɪ] n (US) copain m
budge [bʌdʒ] vt faire bouger; (fig: person) faire changer d'avis ♦ vi bouger; changer d'avis
budgerigar ['bʌdʒərɪgɑː*] n (BRIT) perruche f
budget ['bʌdʒɪt] n budget m ♦ vi: **to ~ for sth** inscrire qch au budget
budgie ['bʌdʒɪ] n (BRIT) n = **budgerigar**
buff [bʌf] adj (couleur f) chamois m ♦ n (inf: enthusiast) mordu(e); **he's a ... =** c'est

un mordu de ...

buffalo ['bʌfələu] (*pl* ~ *or* ~**es**) *n* buffle *m*; (*US*) bison *m*

buffer ['bʌfə*] *n* tampon *m*; (*COMPUT*) mémoire *f* tampon

buffet[1] ['bʌfɪt] *vt* secouer, ébranler

buffet[2] ['bufeɪ] *n* (*in food, BRIT: bar*) buffet *m*; ~ **car** (*BRIT*) *n* (*RAIL*) voiture-buffet *f*

bug [bʌg] *n* (*insect*) punaise *f*; (*: gen*) insecte *m*, bestiole *f*; (*fig: germ*) virus *m*, microbe *m*; (*COMPUT*) erreur *f*; (*fig: spy device*) dispositif *m* d'écoute (électronique) ♦ *vt* garnir de dispositifs d'écoute; (*inf: annoy*) embêter

bugle ['bjuːgl] *n* clairon *m*

build [bɪld] (*pt, pp* **built**) *n* (*of person*) carrure *f*, charpente *f* ♦ *vt* construire, bâtir; ~ **up** *vt* accumuler, amasser; accroître; ~**er** *n* entrepreneur *f*; ~**ing** *n* (*trade*) construction *f*; (*house, structure*) bâtiment *m*, construction; (*offices, flats*) immeuble *m*; ~**ing society** (*BRIT*) *n* société *f* de crédit immobilier

built [bɪlt] *pt, pp of* **build**; ~**-in** *adj* (*cupboard, oven*) encastré(e); (*device*) incorporé(e); intégré(e); ~**-up area** *n* zone urbanisée

bulb [bʌlb] *n* (*BOT*) bulbe *m*, oignon *m*; (*ELEC*) ampoule *f*

bulge [bʌldʒ] *n* renflement *m*, gonflement *m* ♦ *vi* (*pocket, file etc*) être plein(e) à craquer; (*cheeks*) être gonflé(e)

bulk [bʌlk] *n* masse *f*, volume *m*; (*of person*) corpulence *f*; **in** ~ (*COMM*) en vrac; **the** ~ **of** la plus grande *or* grosse partie de; ~**y** *adj* volumineux(euse), encombrant(e)

bull [bul] *n* taureau *m*; (*male elephant/ whale*) mâle *m*; ~**dog** *n* bouledogue *m*

bulldozer ['buldəuzə*] *n* bulldozer *m*

bullet ['bulɪt] *n* balle *f* (*de fusil etc*)

bulletin ['bulɪtɪn] *n* bulletin *m*, communiqué *m*; (*news* ~) (bulletin d')informations *fpl*

bulletproof ['bulɪtpruːf] *adj* (*car*) blindé(e); (*vest etc*) pare-balles *inv*

bullfight ['bulfaɪt] *n* corrida *f*, course *f* de taureaux; ~**er** *n* torero *m*; ~**ing** *n* tauromachie *f*

bullion ['buljən] *n* or *m* or argent en lingots

bull: ~**ock** ['bulək] *n* bœuf *m*; ~**ring** ['bulrɪŋ] *n* arènes *fpl*; ~'**s-eye** ['bulzaɪ] *n* centre *m* (*de la cible*)

bully ['bulɪ] *n* brute *f*, tyran *m* ♦ *vt* tyranniser, rudoyer

bum [bʌm] *n* (*inf: backside*) derrière *m*; (*esp US: tramp*) vagabond(e), traîne-savates *m/f inv*

bumblebee ['bʌmblbiː] *n* bourdon *m*

bump [bʌmp] *n* (*in car: minor accident*) accrochage *m*; (*jolt*) cahot *m*; (*on road etc, on head*) bosse *f* ♦ *vt* heurter, cogner; ~ **into** *vt fus* rentrer dans, tamponner; (*meet*) tomber sur; ~**er** *n* pare-chocs *m inv* ♦ *adj*: ~**er crop/harvest** récolte/moisson exceptionnelle; ~**er cars** *npl* autos tamponneuses

bumpy ['bʌmpɪ] *adj* cahoteux(euse)

bun [bʌn] *n* petit pain au lait; (*of hair*) chignon *m*

bunch [bʌntʃ] *n* (*of flowers*) bouquet *m*; (*of keys*) trousseau *m*; (*of bananas*) régime *m*; (*of people*) groupe *m*; ~**es** *npl* (*in hair*) couettes *fpl*; ~ **of grapes** grappe *f* de raisin

bundle ['bʌndl] *n* paquet *m* ♦ *vt* (*also:* ~ **up**) faire un paquet de; (*put*): **to** ~ **sth/sb into** fourrer *or* enfourner qch/qn dans

bungalow ['bʌŋgələu] *n* bungalow *m*

bungle ['bʌŋgl] *vt* bâcler, gâcher

bunion ['bʌnjən] *n* oignon *m* (*au pied*)

bunk [bʌŋk] *n* couchette *f*; ~ **beds** *npl* lits superposés

bunker ['bʌŋkə*] *n* (*coal store*) soute *f* à charbon; (*MIL, GOLF*) bunker *m*

bunny ['bʌnɪ] *n* (*also:* ~ **rabbit**) Jeannot *m* lapin

bunting ['bʌntɪŋ] *n* pavoisement *m*, drapeaux *mpl*

buoy [bɔɪ] *n* bouée *f*; ~ **up** *vt* faire flotter; (*fig*) soutenir, épauler; ~**ant** *adj* capable de flotter; (*carefree*) gai(e), plein(e) d'entrain; (*economy*) ferme, actif

burden ['bɜːdn] *n* fardeau *m* ♦ *vt* (*trouble*) accabler, surcharger

bureau ['bjuərəu] (*pl* ~**x**) *n* (*BRIT: writing desk*) bureau *m*, secrétaire *m*; (*US: chest of drawers*) commode *f*; (*office*) bureau, office *m*; ~**cracy** [bjuˈrɔkrəsɪ] *n* bureaucratie *f*

burglar ['bɜːglə*] *n* cambrioleur *m*; ~ **alarm** *n* sonnerie *f* d'alarme; ~**y** *n* cambriolage *m*

Burgundy ['bɜːgəndɪ] *n* Bourgogne *f*

burial ['berɪəl] *n* enterrement *m*

burly ['bɜːlɪ] *adj* de forte carrure, costaud(e)

Burma ['bɜːmə] *n* Birmanie *f*

burn [bɜːn] (*pt, pp* **burned** *or* **burnt**) *vt, vi* brûler ♦ *n* brûlure *f*; ~ **down** *vt* incendier, détruire par le feu; ~**er** *n* brûleur *m*; ~**ing** *adj* brûlant(e); (*house*) en flammes; (*ambition*) dévorant(e)

burrow ['bʌrəu] *n* terrier *m* ♦ *vt* creuser

bursary ['bɜːsərɪ] (*BRIT*) *n* bourse *f* (d'études)

burst [bɜːst] (*pt, pp* **burst**) *vt* crever; faire éclater ♦ *vi* (*subj: river: banks etc*) déborder; éclater; (*tyre*) crever ♦ *n* (*of gunfire*) rafale *f* (de tir); (*also:* ~ *pipe*) rupture *f*, fuite *f*; **a** ~ **of enthusiasm/energy** un accès d'enthousiasme/d'énergie; **to** ~ **into flames** s'enflammer soudainement; **to** ~ **out laughing** éclater de rire; **to** ~ **into tears** fondre en larmes; **to be** ~**ing with** être plein (à craquer) de; (*fig*) être débordant(e) de; ~ **into** *vt fus* (*room etc*) faire irruption dans

bury ['berɪ] *vt* enterrer

bus [bʌs, *pl* '-ɪz] (*pl* ~**es**) *n* autobus *m*

bush [bʊʃ] *n* buisson *m*; (*scrubland*) brousse *f*; **to beat about the** ~ tourner autour du pot; ~**y** ['bʊʃɪ] *adj* broussailleux(euse), touffu(e)

busily ['bɪzɪlɪ] *adv* activement

business ['bɪznɪs] *n* (*matter, firm*) affaire *f*; (*trading*) affaires *fpl*; (*job, duty*) travail *m*; **to be away on** ~ être en déplacement d'affaires; **it's none of my** ~ cela ne me regarde pas, ce ne sont pas mes affaires; **he means** ~ il ne plaisante pas, il est sérieux; ~**like** *adj* sérieux(euse); efficace; ~**man** (*irreg*) *n* homme *m* d'affaires; ~ **trip** *n* voyage *m* d'affaires; ~**woman** (*irreg*) *n* femme *f* d'affaires

busker ['bʌskə*] (*BRIT*) *n* musicien ambulant

bus stop *n* arrêt *m* d'autobus

bust [bʌst] *n* buste *m*; (*measurement*) tour *m* de poitrine ♦ *adj* (*inf: broken*) fichu(e), fini(e); **to go** ~ faire faillite

bustle ['bʌsl] *n* remue-ménage *m*, affairement *m* ♦ *vi* s'affairer, se démener; **bustling** *adj* (*town*) bruyant(e), affairé(e)

busy ['bɪzɪ] *adj* occupé(e); (*shop, street*) très fréquenté(e) ♦ *vt*: **to** ~ **o.s.** s'occuper; ~**body** *n* mouche *f* du coche, âme *f* charitable; ~ **signal** (*US*) *n* (*TEL*) tonalité *f* occupé *inv*

─────────────── *KEYWORD*

but [bʌt] *conj* mais; **I'd love to come,** ~ **I'm busy** j'aimerais venir mais je suis occupé ♦ *prep* (*apart from, except*) sauf, excepté; **we've had nothing** ~ **trouble** nous n'avons eu que des ennuis; **no-one** ~ **him can do it** lui seul peut le faire; ~ **for you/ your help** sans toi/ton aide; **anything** ~ **that** tout sauf *or* excepté ça, tout mais pas ça
♦ *adv* (*just, only*) ne ... que; **she's** ~ **a child** elle n'est qu'une enfant; **had I** ~ **known** si seulement j'avais su; **all** ~ **finished** pratiquement terminé

butcher ['bʊtʃə*] *n* boucher *m* ♦ *vt* massacrer; (*cattle etc for meat*) tuer; ~**'s (shop)** *n* boucherie *f*

butler ['bʌtlə*] *n* maître *m* d'hôtel

butt [bʌt] *n* (*large barrel*) gros tonneau; (*of gun*) crosse *f*; (*of cigarette*) mégot *m*; (*BRIT: fig: target*) cible *f* ♦ *vt* donner un coup de tête à; ~ **in** *vi* (*interrupt*) s'immiscer dans la conversation

butter ['bʌtə*] *n* beurre *m* ♦ *vt* beurrer; ~**cup** *n* bouton *m* d'or; ~**fly** *n* papillon *m*; (*SWIMMING: also:* ~**fly stroke**) brasse *f* papillon

buttocks ['bʌtəks] *npl* fesses *fpl*

button ['bʌtn] *n* bouton *m*; (*US: badge*) pin *m* ♦ *vt* (*also:* ~ **up**) boutonner ♦ *vi* se boutonner

buttress ['bʌtrɪs] *n* contrefort *m*

buxom ['bʌksəm] *adj* aux formes avantageuses *or* épanouies

buy [baɪ] (*pt, pp* **bought**) *vt* acheter ♦ *n* achat *m*; **to** ~ **sb sth/sth from sb** acheter qch à qn; **to** ~ **sb a drink** offrir un verre *or* à boire à qn; ~**er** *n* acheteur(euse)

buzz [bʌz] *n* bourdonnement *m*; (*inf: phone call*): **to give sb a** ~ passer un coup *m* de fil à qn ♦ *vi* bourdonner; ~**er** ['bʌzə*] *n* timbre *m* électrique; ~ **word** (*inf*) *n* mot *m* à la mode

─────────────── *KEYWORD*

by [baɪ] *prep* **1** (*referring to cause, agent*) par, de; **killed** ~ **lightning** tué par la foudre; **surrounded** ~ **a fence** entouré d'une barrière; **a painting** ~ **Picasso** un tableau de Picasso
2 (*referring to method, manner, means*): ~ **bus/car** en autobus/voiture; ~ **train** par le *or* en train; **to pay** ~ **cheque** payer par chèque; ~ **saving hard, he ...** à force d'économiser, il ...
3 (*via, through*) par; **we came** ~ **Dover** nous sommes venus par Douvres
4 (*close to, past*) à côté de; **the house** ~ **the school** la maison à côté de l'école; **a holiday** ~ **the sea** des vacances au bord de la mer; **she sat** ~ **his bed** elle était assise à son chevet; **she went** ~ **me** elle est passée à côté de moi; **I go** ~ **the post office every day** je passe devant la poste tous les jours
5 (*with time: not later than*) avant; (: *during*): ~ **daylight** à la lumière du jour; ~ **night** la nuit, de nuit; ~ **4 o'clock** avant 4 heures; ~ **this time tomorrow** d'ici demain à la même heure; ~ **the time I got here it was too late** lorsque je suis arrivé il était déjà trop tard
6 (*amount*) à; ~ **the kilo/metre** au kilo/au mètre; **paid** ~ **the hour** payé à l'heure
7 (*MATH, measure*): **to divide/multiply** ~ **3** diviser/multiplier par 3; **a room 3 metres** ~ **4** une pièce de 3 mètres sur 4; **it's broader** ~ **a metre** c'est plus large d'un mètre; **one** ~ **one** un à un; **little** ~ **little** petit à petit, peu à peu
8 (*according to*) d'après, selon; **it's 3 o'clock** ~ **my watch** il est 3 heures à ma montre; **it's all right** ~ **me** je n'ai rien contre
9: (**all**) ~ **oneself** *etc* tout(e) seul(e)
10: ~ **the way** au fait, à propos
♦ *adv* **1** *see* **go; pass** *etc*
2: ~ **and** ~ un peu plus tard, bientôt; ~ **and large** dans l'ensemble

───────────────

bye(-bye) ['baɪ('baɪ)] *excl* au revoir!, salut!

by(e)-law ['baɪlɔː] n arrêté municipal
by: ~-**election** (BRIT) n élection (législative) partielle; ~**gone** adj passé(e) ♦ n: let ~**gones be** ~**gones** passons l'éponge, oublions le passé; ~**pass** n (route f de) contournement m; (MED) pontage m ♦ vt éviter; ~-**product** n sous-produit m, dérivé m; (fig) conséquence f secondaire, retombée f, ~**stander** ['baɪstændə*] n spectateur(trice), badaud(e)
byte [baɪt] n (COMPUT) octet m
byword ['baɪwɜːd] n: **to be a** ~ **for** être synonyme de (fig)
by-your-leave ['baɪjɔː'liːv] n: **without so much as a** ~ sans même demander la permission

---

C c

C [siː] n (MUS) do m
CA abbr = **chartered accountant**
cab [kæb] n taxi m; (of train, truck) cabine f
cabaret ['kæbəreɪ] n (show) spectacle m de cabaret
cabbage ['kæbɪdʒ] n chou m
cabin ['kæbɪn] n (house) cabane f, hutte f; (on ship) cabine f; (on plane) compartiment m; ~ **cruiser** n cruiser m
cabinet ['kæbɪnɪt] n (POL) cabinet m; (furniture) petit meuble à tiroirs et rayons; (also: display ~) vitrine f, petite armoire vitrée
cable ['keɪbl] n câble m ♦ vt câbler, télégraphier; ~-**car** n téléphérique m; ~ **television** n télévision f par câble
cache [kæʃ] n stock m
cackle ['kækl] vi caqueter
cactus ['kæktəs, pl -taɪ] (pl **cacti**) n cactus m
cadet [kə'det] n (MIL) élève m officier
cadge [kædʒ] (inf) vt: **to** ~ (**from** or **off**) se faire donner (par)
café ['kæfeɪ] n ≈ café(-restaurant) m (sans alcool)
cage [keɪdʒ] n cage f
cagey ['keɪdʒɪ] (inf) adj réticent(e); méfiant(e)
cagoule [kə'guːl] n K-way m (®)
cajole [kə'dʒəʊl] vt couvrir de flatteries or de gentillesses
cake [keɪk] n gâteau m; ~ **of soap** savonnette f; ~**d** adj: ~**d with** raidi(e) par, couvert(e) d'une croûte de
calculate ['kælkjʊleɪt] vt calculer; (estimate:

chances, effect) évaluer; **calculation** [kælkjʊ'leɪʃən] n calcul m; **calculator** n machine f à calculer, calculatrice f; (pocket) calculette f
calendar ['kælɪndə*] n calendrier m; ~ **year** n année civile
calf [kɑːf] (pl **calves**) n (of cow) veau m; (of other animals) petit m; (also: ~-**skin**) veau m, vachette f; (ANAT) mollet m
calibre ['kælɪbə*] (US **caliber**) n calibre m
call [kɔːl] vt appeler; (meeting) convoquer ♦ vi appeler; (visit: also: ~ **in**, ~ **round**) passer ♦ n (shout) appel m, cri m; (also: telephone ~) coup m de téléphone; (visit) visite f; **she's** ~**ed** Suzanne elle s'appelle Suzanne; **to be on** ~ être de permanence; ~ **back** vi (return) repasser; (TEL) rappeler; ~ **for** vt fus (demand) demander; (fetch) passer prendre; ~ **off** vt annuler; ~ **on** vt fus (visit) rendre visite à, passer voir; (request): **to** ~ **on sb to do** inviter qn à faire; ~ **out** vi pousser un cri or des cris; ~ **up** vt (MIL) appeler, mobiliser; (TEL) appeler; ~**box** (BRIT) n (TEL) cabine f téléphonique; ~**er** n (TEL) personne f qui appelle; (visitor) visiteur m; ~ **girl** n call-girl f; ~-**in** (US) n (RADIO, TV: phone-in) programme m à ligne ouverte; ~**ing** n vocation f; (trade, occupation) état m; ~**ing card** (US) n carte f de visite
callous ['kæləs] adj dur(e), insensible
calm [kɑːm] adj calme ♦ n calme m ♦ vt calmer, apaiser; ~ **down** vi se calmer ♦ vt calmer, apaiser
Calor gas ['kælə-] (®) n butane m, butagaz m (®)
calorie ['kælərɪ] n calorie f
calves [kɑːvz] npl of **calf**
camber ['kæmbə*] n (of road) bombement m
Cambodia [kæm'bəʊdjə] n Cambodge m
camcorder ['kæmkɔːdə*] n camescope m
came [keɪm] pt of **come**
camel ['kæməl] n chameau m
camera ['kæmərə] n (PHOT) appareil-photo m; (also: cine-~, movie ~) caméra f; **in** ~ à huis clos; ~**man** (irreg) n caméraman m
camouflage ['kæməflɑːʒ] n camouflage m ♦ vt camoufler
camp [kæmp] n camp m ♦ vi camper ♦ adj (man) efféminé(e)
campaign [kæm'peɪn] n (MIL, POL etc) campagne f ♦ vi faire campagne
camp: ~**bed** (BRIT) n lit m de camp; ~**er** n campeur(euse); (vehicle) camping-car m; ~**ing** n camping m; **to go** ~**ing** faire du camping; ~**site** ['kæmpsaɪt] n campement m, (terrain m de) camping m
campus ['kæmpəs] n campus m
can[1] [kæn] n (of milk, oil, water) bidon m; (tin) boîte f de conserve ♦ vt mettre en conserve

─────────── KEYWORD ───────────

can² [kæn] (*negative* **cannot, can't**; *conditional and pt* **could**) *aux vb* **1** (*be able to*) pouvoir; **you ~ do it if you try** vous pouvez le faire si vous essayez; **I ~'t hear you** je ne t'entends pas

2 (*know how to*) savoir; **I ~ swim/play tennis/drive** je sais nager/jouer au tennis/conduire; **~ you speak French?** parlez-vous français?

3 (*may*) pouvoir; **~ I use your phone?** puis-je me servir de votre téléphone?

4 (*expressing disbelief, puzzlement etc*): **it ~'t be true!** ce n'est pas possible!; **what CAN he want?** qu'est-ce qu'il peut bien vouloir?

5 (*expressing possibility, suggestion etc*): **he could be in the library** il est peut-être dans la bibliothèque; **she could have been delayed** il se peut qu'elle ait été retardée

───────────────────────────

Canada ['kænədə] *n* Canada *m*; **Canadian** [kə'neɪdɪən] *adj* canadien(ne) ♦ *n* Canadien(ne)

canal [kə'næl] *n* canal *m*

canary [kə'nɛərɪ] *n* canari *m*, serin *m*

cancel ['kænsəl] *vt* annuler; (*train*) supprimer; (*party, appointment*) décommander; (*cross out*) barrer, rayer; **~lation** [kænsə'leɪʃən] *n* annulation *f*; suppression *f*

cancer ['kænsə*] *n* (*MED*) cancer *m*; **C~** (*ASTROLOGY*) le Cancer

candid ['kændɪd] *adj* (très) franc(franche), sincère

candidate ['kændɪdeɪt] *n* candidat(e)

candle ['kændl] *n* bougie *f*; (*of tallow*) chandelle *f*; (*in church*) cierge *m*; **~light** *n*: **by ~light** à la lumière d'une bougie; (*dinner*) aux chandelles; **~stick** *n* (*also: ~ holder*) bougeoir *m*; (*bigger, ornate*) chandelier *m*

candour ['kændə*] (*US* **candor**) *n* (grande) franchise *or* sincérité

candy ['kændɪ] *n* sucre candi; (*US*) bonbon *m*; **~-floss** (*BRIT*) *n* barbe à papa

cane [keɪn] *n* canne *f*; (*for furniture, baskets etc*) rotin *m* ♦ *vt* (*BRIT: SCOL*) administrer des coups de bâton à

canister ['kænɪstə*] *n* boîte *f*; (*of gas, pressurized substance*) bombe *f*

cannabis ['kænəbɪs] *n* (*drug*) cannabis *m*

canned [kænd] *adj* (*food*) en boîte, en conserve

cannon ['kænən] (*pl ~ or ~s*) *n* (*gun*) canon *m*

cannot ['kænɒt] = **can not**

canoe [kə'nuː] *n* pirogue *f*; (*SPORT*) canoë *m*

canon ['kænən] *n* (*clergyman*) chanoine *m*; (*standard*) canon *m*

can-opener [-'əʊpnə*] *n* ouvre-boîte *m*

canopy ['kænəpɪ] *n* baldaquin *m*; dais *m*

can't [kɑːnt] = **can not**

cantankerous [kæn'tæŋkərəs] *adj* querelleur(euse), acariâtre

canteen [kæn'tiːn] *n* cantine *f*; (*BRIT: of cutlery*) ménagère *f*

canter ['kæntə*] *vi* (*horse*) aller au petit galop

canvas ['kænvəs] *n* toile *f*

canvass ['kænvəs] *vi* (*POL*): **to ~ for** faire campagne pour ♦ *vt* (*investigate: opinions etc*) sonder

canyon ['kænjən] *n* cañon *m*, gorge (profonde)

cap [kæp] *n* casquette *f*; (*of pen*) capuchon *m*; (*of bottle*) capsule *f*; (*contraceptive: also: Dutch ~*) diaphragme *m*; (*for toy gun*) amorce *f* ♦ *vt* (*outdo*) surpasser; (*put limit on*) plafonner

capability [keɪpə'bɪlɪtɪ] *n* aptitude *f*, capacité *f*

capable ['keɪpəbl] *adj* capable

capacity [kə'pæsɪtɪ] *n* capacité *f*; (*capability*) aptitude *f*; (*of factory*) rendement *m*

cape [keɪp] *n* (*garment*) cape *f*; (*GEO*) cap *m*

caper ['keɪpə*] *n* (*CULIN: gen: ~s*) câpre *f*; (*prank*) farce *f*

capital ['kæpɪtl] *n* (*also: ~ city*) capitale *f*; (*money*) capital *m*; (*also: ~ letter*) majuscule *f*; **~ gains tax** *n* (*COMM*) impôt *m* sur les plus-values; **~ism** *n* capitalisme *m*; **~ist** *adj* capitaliste ♦ *n* capitaliste *m/f*; **~ize** *vi*: **to ~ize on** tirer parti de; **~ punishment** *n* peine capitale

Capricorn ['kæprɪkɔːn] *n* (*ASTROLOGY*) le Capricorne

capsize [kæp'saɪz] *vt* faire chavirer ♦ *vi* chavirer

capsule ['kæpsjuːl] *n* capsule *f*

captain ['kæptɪn] *n* capitaine *m*

caption ['kæpʃən] *n* légende *f*

captive ['kæptɪv] *adj, n* captif(ive)

capture ['kæptʃə*] *vt* capturer, prendre; (*attention*) capter; (*COMPUT*) saisir ♦ *n* capture *f*; (*data ~*) saisie *f* de données

car [kɑː*] *n* voiture *f*, auto *f*; (*RAIL*) wagon *m*, voiture

caramel ['kærəməl] *n* caramel *m*

caravan ['kærəvæn] *n* caravane *f*; **~ site** (*BRIT*) *n* camping *m* pour caravanes

carbohydrate [kɑːbəʊ'haɪdreɪt] *n* hydrate *m* de carbone; (*food*) féculent *m*

carbon ['kɑːbən] *n* carbone *m*; **~ dioxide** *n* gaz *m* carbonique; **~ monoxide** *n* oxyde *m* de carbone; **~ paper** *n* papier *m* carbone

carburettor ['kɑːbjʊretə*] (*US* **carburetor**) *n* carburateur *m*

card [kɑːd] *n* carte *f*; (*material*) carton *m*; **~board** *n* carton *m*; **~ game** *n* jeu *m* de cartes

cardiac ['kɑːdɪæk] *adj* cardiaque

cardigan ['kɑːdɪgən] n cardigan m
cardinal ['kɑːdɪnl] adj cardinal(e) ♦ n cardinal m
card index n fichier m
care [kɛə*] n soin, attention f; (worry) souci m; (charge) charge f, garde f ♦ vi: to ~ about se soucier de, s'intéresser à; (person) être attaché(e) à; ~ of chez, aux bons soins de; in sb's ~ à la garde de qn, confié(e) à qn; to take ~ (to do) faire attention (à faire); to take ~ of s'occuper de; I don't ~ ça m'est bien égal; I couldn't ~ less je m'en fiche complètement (inf); ~ for vt fus s'occuper de; (like) aimer
career [kə'rɪə*] n carrière f ♦ vi (also: ~ along) aller à toute allure; ~ woman (irreg) n femme ambitieuse
care: ~free ['kɛəfriː] adj sans souci, insouciant(e); ~ful ['kɛəful] adj (thorough) soigneux(euse); (cautious) prudent(e); (be) ~ful! (fais) attention!; ~fully adv avec soin, soigneusement; prudemment; ~less ['kɛəlɪs] adj négligent(e); (heedless) insouciant(e); ~r [kɛərə*] n (MED) aide f
caress [kə'res] n caresse f ♦ vt caresser
caretaker ['kɛəteɪkə*] n gardien(ne), concierge m/f
car-ferry ['kɑːferɪ] n (on sea) ferry(-boat) m
cargo ['kɑːgəʊ] (pl ~es) n cargaison f, chargement m
car hire n location f de voitures
Caribbean [kærɪ'biːən] adj: the ~ (Sea) la mer des Antilles or Caraïbes
caring ['kɛərɪŋ] adj (person) bienveillant(e); (society, organization) humanitaire
carnal ['kɑːnl] adj charnel(le)
carnation [kɑː'neɪʃən] n œillet m
carnival ['kɑːnɪvəl] n (public celebration) carnaval m; (US: funfair) fête foraine
carol ['kærl] n: (Christmas) ~ chant m de Noël
carp [kɑːp] n (fish) carpe f; ~ at vt fus critiquer
car park (BRIT) n parking m, parc m de stationnement
carpenter ['kɑːpɪntə*] n charpentier m; **carpentry** ['kɑːpɪntrɪ] n menuiserie f
carpet ['kɑːpɪt] n tapis m ♦ vt recouvrir d'un tapis; ~ slippers npl pantoufles fpl; ~ sweeper n balai m mécanique
car phone n (TEL) téléphone m de voiture
carriage ['kærɪdʒ] n voiture f; (of goods) transport m; (: cost) port m; ~way (BRIT) n (part of road) chaussée f
carrier ['kærɪə*] n transporteur m, camionneur m; (company) entreprise f de transport; (MED) porteur(euse); ~ bag (BRIT) n sac m (en papier or en plastique)
carrot ['kærət] n carotte f
carry ['kærɪ] vt (subj: person) porter; (: vehicle) transporter; (involve: responsibilities etc) comporter, impliquer ♦ vi (sound) porter; to get carried away (fig) s'emballer, s'enthousiasmer; ~ on vi: to ~ on with sth/doing continuer qch/de faire ♦ vt poursuivre; ~ out vt (orders) exécuter; (investigation) mener; ~cot (BRIT) n porte-bébé m; ~-on (inf) n (fuss) histoires fpl
cart [kɑːt] n charrette f ♦ vt (inf) transporter, trimballer (inf)
carton ['kɑːtən] n (box) carton m; (of yogurt) pot m; (of cigarettes) cartouche f
cartoon [kɑː'tuːn] n (PRESS) dessin m (humoristique), caricature f; (BRIT: comic strip) bande dessinée; (CINEMA) dessin animé
cartridge ['kɑːtrɪdʒ] n cartouche f
carve [kɑːv] vt (meat) découper; (wood, stone) tailler, sculpter; ~ up vt découper; (fig: country) morceler; **carving** ['kɑːvɪŋ] n sculpture f; **carving knife** n couteau m à découper
car wash n station f de lavage (de voitures)
case [keɪs] n cas m; (LAW) affaire f, procès m; (box) caisse f, boîte f, étui m; (BRIT: also: suit~) valise f; in ~ of en cas de; in ~ he ... au cas où il ...; just in ~ à tout hasard; in any ~ en tout cas, de toute façon
cash [kæʃ] n argent m; (COMM) argent liquide, espèces fpl ♦ vt encaisser; to pay (in) ~ payer comptant; ~ on delivery payable or paiement à la livraison; ~-book n livre m de caisse; ~ card (BRIT) n carte f de retrait; ~ desk (BRIT) n caisse f; ~ dispenser (BRIT) n distributeur m automatique de billets, billetterie f
cashew [kæ'ʃuː] n (also: ~ nut) noix f de cajou
cashier [kæ'ʃɪə*] n caissier(ère)
cashmere ['kæʃmɪə*] n cachemire m
cash register n caisse (enregistreuse)
casing ['keɪsɪŋ] n revêtement (protecteur), enveloppe (protectrice)
casino [kə'siːnəʊ] n casino m
casket ['kɑːskɪt] n coffret m; (US: coffin) cercueil m
casserole ['kæsərəʊl] n (container) cocotte f; (food) ragoût m (en cocotte)
cassette [kæ'set] n cassette f, musicassette f; ~ player n lecteur m de cassettes; ~ recorder n magnétophone m à cassettes
cast [kɑːst] (pt, pp cast) vt (throw) jeter; (shed) perdre; se dépouiller de; (statue) mouler; (THEATRE): to ~ sb as Hamlet attribuer à qn le rôle de Hamlet ♦ n (THEATRE) distribution f; (also: plaster ~) plâtre m; to ~ one's vote voter; ~ off vi (NAUT) larguer les amarres; (KNITTING) arrêter les mailles; ~ on vi (KNITTING) monter les mailles
castaway ['kɑːstəweɪ] n naufragé(e)
caster sugar ['kɑːstə-] (BRIT) n sucre m semoule

casting vote ['kɑ:stɪŋ-] (*BRIT*) n voix prépondérante (*pour départager*)

cast iron n fonte f

castle ['kɑ:sl] n château (fort); (*CHESS*) tour f

castor ['kɑ:stə*] n (*wheel*) roulette f; ~ **oil** n huile f de ricin

castrate [kæs'treɪt] vt châtrer

casual ['kæʒjul] adj (*by chance*) de hasard, fait(e) au hasard, fortuit(e); (*irregular: work etc*) temporaire; (*unconcerned*) désinvolte; ~**ly** adv avec désinvolture, négligemment; (*dress*) de façon décontractée

casualty ['kæʒjultɪ] n accidenté(e), blessé(e); (*dead*) victime f, mort(e); (*MED: department*) urgences fpl

casual wear n vêtements mpl décontractés

cat [kæt] n chat m

catalogue ['kætəlɔg] (*US* catalog) n catalogue m ♦ vt cataloguer

catalyst ['kætəlɪst] n catalyseur m

catalytic converter [kætə'lɪtɪk kən'vɜ:tə*] n pot m catalytique

catapult ['kætəpʌlt] (*BRIT*) (*sling*) lance-pierres m inv, fronde m

catarrh [kə'tɑ:*] n rhume m chronique, catarrhe m

catastrophe [kə'tæstrəfɪ] n catastrophe f

catch [kætʃ] (*pt, pp* **caught**) vt attraper; (*person: by surprise*) prendre, surprendre; (*understand, hear*) saisir ♦ vi (*fire*) prendre; (*become trapped*) se prendre, s'accrocher ♦ n prise f; (*trick*) attrape f; (*of lock*) loquet m; **to ~ sb's attention** or **eye** attirer l'attention de qn; **to ~ one's breath** retenir son souffle; **to ~ fire** prendre feu; **to ~ sight of** apercevoir; ~ **on** vi saisir; (*grow popular*) prendre; ~ **up** vi se rattraper, combler son retard ♦ vt (*also: ~ up with*) rattraper; ~**ing** adj (*MED*) contagieux(euse); ~**ment area** ['kætʃmənt-] (*BRIT*) n (*SCOL*) secteur m de recrutement; (*of hospital*) circonscription hospitalière; ~ **phrase** n slogan m; expression f (à la mode); ~**y** adj (*tune*) facile à retenir

category ['kætɪgərɪ] n catégorie f

cater ['keɪtə*] vi (*provide food*): **to ~ (for)** préparer des repas (pour), se charger de la restauration (pour); ~ **for** (*BRIT*) vt fus (*needs*) satisfaire, pourvoir à; (*readers, consumers*) s'adresser à, pourvoir aux besoins de; ~**er** n traiteur m; fournisseur m; ~**ing** n restauration f; approvisionnement m, ravitaillement m

caterpillar ['kætəpɪlə*] n chenille f; ~ **track** ® n chenille f

cathedral [kə'θi:drəl] n cathédrale f

catholic ['kæθəlɪk] adj (*tastes*) éclectique, varié(e); **C~** adj catholique ♦ n catholique m/f

Catseye ['kætsaɪ] (®: *BRIT*) n (*AUT*) catardioptre m

cattle ['kætl] npl bétail m

catty ['kætɪ] adj méchant(e)

caucus ['kɔ:kəs] n (*POL: group*) comité local d'un parti politique; (*US: POL*) comité électoral (pour désigner des candidats)

caught [kɔ:t] pt, pp of **catch**

cauliflower ['kɔlɪflauə*] n chou-fleur m

cause [kɔ:z] n cause f ♦ vt causer

caution ['kɔ:ʃən] n prudence f; (*warning*) avertissement m ♦ vt avertir, donner un avertissement à

cautious ['kɔ:ʃəs] adj prudent(e)

cavalry ['kævəlrɪ] n cavalerie f

cave [keɪv] n caverne f, grotte f; ~ **in** vi (*roof etc*) s'effondrer; ~**man** (*irreg*) n homme m des cavernes

caviar(e) ['kævɪɑ:*] n caviar m

cavort [kə'vɔ:t] vi cabrioler, faire des cabrioles

CB n abbr (= *Citizens' Band (Radio)*) CB f

CBI n abbr (= *Confederation of British Industries*) groupement du patronat

cc abbr = **carbon copy; cubic centimetres**

CD n abbr (= *compact disc (player)*) CD m; ~**-ROM** n abbr (= *compact disc read-only memory*) CD-ROM m

cease [si:s] vt, vi cesser; ~**fire** n cessez-le-feu m; ~**less** adj incessant(e), continuel(le)

cedar ['si:də*] n cèdre m

ceiling ['si:lɪŋ] n plafond m

celebrate ['selɪbreɪt] vt, vi célébrer; ~**d** adj célèbre; **celebration** [selɪ'breɪʃən] n célébration f

celery ['selərɪ] n céleri m (à côtes)

cell [sel] n cellule f; (*ELEC*) élément m (de pile)

cellar ['selə*] n cave f

cello ['tʃeləu] n violoncelle m

cellphone [sel'fəun] n téléphone m cellulaire

Celt [kelt, selt] n Celte m/f; ~**ic** ['keltɪk, 'seltɪk] adj celte

cement [sɪ'ment] n ciment m; ~ **mixer** n bétonnière f

cemetery ['semɪtrɪ] n cimetière m

censor ['sensə*] n censeur m ♦ vt censurer; ~**ship** n censure f

censure ['senʃə*] vt blâmer, critiquer

census ['sensəs] n recensement m

cent [sent] n (*US etc: coin*) cent m (= un centième du dollar); *see also* **per**

centenary [sen'ti:nərɪ] n centenaire m

center ['sentə*] (*US*) n = **centre**

centigrade ['sentɪgreɪd] adj centigrade

centimetre ['sentɪmi:tə*] (*US* **centimeter**) n centimètre m

centipede ['sentɪpi:d] n mille-pattes m inv

central ['sentrəl] adj central(e); **C~ America** n Amérique centrale; ~ **heating** n chauffage central; ~ **reservation** (*BRIT*) n (*AUT*) terre-plein central

centre ['sentə*] (*US* **center**) n centre m ♦ vt

centrer; ~-**forward** n (SPORT) avant-centre m; ~-**half** n (SPORT) demi-centre m
century ['sentʃʊrɪ] n siècle m; **20th** ~ XXe siècle
ceramic [sɪ'ræmɪk] adj céramique
cereal ['sɪərɪəl] n céréale f
ceremony ['serɪmənɪ] n cérémonie f; **to stand on** ~ faire des façons
certain ['sɜːtən] adj certain(e); **for** ~ certainement, sûrement; ~**ly** adv certainement; ~**ty** n certitude f
certificate [sə'tɪfɪkɪt] n certificat m
certified mail ['sɜːtɪfaɪd-] (US) n: **by** ~ en recommandé, avec avis de réception
certified public accountant (US) n expert-comptable m
certify ['sɜːtɪfaɪ] vt certifier; (award diploma to) conférer un diplôme etc à; (declare insane) déclarer malade mental(e)
cervical ['sɜːvɪkl] adj: ~ **cancer** cancer m du col de l'utérus; ~ **smear** frottis vaginal
cervix ['sɜːvɪks] n col m de l'utérus
cf. abbr (= compare) cf., voir
CFC n abbr (= chlorofluorocarbon) CFC m (gen pl)
ch. abbr (= chapter) chap.
chafe [tʃeɪf] vt irriter, frotter contre
chain [tʃeɪn] n chaîne f ♦ vt (also: ~ up) enchaîner, attacher (avec une chaîne); ~ **reaction** n réaction f en chaîne; ~-**smoke** vi fumer cigarette sur cigarette; ~ **store** n magasin m à succursales multiples
chair [tʃɛə*] n chaise f; (arm~) fauteuil m; (of university) chaire f; (of meeting, committee) présidence f ♦ vt (meeting) présider; ~**lift** n télésiège m; ~**man** (irreg) n président m
chalet ['ʃæleɪ] n chalet m
chalice ['tʃælɪs] n calice m
chalk ['tʃɔːk] n craie f
challenge ['tʃælɪndʒ] n défi m ♦ vt défier; (statement, right) mettre en question, contester; **to** ~ **sb to do** mettre qn au défi de faire; **challenging** ['tʃælɪndʒɪŋ] adj (tone, look) de défi, provocateur(trice); (task, career) qui représente un défi or une gageure
chamber ['tʃeɪmbə*] n chambre f; ~ **of commerce** chambre de commerce; ~**maid** n femme f de chambre; ~ **music** n musique f de chambre
champagne [ʃæm'peɪn] n champagne m
champion ['tʃæmpɪən] n champion(ne); ~**ship** n championnat m
chance [tʃɑːns] n (opportunity) occasion f, possibilité f; (hope, likelihood) chance f; (risk) risque m ♦ vt: **to** ~ **it** risquer (le coup), essayer ♦ adj fortuit(e), de hasard; **to take a** ~ prendre un risque; **by** ~ par hasard
chancellor ['tʃɑːnsələ*] n chancelier m; **C**~ **of the Exchequer** (BRIT) n chancelier

m de l'Échiquier, ≈ ministre m des Finances
chandelier [ʃændɪ'lɪə*] n lustre m
change [tʃeɪndʒ] vt (alter, replace, COMM: money) changer; (hands, trains, clothes, one's name) changer de; (transform): **to** ~ **sb into** changer or transformer qn en ♦ vi (gen) changer; (one's clothes) se changer; (be transformed): **to** ~ **into** se changer or transformer en ♦ n changement m; (money) monnaie f; **to** ~ **gear** (AUT) changer de vitesse; **to** ~ **one's mind** changer d'avis; **a** ~ **of clothes** des vêtements de rechange; **for a** ~ pour changer; ~**able** adj (weather) variable; ~ **machine** n distributeur de monnaie; ~**over** n (to new system) changement m, passage m
changing ['tʃeɪndʒɪŋ] adj changeant(e); ~ **room** (BRIT) n (in shop) salon m d'essayage; (SPORT) vestiaire m
channel ['tʃænl] n (TV) chaîne f; (navigable passage) chenal m; (irrigation) canal m ♦ vt canaliser; **the (English) C**~ la Manche; **the C**~ **Islands** les îles de la Manche, les îles Anglo-Normandes
chant [tʃɑːnt] n chant m; (REL) psalmodie f ♦ vt chanter, scander
chaos ['keɪɒs] n chaos m
chap [tʃæp] (BRIT: inf) n (man) type m
chapel ['tʃæpəl] n chapelle f; (BRIT: nonconformist ~) église f
chaplain ['tʃæplɪn] n aumônier m
chapped ['tʃæpt] adj (skin, lips) gercé(e)
chapter ['tʃæptə*] n chapitre m
char [tʃɑː*] vt (burn) carboniser
character ['kærɪktə*] n caractère m; (in novel, film) personnage m; (eccentric) numéro m, phénomène m; ~**istic** [kærɪktə'rɪstɪk] adj caractéristique ♦ n caractéristique f
charcoal ['tʃɑːkəʊl] n charbon m de bois; (for drawing) charbon m
charge [tʃɑːdʒ] n (cost) prix (demandé); (accusation) accusation f; (LAW) inculpation f ♦ vt: **to** ~ **sb (with)** inculper qn (de); (battery, enemy) charger; (customer, sum) faire payer ♦ vi foncer; ~**s** npl (costs) frais mpl; **to reverse the** ~**s** (TEL) téléphoner en P.C.V.; **to take** ~ **of** se charger de; **to be in** ~ **of** être responsable de, s'occuper de; **how much do you** ~? combien prenez-vous?; **to** ~ **an expense (up) to sb** mettre une dépense sur le compte de qn; ~ **card** n carte f de client
charity ['tʃærɪtɪ] n charité f; (organization) institution f charitable or de bienfaisance, œuvre f (de charité)
charm [tʃɑːm] n charme m; (on bracelet) breloque f ♦ vt charmer, enchanter; ~**ing** adj charmant(e)
chart [tʃɑːt] n tableau m, diagramme m; graphique m; (map) carte marine ♦ vt dresser or établir la carte de; ~**s** npl (hit pa-

rade) hit-parade *m*

charter ['tʃɑːtə*] *vt* (*plane*) affréter ♦ *n* (*document*) charte *f*; **~ed accountant** (*BRIT*) *n* expert-comptable *m*; **~ flight** *n* charter *m*

chase [tʃeɪs] *vt* poursuivre, pourchasser; (*also*: ~ *away*) chasser ♦ *n* poursuite *f*, chasse *f*

chasm ['kæzəm] *n* gouffre *m*, abîme *m*

chat [tʃæt] *vi* (*also*: have a ~) bavarder, causer ♦ *n* conversation *f*; **~ show** (*BRIT*) *n* causerie télévisée

chatter ['tʃætə*] *vi* (*person*) bavarder; (*animal*) jacasser ♦ *n* bavardage *m*; jacassement *m*; **my teeth are ~ing** je claque des dents; **~box** (*inf*) *n* moulin à paroles

chatty ['tʃætɪ] *adj* (*style*) familier(ère); (*person*) bavard(e)

chauffeur ['ʃəʊfə*] *n* chauffeur *m* (de maître)

chauvinist ['ʃəʊvɪnɪst] *n* (*male* ~) phallocrate *m*; (*nationalist*) chauvin(e)

cheap [tʃiːp] *adj* bon marché *inv*, pas cher(chère); (*joke*) facile, d'un goût douteux; (*poor quality*) à bon marché, de qualité médiocre ♦ *adv* à bon marché, pour pas cher; **~er** *adj* moins cher(chère); **~ly** *adv* à bon marché, à bon compte

cheat [tʃiːt] *vi* tricher ♦ *vt* tromper, duper; (*rob*) **to ~ sb out of sth** escroquer qch à qn ♦ *n* tricheur(euse); escroc *m*

check [tʃek] *vt* vérifier; (*passport, ticket*) contrôler; (*halt*) arrêter; (*restrain*) maîtriser ♦ *n* vérification *f*; contrôle *m*; (*curb*) frein *m*; (*US: bill*) addition *f*; (*pattern: gen pl*) carreaux *mpl*; (*US*) = **cheque** ♦ *adj* (*pattern, cloth*) à carreaux; **~ in** *vi* (*in hotel*) remplir sa fiche (d'hôtel); (*at airport*) se présenter à l'enregistrement ♦ *vt* (*luggage*) (faire) enregistrer; **~ out** *vi* (*in hotel*) régler sa note; **~ up** *vi*: **to ~ up (on sth)** vérifier (qch); **to ~ up on sb** se renseigner sur le compte de qn; **~ered** (*US*) *adj* = **chequered**; **~ers** (*US*) *npl* jeu *m* de dames; **~in (desk)** *n* enregistrement *m*; **~ing account** (*US*) *n* (*current account*) compte courant; **~mate** *n* échec et mat *m*; **~out** *n* (*in shop*) caisse *f*; **~point** *n* contrôle *m*; **~room** (*US*) *n* (*left-luggage office*) consigne *f*; **~up** *n* (*MED*) examen médical, check-up *m*

cheek [tʃiːk] *n* joue *f*; (*impudence*) toupet *m*, culot *m*; **~bone** *n* pommette *f*; **~y** *adj* effronté(e), culotté(e)

cheep [tʃiːp] *vi* piauler

cheer [tʃɪə*] *vt* acclamer, applaudir; (*gladden*) réjouir, réconforter ♦ *vi* applaudir ♦ *n* (*gen pl*) acclamations *fpl*, applaudissements *mpl*; bravos *mpl*, hourras *mpl*; **~s!** à la vôtre!; **~ up** *vi* se dérider, reprendre courage ♦ *vt* remonter le moral à *or* de, dérider; **~ful** *adj* gai(e), joyeux(euse)

cheerio ['tʃɪərɪ'əʊ] (*BRIT*) *excl* salut!, au revoir!

cheese [tʃiːz] *n* fromage *m*; **~board** *n* plateau *m* de fromages

cheetah ['tʃiːtə] *n* guépard *m*

chef [ʃef] *n* chef (cuisinier)

chemical ['kemɪkəl] *adj* chimique ♦ *n* produit *m* chimique

chemist ['kemɪst] *n* (*BRIT: pharmacist*) pharmacien(ne); (*scientist*) chimiste *m/f*; **~ry** *n* chimie *f*; **~'s (shop)** (*BRIT*) *n* pharmacie *f*

cheque [tʃek] (*BRIT*) *n* chèque *m*; **~book** *n* chéquier *m*, carnet *m* de chèques; **~ card** *n* carte *f* (d'identité) bancaire

chequered ['tʃekəd] (*US* **checkered**) *adj* (*fig*) varié(e)

cherish ['tʃerɪʃ] *vt* chérir; **~ed** *adj* (*dream, memory*) cher(chère)

cherry ['tʃerɪ] *n* cerise *f*; (*also*: ~ *tree*) cerisier *m*

chess [tʃes] *n* échecs *mpl*; **~board** *n* échiquier *m*

chest [tʃest] *n* poitrine *f*; (*box*) coffre *m*, caisse *f*; **~ of drawers** *n* commode *f*

chestnut ['tʃesnʌt] *n* châtaigne *f*; (*also*: ~ *tree*) châtaignier *m*

chew [tʃuː] *vt* mâcher; **~ing gum** *n* chewing-gum *m*

chic [ʃiːk] *adj* chic *inv*, élégant(e)

chick [tʃɪk] *n* poussin *m*; (*inf*) nana *f*

chicken ['tʃɪkɪn] *n* poulet *m*; (*inf: coward*) poule mouillée; **~ out** (*inf*) *vi* se dégonfler; **~pox** ['tʃɪkɪnpɒks] *n* varicelle *f*

chicory ['tʃɪkərɪ] *n* (*for coffee*) chicorée *f*; (*salad*) endive

chief [tʃiːf] *n* chef ♦ *adj* principal(e); **~ executive** (*US* **chief executive officer**) *n* directeur(trice) général(e); **~ly** *adv* principalement, surtout

chiffon ['ʃɪfɒn] *n* mousseline *f* de soie

chilblain ['tʃɪlbleɪn] *n* engelure *f*

child [tʃaɪld] (*pl* **~ren**) *n* enfant *m/f*; **~birth** *n* accouchement *m*; **~hood** *n* enfance *f*; **~ish** *adj* puéril(e), enfantin(e); **~like** *adj* d'enfant, innocent(e); **~ minder** (*BRIT*) *n* garde *f* d'enfants

Chile ['tʃɪlɪ] *n* Chili *m*

chill [tʃɪl] *n* (*of water*) froid *m*; (*of air*) fraîcheur *f*; (*MED*) refroidissement *m*, coup *m* de froid ♦ *vt* (*person*) faire frissonner; (*CULIN*) mettre au frais, rafraîchir

chil(l)i ['tʃɪlɪ] *n* piment *m* (rouge)

chilly ['tʃɪlɪ] *adj* froid(e), glacé(e); (*sensitive to cold*) frileux(euse); **to feel ~** avoir froid

chime [tʃaɪm] *n* carillon *m* ♦ *vi* carillonner, sonner

chimney ['tʃɪmnɪ] *n* cheminée *f*; **~ sweep** *n* ramoneur *m*

chimpanzee [tʃɪmpæn'ziː] *n* chimpanzé *m*

chin [tʃɪn] *n* menton *m*

China ['tʃaɪnə] *n* Chine *f*

china ['tʃaɪnə] n porcelaine f; (crockery) (vaisselle f en) porcelaine
Chinese [tʃaɪ'niːz] adj chinois(e) ♦ n inv (person) Chinois(e); (LING) chinois m
chink [tʃɪŋk] n (opening) fente f, fissure f; (noise) tintement m
chip [tʃɪp] n (gen pl: CULIN: BRIT) frite f; (: US: potato ~) chip m; (of wood) copeau m; (of glass, stone) éclat m; (also: micro~) puce f ♦ vt (cup, plate) ébrécher; ~ **in** vi mettre son grain de sel; (contribute) contribuer
chiropodist [kɪ'rɒpədɪst] (BRIT) n pédicure m/f
chirp [tʃɜːp] vi pépier, gazouiller
chisel ['tʃɪzl] n ciseau m
chit [tʃɪt] n mot m, note f
chitchat ['tʃɪttʃæt] n bavardage m
chivalry ['ʃɪvəlrɪ] n esprit m chevaleresque, galanterie f
chives [tʃaɪvz] npl ciboulette f, civette f
chock-a-block ['tʃɒkə'blɒk], **chock-full** [tʃɒk'ful] adj plein(e) à craquer
chocolate ['tʃɒklɪt] n chocolat m
choice [tʃɔɪs] n choix m ♦ adj de choix
choir ['kwaɪə*] n chœur m, chorale f; **~boy** n jeune choriste m
choke [tʃəuk] vi étouffer ♦ vt étrangler; étouffer ♦ n (AUT) starter m; **street ~d with traffic** rue engorgée or embouteillée
cholesterol [kə'lɛstərɒl] n cholestérol m
choose [tʃuːz] (pt chose, pp chosen) vt choisir; **to ~ to do** décider de faire, juger bon de faire
choosy ['tʃuːzɪ] adj: (**to be**) ~ (faire le/la) difficile
chop [tʃɒp] vt (wood) couper (à la hache); (CULIN: also: ~ up) couper (fin), émincer, hacher (en morceaux) ♦ n (CULIN) côtelette f; **~s** npl (jaws) mâchoires fpl
chopper ['tʃɒpə*] n (helicopter) hélicoptère m, hélico m
choppy ['tʃɒpɪ] adj (sea) un peu agité(e)
chopsticks ['tʃɒpstɪks] npl baguettes fpl
chord [kɔːd] n (MUS) accord m
chore [tʃɔː*] n travail m de routine; **household ~s** travaux mpl du ménage
chortle ['tʃɔːtl] vi glousser
chorus ['kɔːrəs] n chœur m; (repeated part of song: also: fig) refrain m
chose [tʃəuz] pt of choose
chosen ['tʃəuzn] pp of choose
Christ [kraɪst] n Christ m
christen ['krɪsn] vt baptiser
Christian ['krɪstɪən] adj, n chrétien(ne); **~ity** [krɪstɪ'ænɪtɪ] n christianisme m; **~ name** n prénom m
Christmas ['krɪsməs] n Noël m or f; **Happy or Merry ~!** joyeux Noël!; ~ **card** n carte f de Noël; ~ **Day** n le jour de Noël; ~ **Eve** n la veille de Noël; la nuit de Noël; ~ **tree** n arbre m de Noël

chrome [krəum] n chrome m
chromium ['krəumɪəm] n chrome m
chronic ['krɒnɪk] adj chronique
chronicle ['krɒnɪkl] n chronique f
chronological [krɒnə'lɒdʒɪkəl] adj chronologique
chrysanthemum [krɪ'sænθəməm] n chrysanthème m
chubby ['tʃʌbɪ] adj potelé(e), rondelet(te)
chuck [tʃʌk] (inf) vt (throw) lancer, jeter; (BRIT: also: ~ up: of job) lâcher; (: person) plaquer; ~ **out** vt flanquer dehors or à la porte; (rubbish) jeter
chuckle ['tʃʌkl] vi glousser
chug [tʃʌg] vi faire teuf-teuf; (also: ~ along) avancer en faisant teuf-teuf
chum [tʃʌm] n copain(copine)
chunk [tʃʌŋk] n gros morceau
church [tʃɜːtʃ] n église f; **~yard** n cimetière m
churn [tʃɜːn] n (for butter) baratte f; (also: milk ~) (grand) bidon à lait; ~ **out** vt débiter
chute [ʃuːt] n glissoire f; (also: rubbish ~) vide-ordures m inv
chutney ['tʃʌtnɪ] n condiment m à base de fruits au vinaigre
CIA (US) n abbr (= Central Intelligence Agency) CIA f
CID (BRIT) n abbr (= Criminal Investigation Department) ≈ P.J. f
cider ['saɪdə*] n cidre m
cigar [sɪ'gɑː*] n cigare m
cigarette [sɪgə'ret] n cigarette f; ~ **case** n étui m à cigarettes; ~ **end** n mégot m
Cinderella [sɪndə'relə] n Cendrillon f
cinders ['sɪndəz] npl cendres fpl
cine-camera ['sɪnɪ'kæmərə] (BRIT) n caméra f
cinema ['sɪnəmə] n cinéma m
cinnamon ['sɪnəmən] n cannelle f
circle ['sɜːkl] n cercle m; (in cinema, theatre) balcon m ♦ vi faire or décrire des cercles ♦ vt (move round) faire le tour de, tourner autour de; (surround) entourer, encercler
circuit ['sɜːkɪt] n circuit m; **~ous** [sɜː'kjuːɪtəs] adj indirect(e), qui fait un détour
circular ['sɜːkjulə*] adj circulaire ♦ n circulaire f
circulate ['sɜːkjuleɪt] vi circuler ♦ vt faire circuler; **circulation** [sɜːkju'leɪʃən] n circulation f; (of newspaper) tirage m
circumflex ['sɜːkəmfleks] n (also: ~ accent) accent m circonflexe
circumstances ['sɜːkəmstənsəz] npl circonstances fpl; (financial condition) moyens mpl, situation financière
circumvent [sɜːkəm'vent] vt (rule, difficulty) tourner
circus ['sɜːkəs] n cirque m
CIS n abbr (= Commonwealth of Indepen-

dent States) CEI f

cistern ['sɪstən] n réservoir m (d'eau); (*in toilet*) réservoir de la chasse d'eau

citizen ['sɪtɪzn] n citoyen(ne); (*resident*): **the ~s of this town** les habitants de cette ville; **~ship** n citoyenneté f

citrus fruit ['sɪtrəs-] n agrume m

city ['sɪtɪ] n ville f, cité f; **the C~** la Cité de Londres (*centre des affaires*)

civic ['sɪvɪk] adj civique; (*authorities*) municipal(e); ~ **centre** (BRIT) n centre administratif (municipal)

civil ['sɪvɪl] adj civil(e); (*polite*) poli(e), courtois(e); (*disobedience, defence*) passif(ive); ~ **engineer** n ingénieur m des travaux publics; **~ian** [sɪ'vɪlɪən] adj, n civil(e)

civilization [sɪvɪlaɪ'zeɪʃən] n civilisation f

civilized ['sɪvɪlaɪzd] adj civilisé(e); (*fig*) où règnent les bonnes manières

civil: ~ **law** n code civil; (*study*) droit civil; ~ **servant** n fonctionnaire m/f; **C~ Service** n fonction publique, administration f; ~ **war** n guerre civile

clad [klæd] adj: ~ **(in)** habillé(e) (de)

claim [kleɪm] vt revendiquer; (*rights, inheritance*) demander, prétendre à; (*assert*) déclarer, prétendre ♦ vi (*for insurance*) faire une déclaration de sinistre ♦ n revendication f; demande f; prétention f, déclaration f; (*right*) droit m, titre m; **~ant** n (ADMIN, LAW) requérant(e)

clairvoyant [kleə'vɔɪənt] n voyant(e), extra-lucide m/f

clam [klæm] n palourde f

clamber ['klæmbə*] vi grimper, se hisser

clammy ['klæmɪ] adj humide (et froid(e)), moite

clamour ['klæmə*] (US clamor) vi: **to ~ for** réclamer à grands cris

clamp [klæmp] n agrafe f, crampon m ♦ vt serrer; (*sth to sth*) fixer; ~ **down on** vt fus sévir or prendre des mesures draconiennes contre

clan [klæn] n clan m

clang [klæŋ] vi émettre un bruit or fracas métallique

clap [klæp] vi applaudir; **~ping** n applaudissements mpl

claret ['klærɪt] n (vin m de) bordeaux m (rouge)

clarinet [klærɪ'net] n clarinette f

clarity ['klærɪtɪ] n clarté f

clash [klæʃ] n choc m; (*fig*) conflit m ♦ vi se heurter; être or entrer en conflit; (*colours*) jurer; (*two events*) tomber en même temps

clasp [klɑːsp] n (*of necklace, bag*) fermoir m; (*hold, embrace*) étreinte f ♦ vt serrer, étreindre

class [klɑːs] n classe f ♦ vt classer, classifier

classic ['klæsɪk] adj classique ♦ n (*author, work*) classique m; **~al** adj classique

classified ['klæsɪfaɪd] adj (*information*) secret(ète); ~ **advertisement** n petite annonce

classmate ['klɑːsmeɪt] n camarade m/f de classe

classroom ['klɑːsrʊm] n (salle f de) classe f

clatter ['klætə*] n cliquetis m ♦ vi cliqueter

clause [klɔːz] n clause f; (LING) proposition f

claw [klɔː] n griffe f; (*of bird of prey*) serre f; (*of lobster*) pince f; ~ **at** vt fus essayer de s'agripper à or griffer

clay [kleɪ] n argile f

clean [kliːn] adj propre; (*clear, smooth*) net(te); (*record, reputation*) sans tache; (*joke, story*) correct(e) ♦ vt nettoyer; ~ **out** vt nettoyer (à fond); ~ **up** vt nettoyer; (*fig*) remettre de l'ordre dans; **~-cut** adj (*person*) net(te), soigné(e); **~er** n (*person*) nettoyeur(euse), femme f de ménage; (*product*) détachant m; **~er's** n (also: dry **~er's**) teinturier m; **~ing** n nettoyage m; **~liness** ['klenlɪnɪs] n propreté f

cleanse [klenz] vt nettoyer; (*purify*) purifier; **~r** n (*for face*) démaquillant m

clean-shaven ['kliːn'ʃeɪvn] adj rasé(e) de près

cleansing department ['klenzɪŋ-] (BRIT) n service m de voirie

clear ['klɪə*] adj clair(e); (*glass, plastic*) transparent(e); (*road, way*) libre, dégagé(e); (*conscience*) net(te) ♦ vt (*room*) débarrasser; (*of people*) faire évacuer; (*cheque*) compenser; (LAW: suspect) innocenter; (*obstacle*) franchir or sauter sans heurter ♦ vi (*weather*) s'éclaircir; (*fog*) se dissiper ♦ adv: ~ **of** à distance de, à l'écart de; **to ~ the table** débarrasser la table, desservir; ~ **up** vt ranger, mettre en ordre; (*mystery*) éclaircir, résoudre; **~ance** n ['klɪərns] (*removal*) déblaiement m; (*permission*) autorisation f; **~-cut** adj clair(e), nettement défini(e); **~ing** n (*in forest*) clairière f; **~ing bank** (BRIT) n banque qui appartient à une chambre de compensation; **~ly** adv clairement; (*evidently*) de toute évidence; **~way** (BRIT) n route f à stationnement interdit

clef [klef] n (MUS) clé f

cleft [kleft] n (*in rock*) crevasse f, fissure f

clench [klentʃ] vt serrer

clergy ['klɜːdʒɪ] n clergé m; **~man** (*irreg*) n ecclésiastique m

clerical ['klerɪkəl] adj de bureau, d'employé de bureau; (REL) clérical(e), du clergé

clerk [klɑːk, (US) klɜːk] n employé m de bureau; (US: salesperson) vendeur(euse)

clever ['klevə*] adj (*mentally*) intelligent(e); (*deft, crafty*) habile, adroit(e); (*device, arrangement*) ingénieux(euse), astucieux(euse)

clew [kluː] (US) n = **clue**

click [klɪk] vi faire un bruit sec or un déclic ♦ vt: **to ~ one's tongue** faire claquer sa langue; **to ~ one's heels** claquer des talons

client ['klaɪənt] n client(e)

cliff [klɪf] n falaise f

climate ['klaɪmɪt] n climat m

climax ['klaɪmæks] n apogée m, point culminant; (*sexual*) orgasme m

climb [klaɪm] vi grimper, monter ♦ vt gravir, escalader, monter sur ♦ n montée f, escalade f; **~-down** n reculade f, dérobade f; **~er** n (*mountaineer*) grimpeur(euse), varappeur(euse); (*plant*) plante grimpante; **~ing** n (*mountaineering*) escalade f, varappe f

clinch [klɪntʃ] vt (*deal*) conclure, sceller

cling [klɪŋ] (pt, pp **clung**) vi: **to ~ (to)** se cramponner (à), s'accrocher (à); (*of clothes*) coller (à)

clinic ['klɪnɪk] n centre médical; **~al** adj clinique; (*attitude*) froid(e), détaché(e)

clink [klɪŋk] vi tinter, cliqueter

clip [klɪp] n (*for hair*) barrette f; (*also: paper ~*) trombone m ♦ vt (*fasten*) attacher; (*hair, nails*) couper; (*hedge*) tailler; **~pers** npl (*for hedge*) sécateur m; (*also: nail ~pers*) coupe-ongles m inv; **~ping** n (*from newspaper*) coupure f de journal

cloak [kləʊk] n grande cape ♦ vt (fig) masquer, cacher; **~room** n (*for coats etc*) vestiaire m; (*BRIT: WC*) toilettes fpl

clock [klɒk] n (*large*) horloge f; (*small*) pendule f; **~ in** (*BRIT*) vi pointer (en arrivant); **~ off** (*BRIT*) vi pointer (en partant); **~ on** (*BRIT*) vi = **clock in**; **~ out** (*BRIT*) vi = **clock off**; **~wise** adv dans le sens des aiguilles d'une montre; **~work** n rouages mpl, mécanisme m; (*of clock*) mouvement m (d'horlogerie) ♦ adj mécanique

clog [klɒg] n sabot m ♦ vt boucher ♦ vi (*also: ~ up*) se boucher

cloister ['klɔɪstə*] n cloître m

close¹ [kləʊs] adj (*near*): **~ (to)** près de), proche (de); (*contact, link*) étroit(e); (*contest*) très serré(e); (*watch*) étroit(e), strict(e); (*examination*) attentif(ive), minutieux(euse); (*weather*) lourd(e), étouffant(e) ♦ adv près, à proximité; **~ to** près de; **~ by** adj proche ♦ adv tout(e) près; **~ at hand** = **by**; **a ~ friend** un ami intime; **to have a ~ shave** (fig) l'échapper belle

close² [kləʊz] vt fermer ♦ vi (*shop etc*) fermer; (*lid, door etc*) se fermer; (*end*) se terminer, se conclure ♦ n (*end*) conclusion f, fin f; **~ down** vt, vi fermer (définitivement)

closed [kləʊzd] adj fermé(e); **~ shop** n organisation f qui n'admet que des travailleurs syndiqués

close-knit ['kləʊs'nɪt] adj (*family, community*) très uni(e)

closely ['kləʊslɪ] adv (*examine, watch*) de près

closet ['klɒzɪt] n (*cupboard*) placard m, réduit m

close-up ['kləʊsʌp] n gros plan

closure ['kləʊʒə*] n fermeture f

clot [klɒt] n (*gen: blood ~*) caillot m; (*inf: person*) ballot m ♦ vi (*blood*) se coaguler

cloth [klɒθ] n (*material*) tissu m, étoffe f; (*also: tea~*) torchon m; lavette f

clothe [kləʊð] vt habiller, vêtir; **~s** npl vêtements mpl, habits mpl; **~s brush** n brosse f à habits; **~s line** n corde f (à linge); **~s peg** (*US* **~s pin**) n pince f à linge

clothing ['kləʊðɪŋ] n = **clothes**

cloud [klaʊd] n nuage m; **~burst** n grosse averse; **~y** adj nuageux(euse), couvert(e); (*liquid*) trouble

clout [klaʊt] vt flanquer une taloche à

clove [kləʊv] n (*CULIN: spice*) clou m de girofle; **~ of garlic** gousse f d'ail

clover ['kləʊvə*] n trèfle m

clown [klaʊn] n clown m ♦ vi (*also: ~ about, ~ around*) faire le clown

cloying ['klɔɪɪŋ] adj (*taste, smell*) écœurant(e)

club [klʌb] n (*society, place: also: golf ~*) club m; (*weapon*) massue f, matraque f ♦ vt matraquer ♦ vi: **to ~ together** s'associer; **~s** npl (*CARDS*) trèfle m; **~ car** (*US*) n (*RAIL*) wagon-restaurant m; **~house** n club m

cluck [klʌk] vi glousser

clue [kluː] n indice m; (*in crosswords*) définition f; **I haven't a ~** je n'en ai pas la moindre idée

clump [klʌmp] n: **~ of trees** bouquet m d'arbres; **a ~ of buildings** un ensemble de bâtiments

clumsy ['klʌmzɪ] adj gauche, maladroit(e)

clung [klʌŋ] pt, pp of **cling**

cluster ['klʌstə*] n (*of people*) (petit) groupe; (*of flowers*) grappe f; (*of stars*) amas m ♦ vi se rassembler

clutch [klʌtʃ] n (*grip, grasp*) étreinte f, prise f; (*AUT*) embrayage m ♦ vt (*grasp*) agripper; (*hold tightly*) serrer fort; (*hold on to*) se cramponner à

clutter ['klʌtə*] vt (*also: ~ up*) encombrer

CND n abbr (= Campaign for Nuclear Disarmament) mouvement pour le désarmement nucléaire

Co. abbr = **county**; **company**

c/o abbr (= care of) c/o, aux bons soins de

coach [kəʊtʃ] n (*bus*) autocar m; (*horse-drawn*) diligence f; (*of train*) voiture f, wagon m; (*SPORT: trainer*) entraîneur(euse); (*SCOL: tutor*) répétiteur(trice) ♦ vt entraîner; (*student*) faire travailler; **~ trip** n excursion f en car

coal [kəʊl] n charbon m; **~ face** n front m de taille; **~field** n bassin houiller

coalition [kəʊə'lɪʃən] n coalition f

coal: ~man ['kəʊlmən] (irreg) n charbonnier m, marchand m de charbon; **~ merchant** n = **~man**; **~mine** ['kəʊlmaɪn] *n* mine *f* de charbon

coarse [kɔːs] *adj* grossier(ère), rude

coast [kəust] *n* côte *f* ♦ *vi* (*car, cycle etc*) descendre en roue libre; **~al** *adj* côtier(ère); **~guard** *n* garde-côte *m*; (*service*) gendarmerie *f* maritime; **~line** *n* côte *f*, littoral *m*

coat [kəut] *n* manteau *m*; (*of animal*) pelage *m*, poil *m*; (*of paint*) couche *f* ♦ *vt* couvrir; **~ hanger** *n* cintre *m*; **~ing** *n* couche *f*, revêtement *m*; **~ of arms** *n* blason *m*, armoiries *fpl*

coax [kəuks] *vt* persuader par des cajoleries

cob [kɔb] *n see* **corn**

cobbler ['kɔblə*] *n* cordonnier *m*

cobbles ['kɔblz] (*also:* **cobblestones**) *npl* pavés (ronds)

cobweb ['kɔbweb] *n* toile *f* d'araignée

cocaine [kə'keɪn] *n* cocaïne *f*

cock [kɔk] *n* (*rooster*) coq *m*; (*male bird*) mâle *m* ♦ *vt* (*gun*) armer; **~erel** *n* jeune coq *m*; **~-eyed** *adj* (*idea, method*) absurde, qui ne tient pas debout

cockle ['kɔkl] *n* coque *f*

cockney ['kɔknɪ] *n* cockney *m*, habitant des quartiers populaires de l'East End de Londres, ≈ faubourien(ne)

cockpit ['kɔkpɪt] *n* (*in aircraft*) poste *m* de pilotage, cockpit *m*

cockroach ['kɔkrəutʃ] *n* cafard *m*

cocktail ['kɔkteɪl] *n* cocktail *m* (*fruit ~ etc*) salade *f*; **~ cabinet** *n* (meuble-)bar *m*; **~ party** *n* cocktail *m*

cocoa ['kəukəu] *n* cacao *m*

coconut ['kəukənʌt] *n* noix *f* de coco

COD *abbr* = **cash on delivery**

cod [kɔd] *n* morue fraîche, cabillaud *m*

code [kəud] *n* code *m*

cod-liver oil ['kɔdlɪvər-] *n* huile *f* de foie de morue

coercion [kəu'ɜːʃən] *n* contrainte *f*

coffee ['kɔfɪ] *n* café *m*; **~ bar** (*BRIT*) *n* café *m*; **~ bean** *n* grain *m* de café; **~ break** *n* pause-café *f*; **~pot** *n* cafetière *f*; **~ table** *n* (petite) table basse

coffin ['kɔfɪn] *n* cercueil *m*

cog [kɔg] *n* dent *f* (d'engrenage); (*wheel*) roue dentée

cogent ['kəudʒənt] *adj* puissant(e), convaincant(e)

coil [kɔɪl] *n* rouleau *m*, bobine *f*; (*contraceptive*) stérilet *m* ♦ *vt* enrouler

coin [kɔɪn] *n* pièce *f* de monnaie ♦ *vt* (*word*) inventer; **~age** *n* monnaie *f*, système *m* monétaire; **~ box** (*BRIT*) *n* cabine *f* téléphonique

coincide [kəuɪn'saɪd] *vi* coïncider; **~nce** [kəu'ɪnsɪdəns] *n* coïncidence *f*

Coke [kəuk] ® *n* coca *m*

coke [kəuk] *n* coke *m*

colander ['kʌləndə*] *n* passoire *f*

cold [kəuld] *adj* froid(e) ♦ *n* froid *m*; (*MED*)

rhume *m*; **it's ~** il fait froid; **to be** *or* **feel ~** (*person*) avoir froid; **to catch ~** prendre *or* attraper froid; **to catch a ~** attraper un rhume; **in ~ blood** de sang-froid; **~-shoulder** *vt* se montrer froid(e) envers, snober; **~ sore** *n* bouton *m* de fièvre

coleslaw ['kəulslɔː] *n* sorte de salade de chou cru

colic ['kɔlɪk] *n* colique(s) *f(pl)*

collapse [kə'læps] *vi* s'effondrer, s'écrouler ♦ *n* effondrement *m*, écroulement *m*; **collapsible** [kə'læpsəbl] *adj* pliant(e); télescopique

collar ['kɔlə*] *n* (*of coat, shirt*) col *m*; (*for animal*) collier *m*; **~bone** *n* clavicule *f*

collateral [kɔ'lætərəl] *n* nantissement *m*

colleague ['kɔliːg] *n* collègue *m/f*

collect [kə'lekt] *vt* rassembler; ramasser; (*as a hobby*) collectionner; (*BRIT: call and pick up*) (passer) prendre; (*mail*) faire la levée de, ramasser; (*money owed*) encaisser; (*donations, subscriptions*) recueillir ♦ *vi* (*people*) se rassembler; (*things*) s'amasser; **to call ~** (*US: TEL*) téléphoner en P.C.V.; **~ion** [kə'lekʃən] *n* collection *f*; (*of mail*) levée *f*; (*for money*) collecte *f*, quête *f*; **~or** [kə'lektə*] *n* collectionneur *m*

college ['kɔlɪdʒ] *n* collège *m*

collide [kə'laɪd] *vi* entrer en collision

collie ['kɔlɪ] *n* (*dog*) colley *m*

colliery ['kɔlɪərɪ] (*BRIT*) *n* mine *f* de charbon, houillère *f*

collision [kə'lɪʒən] *n* collision *f*

colloquial [kə'ləukwɪəl] *adj* familier(ère)

colon ['kəulən] *n* (*sign*) deux-points *m inv*; (*MED*) côlon *m*

colonel ['kɜːnl] *n* colonel *m*

colony ['kɔlənɪ] *n* colonie *f*

colour ['kʌlə*] (*US* **color**) *n* couleur *f* ♦ *vt* (*paint*) peindre; (*dye*) teindre; (*news*) fausser, exagérer ♦ *vi* (*blush*) rougir; **~s** *npl* (*of party, club*) couleurs *fpl*; **~ in** *vt* colorier; **~ bar** *n* discrimination raciale (*dans un établissement*); **~-blind** *adj* daltonien(ne); **~ed** *adj* (*person*) de couleur; (*illustration*) en couleur; **~ film** *n* (*for camera*) pellicule *f* (en) couleur; **~ful** *adj* coloré(e), vif(vive); (*personality*) pittoresque, haut(e) en couleurs; **~ing** *n* colorant *m*; (*complexion*) teint *m*; **~ scheme** *n* combinaison *f* de(s) couleurs; **~ television** *n* télévision *f* (en) couleur

colt [kəult] *n* poulain *m*

column ['kɔləm] *n* colonne *f*; **~ist** ['kɔləmnɪst] *n* chroniqueur(euse)

coma ['kəumə] *n* coma *m*

comb [kəum] *n* peigne *m* ♦ *vt* (*hair*) peigner; (*area*) ratisser, passer au peigne fin

combat ['kɔmbæt] *n* combat *m* ♦ *vt* combattre, lutter contre

combination [kɔmbɪ'neɪʃən] *n* combinaison *f*

combine [vb kəm'baɪn, n 'kɒmbaɪn] vt: **to ~ sth with sth** combiner qch avec qch; (one quality with another) joindre or allier qch à qch ♦ vi s'associer; (CHEM) se combiner ♦ n (ECON) trust m; **~ (harvester)** n moissonneuse-batteuse(-lieuse) f

come [kʌm] (pt came, pp come) vi venir, arriver; **to ~ to** (decision etc) parvenir or arriver à; **to ~ undone/loose** se défaire/desserrer; **~ about** vi se produire, arriver; **~ across** vt fus rencontrer par hasard, tomber sur; **~ along** vi = **to come on**; **~ away** vi partir, s'en aller, se détacher; **~ back** vi revenir; **~ by** vt fus (acquire) obtenir, se procurer; **~ down** vi descendre; (prices) baisser; (buildings) s'écrouler, être démoli(e); **~ forward** vi s'avancer, se présenter, s'annoncer; **~ from** vt fus être originaire de, venir de; **~ in** vi entrer; **~ in for** (criticism etc) être l'objet de; **~ into** vt fus (money) hériter de; **~ off** vi (button) se détacher; (stain) s'enlever; (attempt) réussir; **~ on** vi (pupil, work, project) faire des progrès, s'avancer; (lights, electricity) s'allumer; (central heating) se mettre en marche; **~ on!** viens!, allons!, allez!; **~ out** vi sortir; (book) paraître; (strike) cesser le travail, se mettre en grève; **~ round** vi (after faint, operation) revenir à soi, reprendre connaissance; **~ to** vi revenir à soi; **~ up** vi monter; **~ up against** vt fus (resistance, difficulties) rencontrer; **~ up with** vt fus: **he came up with an idea** il a eu une idée, il a proposé quelque chose; **~ upon** vt fus tomber sur; **~back** ['kʌmbæk] n (THEATRE etc) rentrée f

comedian [kə'miːdɪən] n (in music hall etc) comique m; (THEATRE) comédien m

comedy ['kɒmədɪ] n comédie f

comeuppance [kʌm'ʌpəns] n: **to get one's ~** recevoir ce qu'on mérite

comfort ['kʌmfət] n confort m, bien-être m; (relief) soulagement m, réconfort m ♦ vt consoler, réconforter; **the ~s of home** les commodités fpl de la maison; **~able** adj confortable; (person) à l'aise; (patient) dont l'état est stationnaire; (walk etc) facile; **~ably** adv (sit) confortablement; (live) à l'aise; **~ station** (US) n toilettes fpl

comic ['kɒmɪk] adj (also: **~al**) comique ♦ n comique m; (BRIT: magazine) illustré m; **~ strip** n bande dessinée

coming ['kʌmɪŋ] n arrivée f ♦ adj prochain(e), à venir; **~(s) and going(s)** n(pl) va-et-vient m inv

comma ['kɒmə] n virgule f

command [kə'mɑːnd] n ordre m, commandement m; (MIL: authority) commandement m; (mastery) maîtrise f ♦ vt (troops) commander; **to ~ sb to do** ordonner à qn de faire; **~eer** [kɒmən'dɪə*] vt réquisitionner; **~er** n (MIL) commandant m

commando [kə'mɑːndəʊ] n commando m; membre m d'un commando

commemorate [kə'meməreɪt] vt commémorer

commence [kə'mens] vt, vi commencer

commend [kə'mend] vt louer; (recommend) recommander

commensurate [kə'menʃʊrɪt] adj: **~ with** or **to** en proportion de, proportionné(e) à

comment ['kɒment] n commentaire m ♦ vi: **to ~ (on)** faire des remarques (sur); **"no ~"** "je n'ai rien à dire"; **~ary** ['kɒməntrɪ] n commentaire m; (SPORT) reportage m (en direct); **~ator** ['kɒməntertə*] n commentateur m; reporter m

commerce ['kɒmɜːs] n commerce m

commercial [kə'mɜːʃəl] adj commercial(e) ♦ n (TV, RADIO) annonce f publicitaire, spot m (publicitaire); **~ radio** n radio privée; **~ television** n télévision privée

commiserate [kə'mɪzəreɪt] vi: **to ~ with sb** témoigner de la sympathie pour qn

commission [kə'mɪʃən] n (order for work) commande f; (committee, fee) commission f ♦ vt (work of art) commander, charger un artiste de l'exécution de; **out of ~** (not working) hors service; **~aire** [kəmɪʃə'neə*] (BRIT) n (at shop, cinema etc) portier m (en uniforme); **~er** n (POLICE) préfet m (de police)

commit [kə'mɪt] vt (act) commettre; (resources) consacrer; (to sb's care) confier (à); **to ~ o.s. (to do)** s'engager (à faire); **to ~ suicide** se suicider; **~ment** n engagement m; (obligation) responsabilité(s) f(pl)

committee [kə'mɪtɪ] n comité m

commodity [kə'mɒdɪtɪ] n produit m, marchandise f, article m

common ['kɒmən] adj commun(e); (usual) courant(e) ♦ n terrain communal; **the C~s** npl la chambre des Communes; **in ~** en commun; **~er** n roturier(ière); **~ law** n droit coutumier; **~ly** adv communément, généralement; couramment; **C~ Market** n: **the C~ Market** le Marché commun; **~place** adj banal(e), ordinaire; **~ room** n salle commune; **~ sense** n bon sens; **C~wealth** (BRIT) n: **the C~wealth** le Commonwealth

commotion [kə'məʊʃən] n désordre m, tumulte m

communal ['kɒmjuːnl] adj (life) communautaire; (for common use) communal(e)

commune [n 'kɒmjuːn, vb kə'mjuːn] n (group) communauté f ♦ vi: **to ~ with** communier avec

communicate [kə'mjuːnɪkeɪt] vt, vi communiquer

communication [kəmjuːnɪ'keɪʃən] n communication f; **~ cord** (BRIT) n sonnette f d'alarme

communion [kə'mjuːnɪən] n (also: Holy

C~) communion f

communism ['kɔmjunɪzəm] n communisme m; **communist** ['kɔmjunɪst] adj communiste ♦ n communiste m/f

community [kə'mju:nɪtɪ] n communauté f; ~ **centre** n centre m de loisirs; ~ **chest** (US) n fonds commun; ~ **home** n (school) centre m d'éducation surveillée

commutation ticket [kɔmjuˈteɪʃən-] (US) n carte f d'abonnement

commute [kə'mju:t] vi faire un trajet journalier (de son domicile à son bureau); vt (LAW) commuer; ~r n banlieusard(e) (qui ... see vi)

compact [adj kəm'pækt, n 'kɔmpækt] adj compact(e) ♦ n (also: powder ~) poudrier m; ~ **disc** n disque compact; ~ **disc player** n lecteur m de disque compact

companion [kəm'pænɪən] n compagnon(compagne); ~**ship** n camaraderie f

company ['kʌmpənɪ] n compagnie f; to **keep sb** ~ tenir compagnie à qn; ~ **secretary** (BRIT) n (COMM) secrétaire général (d'une société)

comparative [kəm'pærətɪv] adj (study) comparatif(ive); (relative) relatif(ive); ~**ly** adv (relatively) relativement

compare [kəm'pɛə*] vt: to ~ sth/sb **with/to** comparer qch/qn avec or et/à ♦ vi: to ~ (with) se comparer (à); être comparable (à); **comparison** [kəm'pærɪsn] n comparaison f

compartment [kəm'pɑ:tmənt] n compartiment m

compass ['kʌmpəs] n boussole f; ~**es** npl (GEOM: also: pair of ~es) compas m

compassion [kəm'pæʃən] n compassion f; ~**ate** adj compatissant(e)

compatible [kəm'pætɪbl] adj compatible

compel [kəm'pel] vt contraindre, obliger; ~**ling** adj (fig: argument) irrésistible

compensate ['kɔmpenseɪt] vt indemniser, dédommager ♦ vi: to ~ **for** compenser; **compensation** [kɔmpen'seɪʃn] n compensation f, (money) dédommagement m, indemnité f

compère ['kɔmpɛə*] n (TV) animateur(trice)

compete [kəm'pi:t] vi: to ~ **(with)** rivaliser (avec), faire concurrence (à)

competent ['kɔmpɪtənt] adj compétent(e), capable

competition [kɔmpɪ'tɪʃən] n (contest) compétition f, concours m; (ECON) concurrence f

competitive [kəm'petɪtɪv] adj (ECON) concurrentiel(le); (sport) de compétition; (person) qui a l'esprit de compétition

competitor [kəm'petɪtə*] n concurrent(e)

complacency [kəm'pleɪsnsɪ] n suffisance f, vaine complaisance

complain [kəm'pleɪn] vi: to ~ **(about)** se plaindre (de); (in shop etc) réclamer (au sujet de); to ~ **of** (pain) se plaindre de; ~**t** n plainte f; réclamation f; (MED) affection f

complement [n 'kɔmplɪmənt, vb 'kɔmplɪment] n complément m; (especially of ship's crew etc) effectif complet ♦ vt (enhance) compléter; ~**ary** [kɔmplɪ'mentərɪ] adj complémentaire

complete [kəm'pli:t] adj complet(ète) ♦ vt achever, parachever; (set, group) compléter; (a form) remplir; ~**ly** adv complètement; **completion** [kəm'pli:ʃən] n achèvement m; (of contract) exécution f

complex ['kɔmpleks] adj complexe ♦ n complexe m

complexion [kəm'plekʃən] n (of face) teint m

compliance [kəm'plaɪəns] n (submission) docilité f; (agreement): ~ **with** le fait de se conformer à; **in** ~ **with** en accord avec

complicate ['kɔmplɪkeɪt] vt compliquer; ~**d** adj compliqué(e); **complication** [kɔmplɪ'keɪʃn] n complication f

compliment [n 'kɔmplɪmənt, vb 'kɔmplɪment] n compliment m ♦ vt complimenter; ~**s** npl (respects) compliments mpl, hommages mpl; **to pay sb a** ~ faire or adresser un compliment à qn; ~**ary** [kɔmplɪ'mentərɪ] adj flatteur(euse); (free) (offert(e)) à titre gracieux; ~**ary ticket** n billet m de faveur

comply [kəm'plaɪ] vi: to ~ **with** se soumettre à, se conformer à

component [kəm'pəunənt] n composant m, élément m

compose [kəm'pəuz] vt composer; (form): **to be** ~**d of** se composer de; **to** ~ **o.s.** se calmer, se maîtriser; prendre une contenance; ~**d** adj calme, posé(e); ~**r** n (MUS) compositeur m; **composition** [kɔmpə'zɪʃən] n composition f; **composure** [kəm'pəuʒə*] n calme m, maîtrise f de soi

compound ['kɔmpaund] n composé m; (enclosure) enclos m, enceinte f; ~ **fracture** n fracture compliquée; ~ **interest** n intérêt composé

comprehend [kɔmprɪ'hend] vt comprendre; **comprehension** [kɔmprɪ'henʃən] n compréhension f

comprehensive [kɔmprɪ'hensɪv] adj (très) complet(ète); ~ **policy** n (INSURANCE) assurance f tous risques; ~ **(school)** n (BRIT) n école secondaire polyvalente, ≈ C.E.S. m

compress [vb kəm'pres, n 'kɔmpres] vt comprimer; (text, information) condenser ♦ n (MED) compresse f

comprise [kəm'praɪz] vt (also: be ~d of) comprendre; (constitute) constituer, représenter

compromise ['kɔmprəmaɪz] n compromis m ♦ vt compromettre ♦ vi transiger, accepter un compromis

compulsion [kəm'pʌlʃən] n contrainte f, force f
compulsive [kəm'pʌlsɪv] adj (PSYCH) compulsif(ive); (book, film etc) captivant(e)
compulsory [kəm'pʌlsərɪ] adj obligatoire
computer [kəm'pju:tə*] n ordinateur m; ~ **game** n jeu m vidéo; ~**ize** vt informatiser; ~ **programmer** n programmeur(euse); ~ **programming** n programmation f; ~ **science** n informatique f; **computing** n = ~ **science**
comrade ['kɒmrɪd] n camarade m/f
con [kɒn] vt duper; (cheat) escroquer ♦ n escroquerie f
conceal [kən'si:l] vt cacher, dissimuler
conceit [kən'si:t] n vanité f, suffisance f, prétention f; ~**ed** adj vaniteux(euse), suffisant(e)
conceive [kən'si:v] vt, vi concevoir
concentrate ['kɒnsəntreɪt] vi se concentrer ♦ vt concentrer
concentration [kɒnsən'treɪʃən] n concentration f; ~ **camp** n camp m de concentration
concept ['kɒnsept] n concept m
concern [kən'sɜːn] n affaire f; (COMM) entreprise f, firme f; (anxiety) inquiétude f, souci m ♦ vt concerner; **to be** ~**ed (about)** s'inquiéter (de), être inquiet(e) (au sujet de); ~**ing** prep en ce qui concerne, à propos de
concert ['kɒnsət] n concert m; ~**ed** adj concerté(e); ~ **hall** n salle f de concert
concerto [kən'tʃɜːtəʊ] n concerto m
concession [kən'seʃən] n concession f; **tax** ~ dégrèvement fiscal
conclude [kən'klu:d] vt conclure; **conclusion** [kən'klu:ʒən] n conclusion f; **conclusive** [kən'klu:sɪv] adj concluant(e), définitif(ive)
concoct [kən'kɒkt] vt confectionner, composer; (fig) inventer; ~**ion** [kən'kɒkʃən] n mélange m
concourse ['kɒŋkɔːs] n (hall) hall m, salle f des pas perdus
concrete ['kɒŋkriːt] n béton m ♦ adj concret(ète); (floor etc) en béton
concur [kən'kɜː*] vi (agree) être d'accord
concurrently [kən'kʌrəntlɪ] adv simultanément
concussion [kɒn'kʌʃən] n (MED) commotion (cérébrale)
condemn [kən'dem] vt condamner
condensation [kɒnden'seɪʃən] n condensation f
condense [kən'dens] vi se condenser ♦ vt condenser; ~**d milk** n lait concentré (sucré)
condition [kən'dɪʃən] n condition f; (MED) état m ♦ vt déterminer, conditionner; **on** ~ **that** à condition que +sub, à condition de; ~**al** adj conditionnel(le); ~**er** n (for hair)

baume après-shampooing m; (for fabrics) assouplissant m
condolences [kən'dəʊlənsɪz] npl condoléances fpl
condom ['kɒndəm] n préservatif m
condominium [kɒndə'mɪnɪəm] n (US) (building) immeuble m (en copropriété)
condone [kən'dəʊn] vt fermer les yeux sur, approuver (tacitement)
conducive [kən'dju:sɪv] adj: ~ **to** favorable à, qui contribue à
conduct [n 'kɒndʌkt, vb kən'dʌkt] n conduite f ♦ vt conduire; (MUS) diriger; **to** ~ **o.s.** se conduire, se comporter; ~**ed tour** n voyage organisé; (of building) visite guidée; ~**or** [kən'dʌktə*] n (of orchestra) chef m d'orchestre; (on bus) receveur m; (US: on train) chef m de train; (ELEC) conducteur m; ~**ress** [kən'dʌktrɪs] n (on bus) receveuse f
cone [kəʊn] n cône m; (for ice-cream) cornet m; (BOT) pomme f de pin, cône
confectioner [kən'fekʃənə*] n confiseur(euse); ~'**s (shop)** n confiserie f; ~**y** n confiserie f
confer [kən'fɜː*] vt: **to** ~ **sth on** conférer qch à ♦ vi conférer, s'entretenir
conference ['kɒnfərəns] n conférence f
confess [kən'fes] vt confesser, avouer ♦ vi se confesser; ~**ion** [kən'feʃən] n confession f
confetti [kən'fetɪ] n confettis mpl
confide [kən'faɪd] vi: **to** ~ **in** se confier à
confidence ['kɒnfɪdəns] n confiance f; (also: self-~) assurance f, confiance en soi; (secret) confidence f; **in** ~ (speak, write) en confidence, confidentiellement; ~ **trick** n escroquerie f; **confident** ['kɒnfɪdənt] adj sûr(e), assuré(e); **confidential** [kɒnfɪ'denʃəl] adj confidentiel(le)
confine [kən'faɪn] vt limiter, borner; (shut up) confiner, enfermer; ~**d** adj (space) restreint(e), réduit(e); ~**ment** n emprisonnement m, détention f; ~**s** ['kɒnfaɪnz] npl confins mpl, bornes fpl
confirm [kən'fɜːm] vt confirmer; (appointment) ratifier; ~**ation** [kɒnfə'meɪʃən] n confirmation f; ~**ed** adj invétéré(e), incorrigible
confiscate ['kɒnfɪskeɪt] vt confisquer
conflict [n 'kɒnflɪkt, vb kən'flɪkt] n conflit m, lutte f ♦ vi être or entrer en conflit; (opinions) s'opposer, se heurter; ~**ing** [kən'flɪktɪŋ] adj contradictoire
conform [kən'fɔːm] vi: **to** ~ **(to)** se conformer (à)
confound [kən'faʊnd] vt confondre
confront [kən'frʌnt] vt confronter, mettre en présence; (enemy, danger) affronter, faire face à; ~**ation** [kɒnfrən'teɪʃən] n confrontation f
confuse [kən'fju:z] vt (person) troubler; (si-

tuation) embrouiller; (*one thing with another*) confondre; **~d** adj (*person*) dérouté(e), désorienté(e); **confusing** adj peu clair(e), déroutant(e); **confusion** [kən'fju:ʒən] n confusion f

congeal [kən'dʒi:l] vi (*blood*) se coaguler; (*oil etc*) se figer

congenial [kən'dʒi:nɪəl] adj sympathique, agréable

congested [kən'dʒestɪd] adj (MED) congestionné(e); (*area*) surpeuplé(e); (*road*) bloqué(e)

congestion [kən'dʒestʃən] n congestion f; (*fig*) encombrement m

congratulate [kən'grætjʊleɪt] vt: **to ~ sb (on)** féliciter qn (de); **congratulations** [kəngrætjʊ'leɪʃənz] npl félicitations fpl

congregate ['kɒŋgrɪgeɪt] vi se rassembler, se réunir

congregation [kɒŋgrɪ'geɪʃən] n assemblée f (des fidèles)

congress ['kɒŋgres] n congrès m; **~man** (*irreg*: US) n membre du Congrès

conjunction [kən'dʒʌŋkʃən] n (LING) conjonction f

conjunctivitis [kəndʒʌŋktɪ'vaɪtɪs] n conjonctivite f

conjure ['kʌndʒə*] vi faire des tours de passe-passe; **~ up** vt (*ghost, spirit*) faire apparaître; (*memories*) évoquer; **~r** n prestidigitateur m, illusionniste m/f

conk out [kɒŋk-] (*inf*) vi tomber or rester en panne

con man (*irreg*) n escroc m

connect [kə'nekt] vt joindre, relier; (ELEC) connecter; (TEL: *caller*) mettre en connection (*with* avec); (: *new subscriber*) brancher; (*fig*) établir un rapport entre, faire un rapprochement entre ♦ vi (*train*): **to ~ with** assurer la correspondance avec; **to be ~ed with** (*fig*) avoir un rapport avec; avoir des rapports avec, être en relation avec; **~ion** [kə'nekʃən] n relation f, lien m; (ELEC) connexion f; (*train, plane etc*) correspondance f; (TEL) branchement m, communication f

connive [kə'naɪv] vi: **to ~ at** se faire le complice de

conquer ['kɒŋkə*] vt conquérir; (*feelings*) vaincre, surmonter

conquest ['kɒŋkwest] n conquête f

cons [kɒnz] npl see **convenience; pro**

conscience ['kɒnʃəns] n conscience f; **conscientious** [kɒnʃɪ'enʃəs] adj consciencieux(euse)

conscious ['kɒnʃəs] adj conscient(e); **~ness** n conscience f; (MED) connaissance f

conscript ['kɒnskrɪpt] n conscrit m

consent [kən'sent] n consentement m ♦ vi: **to ~ (to)** consentir (à)

consequence ['kɒnsɪkwəns] n conséquence

f, suites fpl; (*significance*) importance f

consequently ['kɒnsɪkwəntlɪ] adv par conséquent, donc

conservation [kɒnsə'veɪʃən] n préservation f, protection f

conservative [kən'sɜ:vətɪv] adj conservateur(trice); **at a ~ estimate** au bas mot; **C~** (BRIT) adj, n (POL) conservateur(trice)

conservatory [kən'sɜ:vətrɪ] n (*greenhouse*) serre f

conserve [kən'sɜ:v] vt conserver, préserver; (*supplies, energy*) économiser ♦ n confiture f

consider [kən'sɪdə*] vt (*study*) considérer, réfléchir à; (*take into account*) penser à, prendre en considération; (*regard, judge*) considérer, estimer; **to ~ doing sth** envisager de faire qch; **~able** [kən'sɪdərəbl] adj considérable; **~ably** adv nettement; **~ate** [kən'sɪdərɪt] adj prévenant(e), plein(e) d'égards; **~ation** [kənsɪdə'reɪʃən] n considération f; **~ing** [kən'sɪdərɪŋ] prep étant donné

consign [kən'saɪn] vt expédier; (*to sb's care*) confier; (*fig*) livrer; **~ment** n arrivage m, envoi m

consist [kən'sɪst] vi: **to ~ of** consister en, se composer de

consistency [kən'sɪstənsɪ] n consistance f; (*fig*) cohérence f

consistent [kən'sɪstənt] adj logique, cohérent(e)

consolation [kɒnsə'leɪʃən] n consolation f

console ['kɒnsəʊl] n (COMPUT) console f

consonant ['kɒnsənənt] n consonne f

conspicuous [kən'spɪkjʊəs] adj voyant(e), qui attire l'attention

conspiracy [kən'spɪrəsɪ] n conspiration f, complot m

constable ['kʌnstəbl] (BRIT) n ≈ agent m de police, gendarme m; **chief ~** ≈ préfet m de police

constabulary [kən'stæbjʊlərɪ] (BRIT) n ≈ police f, gendarmerie f

constant ['kɒnstənt] adj constant(e); incessant(e); **~ly** adv constamment, sans cesse

constipated ['kɒnstɪpeɪtəd] adj constipé(e); **constipation** [kɒnstɪ'peɪʃən] n constipation f

constituency [kən'stɪtjʊənsɪ] n circonscription électorale

constituent [kən'stɪtjʊənt] n (POL) électeur(trice); (*part*) élément constitutif, composant m

constitution [kɒnstɪ'tju:ʃən] n constitution f; **~al** adj constitutionnel(le)

constraint [kən'streɪnt] n contrainte f

construct [kən'strʌkt] vt construire; **~ion** [kən'strʌkʃən] n construction f; **~ive** adj constructif(ive)

construe [kən'stru:] vt interpréter, expliquer

consul ['kɒnsl] *n* consul *m;* **~ate** ['kɒnsjʊlət] *n* consulat *m*
consult [kən'sʌlt] *vt* consulter; **~ant** *n (MED)* médecin consultant; *(other specialist)* consultant *m,* (expert-) conseil *m;* **~ing room** *(BRIT) n* cabinet *m* de consultation
consume [kən'sju:m] *vt* consommer; **~r** *n* consommateur(trice); **~r goods** *npl* biens *mpl* de consommation; **~r society** *n* société *f* de consommation
consummate ['kɒnsʌmeɪt] *vt* consommer
consumption [kən'sʌmpʃən] *n* consommation *f*
cont. *abbr* (= continued) suite
contact ['kɒntækt] *n* contact *m;* (person) connaissance *f,* relation *f* ♦ *vt* contacter, se mettre en contact or en rapport avec; **~ lenses** *npl* verres *mpl* de contact, lentilles *fpl*
contagious [kən'teɪdʒəs] *adj* contagieux(euse)
contain [kən'teɪn] *vt* contenir; **to ~ o.s.** se contenir, se maîtriser; **~er** *n* récipient *m;* (for shipping etc) container *m*
contaminate [kən'tæmɪneɪt] *vt* contaminer
cont'd *abbr* (= continued) suite
contemplate ['kɒntəmpleɪt] *vt* contempler; (consider) envisager
contemporary [kən'tempərərɪ] *adj* contemporain(e); (design, wallpaper) moderne ♦ *n* contemporain(e)
contempt [kən'tempt] *n* mépris *m,* dédain *m;* **~ of court** *(LAW)* outrage *m* à l'autorité de la justice; **~uous** *adj* dédaigneux(euse), méprisant(e)
contend [kən'tend] *vt:* **to ~ that** soutenir or prétendre que ♦ *vi:* **to ~ with** (compete) rivaliser avec; (struggle) lutter avec; **~er** *n* concurrent(e); *(POL)* candidat(e)
content [adj, vb kən'tent, n 'kɒntent] *adj* content(e), satisfait(e) ♦ *vt* contenter, satisfaire ♦ *n* contenu *m;* (of fat, moisture) teneur *f;* **~s** *npl (of container etc)* contenu *m;* **(table of) ~s** *n* table *f* des matières; **~ed** *adj* content(e), satisfait(e)
contention [kən'tenʃən] *n* dispute *f,* contestation *f;* (argument) assertion *f,* affirmation *f*
contest [n 'kɒntest, vb kən'test] *n* combat *m,* lutte *f;* (competition) concours *m* ♦ *vt* (decision, statement) contester, discuter; (compete for) disputer; **~ant** [kən'testənt] *n* concurrent(e); (in fight) adversaire *m/f*
context ['kɒntekst] *n* contexte *m*
continent ['kɒntɪnənt] *n* continent *m;* **the C~** *(BRIT)* l'Europe continentale; **~al** [kɒntɪ'nentl] *adj* continental(e); **~al quilt** *(BRIT) n* couette *f*
contingency [kən'tɪndʒənsɪ] *n* éventualité *f,* événement imprévu
continual [kən'tɪnjuəl] *adj* continuel(le)
continuation [kəntɪnju'eɪʃən] *n* continua-

tion *f;* (after interruption) reprise *f;* (of story) suite *f*
continue [kən'tɪnju:] *vi, vt* continuer; (after interruption) reprendre, poursuivre
continuity [kɒntɪ'nju:ɪtɪ] *n* continuité *f;* (TV etc) enchaînement *m*
continuous [kən'tɪnjuəs] *adj* continu(e); (LING) progressif(ive); **~ stationery** *n* papier *m* en continu
contort [kən'tɔ:t] *vt* tordre, crisper
contour ['kɒntuə*] *n* contour *m,* profil *m;* (on map: also: **~ line**) courbe *f* de niveau
contraband ['kɒntrəbænd] *n* contrebande *f*
contraceptive [kɒntrə'septɪv] *adj* contraceptif(ive), anticonceptionnel(le) ♦ *n* contraceptif *m*
contract [n 'kɒntrækt, vb kən'trækt] *n* contrat *m* ♦ *vi* (become smaller) se contracter, se resserrer; *(COMM):* **to ~ to do sth** s'engager (par contrat) à faire qch; **~ion** [kən'trækʃən] *n* contraction *f;* **~or** [kən'træktə*] *n* entrepreneur *m*
contradict [kɒntrə'dɪkt] *vt* contredire
contraption [kən'træpʃən] *(pej) n* machin *m,* truc *m*
contrary[1] ['kɒntrərɪ] *adj* contraire, opposé(e) ♦ *n* contraire *m;* **on the ~** au contraire; **unless you hear to the ~** sauf avis contraire
contrary[2] [kən'treərɪ] *adj* (perverse) contrariant(e), entêté(e)
contrast [n 'kɒntrɑ:st, vb kən'trɑ:st] *n* contraste *m* ♦ *vt* mettre en contraste, contraster; **in ~ to** or **with** contrairement à
contravene [kɒntrə'vi:n] *vt* enfreindre, violer, contrevenir à
contribute [kən'trɪbju:t] *vi* contribuer ♦ *vt:* **to ~ £10/an article to** donner 10 livres/un article à; **to ~ to** contribuer à; (newspaper) collaborer à; **contribution** [kɒntrɪ'bju:ʃən] *n* contribution *f;* **contributor** [kən'trɪbjutə*] *n* (to newspaper) collaborateur(trice)
contrive [kən'traɪv] *vi:* **to ~ to do** s'arranger pour faire, trouver le moyen de faire
control [kən'trəul] *vt* maîtriser, commander; (check) contrôler ♦ *n* contrôle *m,* autorité *f;* maîtrise *f;* **~s** *npl (of machine etc)* commandes *fpl;* (on radio, TV) boutons *mpl* de réglage; **everything is under ~** tout va bien, j'ai (or il a etc) la situation en main; **to be in ~ of** être maître de, maîtriser; **the car went out of ~** j'ai (or il a etc) perdu le contrôle du véhicule; **~ panel** *n* tableau *m* de commande; **~ room** *n* salle *f* des commandes; **~ tower** *n (AVIAT)* tour *f* de contrôle
controversial [kɒntrə'vɜ:ʃəl] *adj* (topic) discutable, controversé(e); (person) qui fait beaucoup parler de lui; **controversy** ['kɒntrəvɜ:sɪ] *n* controverse *f,* polémique *f*
convalesce [kɒnvə'les] *vi* relever de maladie, se remettre (d'une maladie)

convector [kən'vɛktə*] *n* (*heater*) radiateur *m* (à convexion)

convene [kən'viːn] *vt* convoquer, assembler ♦ *vi* se réunir, s'assembler

convenience [kən'viːnɪəns] *n* commodité *f*; **at your** ~ quand *or* comme cela vous convient; **all modern** ~**s**, (*BRIT*) **all mod cons** avec tout le confort moderne, tout confort

convenient [kən'viːnɪənt] *adj* commode

convent ['kɒnvənt] *n* couvent *m*

convention [kən'vɛnʃən] *n* convention *f*; ~**al** *adj* conventionnel(le)

conversant [kən'vɜːsənt] *adj*: **to be** ~ **with** s'y connaître en; être au courant de

conversation [kɒnvə'seɪʃən] *n* conversation *f*

converse [*n* 'kɒnvɜːs, *vb* kən'vɜːs] *n* contraire *m*, inverse *m* ♦ *vi* s'entretenir; ~**ly** [kɒn'vɜːslɪ] *adv* inversement, réciproquement

convert [*vb* kən'vɜːt, *n* 'kɒnvɜːt] *vt* (*REL*, *COMM*) convertir; (*alter*) transformer; (*house*) aménager ♦ *n* converti(e); ~**ible** *n* (voiture *f*) décapotable *f*

convey [kən'veɪ] *vt* transporter; (*thanks*) transmettre; (*idea*) communiquer; ~**or belt** *n* convoyeur *m*, tapis roulant

convict [*vb* kən'vɪkt, *n* 'kɒnvɪkt] *vt* déclarer (*or* reconnaître) coupable ♦ *n* forçat *m*, détenu *m*; ~**ion** [kən'vɪkʃən] *n* (*LAW*) condamnation *f*; (*belief*) conviction *f*

convince [kən'vɪns] *vt* convaincre, persuader; **convincing** *adj* persuasif(ive), convaincant(e)

convoluted [kɒnvə'luːtɪd] *adj* (*argument*) compliqué(e)

convulse [kən'vʌls] *vt*: **to be** ~**d with laughter/pain** se tordre de rire/douleur

coo [kuː] *vi* roucouler

cook [kuk] *vt* (faire) cuire ♦ *vi* cuire; (*person*) faire la cuisine ♦ *n* cuisinier(ière); ~**book** *n* livre *m* de cuisine; ~**er** *n* cuisinière *f*; ~**ery** *n* cuisine *f*; ~**ery book** (*BRIT*) *n* = **cookbook**; ~**ie** (*US*) *n* biscuit *m*, petit gâteau sec; ~**ing** *n* cuisine *f*

cool [kuːl] *adj* frais(fraîche); (*calm, unemotional*) calme; (*unfriendly*) froid(e) ♦ *vt, vi* rafraîchir, refroidir

coop [kuːp] *n* poulailler *m*; (*for rabbits*) clapier *m* ♦ *vt*: **to** ~ **up** (*fig*) cloîtrer, enfermer

cooperate [kəu'ɒpəreɪt] *vi* coopérer, collaborer; **cooperation** [kəuɒpə'reɪʃən] *n* coopération *f*, collaboration *f*; **cooperative** [kəu'ɒpərətɪv] *adj* coopératif(ive) ♦ *n* coopérative *f*

coordinate [*vb* kəu'ɔːdɪneɪt, *n* kəu'ɔːdɪnət] *vt* coordonner ♦ *n* (*MATH*) coordonnée *f*; ~**s** *npl* (*clothes*) ensemble *m*, coordonnés *mpl*

co-ownership ['kəu'əunəʃɪp] *n* copropriété *f*

cop [kɒp] (*inf*) *n* flic *m*

cope [kəup] *vi*: **to** ~ **with** faire face à; (*solve*) venir à bout de

copper ['kɒpə*] *n* cuivre *m*; (*BRIT*: *inf*: *policeman*) flic *m*; ~**s** *npl* (*coins*) petite monnaie; ~ **sulphate** *n* sulfate *m* de cuivre

copy ['kɒpɪ] *n* copie *f*; (*of book etc*) exemplaire *m* ♦ *vt* copier; ~**right** *n* droit *m* d'auteur, copyright *m*

coral ['kɒrəl] *n* corail *m*; ~ **reef** *n* récif *m* de corail

cord [kɔːd] *n* corde *f*; (*fabric*) velours côtelé; (*ELEC*) cordon *m*, fil *m*

cordial ['kɔːdɪəl] *adj* cordial(e), chaleureux(euse) ♦ *n* cordial *m*

cordon ['kɔːdn] *n* cordon *m*; ~ **off** *vt* boucler (*par cordon de police*)

corduroy ['kɔːdərɔɪ] *n* velours côtelé

core [kɔː*] *n* noyau *m*; (*of fruit*) trognon *m*, cœur *m*; (*of building, problem*) cœur ♦ *vt* enlever le trognon *or* le cœur de

cork [kɔːk] *n* liège *m*; (*of bottle*) bouchon *m*; ~**screw** *n* tire-bouchon *m*

corn [kɔːn] *n* (*BRIT*: *wheat*) blé *m*; (*US*: *maize*) maïs *m*; (*on foot*) cor *m*; ~ **on the cob** (*CULIN*) épi *m* de maïs; ~**ed beef** ['kɔːnd-] *n* corned-beef *m*

corner ['kɔːnə*] *n* coin *m*; (*AUT*) tournant *m*, virage *m*; (*FOOTBALL*: *also*: ~ **kick**) corner *m* ♦ *vt* acculer, mettre au pied du mur; coincer; (*COMM*: *market*) accaparer ♦ *vi* prendre un virage; ~**stone** *n* pierre *f* angulaire

cornet ['kɔːnɪt] *n* (*MUS*) cornet *m* à pistons; (*BRIT*: *of ice-cream*) cornet (de glace)

cornflakes ['kɔːnfleɪks] *npl* corn-flakes *mpl*

cornflour ['kɔːnflauə*] (*BRIT*), **cornstarch** ['kɔːnstɑːtʃ] (*US*) *n* farine *f* de maïs, maïzena *f* ®

Cornwall ['kɔːnwəl] *n* Cornouailles *f*

corny ['kɔːnɪ] (*inf*) *adj* rebattu(e)

coronary ['kɒrənərɪ] *n* (*also*: ~ *thrombosis*) infarctus *m* (du myocarde), thrombose *f* coronarienne

coronation [kɒrə'neɪʃən] *n* couronnement *m*

coroner ['kɒrənə*] *n* officier chargé de déterminer les causes d'un décès

corporal ['kɔːpərəl] *n* caporal *m*, brigadier *m* ♦ *adj*: ~ **punishment** châtiment corporel

corporate ['kɔːpərɪt] *adj* en commun, collectif(ive); (*COMM*) de l'entreprise

corporation [kɔːpə'reɪʃən] *n* (*of town*) municipalité *f*, conseil municipal; (*COMM*) société *f*

corps [kɔː*, *pl* kɔːz] (*pl* **corps**) *n* corps *m*

corpse [kɔːps] *n* cadavre *m*

correct [kə'rɛkt] *adj* (*accurate*) correct(e), exact(e); (*proper*) correct, convenable ♦ *vt* corriger; ~**ion** [kə'rɛkʃən] *n* correction *f*

correspond [kɒrɪs'pɒnd] *vi* correspondre;

~**ence** n correspondance f; ~**ence course** n cours m par correspondance; ~**ent** n correspondant(e)

corridor ['kɒrɪdɔ:*] n couloir m, corridor m

corrode [kə'rəʊd] vt corroder, ronger ♦ vi se corroder

corrugated ['kɒrəgeɪtɪd] adj plissé(e); ondulé(e); ~ **iron** n tôle ondulée

corrupt [kə'rʌpt] adj corrompu(e) ♦ vt corrompre; ~**ion** [kə'rʌpʃən] n corruption f

Corsica ['kɔ:sɪkə] n Corse f

cosmetic [kɒz'metɪk] n produit m de beauté, cosmétique m

cosset ['kɒsɪt] vt choyer, dorloter

cost [kɒst] (pt, pp cost) n coût m ♦ vi coûter ♦ vt établir or calculer le prix de revient de; ~s npl (COMM) frais mpl; (LAW) dépens mpl; **it** ~**s £5/too much** cela coûte cinq livres/c'est trop cher; **at all** ~**s** coûte que coûte, à tout prix

co-star ['kəʊstɑ:*] n partenaire m/f

cost-effective ['kɒstɪ'fektɪv] adj rentable

costly ['kɒstlɪ] adj coûteux(euse)

cost-of-living ['kɒstəv'lɪvɪŋ] adj: ~ **allowance** indemnité f de vie chère; ~ **index** index m du coût de la vie

cost price (BRIT) n prix coûtant or de revient

costume ['kɒstju:m] n costume m; (lady's suit) tailleur m; (BRIT: also: swimming ~) maillot m (de bain); ~ **jewellery** n bijoux mpl fantaisie

cosy ['kəʊzɪ] (US **cozy**) adj douillet(te); (person) à l'aise, au chaud

cot [kɒt] n (BRIT: child's) lit m d'enfant, petit lit; (US: campbed) lit de camp

cottage ['kɒtɪdʒ] n petite maison (à la campagne), cottage m; ~ **cheese** n fromage blanc (maigre)

cotton ['kɒtn] n coton m; ~ **on** (inf) vi: **to** ~ **on to** piger; ~ **candy** (US) n barbe f à papa; ~ **wool** (BRIT) n ouate f, coton m hydrophile

couch [kaʊtʃ] n canapé m; divan m

couchette [ku:'ʃet] n couchette f

cough [kɒf] vi tousser ♦ n toux f; ~ **drop** n pastille f pour or contre la toux

could [kʊd] pt of **can²**; ~**n't** = **could not**

council ['kaʊnsl] n conseil m; **city** or **town** ~ conseil municipal; ~ **estate** (BRIT) n (zone f de) logements loués à/par la municipalité; ~ **house** (BRIT) n maison f (à loyer modéré) louée par la municipalité; ~**lor** ['kaʊnsɪlə*] n conseiller(ère)

counsel ['kaʊnsl] n (lawyer) avocat(e); (advice) conseil m, consultation f; ~**lor** n conseiller(ère); (US: lawyer) avocat(e)

count [kaʊnt] vt, vi compter ♦ n compte m; (nobleman) comte m; ~ **on** vt fus compter sur; ~**down** n compte m à rebours

countenance ['kaʊntɪnəns] n expression f ♦ vt approuver

counter ['kaʊntə*] n comptoir m; (in post office, bank) guichet m; (in game) jeton m ♦ vt aller à l'encontre de, opposer ♦ adv: ~ **to** contrairement à; ~**act** [kaʊntə'rækt] vt neutraliser, contrebalancer; ~**feit** ['kaʊntəfi:t] n faux m, contrefaçon f ♦ vt contrefaire ♦ adj faux(fausse); ~**foil** ['kaʊntəfɔɪl] n talon m, souche f; ~**mand** ['kaʊntəmɑ:nd] vt annuler; ~**part** ['kaʊntəpɑ:t] n (of person etc) homologue m/f

countess ['kaʊntɪs] n comtesse f

countless ['kaʊntlɪs] adj innombrable

country ['kʌntrɪ] n pays m; (native land) patrie f; (as opposed to town) campagne f; (region) région f, pays; ~ **dancing** (BRIT) n danse f folklorique; ~ **house** n manoir m, (petit) château; ~**man** (irreg) n (compatriot) compatriote m; (country dweller) habitant m de la campagne, campagnard m; ~**side** n campagne f

county ['kaʊntɪ] n comté m

coup [ku:] (pl ~**s**) n beau coup; (also: ~ d'état) coup d'État

couple ['kʌpl] n couple m; **a** ~ **of** deux; (a few) quelques

coupon ['ku:pɒn] n coupon m, bon-prime m, bon-réclame m; (COMM) coupon

courage ['kʌrɪdʒ] n courage m

courier ['kʊrɪə*] n messager m, courrier m; (for tourists) accompagnateur(trice), guide m/f

course [kɔ:s] n cours m; (of ship) route f; (for golf) terrain m; (part of meal) plat m; **first** ~ entrée f; **of** ~ bien sûr; ~ **of action** parti m, ligne f de conduite; ~ **of treatment** (MED) traitement m

court [kɔ:t] n cour f; (LAW) cour, tribunal m; (TENNIS) court m ♦ vt (woman) courtiser, faire la cour à; **to take to** ~ actionner or poursuivre en justice

courteous ['kɜ:tɪəs] adj courtois(e), poli(e)

courtesy ['kɜ:təsɪ] n courtoisie f, politesse f; **(by)** ~ **of** avec l'aimable autorisation de

court: ~**house** ['kɔ:thaʊs] (US) n palais m de justice; ~**ier** ['kɔ:tɪə*] n courtisan m, dame f de cour; ~ **martial** (pl ~**s martial**) n cour martiale, conseil m de guerre; ~**room** ['kɔ:trʊm] n salle f de tribunal; ~**yard** ['kɔ:tjɑ:d] n cour f

cousin ['kʌzn] n cousin(e); **first** ~ cousin(e) germain(e)

cove [kəʊv] n petite baie, anse f

covenant ['kʌvənənt] n engagement m

cover ['kʌvə*] vt couvrir ♦ n couverture f; (of pan) couvercle m; (over furniture) housse f; (shelter) abri m; **to take** ~ se mettre à l'abri; **under** ~ à l'abri; **under** ~ **of darkness** à la faveur de la nuit; **under separate** ~ (COMM) sous pli séparé; **to** ~ **up for sb** couvrir qn; ~**age** n (TV, PRESS) reportage m; ~ **charge** n couvert m (supplément à *payer*); **~ing** *n* couche *f*; **~ing letter** (*US* ~ **letter**) *n* lettre explicative; ~ **note** *n* (*INSURANCE*) police *f* provisoire

covert ['kʌvət] *adj* (*threat*) voilé(e), caché(e); (*glance*) furtif(ive)

cover-up ['kʌvərʌp] *n* tentative *f* pour étouffer une affaire

covet ['kʌvɪt] *vt* convoiter

cow [kaʊ] *n* vache *f* ♦ *vt* effrayer, intimider

coward ['kaʊəd] *n* lâche *m/f*; **~ice** ['kaʊədɪs] *n* lâcheté *f*; **~ly** *adj* lâche

cowboy ['kaʊbɔɪ] *n* cow-boy *m*

cower ['kaʊə*] *vi* se recroqueviller

coy [kɔɪ] *adj* faussement effarouché(e) *or* timide

cozy ['kəʊzɪ] (*US*) *adj* = **cosy**

CPA (*US*) *n abbr* = **certified public accountant**

crab [kræb] *n* crabe *m*; ~ **apple** *n* pomme *f* sauvage

crack [kræk] *n* fente *f*, fissure *f*; fêlure *f*; lézarde *f*; (*noise*) craquement *m*, coup (sec); (*drug*) crack *m* ♦ *vt* fendre, fissurer; fêler; lézarder; (*whip*) faire claquer; (*nut*) casser; (*code*) déchiffrer; (*problem*) résoudre ♦ *adj* (*athlete*) de première classe, d'élite; ~ **down on** *vt fus* mettre un frein à; ~ **up** *vi* être au bout du rouleau, s'effondrer; **~er** *n* (*Christmas ~er*) pétard *m*; (*biscuit*) biscuit *m* (salé)

crackle ['krækl] *vi* crépiter, grésiller

cradle ['kreɪdl] *n* berceau *m*

craft [krɑːft] *n* métier (*artisanal*); (*pl inv*: *boat*) embarcation *f*, barque *f*; (: *plane*) appareil *m*; **~sman** (*irreg*) *n* artisan *m*, ouvrier (*qualifié*); **~smanship** *n* travail *m*; **~y** *adj* rusé(e), malin(igne)

crag [kræg] *n* rocher escarpé

cram [kræm] *vt* (*fill*): **to ~ sth with** bourrer qch de; (*put*): **to ~ sth into** fourrer qch dans ♦ *vi* (*for exams*) bachoter

cramp [kræmp] *n* crampe *f* ♦ *vt* gêner, entraver; **~ed** *adj* à l'étroit, très serré(e)

cranberry ['krænbərɪ] *n* canneberge *f*

crane [kreɪn] *n* grue *f*

crank [kræŋk] *n* manivelle *f*; (*person*) excentrique *m/f*; **~shaft** *n* vilebrequin *m*

cranny ['krænɪ] *n see* **nook**

crash [kræʃ] *n* fracas *m*; (*of car*) collision *f*, (*of plane*) accident *m* ♦ *vt* avoir un accident avec ♦ *vi* (*plane*) s'écraser; (*two cars*) se percuter, s'emboutir; (*COMM*) s'effondrer; **to ~ into** se jeter *or* se fracasser contre; ~ **course** *n* cours intensif; ~ **helmet** *n* casque (*protecteur*); ~ **landing** *n* atterrissage forcé *or* en catastrophe

crate [kreɪt] *n* cageot *m*; (*for bottles*) caisse *f*

cravat(e) [krə'væt] *n* foulard (noué autour du cou)

crave [kreɪv] *vt*, *vi*: **to ~ (for)** avoir une envie irrésistible de

crawl [krɔːl] *vi* ramper; (*vehicle*) avancer au pas ♦ *n* (*SWIMMING*) crawl *m*

crayfish ['kreɪfɪʃ] *n inv* (*freshwater*) écrevisse *f*; (*saltwater*) langoustine *f*

crayon ['kreɪən] *n* crayon *m* (de couleur)

craze [kreɪz] *n* engouement *m*

crazy ['kreɪzɪ] *adj* fou(folle)

creak [kriːk] *vi* grincer; craquer

cream [kriːm] *n* crème *f* ♦ *adj* (*colour*) crème *inv*; ~ **cake** *n* (petit) gâteau à la crème; ~ **cheese** *n* fromage *m* à la crème, fromage blanc; **~y** *adj* crémeux(euse)

crease [kriːs] *n* pli *m* ♦ *vt* froisser, chiffonner ♦ *vi* se froisser, se chiffonner

create [krɪ'eɪt] *vt* créer; **creation** [krɪ'eɪʃən] *n* création *f*; **creative** [krɪ'eɪtɪv] *adj* (*artistic*) créatif(ive); (*ingenious*) ingénieux(euse)

creature ['kriːtʃə*] *n* créature *f*

crèche [kreʃ] *n* garderie *f*, crèche *f*

credence ['kriːdəns] *n*: **to lend** *or* **give ~ to** ajouter foi à

credentials [krɪ'denʃəlz] *npl* (*references*) références *fpl*; (*papers of identity*) pièce *f* d'identité

credit ['kredɪt] *n* crédit *m*; (*recognition*) honneur *m*; *vt* (*COMM*) créditer; (*believe*: *also*: **give ~ to**) ajouter foi à, croire; **~s** *npl* (*CINEMA*, *TV*) générique *m*; **to be in ~** (*person*, *bank account*) être créditeur(trice); **to ~ sb with** (*fig*) prêter *or* attribuer à qn; ~ **card** *n* carte *f* de crédit; **~or** *n* créancier(ière)

creed [kriːd] *n* croyance *f*; credo *m*

creek [kriːk] *n* crique *f*, anse *f*; (*US: stream*) ruisseau *m*, petit cours d'eau

creep [kriːp] (*pt*, *pp* **crept**) *vi* ramper; **~er** *n* plante grimpante; **~y** *adj* (*frightening*) qui fait frissonner, qui donne la chair de poule

cremate [krɪ'meɪt] *vt* incinérer

crematorium [kremə'tɔːrɪəm] (*pl* **~ia**) *n* four *m* crématoire

crêpe [kreɪp] *n* crêpe *m*; ~ **bandage** (*BRIT*) *n* bande *f* Velpeau (®)

crept [krept] *pt*, *pp of* **creep**

crescent ['kresnt] *n* croissant *m*; (*street*) rue *f* (en arc de cercle)

cress [kres] *n* cresson *m*

crest [krest] *n* crête *f*; **~fallen** *adj* déconfit(e), découragé(e)

crevice ['krevɪs] *n* fissure *f*, lézarde *f*, fente *f*

crew [kruː] *n* équipage *m*; (*CINEMA*) équipe *f*; **~-cut** *n*: **to have a ~-cut** avoir les cheveux en brosse; **~-neck** *n* col ras du cou

crib [krɪb] *n* lit *m* d'enfant; (*for baby*) berceau *m* ♦ *vt* (*inf*) copier

crick [krɪk] *n*: ~ **in the neck** torticolis *m*; ~ **in the back** tour *m* de reins

cricket ['krɪkɪt] *n* (*insect*) grillon *m*, cri-cri *m inv*; (*game*) cricket *m*

crime [kraɪm] *n* crime *m*; **criminal** ['krɪmɪnl] *adj*, *n* criminel(le)

crimson ['krɪmzn] adj cramoisi(e)
cringe [krɪndʒ] vi avoir un mouvement de recul
crinkle ['krɪŋkl] vt froisser, chiffonner
cripple ['krɪpl] n boiteux(euse), infirme m/f ♦ vt estropier
crisis ['kraɪsɪs] (pl **crises**) n crise f
crisp [krɪsp] adj croquant(e); (weather) vif(vive); (manner etc) brusque; ~**s** (BRIT) npl (pommes) chips fpl
crisscross ['krɪskrɔs] adj entrecroisé(e)
criterion [kraɪ'tɪərɪən] (pl ~**ia**) n critère m
critic ['krɪtɪk] n critique m; ~**al** adj critique; ~**ally** adv (examine) d'un œil critique; (speak etc) sévèrement; ~**ally ill** gravement malade; ~**ism** ['krɪtɪsɪzəm] n critique f; ~**ize** ['krɪtɪsaɪz] vt critiquer
croak [krəʊk] vi (frog) coasser; (raven) croasser; (person) parler d'une voix rauque
Croatia [krəʊ'eɪʃə] n Croatie f
crochet ['krəʊʃeɪ] n travail m au crochet
crockery ['krɒkərɪ] n vaisselle f
crocodile ['krɒkədaɪl] n crocodile m
crocus ['krəʊkəs] n crocus m
croft [krɒft] (BRIT) n petite ferme
crony ['krəʊnɪ] (inf: pej) n copain(copine)
crook [krʊk] n escroc m; (of shepherd) houlette f; ~**ed** ['krʊkɪd] adj courbé(e), tordu(e); (action) malhonnête
crop [krɒp] n (produce) culture f; (amount produced) récolte f; (riding ~) cravache f ♦ vt (hair) tondre; ~ **up** vi surgir, se présenter, survenir
cross [krɒs] n croix f; (BIO etc) croisement m ♦ vt (street etc) traverser; (arms, legs, BIO) croiser; (cheque) barrer ♦ adj en colère, fâché(e); ~ **out** vt barrer, biffer; ~ **over** vi traverser; ~**bar** n barre (transversale); ~**country (race)** n cross(-country) m; ~**examine** vt (LAW) faire subir un examen contradictoire à; ~**eyed** adj qui louche; ~**fire** n feux croisés; ~**ing** n (sea passage) traversée f; (also: pedestrian ~ing) passage clouté; ~**ing guard** (US) n contractuel(le) qui fait traverser la rue aux enfants; ~ **purposes** npl: **to be at** ~ **purposes with sb** comprendre qn de travers; ~**reference** n renvoi m, référence f; ~**roads** n carrefour m; ~ **section** n (of object) coupe transversale; (in population) échantillon m; ~**walk** (US) n passage clouté; ~**wind** n vent m de travers; ~**word** n mots mpl croisés
crotch [krɒtʃ] n (ANAT, of garment) entrejambes m inv
crouch [krautʃ] vi s'accroupir; se tapir
crow [krəʊ] n (bird) corneille f; (of cock) chant m du coq, cocorico m ♦ vi (cock) chanter
crowbar ['krəʊbɑː*] n levier m
crowd [kraud] n foule f ♦ vt remplir ♦ vi affluer, s'attrouper, s'entasser; **to** ~ **in** entrer

en foule; ~**ed** adj bondé(e), plein(e)
crown [kraun] n couronne f; (of head) sommet m de la tête; (of hill) sommet ♦ vt couronner; ~ **jewels** npl joyaux mpl de la Couronne; ~ **prince** n prince héritier
crow's-feet ['krəʊzfiːt] npl pattes fpl d'oie
crucial ['kruːʃəl] adj crucial(e), décisif(ive)
crucifix ['kruːsɪfɪks] n (REL) crucifix m; ~**ion** [kruːsɪ'fɪkʃən] n (REL) crucifixion f
crude [kruːd] adj (materials) brut(e); non raffiné(e); (fig: basic) rudimentaire, sommaire; (: vulgar) cru(e), grossier(ère); ~ (**oil**) n (pétrole) brut m
cruel ['kruəl] adj cruel(le); ~**ty** n cruauté f
cruise [kruːz] n croisière f ♦ vi (ship) croiser; (car) rouler; ~**r** n croiseur m; (motorboat) yacht m de croisière
crumb [krʌm] n miette f
crumble ['krʌmbl] vt émietter ♦ vi (plaster etc) s'effriter; (land, earth) s'ébouler; (building) s'écrouler, crouler; (fig) s'effondrer; **crumbly** ['krʌmblɪ] adj friable
crumpet ['krʌmpɪt] n petite crêpe (épaisse)
crumple ['krʌmpl] vt froisser, friper
crunch [krʌntʃ] vt croquer; (underfoot) faire craquer or crisser, écraser ♦ n (fig) instant m or moment m critique, moment de vérité; ~**y** adj croquant(e), croustillant(e)
crusade [kruː'seɪd] n croisade f
crush [krʌʃ] n foule f, cohue f; (love): **to have a** ~ **on sb** avoir le béguin pour qn (inf); (drink): **lemon** ~ citron pressé ♦ vt écraser; (crumple) froisser; (fig: hopes) anéantir
crust [krʌst] n croûte f
crutch [krʌtʃ] n béquille f
crux [krʌks] n point crucial
cry [kraɪ] vi pleurer; (shout: also: ~ **out**) crier ♦ n cri m; ~ **off** (inf) vi se dédire; se décommander
cryptic ['krɪptɪk] adj énigmatique
crystal ['krɪstl] n cristal m; ~**clear** adj clair(e) comme de l'eau de roche
cub [kʌb] n petit m (d'un animal); (also: C~ **scout**) louveteau m
Cuba ['kjuːbə] n Cuba m
cubbyhole ['kʌbɪhəul] n cagibi m
cube [kjuːb] n cube m ♦ vt (MATH) élever au cube; **cubic** ['kjuːbɪk] adj cubique; **cubic metre** etc mètre m etc cube; **cubic capacity** n cylindrée f
cubicle ['kjuːbɪkl] n (in hospital) box m; (at pool) cabine f
cuckoo ['kukuː] n coucou m; ~ **clock** n (pendule f à) coucou m
cucumber ['kjuːkʌmbə*] n concombre m
cuddle ['kʌdl] vt câliner, caresser ♦ vi se blottir l'un contre l'autre
cue [kjuː] n (snooker ~) queue f de billard; (THEATRE etc) signal m
cuff [kʌf] n (BRIT: of shirt, coat etc) poignet m, manchette f; (US: of trousers) revers m;

(*blow*) tape f; **off the ~** à l'improviste; **~ links** *npl* boutons *mpl* de manchette

cul-de-sac ['kʌldəsæk] *n* cul-de-sac *m*, impasse *f*

cull [kʌl] *vt* sélectionner ♦ *n* (*of animals*) massacre *m*

culminate ['kʌlmɪneɪt] *vi*: **to ~ in** finir *or* se terminer par; (*end in*) mener à; **culmination** [kʌlmɪ'neɪʃən] *n* point culminant

culottes [kju'lɒts] *npl* jupe-culotte *f*

culprit ['kʌlprɪt] *n* coupable *m/f*

cult [kʌlt] *n* culte *m*

cultivate ['kʌltɪveɪt] *vt* cultiver; **cultivation** [kʌltɪ'veɪʃən] *n* culture *f*

cultural ['kʌltʃərəl] *adj* culturel(le)

culture ['kʌltʃə*] *n* culture *f*; **~d** *adj* (*person*) cultivé(e)

cumbersome ['kʌmbəsəm] *adj* encombrant(e), embarrassant(e)

cunning ['kʌnɪŋ] *n* ruse *f*, astuce *f* ♦ *adj* rusé(e), malin(igne); (*device, idea*) astucieux(euse)

cup [kʌp] *n* tasse *f*; (*as prize*) coupe *f*; (*of bra*) bonnet *m*

cupboard ['kʌbəd] *n* armoire *f*; (*built-in*) placard *m*

cup tie (*BRIT*) *n* match *m* de coupe

curate ['kjʊərɪt] *n* vicaire *m*

curator [kjʊ'reɪtə*] *n* conservateur *m* (*d'un musée etc*)

curb [kɜːb] *vt* refréner, mettre un frein à ♦ *n* (*fig*) frein *m*, restriction *f*; (*US: kerb*) bord *m* du trottoir

curdle ['kɜːdl] *vi* se cailler

cure [kjʊə*] *vt* guérir; (*CULIN: salt*) saler; (: *smoke*) fumer; (: *dry*) sécher ♦ *n* remède *m*

curfew ['kɜːfjuː] *n* couvre-feu *m*

curio ['kjʊərɪəʊ] *n* bibelot *m*, curiosité *f*

curiosity [kjʊərɪ'ɒsɪtɪ] *n* curiosité *f*

curious ['kjʊərɪəs] *adj* curieux(euse)

curl [kɜːl] *n* boucle *f* (de cheveux) ♦ *vt, vi* boucler; (*tightly*) friser; **~ up** *vi* s'enrouler; se pelotonner; **~er** *n* bigoudi *m*, rouleau *m*; **~y** *adj* bouclé(e); frisé(e)

currant ['kʌrənt] *n* (*dried*) raisin *m* de Corinthe, raisin sec; (*bush*) groseiller *m*; (*fruit*) groseille *f*

currency ['kʌrənsɪ] *n* monnaie *f*; **to gain ~** (*fig*) s'accréditer

current ['kʌrənt] *n* courant *m* ♦ *adj* courant(e); **~ account** (*BRIT*) *n* compte courant; **~ affairs** *npl* (questions *fpl* d'actualité *f*; **~ly** *adv* actuellement

curriculum [kə'rɪkjʊləm] (*pl* **~s** *or* **curricula**) *n* programme *m* d'études; **~ vitae** *n* curriculum vitae *m*

curry ['kʌrɪ] *n* curry *m* ♦ *vt*: **to ~ favour with** chercher à s'attirer les bonnes grâces de

curse [kɜːs] *vi* jurer, blasphémer ♦ *vt* maudire ♦ *n* (*spell*) malédiction *f*; (*problem, scourge*) fléau *m*; (*swearword*) juron *m*

cursor ['kɜːsə*] *n* (*COMPUT*) curseur *m*

cursory ['kɜːsərɪ] *adj* superficiel(le), hâtif(ive)

curt [kɜːt] *adj* brusque, sec(sèche)

curtail [kɜː'teɪl] *vt* (*visit etc*) écourter; (*expenses, freedom etc*) réduire

curtain ['kɜːtn] *n* rideau *m*

curts(e)y ['kɜːtsɪ] *vi* faire une révérence

curve [kɜːv] *n* courbe *f*; (*in the road*) tournant *m*, virage *m* ♦ *vi* se courber; (*road*) faire une courbe

cushion ['kʊʃən] *n* coussin *m* ♦ *vt* (*fall, shock*) amortir

custard ['kʌstəd] *n* (*for pouring*) crème anglaise

custody ['kʌstədɪ] *n* (*of child*) garde *f*; **to take sb into ~** (*suspect*) placer qn en détention préventive

custom ['kʌstəm] *n* coutume *f*, usage *m*; (*COMM*) clientèle *f*; **~ary** *adj* habituel(le)

customer ['kʌstəmə*] *n* client(e)

customized ['kʌstəmaɪzd] *adj* (*car etc*) construit(e) sur commande

custom-made ['kʌstəm'meɪd] *adj* (*clothes*) fait(e) sur mesure; (*other goods*) hors série, fait(e) sur commande

customs ['kʌstəmz] *npl* douane *f*; **~ officer** *n* douanier(ière)

cut [kʌt] (*pt, pp* **cut**) *vt* couper; (*meat*) découper; (*reduce*) réduire ♦ *vi* couper ♦ *n* coupure *f*; (*of clothes*) coupe *f*; (*in salary etc*) réduction *f*; (*of meat*) morceau *m*; **to ~ one's hand** se couper la main; **to ~ a tooth** percer une dent; **~ down** *vt fus* (*tree etc*) couper, abattre; (*consumption*) réduire; **~ off** *vt* couper; (*fig*) isoler; **~ out** *vt* découper; (*stop*) arrêter; (*remove*) ôter; **~ up** *vt* (*paper, meat*) découper; **~back** *n* réduction *f*

cute [kjuːt] *adj* mignon(ne), adorable

cuticle remover ['kjuːtɪkl-] *n* (*on nail*) repousse-peaux *m inv*

cutlery ['kʌtlərɪ] *n* couverts *mpl*

cutlet ['kʌtlɪt] *n* côtelette *f*

cut: **~out** *n* (*switch*) coupe-circuit *m inv*; (*cardboard ~out*) découpage *m*; **~-price** (*US* **~-rate**) *adj* au rabais, à prix réduit; **~throat** *n* assassin *m* ♦ *adj* acharné(e)

cutting ['kʌtɪŋ] *adj* tranchant(e), coupant(e); (*fig*) cinglant(e), mordant(e) ♦ *n* (*BRIT: from newspaper*) coupure *f* (de journal); (*from plant*) bouture *f*

CV *n abbr* = **curriculum vitae**

cwt *abbr* = **hundredweight(s)**

cyanide ['saɪənaɪd] *n* cyanure *m*

cycle ['saɪkl] *n* cycle *m*; (*bicycle*) bicyclette *f*, vélo *m* ♦ *vi* faire de la bicyclette; **cycling** ['saɪklɪŋ] *n* cyclisme *m*; **cyclist** ['saɪklɪst] *n* cycliste *m/f*

cygnet ['sɪgnɪt] *n* jeune cygne *m*

cylinder ['sɪlɪndə*] *n* cylindre *m*; **~-head gasket** *n* joint *m* de culasse

cymbals ['sɪmbəlz] *npl* cymbales *fpl*
cynic ['sɪnɪk] *n* cynique *m/f*; **~al** *adj* cynique; **~ism** ['sɪnɪsɪzəm] *n* cynisme *m*
Cypriot ['sɪprɪət] *adj* cypriote, chypriote ♦ *n* Cypriote *m/f*, Chypriote *m/f*
Cyprus ['saɪprəs] *n* Chypre *f*
cyst [sɪst] *n* kyste *m*
cystitis [sɪs'taɪtɪs] *n* cystite *f*
czar [zɑ:*] *n* tsar *m*
Czech [tʃek] *adj* tchèque ♦ *n* Tchèque *m/f*, (*LING*) tchèque *m*
Czechoslovak [tʃekə'sləʊvæk] *adj, n* = **Czechoslovakian**
Czechoslovakia [tʃekəslə'vækɪə] *n* Tchécoslovaquie *f*; **~n** *adj* tchécoslovaque ♦ *n* Tchécoslovaque *m/f*

D d

D [di:] *n* (*MUS*) ré *m*
dab [dæb] *vt* (*eyes, wound*) tamponner; (*paint, cream*) appliquer (par petites touches *or* rapidement)
dabble ['dæbl] *vi*: **to ~ in** faire *or* se mêler *or* s'occuper un peu de
dad [dæd] *n* papa *m*
daddy ['dædɪ] *n* papa *m*
daffodil ['dæfədɪl] *n* jonquille *f*
daft [dɑ:ft] *adj* idiot(e), stupide
dagger ['dægə*] *n* poignard *m*
daily ['deɪlɪ] *adj* quotidien(ne), journalier(ère) ♦ *n* quotidien *m* ♦ *adv* tous les jours
dainty ['deɪntɪ] *adj* délicat(e), mignon(ne)
dairy ['deərɪ] *n* (*BRIT: shop*) crémerie *f*, laiterie *f*; (*on farm*) laiterie *f*; **~ products** *npl* produits laitiers; **~ store** (*US*) *n* crémerie *f*, laiterie *f*
dais ['deɪs] *n* estrade *f*
daisy ['deɪzɪ] *n* pâquerette *f*; **~ wheel** *n* (*on printer*) marguerite *f*
dale [deɪl] *n* vallon *m*
dam [dæm] *n* barrage *m* ♦ *vt* endiguer
damage ['dæmɪdʒ] *n* dégâts *mpl*, dommages *mpl*; (*fig*) tort *m* ♦ *vt* endommager, abîmer; (*fig*) faire du tort à; **~s** *npl* (*LAW*) dommages-intérêts *mpl*
damn [dæm] *vt* condamner; (*curse*) maudire ♦ *n* (*inf*): **I don't give a ~** je m'en fous ♦ *adj* (*inf: also*: **this ~ ...**) ce sacré *or* foutu ...; **~ (it)!** zut!; **~ing** *adj* accablant(e)
damp [dæmp] *adj* humide ♦ *n* humidité *f* ♦ *vt* (*also*: **~en**: *cloth, rag*) humecter; (: *enthu-*

siasm) refroidir
damson ['dæmzən] *n* prune *f* de Damas
dance [dɑ:ns] *n* danse *f*; (*social event*) bal *m* ♦ *vi* danser; **~ hall** *n* salle *f* de bal, dancing *m*; **~r** *n* danseur(euse); **dancing** ['dɑ:nsɪŋ] *n* danse *f*
dandelion ['dændɪlaɪən] *n* pissenlit *m*
dandruff ['dændrəf] *n* pellicules *fpl*
Dane [deɪn] *n* Danois(e)
danger ['deɪndʒə*] *n* danger *m*; **there is a ~ of fire** il y a (un) risque d'incendie; **in ~** en danger; **he was in ~ of falling** il risquait de tomber; **~ous** *adj* dangereux(euse)
dangle ['dæŋgl] *vt* balancer ♦ *vi* pendre
Danish ['deɪnɪʃ] *adj* danois(e) ♦ *n* (*LING*) danois *m*
dapper ['dæpə*] *adj* pimpant(e)
dare [dɛə*] *vt*: **to ~ sb to do** défier qn de faire ♦ *vi*: **to ~ (to) do sth** oser faire qch; **I ~ say** (*I suppose*) il est probable (que); **~devil** *n* casse-cou *m inv*; **daring** ['dɛərɪŋ] *adj* hardi(e), audacieux(euse); (*dress*) osé(e) ♦ *n* audace *f*, hardiesse *f*
dark [dɑ:k] *adj* (*night, room*) obscur(e), sombre; (*colour, complexion*) foncé(e), sombre ♦ *n*: **in the ~** dans le noir; **in the ~ about** (*fig*) ignorant tout de; **after ~** après la tombée de la nuit; **~en** *vt* obscurcir, assombrir ♦ *vi* s'obscurcir, s'assombrir; **~ glasses** *npl* lunettes noires; **~ness** *n* obscurité *f*; **~room** *n* chambre noire
darling ['dɑ:lɪŋ] *adj* chéri(e) ♦ *n* chéri(e); (*favourite*): **to be the ~ of** être la coqueluche de
darn [dɑ:n] *vt* repriser, raccommoder
dart [dɑ:t] *n* fléchette *f*; (*sewing*) pince *f* ♦ *vi*: **to ~ towards** (*also*: **make a ~ towards**) se précipiter *or* s'élancer vers; **~s** *n* (*jeu m de*) fléchettes *fpl*; **to ~ away/along** partir/passer comme une flèche; **~board** *n* cible *f* (de jeu de fléchettes)
dash [dæʃ] *n* (*sign*) tiret *m*; (*small quantity*) goutte *f*, larme *f* ♦ *vt* (*missile*) jeter *or* lancer violemment; (*hopes*) anéantir ♦ *vi*: **to ~ towards** (*also*: **make a ~ towards**) se précipiter *or* se ruer vers; **~ away** *vi* partir à toute allure, filer; **~ off** *vi* = **~ away**
dashboard ['dæʃbɔ:d] *n* (*AUT*) tableau *m* de bord
dashing ['dæʃɪŋ] *adj* fringant(e)
data ['deɪtə] *npl* données *fpl*; **~base** *n* (*COMPUT*) base *f* de données; **~ processing** *n* traitement *m* de données
date [deɪt] *n* date *f*; (*with sb*) rendez-vous *m*; (*fruit*) datte *f* ♦ *vt* dater; (*person*) sortir avec; **~ of birth** date de naissance; **to ~** (*until now*) à ce jour; **out of ~** (*passport*) périmé(e); (*theory etc*) dépassé(e); (*clothes etc*) démodé(e); **up to ~** moderne; (*news*) très récent; **~d** *adj* démodé(e)
daub [dɔ:b] *vt* barbouiller
daughter ['dɔ:tə*] *n* fille *f*; **~-in-law** *n*

belle-fille f, bru f

daunting ['dɔːntɪŋ] *adj* décourageant(e)

dawdle ['dɔːdl] *vi* traîner, lambiner

dawn [dɔːn] *n* aube f, aurore f ♦ *vi* (*day*) se lever, poindre; (*fig*): **it ~ed on him that ...** il lui vint à l'esprit que ...

day [deɪ] *n* jour m; (*as duration*) journée f; (*period of time, age*) époque f, temps m; **the ~ before** la veille, le jour précédent; **the ~ after, the following ~** le lendemain, le jour suivant; **the ~ after tomorrow** après-demain; **the ~ before yesterday** avant-hier; **by ~** de jour; **~break** *n* point m du jour; **~dream** *vi* rêver (tout éveillé); **~light** (lumière f du) jour m; **~ return** (*BRIT*) *n* billet m d'aller-retour (valable pour la journée); **~time** *n* jour m, journée f; **~-to-day** *adj* quotidien(ne); (*event*) journalier(ère)

daze [deɪz] *vt* (*stun*) étourdir ♦ *n*: **in a ~** étourdi(e), hébété(e)

dazzle ['dæzl] *vt* éblouir, aveugler

DC *abbr* (= *direct current*) courant continu

D-day ['diːdeɪ] *n* le jour J

dead [ded] *adj* mort(e); (*numb*) engourdi(e), insensible; (*battery*) à plat; (*telephone*): **the line is ~** la ligne est coupée ♦ *adv* absolument, complètement ♦ *npl*: **the ~** les morts; **he was shot ~** il a été tué d'un coup de revolver; **~ on time** à l'heure pile; **~ tired** éreinté(e), complètement fourbu(e); **to stop ~** s'arrêter pile or net; **~en** *vt* (*blow, sound*) amortir; (*pain*) calmer; **~ end** *n* impasse f; **~ heat** *n* (*SPORT*): **to finish in a ~ heat** terminer ex æquo; **~line** *n* date f or heure f limite; **~lock** *n* (*fig*) impasse f; **~ loss** *n*: **to be a ~ loss** (*inf: person*) n'être bon(ne) à rien; **~ly** *adj* mortel(le); (*weapon*) meurtrier(ère); (*accuracy*) extrême; **~pan** *adj* impassible; **D~ Sea** *n*: **the D~ Sea** la mer Morte

deaf [def] *adj* sourd(e); **~en** *vt* rendre sourd; **~-mute** *n* sourd(e)-muet(te); **~ness** *n* surdité f

deal [diːl] (*pt, pp* dealt) *n* affaire f, marché m ♦ *vt* (*blow*) porter; (*cards*) donner, distribuer; **a great ~ (of)** beaucoup (de); **~ in** *vt fus* faire le commerce de; **~ with** *vt fus* (*person, problem*) s'occuper or se charger de; (*be about: book etc*) traiter de; **~er** *n* marchand m; **~ings** *npl* (*COMM*) transactions fpl; (*relations*) relations fpl, rapports mpl

dean [diːn] *n* (*REL, BRIT: SCOL*) doyen m; (*US*) conseiller(ère) (principal(e)) d'éducation

dear [dɪə*] *adj* cher(chère); (*expensive*) cher, coûteux(euse) ♦ *n*: **my ~** mon cher/ ma chère; **~ me!** mon Dieu!; **D~ Sir/ Madam** (*in letter*) Monsieur/Madame; **D~ Mr/Mrs X** Cher Monsieur/Chère Madame; **~ly** *adv* (*love*) tendrement; (*pay*) cher

death [deθ] *n* mort f; (*fatality*) mort m; (*ADMIN*) décès m; **~ certificate** *n* acte m de décès; **~ly** *adj* de mort; **~ penalty** *n* peine f de mort; **~ rate** *n* (taux m de) mortalité f; **~ toll** *n* nombre m de morts

debar [dɪ'baː*] *vt*: **to ~ sb from doing** interdire à qn de faire

debase [dɪ'beɪs] *vt* (*value*) déprécier, dévaloriser

debatable [dɪ'beɪtəbl] *adj* discutable

debate [dɪ'beɪt] *n* discussion f, débat m ♦ *vt* discuter, débattre

debit ['debɪt] *n* débit m ♦ *vt*: **to ~ a sum to sb** *or* **to sb's account** porter une somme au débit de qn, débiter qn d'une somme; *see also* **direct**

debt [det] *n* dette f; **to be in ~** avoir des dettes, être endetté(e); **~or** *n* débiteur(trice)

debunk [diː'bʌŋk] *vt* (*theory, claim*) montrer le ridicule de

decade ['dekeɪd] *n* décennie f, décade f

decadence ['dekədəns] *n* décadence f

decaffeinated [diː'kæfɪneɪtɪd] *adj* décaféiné(e)

decanter [dɪ'kæntə*] *n* carafe f

decay [dɪ'keɪ] *n* (*of building*) délabrement m; (*also: tooth ~*) carie f (dentaire) ♦ *vi* (*rot*) se décomposer, pourrir; (: *teeth*) se carier

deceased [dɪ'siːst] *n* défunt(e)

deceit [dɪ'siːt] *n* tromperie f, supercherie f; **~ful** *adj* trompeur(euse); **deceive** [dɪ'siːv] *vt* tromper

December [dɪ'sembə*] *n* décembre m

decent ['diːsənt] *adj* décent(e), convenable; **they were very ~ about it** ils se sont montrés très chic

deception [dɪ'sepʃən] *n* tromperie f

deceptive [dɪ'septɪv] *adj* trompeur(euse)

decide [dɪ'saɪd] *vt* (*person*) décider; (*question, argument*) trancher, régler ♦ *vi* se décider, décider; **to ~ to do/that** décider de faire/que; **to ~ on** décider, se décider pour; **~d** *adj* (*resolute*) résolu(e), décidé(e); (*clear, definite*) net(te), marqué(e); **~dly** [dɪ'saɪdɪdlɪ] *adv* résolument; (*distinctly*) incontestablement, nettement

deciduous [dɪ'sɪdjuəs] *adj* à feuilles caduques

decimal ['desɪməl] *adj* décimal(e) ♦ *n* décimale f; **~ point** *n* ≈ virgule f

decipher [dɪ'saɪfə*] *vt* déchiffrer

decision [dɪ'sɪʒən] *n* décision f

decisive [dɪ'saɪsɪv] *adj* décisif(ive); (*person*) décidé(e)

deck [dek] *n* (*NAUT*) pont m; (*of bus*): **top ~** impériale f; (*of cards*) jeu m; (*record ~*) platine f; **~chair** *n* chaise longue

declare [dɪ'kleə*] *vt* déclarer

decline [dɪ'klaɪn] *n* (*decay*) déclin m; (*lessening*) baisse f ♦ *vt* refuser, décliner ♦ *vi*

décliner; (*business*) baisser
decoder [diː'kəʊdə*] *n* (*TV*) décodeur *m*
decorate ['dekəreɪt] *vt* (*adorn, give a medal to*) décorer; (*paint and paper*) peindre et tapisser; **decoration** [dekə'reɪʃən] *n* (*medal etc, adornment*) décoration *f*; **decorator** ['dekəreɪtə*] *n* peintre-décorateur *m*
decoy ['diːkɔɪ] *n* piège *m*; (*person*) compère *m*
decrease [*n* 'diːkriːs, *vb* diː'kriːs] *n*: ~ (**in**) diminution *f* (de) ♦ *vt, vi* diminuer
decree [dɪ'kriː] *n* (*POL, REL*) décret *m*; (*LAW*) arrêt *m*, jugement *m*; ~ **nisi** [-'naɪsaɪ] *n* jugement *m* provisoire de divorce
dedicate ['dedɪkeɪt] *vt* consacrer; (*book etc*) dédier; **dedication** [dedɪ'keɪʃən] *n* (*devotion*) dévouement *m*; (*in book*) dédicace *f*
deduce [dɪ'djuːs] *vt* déduire, conclure
deduct [dɪ'dʌkt] *vt*: **to** ~ **sth** (**from**) déduire qch (de), retrancher qch (de); ~**ion** [dɪ'dʌkʃən] *n* (*deducting, deducing*) déduction *f*; (*from wage etc*) prélèvement *m*, retenue *f*
deed [diːd] *n* action *f*, acte *m*; (*LAW*) acte notarié, contrat *m*
deem [diːm] *vt* (*formal*) juger
deep [diːp] *adj* profond(e); (*voice*) grave ♦ *adv*: **spectators stood 20** ~ il y avait 20 rangs de spectateurs; **4 metres** ~ de 4 mètres de profondeur; ~**en** *vt* approfondir ♦ *vi* (*fig*) s'épaissir; ~**freeze** *n* congélateur *m*; ~**-fry** *vt* faire frire (en friteuse); ~**ly** *adv* profondément; (*interested*) vivement; ~**-sea diver** *n* sous-marin(e); ~**-sea diving** *n* plongée sous-marine; ~**-sea fishing** *n* grande pêche; ~**-seated** *adj* profond(e), profondément enraciné(e)
deer [dɪə*] *n inv*: (**red**) ~ cerf *m*, biche *f*; (**fallow**) ~ daim *m*; (**roe**) ~ chevreuil *m*; ~**skin** *n* daim
deface [dɪ'feɪs] *vt* dégrader; (*notice, poster*) barbouiller
default [dɪ'fɔːlt] *n* (*COMPUT: also:* ~ **value**) valeur *f* par défaut; **by** ~ (*LAW*) par défaut, par contumace; (*SPORT*) par forfait
defeat [dɪ'fiːt] *n* défaite *f* ♦ *vt* (*team, opponents*) battre
defect [*n* 'diːfekt, *vb* dɪ'fekt] *n* défaut *m* ♦ *vi*: **to** ~ **to the enemy/the West** passer à l'ennemi/à l'Ouest; ~**ive** [dɪ'fektɪv] *adj* défectueux(euse)
defence [dɪ'fens] (*US* **defense**) *n* défense *f*; ~**less** *adj* sans défense
defend [dɪ'fend] *vt* défendre; ~**ant** *n* défendeur(deresse); (*in criminal case*) accusé(e), prévenu(e); ~**er** *n* défenseur *m*
defer [dɪ'fɜː*] *vt* (*postpone*) différer, ajourner
defiance [dɪ'faɪəns] *n* défi *m*; **in** ~ **of** au mépris de; **defiant** [dɪ'faɪənt] *adj* provocant(e), de défi; (*person*) rebelle, intraitable
deficiency [dɪ'fɪʃənsɪ] *n* insuffisance *f*, défi-

cience *f*; **deficient** *adj* (*inadequate*) insuffisant(e); **to be deficient in** manquer de
deficit ['defɪsɪt] *n* déficit *m*
defile [*vb* dɪ'faɪl, *n* 'diːfaɪl] *vt* souiller, profaner
define [dɪ'faɪn] *vt* définir
definite ['defɪnɪt] *adj* (*fixed*) défini(e), (bien) déterminé(e); (*clear, obvious*) net(te), manifeste; (*certain*) sûr(e); **he was** ~ **about it** il a été catégorique; ~**ly** *adv* sans aucun doute
definition [defɪ'nɪʃən] *n* définition *f*; (*clearness*) netteté *f*
deflate [diː'fleɪt] *vt* dégonfler
deflect [dɪ'flekt] *vt* détourner, faire dévier
deformed [dɪ'fɔːmd] *adj* difforme
defraud [dɪ'frɔːd] *vt* frauder; **to** ~ **sb of sth** escroquer qch à qn
defrost [diː'frɒst] *vt* dégivrer; (*food*) décongeler; ~**er** (*US*) *n* (*demister*) dispositif *m* anti-buée *inv*
deft [deft] *adj* adroit(e), preste
defunct [dɪ'fʌŋkt] *adj* défunt(e)
defuse [diː'fjuːz] *vt* désamorcer
defy [dɪ'faɪ] *vt* défier; (*efforts etc*) résister à
degenerate [*vb* dɪ'dʒenəreɪt, *adj* dɪ'dʒenərɪt] *vi* dégénérer ♦ *adj* dégénéré(e)
degree [dɪ'griː] *n* degré *m*; (*SCOL*) diplôme *m* (universitaire); **a** (**first**) ~ **in maths** une licence en maths; **by** ~**s** (*gradually*) par degrés; **to some** ~, **to a certain** ~ jusqu'à un certain point, dans une certaine mesure
dehydrated [diːhaɪ'dreɪtɪd] *adj* déshydraté(e); (*milk, eggs*) en poudre
de-ice [diː'aɪs] *vt* (*windscreen*) dégivrer
deign [deɪn] *vi*: **to** ~ **to do** daigner faire
dejected [dɪ'dʒektɪd] *adj* abattu(e), déprimé(e)
delay [dɪ'leɪ] *vt* retarder ♦ *vi* s'attarder ♦ *n* délai *m*, retard *m*; **to be** ~**ed** être en retard
delectable [dɪ'lektəbl] *adj* délicieux(euse)
delegate [*n* 'delɪgɪt, *vb* 'delɪgeɪt] *n* délégué(e) ♦ *vt* déléguer
delete [dɪ'liːt] *vt* rayer, supprimer
deliberate [*adj* dɪ'lɪbərɪt, *vb* dɪ'lɪbəreɪt] *adj* (*intentional*) délibéré(e); (*slow*) mesuré(e) ♦ *vi* délibérer, réfléchir; ~**ly** *adv* (*on purpose*) exprès, délibérément
delicacy ['delɪkəsɪ] *n* délicatesse *f*; (*food*) mets fin *or* délicat, friandise *f*
delicate ['delɪkɪt] *adj* délicat(e)
delicatessen [delɪkə'tesn] *n* épicerie fine
delicious [dɪ'lɪʃəs] *adj* délicieux(euse)
delight [dɪ'laɪt] *n* (grande) joie, grand plaisir ♦ *vt* enchanter; **to take** (**a**) ~ **in** prendre grand plaisir à; ~**ed**: ~**ed** (**at** *or* **with/to do**) ravi(e) (de/de faire); ~**ful** *adj* (*person*) adorable; (*meal, evening*) merveilleux(euse)
delinquent [dɪ'lɪŋkwənt] *adj, n* délinquant(e)
delirious [dɪ'lɪrɪəs] *adj*: **to be** ~ délirer

deliver [dɪ'lɪvə*] *vt* (*mail*) distribuer; (*goods*) livrer; (*message*) remettre; (*speech*) prononcer; (*MED: baby*) mettre au monde; **~y** *n* distribution *f*; livraison *f*; (*of speaker*) élocution *f*; (*MED*) accouchement *m*; **to take ~y of** prendre livraison de

delude [dɪ'luːd] *vt* tromper, leurrer

delusion [dɪ'luːʒən] *n* illusion *f*

delve [delv] *vi*: **to ~ into** fouiller dans; (*subject*) approfondir

demand [dɪ'mɑːnd] *vt* réclamer, exiger ♦ *n* exigence *f*; (*claim*) revendication *f*; (*ECON*) demande *f*; **in ~** demandé(e), recherché(e); **on ~** sur demande; **~ing** *adj* (*person*) exigeant(e); (*work*) astreignant(e)

demean [dɪ'miːn] *vt*: **to ~ o.s.** s'abaisser

demeanour [dɪ'miːnə*] (*US* **demeanor**) *n* comportement *m*; maintien *m*

demented [dɪ'mentɪd] *adj* dément(e), fou(folle)

demise [dɪ'maɪz] *n* mort *f*

demister [diː'mɪstə*] (*BRIT*) *n* (*AUT*) dispositif *m* anti-buée *inv*

demo ['deməʊ] (*inf*) *n abbr* (= *demonstration*) manif *f*

democracy [dɪ'mɒkrəsɪ] *n* démocratie *f*; **democrat** ['deməkræt] *n* démocrate *m/f*; **democratic** [demə'krætɪk] *adj* démocratique

demolish [dɪ'mɒlɪʃ] *vt* démolir

demonstrate ['demənstreɪt] *vt* démontrer, prouver; (*show*) faire une démonstration de ♦ *vi*: **to ~ (for/against)** manifester (en faveur de/contre); **demonstration** [demən'streɪʃən] *n* démonstration *f*, manifestation *f*; **demonstrator** ['demənstreɪtə*] *n* (*POL*) manifestant(e)

demote [dɪ'məʊt] *vt* rétrograder

demure [dɪ'mjʊə*] *adj* sage, réservé(e)

den [den] *n* tanière *f*, antre *m*

denatured alcohol [diː'neɪtʃəd-] (*US*) *n* alcool *m* à brûler

denial [dɪ'naɪəl] *n* démenti *m*; (*refusal*) dénégation *f*

denim ['denɪm] *n* jean *m*; **~s** *npl* (*jeans*) (blue-)jean(s) *m(pl)*

Denmark ['denmɑːk] *n* Danemark *m*

denomination [dɪnɒmɪ'neɪʃən] *n* (*of money*) valeur *f*; (*REL*) confession *f*

denounce [dɪ'naʊns] *vt* dénoncer

dense [dens] *adj* dense; (*stupid*) obtus(e), bouché(e); **~ly** *adv*: **~ly populated** à forte densité de population

density ['densɪtɪ] *n* densité *f*; **double/high-~ diskette** disquette *f* double densité/haute densité

dent [dent] *n* bosse *f* ♦ *vt* (*also*: **make a ~ in**) cabosser

dental ['dentl] *adj* dentaire; **~ surgeon** *n* (chirurgien(ne)) dentiste

dentist ['dentɪst] *n* dentiste *m/f*

dentures ['dentʃəz] *npl* dentier *m sg*

deny [dɪ'naɪ] *vt* nier; (*refuse*) refuser

deodorant [diː'əʊdərənt] *n* déodorant *m*, désodorisant *m*

depart [dɪ'pɑːt] *vi* partir; **to ~ from** (*fig: differ from*) s'écarter de

department [dɪ'pɑːtmənt] *n* (*COMM*) rayon *m*; (*SCOL*) section *f*; (*POL*) ministère *m*, département *m*; **~ store** *n* grand magasin

departure [dɪ'pɑːtʃə*] *n* départ *m*; **a new ~** une nouvelle voie; **~ lounge** *n* (*at airport*) salle *f* d'embarquement

depend [dɪ'pend] *vi*: **to ~ on** dépendre de; (*rely on*) compter sur; **it ~s** cela dépend; **~ing on the result** selon le résultat; **~able** *adj* (*person*) sérieux(euse), sûr(e); (*car, watch*) solide, fiable; **~ant** *n* personne *f* à charge; **~ent** *adj*: **to be ~ent (on)** dépendre (de) ♦ *n* = **dependant**

depict [dɪ'pɪkt] *vt* (*in picture*) représenter; (*in words*) (dé)peindre, décrire

depleted [dɪ'pliːtɪd] *adj* (considérablement) réduit(e) *or* diminué(e)

deport [dɪ'pɔːt] *vt* expulser

deposit [dɪ'pɒzɪt] *n* (*CHEM, COMM, GEO*) dépôt *m*; (*of ore, oil*) gisement *m*; (*part payment*) arrhes *fpl*, acompte *m*; (*on bottle etc*) consigne *f*; (*for hired goods etc*) cautionnement *m*, garantie *f* ♦ *vt* déposer; **~ account** *n* compte *m* sur livret

depot ['depəʊ] *n* dépôt *m*; (*US: RAIL*) gare *f*

depress [dɪ'pres] *vt* déprimer; (*press down*) appuyer sur, abaisser; (*prices, wages*) faire baisser; **~ed** *adj* (*person*) déprimé(e); (*area*) en déclin, touché(e) par le sous-emploi; **~ing** *adj* déprimant(e); **~ion** [dɪ'preʃən] *n* dépression *f*; (*hollow*) creux *m*

deprivation [deprɪ'veɪʃən] *n* privation *f*; (*loss*) perte *f*

deprive [dɪ'praɪv] *vt*: **to ~ sb of** priver qn de; **~d** *adj* déshérité(e)

depth [depθ] *n* profondeur *f*; **in the ~s of despair** au plus profond du désespoir; **to be out of one's ~** avoir perdu pied, nager

deputize ['depjʊtaɪz] *vi*: **to ~ for** assurer l'intérim de

deputy ['depjʊtɪ] *adj* adjoint(e) ♦ *n* (*second in command*) adjoint(e); (*US: also ~ sheriff*) shérif adjoint; **~ head** directeur adjoint, sous-directeur *m*

derail [dɪ'reɪl] *vt*: **to be ~ed** dérailler

deranged [dɪ'reɪndʒd] *adj*: **to be (mentally) ~** avoir le cerveau dérangé

derby ['dɑːbɪ] (*US*) *n* (*bowler hat*) (chapeau *m*) melon *m*

derelict ['derɪlɪkt] *adj* abandonné(e), à l'abandon

derisory [dɪ'raɪsərɪ] *adj* (*sum*) dérisoire; (*smile, person*) moqueur(euse)

derive [dɪ'raɪv] *vt*: **to ~ sth from** tirer qch de; trouver qch dans; **to ~ from** provenir de, dériver de

derogatory [dɪ'rɒgətərɪ] *adj* désobligeant(e); péjoratif(ive)

descend [dɪ'send] *vt, vi* descendre; **to ~ from** descendre de, être issu(e) de; **to ~ to (doing) sth** s'abaisser à (faire) qch; **descent** [dɪ'sent] *n* descente *f*; (*origin*) origine *f*

describe [dɪs'kraɪb] *vt* décrire; **description** [dɪs'krɪpʃən] *n* description *f*; (*sort*) sorte *f*, espèce *f*

desecrate ['desɪkreɪt] *vt* profaner

desert [*n* 'dezət, *vb* dɪ'zɜːt] *n* désert *m* ♦ *vt* déserter, abandonner ♦ *vi* (*MIL*) déserter; **~s** *npl*: **to get one's just ~s** n'avoir que ce qu'on mérite; **~er** *n* déserteur *m*; **~ion** [dɪ'zɜːʃən] *n* (*MIL*) désertion *f*; (*LAW: of spouse*) abandon *m* du domicile conjugal; **~ island** *n* île déserte

deserve [dɪ'zɜːv] *vt* mériter; **deserving** [dɪ'zɜːvɪŋ] *adj* (*person*) méritant(e); (*action, cause*) méritoire

design [dɪ'zaɪn] *n* (*sketch*) plan *m*, dessin *m*; (*layout, shape*) conception *f*, ligne *f*; (*pattern*) dessin *m*, motif(s) *m(pl)*; (*COMM, art*) design *m*, stylisme *m*; (*intention*) dessein *m* ♦ *vt* dessiner; élaborer; **~er** [dɪ'zaɪnə*] *n* (*TECH*) concepteur-projeteur *m*; (*ART*) dessinateur(trice), designer *m*; (*fashion*) styliste *m/f*

desire [dɪ'zaɪə*] *n* désir *m* ♦ *vt* désirer

desk [desk] *n* (*in office*) bureau *m*; (*for pupil*) pupitre *m*; (*BRIT: in shop, restaurant*) caisse *f*; (*in hotel, at airport*) réception *f*

desolate ['desəlɪt] *adj* désolé(e); (*person*) affligé(e)

despair [dɪs'peə*] *n* désespoir *m* ♦ *vi*: **to ~ of** désespérer de

despatch [dɪs'pætʃ] *n, vt* = **dispatch**

desperate ['despərɪt] *adj* désespéré(e); (*criminal*) prêt(e) à tout; **to be ~ for sth/ to do sth** avoir désespérément besoin de qch/de faire qch; **~ly** ['despərɪtlɪ] *adv* désespérément; (*very*) terriblement, extrêmement

desperation [despə'reɪʃən] *n* désespoir *m*; **in (sheer) ~** en désespoir de cause

despicable [dɪs'pɪkəbl] *adj* méprisable

despise [dɪs'paɪz] *vt* mépriser

despite [dɪs'paɪt] *prep* malgré, en dépit de

despondent [dɪs'pɒndənt] *adj* découragé(e), abattu(e)

dessert [dɪ'zɜːt] *n* dessert *m*; **~spoon** *n* cuiller *f* à dessert

destination [destɪ'neɪʃən] *n* destination *f*

destined ['destɪnd] *adj*: **to be ~ to do/for sth** être destiné(e) à faire/à qch

destiny ['destɪnɪ] *n* destinée *f*, destin *m*

destitute ['destɪtjuːt] *adj* indigent(e)

destroy [dɪs'trɔɪ] *vt* détruire; (*injured horse*) abattre; (*dog*) faire piquer; **~er** *n* (*NAUT*) contre-torpilleur *m*

destruction [dɪs'trʌkʃən] *n* destruction *f*

detach [dɪ'tætʃ] *vt* détacher; **~ed** *adj* (*attitude, person*) détaché(e); **~ed house** *n* pa-

villon *m*, maison(nette) (individuelle); **~ment** *n* (*MIL*) détachement *m*; (*fig*) détachement, indifférence *f*

detail ['diːteɪl] *n* détail *m* ♦ *vt* raconter en détail, énumérer; **in ~** en détail; **~ed** *adj* détaillé(e)

detain [dɪ'teɪn] *vt* retenir; (*in captivity*) détenir; (*in hospital*) hospitaliser

detect [dɪ'tekt] *vt* déceler, percevoir; (*MED, POLICE*) dépister; (*MIL, RADAR, TECH*) détecter; **~ion** [dɪ'tekʃən] *n* découverte *f*; **~ive** *n* agent *m* de la sûreté, policier *m*; **private ~ive** détective privé; **~ive story** *n* roman policier

detention [dɪ'tenʃən] *n* détention *f*; (*SCOL*) retenue *f*, consigne *f*

deter [dɪ'tɜː*] *vt* dissuader

detergent [dɪ'tɜːdʒənt] *n* détergent *m*, détersif *m*

deteriorate [dɪ'tɪərɪəreɪt] *vi* se détériorer, se dégrader

determine [dɪ'tɜːmɪn] *vt* déterminer; **to ~ to do** résoudre de faire, se déterminer à faire; **~d** *adj* (*person*) déterminé(e), décidé(e)

deterrent [dɪ'terənt] *n* effet *m* de dissuasion; **force** *f* de dissuasion

detonate ['detəneɪt] *vt* faire détoner *or* exploser

detour ['diːtuə*] *n* détour *m*; (*US: AUT: diversion*) déviation *f*

detract [dɪ'trækt] *vt*: **to ~ from** (*quality, pleasure*) diminuer; (*reputation*) porter atteinte à

detriment ['detrɪmənt] *n*: **to the ~ of** au détriment de, au préjudice de; **~al** [detrɪ'mentl] *adj*: **~al to** préjudiciable *or* nuisible à

devaluation [dɪvæljʊ'eɪʃən] *n* dévaluation *f*

devastate ['devəsteɪt] *vt* (*also fig*) dévaster; **devastating** *adj* dévastateur(trice); (*news*) accablant(e)

develop [dɪ'veləp] *vt* (*gen*) développer; (*disease*) commencer à souffrir de; (*resources*) mettre en valeur, exploiter ♦ *vi* se développer; (*situation, disease: evolve*) évoluer; (*facts, symptoms: appear*) se manifester, se produire; **~ing country** pays *m* en voie de développement; **the machine has ~ed a fault** un problème s'est manifesté dans cette machine; **~er** *n* (*also: property ~er*) promoteur *m*; **~ment** *n* développement *m*; (*of affair, case*) rebondissement *m*, fait(s) nouveau(x)

device [dɪ'vaɪs] *n* (*apparatus*) engin *m*, dispositif *m*

devil ['devl] *n* diable *m*; démon *m*

devious ['diːvɪəs] *adj* (*person*) sournois(e), dissimulé(e)

devise [dɪ'vaɪz] *vt* imaginer, concevoir

devoid [dɪ'vɔɪd] *adj*: **~ of** dépourvu(e) de, dénué(e) de

devolution [diːvəˈluːʃən] n (POL) décentralisation f

devote [dɪˈvəʊt] vt: **to ~ sth to** consacrer qch à; **~d** adj dévoué(e); **to be ~d to** (book etc) être consacré(e) à; (person) être très attaché(e) à; **~e** [dɛvəʊˈtiː] n (REL) adepte m/f, (MUS, SPORT) fervent(e)

devotion [dɪˈvəʊʃən] n dévouement m, attachement m; (REL) dévotion f, piété f

devour [dɪˈvaʊə*] vt dévorer

devout [dɪˈvaʊt] adj pieux(euse), dévot(e)

dew [djuː] n rosée f

diabetes [daɪəˈbiːtiːz] n diabète m; **diabetic** [daɪəˈbɛtɪk] adj diabétique ♦ n diabétique m/f

diabolical [daɪəˈbɒlɪkl] (inf) adj (weather) atroce; (behaviour) infernal(e)

diagnosis [daɪəgˈnəʊsɪs, pl daɪəgˈnəʊsiːz] (pl **diagnoses**) n diagnostic m

diagonal [daɪˈægənl] adj diagonal(e) ♦ n diagonale f

diagram [ˈdaɪəgræm] n diagramme m, schéma m

dial [ˈdaɪəl] n cadran m ♦ vt (number) faire, composer; **~ code** (US) n = **dialling code**

dialect [ˈdaɪəlɛkt] n dialecte m

dialling code [ˈdaɪəlɪŋ-] (BRIT) n indicatif m (téléphonique)

dialling tone [ˈdaɪəlɪŋ-] (BRIT) n tonalité f

dialogue [ˈdaɪəlɒg] n dialogue m

dial tone (US) n = **dialling tone**

diameter [daɪˈæmɪtə*] n diamètre m

diamond [ˈdaɪəmənd] n diamant m; (shape) losange m; **~s** npl (CARDS) carreau m

diaper [ˈdaɪəpə*] (US) n couche f

diaphragm [ˈdaɪəfræm] n diaphragme m

diarrhoea [daɪəˈriːə] (US **diarrhea**) n diarrhée f

diary [ˈdaɪərɪ] n (daily account) journal m; (book) agenda m

dice [daɪs] n inv dé m ♦ vt (CULIN) couper en dés or en cubes

dictate [vb dɪkˈteɪt] vt dicter

dictation [dɪkˈteɪʃən] n dictée f

dictator [dɪkˈteɪtə*] n dictateur m; **~ship** n dictature f

dictionary [ˈdɪkʃənrɪ] n dictionnaire m

did [dɪd] pt of **do**; **~n't** = **did not**

die [daɪ] vi mourir; **to be dying for sth** avoir une envie folle de qch; **to be dying to do sth** mourir d'envie de faire qch; **~ away** vi s'éteindre; **~ down** vi se calmer, s'apaiser; **~ out** vi disparaître

die-hard [ˈdaɪhɑːd] n réactionnaire m/f, jusqu'au-boutiste m/f

diesel [ˈdiːzəl] n (vehicle) diesel m; (also: ~ oil) carburant m diesel, gas-oil m; **~ engine** n moteur m diesel

diet [ˈdaɪət] n alimentation f; (restricted food) régime m ♦ vi (also: be on a ~) suivre un régime

differ [ˈdɪfə*] vi (be different): **to ~ (from)** être différent (de); différer (de); (disagree): **to ~ (from sb over sth)** ne pas être d'accord (avec qn au sujet de qch); **~ence** n différence f; (quarrel) différend m, désaccord m; **~ent** adj différent(e); **~entiate** [dɪfəˈrɛnʃɪeɪt] vi: **to ~entiate (between)** faire une différence (entre)

difficult [ˈdɪfɪkəlt] adj difficile; **~y** n difficulté f

diffident [ˈdɪfɪdənt] adj qui manque de confiance or d'assurance

dig [dɪg] (pt, pp **dug**) vt (hole) creuser; (garden) bêcher ♦ n (prod) coup m de coude; (fig) coup de griffe or de patte; (archeological) fouilles fpl; **~ in** vi (MIL: also: o.s. in) se retrancher; **~ into** vt fus (savings) puiser dans; **to ~ one's nails into sth** enfoncer ses ongles dans qch; **~ up** vt déterrer

digest [vb daɪˈdʒɛst, n ˈdaɪdʒɛst] vt digérer ♦ n sommaire m, résumé m; **~ion** n digestion f

digit [ˈdɪdʒɪt] n (number) chiffre m; (finger) doigt m; **~al** adj digital(e), à affichage numérique or digital; **~al computer** calculateur m numérique

dignified [ˈdɪgnɪfaɪd] adj digne

dignity [ˈdɪgnɪtɪ] n dignité f

digress [daɪˈgrɛs] vi: **to ~ from** s'écarter de, s'éloigner de

digs [dɪgz] (BRIT: inf) npl piaule f, chambre meublée

dilapidated [dɪˈlæpɪdeɪtɪd] adj délabré(e)

dilemma [daɪˈlɛmə] n dilemme m

diligent [ˈdɪlɪdʒənt] adj appliqué(e), assidu(e)

dilute [daɪˈluːt] vt diluer

dim [dɪm] adj (light) faible; (memory, outline) vague, indécis(e); (figure) vague, indistinct(e); (room) sombre; (stupid) borné(e), obtus(e) ♦ vt (light) réduire, baisser; (US: AUT) mettre en code

dime [daɪm] (US) n = **10 cents**

dimension [dɪˈmɛnʃən] n dimension f

diminish [dɪˈmɪnɪʃ] vt, vi diminuer

diminutive [dɪˈmɪnjʊtɪv] adj minuscule, tout(e) petit(e)

dimmers [ˈdɪməz] (US) npl (AUT) phares mpl code inv; feux mpl de position

dimple [ˈdɪmpl] n fossette f

din [dɪn] n vacarme m

dine [daɪn] vi dîner; **~r** n (person) dîneur(euse); (US: restaurant) petit restaurant

dinghy [ˈdɪŋgɪ] n youyou m; (also: rubber ~) canot m pneumatique; (: sailing ~) voilier m, dériveur m

dingy [ˈdɪndʒɪ] adj miteux(euse), minable

dining car [ˈdaɪnɪŋ-] (BRIT) n wagon-restaurant m

dining room [ˈdaɪnɪŋ-] n salle f à manger

dinner [ˈdɪnə*] n dîner m; (lunch) déjeuner

m; (*public*) banquet *m*; ~ **jacket** *n* smoking *m*; ~ **party** *n* dîner *m*; ~ **time** *n* heure *f* du dîner; (*midday*) heure du déjeuner

dint [dɪnt] *n*: **by ~ of (doing)** à force de (faire)

dip [dɪp] *n* déclivité *f*; (*in sea*) baignade *f*, bain *m*; (*CULIN*) ≈ sauce *f* ♦ *vt* tremper, plonger; (*BRIT: AUT: lights*) mettre en code, baisser ♦ *vi* plonger

diploma [dɪ'pləʊmə] *n* diplôme *m*

diplomacy [dɪ'pləʊməsɪ] *n* diplomatie *f*

diplomat ['dɪpləmæt] *n* diplomate *m*; ~**ic** [dɪplə'mætɪk] *adj* diplomatique

dipstick ['dɪpstɪk] *n* (*AUT*) jauge *f* de niveau d'huile

dipswitch ['dɪpswɪtʃ] (*BRIT*) *n* (*AUT*) interrupteur *m* de lumière réduite

dire [daɪə*] *adj* terrible, extrême, affreux(euse)

direct [daɪ'rekt] *adj* direct(e) ♦ *vt* diriger, orienter (*letter, remark*) adresser; (*film, programme*) réaliser; (*play*) mettre en scène; (*order*): **to ~ sb to do sth** ordonner à qn de faire qch ♦ *adv* directement; **can you ~ me to ...?** pouvez-vous m'indiquer le chemin de ...?; ~ **debit** (*BRIT*) *n* prélèvement *m* automatique

direction [dɪ'rekʃən] *n* direction *f*; ~**s** *npl* (*advice*) indications *fpl*; **sense of ~** sens *m* de l'orientation; ~**s for use** mode *m* d'emploi

directly [dɪ'rektlɪ] *adv* (*in a straight line*) directement, tout droit; (*at once*) tout de suite, immédiatement

director [dɪ'rektə*] *n* directeur *m*; (*THEATRE*) metteur *m* en scène; (*CINEMA, TV*) réalisateur(trice)

directory [dɪ'rektərɪ] *n* annuaire *m*; (*COMPUT*) répertoire *m*

dirt [dɜːt] *n* saleté *f*; crasse *f*; (*earth*) terre *f*, boue *f*; ~**-cheap** *adj* très bon marché *inv*; ~**y** *adj* sale ♦ *vt* salir; ~**y trick** coup tordu

disability [dɪsə'bɪlɪtɪ] *n* invalidité *f*, infirmité *f*

disabled [dɪs'eɪbld] *adj* infirme, invalide ♦ *npl*: **the ~** les handicapés

disadvantage [dɪsəd'vɑːntɪdʒ] *n* désavantage *m*, inconvénient *m*

disagree [dɪsə'griː] *vi* (*be different*) ne pas concorder; (*be against, think otherwise*): **to ~ (with)** ne pas être d'accord (avec); ~**able** *adj* désagréable; ~**ment** *n* désaccord *m*, différend *m*

disallow ['dɪsə'laʊ] *vt* rejeter

disappear [dɪsə'pɪə*] *vi* disparaître; ~**ance** *n* disparition *f*

disappoint [dɪsə'pɔɪnt] *vt* décevoir; ~**ed** *adj* déçu(e); ~**ing** *adj* décevant(e); ~**ment** *n* déception *f*

disapproval [dɪsə'pruːvəl] *n* désapprobation *f*

disapprove [dɪsə'pruːv] *vi*: **to ~ (of)** désapprouver

disarmament [dɪs'ɑːməmənt] *n* désarmement *m*

disarray ['dɪsə'reɪ] *n*: **in ~** (*army*) en déroute; (*organization*) en désarroi; (*hair, clothes*) en désordre

disaster [dɪ'zɑːstə*] *n* catastrophe *f*, désastre *m*

disband [dɪs'bænd] *vt* démobiliser; disperser ♦ *vi* se séparer; se disperser

disbelief ['dɪsbə'liːf] *n* incrédulité *f*

disc [dɪsk] *n* disque *m*; (*COMPUT*) = **disk**

discard ['dɪskɑːd] *vt* (*old things*) se débarrasser de; (*fig*) écarter, renoncer à

discern [dɪ'sɜːn] *vt* discerner, distinguer; ~**ing** *adj* perspicace

discharge [*vb* dɪs'tʃɑːdʒ, *n* 'dɪstʃɑːdʒ] *vt* décharger; (*duties*) s'acquitter de; (*patient*) renvoyer (chez lui); (*employee*) congédier, licencier; (*soldier*) rendre à la vie civile, réformer; (*defendant*) relaxer, élargir ♦ *n* décharge *f*; (*dismissal*) renvoi *m*; licenciement *m*; élargissement *m*; (*MED*) écoulement *m*

discipline ['dɪsɪplɪn] *n* discipline *f*

disc jockey *n* disc-jockey *m*

disclaim [dɪs'kleɪm] *vt* nier

disclose [dɪs'kləʊz] *vt* révéler, divulguer; **disclosure** [dɪs'kləʊʒə*] *n* révélation *f*

disco ['dɪskəʊ] *n abbr* = discothèque

discomfort [dɪs'kʌmfət] *n* malaise *m*, gêne *f*; (*lack of comfort*) manque *m* de confort

disconcert [dɪskən'sɜːt] *vt* déconcerter

disconnect ['dɪskə'nekt] *vt* (*ELEC, RADIO, pipe*) débrancher; (*TEL, water*) couper

discontent [dɪskən'tent] *n* mécontentement *m*; ~**ed** *adj* mécontent(e)

discontinue ['dɪskən'tɪnjuː] *vt* cesser, interrompre; "~**d**" (*COMM*) "fin de série"

discord ['dɪskɔːd] *n* discorde *f*, dissension *f*; (*MUS*) dissonance *f*

discotheque ['dɪskəʊtek] *n* discothèque *f*

discount [*n* 'dɪskaʊnt, *vb* dɪs'kaʊnt] *n* remise *f*, rabais *m* ♦ *vt* (*sum*) faire une remise de; (*fig*) ne pas tenir compte de

discourage [dɪs'kʌrɪdʒ] *vt* décourager

discover [dɪs'kʌvə*] *vt* découvrir; ~**y** *n* découverte *f*

discredit [dɪs'kredɪt] *vt* (*idea*) mettre en doute; (*person*) discréditer

discreet [dɪs'kriːt] *adj* discret(ète)

discrepancy [dɪs'krepənsɪ] *n* divergence *f*, contradiction *f*

discretion [dɪ'skreʃən] *n* discrétion *f*; **use your own ~** à vous de juger

discriminate [dɪs'krɪmɪneɪt] *vi*: **to ~ between** établir une distinction entre, faire la différence entre; **to ~ against** pratiquer une discrimination contre; **discriminating** *adj* qui a du discernement; **discrimination** [dɪskrɪmɪ'neɪʃən] *n* discrimination *f*; (*judgment*) discernement *m*

discuss [dɪsˈkʌs] vt discuter de; (*debate*) discuter; **~ion** [dɪsˈkʌʃən] n discussion f

disdain [dɪsˈdeɪn] n dédain m

disease [dɪˈziːz] n maladie f

disembark [dɪsɪmˈbɑːk] vt, vi débarquer

disengage [dɪsɪnˈɡeɪdʒ] vt: **to ~ the clutch** (*AUT*) débrayer

disentangle [dɪsɪnˈtæŋɡl] vt (*wool, wire*) démêler, débrouiller; (*from wreckage*) dégager

disfigure [dɪsˈfɪɡəʳ] vt défigurer

disgrace [dɪsˈɡreɪs] n honte f; (*disfavour*) disgrâce f ♦ vt déshonorer, couvrir de honte; **~ful** adj scandaleux(euse), honteux(euse)

disgruntled [dɪsˈɡrʌntld] adj mécontent(e)

disguise [dɪsˈɡaɪz] n déguisement m ♦ vt déguiser; **in ~** déguisé(e)

disgust [dɪsˈɡʌst] n dégoût m, aversion f ♦ vt dégoûter, écœurer; **~ing** adj dégoûtant(e); révoltant(e)

dish [dɪʃ] n plat m; **to do** or **wash the ~es** faire la vaisselle; **~ out** vt servir, distribuer; **~ up** vt servir; **~cloth** n (*for washing*) lavette f

dishearten [dɪsˈhɑːtn] vt décourager

dishevelled [dɪˈʃevəld] (*US* **disheveled**) adj ébouriffé(e); décoiffé(e); débraillé(e)

dishonest [dɪsˈɒnɪst] adj malhonnête

dishonour [dɪsˈɒnəʳ] (*US* **dishonor**) n déshonneur m; **~able** adj (*behaviour*) déshonorant(e); (*person*) peu honorable

dishtowel [ˈdɪʃtaʊəl] (*US*) n torchon m

dishwasher [ˈdɪʃwɒʃəʳ] n lave-vaisselle m

disillusion [dɪsɪˈluːʒən] vt désabuser, désillusionner

disincentive [dɪsɪnˈsentɪv] n: **to be a ~** être démotivant(e)

disinfect [dɪsɪnˈfekt] vt désinfecter; **~ant** n désinfectant m

disintegrate [dɪsˈɪntɪɡreɪt] vi se désintégrer

disinterested [dɪsˈɪntrɪstɪd] adj désintéressé(e)

disjointed [dɪsˈdʒɔɪntɪd] adj décousu(e), incohérent(e)

disk [dɪsk] n (*COMPUT*) disque m; (: *floppy ~*) disquette f; **single-/double-sided ~** disquette simple/double face; **~ drive** n lecteur m de disquettes; **~ette** [dɪsˈket] n disquette f, disque m souple

dislike [dɪsˈlaɪk] n aversion f, antipathie f ♦ vt ne pas aimer

dislocate [ˈdɪsləʊkeɪt] vt disloquer; déboîter

dislodge [dɪsˈlɒdʒ] vt déplacer, faire bouger

disloyal [ˈdɪsˈlɔɪəl] adj déloyal(e)

dismal [ˈdɪzməl] adj lugubre, maussade

dismantle [dɪsˈmæntl] vt démonter

dismay [dɪsˈmeɪ] n consternation f

dismiss [dɪsˈmɪs] vt congédier, renvoyer; (*soldiers*) faire rompre les rangs à; (*idea*) écarter; (*LAW*): **to ~ a case** rendre une fin de non-recevoir; **~al** n renvoi m

dismount [dɪsˈmaʊnt] vi mettre pied à terre, descendre

disobedient [dɪsəˈbiːdɪənt] adj désobéissant(e)

disobey [ˈdɪsəˈbeɪ] vt désobéir à

disorder [dɪsˈɔːdəʳ] n désordre m; (*rioting*) désordres mpl; (*MED*) troubles mpl; **~ly** [dɪsˈɔːdəlɪ] adj en désordre; désordonné(e)

disorientated [dɪsˈɔːrɪənteɪtɪd] adj désorienté(e)

disown [dɪsˈəʊn] vt renier

disparaging [dɪsˈpærɪdʒɪŋ] adj désobligeant(e)

dispassionate [dɪsˈpæʃnɪt] adj calme, froid(e); impartial(e), objectif(ive)

dispatch [dɪsˈpætʃ] vt expédier, envoyer ♦ n envoi m, expédition f; (*MIL, PRESS*) dépêche f

dispel [dɪsˈpel] vt dissiper, chasser

dispense [dɪsˈpens] vt distribuer, administrer; **~ with** vt fus se passer de; **~r** n (*machine*) distributeur m; **dispensing chemist** (*BRIT*) n pharmacie f

disperse [dɪsˈpɜːs] vt disperser ♦ vi se disperser

dispirited [dɪsˈpɪrɪtɪd] adj découragé(e), déprimé(e)

displace [dɪsˈpleɪs] vt déplacer

display [dɪsˈpleɪ] n étalage m; déploiement m; affichage m; (*screen*) écran m, visuel m; (*of feeling*) manifestation f ♦ vt montrer; (*goods*) mettre à l'étalage, exposer; (*results, departure times*) afficher; (*pej*) faire étalage de

displease [dɪsˈpliːz] vt mécontenter, contrarier; **~d** adj: **~d with** mécontent(e) de; **displeasure** [dɪsˈpleʒəʳ] n mécontentement m

disposable [dɪsˈpəʊzəbl] adj (*pack etc*) jetable, à jeter; (*income*) disponible; **~ nappy** (*BRIT*) n couche f à jeter, couche-culotte f

disposal [dɪsˈpəʊzəl] n (*of goods for sale*) vente f; (*of property*) disposition f, cession f; (*of rubbish*) enlèvement m; destruction f; **at one's ~** à sa disposition

dispose [dɪsˈpəʊz] vt disposer; **~ of** vt fus (*unwanted goods etc*) se débarrasser de, se défaire de; (*problem*) expédier; **~d** [dɪsˈpəʊzd] adj: **to be ~d to do sth** être disposé(e) à faire qch; **disposition** [dɪspəˈzɪʃən] n disposition f; (*temperament*) naturel m

disprove [dɪsˈpruːv] vt réfuter

dispute [dɪsˈpjuːt] n discussion f; (*also: industrial ~*) conflit m ♦ vt contester; (*matter*) discuter; (*victory*) disputer

disqualify [dɪsˈkwɒlɪfaɪ] vt (*SPORT*) disqualifier; **to ~ sb for sth/from doing** rendre qn inapte à qch/à faire

disquiet [dɪsˈkwaɪət] n inquiétude f, trouble m

disregard [dɪsrɪˈɡɑːd] vt ne pas tenir compte de

disrepair ['dɪsrɪ'pɛə*] *n*: **to fall into ~** (*building*) tomber en ruine

disreputable [dɪs'rɛpjʊtəbl] *adj* (*person*) de mauvaise réputation; (*behaviour*) déshonorant(e)

disrespectful [dɪsrɪ'spɛktful] *adj* irrespectueux(euse)

disrupt [dɪs'rʌpt] *vt* (*plans*) déranger; (*conversation*) interrompre

dissatisfied [dɪs'sætɪsfaɪd] *adj*: ~ **(with)** insatisfait(e) (de)

dissect [dɪ'sɛkt] *vt* disséquer

dissent [dɪ'sɛnt] *n* dissentiment *m*, différence *f* d'opinion

dissertation [dɪsə'teɪʃən] *n* mémoire *m*

disservice [dɪs'sɜːvɪs] *n*: **to do sb a ~** rendre un mauvais service à qn

dissimilar ['dɪ'sɪmɪlə*] *adj*: ~ **(to)** dissemblable (à), différent(e) (de)

dissipate ['dɪsɪpeɪt] *vt* dissiper; (*money, efforts*) disperser

dissolute ['dɪsəluːt] *adj* débauché(e), dissolu(e)

dissolve [dɪ'zɒlv] *vt* dissoudre ♦ *vi* se dissoudre, fondre; **to ~ in(to) tears** fondre en larmes

distance ['dɪstəns] *n* distance *f*; **in the ~** au loin

distant ['dɪstənt] *adj* lointain(e), éloigné(e); (*manner*) distant(e), froid(e)

distaste [dɪs'teɪst] *n* dégoût *m*; ~**ful** *adj* déplaisant(e), désagréable

distended [dɪs'tɛndɪd] *adj* (*stomach*) dilaté(e)

distil, (*US*) **distill** [dɪs'tɪl] *vt* distiller; ~**lery** *n* distillerie *f*

distinct [dɪs'tɪŋkt] *adj* distinct(e); (*clear*) marqué(e); **as ~ from** par opposition à; ~**ion** [dɪs'tɪŋkʃən] *n* distinction *f*; (*in exam*) mention *f* très bien; ~**ive** *adj* distinctif(ive)

distinguish [dɪs'tɪŋgwɪʃ] *vt* distinguer; ~**ed** *adj* (*eminent*) distingué(e); ~**ing** *adj* (*feature*) distinctif(ive), caractéristique

distort [dɪs'tɔːt] *vt* déformer

distract [dɪs'trækt] *vt* distraire, déranger; ~**ed** *adj* distrait(e); (*anxious*) éperdu(e), égaré(e); ~**ion** [dɪs'trækʃən] *n* distraction *f*, égarement *m*

distraught [dɪs'trɔːt] *adj* éperdu(e)

distress [dɪs'trɛs] *n* détresse *f* ♦ *vt* affliger; ~**ing** *adj* douloureux(euse), pénible

distribute [dɪs'trɪbjuːt] *vt* distribuer; **distribution** [dɪstrɪ'bjuːʃən] *n* distribution *f*; **distributor** [dɪs'trɪbjʊtə*] *n* distributeur *m*

district ['dɪstrɪkt] *n* (*of country*) région *f*; (*of town*) quartier *m*; (*ADMIN*) district *m*; ~ **attorney** (*US*) *n* ≈ procureur *m* de la République; ~ **nurse** (*BRIT*) *n* infirmière visiteuse

distrust [dɪs'trʌst] *n* méfiance *f* ♦ *vt* se méfier de

disturb [dɪs'tɜːb] *vt* troubler; (*inconvenience*) déranger; ~**ance** *n* dérangement *m*; (*violent event, political event etc*) troubles *mpl*; ~**ed** *adj* (*worried, upset*) agité(e), troublé(e); **to be emotionally ~ed** avoir des problèmes affectifs; ~**ing** *adj* troublant(e), inquiétant(e)

disuse ['dɪs'juːs] *n*: **to fall into ~** tomber en désuétude

disused ['dɪs'juːzd] *adj* désaffecté(e)

ditch [dɪtʃ] *n* fossé *m*; (*irrigation*) rigole *f* ♦ *vt* (*inf*) abandonner; (*person*) plaquer

dither ['dɪðə*] *vi* hésiter

ditto ['dɪtəʊ] *adv* idem

dive [daɪv] *n* plongeon *m*; (*of submarine*) plongée *f* ♦ *vi* plonger; **to ~ into** (*bag, drawer etc*) plonger la main dans; (*shop, car etc*) se précipiter dans; ~**r** *n* plongeur *m*

diversion [daɪ'vɜːʃən] *n* (*BRIT: AUT*) déviation *f*; (*distraction, MIL*) diversion *f*

divert [daɪ'vɜːt] *vt* (*funds, BRIT: traffic*) dévier; (*river, attention*) détourner

divide [dɪ'vaɪd] *vt* diviser; (*separate*) séparer ♦ *vi* se diviser; ~**d highway** (*US*) *n* route *f* à quatre voies

dividend ['dɪvɪdɛnd] *n* dividende *m*

divine [dɪ'vaɪn] *adj* divin(e)

diving ['daɪvɪŋ] *n* plongée (sous-marine); ~ **board** *n* plongeoir *m*

divinity [dɪ'vɪnɪtɪ] *n* divinité *f*; (*SCOL*) théologie *f*

division [dɪ'vɪʒən] *n* division *f*

divorce [dɪ'vɔːs] *n* divorce *m* ♦ *vt* divorcer d'avec; (*dissociate*) séparer; ~**d** *adj* divorcé(e); ~**e** [dɪvɔː'siː] *n* divorcé(e)

D.I.Y. (*BRIT*) *n abbr* = **do-it-yourself**

dizzy ['dɪzɪ] *adj*: **to make sb ~** donner le vertige à qn; **to feel ~** avoir la tête qui tourne

DJ *n abbr* = **disc jockey**

KEYWORD

do [duː] (*pt* **did,** *pp* **done**) *n* (*inf: party etc*) soirée *f*, fête *f*

♦ *vb* **1** (*in negative constructions*) non traduit; **I ~n't understand** je ne comprends pas

2 (*to form questions*) non traduit; **didn't you know?** vous ne le saviez pas?; **why didn't you come?** pourquoi n'êtes-vous pas venu?

3 (*for emphasis, in polite expressions*): **she does seem rather late** je trouve qu'elle est bien en retard; ~ **sit down/help yourself** asseyez-vous/servez-vous je vous en prie

4 (*used to avoid repeating vb*): **she swims better than I ~** elle nage mieux que moi; ~ **you agree? - yes, I ~/no, I ~n't** vous êtes d'accord? - oui/non; **she lives in Glasgow - so ~ I** elle habite Glasgow - moi aussi; **who broke it? - I did** qui l'a cassé? - c'est moi

5 (*in question tags*): **he laughed, didn't he?** il a ri, n'est-ce pas?; **I ~n't know him, ~ I?** je ne le connais pas, je crois
♦ *vt* (*gen: carry out, perform etc*) faire; **what are you ~ing tonight?** qu'est-ce que vous faites ce soir?; **to ~ the cooking/washing-up** faire la cuisine/la vaisselle; **to ~ one's teeth/hair/nails** se brosser les dents/se coiffer/se faire les ongles; **the car was ~ing 100** la voiture faisait du 100 (à l'heure)
♦ *vi* **1** (*act, behave*) faire; **~ as I ~** faites comme moi
2 (*get on, fare*) marcher; **the firm is ~ing well** l'entreprise marche bien; **how ~ you ~?** comment allez-vous?; (*on being introduced*) enchanté(e)!
3 (*suit*) aller; **will it ~?** est-ce que ça ira?
4 (*be sufficient*) suffire, aller; **will £10 ~?** est-ce que 10 livres suffiront?; **that'll ~** ça suffit, ça ira; **that'll ~!** (*in annoyance*) ça va *ou* suffit comme ça!; **to make ~ (with)** se contenter (de)
do away with *vt fus* supprimer
do up *vt* (*laces, dress*) attacher; (*buttons*) boutonner; (*zip*) fermer; (*renovate: room*) refaire; (*: house*) remettre à neuf
do with *vt fus* (*need*): **I could do with a drink/some help** quelque chose à boire/un peu d'aide ne serait pas de refus; (*be connected*): **that has nothing to ~ with you** cela ne vous concerne pas; **I won't have anything to ~ with it** je ne veux pas m'en mêler
do without *vi* s'en passer ♦ *vt fus* se passer de

dock [dɒk] *n* dock *m*; (*LAW*) banc *m* des accusés ♦ *vi* se mettre à quai; (*SPACE*) s'arrimer; **~er** *n* docker *m*; **~yard** *n* chantier *m* de construction navale
doctor ['dɒktə*] *n* médecin *m*, docteur *m*; (*PhD etc*) docteur ♦ *vt* (*drink*) frelater; **D~ of Philosophy** (*degree*) doctorat *m*; (*person*) Docteur *m* en Droit *ou* Lettres *etc*, titulaire *m/f* d'un doctorat
document ['dɒkjʊmənt] *n* document *m*; **~ary** [dɒkjʊ'mentərɪ] *adj* documentaire ♦ *n* documentaire *m*
dodge [dɒdʒ] *n* truc *m*; combine *f* ♦ *vt* esquiver, éviter
dodgems ['dɒdʒəmz] (*BRIT*) *npl* autos tamponneuses
doe [dəʊ] *n* (*deer*) biche *f*; (*rabbit*) lapine *f*
does [dʌz] *vb see* do; **~n't = does not**
dog [dɒg] *n* chien(ne) ♦ *vt* suivre de près, poursuivre, harceler; **~ collar** *n* collier *m* de chien; (*fig*) faux-col *m* d'ecclésiastique; **~-eared** *adj* corné(e)
dogged ['dɒgɪd] *adj* obstiné(e), opiniâtre
dogsbody ['dɒgzbɒdɪ] *n* bonne *f* à tout faire, tâcheron *m*

doings ['duːɪŋz] *npl* activités *fpl*
do-it-yourself ['duːɪtjə'self] *n* bricolage *m*
doldrums ['dɒldrəmz] *npl*: **to be in the ~** avoir le cafard; (*business*) être dans le marasme
dole [dəʊl] *n* (*BRIT: payment*) allocation *f* de chômage; **on the ~** au chômage; **~ out** *vt* donner au compte-goutte
doleful ['dəʊlfʊl] *adj* plaintif(ive), lugubre
doll [dɒl] *n* poupée *f*
dollar ['dɒlə*] *n* dollar *m*
dolled up [dɒld-] (*inf*) *adj*: **(all) ~** sur son trente et un
dolphin ['dɒlfɪn] *n* dauphin *m*
dome [dəʊm] *n* dôme *m*
domestic [də'mestɪk] *adj* (*task, appliances*) ménager(ère); (*of country: trade, situation etc*) intérieur(e); (*animal*) domestique; **~ated** *adj* (*animal*) domestiqué(e); (*husband*) pantouflard(e)
dominate ['dɒmɪneɪt] *vt* dominer
domineering [dɒmɪ'nɪərɪŋ] *adj* dominateur(trice), autoritaire
dominion [də'mɪnɪən] *n* (*territory*) territoire *m*; **to have ~ over** contrôler
domino ['dɒmɪnəʊ] (*pl* **~es**) *n* domino *m*; **~es** *n* (*game*) dominos *mpl*
don [dɒn] (*BRIT*) *n* professeur *m* d'université
donate [də'neɪt] *vt* faire don de, donner
done [dʌn] *pp of* do
donkey ['dɒŋkɪ] *n* âne *m*
donor ['dəʊnə*] *n* (*of blood etc*) donneur(euse); (*to charity*) donateur(trice)
don't [dəʊnt] *vb* = do not
donut (*US*) *n* = doughnut
doodle ['duːdl] *vi* griffonner, gribouiller
doom [duːm] *n* destin *m* ♦ *vt*: **to be ~ed (to failure)** être voué(e) à l'échec; **~sday** *n* le Jugement dernier
door [dɔː*] *n* porte *f*; (*RAIL, car*) portière *f*; **~bell** *n* sonnette *f*; **~handle** *n* poignée *f* de la porte; (*car*) poignée de portière; **~man** (*irreg*) *n* (*in hotel*) portier *m*; **~mat** *n* paillasson *m*; **~step** *n* pas *m* de (la) porte, seuil *m*; **~way** *n* (*embrasure f de la*) porte *f*
dope [dəʊp] *n* (*inf: drug*) drogue *f*; (*: person*) andouille *f* ♦ *vt* (*horse etc*) doper
dopey ['dəʊpɪ] (*inf*) *adj* à moitié endormi(e)
dormant ['dɔːmənt] *adj* assoupi(e), en veilleuse
dormitory ['dɔːmɪtrɪ] *n* dortoir *m*; (*US: building*) résidence *f* universitaire
dormouse ['dɔːmaʊs, *pl* 'dɔːmaɪs] (*pl* **dormice**) *n* loir *m*
dose [dəʊs] *n* dose *f*
doss house ['dɒs-] (*BRIT*) *n* asile *m* de nuit
dot [dɒt] *n* point *m*; (*on material*) pois *m* ♦ *vt*: **~ted with** parsemé(e) de; **on the ~** à l'heure tapante *or* pile
dote [dəʊt]: **to ~ on** *vt fus* être fou(folle)

de

dot-matrix printer [dɒt'meɪtrɪks-] n imprimante matricielle

dotted line n pointillé(s) m(pl)

double ['dʌbl] adj double ♦ adv (twice): **to cost** ~ **(sth)** coûter le double (de qch) or deux fois plus (que qch) ♦ n double m ♦ vt doubler; (fold) plier en deux ♦ vi doubler; ~**s** n (TENNIS) double m; **on** or (BRIT) **at the** ~ au pas de course; ~ **bass** (BRIT) n contrebasse f; ~ **bed** n grand lit; ~ **bend** (BRIT) n virage m en S; ~-**breasted** adj croisé(e); ~**cross** vt doubler, trahir; ~**decker** n autobus m à impériale; ~ **glazing** (BRIT) n double vitrage m; ~ **room** n chambre f pour deux personnes; **doubly** ['dʌblɪ] adv doublement, deux fois plus

doubt [daut] n doute m ♦ vt douter de; **to** ~ **that** douter que; ~**ful** adj douteux(euse); (person) incertain(e); ~**less** adv sans doute, sûrement

dough [dəu] n pâte f; ~**nut** (US **donut**) n beignet m

douse [dauz] vt (drench) tremper, inonder; (extinguish) éteindre

dove [dʌv] n colombe f

Dover ['dəuvə*] n Douvres

dovetail ['dʌvteɪl] vi (fig) concorder

dowdy ['daudɪ] adj démodé(e); mal fagoté(e) (inf)

down [daun] n (soft feathers) duvet m ♦ adv en bas, vers le bas; (on the ground) par terre ♦ prep en bas de; (along) le long de ♦ vt (inf: drink, food) s'envoyer; ~ **with X!** à bas X!; ~-**and-out** n clochard(e); ~-**at-heel** adj éculé(e); (fig) miteux(euse); ~**cast** adj démoralisé(e); ~**fall** n chute f, ruine f; ~**hearted** adj découragé(e); ~**hill** adv: **to go** ~**hill** descendre; (fig) péricliter; ~ **payment** n acompte m; ~**pour** n pluie torrentielle, déluge m; ~**right** adj (lie etc) effronté(e); (refusal) catégorique

Down's syndrome [daunz-] n (MED) trisomie f

down: ~**stairs** adv au rez-de-chaussée; à l'étage inférieur; ~**stream** adv en aval; ~-**to-earth** adj terre à terre inv; ~**town** adv en ville; ~ **under** adv en Australie (or Nouvelle-Zélande); ~**ward** adj, adv vers le bas; ~**wards** adv vers le bas

dowry ['dauri] n dot f

doz. abbr = **dozen**

doze [dəuz] vi sommeiller; ~ **off** vi s'assoupir

dozen ['dʌzn] n douzaine f; **a** ~ **books** une douzaine de livres; ~**s of** des centaines de

Dr. abbr = **doctor; drive**

drab [dræb] adj terne, morne

draft [drɑːft] n ébauche f; (of letter, essay etc) brouillon m; (COMM) traite f; (US: call-up) conscription f ♦ vt faire le brouillon

de or un projet de; (MIL: send) détacher; see also **draught**

draftsman ['drɑːftsmən] (irreg: US) n = **draughtsman**

drag [dræg] vt traîner; (river) draguer ♦ vi traîner ♦ n (inf) casse-pieds m/f; (women's clothing): **in** ~ (en) travesti; ~ **on** vi s'éterniser

dragon ['drægən] n dragon m

dragonfly ['drægənflaɪ] n libellule f

drain [dreɪn] n égout m, canalisation f; (on resources) saignée f ♦ vt (land, marshes etc) drainer, assécher; (vegetables) égoutter; (glass) vider ♦ vi (water) s'écouler; ~**age** n drainage m; système m d'égouts or de canalisations; ~**ing board** (US ~**board**) n égouttoir m; ~**pipe** n tuyau m d'écoulement

drama ['drɑːmə] n (art) théâtre m, art m dramatique; (play) pièce f (de théâtre); (event) drame m; ~**tic** [drə'mætɪk] adj dramatique; spectaculaire; ~**tist** ['dræmətɪst] n auteur m dramatique; ~**tize** vt (events) dramatiser; (adapt: for TV/cinema) adapter pour la télévision/pour l'écran

drank [dræŋk] pt of **drink**

drape [dreɪp] vt draper; ~**s** (US) npl rideaux mpl

drastic ['dræstɪk] adj sévère; énergique; (change) radical(e)

draught [drɑːft] (US **draft**) n courant m d'air; (NAUT) tirant m d'eau; **on** ~ (beer) à la pression; ~**board** (BRIT) n damier m; ~**s** (BRIT) n (jeu m de) dames fpl

draughtsman ['drɑːftsmən] (irreg) n dessinateur(trice) (industriel(le))

draw [drɔː] (pt drew, pp drawn) vt tirer; (tooth) arracher, extraire; (attract) attirer; (picture) dessiner; (line, circle) tracer; (money) retirer; (wages) toucher ♦ vi (SPORT) faire match nul ♦ n match nul; (lottery) tirage m au sort; loterie f; **to** ~ **near** s'approcher; approcher; ~ **out** vi (lengthen) s'allonger ♦ vt (money) retirer; ~ **up** vi (stop) s'arrêter ♦ vt (chair) approcher; (document) établir, dresser; ~**back** n inconvénient m, désavantage m; ~**bridge** n pont-levis m; ~**er** [drɔː*] n tiroir m

drawing ['drɔːɪŋ] n dessin m; ~ **board** n planche f à dessin; ~ **pin** (BRIT) n punaise f; ~ **room** n salon m

drawl [drɔːl] n accent traînant

drawn [drɔːn] pp of **draw**

dread [dred] n terreur f, effroi m ♦ vt redouter, appréhender; ~**ful** adj affreux(euse)

dream [driːm] (pt, pp dreamed or dreamt) n rêve m ♦ vt, vi rêver; ~**y** adj rêveur(euse); (music) langoureux(euse)

dreary ['drɪərɪ] adj morne; monotone

dredge [dredʒ] vt draguer

dregs [dregz] npl lie f

drench [drentʃ] vt tremper

dress [dres] n robe f; (no pl: clothing) habillement m, tenue f ♦ vi s'habiller ♦ vt habiller; (wound) panser; **to get ~ed** s'habiller; **~ up** vi s'habiller; (in fancy ~) se déguiser; **~ circle** (BRIT) n (THEATRE) premier balcon; **~er** n (furniture) vaisselier m; (: US) coiffeuse f, commode f; **~ing** n (MED) pansement m; (CULIN) sauce f, assaisonnement m; **~ing gown** (BRIT) n robe f de chambre; **~ing room** n (THEATRE) loge f; (SPORT) vestiaire m; **~ing table** n coiffeuse f; **~maker** n couturière f; **~ rehearsal** n (répétition) générale f

drew [dru:] pt of **draw**

dribble ['drɪbl] vi (baby) baver ♦ vt (ball) dribbler

dried [draɪd] adj (fruit, beans) sec(sèche); (eggs, milk) en poudre

drier ['draɪə*] n = **dryer**

drift [drɪft] n (of current etc) force f; direction f, mouvement m; (of snow) rafale f; (: on ground) congère f; (general meaning) sens (général) ♦ vi (boat) aller à la dérive, dériver; (sand, snow) s'amonceler, s'entasser; **~wood** n bois flotté

drill [drɪl] n perceuse f; (~ bit) foret m, mèche f; (of dentist) roulette f, fraise f; (MIL) exercice m ♦ vt percer; (troops) entraîner ♦ vi (for oil) faire un or des forage(s)

drink [drɪŋk] n (pt **drank**, pp **drunk**) n boisson f; (alcoholic) verre m ♦ vt, vi boire; **to have a ~** boire quelque chose, boire un verre; (alcoholic) prendre l'apéritif; **a ~ of water** un verre d'eau; **~er** n buveur(euse); **~ing water** n eau f potable

drip [drɪp] n goutte f; (MED) goutte-à-goutte m inv; perfusion f ♦ vi tomber goutte à goutte; (tap) goutter; **~-dry** adj (shirt) sans repassage; **~ping** n graisse f (de rôti)

drive [draɪv] n (pt **drove**, pp **driven**) n promenade f or trajet m en voiture; (also: **~way**) allée f; (energy) dynamisme m, énergie f; (push) effort (concerté), campagne f (also: disk ~) lecteur m de disquettes ♦ vt conduire; (push) chasser, pousser; (TECH: motor, wheel) faire fonctionner; entraîner; (nail, stake etc): **to ~ sth into sth** enfoncer qch dans qch ♦ vi (AUT: at controls) conduire; (: travel) aller en voiture; **left-/right-hand ~** conduite f à gauche/droite; **to ~ sb mad** rendre qn fou(folle); **to ~ sb home/to the airport** reconduire qn chez lui/conduire qn à l'aéroport

drivel ['drɪvl] (inf) n idioties fpl

driver ['draɪvə*] n conducteur(trice); (of taxi, bus) chauffeur m; **~'s license** (US) n permis m de conduire

driveway ['draɪvweɪ] n allée f

driving ['draɪvɪŋ] n conduite f; **~ instructor** n moniteur m d'auto-école; **~ lesson** n leçon f de conduite; **~ licence** (BRIT) n permis m de conduire; **~ school** n auto-

école f; **~ test** n examen m du permis de conduire

drizzle ['drɪzl] n bruine f, crachin m

drone [drəʊn] n bourdonnement m; (male bee) faux bourdon

drool [dru:l] vi baver

droop [dru:p] vi (shoulders) tomber; (head) pencher; (flower) pencher la tête

drop [drɒp] n goutte f; (fall) baisse f; (also: parachute ~) saut m ♦ vt laisser tomber; (voice, eyes, price) baisser; (set down from car) déposer ♦ vi tomber; **~s** npl (MED) gouttes; **~ off** vi (sleep) s'assoupir ♦ vt (passenger) déposer; **~ out** vi (withdraw) se retirer; (student etc) abandonner, décrocher; **~out** n marginal(e); **~per** n compte-gouttes m inv; **~pings** npl crottes fpl

drought [draʊt] n sécheresse f

drove [drəʊv] pt of **drive**

drown [draʊn] vt noyer ♦ vi se noyer

drowsy ['draʊzɪ] adj somnolent(e)

drudgery ['drʌdʒərɪ] n corvée f

drug [drʌg] n médicament m; (narcotic) drogue f ♦ vt droguer; **to be on ~s** se droguer; **~ addict** n toxicomane m/f; **~gist** (US) n pharmacien(ne)-droguiste; **~store** (US) n pharmacie-droguerie f, drugstore m

drum [drʌm] n tambour m; (for oil, petrol) bidon m; **~s** npl (kit) batterie f; **~mer** n (joueur m de) tambour m

drunk [drʌŋk] pp of **drink** ♦ adj ivre, soûl(e) ♦ n (also: **~ard**) ivrogne m/f; **~en** adj (person) ivre, soûl(e); (rage, stupor) ivrogne, d'ivrogne

dry [draɪ] adj sec(sèche); (day) sans pluie; (humour) pince-sans-rire inv; (lake, riverbed, well) à sec ♦ vt sécher; (clothes) faire sécher ♦ vi sécher; **~ up** vi tarir; **~-cleaner's** n teinturerie f; **~er** n séchoir m; (spin-~er) essoreuse f; **~ness** n sécheresse f; **~ rot** n pourriture sèche (du bois)

dual ['djuəl] adj double; **~ carriageway** (BRIT) n route f à quatre voies or à chaussées séparées; **~ purpose** adj à double usage

dubbed [dʌbd] adj (CINEMA) doublé(e)

dubious ['dju:bɪəs] adj hésitant(e), incertain(e); (reputation, company) douteux(euse)

duchess ['dʌtʃɪs] n duchesse f

duck [dʌk] n canard m ♦ vi se baisser vivement, baisser subitement la tête; **~ling** n caneton m

duct [dʌkt] n conduite f, canalisation f; (ANAT) conduit m

dud [dʌd] n (object, tool): **it's a ~** c'est de la camelote, ça ne marche pas ♦ adj **~ cheque** (BRIT) chèque sans provision

due [dju:] adj dû(due); (expected) attendu(e); (fitting) qui convient ♦ n: **to give sb his (or her) ~** être juste envers qn ♦ adv: **north** droit vers le nord; **~s** npl (for club, union) cotisation f; (in harbour) droits mpl (de port); **in ~ course** en temps utile or voulu; finalement; **~ to** dû(due) à; causé(e) par; **he's ~ to finish tomorrow** normalement il doit finir demain

duet [dju:'et] n duo m

duffel bag [dʌtl] n sac m marin

duffel coat n duffel-coat m

dug [dʌg] pt, pp of **dig**

duke [dju:k] n duc m

dull [dʌl] adj terne, morne; (boring) ennuyeux(euse); (sound, pain) sourd(e); (weather, day) gris(e), maussade ♦ vt (pain, grief) atténuer; (mind, senses) engourdir

duly ['dju:lɪ] adv (on time) en temps voulu; (as expected) comme il se doit

dumb [dʌm] adj muet(te); (stupid) bête; **~founded** [dʌm'faundid] adj sidéré(e)

dummy ['dʌmɪ] n (tailor's model) mannequin m; (mock-up) factice m, maquette f; (BRIT: for baby) tétine f ♦ adj faux(fausse), factice

dump [dʌmp] n (also: rubbish dump) décharge (publique); (pej) trou m ♦ vt (put down) déposer; déverser; (get rid of) se débarrasser de; (COMPUT: data) vider, transférer

dumpling ['dʌmplɪŋ] n boulette f (de pâte)

dumpy ['dʌmpɪ] adj boulot(te)

dunce [dʌns] n âne m, cancre m

dune [dju:n] n dune f

dung [dʌŋ] n fumier m

dungarees [dʌŋgə'ri:z] npl salopette f, bleu(s) m(pl)

dungeon ['dʌndʒən] n cachot m

duplex ['dju:pleks] (US) n maison jumelée; (apartment) duplex m

duplicate [n 'dju:plɪkɪt, vb 'dju:plɪkeɪt] n double m ♦ vt faire un double de; (on machine) polycopier; photocopier; **in ~** en deux exemplaires

durable ['djuərəbl] adj durable; (clothes, metal) résistant(e), solide

duration [djuə'reɪʃən] n durée f

duress [djuə'res] n: **under ~** sous la contrainte

during ['djuərɪŋ] prep pendant, au cours de

dusk [dʌsk] n crépuscule m

dust [dʌst] n poussière f ♦ vt (furniture) épousseter, essuyer; (cake etc): **to ~ with** saupoudrer de; **~bin** (BRIT) n poubelle f; **~er** n chiffon m; **~man** (BRIT irreg) n boueux m, éboueur m; **~y** adj poussiéreux(euse)

Dutch [dʌtʃ] adj hollandais(e), néerlandais(e) ♦ n (LING) hollandais m ♦ adv (inf): **to go ~** partager les frais; **the ~** npl (people) les Hollandais; **~man** (irreg) n Hollandais m; **~woman** (irreg) n Hollandaise f

dutiful ['dju:tɪful] adj (child) respectueux(euse)

duty ['dju:tɪ] n devoir m; (tax) droit m, taxe f; **on ~** de service; (at night etc) de garde; **off ~** libre, pas de service or de garde; **~-free** adj exempté(e) de douane, hors taxe inv

duvet ['du:veɪ] (BRIT) n couette f

dwarf [dwɔ:f] (pl **dwarves**) n nain(e) ♦ vt écraser

dwell [dwel] (pt, pp **dwelt**) vi demeurer; **~ on** vt fus s'appesantir sur; **~ing** n habitation f, demeure f

dwindle ['dwɪndl] vi diminuer, décroître

dye [daɪ] n teinture f ♦ vt teindre

dying ['daɪɪŋ] adj mourant(e), agonisant(e)

dyke [daɪk] (BRIT) n digue f

dynamic [daɪ'næmɪk] adj dynamique

dynamite ['daɪnəmaɪt] n dynamite f

dynamo ['daɪnəməu] n dynamo f

dyslexia [dɪs'leksɪə] n dyslexie f

E e

E [i:] n (MUS) mi m

each [i:tʃ] adj chaque ♦ pron chacun(e); **~ other** l'un(e) l'autre; **they hate ~ other** ils se détestent (mutuellement); **you are jealous of ~ other** vous êtes jaloux l'un de l'autre; **they have 2 books ~** ils ont 2 livres chacun

eager ['i:gə*] adj (keen) avide; **to be ~ to do sth** avoir très envie de faire qch; **to be ~ for** désirer vivement, être avide de

eagle ['i:gl] n aigle m

ear [ɪə*] n oreille f; (of corn) épi m; **~ache** n mal m aux oreilles; **~drum** n tympan m

earl [ɜ:l] (BRIT) n comte m

earlier ['ɜ:lɪə*] adj (date etc) plus rapproché(e); (edition, reply etc) plus ancien(ne), antérieur(e) ♦ adv plus tôt

early ['ɜ:lɪ] adv tôt, de bonne heure; (ahead of time) en avance; (near the beginning) au début ♦ adj qui se manifeste (or se fait) tôt or de bonne heure; (work) de jeunesse; (settler, Christian) premier(ère); (reply) rapide; (death) prématuré(e); **to have an ~ night** se coucher tôt or de bonne heure; **in the ~ or ~ in the spring/19th century** au début du printemps/19ème siècle; **~ retirement** n: **to take ~ retirement** prendre sa retraite anticipée

earmark ['ɪəmɑ:k] vt: **to ~ sth for** réserver or destiner qch à

earn [ɜ:n] vt gagner; (COMM: yield) rapporter

earnest ['ɜːnɪst] *adj* sérieux(euse); **in ~** *adv* sérieusement

earnings ['ɜːnɪŋz] *npl* salaire *m*; (*of company*) bénéfices *mpl*

earphones ['ɪəfəʊnz] *npl* écouteurs *mpl*

earring ['ɪərɪŋ] *n* boucle *f* d'oreille

earshot ['ɪəʃɒt] *n*: **within ~** à portée de voix

earth [ɜːθ] *n* (*gen, also* BRIT: ELEC) terre *f* ♦ *vt* relier à la terre; **~enware** *n* poterie *f*; faïence *f*; **~quake** *n* tremblement *m* de terre, séisme *m*; **~y** ['ɜːθɪ] *adj* (*vulgar: humour*) truculent(e)

ease [iːz] *n* facilité *f*, aisance *f*; (*comfort*) bien-être *m* ♦ *vt* (*soothe*) calmer; (*loosen*) relâcher, détendre; **to ~ sth in/out** faire pénétrer/sortir qch délicatement *or* avec douceur; faciliter la pénétration/la sortie de qch; **at ~!** (MIL) repos!; **~ off** *vi* diminuer; (*slow down*) ralentir; **~ up** *vi* = **ease off**

easel ['iːzl] *n* chevalet *m*

easily ['iːzɪlɪ] *adv* facilement

east [iːst] *n* est *m* ♦ *adj* (*wind*) d'est; (*side*) est *inv* ♦ *adv* à l'est, vers l'est; **the E~** l'Orient *m*; (POL) les pays *mpl* de l'Est

Easter ['iːstə*] *n* Pâques *fpl*; **~ egg** *n* œuf *m* de Pâques

east: ~erly ['iːstəlɪ] *adj* (*wind*) d'est; (*direction*) est *inv*; (*point*) à l'est; **~ern** ['iːstən] *adj* de l'est, oriental(e); **~ward(s)** ['iːstwəd(z)] *adv* vers l'est, à l'est

easy ['iːzɪ] *adj* facile; (*manner*) aisé(e) ♦ *adv*: **to take it** *or* **things ~** ne pas se fatiguer; (*not worry*) ne pas (trop) s'en faire; **~ chair** *n* fauteuil *m*; **~-going** *adj* accommodant(e), facile à vivre

eat [iːt] (*pt* **ate**, *pp* **eaten**) *vt, vi* manger; **~ away at** *vt fus* ronger, attaquer; (*savings*) entamer; **~ into** *vt fus* = **eat away at**

eaves [iːvz] *npl* avant-toit *m*

eavesdrop ['iːvzdrɒp] *vi*: **to ~ (on a conversation)** écouter (une conversation) de façon indiscrète

ebb [eb] *n* reflux *m* ♦ *vi* refluer; (*fig: also*: **~ away**) décliner

ebony ['ebənɪ] *n* ébène *f*

EC *n abbr* (= *European Community*) C.E. *f*

eccentric [ɪk'sentrɪk] *adj* excentrique ♦ *n* excentrique *m/f*

echo ['ekəʊ] (*pl* **~es**) *n* écho *m* ♦ *vt* répéter ♦ *vi* résonner, faire écho

eclipse [ɪ'klɪps] *n* éclipse *f*

ecology [ɪ'kɒlədʒɪ] *n* écologie *f*

economic [iːkə'nɒmɪk] *adj* économique; (*business etc*) rentable; **~al** *adj* économique; (*person*) économe; **~s** *n* économie *f* politique ♦ *npl* (*of project, situation*) aspect *m* financier

economize [ɪ'kɒnəmaɪz] *vi* économiser, faire des économies

economy [ɪ'kɒnəmɪ] *n* économie *f*; **~ class** *n* classe *f* touriste; **~ size** *n* format *m* économique

ecstasy ['ekstəsɪ] *n* extase *f*; **ecstatic** *adj* extatique

ECU [eɪ'kjuː] *n abbr* (= *European Currency Unit*) ECU *m*

eczema ['eksɪmə] *n* eczéma *m*

edge [edʒ] *n* bord *m*; (*of knife etc*) tranchant *m*, fil *m* ♦ *vt* border; **on ~** (*fig*) crispé(e), tendu(e); **to ~ away from** s'éloigner furtivement de; **~ways** *adv*: **he couldn't get a word in ~ways** il ne pouvait pas placer un mot

edgy ['edʒɪ] *adj* crispé(e), tendu(e)

edible ['edɪbl] *adj* comestible

edict ['iːdɪkt] *n* décret *m*

Edinburgh ['edɪnbərə] *n* Édimbourg

edit ['edɪt] *vt* (*text, book*) éditer; (*report*) préparer; (*film*) monter; (*broadcast*) réaliser; **~ion** [ɪ'dɪʃən] *n* édition *f*; **~or** *n* (*of column*) rédacteur(trice); (*of newspaper*) rédacteur(trice) en chef; (*of sb's work*) éditeur(trice); **~orial** [edɪ'tɔːrɪəl] *adj* de la rédaction, éditorial(e) ♦ *n* éditorial *m*

educate ['edjʊkeɪt] *vt* (*teach*) instruire; (*instruct*) éduquer

education [edjʊ'keɪʃən] *n* éducation *f*; (*studies*) études *fpl*; (*teaching*) enseignement *m*, instruction *f*; **~al** *adj* (*experience, toy*) pédagogique; (*institution*) scolaire; (*policy*) d'éducation

eel [iːl] *n* anguille *f*

eerie ['ɪərɪ] *adj* inquiétant(e)

effect [ɪ'fekt] *n* effet *m* ♦ *vt* effectuer; **to take ~** (*law*) entrer en vigueur, prendre effet; (*drug*) agir, faire son effet; **in ~** en fait; **~ive** *adj* efficace; (*actual*) véritable; **~ively** *adv* efficacement; (*in reality*) effectivement; **~iveness** *n* efficacité *f*

effeminate [ɪ'femɪnɪt] *adj* efféminé(e)

effervescent [efə'vesnt] *adj* (*drink*) gazeux(euse)

efficiency [ɪ'fɪʃənsɪ] *n* efficacité *f*; (*of machine*) rendement *m*

efficient [ɪ'fɪʃənt] *adj* efficace; (*machine*) qui a un bon rendement

effort ['efət] *n* effort *m*; **~less** *adj* (*style*) aisé(e); (*achievement*) facile

effusive [ɪ'fjuːsɪv] *adj* chaleureux(euse)

e.g. *adv abbr* (= *exempli gratia*) par exemple, p. ex.

egg [eg] *n* œuf *m*; **hard-boiled/soft-boiled ~** œuf dur/à la coque; **~ on** *vt* pousser; **~cup** *n* coquetier *m*; **~plant** *n* (*esp US*) aubergine *f*; **~shell** *n* coquille *f* d'œuf

ego ['iːgəʊ] *n* (*self-esteem*) amour-propre *m*

egotism ['egəʊtɪzəm] *n* égotisme *m*

egotist ['egəʊtɪst] *n* égocentrique *m/f*

Egypt ['iːdʒɪpt] *n* Égypte *f*; **~ian** [ɪ'dʒɪpʃən] *adj* égyptien(ne) ♦ *n* Égyptien(ne)

eiderdown ['aɪdədaʊn] *n* édredon *m*

eight [eɪt] *num* huit; **~een** *num* dix-huit; **~h** [eɪtθ] *num* huitième; **~y** *num* quatre-vingt(s)

Eire ['ɛərə] n République f d'Irlande

either ['aɪðə*] adj l'un ou l'autre; (both, each) chaque ♦ pron: ~ (of them) l'un ou l'autre ♦ adv non plus ♦ conj: ~ **good or bad** ou bon ou mauvais, soit bon soit mauvais; **on ~ side** de chaque côté; **I don't like ~** je n'aime ni l'un ni l'autre; **no, I don't ~** moi non plus

eject [ɪ'dʒɛkt] vt (tenant etc) expulser; (object) éjecter

eke [iːk] : **to ~ out** vt faire durer

elaborate [adj ɪ'læbərɪt, vb ɪ'læbəreɪt] adj compliqué(e), recherché(e) ♦ vt élaborer ♦ vi: **to ~ (on)** entrer dans les détails (de)

elapse [ɪ'læps] vi s'écouler, passer

elastic [ɪ'læstɪk] adj élastique ♦ n élastique m; ~ **band** n élastique m

elated [ɪ'leɪtɪd] adj transporté(e) de joie

elation [ɪ'leɪʃən] n allégresse f

elbow ['ɛlbəʊ] n coude m

elder ['ɛldə*] adj aîné(e) ♦ n (tree) sureau m; **one's ~s** ses aînés; ~**ly** adj âgé(e) ♦ npl: **the ~ly** les personnes âgées

eldest ['ɛldɪst] adj, n: **the ~ (child)** l'aîné(e) (des enfants)

elect [ɪ'lɛkt] vt élire ♦ adj: **the president ~** le président désigné; **to ~ to do** choisir de faire; ~**ion** [ɪ'lɛkʃən] n élection f; ~**ioneering** [ɪlɛkʃə'nɪərɪŋ] n propagande électorale, manœuvres électorales; ~**or** n électeur(trice); ~**orate** n électorat m

electric [ɪ'lɛktrɪk] adj électrique; ~**al** adj électrique; ~ **blanket** n couverture chauffante; ~ **fire** n (BRIT) radiateur m électrique; ~**ian** [ɪlɛk'trɪʃən] n électricien m

electricity [ɪlɛk'trɪsɪtɪ] n électricité f

electrify [ɪ'lɛktrɪfaɪ] vt (RAIL, fence) électrifier; (audience) électriser

electronic [ɪlɛk'trɒnɪk] adj électronique; ~**s** n électronique f

elegant ['ɛlɪgənt] adj élégant(e)

element ['ɛlɪmənt] n (gen) élément m; (of heater, kettle etc) résistance f; ~**ary** [ɛlɪ'mɛntərɪ] adj élémentaire; (school, education) primaire

elephant ['ɛlɪfənt] n éléphant m

elevation [ɛlɪ'veɪʃən] n (raising, promotion) avancement m, promotion f; (height) hauteur f

elevator ['ɛlɪveɪtə*] n (in warehouse etc) élévateur m, monte-charge m inv; (US: lift) ascenseur m

eleven [ɪ'lɛvn] num onze; ~**ses** npl ≈ pause-café f; ~**th** num onzième

elicit [ɪ'lɪsɪt] vt: **to ~ (from)** obtenir (de), arracher (à)

eligible ['ɛlɪdʒəbl] adj: **to be ~ for** remplir les conditions requises pour; **an ~ young man/woman** un beau parti

elm [ɛlm] n orme m

elongated ['iːlɒŋgeɪtɪd] adj allongé(e)

elope [ɪ'ləʊp] vi (lovers) s'enfuir (ensemble); ~**ment** [ɪləʊpmənt] n fugue amoureuse

eloquent ['ɛləkwənt] adj éloquent(e)

else [ɛls] adv d'autre; **something ~** quelque chose d'autre, autre chose; **somewhere ~** ailleurs, autre part; **everywhere ~** partout ailleurs; **nobody ~** personne d'autre; **where ~?** à quel autre endroit?; **little ~** pas grand-chose d'autre; ~**where** adv ailleurs, autre part

elude [ɪ'luːd] vt échapper à

elusive [ɪ'luːsɪv] adj insaisissable

emaciated [ɪ'meɪsɪeɪtɪd] adj émacié(e), décharné(e)

emancipate [ɪ'mænsɪpeɪt] vt émanciper

embankment [ɪm'bæŋkmənt] n (of road, railway) remblai m, talus m; (of river) berge f, quai m

embark [ɪm'bɑːk] vi embarquer; **to ~ on** (journey) entreprendre; (fig) se lancer or s'embarquer dans; ~**ation** [ɛmbɑː'keɪʃən] n embarquement m

embarrass [ɪm'bærəs] vt embarrasser, gêner; ~**ed** adj gêné(e); ~**ing** adj gênant(e), embarrassant(e); ~**ment** n embarras m, gêne f

embassy ['ɛmbəsɪ] n ambassade f

embedded [ɪm'bɛdɪd] adj enfoncé(e)

embellish [ɪm'bɛlɪʃ] vt orner, décorer; (fig: account) enjoliver

embers ['ɛmbəz] npl braise f

embezzle [ɪm'bɛzl] vt détourner

embezzlement [ɪm'bɛzlmənt] n détournement m de fonds

embitter [ɪm'bɪtə*] vt (person) aigrir; (relations) envenimer

embody [ɪm'bɒdɪ] vt (features) réunir, comprendre; (ideas) formuler, exprimer

embossed [ɪm'bɒst] adj (metal) estampé(e); (leather) frappé(e); ~ **wallpaper** papier gaufré

embrace [ɪm'breɪs] vt embrasser, étreindre; (include) embrasser ♦ vi s'étreindre, s'embrasser ♦ n étreinte f

embroider [ɪm'brɔɪdə*] vt broder; ~**y** n broderie f

emerald ['ɛmərəld] n émeraude f

emerge [ɪ'mɜːdʒ] vi apparaître; (from room, car) surgir; (from sleep, imprisonment) sortir

emergency [ɪ'mɜːdʒənsɪ] n urgence f; **in an ~** en cas d'urgence; ~ **cord** n sonnette f d'alarme; ~ **exit** n sortie f de secours; ~ **landing** n atterrissage forcé; ~ **services** npl: **the ~ services** (fire, police, ambulance) les services mpl d'urgence

emergent [ɪ'mɜːdʒənt] adj (nation) en voie de développement; (group) en développement

emery board ['ɛmərɪ-] n lime f à ongles (en carton émerisé)

emigrate ['ɛmɪgreɪt] vi émigrer

eminent ['ɛmɪnənt] adj éminent(e)

emissions [ɪ'mɪʃənz] npl émissions fpl

emit [ɪ'mɪt] vt émettre

emotion [ɪ'məʊʃən] n émotion f; **~al** adj (person) émotif(ive), très sensible; (needs, exhaustion) affectif(ive); (scene) émouvant(e); (tone, speech) qui fait appel aux sentiments

emotive [ɪ'məʊtɪv] adj chargé(e) d'émotion; (subject) sensible

emperor ['empərə*] n empereur m

emphasis ['emfəsɪs] (pl **-ases**) n (stress) accent m; (importance) insistance f

emphasize ['emfəsaɪz] vt (syllable, word, point) appuyer or insister sur; (feature) souligner, accentuer

emphatic [ɪm'fætɪk] adj (strong) énergique, vigoureux(euse); (unambiguous, clear) catégorique; **~ally** [ɪm'fætɪkəlɪ] adv avec vigueur or énergie; catégoriquement

empire ['empaɪə*] n empire m

employ [ɪm'plɔɪ] vt employer; **~ee** n employé(e) f; **~er** n employeur(euse); **~ment** n emploi m; **~ment agency** n agence f or bureau m de placement

empower [ɪm'paʊə*] vt: **to ~ sb to do** autoriser or habiliter qn à faire

empress ['emprɪs] n impératrice f

emptiness ['emptɪnəs] n (of area, region) aspect m désertique; (of life) vide m, vacuité f

empty ['emptɪ] adj vide; (threat, promise) en l'air, vain(e) ♦ vt vider ♦ vi se vider; (liquid) s'écouler; **~-handed** adj les mains vides

emulate ['emjʊleɪt] vt rivaliser avec, imiter

emulsion [ɪ'mʌlʃən] n émulsion f; **~ (paint)** n peinture mate

enable [ɪ'neɪbl] vt: **to ~ sb to do** permettre à qn de faire

enact [ɪn'ækt] vt (law) promulguer; (play) jouer

enamel [ɪ'næməl] n émail m; (also: **~ paint**) peinture laquée

enamoured [ɪn'æməd] adj: **to be ~ of** être entiché(e) de

encased [ɪn'keɪst] adj: **~ in** enfermé(e) or enchâssé(e) dans

enchant [ɪn'tʃɑːnt] vt enchanter; **~ing** adj ravissant(e), enchanteur(teresse)

encl. abbr = **enclosed**

enclose [ɪn'kləʊz] vt (land) clôturer; (space, object) entourer; (letter etc): **to ~ (with)** joindre (à); **please find ~d** veuillez trouver ci-joint

enclosure [ɪn'kləʊʒə*] n enceinte f

encompass [ɪn'kʌmpəs] vt (include) contenir, inclure

encore ['ɒŋkɔː*] excl bis ♦ n bis m

encounter [ɪn'kaʊntə*] n rencontre f ♦ vt rencontrer

encourage [ɪn'kʌrɪdʒ] vt encourager; **~ment** n encouragement m

encroach [ɪn'krəʊtʃ] vi: **to ~ (up)on** empiéter sur

encyclop(a)edia [ensaɪkləʊ'piːdɪə] n encyclopédie f

end [end] n (gen, also: aim) fin f; (of table, street, rope etc) bout m, extrémité f ♦ vt terminer; (also: **bring to an ~**, **put an ~ to**) mettre fin à ♦ vi se terminer, finir; **in the ~** finalement; **on ~** (object) debout, dressé(e); **to stand on ~** (hair) se dresser sur la tête; **for hours on ~** pendant des heures et des heures; **~ up** vi: **to ~ up in** (condition) finir or se terminer par; (place) finir or aboutir à

endanger [ɪn'deɪndʒə*] vt mettre en danger

endearing [ɪn'dɪərɪŋ] adj attachant(e)

endeavour [ɪn'devə*] (US **endeavor**) n tentative f, effort m ♦ vi: **to ~ to do** tenter or s'efforcer de faire

ending ['endɪŋ] n dénouement m, fin f; (LING) terminaison f

endive ['endaɪv] n chicorée f; (smooth) endive f

endless ['endlɪs] adj sans fin, interminable

endorse [ɪn'dɔːs] vt (cheque) endosser; (approve) appuyer, approuver, sanctionner; **~ment** n (approval) appui m, aval m; (BRIT: on driving licence) contravention portée au permis de conduire

endow [ɪn'daʊ] vt: **to ~ (with)** doter (de)

endure [ɪn'djʊə*] vt supporter, endurer ♦ vi durer

enemy ['enɪmɪ] adj, n ennemi(e)

energetic [enə'dʒetɪk] adj énergique; (activity) qui fait se dépenser (physiquement)

energy ['enədʒɪ] n énergie f

enforce [ɪn'fɔːs] vt (LAW) appliquer, faire respecter

engage [ɪn'geɪdʒ] vt engager; (attention etc) retenir ♦ vi (TECH) s'enclencher, s'engrener; **to ~ in** se lancer dans; **~d** adj (BRIT: busy, in use) occupé(e); (betrothed) fiancé(e); **to get ~d** se fiancer; **~d tone** n (TEL) tonalité f occupé inv or pas libre; **~ment** n obligation f, engagement m; rendez-vous m inv; (to marry) fiançailles fpl; **~ment ring** n bague f de fiançailles

engaging [ɪn'geɪdʒɪŋ] adj engageant(e), attirant(e)

engender [ɪn'dʒendə*] vt produire, causer

engine ['endʒɪn] n (AUT) moteur m; (RAIL) locomotive f; **~ driver** n mécanicien m

engineer [endʒɪ'nɪə*] n ingénieur m; (BRIT: repairer) dépanneur m; (NAVY, US RAIL) mécanicien m; **~ing** [-'nɪərɪŋ] n engineering m, ingénierie f; (of bridges, ships) génie m; (of machine) mécanique f

England ['ɪŋglənd] n Angleterre f

English ['ɪŋglɪʃ] adj anglais(e) ♦ n (LING) anglais m; **the ~** npl (people) les Anglais; **the ~ Channel** la Manche; **~man** (irreg) n Anglais; **~woman** (irreg) n Anglaise f

engraving [ɪnˈgreɪvɪŋ] n gravure f
engrossed [ɪnˈgrəʊst] adj: ~ **in** absorbé(e) par, plongé(e) dans
engulf [ɪnˈgʌlf] vt engloutir
enhance [ɪnˈhɑːns] vt rehausser, mettre en valeur
enjoy [ɪnˈdʒɔɪ] vt aimer, prendre plaisir à; (have: health, fortune) jouir de; (: success) connaître; **to ~ o.s.** s'amuser; **~able** adj agréable; **~ment** n plaisir m
enlarge [ɪnˈlɑːdʒ] vt accroître, (PHOT) agrandir ♦ vi: **to ~ on** (subject) s'étendre sur; **~ment** n (PHOT) agrandissement m
enlighten [ɪnˈlaɪtn] vt éclairer; **~ed** adj éclairé(e); **~ment** n: the E~ment (HISTORY) ≈ le Siècle des lumières
enlist [ɪnˈlɪst] vt recruter; (support) s'assurer ♦ vi s'engager
enmity [ˈenmɪtɪ] n inimitié f
enormous [ɪˈnɔːməs] adj énorme
enough [ɪˈnʌf] adj, pron: ~ **time/books** assez or suffisamment de temps/livres ♦ adv: **big ~** assez or suffisamment grand; **have you got ~?** en avez-vous assez?; **he has not worked ~** il n'a pas assez or suffisamment travaillé; **~ to eat** assez à manger; **~!** assez!, ça suffit!; **that's ~, thanks** cela suffit or c'est assez, merci; **I've had ~ of him** j'en ai assez de lui; **... which, funnily** or **oddly ~** ... qui, chose curieuse
enquire [ɪnˈkwaɪə*] vt, vi = **inquire**
enrage [ɪnˈreɪdʒ] vt mettre en fureur or en rage, rendre furieux(euse)
enrol [ɪnˈrəʊl] (US **-l**) vt inscrire ♦ vi s'inscrire; **~ment** (US **-lment**) n inscription f
ensue [ɪnˈsjuː] vi s'ensuivre, résulter
ensure [ɪnˈʃʊə*] vt assurer; garantir; **to ~ that** s'assurer que
entail [ɪnˈteɪl] vt entraîner, occasionner
entangled [ɪnˈtæŋgld] adj: **to become ~ (in)** s'empêtrer (dans)
enter [ˈentə*] vt (room) entrer dans, pénétrer dans; (club, army) entrer à; (competition) s'inscrire à or pour; (sb for a competition) (faire) inscrire; (write down) inscrire, noter; (COMPUT) entrer, introduire ♦ vi entrer; ~ **for** vt fus s'inscrire à, se présenter pour or à; ~ **into** vt fus (explanation) se lancer dans; (discussion, negotiations) entamer; (agreement) conclure
enterprise [ˈentəpraɪz] n entreprise f; (initiative) (esprit m d')initiative f; **free ~** libre entreprise; **private ~** entreprise privée
enterprising [ˈentəpraɪzɪŋ] adj entreprenant(e), dynamique; (scheme) audacieux(euse)
entertain [entəˈteɪn] vt amuser, distraire; (invite) recevoir (à dîner); (idea, plan) envisager; **~er** n artiste m/f de variétés; **~ing** adj amusant(e), distrayant(e); **~ment** n (amusement) divertissement m, amusement m; (show) spectacle m

enthralled [ɪnˈθrɔːld] adj captivé(e)
enthusiasm [ɪnˈθuːzɪæzəm] n enthousiasme m
enthusiast [ɪnˈθuːzɪæst] n enthousiaste m/f; **~ic** [ɪnθuːzɪˈæstɪk] adj enthousiaste; **to be ~ic about** être enthousiasmé(e) par
entice [ɪnˈtaɪs] vt attirer, séduire
entire [ɪnˈtaɪə*] adj (tout) entier(ère); **~ly** adv entièrement, complètement; **~ty** [ɪnˈtaɪərətɪ] n: **in its ~ty** dans sa totalité
entitle [ɪnˈtaɪtl] vt: **to ~ sb to sth** donner droit à qch à qn; **~d** adj (book) intitulé(e); **to be ~d to do** avoir le droit de or être habilité à faire
entrance [n ˈentrəns, vb ɪnˈtrɑːns] n entrée f ♦ vt enchanter, ravir; **to gain ~ to** (university etc) être admis à; ~ **examination** n examen m d'entrée; ~ **fee** n (to museum etc) prix m d'entrée; (to join club etc) droit m d'inscription; ~ **ramp** (US) n (AUT) bretelle f d'accès
entrant [ˈentrənt] n participant(e); concurrent(e); (BRIT: in exam) candidat(e)
entrenched [ɪnˈtrentʃt] adj retranché(e); (ideas) arrêté(e)
entrepreneur [ɒntrəprəˈnɜː*] n entrepreneur m
entrust [ɪnˈtrʌst] vt: **to ~ sth to** confier qch à
entry [ˈentrɪ] n entrée f; (in register) inscription f; **no ~** défense d'entrer, entrée interdite; (AUT) sens interdit; ~ **form** n feuille f d'inscription; ~ **phone** n (BRIT) interphone m
enunciate [ɪˈnʌnsɪeɪt] vt énoncer; (word) articuler, prononcer
envelop [ɪnˈveləp] vt envelopper
envelope [ˈenvələʊp] n enveloppe f
envious [ˈenvɪəs] adj envieux(euse)
environment [ɪnˈvaɪərənmənt] n environnement m; (social, moral) milieu m; **~al** [ɪnvaɪərənˈmentl] adj écologique; du milieu; **~-friendly** adj écologique
envisage [ɪnˈvɪzɪdʒ] vt (foresee) prévoir
envoy [ˈenvɔɪ] n (diplomat) ministre m plénipotentiaire
envy [ˈenvɪ] n envie f ♦ vt envier; **to ~ sb sth** envier qch à qn
epic [ˈepɪk] n épopée f ♦ adj épique
epidemic [epɪˈdemɪk] n épidémie f
epilepsy [ˈepɪlepsɪ] n épilepsie f
episode [ˈepɪsəʊd] n épisode m
epitome [ɪˈpɪtəmɪ] n modèle m; **epitomize** [ɪˈpɪtəmaɪz] vt incarner
equable [ˈekwəbl] adj égal(e); de tempérament égal
equal [ˈiːkwl] adj égal(e) ♦ n égal(e) ♦ vt égaler; ~ **to** (task) à la hauteur de; **~ity** [iːˈkwɒlɪtɪ] n égalité f; **~ize** vi (SPORT) égaliser; **~ly** adv également; (just as) tout aussi
equanimity [ekwəˈnɪmɪtɪ] n égalité f d'hu-

meur

equate [ɪ'kweɪt] *vt*: **to ~ sth with** comparer qch à; assimiler qch à; **equation** [ɪ'kweɪʒən] *n* (*MATH*) équation *f*

equator [ɪ'kweɪtə*] *n* équateur *m*

equilibrium [i:kwɪ'lɪbrɪəm] *n* équilibre *m*

equip [ɪ'kwɪp] *vt*: **to ~ (with)** équiper (de); **to be well ~ped** (*office etc*) être bien équipé(e); **he is well ~ped for the job** il a les compétences requises pour ce travail; **~ment** *n* équipement *m*; (*electrical etc*) appareillage *m*, installation *f*

equities ['ekwɪtɪz] (*BRIT*) *npl* (*COMM*) actions cotées en Bourse

equivalent [ɪ'kwɪvələnt] *adj*: **~ (to)** équivalent(e) (à) ♦ *n* équivalent *m*

equivocal [ɪ'kwɪvəkəl] *adj* équivoque; (*open to suspicion*) douteux (euse)

era ['ɪərə] *n* ère *f*, époque *f*

eradicate [ɪ'rædɪkeɪt] *vt* éliminer

erase [ɪ'reɪz] *vt* effacer; **~r** *n* gomme *f*

erect [ɪ'rekt] *adj* droit(e) ♦ *vt* construire; (*monument*) ériger; élever; (*tent etc*) dresser; **~ion** [ɪ'rekʃən] *n* érection *f*

ERM *n abbr* (= *Exchange Rate Mechanism*) SME *m*

erode [ɪ'rəud] *vt* éroder; (*metal*) ronger

erotic [ɪ'rɒtɪk] *adj* érotique

err [ɜ:*] *vi* (*formal: make a mistake*) se tromper

errand ['erənd] *n* course *f*, commission *f*

erratic [ɪ'rætɪk] *adj* irrégulier(ère); inconstant(e)

error ['erə*] *n* erreur *f*

erupt [ɪ'rʌpt] *vi* entrer en éruption; (*fig*) éclater; **~ion** [ɪ'rʌpʃən] *n* éruption *f*

escalate ['eskəleɪt] *vi* s'intensifier

escalator ['eskəleɪtə*] *n* escalier roulant

escapade [eskə'peɪd] *n* fredaine *f*; équipée *f*

escape [ɪs'keɪp] *n* fuite *f*; (*from prison*) évasion *f* ♦ *vi* s'échapper, fuir; (*from jail*) s'évader; (*fig*) s'en tirer; (*leak*) s'échapper ♦ *vt* échapper à; **to ~ from** (*person*) échapper à; (*place*) s'échapper de; (*fig*) fuir; **escapism** [-ɪzəm] *n* (*fig*) évasion *f*

escort [*n* 'eskɔ:t, *vb* ɪs'kɔ:t] *n* escorte *f* ♦ *vt* escorter

Eskimo ['eskɪməu] *n* Esquimau(de)

esophagus [i:'sɒfəgəs] (*US*) *n* = **oesophagus**

especially [ɪs'peʃəlɪ] *adv* (*particularly*) particulièrement; (*above all*) surtout

espionage ['espɪənɑ:ʒ] *n* espionnage *m*

Esquire [ɪs'kwaɪə*] *n*: **J Brown, ~** Monsieur J. Brown

essay ['eseɪ] *n* (*SCOL*) dissertation *f*; (*LITERATURE*) essai *m*

essence ['esəns] *n* essence *f*

essential [ɪ'senʃəl] *adj* essentiel(le); (*basic*) fondamental(e) ♦ *n*: **~s** éléments essentiels; **~ly** *adv* essentiellement

establish [ɪs'tæblɪʃ] *vt* établir; (*business*) fonder, créer; (*one's power etc*) asseoir, affermir; **~ed** *adj* bien établi(e); **~ment** *n* établissement *m*; (*founding*) création *f*; **the E~ment** les pouvoirs établis; l'ordre établi; les milieux dirigeants

estate [ɪs'teɪt] *n* (*land*) domaine *m*, propriété *f*; (*LAW*) biens *mpl*, succession *f*; (*BRIT: also: housing ~*) lotissement *m*, cité *f*; **~ agent** *n* agent immobilier; **~ car** (*BRIT*) *n* break *m*

esteem [ɪs'ti:m] *n* estime *f*

esthetic [ɪs'θetɪk] (*US*) *adj* = **aesthetic**

estimate [*n* 'estɪmət, *vb* 'estɪmeɪt] *n* estimation *f*; (*COMM*) devis *m* ♦ *vt* estimer; **estimation** [estɪ'meɪʃən] *n* opinion *f*; (*calculation*) estimation *f*

estranged [ɪ'streɪndʒd] *adj* séparé(e); **dont on s'est séparé(e)**

etc. *abbr* (= *et cetera*) etc

etching ['etʃɪŋ] *n* eau-forte *f*

eternal [ɪ'tɜ:nl] *adj* éternel(le)

eternity [ɪ'tɜ:nɪtɪ] *n* éternité *f*

ethical ['eθɪkəl] *adj* moral(e); **ethics** ['eθɪks] *n* éthique *f* ♦ *npl* moralité *f*

Ethiopia [i:θɪ'əupɪə] *n* Éthiopie *f*

ethnic ['eθnɪk] *adj* ethnique; (*music etc*) folklorique

ethos ['i:θɒs] *n* génie *m*

etiquette ['etɪket] *n* convenances *fpl*, étiquette *f*

Eurocheque ['juərəu'tʃek] *n* eurochèque *m*

Europe ['juərəp] *n* Europe *f*; **~an** [juərə'pi:ən] *adj* européen(ne) ♦ *n* Européen(ne)

evacuate [ɪ'vækjueɪt] *vt* évacuer

evade [ɪ'veɪd] *vt* échapper à; (*question etc*) éluder; (*duties*) se dérober à; **to ~ tax** frauder le fisc

evaporate [ɪ'væpəreɪt] *vi* s'évaporer; **~d milk** *n* lait condensé non sucré

evasion [ɪ'veɪʒən] *n* dérobade *f*; **tax ~** fraude fiscale

eve [i:v] *n*: **on the ~ of** à la veille de

even ['i:vən] *adj* (*level, smooth*) régulier(ère); (*equal*) égal(e); (*number*) pair(e) ♦ *adv* même; **~ if** même si *+indic*; **~ though** alors même que *+cond*; **~ more** encore plus; **~ so** quand même; **not ~** pas même; **to get ~ with sb** prendre sa revanche sur qn; **~ out** *vi* s'égaliser

evening ['i:vnɪŋ] *n* soir *m*; (*as duration, event*) soirée *f*; **in the ~** le soir; **~ class** *n* cours *m* du soir; **~ dress** *n* tenue *f* de soirée

event [ɪ'vent] *n* événement *m*; (*SPORT*) épreuve *f*; **in the ~ of** en cas de; **~ful** *adj* mouvementé(e)

eventual [ɪ'ventʃuəl] *adj* final(e); **~ity** [ɪventʃu'ælɪtɪ] *n* possibilité *f*, éventualité *f*; **~ly** *adv* finalement

ever ['evə*] *adv* jamais; (*at all times*) toujours; **the best** ~ le meilleur qu'on ait jamais vu; **have you** ~ **seen it?** l'as-tu déjà vu?, as-tu eu l'occasion *or* t'est-il arrivé de le voir?; **why** ~ **not?** mais enfin, pourquoi pas?; ~ **since** *adv* depuis ♦ *conj* depuis que; ~**green** *n* arbre *m* à feuilles persistantes; ~**lasting** *adj* éternel(le)

every ['evrɪ] *adj* chaque; ~ **day** tous les jours, chaque jour; ~ **other/third day** tous les deux/trois jours; ~ **other car** une voiture sur deux; ~ **now and then** de temps en temps; ~**body** *pron* tout le monde, tous *pl*; ~**day** *adj* quotidien(ne); de tous les jours; ~**one** *pron* = **everybody**; ~**thing** *pron* tout; ~**where** *adv* partout

evict [ɪ'vɪkt] *vt* expulser; ~**ion** [ɪ'vɪkʃən] *n* expulsion *f*

evidence ['evɪdəns] *n* (*proof*) preuve(s) *f(pl)*; (*of witness*) témoignage *m*; (*sign*): **to show** ~ **of** présenter des signes de; **to give** ~ témoigner, déposer

evident ['evɪdənt] *adj* évident(e); ~**ly** *adv* de toute évidence; (*apparently*) apparemment

evil ['iːvl] *adj* mauvais(e) ♦ *n* mal *m*

evoke [ɪ'vəuk] *vt* évoquer

evolution [iːvə'luːʃən] *n* évolution *f*

evolve [ɪ'vɔlv] *vt* élaborer ♦ *vi* évoluer

ewe [juː] *n* brebis *f*

ex- [eks] *prefix* ex-

exact [ɪg'zækt] *adj* exact(e) ♦ *vt*: **to** ~ **sth (from)** extorquer qch (à); exiger qch (de); ~**ing** *adj* exigeant(e); (*work*) astreignant(e); ~**ly** *adv* exactement

exaggerate [ɪg'zædʒəreɪt] *vt*, *vi* exagérer; **exaggeration** [ɪgzædʒə'reɪʃən] *n* exagération *f*

exalted [ɪg'zɔːltɪd] *adj* (*prominent*) élevé(e); (: *person*) haut placé(e)

exam [ɪg'zæm] *n abbr* (SCOL) = **examination**

examination [ɪgzæmɪ'neɪʃən] *n* (SCOL, MED) examen *m*

examine [ɪg'zæmɪn] *vt* (*gen*) examiner; (SCOL: *person*) interroger; ~**r** *n* examinateur(trice)

example [ɪg'zɑːmpl] *n* exemple *m*; **for** ~ par exemple

exasperate [ɪg'zɑːspəreɪt] *vt* exaspérer; **exasperation** [ɪgzɑːspə'reɪʃən] *n* exaspération *f*, irritation *f*

excavate ['ekskəveɪt] *vt* excaver; **excavation** [ekskə'veɪʃən] *n* fouilles *fpl*

exceed [ɪk'siːd] *vt* dépasser; (*one's powers*) outrepasser; ~**ingly** *adv* extrêmement

excellent ['eksələnt] *adj* excellent(e)

except [ɪk'sept] *prep* (*also*: ~ **for**, ~**ing**) sauf, excepté ♦ *vt* excepter; ~ **if/when** sauf si/quand; ~ **that** sauf que, si ce n'est que; ~**ion** [ɪk'sepʃən] *n* exception *f*; **to take** ~**ion to** s'offusquer de; ~**ional** [ɪk'sepʃənl] *adj* exceptionnel(le)

excerpt ['eksɜːpt] *n* extrait *m*

excess [ek'ses] *n* excès *m*; ~ **baggage** *n* excédent *m* de bagages; ~ **fare** (BRIT) *n* supplément *m*; ~**ive** *adj* excessif(ive)

exchange [ɪks'tʃeɪndʒ] *n* échange *m*; (*also*: *telephone* ~) central *m* ♦ *vt*: **to** ~ **(for)** échanger (contre); ~ **rate** *n* taux *m* de change

Exchequer [ɪks'tʃekə*] (BRIT) *n*: **the** ~ l'Échiquier *m*, ≈ le ministère des Finances

excise [*n* 'eksaɪz, *vb* ek'saɪz] *n* taxe *f* ♦ *vt* exciser

excite [ɪk'saɪt] *vt* exciter; **to get** ~**d** s'exciter; ~**ment** *n* excitation *f*; **exciting** *adj* passionnant(e)

exclaim [ɪks'kleɪm] *vi* s'exclamer; **exclamation** [eksklə'meɪʃən] *n* exclamation *f*; **exclamation mark** *n* point *m* d'exclamation

exclude [ɪks'kluːd] *vt* exclure

exclusive [ɪks'kluːsɪv] *adj* exclusif(ive); (*club, district*) sélect(e); (*item of news*) en exclusivité; ~ **of VAT** TVA non comprise; **mutually** ~ qui s'excluent l'un(e) l'autre

excruciating [ɪks'kruːʃɪeɪtɪŋ] *adj* atroce

excursion [ɪks'kɜːʃən] *n* excursion *f*

excuse [*n* ɪks'kjuːs, *vb* ɪks'kjuːz] *n* excuse *f* ♦ *vt* excuser; **to** ~ **sb from** (*activity*) dispenser qn de; ~ **me!** excusez-moi!, pardon!; **now if you will** ~ **me**, ... maintenant, si vous (le) permettez ...

ex-directory ['eksdaɪ'rektərɪ] (BRIT) *adj* sur la liste rouge

execute ['eksɪkjuːt] *vt* exécuter

execution [eksɪ'kjuːʃən] *n* exécution *f*; ~**er** *n* bourreau *m*

executive [ɪg'zekjʊtɪv] *n* (COMM) cadre *m*; (*of organization, political party*) bureau *m* ♦ *adj* exécutif(ive)

exemplify [ɪg'zemplɪfaɪ] *vt* illustrer; (*typify*) incarner

exempt [ɪg'zempt] *adj*: ~ **from** exempté(e) *or* dispensé(e) de ♦ *vt*: **to** ~ **sb from** exempter *or* dispenser qn de

exercise ['eksəsaɪz] *n* exercice *m* ♦ *vt* exercer; (*patience etc*) faire preuve de; (*dog*) promener ♦ *vi* prendre de l'exercice; ~ **bike** *n* vélo *m* d'appartement; ~ **book** *n* cahier *m*

exert [ɪg'zɜːt] *vt* exercer, employer; **to** ~ **o.s.** se dépenser; ~**ion** [ɪg'zɜːʃən] *n* effort *m*

exhale [eks'heɪl] *vt* exhaler ♦ *vi* expirer

exhaust [ɪg'zɔːst] *n* (*also*: ~ *fumes*) gaz *mpl* d'échappement; (: ~ *pipe*) tuyau *m* d'échappement ♦ *vt* épuiser; ~**ed** *adj* épuisé(e); ~**ion** [ɪg'zɔːstʃən] *n* épuisement *m*; **nervous** ~**ion** fatigue nerveuse; surmenage mental; ~**ive** *adj* très complet(ète)

exhibit [ɪg'zɪbɪt] *n* (ART) pièce exposée, objet exposé; (LAW) pièce à conviction ♦ *vt* exposer; (*courage, skill*) faire preuve de;

~ion [eksɪ'bɪʃən] n exposition f; (of ill-temper, talent etc) démonstration f
exhilarating [ɪg'zɪləreɪtɪŋ] adj grisant(e); stimulant(e)
exile ['eksaɪl] n exil m; (person) exilé(e) ♦ vt exiler
exist [ɪg'zɪst] vi exister; **~ence** n existence f; **~ing** adj actuel(le)
exit ['eksɪt] n sortie f ♦ vi (COMPUT, THEATRE) sortir; **~ ramp** n (AUT) bretelle f d'accès
exodus ['eksədəs] n exode m
exonerate [ɪg'zɒnəreɪt] vt: **to ~ from** disculper de
exotic [ɪg'zɒtɪk] adj exotique
expand [ɪks'pænd] vt agrandir; accroître ♦ vi (trade etc) se développer, s'accroître; (gas, metal) se dilater
expanse [ɪks'pæns] n étendue f
expansion [ɪks'pænʃən] n développement m, accroissement m
expect [ɪks'pekt] vt (anticipate) s'attendre à, s'attendre à ce que +sub; (count on) compter sur, escompter; (require) demander, exiger; (suppose) supposer; (await, also baby) attendre ♦ vi: **to be ~ing** être enceinte; **~ancy** n (anticipation) attente f; **life ~ancy** espérance f de vie; **~ant mother** n future maman; **~ation** [ekspek'teɪʃən] n attente f; espérance(s) f(pl)
expedient [ɪks'piːdɪənt] adj indiqué(e), opportun(e) ♦ n expédient m
expedition [ekspɪ'dɪʃən] n expédition f
expel [ɪks'pel] vt chasser, expulser; (SCOL) renvoyer
expend [ɪks'pend] vt consacrer; (money) dépenser; **~able** adj remplaçable; **~iture** [ɪk'spendɪtʃə*] n dépense f, dépenses fpl
expense [ɪks'pens] n dépense f, frais mpl; (high cost) coût m; **~s** npl (COMM) frais mpl; **at the ~ of** aux dépens de; **~ account** n (note f de) frais mpl
expensive [ɪks'pensɪv] adj cher(chère), coûteux(euse); **to be ~** coûter cher
experience [ɪks'pɪərɪəns] n expérience f ♦ vt connaître, faire l'expérience de; (feeling) éprouver; **~d** adj expérimenté(e)
experiment [n ɪks'perɪmənt, vb ɪks'perɪment] n expérience f ♦ vi faire une expérience; **to ~ with** expérimenter
expert ['ekspɜːt] adj expert(e) ♦ n expert m; **~ise** [ekspə'tiːz] n (grande) compétence f
expire [ɪks'paɪə*] vi expirer; **expiry** n expiration f
explain [ɪks'pleɪn] vt expliquer; **explanation** [eksplə'neɪʃən] n explication f; **explanatory** [ɪks'plænətərɪ] adj explicatif(ive)
explicit [ɪks'plɪsɪt] adj explicite; (definite) formel(le)
explode [ɪks'pləʊd] vi exploser
exploit [n 'eksplɔɪt, vb ɪks'plɔɪt] n exploit m ♦ vt exploiter; **~ation** [eksplɔɪ'teɪʃən] n ex-

ploitation f
exploratory [eks'plɒrətərɪ] adj (expedition) d'exploration; (fig: talks) préliminaire; **~ operation** n (MED) sondage m
explore [ɪks'plɔː*] vt explorer; (possibilities) étudier, examiner; **~r** n explorateur(trice)
explosion [ɪks'pləʊʒən] n explosion f; **explosive** [ɪks'pləʊzɪv] adj explosif(ive) ♦ n explosif m
exponent [eks'pəʊnənt] n (of school of thought etc) interprète m, représentant m
export [vb eks'pɔːt, n 'ekspɔːt] vt exporter ♦ n exportation f ♦ cpd d'exportation; **~er** n exportateur m
expose [ɪks'pəʊz] vt exposer; (unmask) démasquer, dévoiler; **~d** [ɪks'pəʊzd] adj (position, house) exposé(e)
exposure [ɪks'pəʊʒə*] n exposition f; (publicity) couverture f; (PHOT) (temps m de) pose f; (: shot) pose; **to die from ~** (MED) mourir de froid; **~ meter** n posemètre m
express [ɪks'pres] adj (definite) formel(le), exprès(esse); (BRIT: letter etc) exprès inv ♦ n (train) rapide m; (bus) car m express ♦ vt exprimer; **~ion** [ɪks'preʃən] n expression f; **~ly** adv expressément, formellement; **~way** (US) n (urban motorway) voie f express (à plusieurs files)
exquisite [eks'kwɪzɪt] adj exquis(e)
extend [ɪks'tend] vt (visit, street) prolonger; (building) agrandir; (offer) présenter, offrir; (hand, arm) tendre ♦ vi s'étendre
extension [ɪks'tenʃən] n prolongation f; agrandissement m; (building) annexe f; (to wire, table) rallonge f; (telephone: in offices) poste m; (: in private house) téléphone m supplémentaire
extensive [ɪks'tensɪv] adj étendu(e), vaste; (damage, alterations) considérable; (inquiries) approfondi(e); **~ly** adv: **he's travelled ~ly** il a beaucoup voyagé
extent [ɪks'tent] n étendue f; **to some ~** dans une certaine mesure; **to what ~?** dans quelle mesure?, jusqu'à quel point?; **to the ~ of ...** au point de ...; **to such an ~ that ...** à tel point que ...
extenuating [eks'tenjʊeɪtɪŋ] adj: **~ circumstances** circonstances atténuantes
exterior [eks'tɪərɪə*] adj extérieur(e) ♦ n extérieur m; dehors m
external [eks'tɜːnl] adj externe
extinct [ɪks'tɪŋkt] adj éteint(e)
extinguish [ɪks'tɪŋgwɪʃ] vt éteindre; **~er** n (also: fire ~er) extincteur m
extort [ɪks'tɔːt] vt: **to ~ sth (from)** extorquer qch (à); **~ionate** [ɪks'tɔːʃənɪt] adj exorbitant(e)
extra ['ekstrə] adj supplémentaire, de plus ♦ adv (in addition) en plus ♦ n supplément m; (perk) à-côté m; (THEATRE) figurant(e) ♦ prefix extra...
extract [vb ɪks'trækt, n 'ekstrækt] vt extrai-

re; (*tooth*) arracher; (*money, promise*) soutirer ♦ n extrait m
extracurricular ['ekstrəkə'rıkjələ*] *adj* parascolaire
extradite ['ekstrədaıt] *vt* extrader
extra: ~marital [ekstrə'mærıtl] *adj* extraconjugal(e); **~mural** [ekstrə'mjʊərl] *adj* hors faculté *inv*; (*lecture*) public(que); **~ordinary** [ıks'trɔːdnrı] *adj* extraordinaire
extravagance [ıks'trævəgəns] *n* prodigalités *fpl*; (*thing bought*) folie f, dépense excessive; **extravagant** [ıks'trævəgənt] *adj* extravagant(e); (*in spending: person*) prodigue, dépensier(ère); (: *tastes*) dispendieux(euse)
extreme [ıks'triːm] *adj* extrême ♦ n extrême m; **~ly** *adv* extrêmement
extricate ['ekstrıkeıt] *vt*: **to ~ sth (from)** dégager qch (de)
extrovert ['ekstrəʊvəːt] *n* extraverti(e)
eye [aı] *n* œil m (*pl* yeux); (*of needle*) trou m, chas m ♦ vt examiner; **to keep an ~ on** surveiller; **~ball** n globe m oculaire; **~bath** (*BRIT*) n œillère f (*pour bains d'œil*); **~brow** n sourcil m; **~brow pencil** n crayon m à sourcils; **~drops** *npl* gouttes *fpl* pour les yeux; **~lash** n cil m; **~lid** n paupière f; **~liner** n eye-liner m; **~-opener** n révélation f; **~shadow** n ombre f à paupières; **~sight** n vue f; **~sore** n horreur f; **~ witness** n témoin m oculaire

— F f

F [ef] *n* (*MUS*) fa m ♦ *abbr* = Fahrenheit
fable ['feıbl] *n* fable f
fabric ['fæbrɪk] *n* tissu m
fabrication [fæbrɪ'keɪʃən] *n* (*lies*) invention(s) f(*pl*), fabulation f; (*making*) fabrication f
fabulous ['fæbjʊləs] *adj* fabuleux(euse); (*inf: super*) formidable
face [feɪs] *n* visage m, figure f; (*expression*) expression f; (*of clock*) cadran m; (*of cliff*) paroi f; (*of mountain*) face f; (*of building*) façade f ♦ vt faire face à; **~ down** (*person*) à plat ventre; (*card*) face en dessous; **to lose/save ~** perdre/sauver la face; **to make or pull a ~** faire une grimace; **in the ~ of** (*difficulties etc*) face à, devant; **on the ~ of it** à première vue; **~ to ~** face à face; **~ up to** *vt fus* faire face à, affronter; **~ cloth** (*BRIT*) n gant m de toilette; **~ cream** n crème f pour le visage; **~ lift** n

lifting m; (*of building etc*) ravalement m, retapage m; **~ powder** n poudre f de riz; **~ value** n (*of coin*) valeur nominale; **to take sth at ~ value** (*fig*) prendre qch pour argent comptant
facilities [fə'sɪlɪtɪz] *npl* installations *fpl*, équipement m; **credit ~** facilités *fpl* de paiement
facing ['feɪsɪŋ] *prep* face à, en face de
facsimile [fæk'sɪmɪlɪ] *n* (*exact replica*) facsimilé m; (*fax*) télécopie f
fact [fækt] *n* fait m; **in ~** en fait
factor ['fæktə*] *n* facteur m
factory ['fæktərɪ] *n* usine f, fabrique f
factual ['fæktjʊəl] *adj* basé(e) sur les faits
faculty ['fækltɪ] *n* faculté f; (*US: teaching staff*) corps enseignant
fad [fæd] *n* (*craze*) engouement m
fade [feɪd] *vi* se décolorer, passer; (*light, sound*) s'affaiblir; (*flower*) se faner
fag [fæg] (*BRIT: inf*) n (*cigarette*) sèche f
fail [feɪl] *vt* (*exam*) échouer à; (*candidate*) recaler; (*subj: courage, memory*) faire défaut à ♦ vi échouer; (*brakes*) lâcher; (*eyesight, health, light*) baisser, s'affaiblir; **to ~ to do sth** (*neglect*) négliger de faire qch; (*be unable*) ne pas arriver *or* parvenir à faire qch; **without ~** à coup sûr; sans faute; **~ing** n défaut m ♦ prep faute de; **~ure** n échec m; (*person*) raté(e); (*mechanical etc*) défaillance f
faint [feɪnt] *adj* faible; (*recollection*) vague; (*mark*) à peine visible ♦ n évanouissement m ♦ vi s'évanouir; **to feel ~** défaillir
fair [feə*] *adj* équitable, juste, impartial(e); (*hair*) blond(e); (*skin, complexion*) pâle, blanc(blanche); (*weather*) beau(belle); (*good enough*) assez bon(ne); (*sizeable*) considérable ♦ adv: **to play ~** jouer franc-jeu ♦ n foire f; (*BRIT: fun~*) fête (foraine); **~ly** *adv* équitablement; (*quite*) assez; **~ness** n justice f, équité f, impartialité f
fairy ['feərɪ] *n* fée f; **~ tale** n conte m de fées
faith [feɪθ] *n* foi f; (*trust*) confiance f; (*specific religion*) religion f; **~ful** *adj* fidèle; **~fully** *adv* see **yours**
fake [feɪk] *n* (*painting etc*) faux m; (*person*) imposteur m ♦ adj faux(fausse) ♦ vt simuler; (*painting*) faire un faux de
falcon ['fɔːlkən] *n* faucon m
fall [fɔːl] (*pt* fell, *pp* fallen) *n* chute f; (*US: autumn*) automne m ♦ vi tomber; (*price, temperature, dollar*) baisser; **~s** *npl* (*waterfall*) chute f d'eau, cascade f; **to ~ flat** (*on one's face*) tomber de tout son long, s'étaler; (*joke*) tomber à plat; (*plan*) échouer; **~ back** vi reculer, se retirer; **~ back on** *vt fus* se rabattre sur; **~ behind** *vi* prendre du retard; **~ down** *vi* (*person*) tomber; (*building*) s'effondrer, s'écrouler; **~ for** *vt fus* (*trick, story etc*) se laisser prendre à;

(*person*) tomber amoureux de; ~ **in** *vi* s'effondrer; (*MIL*) se mettre en rangs; ~ **off** *vi* tomber; (*diminish*) baisser, diminuer; ~ **out** *vi* (*hair, teeth*) tomber; (*MIL*) rompre les rangs; (*friends etc*) se brouiller; ~ **through** *vi* (*plan, project*) tomber à l'eau

fallacy ['fæləsɪ] *n* erreur *f*, illusion *f*

fallout ['fɔːlaut] *n* retombées (radioactives); ~ **shelter** *n* abri *m* antiatomique

fallow ['fæləu] *adj* en jachère; en friche

false [fɔːls] *adj* faux(fausse); ~ **alarm** *n* fausse alerte; ~ **pretences** *npl*: **under** ~ **pretences** sous un faux prétexte; ~ **teeth** (*BRIT*) *npl* fausses dents

falter ['fɔːltə*] *vi* chanceler, vaciller

fame [feɪm] *n* renommée *f*, renom *m*

familiar [fə'mɪlɪə*] *adj* familier(ère); **to be** ~ **with** (*subject*) connaître

family ['fæmɪlɪ] *n* famille *f* ♦ *cpd* (*business, doctor etc*) de famille; **has he any ~?** (*children*) a-t-il des enfants?

famine ['fæmɪn] *n* famine *f*

famished ['fæmɪʃt] (*inf*) *adj* affamé(e)

famous ['feɪməs] *adj* célèbre; **~ly** *adv* (*get on*) fameusement, à merveille

fan [fæn] *n* (*folding*) éventail *m*; (*ELEC*) ventilateur *m*; (*of person*) fan *m*, admirateur(trice); (*of team, sport etc*) supporter *m/f* ♦ *vt* éventer; (*fire, quarrel*) attiser; ~ **out** *vi* se déployer (en éventail)

fanatic [fə'nætɪk] *n* fanatique *m/f*

fan belt *n* courroie *f* de ventilateur

fanciful ['fænsɪful] *adj* fantaisiste

fancy ['fænsɪ] *n* fantaisie *f*, envie *f*; imagination *f* ♦ *adj* (*de*) fantaisie *inv* ♦ *vt* (*feel like, want*) avoir envie de; (*imagine, think*) imaginer; **to take a ~ to** se prendre d'affection pour; s'enticher de; **he fancies her** (*inf*) elle lui plaît; ~ **dress** *n* déguisement *m*, travesti *m*; **~-dress ball** *n* bal masqué *or* costumé

fang [fæŋ] *n* croc *m*; (*of snake*) crochet *m*

fantastic [fæn'tæstɪk] *adj* fantastique

fantasy ['fæntəzɪ] *n* imagination *f*, fantaisie *f*; (*dream*) chimère *f*

far [fɑː*] *adj* lointain(e), éloigné(e) ♦ *adv* loin; ~ **away** *or* **off** au loin, dans le lointain; **at the ~ side/end** à l'autre côté/bout; ~ **better** beaucoup mieux; ~ **from** loin de; **by** ~ de loin, de beaucoup; **go as** ~ **as the farm** allez jusqu'à la ferme; **as** ~ **as I know** pour autant que je sache; **as** ~ **as I know** pour autant que je sache; **how** ~ **is it to ...?** combien y a-t-il jusqu'à ...?; **how** ~ **have you got?** où en êtes-vous?; **~away** *adj* lointain(e); (*look*) distrait(e)

farce [fɑːs] *n* farce *f*

farcical ['fɑːsɪkəl] *adj* grotesque

fare [fɛə*] *n* (*on trains, buses*) prix *m* du billet; (*in taxi*) prix de la course; (*food*) table *f*, chère *f*; **half ~** demi-tarif; **full ~** plein tarif

Far East *n*: **the ~** l'Extrême-Orient *m*

farewell [fɛə'wel] *excl* adieu ♦ *n* adieu

farm [fɑːm] *n* ferme *f* ♦ *vt* cultiver; **~er** *n* fermier(ère); cultivateur(trice); **~hand** *n* ouvrier(ère) agricole; **~house** *n* (maison *f* de) ferme *f*; **~ing** *n* agriculture *f*; (*of animals*) élevage *m*; **~land** *n* terres cultivées; ~ **worker** *n* = **farmhand**; **~yard** *n* cour *f* de ferme

far-reaching ['fɑː'riːtʃɪŋ] *adj* d'une grande portée

fart [fɑːt] (*inf!*) *vi* péter

farther ['fɑːðə*] *adv* plus loin ♦ *adj* plus éloigné(e), plus lointain(e)

farthest ['fɑːðɪst] *superl of* **far**

fascinate ['fæsɪneɪt] *vt* fasciner; **fascinating** *adj* fascinant(e)

fascism ['fæʃɪzəm] *n* fascisme *m*

fashion ['fæʃən] *n* mode *f*; (*manner*) façon *f*, manière *f* ♦ *vt* façonner; **in** ~ à la mode; **out of** ~ démodé(e); **~able** *adj* à la mode; ~ **show** *n* défilé *m* de mannequins *or* de mode

fast [fɑːst] *adj* rapide; (*clock*): **to be** ~ avancer; (*dye, colour*) grand *or* bon teint *inv* ♦ *adv* vite, rapidement; (*stuck, held*) solidement ♦ *n* jeûne *m* ♦ *vi* jeûner; ~ **asleep** profondément endormi

fasten ['fɑːsn] *vt* attacher, fixer; (*coat*) attacher, fermer ♦ *vi* se fermer, s'attacher; **~er** *n* attache *f*; **~ing** *n* = **fastener**

fast food *n* fast food *m*, restauration *f* rapide

fastidious [fæs'tɪdɪəs] *adj* exigeant(e), difficile

fat [fæt] *adj* gros(se) ♦ *n* graisse *f*; (*on meat*) gras *m*; (*for cooking*) matière grasse

fatal ['feɪtl] *adj* (*injury etc*) mortel(le); (*mistake*) fatal(e); **~ity** [fə'tælɪtɪ] *n* (*road death etc*) victime *f*, décès *m*

fate [feɪt] *n* destin *m*; (*of person*) sort *m*; **~ful** *adj* fatidique

father ['fɑːðə*] *n* père *m*; **~-in-law** *n* beau-père *m*; **~ly** *adj* paternel(le)

fathom ['fæðəm] *n* brasse *f* (= *1828 mm*) ♦ *vt* (*mystery*) sonder, pénétrer

fatigue [fə'tiːg] *n* fatigue *f*

fatten ['fætn] *vt, vi* engraisser

fatty ['fætɪ] *adj* (*food*) gras(se) ♦ *n* (*inf*) gros(se)

fatuous ['fætjuəs] *adj* stupide

faucet ['fɔːsɪt] (*US*) *n* robinet *m*

fault [fɔːlt] *n* faute *f*; (*defect*) défaut *m*; (*GEO*) faille *f* ♦ *vt* trouver des défauts à; **it's my ~** c'est de ma faute; **to find ~ with** trouver à redire *or* à critiquer à; **at ~** fautif(ive), coupable; **~y** *adj* défectueux(euse)

fauna ['fɔːnə] *n* faune *f*

faux pas ['fəu'pɑː] *n inv* impair *m*, bévue *f*, gaffe *f*

favour ['feɪvə*] (*US* favor) *n* faveur *f*; (*help*) service *m* ♦ *vt* (*proposition*) être en faveur de; (*pupil etc*) favoriser; (*team, horse*) donner gagnant; **to do sb a ~** rendre un service à qn; **to find ~ with** trouver grâce aux yeux de; **in ~ of** en faveur de; **~able** adj favorable; **~ite** ['feɪvərɪt] adj, n favori(te)

fawn [fɔ:n] n faon m ♦ adj (also: **~-coloured**) fauve ♦ vi: **to ~ (up)on** flatter servilement

fax [fæks] n (document) télécopie f; (machine) télécopieur m ♦ vt envoyer par télécopie

FBI ['efbi:'aɪ] n abbr (US: = Federal Bureau of Investigation) F.B.I. m

fear [fɪə*] n crainte f, peur f ♦ vt craindre; **for ~ of** de peur que +sub, de peur de +infin; **~ful** adj craintif(ive); (sight, noise) affreux(euse), épouvantable; **~less** adj intrépide

feasible ['fi:zəbl] adj faisable, réalisable

feast [fi:st] n festin m, banquet m; (REL: also: **~ day**) fête f ♦ vi festoyer

feat [fi:t] n exploit m, prouesse f

feather ['feðə*] n plume f

feature ['fi:tʃə*] n caractéristique f; (article) chronique f, rubrique f ♦ vt (subj: film) avoir pour vedette(s) ♦ vi: **to ~ in** figurer (en bonne place) dans; (in film) jouer dans; **~s** npl (of face) traits mpl; **~ film** n long métrage

February ['februəri] n février m

fed [fed] pt, pp of **feed**

federal ['fedərəl] adj fédéral(e)

fed up adj: **to be ~** en avoir marre, en avoir plein le dos

fee [fi:] n rémunération f; (of doctor, lawyer) honoraires mpl; (for examination) droits mpl; **school ~s** frais mpl de scolarité

feeble ['fi:bl] adj faible; (pathetic: attempt, excuse) pauvre; (:joke) piteux(euse)

feed [fi:d] (pt, pp **fed**) n (of baby) tétée f; (of animal) fourrage m; pâture f; (on printer) mécanisme m d'alimentation ♦ vt (person) nourrir; (BRIT: baby) allaiter; (: with bottle) donner le biberon à; (horse etc) donner à manger à; (machine) alimenter; (data, information): **to ~ sth into** fournir qch à; **~ on** vt fus se nourrir de; **~back** n feed-back m inv; **~ing bottle** (BRIT) n biberon m

feel [fi:l] (pt, pp **felt**) n sensation f; (impression) impression f ♦ vt toucher; (explore) tâter, palper; (cold, pain) sentir; (grief, anger) ressentir, éprouver; (think, believe) trouver; **to ~ hungry/cold** avoir faim/froid; **to ~ lonely/better** se sentir seul/mieux; **I don't ~ well** je ne me sens pas bien; **it ~s soft** c'est doux(douce) au toucher; **to ~ like** (want) avoir envie de; **~ about** vi fouiller, tâtonner; **~er** n (of insect) antenne f; **to put out ~ers** or a **~er** tâter le terrain; **~ing** n (physical) sensation f, (emotional) sentiment m

feet [fi:t] npl of **foot**

feign [feɪn] vt feindre, simuler

fell [fel] pt of **fall** ♦ vt (tree, person) abattre

fellow ['feləʊ] n type m; (comrade) compagnon m; (of learned society) membre m ♦ cpd: **their ~ prisoners/students** leurs camarades prisonniers/d'étude; **~ citizen** n concitoyen(ne) m/f; **~ countryman** (irreg) n compatriote m; **~ men** npl semblables mpl; **~ship** n (society) association f; (comradeship) amitié f, camaraderie f; (grant) sorte de bourse universitaire

felony ['feləni] n crime m, forfait m

felt [felt] pt, pp of **feel** ♦ n feutre m; **~-tip pen** n stylo-feutre m

female ['fi:meɪl] n (ZOOL) femelle f; (pej: woman) bonne femme ♦ adj (BIO) femelle; (sex, character) féminin(e); (vote etc) des femmes

feminine ['feminin] adj féminin(e)

feminist ['feminist] n féministe m/f

fence [fens] n barrière f ♦ vt (also: **~ in**) clôturer ♦ vi faire de l'escrime; **fencing** ['fensɪŋ] n escrime m

fend [fend] vi: **to ~ for o.s.** se débrouiller (tout seul); **~ off** vt (attack etc) parer

fender ['fendə*] n garde-feu m inv; (on boat) défense f; (US: of car) aile f

ferment [vb fə'ment, n 'fɜ:ment] vi fermenter ♦ n agitation f, effervescence f

fern [fɜ:n] n fougère f

ferocious [fə'rəʊʃəs] adj féroce

ferret ['ferɪt] n furet m

ferry ['feri] n (small) bac m; (large: also: **~boat**) ferry(-boat) m ♦ vt transporter

fertile ['fɜ:taɪl] adj fertile; (BIO) fécond(e); **fertilizer** ['fɜ:tɪlaɪzə*] n engrais m

fester ['festə*] vi suppurer

festival ['festɪvəl] n (REL) fête f; (ART, MUS) festival m

festive ['festɪv] adj de fête; **the ~ season** (BRIT: Christmas) la période des fêtes; **festivities** [fes'tɪvɪtɪz] npl réjouissances fpl

festoon [fes'tu:n] vt: **to ~ with** orner de

fetch [fetʃ] vt aller chercher; (sell for) rapporter

fetching ['fetʃɪŋ] adj charmant(e)

fête [feɪt] n fête f, kermesse f

fetish ['fetɪʃ] n: **to make a ~ of** être obsédé(e) par

feud [fju:d] n dispute f, dissension f

fever ['fi:və*] n fièvre f; **~ish** adj fiévreux(euse), fébrile

few [fju:] adj (not many) peu de; **a ~** adj quelques ♦ pron quelques-uns(unes); **~er** adj moins de; moins (nombreux); **~est** adj le moins (de)

fiancé, e [fɪ'ã:nseɪ] n fiancé(e) m/f

fib [fɪb] n bobard m

fibre ['faɪbə*] (US fiber) n fibre f; **~-glass** (®) n fibre de verre

fickle ['fɪkl] adj inconstant(e), volage, capricieux(euse)

fiction ['fɪkʃən] n romans mpl, littérature f

romanesque; (*invention*) fiction *f*; ~**al** *adj* fictif(ive)

fictitious [fɪk'tɪʃəs] *adj* fictif(ive), imaginaire

fiddle ['fɪdl] *n* (*MUS*) violon *m*; (*cheating*) combine *f*; escroquerie *f* ♦ *vt* (*BRIT: accounts*) falsifier, maquiller; ~ **with** *vt fus* tripoter

fidget ['fɪdʒɪt] *vi* se trémousser, remuer

field [fiːld] *n* champ *m*; (*fig*) domaine *m*, champ; (*SPORT: ground*) terrain *m*; ~ **marshal** *n* maréchal *m*; ~**work** *n* travaux *mpl* pratiques (sur le terrain)

fiend [fiːnd] *n* démon *m*; ~**ish** *adj* diabolique, abominable

fierce [fɪəs] *adj* (*look, animal*) féroce, sauvage; (*wind, attack, person*) (très) violent(e); (*fighting, enemy*) acharné(e)

fiery ['faɪərɪ] *adj* ardent(e), brûlant(e); (*temperament*) fougueux(euse)

fifteen [fɪf'tiːn] *num* quinze

fifth [fɪfθ] *num* cinquième

fifty ['fɪftɪ] *num* cinquante; ~-**fifty** *adj*: a ~-**fifty chance** *etc* une chance *etc* sur deux ♦ *adv* moitié-moitié

fig [fɪg] *n* figue *f*

fight [faɪt] *n* (*pt, pp* **fought**) *n* (*MIL*) combat *m*; (*between persons*) bagarre *f*; (*against cancer etc*) lutte *f* ♦ *vt* se battre contre; (*cancer, alcoholism, emotion*) combattre, lutter contre; (*election*) se présenter à ♦ *vi* se battre; ~**er** *n* (*fig*) lutteur *m*; (*plane*) chasseur *m*; ~**ing** *n* combats *mpl* (*brawl*) bagarres *fpl*

figment ['fɪgmənt] *n*: **a** ~ **of the imagination** une invention

figurative ['fɪgərətɪv] *adj* figuré(e)

figure ['fɪgə*] *n* figure *f*; (*number, cipher*) chiffre *m*; (*body, outline*) silhouette *f*; (*shape*) ligne *f*, formes *fpl* ♦ *vt* (*think: esp US*) supposer ♦ *vi* (*appear*) figurer; ~ **out** *vt* (*work out*) calculer; ~**head** *n* (*NAUT*) figure *f* de proue; (*pej*) prête-nom *m*; ~ **of speech** *n* figure *f* de rhétorique

file [faɪl] *n* (*dossier*) dossier *m*; (*folder*) dossier, chemise *f*; (: *with hinges*) classeur *m*; (*COMPUT*) fichier *m*; (*row*) file *f*; (*tool*) lime *f* ♦ *vt* (*nails, wood*) limer; (*papers*) classer; (*LAW: claim*) faire enregistrer; déposer ♦ *vi*: **to** ~ **in/out** entrer/sortir l'un derrière l'autre; **to** ~ **for divorce** faire une demande en divorce; **filing cabinet** *n* classeur *m* (*meuble*)

fill [fɪl] *vt* remplir; (*need*) répondre à ♦ *n*: **to eat one's** ~ manger à sa faim; **to** ~ **with** remplir de; ~ **in** *vt* (*hole*) boucher; (*form*) remplir; ~ **up** *vt* remplir; ~ **it up, please** (*AUT*) le plein, s'il vous plaît

fillet ['fɪlɪt] *n* filet *m*; ~ **steak** *n* filet *m* de bœuf, tournedos *m*

filling ['fɪlɪŋ] *n* (*CULIN*) garniture *f*, farce *f*; (*for tooth*) plombage *m*; ~ **station** *n* station-service *f*

film [fɪlm] *n* film *m*; (*PHOT*) pellicule *f*, film; (*of powder, liquid*) couche *f*, pellicule ♦ *vt* (*scene*) filmer ♦ *vi* tourner; ~ **star** *n* vedette *f* de cinéma

filter ['fɪltə*] *n* filtre *m* ♦ *vt* filtrer; ~ **lane** *n* (*AUT*) voie *f* de sortie; ~-**tipped** *adj* à bout filtre

filth [fɪlθ] *n* saleté *f*; ~**y** *adj* sale, dégoûtant(e); (*language*) ordurier(ère)

fin [fɪn] *n* (*of fish*) nageoire *f*

final ['faɪnl] *adj* final(e); (*definitive*) définitif(ive) ♦ *n* (*SPORT*) finale *f*; ~**s** *npl* (*SCOL*) examens *mpl* de dernière année; ~**e** [fɪ'nɑːlɪ] *n* finale *m*; ~**ize** *vt* mettre au point; ~**ly** *adv* (*eventually*) enfin, finalement; (*lastly*) en dernier lieu

finance [faɪ'næns] *n* finance *f* ♦ *vt* financer; ~**s** *npl* (*financial position*) finances *fpl*; **financial** [faɪ'nænʃəl] *adj* financier(ère)

find [faɪnd] (*pt, pp* **found**) *vt* trouver; (*lost object*) retrouver ♦ *n* trouvaille *f*, découverte *f*; **to** ~ **sb guilty** (*LAW*) déclarer qn coupable; ~ **out** *vt* (*truth, secret*) découvrir; (*person*) démasquer ♦ *vi*: **to** ~ **out about** (*make enquiries*) se renseigner; (*by chance*) apprendre; ~**ings** *npl* (*LAW*) conclusions *fpl*, verdict *m*; (*of report*) conclusions

fine [faɪn] *adj* (*excellent*) excellent(e); (*thin, not coarse, subtle*) fin(e); (*weather*) beau(belle) ♦ *adv* (*well*) très bien ♦ *n* (*LAW*) amende *f*; contravention *f* ♦ *vt* (*LAW*) condamner à une amende; donner une contravention à; **to be** ~ (*person*) aller bien; (*weather*) être beau; ~ **arts** *npl* beaux-arts *mpl*

finery ['faɪnərɪ] *n* parure *f*

finger ['fɪŋgə*] *n* doigt *m* ♦ *vt* palper, toucher; **little** ~ auriculaire *m*, petit doigt; **index** ~ index *m*; ~**nail** *n* ongle *m* (de la main); ~**print** *n* empreinte digitale; ~**tip** *n* bout *m* du doigt

finicky ['fɪnɪkɪ] *adj* tatillon(ne), méticuleux(euse); minutieux(euse)

finish ['fɪnɪʃ] *n* fin *f*; (*SPORT*) arrivée *f*; (*polish etc*) finition *f* ♦ *vt* finir, terminer ♦ *vi* finir, se terminer; **to** ~ **doing sth** finir de faire qch; **to** ~ **third** arriver or terminer troisième; ~ **off** *vt* finir, terminer; (*kill*) achever; ~ **up** *vi, vt* finir; ~**ing line** *n* ligne *f* d'arrivée; ~**ing school** *n* institution privée (*pour jeunes filles*)

finite ['faɪnaɪt] *adj* fini(e); (*verb*) conjugué(e)

Finland ['fɪnlənd] *n* Finlande *f*

Finn [fɪn] *n* Finnois(e); Finlandais(e); ~**ish** *adj* finnois(e), finlandais(e) ♦ *n* (*LING*) finnois *m*

fir [fɜː*] *n* sapin *m*

fire [faɪə*] *n* feu *m*; (*accidental*) incendie *m*; (*heater*) radiateur *m* ♦ *vt* (*discharge*): **to** ~ **a gun** tirer un coup de feu; (*fig*) enflammer, animer; (*inf*: *dismiss*) mettre à la porte, renvoyer ♦ *vi* (*shoot*) tirer, faire feu; **on ~ en feu**; ~ **alarm** *n* avertisseur *m* d'incendie; ~**arm** *n* arme *f* à feu; ~ **brigade** *n* (sapeurs-)pompiers *mpl*; ~ **department** (*US*) *n* = **fire brigade**; ~ **engine** *n* (*vehicle*) voiture *f* des pompiers; ~ **escape** *n* escalier *m* de secours; ~ **extinguisher** *n* extincteur *m*; ~**man** *n* pompier *m*; ~**place** *n* cheminée *f*; ~**side** *n* foyer *m*, coin du feu; ~ **station** *n* caserne *f* de pompiers; ~**wood** *n* bois *m* de chauffage; ~**works** *npl* feux *mpl* d'artifice; (*display*) feu(x) d'artifice

firing squad ['faɪərɪŋ-] *n* peloton *m* d'exécution

firm [fɜːm] *adj* ferme ♦ *n* compagnie *f*, firme *f*

first [fɜːst] *adj* premier(ère) ♦ *adv* (*before all others*) le premier, la première; (*before all other things*) en premier, d'abord; (*when listing reasons etc*) en premier lieu, premièrement ♦ *n* (*person*: *in race*) premier(ère); (*BRIT*: *SCOL*) mention *f* très bien; (*AUT*) première *f*; **at ~** au commencement, au début; ~ **of all** tout d'abord, pour commencer; ~ **aid** *n* premiers secours or soins; ~**-aid kit** *n* trousse *f* à pharmacie; ~**-class** *adj* de première classe; (*excellent*) excellent(e), exceptionnel(le); ~**-hand** *adj* de première main; ~ **lady** (*US*) *n* femme *f* du président; ~**ly** *adv* premièrement, en premier lieu; ~ **name** *n* prénom *m*; ~**-rate** *adj* excellent(e)

fish [fɪʃ] *n inv* poisson *m* ♦ *vt*, *vi* pêcher; **to go ~ing** aller à la pêche; ~**erman** *n* pêcheur *m*; ~ **farm** *n* établissement *m* piscicole; ~ **fingers** (*BRIT*) *npl* bâtonnets de poisson (congelés); ~**ing boat** *n* barque *f* or bateau *m* de pêche; ~**ing line** *n* ligne *f* (de pêche); ~**ing rod** *n* canne *f* à pêche; ~**monger's (shop)** *n* poissonnerie *f*; ~ **sticks** (*US*) *npl* = **fish fingers**; ~**y** (*inf*) *adj* suspect(e), louche

fist [fɪst] *n* poing *m*

fit [fɪt] *adj* (*healthy*) en bonne forme; (*proper*) convenable; approprié(e) ♦ *vt* (*subj*: *clothes*) aller à; (*put in, attach*) installer, poser; adapter; (*equip*) équiper, garnir, munir; (*suit*) convenir à ♦ *vi* (*clothes*) aller; (*parts*) s'adapter; (*in space, gap*) entrer, s'adapter ♦ *n* (*MED*) accès *m*, crise *f*; (*of anger*) accès; (*of hysterics, jealousy*) crise; ~ **to** en état de; ~ **for** digne de; apte à; ~ **of coughing** quinte *f* de toux; **a ~ of giggles** le fou rire; **this dress is a good ~** cette robe (me) va très bien; **by ~s and starts** par à-coups; ~ **in** *vi* s'accorder; s'adapter; ~**ful** *adj* (*sleep*) agité(e); ~**ment** *n* meuble encastré, élément *m*; ~**ness** *n* (*MED*) forme *f* physique; ~**ted carpet** *n* moquette *f*, tapis *m*; ~**ted kitchen** (*BRIT*) *n* cuisine équipée; ~**ter** *n* monteur

m; ~**ting** *adj* approprié(e) ♦ *n* (*of dress*) essayage *m*; (*of piece of equipment*) pose *f*, installation *f*; ~**tings** *npl* (*in building*) installations *fpl*; ~**ting room** *n* cabine *f* d'essayage

five [faɪv] *num* cinq; ~**r** (*BRIT*) *n* billet *m* de cinq livres; (*US*) billet de cinq dollars

fix [fɪks] *vt* (*date, amount etc*) fixer; (*organize*) arranger; (*mend*) réparer; (*meal, drink*) préparer ♦ *n*: **to be in a ~** être dans le pétrin; ~ **up** *vt* (*meeting*) arranger; **to ~ sb up with sth** faire avoir qch à qn; ~**ation** [fɪk'seɪʃən] *n* (*PSYCH*) fixation *f*; (*fig*) obsession *f*; ~**ed** [fɪkst] *adj* (*prices etc*) fixe; (*smile*) figé(e); ~**ture** ['fɪkstʃə*] *n* installation *f* (fixe); (*SPORT*) rencontre *f* (au programme)

fizzle ['fɪzl-] *vi*: ~ **out** *vi* (*interest*) s'estomper; (*strike, film*) se terminer en queue de poisson

fizzy ['fɪzɪ] *adj* pétillant(e); gazeux(euse)

flabbergasted ['flæbəgɑːstɪd] *adj* sidéré(e), ahuri(e)

flabby ['flæbɪ] *adj* mou(molle)

flag [flæg] *n* drapeau *m*; (*also*: ~**stone**) dalle *f* ♦ *vi* faiblir; fléchir; ~ **down** *vt* héler, faire signe (de s'arrêter) à; ~**pole** ['flægpəul] *n* mât *m*; ~**ship** *n* vaisseau *m* amiral; (*fig*) produit *m* vedette

flair [flɛə*] *n* flair *m*

flak [flæk] *n* (*MIL*) tir antiaérien; (*inf*: *criticism*) critiques *fpl*

flake [fleɪk] *n* (*of rust, paint*) écaille *f*; (*of snow, soap powder*) flocon *m* ♦ *vi* (*also*: ~ **off**) s'écailler

flamboyant [flæm'bɔɪənt] *adj* flamboyant(e), éclatant(e); (*person*) haut(e) en couleur

flame [fleɪm] *n* flamme *f*

flamingo [flə'mɪŋgəu] *n* flamant *m* (rose)

flammable ['flæməbl] *adj* inflammable

flan [flæn] (*BRIT*) *n* tarte *f*

flank [flæŋk] *n* flanc *m* ♦ *vt* flanquer

flannel ['flænl] *n* (*fabric*) flanelle *f*; (*BRIT*: *also*: *face* ~) gant *m* de toilette; ~**s** *npl* (*trousers*) pantalon *m* de flanelle

flap [flæp] *n* (*of pocket, envelope*) rabat *m* ♦ *vt* (*wings*) battre (de) ♦ *vi* (*sail, flag*) claquer; (*inf*: *also*: **be in a ~**) paniquer

flare [flɛə*] *n* (*signal*) signal lumineux; (*in skirt etc*) évasement *m*; ~ **up** *vi* s'embraser; (*fig*: *person*) se mettre en colère, s'emporter; (*: revolt etc*) éclater

flash [flæʃ] *n* éclair *m*; (*also*: *news* ~) flash *m* (d'information); (*PHOT*) flash *m* ♦ *vt* (*light*) projeter; (*send*: *message*) câbler; (*look*) jeter; (*smile*) lancer ♦ *vi* (*light*) clignoter; **a ~ of lightning** un éclair; **in a ~** en un clin d'œil; **to ~ one's headlights** faire un appel de phares; **to ~ by** or **past** (*person*) passer comme un éclair (devant); ~**bulb** *n* ampoule *f* de flash; ~**cube** *n* cube-flash *m*; ~**light** *n* lampe *f* de poche

flashy ['flæʃɪ] (*pej*) *adj* tape-à-l'œil *inv*, tapageur(euse)

flask [flɑːsk] *n* flacon *m*, bouteille *f*; (**vacuum**) ~ thermos *m* or *f* ®

flat [flæt] *adj* plat(e); (*tyre*) dégonflé(e), à plat; (*beer*) éventé(e); (*denial*) catégorique; (*MUS*) bémol *inv*; (: *voice*) faux(fausse); (*fee, rate*) fixe ♦ *n* (*BRIT: apartment*) appartement *m*; (*AUT*) crevaison *f*; (*MUS*) bémol *m*; **to work ~ out** travailler d'arrache-pied; **~ly** *adv* catégoriquement; **~ten** *vt* (*also*: **~ten out**) aplatir; (*crop*) coucher; (*building(s)*) raser

flatter ['flætə*] *vt* flatter; **~ing** *adj* flatteur(euse); **~y** *n* flatterie *f*

flaunt [flɔːnt] *vt* faire étalage de

flavour ['fleɪvə*] (*US* **flavor**) *n* goût *m*, saveur *f*; (*of ice cream etc*) parfum *m* ♦ *vt* parfumer; **vanilla-flavoured** à l'arôme de vanille, à la vanille; **~ing** *n* arôme *m*

flaw [flɔː] *n* défaut *m*; **~less** *adj* sans défaut

flax [flæks] *n* lin *m*; **~en** *adj* blond(e)

flea [fliː] *n* puce *f*

fleck [flek] *n* tacheture *f*, moucheture *f*

flee [fliː] (*pt, pp* **fled**) *vt* fuir ♦ *vi* fuir, s'enfuir

fleece [fliːs] *n* toison *f* ♦ *vt* (*inf*) voler, filouter

fleet [fliːt] *n* flotte *f*; (*of lorries etc*) parc *m*, convoi *m*

fleeting ['fliːtɪŋ] *adj* fugace, fugitif(ive); (*visit*) très bref(brève)

Flemish ['flemɪʃ] *adj* flamand(e)

flesh [fleʃ] *n* chair *f*; ~ **wound** *n* blessure superficielle

flew [fluː] *pt of* **fly**

flex [fleks] *n* fil *m* or câble *m* électrique ♦ *vt* (*knee*) fléchir; (*muscles*) tendre

flexible *adj* flexible

flick [flɪk] *n* petite tape; chiquenaude *f*; (*of duster*) petit coup ♦ *vt* donner un petit coup à; (*switch*) appuyer sur; ~ **through** *vt fus* feuilleter

flicker ['flɪkə*] *vi* (*light*) vaciller; **his eyelids ~ed** il a cillé

flier ['flaɪə*] *n* aviateur *m*

flight [flaɪt] *n* vol *m*; (*escape*) fuite *f*; (*also*: ~ **of steps**) escalier *m*; ~ **attendant** (*US*) *n* steward *m*, hôtesse *f* de l'air; ~ **deck** *n* (*AVIAT*) poste *m* de pilotage; (*NAUT*) pont *m* d'envol

flimsy ['flɪmzɪ] *adj* peu solide; (*clothes*) trop léger(ère); (*excuse*) pauvre, mince

flinch [flɪntʃ] *vi* tressaillir; **to ~ from** se dérober à, reculer devant

fling [flɪŋ] (*pt, pp* **flung**) *vt* jeter, lancer

flint [flɪnt] *n* silex *m*; (*in lighter*) pierre *f* (à briquet)

flip [flɪp] *vt* (*throw*) lancer (d'une chiquenaude); **to ~ a coin** jouer à pile ou face; **to ~ sth over** retourner qch

flippant ['flɪpənt] *adj* désinvolte, irrévérencieux(euse)

flipper ['flɪpə*] *n* (*of seal etc*) nageoire *f*; (*for swimming*) palme *f*

flirt [flɜːt] *vi* flirter ♦ *n* flirteur(euse) *m/f*

flit [flɪt] *vi* voleter

float [fləut] *n* flotteur *m*; (*in procession*) char *m*; (*money*) réserve *f* ♦ *vi* flotter

flock [flɒk] *n* troupeau *m*; (*of birds*) vol *m*; (*REL*) ouailles *fpl* ♦ *vi*: **to ~ to** se rendre en masse à

flog [flɒg] *vt* fouetter

flood [flʌd] *n* inondation *f*; (*of letters, refugees etc*) flot *m* ♦ *vt* inonder ♦ *vi* (*people*): **to ~ into** envahir; **~ing** *n* inondation *f*; **~light** *n* projecteur *m*

floor [flɔː*] *n* sol *m*; (*storey*) étage *m*; (*of sea, valley*) fond *m* ♦ *vt* (*subj: question*) déconcentrer; (: *blow*) terrasser; **on the ~** par terre; **ground ~**, (*US*) **first ~** rez-de-chaussée *m inv*; **first ~**, (*US*) **second ~** premier étage; **~board** *n* planche *f* (*du plancher*); ~ **show** *n* spectacle *m* de variétés

flop [flɒp] *n* fiasco *m* ♦ *vi* être un fiasco; (*fall: into chair*) s'affaler, s'effondrer

floppy ['flɒpɪ] *adj* lâche, flottant(e); ~ (**disk**) *n* (*COMPUT*) disquette *f*

flora ['flɔːrə] *n* flore *f*

floral ['flɔːrəl] *adj* (*dress*) à fleurs

florid ['flɒrɪd] *adj* (*complexion*) coloré(e); (*style*) plein(e) de fioritures

florist ['flɒrɪst] *n* fleuriste *m/f*

flounce [flauns] *n*: **to ~ out** sortir dans un mouvement d'humeur

flounder ['flaundə*] *vi* patauger ♦ *n* (*ZOOL*) flet *m*

flour ['flauə*] *n* farine *f*

flourish ['flʌrɪʃ] *vi* prospérer ♦ *n* (*gesture*) moulinet *m*

flout [flaut] *vt* se moquer de, faire fi de

flow [fləu] *n* (*ELEC, of river*) courant *m*; (*of blood in veins*) circulation *f*; (*of tide*) flux *m*; (*of orders, data*) flot *m* ♦ *vi* couler; (*traffic*) s'écouler; (*robes, hair*) flotter; **the ~ of traffic** l'écoulement *m* de la circulation; ~ **chart** *n* organigramme *m*

flower ['flauə*] *n* fleur *f* ♦ *vi* fleurir; ~ **bed** *n* plate-bande *f*; **~pot** *n* pot *m* (de fleurs); **~y** *adj* fleuri(e)

flown [fləun] *pp of* **fly**

flu [fluː] *n* grippe *f*

fluctuate ['flʌktjueɪt] *vi* varier, fluctuer

fluent ['fluːənt] *adj* (*speech*) coulant(e), aisé(e); **he speaks ~ French, he's ~ in French** il parle couramment le français

fluff [flʌf] *n* duvet *m*; (*on jacket, carpet*) peluche *f*; **~y** *adj* duveteux(euse); (*toy*) en peluche

fluid ['fluːɪd] *adj* fluide ♦ *n* fluide *m*

fluke [fluːk] (*inf*) *n* (*luck*) coup *m* de veine

flung [flʌŋ] *pt, pp of* **fling**

fluoride ['flʊəraɪd] n fluorure f; ~ **toothpaste** n dentifrice m au fluor

flurry ['flʌrɪ] n (of snow) rafale f, bourrasque f; ~ **of activity/excitement** affairement m/excitation f soudain(e)

flush [flʌʃ] n (on face) rougeur f; (fig: of youth, beauty etc) éclat m ♦ vt nettoyer à grande eau ♦ vi rougir ♦ adj: ~ **with** au ras de, de niveau avec; **to ~ the toilet** tirer la chasse (d'eau); ~ **out** vt (game, birds) débusquer; ~**ed** adj (tout(e)) rouge

flustered ['flʌstəd] adj énervé(e)

flute [fluːt] n flûte f

flutter ['flʌtə*] n (of panic, excitement) agitation f; (of wings) battement m ♦ vi (bird) battre des ailes, voleter

flux [flʌks] n: **in a state of ~** fluctuant sans cesse

fly [flaɪ] (pt **flew**, pp **flown**) n (insect) mouche f; (on trousers: also: **flies**) braguette f ♦ vt piloter; (passengers, cargo) transporter (par avion); (distances) parcourir ♦ vi voler; (passengers) aller en avion; (escape) s'enfuir, fuir; (flag) se déployer; ~ **away** vi (bird, insect) s'envoler; ~ **off** vi = **fly away**; ~**ing** n (activity) aviation f; (action) vol m ♦ adj: **a ~ing visit** une visite éclair; **with ~ing colours** haut la main; ~**ing saucer** n soucoupe volante; ~**ing start** n: **to get off to a ~ing start** prendre un excellent départ; ~**over** (BRIT) n (bridge) saut-de-mouton m; ~**sheet** n (for tent) double toit m

foal [fəʊl] n poulain m

foam [fəʊm] n écume f; (on beer) mousse f; (also: ~ **rubber**) caoutchouc m mousse ♦ vi (liquid) écumer; (soapy water) mousser

fob [fɒb] vt: **to ~ sb off** se débarrasser de qn

focal point ['fəʊkəl-] n (fig) point central

focus ['fəʊkəs] (pl ~**es**) n foyer m; (of interest) centre m ♦ vt (field glasses etc) mettre au point ♦ vi: **to ~ (on)** (with camera) régler la mise au point (sur); (person) fixer son regard (sur); **out of/in ~** (picture) flou(e)/net(te); (camera) pas au point/au point

fodder ['fɒdə*] n fourrage m

foe [fəʊ] n ennemi m

fog [fɒg] n brouillard m; ~**gy** adj: **it's ~gy** il y a du brouillard; ~ **lamp** n (AUT) phare m antibrouillard; ~ **light** (US) n = **fog lamp**

foil [fɔɪl] vt déjouer, contrecarrer ♦ n feuille f de métal; (kitchen ~) papier m d'alu(minium); (complement) repoussoir m; (FENCING) fleuret m

fold [fəʊld] n (bend, crease) pli m; (AGR) parc m à moutons; (fig) bercail m ♦ vt plier; (arms) croiser; ~ **up** vi (map, table etc) se plier; (business) fermer boutique ♦ vt (map, clothes) plier; ~**er** n (for papers)

chemise f; (: with hinges) classeur m; ~**ing** adj (chair, bed) pliant(e)

foliage ['fəʊlɪɪdʒ] n feuillage m

folk [fəʊk] npl gens mpl ♦ cpd folklorique; ~**s** npl (parents) parents mpl; ~**lore** ['fəʊklɔː*] n folklore m; ~ **song** n chanson f folklorique

follow ['fɒləʊ] vt suivre ♦ vi suivre; (result) s'ensuivre; **to ~ suit** (fig) faire de même; ~ **up** vt (letter, offer) donner suite à; (case) suivre; ~**er** n disciple m/f, partisan(e); ~**ing** adj suivant(e) ♦ n partisans mpl, disciples mpl

folly ['fɒlɪ] n inconscience f; folie f

fond [fɒnd] adj (memory, look) tendre; (hopes, dreams) un peu fou(folle); **to be ~ of** aimer beaucoup

fondle ['fɒndl] vt caresser

font [fɒnt] n (in church: for baptism) fonts baptismaux; (TYP) fonte f

food [fuːd] n nourriture f; ~ **mixer** n mixer m; ~ **poisoning** n intoxication f alimentaire; ~ **processor** n robot m de cuisine; ~**stuffs** npl denrées fpl alimentaires

fool [fuːl] n idiot(e); (CULIN) mousse f de fruits ♦ vt berner, duper ♦ vi faire l'idiot or l'imbécile; ~**hardy** adj téméraire, imprudent(e); ~**ish** adj idiot(e), stupide; (rash) imprudent(e); insensé; ~**proof** adj (plan etc) infaillible

foot [fʊt] (pl **feet**) n pied m; (of animal) patte f; (measure) pied (= 30,48 cm; 12 inches) ♦ vt (bill) payer; **on ~** à pied; ~**age** n (CINEMA: length) ≈ métrage m; (: material) séquences fpl; ~**ball** n ballon m (de football); (sport: BRIT) football m, foot m; (: US) football américain; ~**ball player** (BRIT) n (also: **footballer**) joueur m de football; ~**brake** n frein m à pédale; ~**bridge** n passerelle f; ~**hills** npl contreforts mpl; ~**hold** n prise f (de pied); ~**ing** n (fig) position f; **to lose one's ~ing** perdre pied; ~**lights** npl rampe f; ~**man** (irreg) n valet m de pied; ~**note** n note f (en bas de page); ~**path** n sentier m; (in street) trottoir m; ~**print** n trace f (de pas); ~**step** n pas m; ~**wear** n chaussure(s) f(pl)

─────────── *KEYWORD*

for [fɔː*] prep **1** (indicating destination, intention, purpose) pour; **the train ~ London** le train pour or (à destination) de Londres; **he went ~ the paper** il est allé chercher le journal; **it's time ~ lunch** c'est l'heure du déjeuner; **what's it ~?** ça sert à quoi?; **what ~?** (why) pourquoi?

2 (on behalf of, representing) pour; **the MP ~ Hove** le député de Hove; **to work ~ sb/sth** travailler pour qn/qch; **G ~ George** G comme Georges

3 (because of) pour; ~ **this reason** pour cette raison; ~ **fear of being criticized** de

peur d'être critiqué
4 (*with regard to*) pour; **it's cold ~ July** il fait froid pour juillet; **a gift ~ languages** un don pour les langues
5 (*in exchange for*): **I sold it ~ £5** je l'ai vendu 5 livres; **to pay 50 pence ~ a ticket** payer un billet 50 pence
6 (*in favour of*) pour; **are you ~ or against us?** êtes-vous pour ou contre nous?
7 (*referring to distance*) pendant, sur; **there are roadworks ~ 5 km** il y a des travaux sur 5 km; **we walked ~ miles** nous avons marché pendant des kilomètres
8 (*referring to time*) pendant; depuis; pour; **he was away ~ 2 years** il a été absent pendant 2 ans; **she will be away ~ a month** elle sera absente (pendant) un mois; **I have known her ~ years** je la connais depuis des années; **can you do it ~ tomorrow?** est-ce que tu peux le faire pour demain?
9 (*with infinitive clauses*): **it is not ~ me to decide** ce n'est pas à moi de décider; **it would be best ~ you to leave** le mieux serait que vous partiez; **there is still time ~ you to do it** vous avez encore le temps de le faire; **~ this to be possible ...** pour que cela soit possible ...
10 (*in spite of*): **~ all his work/efforts** malgré tout son travail/tous ses efforts; **~ all his complaints, he's very fond of her** il a beau se plaindre, il l'aime beaucoup
♦ *conj* (*since, as: rather formal*) car

forage ['fɒrɪdʒ] *vi* fourrager
foray ['fɒreɪ] *n* incursion *f*
forbid [fə'bɪd] (*pt* **forbad(e)**, *pp* **forbidden**) *vt* défendre, interdire; **to ~ sb to do sth** défendre *or* interdire à qn de faire; **~ding** *adj* sévère, sombre
force [fɔːs] *n* force *f* ♦ *vt* forcer; (*push*) pousser (de force); **the F~s** *npl* (*MIL*) l'armée *f*; **in ~** en vigueur; **~-feed** *vt* nourrir de force; **~ful** *adj* énergique, volontaire
forcibly ['fɔːsəblɪ] *adv* par la force, de force; (*express*) énergiquement
ford [fɔːd] *n* gué *m*
fore [fɔː*] *n*: **to come to the ~** se faire remarquer
fore: **~arm** ['fɔːrɑːm] *n* avant-bras *m inv*; **~boding** [fɔː'bəʊdɪŋ] *n* pressentiment *m* (néfaste); **~cast** ['fɔːkɑːst] (*irreg: like* **cast**) *n* prévision *f* ♦ *vt* prévoir; **~court** ['fɔːkɔːt] *n* (*of garage*) devant *m*; **~fathers** ['fɔːfɑːðəz] *npl* ancêtres *mpl*; **~finger** ['fɔːfɪŋgə*] *n* index *m*
forefront ['fɔːfrʌnt] *n*: **in the ~ of** au premier rang *or* plan de
forego [fɔː'gəʊ] (*irreg: like* **go**) *vt* renoncer à; **~ne** ['fɔːgɒn] *adj*: **it's a ~ne conclusion** c'est couru d'avance
foreground ['fɔːgraʊnd] *n* premier plan

forehead ['fɒrɪd] *n* front *m*
foreign ['fɒrɪn] *adj* étranger(ère); (*trade*) extérieur(e); **~er** *n* étranger(ère); **~ exchange** *n* change *m*; **F~ Office** (*BRIT*) *n* ministère *m* des affaires étrangères; **F~ Secretary** (*BRIT*) *n* ministre *m* des affaires étrangères
foreleg ['fɔːleg] *n* (*cat, dog*) patte *f* de devant; (*horse*) jambe antérieure
foreman ['fɔːmən] (*irreg*) *n* (*factory, building site*) contremaître *m*, chef *m* d'équipe
foremost ['fɔːməʊst] *adj* le(la) plus en vue; premier(ère) ♦ *adv*: **first and ~** avant tout, tout d'abord
forensic [fə'rɛnsɪk] *adj*: **~ medicine** médecine légale; **~ scientist** *n* médecin *m* légiste
forerunner ['fɔːrʌnə*] *n* précurseur *m*
foresee [fɔː'siː] (*irreg: like* **see**) *vt* prévoir; **~able** *adj* prévisible
foreshadow [fɔː'ʃædəʊ] *vt* présager, annoncer, laisser prévoir
foresight ['fɔːsaɪt] *n* prévoyance *f*
forest ['fɒrɪst] *n* forêt *f*
forestall [fɔː'stɔːl] *vt* devancer
forestry ['fɒrɪstrɪ] *n* sylviculture *f*
foretaste ['fɔːteɪst] *n* avant-goût *m*
foretell [fɔː'tel] (*irreg: like* **tell**) *vt* prédire
foretold [fɔː'təʊld] *pt, pp of* **foretell**
forever [fə'rɛvə*] *adv* pour toujours; (*fig*) continuellement
forewent [fɔː'went] *pt of* **forego**
foreword ['fɔːwɜːd] *n* avant-propos *m inv*
forfeit ['fɔːfɪt] *vt* (*lose*) perdre
forgave [fə'geɪv] *pt of* **forgive**
forge [fɔːdʒ] *n* forge *f* ♦ *vt* (*signature*) contrefaire; (*wrought iron*) forger; **to ~ money** (*BRIT*) fabriquer de la fausse monnaie; **~ ahead** *vi* pousser de l'avant, prendre de l'avance; **~r** *n* faussaire *m*; **~ry** *n* faux *m*, contrefaçon *f*
forget [fə'get] (*pt* **forgot**, *pp* **forgotten**) *vt, vi* oublier; **~ful** *adj* distrait(e), étourdi(e); **~-me-not** *n* myosotis *m*
forgive [fə'gɪv] (*pt* **forgave**, *pp* **forgiven**) *vt* pardonner; **to ~ sb for sth/for doing sth** pardonner qch à qn/à qn de faire qch; **~ness** *n* pardon *m*
forgo [fɔː'gəʊ] (*pt* **forwent**, *pp* **forgone**) *vt* = **forego**
fork [fɔːk] *n* (*for eating*) fourchette *f*; (*for gardening*) fourche *f*; (*of roads*) bifurcation *f*; (*of railways*) embranchement *m* ♦ *vi* (*road*) bifurquer; **~ out** *vt* (*inf*) allonger; **~-lift truck** *n* chariot élévateur
forlorn [fə'lɔːn] *adj* (*deserted*) abandonné(e); (*attempt, hope*) désespéré(e)
form [fɔːm] *n* forme *f*; (*SCOL*) classe *f*; (*questionnaire*) formulaire *m* ♦ *vt* former; (*habit*) contracter; **in top ~** en pleine forme
formal ['fɔːməl] *adj* (*offer, receipt*) en bonne et due forme; (*person*) cérémonieux(euse);

(*dinner*) officiel(le); (*clothes*) de soirée; (*garden*) à la française; (*education*) à proprement parler; ~**ly** *adv* officiellement; cérémonieusement

format ['fɔːmæt] *n* format *m* ♦ *vt* (COMPUT) formater

formative ['fɔːmətɪv] *adj*: ~ **years** années *fpl* d'apprentissage or de formation

former ['fɔːmə*] *adj* ancien(ne) (*before n*), précédent(e); **the** ~ ... **the latter** le premier ... le second, celui-là ... celui-ci; ~**ly** *adv* autrefois

formidable ['fɔːmɪdəbl] *adj* redoutable

formula ['fɔːmjʊlə] (*pl* ~**s** *or* **formulae**) *n* formule *f*

forsake [fə'seɪk] (*pt* **forsook**, *pp* **forsaken**) *vt* abandonner

fort [fɔːt] *n* fort *m*

forte ['fɔːtɪ] *n* (point) fort *m*

forth [fɔːθ] *adv* en avant; **to go back and** ~ aller et venir; **and so** ~ et ainsi de suite; ~**coming** *adj* (*event*) qui va avoir lieu prochainement; (*character*) ouvert(e), communicatif(ive); (*available*) disponible; ~**right** *adj* franc(franche), direct(e); ~**with** *adv* sur-le-champ

fortify ['fɔːtɪfaɪ] *vt* fortifier

fortitude ['fɔːtɪtjuːd] *n* courage *m*

fortnight ['fɔːtnaɪt] (BRIT) *n* quinzaine *f*, quinze jours *mpl*; ~**ly** (BRIT) *adj* bimensuel(le) ♦ *adv* tous les quinze jours

fortunate ['fɔːtʃənɪt] *adj* heureux(euse); (*person*) chanceux(euse); **it is** ~ **that** c'est une chance que; ~**ly** *adv* heureusement

fortune ['fɔːtʃən] *n* chance *f*; (*wealth*) fortune *f*; ~**-teller** *n* diseuse *f* de bonne aventure

forty ['fɔːtɪ] *num* quarante

forward ['fɔːwəd] *adj* (*ahead of schedule*) en avance; (*movement, position*) en avant, vers l'avant; (*not shy*) direct(e); effronté(e) ♦ *n* (SPORT) avant *m* ♦ *vt* (*letter*) faire suivre; (*parcel, goods*) expédier; (*fig*) promouvoir, favoriser; ~**(s)** *adv* en avant; **to move** ~ avancer

fossil ['fɔsl] *n* fossile *m*

foster ['fɔstə*] *vt* encourager, favoriser; (*child*) élever (*sans obligation d'adopter*); ~ **child** *n* enfant adoptif(ive)

fought [fɔːt] *pt, pp of* **fight**

foul [faʊl] *adj* (*weather, smell, food*) infect(e); (*language*) ordurier(ère) ♦ *n* (SPORT) faute *f* ♦ *vt* (*dirty*) salir, encrasser; **he's got a** ~ **temper** il a un caractère de chien; ~ **play** *n* (LAW) acte criminel

found [faʊnd] *pt, pp of* **find** ♦ *vt* (*establish*) fonder; ~**ation** [faʊn'deɪʃən] *n* (*act*) fondation *f*; (*base*) fondement *m*; (*also*: ~**ation cream**) fond *m* de teint; ~**ations** *npl* (*of building*) fondations *fpl*

founder ['faʊndə*] *n* fondateur *m* ♦ *vi* couler, sombrer

foundry ['faʊndrɪ] *n* fonderie *f*

fountain ['faʊntɪn] *n* fontaine *f*; ~ **pen** *n* stylo *m* (à encre)

four [fɔː*] *num* quatre; **on all** ~**s** à quatre pattes; ~**-poster** *n* (*also*: ~**-poster bed**) lit *m* à baldaquin; ~**some** *n* (*game*) partie *f* à quatre; (*outing*) sortie *f* à quatre

fourteen [fɔː'tiːn] *num* quatorze

fourth [fɔːθ] *num* quatrième

fowl [faʊl] *n* volaille *f*

fox [fɔks] *n* renard *m* ♦ *vt* mystifier

foyer ['fɔɪeɪ] *n* (*hotel*) hall *m*; (THEATRE) foyer *m*

fraction ['frækʃən] *n* fraction *f*

fracture ['fræktʃə*] *n* fracture *f*

fragile ['frædʒaɪl] *adj* fragile

fragment ['frægmənt] *n* fragment *m*

fragrant ['freɪgrənt] *adj* parfumé(e), odorant(e)

frail [freɪl] *adj* fragile, délicat(e)

frame [freɪm] *n* charpente *f*; (*of picture, bicycle*) cadre *m*; (*of door, window*) encadrement *m*, chambranle *m*; (*of spectacles*: *also*: ~**s**) monture *f* ♦ *vt* encadrer; ~ **of mind** disposition *f* d'esprit; ~**work** *n* structure *f*

France [frɑːns] *n* France *f*

franchise ['fræntʃaɪz] *n* (POL) droit *m* de vote; (COMM) franchise *f*

frank [fræŋk] *adj* franc(franche) ♦ *vt* (*letter*) affranchir; ~**ly** *adv* franchement

frantic ['fræntɪk] *adj* (*hectic*) frénétique; (*distraught*) hors de soi

fraternity [frə'tɜːnɪtɪ] *n* (*spirit*) fraternité *f*; (*club*) communauté *f*, confrérie *f*

fraud [frɔːd] *n* supercherie *f*, fraude *f*, tromperie *f*; (*person*) imposteur *m*

fraught [frɔːt] *adj*: ~ **with** chargé(e) de, plein(e) de

fray [freɪ] *n* bagarre *f* ♦ *vi* s'effilocher; **tempers were** ~**ed** les gens commençaient à s'énerver

freak [friːk] *n* (*also cpd*) phénomène *m*, créature *or* événement exceptionnel(le) par sa rareté

freckle ['frekl] *n* tache *f* de rousseur

free [friː] *adj* libre; (*gratis*) gratuit(e) ♦ *vt* (*prisoner etc*) libérer; (*jammed object or person*) dégager; ~ **(of charge)**, **for** ~ gratuitement; ~**dom** ['friːdəm] *n* liberté *f*; ~**-for-all** *n* mêlée générale; ~ **gift** *n* prime *f*; ~**hold** *n* propriété foncière libre; ~ **kick** *n* coup franc; ~**lance** *adj* indépendant(e); ~**ly** *adv* librement; (*liberally*) libéralement; **F**~**mason** *n* franc-maçon *m*; **F**~**post** (®) *n* port payé; ~**-range** *adj* (*hen, eggs*) de ferme; ~ **trade** *n* libre-échange *m*; ~**way** (US) *n* autoroute *f*; ~ **will** *n* libre arbitre *m*; **of one's own** ~ **will** de son plein gré

freeze [friːz] (*pt* **froze**, *pp* **frozen**) *vi* geler ♦ *vt* geler; (*food*) congeler; (*prices, salaries*) bloquer, geler ♦ *n* gel *m*; (*fig*) blocage *m*; ~**-dried** *adj* lyophilisé(e); ~**r** *n* congélateur *m*

freezing ['fri:zɪŋ] *adj*: ~ **(cold)** *(weather, water)* glacial(e) ♦ *n* **3 degrees below** ~ 3 degrés au-dessous de zéro; ~ **point** *n* point *m* de congélation

freight [freɪt] *n (goods)* fret *m*, cargaison *f*; *(money charged)* fret, prix *m* du transport; ~ **train** *n* train *m* de marchandises

French [frentʃ] *adj* français(e) ♦ *n* (LING) français *m*; **the** ~ *npl (people)* les Français; ~ **bean** *n* haricot vert; ~ **fried (potatoes),** ~ **fries** *(US) npl* (pommes de terre *fpl*) frites *fpl*; ~**man** *(irreg) n* Français *m*; ~ **window** *n* porte-fenêtre *f*; ~**woman** *(irreg) n* Française *f*

frenzy ['frenzɪ] *n* frénésie *f*

frequency ['fri:kwənsɪ] *n* fréquence *f*

frequent [*adj* 'fri:kwənt, *vb* frɪ'kwent] *adj* fréquent(e) ♦ *vt* fréquenter; ~**ly** *adv* fréquemment

fresh [freʃ] *adj* frais(fraîche); *(new)* nouveau(nouvelle); *(cheeky)* familier(ère), culotté(e); ~**en** *vi (wind, air)* fraîchir; ~**en up** *vi* faire un brin de toilette; ~**er** *(BRIT: inf) n (SCOL)* bizuth *m*, étudiant(e) de 1ère année; ~**ly** *adv* nouvellement, récemment; ~**man** *(US: irreg) n* = **fresher**; ~**ness** *n* fraîcheur *f*; ~**water** *adj (fish)* d'eau douce

fret [fret] *vi* s'agiter, se tracasser

friar ['fraɪə*] *n* moine *m*, frère *m*

friction ['frɪkʃən] *n* friction *f*

Friday ['fraɪdeɪ] *n* vendredi *m*

fridge [frɪdʒ] *(BRIT) n* frigo *m*, frigidaire *m* (®)

fried [fraɪd] *adj* frit(e); ~ **egg** œuf *m* sur le plat

friend [frend] *n* ami(e); ~**ly** *adj* amical(e); gentil(le); *(place)* accueillant(e); ~**ship** *n* amitié *f*

frieze [fri:z] *n* frise *f*

fright [fraɪt] *n* peur *f*, effroi *m*; **to take** ~ prendre peur, s'effrayer; ~**en** *vt* effrayer, faire peur à; ~**ened** *adj*: **to be** ~**ened (of)** avoir peur (de); ~**ening** *adj* effrayant(e); ~**ful** *adj* affreux(euse)

frigid ['frɪdʒɪd] *adj (woman)* frigide

frill [frɪl] *n (of dress)* volant *m*; *(of shirt)* jabot *m*

fringe [frɪndʒ] *n (BRIT: of hair)* frange *f*; *(edge: of forest etc)* bordure *f*; ~ **benefits** *npl* avantages sociaux *or* en nature

frisk [frɪsk] *vt* fouiller

fritter ['frɪtə*] *n* beignet *m*; ~ **away** *vt* gaspiller

frivolous ['frɪvələs] *adj* frivole

frizzy ['frɪzɪ] *adj* crépu(e)

fro [frəʊ] *adv*: **to go to and** ~ aller et venir

frock [frɒk] *n* robe *f*

frog [frɒg] *n* grenouille *f*; ~**man** *n* homme-grenouille *m*

frolic ['frɒlɪk] *vi* folâtrer, batifoler

from [frɒm] *prep* **1** *(indicating starting place, origin etc)* de; **where do you come** ~**?**, **where are you** ~**?** d'où venez-vous?; ~ **London to Paris** de Londres à Paris; **a letter** ~ **my sister** une lettre de ma sœur; **to drink** ~ **the bottle** boire à (même) la bouteille

2 *(indicating time)* (à partir) de; ~ **one o'clock to** *or* **until** *or* **till two** d'une heure à deux heures; ~ **January (on)** à partir de janvier

3 *(indicating distance)* de; **the hotel is one kilometre** ~ **the beach** l'hôtel est à un kilomètre de la plage

4 *(indicating price, number etc)* de; **the interest rate was increased** ~ **9% to 10%** le taux d'intérêt a augmenté de 9 à 10%

5 *(indicating difference)* de; **he can't tell red** ~ **green** il ne peut pas distinguer le rouge du vert

6 *(because of, on the basis of)*: ~ **what he says** d'après ce qu'il dit; **weak** ~ **hunger** affaibli par la faim

front [frʌnt] *n (of house, dress)* devant *m*; *(of coach, train)* avant *m*; *(promenade: also: sea* ~*)* bord *m* de mer; *(MIL, METEOROLOGY)* front *m*; *(fig: appearances)* contenance *f*, façade *f* ♦ *adj* de devant; *(seat)* avant *inv*; **in** ~ **(of)** devant; ~**age** ['frʌntɪdʒ] *n (of building)* façade *f*; ~ **door** *n* porte *f* d'entrée; *(of car)* portière *f* avant; ~**ier** ['frʌntɪə*] *n* frontière *f*; ~ **page** *n* première page; ~ **room** *(BRIT) n* pièce *f* de devant, salon *m*; ~**-wheel drive** *n* traction *f* avant

frost [frɒst] *n* gel *m*, gelée *f*; *(also: hoar*~*)* givre *m*; ~**bite** *n* gelures *fpl*; ~**ed** *adj (glass)* dépoli(e); ~**y** *adj (weather, welcome)* glacial(e)

froth [frɒθ] *n* mousse *f*; écume *f*

frown [fraʊn] *vi* froncer les sourcils

froze [frəʊz] *pt of* **freeze**

frozen ['frəʊzn] *pp of* **freeze**

fruit [fru:t] *n inv* fruit *m*; ~**erer** *n* fruitier *m*, marchand(e) de fruits; ~**ful** *adj (fig)* fructueux(euse); ~**ion** [fru:'ɪʃən] *n*: **to come to** ~**ion** se réaliser; ~ **juice** *n* jus *m* de fruit; ~ **machine** *(BRIT) n* machine *f* à sous; ~ **salad** *n* salade *f* de fruits

frustrate [frʌs'treɪt] *vt* frustrer

fry [fraɪ] *(pt, pp* **fried)** *vt* (faire) frire; *see also* **small**; ~**ing pan** *n* poêle *f* (à frire)

ft. *abbr* = **foot**; **feet**

fuddy-duddy ['fʌdɪdʌdɪ] *(pej) n* vieux schnock

fudge [fʌdʒ] *n (CULIN)* caramel *m*

fuel [fjʊəl] *n (for heating)* combustible *m*; *(for propelling)* carburant *m*; ~ **oil** *n* mazout *m*; ~ **tank** *n (in vehicle)* réservoir *m*

fugitive ['fju:dʒɪtɪv] *n* fugitif(ive)

fulfil [fʊl'fɪl] (*US* **~l**) *vt* (*function, condition*) remplir; (*order*) exécuter; (*wish, desire*) satisfaire, réaliser; (*skirt*) ample, large ♦ *adv*: **to know ~ well that** savoir fort bien que; **I'm ~ (up)** j'ai bien mangé; **a ~ two hours** deux bonnes heures; **at ~ speed** à toute vitesse; **in ~** (*reproduce, quote*) intégralement; (*write*) en toutes lettres; **~ employment** plein emploi; **to pay in ~** tout payer; **~-length** *adj* (*film*) long métrage; (*portrait, mirror*) en pied; (*coat*) long(ue); **~ moon** *n* pleine lune; **~-scale** *adj* (*attack, war*) complet(ète), total(e); (*model*) grandeur nature *inv*; **~ stop** *n* point *m*; **~-time** *adj, adv* (*work*) à plein temps; **~y** *adv* entièrement, complètement; (*at least*) au moins; **~y-fledged** *adj* (*teacher, barrister*) diplômé(e); (*citizen, member*) à part entière

fumble ['fʌmbl] *vi*: **~ with** tripoter

fume [fjuːm] *vi* rager; **~s** *npl* vapeurs *fpl*, émanations *fpl*, gaz *mpl*

fun [fʌn] *n* amusement *m*, divertissement *m*; **to have ~** s'amuser; **for ~** pour rire; **to make ~ of** se moquer de

function ['fʌŋkʃən] *n* fonction *f*; (*social occasion*) cérémonie *f*, soirée officielle ♦ *vi* fonctionner; **~al** *adj* fonctionnel(le)

fund [fʌnd] *n* caisse *f*, fonds *m*; (*source, store*) source *f*, mine *f*; **~s** *npl* (*money*) fonds *mpl*

fundamental [fʌndə'mentl] *adj* fondamental(e)

funeral ['fjuːnərəl] *n* enterrement *m*, obsèques *fpl*; **~ parlour** *n* entreprise *f* de pompes funèbres; **~ service** *n* service *m* funèbre

funfair ['fʌnfeə*] (*BRIT*) *n* fête (foraine)

fungus ['fʌŋgəs] (*pl* **fungi**) *n* champignon *m*; (*mould*) moisissure *f*

funnel ['fʌnl] *n* entonnoir *m*; (*of ship*) cheminée *f*

funny ['fʌnɪ] *adj* amusant(e), drôle; (*strange*) curieux(euse), bizarre

fur [fɜː*] *n* fourrure *f*; (*BRIT: in kettle etc*) (dépôt *m* de) tartre *m*; **~ coat** *n* manteau *m* de fourrure

furious ['fjʊərɪəs] *adj* furieux(euse); (*effort*) acharné(e)

furlong ['fɜːlɒŋ] *n* = 201,17 m

furlough ['fɜːləʊ] *n* permission *f*, congé *m*

furnace ['fɜːnɪs] *n* fourneau *m*

furnish ['fɜːnɪʃ] *vt* meubler; (*supply*): **to ~ sb with sth** fournir qch à qn; **~ings** *npl* mobilier *m*, ameublement *m*

furniture ['fɜːnɪtʃə*] *n* meubles *mpl*, mobilier *m*; **piece of ~** meuble *m*

furrow ['fʌrəʊ] *n* sillon *m*

furry ['fɜːrɪ] *adj* (*animal*) à fourrure; (*toy*) en peluche

further ['fɜːðə*] *adj* (*additional*) supplémentaire, autre; nouveau (nouvelle) ♦ *adv* plus loin; (*more*) davantage; (*moreover*) de plus ♦ *vt* faire avancer *or* progresser, promouvoir; **~ education** *n* enseignement *m* postscolaire; **~more** *adv* de plus, en outre

furthest ['fɜːðɪst] *superl of* **far**

fury ['fjʊərɪ] *n* fureur *f*

fuse [fjuːz] (*US* **fuze**) *n* fusible *m*; (*for bomb etc*) amorce *f*, détonateur *m* ♦ *vt, vi* (*metal*) fondre; **to ~ the lights** (*BRIT*) faire sauter les plombs; **~ box** *n* boîte *f* à fusibles

fuss [fʌs] *n* (*excitement*) agitation *f*; (*complaining*) histoire(s) *f(pl)*; **to make a ~** faire des histoires; **to make a ~ of sb** être aux petits soins pour qn; **~y** *adj* (*person*) tatillon(ne), difficile; (*dress, style*) tarabiscoté(e)

future ['fjuːtʃə*] *adj* futur(e) ♦ *n* avenir *m*; (*LING*) futur *m*; **in ~** à l'avenir

fuze [fjuːz] (*US*) *n, vt, vi* = **fuse**

fuzzy ['fʌzɪ] *adj* (*PHOT*) flou(e); (*hair*) crépu(e)

G g

G [dʒiː] *n* (*MUS*) sol *m*

G7 *n abbr* (= *Group of 7*) le groupe des 7

gabble ['gæbl] *vi* bredouiller

gable ['geɪbl] *n* pignon *m*

gadget ['gædʒɪt] *n* gadget *m*

Gaelic ['geɪlɪk] *adj* gaélique ♦ *n* (*LING*) gaélique *m*

gag [gæg] *n* (*on mouth*) bâillon *m*; (*joke*) gag *m* ♦ *vt* bâillonner

gaiety ['geɪətɪ] *n* gaieté *f*

gain [geɪn] *n* (*improvement*) gain *m*; (*profit*) gain, profit *m*; (*increase*): **~ (in)** augmentation *f* (de) ♦ *vt* gagner ♦ *vi* (*watch*) avancer; **to ~ 3 lbs (in weight)** prendre 3 livres; **to ~ on sb** (*catch up*) rattraper qn; **to ~ from/by** gagner de/à

gait [geɪt] *n* démarche *f*

gal. *abbr* = **gallon**

gale [geɪl] *n* rafale *f* de vent; coup *m* de vent

gallant ['gælənt] *adj* vaillant(e), brave; (*towards ladies*) galant

gall bladder ['gɔːl-] *n* vésicule *f* biliaire

gallery ['gælərɪ] *n* galerie *f*; (*also*: **art ~**) musée *m*; (*: private*) galerie

galley ['gælɪ] *n* (*ship's kitchen*) cambuse *f*

gallon ['gælən] *n* gallon *m* (*BRIT = 4,5 l; US*

= 3,8 *l*)

gallop ['gæləp] *n* galop *m* ♦ *vi* galoper

gallows ['gæləuz] *n* potence *f*

gallstone ['gɔːlstəun] *n* calcul *m* biliaire

galore [gə'lɔː*] *adv* en abondance, à gogo

Gambia *n*: **(The)** ~ la Gambie

gambit ['gæmbɪt] *n* (*fig*): **(opening)** ~ manœuvre *f* stratégique

gamble ['gæmbl] *n* pari *m*, risque calculé ♦ *vt*, *vi* jouer; **to** ~ **on** (*fig*) miser sur; ~**r** *n* joueur *m*; **gambling** ['gæmblɪŋ] *n* jeu *m*

game [geɪm] *n* jeu *m*; (*match*) match *m*; (*strategy, scheme*) plan *m*; projet *m*; (*HUNTING*) gibier *m* ♦ *adj* (*willing*): **to be** ~ **(for)** être prêt(e) (à *or* pour); **big** ~ gros gibier; ~**keeper** *n* garde-chasse *m*

gammon ['gæmən] *n* (*bacon*) quartier *m* de lard fumé; (*ham*) jambon fumé

gamut ['gæmət] *n* gamme *f*

gang [gæŋ] *n* bande *f*, (*of workmen*) équipe *f*; ~ **up** *vi*: **to** ~ **up on sb** se liguer contre qn; ~**ster** ['gæŋstə*] *n* gangster *m*; ~**way** *n* passerelle *f*, (*BRIT*: *of bus, plane*) couloir central; (: *in cinema*) allée centrale

gaol [dʒeɪl] (*BRIT*) *n* = **jail**

gap [gæp] *n* trou *m*; (*in time*) intervalle *m*; (*difference*): ~ **between** écart *m* entre

gape [geɪp] *vi* (*person*) être *or* rester bouche bée; (*hole, shirt*) être ouvert(e); **gaping** ['geɪpɪŋ] *adj* (*hole*) béant(e)

garage ['gærɑːʒ] *n* garage *m*

garbage ['gɑːbɪdʒ] *n* (*US: rubbish*) ordures *fpl*, détritus *mpl*; (*inf: nonsense*) foutaises *fpl*; ~ **can** (*US*) *n* poubelle *f*, boîte *f* à ordures

garbled ['gɑːbld] *adj* (*account, message*) embrouillé(e)

garden ['gɑːdn] *n* jardin *m*; ~**s** *npl* jardin public; ~**er** *n* jardinier *m*; ~**ing** *n* jardinage *m*

gargle ['gɑːgl] *vi* se gargariser

garish ['gɛərɪʃ] *adj* criard(e), voyant(e); (*light*) cru(e)

garland ['gɑːlənd] *n* guirlande *f*, couronne *f*

garlic ['gɑːlɪk] *n* ail *m*

garment ['gɑːmənt] *n* vêtement *m*

garrison ['gærɪsən] *n* garnison *f*

garrulous ['gærʊləs] *adj* volubile, loquace

garter ['gɑːtə*] *n* jarretière *f*, (*US*) jarretelle *f*

gas [gæs] *n* gaz *m*; (*US*: ~*oline*) essence *f* ♦ *vt* asphyxier; ~ **cooker** (*BRIT*) *n* cuisinière *f* à gaz; ~ **cylinder** *n* bouteille *f* de gaz; ~ **fire** (*BRIT*) *n* radiateur *m* à gaz

gash [gæʃ] *n* entaille *f*; (*on face*) balafre *f*

gasket ['gæskɪt] *n* (*AUT*) joint *m* de culasse

gas mask *n* masque *m* à gaz

gas meter *n* compteur *m* à gaz

gasoline ['gæsəliːn] (*US*) *n* essence *f*

gasp [gɑːsp] *vi* haleter; ~ **out** *vt* (*say*) dire dans un souffle *or* d'une voix entrecoupée

gas station (*US*) *n* station-service *f*

gas tap *n* bouton *m* (de cuisinière à gaz); (*on pipe*) robinet *m* à gaz

gastric *adj* gastrique; ~ **flu** grippe *f* intestinale

gate [geɪt] *n* (*of garden*) portail *m*; (*of field*) barrière *f*; (*of building, at airport*) porte *f*; ~**crash** *vt* s'introduire sans invitation dans; ~**way** *n* porte *f*

gather ['gæðə*] *vt* (*flowers, fruit*) cueillir; (*pick up*) ramasser; (*assemble*) rassembler, réunir; recueillir; (*understand*) comprendre; (*SEWING*) froncer ♦ *vi* (*assemble*) se rassembler; **to** ~ **speed** prendre de la vitesse; ~**ing** *n* rassemblement *m*

gaudy ['gɔːdɪ] *adj* voyant(e)

gauge [geɪdʒ] *n* (*instrument*) jauge *f* ♦ *vt* jauger

gaunt [gɔːnt] *adj* (*thin*) décharné(e); (*grim, desolate*) désolé(e)

gauntlet ['gɔːntlɪt] *n* (*glove*) gant *m*; (*fig*): **to run the** ~ **through an angry crowd** se frayer un passage à travers une foule hostile; **to throw down the** ~ jeter le gant

gauze [gɔːz] *n* gaze *f*

gave [geɪv] *pt of* **give**

gay [geɪ] *adj* (*homosexual*) homosexuel(le); (*cheerful*) gai(e), réjoui(e); (*colour etc*) gai, vif(vive)

gaze [geɪz] *n* regard *m* fixe ♦ *vi*: **to** ~ **at** fixer du regard

gazump (*BRIT*) *vi* revenir sur une promesse de vente (pour accepter une offre plus intéressante)

GB *abbr* = **Great Britain**

GCE *n abbr* (*BRIT*) = **General Certificate of Education**

GCSE *n abbr* (*BRIT*) = **General Certificate of Secondary Education**

gear [gɪə*] *n* matériel *m*, équipement *m*; attirail *m*; (*TECH*) engrenage *m*; (*AUT*) vitesse *f* ♦ *vt* (*fig: adapt*): **to** ~ **sth to** adapter qch à; **top** (*or US* **high**) ~ quatrième (*or* cinquième) vitesse; **low** ~ première vitesse; **in** ~ en prise; ~ **box** *n* boîte *f* de vitesses; ~ **lever** (*US* ~ **shift**) *n* levier *m* de vitesse

geese [giːs] *npl of* **goose**

gel [dʒel] *n* gel *m*

gelignite ['dʒelɪgnaɪt] *n* plastic *m*

gem [dʒem] *n* pierre précieuse

Gemini ['dʒemɪniː] *n* les Gémeaux *mpl*

gender ['dʒendə*] *n* genre *m*

general ['dʒenərəl] *n* général *m* ♦ *adj* général(e); **in** ~ en général; ~ **delivery** *n* poste restante; ~ **election** *n* élection(s) législative(s); ~**ly** *adv* généralement; ~ **practitioner** *n* généraliste *m/f*

generate ['dʒenəreɪt] *vt* engendrer; (*electricity etc*) produire

generation [dʒenə'reɪʃən] *n* génération *f*, (*of electricity etc*) production *f*

generator ['dʒenəreɪtə*] *n* générateur *m*

generosity [dʒenə'rɒsɪtɪ] *n* générosité *f*,

generous ['dʒenərəs] *adj* généreux(euse); (*copious*) copieux(euse)

genetic engineering [dʒɪ'netɪk-] *n* ingénierie *f* génétique

genetics [dʒɪ'netɪks] *n* génétique *f*

Geneva [dʒɪ'niːvə] *n* Genève

genial ['dʒiːnɪəl] *adj* cordial(e), chaleureux(euse)

genitals ['dʒenɪtlz] *npl* organes génitaux

genius ['dʒiːnɪəs] *n* génie *m*

genteel [dʒen'tiːl] *adj* de bon ton, distingué(e)

gentle ['dʒentl] *adj* doux(douce)

gentleman ['dʒentlmən] *n* monsieur *m*; (*well-bred man*) gentleman *m*

gently ['dʒentlɪ] *adv* doucement

gentry ['dʒentrɪ] *n inv*: **the ~** la petite noblesse

gents [dʒents] *n* W.-C. *mpl* (pour hommes)

genuine ['dʒenjuɪn] *adj* véritable, authentique; (*person*) sincère

geography [dʒɪ'ɒgrəfɪ] *n* géographie *f*

geology [dʒɪ'ɒlədʒɪ] *n* géologie *f*

geometric(al) [dʒɪə'metrɪk(l)] *adj* géométrique

geometry [dʒɪ'ɒmɪtrɪ] *n* géométrie *f*

geranium [dʒɪ'reɪnɪəm] *n* géranium *m*

geriatric [dʒerɪ'ætrɪk] *adj* gériatrique

germ [dʒɜːm] *n* (*MED*) microbe *m*

German ['dʒɜːmən] *adj* allemand(e) ♦ *n* Allemand(e); (*LING*) allemand *m*; **~ measles** (*BRIT*) *n* rubéole *f*

Germany ['dʒɜːmənɪ] *n* Allemagne *f*

gesture ['dʒestʃə*] *n* geste *m*

─────── **KEYWORD** ───────

get [get] (*pt, pp* **got**, *pp* **gotten** (*US*)) *vi* **1** (*become, be*) devenir; **to ~ old/tired** devenir vieux/fatigué, vieillir *or* fatiguer; **to ~ drunk** s'enivrer; **to ~ killed** se faire tuer; **when do I ~ paid?** quand est-ce que je serai payé?; **it's ~ting late** il se fait tard

2 (*go*): **to ~ to/from** aller à/de; **to ~ home** rentrer chez soi; **how did you ~ here?** comment es-tu arrivé ici?

3 (*begin*) commencer *or* se mettre à; **I'm ~ting to like him** je commence à l'apprécier; **let's ~ going** *or* **started** allons-y

4 (*modal aux vb*): **you've got to do it** il faut que vous le fassiez; **I've got to tell the police** je dois le dire à la police

♦ *vt* **1**: **to ~ sth done** (*do*) faire qch; (*have done*) faire faire qch; **to ~ one's hair cut** se faire couper les cheveux; **to ~ sb to do sth** faire faire qch à qn; **to ~ sb drunk** enivrer qn

2 (*obtain: money, permission, results*) obtenir, avoir; (*find: job, flat*) trouver; (*fetch: person, doctor, object*) aller chercher; **to ~ sth for sb** procurer qch à qn; **~ me Mr Jones, please** (*on phone*) passez-moi Mr Jones, s'il vous plaît; **can I ~ you a drink?**

est-ce que je peux vous servir à boire?

3 (*receive: present, letter*) recevoir, avoir; (*acquire: reputation*) avoir; (: *prize*) obtenir; **what did you ~ for your birthday?** qu'est-ce que tu as eu pour ton anniversaire?

4 (*catch*) prendre, saisir, attraper; (*hit: target etc*) atteindre; **to ~ sb by the arm/throat** prendre *or* saisir *or* attraper qn par le bras/à la gorge; **~ him!** arrête-le!

5 (*take, move*) faire parvenir; **do you think we'll ~ it through the door?** on arrivera à le faire passer par la porte?; **I'll ~ you there somehow** je me débrouillerai pour t'y emmener

6 (*catch, take: plane, bus etc*) prendre

7 (*understand*) comprendre, saisir; (*hear*) entendre; **I've got it!** j'ai compris!; **I didn't ~ your name** je n'ai pas entendu votre nom

8 (*have, possess*): **to have got** avoir; **how many have you got?** vous en avez combien?

get about *vi* se déplacer; (*news*) se répandre

get along *vi* (*agree*) s'entendre; (*depart*) s'en aller; (*manage*) = **get by**

get at *vt fus* (*attack*) s'en prendre à; (*reach*) attraper, atteindre

get away *vi* partir, s'en aller; (*escape*) s'échapper

get away with *vt fus* en être quitte pour; se faire passer *or* pardonner

get back *vi* (*return*) rentrer ♦ *vt* récupérer, recouvrer

get by *vi* (*pass*) passer; (*manage*) se débrouiller

get down *vi, vt fus* descendre ♦ *vt* descendre; (*depress*) déprimer

get down to *vt fus* (*work*) se mettre à (faire)

get in *vi* rentrer; (*train*) arriver; **get into** *vt fus* entrer dans; (*car, train etc*) monter dans; (*clothes*) mettre, enfiler, endosser; **to get into bed/a rage** se mettre au lit/en colère

get off *vi* (*from train etc*) descendre; (*depart: person, car*) s'en aller; (*escape*) s'en tirer ♦ *vt* (*remove: clothes, stain*) enlever ♦ *vt fus* (*train, bus*) descendre de

get on *vi* (*at exam etc*) se débrouiller; (*agree*): **to get on (with)** s'entendre (avec) ♦ *vt fus* monter dans; (*horse*) monter sur

get out *vi* sortir; (*of vehicle*) descendre ♦ *vt* sortir

get out of *vt fus* sortir de; (*duty etc*) échapper à, se soustraire à

get over *vt fus* (*illness*) se remettre de

get round *vt fus* contourner; (*fig: person*) entortiller

get through *vi* (*TEL*) avoir la communication; **to get through to sb** atteindre qn

get together *vi* se réunir ♦ *vt* assembler
get up *vi* (*rise*) se lever ♦ *vt fus* monter
get up to *vt fus* (*reach*) arriver à; (*prank etc*) faire

getaway ['getəweɪ] *n*: **to make one's ~** filer
geyser ['giːzə*] *n* (GEO) geyser *m*; (BRIT: *water heater*) chauffe-eau *m inv*
Ghana ['gɑːnə] *n* Ghana *m*
ghastly ['gɑːstlɪ] *adj* atroce, horrible; (*pale*) livide, blême
gherkin ['gɜːkɪn] *n* cornichon *m*
ghetto blaster ['getəʊ-] *n* stéréo *f* portable
ghost [gəʊst] *n* fantôme *m*, revenant *m*
giant ['dʒaɪənt] *n* géant(e) ♦ *adj* géant(e), énorme
gibberish ['dʒɪbərɪʃ] *n* charabia *m*
giblets ['dʒɪblɪts] *npl* abats *mpl*
Gibraltar [dʒɪ'brɔːltə*] *n* Gibraltar *m*
giddy ['gɪdɪ] *adj* (*dizzy*): **to be** or **feel ~** avoir le vertige
gift [gɪft] *n* cadeau *m*; (*donation, ability*) don *m*; ~**ed** *adj* doué(e); ~ **token** *n* chèque-cadeau *m*
gigantic [dʒaɪ'gæntɪk] *adj* gigantesque
giggle ['gɪgl] *vi* pouffer (de rire), rire sottement
gill [dʒɪl] *n* (*measure*) = 0.25 pints (BRIT = 0.15 l, US = 0.12 l)
gills [gɪlz] *npl* (*of fish*) ouïes *fpl*, branchies *fpl*
gilt [gɪlt] *adj* doré(e) ♦ *n* dorure *f*; ~**-edged** *adj* (COMM) de premier ordre
gimmick ['gɪmɪk] *n* truc *m*
gin [dʒɪn] *n* (*liquor*) gin *m*
ginger ['dʒɪndʒə*] *n* gingembre *m*; ~ **ale** *n* boisson gazeuse au gingembre; ~ **beer** *n* = ginger ale; ~**bread** *n* pain *m* d'épices
gingerly ['dʒɪndʒəlɪ] *adv* avec précaution
gipsy ['dʒɪpsɪ] *n* = **gypsy**
giraffe [dʒɪ'rɑːf] *n* girafe *f*
girder ['gɜːdə*] *n* poutrelle *f*
girdle ['gɜːdl] *n* (*corset*) gaine *f*
girl [gɜːl] *n* fille *f*, fillette *f*; (*young unmarried woman*) jeune fille; (*daughter*) fille; **an English ~** une jeune Anglaise; ~**friend** *n* (*of girl*) amie *f*; (*of boy*) petite amie; ~**ish** *adj* de petite or de jeune fille; (*for a boy*) efféminé(e)
giro ['dʒaɪrəʊ] *n* (*bank ~*) virement *m* bancaire; (*post office ~*) mandat *m*; (BRIT: *welfare cheque*) mandat d'allocation chômage
girth [gɜːθ] *n* circonférence *f*; (*of horse*) sangle *f*
gist [dʒɪst] *n* essentiel *m*
give [gɪv] (*pt* gave, *pp* given) *vt* donner ♦ *vi* (*break*) céder; (*stretch: fabric*) se prêter; **to ~ sb sth**, ~ **sth to sb** donner qch à qn; **to ~ a cry/sigh** pousser un cri/un soupir; ~ **away** *vt* donner; (~ *free*) faire cadeau de; (*betray*) donner, trahir; (*disclose*) révé-

ler; (*bride*) conduire à l'autel; ~ **back** *vt* rendre; ~ **in** *vi* céder ♦ *vt* donner; ~ **off** *vt* dégager; ~ **out** *vt* distribuer; annoncer; ~ **up** *vi* renoncer ♦ *vt* renoncer à; **to ~ up smoking** arrêter de fumer; **to ~ o.s. up** se rendre; ~ **way** (BRIT) *vi* céder; (AUT) céder la priorité
glacier ['glæsɪə*] *n* glacier *m*
glad [glæd] *adj* content(e); ~**ly** *adv* volontiers
glamorous ['glæmərəs] *adj* (*person*) séduisant(e); (*job*) prestigieux(euse)
glamour ['glæmə*] *n* éclat *m*, prestige *m*
glance [glɑːns] *n* coup *m* d'œil ♦ *vi*: **to ~ at** jeter un coup d'œil à; ~ **off** *vt fus* (*bullet*) ricocher sur; **glancing** ['glɑːnsɪŋ] *adj* (*blow*) oblique
gland [glænd] *n* glande *f*
glare [gleə*] *n* (*of anger*) regard furieux; (*of light*) lumière éblouissante; (*of publicity*) feux *mpl* ♦ *vi* briller d'un éclat aveuglant; **to ~ at** lancer un regard furieux à; **glaring** ['gleərɪŋ] *adj* (*mistake*) criant(e), qui saute aux yeux
glass [glɑːs] *n* verre *m*; ~**es** *npl* (*spectacles*) lunettes *fpl*; ~**house** (BRIT) *n* (*for plants*) serre *f*; ~**ware** *n* verrerie *f*
glaze [gleɪz] *vt* (*door, window*) vitrer; (*pottery*) vernir ♦ *n* (*on pottery*) vernis *m*; ~**d** *adj* (*pottery*) verni(e); (*eyes*) vitreux(euse); **glazier** ['gleɪzɪə*] *n* vitrier *m*
gleam [gliːm] *vi* luire, briller
glean [gliːn] *vt* (*information*) glaner
glee [gliː] *n* joie *f*
glib [glɪb] *adj* (*person*) qui a du bagou; (*response*) désinvolte, facile
glide [glaɪd] *vi* glisser; (AVIAT, *birds*) planer; ~**r** *n* (AVIAT) planeur *m*; **gliding** ['glaɪdɪŋ] *n* (SPORT) vol *m* à voile
glimmer ['glɪmə*] *n* lueur *f*
glimpse [glɪmps] *n* vision passagère, aperçu *m* ♦ *vt* entrevoir, apercevoir
glint [glɪnt] *vi* étinceler
glisten ['glɪsn] *vi* briller, luire
glitter ['glɪtə*] *vi* scintiller, briller
gloat [gləʊt] *vi*: **to ~ (over)** jubiler (à propos de)
global ['gləʊbl] *adj* mondial(e)
globe [gləʊb] *n* globe *m*
gloom [gluːm] *n* obscurité *f*; (*sadness*) tristesse *f*, mélancolie *f*; ~**y** *adj* sombre, triste, lugubre
glorious ['glɔːrɪəs] *adj* glorieux(euse); splendide
glory ['glɔːrɪ] *n* gloire *f*; (*splendour*) splendeur *f*
gloss [glɒs] *n* (*shine*) brillant *m*, vernis *m*; (*also*: ~ *paint*) peinture brillante or laquée; ~ **over** *vt fus* glisser sur
glossary ['glɒsərɪ] *n* glossaire *m*
glossy ['glɒsɪ] *adj* brillant(e); ~ **magazine** magazine *m* de luxe

glove [glʌv] n gant m; ~ **compartment** n (AUT) boîte f à gants, vide-poches m inv
glow [gləʊ] vi rougeoyer; (face) rayonner; (eyes) briller
glower ['glaʊə*] vi: **to ~ (at)** lancer des regards mauvais (à)
glucose ['gluːkəʊz] n glucose m
glue [gluː] n colle f ♦ vt coller
glum [glʌm] adj sombre, morne
glut [glʌt] n surabondance f
glutton ['glʌtn] n glouton(ne); **a ~ for work** un bourreau de travail; **a ~ for punishment** un masochiste (fig)
gnarled [nɑːld] adj noueux(euse)
gnat [næt] n moucheron m
gnaw [nɔː] vt ronger
go [gəʊ] (pt went, pp gone; pl ~es) vi aller; (depart) partir, s'en aller; (work) marcher; (be sold): **to ~ for £10** se vendre 10 livres; (fit, suit): **to ~ with** aller avec; (become): **to ~ pale/mouldy** pâlir/moisir; (break etc) céder ♦ n: **to have a ~ (at)** essayer (de faire); **to be on the ~** être en mouvement; **whose ~ is it?** à qui est-ce de jouer?; **he's ~ing to do** il va faire, il est sur le point de faire; **to ~ for a walk** aller se promener; **to ~ dancing** aller danser; **how did it ~?** comment est-ce que ça s'est passé?; **to ~ round the back/by the shop** passer par derrière/devant le magasin; ~ **about** vi (rumour) se répandre ♦ vt fus: **how do I ~ about this?** comment dois-je m'y prendre (pour faire ceci)?; ~ **ahead** vi (make progress) avancer; (get going) y aller; ~ **along** vi aller, avancer ♦ vt fus longer, parcourir; ~ **away** vi partir, s'en aller; ~ **back** vi rentrer; revenir; (go again) retourner; ~ **back on** vt fus (promise) revenir sur; ~ **by** vi (years, time) passer, s'écouler ♦ vt fus s'en tenir à; en croire; ~ **down** vi descendre; (ship) couler; (sun) se coucher ♦ vt fus descendre; ~ **for** vt fus (fetch) aller chercher; (like) aimer; (attack) s'en prendre à, attaquer; ~ **in** vi entrer; ~ **in for** vt fus (competition) se présenter à; (like) aimer; ~ **into** vt fus entrer dans; (investigate) étudier, examiner; (embark on) se lancer dans; ~ **off** vi partir, s'en aller; (food) se gâter; (explode) sauter; (event) se dérouler ♦ vt fus ne plus aimer; **the gun went off** le coup est parti; ~ **on** vi continuer; (happen) se passer; **to ~ on doing** continuer à faire; ~ **out** vi sortir; (fire, light) s'éteindre; ~ **over** vt fus (check) revoir, vérifier; ~ **through** vt fus (town etc) traverser; ~ **up** vi monter; (price) augmenter ♦ vt fus gravir; ~ **without** vt fus se passer de
goad [gəʊd] vt aiguillonner
go-ahead ['gəʊəhed] adj dynamique, entreprenant(e) ♦ n feu vert
goal [gəʊl] n but m; ~**keeper** n gardien m de but; ~**post** n poteau m de but

goat [gəʊt] n chèvre f
gobble ['gɒbl] vt (also: ~ down, ~ up) engloutir
go-between ['gəʊ-] n intermédiaire m/f
god [gɒd] n dieu m; **G~** n Dieu m; ~**child** n filleul(e); ~**daughter** n filleule f; ~**dess** n déesse f; ~**father** n parrain m; ~**forsaken** adj maudit(e); ~**mother** n marraine f; ~**send** n aubaine f; ~**son** n filleul m
goggles ['gɒglz] npl (for skiing etc) lunettes protectrices
going ['gəʊɪŋ] n (conditions) état m du terrain ♦ adj: **the ~ rate** le tarif (en vigueur)
gold [gəʊld] n or m ♦ adj en or; (reserves) d'or; ~**en** adj (made of gold) en or; (gold in colour) doré(e); ~**fish** n poisson m rouge; ~-**plated** adj plaqué(e or inv); ~**smith** n orfèvre m
golf [gɒlf] n golf m; ~ **ball** n balle f de golf; (on typewriter) boule f; ~ **club** n club m de golf; (stick) club m, crosse f de golf; ~ **course** n (terrain m de) golf m; ~**er** n joueur(euse) de golf
gone [gɒn] pp of go
gong [gɒŋ] n gong m
good [gʊd] adj bon(ne); (kind) gentil(le); (child) sage ♦ n bien m; ~**s** npl (COMM) marchandises fpl, articles mpl; ~!, très bien!; **to be ~ at** être bon en; **to be ~ for** être bon pour; **would you be ~ enough to ...?** auriez-vous la bonté or l'amabilité de ...?; **a ~ deal (of)** beaucoup (de); **a ~ many** beaucoup (de); **to make ~** vi (succeed) faire son chemin, réussir ♦ vt (deficit) combler; (losses) compenser; **it's no ~ complaining** cela ne sert à rien de se plaindre; **for ~** pour de bon, une fois pour toutes; ~ **morning/afternoon!** bonjour!; ~ **evening!** bonsoir!; ~ **night!** bonsoir!; (on going to bed) bonne nuit!; ~**bye** excl au revoir!; **G~ Friday** n Vendredi saint; ~-**looking** adj beau(belle), bien inv; ~-**natured** adj (person) qui a un bon naturel; ~**ness** n (of person) bonté f; **for ~ness sake!** je vous en prie!; ~**ness gracious!** mon Dieu!; ~**s train** (BRIT) n train m de marchandises; ~**will** n bonne volonté
goose [guːs] (pl geese) n oie f
gooseberry ['gʊzbərɪ] n groseille f à maquereau; **to play ~** (BRIT) tenir la chandelle
gooseflesh ['guːsfleʃ] n, **goose pimples** npl chair f de poule
gore [gɔː*] vt encorner ♦ n sang m
gorge [gɔːdʒ] n gorge f ♦ vt: **to ~ o.s. (on)** se gorger (de)
gorgeous ['gɔːdʒəs] adj splendide, superbe
gorilla [gə'rɪlə] n gorille m
gorse [gɔːs] n ajoncs mpl
gory ['gɔːrɪ] adj sanglant(e); (details) horrible

go-slow ['gəʊ'sləʊ] (*BRIT*) *n* grève perlée
gospel ['gɒspəl] *n* évangile *m*
gossip ['gɒsɪp] *n* (*chat*) bavardages *mpl*; commérage *m*, cancans *mpl*; (*person*) commère *f* ♦ *vi* bavarder; (*maliciously*) cancaner, faire des commérages
got [gɒt] *pt, pp of* **get**
gotten ['gɒtn] (*US*) *pp of* **get**
gout [gaʊt] *n* goutte *f*
govern ['gʌvən] *vt* gouverner; **~ess** ['gʌvənɪs] *n* gouvernante *f*; **~ment** ['gʌvnmənt] *n* gouvernement *m*; (*BRIT: ministers*) ministère *m*; **~or** ['gʌvənə*] *n* (*of state, bank*) gouverneur *m*; (*of school, hospital*) ≈ membre *m/f* du conseil d'établissement; (*BRIT: of prison*) directeur(trice)
gown [gaʊn] *n* robe *f*; (*of teacher, BRIT: of judge*) toge *f*
GP *n abbr* = **general practitioner**
grab [græb] *vt* saisir, empoigner ♦ *vi*: **to ~ at** essayer de saisir
grace [greɪs] *n* grâce *f* ♦ *vt* honorer; (*adorn*) orner; **~ 5 days'** ~ cinq jours de répit; **~ful** *adj* gracieux(euse), élégant(e); **gracious** ['greɪʃəs] *adj* bienveillant(e)
grade [greɪd] *n* (*COMM*) qualité; *f* (*in hierarchy*) catégorie *f*, grade *m*, échelon *m*; (*SCOL*) note *f*; (*US: school class*) classe *f* ♦ *vt* classer; **~ crossing** (*US*) *n* passage *m* à niveau; **~ school** (*US*) *n* école *f* primaire
gradient ['greɪdɪənt] *n* inclinaison *f*, pente *f*
gradual ['grædjʊəl] *adj* graduel(le), progressif(ive); **~ly** *adv* peu à peu, graduellement
graduate [*n* 'grædjʊɪt, *vb* 'grædjʊeɪt] *n* diplômé(e), licencié(e); (*US: of high school*) bachelier(ère) ♦ *vi* obtenir son diplôme; (*US*) obtenir son baccalauréat; **graduation** [grædjʊ'eɪʃən] *n* (cérémonie *f* de) remise *f* des diplômes
graffiti [grə'fiːtɪ] *npl* graffiti *mpl*
graft [grɑːft] *n* (*AGR, MED*) greffe *f*; (*bribery*) corruption *f* ♦ *vt* greffer; **hard ~** (*BRIT: inf*) boulot acharné
grain [greɪn] *n* grain *m*
gram [græm] *n* gramme *m*
grammar ['græmə*] *n* grammaire *f*; **~ school** (*BRIT*) *n* ≈ lycée *m*; **grammatical** [grə'mætɪkl] *adj* grammatical(e)
gramme [græm] *n* = **gram**
grand [grænd] *adj* magnifique, splendide; (*gesture etc*) noble; **~children** *npl* petits-enfants *mpl*; **~dad** (*inf*) *n* grand-papa *m*; **~daughter** *n* petite-fille *f*; **~father** *n* grand-père *m*; **~ma** (*inf*) *n* grand-maman *f*; **~mother** *n* grand-mère *f*; **~pa** (*inf*) *n* = **~dad**; **~parents** *npl* grands-parents *mpl*; **~ piano** *n* piano *m* à queue; **~son** *n* petit-fils *m*; **~stand** (*SPORT*) tribune *f*
granite ['grænɪt] *n* granit *m*
granny ['grænɪ] (*inf*) *n* grand-maman *f*
grant [grɑːnt] *vt* accorder; (*a request*) accéder à; (*admit*) concéder ♦ *n* (*SCOL*) bourse

f; (*ADMIN*) subside *m*, subvention *f*; **to take it for ~ed that** trouver tout naturel que +*sub*; **to take sb for ~ed** considérer qn comme faisant partie du décor
granulated sugar ['grænjʊleɪtɪd-] *n* sucre *m* en poudre
grape [greɪp] *n* raisin *m*; **~fruit** ['greɪpfruːt] *n* pamplemousse *m*
graph [grɑːf] *n* graphique *m*; **~ic** ['græfɪk] *adj* graphique; (*account, description*) vivant(e); **~ics** *n* arts *mpl* graphiques; graphisme *m* ♦ *npl* représentations *fpl* graphiques
grapple ['græpl] *vi*: **to ~ with** être aux prises avec
grasp [grɑːsp] *vt* saisir ♦ *n* (*grip*) prise *f*; (*understanding*) compréhension *f*, connaissance *f*; **~ing** *adj* cupide
grass [grɑːs] *n* herbe *f*; (*lawn*) gazon *m*; **~hopper** *n* sauterelle *f*; **~-roots** *adj* de la base, du peuple
grate [greɪt] *n* grille *f* de cheminée ♦ *vi* grincer ♦ *vt* (*CULIN*) râper
grateful ['greɪtfʊl] *adj* reconnaissant(e)
grater ['greɪtə*] *n* râpe *f*
gratifying ['grætɪfaɪɪŋ] *adj* agréable
grating ['greɪtɪŋ] *n* (*iron bars*) grille *f* ♦ *adj* (*noise*) grinçant(e)
gratitude ['grætɪtjuːd] *n* gratitude *f*
gratuity [grə'tjuːɪtɪ] *n* pourboire *m*
grave [greɪv] *n* tombe *f* ♦ *adj* grave, sérieux(euse)
gravel ['grævəl] *n* gravier *m*
gravestone ['greɪvstəʊn] *n* pierre tombale
graveyard ['greɪvjɑːd] *n* cimetière *m*
gravity ['grævɪtɪ] *n* (*PHYSICS*) gravité *f*; pesanteur *f*; (*seriousness*) gravité *f*
gravy ['greɪvɪ] *n* jus *m* (de viande); sauce *f*
gray [greɪ] (*US*) *adj* = **grey**
graze [greɪz] *vi* paître, brouter ♦ *vt* (*touch lightly*) frôler, effleurer; (*scrape*) écorcher ♦ *n* écorchure *f*
grease [griːs] *n* (*fat*) graisse *f*; (*lubricant*) lubrifiant *m* ♦ *vt* graisser; lubrifier; **~proof paper** (*BRIT*) *n* papier sulfurisé; **greasy** ['griːsɪ] *adj* gras(se), graisseux(euse)
great [greɪt] *adj* grand(e); (*inf*) formidable; **G~ Britain** *n* Grande-Bretagne *f*; **~-grandfather** *n* arrière-grand-père *m*; **~-grandmother** *n* arrière-grand-mère *f*; **~ly** *adv* très, grandement; (*with verbs*) beaucoup; **~ness** *n* grandeur *f*
Greece [griːs] *n* Grèce *f*
greed [griːd] *n* (*also: ~iness*) avidité *f*; (*for food*) gourmandise *f*, gloutonnerie *f*; **~y** *adj* avide; gourmand(e), glouton(ne)
Greek [griːk] *adj* grec(grecque) ♦ *n* Grec(Grecque); (*LING*) grec *m*
green [griːn] *adj* vert(e); (*inexperienced*) (bien) jeune, naïf(naïve); (*POL*) vert(e), écologiste; (*ecological*) écologique ♦ *n* vert *m*; (*stretch of grass*) pelouse *f*; **~s** *npl* (*vegeta-*

bles) légumes verts; (*POL*): **the G~s** les Verts *mpl*; **The G~ Party** (*BRIT*: *POL*) le parti écologiste; ~ **belt** *n* (*round town*) ceinture verte; ~ **card** *n* (*AUT*) carte verte; (*US*) permis *m* de travail; ~**ery** *n* verdure *f*; ~**grocer** (*BRIT*) *n* marchand *m* de fruits et légumes; ~**house** *n* serre *f*; ~**house effect** *n* effet *m* de serre; ~**house gas** *n* gas *m* à effet de serre; ~**ish** *adj* verdâtre

Greenland ['griːnlənd] *n* Groenland *m*

greet [griːt] *vt* accueillir; ~**ing** *n* salutation *f*; ~**ing(s) card** *n* carte *f* de vœux

gregarious [grɪ'geərɪəs] *adj* (*person*) sociable

grenade [grɪ'neɪd] *n* grenade *f*

grew [gruː] *pt of* **grow**

grey [greɪ] (*US* **gray**) *adj* gris(e); (*dismal*) sombre; ~**-haired** *adj* grisonnant(e); ~**hound** *n* lévrier *m*

grid [grɪd] *n* grille *f*; (*ELEC*) réseau *m*

grief [griːf] *n* chagrin *m*, douleur *f*

grievance ['griːvəns] *n* doléance *f*, grief *m*

grieve [griːv] *vi* avoir du chagrin; se désoler ♦ *vt* faire de la peine à, affliger; **to ~ for** *sb* (*dead person*) pleurer qn

grievous ['griːvəs] *adj* (*LAW*): ~ **bodily harm** coups *mpl* et blessures *fpl*

grill [grɪl] *n* (*on cooker*) gril *m*; (*food: also mixed ~*) grillade(s) *f(pl)* ♦ *vt* (*BRIT*) griller; (*inf: question*) cuisiner

grille [grɪl] *n* grille *f*, grillage *m*; (*AUT*) calandre *f*

grim [grɪm] *adj* sinistre, lugubre; (*serious, stern*) sévère

grimace [grɪ'meɪs] *n* grimace *f* ♦ *vi* grimacer, faire une grimace

grime [graɪm] *n* crasse *f*, saleté *f*

grin [grɪn] *n* large sourire *m* ♦ *vi* sourire

grind [graɪnd] (*pt, pp* **ground**) *vt* écraser; (*coffee, pepper etc*) moudre; (*US: meat*) hacher; (*make sharp*) aiguiser ♦ *n* (*work*) corvée *f*

grip [grɪp] *n* (*hold*) prise *f*, étreinte *f*; (*control*) emprise *f*; (*grasp*) connaissance *f*; (*handle*) poignée *f*; (*holdall*) sac *m* de voyage ♦ *vt* saisir, empoigner; **to come to ~s with** en venir aux prises avec; ~**ping** *adj* prenant(e), palpitant(e)

grisly ['grɪzlɪ] *adj* sinistre, macabre

gristle ['grɪsl] *n* cartilage *m*

grit [grɪt] *n* gravillon *m*; (*courage*) cran *m* ♦ *vt* (*road*) sabler; **to ~ one's teeth** serrer les dents

groan [grəʊn] *n* (*of pain*) gémissement *m* ♦ *vi* gémir

grocer ['grəʊsə*] *n* épicier *m*; ~**ies** *npl* provisions *fpl*; ~**'s (shop)** *n* épicerie *f*

groin [grɔɪn] *n* aine *f*

groom [gruːm] *n* palefrenier *m*; (*also: bride~*) marié *m* ♦ *vt* (*horse*) panser; (*fig*): **to ~ sb for** former qn pour; **well-groomed** très soigné(e)

groove [gruːv] *n* rainure *f*

grope [grəʊp] *vi*: **to ~ for** chercher à tâtons

gross [grəʊs] *adj* grossier(ère); (*COMM*) brut(e); ~**ly** *adv* (*greatly*) très, grandement

grotto ['grɒtəʊ] *n* grotte *f*

grotty ['grɒtɪ] (*inf*) *adj* minable, affreux(euse)

ground [graʊnd] *pt, pp of* **grind** ♦ *n* sol *m*, terre *f*; (*land*) terrain *m*, terres *fpl*; (*SPORT*) terrain; (*US: also: ~s*) raison *f* ♦ *vt* (*plane*) empêcher de décoller, retenir au sol; (*US: ELEC*) équiper d'une prise de terre; ~**s** *npl* (*of coffee etc*) marc *m*; (*gardens etc*) parc *m*, domaine *m*; **on the ~, to the ~** par terre; **to gain/lose ~** gagner/perdre du terrain; ~ **cloth** (*US*) *n* = **groundsheet**; ~**ing** *n* (*in education*) connaissances *fpl* de base; ~**less** *adj* sans fondement; ~**sheet** (*BRIT*) *n* tapis *m* de sol; ~ **staff** *n* personnel *m* au sol; ~**swell** *n* lame *f* or vague *f* de fond; ~**work** *n* préparation *f*

group [gruːp] *n* groupe *m* ♦ *vt* (*also: ~ together*) grouper ♦ *vi* se grouper

grouse [graʊs] *n inv* (*bird*) grouse *f* ♦ *vi* (*complain*) rouspéter, râler

grove [grəʊv] *n* bosquet *m*

grovel ['grɒvl] *vi* (*fig*) ramper

grow [grəʊ] (*pt* **grew**, *pp* **grown**) *vi* pousser, croître; (*person*) grandir; (*increase*) augmenter, se développer; (*become*): **to ~ rich/weak** s'enrichir/s'affaiblir; (*develop*): **he's ~n out of his jacket** sa veste est (devenue) trop petite pour lui; **he'll ~ out of it!** ça lui passera! ♦ *vt* cultiver, faire pousser; (*beard*) laisser pousser; ~ **up** *vi* grandir; ~**er** *n* producteur *m*; ~**ing** *adj* (*fear, amount*) croissant(e), grandissant(e)

growl [graʊl] *vi* grogner

grown [grəʊn] *pp of* **grow**; ~**-up** *n* adulte *m/f*, grande personne

growth [grəʊθ] *n* croissance *f*, développement *m*; (*what has grown*) pousse *f*, poussée *f*; (*MED*) grosseur *f*, tumeur *f*

grub [grʌb] *n* larve *f*; (*inf: food*) bouffe *f*

grubby ['grʌbɪ] *adj* crasseux(euse)

grudge [grʌdʒ] *n* rancune *f* ♦ *vt*: **to ~ sb sth** (*in giving*) donner qch à qn à contrecœur; (*resent*) reprocher qch à qn; **to bear sb a ~ (for)** garder rancune *or* en vouloir à qn (de)

gruelling ['grʊəlɪŋ] (*US* **grueling**) *adj* exténuant(e)

gruesome ['gruːsəm] *adj* horrible

gruff [grʌf] *adj* bourru(e)

grumble ['grʌmbl] *vi* rouspéter, ronchonner

grumpy ['grʌmpɪ] *adj* grincheux(euse)

grunt [grʌnt] *vi* grogner

G-string ['dʒiː-] *n* (*garment*) cache-sexe *m* inv

guarantee [gærən'tiː] n garantie f ♦ vt garantir

guard [gɑːd] n garde f; (one man) garde m; (BRIT: RAIL) chef m de train; (on machine) dispositif m de sûreté; (also: fire~) garde-feu m ♦ vt garder, surveiller; (protect): **to ~ (against** or **from)** protéger (contre); **~ against** vt (prevent) empêcher, se protéger de; **~ed** adj (fig) prudent(e); **~ian** n gardien(ne); (of minor) tuteur(trice); **~'s van** (BRIT) n (RAIL) fourgon m

guerrilla [gə'rɪlə] n guérillero m

guess [ges] vt deviner; (estimate) évaluer; (US) croire, penser ♦ vi deviner ♦ n supposition f, hypothèse f; **to take** or **have a ~** essayer de deviner; **~work** n hypothèse f

guest [gest] n invité(e); (in hotel) client(e); **~-house** n pension f; **~ room** n chambre f d'amis

guffaw [gʌ'fɔː] vi pouffer de rire

guidance ['gaɪdəns] n conseils mpl

guide [gaɪd] n (person, book etc) guide m; (BRIT: also: girl ~) guide f ♦ vt guider; **~book** n guide m; **~ dog** n chien m d'aveugle; **~lines** npl (fig) instructions (générales), conseils mpl

guild [gɪld] n corporation f; cercle m, association f

guile [gaɪl] n astuce f

guillotine [gɪlə'tiːn] n guillotine f

guilt [gɪlt] n culpabilité f; **~y** adj coupable

guinea pig ['gɪnɪ-] n cobaye m

guise [gaɪz] n aspect m, apparence f

guitar [gɪ'tɑː*] n guitare f

gulf [gʌlf] n golfe m; (abyss) gouffre m

gull [gʌl] n mouette f; (larger) goéland m

gullet ['gʌlɪt] n gosier m

gullible ['gʌlɪbl] adj crédule

gully ['gʌlɪ] n ravin m; ravine f; couloir m

gulp [gʌlp] vi avaler sa salive ♦ vt (also: ~ down) avaler

gum [gʌm] n (ANAT) gencive f; (glue) colle f; (sweet: also ~drop) boule f de gomme; (also: chewing ~) chewing-gum m ♦ vt coller; **~boots** (BRIT) npl bottes fpl en caoutchouc

gun [gʌn] n (small) revolver m, pistolet m; (rifle) fusil m, carabine f; (cannon) canon m; **~boat** n canonnière f; **~fire** n fusillade f; **~man** n bandit armé; **~point** n: **at ~point** sous la menace du pistolet (or fusil); **~powder** n poudre f à canon; **~shot** n coup m de feu

gurgle ['gɜːgl] vi gargouiller; (baby) gazouiller

gush [gʌʃ] vi jaillir; (fig) se répandre en effusions

gust [gʌst] n (of wind) rafale f; (of smoke) bouffée f

gusto ['gʌstəu] n enthousiasme m

gut [gʌt] n intestin m, boyau m; **~s** npl (inf: courage) cran m

gutter ['gʌtə*] n (in street) caniveau m; (of roof) gouttière f

guy [gaɪ] n (inf: man) type m; (also: ~rope) corde f; (BRIT: figure) effigie de Guy Fawkes (brûlée en plein air le 5 novembre)

guzzle ['gʌzl] vt avaler gloutonnement

gym [dʒɪm] n (also: ~nasium) gymnase m; (also: ~nastics) gym f; **~nast** ['dʒɪmnæst] n gymnaste m/f; **~nastics** [dʒɪm'næstɪks] n, npl gymnastique f; **~ shoes** npl chaussures fpl de gym; **~slip** (BRIT) n tunique f (d'écolière)

gynaecologist [gaɪnɪ'kɒlədʒɪst] (US **gynecologist**) n gynécologue m/f

gypsy ['dʒɪpsɪ] n gitan(e), bohémien(ne)

H h

haberdashery [hæbə'dæʃərɪ] (BRIT) n mercerie f

habit ['hæbɪt] n habitude f; (REL: costume) habit m

habitual [hə'bɪtjuəl] adj habituel(le); (drinker, liar) invétéré(e)

hack [hæk] vt hacher, tailler ♦ n (pej: writer) nègre m; **~er** n (COMPUT) pirate m (informatique); (: enthusiast) passionné(e) m/f des ordinateurs

hackneyed ['hæknɪd] adj usé(e), rebattu(e)

had [hæd] pt, pp of **have**

haddock ['hædək] (pl ~ or ~s) n églefin m; **smoked ~** haddock m

hadn't ['hædnt] = **had not**

haemorrhage ['hemərɪdʒ] (US **hemorrhage**) n hémorragie f

haemorroids ['hemərɔɪdz] (US **hemorroids**) npl hémorroïdes fpl

haggle ['hægl] vi marchander

Hague [heɪg] n: **The ~** La Haye

hail [heɪl] n grêle f ♦ vt (call) héler; (acclaim) acclamer ♦ vi grêler; **~stone** n grêlon m

hair [heə*] n cheveux mpl; (of animal) pelage m; (single hair: on head) cheveu m; (: on body; of animal) poil m; **to do one's ~** se coiffer; **~brush** n brosse f à cheveux; **~cut** n coupe f (de cheveux); **~do** n coiffure f; **~dresser** n coiffeur(euse); **~dresser's** n salon m de coiffure, coiffeur m; **~ dryer** n sèche-cheveux m; **~grip** n pince f à cheveux; **~net** n filet m à cheveux; **~piece** n perruque f; **~pin** n épingle f à cheveux; **~pin bend** (US **~pin curve**) n virage *m* en épingle à cheveux; ~**-raising** *adj* à (vous) faire dresser les cheveux sur la tête; ~ **removing cream** *n* crème *f* dépilatoire; ~ **spray** *n* laque *f* (pour les cheveux); ~**style** *n* coiffure *f*; ~**y** *adj* poilu(e); (*inf: fig*) effrayant(e)

hake [heɪk] (*pl* ~ *or* ~**s**) *n* colin *m*, merlu *m*

half [hɑːf] (*pl* **halves**) *n* moitié *f*; (*of beer: also:* ~ **pint**) ≈ demi *m*; (*RAIL, bus also:* ~ *fare*) demi-tarif *m* ♦ *adj* demi(e) ♦ *adv* (à) moitié, à demi; ~ **a dozen** une demi-douzaine; ~ **a pound** une demi-livre, ≈ 250 g; **two and a** ~ deux et demi; **to cut sth in** ~ couper qch en deux; ~**-baked** *adj* (*plan*) qui ne tient pas debout; ~**-caste** *n* métis(se); ~**-hearted** *adj* tiède, sans enthousiasme; ~**-hour** *n* demi-heure *f*; **half-mast: at** ~**-mast** *adv* (*flag*) en berne; ~**penny** ['heɪpnɪ] (*BRIT*) *n* demi-penny *m*; ~**-price** *adj, adv:* (**at**) ~**-price** à moitié prix; ~ **term** (*BRIT*) *n* (*SCOL*) congé *m* de demi-trimestre; ~**-time** *n* mi-temps *f*; ~**way** *adv* à mi-chemin

hall [hɔːl] *n* salle *f*, (*entrance way*) hall *m*, entrée *f*

hallmark ['hɔːlmɑːk] *n* poinçon *m*; (*fig*) marque *f*

hallo [hʌ'ləʊ] *excl* = **hello**

hall of residence (*BRIT: pl* **halls of residence**) *n* résidence *f* universitaire

Hallowe'en ['hæləʊ'iːn] *n* veille *f* de la Toussaint

hallucination [həluːsɪ'neɪʃən] *n* hallucination *f*

hallway ['hɔːlweɪ] *n* vestibule *m*

halo ['heɪləʊ] *n* (*of saint etc*) auréole *f*

halt [hɔːlt] *n* halte *f*, arrêt *m* ♦ *vt* (*progress etc*) interrompre ♦ *vi* faire halte, s'arrêter

halve [hɑːv] *vt* (*apple etc*) partager *or* diviser en deux; (*expense*) réduire de moitié; ~**s** [hɑːvz] *npl of* **half**

ham [hæm] *n* jambon *m*

hamburger ['hæmbɜːgə*] *n* hamburger *m*

hamlet ['hæmlɪt] *n* hameau *m*

hammer ['hæmə*] *n* marteau *m* ♦ *vt* (*nail*) enfoncer; (*fig*) démolir ♦ *vi* (*on door*) frapper à coups redoublés; **to** ~ **an idea into sb** faire entrer de force une idée dans la tête de qn

hammock ['hæmək] *n* hamac *m*

hamper ['hæmpə*] *vt* gêner ♦ *n* panier *m* (d'osier)

hamster ['hæmstə*] *n* hamster *m*

hand [hænd] *n* main *f*; (*of clock*) aiguille *f*; (*handwriting*) écriture *f*; (*worker*) ouvrier(ère); (*at cards*) jeu *m* ♦ *vt* passer, donner; **to give** *or* **lend sb a** ~ donner un coup de main à qn; **at** ~ à portée de la main; **in** ~ (*time*) à disposition; (*job, situation*) en main; **to be on** ~ (*person*) être disponible; (*emergency services*) se tenir prêt(e) (à intervenir); **to** ~ (*information etc*) sous la main, à portée de la main; **on the one** ~ ..., **on the other** ~ d'une part ..., d'autre part; ~ **in** *vt* remettre; ~ **out** *vt* distribuer; ~ **over** *vt* transmettre; céder; ~**bag** *n* sac *m* à main; ~**book** *n* manuel *m*; ~**brake** *n* frein *m* à main; ~**cuffs** *npl* menottes *fpl*; ~**ful** *n* poignée *f*

handicap ['hændɪkæp] *n* handicap *m* ♦ *vt* handicaper; **mentally/physically** ~**ped** handicapé(e) mentalement/physiquement

handicraft ['hændɪkrɑːft] *n* (*travail m* d')artisanat *m*, technique artisanale; (*object*) objet artisanal

handiwork ['hændɪwɜːk] *n* ouvrage *m*

handkerchief ['hæŋkətʃɪf] *n* mouchoir *m*

handle ['hændl] *n* (*of door etc*) poignée *f*; (*of cup etc*) anse *f*; (*of knife etc*) manche *m*; (*of saucepan*) queue *f*; (*for winding*) manivelle *f* ♦ *vt* toucher, manier; (*deal with*) s'occuper de; (*treat: people*) prendre; "~ **with care**" "fragile"; **to fly off the** ~ s'énerver; ~**bar(s)** *n(pl)* guidon *m*

hand: ~**-luggage** *n* bagages *mpl* à main; ~**made** *adj* fait(e) à la main; ~**out** *n* (*from government, parents*) aide *f*, don *m*; (*leaflet*) documentation *f*, prospectus *m*; (*summary of lecture*) polycopié *m*; ~**rail** *n* rampe *f*, main courante; ~**shake** *n* poignée *f* de main

handsome ['hænsəm] *adj* beau (belle); (*profit, return*) considérable

handwriting ['hændraɪtɪŋ] *n* écriture *f*

handy ['hændɪ] *adj* (*person*) adroit(e); (*close at hand*) sous la main; (*convenient*) pratique; ~**man** ['hændɪmæn] (*irreg*) *n* bricoleur *m*; (*servant*) homme *m* à tout faire

hang [hæŋ] (*pt, pp* **hung**) *vt* accrocher; (*criminal: pt, pp:* **hanged**) pendre ♦ *vi* pendre; (*hair, drapery*) tomber; **to get the** ~ **of (doing) sth** (*inf*) attraper le coup pour faire qch; ~ **about** *vi* traîner; = **hang about**; ~ **on** *vi* (*wait*) attendre; ~ **up** *vi* (*TEL*): **to** ~ **up (on sb)** raccrocher (au nez de qn) ♦ *vt* (*coat, painting etc*) accrocher, suspendre

hangar ['hæŋə*] *n* hangar *m*

hanger ['hæŋə*] *n* cintre *m*, portemanteau *m*; ~**-on** ['hæŋər'ɒn] *n* parasite *m*

hang: ~**-gliding** ['hæŋglaɪdɪŋ] *n* deltaplane *m*, vol *m* libre; ~**over** ['hæŋəʊvə*] *n* (*after drinking*) gueule *f* de bois; ~**-up** ['hæŋʌp] *n* complexe *m*

hanker ['hæŋkə*] *vi:* **to** ~ **after** avoir envie de

hankie, hanky ['hæŋkɪ] *n abbr* = **handkerchief**

haphazard ['hæp'hæzəd] *adj* fait(e) au hasard, fait(e) au petit bonheur

happen ['hæpən] *vi* arriver; se passer, se produire; **if it so** ~**s that** il se trouve que; **as it** ~**s** justement; ~**ing** *n* événement *m*

happily ['hæpɪlɪ] *adv* heureusement; (*cheerfully*) joyeusement

happiness ['hæpɪnɪs] *n* bonheur *m*

happy ['hæpɪ] *adj* heureux(euse); ~ **with** (*arrangements etc*) satisfait(e) de; **to be** ~ **to do** faire volontiers; ~ **birthday!** bon anniversaire!; ~**-go-lucky** *adj* insouciant(e)

harass ['hærəs] *vt* accabler, tourmenter; ~**ment** *n* tracasseries *fpl*

harbour ['hɑːbə*] (*US* **harbor**) *n* port *m* ♦ *vt* héberger, abriter; (*hope, fear etc*) entretenir

hard [hɑːd] *adj* dur(e); (*question, problem*) difficile, dur(e); (*facts, evidence*) concret(ète) ♦ *adv* (*work*) dur; (*think, try*) sérieusement; **to look** ~ **at** regarder fixement; (*thing*) regarder de près; **no** ~ **feelings!** sans rancune!; **to be** ~ **of hearing** être dur(e) d'oreille; **to be** ~ **done by** être traité(e) injustement; ~**back** *n* livre relié; ~ **cash** *n* espèces *fpl*; ~ **disk** *n* (COMPUT) disque dur; ~**en** *vt* durcir; (*fig*) endurcir ♦ *vi* durcir; ~**-headed** *adj* réaliste; décidé(e); ~ **labour** *n* travaux forcés

hardly ['hɑːdlɪ] *adv* (*scarcely, no sooner*) à peine; ~ **anywhere/ever** presque nulle part/jamais

hard: ~**ship** *n* épreuves *fpl*; ~ **up** (*inf*) fauché(e); ~**ware** *n* quincaillerie *f*; (COMPUT, MIL) matériel *m*; ~**ware shop** *n* quincaillerie *f*; ~**-wearing** *adj* solide; ~**-working** *adj* travailleur(euse)

hardy ['hɑːdɪ] *adj* robuste; (*plant*) résistant(e) au gel

hare [hɛə*] *n* lièvre *m*; ~**-brained** *adj* farfelu(e)

harm [hɑːm] *n* mal *m*; (*wrong*) tort *m* ♦ *vt* (*person*) faire du mal *or* du tort à; (*thing*) endommager; **out of** ~**'s way** à l'abri du danger, en lieu sûr; ~**ful** *adj* nuisible; ~**less** *adj* inoffensif(ive); sans méchanceté

harmony ['hɑːmənɪ] *n* harmonie *f*

harness ['hɑːnɪs] *n* harnais *m*; (*safety* ~) harnais de sécurité ♦ *vt* (*horse*) harnacher; (*resources*) exploiter

harp [hɑːp] *n* harpe *f* ♦ *vi*: **to** ~ **on about** rabâcher

harrowing ['hærəʊɪŋ] *adj* déchirant(e), très pénible

harsh [hɑːʃ] *adj* (*hard*) dur(e); (*severe*) sévère; (*unpleasant: sound*) discordant(e); (: *light*) cru(e)

harvest ['hɑːvɪst] *n* (*of corn*) moisson *f*; (*of fruit*) récolte *f*; (*of grapes*) vendange *f* ♦ *vt* moissonner; récolter; vendanger

has [hæz] *vb see* **have**

hash [hæʃ] *n* (CULIN) hachis *m*; (*fig: mess*) gâchis *m*

hasn't ['hæznt] = **has not**

hassle ['hæsl] *n* (*inf: bother*) histoires *fpl*, tracas *mpl*

haste [heɪst] *n* hâte *f*; précipitation *f*; ~**n** ['heɪsn] *vt* hâter, accélérer ♦ *vi* se hâter, s'empresser; **hastily** *adv* à la hâte; précipitamment; **hasty** ['heɪstɪ] *adj* hâtif(ive); précipité(e)

hat [hæt] *n* chapeau *m*

hatch [hætʃ] *n* (NAUT: *also*: ~*way*) écoutille *f*; (*also*: service ~) passe-plats *m inv* ♦ *vi* éclore

hatchback ['hætʃbæk] *n* (AUT) modèle *m* avec hayon arrière

hatchet ['hætʃɪt] *n* hachette *f*

hate [heɪt] *vt* haïr, détester ♦ *n* haine *f*; ~**ful** *adj* odieux(euse), détestable; **hatred** ['heɪtrɪd] *n* haine *f*

haughty ['hɔːtɪ] *adj* hautain(e), arrogant(e)

haul [hɔːl] *vt* traîner, tirer ♦ *n* (*of fish*) prise *f*; (*of stolen goods etc*) butin *m*; ~**age** *n* transport routier; (*costs*) frais *mpl* de transport; ~**ier** (*US* **hauler**) *n* (*company*) transporteur (routier); (*driver*) camionneur *m*

haunch [hɔːntʃ] *n* hanche *f*; (*of meat*) cuissot *m*

haunt [hɔːnt] *vt* hanter ♦ *n* repaire *m*

— KEYWORD

have [hæv] (*pt, pp* **had**) *aux vb* **1** (*gen*) avoir; être; **to** ~ **arrived/gone** être arrivé(e)/allé(e); **to** ~ **eaten/slept** avoir mangé/dormi; **he has been promoted** il a eu une promotion

2 (*in tag questions*): **you've done it,** ~**n't you?** vous l'avez fait, n'est-ce pas?

3 (*in short answers and questions*): **no I** ~**n't/yes we have!** mais non!/mais si!; **so I** ~! ah oui!, oui c'est vrai!; **I've been there before,** ~ **you?** j'y suis déjà allé, et vous?

♦ *modal aux vb* (*be obliged*): **to** ~ (**got**) **to do sth** devoir faire qch; être obligé(e) de faire qch; **she has (got) to do it** elle doit le faire, il faut qu'elle le fasse; **you** ~**n't to tell her** vous ne devez pas le lui dire

♦ *vt* **1** (*possess, obtain*) avoir; **he has (got) blue eyes/dark hair** il a les yeux bleus/les cheveux bruns; **may I** ~ **your address?** puis-je avoir votre adresse?

2 (+*noun: take, hold etc*): **to** ~ **breakfast/a bath/a shower** prendre le petit déjeuner/un bain/une douche; **to** ~ **dinner/lunch** dîner/déjeuner; **to** ~ **a swim** nager; **to** ~ **a meeting** se réunir; **to** ~ **a party** organiser une fête

3: **to** ~ **sth done** faire faire qch; **to** ~ **one's hair cut** se faire couper les cheveux; **to** ~ **sb do sth** faire faire qch à qn

4 (*experience, suffer*) avoir; **to** ~ **a cold/flu** avoir un rhume/la grippe; **to** ~ **an operation** se faire opérer

5 (*inf: dupe*) avoir; **he's been had** il s'est fait avoir *or* rouler

have out *vt*: **to have it out with sb** (*settle a problem etc*) s'expliquer (franchement) avec qn

haven ['heɪvn] n port m; (fig) havre m

haven't ['hævnt] = **have not**

havoc ['hævək] n ravages mpl

hawk [hɔːk] n faucon m

hay [heɪ] n foin m; ~ **fever** n rhume m des foins; ~**stack** n meule f de foin

haywire ['heɪwaɪə*] (inf) adj: **to go** ~ (machine) se détraquer; (plans) mal tourner

hazard ['hæzəd] n (danger) danger m, risque m ♦ vt risquer, hasarder; ~ (**warning**) **lights** npl (AUT) feux mpl de détresse

haze [heɪz] n brume f

hazelnut ['heɪzlnʌt] n noisette f

hazy ['heɪzɪ] adj brumeux(euse); (idea) vague

he [hiː] pron il; **it is** ~ **who** ... c'est lui qui ...

head [hed] n tête f; (leader) chef m; (of school) directeur(trice) ♦ vt (list) être en tête de; (group) être à la tête de; ~**s (or tails)** pile (ou face); ~ **first** la tête la première; ~ **over heels in love** follement or éperdument amoureux(euse); **to** ~ **a ball** faire une tête; ~ **for** vt fus se diriger vers; ~**ache** n mal m de tête; ~**dress** (BRIT) n (of Red Indian etc) coiffure f; ~**ing** n titre m; ~**lamp** (BRIT) n = **headlight**; ~**land** n promontoire m, cap m; ~**light** n phare m; ~**line** n titre m; ~**long** adv (fall) la tête la première; (rush) tête baissée; ~**master** n directeur m; ~**mistress** n directrice f; ~ **office** n bureau central, siège m; ~**-on** adj (collision) de plein fouet; (confrontation) en face à face; ~**phones** npl casque m (à écouteurs); ~**quarters** npl bureau or siège central; (MIL) quartier général; ~**rest** n appui-tête m; ~**room** n (in car) hauteur f de plafond; (under bridge) hauteur limite; ~**scarf** n foulard m; ~**strong** adj têtu(e), entêté(e); ~ **waiter** n maître m d'hôtel; ~**way** n: **to make** ~**way** avancer, faire des progrès; ~**wind** n vent m contraire; (NAUT) vent debout; ~**y** adj capiteux(euse); enivrant(e); (experience) grisant(e)

heal [hiːl] vt, vi guérir

health [helθ] n santé f; ~ **food** n aliment(s) naturel(s); ~ **food shop** n magasin m diététique; **H**~ **Service** (BRIT) n: **the H**~ **Service** ≈ la Sécurité sociale; ~**y** adj (person) en bonne santé; (climate, food, attitude etc) sain(e), bon(ne) pour la santé

heap [hiːp] n tas m ♦ vt: **to** ~ (**up**) entasser, amonceler; **she** ~**ed her plate with cakes** elle a chargé son assiette de gâteaux

hear [hɪə*] (pt, pp **heard**) vt entendre; (news) apprendre ♦ vi entendre; **to** ~ **about** entendre parler de; avoir des nouvelles de; **to** ~ **from sb** recevoir or avoir des nouvelles de qn; ~**ing** ['hɪərɪŋ] n (sense) ouïe f; (of witnesses) audition f; (of a case)

audience f; ~**ing aid** n appareil m acoustique; ~**say** ['hɪəseɪ]: **by** ~**say** adv par ouï-dire m

hearse [hɜːs] n corbillard m

heart [hɑːt] n cœur m; ~**s** npl (CARDS) cœur; **to lose/take** ~ perdre/prendre courage; **at** ~ au fond; **by** ~ (learn, know) par cœur; ~ **attack** n crise f cardiaque; ~**beat** n battement m du cœur; ~**breaking** adj déchirant(e), qui fend le cœur; ~**broken** adj: **to be** ~**broken** avoir beaucoup de chagrin or le cœur brisé; ~**burn** n brûlures fpl d'estomac; ~ **failure** n arrêt m du cœur; ~**felt** adj sincère

hearth [hɑːθ] n foyer m, cheminée f

heartily ['hɑːtɪlɪ] adv chaleureusement; (laugh) de bon cœur; (eat) de bon appétit; **to agree** ~ être entièrement d'accord

heartland ['hɑːtlænd] n (of country, region) centre m

hearty ['hɑːtɪ] adj chaleureux(euse); (appetite) robuste; (dislike) cordial(e)

heat [hiːt] n chaleur f; (fig) feu m, agitation f; (SPORT: also: qualifying ~) éliminatoire f ♦ vt chauffer; ~ **up** vi (water) chauffer; (room) se réchauffer ♦ vt réchauffer; ~**ed** adj chauffé(e); (fig) passionné(e), échauffé(e); ~**er** n appareil m de chauffage; radiateur m; (in car) chauffage m; (water ~) chauffe-eau m

heath [hiːθ] (BRIT) n lande f

heather ['heðə*] n bruyère f

heating ['hiːtɪŋ] n chauffage m

heatstroke ['hiːtstrəʊk] n (MED) coup m de chaleur

heatwave n vague f de chaleur

heave [hiːv] vt soulever (avec effort); (drag) traîner ♦ vi se soulever; (retch) avoir un haut-le-cœur; **to** ~ **a sigh** pousser un soupir

heaven ['hevn] n ciel m, paradis m; (fig) paradis; ~**ly** adj céleste, divin(e)

heavily ['hevɪlɪ] adv lourdement; (drink, smoke) beaucoup; (sleep, sigh) profondément

heavy ['hevɪ] adj lourd(e); (work, sea, rain, eater) gros(se); (snow) beaucoup de; (drinker, smoker) grand(e); (breathing) bruyant(e); (schedule, week) chargé(e); ~ **goods vehicle** n poids lourd; ~**weight** n (SPORT) poids lourd

Hebrew ['hiːbruː] adj hébraïque ♦ n (LING) hébreu m

Hebrides ['hebrɪdiːz] npl: **the** ~ les Hébrides fpl

heckle ['hekl] vt interpeller (un orateur)

hectic ['hektɪk] adj agité(e), trépidant(e)

he'd [hiːd] = **he would**; **he had**

hedge [hedʒ] n haie f ♦ vi se dérober; **to** ~ **one's bets** (fig) se couvrir

hedgehog ['hedʒhɒg] n hérisson m

heed [hiːd] vt (also: **take** ~ **of**) tenir compte

de; ~**less** *adj* insouciant(e)
heel [hiːl] *n* talon *m* ♦ *vt* (*shoe*) retalonner
hefty ['heftɪ] *adj* (*person*) costaud(e); (*parcel*) lourd(e); (*profit*) gros(se)
heifer ['hefə*] *n* génisse *f*
height [haɪt] *n* (*of person*) taille *f*, grandeur *f*; (*of object*) hauteur *f*; (*of plane, mountain*) altitude *f*; (*high ground*) hauteur *f*, éminence *f*; (*fig: of glory*) sommet *m*; (: *of luxury, stupidity*) comble *m*; ~**en** *vt* (*fig*) augmenter
heir [ɛə*] *n* héritier *m*; ~**ess** ['ɛərɪs] *n* héritière *f*; ~**loom** *n* héritage *m*, meuble *m* (*or* bijou *m* *or* tableau *m*) de famille
held [held] *pt, pp of* **hold**
helicopter ['helɪkɒptə*] *n* hélicoptère *m*
hell [hel] *n* enfer *m*; ~! (*infl*) merde!
he'll [hiːl] = **he will; he shall**
hellish ['helɪʃ] (*inf*) *adj* infernal(e)
hello [hʌˈləʊ] *excl* bonjour!; (*to attract attention*) hé!; (*surprise*) tiens!
helm [helm] *n* (NAUT) barre *f*
helmet ['helmɪt] *n* casque *m*
help [help] *n* aide *f*, (*cleaner*) femme *f* de ménage ♦ *vt* aider; ~! au secours!; ~ **yourself** servez-vous; **he can't** ~ **it** il n'y peut rien; ~**er** *n* aide *m/f*, assistant(e); ~**ful** *adj* serviable, obligeant(e); (*useful*) utile; ~**ing** *n* portion *f*; ~**less** *adj* impuissant(e); (*defenceless*) faible
hem [hem] *n* ourlet *m* ♦ *vt* ourler; ~ **in** *vt* cerner
hemorrhage ['hemərɪdʒ] (US) *n* = **haemorrhage**
hemorrhoids ['hemərɔɪdz] (US) *npl* = **haemorrhoids**
hen [hen] *n* poule *f*
hence [hens] *adv* (*therefore*) d'où, de là; **2 years** ~ d'ici 2 ans, dans 2 ans; ~**forth** *adv* dorénavant
henchman ['hentʃmən] (*pej: irreg*) *n* acolyte *m*
her [hɜː*] *pron* (*direct*) la, l'; (*indirect*) lui; (*stressed, after prep*) elle ♦ *adj* son(sa), ses *pl*; *see also* **me; my**
herald ['herəld] *n* héraut *m* ♦ *vt* annoncer; ~**ry** ['herəldrɪ] *n* (*study*) héraldique *f*; (*coat of arms*) blason *m*
herb [hɜːb] *n* herbe *f*
herd [hɜːd] *n* troupeau *m*
here [hɪə*] *adv* ici; (*time*) alors ♦ *excl* tiens!, tenez!; ~! présent!; ~ **is,** ~ **are** voici; ~ **he/she is!** le/la voici!; ~**after** *adv* après, plus tard; ~**by** *adv* (*formal: in letter*) par la présente
hereditary [hɪˈredɪtərɪ] *adj* héréditaire
heresy ['herəsɪ] *n* hérésie *f*
heritage ['herɪtɪdʒ] *n* (*of country*) patrimoine *m*
hermit ['hɜːmɪt] *n* ermite *m*
hernia ['hɜːnɪə] *n* hernie *f*
hero ['hɪərəʊ] (*pl* ~**es**) *n* héros *m*
heroin ['herəʊɪn] *n* héroïne *f*

heroine ['herəʊɪn] *n* héroïne *f*
heron ['herən] *n* héron *m*
herring ['herɪŋ] *n* hareng *m*
hers [hɜːz] *pron* le(la) sien(ne), les siens(siennes); *see also* **mine[1]**
herself [hɜːˈself] *pron* (*reflexive*) se; (*emphatic*) elle-même; (*after prep*) elle; *see also* **oneself**
he's [hiːz] = **he is; he has**
hesitant ['hezɪtənt] *adj* hésitant(e), indécis(e)
hesitate ['hezɪteɪt] *vi* hésiter; **hesitation** [hezɪˈteɪʃən] *n* hésitation *f*
hew [hjuː] (*pp* **hewed** *or* **hewn**) *vt* (*stone*) tailler; (*wood*) couper
heyday ['heɪdeɪ] *n*: **the** ~ **of** l'âge *m* d'or de, les beaux jours de
HGV *n abbr* = **heavy goods vehicle**
hi [haɪ] *excl* salut!; (*to attract attention*) hé!
hiatus [haɪˈeɪtəs] *n* (*gap*) lacune *f*; (*interruption*) pause *f*
hibernate ['haɪbəneɪt] *vi* hiberner
hiccough, hiccup ['hɪkʌp] *vi* hoqueter; ~**s** *npl* hoquet *m*
hide [haɪd] (*pt* **hid**, *pp* **hidden**) *n* (*skin*) peau *f* ♦ *vt* cacher; *vi*: **to** ~ (**from sb**) se cacher (de qn); ~**-and-seek** *n* cache-cache *m*; ~**away** *n* cachette *f*
hideous ['hɪdɪəs] *adj* hideux(euse)
hiding ['haɪdɪŋ] *n* (*beating*) correction *f*, volée *f* de coups; **to be in** ~ (*concealed*) se tenir caché(e)
hierarchy ['haɪərɑːkɪ] *n* hiérarchie *f*
hi-fi ['haɪfaɪ] *n* hi-fi *f inv* ♦ *adj* hi-fi *inv*
high [haɪ] *adj* haut(e); (*speed, respect, number*) grand(e); (*price*) élevé(e); (*wind*) fort(e), violent(e); (*voice*) aigu(aiguë) ♦ *adv* haut; **20 m** ~ haut(e) de 20 m; ~**brow** *adj, n* intellectuel(le); ~**chair** *n* (*child's*) chaise haute; ~**er education** *n* études supérieures; ~**handed** *adj* très autoritaire; très cavalier(ère); ~ **jump** *n* (SPORT) saut *m* en hauteur; ~**lands** *npl*: **the H~lands** les Highlands *mpl*; ~**light** *n* (*fig: of event*) point culminant ♦ *vt* faire ressortir, souligner; ~**lights** *npl* (*in hair*) reflets *mpl*; ~**ly** *adv* très, fort, hautement; **to speak/think** ~**ly of sb** dire/penser beaucoup de bien de qn; ~**ly paid** *adj* très bien payé(e); ~**ly strung** *adj* nerveux(euse), toujours tendu(e); ~**ness** *n*: **Her** (*or* **His**) **H~ness** Son Altesse *f*; ~**-pitched** *adj* aigu(aiguë); ~**-rise** *adj*: ~**-rise block**, ~**-rise flats** tour *f* (d'habitation); ~ **school** *n* lycée *m*; (US) établissement *m* d'enseignement supérieur; ~ **season** (BRIT) *n* haute saison; ~ **street** (BRIT) *n* grand-rue *f*; ~**way** ['haɪweɪ] *n* route nationale; **H~way Code** (BRIT) *n* code *m* de la route
hijack ['haɪdʒæk] *vt* (*plane*) détourner; ~**er** *n* pirate *m* de l'air
hike [haɪk] *vi* aller *or* faire des excursions à

pied ♦ *n* excursion *f* à pied, randonnée *f*; ~**r** *n* promeneur(euse), excursionniste *m/f*

hilarious [hɪ'lɛərɪəs] *adj* (*account, event*) désopilant(e)

hill [hɪl] *n* colline *f*; (*fairly high*) montagne *f*; (*on road*) côte *f*; ~**side** *n* (flanc *m* de) coteau *m*; ~**y** *adj* vallonné(e); montagneux(euse)

hilt [hɪlt] *n* (*of sword*) garde *f*; **to the ~** (*fig: support*) à fond

him [hɪm] *pron* (*direct*) le, l'; (*stressed, indirect, after prep*) lui; *see also* **me**; ~**self** [hɪm'sɛlf] *pron* (*reflexive*) se; (*emphatic*) lui-même; (*after prep*) lui; *see also* **oneself**

hind [haɪnd] *adj* de derrière

hinder ['hɪndə*] *vt* gêner; (*delay*) retarder; **hindrance** ['hɪndrəns] *n* gêne *f*, obstacle *m*

hindsight ['haɪndsaɪt] *n*: **with ~** avec du recul, rétrospectivement

Hindu ['hɪndu:] *adj* hindou(e)

hinge [hɪndʒ] *n* charnière *f* ♦ *vi* (*fig*): **to ~ on** dépendre de

hint [hɪnt] *n* allusion *f*; (*advice*) conseil *m* ♦ *vt*: **to ~ that** insinuer que ♦ *vi*: **to ~ at** faire une allusion à

hip [hɪp] *n* hanche *f*

hippopotamus [hɪpə'pɒtəməs] (*pl* ~**es** *or* **hippopotami**) *n* hippopotame *m*

hire ['haɪə*] *vt* (*BRIT: equipment*) louer; (*worker*) embaucher, engager ♦ *n* location *f*; **for ~** à louer; (*taxi*) libre; ~ **purchase** (*BRIT*) *n* achat *m* (*or* vente *f*) à tempérament *or* crédit

his [hɪz] *pron* le(la) sien(ne), les siens(siennes) ♦ *adj* son(sa), ses *pl*; *see also* **my**; **mine**[1]

hiss [hɪs] *vi* siffler

historic [hɪs'tɒrɪk] *adj* historique

historical [hɪs'tɒrɪkəl] *adj* historique

history ['hɪstərɪ] *n* histoire *f*

hit [hɪt] (*pt, pp* **hit**) *vt* frapper; (*reach: target*) atteindre, toucher; (*collide with: car*) entrer en collision avec, heurter; (*fig: affect*) toucher ♦ *n* coup *m*; (*success*) succès *m*; (*: song*) tube *m*; **to ~ it off with sb** bien s'entendre avec qn; ~**-and-run driver** *n* chauffard *m* (coupable du délit de fuite)

hitch [hɪtʃ] *vt* (*fasten*) accrocher, attacher; (*also*: ~ **up**) remonter d'une saccade ♦ *n* (*difficulty*) anicroche *f*, contretemps *m*; **to ~ a lift** faire du stop

hitchhike ['hɪtʃhaɪk] *vi* faire de l'auto-stop; ~**r** *n* auto-stoppeur(euse)

hi-tech ['haɪ'tɛk] *adj* de pointe

hitherto ['hɪðə'tu:] *adv* jusqu'ici

HIV: ~**-negative**/**-positive** *adj* séro-négatif (ive)/-positif(ive)

hive [haɪv] *n* ruche *f*; ~ **off** (*inf*) *vt* mettre à part, séparer

HMS *abbr* = **Her (His) Majesty's Ship**

hoard [hɔ:d] *n* (*of food*) provisions *fpl*, réserves *fpl*; (*of money*) trésor *m* ♦ *vt* amasser; ~**ing** ['hɔ:dɪŋ] (*BRIT*) *n* (*for posters*) panneau *m* d'affichage *or* publicitaire

hoarse [hɔ:s] *adj* enroué(e)

hoax [həʊks] *n* canular *m*

hob [hɒb] *n* plaque (chauffante)

hobble ['hɒbl] *vi* boitiller

hobby ['hɒbɪ] *n* passe-temps favori; ~-**horse** *n* (*fig*) dada *m*

hobo ['həʊbəʊ] (*US*) *n* vagabond *m*

hockey ['hɒkɪ] *n* hockey *m*

hog [hɒg] *n* porc (châtré) ♦ *vt* (*fig*) accaparer; **to go the whole ~** aller jusqu'au bout

hoist [hɔɪst] *n* (*apparatus*) palan *m* ♦ *vt* hisser

hold [həʊld] (*pt, pp* **held**) *vt* tenir; (*contain*) contenir; (*believe*) considérer; (*possess*) avoir; (*detain*) détenir ♦ *vi* (*withstand pressure*) tenir (bon); (*be valid*) valoir ♦ *vt* (*also fig*) prise *f*; (*NAUT*) cale *f*; ~ **the line!** (*TEL*) ne quittez pas!; **to ~ one's own** (*fig*) (bien) se défendre; **to catch** *or* **get** (**a**) ~ **of** saisir; **to get** ~ **of** (*fig*) trouver; ~ **back** *vt* retenir; (*secret*) taire; ~ **down** *vt* (*person*) maintenir à terre; (*job*) occuper; ~ **off** *vt* tenir à distance; ~ **on** *vi* tenir bon; (*wait*) attendre; ~ **on!** (*TEL*) ne quittez pas!; ~ **on to** *vt fus* se cramponner à; (*keep*) conserver, garder; ~ **out** *vt* offrir ♦ *vi* (*resist*) tenir bon; ~ **up** *vt* (*raise*) lever; (*support*) soutenir; (*delay*) retarder; (*rob*) braquer; ~**all** (*BRIT*) *n* fourre-tout *m inv*; ~**er** *n* (*of ticket, record*) détenteur(trice); (*of office, title etc*) titulaire *m/f*; (*container*) support *m*; ~**ing** *n* (*share*) intérêts *mpl*; (*farm*) ferme *f*; ~-**up** *n* (*robbery*) hold-up *m*; (*delay*) retard *m*; (*BRIT: in traffic*) bouchon *m*

hole [həʊl] *n* trou *m*

holiday ['hɒlədɪ] *n* vacances *fpl*; (*day off*) jour *m* de congé; (*public*) jour férié; **on ~** en congé; ~ **camp** *n* (*also*: ~ *centre*) camp *m* de vacances; ~-**maker** (*BRIT*) *n* vacancier(ère); ~ **resort** *n* centre *m* de villégiature *or* de vacances

Holland ['hɒlənd] *n* Hollande *f*

hollow ['hɒləʊ] *adj* creux(euse) ♦ *n* creux *m* ♦ *vt*: **to ~ out** creuser, évider

holly ['hɒlɪ] *n* houx *m*

holocaust ['hɒləkɔ:st] *n* holocauste *m*

holster ['həʊlstə*] *n* étui *m* de revolver

holy ['həʊlɪ] *adj* saint(e); (*bread, water*) bénit(e); (*ground*) sacré(e); **H~ Ghost** *m* Saint-Esprit *m*

homage ['hɒmɪdʒ] *n* hommage *m*; **to pay ~ to** rendre hommage à

home [həʊm] *n* foyer *m*, maison *f*; (*country*) pays natal, patrie *f*; (*institution*) maison ♦ *adj* de famille; (*ECON, POL*) national(e), intérieur(e); (*SPORT: game*) sur leur (*or* notre) terrain; (*team*) qui reçoit ♦ *adv* chez soi, à la maison; au pays natal; (*right in: nail etc*) à fond; **at ~** chez soi, à la maison; **make yourself at ~** faites comme chez vous; ~ **address** n domicile permanent; ~**land** n patrie f; ~**less** adj sans foyer; sans abri; ~**ly** adj (plain) simple, sans prétention; ~**made** adj fait(e) à la maison; **H~ Office** (BRIT) n ministère m de l'Intérieur; ~ **rule** n autonomie f; **H~ Secretary** (BRIT) n ministre m de l'Intérieur; ~**sick** adj: **to be** ~**sick** avoir le mal du pays; s'ennuyer de sa famille; ~ **town** n ville natale; ~**ward** adj (journey) du retour; ~**work** n devoirs mpl

homogeneous [hɒmə'dʒiːnɪəs] adj homogène

homosexual ['hɒməʊ'seksjʊəl] adj, n homosexuel(le)

honest ['ɒnɪst] adj honnête; (sincere) franc(franche); ~**ly** adv honnêtement; franchement; ~**y** n honnêteté f

honey ['hʌnɪ] n miel m; ~**comb** n rayon m de miel; ~**moon** n lune f de miel, voyage m de noces; ~**suckle** ['hʌnɪsʌkl] (BOT) n chèvrefeuille m

honk [hɒŋk] vi (AUT) klaxonner

honorary ['ɒnərərɪ] adj honoraire; (duty, title) honorifique

honour ['ɒnə*] (US **honor**) vt honorer ♦ n honneur m; **hono(u)rable** adj honorable; **hono(u)rs degree** n (SCOL) licence avec mention

hood [hʊd] n capuchon m; (of cooker) hotte f; (AUT: BRIT) capote f; (: US) capot m

hoof [huːf] (pl **hooves**) n sabot m

hook [hʊk] n crochet m; (on dress) agrafe f; (for fishing) hameçon m ♦ vt accrocher; (fish) prendre

hooligan ['huːlɪgən] n voyou m

hoop [huːp] n cerceau m

hooray [huːˈreɪ] excl hourra

hoot [huːt] vi (AUT) klaxonner; (siren) mugir; (owl) hululer; ~**er** n (BRIT: AUT) klaxon m; (NAUT, factory) sirène f

Hoover ['huːvə*] (®:BRIT) n aspirateur m ♦ vt: **h~** passer l'aspirateur dans or sur

hooves [huːvz] npl of **hoof**

hop [hɒp] vi (on one foot) sauter à cloche-pied; (bird) sautiller

hope [həʊp] vt, vi espérer ♦ n espoir m; **I** ~ **so** je l'espère; **I** ~ **not** j'espère que non; ~**ful** adj (person) plein(e) d'espoir; (situation) prometteur(euse), encourageant(e); ~**fully** adv (expectantly) avec espoir, avec optimisme; (one hopes) avec un peu de chance; ~**less** adj désespéré(e), (useless) nul(le)

hops [hɒps] npl houblon m

horizon [hə'raɪzn] n horizon m; ~**tal** [hɒrɪˈzɒntl] adj horizontal(e)

horn [hɔːn] n corne f; (MUS: also: French ~) cor m; (AUT) klaxon m

hornet ['hɔːnɪt] n frelon m

horny ['hɔːnɪ] (inf) adj (aroused) en rut, excité(e)

horoscope ['hɒrəskəʊp] n horoscope m

horrendous [hə'rendəs] adj horrible, affreux(euse)

horrible ['hɒrɪbl] adj horrible, affreux(euse)

horrid ['hɒrɪd] adj épouvantable

horrify ['hɒrɪfaɪ] vt horrifier

horror ['hɒrə*] n horreur f; ~ **film** n film m d'épouvante

hors d'œuvre [ɔːˈdɜːvrə] n (CULIN) hors-d'œuvre m inv

horse [hɔːs] n cheval m; ~**back** n: **on** ~**back** à cheval; ~ **chestnut** n marron m (d'Inde); ~**man** (irreg) n cavalier m; ~**power** n puissance f (en chevaux); ~**racing** n courses fpl de chevaux; ~**radish** n raifort m; ~**shoe** n fer m à cheval

hose [həʊz] n (also: ~**pipe**) tuyau m; (: garden ~) tuyau d'arrosage

hospitable [hɒs'pɪtəbl] adj hospitalier(ère)

hospital ['hɒspɪtl] n hôpital m; **in** ~ à l'hôpital

hospitality [hɒspɪ'tælɪtɪ] n hospitalité f

host [həʊst] n hôte m; (TV, RADIO) animateur(trice); (REL) hostie f; (large number): **a** ~ **of** une foule de

hostage ['hɒstɪdʒ] n otage m

hostel ['hɒstəl] n foyer m; (also: youth ~) auberge f de jeunesse

hostess ['həʊstes] n hôtesse f; (TV, RADIO) animatrice f

hostile ['hɒstaɪl] adj hostile; **hostility** [hɒs'tɪlɪtɪ] n hostilité f

hot [hɒt] adj chaud(e); (as opposed to only warm) très chaud; (spicy) fort(e); (contest etc) acharné(e); (temper) passionné(e); **to be** ~ (person) avoir chaud; (object) être (très) chaud; **it is** ~ (weather) il fait chaud; ~**bed** n (fig) foyer m, pépinière f; ~ **dog** n hot-dog m

hotel [həʊ'tel] n hôtel m

hot: ~**-headed** adj impétueux(euse); ~**house** n serre (chaude); ~**line** n (POL) téléphone m rouge, ligne directe; ~**ly** adv passionnément, violemment; ~**plate** n (on cooker) plaque chauffante; ~**-water bottle** n bouillotte f

hound [haʊnd] vt poursuivre avec acharnement ♦ n chien courant

hour ['aʊə*] n heure f; ~**ly** adj, adv toutes les heures; (rate) horaire

house [n haʊs, pl 'haʊzɪz, vb haʊz] n maison f; (POL) chambre f; (THEATRE) salle f; auditoire m ♦ vt (person) loger, héberger; (objects) abriter; **on the** ~ (fig) aux frais de la maison; ~ **arrest** n assignation f à résidence; ~**boat** n bateau m (aménagé en habitation); ~**bound** adj confiné(e) chez soi; ~**breaking** n cambriolage m (avec effraction); ~**coat** n peignoir m; ~**hold** n (persons) famille f, maisonnée f; (ADMIN etc) ménage m; ~**keeper** n gouvernante f; ~**keeping** n (work) ménage m; ~**keeping**

(money) argent *m* du ménage; **~-warming (party)** *n* pendaison *f* de crémaillère; **~wife** (*irreg*) *n* ménagère *f*; femme *f* au foyer; **~work** *n* (travaux *mpl* du) ménage *m*

housing ['hauzɪŋ] *n* logement *m*; **~ development, ~ estate** *n* lotissement *m*

hovel ['hɒvəl] *n* taudis *m*

hover ['hɒvə*] *vi* planer; **~craft** *n* aéroglisseur *m*

how [hau] *adv* comment; **~ are you?** comment allez-vous?; **~ do you do?** bonjour; enchanté(e); **~ far is it to?** combien y a-t-il jusqu'à ...?; **~ long have you been here?** depuis combien de temps êtes-vous là?; **~ lovely!** que *or* comme c'est joli!; **~ many/much?** combien?; **~ many people/much milk?** combien de gens/lait?; **~ old are you?** quel âge avez-vous?

however [hau'evə*] *adv* de quelque façon *or* manière que +*subj*; (+*adj*) quelque *or* si ... que +*subj*; (*in questions*) comment ♦ *conj* pourtant, cependant

howl [haul] *vi* hurler

H.P. *abbr* = **hire purchase**

h.p. *abbr* = **horsepower**

HQ *abbr* = **headquarters**

hub [hʌb] *n* (*of wheel*) moyeu *m*; (*fig*) centre *m*, foyer *m*

hubbub ['hʌbʌb] *n* brouhaha *m*

hubcap ['hʌbkæp] *n* enjoliveur *m*

huddle ['hʌdl] *vi*: **to ~ together** se blottir les uns contre les autres

hue [hju:] *n* teinte *f*, nuance *f*, **~ and cry** *n* tollé *m* (général), clameur *f*

huff [hʌf] *n*: **in a ~** fâché(e)

hug [hʌg] *vt* serrer dans ses bras; (*shore, kerb*) serrer

huge [hju:dʒ] *adj* énorme, immense

hulk [hʌlk] *n* (*ship*) épave *f*; (*car, building*) carcasse *f*; (*person*) mastodonte *m*

hull [hʌl] *n* coque *f*

hullo [hʌ'ləu] *excl* = **hello**

hum [hʌm] *vt* (*tune*) fredonner ♦ *vi* fredonner; (*insect*) bourdonner; (*plane, tool*) vrombir

human ['hju:mən] *adj* humain(e) ♦ *n* **~ (being)** être humain; **~e** [hju:'meɪn] *adj* humain(e), humanitaire; **~itarian** [hju:mænɪ'tɛərɪən] *adj* humanitaire; **~ity** [hju:'mænɪtɪ] *n* humanité *f*

humble ['hʌmbl] *adj* humble, modeste ♦ *vt* humilier

humbug ['hʌmbʌg] *n* fumisterie *f*; (*BRIT*) bonbon *m* à la menthe

humdrum ['hʌmdrʌm] *adj* monotone, banal(e)

humid ['hju:mɪd] *adj* humide

humiliate [hju:'mɪlɪeɪt] *vt* humilier; **humiliation** *n* humiliation *f*

humorous ['hju:mərəs] *adj* humoristique; (*person*) plein(e) d'humour

humour ['hju:mə*] (*US* **humor**) *n* humour *m*; (*mood*) humeur *f* ♦ *vt* (*person*) faire plaisir à; se prêter aux caprices de

hump [hʌmp] *n* bosse *f*

humpbacked ['hʌmpbækt] *adj*: **~ bridge** pont *m* en dos d'âne

hunch [hʌntʃ] *n* (*premonition*) intuition *f*; **~back** *n* bossu(e); **~ed** *adj* voûté(e)

hundred ['hʌndrəd] *num* cent; **~s of** des centaines de; **~weight** *n* (*BRIT*) = 50.8 kg; (*US*) = 45.3 kg

hung [hʌŋ] *pt, pp of* **hang**

Hungary ['hʌŋgərɪ] *n* Hongrie *f*

hunger ['hʌŋgə*] *n* faim *f* ♦ *vi*: **to ~ for** avoir faim de, désirer ardemment

hungry ['hʌŋgrɪ] *adj* affamé(e); (*keen*): **~ for** avide de; **to be ~** avoir faim

hunk [hʌŋk] *n* (*of bread etc*) gros morceau

hunt [hʌnt] *vt* chasser; (*criminal*) pourchasser ♦ *vi* chasser; (*search*): **to ~ for** chercher (partout) ♦ *n* chasse *f*; **~er** *n* chasseur *m*; **~ing** *n* chasse *f*

hurdle ['hɜ:dl] *n* (*SPORT*) haie *f*; (*fig*) obstacle *m*

hurl [hɜ:l] *vt* lancer (avec violence); (*abuse, insults*) lancer

hurrah [hu'rɑ:] *excl* = **hooray**

hurray [hu'reɪ] *excl* = **hooray**

hurricane ['hʌrɪkən] *n* ouragan *m*

hurried ['hʌrɪd] *adj* pressé(e), précipité(e); (*work*) fait(e) à la hâte; **~ly** *adv* précipitamment, à la hâte

hurry ['hʌrɪ] (*vb: also:* **~ up**) *n* hâte *f*, précipitation *f* ♦ *vi* se presser, se dépêcher ♦ *vt* (*person*) faire presser, faire se dépêcher; (*work*) presser; **to be in a ~** être pressé(e); **to do sth in a ~** faire qch en vitesse; **to ~ in/out** entrer/sortir précipitamment

hurt [hɜ:t] (*pt, pp* **hurt**) *vt* (*cause pain to*) faire mal à; (*injure, fig*) blesser ♦ *vi* faire mal ♦ *adj* blessé(e); **~ful** *adj* (*remark*) blessant(e)

hurtle ['hɜ:tl] *vi*: **to ~ past** passer en trombe; **to ~ down** dégringoler

husband ['hʌzbənd] *n* mari *m*

hush [hʌʃ] *n* calme *m*, silence *m* ♦ *vt* faire taire; **~! chut!**; **~ up** *vt* (*scandal*) étouffer

husk [hʌsk] *n* (*of wheat*) balle *f*; (*of rice, maize*) enveloppe *f*

husky ['hʌskɪ] *adj* rauque ♦ *n* chien *m* esquimau *or* de traîneau

hustle ['hʌsl] *vt* pousser, bousculer ♦ *n*: **~ and bustle** tourbillon *m* (d'activité)

hut [hʌt] *n* hutte *f*; (*shed*) cabane *f*

hutch [hʌtʃ] *n* clapier *m*

hyacinth ['haɪəsɪnθ] *n* jacinthe *f*

hydrant ['haɪdrənt] *n* (*also:* **fire ~**) bouche *f* d'incendie

hydraulic [haɪ'drɒlɪk] *adj* hydraulique

hydroelectric [haɪdrəʊ'lektrɪk] *adj* hydro-électrique

hydrofoil ['haɪdrəʊfɔɪl] *n* hydrofoil *m*

hydrogen ['haɪdrɪdʒən] *n* hydrogène *m*
hyena [haɪ'iːnə] *n* hyène *f*
hygiene ['haɪdʒiːn] *n* hygiène *f*
hymn [hɪm] *n* hymne *m*; cantique *m*
hype [haɪp] (*inf*) *n* battage *m* publicitaire
hypermarket ['haɪpəˈmɑːkɪt] (*BRIT*) *n* hypermarché *m*
hyphen ['haɪfən] *n* trait *m* d'union
hypnotize ['hɪpnətaɪz] *vt* hypnotiser
hypocrisy [hɪ'pɒkrɪsɪ] *n* hypocrisie *f*; **hypocrite** ['hɪpəkrɪt] *n* hypocrite *m/f*; **hypocritical** *adj* hypocrite
hypothesis [haɪ'pɒθɪsɪs] (*pl* ~es) *n* hypothèse *f*
hysterical [hɪs'terɪkəl] *adj* hystérique; (*funny*) hilarant(e); ~ **laughter** fou rire *m*
hysterics [hɪs'terɪks] *npl*: **to be in/have** ~ (*anger, panic*) avoir une crise de nerfs; (*laughter*) attraper un fou rire

I i

I [aɪ] *pron* je; (*before vowel*) j'; (*stressed*) moi
ice [aɪs] *n* glace *f*; (*on road*) verglas *m* ♦ *vt* (*cake*) glacer ♦ *vi* (*also*: ~ *over*, ~ *up*) geler; (: *window*) se givrer; ~**berg** *n* iceberg *m*; ~**box** *n* (*US*) réfrigérateur *m*; (*BRIT*) compartiment *m* à glace; (*insulated box*) glacière *f*; ~ **cream** *n* glace *f*; ~ **cube** *n* glaçon *m*; ~**d** *adj* glacé(e); ~ **hockey** *n* hockey *m* sur glace; **i~land** ['aɪslənd] *n* Islande *f* ♦ *vi* (*BRIT*) esquimau *m* (glace); ~ **rink** *n* patinoire *f*; ~**-skating** *n* patinage *m* (sur glace)
icicle ['aɪsɪkl] *n* glaçon *m* (*naturel*)
icing ['aɪsɪŋ] *n* (*CULIN*) glace *f*, ~ **sugar** (*BRIT*) *n* sucre *m* glace
icy ['aɪsɪ] *adj* glacé(e); (*road*) verglacé(e); (*weather, temperature*) glacial(e)
I'd [aɪd] = I would; I had
idea [aɪ'dɪə] *n* idée *f*
ideal [aɪ'dɪəl] *n* idéal *m* ♦ *adj* idéal(e)
identical [aɪ'dentɪkəl] *adj* identique
identification [aɪdentɪfɪ'keɪʃən] *n* identification *f*; **means of** ~ pièce *f* d'identité
identify [aɪ'dentɪfaɪ] *vt* identifier
Identikit picture [aɪ'dentɪkɪt-] ® *n* portrait-robot *m*
identity [aɪ'dentɪtɪ] *n* identité *f*, ~ **card** *n* carte *f* d'identité
ideology [aɪdɪ'ɒlədʒɪ] *n* idéologie *f*
idiom ['ɪdɪəm] *n* expression *f* idiomatique; (*style*) style *m*

idiosyncrasy [ɪdɪəˈsɪŋkrəsɪ] *n* (*of person*) particularité *f*, petite manie
idiot ['ɪdɪət] *n* idiot(e), imbécile *m/f*; ~**ic** [ɪdɪ'ɒtɪk] *adj* idiot(e), bête, stupide
idle ['aɪdl] *adj* sans occupation, désœuvré(e); (*lazy*) oisif(ive), paresseux(euse); (*unemployed*) au chômage; (*question, pleasures*) vain(e), futile ♦ *vi* (*engine*) tourner au ralenti; **to lie** ~ être arrêté(e), ne pas fonctionner; ~ **away** *vt*: **to** ~ **away the time** passer son temps à ne rien faire
idol ['aɪdl] *n* idole *f*; ~**ize** *vt* idolâtrer, adorer
i.e. *adv abbr* (= *id est*) c'est-à-dire
if [ɪf] *conj* si; ~ **so** si c'est le cas; ~ **not** sinon; ~ **only** si seulement
ignite [ɪg'naɪt] *vt* mettre le feu à, enflammer ♦ *vi* s'enflammer
ignition [ɪg'nɪʃən] *n* (*AUT*) allumage *m*; **to switch on/off the** ~ mettre/couper le contact; ~ **key** *n* clé *f* de contact
ignorant ['ɪgnərənt] *adj* ignorant(e); **to be** ~ **of** (*subject*) ne rien connaître à; (*events*) ne pas être au courant de
ignore [ɪg'nɔː*] *vt* ne tenir aucun compte de; (*person*) faire semblant de ne pas reconnaître, ignorer; (*fact*) méconnaître
ill [ɪl] *adj* (*sick*) malade; (*bad*) mauvais(e) ♦ *n* mal *m* ♦ *adv*: **to speak/think** ~ **of** dire/penser du mal de; ~**s** *npl* (*misfortunes*) maux *mpl*, malheurs *mpl*; **to be taken** ~ tomber malade; ~**-advised** *adj* (*decision*) peu judicieux(euse); (*person*) malavisé(e); ~**-at-ease** *adj* mal à l'aise
I'll [aɪl] = I will; I shall
illegal [ɪ'liːgəl] *adj* illégal(e)
illegible [ɪ'ledʒəbl] *adj* illisible
illegitimate [ɪlɪ'dʒɪtɪmət] *adj* illégitime
ill: ~-fated [ɪl'feɪtɪd] *adj* malheureux(euse); (*day*) néfaste; ~ **feeling** *n* ressentiment *m*, rancune *f*
illiterate [ɪ'lɪtərət] *adj* illettré(e); (*letter*) plein(e) de fautes
ill: ~-mannered [ɪl'mænəd] *adj* (*child*) mal élevé(e); ~**ness** ['ɪlnəs] *n* maladie *f*, ~**treat** ['ɪl'triːt] *vt* maltraiter
illuminate [ɪ'luːmɪneɪt] *vt* (*room, street*) éclairer; (*for special effect*) illuminer; **illumination** [ɪluːmɪ'neɪʃən] *n* éclairage *m*; illumination *f*
illusion [ɪ'luːʒən] *n* illusion *f*
illustrate ['ɪləstreɪt] *vt* illustrer; **illustration** [ɪləs'treɪʃən] *n* illustration *f*
ill will *n* malveillance *f*
I'm [aɪm] = I am
image ['ɪmɪdʒ] *n* image *f*; (*public face*) image de marque; ~**ry** *n* images *fpl*
imaginary [ɪ'mædʒɪnərɪ] *adj* imaginaire
imagination [ɪmædʒɪ'neɪʃən] *n* imagination *f*
imaginative [ɪ'mædʒɪnətɪv] *adj* imaginatif(ive); (*person*) plein(e) d'imagination

imagine [ɪˈmædʒɪn] vt imaginer, s'imaginer; (suppose) imaginer, supposer

imbalance [ɪmˈbæləns] n déséquilibre m

imbue [ɪmˈbjuː] vt: **to ~ sb/sth with** imprégner qn/qch de

imitate [ˈɪmɪteɪt] vt imiter; **imitation** [ɪmɪˈteɪʃən] n imitation f

immaculate [ɪˈmækjulɪt] adj impeccable; (REL) immaculé(e)

immaterial [ɪməˈtɪərɪəl] adj sans importance, insignifiant(e)

immature [ɪməˈtjuə*] adj (fruit) (qui n'est pas mûr(e); (person) qui manque de maturité

immediate [ɪˈmiːdɪət] adj immédiat(e); **~ly** adv (at once) immédiatement; **~ly next to** juste à côté de

immense [ɪˈmens] adj immense; énorme

immerse [ɪˈmɜːs] vt immerger, plonger; **immersion heater** [ɪˈmɜːʃən-] (BRIT) n chauffe-eau m électrique

immigrant [ˈɪmɪɡrənt] n immigrant(e); immigré(e); **immigration** [ɪmɪˈɡreɪʃən] n immigration f

imminent [ˈɪmɪnənt] adj imminent(e)

immoral [ɪˈmɒrəl] adj immoral(e)

immortal [ɪˈmɔːtl] adj, n immortel(le)

immune [ɪˈmjuːn] adj: **~ (to)** immunisé(e) (contre); (fig) à l'abri de; **immunity** [ɪˈmjuːnɪtɪ] n immunité f

imp [ɪmp] n lutin m; (child) petit diable

impact [ˈɪmpækt] n choc m, impact m; (fig) impact

impair [ɪmˈpeə*] vt détériorer, diminuer

impart [ɪmˈpɑːt] vt communiquer, transmettre; (flavour) donner

impartial [ɪmˈpɑːʃəl] adj impartial(e)

impassable [ɪmˈpɑːsəbl] adj infranchissable; (road) impraticable

impassive [ɪmˈpæsɪv] adj impassible

impatience [ɪmˈpeɪʃəns] n impatience f

impatient [ɪmˈpeɪʃənt] adj impatient(e); **to get** or **grow ~** s'impatienter

impeccable [ɪmˈpekəbl] adj impeccable, parfait(e)

impede [ɪmˈpiːd] vt gêner

impediment [ɪmˈpedɪmənt] n obstacle m; (also: speech ~) défaut m d'élocution

impending [ɪmˈpendɪŋ] adj imminent(e)

imperative [ɪmˈperətɪv] adj (need) urgent(e), pressant(e); (tone) impérieux(euse) ♦ n (LING) impératif m

imperfect [ɪmˈpɜːfɪkt] adj imparfait(e); (goods etc) défectueux(euse)

imperial [ɪmˈpɪərɪəl] adj impérial(e); (BRIT: measure) légal(e)

impersonal [ɪmˈpɜːsnl] adj impersonnel(le)

impersonate [ɪmˈpɜːsəneɪt] vt se faire passer pour; (THEATRE) imiter

impertinent [ɪmˈpɜːtɪnənt] adj impertinent(e), insolent(e)

impervious [ɪmˈpɜːvɪəs] adj (fig): **~ to** insensible à

impetuous [ɪmˈpetjuəs] adj impétueux(euse), fougueux(euse)

impetus [ˈɪmpɪtəs] n impulsion f; (of runner) élan m

impinge [ɪmˈpɪndʒ]: **to ~ on** vt fus (person) affecter, toucher; (rights) empiéter sur

implement [n ˈɪmplɪmənt, vb ˈɪmplɪment] n outil m, instrument m; (for cooking) ustensile m ♦ vt exécuter

implicit [ɪmˈplɪsɪt] adj implicite; (complete) absolu(e), sans réserve

imply [ɪmˈplaɪ] vt suggérer, laisser entendre; indiquer, supposer

impolite [ɪmpəˈlaɪt] adj impoli(e)

import [vb ɪmˈpɔːt, n ˈɪmpɔːt] vt importer ♦ n (COMM) importation f

importance [ɪmˈpɔːtəns] n importance f

important [ɪmˈpɔːtənt] adj important(e)

importer [ɪmˈpɔːtə*] n importateur(trice)

impose [ɪmˈpəʊz] vt imposer ♦ vi: **to ~ on sb** abuser de la gentillesse de qn; **imposing** [ɪmˈpəʊzɪŋ] adj imposant(e), impressionnant(e); **imposition** [ɪmpəˈzɪʃən] n (of tax etc) imposition f; **to be an imposition on** (person) abuser de la gentillesse or la bonté de

impossible [ɪmˈpɒsəbl] adj impossible

impotent [ˈɪmpətənt] adj impuissant(e)

impound [ɪmˈpaʊnd] vt confisquer, saisir

impoverished [ɪmˈpɒvərɪʃt] adj appauvri(e), pauvre

impractical [ɪmˈpræktɪkəl] adj pas pratique; (person) qui manque d'esprit pratique

impregnable [ɪmˈpreɡnəbl] adj (fortress) imprenable

impress [ɪmˈpres] vt impressionner, faire impression sur; (mark) imprimer, marquer; **to ~ sth on sb** faire bien comprendre qch à qn

impression [ɪmˈpreʃən] n impression f; (of stamp, seal) empreinte f; (imitation) imitation f; **to be under the ~ that** avoir l'impression que; **~ist** n (ART) impressionniste m/f; (entertainer) imitateur(trice) m/f

impressive [ɪmˈpresɪv] adj impressionnant(e)

imprint [ˈɪmprɪnt] n (outline) marque f, empreinte f

imprison [ɪmˈprɪzn] vt emprisonner, mettre en prison

improbable [ɪmˈprɒbəbl] adj improbable; (excuse) peu plausible

improper [ɪmˈprɒpə*] adj (unsuitable) déplacé(e), de mauvais goût; indécent(e); (dishonest) malhonnête

improve [ɪmˈpruːv] vt améliorer ♦ vi s'améliorer; (pupil etc) faire des progrès; **~ment** n amélioration f (in de); progrès m

improvise [ˈɪmprəvaɪz] vt, vi improviser

impudent [ˈɪmpjudənt] adj impudent(e)

impulse [ˈɪmpʌls] n impulsion f; **on ~** impulsivement, sur un coup de tête; **impulsive** [ɪm'pʌlsɪv] *adj* impulsif(ive)

───────── *KEYWORD*

in [ɪn] *prep* **1** (*indicating place, position*) dans; ~ **the house/the fridge** dans la maison/le frigo; ~ **the garden** dans le *or* au jardin; ~ **town** en ville; ~ **the country** à la campagne; ~ **school** à l'école; ~ **here/there** ici/là
2 (*with place names: of town, region, country*): ~ **London** à Londres; ~ **England** en Angleterre; ~ **Japan** au Japon; ~ **the United States** aux États-Unis
3 (*indicating time: during*): ~ **spring** au printemps; ~ **summer** en été; ~ **May/1992** en mai/1992; ~ **the afternoon** (dans) l'après-midi; **at 4 o'clock ~ the afternoon** à 4 heures de l'après-midi
4 (*indicating time: in the space of*) en; (: *future*) dans; **I did it ~ 3 hours/days** je l'ai fait en 3 heures/jours; **I'll see you ~ 2 weeks** *or* ~ **2 weeks' time** je te verrai dans 2 semaines
5 (*indicating manner etc*) à; ~ **a loud/soft voice** à voix haute/basse; ~ **pencil** au crayon; ~ **French** en français; **the boy ~ the blue shirt** le garçon à *or* avec la chemise bleue
6 (*indicating circumstances*): ~ **the sun** au soleil; ~ **the shade** à l'ombre; ~ **the rain** sous la pluie
7 (*indicating mood, state*): ~ **tears** en larmes; ~ **anger** sous le coup de la colère; ~ **despair** au désespoir; ~ **good condition** en bon état; **to live ~ luxury** vivre dans le luxe
8 (*with ratios, numbers*): **1 ~ 10** (*households*), **1** (*household*) ~ **10** 1 (ménage) sur 10; **20 pence ~ the pound** 20 pence par livre sterling; **they lined up ~ twos** ils se mirent en rangs (deux) par deux; ~ **hundreds** par centaines
9 (*referring to people, works*) chez; **the disease is common ~ children** c'est une maladie courante chez les enfants; ~ **(the works of) Dickens** chez Dickens, dans (l'œuvre de) Dickens
10 (*indicating profession etc*) dans; **to be ~ teaching** être dans l'enseignement
11 (*after superlative*) de; **the best pupil ~ the class** le meilleur élève de la classe
12 (*with present participle*): ~ **saying this** en disant ceci
♦ *adv*: **to be ~** (*person: at home, work*) être là; (*train, ship, plane*) être arrivé(e); (*in fashion*) être à la mode; **to ask sb ~** inviter qn à entrer; **to run/limp** *etc* ~ entrer en courant/boitant *etc*
♦ *n*: **the ~s and outs (of)** (*of proposal, situation etc*) les tenants et aboutissants (de)

in. *abbr* = **inch**
inability [ɪnə'bɪlɪtɪ] *n* incapacité *f*
inaccurate [ɪn'ækjʊrɪt] *adj* inexact(e); (*person*) qui manque de précision
inadequate [ɪn'ædɪkwət] *adj* insuffisant(e), inadéquat(e)
inadvertently [ɪnəd'vɜːtəntlɪ] *adv* par mégarde
inadvisable [ɪnəd'vaɪzəbl] *adj* (*action*) à déconseiller
inane [ɪ'neɪn] *adj* inepte, stupide
inanimate [ɪn'ænɪmət] *adj* inanimé(e)
inappropriate [ɪnə'prəʊprɪət] *adj* inopportun(e), mal à propos; (*word, expression*) impropre
inarticulate [ɪnɑː'tɪkjʊlət] *adj* (*person*) qui s'exprime mal; (*speech*) indistinct(e)
inasmuch as [ɪnəz'mʌtʃəz] *adv* (*insofar as*) dans la mesure où; (*seeing that*) attendu que
inauguration [ɪnɔːgju'reɪʃən] *n* inauguration *f*; (*of president*) investiture *f*
inborn ['ɪnbɔːn] *adj* (*quality*) inné(e)
inbred ['ɪn'bred] *adj* inné(e), naturel(le); (*family*) consanguin(e)
Inc. *abbr* = **incorporated**
incapable [ɪn'keɪpəbl] *adj* incapable
incapacitate [ɪnkə'pæsɪteɪt] *vt*: **to ~ sb from doing** rendre qn incapable de faire
incense [*n* 'ɪnsens, *vb* ɪn'sens] *n* encens *m* ♦ *vt* (*anger*) mettre en colère
incentive [ɪn'sentɪv] *n* encouragement *m*, raison *f* de se donner de la peine
incessant [ɪn'sesnt] *adj* incessant(e); ~**ly** *adv* sans cesse, constamment
inch [ɪntʃ] *n* pouce *m* (= 25 mm; 12 in a foot); **within an ~ of** à deux doigts de; **he didn't give an ~** (*fig*) il n'a pas voulu céder d'un pouce; ~ **forward** *vi* avancer petit à petit
incident ['ɪnsɪdənt] *n* incident *m*
incidental [ɪnsɪ'dentl] *adj* (*additional*) accessoire; ~ **to** qui accompagne; ~**ly** *adv* (*by the way*) à propos
inclination [ɪnklɪ'neɪʃən] *n* (*fig*) inclination *f*
incline [*n* 'ɪnklaɪn, *vb* ɪn'klaɪn] *n* pente *f* ♦ *vt* incliner ♦ *vi* (*surface*) s'incliner; **to be ~d to do** avoir tendance à faire
include [ɪn'kluːd] *vt* inclure, comprendre; **including** [ɪn'kluːdɪŋ] *prep* y compris
inclusive [ɪn'kluːsɪv] *adj* inclus(e), compris(e); ~ **of tax** *etc* taxes *etc* comprises
income ['ɪnkʌm] *n* revenu *m*; ~ **tax** *n* impôt *m* sur le revenu
incoming ['ɪnkʌmɪŋ] *adj* qui arrive; (*president*) entrant(e); ~ **mail** courrier *m* du jour; ~ **tide** marée montante
incompetent [ɪn'kɒmpɪtənt] *adj* incompétent(e), incapable

incomplete [ɪnkəm'pliːt] *adj* incomplet(ète)
incongruous [ɪn'kɒŋgruəs] *adj* incongru(e)
inconsiderate [ɪnkən'sɪdərɪt] *adj* (*person*) qui manque d'égards; (*action*) inconsidéré(e)
inconsistency [ɪnkən'sɪstənsɪ] *n* (*of actions etc*) inconséquence *f*; (*of work*) irrégularité *f*; (*of statement etc*) incohérence *f*
inconsistent [ɪnkən'sɪstənt] *adj* inconséquent(e); irrégulier(ère); peu cohérent(e); ~ **with** incompatible avec
inconspicuous [ɪnkən'spɪkjuəs] *adj* qui passe inaperçu(e); (*colour, dress*) discret(ète)
inconvenience [ɪnkən'viːnɪəns] *n* inconvénient *m*; (*trouble*) dérangement *m* ♦ *vt* déranger
inconvenient [ɪnkən'viːnɪənt] *adj* (*house*) malcommode; (*time, place*) mal choisi(e), qui ne convient pas; (*visitor*) importun(e)
incorporate [ɪn'kɔːpəreɪt] *vt* incorporer; (*contain*) contenir; ~**d company** (*US*) *n* ≈ société *f* anonyme
incorrect [ɪnkə'rekt] *adj* incorrect(e)
increase [*n* 'ɪnkriːs, *vb* ɪn'kriːs] *n* augmentation *f* ♦ *vi, vt* augmenter; **increasing** [ɪn'kriːsɪŋ] *adj* (*number*) croissant(e); **increasingly** [ɪn'kriːsɪŋlɪ] *adv* de plus en plus
incredible [ɪn'kredəbl] *adj* incroyable
incredulous [ɪn'kredjuləs] *adj* incrédule
incubator ['ɪnkjubeɪtə*] *n* (*for babies*) couveuse *f*
incumbent [ɪn'kʌmbənt] *n* (*president*) président *m* en exercice; (*REL*) titulaire *m/f* ♦ *adj*: **it is ~ on him to ...** il lui incombe *or* appartient de ...
incur [ɪn'kɜː*] *vt* (*expenses*) encourir; (*anger, risk*) s'exposer à; (*debt*) contracter; (*loss*) subir
indebted [ɪn'detɪd] *adj*: **to be ~ to sb (for)** être redevable à qn (de)
indecent [ɪn'diːsnt] *adj* indécent(e), inconvenant(e); ~ **assault** (*BRIT*) *n* attentat *m* à la pudeur; ~ **exposure** *n* outrage *m* (public) à la pudeur
indecisive [ɪndɪ'saɪsɪv] *adj* (*person*) indécis(e)
indeed [ɪn'diːd] *adv* vraiment; en effet; (*furthermore*) d'ailleurs; **yes ~!** certainement!
indefinitely [ɪn'defɪnɪtlɪ] *adv* (*wait*) indéfiniment
indemnity [ɪn'demnɪtɪ] *n* (*safeguard*) assurance *f*, garantie *f*; (*compensation*) indemnité *f*
independence [ɪndɪ'pendəns] *n* indépendance *f*; **independent** [ɪndɪ'pendənt] *adj* indépendant(e); (*school*) privé(e); (*radio*) libre
index ['ɪndeks] *n* (*pl*: ~**es**: *in book*) index *m*; (: *in library etc*) catalogue *m*; (*pl*: *indices*: *ratio, sign*) indice *m*; ~ **card** *n* fiche *f*; ~**-finger** *n* index *m*; ~**-linked** *adj* indexé(e)

India ['ɪndɪə] *n* Inde *f*; ~**n** *adj* indien(ne) ♦ *n* Indien(ne); **(American)** ~**n** Indien(ne) (d'Amérique)
indicate ['ɪndɪkeɪt] *vt* indiquer; **indication** [ɪndɪ'keɪʃən] *n* indication *f*, signe *m*; **indicative** [ɪn'dɪkətɪv] *adj*: **indicative of** symptomatique de ♦ *n* (*LING*) indicatif *m*; **indicator** ['ɪndɪkeɪtə*] *n* (*sign*) indicateur *m*; (*AUT*) clignotant *m*
indices ['ɪndɪsiːz] *npl of* **index**
indictment [ɪn'daɪtmənt] *n* accusation *f*
indifferent [ɪn'dɪfrənt] *adj* indifférent(e); (*poor*) médiocre, quelconque
indigenous [ɪn'dɪdʒɪnəs] *adj* indigène
indigestion [ɪndɪ'dʒestʃən] *n* indigestion *f*, mauvaise digestion
indignant [ɪn'dɪgnənt] *adj*: ~ **(at sth/with sb)** indigné(e) (de qch/contre qn)
indignity [ɪn'dɪgnɪtɪ] *n* indignité *f*, affront *m*
indirect [ɪndɪ'rekt] *adj* indirect(e)
indiscreet [ɪndɪs'kriːt] *adj* indiscret(ète); (*rash*) imprudent(e)
indiscriminate [ɪndɪs'krɪmɪnət] *adj* (*person*) qui manque de discernement; (*killings*) commis(e) au hasard
indisputable [ɪndɪs'pjuːtəbl] *adj* incontestable, indiscutable
individual [ɪndɪ'vɪdjuəl] *n* individu *m* ♦ *adj* individuel(le); (*characteristic*) particulier(ère), original(e)
indoctrination [ɪndɒktrɪ'neɪʃən] *n* endoctrinement *m*
Indonesia [ɪndəʊ'niːzɪə] *n* Indonésie *f*
indoor ['ɪndɔː*] *adj* (*plant*) d'appartement; (*swimming pool*) couvert(e); (*sport, games*) pratiqué(e) en salle; ~**s** [ɪn'dɔːz] *adv* à l'intérieur
induce [ɪn'djuːs] *vt* (*persuade*) persuader; (*bring about*) provoquer; ~**ment** *n* (*incentive*) récompense *f*; (*pej: bribe*) pot-de-vin *m*
indulge [ɪn'dʌldʒ] *vt* (*whim*) céder à, satisfaire; (*child*) gâter ♦ *vi*: **to ~ in sth** (*luxury*) se permettre qch; (*fantasies etc*) se livrer à qch; ~**nce** *n* fantaisie *f* (que l'on s'offre); (*leniency*) indulgence *f*; ~**nt** *adj* indulgent(e)
industrial [ɪn'dʌstrɪəl] *adj* industriel(le); (*injury*) du travail; ~ **action** *n* action revendicative; ~ **estate** (*BRIT*) *n* zone industrielle; ~**ist** *n* industriel *m*; ~ **park** (*US*) *n* = **industrial estate**
industrious [ɪn'dʌstrɪəs] *adj* travailleur(euse)
industry ['ɪndəstrɪ] *n* industrie *f*; (*diligence*) zèle *m*, application *f*
inebriated [ɪ'niːbrɪeɪtɪd] *adj* ivre
inedible [ɪn'edɪbl] *adj* immangeable; (*plant etc*) non comestible
ineffective [ɪnɪ'fektɪv], **ineffectual** [ɪnɪ'fektjuəl] *adj* inefficace

inefficient [ɪnɪ'fɪʃənt] *adj* inefficace
inequality [ɪnɪ'kwɒlɪtɪ] *n* inégalité *f*
inescapable [ɪnɪs'keɪpəbl] *adj* inéluctable, inévitable
inevitable [ɪn'evɪtəbl] *adj* inévitable; **inevitably** *adv* inévitablement
inexhaustible [ɪnɪg'zɔːstəbl] *adj* inépuisable
inexpensive [ɪnɪks'pensɪv] *adj* bon marché *inv*
inexperienced [ɪnɪks'pɪərɪənst] *adj* inexpérimenté(e)
infallible [ɪn'fæləbl] *adj* infaillible
infamous ['ɪnfəməs] *adj* infâme, abominable
infancy ['ɪnfənsɪ] *n* petite enfance, bas âge
infant ['ɪnfənt] *n* (*baby*) nourrisson *m*; (*young child*) petit(e) enfant; **~ school** (*BRIT*) *n* classes *fpl* préparatoires (*entre 5 et 7 ans*)
infatuated [ɪn'fætjʊeɪtɪd] *adj*: **~ with** entiché(e) de; **infatuation** [ɪnfætjʊ'eɪʃən] *n* engouement *m*
infect [ɪn'fekt] *vt* infecter, contaminer; **~ion** [ɪn'fekʃən] *n* infection *f*, (*contagion*) contagion *f*; **~ious** [ɪn'fekʃəs] *adj* infectieux(euse); (*also fig*) contagieux(euse)
infer [ɪn'fɜː*] *vt* conclure, déduire; (*imply*) suggérer
inferior [ɪn'fɪərɪə*] *adj* inférieur(e); (*goods*) de qualité inférieure ♦ *n* inférieur(e); (*in rank*) subalterne *m/f*; **~ity** [ɪnfɪərɪ'ɔrɪtɪ] *n* infériorité *f*; **~ity complex** *n* complexe *m* d'infériorité
inferno [ɪn'fɜːnəʊ] (*blaze*) brasier *m*
infertile [ɪn'fɜːtaɪl] *adj* stérile
infighting ['ɪnfaɪtɪŋ] *n* querelles *fpl* internes
infinite ['ɪnfɪnɪt] *adj* infini(e)
infinitive [ɪn'fɪnɪtɪv] *n* infinitif *m*
infinity [ɪn'fɪnɪtɪ] *n* infinité *f*; (*also MATH*) infini *m*
infirmary [ɪn'fɜːmərɪ] *n* (*hospital*) hôpital *m*
inflamed [ɪn'fleɪmd] *adj* enflammé(e)
inflammable [ɪn'flæməbl] (*BRIT*) *adj* inflammable
inflammation [ɪnflə'meɪʃən] *n* inflammation *f*
inflatable [ɪn'fleɪtəbl] *adj* gonflable
inflate [ɪn'fleɪt] *vt* (*tyre, balloon*) gonfler; (*price*) faire monter; **inflation** [ɪn'fleɪʃən] (*ECON*) *n* inflation *f*; **inflationary** [ɪn'fleɪʃnərɪ] *adj* inflationniste
inflict [ɪn'flɪkt] *vt*: **to ~ on** infliger à
influence ['ɪnflʊəns] *n* influence *f* ♦ *vt* influencer; **under the ~ of alcohol** en état d'ébriété; **influential** [ɪnflʊ'enʃəl] *adj* influent(e)
influenza [ɪnflʊ'enzə] *n* grippe *f*
influx ['ɪnflʌks] *n* afflux *m*
inform [ɪn'fɔːm] *vt*: **to ~ sb (of)** informer *or* avertir qn (de) ♦ *vi*: **to ~ on sb** dénoncer qn

informal [ɪn'fɔːməl] *adj* (*person, manner, party*) simple; (*visit, discussion*) dénué(e) de formalités; (*announcement, invitation*) non officiel(le); (*colloquial*) familier(ère); **~ity** [ɪnfɔː'mælɪtɪ] *n* simplicité *f*, absence *f* de cérémonie; caractère non officiel
informant [ɪn'fɔːmənt] *n* informateur(trice)
information [ɪnfə'meɪʃən] *n* information *f*, renseignements *mpl*; (*knowledge*) connaissances *fpl*; **a piece of ~** un renseignement; **~ office** *n* bureau *m* de renseignements
informative [ɪn'fɔːmətɪv] *adj* instructif(ive)
informer [ɪn'fɔːmə*] *n* (*also: police ~*) indicateur(trice)
infringe [ɪn'frɪndʒ] *vt* enfreindre ♦ *vi*: **to ~ on** empiéter sur; **~ment** *n*: **~ment (of)** infraction *f* (à)
infuriating [ɪn'fjʊərɪeɪtɪŋ] *adj* exaspérant(e)
ingenious [ɪn'dʒiːnɪəs] *adj* ingénieux(euse); **ingenuity** [ɪndʒɪ'njuːɪtɪ] *n* ingéniosité *f*
ingenuous [ɪn'dʒenjʊəs] *adj* naïf(naïve), ingénu(e)
ingot ['ɪŋgət] *n* lingot *m*
ingrained [ɪn'greɪnd] *adj* enraciné(e)
ingratiate [ɪn'greɪʃɪeɪt] *vt*: **to ~ o.s. with** s'insinuer dans les bonnes grâces de, se faire bien voir de
ingredient [ɪn'griːdɪənt] *n* ingrédient *m*; (*fig*) élément *m*
inhabit [ɪn'hæbɪt] *vt* habiter; **~ant** [ɪn'hæbɪtnt] *n* habitant(e)
inhale [ɪn'heɪl] *vt* respirer; (*smoke*) avaler ♦ *vi* aspirer; (*in smoking*) avaler la fumée
inherent [ɪn'hɪərənt] *adj*: **~ (in or to)** inhérent(e) (à)
inherit [ɪn'herɪt] *vt* hériter (de); **~ance** *n* héritage *m*
inhibit [ɪn'hɪbɪt] *vt* (*PSYCH*) inhiber; (*growth*) freiner; **~ion** [ɪnhɪ'bɪʃən] *n* inhibition *f*
inhuman [ɪn'hjuːmən] *adj* inhumain(e)
initial [ɪ'nɪʃəl] *adj* initial(e) ♦ *n* initiale *f* ♦ *vt* parafer; **~s** *npl* (*letters*) initiales *fpl*; (*as signature*) parafe *m*; **~ly** *adv* initialement, au début
initiate [ɪ'nɪʃɪeɪt] *vt* (*start*) entreprendre; amorcer; lancer; (*person*) initier; **to ~ proceedings against sb** intenter une action à qn
initiative [ɪ'nɪʃətɪv] *n* initiative *f*
inject [ɪn'dʒekt] *vt* injecter; (*person*): **to ~ sb with sth** faire une piqûre de qch à qn; **~ion** [ɪn'dʒekʃən] *n* injection *f*, piqûre *f*
injure ['ɪndʒə*] *vt* blesser; (*reputation etc*) compromettre; **~d** *adj* blessé(e); **injury** ['ɪndʒərɪ] *n* blessure *f*; **injury time** *n* (*SPORT*) arrêts *mpl* de jeu
injustice [ɪn'dʒʌstɪs] *n* injustice *f*
ink [ɪŋk] *n* encre *f*
inkling ['ɪŋklɪŋ] *n*: **to have an/no ~ of** avoir une (vague) idée de/n'avoir aucune idée de

inlaid ['ɪn'leɪd] *adj* incrusté(e); (*table* etc) marqueté(e)

inland [*adj* 'ɪnlənd, *adv* 'ɪnlænd] *adj* intérieur(e) ♦ *adv* à l'intérieur, dans les terres; **I~ Revenue** (*BRIT*) *n* fisc *m*

in-laws ['ɪnlɔːz] *npl* beaux-parents *mpl*; belle famille

inlet ['ɪnlet] *n* (*GEO*) crique *f*

inmate ['ɪnmeɪt] *n* (*in prison*) détenu(e); (*in asylum*) interné(e)

inn [ɪn] *n* auberge *f*

innate [ɪ'neɪt] *adj* inné(e)

inner ['ɪnə*] *adj* intérieur(e); **~ city** *n* centre *m* de zone urbaine; **~ tube** *n* (*of tyre*) chambre *f* à air

innings ['ɪnɪŋz] *n* (*CRICKET*) tour *m* de batte

innocent ['ɪnəsnt] *adj* innocent(e)

innocuous [ɪ'nɒkjʊəs] *adj* inoffensif(ive)

innuendo [ɪnjuˈendəʊ] (*pl* ~**es**) *n* insinuation *f*, allusion (malveillante)

innumerable [ɪ'njuːmərəbl] *adj* innombrable

inordinately [ɪ'nɔːdɪnɪtlɪ] *adv* démesurément

inpatient ['ɪnpeɪʃənt] *n* malade hospitalisé(e)

input ['ɪnpʊt] *n* (*resources*) ressources *fpl*; (*COMPUT*) entrée *f* (de données); (: *data*) données *fpl*

inquest ['ɪnkwest] *n* enquête *f*; (**coroner's**) ~ enquête judiciaire

inquire [ɪn'kwaɪə*] *vi* demander ♦ *vt* demander; **to ~ about** se renseigner sur; **~ into** *vt fus* faire une enquête sur; **inquiry** [ɪn'kwaɪərɪ] *n* demande *f* de renseignements; (*investigation*) enquête *f*, investigation *f*; **inquiry office** (*BRIT*) *n* bureau *m* de renseignements

inquisitive [ɪn'kwɪzɪtɪv] *adj* curieux(euse)

inroads ['ɪnrəʊdz] *npl*: **to make ~ into** (*savings* etc) entamer

ins *abbr* = **inches**

insane [ɪn'seɪn] *adj* fou(folle); (*MED*) aliéné(e); **insanity** [ɪn'sænɪtɪ] *n* folie *f*; (*MED*) aliénation (mentale)

inscription [ɪn'skrɪpʃən] *n* inscription *f*; (*in book*) dédicace *f*

inscrutable [ɪn'skruːtəbl] *adj* impénétrable; (*comment*) obscur(e)

insect ['ɪnsekt] *n* insecte *m*; **~icide** [ɪn'sektɪsaɪd] *n* insecticide *m*

insecure [ɪnsɪ'kjʊə*] *adj* peu solide; peu sûr(e); (*person*) anxieux(euse)

insensitive [ɪn'sensɪtɪv] *adj* insensible

insert [ɪn'sɜːt] *vt* insérer; **~ion** [ɪn'sɜːʃən] *n* insertion *f*

in-service ['ɪn'sɜːvɪs] *adj* (*training*) continu(e), en cours d'emploi; (*course*) de perfectionnement; de recyclage

inshore ['ɪn'ʃɔː*] *adj* côtier(ère) ♦ *adv* près de la côte; (*move*) vers la côte

inside ['ɪn'saɪd] *n* intérieur *m* ♦ *adj* intérieur(e) ♦ *adv* à l'intérieur, dedans ♦ *prep* à l'intérieur de; (*of time*): **~ 10 minutes** en moins de 10 minutes; **~s** *npl* (*inf*) intestins *mpl*; **~ information** *n* renseignements obtenus à la source; **~ lane** *n* (*AUT*: *BRIT*) voie *f* de gauche; (: *US, Europe* etc) voie de droite; **~ out** *adv* à l'envers; (*know*) à fond

insider dealing, insider trading *n* (*St Ex*) délit *m* d'initié

insight ['ɪnsaɪt] *n* perspicacité *f*; (*glimpse, idea*) aperçu *m*

insignificant [ɪnsɪg'nɪfɪkənt] *adj* insignifiant(e)

insincere [ɪnsɪn'sɪə*] *adj* hypocrite

insinuate [ɪn'sɪnjʊeɪt] *vt* insinuer

insist [ɪn'sɪst] *vi* insister; **to ~ on doing** insister pour faire; **to ~ on sth** exiger qch; **to ~ that** insister pour que; (*claim*) maintenir *or* soutenir que; **~ent** *adj* insistant(e), pressant(e); (*noise, action*) ininterrompu(e)

insole ['ɪnsəʊl] *n* (*removable*) semelle intérieure

insolent ['ɪnsələnt] *adj* insolent(e)

insolvent [ɪn'sɒlvənt] *adj* insolvable

insomnia [ɪn'sɒmnɪə] *n* insomnie *f*

inspect [ɪn'spekt] *vt* inspecter; (*ticket*) contrôler; **~ion** [ɪn'spekʃən] *n* inspection *f*, contrôle *m*; **~or** *n* inspecteur(trice); (*BRIT*: *on buses, trains*) contrôleur(euse)

inspire [ɪn'spaɪə*] *vt* inspirer

install [ɪn'stɔːl] *vt* installer; **~ation** [ɪnstə'leɪʃən] *n* installation *f*

instalment [ɪn'stɔːlmənt] (*US* **installment**) *n* acompte *m*, versement partiel; (*of TV serial* etc) épisode *m*; **in ~s** (*pay*) à tempérament; (*receive*) en plusieurs fois

instance ['ɪnstəns] *n* exemple *m*; **for ~** par exemple; **in the first ~** tout d'abord, en premier lieu

instant ['ɪnstənt] *n* instant *m* ♦ *adj* immédiat(e); (*coffee, food*) instantané(e), en poudre; **~ly** *adv* immédiatement, tout de suite

instead [ɪn'sted] *adv* au lieu de cela; **~ of** au lieu de; **~ of sb** à la place de qn

instep ['ɪnstep] *n* cou-de-pied *m*; (*of shoe*) cambrure *f*

instigate ['ɪnstɪgeɪt] *vt* (*rebellion*) fomenter, provoquer; (*talks* etc) promouvoir

instil [ɪn'stɪl] *vt*: **to ~ (into)** inculquer (à); (*courage*) insuffler (à)

instinct ['ɪnstɪŋkt] *n* instinct *m*

institute ['ɪnstɪtjuːt] *n* institut *m* ♦ *vt* instituer, établir; (*inquiry*) ouvrir; (*proceedings*) entamer

institution [ɪnstɪ'tjuːʃən] *n* institution *f*; (*educational*) établissement *m* (scolaire); (*mental home*) établissement (psychiatrique)

instruct [ɪn'strʌkt] *vt*: **to ~ sb in sth** enseigner qch à qn; **to ~ sb to do** charger qn *or* ordonner à qn de faire; **~ion** [ɪn'strʌkʃən] *n* instruction *f*; **~ions** *npl* (*or-*

ders) directives *fpl*; ~**ions (for use)** mode *m* d'emploi; ~**or** *n* professeur *m*; (*for skiing, driving*) moniteur *m*

instrument ['ɪnstrʊmənt] *n* instrument *m*; ~**al** [ɪnstrʊ'mentl] *adj*: **to be** ~**al in** contribuer à; ~ **panel** *n* tableau *m* de bord

insufficient [ɪnsə'fɪʃənt] *adj* insuffisant(e)

insular ['ɪnsjʊlə*] *adj* (*outlook*) borné(e); (*person*) aux vues étroites

insulate ['ɪnsjʊleɪt] *vt* isoler; (*against sound*) insonoriser; **insulating tape** *n* ruban isolant; **insulation** [ɪnsjʊ'leɪʃən] *n* isolation *f*; insonorisation *f*

insulin ['ɪnsjʊlɪn] *n* insuline *f*

insult [*n* 'ɪnsʌlt, *vb* ɪn'sʌlt] *n* insulte *f*, affront *m* ♦ *vt* insulter, faire affront à

insurance [ɪn'ʃʊərəns] *n* assurance *f*; **fire/ life** ~ assurance-incendie/-vie; ~ **policy** *n* police *f* d'assurance

insure [ɪn'ʃʊə*] *vt* assurer; **to** ~ **(o.s.) against** (*fig*) parer à

intact [ɪn'tækt] *adj* intact(e)

intake ['ɪnteɪk] *n* (*of food, oxygen*) consommation *f*; (*BRIT: SCOL*): **an** ~ **of 200 a year** 200 admissions *fpl* par an

integral ['ɪntɪɡrəl] *adj* (*part*) intégrant(e)

integrate ['ɪntɪɡreɪt] *vt* intégrer ♦ *vi* s'intégrer

intellect ['ɪntɪlekt] *n* intelligence *f*; ~**ual** [ɪntɪ'lektjʊəl] *adj, n* intellectuel(le)

intelligence [ɪn'telɪdʒəns] *n* intelligence *f*; (*MIL etc*) informations *fpl*, renseignements *mpl*; ~ **service** *n* services secrets; **intelligent** [ɪn'telɪdʒənt] *adj* intelligent(e)

intend [ɪn'tend] *vt* (*gift etc*): **to** ~ **sth for** destiner qch à; **to** ~ **to do** avoir l'intention de faire; ~**ed** *adj* (*journey*) projeté(e); (*effect*) voulu(e); (*insult*) intentionnel(le)

intense [ɪn'tens] *adj* intense; (*person*) véhément(e); ~**ly** *adv* intensément; profondément

intensive [ɪn'tensɪv] *adj* intensif(ive); ~ **care unit** *n* service *m* de réanimation

intent [ɪn'tent] *n* intention *f* ♦ *adj* attentif(ive); (*absorbed*): ~ **(on)** absorbé(e) (par); **to all** ~**s and purposes** en fait, pratiquement; **to be** ~ **on doing sth** être (bien) décidé à faire qch

intention [ɪn'tenʃən] *n* intention *f*; ~**al** *adj* intentionnel(le), délibéré(e)

intently [ɪn'tentlɪ] *adv* attentivement

interact [ɪntər'ækt] *vi* avoir une action réciproque; (*people*) communiquer; ~**ive** *adj* (*COMPUT*) interactif(ive)

interchange [*n* 'ɪntətʃeɪndʒ, *vb* ɪntə'tʃeɪndʒ] *n* (*exchange*) échange *m*; (*on motorway*) échangeur *m*; ~**able** [ɪntə'tʃeɪndʒəbl] *adj* interchangeable

intercom ['ɪntəkɔm] *n* interphone *m*

intercourse ['ɪntəkɔːs] *n* (*sexual*) rapports *mpl*

interest ['ɪntrest] *n* intérêt *m*; (*pastime*):

my main ~ ce qui m'intéresse le plus; (*COMM*) intérêts *mpl* ♦ *vt* intéresser; **to be** ~**ed in sth** s'intéresser à qch; **I am** ~**ed in going** ça m'intéresse d'y aller; ~**ing** *adj* intéressant(e); ~ **rate** *n* taux *m* d'intérêt

interface ['ɪntəfeɪs] *n* (*COMPUT*) interface *f*

interfere [ɪntə'fɪə*] *vi*: **to** ~ **in** (*quarrel*) s'immiscer dans; (*other people's business*) se mêler de; **to** ~ **with** (*object*) toucher à; (*plans*) contrecarrer; (*duty*) être en conflit avec; ~**nce** [ɪntə'fɪərəns] *n* ingérance *f*; (*RADIO, TV*) parasites *mpl*

interim ['ɪntərɪm] *adj* provisoire ♦ *n*: **in the** ~ dans l'intérim, entre-temps

interior [ɪn'tɪərɪə*] *n* intérieur *m* ♦ *adj* intérieur(e); (*minister, department*) de l'Intérieur; ~ **designer** *n* styliste *m/f*, designer *m/f*

interjection [ɪntə'dʒekʃən] *n* (*interruption*) interruption *f*; (*LING*) interjection *f*

interlock [ɪntə'lɔk] *vi* s'enclencher

interlude ['ɪntəluːd] *n* intervalle *m*; (*THEATRE*) intermède *m*

intermediate [ɪntə'miːdɪət] *adj* intermédiaire; (*SCOL: course, level*) moyen(ne)

intermission [ɪntə'mɪʃən] *n* pause *f*; (*THEATRE, CINEMA*) entracte *m*

intern [*vb* ɪn'tɜːn, *n* 'ɪntɜːn] *vt* interner ♦ *n* (*US*) interne *m/f*

internal [ɪn'tɜːnl] *adj* interne; (*politics*) intérieur(e); ~**ly** *adv*: **"not to be taken** ~**ly"** "pour usage externe"; **I**~ **Revenue Service** (*US*) *n* fisc *m*

international [ɪntə'næʃnəl] *adj* international(e)

interplay ['ɪntəpleɪ] *n* effet *m* réciproque, interaction *f*

interpret [ɪn'tɜːprɪt] *vt* interpréter ♦ *vi* servir d'interprète; ~**er** *n* interprète *m/f*

interrelated [ɪntərɪ'leɪtɪd] *adj* en corrélation, en rapport étroit

interrogate [ɪn'terəgeɪt] *vt* interroger; (*suspect etc*) soumettre à un interrogatoire; **interrogation** [ɪnterə'geɪʃən] *n* interrogation *f*, interrogatoire *m*

interrupt [ɪntə'rʌpt] *vt, vi* interrompre; ~**ion** *n* interruption *f*

intersect [ɪntə'sekt] *vi* (*roads*) se croiser, se couper; ~**ion** [ɪntə'sekʃən] *n* (*of roads*) croisement *m*

intersperse [ɪntə'spɜːs] *vt*: **to** ~ **with** parsemer de

intertwine [ɪntə'twaɪn] *vi* s'entrelacer

interval ['ɪntəvəl] *n* intervalle *m*; (*BRIT: THEATRE*) entracte *m*; (: *SPORT*) mi-temps *f*; **at** ~**s** par intervalles

intervene [ɪntə'viːn] *vi* (*person*) intervenir; (*event*) survenir; (*time*) s'écouler (entretemps); **intervention** [ɪntə'venʃən] *n* intervention *f*

interview ['ɪntəvjuː] *n* (*RADIO, TV etc*) interview *f*; (*for job*) entrevue *f* ♦ *vt* interviewer; avoir une entrevue avec; **~er** n (*RADIO, TV*) interviewer m

intestine [ɪnˈtestɪn] n intestin m

intimacy [ˈɪntɪməsɪ] n intimité f

intimate [adj ˈɪntɪmət, vb ˈɪntɪmeɪt] adj intime; (*friendship*) profond(e); (*knowledge*) approfondi(e) ♦ vt (*hint*) suggérer, laisser entendre

into [ˈɪntʊ] prep dans; **~ pieces/French** en morceaux/français

intolerant [ɪnˈtɒlərənt] adj: **~ (of)** intolérant(e) (de)

intoxicated [ɪnˈtɒksɪkeɪtɪd] adj (*drunk*) ivre; **intoxication** [ɪntɒksɪˈkeɪʃən] n ivresse f

intractable [ɪnˈtræktəbl] adj (*child*) indocile, insoumis(e); (*problem*) insoluble

intransitive [ɪnˈtrænsɪtɪv] adj intransitif(ive)

intravenous [ɪntrəˈviːnəs] adj intraveineux(euse)

in-tray [ˈɪntreɪ] n courrier m "arrivée"

intricate [ˈɪntrɪkət] adj complexe, compliqué(e)

intrigue [ɪnˈtriːg] n intrigue f ♦ vt intriguer; **intriguing** [ɪnˈtriːgɪŋ] adj fascinant(e)

intrinsic [ɪnˈtrɪnsɪk] adj intrinsèque

introduce [ɪntrəˈdjuːs] vt introduire; (*TV show, people to each other*) présenter; **to ~ sb to** (*pastime, technique*) initier qn à; **introduction** [ɪntrəˈdʌkʃən] n introduction f; (*of person*) présentation f; (*to new experience*) initiation f; **introductory** [ɪntrəˈdʌktərɪ] adj préliminaire, d'introduction; **introductory offer** n (*COMM*) offre f de lancement

intrude [ɪnˈtruːd] vi (*person*) être importun(e); **to ~ on** (*conversation etc*) s'immiscer dans; **~r** n intrus(e)

intuition [ɪntjuːˈɪʃən] n intuition f

inundate [ˈɪnʌndeɪt] vt: **to ~ with** inonder de

invade [ɪnˈveɪd] vt envahir

invalid [n ˈɪnvəlɪd, adj ɪnˈvælɪd] n malade m/f; (*with disability*) invalide m/f ♦ adj (*not valid*) non valide or valable

invaluable [ɪnˈvæljʊəbl] adj inestimable, inappréciable

invariably [ɪnˈvɛərɪəblɪ] adv invariablement; toujours

invent [ɪnˈvent] vt inventer; **~ion** [ɪnˈvenʃən] n invention f; **~ive** adj inventif(ive); **~or** n inventeur(trice)

inventory [ˈɪnvəntrɪ] n inventaire m

invert [ɪnˈvɜːt] vt intervertir; (*cup, object*) retourner; **~ed commas** (*BRIT*) npl guillemets mpl

invest [ɪnˈvest] vt investir ♦ vi: **to ~ in sth** placer son argent dans qch; (*fig*) s'offrir qch

investigate [ɪnˈvestɪgeɪt] vt (*crime etc*) faire une enquête sur; **investigation** [ɪnvestɪˈgeɪʃən] n (*of crime*) enquête f

investment [ɪnˈvestmənt] n investissement m, placement m

investor [ɪnˈvestə*] n investisseur m; actionnaire m/f

invigilator [ɪnˈvɪdʒɪleɪtə*] n surveillant(e)

invigorating [ɪnˈvɪgəreɪtɪŋ] adj vivifiant(e); (*fig*) stimulant(e)

invisible [ɪnˈvɪzəbl] adj invisible

invitation [ɪnvɪˈteɪʃən] n invitation f

invite [ɪnˈvaɪt] vt inviter; (*opinions etc*) demander; **inviting** [ɪnˈvaɪtɪŋ] adj engageant(e), attrayant(e)

invoice [ˈɪnvɔɪs] n facture f

involuntary [ɪnˈvɒləntrɪ] adj involontaire

involve [ɪnˈvɒlv] vt (*entail*) entraîner, nécessiter; (*concern*) concerner; (*associate*): **to ~ sb (in)** impliquer qn (dans), mêler qn (à); faire participer qn (à); **~d** adj (*complicated*) complexe; **to be ~d in** participer à; (*engrossed*) être absorbé(e) par; **~ment** n: **~ment (in)** participation f (à); rôle n (dans); (*enthusiasm*) enthousiasme m (pour)

inward [ˈɪnwəd] adj (*thought, feeling*) profond(e), intime; (*movement*) vers l'intérieur; **~(s)** adv vers l'intérieur

I/O abbr (*COMPUT*: = *input/output*) E/S

iodine [ˈaɪədiːn] n iode m

iota [aɪˈəʊtə] n (*fig*) brin m, grain m

IOU n abbr (= *I owe you*) reconnaissance f de dette

IQ n abbr (= *intelligence quotient*) Q.I. m

IRA n abbr (= *Irish Republican Army*) IRA f

Iran [ɪˈrɑːn] n Iran m

Iraq [ɪˈrɑːk] n Irak m

irate [aɪˈreɪt] adj courroucé(e)

Ireland [ˈaɪələnd] n Irlande f

iris [ˈaɪrɪs] (*pl* **~es**) n iris m

Irish [ˈaɪrɪʃ] adj irlandais(e) ♦ npl: **the ~** les Irlandais; **~man** (*irreg*) n Irlandais m; **~ Sea** n mer f d'Irlande; **~woman** (*irreg*) n Irlandaise f

iron [ˈaɪən] n fer m; (*for clothes*) fer m à repasser ♦ cpd de or en fer; (*fig*) de fer ♦ vt (*clothes*) repasser; **~ out** vt (*fig*) aplanir; faire disparaître; **the I~ Curtain** n le rideau de fer

ironic(al) [aɪˈrɒnɪk(əl)] adj ironique

ironing [ˈaɪənɪŋ] n repassage m; **~ board** n planche f à repasser

ironmonger's (shop) [ˈaɪənmʌŋgəz-] n quincaillerie f

irony [ˈaɪərənɪ] n ironie f

irrational [ɪˈræʃənl] adj irrationnel(le)

irregular [ɪˈregjʊlə*] adj irrégulier(ère); (*surface*) inégal(e)

irrelevant [ɪˈreləvənt] adj sans rapport, hors de propos

irresistible [ɪrɪˈzɪstəbl] adj irrésistible

irrespective [ɪrɪˈspektɪv]: **~ of** prep sans tenir compte de

irresponsible [ɪrɪˈspɒnsəbl] adj (*act*) irréfléchi(e); (*person*) irresponsable, inconscient(e)

irrigate ['ɪrɪgeɪt] vt irriguer; **irrigation** [ɪrɪ'geɪʃən] n irrigation f
irritate ['ɪrɪteɪt] vt irriter; **irritating** adj irritant(e); **irritation** [ɪrɪ'teɪʃən] n irritation f
IRS n abbr = Internal Revenue Service
is [ɪz] vb see **be**
Islam ['ɪzlɑːm] n Islam m
island ['aɪlənd] n île f; **~er** n habitant(e) d'une île, insulaire m/f
isle [aɪl] n île f
isn't ['ɪznt] = **is not**
isolate ['aɪsəʊleɪt] vt isoler; **~d** adj isolé(e); **isolation** [aɪsəʊ'leɪʃən] n isolation f
Israel ['ɪzreɪəl] n Israël m; **~i** [ɪz'reɪlɪ] adj israélien(ne) ♦ n Israélien(ne)
issue ['ɪʃuː] n question f, problème m; (of book) publication f, parution f; (of banknotes etc) émission f; (of newspaper etc) numéro m ♦ vt (rations, equipment) distribuer; (statement) publier, faire; (banknotes etc) émettre, mettre en circulation; **at ~** en jeu, en cause; **to take ~ with sb (over)** exprimer son désaccord avec qn (sur); **to make an ~ of sth** faire une montagne de qch

──────────── KEYWORD

it [ɪt] pron **1** (specific: subject) il(elle); (: direct object) le(la, l'); (: indirect object) lui; **~'s on the table** c'est or il (or elle) est sur la table; **about/from/of ~** en; **I spoke to him about ~** je lui en ai parlé; **what did you learn from ~?** qu'est-ce que vous en avez retiré?; **I'm proud of ~** j'en suis fier; **in/to ~** y; **put the book in ~** mettez-y le livre; **he agreed to ~** il y a consenti; **did you go to ~?** (party, concert etc) est-ce que vous y êtes allé(s)?
2 (impersonal) il; ce; **~'s raining** il pleut; **~'s Friday tomorrow** demain c'est vendredi or nous sommes vendredi; **~'s 6 o'clock** il est 6 heures; **who is ~? - ~'s me** qui est-ce? - c'est moi

──────────────

Italian [ɪ'tæljən] adj italien(ne) ♦ n Italien(ne); (LING) italien m
italics [ɪ'tælɪks] npl italiques fpl
Italy ['ɪtəlɪ] n Italie f
itch [ɪtʃ] n démangeaison f ♦ vi (person) éprouver des démangeaisons; (part of body) démanger; **I'm ~ing to do** l'envie me démange de faire; **~y** adj qui démange; **to be ~y** avoir des démangeaisons
it'd ['ɪtd] = **it would; it had**
item ['aɪtəm] n article m; (on agenda) question f, point m; (also: news ~) nouvelle f; **~ize** vt détailler, faire une liste de
itinerary [aɪ'tɪnərərɪ] n itinéraire m
it: **~'ll** ['ɪtl] = **it will; it shall; ~s** [ɪts] adj son(sa), ses pl; **~'s** [ɪts] = **it is; it has; ~self** [ɪt'self] pron (reflexive) se; (emphatic) lui-même(elle-même)
ITV n abbr (BRIT: = Independent Television)

chaîne privée
IUD n abbr (= intra-uterine device) DIU m, stérilet m
I've [aɪv] = **I have**
ivory ['aɪvərɪ] n ivoire m
ivy ['aɪvɪ] n lierre m

──────────── *J j*

jab [dʒæb] vt: **to ~ sth into** enfoncer or planter qch dans ♦ n (inf: injection) piqûre f
jack [dʒæk] n (AUT) cric m; (CARDS) valet m; **~ up** vt soulever (au cric)
jackal ['dʒækəl] n chacal m
jackdaw ['dʒækdɔː] n choucas m
jacket ['dʒækɪt] n veste f, veston m; (of book) jaquette f, couverture f
jackknife ['dʒæknaɪf] vi: **the lorry ~d** la remorque (du camion) s'est mise en travers
jack plug n (ELEC) prise jack mâle f
jackpot ['dʒækpɒt] n gros lot
jaded ['dʒeɪdɪd] adj éreinté(e), fatigué(e)
jagged ['dʒægɪd] adj dentelé(e)
jail [dʒeɪl] n prison f ♦ vt emprisonner, mettre en prison
jam [dʒæm] n confiture f; (also: traffic ~) embouteillage m ♦ vt (passage etc) encombrer, obstruer; (mechanism, drawer etc) bloquer, coincer; (RADIO) brouiller ♦ vi se coincer, se bloquer; (gun) s'enrayer; **to be in a ~** (inf) être dans le pétrin; **to ~ sth into** entasser qch dans; enfoncer qch dans
jangle ['dʒæŋgl] vi cliqueter
janitor ['dʒænɪtə*] n concierge m
January ['dʒænjʊərɪ] n janvier m
Japan [dʒə'pæn] n Japon m; **~ese** adj [dʒæpə'niːz] japonais(e) ♦ n inv Japonais(e); (LING) japonais m
jar [dʒɑː*] n (stone, earthenware) pot m; (glass) bocal m ♦ vi (sound discordant) produire un son grinçant or discordant; (colours etc) jurer
jargon ['dʒɑːgən] n jargon m
jaundice ['dʒɔːndɪs] n jaunisse f; **~d** adj (fig) envieux(euse), désapprobateur(trice)
javelin ['dʒævlɪn] n javelot m
jaw [dʒɔː] n mâchoire f
jay [dʒeɪ] n geai m; **~walker** ['dʒeɪwɔːkə*] n piéton indiscipliné
jazz [dʒæz] n jazz m; **~ up** vt animer, égayer
jealous ['dʒeləs] adj jaloux(ouse); **~y** n jalousie f

jeans [dʒiːnz] *npl* jean *m*
jeer [dʒɪə*] *vi*: **to ~ (at)** se moquer cruellement (de), railler
jelly ['dʒelɪ] *n* gelée *f*; **~fish** *n* méduse *f*
jeopardy ['dʒepədɪ] *n*: **to be in ~** être en danger *or* péril
jerk [dʒɜːk] *n* secousse *f*; saccade *f*; sursaut *m*, spasme *m*; (*inf*: *idiot*) pauvre type *m* ♦ *vt* (*pull*) tirer brusquement ♦ *vi* (*vehicles*) cahoter
jersey ['dʒɜːzɪ] *n* (*pullover*) tricot *m*; (*fabric*) jersey *m*
Jesus ['dʒiːzəs] *n* Jésus
jet [dʒet] *n* (*gas, liquid*) jet *m*; (*AVIAT*) avion *m* à réaction, jet *m*; **~-black** *adj* (d'un noir) de jais; **~ engine** *n* moteur *m* à réaction; **~ lag** *n* (fatigue due au) décalage *m* horaire
jettison ['dʒetɪsn] *vt* jeter par-dessus bord
jetty ['dʒetɪ] *n* jetée *f*, digue *f*
Jew [dʒuː] *n* Juif *m*
jewel ['dʒuːəl] *n* bijou *m*, joyau *m*; (*in watch*) rubis *m*; **~ler** (*US* **~er**) *n* bijoutier(ère), joaillier *m*; **~ler's (shop)** *n* bijouterie *f*, joaillerie *f*; **~lery** (*US* **~ry**) *n* bijoux *mpl*
Jewess ['dʒuːɪs] *n* Juive *f*
Jewish ['dʒuːɪʃ] *adj* juif(juive)
jibe [dʒaɪb] *n* sarcasme *m*
jiffy ['dʒɪfɪ] (*inf*) *n*: **in a ~** en un clin d'œil
jigsaw ['dʒɪgsɔː] *n* (*also*: **~ puzzle**) puzzle *m*
jilt [dʒɪlt] *vt* laisser tomber, plaquer
jingle ['dʒɪŋgl] *n* (*for advert*) couplet *m* publicitaire ♦ *vi* cliqueter, tinter
jinx [dʒɪŋks] (*inf*) *n* (mauvais) sort *m*
jitters ['dʒɪtəz] (*inf*) *npl*: **to get the ~** (*inf*) avoir la trouille *or* la frousse
job [dʒɒb] *n* (*chore, task*) travail *m*, tâche *f*; (*employment*) emploi *m*, poste *m*, place *f*; **it's a good ~ that ...** c'est heureux *or* c'est une chance que ...; **just the ~!** (c'est) juste *or* exactement ce qu'il faut!; **~ centre** (*BRIT*) *n* agence *f* pour l'emploi; **~less** *adj* sans travail, au chômage
jockey ['dʒɒkɪ] *n* jockey *m* ♦ *vi*: **to ~ for position** manœuvrer pour être bien placé
jocular ['dʒɒkjʊlə*] *adj* jovial(e), enjoué(e); facétieux(euse)
jog [dʒɒg] *vt* secouer ♦ *vi* (*SPORT*) faire du jogging; **to ~ sb's memory** rafraîchir la mémoire de qn; **~ along** *vi* cheminer; trotter; **~ging** *n* jogging *m*
join [dʒɔɪn] *vt* (*put together*) unir, assembler; (*become member of*) s'inscrire à; (*meet*) rejoindre, retrouver; (*queue*) se joindre à ♦ *vi* (*roads, rivers*) se rejoindre, se rencontrer ♦ *n* raccord *m*; **~ in** *vi* se mettre de la partie, participer ♦ *vt fus* participer à, se mêler à; **~ up** *vi* (*meet*) se rejoindre; (*MIL*) s'engager; **~er** ['dʒɔɪnə*] (*BRIT*) *n* menuisier *m*

joint [dʒɔɪnt] *n* (*TECH*) jointure *f*; joint *m*; (*ANAT*) articulation *f*, jointure; (*BRIT*: *CULIN*) rôti *m*; (*inf*: *place*) boîte *f*; (: *of cannabis*) joint *m* ♦ *adj* commun(e); **~ account** *n* (*with bank etc*) compte joint
joke [dʒəʊk] *n* plaisanterie *f*; (*also*: *practical ~*) farce *f* ♦ *vi* plaisanter; **to play a ~ on** jouer un tour à, faire une farce à; **~r** *n* (*CARDS*) joker *m*
jolly ['dʒɒlɪ] *adj* gai(e), enjoué(e); (*enjoyable*) amusant(e), plaisant(e) ♦ *adv* (*BRIT*: *inf*) rudement, drôlement
jolt [dʒəʊlt] *n* cahot *m*, secousse *f*; (*shock*) choc *m* ♦ *vt* cahoter, secouer
Jordan ['dʒɔːdən] *n* (*country*) Jordanie *f*
jostle ['dʒɒsl] *vt* bousculer, pousser
jot [dʒɒt] *n*: **not one ~** pas un brin; **~ down** *vt* noter; **~ter** (*BRIT*) *n* cahier *m* (de brouillon); (*pad*) bloc-notes *m*
journal ['dʒɜːnl] *n* journal *m*; **~ism** *n* journalisme *m*; **~ist** *n* journaliste *m/f*
journey ['dʒɜːnɪ] *n* voyage *m*; (*distance covered*) trajet *m*
joy [dʒɔɪ] *n* joie *f*; **~ful** *adj* joyeux(euse); **~rider** *n* personne qui fait une virée dans une voiture volée; **~stick** *n* (*AVIAT*, *COMPUT*) manche *m* à balai
JP *n abbr* = **Justice of the Peace**
Jr *abbr* = **junior**
jubilant ['dʒuːbɪlənt] *adj* triomphant(e); réjoui(e)
judge [dʒʌdʒ] *n* juge *m* ♦ *vt* juger; **judg(e)ment** *n* jugement *m*
judicial [dʒuː'dɪʃəl] *adj* judiciaire
judiciary [dʒuː'dɪʃɪərɪ] *n* (*pouvoir m*) judiciaire *m*
judo ['dʒuːdəʊ] *n* judo *m*
jug [dʒʌg] *n* pot *m*, cruche *f*
juggernaut ['dʒʌgənɔːt] (*BRIT*) *n* (*huge truck*) énorme poids lourd
juggle ['dʒʌgl] *vi* jongler; **~r** *n* jongleur *m*
Jugoslav *etc* = **Yugoslav** *etc*
juice [dʒuːs] *n* jus *m*; **juicy** ['dʒuːsɪ] *adj* juteux(euse)
jukebox ['dʒuːkbɒks] *n* juke-box *m*
July [dʒuː'laɪ] *n* juillet *m*
jumble ['dʒʌmbl] *n* fouillis *m* ♦ *vt* (*also*: *~ up*) mélanger, brouiller; **~ sale** (*BRIT*) *n* vente *f* de charité
jumbo (jet) ['dʒʌmbəʊ-] *n* jumbo-jet *m*, gros porteur
jump [dʒʌmp] *vi* sauter, bondir; (*start*) sursauter; (*increase*) monter en flèche ♦ *vt* sauter, franchir ♦ *n* saut *m*, bond *m*; sursaut *m*; **to ~ the queue** (*BRIT*) passer avant son tour
jumper ['dʒʌmpə*] *n* (*BRIT*: *pullover*) pullover *m*; (*US*: *dress*) robe-chasuble *f*
jumper cables (*US*), **jump leads** (*BRIT*) *npl* câbles *mpl* de démarrage
jumpy ['dʒʌmpɪ] *adj* nerveux(euse), agité(e)
Jun. *abbr* = **junior**

junction ['dʒʌŋkʃən] (*BRIT*) *n* (*of roads*) carrefour *m*; (*of rails*) embranchement *m*

juncture ['dʒʌŋktʃə*] *n*: **at this ~** à ce moment-là, sur ces entrefaites

June [dʒu:n] *n* juin *m*

jungle ['dʒʌŋgl] *n* jungle *f*

junior ['dʒu:nɪə*] *adj, n*: **he's ~ to me (by 2 years), he's my ~ (by 2 years)** il est mon cadet (de 2 ans), il est plus jeune que moi (de 2 ans); **he's ~ to me** (*seniority*) il est en dessous de moi (dans la hiérarchie), j'ai plus d'ancienneté que lui; **~ school** (*BRIT*) *n* ≈ école f primaire

junk [dʒʌŋk] *n* (*rubbish*) camelote *f*; (*cheap goods*) bric-à-brac *m inv*; **~ food** *n* aliments *mpl* sans grande valeur nutritive; **~ mail** *n* prospectus *mpl* (*non sollicités*); **~ shop** *n* (*boutique f de*) brocanteur *m*

Junr *abbr* = **junior**

juror ['dʒuərə*] *n* juré *m*

jury ['dʒuərɪ] *n* jury *m*

just [dʒʌst] *adj* juste ♦ *adv*: **he's ~ done it/left** il vient de le faire/partir; **~ right/ two o'clock** exactement *or* juste ce qu'il faut/deux heures; **she's ~ as clever as you** elle est tout aussi intelligente que vous; **it's ~ as well (that)** ... heureusement que ...; **~ as he was leaving** au moment *or* à l'instant précis où il partait; **~ before/ enough/here** juste avant/assez/ici; **it's ~ me/a mistake** ce n'est que moi/(rien) qu'une erreur; **~ missed/caught** manqué/ attrapé de justesse; **~ listen to this!** écoutez un peu ça!

justice ['dʒʌstɪs] *n* justice *f*; (*US: judge*) juge *m* de la Cour suprême; **J~ of the Peace** *n* juge *m* de paix

justify ['dʒʌstɪfaɪ] *vt* justifier

jut [dʒʌt] *vi* (*also:* **~ out**) dépasser, faire saillie

juvenile ['dʒu:vənaɪl] *adj* juvénile; (*court, books*) pour enfants ♦ *n* adolescent(e)

K k

K *abbr* (= *one thousand*) K; (= *kilobyte*) Ko

kangaroo [kæŋgə'ru:] *n* kangourou *m*

karate [kə'rɑ:tɪ] *n* karaté *m*

kebab [kə'bæb] *n* kébab *m*

keel [ki:l] *n* quille *f*

keen [ki:n] *adj* (*eager*) plein(e) d'enthousiasme; (*interest, desire, competition*) vif(vive); (*eye, intelligence*) pénétrant(e);

(*edge*) effilé(e); **to be ~ to do** *or* **on doing sth** désirer vivement faire qch, tenir beaucoup à faire qch; **to be ~ on sth/sb** aimer beaucoup qch/qn

keep [ki:p] (*pt, pp* **kept**) *vt* (*retain, preserve*) garder; (*detain*) retenir; (*shop, accounts, diary, promise*) tenir; (*house*) avoir; (*support*) entretenir; (*chickens, bees etc*) élever ♦ *vi* (*remain*) rester; (*food*) se conserver ♦ *n* (*of castle*) donjon *m*; (*food etc*): **enough for his ~** assez pour (assurer) sa subsistance; (*inf*): **for ~s** pour de bon, pour toujours; **to ~ doing sth** ne pas arrêter de faire qch; **to ~ sb from doing** empêcher qn de faire *or* que qn ne fasse; **to ~ sb happy/a place tidy** faire que qn soit content/qu'un endroit reste propre; **to ~ sth to o.s.** garder qch pour soi, tenir qch secret; **to ~ sth (back) from sb** cacher qch à qn; **to ~ time** (*clock*) être à l'heure, ne pas retarder; **well kept** bien entretenu(e); **~ on** *vi*: **to ~ on doing** continuer à faire; **don't ~ on about it!** arrête (d'en parler)!; **~ out** *vt* empêcher d'entrer; **"~ out"** "défense d'entrer"; **~ up** *vt* continuer, maintenir ♦ *vi*: **to ~ up with sb** (*in race etc*) aller aussi vite que qn; (*in work etc*) se maintenir au niveau de qn; **~er** *n* gardien(ne); **~-fit** *n* gymnastique *f* d'entretien; **~ing** *n* (*care*) garde *f*; **in ~ing with** en accord avec; **~sake** *n* souvenir *m*

kennel ['kɛnl] *n* niche *f*; **~s** *npl* (*boarding ~s*) chenil *m*

kerb [kɜ:b] (*BRIT*) *n* bordure *f* du trottoir

kernel ['kɜ:nl] *n* (*of nut*) amande *f*; (*fig*) noyau *m*

kettle ['kɛtl] *n* bouilloire *f*; **~drum** *n* timbale *f*

key [ki:] *n* (*gen, MUS*) clé *f*; (*of piano, typewriter*) touche *f* ♦ *cpd* clé ♦ *vt* (*also: ~ in*) introduire (au clavier), saisir; **~board** *n* clavier *m*; **~ed up** *adj* (*person*) surexcité(e); **~hole** *n* trou *m* de la serrure; **~note** *n* (*of speech*) note dominante; (*MUS*) tonique *f*; **~ ring** *n* porte-clés *m*

khaki ['kɑ:kɪ] *n* kaki *m*

kick [kɪk] *vt* donner un coup de pied à ♦ *vi* (*horse*) ruer ♦ *n* coup *m* de pied; (*thrill*): **he does it for ~s** il le fait parce que ça l'excite, il le fait pour le plaisir; **to ~ the habit** (*inf*) arrêter; **~ off** *vi* (*SPORT*) donner le coup d'envoi

kid [kɪd] *n* (*inf: child*) gamin(e), gosse *m/f*; (*animal, leather*) chevreau *m* ♦ *vi* (*inf*) plaisanter, blaguer

kidnap ['kɪdnæp] *vt* enlever, kidnapper; **~per** *n* ravisseur(euse); **~ping** *n* enlèvement *m*

kidney ['kɪdnɪ] *n* (*ANAT*) rein *m*; (*CULIN*) rognon *m*

kill [kɪl] *vt* tuer ♦ *n* mise *f* à mort; **~er** *n* tueur(euse); meurtrier(ère); **~ing** *n* meurtre *m*; (*of group of people*) tuerie *f*, massacre *m*; **to make a ~ing** (*inf*) réussir un beau coup (de filet); **~joy** *n* rabat-joie *m/f*

kiln [kɪln] *n* four *m*

kilo ['kiːləʊ] *n* kilo *m*; **~byte** *n* (*COMPUT*) kilo-octet *m*; **~gram(me)** ['kɪləʊgræm] *n* kilogramme *m*; **~metre** ['kɪləmiːtə*] (*US* **~meter**) *n* kilomètre *m*; **~watt** *n* kilowatt *m*

kilt [kɪlt] *n* kilt *m*

kin [kɪn] *n see* **next**; **kith**

kind [kaɪnd] *adj* gentil(le), aimable ♦ *n* sorte *f*, espèce *f*, genre *m*; **to be two of a ~** se ressembler; **in ~** (*COMM*) en nature

kindergarten ['kɪndəgɑːtn] *n* jardin *m* d'enfants

kind-hearted ['kaɪnd'hɑːtɪd] *adj* bon(bonne)

kindle ['kɪndl] *vt* allumer, enflammer

kindly ['kaɪndlɪ] *adj* bienveillant(e), plein(e) de gentillesse ♦ *adv* avec bonté; **will you ~ ...!** auriez-vous la bonté *or* l'obligeance de ...?

kindness ['kaɪndnəs] *n* bonté *f*, gentillesse *f*

kindred ['kɪndrɪd] *adj*: **~ spirit** âme *f* sœur

kinetic [kɪ'netɪk] *adj* cinétique

king [kɪŋ] *n* roi *m*; **~dom** *n* royaume *m*; **~fisher** *n* martin-pêcheur *m*; **~-size bed** *n* grand lit (*de 1,95 m de large*); **~-size(d)** *adj* format géant *inv*; (*cigarettes*) long(longue)

kinky ['kɪŋkɪ] (*pej*) *adj* (*person*) excentrique; (*sexually*) aux goûts spéciaux

kiosk ['kiːɒsk] *n* kiosque *m*; (*BRIT: TEL*) cabine *f* (téléphonique)

kipper ['kɪpə*] *n* hareng fumé et salé

kiss [kɪs] *n* baiser *m* ♦ *vt* embrasser; **to ~ (each other)** s'embrasser; **~ of life** (*BRIT*) *n* bouche à bouche *m*

kit [kɪt] *n* équipement *m*, matériel *m*; (*set of tools etc*) trousse *f*; (*for assembly*) kit *m*

kitchen ['kɪtʃɪn] *n* cuisine *f*; **~ sink** *n* évier *m*

kite [kaɪt] *n* (*toy*) cerf-volant *m*

kith [kɪθ] *n*: **~ and kin** parents et amis *mpl*

kitten ['kɪtn] *n* chaton *m*, petit chat

kitty ['kɪtɪ] *n* (*money*) cagnotte *f*

knack [næk] *n*: **to have the ~ of doing** avoir le coup pour faire

knapsack ['næpsæk] *n* musette *f*

knead [niːd] *vt* pétrir

knee [niː] *n* genou *m*; **~cap** *n* rotule *f*

kneel [niːl] (*pt, pp* **knelt**) *vi* (*also*: **~ down**) s'agenouiller

knew [njuː] *pt of* **know**

knickers ['nɪkəz] (*BRIT*) *npl* culotte *f* (de femme)

knife [naɪf] (*pl* **knives**) *n* couteau *m* ♦ *vt* poignarder, frapper d'un coup de couteau

knight [naɪt] *n* chevalier *m*; (*CHESS*) cavalier *m*; **~hood** (*BRIT*) *n* (*title*): **to get a ~hood** être fait chevalier

knit [nɪt] *vt* tricoter ♦ *vi* tricoter; (*broken*

bones) se ressouder; **to ~ one's brows** froncer les sourcils; **~ting** *n* tricot *m*; **~ting needle** *n* aiguille *f* à tricoter; **~wear** *n* tricots *mpl*, lainages *mpl*

knives [naɪvz] *npl of* **knife**

knob [nɒb] *n* bouton *m*

knock [nɒk] *vt* frapper; (*bump into*) heurter; (*inf*) dénigrer ♦ *vi* (*at door etc*): **to ~ at** *or* **on frapper à** ♦ *n* coup *m*; **~ down** *vt* renverser; **~ off** *vi* (*inf: finish*) s'arrêter (de travailler) ♦ *vt* (*from price*) faire un rabais de; (*inf: steal*) piquer; **~ out** *vt* assommer; (*BOXING*) mettre k.-o.; (*defeat*) éliminer; **~ over** *vt* renverser, faire tomber; **~er** *n* (*on door*) heurtoir *m*; **~out** *n* (*BOXING*) knock-out *m*, K.-O. *m*; **~out competition** *n* compétition *f* avec épreuves éliminatoires

knot [nɒt] *n* (*gen*) nœud *m* ♦ *vt* nouer; **~ty** *adj* (*fig*) épineux(euse)

know [nəʊ] (*pt* **knew**, *pp* **known**) *vt* savoir; (*person, place*) connaître; **to ~ how to do** savoir (comment) faire; **to ~ how to swim** savoir nager; **to ~ about** *or* **of sth** être au courant de qch; **to ~ about** *or* **of sb** avoir entendu parler de qn; **~-all** (*pej*) *n* je-sais-tout *m/f*; **~-how** *n* savoir-faire *m*; **~ing** *adj* (*look etc*) entendu(e); **~ingly** *adv* sciemment; (*smile, look*) d'un air entendu

knowledge ['nɒlɪdʒ] *n* connaissance *f*; (*learning*) connaissances, savoir *m*; **~able** *adj* bien informé(e)

knuckle ['nʌkl] *n* articulation *f* (des doigts), jointure *f*

Koran [kɔː'rɑːn] *n* Coran *m*

Korea [kə'rɪə] *n* Corée *f*

kosher ['kəʊʃə*] *adj* kascher *inv*

L l

L *abbr* (= *lake, large*) L; (= *left*) g; (= *BRIT: AUT*: = *learner*) signale un conducteur débutant

lab [læb] *n abbr* (= *laboratory*) labo *m*

label ['leɪbl] *n* étiquette *f* ♦ *vt* étiqueter

labor etc (*US*) = **labour** etc

laboratory [lə'bɒrətərɪ] *n* laboratoire *m*

labour ['leɪbə*] (*US* **labor**) *n* travail *m*; (*workforce*) main-d'œuvre *f* ♦ *vi*: **to ~ (at)** travailler dur (à), peiner (sur) ♦ *vt*: **to ~ a point** insister sur un point; **in ~** (*MED*) en travail, en train d'accoucher; **L~, the L~ party** (*BRIT*) le parti travailliste, les travaillistes *mpl*; **~ed** *adj* (*breathing*) pénible, difficile; **~er** n manœuvre m; **farm ~er** ouvrier m agricole

lace [leɪs] n dentelle f; (of shoe etc) lacet m ♦ vt (shoe: also: ~ **up**) lacer

lack [læk] n manque m ♦ vt manquer de; **through** or **for ~** of faute de, par manque de; **to be ~ing** manquer, faire défaut; **to be ~ing in** manquer de

lacquer ['lækə*] n laque f

lad [læd] n garçon m, gars m

ladder ['lædə*] n échelle f; (BRIT: in tights) maille filée

laden ['leɪdn] adj: ~ **(with)** chargé(e) (de)

ladle ['leɪdl] n louche f

lady ['leɪdɪ] n dame f; (in address): **ladies and gentlemen** Mesdames (et) Messieurs; **young ~** jeune fille f; (married) jeune femme f; **the ladies' (room)** les toilettes fpl (pour dames); **~bird** n coccinelle f; **~bug** (US) n = ladybird; **~like** adj distingué(e); **~ship** n: **your ~ship** Madame la comtesse (or la baronne etc)

lag [læg] n retard m ♦ vi (also: ~ **behind**) rester en arrière, traîner; (fig) rester en traîne ♦ vt (pipes) calorifuger

lager ['lɑːgə*] n bière blonde

lagoon [lə'guːn] n lagune f

laid [leɪd] pt, pp of **lay**; **~-back** (inf) adj relaxe, décontracté(e); ~ **up** adj alité(e)

lain [leɪn] pp of **lie**

lake [leɪk] n lac m

lamb [læm] n agneau m; ~ **chop** côtelette f d'agneau

lame [leɪm] adj boiteux(euse)

lament [lə'ment] n lamentation f ♦ vt pleurer, se lamenter sur

laminated ['læmɪneɪtɪd] adj laminé(e); (windscreen) (en verre) feuilleté

lamp [læmp] n lampe f; **~post** (BRIT) n réverbère m; **~shade** n abat-jour m inv

lance [lɑːns] vt (MED) inciser

land [lænd] n (as opposed to sea) terre f (ferme); (soil) terre; terrain m; (estate) terre(s), domaine(s) m(pl); (country) pays m ♦ vi (AVIAT) atterrir; (fig) (re)tomber ♦ vt (passengers, goods) débarquer; **to ~ sb with sth** (inf) coller qch à qn; ~ **up** vi atterrir, (finir par) se retrouver; **~fill site** n décharge f; **~ing** n (AVIAT) atterrissage m; (of staircase) palier m; (of troops) débarquement m; **~ing gear** n train m d'atterrissage; **~ing strip** n piste f d'atterrissage; **~lady** n propriétaire f, logeuse f; (of pub) patronne f; **~locked** adj sans littoral; **~lord** n propriétaire m, logeur m; (of pub etc) patron m; **~mark** n (point m de) repère m; **to be a ~mark** (fig) faire date et époque; **~owner** n propriétaire foncier or terrien; **~scape** ['lændskeɪp] n paysage m; **~scape gardener** n jardinier(ière) paysagiste; **~slide** n (GEO) glissement m (de terrain); (fig: POL) raz-de-

marée (électoral)

lane [leɪn] n (in country) chemin m; (AUT) voie f; file f; (in race) couloir m

language ['læŋgwɪdʒ] n langue f; (way one speaks) langage m; **bad ~** grossièretés fpl, langage grossier; ~ **laboratory** n laboratoire m de langues

lank [læŋk] adj (hair) raide et terne

lanky ['læŋkɪ] adj grand(e) et maigre, efflanqué(e)

lantern ['læntən] n lanterne f

lap [læp] n (of track) tour m (de piste); (of body): **in** or **on one's ~** sur les genoux ♦ vt (also: ~ **up**) laper ♦ vi (waves) clapoter; ~ **up** vt (fig) accepter béatement, gober

lapel [lə'pel] n revers m

Lapland ['læplænd] n Laponie f

lapse [læps] n défaillance f; (in behaviour) écart m de conduite ♦ vi (LAW) cesser d'être en vigueur; (contract) expirer; **to ~ into bad habits** prendre de mauvaises habitudes; ~ **of time** laps m de temps, intervalle m

laptop (computer) ['læptɒp-] n portable m

larceny ['lɑːsənɪ] n vol m

larch [lɑːtʃ] n mélèze m

lard [lɑːd] n saindoux m

larder ['lɑːdə*] n garde-manger m inv

large [lɑːdʒ] adj grand(e); (person, animal) gros(se); **at ~** (free) en liberté; (generally) en général; see also **by**; **~ly** adv en grande partie; (principally) surtout; **~-scale** adj (action) d'envergure; (map) à grande échelle

lark [lɑːk] n (bird) alouette f; (joke) blague f, farce f; ~ **about** vi faire l'idiot, rigoler

laryngitis [lærɪn'dʒaɪtɪs] n laryngite f

laser ['leɪzə*] n laser m; ~ **printer** n imprimante f laser

lash [læʃ] n coup m de fouet; (also: eye~) cil m ♦ vt fouetter; (tie) attacher; ~ **out** vi: **to ~ out at** or **against** attaquer violemment

lass [læs] (BRIT) n (jeune) fille f

lasso [læ'suː] n lasso m

last [lɑːst] adj dernier(ère) ♦ adv en dernier; (finally) finalement ♦ vi durer; ~ **week** la semaine dernière; ~ **night** (evening) hier soir; (night) la nuit dernière; **at ~** enfin; ~ **but one** avant-dernier(ère); **~-ditch** adj (attempt) ultime, désespéré(e); **~ing** adj durable; **~ly** adv en dernier lieu, pour finir; **~-minute** adj de dernière minute

latch [lætʃ] n loquet m

late [leɪt] adj (not on time) en retard; (far on in day etc) tardif(ive); (edition, delivery) dernier(ière); (former) ancien(ne) ♦ adv tard; (behind time, schedule) en retard; **of ~** dernièrement; **in ~ May** vers la fin (du mois) de mai, fin mai; **the ~ Mr X** feu M. X; **~comer** n retardataire m/f; **~ly** adv récemment; **~r** ['leɪtə*] *adj* (*date etc*) ultérieur(e); (*version etc*) plus récent(e) ♦ *adv* plus tard; **~r on** plus tard; **~st** ['leɪtɪst] *adj* tout(e) dernier(ère); **at the ~st** au plus tard

lathe [leɪð] *n* tour *m*

lather ['lɑːðə*] *n* mousse *f* (de savon) ♦ *vt* savonner

Latin ['lætɪn] *n* latin *m* ♦ *adj* latin(e); **~ America** *n* Amérique latine; **~ American** *adj* latino-américain(e)

latitude ['lætɪtjuːd] *n* latitude *f*

latter ['lætə*] *adj* deuxième, dernier(ère) ♦ *n*: **the ~** ce dernier, celui-ci; **~ly** *adv* dernièrement, récemment

laudable ['lɔːdəbl] *adj* louable

laugh [lɑːf] *n* rire *m* ♦ *vi* rire; **~ at** *vt fus* se moquer de; rire de; **~ off** *vt* écarter par une plaisanterie *or* par une boutade; **~able** *adj* risible, ridicule; **~ing stock** *n*: **the ~ing stock of** la risée de; **~ter** *n* rire *m*; rires *mpl*

launch [lɔːntʃ] *n* lancement *m*; (*motorboat*) vedette *f* ♦ *vt* lancer; **~ into** *vt fus* se lancer dans

Launderette [lɔːn'dret] (*BRIT*: ®), **Laundromat** ['lɔːndrəmæt] (*US*: ®) *n* laverie *f* (automatique)

laundry ['lɔːndrɪ] *n* (*clothes*) linge *m*; (*business*) blanchisserie *f*; (*room*) buanderie *f*

laureate ['lɔːrɪət] *adj see* **poet**

laurel ['lɒrəl] *n* laurier *m*

lava ['lɑːvə] *n* lave *f*

lavatory ['lævətrɪ] *n* toilettes *fpl*

lavender ['lævɪndə*] *n* lavande *f*

lavish ['lævɪʃ] *adj* (*amount*) copieux(euse), (*person*): **~ with** prodigue de ♦ *vt*: **to ~ sth on sb** prodiguer qch à qn; (*money*) dépenser qch sans compter pour qn/qch

law [lɔː] *n* loi *f*; (*science*) droit *m*; **~-abiding** *adj* respectueux(euse) des lois; **~ and order** *n* l'ordre public; **~ court** *n* tribunal *m*, cour *f* de justice; **~ful** *adj* légal(e); **~less** *adj* (*action*) illégal(e)

lawn [lɔːn] *n* pelouse *f*; **~mower** *n* tondeuse *f* à gazon; **~ tennis** *n* tennis *m*

law school (*US*) *n* faculté *f* de droit

lawsuit ['lɔːsuːt] *n* procès *m*

lawyer ['lɔːjə*] *n* (*consultant, with company*) juriste *m*; (*for sales, wills etc*) notaire *m*; (*partner, in court*) avocat *m*

lax [læks] *adj* relâché(e)

laxative ['læksətɪv] *n* laxatif *m*

lay [leɪ] (*pt, pp* **laid**) *pt of* **lie** ♦ *adj* laïque; (*not expert*) profane ♦ *vt* poser, mettre; (*eggs*) pondre; **to ~ the table** mettre la table; **~ aside** *vt* mettre de côté; **~ by** *vt* = **lay aside**; **~ down** *vt* poser; **to ~ down the law** faire la loi; **to ~ down one's life** sacrifier sa vie; **~ off** *vt* (*workers*) licencier; **~ on** *vt* (*provide*) fournir; **~ out** *vt* (*display*) disposer, étaler; **~about** (*inf*) *n* fai-

néant(e); **~-by** (*BRIT*) *n* aire *f* de stationnement (sur le bas-côté)

layer ['leɪə*] *n* couche *f*

layman ['leɪmən] (*irreg*) *n* profane *m*

layout ['leɪaʊt] *n* disposition *f*, plan *m*, agencement *m*; (*PRESS*) mise *f* en page

laze [leɪz] *vi* (*also*: **~ about**) paresser

lazy ['leɪzɪ] *adj* paresseux(euse)

lb *abbr* = **pound** (*weight*)

lead¹ [liːd] (*pt, pp* **led**) *n* (*distance, time ahead*) avance *f*; (*clue*) piste *f*; (*THEATRE*) rôle principal; (*ELEC*) fil *m*; (*for dog*) laisse *f* ♦ *vt* mener, conduire; (*be leader of*) être à la tête de ♦ *vi* (*street etc*) mener, conduire; (*SPORT*) mener, être en tête; **in the ~** en tête; **to ~ the way** montrer le chemin; **~ away** *vt* emmener; **~ back** *vt*: **to ~ back to** ramener à; **~ on** *vt* (*tease*) faire marcher; **~ to** *vt fus* mener à; conduire à; **~ up to** *vt fus* conduire à

lead² [led] *n* (*metal*) plomb *m*; (*in pencil*) mine *f*; **~en** ['ledn] *adj* (*sky, sea*) de plomb

leader ['liːdə*] *n* chef *m*; dirigeant(e), leader *m*; (*SPORT: in league*) leader; (: *in race*) coureur *m* de tête; **~ship** *n* direction *f*; (*quality*) qualités *fpl* de chef

lead-free ['led'friː] *adj* (*petrol*) sans plomb

leading ['liːdɪŋ] *adj* principal(e); de premier plan; (*in race*) de tête; **~ lady** *n* (*THEATRE*) vedette (féminine); **~ light** *n* (*person*) vedette *f*, sommité *f*; **~ man** (*irreg*) *n* vedette (masculine)

lead singer [liːd-] *n* (*in pop group*) (chanteur *m*) vedette *f*

leaf [liːf] (*pl* **leaves**) *n* feuille *f* ♦ *vi*: **to ~ through** feuilleter; **to turn over a new ~** changer de conduite *or* d'existence

leaflet ['liːflɪt] *n* prospectus *m*, brochure *f*; (*POL, REL*) tract *m*

league [liːg] *n* ligue *f*; (*FOOTBALL*) championnat *m*; **to be in ~ with** avoir partie liée avec, être de mèche avec

leak [liːk] *n* fuite *f* ♦ *vi* (*pipe, liquid etc*) fuir; (*shoes*) prendre l'eau; (*ship*) faire eau ♦ *vt* (*information*) divulguer

lean [liːn] (*pt, pp* **leaned** *or* **leant**) *adj* maigre ♦ *vt*: **to ~ sth on sth** appuyer qch sur qch ♦ *vi* (*slope*) pencher; (*rest*): **to ~ against** s'appuyer contre; être appuyé(e) contre; **to ~ on** s'appuyer sur; **to ~ back/forward** se pencher en arrière/avant; **~ out** *vi* se pencher au dehors; **~ over** *vi* se pencher; **~ing** *n*: **~ing (towards)** tendance *f* (à), penchant *m* (pour)

leap [liːp] (*pt, pp* **leaped** *or* **leapt**) *n* bond *m*, saut *m* ♦ *vi* bondir, sauter; **~frog** *n* saute-mouton *m*; **~ year** *n* année *f* bissextile

learn [lɜːn] (*pt, pp* **~ed** *or* **learnt**) *vt, vi* apprendre; **to ~ to do sth** apprendre à faire qch; **to ~ about** *or* **of sth** (*hear, read*) apprendre qch; **~ed** ['lɜːnɪd] *adj* érudit(e), savant(e); **~er** (BRIT) n (also: **~er driver**) (conducteur(trice)) débutant(e); **~ing** n (knowledge) savoir m

lease [li:s] n bail m ♦ vt louer à bail

leash [li:ʃ] n laisse f

least [li:st] adj: **the ~** (+noun) le(la) plus petit(e), le(la) moindre; (: smallest amount of) le moins de ♦ adv (+verb) le moins; (+adj): **the ~** le(la) moins; **at ~** au moins; (or rather): **the ~** du moins; **not in the ~** pas le moins du monde

leather ['leðə*] n cuir m

leave [li:v] (pt, pp **left**) vt laisser; (go away from) quitter; (forget) oublier ♦ vi partir, s'en aller ♦ n (time off) congé m; (MIL also: consent) permission f; **to be left** rester; **there's some milk left over** il reste du lait; **on ~** en permission; **~ behind** vt (person, object) laisser; (forget) oublier; **~ out** vt oublier, omettre; **~ of absence** n congé exceptionnel; (MIL) permission spéciale

leaves [li:vz] npl of **leaf**

Lebanon ['lebənən] n Liban m

lecherous ['letʃərəs] (pej) adj lubrique

lecture ['lektʃə*] n conférence f; (SCOL) cours m ♦ vi donner des cours; enseigner ♦ vt (scold) sermonner, réprimander; **to give a ~ on** faire une conférence sur; donner un cours sur; **~r** ['lektʃərə*] (BRIT) n (at university) professeur m (d'université)

led [led] pt, pp of **lead**

ledge [ledʒ] n (of window, on wall) rebord m; (of mountain) saillie f, corniche f

ledger ['ledʒə*] n (COMM) registre m, grand livre

leech [li:tʃ] n (also fig) sangsue f

leek [li:k] n poireau m

leer [lɪə*] vi: **to ~ at sb** regarder qn d'un air mauvais or concupiscent

leeway ['li:weɪ] n (fig): **to have some ~** avoir une certaine liberté d'action

left [left] pt, pp of **leave** ♦ adj (not right) gauche ♦ n gauche f ♦ adv à gauche; **on the ~, to the ~** à gauche; **the L~** (POL) la gauche; **~-handed** adj gaucher(ère); **~-hand side** n gauche f, côté m gauche; **~-luggage (office)** (BRIT) n consigne f; **~overs** npl restes mpl; **~-wing** adj (POL) de gauche

leg [leg] n jambe f; (of animal) patte f; (of furniture) pied m; (CULIN: of chicken, pork) cuisse f; (: of lamb) gigot m; (of journey) étape f; **1st/2nd ~** (SPORT) match m aller/retour

legacy ['legəsɪ] n héritage m, legs m

legal ['li:gəl] adj légal(e); **~ holiday** (US) n jour férié m; **~ tender** n monnaie légale

legend ['ledʒənd] n légende f

legible ['ledʒəbl] adj lisible

legislation [ledʒɪs'leɪʃən] n législation f; **legislature** ['ledʒɪsleɪtʃə*] n (corps) m législatif

legitimate [lɪ'dʒɪtɪmət] adj légitime

leg-room ['legrum] n place f pour les jambes

leisure ['leʒə*] n loisir m, temps m libre; loisirs mpl; **at ~** (tout) à loisir; à tête reposée; **~ centre** n centre m de loisirs; **~ly** adj tranquille; fait(e) sans se presser

lemon ['lemən] n citron m; **~ade** n limonade f; **~ tea** n thé m au citron

lend [lend] (pt, pp **lent**) vt: **to ~ sth (to sb)** prêter qch (à qn)

length [leŋθ] n longueur f; (section: of road, pipe etc) morceau m, bout m; (of time) durée f; **at ~** (at last) enfin, à la fin; (lengthily) longuement; **~en** vt allonger, prolonger ♦ vi s'allonger; **~ways** adv dans le sens de la longueur, en long; **~y** adj (très) long(longue)

lenient ['li:nɪənt] adj indulgent(e), clément(e)

lens [lenz] n lentille f; (of spectacles) verre m; (of camera) objectif m

Lent [lent] n Carême m

lent [lent] pt, pp of **lend**

lentil ['lentl] n lentille f

Leo ['li:əu] n le Lion

leotard ['li:əta:d] n maillot m (de danseur etc), collant m

leprosy ['leprəsɪ] n lèpre f

lesbian ['lezbɪən] n lesbienne f

less [les] adj moins de ♦ pron, adv moins ♦ prep moins; **~ than that/you** moins que cela/vous; **~ than half** moins de la moitié; **~ than ever** moins que jamais; **~ and ~** de moins en moins; **the ~ he works ...** moins il travaille ...

lessen ['lesn] vi diminuer, s'atténuer ♦ vt diminuer, réduire, atténuer

lesser ['lesə*] adj moindre; **to a ~ extent** à un degré moindre

lesson ['lesn] n leçon f; **to teach sb a ~** (fig) donner une bonne leçon à qn

lest [lest] conj de peur que +sub

let [let] (pt, pp **let**) vt laisser; (BRIT: lease) louer; **to ~ sb do sth** laisser qn faire qch; **to ~ sb know sth** faire savoir qch à qn, prévenir qn de qch; **~'s go** allons-y; **~ him come** qu'il vienne; **"to ~"** "à louer"; **~ down** vt (tyre) dégonfler; (person) décevoir, faire faux bond à; **~ go** vi lâcher prise ♦ vt lâcher; **~ in** vt laisser entrer; (visitor etc) faire entrer; **~ off** vt (culprit) ne pas punir; (firework etc) faire partir; **~ on** (inf) vi dire; **~ out** vt laisser sortir; (scream) laisser échapper; **~ up** vi diminuer; (cease) s'arrêter

lethal ['li:θəl] adj mortel(le), fatal(e)

letter ['letə*] n lettre f; **~ bomb** n lettre piégée; **~box** (BRIT) n boîte f aux or à lettres; **~ing** n lettres fpl; caractères mpl

lettuce ['letɪs] n laitue f, salade f

let-up ['letʌp] n répit m, arrêt m

leukaemia [luːˈkiːmɪə] (*US* **leukemia**) *n* leucémie *f*

level [ˈlɛvl] *adj* plat(e), plan(e), uni(e); horizontal(e) ♦ *n* niveau *m* ♦ *vt* niveler, aplanir; **to be ~ with** être au même niveau que; **to draw ~ with** (*person, vehicle*) arriver à la hauteur de; **"A" ~s** (*BRIT*) ≈ baccalauréat *m*; **"O" ~s** (*BRIT*) ≈ B.E.P.C.; **on the ~** (*fig*: *honest*) régulier(ère); **~ off** *vi* (*prices etc*) se stabiliser; **~ out** *vi* = level off; **~ crossing** (*BRIT*) *n* passage *m* à niveau; **~-headed** *adj* équilibré(e)

lever [ˈliːvə*] *n* levier *m*; **~age** *n*: **~age (on** *or* **with)** prise *f* (sur)

levity [ˈlɛvɪtɪ] *n* légèreté *f*

levy [ˈlɛvɪ] *n* taxe *f*, impôt *m* ♦ *vt* prélever, imposer; percevoir

lewd [luːd] *adj* obscène, lubrique

liability [laɪəˈbɪlɪtɪ] *n* responsabilité *f*; (*handicap*) handicap *m*; **liabilities** *npl* (*on balance sheet*) passif *m*

liable [ˈlaɪəbl] *adj* (*subject*): **~ to** sujet(te) à; passible de; (*responsible*): **~ (for)** responsable (de); (*likely*): **~ to do** susceptible de faire

liaise [lɪˈeɪz] *vi*: **to ~ with** assurer la liaison avec; **liaison** [liːˈeɪzɒn] *n* liaison *f*

liar [ˈlaɪə*] *n* menteur(euse)

libel [ˈlaɪbəl] *n* diffamation *f*; (*document*) écrit *m* diffamatoire ♦ *vt* diffamer

liberal [ˈlɪbərəl] *adj* libéral(e); (*generous*): **~ with** prodigue de, généreux(euse) avec; **the L~ Democrats** (*BRIT*) le parti libéral-démocrate

liberation [lɪbəˈreɪʃən] *n* libération *f*

liberty [ˈlɪbətɪ] *n* liberté *f*; **to be at ~ to do** être libre de faire

Libra [ˈliːbrə] *n* la Balance

librarian [laɪˈbrɛərɪən] *n* bibliothécaire *m/f*

library [ˈlaɪbrərɪ] *n* bibliothèque *f*

libretto [lɪˈbretəʊ] *n* livret *m*

Libya [ˈlɪbɪə] *n* Libye *f*

lice [laɪs] *npl of* **louse**

licence [ˈlaɪsəns] (*US* **license**) *n* autorisation *f*, permis *m*; (*RADIO, TV*) redevance *f*; **driving ~,** (*US*) **driver's license** permis *m* (de conduire); **~ number** *n* numéro *m* d'immatriculation; **~ plate** *n* plaque *f* minéralogique

license [ˈlaɪsəns] *n* (*US*) = **licence** ♦ *vt* donner une licence à; **~d** *adj* (*car*) muni(e) de la vignette; (*to sell alcohol*) patenté(e) pour la vente des spiritueux, qui a une licence de débit de boissons

lick [lɪk] *vt* lécher; (*inf: defeat*) écraser; **to ~ one's lips** (*fig*) se frotter les mains

licorice [ˈlɪkərɪs] (*US*) *n* = **liquorice**

lid [lɪd] *n* couvercle *m*; (*eye~*) paupière *f*

lie [laɪ] (*pt* **lay**, *pp* **lain**) *vi* (*rest*) être étendu(e) *or* allongé(e) *or* couché(e); (*in grave*) être enterré(e), reposer; (*be situated*) se trouver, être; (*be untruthful*: *pt, pp* **lied**) mentir ♦ *n* mensonge *m*; **to ~ low** (*fig*) se cacher; **~ about** *vi* traîner; **~ around** *vi* = **lie about**; **~-down** (*BRIT*) *n*: **to have a ~-down** s'allonger, se reposer; **~-in** (*BRIT*) *n*: **to have a ~-in** faire la grasse matinée

lieutenant [lefˈtɛnənt, (*US*) luːˈtɛnənt] *n* lieutenant *m*

life [laɪf] (*pl* **lives**) *n* vie *f*; **to come to ~** (*fig*) s'animer; **~ assurance** (*BRIT*) *n* = **life insurance**; **~belt** (*BRIT*) *n* bouée *f* de sauvetage; **~boat** *n* canot *m* *or* chaloupe *f* de sauvetage; **~buoy** *n* bouée *f* de sauvetage; **~guard** *n* surveillant *m* de baignade; **~ insurance** *n* assurance-vie *f*; **~ jacket** *n* gilet *m* *or* ceinture *f* de sauvetage; **~less** *adj* sans vie, inanimé(e); (*dull*) qui manque de vie *or* de vigueur; **~like** *adj* qui semble vrai(e) *or* vivant(e); (*painting*) réaliste; **~line** *n*: **it was his ~line** ça l'a sauvé; **~long** *adj* de toute une vie, de toujours; **~ preserver** (*US*) *n* = **lifebelt** *or* **life jacket**; **~ sentence** *n* condamnation *f* à perpétuité; **~-size(d)** *adj* grandeur nature *inv*; **~ span** *n* (durée *f* de) vie *f*; **~ style** *n* style *m* *or* mode *m* de vie; **~-support system** *n* (*MED*) respirateur artificiel; **~time** *n* vie *f*; **in his ~time** de son vivant

lift [lɪft] *vt* soulever, lever; (*end*) supprimer, lever ♦ *vi* (*fog*) se lever ♦ *n* (*BRIT*: *elevator*) ascenseur *m*; **to give sb a ~** (: *AUT*) emmener *or* prendre qn en voiture; **~-off** *n* décollage *m*

light [laɪt] (*pt, pp* **lit**) *n* lumière *f*; (*lamp*) lampe *f*; (*AUT*: *rear ~*) feu *m*; (: *head~*) phare *m*; (*for cigarette etc*): **have you got a ~?** avez-vous du feu? ♦ *vt* (*candle, cigarette, fire*) allumer; (*room*) éclairer ♦ *adj* (*room, colour*) clair(e); (*not heavy*) léger(ère); (*not strenuous*) peu fatigant(e); **~s** *npl* (*AUT*: *traffic ~s*) feux *mpl*; **to come to ~** être dévoilé(e) *or* découvert(e); **~ up** *vi* (*face*) s'éclairer ♦ *vt* (*illuminate*) éclairer, illuminer; **~ bulb** *n* ampoule *f*; **~en** *vt* (*make less heavy*) alléger; **~er** *n* (*also*: *cigarette ~er*) briquet *m*; **~-headed** *adj* étourdi(e); (*excited*) grisé(e); **~-hearted** *adj* gai(e), joyeux(euse), enjoué(e); **~house** *n* phare *m*; **~ing** *n* (*on road*) éclairage *m*; (*in theatre*) éclairages *mpl*; **~ly** *adv* légèrement; **to get off ~ly** s'en tirer à bon compte; **~ness** *n* (*in weight*) légèreté *f*

lightning [ˈlaɪtnɪŋ] *n* éclair *m*, foudre *f*; **~ conductor** *n* paratonnerre *m*; **~ rod** (*US*) *n* = **lightning conductor**

light pen *n* crayon *m* optique

lightweight [ˈlaɪtweɪt] *adj* (*suit*) léger(ère) ♦ *n* (*BOXING*) poids léger

like [laɪk] *vt* aimer (bien) ♦ *prep* comme ♦ *adj* semblable, pareil(le) ♦ *n*: **and the ~** et d'autres du même genre; **his ~s and dislikes** ses goûts *mpl* *or* préférences *fpl*; **I would ~, I'd ~** je voudrais, j'aimerais;

would you ~ a coffee? voulez-vous du café?; **to be/look ~ sb/sth** ressembler à qn/ qch; **what does it look ~?** de quoi est-ce que ça a l'air?; **what does it taste ~?** quel goût est-ce que ça a?; **that's just ~ him** c'est bien de lui, ça lui ressemble; **do it ~ this** fais-le comme ceci; **it's nothing ~ ...** ce n'est pas du tout comme ...; **~able** adj sympathique, agréable

likelihood ['laɪklɪhʊd] n probabilité f

likely ['laɪklɪ] adj probable; plausible; **he's ~ to leave** il va sûrement partir, il risque fort de partir; **not ~!** (inf) pas de danger!

likeness ['laɪknɪs] n ressemblance f; **that's a good ~** c'est très ressemblant

likewise ['laɪkwaɪz] adv de même, pareillement

liking ['laɪkɪŋ] n (for person) affection f; (for thing) penchant m, goût m

lilac ['laɪlək] n lilas m

lily ['lɪlɪ] n lis m; **~ of the valley** n muguet m

limb [lɪm] n membre m

limber up ['lɪmbə*-] vi se dégourdir, faire des exercices d'assouplissement

limbo ['lɪmbəʊ] n: **to be in ~** (fig) être tombé(e) dans l'oubli

lime [laɪm] n (tree) tilleul m; (fruit) lime f, citron vert; (GEO) chaux f

limelight ['laɪmlaɪt] n: **in the ~** (fig) en vedette, au premier plan

limerick ['lɪmərɪk] n poème m humoristique (de 5 vers)

limestone ['laɪmstəʊn] n pierre f à chaux; (GEO) calcaire m

limit ['lɪmɪt] n limite f ♦ vt limiter; **~ed** adj limité(e), restreint(e); **to be ~ed to** se limiter à, ne concerner que; **~ed (liability) company** (BRIT) n ≈ société f anonyme

limp [lɪmp] n: **to have a ~** boiter ♦ vi boiter ♦ adj mou(molle)

limpet ['lɪmpɪt] n patelle f

line [laɪn] n ligne f; (stroke) trait m; (wrinkle) ride f; (rope) corde f; (wire) fil m; (of poem) vers m; (row, series) rangée f; (of people) file f, queue f; (railway track) voie f; (COMM: series of goods) article(s) m(pl); (work) métier m, type m d'activité; (attitude, policy) position f ♦ vt: **to ~ (with)** (clothes) doubler (de); (box) garnir or tapisser (de); (subj: trees, crowd) border; **in a ~** aligné(e); **in his ~ of business** dans sa partie, dans son rayon; **in ~ with** en accord avec; **~ up** vi s'aligner, se mettre en rang(s) ♦ vt aligner; (event) prévoir, préparer

lined [laɪnd] adj (face) ridé(e), marqué(e); (paper) réglé(e)

linen ['lɪnɪn] n linge m (de maison); (cloth) lin m

liner ['laɪnə*] n paquebot m (de ligne); (for bin) sac m à poubelle

linesman ['laɪnzmən] (irreg) n juge m de ligne

touche; (TENNIS) juge m de ligne

line-up ['laɪnʌp] n (US: queue) file f; (SPORT) (composition f de l')équipe f

linger ['lɪŋgə*] vi s'attarder; traîner; (smell, tradition) persister

lingo ['lɪŋgəʊ] (inf: pl ~es) n pej jargon m

linguist ['lɪŋgwɪst] n: **to be a good ~** être doué(e) par les langues

linguistics [lɪŋ'gwɪstɪks] n linguistique f

lining ['laɪnɪŋ] n doublure f

link [lɪŋk] n lien m, rapport m; (of a chain) maillon m ♦ vt relier, lier, unir; **~s** npl (GOLF) (terrain m de) golf m; **~ up** vt relier ♦ vi se rejoindre; s'associer

lino ['laɪnəʊ] n = **linoleum**

linoleum [lɪ'nəʊlɪəm] n linoléum m

lion ['laɪən] n lion m; **~ess** n lionne f

lip [lɪp] n lèvre f; **~-read** vi lire sur les lèvres; **~ salve** n pommade f rosat or pour les lèvres; **~ service** n: **to pay ~ service to sth** ne reconnaître le mérite de qch que pour la forme; **~stick** n rouge m à lèvres

liqueur [lɪ'kjʊə*] n liqueur f

liquid ['lɪkwɪd] adj liquide ♦ n liquide m; **~ize** ['lɪkwɪdaɪz] vt (CULIN) passer au mixer; **~izer** n mixer m

liquor ['lɪkə*] (US) n spiritueux m, alcool m

liquorice ['lɪkərɪs] (BRIT) n réglisse f

liquor store (US) n magasin m de vins et spiritueux

lisp [lɪsp] vi zézayer

list [lɪst] n liste f ♦ vt (write down) faire une or la liste de; (mention) énumérer; **~ed building** (BRIT) n monument classé

listen ['lɪsn] vi écouter; **to ~ to** écouter; **~er** n auditeur(trice)

listless ['lɪstləs] adj indolent(e), apathique

lit [lɪt] pt, pp of **light**

liter ['liːtə*] (US) n = **litre**

literacy ['lɪtərəsɪ] n degré m d'alphabétisation, fait m de savoir lire et écrire

literal ['lɪtərəl] adj littéral(e); **~ly** adv littéralement; (really) réellement

literary ['lɪtərərɪ] adj littéraire

literate ['lɪtərət] adj qui sait lire et écrire, instruit(e)

literature ['lɪtrɪtʃə*] n littérature f; (brochures etc) documentation f

lithe [laɪð] adj agile, souple

litigation [lɪtɪ'geɪʃən] n litige m; contentieux m

litre ['liːtə*] (US liter) n litre m

litter ['lɪtə*] n (rubbish) détritus mpl, ordures fpl; (young animals) portée f; **~ bin** (BRIT) n boîte f à ordures, poubelle f; **~ed** adj: **~ed with** jonché(e) de, couvert(e) de

little ['lɪtl] adj (small) petit(e) ♦ adv peu; **~ milk/time** peu de lait/temps; **a ~** un peu (de); **a ~ bit** un peu; **~ by ~** petit à petit, peu à peu

live¹ [laɪv] adj (animal) vivant(e), en vie;

(*wire*) sous tension; (*bullet, bomb*) non explosé(e); (*broadcast*) en direct; (*performance*) en public

live² [lɪv] *vi* vivre; (*reside*) vivre, habiter; ~ **down** *vt* faire oublier (avec le temps); ~ **on** *vt fus* vivre de; ~ to**gether** *vi* vivre ensemble, cohabiter; ~ **up to** *vt fus* se montrer à la hauteur de

livelihood [ˈlaɪvlɪhʊd] *n* moyens *mpl* d'existence

lively [ˈlaɪvlɪ] *adj* vif(vive), plein(e) d'entrain; (*place, book*) vivant(e)

liven up [ˈlaɪvn-] *vt* animer ♦ *vi* s'animer

liver [ˈlɪvə*] *n* foie *m*

lives [laɪvz] *npl of* **life**

livestock [ˈlaɪvstɔk] *n* bétail *m*, cheptel *m*

livid [ˈlɪvɪd] *adj* livide, blafard(e); (*inf: furious*) furieux(euse), furibond(e)

living [ˈlɪvɪŋ] *adj* vivant(e), en vie ♦ *n*: **to earn** *or* **make a** ~ gagner sa vie; ~ **conditions** *fpl* conditions *fpl* de vie; ~ **room** *n* salle *f* de séjour; ~ **standards** *npl* niveau *m* de vie; ~ **wage** *n* salaire *m* permettant de vivre (décemment)

lizard [ˈlɪzəd] *n* lézard *m*

load [ləʊd] *n* (*weight*) poids *m*; (*thing carried*) chargement *m*, charge *f* ♦ *vt* (*also: ~ up*): **to** ~ **(with)** charger (de); (*gun, camera*) charger (avec); (*COMPUT*) charger; **a** ~ **of**, ~**s of** (*fig*) un *or* des tas de, des masses de; **to talk a** ~ **of rubbish** dire des bêtises; ~**ed** *adj* (*question*) insidieux(euse); (*inf: rich*) bourré(e) de fric

loaf [ləʊf] (*pl* **loaves**) *n* pain *m*, miche *f*

loan [ləʊn] *n* prêt *m* ♦ *vt* prêter; **on** ~ prêté(e), en prêt

loath [ləʊθ] *adj*: **to be** ~ **to do** répugner à faire

loathe [ləʊð] *vt* détester, avoir en horreur

loaves [ləʊvz] *npl of* **loaf**

lobby [ˈlɔbɪ] *n* hall *m*, entrée *f*; (*POL*) groupe *m* de pression, lobby *m* ♦ *vt* faire pression sur

lobster [ˈlɔbstə*] *n* homard *m*

local [ˈləʊkəl] *adj* local(e) ♦ *n* (*BRIT: pub*) pub *m* or café *m* du coin; **the** ~**s** *npl* (*inhabitants*) les gens *mpl* du pays *or* du coin; ~ **anaesthetic** *n* anesthésie locale; ~ **call** *n* communication urbaine; ~ **government** *n* administration locale *or* municipale; ~**ity** [ləʊˈkælɪtɪ] *n* région *f*, environs *mpl*; (*position*) lieu *m*

locate [ləʊˈkeɪt] *vt* (*find*) trouver, repérer; (*situate*): **to be** ~**d** **in** être situé(e) à *or* en

location [ləʊˈkeɪʃən] *n* emplacement *m*; **on** ~ (*CINEMA*) en extérieur

loch [lɔx] *n* lac *m*, loch *m*

lock [lɔk] *n* (*of door, box*) serrure *f*; (*of canal*) écluse *f*; (*of hair*) mèche *f*, boucle *f* ♦ *vt* (*with key*) fermer à clé ♦ *vi* (*door etc*) fermer à clé; (*wheels*) se bloquer; ~ **in** *vt* enfermer; ~ **out** *vt* enfermer dehors; (*delibe-*

rately) mettre à la porte; ~ **up** *vt* (*person*) enfermer; (*house*) fermer à clé ♦ *vi* tout fermer (à clé)

locker [ˈlɔkə*] *n* casier *m*; (*in station*) consigne *f* automatique

locket [ˈlɔkɪt] *n* médaillon *m*

locksmith [ˈlɔksmɪθ] *n* serrurier *m*

lockup [ˈlɔkʌp] *n* (*prison*) prison *f*

locum [ˈləʊkəm] *n* (*MED*) suppléant(e) (de médecin)

lodge [lɔdʒ] *n* pavillon *m* (de gardien); (*hunting* ~) pavillon de chasse ♦ *vi* (*person*): **to** ~ **(with)** être logé(e) (chez), être en pension (chez); (*bullet*) se loger ♦ *vt*: **to** ~ **a complaint** porter plainte; ~**r** *n* locataire *m/f*; (*with meals*) pensionnaire *m/f*; **lodgings** [ˈlɔdʒɪŋz] *npl* chambre *f*; meublé *m*

loft [lɔft] *n* grenier *m*

lofty [ˈlɔftɪ] *adj* (*noble*) noble, élevé(e); (*haughty*) hautain(e)

log [lɔg] *n* (*of wood*) bûche *f*; (*book*) = **logbook** ♦ *vt* (*record*) noter

logbook [ˈlɔgbʊk] *n* (*NAUT*) livre *m* *or* journal *m* de bord; (*AVIAT*) carnet *m* de vol; (*of car*) ≈ carte grise

loggerheads [ˈlɔgəhedz] *npl*: **at** ~ **(with)** à couteaux tirés (avec)

logic [ˈlɔdʒɪk] *n* logique *f*; ~**al** *adj* logique

loin [lɔɪn] *n* (*CULIN*) filet *m*, longe *f*

loiter [ˈlɔɪtə*] *vi* traîner

loll [lɔl] *vi* (*also: ~ about*) se prélasser, fainéanter

lollipop [ˈlɔlɪpɔp] *n* sucette *f*; ~ **man/lady** (*BRIT: irreg*) *n* contractuel(le) qui fait traverser la rue aux enfants

London [ˈlʌndən] *n* Londres *m*; ~**er** *n* Londonien(ne)

lone [ləʊn] *adj* solitaire

loneliness [ˈləʊnlɪnəs] *n* solitude *f*, isolement *m*; **lonely** [ˈləʊnlɪ] *adj* seul(e); solitaire, isolé(e)

long [lɔŋ] *adj* long(longue) ♦ *adv* longtemps ♦ *vi*: **to** ~ **for sth** avoir très envie de qch; attendre qch avec impatience; **so** *or* **as** ~ **as** pourvu que; **don't be** ~! dépêchez-vous!; **how** ~ **is this river/course?** quelle est la longueur de ce fleuve/la durée de ce cours?; **6 metres** ~ (long) de 6 mètres; **6 months** ~ qui dure 6 mois, de 6 mois; **all night** ~ toute la nuit; **he no** ~**er comes** il ne vient plus; ~ **before/after** longtemps avant/après; **before** ~ (+*future*) avant peu, dans peu de temps; (+*past*) peu de temps après; **at** ~ **last** enfin; ~**-distance** *adj* (*call*) interurbain(e); ~**hand** *n* écriture normale *or* courante; ~**ing** *n* désir *m*, envie *f*, nostalgie *f*

longitude [ˈlɔŋgɪtjuːd] *n* longitude *f*

long: ~ **jump** *n* saut *m* en longueur; ~**-life** *adj* longue durée *inv*; (*milk*) upérisé(e); ~**-lost** *adj* (*person*) perdu(e) de vue depuis longtemps; ~**-playing record** *n* (disque *m*)

33 tours *inv*; ~-**range** *adj* à longue portée; ~-**sighted** *adj* (MED) presbyte; ~-**standing** *adj* de longue date; ~-**suffering** *adj* empreint(e) d'une patience résignée; extrêmement patient(e); ~-**term** *adj* à long terme; ~-**wave** *n* grandes ondes; ~-**winded** *adj* intarissable, interminable

loo [luː] *n* (BRIT: *inf*) n W.-C. *mpl*, petit coin

look [luk] *vi* regarder; (*seem*) sembler, paraître, avoir l'air; (*building etc*): **to** ~ **south/(out) onto the sea** donner au sud/ sur la mer ♦ *n* regard *m*; (*appearance*) air *m*, allure *f*, aspect *m*; ~**s** *npl* (*good* ~**s**) physique *m*, beauté *f*; **to have a** ~ regarder; ~**!** regardez!; ~ **(here)!** (*annoyance*) écoutez!; ~ **after** *vt fus* (*care for, deal with*) s'occuper de; ~ **at** *vt fus*, regarder (*problem etc*) examiner; ~ **back** *vi*: **to** ~ **back on** (*event etc*) évoquer, repenser à; ~ **down on** *vt fus* (*fig*) regarder de haut, dédaigner; ~ **for** *vt fus* chercher; ~ **forward to** *vt fus* attendre avec impatience; **we** ~ **forward to hearing from you** (*in letter*) dans l'attente de vous lire; ~ **into** *vt fus* examiner, étudier; ~ **on** *vi* regarder (en spectateur); ~ **out** *vi* (*beware*): **to** ~ **out (for)** prendre garde (à), faire attention (à); ~ **out for** *vt fus* être à la recherche de; guetter; ~ **round** *vi* regarder derrière soi, se retourner; ~ **to** *vt fus* (*rely on*) compter sur; ~ **up** *vi* lever les yeux; (*improve*) s'améliorer ♦ *vt* (*word, name*) chercher; ~ **up to** *vt fus* avoir du respect pour; ~**out** *n* poste *m* de guet; (*person*) guetteur *m*; **to be on the** ~**out (for)** guetter

loom [luːm] *vi* (*also*: ~ **up**) surgir; (*approach: event etc*) être imminent(e); (*threaten*) menacer ♦ *n* (*for weaving*) métier *m* à tisser

loony ['luːnɪ] (*inf*) *adj, n* timbré(e), cinglé(e)

loop [luːp] *n* boucle *f*; ~**hole** *n* (*fig*) porte *f* de sortie; échappatoire *f*

loose [luːs] *adj* (*knot, screw*) desserré(e); (*clothes*) ample, lâche; (*hair*) dénoué(e), épars(e); (*not firmly fixed*) pas solide; (*morals, discipline*) relâché(e) ♦ *n*: **on the** ~ en liberté; ~ **change** *n* petite monnaie; ~ **chippings** *npl* (*on road*) gravillons *mpl*; ~ **end** *n*: **to be at a** ~ **end** *or* (US) **at** ~ **ends** ne pas trop savoir quoi faire; ~**ly** *adv* sans serrer; (*imprecisely*) approximativement; ~**n** *vt* desserrer

loot [luːt] *n* (*inf: money*) pognon *m*, fric *m* ♦ *vt* piller

lopsided ['lɒp'saɪdɪd] *adj* de travers, asymétrique

lord [lɔːd] *n* seigneur *m*; **L**~ **Smith** lord Smith; **the L**~ le Seigneur; **good L**~**!** mon Dieu!; **the (House of) L**~**s** (BRIT) la Chambre des lords; **my L**~ = **your lordship**; **L**~**ship** *n*: **your L**~**ship** Monsieur le comte (*or* le baron *or* le juge); (*to bishop*) Monsei-

gneur

lore [lɔː*] *n* tradition(s) *f(pl)*

lorry ['lɒrɪ] (BRIT) *n* camion *m*; ~ **driver** (BRIT) *n* camionneur *m*, routier *m*

lose [luːz] (*pt, pp* **lost**) *vt, vi* perdre; **to** ~ **(time)** (*clock*) retarder; **to get lost** *vi* se perdre; ~**r** *n* perdant(e)

loss [lɒs] *n* perte *f*; **to be at a** ~ être perplexe *or* embarrassé(e)

lost [lɒst] *pt, pp* *of* **lose** ♦ *adj* perdu(e); ~ **and found** (US), ~ **property** *n* objets trouvés

lot [lɒt] *n* (*set*) lot *m*; **the** ~ le tout; **a** ~ **(of)** beaucoup (de); ~**s of** des tas de; **to draw** ~**s (for sth)** tirer (qch) au sort

lotion ['ləʊʃən] *n* lotion *f*

lottery ['lɒtərɪ] *n* loterie *f*

loud [laud] *adj* bruyant(e), sonore; (*voice*) fort(e); (*support, condemnation*) vigoureux(euse); (*gaudy*) voyant(e), tapageur(euse) ♦ *adv* (*speak etc*) fort; **out** ~ tout haut; ~-**hailer** (BRIT) *n* porte-voix *m inv*; ~**ly** *adv* fort, bruyamment; ~ **speaker** *n* haut-parleur *m*

lounge [laundʒ] *n* salon *m*; (*at airport*) salle *f*, (BRIT: *also*: ~ **bar**) (salle de) café *m* or bar *m* ♦ *vi* (*also*: ~ *about or around*) se prélasser, paresser; ~ **suit** (BRIT) *n* complet *m*; (*on invitation*) "tenue de ville"

louse [laus] (*pl* **lice**) *n* pou *m*

lousy ['lauzɪ] (*inf*) *adj* infect(e), moche; **I feel** ~ je suis mal fichu(e)

lout [laut] *n* rustre *m*, butor *m*

lovable ['lʌvəbl] *adj* adorable; très sympathique

love [lʌv] *n* amour *m* ♦ *vt* aimer; (*caringly, kindly*) aimer beaucoup; "~ **(from) Anne**" "affectueusement, Anne"; **I** ~ **chocolate** j'adore le chocolat; **to be/fall in** ~ **with** être/tomber amoureux(euse) de; **to make** ~ faire l'amour; "**15** ~**"** (TENNIS) "15 à rien *or* zéro"; ~ **affair** *n* liaison (amoureuse); ~ **life** *n* vie sentimentale

lovely ['lʌvlɪ] *adj* (très) joli(e), ravissant(e); (*delightful: person*) charmant(e); (*holiday etc*) (très) agréable

lover ['lʌvə*] *n* amant *m*; (*person in love*) amoureux(euse); (*amateur*): **a** ~ **of** un amateur de; un(e) amoureux(euse) de

loving ['lʌvɪŋ] *adj* affectueux(euse), tendre

low [ləʊ] *adj* bas(basse); (*quality*) mauvais(e), inférieur(e); (*person: depressed*) déprimé(e); (: *ill*) bas(basse), affaibli(e) ♦ *adv* bas ♦ *n* (METEOROLOGY) dépression *f*; **to be** ♦ **on** être à court de; **to feel** ~ se sentir déprimé(e); **to reach an all-time** ~ être au plus bas; ~-**alcohol** *adj* peu alcoolisé(e); ~-**cut** *adj* (*dress*) décolleté(e)

lower ['ləʊə*] *adj* inférieur(e) ♦ *vt* abaisser, baisser

low: ~-**fat** *adj* maigre; ~**lands** *npl* (GEO) plaines *fpl*; ~**ly** *adj* humble, modeste

loyalty ['lɔɪəltɪ] n loyauté f, fidélité f
lozenge ['lɒzɪndʒ] n (MED) pastille f
LP n abbr = **long-playing record**
L-plates ['elpleɪts] (BRIT) npl plaques fpl d'apprenti conducteur
Ltd abbr (= limited) ≈ S.A.
lubricant ['luːbrɪkənt] n lubrifiant m
lubricate ['luːbrɪkeɪt] vt lubrifier, graisser
luck [lʌk] n chance f; **bad** ~ malchance f, malheur m; **bad** or **hard** or **tough** ~! pas de chance!; **good** ~! bonne chance!; ~**ily** adv heureusement, par bonheur; ~**y** adj (person) qui a de la chance; (coincidence, event) heureux(euse); (object) porte-bonheur inv
ludicrous ['luːdɪkrəs] adj ridicule, absurde
lug [lʌg] (inf) vt traîner, tirer
luggage ['lʌgɪdʒ] n bagages mpl; ~ **rack** n (on car) galerie f
lukewarm ['luːkwɔːm] adj tiède
lull [lʌl] n accalmie f; (in conversation) pause f ♦ vt: **to** ~ **sb to sleep** bercer qn pour qu'il s'endorme; **to be ~ed into a false sense of security** s'endormir dans une fausse sécurité
lullaby ['lʌləbaɪ] n berceuse f
lumbago [lʌm'beɪgəu] n lumbago m
lumber ['lʌmbə*] n (wood) bois m de charpente; (junk) bric-à-brac m inv ♦ vt: **to be ~ed with** (inf) se farcir; ~**jack** n bûcheron m
luminous ['luːmɪnəs] adj lumineux(euse)
lump [lʌmp] n morceau m; (swelling) grosseur f ♦ vt: **to** ~ **together** réunir, mettre en tas; ~ **sum** n somme globale or forfaitaire; ~**y** adj (sauce) avec des grumeaux; (bed) défoncé(e), peu confortable
lunar ['luːnə*] adj lunaire
lunatic ['luːnətɪk] adj fou(folle), cinglé(e) (inf)
lunch [lʌntʃ] n déjeuner m
luncheon ['lʌntʃən] n déjeuner m (chic); ~ **meat** n sorte de mortadelle; ~ **voucher** (BRIT) n chèque-repas m
lung [lʌŋ] n poumon m
lunge [lʌndʒ] vi (also: ~ **forward**) faire un mouvement brusque en avant; **to** ~ **at** envoyer or assener un coup à
lurch [lɜːtʃ] vi vaciller, tituber ♦ n écart m brusque; **to leave sb in the** ~ laisser qn se débrouiller or se dépêtrer tout(e) seul(e)
lure [ljuə*] n (attraction) attrait m, charme m ♦ vt attirer or persuader par la ruse
lurid ['ljuərɪd] adj affreux(euse), atroce; (pej: colour, dress) criard(e)
lurk [lɜːk] vi se tapir, se cacher
luscious ['lʌʃəs] adj succulent(e); appétissant(e)
lush [lʌʃ] adj luxuriant(e)
lust [lʌst] n (sexual) luxure f; lubricité f; désir m; (fig): ~ **for** soif f de; ~ **after,** ~ **for** vt fus (sexually) convoiter, désirer; ~**y**

['lʌstɪ] adj vigoureux(euse), robuste
Luxembourg ['lʌksəmbɜːg] n Luxembourg m
luxurious [lʌg'zjuərɪəs] adj luxueux(euse); **luxury** ['lʌkʃərɪ] n luxe m ♦ cpd de luxe
lying ['laɪɪŋ] n mensonge(s) m(pl) ♦ vb see lie
lyrical adj lyrique
lyrics ['lɪrɪks] npl (of song) paroles fpl

M m

m. abbr = **metre**; **mile**; **million**
M.A. abbr = **Master of Arts**
mac [mæk] (BRIT) n imper(méable) m
macaroni [mækə'rəunɪ] n macaroni mpl
machine [mə'ʃiːn] n machine f ♦ vt (TECH) façonner à la machine; (dress etc) coudre à la machine; ~ **gun** n mitrailleuse f; ~ **language** n (COMPUT) langage-machine m; ~**ry** n machinerie f, machines fpl; (fig) mécanisme(s) m(pl)
mackerel ['mækrəl] n inv maquereau m
mackintosh ['mækɪntɒʃ] (BRIT) n imperméable m
mad [mæd] adj fou(folle); (foolish) insensé(e); (angry) furieux(euse); (keen): **to be** ~ **about** être fou(folle) de
madam ['mædəm] n madame f
madden ['mædn] vt exaspérer
made [meɪd] pt, pp of **make**
Madeira [mə'dɪərə] n (GEO) Madère f; (wine) madère m
made-to-measure ['meɪdtə'meʒə*] (BRIT) adj fait(e) sur mesure
madly ['mædlɪ] adv follement; ~ **in love** éperdument amoureux(euse)
madman ['mædmən] (irreg) n fou m
madness ['mædnəs] n folie f
magazine ['mægəziːn] n (PRESS) magazine m, revue f; (RADIO, TV: also: ~ **programme**) magazine
maggot ['mægət] n ver m, asticot m
magic ['mædʒɪk] n magie f ♦ adj magique; ~**al** adj magique; (experience, evening) merveilleux(euse); ~**ian** [mə'dʒɪʃən] n magicien (ne); (conjurer) prestidigitateur m
magistrate ['mædʒɪstreɪt] n magistrat m; juge m
magnet ['mægnɪt] n aimant m; ~**ic** [mæg'netɪk] adj magnétique
magnificent [mæg'nɪfɪsənt] adj superbe, magnifique; (splendid: robe, building) somp-

tueux(euse), magnifique
magnify ['mægnɪfaɪ] *vt* grossir; (*sound*) amplifier; ~**ing glass** *n* loupe *f*
magnitude ['mægnɪtjuːd] *n* ampleur *f*
magpie ['mægpaɪ] *n* pie *f*
mahogany [mə'hɒɡənɪ] *n* acajou *m*
maid [meɪd] *n* bonne *f*; **old** ~ (*pej*) vieille fille
maiden ['meɪdn] *n* jeune fille *f* ♦ *adj* (*aunt etc*) non mariée; (*speech, voyage*) inaugural(e); ~ **name** *n* nom *m* de jeune fille
mail [meɪl] *n* poste *f*; (*letters*) courrier *m* ♦ *vt* envoyer (par la poste); ~**box** (*US*) *n* boîte *f* aux lettres; ~**ing list** *n* liste *f* d'adresses; ~**-order** *n* vente *f* or achat *m* par correspondance
maim [meɪm] *vt* mutiler
main [meɪn] *adj* principal(e) ♦ *n*: **the** ~(**s**) *n(pl)* (*gas, water*) conduite principale, canalisation *f*; **the** ~**s** *npl* (*ELEC*) le secteur; **in the** ~ dans l'ensemble; ~**frame** *n* (*COMPUT*) (gros) ordinateur, unité centrale; ~**land** *n* continent *m*; ~**ly** *adv* principalement, surtout; ~ **road** *n* grand-route *f*; ~**stay** *n* (*fig*) pilier *m*; ~**stream** *n* courant principal
maintain [meɪn'teɪn] *vt* entretenir; (*continue*) maintenir; (*affirm*) soutenir; **maintenance** ['meɪntənəns] *n* entretien *m*; (*alimony*) pension *f* alimentaire
maize [meɪz] *n* maïs *m*
majestic [mə'dʒestɪk] *adj* majestueux(euse)
majesty ['mædʒɪstɪ] *n* majesté *f*
major ['meɪdʒə*] *n* (*MIL*) commandant *m* ♦ *adj* (*important*) important(e); (*most important*) principal(e); (*MUS*) majeur
Majorca [mə'jɔːkə] *n* Majorque *f*
majority [mə'dʒɒrɪtɪ] *n* majorité *f*
make [meɪk] *vt* faire; (*manufacture*) faire, fabriquer; (*earn*) gagner; (*cause to be*): **to** ~ **sb sad etc** rendre qn triste etc; (*force*): **to** ~ **sb do sth** obliger qn à faire qch, faire faire qch à qn; (*equal*): **2 and 2** ~ **4** 2 et 2 font 4 ♦ *n* fabrication *f*; (*brand*) marque *f*; **to** ~ **a fool of sb** (*ridicule*) ridiculiser qn; (*trick*) avoir or duper qn; **to** ~ **a profit** faire un or des bénéfice(s); **to** ~ **a loss** essuyer une perte; **to** ~ **it** (*arrive*) arriver; (*achieve sth*) parvenir à qch, réussir; **what time do you** ~ **it?** quelle heure avez-vous?; **to** ~ **do with** se contenter de; se débrouiller avec; ~ **for** *vt fus* se diriger vers; ~ **out** *vt* (*write out: cheque*) faire; (*decipher*) déchiffrer; (*understand*) comprendre; (*see*) distinguer; ~ **up** *vt* (*constitute*) constituer; (*invent*) inventer, imaginer; (*parcel, bed*) faire ♦ *vi* se réconcilier; (*with cosmetics*) se maquiller; ~ **up for** *vt fus* compenser; ~**-believe** *n*: **it's just** ~-**believe** (*game*) c'est pour faire semblant; (*invention*) c'est de l'invention pure; ~**r** *n* fabricant *m*; ~**shift** *adj* provisoire,

improvisé(e); ~-**up** *n* maquillage *m*; ~-**up remover** *n* démaquillant *m*
making ['meɪkɪŋ] *n* (*fig*): **in the** ~ en formation *or* gestation; **to have the** ~**s of** (*actor, athlete etc*) avoir l'étoffe de
malaria [mə'lɛərɪə] *n* malaria *f*
Malaysia [mə'leɪzɪə] *n* Malaisie *f*
male [meɪl] *n* (*BIO*) mâle *m* ♦ *adj* mâle; (*sex, attitude*) masculin(e); (*child etc*) du sexe masculin
malevolent [mə'levələnt] *adj* malveillant(e)
malfunction [mæl'fʌŋkʃən] *n* fonctionnement défectueux
malice ['mælɪs] *n* méchanceté *f*, malveillance *f*; **malicious** [mə'lɪʃəs] *adj* méchant(e), malveillant(e)
malign [mə'laɪn] *vt* diffamer, calomnier
malignant [mə'lɪɡnənt] *adj* (*MED*) malin(igne)
mall [mɔːl] *n* (*also: shopping* ~) centre commercial
mallet ['mælɪt] *n* maillet *m*
malpractice [mæl'præktɪs] *n* faute professionnelle; négligence *f*
malt [mɔːlt] *n* malt *m* ♦ *cpd* (*also:* ~ *whisky*) pur malt
Malta ['mɔːltə] *n* Malte *f*
mammal ['mæməl] *n* mammifère *m*
mammoth ['mæməθ] *n* mammouth *m* ♦ *adj* géant(e), monstre
man [mæn] (*pl* **men**) *n* homme *m* ♦ *vt* (*NAUT: ship*) garnir d'hommes; (*MIL: gun*) servir; (*: post*) être de service à; (*machine*) assurer le fonctionnement de; **an old** ~ un vieillard; ~ **and wife** mari et femme
manage ['mænɪdʒ] *vi* se débrouiller ♦ *vt* (*be in charge of*) s'occuper de; (*: business etc*) gérer; (*control: ship*) manier, manœuvrer; (*: person*) savoir s'y prendre avec; **to** ~ **to do** réussir à faire; ~**able** *adj* (*task*) faisable; (*number*) raisonnable; ~**ment** *n* gestion *f*, administration *f*, direction *f*; ~**r** *n* directeur *m*; administrateur *m*; (*SPORT*) manager *m*; (*of artist*) impresario *m*; ~**ress** [mænɪdʒə'res] *n* directrice *f*, gérante *f*; ~**rial** [mænə'dʒɪərɪəl] *adj* directorial(e); (*skills*) de cadre, de gestion; **managing director** ['mænɪdʒɪŋ] *n* directeur général
mandarin ['mændərɪn] *n* (*also:* ~ *orange*) mandarine *f*; (*person*) mandarin *m*
mandatory ['mændətərɪ] *adj* obligatoire
mane [meɪn] *n* crinière *f*
maneuver (*US*) *vt, vi, n* = **manoeuvre**
manfully ['mænfʊlɪ] *adv* vaillamment
mangle ['mæŋɡl] *vt* déchiqueter; mutiler
mango ['mæŋɡəʊ] (*pl* ~**es**) *n* mangue *f*
mangy ['meɪndʒɪ] *adj* galeux(euse)
manhandle ['mænhændl] *vt* malmener
man: ~**hole** ['mænhəʊl] *n* trou *m* d'homme; ~**hood** ['mænhʊd] *n* âge *m* d'homme; virilité *f*; ~**-hour** ['mæn'aʊə*] *n* heure *f* de main-d'œuvre; ~**hunt** ['mænhʌnt] *n* (*POLI-*

CE) chasse f à l'homme

mania ['meɪnɪə] n manie f; ~**c** ['meɪnɪæk] n maniaque m/f; (fig) fou(folle) m/f; **manic** ['mænɪk] adj maniaque

manicure ['mænɪkjʊə*] n manucure f; ~ **set** n trousse f à ongles

manifest ['mænɪfest] vt manifester ♦ adj manifeste, évident(e)

manifesto [mænɪ'festəʊ] n manifeste m

manipulate [mə'nɪpjʊleɪt] vt manipuler; (system, situation) exploiter

man: ~**kind** [mæn'kaɪnd] n humanité f, genre humain; ~**ly** ['mænlɪ] adj viril(e); ~-**made** ['mæn'meɪd] adj artificiel(le); (fibre) synthétique

manner ['mænə*] n manière f, façon f; (behaviour) attitude f, comportement m; (sort): **all** ~ **of** toutes sortes de; ~**s** npl (behaviour) manières; ~**ism** n particularité f de langage (or de comportement), tic m

manoeuvre [mə'nu:və*] (US **maneuver**) vt (move) manœuvrer; (manipulate: person) manipuler; (: situation) exploiter ♦ vi manœuvrer ♦ n manœuvre f

manor ['mænə*] n (also: ~ **house**) manoir m

manpower ['mænpaʊə*] n main-d'œuvre f

mansion ['mænʃən] n château m, manoir m

manslaughter ['mænslɔ:tə*] n homicide m involontaire

mantelpiece ['mæntlpi:s] n cheminée f

manual ['mænjʊəl] adj manuel(le) ♦ n manuel m

manufacture [mænjʊ'fæktʃə*] vt fabriquer ♦ n fabrication f; ~**r** n fabricant m

manure [mə'njʊə*] n fumier m

manuscript ['mænjʊskrɪpt] n manuscrit m

many ['menɪ] adj beaucoup de, de nombreux(euses) ♦ pron beaucoup, un grand nombre; **a great** ~ un grand nombre (de); ~ **a** ... bien des ..., plus d'un(e) ...

map [mæp] n carte f; (of town) plan m; ~ **out** vt tracer; (task) planifier

maple ['meɪpl] n érable m

mar [mɑ:*] vt gâcher, gâter

marathon ['mærəθən] n marathon m

marble ['mɑ:bl] n marbre m; (toy) bille f

March [mɑ:tʃ] n mars m

march [mɑ:tʃ] vi marcher au pas; (fig: protesters) défiler ♦ n marche f; (demonstration) manifestation f

mare [mɛə*] n jument f

margarine [mɑ:dʒə'ri:n] n margarine f

margin ['mɑ:dʒɪn] n marge f; ~**al** (seat) n (POL) siège disputé

marigold ['mærɪgəʊld] n souci m

marijuana [mærɪ'wɑ:nə] n marijuana f

marina [mə'ri:nə] n (harbour) marina f

marine [mə'ri:n] adj marin(e) ♦ n fusilier marin; (US) marine m; ~ **engineer** n ingénieur m en génie maritime

marital ['mærɪtl] adj matrimonial(e); ~ **status** situation f de famille

marjoram ['mɑ:dʒərəm] n marjolaine f

mark [mɑ:k] n marque f; (of skid etc) trace f; (BRIT: SCOL) note f; (currency) mark m ♦ vt marquer; (stain) tacher; (BRIT: SCOL) noter; corriger; **to** ~ **time** marquer le pas; ~**er** n (sign) jalon m; (bookmark) signet m

market ['mɑ:kɪt] n marché m ♦ vt (COMM) commercialiser; ~ **garden** (BRIT) n jardin maraîcher; ~**ing** n marketing m; ~**place** n place f du marché; (COMM) marché m; ~ **research** n étude f de marché

marksman ['mɑ:ksmən] (irreg) n tireur m d'élite

marmalade ['mɑ:məleɪd] n confiture f d'oranges

maroon [mə'ru:n] vt: **to be** ~**ed** être abandonné(e); (fig) être bloqué(e) ♦ adj bordeaux inv

marquee [mɑ:'ki:] n chapiteau m

marriage ['mærɪdʒ] n mariage m; ~ **bureau** n agence f matrimoniale; ~ **certificate** n extrait m d'acte de mariage

married ['mærɪd] adj marié(e); (life, love) conjugal(e)

marrow ['mærəʊ] n moelle f; (vegetable) courge f

marry ['mærɪ] vt épouser, se marier avec; (subj: father, priest etc) marier ♦ vi (also: get married) se marier

Mars [mɑ:z] n (planet) Mars f

marsh [mɑ:ʃ] n marais m, marécage m

marshal ['mɑ:ʃəl] n maréchal m; (US: fire, police) ≈ capitaine m; (SPORT) membre m du service d'ordre ♦ vt rassembler

marshy ['mɑ:ʃɪ] adj marécageux(euse)

martyr ['mɑ:tə*] n martyr(e); ~**dom** n martyre m

marvel ['mɑ:vəl] n merveille f ♦ vi: **to** ~ **(at)** s'émerveiller (de); ~**lous** (US ~**ous**) adj merveilleux(euse)

Marxist ['mɑ:ksɪst] adj marxiste ♦ n marxiste m/f

marzipan [mɑ:zɪ'pæn] n pâte f d'amandes

mascara [mæs'kɑ:rə] n mascara m

masculine ['mæskjʊlɪn] adj masculin(e)

mash [mæʃ] vt écraser, réduire en purée; ~**ed potatoes** npl purée f de pommes de terre

mask [mɑ:sk] n masque m ♦ vt masquer

mason ['meɪsn] n (also: stone~) maçon m; (: free~) franc-maçon m; ~**ry** n maçonnerie f

masquerade [mæskə'reɪd] vi: **to** ~ **as** se faire passer pour

mass [mæs] n multitude f, masse f; (PHYSICS) masse; (REL) messe f ♦ cpd (communication) de masse; (unemployment) massif(ive) ♦ vi se masser; **the** ~**es** les masses; ~**es of** des tas de

massacre ['mæsəkə*] n massacre m

massage ['mæsɑːʒ] n massage m ♦ vt masser

massive ['mæsɪv] adj énorme, massif(ive)

mass media n inv mass-media mpl

mass production n fabrication f en série

mast [mɑːst] n mât m; (RADIO) pylône m

master ['mɑːstə*] n maître m; (in secondary school) professeur m; (title for boys): M~ X Monsieur X ♦ vt maîtriser; (learn) apprendre à fond; ~ly adj magistral(e); ~mind n esprit supérieur ♦ vt diriger, être le cerveau de; M~ of Arts/Science n ≈ maîtrise f (en lettres/sciences); ~piece n chef-d'œuvre m; ~plan n stratégie f d'ensemble; ~y n maîtrise f; connaissance parfaite

mat [mæt] n petit tapis; (also: door~) paillasson m; (: table~) napperon m ♦ adj = matt

match [mætʃ] n allumette f; (fig) égal(e) m; (game) match m, partie f; (fig) égal(e) ♦ vt (also: ~ up) sortir; (go well with) aller bien avec, s'assortir; (equal) égaler, valoir ♦ vi être assorti(e); to be a good ~ être bien assorti(e); ~box n boîte f d'allumettes; ~ing adj assorti(e)

mate [meɪt] n (inf) copain(copine); (animal) partenaire m/f, mâle/femelle; (in merchant navy) second m ♦ vi s'accoupler

material [mə'tɪərɪəl] n (substance) matière f, matériau m; (cloth) tissu m, étoffe f; (information, data) données fpl ♦ adj matériel(le); (relevant: evidence) pertinent(e); ~s npl (equipment) matériaux mpl

maternal [mə'tɜːnl] adj maternel(le)

maternity [mə'tɜːnɪtɪ] n maternité f; ~ dress n robe f de grossesse; ~ hospital n maternité f

mathematical [mæθə'mætɪkl] adj mathématique; **mathematics** [mæθə'mætɪks] n mathématiques fpl

maths [mæθs] (US **math**) n math(s) fpl

matinée ['mætɪneɪ] n matinée f

mating call ['meɪtɪŋ-] n appel m du mâle

matrices ['meɪtrɪsiːz] npl of matrix

matriculation [mətrɪkju'leɪʃən] n inscription f

matrimonial [mætrɪ'məʊnɪəl] adj matrimonial(e), conjugal(e)

matrimony ['mætrɪmənɪ] n mariage m

matrix ['meɪtrɪks] (pl **matrices**) n matrice f

matron ['meɪtrən] n (in hospital) infirmière-chef f; (in school) infirmière

mat(t) [mæt] adj mat(e)

matted ['mætɪd] adj emmêlé(e)

matter ['mætə*] n question f; (PHYSICS) matière f; (content) contenu m, fond m; (MED: pus) pus m ♦ vi importer; ~s npl (affairs, situation) la situation; **it doesn't ~** cela n'a pas d'importance; (I don't mind) cela ne fait rien; **what's the ~?** qu'est-ce qu'il y a?, qu'est-ce qui ne va pas?; **no ~ what** quoiqu'il arrive; **as a ~ of course**

tout naturellement; **as a ~ of fact** en fait; ~-of-fact adj terre à terre; (voice) neutre

mattress ['mætrəs] n matelas m

mature [mə'tjʊə*] adj mûr(e); (cheese) fait(e); (wine) arrivé(e) à maturité ♦ vi (person) mûrir; (wine, cheese) se faire

maul [mɔːl] vt lacérer

mausoleum [mɔːsə'lɪəm] n mausolée m

mauve [məʊv] adj mauve

maverick ['mævərɪk] n (fig) non-conformiste m/f

maximum ['mæksɪməm] (pl **maxima**) adj maximum ♦ n maximum m

May [meɪ] n mai m; ~ **Day** n le Premier Mai; see also **mayday**

may [meɪ] (conditional **might**) vi (indicating possibility): **he ~ come** il se peut qu'il vienne; (be allowed to): ~ **I smoke?** puis-je fumer?; (wishes): ~ **God bless you!** (que) Dieu vous bénisse!; **you ~ as well go** à votre place, je partirais

maybe ['meɪbiː] adv peut-être; ~ **he'll ...** peut-être qu'il ...

mayday ['meɪdeɪ] n SOS m

mayhem ['meɪhem] n grabuge m

mayonnaise [meɪə'neɪz] n mayonnaise f

mayor [mɛə*] n maire m; ~**ess** n épouse f du maire

maze [meɪz] n labyrinthe m, dédale m

MD n abbr (= Doctor of Medicine) titre universitaire; = **managing director**

me [miː] pron me, m' +vowel; (stressed, after prep) moi; **he heard ~** il m'a entendu(e); **give ~ a book** donnez-moi un livre; **after ~** après moi

meadow ['medəʊ] n prairie f, pré m

meagre ['miːgə*] (US **meager**) adj maigre

meal [miːl] n repas m; (flour) farine f; ~**time** n l'heure f du repas

mean [miːn] (pt, pp **meant**) adj (with money) avare, radin(e); (unkind) méchant(e); (shabby) misérable; (average) moyen(ne) ♦ vt signifier, vouloir dire; (refer to) faire allusion à, parler de; (intend): **to ~ to do** avoir l'intention de faire ♦ n moyenne f; ~**s** npl (way, money) moyens mpl; **by ~s of** par l'intermédiaire de; au moyen de; **by all ~s!** je vous en prie!; **to be ~t for sb/sth** être destiné(e) à qn/qch; **do you ~ it?** vous êtes sérieux?; **what do you ~?** que voulez-vous dire?

meander [mɪ'ændə*] vi faire des méandres

meaning ['miːnɪŋ] n signification f, sens m; ~**ful** adj significatif(ive); (relationship, occasion) important(e); ~**less** adj dénué(e) de sens

meanness ['miːnnɪs] n (with money) avarice f; (unkindness) méchanceté f; (shabbiness) médiocrité f

meant [ment] pt, pp of **mean**

meantime ['miːn'taɪm] adv (also: in the ~) pendant ce temps

meanwhile → merciful

meanwhile ['mi:nwaɪl] *adv* = **meantime**
measles ['mi:zlz] *n* rougeole *f*
measly ['mi:zlɪ] (*inf*) *adj* minable
measure ['meʒə*] *vt, vi* mesurer ♦ *n* mesure *f*; (*ruler*) règle (graduée); ~**ments** *npl* mesures *fpl*; **chest/hip** ~**ment** tour *m* de poitrine/hanches
meat [mi:t] *n* viande *f*; ~**ball** *n* boulette *f* de viande
Mecca ['mekə] *n* la Mecque
mechanic [mɪ'kænɪk] *n* mécanicien *m*; ~**al** *adj* mécanique; ~**s** *n* (*PHYSICS*) mécanique *f* ♦ *npl* (*of reading, government etc*) mécanisme *m*
mechanism ['mekənɪzəm] *n* mécanisme *m*
medal ['medl] *n* médaille *f*; ~**lion** *n* médaillon *m*; ~**list** (*US* ~**ist**) *n* (*SPORT*) médaillé(e)
meddle ['medl] *vi*: **to** ~ **in** se mêler de, s'occuper de; **to** ~ **with** toucher à
media ['mi:dɪə] *npl* media *mpl*
mediaeval [medɪ'i:vəl] *adj* = **medieval**
median ['mi:dɪən] (*US*) *n* (*also*: ~ **strip**) bande médiane
mediate ['mi:dɪeɪt] *vi* servir d'intermédiaire
Medicaid ['medɪkeɪd] (®:*US*) *n* assistance médicale aux indigents
medical ['medɪkəl] *adj* médical(e) ♦ *n* visite médicale
Medicare ['medɪkeə*] (®:*US*) *n* assistance médicale aux personnes âgées
medication [medɪ'keɪʃən] *n* (*drugs*) médicaments *mpl*
medicine ['medsɪn] *n* médecine *f*; (*drug*) médicament *m*
medieval [medɪ'i:vəl] *adj* médiéval(e)
mediocre [mi:dɪ'əʊkə*] *adj* médiocre
meditate ['medɪteɪt] *vi* méditer
Mediterranean [medɪtə'reɪnɪən] *adj* méditerranéen(ne); **the** ~ (**Sea**) la (mer) Méditerranée
medium ['mi:dɪəm] (*pl* **media**) *adj* moyen(ne) ♦ *n* (*means*) moyen *m*; (*pl mediums: person*) médium *m*; **the happy** ~ le juste milieu; ~ **wave** *n* ondes moyennes
medley ['medlɪ] *n* mélange *m*; (*MUS*) pot-pourri *m*
meek [mi:k] *adj* doux(douce), humble
meet [mi:t] (*pt, pp* **met**) *vt* rencontrer; (*by arrangement*) retrouver, rejoindre; (*for the first time*) faire la connaissance de; (*go and fetch*): **I'll** ~ **you at the station** j'irai te chercher à la gare; (*opponent, danger*) faire face à; (*obligations*) satisfaire à ♦ *vi* (*friends*) se rencontrer, se retrouver; (*in session*) se réunir; (*join: lines, roads*) se rejoindre; ~ **with** *vt fus* rencontrer; ~**ing** *n* rencontre *f*; (*session: of club etc*) réunion *f*; (*POL*) meeting *m*; **she's at a** ~**ing** (*COMM*) elle est en conférence
megabyte ['megəbaɪt] *n* (*COMPUT*) mégaoctet *m*

megaphone ['megəfəʊn] *n* porte-voix *m inv*
melancholy ['melənkəlɪ] *n* mélancolie *f* ♦ *adj* mélancolique
mellow ['meləʊ] *adj* velouté(e); doux(douce); (*sound*) mélodieux(euse) ♦ *vi* (*person*) s'adoucir
melody ['melədɪ] *n* mélodie *f*
melon ['melən] *n* melon *m*
melt [melt] *vi* fondre ♦ *vt* faire fondre; (*metal*) fondre; ~ **away** *vi* fondre complètement; ~ **down** *vt* fondre; ~**down** *n* fusion *f* (du cœur d'un réacteur nucléaire); ~**ing pot** *n* (*fig*) creuset *m*
member ['membə*] *n* membre *m*; **M~ of Parliament** (*BRIT*) député *m*; **M~ of the European Parliament** Eurodéputé *m*; ~**ship** *n* adhésion *f*; statut *m* de membre; (*members*) membres *mpl*, adhérents *mpl*; ~**ship card** *n* carte *f* de membre
memento [mə'mentəʊ] *n* souvenir *m*
memo ['meməʊ] *n* note *f* (de service)
memoirs ['memwɑ:z] *npl* mémoires *mpl*
memorandum [memə'rændəm] (*pl* **memoranda**) *n* note *f* (de service)
memorial [mɪ'mɔ:rɪəl] *n* mémorial *m* ♦ *adj* commémoratif(ive)
memorize ['meməraɪz] *vt* apprendre par cœur; retenir
memory ['memərɪ] *n* mémoire *f*; (*recollection*) souvenir *m*
men [men] *npl of* **man**
menace ['menɪs] *n* menace *f*; (*nuisance*) plaie *f* ♦ *vt* menacer; **menacing** *adj* menaçant(e)
mend [mend] *vt* réparer; (*darn*) raccommoder, repriser ♦ *n*: **on the** ~ en voie de guérison; **to** ~ **one's ways** s'amender; ~**ing** *n* réparation *f*; (*clothes*) raccommodage *m*
menial ['mi:nɪəl] *adj* subalterne
meningitis [menɪn'dʒaɪtɪs] *n* méningite *f*
menopause ['menəʊpɔ:z] *n* ménopause *f*
menstruation [menstrʊ'eɪʃən] *n* menstruation *f*
mental ['mentl] *adj* mental(e); ~**ity** [men'tælɪtɪ] *n* mentalité *f*
mention ['menʃən] *n* mention *f* ♦ *vt* mentionner, faire mention de; **don't** ~ **it!** je vous en prie, il n'y a pas de quoi!
menu ['menju:] *n* (*set* ~, *COMPUT*) menu *m*; (*list of dishes*) carte *f*
MEP *n abbr* = **Member of the European Parliament**
mercenary ['mɜ:sɪnərɪ] *adj* intéressé(e), mercenaire ♦ *n* mercenaire *m*
merchandise ['mɜ:tʃəndaɪz] *n* marchandises *fpl*
merchant ['mɜ:tʃənt] *n* négociant *m*, marchand *m*; ~ **bank** (*BRIT*) *n* banque *f* d'affaires; ~ **navy** (*US* ~ **marine**) *n* marine marchande
merciful ['mɜ:sɪfʊl] *adj* miséricor-

dieux(euse), clément(e); **a ~ release** une délivrance

merciless ['mɜːsɪləs] *adj* impitoyable, sans pitié

mercury ['mɜːkjurɪ] *n* mercure *m*

mercy ['mɜːsɪ] *n* pitié *f*, indulgence *f*; *(REL)* miséricorde *f*; **at the ~ of** à la merci de

mere [mɪə*] *adj* simple; *(chance)* pur(e); **a ~ two hours** seulement deux heures; **~ly** *adv* simplement, purement

merge [mɜːdʒ] *vt* unir ♦ *vi (colours, shapes, sounds)* se mêler; *(roads)* se joindre; *(COMM)* fusionner; **~r** *n (COMM)* fusion *f*

meringue [mə'ræŋ] *n* meringue *f*

merit ['merɪt] *n* mérite *m*, valeur *f*

mermaid ['mɜːmeɪd] *n* sirène *f*

merry ['merɪ] *adj* gai(e); **M~ Christmas!** Joyeux Noël!; **~-go-round** *n* manège *m*

mesh [meʃ] *n* maille *f*

mesmerize ['mezməraɪz] *vt* hypnotiser; fasciner

mess [mes] *n* désordre *m*, fouillis *m*, pagaille *f*; *(muddle: of situation)* gâchis *m*; *(dirt)* saleté *f*; *(MIL)* mess *m*, cantine *f*; **~ about** *(inf) vi* perdre son temps; **~ about with** *(inf) vt fus* tripoter; **~ around** *(inf) vi* = **mess about**; **~ around with** *vt fus* = **mess about with**; **~ up** *vt (dirty)* salir; *(spoil)* gâcher

message ['mesɪdʒ] *n* message *m*

messenger ['mesɪndʒə*] *n* messager *m*

Messrs ['mesəz] *abbr (on letters)* MM

messy ['mesɪ] *adj* sale; en désordre

met [met] *pt, pp of* **meet**

metal ['metl] *n* métal *m*; **~lic** *adj* métallique

meteorology [miːtɪə'rɒlədʒɪ] *n* météorologie *f*

mete out [miːt-] *vt* infliger; *(justice)* rendre

meter ['miːtə*] *n (instrument)* compteur *m*; *(also: parking ~)* parcomètre *m*; *(US: unit)* = **metre**

method ['meθəd] *n* méthode *f*; **~ical** *adj* méthodique; **M~ist** ['meθədɪst] *n* méthodiste *m/f*

meths [meθs] *(BRIT)*, **methylated spirit** ['meθɪleɪtɪd-] *(BRIT) n* alcool *m* à brûler

metre ['miːtə*] *(US* **meter)** *n* mètre *m*

metric ['metrɪk] *adj* métrique

metropolitan [metrə'pɒlɪtən] *adj* métropolitain(e); **the M~ Police** *(BRIT)* la police londonienne

mettle ['metl] *n*: **to be on one's ~** être d'attaque

mew [mjuː] *vi (cat)* miauler

mews [mjuːz] *(BRIT) n*: **~ cottage** cottage aménagé dans une ancienne écurie

Mexico ['meksɪkəu] *n* Mexique *m*

miaow [miː'au] *vi* miauler

mice [maɪs] *npl of* **mouse**

micro ['maɪkrəu] *n (also: ~computer)* micro-ordinateur *m*

microchip ['maɪkrəutʃɪp] *n* puce *f*

microphone ['maɪkrəfəun] *n* microphone *m*

microscope ['maɪkrəskəup] *n* microscope *m*

microwave ['maɪkrəuweɪv] *n (also: ~ oven)* four *m* à micro-ondes

mid [mɪd] *adj*: **in ~ May** à la mi-mai; **~ afternoon** le milieu de l'après-midi; **in ~ air** en plein ciel; **~day** *n* midi *m*

middle ['mɪdl] *n* milieu *m*; *(waist)* taille *f* ♦ *adj* du milieu; *(average)* moyen(ne); **in the ~ of the night** au milieu de la nuit; **~-aged** *adj* d'un certain âge; **M~ Ages** *npl*: **the M~ Ages** le moyen âge; **~-class** *adj* ≈ bourgeois(e); **~ class(es)** *n(pl)*: **the ~ class(es)** ≈ les classes moyennes; **M~ East** *n* Proche-Orient *m*, Moyen-Orient *m*; **~man** *(irreg) n* intermédiaire *m*; **~ name** *n* deuxième nom *m*; **~-of-the-road** *adj (politician)* modéré(e); *(music)* neutre; **~weight** *n (BOXING)* poids moyen; **middling** ['mɪdlɪŋ] *adj* moyen(ne)

midge [mɪdʒ] *n* moucheron *m*

midget ['mɪdʒɪt] *n* nain(e)

Midlands ['mɪdləndz] *npl* comtés du centre de l'Angleterre

midnight ['mɪdnaɪt] *n* minuit *m*

midriff ['mɪdrɪf] *n* estomac *m*, taille *f*

midst [mɪdst] *n*: **in the ~ of** au milieu de

midsummer ['mɪd'sʌmə*] *n* milieu *m* de l'été

midway ['mɪd'weɪ] *adj, adv*: **~ (between)** à mi-chemin (entre); **~ through ...** au milieu de ..., en plein(e) ...

midweek ['mɪd'wiːk] *n* milieu *m* de la semaine

midwife ['mɪdwaɪf] *(pl* **midwives)** *n* sage-femme *f*

midwinter ['mɪd'wɪntə*] *n*: **in ~** en plein hiver

might [maɪt] *vb see* **may** ♦ *n* puissance *f*, force *f*; **~y** *adj* puissant(e)

migraine ['miːɡreɪn] *n* migraine *f*

migrant ['maɪɡrənt] *adj (bird)* migrateur(trice); *(worker)* saisonnier(ère)

migrate [maɪ'ɡreɪt] *vi* émigrer

mike [maɪk] *n abbr (= microphone)* micro *m*

mild [maɪld] *adj* doux(douce); *(reproach, infection)* léger(ère); *(illness)* bénin(igne); *(interest)* modéré(e); *(taste)* peu relevé(e)

mildly ['maɪldlɪ] *adv* doucement; légèrement; **to put it ~** c'est le moins qu'on puisse dire

mile [maɪl] *n* mi(l)le *m* (= 1609 m); **~age** *n* distance *f* en milles, ≈ kilométrage *m*; **~ometer** [maɪ'lɒmɪtə*] *n* compteur *m* (kilométrique); **~stone** *n* borne *f*; *(fig)* jalon *m*

militant ['mɪlɪtnt] *adj* militant(e)

military ['mɪlɪtərɪ] *adj* militaire

militate ['mɪlɪteɪt] *vi*: **to ~ against** (*prevent*) empêcher

militia [mɪ'lɪʃə] *n* milice(s) *f(pl)*

milk [mɪlk] *n* lait *m* ♦ *vt* (*cow*) traire; (*fig: person*) dépouiller, plumer; (: *situation*) exploiter à fond; **~ chocolate** *n* chocolat *m* au lait; **~man** (*irreg*) *n* laitier *m*; **~ shake** *n* milk-shake *m*; **~y** *adj* (*drink*) au lait; (*colour*) laiteux(euse); **M~y Way** *n* voie lactée

mill [mɪl] *n* moulin *m*; (*steel ~*) aciérie *f*; (*spinning ~*) filature *f*; (*flour ~*) minoterie *f* ♦ *vt* moudre, broyer ♦ *vi* (*also: ~ about*) grouiller; **~er** *n* meunier *m*

milligram(me) ['mɪlɪɡræm] *n* milligramme *m*

millimetre ['mɪlɪmiːtə*] (*US* **millimeter**) *n* millimètre *m*

millinery ['mɪlɪnərɪ] *n* chapellerie *f*

million ['mɪljən] *n* million *m*; **~aire** [mɪljə'nɛə*] *n* millionnaire *m*

milometer [maɪ'lɒmɪtə*] *n* ≈ compteur *m* kilométrique

mime [maɪm] *n* mime *m* ♦ *vt, vi* mimer

mimic ['mɪmɪk] *n* imitateur(trice) ♦ *vt* imiter, contrefaire

min. *abbr* = **minute(s); minimum**

mince [mɪns] *vt* hacher ♦ *vi* (*in walking*) marcher à petits pas maniérés ♦ *n* (*BRIT: CULIN*) viande hachée, hachis *m*; **~meat** *n* (*fruit*) hachis de fruits secs utilisé en pâtisserie; (*US: meat*) viande hachée, hachis; **~ pie** *n* (*sweet*) sorte de tarte aux fruits secs; **~r** *n* hachoir *m*

mind [maɪnd] *n* esprit *m* ♦ *vt* (*attend to, look after*) s'occuper de; (*be careful*) faire attention à; (*object to*): **I don't ~ the noise** le bruit ne me dérange pas; **I don't ~ cela** ne me dérange pas; **it is on my ~** cela me préoccupe; **to my ~** à mon avis *or* sens; **to be out of one's ~** ne plus avoir toute sa raison; **to keep** *or* **bear sth in ~** tenir compte de qch; **to make up one's ~** se décider; **~ you, ... remarquez ...; never ~** ça ne fait rien; (*don't worry*) ne vous en faites pas; **"~ the step" "attention à la marche"**; **~er** *n* (*child-~er*) gardienne *f*; (*inf: bodyguard*) ange gardien (*fig*); **~ful** *adj*: **~ful of** attentif(ive) à, soucieux(euse) de; **~less** *adj* irréfléchi(e); (*boring: job*) idiot(e)

mine[1] [maɪn] *pron* le(la) mien(ne), les miens(miennes) ♦ *adj*: **this book is mine** ce livre est à moi

mine[2] [maɪn] *n* mine *f* ♦ *vt* (*coal*) extraire; (*ship, beach*) miner; **~field** *n* champ *m* de mines; (*fig*) situation (très délicate); **~r** *n* mineur *m*

mineral ['mɪnərəl] *adj* minéral(e) ♦ *n* minéral *m*; **~s** *npl* (*BRIT: soft drinks*) boissons gazeuses; **~ water** *n* eau minérale

mingle ['mɪŋɡl] *vi*: **to ~ with** se mêler à

miniature ['mɪnɪtʃə*] *adj* (en) miniature ♦

n miniature *f*

minibus ['mɪnɪbʌs] *n* minibus *m*

minim ['mɪnɪm] *n* (*MUS*) blanche *f*

minimal ['mɪnɪməl] *adj* minime

minimize ['mɪnɪmaɪz] *vt* (*reduce*) réduire au minimum; (*play down*) minimiser

minimum ['mɪnɪməm] (*pl* **minima**) *adj, n* minimum *m*

mining ['maɪnɪŋ] *n* exploitation minière

miniskirt ['mɪnɪskɜːt] *n* mini-jupe *f*

minister ['mɪnɪstə*] *n* (*BRIT: POL*) ministre *m*; (*REL*) pasteur *m* ♦ *vi*: **to ~ to sb's needs** pourvoir aux besoins de qn; **~ial** [mɪnɪs'tɪərɪəl] (*BRIT*) *adj* (*POL*) ministériel(le)

ministry ['mɪnɪstrɪ] *n* (*BRIT: POL*) ministère *m*; (*REL*): **to go into the ~** devenir pasteur

mink [mɪŋk] *n* vison *m*

minor ['maɪnə*] *adj* petit(e), de peu d'importance; (*MUS, poet, problem*) mineur(e) ♦ *n* (*LAW*) mineur(e)

minority [maɪ'nɒrɪtɪ] *n* minorité *f*

mint [mɪnt] *n* (*plant*) menthe *f*; (*sweet*) bonbon *m* à la menthe ♦ *vt* (*coins*) battre; **the (Royal) M~, (*US*) the (US) M~** ≈ l'Hôtel *m* de la Monnaie; **in ~ condition** à l'état de neuf

minus ['maɪnəs] *n* (*also: ~ sign*) signe *m* moins ♦ *prep* moins

minute[1] [maɪ'njuːt] *adj* minuscule; (*detail, search*) minutieux(euse)

minute[2] ['mɪnɪt] *n* minute *f*; **~s** *npl* (*official record*) procès-verbal, compte rendu

miracle ['mɪrəkl] *n* miracle *m*

mirage ['mɪrɑːʒ] *n* mirage *m*

mirror ['mɪrə*] *n* miroir *m*, glace *f*; (*in car*) rétroviseur *m*

mirth [mɜːθ] *n* gaieté *f*

misadventure [mɪsəd'ventʃə*] *n* mésaventure *f*

misapprehension ['mɪsæprɪ'henʃən] *n* malentendu *m*, méprise *f*

misappropriate [mɪsə'prəʊprɪeɪt] *vt* détourner

misbehave ['mɪsbɪ'heɪv] *vi* se conduire mal

miscalculate [mɪs'kælkjʊleɪt] *vt* mal calculer

miscarriage ['mɪskærɪdʒ] *n* (*MED*) fausse couche; **~ of justice** erreur *f* judiciaire

miscellaneous [mɪsɪ'leɪnɪəs] *adj* (*items*) divers(es); (*selection*) varié(e)

mischief ['mɪstʃɪf] *n* (*naughtiness*) sottises *fpl*; (*fun*) farce *f*; (*playfulness*) espièglerie *f*; (*maliciousness*) méchanceté *f*; **mischievous** ['mɪstʃɪvəs] *adj* (*playful, naughty*) coquin(e), espiègle

misconception ['mɪskən'sepʃən] *n* idée fausse

misconduct [mɪs'kɒndʌkt] *n* inconduite *f*; **professional ~** faute professionnelle

misdemeanour [mɪsdɪ'miːnə*] (*US* **misdemeanor**) *n* écart *m* de conduite; infraction *f*

miser ['maizə*] *n* avare *m/f*

miserable ['mizərəbl] *adj* (*person, expression*) malheureux(euse); (*conditions*) misérable; (*weather*) maussade; (*offer, donation*) minable; (*failure*) pitoyable

miserly ['maizəli] *adj* avare

misery ['mizəri] *n* (*unhappiness*) tristesse *f*; (*pain*) souffrances *fpl*; (*wretchedness*) misère *f*

misfire ['mis'faiə*] *vi* rater

misfit ['misfit] *n* (*person*) inadapté(e)

misfortune [mis'fɔːtʃən] *n* malchance *f*, malheur *m*

misgiving [mis'givŋ] *n* (*apprehension*) craintes *fpl*; **to have ~s about** avoir des doutes quant à

misguided ['mis'gaidid] *adj* malavisé(e)

mishandle ['mis'hændl] *vt* (*mismanage*) mal s'y prendre pour faire *or* résoudre *etc*

mishap ['mishæp] *n* mésaventure *f*

misinform [misin'fɔːm] *vt* mal renseigner

misinterpret ['misin'tɜːprit] *vt* mal interpréter

misjudge ['mis'dʒʌdʒ] *vt* méjuger

mislay [mis'lei] (*irreg: like* lay) *vt* égarer

mislead [mis'liːd] (*irreg: like* lead) *vt* induire en erreur; **~ing** *adj* trompeur(euse)

mismanage [mis'mænidʒ] *vt* mal gérer

misnomer ['mis'nəumə*] *n* terme *or* qualificatif trompeur *or* peu approprié

misplace ['mis'pleis] *vt* égarer

misprint ['misprint] *n* faute *f* d'impression

Miss [mis] *n* Mademoiselle

miss [mis] *vt* (*fail to get, attend or see*) manquer, rater; (*regret the absence of*): **I ~ him/it** il/cela me manque ♦ *vi* manquer ♦ *n* (*shot*) coup manqué; **~ out** (*BRIT*) *vt* oublier

misshapen ['mis'ʃeipən] *adj* difforme

missile ['misail] *n* (*MIL*) missile *m*; (*object thrown*) projectile *m*

missing ['misŋ] *adj* manquant(e); (*after escape, disaster: person*) disparu(e); **to go ~** disparaître; **to be ~** avoir disparu

mission ['miʃən] *n* mission *f*; **~ary** *n* missionnaire *m/f*

misspent ['mis'spent] *adj*: **his ~ youth** sa folle jeunesse

mist [mist] *n* (*light*) brume *f*; (*heavy*) brouillard *m* ♦ *vi* (*also: ~ over: eyes*) s'embuer; **~ over** *vi* (*windows etc*) s'embuer; **~ up** *vi* = mist over

mistake [mis'teik] (*irreg: like* take) *n* erreur *f*, faute *f* ♦ *vt* (*meaning, remark*) mal comprendre; se méprendre sur; **to make a ~** se tromper, faire une erreur; **by ~** par erreur, par inadvertance; **to ~ for** prendre pour; **~n** *pp of* **mistake** ♦ *adj* (*idea etc*) erroné(e); **to be ~n** faire erreur, se tromper

mister ['mistə*] *n* (*inf*) Monsieur *m*; *see also* **Mr**

mistletoe ['misltəu] *n* gui *m*

mistook [mis'tuk] *pt of* **mistake**

mistress ['mistris] *n* maîtresse *f*; (*BRIT: in primary school*) institutrice *f*; (*: in secondary school*) professeur *m*

mistrust [mis'trʌst] *vt* se méfier de

misty ['misti] *adj* brumeux(euse); (*glasses, window*) embué(e)

misunderstand ['misʌndə'stænd] (*irreg*) *vt, vi* mal comprendre; **~ing** *n* méprise *f*, malentendu *m*

misuse [*n* 'mis'juːs, *vb* 'mis'juːz] *n* mauvais emploi; (*of power*) abus *m* ♦ *vt* mal employer; abuser de; **~ of funds** détournement *m* de fonds

mitigate ['mitigeit] *vt* atténuer

mitt(en) ['mit(n)] *n* mitaine *f*; moufle *f*

mix [miks] *vt* mélanger; (*sauce, drink etc*) préparer ♦ *vi* se mélanger; (*socialize*): **he doesn't ~ well** il est peu sociable ♦ *n* mélange *m*; **to ~ with** (*people*) fréquenter; **~ up** *vt* mélanger; (*confuse*) confondre; **~ed** *adj* (*feelings, reactions*) contradictoire; (*salad*) mélangé(e); (*school, marriage*) mixte; **~ed grill** *n* assortiment *m* de grillades; **~ed-up** *adj* (*confused*) désorienté(e), embrouillé(e); **~er** *n* (*for food*) batteur *m*, mixer *m*; (*person*): **he is a good ~er** il est très liant; **~ture** *n* assortiment *m*, mélange *m*; (*MED*) préparation *f*; **~-up** *n* confusion *f*

mm *abbr* (= *millimeter*) mm

moan [məun] *n* gémissement *m* ♦ *vi* gémir; (*inf: complain*): **to ~ (about)** se plaindre (de)

moat [məut] *n* fossé *m*, douves *fpl*

mob [mɔb] *n* foule *f*; (*disorderly*) cohue *f* ♦ *vt* assaillir

mobile ['məubail] *adj* mobile ♦ *n* mobile *m*; **~ home** *n* (grande) caravane; **~ phone** *n* téléphone portatif

mock [mɔk] *vt* ridiculiser; (*laugh at*) se moquer de ♦ *adj* faux(fausse); **~ exam** examen blanc; **~ery** *n* moquerie *f*, raillerie *f*; **to make a ~ery of** tourner en dérision; **~-up** *n* maquette *f*

mod [mɔd] *adj see* **convenience**

mode [məud] *n* mode *m*

model ['mɔdl] *n* modèle *m*; (*person: for fashion*) mannequin *m*; (*: for artist*) modèle ♦ *vt* (*with clay etc*) modeler ♦ *vi* travailler comme mannequin ♦ *adj* (*railway: toy*) modèle réduit *inv*; (*child, factory*) modèle; **to ~ clothes** présenter des vêtements; **to ~ o.s. on** imiter

modem ['məudem] *n* (*COMPUT*) modem *m*

moderate [*adj, n* 'mɔdərət, *vb* 'mɔdəreit] *adj* modéré(e); (*amount, change*) peu important(e) ♦ *vi* se calmer ♦ *vt* modérer

modern ['mɔdən] *adj* moderne; **~ize** *vt* moderniser

modest ['mɔdist] *adj* modeste; **~y** *n* mo-

destie f

modicum ['mɒdɪkəm] n: **a ~ of** un minimum de

modify ['mɒdɪfaɪ] vt modifier

mogul ['məʊgəl] n (fig) nabab m

mohair ['məʊhɛə*] n mohair m

moist [mɔɪst] adj humide, moite; **~en** ['mɔɪsən] vt humecter, mouiller légèrement; **~ure** ['mɔɪstʃə*] n humidité f; **~urizer** ['mɔɪstʃəraɪzə*] n produit hydratant

molar ['məʊlə*] n molaire f

molasses [məʊ'læsɪz] n mélasse f

mold [məʊld] (US) n, vt = **mould**

mole [məʊl] n (animal, fig: spy) taupe f; (spot) grain m de beauté

molest [məʊ'lest] vt (harass) molester; (JUR: sexually) attenter à la pudeur de

mollycoddle ['mɒlɪkɒdl] vt chouchouter, couver

molt [məʊlt] (US) vi = **moult**

molten ['məʊltən] adj fondu(e); (rock) en fusion

mom [mɒm] (US) n = **mum**

moment ['məʊmənt] n moment m, instant m; **at the ~** en ce moment; **at that ~** à ce moment-là; **~ary** adj momentané(e), passager(ère); **~ous** [məʊ'mentəs] adj important(e), capital(e)

momentum [məʊ'mentəm] n élan m, vitesse acquise; (fig) dynamique f; **to gather ~** prendre de la vitesse

mommy ['mɒmɪ] (US) n = **mummy**

Monaco ['mɒnəkəʊ] n Monaco m

monarch ['mɒnək] n monarque m; **~y** n monarchie f

monastery ['mɒnəstrɪ] n monastère m

Monday ['mʌndeɪ] n lundi m

monetary ['mʌnɪtərɪ] adj monétaire

money ['mʌnɪ] n argent m; **to make ~** gagner de l'argent; **~ order** n mandat m; **~-spinner** (inf) n mine f d'or (fig)

mongrel ['mʌŋgrəl] n (dog) bâtard m

monitor ['mɒnɪtə*] n (TV, COMPUT) moniteur m ♦ vt contrôler; (broadcast) être à l'écoute de; (progress) suivre de près

monk [mʌŋk] n moine m

monkey ['mʌŋkɪ] n singe m; **~ nut** (BRIT) n cacahuète f; **~ wrench** n clé f à molette

monopoly [mə'nɒpəlɪ] n monopole m

monotonous [mə'nɒtənəs] adj monotone

monsoon [mɒn'suːn] n mousson f

monster ['mɒnstə*] n monstre m

monstrous ['mɒnstrəs] adj monstrueux(euse); (huge) gigantesque

month [mʌnθ] n mois m; **~ly** adj mensuel(le) ♦ adv mensuellement

monument ['mɒnjʊmənt] n monument m

moo [muː] vi meugler, beugler

mood [muːd] n humeur f, disposition f; **to be in a good/bad ~** être de bonne/ mauvaise humeur; **~y** adj (variable) d'humeur changeante, lunatique; (sullen) morose, maussade

moon [muːn] n lune f; **~light** n clair m de lune; **~lighting** n travail m au noir; **~lit** adj: **a ~lit night** une nuit de lune

moor [mʊə*] n lande f ♦ vt (ship) amarrer ♦ vi mouiller; **~land** ['mʊələnd] n lande f

moose [muːs] n inv élan m

mop [mɒp] n balai m à laver; (for dishes) lavette f (à vaisselle) ♦ vt essuyer; **~ of hair** tignasse f; **~ up** vt éponger

mope [məʊp] vi avoir le cafard, se morfondre

moped ['məʊped] n cyclomoteur m

moral ['mɒrəl] adj moral(e) ♦ n morale f; **~s** npl (attitude, behaviour) moralité f

morale [mɒ'rɑːl] n moral m

morality [mə'rælɪtɪ] n moralité f

morass [mə'ræs] n marais m, marécage m

KEYWORD

more [mɔː*] adj **1** (greater in number etc) plus (de), davantage; **~ people/work (than)** plus de gens/de travail (que)
2 (additional) encore (de); **do you want (some) ~ tea?** voulez-vous encore du thé?; **I have no** or **I don't have any ~ money** je n'ai plus d'argent; **it'll take a few ~ weeks** ça prendra encore quelques semaines
♦ pron plus, davantage; **~ than 10** plus de 10; **it cost ~ than we expected** cela a coûté plus que prévu; **I want ~** j'en veux plus or davantage; **is there any ~?** est-ce qu'il en reste?; **there's no ~** il n'y en a plus; **a little ~** un peu plus; **many/much ~** beaucoup plus, bien davantage
♦ adv: **~ dangerous/easily (than)** plus dangereux/facilement (que); **~ and ~ expensive** de plus en plus cher; **~ or less** plus ou moins; **~ than ever** plus que jamais

---

moreover [mɔː'rəʊvə*] adv de plus

morning ['mɔːnɪŋ] n matin m; matinée f ♦ cpd matinal(e); (paper) du matin; **in the ~** le matin; **7 o'clock in the ~** 7 heures du matin; **~ sickness** n nausées matinales

Morocco [mə'rɒkəʊ] n Maroc m

moron ['mɔːrɒn] (inf) n idiot(e)

Morse [mɔːs] n: **~ (code)** morse m

morsel ['mɔːsl] n bouchée f

mortar ['mɔːtə*] n mortier m

mortgage ['mɔːgɪdʒ] n hypothèque f; (loan) prêt m (or crédit m) hypothécaire ♦ vt hypothéquer; **~ company** (US) n société f de crédit immobilier

mortuary ['mɔːtjʊərɪ] n morgue f

mosaic [məʊ'zeɪɪk] n mosaïque f

Moscow ['mɒskəʊ] n Moscou

Moslem ['mɒzləm] adj, n = **Muslim**

mosque [mɒsk] n mosquée f
mosquito [mɒs'ki:təʊ] (pl ~es) n moustique m
moss [mɒs] n mousse f
most [məʊst] adj la plupart de; le plus de ♦ pron la plupart ♦ adv le plus; (very) très, extrêmement; **the ~** (also: + adjective) le plus; **~ of** la plus grande partie de; **~ of them** la plupart d'entre eux; **I saw (the) ~** j'en ai vu la plupart; c'est moi qui en ai vu le plus; **at the (very) ~** au plus; **to make the ~ of** profiter au maximum de; **~ly** adv (chiefly) surtout, (usually) généralement
MOT n abbr (BRIT: = Ministry of Transport): **the ~ (test)** la visite technique (annuelle) obligatoire des véhicules à moteur
motel [məʊ'tel] n motel m
moth [mɒθ] n papillon m de nuit; (in clothes) mite f; **~ball** n boule f de naphtaline
mother ['mʌðə*] n mère f ♦ vt (act as mother to) servir de mère à; (pamper, protect) materner; **~ country** mère patrie; **~hood** n maternité f; **~-in-law** n belle-mère f; **~ly** adj maternel(le); **~-of-pearl** n nacre f; **~-to-be** n future maman; **~ tongue** n langue maternelle
motion ['məʊʃən] n mouvement m; (gesture) geste m; (at meeting) motion f ♦ vt, vi: **to ~ (to) sb to do** faire signe à qn de faire; **~less** adj immobile, sans mouvement; **~ picture** n film m
motivated ['məʊtɪveɪtɪd] adj motivé(e)
motive ['məʊtɪv] n motif m, mobile m
motley ['mɒtlɪ] adj hétéroclite
motor ['məʊtə*] n moteur m; (BRIT: inf: vehicle) auto f ♦ cpd (industry, vehicle) automobile; **~bike** n moto f; **~boat** n bateau m à moteur; **~car** (BRIT) n automobile f; **~cycle** n vélomoteur m; **~cycle racing** n course f de motos; **~cyclist** n motocycliste m/f; **~ing** (BRIT) n tourisme m automobile; **~ist** ['məʊtərɪst] n automobiliste m/f; **~ mechanic** n mécanicien m garagiste; **~ racing** (BRIT) n course f automobile; **~ trade** n secteur m de l'automobile; **~way** (BRIT) n autoroute f
mottled ['mɒtld] adj tacheté(e), marbré(e)
motto ['mɒtəʊ] (pl ~es) n devise f
mould [məʊld] (US **mold**) n moule m; (mildew) moisissure f ♦ vt mouler, modeler; (fig) façonner; **mo(u)ldy** adj moisi(e); (smell) de moisi
moult [məʊlt] (US **molt**) vi muer
mound [maʊnd] n monticule m, tertre m; (heap) monceau m, tas m
mount [maʊnt] n mont m, montagne f ♦ vt monter ♦ vi (inflation, tension) augmenter; (also: **~ up**: problems etc) s'accumuler; **~ up** vi (bills, costs, savings) s'accumuler
mountain ['maʊntɪn] n montagne f ♦ cpd de montagne; **~ bike** n VTT m, vélo tout-terrain; **~eer** [maʊntɪ'nɪə*] n alpiniste m/f;

~eering n alpinisme m; **~ous** adj montagneux(euse); **~ rescue team** n équipe f de secours en montagne; **~side** n flanc m or versant m de la montagne
mourn [mɔ:n] vt pleurer ♦ vi: **to ~ (for)** (person) pleurer (la mort de); **~er** n parent(e) or ami(e) du défunt; personne f en deuil; **~ful** adj triste, lugubre; **~ing** n deuil m; **in ~ing** en deuil
mouse [maʊs] (pl **mice**) n (also COMPUT) souris f; **~trap** n souricière f
mousse [mu:s] n mousse f
moustache [məs'tɑ:ʃ] (US **mustache**) n moustache(s) f(pl)
mousy ['maʊsɪ] adj (hair) d'un châtain terne
mouth [maʊθ, pl maʊðz] (pl ~s) n bouche f; (of dog, cat) gueule f; (of river) embouchure f; (of hole, cave) ouverture f; **~ful** n bouchée f; **~ organ** n harmonica m; **~piece** n (of musical instrument) embouchure f; (spokesman) porte-parole m inv; **~wash** n eau f dentifrice; **~-watering** adj qui met l'eau à la bouche
movable ['mu:vəbl] adj mobile
move [mu:v] n (movement) mouvement m; (in game) coup m; (: turn to play) tour m; (change: of house) déménagement m; (: of job) changement m d'emploi ♦ vt déplacer, bouger; (emotionally) émouvoir; (POL: resolution etc) proposer; (in game) jouer ♦ vi (gen) bouger, remuer; (traffic) circuler; (also: ~ house) déménager; (situation) progresser; **that was a good ~** bien joué!; **to ~ sb to do sth** pousser or inciter qn à faire qch; **to get a ~ on** se dépêcher, se remuer; **~ about** vi (fidget) remuer; (travel) voyager, se déplacer; (change residence, job) ne pas rester au même endroit; **~ along** vi se pousser; **~ around** vi = **move about**; **~ away** vi s'en aller; **~ back** vi revenir, retourner; **~ forward** vi avancer; **~ in** vi (to a house) emménager; (police, soldiers) intervenir; **~ on** vi se remettre en route; **~ out** vi (of house) déménager; **~ over** vi se pousser, se déplacer; **~ up** vi (pupil) passer dans la classe supérieure; (employee) avoir de l'avancement; **~able** adj = **movable**
movement ['mu:vmənt] n mouvement m
movie ['mu:vɪ] n film m; **the ~s** le cinéma; **~ camera** n caméra f
moving ['mu:vɪŋ] adj en mouvement; (emotional) émouvant(e)
mow [məʊ] (pt **mowed**, pp **mowed** or **mown**) vt faucher; (lawn) tondre; **~ down** vt faucher; **~er** n (also: **lawnmower**) tondeuse f à gazon
MP n abbr = **Member of Parliament**
mph abbr = **miles per hour**
Mr ['mɪstə*] (US **Mr.**) n: **~ Smith** Monsieur Smith, M. Smith
Mrs ['mɪsɪz] (US **Mrs.**) n: **~ Smith** Madame

Smith, Mme Smith
Ms [mɪz] (US **Ms.**) n (= Miss or Mrs): ~ Smith ≈ Madame Smith, Mme Smith
MSc abbr = Master of Science
much [mʌtʃ] adj beaucoup de ♦ adv, n, pron beaucoup; **how ~ is it?** combien est-ce que ça coûte?; **too ~** trop (de); **as ~ as** autant de
muck [mʌk] n (dirt) saleté f; ~ **about** (or) **around** (inf) vi faire l'imbécile; ~ **up** (inf) vt (exam, interview) se planter à (fam); ~**y** adj (très) sale; (book, film) cochon(ne)
mud [mʌd] n boue f
muddle [mʌdl] n (mess) pagaille f, désordre m; (mix-up) confusion f ♦ vt (also: ~ **up**) embrouiller; ~ **through** vi se débrouiller
muddy [mʌdɪ] adj boueux(euse); **mudguard** [mʌdgɑːd] n garde-boue m inv
muffin [mʌfɪn] n muffin m
muffle [mʌfl] vt (sound) assourdir, étouffer; (against cold) emmitoufler; ~**d** adj (sound) étouffé(e); (person) emmitouflé(e); ~**r** (US) n (AUT) silencieux m
mug [mʌg] n (cup) grande tasse (sans soucoupe); (: for beer) chope f; (inf: face) bouille f; (: fool) poire f ♦ vt (assault) agresser; ~**ging** n agression f
muggy [mʌgɪ] adj lourd(e), moite
mule [mjuːl] n mule f
mull over [mʌl-] vt réfléchir à
multi-level [mʌltɪlevl] (US) adj = multistorey
multiple [mʌltɪpl] adj multiple ♦ n multiple m; ~ **sclerosis** n sclérose f en plaques
multiplication [mʌltɪplɪˈkeɪʃən] n multiplication f; **multiply** [mʌltɪplaɪ] vt multiplier ♦ vi se multiplier
multistorey [mʌltɪˈstɔːrɪ] (BRIT) adj (building) à étages; (car park) à étages or niveaux multiples
mum [mʌm] (BRIT: inf) n maman f ♦ adj: **to keep ~** ne pas souffler mot
mumble [mʌmbl] vt, vi marmotter, marmonner
mummy [mʌmɪ] n (BRIT: mother) maman f; (embalmed) momie f
mumps [mʌmps] n oreillons mpl
munch [mʌntʃ] vt, vi mâcher
mundane [mʌnˈdeɪn] adj banal(e), terre à terre inv
municipal [mjuːˈnɪsɪpəl] adj municipal(e)
murder [mɜːdə*] n meurtre m, assassinat m ♦ vt assassiner; ~**ous** adj meurtrier(ère)
murky [mɜːkɪ] adj sombre, ténébreux(euse); (water) trouble
murmur [mɜːmə*] n murmure m ♦ vt, vi murmurer
muscle [mʌsl] n muscle m; (fig) force f; ~ **in** vi (on territory) envahir; (on success) ex-

ploiter
muscular [mʌskjʊlə*] adj musculaire; (person, arm) musclé(e)
muse [mjuːz] vi méditer, songer
museum [mjuːˈzɪəm] n musée m
mushroom [mʌʃrʊm] n champignon m ♦ vi pousser comme un champignon
music [mjuːzɪk] n musique f; ~**al** adj musical(e); (person) musicien(ne) ♦ n (show) comédie musicale; ~**al instrument** n instrument m de musique; ~**ian** [mjuːˈzɪʃən] n musicien(ne)
Muslim [mʌzlɪm] adj, n musulman(e)
muslin [mʌzlɪn] n mousseline f
mussel [mʌsl] n moule f
must [mʌst] aux vb (obligation): **I ~ do it** je dois le faire, il faut que je le fasse; (probability): **he ~ be there by now** il doit y être maintenant, il y est probablement maintenant; (suggestion, invitation): **you ~ come and see me** il faut que vous veniez me voir; (indicating sth unwelcome): **why ~ he behave so badly?** qu'est-ce qui le pousse à se conduire si mal? ♦ n nécessité f, impératif m; **it's a ~** c'est indispensable
mustache [mʌstæʃ] (US) n = moustache
mustard [mʌstəd] n moutarde f
muster [mʌstə*] vt rassembler
mustn't [mʌsnt] = must not
mute [mjuːt] adj muet(te)
muted [mjuːtɪd] adj (colour) sourd(e); (reaction) voilé(e)
mutiny [mjuːtɪnɪ] n mutinerie f ♦ vi se mutiner
mutter [mʌtə*] vt, vi marmonner, marmotter
mutton [mʌtn] n mouton m
mutual [mjuːtjʊəl] adj mutuel(le), réciproque; (benefit, interest) commun(e); ~**ly** adv mutuellement
muzzle [mʌzl] n museau m; (protective device) muselière f; (of gun) gueule f ♦ vt museler
my [maɪ] adj mon(ma), mes pl; ~ **house/car/gloves** ma maison/mon auto/mes gants; **I've washed ~ hair/cut ~ finger** je me suis lavé les cheveux/coupé le doigt; ~**self** [maɪˈself] pron (reflexive) me; (emphatic) moi-même; (after prep) moi; see also oneself
mysterious [mɪsˈtɪərɪəs] adj mystérieux(euse)
mystery [mɪstərɪ] n mystère m
mystify [mɪstɪfaɪ] vt mystifier; (puzzle) ébahir
myth [mɪθ] n mythe m; ~**ology** [mɪˈθɒlədʒɪ] n mythologie f

N n

n/a *abbr* = **not applicable**

nag [næg] *vt* (*scold*) être toujours après, reprendre sans arrêt; ~**ging** *adj* (*doubt, pain*) persistant(e)

nail [neɪl] *n* (*human*) ongle *m*; (*metal*) clou *m* ♦ *vt* clouer; **to ~ sb down to a date/ price** contraindre qn à accepter *or* donner une date/un prix; ~**brush** *n* brosse *f* à ongles; ~**file** *n* lime *f* à ongles; ~ **polish** *n* vernis *m* à ongles; ~ **polish remover** *n* dissolvant *m*; ~ **scissors** *npl* ciseaux *mpl* à ongles; ~ **varnish** (*BRIT*) *n* = **nail polish**

naïve [naɪˈiːv] *adj* naïf(ïve)

naked [ˈneɪkɪd] *adj* nu(e)

name [neɪm] *n* nom *m*; (*reputation*) réputation *f* ♦ *vt* nommer; (*identify: accomplice etc*) citer; (*price, date*) fixer, donner; **by ~** par son nom; **in the ~ of** au nom de; **what's your ~?** comment vous appelez-vous?; ~**less** *adj* sans nom; (*witness, contributor*) anonyme; ~**ly** *adv* à savoir; ~**sake** *n* homonyme *m*

nanny [ˈnænɪ] *n* bonne *f* d'enfants

nap [næp] *n* (*sleep*) (petit) somme ♦ *vi*: **to be caught** ~**ping** être pris à l'improviste *or* en défaut

nape [neɪp] *n*: ~ **of the neck** nuque *f*

napkin [ˈnæpkɪn] *n* serviette *f* (de table)

nappy [ˈnæpɪ] (*BRIT*) *n* couche *f* (*gen pl*); ~ **rash** *n*: **to have a ~ rash** avoir les fesses rouges

narcissus [nɑːˈsɪsəs, *pl* nɑːˈsɪsaɪ] (*pl* **narcissi**) *n* narcisse *m*

narcotic [nɑːˈkɒtɪk] *n* (*drug*) stupéfiant *m*; (*MED*) narcotique *m*

narrative [ˈnærətɪv] *n* récit *m*

narrow [ˈnærəʊ] *adj* étroit(e); (*fig*) restreint(e), limité(e) ♦ *vi* (*road*) devenir plus étroit, se rétrécir; (*gap, difference*) se réduire; **to have a ~ escape** l'échapper belle; **to ~ sth down** to réduire qch à; ~**ly** *adv*: **he ~ly missed injury/the tree** il a failli se blesser/rentrer dans l'arbre; ~-**minded** *adj* à l'esprit étroit, borné(e); (*attitude*) borné

nasty [ˈnɑːstɪ] *adj* (*person: malicious*) méchant(e); (: *rude*) très désagréable; (*smell*) dégoûtant(e); (*wound, situation, disease*) mauvais(e)

nation [ˈneɪʃən] *n* nation *f*

national [ˈnæʃənl] *adj* national(e) ♦ *n* (*abroad*) ressortissant(e); (*when home*) national(e); ~ **dress** *n* costume national; **N~ Health Service** (*BRIT*) *n* service national de santé, ≈ Sécurité Sociale; **N~ Insurance** (*BRIT*) *n* ≈ Sécurité Sociale; ~**ism** [ˈnæʃnəlɪzəm] *n* nationalisme *m*; ~**ist** [ˈnæʃnəlɪst] *adj* nationaliste ♦ *n* nationaliste *m/f*; ~**ity** [næʃəˈnælɪtɪ] *n* nationalité *f*; ~**ize** *vt* nationaliser; ~**ly** *adv* (*as a nation*) du point de vue national; (*nationwide*) dans le pays entier

nationwide [ˈneɪʃənwaɪd] *adj* s'étendant à l'ensemble du pays; (*problem*) à l'échelle du pays entier ♦ *adv* à travers *or* dans tout le pays

native [ˈneɪtɪv] *n* autochtone *m/f*, habitant(e) du pays ♦ *adj* du pays, indigène; (*country*) natal(e); (*ability*) inné(e); **a ~ of Russia** une personne originaire de Russie; **a ~ speaker of French** une personne de langue maternelle française; ~ **language** *n* langue maternelle

NATO [ˈneɪtəʊ] *n abbr* (= *North Atlantic Treaty Organization*) OTAN *f*

natural [ˈnætʃrəl] *adj* naturel(le); ~ **gas** *n* gaz naturel; ~**ize** *vt* naturaliser; (*plant*) acclimater; **to become ~ized** (*person*) se faire naturaliser; ~**ly** *adv* naturellement

nature [ˈneɪtʃə*] *n* nature *f*; **by ~** par tempérament, de nature

naught [nɔːt] *n* = **nought**

naughty [ˈnɔːtɪ] *adj* (*child*) vilain(e), pas sage

nausea [ˈnɔːsɪə] *n* nausée *f*; **nauseate** [ˈnɔːsɪeɪt] *vt* écœurer, donner la nausée à

naval [ˈneɪvl] *adj* naval(e); ~ **officer** *n* officier *m* de marine

nave [neɪv] *n* nef *f*

navel [ˈneɪvl] *n* nombril *m*

navigate [ˈnævɪgeɪt] *vt* (*steer*) diriger; (*plot course*) naviguer ♦ *vi* naviguer; **navigation** [nævɪˈgeɪʃən] *n* navigation *f*

navvy [ˈnævɪ] (*BRIT*) *n* terrassier *m*

navy [ˈneɪvɪ] *n* marine *f*; ~(-**blue**) *adj* bleu marine *inv*

Nazi [ˈnɑːtsɪ] *n* Nazi(e)

NB *abbr* (= *nota bene*) NB

near [nɪə*] *adj* proche ♦ *adv* près ♦ *prep* (*also*: ~ **to**) près de ♦ *vt* approcher de; ~**by** *adj* proche ♦ *adv* tout près, à proximité; ~**ly** *adv* presque; **I ~ly fell** j'ai failli tomber; ~ **miss** *n* (*AVIAT*) quasi-collision *f*; **that was a ~ miss** (*gen*) il s'en est fallu de peu; (*of shot*) c'est passé très près; ~**side** *n* (*AUT: BRIT*) côté *m* gauche; (: *in US, Europe*) côté droit; ~-**sighted** *adj* myope

neat [niːt] *adj* (*person, work*) soigné(e); (*room etc*) bien tenu(e) *or* rangé(e); (*skilful*) habile; (*spirits*) pur(e); ~**ly** *adv* avec soin *or* ordre; habilement

necessarily [ˈnesɪsərɪlɪ] *adv* nécessairement

necessary ['nesɪsərɪ] *adj* nécessaire
necessity [nɪ'sesɪtɪ] *n* nécessité *f*; (*thing needed*) chose nécessaire *or* essentielle; **necessities** [*pl*] *npl* nécessaire *m*
neck [nek] *n* cou *m*; (*of animal, garment*) encolure *f*; (*of bottle*) goulot *m* ♦ *vi* (*inf*) se peloter; ~ **and** ~ à égalité; **~lace** ['neklɪs] *n* collier *m*; **~line** *n* encolure *f*; **~tie** *n* cravate *f*
need [niːd] *n* besoin *m* ♦ *vt* avoir besoin de; **to** ~ **to do** devoir faire; avoir besoin de faire; **you don't** ~ **to go** vous n'avez pas besoin *or* vous n'êtes pas obligé de partir
needle ['niːdl] *n* aiguille *f* ♦ *vt* asticoter, tourmenter
needless ['niːdlɪs] *adj* inutile
needlework ['niːdlwɜːk] *n* (*activity*) travaux *mpl* d'aiguille; (*object(s)*) ouvrage *m*
needn't ['niːdnt] = **need not**
needy ['niːdɪ] *adj* nécessiteux(euse)
negative ['negətɪv] *n* (PHOT, ELEC) négatif *m*; (LING) terme *m* de négation ♦ *adj* négatif(ive)
neglect [nɪ'glekt] *vt* négliger ♦ *n* (*of person, duty, garden*) le fait de négliger; (*state*) abandon *m*
negligee ['negliʒeɪ] *n* déshabillé *m*
negotiate [nɪ'gəʊʃɪeɪt] *vi, vt* négocier; **negotiation** [nɪgəʊʃɪ'eɪʃən] *n* négociation *f*, pourparlers *mpl*
Negro ['niːgrəʊ] (!; *pl* ~**es**) *n* Noir(e)
neigh [neɪ] *vi* hennir
neighbour ['neɪbə*] (*US* **neighbor**) *n* voisin(e); **~hood** *n* (*place*) quartier *m*; (*people*) voisinage *m*; **~ing** *adj* voisin(e), avoisinant(e); **~ly** *adj* obligeant(e); (*action etc*) amical(e)
neither ['naɪðə*] *adj, pron* aucun(e) (des deux), ni l'un(e) ni l'autre ♦ *conj*: **I didn't move and** ~ **did Claude** je n'ai pas bougé, (et) Claude non plus; ..., ~ **did I refuse ...,** (et *or* mais) je n'ai pas non plus refusé ... ♦ *adv*: ~ **good nor bad** ni bon ni mauvais
neon ['niːɒn] *n* néon *m*; ~ **light** *n* lampe *f* au néon
nephew ['nefjuː] *n* neveu *m*
nerve [nɜːv] *n* nerf *m*; (*fig: courage*) sang-froid *m*, courage *m*; (: *impudence*) aplomb *m*, toupet *m*; **to have a fit of** ~**s** avoir le trac; **~-racking** *adj* angoissant(e)
nervous ['nɜːvəs] *adj* nerveux(euse); (*anxious*) inquiet(ète), plein(e) d'appréhension; (*timid*) intimidé(e); ~ **breakdown** *n* dépression nerveuse
nest [nest] *n* nid *m* ♦ *vi* (se) nicher, faire son nid; ~ **egg** *n* (*fig*) bas *m* de laine, magot *m*
nestle ['nesl] *vi* se blottir
net [net] *n* filet *m* ♦ *adj* net(te) ♦ *vt* (*fish etc*) prendre au filet; (*profit*) rapporter; **~ball** *n* netball *m*; ~ **curtains** *npl* voilages

mpl
Netherlands ['neðələndz] *npl*: **the** ~ les Pays-Bas *mpl*
nett [net] *adj* = **net**
netting ['netɪŋ] *n* (*for fence etc*) treillis *m*, grillage *m*
nettle ['netl] *n* ortie *f*
network ['netwɜːk] *n* réseau *m*
neurotic [njʊə'rɒtɪk] *adj, n* névrosé(e)
neuter ['njuːtə*] *adj* neutre ♦ *vt* (*cat etc*) châtrer, couper
neutral ['njuːtrəl] *adj* neutre ♦ *n* (AUT) point mort; **~ize** *vt* neutraliser
never ['nevə*] *adv* (ne ...) jamais; ~ **again** plus jamais; ~ **in my life** jamais de ma vie; *see also* **mind**; **~-ending** *adj* interminable; **~theless** [nevəðə'les] *adv* néanmoins, malgré tout
new [njuː] *adj* nouveau(nouvelle); (*brand new*) neuf(neuve); **~born** *adj* nouveau-né(e); **~comer** ['njuːkʌmə*] *n* nouveau venu/nouvelle venue; **~-fangled** (*pej*) *adj* ultramoderne (et farfelu(e)); **~-found** *adj* (*enthusiasm*) de fraîche date; (*friend*) nouveau(nouvelle); **~ly** *adv* nouvellement, récemment; **~ly-weds** *npl* jeunes mariés *mpl*
news [njuːz] *n* nouvelle(s) *f(pl)*; (RADIO, TV) informations *fpl*, actualités *fpl*; **a piece of** ~ une nouvelle; ~ **agency** *n* agence *f* de presse; **~agent** (BRIT) *n* marchand *m* de journaux; **~caster** *n* présentateur(trice); **~dealer** (*US*) *n* = **newsagent**; ~ **flash** *n* flash *m* d'information; **~letter** *n* bulletin *m*; **~paper** *n* journal *m*; **~print** *n* papier *m* (de) journal; **~reader** *n* = **newscaster**; **~reel** *n* actualités (filmées) *fpl*; ~ **stand** *n* kiosque *m* à journaux
newt [njuːt] *n* triton *m*
New Year *n* Nouvel An; ~**'s Day** *n* le jour de l'An; ~**'s Eve** *n* la Saint-Sylvestre
New Zealand [-'ziːlənd] *n* la Nouvelle-Zélande; **~er** *n* Néo-zélandais(e)
next [nekst] *adj* (*seat, room*) voisin(e), d'à côté; (*meeting, bus stop*) suivant(e); (*in time*) prochain(e) ♦ *adv* (*place*) à côté; (*time*) la fois suivante, la prochaine fois; (*afterwards*) ensuite; **the** ~ **day** le lendemain, le jour suivant *or* d'après; ~ **year** l'année prochaine; ~ **time** la prochaine fois; **to** ~ **to** à côté de; ~ **to nothing** presque rien; ~, **please!** (*at doctor's etc*) au suivant!; ~ **door** *adv* à côté ♦ *adj* d'à côté; **~-of-kin** *n* parent *m* le plus proche
NHS *n abbr* = **National Health Service**
nib [nɪb] *n* (bec *m* de) plume *f*
nibble ['nɪbl] *vt* grignoter
nice [naɪs] *adj* (*pleasant, likeable*) agréable; (*pretty*) joli(e); (*kind*) gentil(le); **~ly** *adv* agréablement; joliment; gentiment
niceties ['naɪsɪtɪz] *npl* subtilités *fpl*
nick [nɪk] *n* (*indentation*) encoche *f*; (*wound*) entaille *f* ♦ *vt* (BRIT: *inf*) faucher,

piquer; **in the ~ of time** juste à temps

nickel ['nɪkl] *n* nickel *m*; (*US*) pièce *f* de 5 cents

nickname ['nɪkneɪm] *n* surnom *m* ♦ *vt* surnommer

niece [niːs] *n* nièce *f*

Nigeria [naɪ'dʒɪərɪə] *n* Nigéria *m or f*

niggling ['nɪɡlɪŋ] *adj* (*person*) tatillon(ne); (*detail*) insignifiant(e); (*doubts, injury*) persistant(e)

night [naɪt] *n* nuit *f*; (*evening*) soir *m*; **at ~** la nuit; **by ~** de nuit; **the ~ before last** avant-hier soir; **~cap** *n* boisson prise avant le coucher; **~ club** *n* boîte *f* de nuit; **~dress** *n* chemise *f* de nuit; **~fall** *n* tombée *f* de la nuit; **~gown** *n* chemise *f* de nuit; **~ie** ['naɪtɪ] *n* chemise *f* de nuit; **~ingale** ['naɪtɪŋɡeɪl] *n* rossignol *m*; **~life** ['naɪtlaɪf] *n* vie *f* nocturne; **~ly** ['naɪtlɪ] *adj* de chaque nuit *or* soir; (*by night*) nocturne ♦ *adv* chaque nuit *or* soir; **~mare** ['naɪtmɛə*] *n* cauchemar *m*; **~ porter** *n* gardien *m* de nuit, concierge *m* de service la nuit; **~ school** *n* cours *mpl* du soir; **~ shift** *n* équipe *f* de nuit; **~-time** *n* nuit *f*; **~ watchman** *n* veilleur *m* or gardien *m* de nuit

nil [nɪl] *n* rien *m*; (*BRIT: SPORT*) zéro *m*

Nile [naɪl] *n*: **the ~** le Nil

nimble ['nɪmbl] *adj* agile

nine [naɪn] *num* neuf; **~teen** *num* dix-neuf; **~ty** *num* quatre-vingt-dix

ninth [naɪnθ] *num* neuvième

nip [nɪp] *vt* pincer

nipple ['nɪpl] *n* (*ANAT*) mamelon *m*, bout *m* du sein

nitrogen ['naɪtrədʒən] *n* azote *m*

--- KEYWORD

no [nəʊ] (*pl* **~es**) *adv* (*opposite of "yes"*) non; **are you coming? - ~ (I'm not)** est-ce que vous venez? - non; **would you like some more? - ~ thank you** vous en voulez encore? - non merci
♦ *adj* (*not any*) pas de, aucun(e) (*used with "ne"*); **I have ~ money/books** je n'ai pas d'argent/de livres; **~ student would have done it** aucun étudiant ne l'aurait fait; **"~ smoking"** "défense de fumer"; **"~ dogs"** "les chiens ne sont pas admis"
♦ *n* non *m*

nobility [nəʊ'bɪlɪtɪ] *n* noblesse *f*

noble ['nəʊbl] *adj* noble

nobody ['nəʊbədɪ] *pron* personne

nod [nɒd] *vi* faire un signe de tête (*affirmatif ou amical*); (*sleep*) somnoler ♦ *vt*: **to ~ one's head** faire un signe de (la) tête; (*in agreement*) faire signe que oui ♦ *n* signe *m* de (la) tête; **~ off** *vi* s'assoupir

noise [nɔɪz] *n* bruit *m*; **noisy** ['nɔɪzɪ] *adj* bruyant(e)

nominal ['nɒmɪnl] *adj* (*rent, leader*) symbolique

nominate ['nɒmɪneɪt] *vt* (*propose*) proposer; (*appoint*) nommer; **nominee** [nɒmɪ'niː] *n* candidat agréé; personne nommée

non... *prefix* non-; **~alcoholic** *adj* non-alcoolisé(e); **~committal** *adj* évasif(ive)

nondescript ['nɒndɪskrɪpt] *adj* quelconque, indéfinissable

none [nʌn] *pron* aucun(e); **~ of you** aucun d'entre vous, personne parmi vous; **I've ~ left** je n'en ai plus; **he's ~ the worse for it** il ne s'en porte pas plus mal

nonentity [nɒ'nentɪtɪ] *n* personne insignifiante

nonetheless ['nʌnðə'les] *adv* néanmoins

non-existent [nɒnɪɡ'zɪstənt] *adj* inexistant(e)

non-fiction [nɒn'fɪkʃən] *n* littérature *f* non-romanesque

nonplussed ['nɒn'plʌst] *adj* perplexe

nonsense ['nɒnsəns] *n* absurdités *fpl*, idioties *fpl*; **~!** ne dites pas d'idioties!

non: **~-smoker** *n* non-fumeur *m*; **~-stick** *adj* qui n'attache pas; **~-stop** *adj* direct(e), sans arrêt (*or* escale) ♦ *adv* sans arrêt

noodles ['nuːdlz] *npl* nouilles *fpl*

nook [nʊk] *n*: **~s and crannies** recoins *mpl*

noon [nuːn] *n* midi *m*

no one ['nəʊwʌn] *pron* = **nobody**

noose [nuːs] *n* nœud coulant; (*hangman's*) corde *f*

nor [nɔː*] *conj* = **neither** ♦ *adv see* **neither**

norm [nɔːm] *n* norme *f*

normal ['nɔːməl] *adj* normal(e); **~ly** *adv* normalement

Normandy ['nɔːməndɪ] *n* Normandie *f*

north [nɔːθ] *n* nord *m* ♦ *adj* du nord, nord *inv* ♦ *adv* au *or* vers le nord; **N~ America** *n* Amérique *f* du Nord; **~-east** *n* nord-est *m*; **~erly** ['nɔːðəlɪ] *adj* du nord; **~ern** ['nɔːðən] *adj* du nord, septentrional(e); **N~ern Ireland** *n* Irlande *f* du Nord; **N~ Pole** *n* pôle *m* Nord; **N~ Sea** *n* mer *f* du Nord; **~ward(s)** ['nɔːθwəd(z)] *adv* vers le nord; **~-west** *n* nord-ouest *m*

Norway ['nɔːweɪ] *n* Norvège *f*

Norwegian [nɔː'wiːdʒən] *adj* norvégien(ne) ♦ *n* Norvégien(ne); (*LING*) norvégien *m*

nose [nəʊz] *n* nez *m*; **~ about, around** *vi* fouiner *or* fureter (partout); **~bleed** *n* saignement *m* du nez; **~-dive** *n* (descente *f* en) piqué *m*; **~y** (*inf*) *adj* = **nosy**

nostalgia [nɔs'tældʒɪə] *n* nostalgie *f*

nostril ['nɒstrɪl] *n* narine *f*; (*of horse*) naseau *m*

nosy ['nəʊzɪ] (*inf*) *adj* curieux(euse)

not [nɒt] *adv* (ne ...) pas; **he is ~** *or* **isn't here** il n'est pas ici; **you must ~** *or* **you mustn't do that** tu ne dois pas faire ça; **it's too late, isn't it** *or* **is it ~?** c'est trop tard, n'est-ce pas?; **~ yet/now** pas encore/maintenant; see also **all**; **only**

notably ['nəʊtəblɪ] adv (particularly) en particulier; (markedly) spécialement

notary ['nəʊtərɪ] n notaire m

notch [nɒtʃ] n encoche f

note [nəʊt] n note f; (letter) mot m; (banknote) billet m ♦ vt (also: ~ **down**) noter; (observe) constater; **~book** n carnet m; **~d** ['nəʊtɪd] adj réputé(e); **~pad** n bloc-notes m; **~paper** n papier m à lettres

nothing ['nʌθɪŋ] n rien m; **he does** ~ il ne fait rien; ~ **new** rien de nouveau; **for** ~ pour rien

notice ['nəʊtɪs] n (announcement, warning) avis m; (period of time) délai m; (resignation) démission f; (dismissal) congé m ♦ vt remarquer, s'apercevoir de; **to take** ~ **of** prêter attention à; **to bring sth to sb's** ~ porter qch à la connaissance de qn; **at short** ~ dans un délai très court; **until further** ~ jusqu'à nouvel ordre; **to hand in one's** ~ donner sa démission, démissionner; **~able** adj visible; ~ **board** (BRIT) n panneau m d'affichage

notify ['nəʊtɪfaɪ] vt: **to** ~ **sth to sb** notifier qch à qn; **to** ~ **sb (of sth)** avertir qn (de qch)

notion ['nəʊʃən] n idée f; (concept) notion f

notorious [nəʊ'tɔ:rɪəs] adj notoire (souvent en mal)

notwithstanding [nɒtwɪθ'stændɪŋ] adv néanmoins ♦ prep en dépit de

nought [nɔ:t] n zéro m

noun [naʊn] n nom m

nourish ['nʌrɪʃ] vt nourrir; **~ing** adj nourrissant(e); **~ment** n nourriture f

novel ['nɒvəl] n roman m ♦ adj nouveau(nouvelle), original(e); **~ist** n romancier m; **~ty** n nouveauté f

November [nəʊ'vɛmbə*] n novembre m

now [naʊ] adv maintenant ♦ conj: ~ **(that)** maintenant que; **right** ~ tout de suite; **by** ~ à l'heure qu'il est; **just** ~: **that's the fashion just** ~ c'est la mode en ce moment; ~ **and then**, ~ **and again** de temps en temps; **from** ~ **on** dorénavant; **~adays** ['naʊədeɪz] adv de nos jours

nowhere ['nəʊwɛə*] adv nulle part

nozzle ['nɒzl] n (of hose etc) ajutage m; (of vacuum cleaner) suceur m

nuclear ['nju:klɪə*] adj nucléaire

nucleus ['nju:klɪəs, pl 'nju:klɪaɪ] (pl **nuclei**) n noyau m

nude [nju:d] adj nu(e) ♦ n nu m; **in the** ~ (tout(e)) nu(e)

nudge [nʌdʒ] vt donner un (petit) coup de coude à

nudist ['nju:dɪst] n nudiste m/f

nuisance ['nju:sns] n: **it's a** ~ c'est (très) embêtant; **he's a** ~ il est assommant or casse-pieds; **what a** ~! quelle barbe!

null [nʌl] adj: ~ **and void** nul(le) et non avenu(e)

numb [nʌm] adj engourdi(e); (with fear) paralysé(e)

number ['nʌmbə*] n nombre m; (numeral) chiffre m; (of house, bank account etc) numéro m ♦ vt numéroter; (amount to) compter; **a** ~ **of** un certain nombre de; **to be ~ed among** compter parmi; **they were seven in** ~ ils étaient (au nombre de) sept; ~ **plate** n (AUT) plaque f minéralogique or d'immatriculation

numeral ['nju:mərəl] n chiffre m

numerate ['nju:mərɪt] (BRIT) adj: **to be** ~ avoir des notions d'arithmétique

numerical [nju:'merɪkəl] adj numérique

numerous ['nju:mərəs] adj nombreux(euse)

nun [nʌn] n religieuse f, sœur f

nurse [nɜ:s] n infirmière f ♦ vt (patient, cold) soigner

nursery ['nɜ:sərɪ] n (room) nursery f; (institution) crèche f; (for plants) pépinière f; ~ **rhyme** n comptine f, chansonnette f pour enfants; ~ **school** n école maternelle; ~ **slope** n (SKI) piste f pour débutants

nursing ['nɜ:sɪŋ] n (profession) profession f d'infirmière; (care) soins mpl; ~ **home** n clinique f, maison f de convalescence; ~ **mother** n mère f qui allaite

nut [nʌt] n (of metal) écrou m; (fruit) noix f, noisette f, cacahuète f; **~crackers** ['nʌtkrækəz] npl casse-noix m inv, casse-noisette(s) m

nutmeg ['nʌtmeg] n (noix f) muscade f

nutritious [nju:'trɪʃəs] adj nutritif(ive), nourrissant(e)

nuts (inf) adj dingue

nutshell ['nʌtʃel] n: **in a** ~ en un mot

nylon ['naɪlɒn] n nylon m ♦ adj de or en nylon

O o

oak [əʊk] n chêne m ♦ adj de or en (bois de) chêne

OAP (BRIT) n abbr = **old age pensioner**

oar [ɔ:*] n aviron m, rame f

oasis [əʊ'eɪsɪs, pl əʊ'eɪsi:z] (pl **oases**) n oasis f

oath [əʊθ] n serment m; (swear word) juron m; **under** ~, (BRIT) **on** ~ sous serment

oatmeal ['əʊtmi:l] n flocons mpl d'avoine

oats [əʊts] n avoine f

obedience [ə'bi:dɪəns] n obéissance f; **ob-**

edient [ə'biːdɪənt] *adj* obéissant(e)
obey [ə'beɪ] *vt* obéir à; (*instructions*) se conformer à
obituary [ə'bɪtjʊərɪ] *n* nécrologie *f*
object [*n* 'ɒbdʒɪkt, *vb* əb'dʒekt] *n* objet *m*; (*purpose*) but *m*, objet; (*LING*) complément *m* d'objet ♦ *vi*: **to ~ to** (*attitude*) désapprouver; (*proposal*) protester contre; **expense is no ~** l'argent n'est pas un problème; **he ~ed that ...** il a fait valoir *or* a objecté que ...; **I ~!** je proteste!; **~ion** [əb'dʒekʃən] *n* objection *f*; **~ionable** [əb'dʒekʃnəbl] *adj* très désagréable; (*language*) choquant(e); **~ive** [əb'dʒektɪv] *n* objectif *m* ♦ *adj* objectif(ive)
obligation [ɒblɪ'ɡeɪʃən] *n* obligation *f*, devoir *m*; **without ~** sans engagement
oblige [ə'blaɪdʒ] *vt* (*force*): **to ~ sb to do** obliger *or* forcer qn à faire; (*do a favour*) rendre service à, obliger; **to be ~d to sb for sth** être obligé(e) à qn de qch; **obliging** [ə'blaɪdʒɪŋ] *adj* obligeant(e), serviable
oblique [ə'bliːk] *adj* oblique; (*allusion*) indirect(e)
obliterate [ə'blɪtəreɪt] *vt* effacer
oblivion [ə'blɪvɪən] *n* oubli *m*; **oblivious** [ə'blɪvɪəs] *adj*: **oblivious of** oublieux(euse) de
oblong ['ɒblɒŋ] *adj* oblong(ue) ♦ *n* rectangle *m*
obnoxious [əb'nɒkʃəs] *adj* odieux (euse); (*smell*) nauséabond(e)
oboe ['əʊbəʊ] *n* hautbois *m*
obscene [əb'siːn] *adj* obscène
obscure [əb'skjʊə*] *adj* obscur(e) ♦ *vt* obscurcir; (*hide: sun*) cacher
observant [əb'zɜːvənt] *adj* observateur(trice)
observation [ɒbzə'veɪʃən] *n* (*remark*) observation *f*; (*watching*) surveillance *f*; **observatory** [əb'zɜːvətrɪ] *n* observatoire *m*
observe [əb'zɜːv] *vt* observer; (*remark*) faire observer *or* remarquer; **~r** *n* observateur(trice)
obsess [əb'ses] *vt* obséder; **~ive** *adj* obsédant(e)
obsolescence [ɒbsə'lesns] *n* vieillissement *m*
obsolete ['ɒbsəliːt] *adj* dépassé(e); démodé(e)
obstacle ['ɒbstəkl] *n* obstacle *m*; **~ race** *n* course *f* d'obstacles
obstinate ['ɒbstɪnət] *adj* obstiné(e)
obstruct [əb'strʌkt] *vt* (*block*) boucher, obstruer; (*hinder*) entraver
obtain [əb'teɪn] *vt* obtenir; **~able** *adj* qu'on peut obtenir
obvious ['ɒbvɪəs] *adj* évident(e), manifeste; **~ly** *adv* manifestement; **~ly not!** bien sûr que non!
occasion [ə'keɪʒən] *n* occasion *f*; (*event*) événement *m*; **~al** *adj* pris(e) *or* fait(e) *etc*

de temps en temps; occasionnel(le); **~ally** *adv* de temps en temps, quelquefois
occupation [ɒkjʊ'peɪʃən] *n* occupation *f*; (*job*) métier *m*, profession *f*; **~al hazard** *n* risque *m* du métier
occupier ['ɒkjʊpaɪə*] *n* occupant(e)
occupy ['ɒkjʊpaɪ] *vt* occuper; **to ~ o.s. in** *or* **with doing** s'occuper à faire
occur [ə'kɜː*] *vi* (*event*) se produire; (*phenomenon, error*) se rencontrer; **to ~ to sb** venir à l'esprit de qn; **~rence** *n* (*existence*) présence *f*, existence *f*; (*event*) cas *m*, fait *m*
ocean ['əʊʃən] *n* océan *m*; **~-going** *adj* de haute mer
o'clock [ə'klɒk] *adv*: **it is 5 ~** il est 5 heures
OCR *n abbr* = optical character reader; optical character recognition
October [ɒk'təʊbə*] *n* octobre *m*
octopus ['ɒktəpəs] *n* pieuvre *f*
odd [ɒd] *adj* (*strange*) bizarre, curieux(euse); (*number*) impair(e); (*not of a set*) dépareillé(e); **60-odd** 60 et quelques; **at ~ times** de temps en temps; **the ~ one out** l'exception *f*; **~ity** *n* (*person*) excentrique *m/f*; (*thing*) curiosité *f*; **~-job man** *n* homme *m* à tout faire; **~ jobs** *npl* petits travaux divers; **~ly** *adv* bizarrement, curieusement; **~ments** *npl* (*COMM*) fins *fpl* de série; **~s** *npl* (*in betting*) cote *f*; **it makes no ~s** cela n'a pas d'importance; **at ~s** en désaccord; **~s and ends** de petites choses
odour ['əʊdə*] (*US* **odor**) *n* odeur *f*

――――――――― *KEYWORD*

of [ɒv, əv] *prep* **1** (*gen*) de; **a friend ~ ours** un de nos amis; **a boy ~ 10** un garçon de 10 ans; **that was kind ~ you** c'était gentil de votre part
2 (*expressing quantity, amount, dates etc*) de; **a kilo ~ flour** un kilo de farine; **how much ~ this do you need?** combien vous en faut-il?; **there were 3 ~ them** (*people*) ils étaient 3; (*objects*) il y en avait 3; **3 ~ us went** 3 d'entre nous y sont allé(e)s; **the 5th ~ July** le 5 juillet
3 (*from, out of*) en, de; **a statue ~ marble** une statue de *or* en marbre; **made ~ wood** (fait) en bois

off [ɒf] *adj, adv* (*engine*) coupé(e); (*tap*) fermé(e); (*BRIT: food: bad*) mauvais(e); (: *milk*) tourné(e); (*absent*) absent(e); (*cancelled*) annulé(e) ♦ *prep* de; sur; **to be ~** (*to leave*) partir, s'en aller; **to be ~ sick** être absent pour cause de maladie; **a day ~** un jour de congé; **to have an ~ day** n'être pas en forme; **he had his coat ~** il avait enlevé son manteau; **10% ~** (*COMM*) 10% de rabais; **~ the coast** au large de la côte; **I'm ~ meat** je ne mange plus de viande, je n'aime plus la viande; **on the ~ chance** à tout hasard

offal ['ɒfəl] *n* (*CULIN*) abats *mpl*

off-colour ['ɒf'kʌləʳ] (*US* **off-color**) (*BRIT*) *adj* (*ill*) malade, mal fichu(e)

offence [ə'fɛns] (*US* **offense**) *n* (*crime*) délit *m*, infraction *f*; **to take ~ at** se vexer de, s'offenser de

offend [ə'fɛnd] *vt* (*person*) offenser, blesser; **~er** *n* délinquant(e)

offense [ə'fɛns] (*US*) *n* = **offence**

offensive [ə'fɛnsɪv] *adj* offensant(e), choquant(e); (*smell etc*) très déplaisant(e); (*weapon*) offensif(ive) ♦ *n* (*MIL*) offensive *f*

offer ['ɒfəʳ] *n* offre *f*, proposition *f* ♦ *vt* offrir, proposer; **"on ~"** (*COMM*) "en promotion"; **~ing** *n* offrande *f*

offhand ['ɒf'hænd] *adj* désinvolte ♦ *adv* spontanément

office ['ɒfɪs] *n* (*place, room*) bureau *m*; (*position*) charge *f*, fonction *f*; **doctor's ~** (*US*) cabinet (médical); **to take ~** entrer en fonctions; **~ automation** *n* bureautique *f*; **~ block** (*US* **~ building**) *n* immeuble *m* de bureaux; **~ hours** *npl* heures *fpl* de bureau; (*US*: *MED*) heures de consultation

officer ['ɒfɪsəʳ] *n* (*MIL etc*) officier *m*; (*also*: *police ~*) agent *m* (de police); (*of organization*) membre *m* du bureau directeur

office worker *n* employé(e) de bureau

official [ə'fɪʃəl] *adj* officiel(le) ♦ *n* officiel *m*; (*civil servant*) fonctionnaire *m/f*; employé(e); **~dom** *n* administration *f*, bureaucratie *f*

officiate [ə'fɪʃɪeɪt] *vi* (*REL*) officier; **to ~ at a marriage** célébrer un mariage

officious [ə'fɪʃəs] *adj* trop empressé(e)

offing ['ɒfɪŋ] *n*: **in the ~** (*fig*) en perspective

off: **~-licence** (*BRIT*) *n* (*shop*) débit *m* de vins et de spiritueux; **~-line** *adj*, *adv* (*COMPUT*) (en mode) autonome; (: *switched off*) non connecté(e); **~-peak** *adj* aux heures creuses; (*electricity, heating, ticket*) au tarif heures creuses; **~-putting** (*BRIT*) *adj* (*remark*) rébarbatif(ive); (*person*) rebutant(e), peu engageant(e); **~-season** *adj, adv* hors-saison *inv*

offset ['ɒfsɛt] (*irreg*) *vt* (*counteract*) contrebalancer, compenser

offshoot ['ɒfʃuːt] *n* (*fig*) ramification *f*, antenne *f*

offshore ['ɒf'ʃɔːʳ] *adj* (*breeze*) de terre; (*fishing*) côtier(ère)

offside ['ɒf'saɪd] *adj* (*SPORT*) hors jeu; (*AUT*: *with right-hand drive*) de droite; (: *with left-hand drive*) de gauche

offspring ['ɒfsprɪŋ] *n inv* progéniture *f*

off: **~stage** *adv* dans les coulisses; **~-the-peg** (*US* **~-the-rack**) *adv* en prêt-à-porter; **~-white** *adj* blanc cassé *inv*

often ['ɒfən] *adv* souvent; **how ~ do you go?** vous y allez tous les combien?; **how ~ have you gone there?** vous y êtes allé combien de fois?

ogle ['əʊgl] *vt* lorgner

oh [əʊ] *excl* ô!, oh!, ah!

oil [ɔɪl] *n* huile *f*; (*petroleum*) pétrole *m*; (*for central heating*) mazout *m* ♦ *vt* (*machine*) graisser; **~can** *n* burette *f* de graissage; (*for storing*) bidon *m* à huile; **~field** *n* gisement *m* de pétrole; **~ filter** *n* (*AUT*) filtre *m* à huile; **~ painting** *n* peinture *f* à l'huile; **~ refinery** *n* raffinerie *f*; **~ rig** *n* derrick *m*; (*at sea*) plate-forme pétrolière; **~skins** *npl* ciré *m*; **~ tanker** *n* (*ship*) pétrolier *m*; (*truck*) camion-citerne *m*; **~ well** *n* puits *m* de pétrole; **~y** *adj* huileux(euse); (*food*) gras(se)

ointment ['ɔɪntmənt] *n* onguent *m*

O.K., okay ['əʊ'keɪ] *excl* d'accord! ♦ *adj* (*average*) pas mal ♦ *vt* approuver, donner son accord à; **is it ~?, are you ~?** ça va?

old [əʊld] *adj* vieux(vieille); (*person*) vieux, âgé(e); (*former*) ancien(ne), vieux; **how ~ are you?** quel âge avez-vous?; **he's 10 years ~** il a 10 ans, il est âgé de 10 ans; **~er brother/sister** frère/sœur aîné(e); **~ age** *n* vieillesse *f*; **~ age pensioner** (*BRIT*) *n* retraité(e); **~-fashioned** *adj* démodé(e); (*person*) vieux jeu *inv*

olive ['ɒlɪv] *n* (*fruit*) olive *f*; (*tree*) olivier *m* ♦ *adj* (*also*: *~-green*) (vert) olive *inv*; **~ oil** *n* huile *f* d'olive

Olympic [əʊ'lɪmpɪk] *adj* olympique; **the ~ Games, the ~s** les Jeux *mpl* olympiques

omelet(te) ['ɒmlɪt] *n* omelette *f*

omen ['əʊmən] *n* présage *m*

ominous ['ɒmɪnəs] *adj* menaçant(e), inquiétant(e); (*event*) de mauvais augure

omit [əʊ'mɪt] *vt* omettre; **to ~ to do** omettre de faire

KEYWORD

on [ɒn] *prep* **1** (*indicating position*) sur; **~ the table** sur la table; **~ the wall** sur le *or* au mur; **~ the left** à gauche

2 (*indicating means, method, condition etc*): **~ foot** à pied; **~ the train/plane** (*be*) dans le train/l'avion; (*go*) en train/avion; **~ the telephone/radio/television** au téléphone/à la radio/à la télévision; **to be ~ drugs** se droguer; **~ holiday** en vacances

3 (*referring to time*): **~ Friday** vendredi; **~ Fridays** le vendredi; **~ June 20th** le 20 juin; **a week ~ Friday** vendredi en huit; **~ arrival** à l'arrivée; **~ seeing this** en voyant cela

4 (*about, concerning*) sur, de; **a book ~ Balzac/physics** un livre sur Balzac/de physique

♦ *adv* **1** (*referring to dress, covering*): **to have one's coat ~** avoir (mis) son manteau; **to put one's coat ~** mettre son manteau; **what's she got ~?** qu'est-ce qu'elle

porte?; **screw the lid ~ tightly** vissez bien le couvercle
2 (*further, continuously*): **to walk** *etc* ~ continuer à marcher *etc*; ~ **and off** de temps à autre
♦ *adj* **1** (*in operation: machine*) en marche; (: *radio, TV, light*) allumé(e); (: *tap, gas*) ouvert(e); (: *brakes*) mis(e); **is the meeting still ~?** (*not cancelled*) est-ce que la réunion a bien lieu?; (*in progress*) la réunion dure-t-elle encore?; **when is this film ~?** quand passe ce film?
2 (*inf*): **that's not ~!** (*not acceptable*) cela ne se fait pas!; (*not possible*) pas question!

once [wʌns] *adv* une fois; (*formerly*) autrefois ♦ *conj* une fois que; ~ **he had left/it was done** une fois qu'il fut parti/que ce fut terminé; **at** ~ tout de suite, immédiatement; (*simultaneously*) à la fois; ~ **a week** une fois par semaine; ~ **more** encore une fois; ~ **and for all** une fois pour toutes; ~ **upon a time** il y avait une fois, il était une fois

oncoming [ˈɒnkʌmɪŋ] *adj* (*traffic*) venant en sens inverse

───────────── *KEYWORD*

one [wʌn] *num* un(e); ~ **hundred and fifty** cent cinquante; ~ **day** un jour
♦ *adj* **1** (*sole*) seul(e), unique; **the ~ book which** l'unique *or* le seul livre qui; **the ~ man who** le seul (homme) qui
2 (*same*) même; **they came in the ~ car** ils sont venus dans la même voiture
♦ *pron* **1**: **this** ~ celui-ci(celle-ci); **that** ~ celui-là(celle-là); **I've already got ~/a red** ~ j'en ai déjà un(e)/un(e) rouge; ~ **by** ~ un(e) à *or* par une(e)
2: ~ **another** l'un(e) l'autre; **to look at** ~ **another** se regarder
3 (*impersonal*) on; ~ **never knows** on ne sait jamais; **to cut ~'s finger** se couper le doigt

one: ~-**day excursion** (*US*) *n* billet *m* d'aller-retour (valable pour la journée); ~-**man** *adj* (*business*) dirigé(e) *etc* par un seul homme; ~-**man band** *n* homme-orchestre *m*; ~-**off** (*BRIT: inf*) *n* exemplaire *m* unique
oneself [wʌnˈself] *pron* (*reflexive*) se; (*after prep*) soi(-même); (*emphatic*) soi-même; **to hurt** ~ se faire mal; **to keep sth for** ~ garder qch pour soi; **to talk to** ~ se parler à soi-même
one: ~-**sided** *adj* (*argument*) unilatéral; ~-**to**-~ *adj* (*relationship*) univoque; ~-**upmanship** *n*: **the art of** ~-**upmanship** l'art de faire mieux que les autres; ~-**way** *adj* (*street, traffic*) à sens unique
ongoing [ˈɒngəʊɪŋ] *adj* en cours; (*relationship*) suivi(e)

onion [ˈʌnjən] *n* oignon *m*
on-line [ˈɒnˈlaɪn] *adj, adv* (*COMPUT*) en ligne; (: *switched on*) connecté(e)
onlooker [ˈɒnlʊkə*] *n* spectateur(trice)
only [ˈəʊnlɪ] *adv* seulement ♦ *adj* seul(e), unique ♦ *conj* seulement, mais; **an** ~ **child** un enfant unique; **not** ~ ... **but also** non seulement ... mais aussi
onset [ˈɒnset] *n* début *m*; (*of winter, old age*) approche *f*
onshore [ˈɒnʃɔ:*] *adj* (*wind*) du large
onslaught [ˈɒnslɔ:t] *n* attaque *f*, assaut *m*
onto [ˈɒntu] *prep* = **on to**
onus [ˈəʊnəs] *n* responsabilité *f*
onward(s) [ˈɒnwəd(z)] *adv* (*move*) en avant; **from that time** ~ à partir de ce moment
ooze [u:z] *vi* suinter
opaque [əʊˈpeɪk] *adj* opaque
OPEC [ˈəʊpek] *n abbr* (= *Organization of Petroleum Exporting Countries*) O.P.E.P. *f*
open [ˈəʊpən] *adj* ouvert(e); (*car*) découvert(e); (*road, view*) dégagé(e); (*meeting*) public(ique); (*admiration*) manifeste ♦ *vt* ouvrir ♦ *vi* (*flower, eyes, door, debate*) s'ouvrir; (*shop, bank, museum*) ouvrir; (*book etc: commence*) commencer, débuter; **in the** ~ (**air**) en plein air; ~ **on to** *vt fus* (*subj: room, door*) donner sur; ~ **up** *vt* ouvrir; (*blocked road*) dégager ♦ *vi* s'ouvrir; ~**ing** *n* ouverture *f*; (*opportunity*) occasion *f* ♦ *adj* (*remarks*) préliminaire; ~**ly** *adv* ouvertement; ~-**minded** *adj* à l'esprit ouvert; ~-**necked** *adj* à col ouvert; ~-**plan** *adj* sans cloisons
opera [ˈɒpərə] *n* opéra *m*; ~ **singer** *n* chanteur(euse) d'opéra
operate [ˈɒpəreɪt] *vt* (*machine*) faire marcher, faire fonctionner ♦ *vi* fonctionner; (*MED*): **to** ~ (**on sb**) opérer (qn)
operatic [ɒpəˈrætɪk] *adj* d'opéra
operating: ~-**table** *n* table *f* d'opération; ~ **theatre** *n* salle *f* d'opération
operation [ɒpəˈreɪʃən] *n* opération *f*; (*of machine*) fonctionnement *m*; **to be in** ~ (*system, law*) être en vigueur; **to have an** ~ (*MED*) se faire opérer
operative [ˈɒpərətɪv] *adj* (*measure*) en vigueur
operator [ˈɒpəreɪtə*] *n* (*of machine*) opérateur(trice); (*TEL*) téléphoniste *m/f*
opinion [əˈpɪnjən] *n* opinion *f*, avis *m*; **in my** ~ à mon avis; ~**ated** *adj* aux idées bien arrêtées; ~ **poll** *n* sondage *m* (d'opinion)
opponent [əˈpəʊnənt] *n* adversaire *m/f*
opportunity [ɒpəˈtju:nɪtɪ] *n* occasion *f*; **to take the** ~ **of doing** profiter de l'occasion pour faire; en profiter pour faire
oppose [əˈpəʊz] *vt* s'opposer à; ~**d to** opposé(e) à; **as** ~**d to** par opposition à; **opposing** [əˈpəʊzɪŋ] *adj* (*side*) opposé(e)

opposite ['ɒpəzɪt] adj opposé(e); (house etc) d'en face ♦ adv en face ♦ prep en face de ♦ n opposé m, contraire m; **the ~ sex** l'autre sexe, le sexe opposé

opposition [ɒpə'zɪʃən] n opposition f

oppress [ə'pres] vt opprimer

oppressive adj (political regime) oppressif(ive); (weather) lourd(e); (heat) accablant(e)

opt [ɒpt] vi: **to ~ for** opter pour; **to ~ to do** choisir de faire; **~ out** vi: **to ~ out of** choisir de ne pas participer à or de ne pas faire

optical ['ɒptɪkəl] adj optique; (instrument) d'optique; **~ character recognition/reader** n lecture f/lecteur m optique

optician [ɒp'tɪʃən] n opticien(ne)

optimist ['ɒptɪmɪst] n optimiste m/f; **~ic** adj optimiste

option ['ɒpʃən] n choix m, option f; (SCOL) matière f à option; (COMM) option; **~al** adj facultatif(ive); (COMM) en option

or [ɔː*] conj ou; (with negative): **he hasn't seen ~ heard anything** il n'a rien vu ni entendu; **~ else** sinon; ou bien

oral ['ɔːrəl] adj oral(e) ♦ n oral m

orange ['ɒrɪndʒ] n (fruit) orange f ♦ adj orange inv

orator ['ɒrətə*] n orateur(trice)

orbit ['ɔːbɪt] n orbite f ♦ vt graviter autour de

orchard ['ɔːtʃəd] n verger m

orchestra ['ɔːkɪstrə] n orchestre m; (US: seating) (fauteuils mpl d')orchestre

orchid ['ɔːkɪd] n orchidée f

ordain [ɔː'deɪn] vt (REL) ordonner

ordeal [ɔː'diːl] n épreuve f

order ['ɔːdə*] n ordre m; (COMM) commande f ♦ vt ordonner; (COMM) commander; **in ~** en ordre; (document) en règle; **in (working) ~** en état de marche; **out of ~** (not in correct order) en désordre; (not working) en dérangement; **in ~ to do/that** pour faire/que +sub; **on ~** (COMM) en commande; **to ~ sb to do** ordonner à qn de faire; **~ form** n bon m de commande; **~ly** n (MIL) ordonnance f; (MED) garçon m de salle ♦ adj (room) en ordre; (person) qui a de l'ordre

ordinary ['ɔːdnrɪ] adj ordinaire, normal(e); (pej) ordinaire, quelconque; **out of the ~** exceptionnel(le)

Ordnance Survey map n ≈ carte f d'Etat-Major

ore [ɔː*] n minerai m

organ ['ɔːgən] n organe m; (MUS) orgue m, orgues fpl; **~ic** [ɔː'gænɪk] adj organique

organization [ɔːgənaɪ'zeɪʃən] n organisation f

organize ['ɔːgənaɪz] vt organiser; **~r** n organisateur(trice)

orgasm ['ɔːgæzəm] n orgasme m

Orient ['ɔːrɪənt] n: **the ~** l'Orient m; **o~al** [ɔːrɪ'entəl] adj oriental(e)

origin ['ɒrɪdʒɪn] n origine f

original [ə'rɪdʒɪnl] adj original(e); (earliest) originel(le) ♦ n original m; **~ly** adv (at first) à l'origine

originate [ə'rɪdʒɪneɪt] vi: **to ~ from** (person) être originaire de; (suggestion) provenir de; **to ~ in** prendre naissance dans; avoir son origine dans

Orkneys ['ɔːknɪz] npl: **the ~** (also: the Orkney Islands) les Orcades fpl

ornament ['ɔːnəmənt] n ornement m; (trinket) bibelot m; **~al** [ɔːnə'mentl] adj décoratif(ive); (garden) d'agrément

ornate [ɔː'neɪt] adj très orné(e)

orphan ['ɔːfn] n orphelin(e); **~age** n orphelinat m

orthopaedic [ɔːθəʊ'piːdɪk] (US orthopedic) adj orthopédique

ostensibly [ɒs'tensəblɪ] adv en apparence

ostentatious [ɒsten'teɪʃəs] adj prétentieux(euse)

ostracize ['ɒstrəsaɪz] vt frapper d'ostracisme

ostrich ['ɒstrɪtʃ] n autruche f

other ['ʌðə*] adj autre ♦ pron: **the ~ (one)** l'autre; **~s** (= people) d'autres; **~ than** autrement que; à part; **~wise** adv, conj autrement

otter ['ɒtə*] n loutre f

ouch [aʊtʃ] excl aïe!

ought [ɔːt] (pt ought) aux vb: **I ~ to do it** je devrais le faire, il faudrait que je le fasse; **this ~ to have been corrected** cela aurait dû être corrigé; **he ~ to win** il devrait gagner

ounce [aʊns] n once f (= 28.35g; 16 in a pound)

our [aʊə*] adj notre, nos pl; see also **my**; **~s** pron le(la) nôtre, les nôtres; see also **mine**[1]; **~selves** pron pl (reflexive, after preposition) nous; (emphatic) nous-mêmes; see also **oneself**

oust [aʊst] vt évincer

out [aʊt] adv dehors; (published, not at home etc) sorti(e); (light, fire) éteint(e); **~ here** ici; **~ there** là-bas; **he's ~** (absent) il est sorti; (unconscious) il est sans connaissance; **to be ~ in one's calculations** s'être trompé dans ses calculs; **to run/back etc ~** sortir en courant/en reculant etc; **~ loud** à haute voix; **~ of** (outside) en dehors de; (because of: anger etc) par; (from among): **~ of 10** sur 10; **~ of** (without): **~ of petrol** sans essence, à court d'essence; **~ of order** (machine) en panne; (TEL: line) en dérangement; **~-and-out** adj (liar, thief etc) véritable

outback ['aʊtbæk] n (in Australia): **the ~** l'intérieur m

outboard ['aʊtbɔːd] n (also: ~ motor) (mo-

teur *m*) hors-bord *m*;
out: ~**break** ['autbreɪk] *n* (*of war, disease*) début *m*; (*of violence*) éruption *f*; ~**burst** ['autbɜːst] *n* explosion *f*, accès *m*; ~**cast** ['autkɑːst] *n* exilé(e); (*socially*) paria *m*; ~**come** ['autkʌm] *n* issue *f*, résultat *m*; ~**crop** ['autkrɒp] *n* (*of rock*) affleurement *m*; ~**cry** ['autkraɪ] *n* tollé (général); ~**dated** [aut'deɪtɪd] *adj* démodé(e); ~**do** [aut'duː] (*irreg*) *vt* surpasser

outdoor ['autdɔː*] *adj* de *or* en plein air; ~**s** *adv* dehors; au grand air

outer ['autə*] *adj* extérieur(e); ~ **space** *n* espace *m* cosmique

outfit ['autfɪt] *n* (*clothes*) tenue *f*

outgoing ['autgəuɪŋ] *adj* (*character*) ouvert(e), extraverti(e); (*retiring*) sortant(e); ~**s** (*BRIT*) *npl* (*expenses*) dépenses *fpl*

outgrow [aut'grəu] (*irreg*) *vt* (*clothes*) devenir trop grand(e) pour

outhouse ['authaus] *n* appentis *m*, remise *f*

outing ['autɪŋ] *n* sortie *f*, excursion *f*

outlandish [aut'lændɪʃ] *adj* étrange

outlaw ['autlɔː] *n* hors-la-loi *m inv* ♦ *vt* mettre hors-la-loi

outlay ['autleɪ] *n* dépenses *fpl*; (*investment*) mise *f* de fonds

outlet ['autlet] *n* (*for liquid etc*) issue *f*, sortie *f*; (*US: ELEC*) prise *f* de courant; (*also: retail* ~) point *m* de vente

outline ['autlaɪn] *n* (*shape*) contour *m*; (*summary*) esquisse *f*, grandes lignes ♦ *vt* (*fig: theory, plan*) exposer à grands traits

out: ~**live** [aut'lɪv] *vt* survivre à; ~**look** ['autluk] *n* perspective *f*; ~**lying** ['autlaɪɪŋ] *adj* écarté(e); ~**moded** [aut'məudɪd] *adj* démodé(e); dépassé(e); ~**number** [aut'nʌmbə*] *vt* surpasser en nombre

out-of-date [autəv'deɪt] *adj* (*passport*) périmé(e); (*theory etc*) dépassé(e); (*clothes etc*) démodé(e)

out-of-the-way [autəvðə'weɪ] *adj* (*place*) loin de tout

outpatient ['autpeɪʃənt] *n* malade *m/f* en consultation externe

outpost ['autpəust] *n* avant-poste *m*

output ['autput] *n* rendement *m*, production *f*; (*COMPUT*) sortie *f*

outrage ['autreɪdʒ] *n* (*anger*) indignation *f*; (*violent act*) atrocité *f*; (*scandal*) scandale *m* ♦ *vt* outrager; ~**ous** [aut'reɪdʒəs] *adj* atroce; scandaleux(euse)

outright [*adv* 'autraɪt, *adj* aut'raɪt] *adv* complètement; (*deny, refuse*) catégoriquement; (*ask*) carrément; (*kill*) sur le coup ♦ *adj* complet(ète); catégorique

outset ['autset] *n* début *m*

outside [aut'saɪd] *n* extérieur *m* ♦ *adj* extérieur(e) ♦ *adv* (au) dehors, à l'extérieur ♦ *prep* hors de, à l'extérieur de; **at the** ~ (*fig*) au plus *or* maximum; ~ **lane** *n* (*AUT: in Britain*) voie *f* de droite; (*: in US, Europe*)

voie de gauche; ~ **line** *n* (*TEL*) ligne extérieure; ~**r** *n* (*stranger*) étranger(ère)

out: ~**size** ['autsaɪz] *adj* énorme; (*clothes*) grande taille *inv*; ~**skirts** ['autskɜːts] *npl* faubourgs *mpl*; ~**spoken** [aut'spəukən] *adj* très franc(franche)

outstanding [aut'stændɪŋ] *adj* remarquable, exceptionnel(le); (*unfinished*) en suspens; (*debt*) impayé(e); (*problem*) non réglé(e)

outstay [aut'steɪ] *vt*: **to** ~ **one's welcome** abuser de l'hospitalité de son hôte

out: ~**stretched** ['autstretʃt] *adj* (*hand*) tendu(e); ~**strip** [aut'strɪp] *vt* (*competitors, demand*) dépasser; ~ **tray** *n* courrier *m* "départ"

outward ['autwəd] *adj* (*sign, appearances*) extérieur(e); (*journey*) (d')aller; ~**ly** *adv* extérieurement; en apparence

outweigh [aut'weɪ] *vt* l'emporter sur

outwit [aut'wɪt] *vt* se montrer plus malin que

oval ['əuvəl] *adj* ovale ♦ *n* ovale *m*

ovary ['əuvərɪ] *n* ovaire *m*

oven ['ʌvn] *n* four *m*; ~**proof** *adj* allant au four

over ['əuvə*] *adv* (par-)dessus ♦ *adj* (*finished*) fini(e), terminé(e); (*too much*) en plus ♦ *prep* sur; par-dessus; (*above*) au-dessus de; (*on the other side of*) de l'autre côté de; (*more than*) plus de; (*during*) pendant; ~ **here** ici; ~ **there** là-bas; **all** ~ (*everywhere*) partout; (*finished*) fini(e); ~ **and** ~ (**again**) à plusieurs reprises; ~ **and above** en plus de; **to ask sb** ~ inviter qn (à passer)

overall [*adj, n* 'əuvərɔːl, *adv* əuvər'ɔːl] *adj* (*length, cost etc*) total(e); (*study*) d'ensemble ♦ *n* (*BRIT*) blouse *f* ♦ *adv* dans l'ensemble, en général; ~**s** *npl* bleus *mpl* (de travail)

overawe [əuvər'ɔː] *vt* impressionner

over: ~**balance** [əuvə'bæləns] *vi* basculer; ~**bearing** [əuvə'bɛərɪŋ] *adj* impérieux(euse), autoritaire; ~**board** ['əuvəbɔːd] *adv* (*NAUT*) par-dessus bord; ~**book** [əuvə'buk] *vt* faire du surbooking; ~**cast** ['əuvəkɑːst] *adj* couvert(e)

overcharge ['əuvə'tʃɑːdʒ] *vt*: **to** ~ **sb for sth** faire payer qch trop cher à qn

overcoat ['əuvəkəut] *n* pardessus *m*

overcome [əuvə'kʌm] (*irreg*) *vt* (*defeat*) triompher de; (*difficulty*) surmonter

overcrowded [əuvə'kraudɪd] *adj* bondé(e)

overdo [əuvə'duː] (*irreg*) *vt* exagérer; (*overcook*) trop cuire; **to** ~ **it** (*work etc*) se surmener

overdose ['əuvədəus] *n* dose excessive

overdraft ['əuvədrɑːft] *n* découvert *m*; **overdrawn** ['əuvə'drɔːn] *adj* (*account*) à découvert; (*person*) dont le compte est à découvert

overdue ['əuvə'djuː] *adj* en retard; (*change,*

reform) qui tarde

overestimate [əuvər'ɛstɪmeɪt] *vt* surestimer

overexcited [əuvərɪk'saɪtɪd] *adj* surexcité(e)

overflow [*vb* əuvə'fləu, *n* 'əuvəfləu] *vi* déborder ♦ *n* (*also:* ~ *pipe*) tuyau *m* d'écoulement, trop-plein *m*

overgrown ['əuvə'grəun] *adj* (*garden*) envahi(e) par la végétation

overhaul [*vb* əuvə'hɔːl, *n* 'əuvəhɔːl] *vt* réviser ♦ *n* révision *f*

overhead [*adv* əuvə'hed, *adj*, *n* 'əuvəhed] *adv* au-dessus ♦ *adj* aérien(ne); (*lighting*) vertical(e) ♦ ~**s** *npl*, (*US*) *n* frais généraux

overhear [əuvə'hɪə*] (*irreg*) *vt* entendre (par hasard)

overheat [əuvə'hiːt] *vi* (*engine*) chauffer

overjoyed [əuvə'dʒɔɪd] *adj:* ~ **(at)** ravi(e) (de), enchanté(e) (de)

overkill ['əuvəkɪl] *n:* **that would be** ~ ce serait trop

overland *adj*, *adv* par voie de terre

overlap [*vb* əuvə'læp, *n* 'əuvəlæp] *vi* se chevaucher

overleaf [əuvə'liːf] *adv* au verso

overload [əuvə'ləud] *vt* surcharger

overlook [əuvə'luk] *vt* (*have view of*) donner sur; (*miss: by mistake*) oublier; (*forgive*) fermer les yeux sur

overnight [*adv* 'əuvə'naɪt, *adj* 'əuvənaɪt] *adv* (*happen*) durant la nuit; (*fig*) soudain ♦ *adj* d'une (*or* de) nuit; **he stayed there** ~ il y a passé la nuit

overpass *n* pont autoroutier

overpower [əuvə'pauə*] *vt* vaincre; (*fig*) accabler; ~**ing** *adj* (*heat, stench*) suffocant(e)

overrate ['əuvə'reɪt] *vt* surestimer

override [əuvə'raɪd] (*irreg: like* ride) *vt* (*order, objection*) passer outre à; **overriding** [əuvə'raɪdɪŋ] *adj* prépondérant(e)

overrule [əuvə'ruːl] *vt* (*decision*) annuler; (*claim*) rejeter; (*person*) rejeter l'avis de

overrun [əuvə'rʌn] (*irreg: like* run) *vt* (*country*) occuper; (*time limit*) dépasser

overseas ['əuvə'siːz] *adv* outre-mer; (*abroad*) à l'étranger ♦ *adj* (*trade*) extérieur(e); (*visitor*) étranger(ère)

overshadow [əuvə'ʃædəu] *vt* (*fig*) éclipser

oversight ['əuvəsaɪt] *n* omission *f*, oubli *m*

oversleep ['əuvə'sliːp] (*irreg*) *vi* se réveiller (trop) tard

overstate *vt* exagérer

overstep [əuvə'step] *vt:* **to** ~ **the mark** dépasser la mesure

overt [əu'vəːt] *adj* non dissimulé(e)

overtake [əuvə'teɪk] (*irreg*) *vt* (*AUT*) dépasser, doubler

overthrow [əuvə'θrəu] (*irreg*) *vt* (*government*) renverser

overtime ['əuvətaɪm] *n* heures *fpl* supplémentaires

overtone ['əuvətəun] *n* (*also:* ~**s**) note *f*, sous-entendus *mpl*

overture ['əuvətʃuə*] *n* (*MUS, fig*) ouverture *f*

overturn [əuvə'təːn] *vt* renverser ♦ *vi* se retourner

overweight ['əuvə'weɪt] *adj* (*person*) trop gros(se)

overwhelm [əuvə'welm] *vt* (*subj: emotion*) accabler; (*enemy, opponent*) écraser; ~**ing** *adj* (*victory, defeat*) écrasant(e); (*desire*) irrésistible

overwork ['əuvə'wəːk] *n* surmenage *m*

overwrought ['əuvə'rɔːt] *adj* excédé(e)

owe [əu] *vt:* **to** ~ **sb sth**, **to** ~ **sth to sb** devoir qch à qn; **owing to** ['əuɪŋ-] *prep* à cause de, en raison de

owl [aul] *n* hibou *m*

own [əun] *vt* posséder ♦ *adj* propre; **a room of my** ~ une chambre à moi, ma propre chambre; **to get one's** ~ **back** prendre sa revanche; **on one's** ~ tout(e) seul(e); ~ **up** *vi* avouer; ~**er** *n* propriétaire *m/f*; ~**ership** *n* possession *f*

ox [ɒks] (*pl* **oxen**) *n* bœuf *m*

oxtail ['ɒksteɪl] *n:* ~ **soup** soupe *f* à la queue de bœuf

oxygen ['ɒksɪdʒən] *n* oxygène *m*; ~ **mask** *n* masque *m* à oxygène

oyster ['ɔɪstə*] *n* huître *f*

oz. *abbr* = **ounce(s)**

ozone hole *n* trou *m* d'ozone

ozone layer *n* couche *f* d'ozone

P p

p [piː] *abbr* = **penny; pence**

PA *n abbr* = **personal assistant; public address system**

pa [pɑː] (*inf*) *n* papa *m*

p.a. *abbr* = **per annum**

pace [peɪs] *n* pas *m*; (*speed*) allure *f*; vitesse *f* ♦ *vi:* **to** ~ **up and down** faire les cent pas; **to keep** ~ **with** aller à la même vitesse que; ~**maker** *n* (*MED*) stimulateur *m* cardiaque; (*SPORT: also:* **pacesetter**) meneur(euse) de train

Pacific *n:* **the** ~ **(Ocean)** le Pacifique, l'océan *m* Pacifique

pack [pæk] *n* (*packet; US: of cigarettes*) paquet *m*; (*of hounds*) meute *f*; (*of thieves etc*) bande *f*; (*back pack*) sac *m* à dos; (*of cards*) jeu *m* ♦ *vt* (*goods*) empaqueter, emballer; (*box*) remplir; (*cram*) entasser; **to** ~ **one's**

suitcase faire sa valise; **to ~ (one's bags)** faire ses bagages; **to ~ sb off** to expédier qn à; **~ it in!** laisse tomber!, écrase!

package ['pækɪdʒ] n paquet m; (also: ~ **deal**) forfait m; **~ tour** (BRIT) n voyage organisé

packed lunch ['pækt-] (BRIT) n repas froid

packet ['pækɪt] n paquet m

packing ['pækɪŋ] n emballage m; **~ case** n caisse f (d'emballage)

pact [pækt] n pacte m; traité m

pad [pæd] n bloc(-notes) m; (to prevent friction) tampon m; (inf: home) piaule f ♦ vt rembourrer; **~ding** n rembourrage m

paddle ['pædl] n (oar) pagaie f; (US: for table tennis) raquette f de ping-pong ♦ vt: **to ~ a canoe** etc pagayer ♦ vi barboter, faire trempette; **~ steamer** n bateau m à aubes; **paddling pool** (BRIT) n petit bassin

paddock ['pædək] n enclos m; (RACING) paddock m

paddy field ['pædɪ-] n rizière f

padlock ['pædlɒk] n cadenas m

paediatrics [piːdɪ'ætrɪks] (US **pediatrics**) n pédiatrie f

pagan ['peɪgən] adj, n païen(ne)

page [peɪdʒ] n (of book) page f; (also: ~ **boy**) groom m, chasseur m; (at wedding) garçon m d'honneur ♦ vt (in hotel etc) (faire) appeler

pageant ['pædʒənt] n spectacle m historique; **~ry** n apparat m, pompe f

pager, paging device n (TEL) récepteur m d'appels

paid [peɪd] pt, pp of **pay** ♦ adj (work, official) rémunéré(e); (holiday) payé(e); **to put ~ to** (BRIT) mettre fin à, régler; **~ gunman** n tueur m à gages

pail [peɪl] n seau m

pain [peɪn] n douleur f; **to be in ~** souffrir, avoir mal; **to take ~s to do** se donner du mal pour faire; **~ed** adj peiné(e), chagrin(e); **~ful** adj douloureux(euse); (fig) difficile, pénible; **~fully** adv (fig: very) terriblement; **~killer** n analgésique m; **~less** adj indolore

painstaking ['peɪnzteɪkɪŋ] adj (person) soigneux(euse); (work) soigné(e)

paint [peɪnt] n peinture f ♦ vt peindre; **to ~ the door blue** peindre la porte en bleu; **~brush** n pinceau m; **~er** n peintre m; **~ing** n peinture f; (picture) tableau m; **~work** n peinture f

pair [pɛə*] n (of shoes, gloves etc) paire f; (of people) couple m; **~ of scissors** (paire de) ciseaux mpl; **~ of trousers** pantalon m

pajamas [pə'dʒɑːməz] (US) npl pyjama(s) m(pl)

Pakistan [pɑːkɪ'stɑːn] n Pakistan m; **~i** adj pakistanais(e) ♦ n Pakistanais(e)

pal [pæl] (inf) n copain(copine)

palace ['pæləs] n palais m

palatable ['pælətəbl] adj bon(bonne), agréable au goût

palate ['pælɪt] n palais m (ANAT)

pale [peɪl] adj pâle ♦ n: **beyond the ~** (behaviour) inacceptable; **to grow ~** pâlir

Palestine ['pælɪstaɪn] n Palestine f; **Palestinian** adj palestinien(ne) ♦ n Palestinien(ne)

palette ['pælɪt] n palette f

pall [pɔːl] n (of smoke) voile m ♦ vi devenir lassant(e)

pallet ['pælɪt] n (for goods) palette f

pallid ['pælɪd] adj blême

palm [pɑːm] n (of hand) paume f; (also: ~ **tree**) palmier m ♦ vt: **to ~ sth off on sb** (inf) refiler qch à qn; **P~ Sunday** n le dimanche des Rameaux

palpable ['pælpəbl] adj évident(e), manifeste

paltry ['pɔːltrɪ] adj dérisoire

pamper ['pæmpə*] vt gâter, dorloter

pamphlet ['pæmflət] n brochure f

pan [pæn] n (also: **sauce~**) casserole f; (: **frying ~**) poêle f

pancake ['pænkeɪk] n crêpe f

panda ['pændə] n panda m; **~ car** (BRIT) n ≈ voiture f pie inv (de police)

pandemonium [pændɪ'məʊnɪəm] n tohubohu m

pander ['pændə*] vi: **to ~ to** flatter bassement; obéir servilement à

pane [peɪn] n carreau m, vitre f

panel ['pænl] n (of wood, cloth etc) panneau m; (RADIO, TV) experts mpl; (for interview, exams) jury m; **~ling** (US **~ing**) n boiseries fpl

pang [pæŋ] n: **~s of remorse/jealousy** affres mpl du remords/de la jalousie; **~s of hunger/conscience** tiraillements mpl d'estomac/de la conscience

panic ['pænɪk] n panique f, affolement m ♦ vi s'affoler, paniquer; **~ky** adj (person) qui panique or s'affole facilement; **~-stricken** adj affolé(e)

pansy ['pænzɪ] n (BOT) pensée f; (inf: pej) tapette f, pédé m

pant [pænt] vi haleter

panther ['pænθə*] n panthère f

panties ['pæntɪz] npl slip m

pantomime ['pæntəmaɪm] (BRIT) n spectacle m de Noël

pantry ['pæntrɪ] n garde-manger m inv

pants [pænts] npl (BRIT: woman's) slip m; (: man's) slip m, caleçon m; (US: trousers) pantalon m

pantyhose ['pæntɪhəʊz] (US) npl collant m

paper ['peɪpə*] n papier m; (also: **wall~**) papier peint; (: news~) journal m; (academic essay) article m; (exam) épreuve écrite ♦ adj en or de papier ♦ vt tapisser (de papier peint); **~s** npl (also: identity ~s) papiers (d'identité); **~back** n livre m de poche; livre broché or non relié; **~ bag** n sac

m en papier; ~ **clip** *n* trombone *m*; ~
hankie *n* mouchoir *m* en papier; ~**weight**
n presse-papiers *m inv*; ~**work** *n* papiers
mpl; (*pej*) paperasserie *f*

par [pɑː*] *n* pair *m*; (*GOLF*) normale *f* du
parcours; **on a ~ with** à égalité avec, au
même niveau que

parable ['pærəbl] *n* parabole *f* (*REL*)

parachute ['pærəʃuːt] *n* parachute *m*

parade [pə'reɪd] *n* défilé *m* ♦ *vt* (*fig*) faire
étalage de ♦ *vi* défiler

paradise ['pærədaɪs] *n* paradis *m*

paradox ['pærədɒks] *n* paradoxe *m*; ~**ical-
ly** [pærə'dɒksɪkəlɪ] *adv* paradoxalement

paraffin ['pærəfɪn] (*BRIT*) *n* (*also*: ~ **oil**) pétrole (lampant)

paragon ['pærəgən] *n* modèle *m*

paragraph ['pærəgrɑːf] *n* paragraphe *m*

parallel ['pærəlel] *adj* parallèle; (*fig*) semblable ♦ *n* (*line*) parallèle *f*; (*fig, GEO*) parallèle *m*

paralyse ['pærəlaɪz] (*BRIT*) *vt* paralyser

paralysis [pə'rælɪsɪs] *n* paralysie *f*

paralyze ['pærəlaɪz] (*US*) *vt* = **paralyse**

paramount ['pærəmaʊnt] *adj*: **of ~ importance** de la plus haute *or* grande importance

paranoid ['pærənɔɪd] *adj* (*PSYCH*) para-
noïaque

paraphernalia ['pærəfə'neɪlɪə] *n* attirail *m*

parasol ['pærəsɒl] *n* ombrelle *f*; (*over table*)
parasol *m*

paratrooper ['pærətruːpə*] *n* parachutiste
m (*soldat*)

parcel ['pɑːsl] *n* paquet *m*, colis *m* ♦ *vt*
(*also*: ~ **up**) empaqueter

parch [pɑːtʃ] *vt* dessécher; ~**ed** *adj* (*person*) assoiffé(e)

parchment ['pɑːtʃmənt] *n* parchemin *m*

pardon ['pɑːdn] *n* pardon *m*; grâce *f* ♦ *vt*
pardonner à; ~ **me!, I beg your** ~**!** pardon!, je suis désolé!; (**I beg your**) ~**?**, (*US*)
~ **me?** pardon?

parent ['pɛərənt] *n* père *m* *or* mère *f*; ~**s**
npl parents *mpl*

Paris ['pærɪs] *n* Paris

parish ['pærɪʃ] *n* paroisse *f*; (*BRIT*: *civil*) ≈
commune *f*

Parisian [pə'rɪzɪən] *adj* parisien(ne) ♦ *n* Pa-
risien(ne)

park [pɑːk] *n* parc *m*, jardin public ♦ *vt* garer ♦ *vi* se garer

parking ['pɑːkɪŋ] *n* stationnement *m*; "**no
~**" "stationnement interdit"; ~ **lot** (*US*) *n*
parking *m*, parc *m* de stationnement; ~
meter *n* parcomètre *m*; ~ **ticket** *n* P.V. *m*

parlance ['pɑːləns] *n* langage *m*

parliament ['pɑːləmənt] *n* parlement *m*;
~**ary** [pɑːlə'mentərɪ] *adj* parlementaire

parlour ['pɑːlə*] (*US* **parlor**) *n* salon *m*

parochial [pə'rəʊkɪəl] (*pej*) *adj* à l'esprit de
clocher

parody ['pærədɪ] *n* parodie *f*

parole [pə'rəʊl] *n*: **on** ~ en liberté condi-
tionnelle

parrot ['pærət] *n* perroquet *m*

parry ['pærɪ] *vt* (*blow*) esquiver

parsley ['pɑːslɪ] *n* persil *m*

parsnip ['pɑːsnɪp] *n* panais *m*

parson ['pɑːsn] *n* ecclésiastique *m*; (*Church
of England*) pasteur *m*

part [pɑːt] *n* partie *f*; (*of machine*) pièce *f*;
(*THEATRE etc*) rôle *m*; (*of serial*) épisode *m*;
(*US*: *in hair*) raie *f* ♦ *adv* = **partly** ♦ *vt* séparer ♦ *vi* (*people*) se séparer; (*crowd*) s'ouvrir; **to take ~ in** participer à, prendre part
à; **to take sth in good** ~ prendre qch du
bon côté; **to take sb's** ~ prendre le parti
de qn, prendre parti pour qn; **for my** ~ en
ce qui me concerne; **for the most** ~ dans
la plupart des cas; ~ **with** *vt fus* se séparer
de; ~ **exchange** (*BRIT*) *n*: **in** ~ **exchange**
en reprise

partial ['pɑːʃəl] *adj* (*not complete*) par-
tiel(le); **to be** ~ **to** avoir un faible pour

participate [pɑː'tɪsɪpeɪt] *vi*: **to** ~ (**in**) participer à, prendre part (à); **participation**
[pɑːtɪsɪ'peɪʃən] *n* participation *f*

participle ['pɑːtɪsɪpl] *n* participe *m*

particle ['pɑːtɪkl] *n* particule *f*

particular [pə'tɪkjʊlə*] *adj* particulier(ère);
(*special*) spécial(e); (*fussy*) difficile; méti-
culeux(euse); ~**s** *npl* (*details*) détails *mpl*;
(*personal*) nom, adresse etc; **in** ~ en particulier; ~**ly** *adv* particulièrement

parting ['pɑːtɪŋ] *n* séparation *f*; (*BRIT*: *in
hair*) raie *f* ♦ *adj* d'adieu

partisan [pɑːtɪ'zæn] *n* partisan(e) ♦ *adj* par-
tisan(e); de parti

partition [pɑː'tɪʃən] *n* (*wall*) cloison *f*;
(*POL*) partition *f*, division *f*

partly ['pɑːtlɪ] *adv* en partie, partiellement

partner ['pɑːtnə*] *n* partenaire *m/f*; (*in marriage*) conjoint(e); (*boyfriend, girlfriend*)
ami(e); (*COMM*) associé(e); (*at dance*) cava-
lier(ère); ~**ship** *n* association *f*

partridge ['pɑːtrɪdʒ] *n* perdrix *f*

part-time ['pɑːt'taɪm] *adj, adv* à mi-temps,
à temps partiel

party ['pɑːtɪ] *n* (*POL*) parti *m*; (*group*) groupe *m*; (*LAW*) partie *f*; (*celebration*) réception
f; soirée *f*; fête *f* ♦ *cpd* (*POL*) de or du parti;
~ **dress** *n* robe habillée; ~ **line** *n* (*TEL*) ligne partagée

pass [pɑːs] *vt* passer; (*place*) passer devant;
(*friend*) croiser; (*overtake*) dépasser; (*exam*)
être reçu(e) à, réussir; (*approve*) approuver,
accepter ♦ *vi* passer; (*SCOL*) être reçu(e) or
admis(e), réussir ♦ *n* (*permit*) laissez-passer
m inv; carte *f* d'accès or d'abonnement; (*in
mountains*) col *m*; (*SPORT*) passe *f*; (*SCOL*:
also: ~ **mark**): **to get a** ~ être reçu(e) (sans
mention); **to make a** ~ **at sb** (*inf*) faire des
avances à qn; ~ **away** *vi* mourir; ~ **by** *vi*

passer ♦ *vt* négliger; ~ **on** *vt* (*news, object*) transmettre; (*illness*) passer; ~ **out** *vi* s'évanouir; ~ **up** *vt* (*opportunity*) laisser passer; ~**able** *adj* (*road*) praticable; (*work*) acceptable

passage ['pæsɪdʒ] *n* (*also*: ~**way**) couloir *m*; (*gen, in book*) passage *m*; (*by boat*) traversée *f*

passbook ['pɑːsbʊk] *n* livret *m*

passenger ['pæsɪndʒə*] *n* passager(ère)

passer-by ['pɑːsə'baɪ] (*pl* ~**s-by**) *n* passant(e)

passing ['pɑːsɪŋ] *adj* (*fig*) passager(ère); **in** ~ en passant

passing place *n* (*AUT*) aire *f* de croisement

passion ['pæʃən] *n* passion *f*; ~**ate** *adj* passionné(e)

passive ['pæsɪv] *adj* (*also LING*) passif(ive); ~ **smoking** *n* tabagisme *m* passif

Passover ['pɑːsəʊvə*] *n* Pâque *f* (*juive*)

passport ['pɑːspɔːt] *n* passeport *m*; ~ **control** *n* contrôle *m* des passeports

password ['pɑːswɜːd] *n* mot *m* de passe

past [pɑːst] *prep* (*in front of*) devant; (*further than*) au delà de, plus loin que; après; (*later than*) après ♦ *adj* passé(e); (*president etc*) ancien(ne) ♦ *n* passé *m*; **he's** ~ **forty** il a dépassé la quarantaine, il a plus de *or* passé quarante ans; **for the** ~ **few/3 days** depuis quelques/3 jours; **ces** derniers/3 derniers jours; **ten/quarter** ~ **eight** huit heures dix/un *or* et quart

pasta ['pæstə] *n* pâtes *fpl*

paste [peɪst] *n* pâte *f*; (*meat* ~) pâté *m* (à tartiner); (*tomato* ~) purée *f*, concentré *m*; (*glue*) colle *f* (de pâte) ♦ *vt* coller

pasteurized ['pæstəraɪzd] *adj* pasteurisé(e)

pastille ['pæstl] *n* pastille *f*

pastime ['pɑːstaɪm] *n* passe-temps *m inv*

pastry ['peɪstrɪ] *n* pâte *f*; (*cake*) pâtisserie *f*

pasture ['pɑːstʃə*] *n* pâturage *m*

pasty [*n* 'pæstɪ, *adj* 'peɪstɪ] *n* petit pâté (en croûte) ♦ *adj* (*complexion*) terreux(euse)

pâté ['pæteɪ] *n* pâté *m*, terrine *f*

patent ['peɪtənt] *n* brevet *m* (d'invention) ♦ *vt* faire breveter ♦ *adj* patent(e), manifeste; ~ **leather** *n* cuir verni

paternal [pə'tɜːnl] *adj* paternel(le)

path [pɑːθ] *n* chemin *m*, sentier *m*; (*in garden*) allée *f*; (*trajectory*) trajectoire *f*

pathetic [pə'θetɪk] *adj* (*pitiful*) pitoyable; (*very bad*) lamentable, minable

pathological [pæθə'lɒdʒɪkl] *adj* pathologique

pathos ['peɪθɒs] *n* pathétique *m*

pathway ['pɑːθweɪ] *n* sentier *m*, passage *m*

patience ['peɪʃəns] *n* patience *f*; (*BRIT: CARDS*) réussite *f*

patient ['peɪʃənt] *n* patient(e); malade *m/f* ♦ *adj* patient(e)

patriotic [pætrɪ'ɒtɪk] *adj* patriotique; (*person*) patriote

patrol [pə'trəul] *n* patrouille *f* ♦ *vt* patrouiller dans; ~ **car** *n* voiture *f* de police; ~**man** (*irreg: US*) *n* agent *m* de police

patron ['peɪtrən] *n* (*in shop*) client(e); (*of charity*) patron(ne); ~ **of the arts** mécène *m*; ~**ize** *vt* (*pej*) traiter avec condescendance; (*shop, club*) être (un) client *or* un habitué de

patter ['pætə*] *n* crépitement *m*, tapotement *m*; (*sales talk*) boniment *m*

pattern ['pætən] *n* (*design*) motif *m*; (*SEWING*) patron *m*

paunch [pɔːntʃ] *n* gros ventre, bedaine *f*

pauper ['pɔːpə*] *n* indigent(e)

pause [pɔːz] *n* pause *f*, arrêt *m* ♦ *vi* faire une pause, s'arrêter

pave [peɪv] *vt* paver, daller; **to** ~ **the way for** ouvrir la voie à; ~**ment** ['peɪvmənt] (*BRIT*) *n* trottoir *m*

pavilion [pə'vɪlɪən] *n* pavillon *m*; tente *f*

paving ['peɪvɪŋ] *n* (*material*) pavé *m*, dalle *f*; ~ **stone** *n* pavé *m*

paw [pɔː] *n* patte *f*

pawn [pɔːn] *n* (*CHESS, also fig*) pion *m* ♦ *vt* mettre en gage; ~**broker** *n* prêteur *m* sur gages; ~**shop** *n* mont-de-piété *m*

pay [peɪ] (*pt, pp* **paid**) *n* salaire *m*; paie *f* ♦ *vt* payer ♦ *vi* payer; (*be profitable*) être rentable; **to** ~ **attention (to)** prêter attention (à); **to** ~ **sb a visit** rendre visite à qn; **to** ~ **one's respects to sb** présenter ses respects à qn; ~ **back** *vt* rembourser; ~ **for** *vt fus* payer; ~ **in** *vt* verser; ~ **off** *vt* régler, acquitter; (*person*) rembourser ♦ *vi* (*scheme, decision*) se révéler payant(e); ~ **up** *vt* (*money*) payer; ~**able** *adj*: ~**able to sb** (*cheque*) à l'ordre de qn; ~**ee** [peɪ'iː] *n* bénéficiaire *m/f*; ~ **envelope** (*US*) *n* = **pay packet**; ~**ment** *n* paiement *m*; **monthly** ~**ment** mensualité *f*; ~ **packet** (*BRIT*) *n* paie *f*; ~ **phone** *n* cabine *f* téléphonique, téléphone public; ~**roll** *n* registre *m* du personnel; ~ **slip** (*BRIT*) *n* bulletin *m* de paie; ~ **television** *n* chaînes *fpl* payantes

PC *n abbr* = **personal computer**

p.c. *abbr* = **per cent**

pea [piː] *n* (*petit*) pois

peace [piːs] *n* paix *f*; (*calm*) calme *m*, tranquillité *f*; ~**ful** *adj* paisible, calme

peach [piːtʃ] *n* pêche *f*

peacock ['piːkɒk] *n* paon *m*

peak [piːk] *n* (*mountain*) pic *m*, cime *f*; (*of*

cap) visière f; (*fig: highest level*) maximum m; (: *of career, fame*) apogée m; **~ hours** npl heures fpl de pointe

peal [piːl] n (*of bells*) carillon m; **~ of laughter** éclat m de rire

peanut ['piːnʌt] n arachide f, cacahuète f

pear [pɛə*] n poire f

pearl [pɜːl] n perle f

peasant ['pɛznt] n paysan(ne)

peat [piːt] n tourbe f

pebble ['pɛbl] n caillou m, galet m

peck [pɛk] vt (*also*: **~ at**) donner un coup de bec à ♦ n coup m de bec; (*kiss*) bise f; **~ing order** n ordre m des préséances; **~ish** (*BRIT: inf*) adj: **I feel ~ish** je mangerais bien quelque chose

peculiar [pɪˈkjuːlɪə*] adj étrange, bizarre, curieux(euse); **~ to** particulier(ère) à

pedal ['pɛdl] n pédale f ♦ vi pédaler

pedantic [pɪˈdæntɪk] adj pédant(e)

peddler ['pɛdlə*] n (*of drugs*) revendeur(euse)

pedestal ['pɛdɪstl] n piédestal m

pedestrian [pɪˈdɛstrɪən] n piéton m; **~ crossing** (*BRIT*) n passage clouté

pediatrics [piːdɪˈætrɪks] (*US*) n = **paediatrics**

pedigree ['pɛdɪgriː] n ascendance f; (*of animal*) pedigree m ♦ cpd (*animal*) de race

pee [piː] (*inf*) vi faire pipi, pisser

peek [piːk] vi jeter un coup d'œil (furtif)

peel [piːl] n pelure f, épluchure f; (*of orange, lemon*) écorce f ♦ vt peler, éplucher ♦ vi (*paint etc*) s'écailler; (*wallpaper*) se décoller; (*skin*) peler

peep [piːp] n (*BRIT: look*) coup d'œil furtif; (*sound*) pépiement m m ♦ vi (*BRIT*) jeter un coup d'œil (furtif); **~ out** (*BRIT*) vi se montrer (furtivement); **~hole** n judas m

peer [pɪə*] vi: **to ~ at** regarder attentivement, scruter ♦ n (*noble*) pair m; (*equal*) pair, égal(e); **~age** n pairie f

peeved [piːvd] adj irrité(e), fâché(e)

peg [pɛg] n (*for coat etc*) patère f; (*BRIT: also: clothes ~*) pince f à linge

Peking [piːˈkɪŋ] n Pékin; **Pekin(g)ese** [piːkɪˈniːz] n (*dog*) pékinois m

pelican ['pɛlɪkən] n pélican m; **~ crossing** (*BRIT*) n (*AUT*) feu m à commande manuelle

pellet ['pɛlɪt] n boulette f; (*of lead*) plomb m

pelt [pɛlt] vt: **to ~ sb (with)** bombarder qn (de) ♦ vi (*rain*) tomber à seaux; (*inf: run*) courir à toutes jambes ♦ n peau f

pelvis ['pɛlvɪs] n bassin m

pen [pɛn] n (*for writing*) stylo m; (*for sheep*) parc m

penal ['piːnl] adj pénal(e); (*system, colony*) pénitentiaire; **~ize** vt pénaliser

penalty ['pɛnltɪ] n pénalité f; sanction f; (*fine*) amende f; (*SPORT*) pénalisation f;

(*FOOTBALL*) penalty m; (*RUGBY*) pénalité f

penance ['pɛnəns] n pénitence f

pence [pɛns] (*BRIT*) npl of **penny**

pencil ['pɛnsl] n crayon m; **~ case** n trousse f (d'écolier); **~ sharpener** n taille-crayon(s) m inv

pendant ['pɛndənt] n pendentif m

pending ['pɛndɪŋ] prep en attendant ♦ adj en suspens

pendulum ['pɛndjʊləm] n (*of clock*) balancier m

penetrate ['pɛnɪtreɪt] vt pénétrer dans; pénétrer

penfriend ['pɛnfrɛnd] (*BRIT*) n correspondant(e)

penguin ['pɛŋgwɪn] n pingouin m

penicillin [pɛnɪˈsɪlɪn] n pénicilline f

peninsula [pɪˈnɪnsjʊlə] n péninsule f

penis ['piːnɪs] n pénis m, verge f

penitentiary [pɛnɪˈtɛnʃərɪ] n prison f

penknife ['pɛnnaɪf] n canif m

pen name n nom m de plume, pseudonyme m

penniless ['pɛnɪləs] adj sans le sou

penny ['pɛnɪ] (*pl* **pennies** or (*BRIT*) **pence**) n penny m; (*US*) = **cent**

penpal ['pɛnpæl] n correspondant(e)

pension ['pɛnʃən] n pension f; (*from company*) retraite f; **~er** (*BRIT*) n retraité(e); **~ fund** n caisse f de pension

Pentecost ['pɛntɪkɒst] n Pentecôte f

penthouse ['pɛnthaʊs] n appartement m (de luxe) (en attique)

pent-up ['pɛntʌp] adj (*feelings*) refoulé(e)

penultimate [pɪˈnʌltɪmɪt] adj avant-dernier(ère)

people ['piːpl] npl gens mpl; personnes fpl; (*inhabitants*) population f; (*POL*) peuple m ♦ n (*nation, race*) peuple m; **several ~ came** plusieurs personnes sont venues; **~ say that ...** on dit que ...

pep [pɛp] (*inf*) n entrain m, dynamisme m; **~ up** vt remonter

pepper ['pɛpə*] n poivre m; (*vegetable*) poivron m ♦ vt (*fig*): **to ~ with** bombarder de; **~mint** n (*sweet*) pastille f de menthe

peptalk ['pɛptɔːk] (*inf*) n (*petit*) discours d'encouragement

per [pɜː*] prep par; **~ hour** (*miles etc*) à l'heure; (*fee*) (de) l'heure; **~ kilo** etc le kilo etc; **~ annum** adv par an; **~ capita** adj, adv par personne, par habitant

perceive [pəˈsiːv] vt percevoir; (*notice*) remarquer, s'apercevoir de

per cent [pəˈsɛnt] adv pour cent

percentage [pəˈsɛntɪdʒ] n pourcentage m

perception [pəˈsɛpʃən] n perception f; (*insight*) perspicacité f

perceptive [pəˈsɛptɪv] adj pénétrant(e); (*person*) perspicace

perch [pɜːtʃ] n (*fish*) perche f; (*for bird*) perchoir m ♦ vi: **to ~ on** se percher sur

percolator ['pɜːkəleɪtə*] n cafetière f (électrique)

perennial [pə'renɪəl] adj perpétuel(le); (BOT) vivace

perfect [adj, n 'pɜːfɪkt, vb pə'fekt] adj parfait(e) ♦ n (also: ~ tense) parfait m ♦ vt parfaire; mettre au point; ~ly adv parfaitement

perforate ['pɜːfəreɪt] vt perforer, percer; **perforation** [pɜːfə'reɪʃən] n perforation f

perform [pə'fɔːm] vt (carry out) exécuter; (concert etc) jouer, donner ♦ vi jouer; ~ance n représentation f, spectacle m; (of an artist) interprétation f, (SPORT) performance f; (of car, engine) fonctionnement m; (of company, economy) résultats mpl; ~er n artiste m/f, interprète m/f

perfume ['pɜːfjuːm] n parfum m

perfunctory [pə'fʌŋktərɪ] adj négligent(e), pour la forme

perhaps [pə'hæps] adv peut-être

peril ['perɪl] n péril m

perimeter [pə'rɪmɪtə*] n périmètre m

period ['pɪərɪəd] n période f; (HISTORY) époque f; (SCOL) cours m; (full stop) point m; (MED) règles fpl ♦ adj (costume, furniture) d'époque; ~ic(al) [pɪərɪ'ɒdɪk(əl)] adj périodique; ~ical n périodique m

peripheral [pə'rɪfərəl] adj périphérique ♦ n (COMPUT) périphérique m

perish ['perɪʃ] vi périr; (decay) se détériorer; ~able adj périssable

perjury ['pɜːdʒərɪ] n parjure m, faux serment

perk [pɜːk] n avantage m; accessoire, à-côté m; ~ up vi (cheer up) se ragaillardir; ~y adj (cheerful) guilleret(te)

perm [pɜːm] n (for hair) permanente f

permanent ['pɜːmənənt] adj permanent(e)

permeate ['pɜːmɪeɪt] vi s'infiltrer ♦ vt s'infiltrer dans; pénétrer

permissible [pə'mɪsɪbl] adj permis(e), acceptable

permission [pə'mɪʃən] n permission f, autorisation f

permissive [pə'mɪsɪv] adj tolérant(e), permissif(ive)

permit [n 'pɜːmɪt, vb pə'mɪt] n permis m ♦ vt permettre

perpendicular [pɜːpən'dɪkjulə*] adj perpendiculaire

perplex [pə'pleks] vt (person) rendre perplexe

persecute ['pɜːsɪkjuːt] vt persécuter

persevere [pɜːsɪ'vɪə*] vi persévérer

Persian ['pɜːʃən] adj persan(e) ♦ n (LING) persan m; **the** (~) **Gulf** le golfe Persique

persist [pə'sɪst] vi: **to** ~ (**in doing**) persister or s'obstiner (à faire); ~ent adj persistant(e), tenace

person ['pɜːsn] n personne f; **in** ~ en personne; ~al adj personnel(le); ~al assis-

tant n secrétaire privé(e); ~al **call** n communication privée; ~al **column** n annonces personnelles; ~al **computer** n ordinateur personnel; ~ality [pɜːsə'nælɪtɪ] n personnalité f; ~ally adv personnellement; **to take sth** ~ally se sentir visé(e) (par qch); ~al **organizer** n filofax m (®); ~al **stereo** n balladeur m

personnel [pɜːsə'nel] n personnel m

perspective [pə'spektɪv] n perspective f; **to get things into** ~ faire la part des choses

Perspex ['pɜːspeks] ® n plexiglas m (®)

perspiration [pɜːspə'reɪʃən] n transpiration f

persuade [pə'sweɪd] vt: **to** ~ **sb to do sth** persuader qn de faire qch

persuasion [pə'sweɪʒən] n persuasion f; (creed) religion f

pertaining [pɜː'teɪnɪŋ] : ~ **to** prep relatif(ive) à

peruse [pə'ruːz] vt lire (attentivement)

pervade [pɜː'veɪd] vt se répandre dans, envahir

perverse [pə'vɜːs] adj pervers(e); (contrary) contrariant(e); **pervert** [n 'pɜːvɜːt, vb pə'vɜːt] n perverti(e) ♦ vt pervertir; (words) déformer

pessimist ['pesɪmɪst] n pessimiste m/f; ~ic [pesɪ'mɪstɪk] adj pessimiste

pest [pest] n animal m (or insecte m) nuisible; (fig) fléau m

pester ['pestə*] vt importuner, harceler

pet [pet] n animal familier ♦ cpd (favourite) favori(te) ♦ vt (stroke) caresser, câliner ♦ vi (inf) se peloter; **teacher's** ~ chouchou m du professeur; ~ **hate** bête noire

petal ['petl] n pétale m

peter out ['piːtə-] vi (stream, conversation) tarir; (meeting) tourner court; (road) se perdre

petite [pə'tiːt] adj menu(e)

petition [pə'tɪʃən] n pétition f

petrified ['petrɪfaɪd] adj (fig) mort(e) de peur

petrol ['petrəl] (BRIT) n essence f; **two-star** ~ essence f ordinaire; **four-star** ~ super m; ~ **can** n bidon m à essence

petroleum [pɪ'trəulɪəm] n pétrole m

petrol: ~ **pump** (BRIT) n pompe f à essence; ~ **station** (BRIT) n station-service f; ~ **tank** (BRIT) n réservoir m (d'essence)

petticoat ['petɪkəut] n combinaison f

petty ['petɪ] adj (mean) mesquin(e); (unimportant) insignifiant(e), sans importance; ~ **cash** n caisse f des dépenses courantes; ~ **officer** n second-maître m

petulant ['petjulənt] adj boudeur(euse), irritable

pew [pjuː] n banc m (d'église)

pewter ['pjuːtə*] n étain m

phantom ['fæntəm] n fantôme m

pharmacy ['fɑːməsɪ] n pharmacie f

phase [feɪz] n phase f ♦ vt: **to ~ sth in/out** introduire/supprimer qch progressivement

PhD abbr = **Doctor of Philosophy** n (title) ≈ docteur m (en droit or lettres etc) ≈ doctorat m; titulaire m/f d'un doctorat

pheasant ['feznt] n faisan m

phenomenon [fɪ'nɒmɪnən] (pl **phenomena**) n phénomène m

philosophical [fɪlə'sɔfɪkl] adj philosophique

philosophy [fɪ'lɒsəfɪ] n philosophie f

phobia ['fəʊbjə] n phobie f

phone [fəʊn] n téléphone m ♦ vt téléphoner; **to be on the ~** avoir le téléphone; (be calling) être au téléphone; **~ back** vt, vi rappeler; **~ up** vt téléphoner à ♦ vi téléphoner; **~ book** n annuaire m; **~ booth** n = **phone box**; **~ box** (BRIT) n cabine f téléphonique; **~ call** n coup m de fil or de téléphone; **~card** n carte f de téléphone; **~-in** (BRIT) n (RADIO, TV) programme m à ligne ouverte

phonetics [fə'netɪks] n phonétique f

phoney ['fəʊnɪ] adj faux(fausse), factice; (person) pas franc(he), poseur(euse)

photo ['fəʊtəʊ] n photo f

photo...: **~copier** [-'kɒpɪə*] n photocopieuse f; **~copy** [-kɒpɪ] n photocopie f ♦ vt photocopier; **~graph** [-grɑːf] n photographie f ♦ vt photographier; **~grapher** [-grəfə*] n photographe m/f; **~graphy** [-grəfɪ] n photographie f

phrase [freɪz] n expression f; (LING) locution f ♦ vt exprimer; **~ book** n recueil m d'expressions (pour touristes)

physical ['fɪzɪkəl] adj physique; **~ education** n éducation f physique; **~ly** adv physiquement

physician [fɪ'zɪʃən] n médecin m

physicist ['fɪzɪsɪst] n physicien(ne)

physics ['fɪzɪks] n physique f

physiotherapy [fɪzɪə'θerəpɪ] n kinésithérapie f

physique [fɪ'ziːk] n physique m; constitution f

pianist ['pɪənɪst] n pianiste m/f

piano [pɪ'ænəʊ] n piano m

pick [pɪk] n (tool: also: **~axe**) pic m, pioche f ♦ vt choisir; (fruit etc) cueillir; (remove) prendre; (lock) forcer; **take your ~** faites votre choix; **the ~ of** le(la) meilleur(e) de; **to ~ one's nose** se mettre les doigts dans le nez; **to ~ one's teeth** se curer les dents; **to ~ a quarrel with sb** chercher noise à qn; **~ at** vt fus: **to ~ at one's food** manger du bout des dents, chipoter; **~ on** vt fus (person) harceler; **~ out** vt choisir; (distinguish) distinguer; **~ up** vi (improve) s'améliorer ♦ vt ramasser; (collect) passer prendre; (AUT: give lift to) prendre, emmener; (learn) apprendre; (RADIO) capter; **to ~ up speed** prendre de la vitesse; **to ~**

o.s. up se relever

picket ['pɪkɪt] n (in strike) piquet m de grève ♦ vt mettre un piquet de grève devant

pickle ['pɪkl] n (also: **~s**: as condiment) pickles mpl, petits légumes macérés dans du vinaigre ♦ vt conserver dans du vinaigre or dans de la saumure; **to be in a ~** (mess) être dans le pétrin

pickpocket ['pɪkpɒkɪt] n pickpocket m

pick-up ['pɪkʌp] n (small truck) pick-up m inv

picnic ['pɪknɪk] n pique-nique m

picture ['pɪktʃə*] n image f; (painting) peinture f, tableau m; (etching) gravure f; (photograph) photo(graphie) f; (drawing) dessin m; (film) film m; (fig) description f, tableau m ♦ vt se représenter; **the ~s** (BRIT: inf) le cinéma; **~ book** n livre m d'images

picturesque [pɪktʃə'resk] adj pittoresque

pie [paɪ] n tourte f; (of fruit) tarte f; (of meat) pâté m en croûte

piece [piːs] n morceau m; (item): **a ~ of furniture/advice** un meuble/conseil ♦ vt: **to ~ together** rassembler; **to take to ~s** démonter; **~meal** adv (irregularly) au coup par coup; (bit by bit) par bouts; **~work** n travail m aux pièces

pie chart n graphique m circulaire, camembert m

pier [pɪə*] n jetée f

pierce [pɪəs] vt percer, transpercer

pig [pɪg] n cochon m, porc m

pigeon ['pɪdʒən] n pigeon m; **~hole** n casier m

piggy bank ['pɪgɪ-] n tirelire f

pig: **~-headed** [-'hedɪd] adj entêté(e), têtu(e); **~let** n porcelet m, petit cochon; **~skin** [-skɪn] n peau m de porc; **~sty** [-staɪ] n porcherie f; **~tail** [-teɪl] n natte f, tresse f

pike [paɪk] n (fish) brochet m

pilchard ['pɪltʃəd] n pilchard m (sorte de sardine)

pile [paɪl] n (pillar, of books) pile f; (heap) tas m; (of carpet) poils mpl ♦ vt (also: **~ up**) empiler, entasser ♦ vi (also: **~up**) s'entasser, s'accumuler; **to ~ into** (car) s'entasser dans

piles [paɪlz] npl hémorroïdes fpl

pile-up ['paɪlʌp] n (AUT) télescopage m, collision f en série

pilfering ['pɪlfərɪŋ] n chapardage m

pilgrim ['pɪlgrɪm] n pèlerin m

pill [pɪl] n pilule f

pillage ['pɪlɪdʒ] vt piller

pillar ['pɪlə*] n pilier m; **~ box** (BRIT) n boîte f aux lettres

pillion ['pɪljən] n: **to ride ~** (on motorcycle) monter derrière

pillow ['pɪləʊ] n oreiller m; **~case** n taie f d'oreiller

pilot ['paɪlət] n pilote m ♦ cpd (scheme etc)

pilote, expérimental(e) ♦ vt piloter; ~ **light**
n veilleuse f

pimp [pɪmp] n souteneur m, maquereau m

pimple ['pɪmpl] n bouton m

pin [pɪn] n épingle f; (TECH) cheville f ♦ vt
épingler; ~**s and needles** fourmis fpl; **to ~
sb down** (fig) obliger qn à répondre; **to ~
sth on sb** (fig) mettre qch sur le dos de qn

pinafore ['pɪnəfɔ:*] n tablier m

pinball ['pɪnbɔ:l] n flipper m

pincers ['pɪnsəz] npl tenailles fpl; (of crab
etc) pinces fpl

pinch [pɪntʃ] n (of salt etc) pincée f ♦ vt
pincer; (inf: steal) piquer, chiper; **at a ~** à
la rigueur

pincushion ['pɪnkʊʃən] n pelote f à épingles

pine [paɪn] n (also: ~ **tree**) pin m ♦ vi: **to ~
for** s'ennuyer de, désirer ardemment; ~
away vi dépérir

pineapple ['paɪnæpl] n ananas m

ping [pɪŋ] n (noise) tintement m; ~**-pong**
(®) n ping-pong m (®)

pink [pɪŋk] adj rose ♦ n (colour) rose m;
(BOT) œillet m, mignardise f

PIN (number) n code m confidentiel

pinpoint ['pɪnpɔɪnt] vt indiquer or localiser
(avec précision); (problem) mettre le doigt
sur

pint [paɪnt] n pinte f (BRIT = 0.57l; US =
0.47l); (BRIT: inf) ≈ demi m

pioneer [paɪə'nɪə*] n pionnier m

pious ['paɪəs] adj pieux(euse)

pip [pɪp] n (seed) pépin m; **the ~s** npl
(BRIT: time signal on radio) le(s) top(s) so-
nore(s)

pipe [paɪp] n tuyau m, conduite f; (for smoking) pipe f ♦ vt amener par tuyau; ~**s** npl
(also: bag~s) cornemuse f; ~ **down** (inf) vi
se taire; ~ **cleaner** n cure-pipe m; ~
dream n chimère f, château m en Espagne;
~**line** n pipe-line m; ~**r** n joueur(euse) de
cornemuse

piping ['paɪpɪŋ] adv: ~ **hot** très chaud(e)

pique [pi:k] n dépit m

pirate ['paɪərɪt] n pirate m

Pisces ['paɪsi:z] n les Poissons mpl

piss [pɪs] (inf!) vi pisser; ~**ed** (inf!) adj
(drunk) bourré(e)

pistol ['pɪstl] n pistolet m

piston ['pɪstən] n piston m

pit [pɪt] n trou m, fosse f; (also: coal ~)
puits m de mine; (quarry) carrière f ♦ vt: **to
~ one's wits against sb** se mesurer à qn;
~**s** npl (AUT) aire f de service

pitch [pɪtʃ] n (MUS) ton m; (BRIT: SPORT)
terrain m; (tar) poix f; (fig) degré m; point
m ♦ vt (throw) lancer ♦ vi (fall) tomber; **to
~ a tent** dresser une tente; ~**-black** adj
noir(e) (comme du cirage); ~**ed battle** n
bataille rangée

piteous ['pɪtɪəs] adj pitoyable

pitfall ['pɪtfɔ:l] n piège m

pith [pɪθ] n (of orange etc) intérieur m de
l'écorce

pithy ['pɪθɪ] adj piquant(e)

pitiful ['pɪtɪfʊl] adj (touching) pitoyable

pitiless ['pɪtɪləs] adj impitoyable

pittance ['pɪtəns] n salaire m de misère

pity ['pɪtɪ] n pitié f ♦ vt plaindre; **what a
~!** quel dommage!

pizza ['pi:tsə] n pizza f

placard ['plækɑ:d] n affiche f; (in march)
pancarte f

placate [plə'keɪt] vt apaiser, calmer

place [pleɪs] n endroit m, lieu m; (proper
position, job, rank, seat) place f; (home):
at/to his ~ chez lui ♦ vt (object) placer,
mettre; (identify) situer; reconnaître; **to
take ~** avoir lieu; **out of ~** (not suitable)
déplacé(e), inopportun(e); **to change ~s
with sb** changer de place avec qn; **in the
first ~** d'abord, en premier

plague [pleɪg] n fléau m; (MED) peste f ♦ vt
(fig) tourmenter

plaice [pleɪs] n inv carrelet m

plaid [plæd] n tissu écossais

plain [pleɪn] adj (in one colour) uni(e); (simple) simple; (clear) clair(e), évident(e); (not
handsome) quelconque, ordinaire ♦ adv
franchement, carrément ♦ n plaine f; ~
chocolate n chocolat m à croquer; ~
clothes adj (police officer) en civil; ~**ly**
adv clairement; (frankly) carrément, sans
détours

plaintiff ['pleɪntɪf] n plaignant(e)

plait [plæt] n tresse f, natte f

plan [plæn] n plan m; (scheme) projet m ♦
vt (think in advance) projeter; (prepare) organiser; (house) dresser les plans de,
concevoir ♦ vi faire des projets; **to ~ to do**
prévoir de faire

plane [pleɪn] n (AVIAT) avion m; (ART,
MATH etc) plan m; (fig) niveau m, plan;
(tool) rabot m; (also: ~ **tree**) platane m ♦ vt
raboter

planet ['plænɪt] n planète f

plank [plæŋk] n planche f

planner ['plænə*] n planificateur(trice);
(town ~) urbaniste m/f

planning ['plænɪŋ] n planification f; **family
~** planning familial; ~ **permission** n permis m de construire

plant [plɑ:nt] n plante f; (machinery) matériel m; (factory) usine f ♦ vt planter; (bomb)
poser; (microphone, incriminating evidence)
cacher

plaster ['plɑ:stə*] n plâtre m; (also: ~ of
Paris) plâtre à mouler; (BRIT: also: sticking
~) pansement adhésif ♦ vt plâtrer; (cover):
to ~ with couvrir de; ~**ed** (inf) adj soûl(e)

plastic ['plæstɪk] n plastique m ♦ adj (made
of ~) en plastique; ~ **bag** n sac m en plastique

Plasticine ['plæstɪsiːn] (®) *n* pâte *f* à modeler

plastic surgery *n* chirurgie *f* esthétique

plate [pleɪt] *n* (*dish*) assiette *f*; (*in book*) gravure *f*, planche *f*; (*dental ~*) dentier *m*

plateau ['plætəʊ] (*pl* ~**s** *or* ~**x**) *n* plateau *m*

plate glass *n* verre *m* (de vitrine)

platform ['plætfɔːm] *n* plate-forme *f*; (*at meeting*) tribune *f*; (*stage*) estrade *f*; (*RAIL*) quai *m*

platinum ['plætɪnəm] *n* platine *m*

platter ['plætə*] *n* plat *m*

plausible ['plɔːzɪbl] *adj* plausible; (*person*) convaincant(e)

play [pleɪ] *n* (*THEATRE*) pièce *f* (de théâtre) ♦ *vt* (*game*) jouer à; (*team, opponent*) jouer contre; (*instrument*) jouer de; (*part, piece of music, note*) jouer; (*record etc*) passer ♦ *vi* jouer; **to ~ safe** ne prendre aucun risque; **~ down** *vt* minimiser; **~ up** *vi* (*cause trouble*) faire des siennes; **~boy** *n* playboy *m*; **~er** *n* joueur(euse); (*THEATRE*) acteur(trice); (*MUS*) musicien(ne); **~ful** *adj* enjoué(e); **~ground** *n* cour *f* de récréation; (*in park*) aire *f* de jeux; **~group** *n* garderie *f*; **~ing card** *n* carte *f* à jouer; **~ing field** *n* terrain *m* de sport; **~mate** *n* camarade *m/f*, copain(copine); **~-off** *n* (*SPORT*) belle *f*; **~pen** *n* parc *m* (pour bébé); **~thing** *n* jouet *m*; **~time** *n* récréation *f*; **~wright** *n* dramaturge *m*

plc *abbr* (= *public limited company*) ≈ SARL *f*

plea [pliː] *n* (*request*) appel *m*; (*LAW*) défense *f*

plead [pliːd] *vt* plaider; (*give as excuse*) invoquer ♦ *vi* (*LAW*) plaider; (*beg*): **to ~ with sb** implorer qn

pleasant ['plɛznt] *adj* agréable; **~ries** *npl* (*polite remarks*) civilités *fpl*

please [pliːz] *excl* s'il te (*or* vous) plaît ♦ *vt* plaire à ♦ *vi* plaire; (*think fit*): **do as you ~** faites comme il vous plaira; **~ yourself!** à ta (*or* votre) guise!; **~d** *adj*: **~d (with)** content(e) (de); **~d to meet you** enchanté (de faire votre connaissance); **pleasing** ['pliːzɪŋ] *adj* plaisant(e), qui fait plaisir

pleasure ['plɛʒə*] *n* plaisir *m*; "**it's a ~**" "je vous en prie"; **~ boat** *n* bateau *m* de plaisance

pleat [pliːt] *n* pli *m*

pledge [plɛdʒ] *n* (*promise*) promesse *f* ♦ *vt* engager; promettre

plentiful ['plɛntɪfʊl] *adj* abondant(e), copieux(euse)

plenty ['plɛntɪ] *n*: **~ of** beaucoup de; (*bien*) assez de

pliable ['plaɪəbl] *adj* flexible; (*person*) malléable

pliers ['plaɪəz] *npl* pinces *fpl*

plight [plaɪt] *n* situation *f* critique

plimsolls ['plɪmsəlz] (*BRIT*) *npl* chaussures

fpl de tennis, tennis *mpl*

plinth [plɪnθ] *n* (*of statue*) socle *m*

PLO *n abbr* (= *Palestine Liberation Organization*) OLP *f*

plod [plɒd] *vi* avancer péniblement; (*fig*) peiner

plonk [plɒŋk] (*inf*) *n* (*BRIT: wine*) pinard *m*, piquette *f* ♦ *vt*: **to ~ sth down** poser brusquement qch

plot [plɒt] *n* complot *m*, conspiration *f*; (*of story, play*) intrigue *f*; (*of land*) lot *m* de terrain, lopin *m* ♦ *vt* (*sb's downfall*) comploter; (*mark out*) pointer; relever, déterminer ♦ *vi* comploter

plough [plaʊ] (*US* **plow**) *n* charrue *f* ♦ *vt* (*earth*) labourer; **to ~ money into** investir dans; **~ through** *vt fus* (*snow etc*) avancer péniblement dans; **~man's lunch** (*BRIT*) *n* assiette froide avec du pain, du fromage et des pickles

ploy [plɔɪ] *n* stratagème *m*

pluck [plʌk] *vt* (*fruit*) cueillir; (*musical instrument*) pincer; (*bird*) plumer; (*eyebrow*) épiler ♦ *n* courage *m*, cran *m*; **to ~ up courage** prendre son courage à deux mains

plug [plʌg] *n* (*ELEC*) prise *f* de courant; (*stopper*) bouchon *m*, bonde *f*; (*AUT: also: spark(ing) ~*) bougie *f* ♦ *vt* (*hole*) boucher; (*inf: advertise*) faire du battage pour; **~ in** *vt* (*ELEC*) brancher

plum [plʌm] *n* (*fruit*) prune *f* ♦ *cpd*: **~ job** (*inf*) travail *m* en or

plumb [plʌm] *vt*: **to ~ the depths** (*fig*) toucher le fond (du désespoir)

plumber ['plʌmə*] *n* plombier *m*

plumbing ['plʌmɪŋ] *n* (*trade*) plomberie *f*; (*piping*) tuyauterie *f*

plummet ['plʌmɪt] *vi*: **to ~ (down)** plonger, dégringoler

plump [plʌmp] *adj* rondelet(te), dodu(e), bien en chair ♦ *vi*: **to ~ for** (*col: choose*) se décider pour

plunder ['plʌndə*] *n* pillage *m* (*loot*) butin *m* ♦ *vt* piller

plunge [plʌndʒ] *n* plongeon *m*; (*fig*) chute *f* ♦ *vt* plonger ♦ *vi* (*dive*) plonger (*fall*) tomber, dégringoler; **to take the ~** se jeter à l'eau; **~r** *n* (*for drain*) (déboucher *m* à) ventouse *f*; **plunging** *adj*: **plunging neckline** décolleté plongeant

pluperfect [pluːˈpɜːfɪkt] *n* plus-que-parfait *m*

plural ['plʊərəl] *adj* pluriel(le) ♦ *n* pluriel *m*

plus [plʌs] *n* (*also*: **~ sign**) signe *m* plus ♦ *prep* plus; **ten/twenty ~** plus de dix/vingt

plush [plʌʃ] *adj* somptueux(euse)

ply [plaɪ] *vt* (*a trade*) exercer ♦ *vi* (*ship*) faire la navette ♦ *n* (*of wool, rope*) fil *m*, brin *m*; **to ~ sb with drink** donner continuellement à boire à qn; **to ~ sb with questions** presser qn de questions; **~wood** *n* contre-plaqué *m*

PM *abbr* = Prime Minister

p.m. *adv abbr* (= *post meridiem*) de l'après-midi

pneumatic drill [nju:'mætɪk-] *n* marteau-piqueur *m*

pneumonia [nju:'məʊnɪə] *n* pneumonie *f*

poach [pəʊtʃ] *vt* (*cook*) pocher; (*steal*) pêcher (*or* chasser) sans permis ♦ *vi* braconner; ~**ed egg** *n* œuf poché; ~**er** *n* braconnier *m*

P.O. Box *n abbr* = Post Office Box

pocket ['pɒkɪt] *n* poche *f* ♦ *vt* empocher; **to be out of** ~ (*BRIT*) en être de sa poche; ~**book** (*US*) *n* (*wallet*) portefeuille *m*; ~ **knife** *n* canif *m*; ~ **money** *n* argent *m* de poche

pod [pɒd] *n* cosse *f*

podgy ['pɒdʒɪ] *adj* rondelet(te)

podiatrist [pɒ'di:ətrɪst] (*US*) *n* pédicure *m/f*, podologue *m/f*

poem ['pəʊəm] *n* poème *m*

poet ['pəʊɪt] *n* poète *m*; ~**ic** *adj* poétique; ~ **laureate** *n* poète lauréat (*nommé par la Cour royal*); ~**ry** *n* poésie *f*

poignant ['pɔɪnjənt] *adj* poignant(e); (*sharp*) vif(vive)

point [pɔɪnt] *n* point *m*; (*tip*) pointe *f*; (*in time*) moment *m*; (*in space*) endroit *m*; (*subject, idea*) point, sujet *m*; (*purpose*) sens *m*; (*ELEC*) prise *f*; (*also: decimal* ~): **2 ~ 3 (2.3)** 2 virgule 3 (2,3) ♦ *vt* (*show*) indiquer; (*gun etc*): **to** ~ **sth at** braquer *or* diriger qch sur ♦ *vi*: **to** ~ **at** montrer du doigt; ~**s** *npl* (*AUT*) vis platinées; (*RAIL*) aiguillage *m*; **to be on the** ~ **of doing sth** être sur le point de faire qch; **to make a** ~ **of doing** ne pas manquer de faire; **to get the** ~ comprendre, saisir; **to miss the** ~ ne pas comprendre; **to come to the** ~ en venir au fait; **there's no** ~ (**in doing**) cela ne sert à rien (de faire); ~ **out** *vt* faire remarquer, souligner; ~ **to** *vt fus* (*fig*) indiquer; ~**-blank** *adv* (*fig*) catégoriquement; (*also: at* ~*-blank range*) à bout portant; ~**ed** *adj* (*shape*) pointu(e); (*remark*) plein(e) de sous-entendus; ~**er** *n* (*needle*) aiguille *f*; (*piece of advice*) conseil *m*; (*clue*) indice *m*; ~**less** *adj* inutile, vain(e); ~ **of view** *n* point *m* de vue

poise [pɔɪz] *n* (*composure*) calme *m*

poison ['pɔɪzn] *n* poison *m* ♦ *vt* empoisonner; ~**ous** *adj* (*snake*) venimeux(euse); (*plant*) vénéneux(euse); (*fumes etc*) toxique

poke [pəʊk] *vt* (*fire*) tisonner; (*jab with finger, stick etc*) piquer; (*put*): **to** ~ **sth in(to)** fourrer *or* enfoncer qch dans; ~ **about** *vi* fureter

poker ['pəʊkə*] *n* tisonnier *m*; (*CARDS*) poker *m*

poky ['pəʊkɪ] *adj* exigu(ë)

Poland ['pəʊlənd] *n* Pologne *f*

polar ['pəʊlə*] *adj* polaire; ~ **bear** *n* ours blanc

Pole [pəʊl] *n* Polonais(e)

pole [pəʊl] *n* poteau *m*; (*of wood*) mât *m*, perche *f*; (*GEO*) pôle *m*; ~ **bean** (*US*) *n* haricot *m* (à rames); ~ **vault** *n* saut *m* à la perche

police [pə'li:s] *npl* police *f* ♦ *vt* maintenir l'ordre dans; ~ **car** *n* voiture *f* de police; ~**man** (*irreg*) *n* agent *m* de police, policier *m*; ~ **station** *n* commissariat *m* de police; ~**woman** (*irreg*) *n* femme-agent *f*

policy ['pɒlɪsɪ] *n* politique *f*; (*also: insurance* ~) police *f* (d'assurance)

polio ['pəʊlɪəʊ] *n* polio *f*

Polish ['pəʊlɪʃ] *adj* polonais(e) ♦ *n* (*LING*) polonais *m*

polish ['pɒlɪʃ] *n* (*for shoes*) cirage *m*; (*for floor*) cire *f*, encaustique *f*; (*shine*) éclat *m*, poli *m*; (*fig: refinement*) raffinement *m* ♦ *vt* (*put polish on shoes, wood*) cirer; (*make shiny*) astiquer, faire briller; ~ **off** *vt* (*work*) expédier; (*food*) liquider; ~**ed** *adj* (*fig*) raffiné(e)

polite [pə'laɪt] *adj* poli(e); **in** ~ **society** dans la bonne société; ~**ness** *n* politesse *f*

political [pə'lɪtɪkəl] *adj* politique

politician [pɒlɪ'tɪʃən] *n* homme *m* politique, politicien *m*

politics ['pɒlɪtɪks] *npl* politique *f*

poll [pəʊl] *n* scrutin, vote *m*; (*also: opinion* ~) sondage *m* (d'opinion) ♦ *vt* obtenir

pollen ['pɒlən] *n* pollen *m*

polling day ['pəʊlɪŋ-] (*BRIT*) *n* jour *m* des élections

polling station (*BRIT*) *n* bureau *m* de vote

pollute [pə'lu:t] *vt* polluer; **pollution** *n* pollution *f*

polo ['pəʊləʊ] *n* polo *m*; ~-**necked** *adj* à col roulé; ~ **shirt** *n* polo *m*

poltergeist ['pɔltəgaɪst] *n* esprit frappeur

polyester [pɒlɪ'ɛstə*] *n* polyester *m*

polytechnic [pɒlɪ'tɛknɪk] (*BRIT*) *n* (*college*) I.U.T. *m*, Institut *m* Universitaire de Technologie

polythene ['pɒlɪθi:n] *n* polyéthylène *m*; ~ **bag** *n* sac *m* en plastique

pomegranate ['pɒməgrænɪt] *n* grenade *f*

pomp [pɒmp] *n* pompe *f*, faste *f*, apparat *m*; ~**ous** ['pɒmpəs] *adj* pompeux(euse)

pond [pɒnd] *n* étang *m*; mare *f*

ponder ['pɒndə*] *vt* considérer, peser; ~**ous** *adj* pesant(e), lourd(e)

pong [pɒŋ] (*BRIT: inf*) *n* puanteur *f*

pony ['pəʊnɪ] *n* poney *m*; ~**tail** *n* queue *f* de cheval; ~ **trekking** (*BRIT*) *n* randonnée *f* à cheval

poodle ['pu:dl] *n* caniche *m*

pool [pu:l] *n* (*of rain*) flaque *f*; (*pond*) mare *f*; (*also: swimming* ~) piscine *f*; (*billiards*) poule *f* ♦ *vt* mettre en commun; ~**s** *npl* (*football pools*) ≈ loto sportif

poor [pʊə*] *adj* pauvre; (*mediocre*) médiocre, faible, mauvais(e) ♦ *npl*: **the ~** les pauvres *mpl*; **~ly** *adj* souffrant(e), malade ♦ *adv* mal; médiocrement

pop [pɒp] *n* (MUS) musique *f* pop; (*drink*) boisson gazeuse; (US: *inf: father*) papa *m*; (*noise*) bruit sec ♦ *vt* (*put*) mettre (rapidement) ♦ *vi* éclater; (*cork*) sauter; **~ in** *vi* entrer en passant; **~ out** *vi* sortir (brièvement); **~ up** *vi* apparaître, surgir

pope [pəʊp] *n* pape *m*

poplar ['pɒplə*] *n* peuplier *m*

popper ['pɒpə*] (BRIT: *inf*) *n* bouton-pression *m*

poppy ['pɒpɪ] *n* coquelicot *m*; pavot *m*

Popsicle ['pɒpsɪkl] (®: US) *n* esquimau *m* (*glace*)

popular ['pɒpjʊlə*] *adj* populaire; (*fashionable*) à la mode

population [pɒpjʊ'leɪʃən] *n* population *f*

porcelain ['pɔːslɪn] *n* porcelaine *f*

porch [pɔːtʃ] *n* porche *m*; (US) véranda *f*

porcupine ['pɔːkjʊpaɪn] *n* porc-épic *m*

pore [pɔː*] *n* pore *m* ♦ *vi*: **to ~ over** s'absorber dans, être plongé(e) dans

pork [pɔːk] *n* porc *m*

pornography [pɔː'nɒgrəfɪ] *n* pornographie *f*

porpoise ['pɔːpəs] *n* marsouin *m*

porridge ['pɒrɪdʒ] *n* porridge *m*

port [pɔːt] *n* (*harbour*) port *m*; (NAUT: *left side*) bâbord *m*; (*wine*) porto *m*; **~ of call** escale *f*

portable ['pɔːtəbl] *adj* portatif(ive)

porter ['pɔːtə*] *n* (*for luggage*) porteur *m*; (*doorkeeper*) gardien(ne); portier *m*

portfolio [pɔːt'fəʊlɪəʊ] *n* portefeuille *m*; (*of artist*) portfolio *m*

porthole ['pɔːthəʊl] *n* hublot *m*

portion ['pɔːʃən] *n* portion *f*, part *f*

portly ['pɔːtlɪ] *adj* corpulent(e)

portrait ['pɔːtrɪt] *n* portrait *m*

portray [pɔː'treɪ] *vt* faire le portrait de; (*in writing*) dépeindre, représenter; (*subj: actor*) jouer; **~al** *n* portrait *m*, représentation *f*

Portugal ['pɔːtjʊgəl] *n* Portugal *m*

Portuguese [pɔːtjʊ'giːz] *adj* portugais(e) ♦ *n inv* Portugais(e); (LING) portugais *m*

pose [pəʊz] *n* pose *f* ♦ *vi* (*pretend*): **to ~ as** se poser en ♦ *vt* poser; (*problem*) créer

posh [pɒʃ] (*inf*) *adj* chic *inv*

position [pə'zɪʃən] *n* position *f*; (*job*) situation *f* ♦ *vt* placer

positive ['pɒzɪtɪv] *adj* positif(ive); (*certain*) sûr(e), certain(e); (*definite*) formel(le), catégorique

posse ['pɒsɪ] (US) *n* détachement *m*

possess [pə'zɛs] *vt* posséder; **~ion** [pə'zɛʃən] *n* possession *f*

possibility [pɒsə'bɪlɪtɪ] *n* possibilité *f*; éventualité *f*

possible ['pɒsəbl] *adj* possible; **as big as ~** aussi gros que possible

possibly ['pɒsəblɪ] *adv* (*perhaps*) peut-être; **if you ~ can** si cela vous est possible; **I cannot ~ come** il m'est impossible de venir

post [pəʊst] *n* poste *f*; (BRIT: *letters, delivery*) courrier *m*; (*job, situation, MIL*) poste *m*; (*pole*) poteau *m* ♦ *vt* (BRIT: *send by ~*) poster; (: *appoint*): **to ~ to** affecter à; **~age** *n* tarifs *mpl* d'affranchissement; **~al** **order** *n* mandat(-poste) *m*; **~box** (BRIT) *n* boîte *f* aux lettres; **~card** *n* carte postale; **~code** (BRIT) *n* code postal

poster ['pəʊstə*] *n* affiche *f*

poste restante ['pəʊst'rɛstɑːnt] (BRIT) *n* poste restante *f*

postgraduate ['pəʊst'grædjuɪt] *n* ≈ étudiant(e) de troisième cycle

posthumous ['pɒstjʊməs] *adj* posthume

postman ['pəʊstmən] (*irreg*) *n* facteur *m*

postmark ['pəʊstmɑːk] *n* cachet *m* (de la poste)

postmortem ['pəʊst'mɔːtəm] *n* autopsie *f*

post office *n* (*building*) poste *f*; (*organization*): **the Post Office** les Postes; **Post Office Box** *n* boîte postale

postpone [pə'spəʊn] *vt* remettre (à plus tard)

posture ['pɒstʃə*] *n* posture *f*; (*fig*) attitude *f*

postwar ['pəʊst'wɔː*] *adj* d'après-guerre

posy ['pəʊzɪ] *n* petit bouquet

pot [pɒt] *n* pot *m*; (*for cooking*) marmite *f*, casserole *f*; (*tea~*) théière *f*; (*coffee~*) cafetière *f*; (*inf: marijuana*) herbe *f* ♦ *vt* (*plant*) mettre en pot; **to go to ~** (*inf: work, performance*) aller à vau-l'eau

potato [pə'teɪtəʊ] (*pl* **~es**) *n* pomme *f* de terre; **~ peeler** *n* épluche-légumes *m inv*

potent ['pəʊtənt] *adj* puissant(e); (*drink*) fort(e), très alcoolisé(e); (*man*) viril

potential [pəʊ'tɛnʃəl] *adj* potentiel(le) ♦ *n* potentiel *m*

pothole ['pɒthəʊl] *n* (*in road*) nid *m* de poule; (BRIT: *underground*) gouffre *m*, caverne *f*; **potholing** ['pɒthəʊlɪŋ] (BRIT) *n*: **to go potholing** faire de la spéléologie

potluck ['pɒt'lʌk] *n*: **to take ~** tenter sa chance

potted ['pɒtɪd] *adj* (*food*) en conserve; (*plant*) en pot; (*abbreviated*) abrégé(e)

potter ['pɒtə*] *n* potier *m* ♦ *vi*: **to ~ around**, **~ about** (BRIT) bricoler; **~y** *n* poterie *f*

potty ['pɒtɪ] *adj* (*inf: mad*) dingue ♦ *n* (*child's*) pot *m*

pouch [paʊtʃ] *n* (ZOOL) poche *f*; (*for tobacco*) blague *f*; (*for money*) bourse *f*

poultry ['pəʊltrɪ] *n* volaille *f*

pounce [paʊns] *vi*: **to ~ (on)** bondir (sur), sauter (sur)

pound [paʊnd] *n* (*unit of money*) livre *f*; (*unit of weight*) livre ♦ *vt* (*beat*) bourrer de coups, marteler; (*crush*) piler, pulvériser ♦ *vi* (*heart*) battre violemment, taper

pour [pɔː*] *vt* verser ♦ *vi* couler à flots; **to ~ (with rain)** pleuvoir à verse; **to ~ sb a drink** verser *or* servir à boire à qn; **~ away** *vt* vider; **~ in** *vi* (*people*) affluer, se précipiter; (*news, letters etc*) arriver en masse; **~ off** *vt* = **pour away**; **~ out** *vi* (*people*) sortir en masse ♦ *vt* vider; (*fig*) déverser; (*serve: a drink*) verser; **~ing** *adj*: **~ing rain** pluie torrentielle

pout [paut] *vi* faire la moue

poverty ['pɒvətɪ] *n* pauvreté *f*, misère *f*; **~-stricken** *adj* pauvre, déshérité(e)

powder ['paudə*] *n* poudre *f* ♦ *vt*: **to ~ one's face** se poudrer; **~ compact** *n* poudrier *m*; **~ed milk** *n* lait *m* en poudre; **~ puff** *n* houppette *f*; **~ room** *n* toilettes *fpl* (pour dames)

power ['pauə*] *n* (*strength*) puissance *f*, force *f*; (*ability, authority*) pouvoir *m*; (*of speech, thought*) faculté *f*; (*ELEC*) courant *m*; **to be in ~** (*POL etc*) être au pouvoir; **~ cut** *n* coupure *f* de courant; **~ed** *adj*: **~ed by** actionné(e) par, fonctionnant à; **~ failure** *n* panne *f* de courant; **~ful** *adj* puissant(e); **~less** *adj* impuissant(e); **~ point** (*BRIT*) *n* prise *f* de courant; **~ station** *n* centrale *f* électrique

p.p. *abbr* (= *per procurationem*): **~ J. Smith** pour M. J. Smith

PR *n abbr* = **public relations**

practical ['præktɪkəl] *adj* pratique; **~ities** *npl* (*of situation*) aspect *m* pratique; **~ity** (*no pl*) *n* (*of person*) sens *m* pratique; **~ joke** *n* farce *f*, attrape *f*; **~ly** *adv* (*almost*) pratiquement

practice ['præktɪs] *n* pratique *f*; (*of profession*) exercice *m*; (*at football etc*) entraînement *m*; (*business*) cabinet *m* ♦ *vt, vi* (*US*) = **practise**; **in ~** (*in reality*) en pratique; **out of ~** rouillé(e)

practise ['præktɪs] (*US* **practice**) *vt* (*musical instrument*) travailler; (*train for: sport*) s'entraîner à; (*a sport, religion*) pratiquer; (*profession*) exercer ♦ *vi* s'exercer, travailler; (*train*) s'entraîner; (*lawyer, doctor*) exercer; **practising** ['præktɪsɪŋ] *adj* (*Christian etc*) pratiquant(e); (*lawyer*) en exercice

practitioner [præk'tɪʃənə*] *n* praticien(ne)

prairie ['preərɪ] *n* steppe *f*, prairie *f*

praise [preɪz] *n* éloge(s) *m(pl)*, louange(s) *f(pl)* ♦ *vt* louer, faire l'éloge de; **~worthy** *adj* digne d'éloges

pram [præm] (*BRIT*) *n* landau *m*, voiture *f* d'enfant

prance [prɑːns] *vi* (*also: to ~ about: person*) se pavaner

prank [præŋk] *n* farce *f*

prawn [prɔːn] *n* crevette *f* (rose)

pray [preɪ] *vi* prier; **~er** [preə*] *n* prière *f*

preach [priːtʃ] *vt, vi* prêcher

precaution [prɪ'kɔːʃən] *n* précaution *f*

precede [prɪ'siːd] *vt* précéder

precedent ['presɪdənt] *n* précédent *m*

precinct ['priːsɪŋkt] *n* (*US*) circonscription *f*, arrondissement *m*; **~s** *npl* (*neighbourhood*) alentours *mpl*, environs *mpl*; **pedestrian ~** (*BRIT*) zone piétonnière; **shopping ~** (*BRIT*) centre commercial

precious ['preʃəs] *adj* précieux(euse)

precipitate [*vb* prɪ'sɪpɪteɪt] *vt* précipiter

precise [prɪ'saɪs] *adj* précis(e); **~ly** *adv* précisément

preclude [prɪ'kluːd] *vt* exclure

precocious [prɪ'kəuʃəs] *adj* précoce

precondition ['priːkən'dɪʃən] *n* condition *f* nécessaire

predecessor ['priːdɪsesə*] *n* prédécesseur *m*

predicament [prɪ'dɪkəmənt] *n* situation *f* difficile

predict [prɪ'dɪkt] *vt* prédire; **~able** *adj* prévisible

predominantly [prɪ'dɒmɪnəntlɪ] *adv* en majeure partie; surtout

preempt *vt* anticiper, devancer

preen [priːn] *vt*: **to ~ itself** (*bird*) se lisser les plumes; **to ~ o.s.** s'admirer

prefab ['priːfæb] *n* bâtiment préfabriqué

preface ['prefɪs] *n* préface *f*

prefect ['priːfekt] (*BRIT*) *n* (*in school*) élève chargé(e) de certaines fonctions de discipline

prefer [prɪ'fɜː*] *vt* préférer; **~ably** *adv* de préférence; **~ence** *n* préférence *f*; **~ential** *adj*: **~ential treatment** traitement *m* de faveur *or* préférentiel

prefix ['priːfɪks] *n* préfixe *m*

pregnancy ['pregnənsɪ] *n* grossesse *f*

pregnant ['pregnənt] *adj* enceinte; (*animal*) pleine

prehistoric ['priːhɪs'tɔrɪk] *adj* préhistorique

prejudice ['predʒudɪs] *n* préjugé *m*; **~d** *adj* (*person*) plein(e) de préjugés; (*in a matter*) partial(e)

premarital ['priː'mærɪtl] *adj* avant le mariage

premature ['premətʃuə*] *adj* prématuré(e)

premier ['premɪə*] *adj* premier(ère), principal(e) ♦ *n* (*POL*) Premier ministre

première ['premɪ'eə*] *n* première *f*

premise ['premɪs] *n* prémisse *f*; **~s** *npl* (*building*) locaux *mpl*; **on the ~s** sur les lieux; sur place

premium ['priːmɪəm] *n* prime *f*; **to be at a ~** faire prime; **~ bond** (*BRIT*) *n* bon *m* à lot, obligation *f* à prime

premonition [premə'nɪʃən] *n* prémonition *f*

preoccupied [priː'ɒkjupaɪd] *adj* préoccupé(e)

prep [prep] *n* (*SCOL: study*) étude *f*

prepaid ['priː'peɪd] adj payé(e) d'avance
preparation ['prepə'reɪʃən] n préparation f;
~s npl (for trip, war) préparatifs mpl
preparatory [prɪ'pærətərɪ] adj préliminaire;
~ **school** (BRIT) n école primaire privée
prepare [prɪ'pɛə*] vt préparer ♦ vi: to ~
for se préparer à; ~**d** to prêt(e) à
preposition [prepə'zɪʃən] n préposition f
preposterous [prɪ'pɒstərəs] adj absurde
prep school n = preparatory school
prerequisite ['priː'rekwɪzɪt] n condition f
préalable
prescribe [prɪs'kraɪb] vt prescrire
prescription [prɪs'krɪpʃən] n (MED) ordonnance f; (: medicine) médicament (obtenu
sur ordonnance)
presence ['prezns] n présence f; ~ **of mind**
présence d'esprit
present [adj, n 'preznt, vb prɪ'zent] adj pré-
sent(e) ♦ n (gift) cadeau m; (actuality) présent m ♦ vt présenter; (prize, medal) remettre; (give): **to** ~ **sb with sth** or **sth to sb**
offrir qch à qn; **to give sb a** ~ offrir un
cadeau à qn; **at** ~ en ce moment; ~**ation**
n présentation f; (ceremony) remise f du cadeau (or de la médaille etc); ~**-day** adj
contemporain(e), actuel(le); ~**er** n (RADIO,
TV) présentateur(trice); ~**ly** adv (with verb
in past) peu après; (soon) tout à l'heure,
bientôt; (at present) en ce moment
preservative [prɪ'zɜːvətɪv] n agent m de
conservation
preserve [prɪ'zɜːv] vt (keep safe) préserver,
protéger; (maintain) conserver, garder;
(food) mettre en conserve ♦ n (often pl:
jam) confiture f
president ['prezɪdənt] n président(e); ~**ial**
adj présidentiel(le)
press [pres] n presse f; (for wine) pressoir
m ♦ vt (squeeze) presser, serrer; (push) appuyer sur; (clothes: iron) repasser; (put pressure on) faire pression sur; (insist): **to** ~
sth on sb presser qn d'accepter qch ♦ vi
appuyer, peser; **to** ~ **for sth** faire pression
pour obtenir qch; **we are** ~**ed for time/
money** le temps/l'argent nous manque; ~
on vi continuer; ~ **conference** n conférence f de presse; ~**ing** adj urgent(e), pres-
sant(e); ~ **stud** (BRIT) n bouton-pression
m; ~**-up** (BRIT) n traction f
pressure ['preʃə*] n pression f; (stress) tension f; **to put** ~ **on sb (to do)** faire pression sur qn (pour qu'il/elle fasse); ~
cooker n cocotte-minute f; ~ **gauge** n
manomètre m; ~ **group** n groupe m de
pression
prestige [pres'tiːʒ] n prestige m
presumably [prɪ'zjuːməblɪ] adv vraisembla-
blement
presume [prɪ'zjuːm] vt présumer, supposer
pretence [prɪ'tens] (US **pretense**) n (claim)
prétention f; **under false** ~**s** sous des pré-

textes fallacieux
pretend [prɪ'tend] vt (feign) feindre, simuler ♦ vi faire semblant
pretext ['priːtekst] n prétexte m
pretty ['prɪtɪ] adj joli(e) ♦ adv assez
prevail [prɪ'veɪl] vi (be usual) avoir cours;
(win) l'emporter, prévaloir; ~**ing** adj domi-
nant(e)
prevalent ['prevələnt] adj répandu(e), cou-
rant(e)
prevent [prɪ'vent] vt: **to** ~ **(from doing)**
empêcher (de faire); ~**ive** adj = **preven-
tive**; ~**ive** adj préventif(ive)
preview ['priːvjuː] n (of film etc) avant-
première f
previous ['priːvɪəs] adj précédent(e); anté-
rieur(e); ~**ly** adv précédemment, auparavant
prewar ['priː'wɔː*] adj d'avant-guerre
prey [preɪ] n proie f ♦ vi: **to** ~ **on** s'attaquer à; **it was** ~**ing on his mind** cela le
travaillait
price [praɪs] n prix m ♦ vt (goods) fixer le
prix de; ~**less** adj sans prix, inestimable;
~ **list** n liste f des prix, tarif m
prick [prɪk] n piqûre f ♦ vt piquer; **to** ~ **up**
one's ears dresser or tendre l'oreille
prickle ['prɪkl] n (of plant) épine f; (sensation) picotement m; **prickly** ['prɪklɪ] adj pi-
quant(e), épineux(euse); **prickly heat** n
fièvre f miliaire
pride [praɪd] n orgueil m; fierté f ♦ vt: **to** ~
o.s. on se flatter de; s'enorgueillir de
priest [priːst] n prêtre m; ~**hood** n prêtrise
f, sacerdoce m
prim [prɪm] adj collet monté inv, guindé(e)
primarily ['praɪmərɪlɪ] adv principalement,
essentiellement
primary ['praɪmərɪ] adj (first in importance)
premier(ère), primordial(e), principal(e) ♦ n
(US: election) (élection f) primaire f; ~
school (BRIT) n école primaire f
prime [praɪm] adj primordial(e), fondamen-
tal(e); (excellent) excellent(e) ♦ n: **in the** ~
of life dans la fleur de l'âge ♦ vt (wood) apprêter; (fig) mettre au courant; **P~ Minister** n Premier ministre m
primeval [praɪ'miːvəl] adj primitif(ive); ~
forest forêt f vierge
primitive ['prɪmɪtɪv] adj primitif(ive)
primrose ['prɪmrəʊz] n primevère f
primus (stove) ['praɪməs-] (®:BRIT) n réchaud m de camping
prince [prɪns] n prince m
princess [prɪn'ses] n princesse f
principal ['prɪnsəpl] adj principal(e) ♦ n
(headmaster) directeur(trice), principal m
principle ['prɪnsəpl] n principe m; **in/on** ~
en/par principe
print [prɪnt] n (mark) empreinte f; (letters)
caractères mpl; (ART) gravure f, estampe f;
(: photograph) photo f ♦ vt imprimer;

(*publish*) publier; (*write in block letters*) écrire en caractères d'imprimerie; **out of** ~ épuisé(e); ~**ed matter** *n* imprimé(s) *m(pl)*; ~**er** *n* imprimeur *m*; (*machine*) imprimante *f*; ~**ing** *n* impression *f*; ~**-out** *n* copie *f* papier

prior ['praɪə*] *adj* antérieur(e), précédent(e); (*more important*) prioritaire ♦ *adv*: ~ **to doing** avant de faire

priority [praɪ'ɒrɪtɪ] *n* priorité *f*

prise [praɪz] *vt*: **to** ~ **open** forcer

prison ['prɪzn] *n* prison *f* ♦ *cpd* pénitentiaire; ~**er** *n* prisonnier(ère)

pristine ['prɪstiːn] *adj* parfait(e)

privacy ['prɪvəsɪ] *n* intimité *f*, solitude *f*

private ['praɪvɪt] *adj* privé(e); (*personal*) personnel(le); (*house, lesson*) particulier(ère); (*quiet: place*) tranquille; (*reserved: person*) secret(ète) ♦ *n* soldat *m* de deuxième classe; "**~**" (*on envelope*) "personnelle"; **in** ~ en privé; ~ **enterprise** *n* l'entreprise privée; ~ **eye** *n* détective privé; ~ **property** *n* propriété privée; **privatize** *vt* privatiser

privet ['prɪvɪt] *n* troène *m*

privilege ['prɪvɪlɪdʒ] *n* privilège *m*

privy ['prɪvɪ] *adj*: **to be** ~ **to** être au courant de

prize [praɪz] *n* prix *m* ♦ *adj* (*example, idiot*) parfait(e); (*bull, novel*) primé(e) ♦ *vt* priser, faire grand cas de; ~**-giving** *n* distribution *f* des prix; ~**winner** *n* gagnant(e)

pro [prəu] *n* (*SPORT*) professionnel(le); **the** ~**s and cons** le pour et le contre

probability [prɒbə'bɪlɪtɪ] *n* probabilité *f*; **probable** ['prɒbəbl] *adj* probable; **probably** *adv* probablement

probation [prə'beɪʃən] *n*: **on** ~ (*LAW*) en liberté surveillée, en sursis; (*employee*) à l'essai

probe [prəub] *n* (*MED, SPACE*) sonde *f*; (*enquiry*) enquête *f*, investigation *f* ♦ *vt* sonder, explorer

problem ['prɒbləm] *n* problème *m*

procedure [prə'siːdʒə*] *n* (*ADMIN, LAW*) procédure *f*; (*method*) marche *f* à suivre, façon *f* de procéder

proceed [prə'siːd] *vi* continuer; (*go forward*) avancer; **to** ~ (**with**) continuer, poursuivre; **to** ~ **to do** se mettre à faire; ~**ings** *npl* (*LAW*) poursuites *fpl*; (*meeting*) réunion *f*, séance *f*; ~**s** ['prəusiːdz] *npl* produit *m*, recette *f*

process ['prəuses] *n* processus *m*; (*method*) procédé *m* ♦ *vt* traiter; ~**ing** *n* (*PHOT*) développement *m*; ~**ion** [prə'seʃən] *n* défilé *m*, cortège *m*; (*REL*) procession *f*; **funeral** ~**ion** (*on foot*) cortège *m* funèbre; (*in cars*) convoi *m* mortuaire

proclaim [prə'kleɪm] *vt* déclarer, proclamer

procrastinate [prəu'kræstɪneɪt] *vi* faire traîner les choses, vouloir tout remettre au lendemain

procure [prə'kjuə*] *vt* obtenir

prod [prɒd] *vt* pousser

prodigal ['prɒdɪgəl] *adj* prodigue

prodigy ['prɒdɪdʒɪ] *n* prodige *m*

produce [*n* 'prɒdjuːs, *vb* prə'djuːs] *n* (*AGR*) produits *mpl* ♦ *vt* produire; (*to show*) présenter; (*cause*) provoquer, causer; (*THEATRE*) monter, mettre en scène; ~**r** *n* producteur *m*; (*THEATRE*) metteur *m* en scène

product ['prɒdʌkt] *n* produit *m*

production [prə'dʌkʃən] *n* production *f*; (*THEATRE*) mise *f* en scène; ~ **line** *n* chaîne *f* (de fabrication)

productivity [prɒdʌk'tɪvɪtɪ] *n* productivité *f*

profession [prə'feʃən] *n* profession *f*; ~**al** *n* professionnel(le) ♦ *adj* professionnel(le); (*work*) de professionnel

professor [prə'fesə*] *n* professeur *m* (*titulaire d'une chaire*)

proficiency [prə'fɪʃənsɪ] *n* compétence *f*, aptitude *f*

profile ['prəufaɪl] *n* profil *m*

profit ['prɒfɪt] *n* bénéfice *m*; profit *m* ♦ *vi*: **to** ~ (**by** *or* **from**) profiter (de); ~**able** *adj* lucratif(ive), rentable

profound [prə'faund] *adj* profond(e)

profusely [prə'fjuːslɪ] *adv* abondamment; avec effusion

prognosis [prɒg'nəusɪs] (*pl* **prognoses**) *n* pronostic *m*

programme ['prəugræm] (*US* **program**) *n* programme *m*; (*RADIO, TV*) émission *f* ♦ *vt* programmer; ~**r** (*US* **programer**) *n* programmeur(euse)

progress [*n* 'prəugres, *vb* prə'gres] *n* progrès *m(pl)* ♦ *vi* progresser, avancer; **in** ~ en cours; ~**ive** *adj* progressif(ive); (*person*) progressiste

prohibit [prə'hɪbɪt] *vt* interdire, défendre

project [*n* 'prɒdʒekt, *vb* prə'dʒekt] *n* (*plan*) projet *m*, plan *m*; (*venture*) opération *f*, entreprise *f*; (*research*) étude *f*, dossier *m* ♦ *vt* projeter ♦ *vi* (*stick out*) faire saillie, s'avancer; ~**ion** [prə'dʒekʃən] *n* projection *f*; (*overhang*) saillie *f*; ~**or** [prə'dʒektə*] *n* projecteur *m*

prolong [prə'lɒŋ] *vt* prolonger

prom [prɒm] *n abbr* = **promenade**; (*US: ball*) bal *m* d'étudiants

promenade [prɒmɪ'nɑːd] *n* (*by sea*) esplanade *f*, promenade *f*; ~ **concert** (*BRIT*) *n* concert *m* populaire (de musique classique)

prominent ['prɒmɪnənt] *adj* (*standing out*) proéminent(e); (*important*) important(e)

promiscuous [prə'mɪskjuəs] *adj* (*sexually*) de mœurs légères

promise ['prɒmɪs] *n* promesse *f* ♦ *vt, vi* promettre; **promising** ['prɒmɪsɪŋ] *adj* prometteur(euse)

promote [prə'məut] *vt* promouvoir; (*new product*) faire la promotion de; ~**r** *n* (*of* *event*) organisateur(trice); (*of cause, idea*) promoteur(trice); **promotion** [prə'məʊʃen] *n* promotion *f*

prompt [prɒmpt] *adj* rapide ♦ *adv* (*punctually*) à l'heure ♦ *n* (*COMPUT*) message *m* (de guidage) ♦ *vt* provoquer; (*person*) inciter, pousser; (*THEATRE*) souffler (son rôle *or* ses répliques) à; ~**ly** *adv* rapidement, sans délai; ponctuellement

prone [prəʊn] *adj* (*lying*) couché(e) (face contre terre); ~ **to** enclin(e) à

prong [prɒŋ] *n* (*of fork*) dent *f*

pronoun [ˈprəʊnaʊn] *n* pronom *m*

pronounce [prəˈnaʊns] *vt* prononcer

pronunciation [prənʌnsɪˈeɪʃən] *n* prononciation *f*

proof [pruːf] *n* preuve *f*; (*TYP*) épreuve *f* ♦ *adj*: ~ **against** à l'épreuve de

prop [prɒp] *n* support *m*, étai *m*; (*fig*) soutien *m* ♦ *vt* (*also:* ~ *up*) étayer, soutenir; (*lean*): **to** ~ **sth against** appuyer qch contre *or* à

propaganda [prɒpəˈgændə] *n* propagande *f*

propel [prəˈpel] *vt* propulser, faire avancer; ~**ler** *n* hélice *f*

propensity [prəˈpensɪtɪ] *n*: **a** ~ **for** *or* **to/to do** une propension à/à faire

proper [ˈprɒpə*] *adj* (*suited, right*) approprié(e), bon(bonne); (*seemly*) correct(e), convenable; (*authentic*) vrai(e), véritable; (*referring to place*): **the village** ~ le village proprement dit; ~**ly** *adv* correctement, convenablement; ~ **noun** *n* nom *m* propre

property [ˈprɒpətɪ] *n* propriété *f*; (*things owned*) biens *mpl*; propriété(s) *f(pl)*; (*land*) terres *fpl*

prophecy [ˈprɒfɪsɪ] *n* prophétie *f*

prophesy [ˈprɒfɪsaɪ] *vt* prédire

prophet [ˈprɒfɪt] *n* prophète *m*

proportion [prəˈpɔːʃən] *n* proportion *f*; (*share*) part *f*, partie *f*; ~**al**, ~**ate** *adj* proportionnel(le)

proposal [prəˈpəʊzl] *n* proposition *f*, offre *f*; (*plan*) projet *m*; (*of marriage*) demande *f* en mariage

propose [prəˈpəʊz] *vt* proposer, suggérer ♦ *vi* faire sa demande en mariage; **to** ~ **to do** avoir l'intention de faire; **proposition** [prɒpəˈzɪʃən] *n* proposition *f*

propriety [prəˈpraɪətɪ] *n* (*seemliness*) bienséance *f*, convenance *f*

prose [prəʊz] *n* (*not poetry*) prose *f*

prosecute [ˈprɒsɪkjuːt] *vt* poursuivre; **prosecution** [prɒsɪˈkjuːʃən] *n* poursuites *fpl* judiciaires; (*accusing side*) partie plaignante; **prosecutor** [ˈprɒsɪkjuːtə*] *n* (*US: plaintiff*) plaignant(e); (*also: public* ~) procureur *m*, ministère public

prospect [*n* ˈprɒspekt, *vb* prəˈspekt] *n* perspective *f* ♦ *vt, vi* prospecter; ~**s** *npl* (*for work etc*) possibilités *fpl* d'avenir, débouchés *mpl*; ~**ing** *n* (*for gold, oil etc*) pros-

pection *f*; ~**ive** *adj* (*possible*) éventuel(le); (*future*) futur(e)

prospectus [prəˈspektəs] *n* prospectus *m*

prosperity [prɒˈsperɪtɪ] *n* prospérité *f*

prostitute [ˈprɒstɪtjuːt] *n* prostitué(e)

protect [prəˈtekt] *vt* protéger; ~**ion** *n* protection *f*; ~**ive** *adj* protecteur(trice); (*clothing*) de protection

protein [ˈprəʊtiːn] *n* protéine *f*

protest [*n* ˈprəʊtest, *vb* prəˈtest] *n* protestation *f* ♦ *vi, vt*: **to** ~ (**that**) protester (que)

Protestant [ˈprɒtɪstənt] *adj, n* protestant(e)

protester [prəˈtestə*] *n* manifestant(e)

protracted [prəˈtræktɪd] *adj* prolongé(e)

protrude [prəˈtruːd] *vi* avancer, dépasser

proud [praʊd] *adj* fier(ère); (*pej*) orgueilleux(euse)

prove [pruːv] *vt* prouver, démontrer ♦ *vi*: **to** ~ (**to be**) **correct** *etc* s'avérer juste *etc*; **to** ~ **o.s.** montrer ce dont on est capable

proverb [ˈprɒvɜːb] *n* proverbe *m*

provide [prəˈvaɪd] *vt* fournir; **to** ~ **sb with sth** fournir qch à qn; ~ **for** *vt fus* (*person*) subvenir aux besoins de; (*future event*) prévoir; ~**d** (**that**) *conj* à condition que +*sub*; **providing** [prəˈvaɪdɪŋ] *conj*: **providing (that)** à condition que +*sub*

province [ˈprɒvɪns] *n* province *f*; (*fig*) domaine *m*; **provincial** [prəˈvɪnʃəl] *adj* provincial(e)

provision [prəˈvɪʒən] *n* (*supplying*) fourniture *f*; approvisionnement *m*; (*stipulation*) disposition *f*; ~**s** *npl* (*food*) provisions *fpl*; ~**al** *adj* provisoire

proviso [prəˈvaɪzəʊ] *n* condition *f*

provocative [prəˈvɒkətɪv] *adj* provocateur(trice), provocant(e)

provoke [prəˈvəʊk] *vt* provoquer

prow [praʊ] *n* proue *f*

prowess [ˈpraʊes] *n* prouesse *f*

prowl [praʊl] *vi* (*also:* ~ *about*, ~ *around*) rôder ♦ *n*: **on the** ~ à l'affût; ~**er** ♦ *n* rôdeur(euse)

proxy [ˈprɒksɪ] *n* procuration *f*

prudent [ˈpruːdənt] *adj* prudent(e)

prune [pruːn] *n* pruneau *m* ♦ *vt* élaguer

pry [praɪ] *vi*: **to** ~ **into** fourrer son nez dans

PS *n abbr* (= *postscript*) p.s.

psalm [sɑːm] *n* psaume *m*

pseudo- [ˈsjuːdəʊ] *prefix* pseudo-; ~**nym** [ˈsjuːdənɪm] *n* pseudonyme *m*

psyche [ˈsaɪkɪ] *n* psychisme *m*

psychiatrist [saɪˈkaɪətrɪst] *n* psychiatre *m/f*

psychic [ˈsaɪkɪk] *adj* (*also:* ~*al*) (méta)psychique; (*person*) doué(e) d'un sixième sens

psychoanalyst [saɪkəʊˈænəlɪst] *n* psychanalyste *m/f*

psychological [saɪkəˈlɒdʒɪkəl] *adj* psychologique; **psychologist** [saɪˈkɒlədʒɪst] *n* psychologue *m/f*; **psychology** [saɪˈkɒlədʒɪ] *n* psychologie f

PTO abbr (= please turn over) T.S.V.P.

pub [pʌb] n (= public house) pub m

public ['pʌblɪk] adj public(ique) ♦ n public m; **in** ~ en public; **to make** ~ rendre public; ~ **address system** n (système m de) sonorisation f; hauts-parleurs mpl

publican ['pʌblɪkən] n patron m de pub

public: ~ **company** n société f anonyme (cotée en Bourse); ~ **convenience** (BRIT) n toilettes fpl; ~ **holiday** n jour férié; ~ **house** (BRIT) n pub m

publicity [pʌb'lɪsɪtɪ] n publicité f

publicize ['pʌblɪsaɪz] vt faire connaître, rendre public(ique)

public: ~ **opinion** n opinion publique; ~ **relations** n relations publiques; ~ **school** n (BRIT) école (secondaire) privée; (US) école publique; ~**-spirited** adj qui fait preuve de civisme; ~ **transport** n transports mpl en commun

publish ['pʌblɪʃ] vt publier; ~**er** n éditeur m; ~**ing** n édition f

pucker ['pʌkə*] vt plisser

pudding ['pʊdɪŋ] n pudding m; (BRIT: sweet) dessert m, entremets m; **black** ~, (US) **blood** ~ boudin (noir)

puddle ['pʌdl] n flaque f (d'eau)

puff [pʌf] n bouffée f ♦ vt: **to** ~ **one's pipe** tirer sur sa pipe ♦ vi (pant) haleter; ~ **out** vt (fill with air) gonfler; ~**ed (out)** (inf) adj (out of breath) tout(e) essoufflé(e); ~ **pastry** (US ~ **paste**) n pâte feuilletée; ~**y** adj bouffi(e), boursouflé(e)

pull [pʊl] n (tug): **to give sth a** ~ tirer sur qch ♦ vt tirer; (trigger) presser ♦ vi tirer; **to** ~ **to pieces** mettre en morceaux; **to** ~ **one's punches** ménager son adversaire; **to** ~ **one's weight** faire sa part (du travail); **to** ~ **o.s. together** se ressaisir; **to** ~ **sb's leg** (fig) faire marcher qn; ~ **apart** vt (break) mettre en pièces, démantibuler; ~ **down** vt (house) démolir; ~ **in** vi (AUT) entrer; (RAIL) entrer en gare; ~ **off** vt enlever, ôter; (deal etc) mener à bien, conclure; ~ **out** vi démarrer, partir ♦ vt sortir; arracher; ~ **over** vi (AUT) se ranger; ~ **through** vi s'en sortir; ~ **up** vi (stop) s'arrêter ♦ vt remonter; (uproot) déraciner, arracher

pulley ['pʊlɪ] n poulie f

pullover ['pʊləʊvə*] n pull(-over) m, tricot m

pulp [pʌlp] n (of fruit) pulpe f

pulpit ['pʊlpɪt] n chaire f

pulsate [pʌl'seɪt] vi battre, palpiter; (music) vibrer

pulse [pʌls] n (of blood) pouls m; (of heart) battement m; (of music, engine) vibrations fpl; (BOT, CULIN) légume sec

pump [pʌmp] n pompe f; (shoe) escarpin m ♦ vt pomper; ~ **up** vt gonfler

pumpkin ['pʌmpkɪn] n potiron m, citrouille f

pun [pʌn] n jeu m de mots, calembour m

punch [pʌntʃ] n (blow) coup m de poing; (tool) poinçon m; (drink) punch m ♦ vt (hit): **to** ~ **sb/sth** donner un coup de poing à qn/sur qch; ~**line** n (of joke) conclusion f; ~**-up** (BRIT: inf) n bagarre f

punctual ['pʌŋktjʊəl] adj ponctuel(le)

punctuation [pʌŋktjʊ'eɪʃən] n ponctuation f

puncture ['pʌŋktʃə*] n crevaison f

pundit ['pʌndɪt] n individu m qui pontifie, pontife m

pungent ['pʌndʒənt] adj piquant(e), âcre

punish ['pʌnɪʃ] vt punir; ~**ment** n punition f, châtiment m

punk [pʌŋk] n (also: ~ **rocker**) punk m/f; (: ~ **rock**) le punk rock; (US: inf: hoodlum) voyou m

punt [pʌnt] n (boat) bachot m

punter ['pʌntə*] n (BRIT) n (gambler) parieur(euse); (inf): **the** ~**s** le public

puny ['pjuːnɪ] adj chétif(ive); (effort) piteux(euse)

pup [pʌp] n chiot m

pupil ['pjuːpl] n (SCOL) élève m/f; (of eye) pupille f

puppet ['pʌpɪt] n marionnette f, pantin m

puppy ['pʌpɪ] n chiot m, jeune chien(ne)

purchase ['pɜːtʃɪs] n achat m ♦ vt acheter; ~**r** n acheteur(euse)

pure [pjʊə*] adj pur(e); ~**ly** ['pjʊəlɪ] adv purement

purge [pɜːdʒ] n purge f

purple ['pɜːpl] adj violet(te); (face) cramoisi(e)

purport [pɜː'pɔːt] vi: **to** ~ **to be/do** prétendre être/faire

purpose ['pɜːpəs] n intention f, but m; **on** ~ exprès; ~**ful** adj déterminé(e), résolu(e)

purr [pɜː*] vi ronronner

purse [pɜːs] n (BRIT: for money) portemonnaie m inv; (US: handbag) sac m à main ♦ vt serrer, pincer

purser ['pɜːsə*] n (NAUT) commissaire m du bord

pursue [pə'sjuː] vt poursuivre

pursuit [pə'sjuːt] n poursuite f; (occupation) occupation f, activité f

push [pʊʃ] n poussée f ♦ vt pousser; (button) appuyer sur; (thrust): **to** ~ **sth (into)** enfoncer qch (dans); (product) faire de la publicité pour ♦ vi pousser; (demand): **to** ~ **for** exiger, demander avec insistance; ~ **aside** vt écarter; ~ **off** (inf) vi filer, ficher le camp; ~ **on** vi (continue) continuer; ~ **through** vi se frayer un chemin ♦ vt (measure) faire accepter; ~ **up** vt (total, prices) faire monter; ~**chair** n (BRIT) poussette f; ~**er** n (drug ~er) revendeur(euse) (de drogue), ravitailleur(euse) (en drogue); ~**over**

(inf) n: **it's a ~over** c'est un jeu d'enfant; **~-up** (US) n traction f; **~y** (pej) adj arriviste

puss [pus] (inf) n minet m

pussy (cat) ['pusi (kæt)] (inf) n minet m

put [put] (pt, pp put) vt mettre, poser, placer; (say) dire, exprimer; (a question) poser; (case, view) exposer, présenter; (estimate) estimer; **~ about** vt (rumour) faire courir; **~ across** vt (ideas etc) communiquer; **~ away** vt (store) ranger; **~ back** vt (replace) remettre, replacer; (postpone) remettre; (delay) retarder; **~ by** vt (money) mettre de côté, économiser; **~ down** vt (parcel etc) poser, déposer; (in writing) mettre par écrit, inscrire; (suppress: revolt etc) réprimer, faire cesser; (animal) abattre; (dog, cat) faire piquer; (attribute) attribuer; **~ forward** vt (ideas) avancer; **~ in** vt (gas, electricity) installer; (application, complaint) soumettre; (time, effort) consacrer; **~ off** vt (light etc) éteindre; (postpone) remettre à plus tard, ajourner; (discourage) dissuader; **~ on** vt (clothes, lipstick, record) mettre; (light etc) allumer; (play etc) monter; (food: cook) mettre à cuire or à chauffer; (gain): **to ~ on weight** prendre du poids, grossir; **to ~ the brakes on** freiner; **to ~ the kettle on** mettre l'eau à chauffer; **~ out** vt (take out) mettre dehors; (one's hand) tendre; (light etc) éteindre; (person: inconvenience) déranger, gêner; **~ through** vt (TEL: call) passer; (: person) mettre en communication; (plan) faire accepter; **~ up** vt (raise) lever, relever, remonter; (pin up) afficher; (hang) accrocher; (build) construire, ériger; (tent) monter; (umbrella) ouvrir; (increase) augmenter; (accommodate) loger; **~ up with** vt fus supporter

putt [pʌt] n coup roulé; **~ing green** n green m

putty ['pʌti] n mastic m

put-up ['putʌp] (BRIT) adj: **~ job** coup monté

puzzle ['pʌzl] n énigme f, mystère m; (jigsaw) puzzle m ♦ vt intriguer, rendre perplexe ♦ vi se creuser la tête; **puzzling** adj déconcertant(e)

pyjamas [pɪ'dʒɑːməz] (BRIT) npl pyjama(s) m(pl)

pyramid ['pɪrəmɪd] n pyramide f

Pyrenees [pɪrɪ'niːz] npl: **the ~** les Pyrénées fpl

Q q

quack [kwæk] n (of duck) coin-coin m inv; (pej: doctor) charlatan m

quad [kwɒd] n abbr = **quadrangle** ♦ abbr = **quadruplet**

quadrangle ['kwɒdræŋgl] n (courtyard) cour f

quadruple [kwɒ'druːpl] vt, vi quadrupler; **~ts** [kwɒ'druːpləts] npl quadruplés

quagmire ['kwægmaɪə*] n bourbier m

quail [kweɪl] n (ZOOL) caille f ♦ vi: **to ~ at or before** reculer devant

quaint [kweɪnt] adj bizarre; (house, village) au charme vieillot, pittoresque

quake [kweɪk] vi trembler

qualification [kwɒlɪfɪ'keɪʃən] n (often pl: degree etc) diplôme m; (: training) qualification(s) f(pl), expérience f; (ability) compétence(s) f(pl); (limitation) réserve f, restriction f

qualified ['kwɒlɪfaɪd] adj (trained) qualifié(e); (professionally) diplômé(e); (fit, competent) compétent(e), qualifié(e); (limited) conditionnel(le)

qualify ['kwɒlɪfaɪ] vt qualifier; (modify) atténuer, nuancer ♦ vi: **to ~ (as)** obtenir son diplôme (de); **to ~ (for)** remplir les conditions requises (pour); (SPORT) se qualifier (pour)

quality ['kwɒlɪtɪ] n qualité f

qualm [kwɑːm] n doute m; scrupule m

quandary ['kwɒndərɪ] n: **in a ~** devant un dilemme, dans l'embarras

quantity ['kwɒntɪtɪ] n quantité f; **~ surveyor** n métreur m vérificateur

quarantine ['kwɒrəntiːn] n quarantaine f

quarrel ['kwɒrəl] n querelle f, dispute f ♦ vi se disputer, se quereller; **~some** adj querelleur(euse)

quarry ['kwɒrɪ] n (for stone) carrière f; (animal) proie f, gibier m

quart [kwɔːt] n ≈ litre m

quarter ['kwɔːtə*] n quart m; (US: coin: 25 cents) quart de dollar; (of year) trimestre m; (district) quartier m ♦ vt (divide) partager en quartiers or en quatre; **~s** npl (living ~) logement m; (MIL) quartiers mpl, cantonnement m; **a ~ of an hour** un quart d'heure; **~ final** n quart m de finale; **~ly** adj trimestriel(le) ♦ adv tous les trois mois

quartet(te) [kwɔː'tet] *n* quatuor *m*; *(jazz players)* quartette *m*

quartz [kwɔːts] *n* quartz *m*

quash [kwɒʃ] *vt (verdict)* annuler

quaver ['kweɪvə*] *n (BRIT: MUS)* croche *f* ♦ *vi* trembler

quay [kiː] *n (also: ~side)* quai *m*

queasy ['kwiːzɪ] *adj*: **to feel ~** avoir mal au cœur

queen [kwiːn] *n* reine *f*; *(CARDS etc)* dame *f*; **~ mother** *n* reine mère *f*

queer [kwɪə*] *adj* étrange, curieux(euse); *(suspicious)* louche ♦ *n (infl)* homosexuel *m*

quell [kwel] *vt* réprimer, étouffer

quench [kwentʃ] *vt*: **to ~ one's thirst** se désaltérer

querulous ['kwerʊləs] *adj (person)* récriminateur(trice); *(voice)* plaintif(ive)

query ['kwɪərɪ] *n* question *f* ♦ *vt* remettre en question, mettre en doute

quest [kwest] *n* recherche *f*, quête *f*

question ['kwestʃən] *n* question *f* ♦ *vt (person)* interroger; *(plan, idea)* remettre en question, mettre en doute; **beyond ~** sans aucun doute; **out of the ~** hors de question; **~able** *adj* discutable; **~ mark** *n* point *m* d'interrogation; **~naire** [kwestʃə'nɛə*] *n* questionnaire *m*

queue [kjuː] *(BRIT)* *n* queue *f*, file *f* ♦ *vi (also: ~ up)* faire la queue

quibble ['kwɪbl] *vi*: **~ (about)** *or* **(over)** *or* **(with sth)** ergoter (sur qch)

quick [kwɪk] *adj* rapide; *(agile)* agile, vif(vive) ♦ *n*: **cut to the ~** *(fig)* touché(e) au vif; **be ~!** dépêche-toi!; **~en** *vt* accélérer, presser ♦ *vi* s'accélérer, devenir plus rapide; **~ly** *adv* vite, rapidement; **~sand** *n* sables mouvants; **~-witted** *adj* à l'esprit vif

quid [kwɪd] *(BRIT: inf)* *n, pl inv* livre *f*

quiet ['kwaɪət] *adj* tranquille, calme; *(voice)* bas(se); *(ceremony, colour)* discret(ète) ♦ *n* tranquillité *f*, calme *m*; *(silence)* silence *m* ♦ *vt, vi (US)* = **quieten**; **keep ~!** tais-toi!; **~en** *vi (also: ~ down)* se calmer, s'apaiser ♦ *vt* calmer, apaiser; **~ly** *adv* tranquillement, calmement; *(silently)* silencieusement; **~ness** *n* tranquillité *f*, calme *m*; *(silence)* silence *m*

quilt [kwɪlt] *n* édredon *m*; *(continental ~)* couette *f*

quin [kwɪn] *n abbr* = **quintuplet**

quintuplets [kwɪn'tjuːplɪts] *npl* quintuplé(e)s

quip [kwɪp] *n* remarque piquante *or* spirituelle, pointe *f*

quirk [kwɜːk] *n* bizarrerie *f*

quit [kwɪt] *(pt, pp ~ or ~ted)* *vt* quitter; *(smoking, grumbling)* arrêter de ♦ *vi (give up)* abandonner, renoncer; *(resign)* démissionner

quite [kwaɪt] *adv (rather)* assez, plutôt; *(en-tirely)* complètement, tout à fait; *(following a negative = almost)*: **that's not ~ big enough** ce n'est pas tout à fait assez grand; **I ~ understand** je comprends très bien; **~ a few of them** un assez grand nombre d'entre eux; **~ (so)!** exactement!

quits [kwɪts] *adj*: **~ (with)** quitte (envers); **let's call it ~** restons-en là

quiver ['kwɪvə*] *vi* trembler, frémir

quiz [kwɪz] *n (game)* jeu-concours *m* ♦ *vt* interroger; **~zical** *adj* narquois(e)

quota ['kwəʊtə] *n* quota *m*

quotation [kwəʊ'teɪʃən] *n* citation *f*; *(esti-mate)* devis *m*; **~ marks** *npl* guillemets *mpl*

quote [kwəʊt] *n* citation *f*; *(estimate)* devis *m* ♦ *vt* citer; *(price)* indiquer; **~s** *npl* guillemets *mpl*

R r

rabbi ['ræbaɪ] *n* rabbin *m*

rabbit ['ræbɪt] *n* lapin *m*; **~ hutch** *n* clapier *m*

rabble ['ræbl] *(pej)* *n* populace *f*

rabies ['reɪbiːz] *n* rage *f*

RAC *n abbr (BRIT)* = Royal Automobile Club

rac(c)oon [rə'kuːn] *n* raton laveur

race [reɪs] *n (species)* race *f*; *(competition, rush)* course *f* ♦ *vt (horse)* faire courir ♦ *vi (compete)* faire la course, courir; *(hurry)* aller à toute vitesse, courir; *(engine)* s'emballer; *(pulse)* augmenter; **~ car** *(US)* *n* = **racing car**; **~ car driver** *(US)* *n* = **racing driver**; **~course** *n* champ *m* de courses; **~horse** *n* cheval *m* de course; **~track** *n* piste *f*

racial ['reɪʃəl] *adj* racial(e)

racing ['reɪsɪŋ] *n* courses *fpl*; **~ car** *(BRIT)* *n* voiture *f* de course; **~ driver** *(BRIT)* *n* pilote *m* de course

racism ['reɪsɪzəm] *n* racisme *m*; **racist** *adj* raciste ♦ *n* raciste *m/f*

rack [ræk] *n (for guns, tools)* râtelier *m*; *(also: luggage ~)* porte-bagages *m inv*, filet *m* à bagages; *(: roof ~)* galerie *f*; *(dish ~)* égouttoir *m* ♦ *vt* tourmenter; **to ~ one's brains** se creuser la cervelle

racket ['rækɪt] *n (for tennis)* raquette *f*; *(noise)* tapage *m*; vacarme *m*; *(swindle)* escroquerie *f*

racquet ['rækɪt] *n* raquette *f*

racy ['reɪsɪ] adj plein(e) de verve; (slightly indecent) osé(e)

radar ['reɪdɑ:*] n radar m

radial ['reɪdɪəl] adj (also: ~-ply) à carcasse radiale

radiant ['reɪdɪənt] adj rayonnant(e)

radiate ['reɪdɪeɪt] vt (heat) émettre, dégager; (emotion) rayonner de ♦ vi (lines) rayonner

radiation [reɪdɪ'eɪʃən] n rayonnement m; (radioactive) radiation f

radiator ['reɪdɪeɪtə*] n radiateur m

radical ['rædɪkəl] adj radical(e)

radii ['reɪdɪaɪ] npl of radius

radio ['reɪdɪəu] n radio f ♦ vt appeler par radio; on the ~ à la radio; ~active [reɪdɪəu'æktɪv] adj radioactif(ive); ~ station n station f de radio

radish ['rædɪʃ] n radis m

radius ['reɪdɪəs] (pl radii) n rayon m

RAF n abbr = Royal Air Force

raffle ['ræfl] n tombola f

raft [rɑ:ft] n (craft; also: life ~) radeau m

rafter ['rɑ:ftə*] n chevron m

rag [ræg] n chiffon m; (pej: newspaper) feuille f de chou, torchon m; (student ~) attractions organisées au profit d'œuvres de charité; ~s npl (torn clothes etc) haillons mpl; ~ doll n poupée f de chiffon

rage [reɪdʒ] n (fury) rage f, fureur f ♦ vi (person) être fou(folle) de rage; (storm) faire rage, être déchaîné(e); it's all the ~ cela fait fureur

ragged ['rægɪd] adj (edge) inégal(e); (clothes) en loques; (appearance) déguenillé(e)

raid [reɪd] n (attack, also: MIL) raid m; (criminal) hold-up m inv; (by police) descente f, rafle f ♦ vt faire un raid sur or un hold-up or une descente dans

rail [reɪl] n (on stairs) rampe f; (on bridge, balcony) balustrade f; (of ship) bastingage m; ~s npl (track) rails mpl, voie ferrée; by ~ par chemin de fer, en train; ~ing(s) n(pl) grille f; ~road (US), ~way (BRIT) n (track) voie ferrée; (company) chemin m de fer; ~way line (BRIT) n ligne f de chemin de fer; ~wayman (BRIT: irreg) n cheminot m; ~way station (BRIT) n gare f

rain [reɪn] n pluie f ♦ vi pleuvoir; in the ~ sous la pluie; it's ~ing il pleut; ~bow n arc-en-ciel m; ~coat n imperméable m; ~drop n goutte f de pluie; ~fall n chute f de pluie; (measurement) hauteur f des précipitations; ~forest n forêt f tropicale humide; ~y adj pluvieux(euse)

raise [reɪz] n augmentation f ♦ vt (lift) lever; hausser; (increase) augmenter; (morale) remonter; (standards) améliorer; (question, doubt) provoquer, soulever; (cattle, family) élever; (crop) faire pousser; (funds) rassembler; (loan) obtenir; (army) lever; to ~ one's voice élever la voix

raisin ['reɪzən] n raisin sec

rake [reɪk] n (tool) râteau m ♦ vt (garden, leaves) ratisser; (with machine gun) balayer

rally ['rælɪ] n (POL etc) meeting m, rassemblement m; (AUT) rallye m; (TENNIS) échange m ♦ vt (support) gagner ♦ vi (sick person) aller mieux; (Stock Exchange) reprendre; ~ round vt fus venir en aide à

RAM [ræm] n abbr (= random access memory) mémoire vive

ram [ræm] n bélier m ♦ vt enfoncer; (crash into) emboutir; percuter

ramble ['ræmbl] n randonnée f ♦ vi (walk) se promener, faire une randonnée; (talk: also: ~ on) discourir, pérorer; ~r n promeneur(euse), randonneur(euse); (BOT) rosier grimpant; rambling ['ræmblɪŋ] adj (speech) décousu(e); (house) plein(e) de coins et de recoins; (BOT) grimpant(e)

ramp [ræmp] n (incline) rampe f; dénivellation f; on ~, off ~ (US: AUT) bretelle f d'accès

rampage [ræm'peɪdʒ] n: to be on the ~ se déchaîner

rampant ['ræmpənt] adj (disease etc) qui sévit

ramshackle ['ræmʃækl] adj (house) délabré(e); (car etc) déglingué(e)

ran [ræn] pt of run

ranch [rɑ:ntʃ] n ranch m; ~er n propriétaire m de ranch

rancid ['rænsɪd] adj rance

rancour ['ræŋkə*] (US rancor) n rancune f

random ['rændəm] adj fait(e) or établi(e) au hasard; (MATH) aléatoire ♦ n: at ~ au hasard; ~ access n (COMPUT) accès sélectif

randy ['rændɪ] (BRIT: inf) adj excité(e); lubrique

rang [ræŋ] pt of ring

range [reɪndʒ] n (of mountains) chaîne f; (of missile, voice) portée f; (of products) choix m, gamme f; (MIL: also: shooting ~) champ m de tir; (indoor) stand m de tir; (also: kitchen ~) fourneau m (de cuisine) ♦ vt (place in a line) mettre en rang, ranger ♦ vi: to ~ over couvrir; to ~ from ... to aller de ... à; a ~ of (series: of proposals etc) divers(e)

ranger ['reɪndʒə*] n garde forestier

rank [ræŋk] n rang m; (MIL) grade m; (BRIT: also: taxi ~) station f de taxis ♦ vi: to ~ among compter or se classer parmi ♦ adj (stinking) fétide, puant(e); the ~ and file (fig) la masse, la base

rankle ['ræŋkl] vi (insult) rester sur le cœur

ransack ['rænsæk] vt fouiller (à fond); (plunder) piller

ransom ['rænsəm] n rançon f; to hold to ~ (fig) exercer un chantage sur

rant [rænt] vi fulminer

rap [ræp] vt frapper sur or à; taper sur; n: (music) rap m

rape [reɪp] n viol m; (BOT) colza m ♦ vt

violer; **~(seed) oil** *n* huile *f* de colza
rapid ['ræpɪd] *adj* rapide; **~s** *npl* (*GEO*) rapides *mpl*
rapist ['reɪpɪst] *n* violeur *m*
rapport [ræ'pɔ:*] *n* entente *f*
rapture ['ræptʃə*] *n* extase *f*, ravissement *m*; **rapturous** ['ræptʃərəs] *adj* enthousiaste, frénétique
rare [rɛə*] *adj* rare; (*CULIN*: *steak*) saignant(e)
raring ['rɛərɪŋ] *adj*: ~ **to go** (*inf*) très impatient(e) de commencer
rascal ['rɑ:skəl] *n* vaurien *m*
rash [ræʃ] *adj* imprudent(e), irréfléchi(e) ♦ *n* (*MED*) rougeur *f*, éruption *f*, (*spate: of events*) série (noire)
rasher ['ræʃə*] *n* fine tranche (de lard)
raspberry ['rɑːzbərɪ] *n* framboise *f*; ~ **bush** *n* framboisier *m*
rasping ['rɑːspɪŋ] *adj*: ~ **noise** grincement *m*
rat [ræt] *n* rat *m*
rate [reɪt] *n* taux *m*; (*speed*) vitesse *f*, rythme *m*; (*price*) tarif *m* ♦ *vt* classer; évaluer; **~s** *npl* (*BRIT*: *tax*) impôts locaux; (*fees*) tarifs *mpl*; **to ~ sb/sth as** considérer qn/qch comme; **~able value** (*BRIT*) *n* valeur locative imposable; **~payer** (*BRIT*) *n* contribuable *m/f* (*payant les impôts locaux*)
rather ['rɑːðə*] *adv* plutôt; **it's ~ expensive** c'est assez cher; (*too much*) c'est un peu cher; **there's ~ a lot** il y en a beaucoup; **I would ~ or I'd ~ go** j'aimerais mieux *or* je préférerais partir
rating ['reɪtɪŋ] *n* (*assessment*) évaluation *f*, (*score*) classement *m*; (*NAUT*: *BRIT*: *sailor*) matelot *m*; **~s** *npl* (*RADIO*, *TV*) indice *m* d'écoute
ratio ['reɪʃɪəʊ] *n* proportion *f*
ration ['ræʃən] *n* (*gen pl*) ration(s) *f(pl)*
rational ['ræʃənl] *adj* raisonnable, sensé(e); (*solution, reasoning*) logique; **~e** [ræʃə'nɑːl] *n* raisonnement *m*; **~ize** ['ræʃnəlaɪz] *vt* rationaliser; (*conduct*) essayer d'expliquer *or* de motiver
rat race *n* foire *f* d'empoigne
rattle ['rætl] *n* (*of door, window*) battement *m*; (*of coins, chain*) cliquetis *m*; (*of train, engine*) bruit *m* de ferraille; (*object: for baby*) hochet *m* ♦ *vi* cliqueter; (*car, bus*): **to ~ along** rouler dans un bruit de ferraille ♦ *vt* agiter (bruyamment); (*unnerve*) décontenancer; **~snake** *n* serpent *m* à sonnettes
raucous ['rɔːkəs] *adj* rauque; (*noisy*) bruyant(e), tapageur(euse)
rave [reɪv] *vi* (*in anger*) s'emporter; (*with enthusiasm*) s'extasier; (*MED*) délirer
raven ['reɪvn] *n* corbeau *m*
ravenous ['rævənəs] *adj* affamé(e)
ravine [rə'viːn] *n* ravin *m*
raving ['reɪvɪŋ] *adj*: ~ **lunatic** *n* fou(folle) furieux(euse)

ravishing ['rævɪʃɪŋ] *adj* enchanteur(eresse)
raw [rɔː] *adj* (*uncooked*) cru(e); (*not processed*) brut(e); (*sore*) à vif, irrité(e); (*inexperienced*) inexpérimenté(e); (*weather, day*) froid(e) et humide; ~ **deal** (*inf*) *n* sale coup *m*; ~ **material** *n* matière première
ray [reɪ] *n* rayon *m*; ~ **of hope** lueur *f* d'espoir
raze [reɪz] *vt* (*also*: ~ **to the ground**) raser, détruire
razor ['reɪzə*] *n* rasoir *m*; ~ **blade** *n* lame *f* de rasoir
Rd *abbr* = **road**
re [riː] *prep* concernant
reach [riːtʃ] *n* portée *f*, atteinte *f*; (*of river etc*) étendue *f* ♦ *vt* atteindre; (*conclusion, decision*) parvenir à ♦ *vi* s'étendre, étendre le bras; **out of/within ~** hors de/à portée; **within ~ of the shops** pas trop loin des *or* à proximité des magasins; ~ **out** *vt* tendre ♦ *vi*: **to ~ out (for)** allonger le bras (pour prendre)
react [riː'ækt] *vi* réagir; **~ion** [riː'ækʃən] *n* réaction *f*
reactor [riː'æktə*] *n* réacteur *m*
read¹ [riːd] (*pt, pp* **read**) *vi* lire ♦ *vt* lire; (*understand*) comprendre, interpréter; (*study*) étudier; (*meter*) relever; ~ **out** *vt* lire à haute voix; **~able** *adj* facile *or* agréable à lire; (*writing*) lisible; **~er** *n* lecteur(trice); (*book*) livre *m* de lecture; (*BRIT*: *at university*) chargé(e) d'enseignement; **~ership** *n* (*of paper etc*) nombre *m* de) lecteurs *mpl*
read² [red] *pt, pp of* **read¹**
readily ['redɪlɪ] *adv* volontiers, avec empressement; (*easily*) facilement
readiness ['redɪnəs] *n* empressement *m*; **in ~** (*prepared*) prêt(e)
reading ['riːdɪŋ] *n* lecture *f*; (*understanding*) interprétation *f*; (*on instrument*) indications *fpl*
ready ['redɪ] *adj* prêt(e); (*willing*) prêt, disposé(e); (*available*) disponible ♦ *n*: **at the ~** (*MIL*) prêt à faire feu; **to get ~** se préparer ♦ *vt* préparer; **~-made** *adj* tout(e) fait(e); ~ **money** *n* (argent *m*) liquide *m*; **~-to-wear** *adj* prêt(e) à porter
real [rɪəl] *adj* véritable; réel(le); **in ~ terms** dans la réalité; ~ **estate** *n* biens fonciers *or* immobiliers; **~istic** *adj* réaliste; **~ity** [rɪ'ælɪtɪ] *n* réalité *f*
realization [rɪələ'zeɪʃən] *n* (*awareness*) prise *f* de conscience; (*fulfilment; also: of asset*) réalisation *f*
realize ['rɪəlaɪz] *vt* (*understand*) se rendre compte de; (*a project, COMM*: *asset*) réaliser
really ['rɪəlɪ] *adv* vraiment; ~? vraiment?, c'est vrai?
realm [relm] *n* royaume *m*; (*fig*) domaine *m*
realtor ['rɪəltɔː*] *n* (®*:US*) agent immobilier
reap [riːp] *vt* moissonner; (*fig*) récolter

reappear ['ri:ə'pɪə*] vi réapparaître, reparaître

rear [rɪə*] adj de derrière, arrière inv; (AUT: wheel etc) arrière ♦ n arrière m ♦ vt (cattle, family) élever ♦ vi (also: ~ up: animal) se cabrer; **~guard** n (MIL) arrière-garde f

rear-view mirror ['rɪəvjuː-] n (AUT) rétroviseur m

reason ['riːzn] n raison f ♦ vi: **to ~ with sb** raisonner qn, faire entendre raison à qn; **to have ~ to think** avoir lieu de penser; **it stands to ~ that** il va sans dire que; **~able** adj raisonnable; (not bad) acceptable; **~ably** adv raisonnablement; **~ing** n raisonnement m

reassurance ['ri:ə'ʃʊərəns] n réconfort m; (factual) assurance f, garantie f; **reassure** ['ri:ə'ʃʊə*] vt rassurer

rebate ['ri:beɪt] n (on tax etc) dégrèvement m

rebel [n 'rebl, vb rɪ'bel] n rebelle m/f ♦ vi se rebeller, se révolter; **~lious** adj rebelle

rebound [vb rɪ'baʊnd, n 'ri:baʊnd] vi (ball) rebondir ♦ n rebond m; **to marry on the ~** se marier immédiatement après une déception amoureuse

rebuff [rɪ'bʌf] n rebuffade f

rebuke [rɪ'bjuːk] vt réprimander

rebut [rɪ'bʌt] vt réfuter

recall [rɪ'kɔːl] vt rappeler; (remember) se rappeler, se souvenir de ♦ n rappel m; (ability to remember) mémoire f

recant [rɪ'kænt] vi se rétracter; (REL) abjurer

recap ['ri:kæp], **recapitulate** [ri:kə'pɪtjuleɪt] vt, vi récapituler

rec'd abbr = **received**

recede [rɪ'si:d] vi (tide) descendre; (disappear) disparaître peu à peu; (memory, hope) s'estomper; **receding** [rɪ'si:dɪŋ] adj (chin) fuyant(e); **receding hairline** front dégarni

receipt [rɪ'si:t] n (document) reçu m; (for parcel etc) accusé m de réception; (act of receiving) réception f; **~s** npl (COMM) recettes fpl

receive [rɪ'si:v] vt recevoir

receiver [rɪ'si:və*] n (TEL) récepteur m, combiné m; (RADIO) récepteur m; (of stolen goods) receleur m; (LAW) administrateur m judiciaire

recent ['ri:snt] adj récent(e); **~ly** adv récemment

receptacle [rɪ'septəkl] n récipient m

reception [rɪ'sepʃən] n réception f; (welcome) accueil m, réception; **~ desk** n réception f; **~ist** n réceptionniste m/f

recess [rɪ'ses] n (in room) renfoncement m, alcôve f; (secret place) recoin m; (POL etc: holiday) vacances fpl

recession [rɪ'seʃən] n récession f

recipe ['resɪpɪ] n recette f

recipient [rɪ'sɪpɪənt] n (of payment) bénéficiaire m/f; (of letter) destinataire m/f

recital [rɪ'saɪtl] n récital m

recite [rɪ'saɪt] vt (poem) réciter

reckless ['rekləs] adj (driver etc) imprudent(e)

reckon ['rekən] vt (count) calculer, compter; (think): **I ~ that ...** je pense que ...; **~ on** vt fus compter sur, s'attendre à; **~ing** n compte m, calcul m; estimation f

reclaim [rɪ'kleɪm] vt (demand back) réclamer (le remboursement or la restitution de); (land: from sea) assécher; (waste materials) récupérer

recline [rɪ'klaɪn] vi être allongé(e) or étendu(e); **reclining** [rɪ'klaɪnɪŋ] adj (seat) à dossier réglable

recluse [rɪ'kluːs] n reclus(e), ermite m

recognition [rekəg'nɪʃən] n reconnaissance f; **to gain ~** être reconnu(e); **transformed beyond ~** méconnaissable

recognize ['rekəgnaɪz] vt: **to ~ (by/as)** reconnaître (à/comme étant)

recoil [rɪ'kɔɪl] vi (person): **to ~ (from sth/ doing sth)** reculer (devant qch/l'idée de faire qch) ♦ n (of gun) recul m

recollect [rekə'lekt] vt se rappeler, se souvenir de; **~ion** [rekə'lekʃən] n souvenir m

recommend [rekə'mend] vt recommander

reconcile ['rekənsaɪl] vt (two people) réconcilier; (two facts) concilier, accorder; **to ~ o.s. to** se résigner à

recondition ['ri:kən'dɪʃən] vt remettre à neuf; réviser entièrement

reconnoitre [rekə'nɔɪtə*] (US **reconnoiter**) vt (MIL) reconnaître

reconstruct ['ri:kən'strʌkt] vt (building) reconstruire; (crime, policy, system) reconstituer

record [n 'rekɔːd, vb rɪ'kɔːd] n rapport m, récit m; (of meeting etc) procès-verbal m; (register) registre m; (file) dossier m; (also: criminal ~) casier m judiciaire; (MUS: disc) disque m; (SPORT) record m; (COMPUT) article m ♦ vt (set down) noter; (MUS: song etc) enregistrer; **in ~ time** en un temps record inv; **off the ~** adj officieux(euse) ♦ adv officieusement; **~ card** n (in file) fiche f; **~ed delivery** [rɪ'kɔːdɪd-] n (BRIT: POST): **~ed delivery letter** etc lettre etc recommandée; **~er** [rɪ'kɔːdə*] n (MUS) flûte f à bec; **~ holder** n (SPORT) détenteur(trice) du record; **~ing** [rɪ'kɔːdɪŋ] n (MUS) enregistrement m; **~ player** n tourne-disque m

recount [rɪ'kaʊnt] vt raconter

re-count ['ri:kaʊnt] n (POL: of votes) deuxième compte m ♦ vt recompter

recoup [rɪ'ku:p] vt: **to ~ one's losses** récupérer ce qu'on a perdu, se refaire

recourse [rɪ'kɔːs] n: **to have ~ to** avoir recours à

recover [rɪ'kʌvə*] vt récupérer ♦ vi: **to ~ (from)** (illness) se rétablir (de); (from shock) se remettre (de); **~y** [rɪ'kʌvərɪ] n récupération f; rétablissement m; (ECON) redressement m

recreation [rekrɪ'eɪʃən] n récréation f, détente f; **~al** adj pour la détente, récréatif(ive)

recruit [rɪ'kruːt] n recrue f ♦ vt recruter

rectangle ['rektæŋgl] n rectangle m; **rectangular** [rek'tæŋgjulə*] adj rectangulaire

rectify ['rektɪfaɪ] vt (error) rectifier, corriger

rector ['rektə*] n (REL) pasteur m

recuperate [rɪ'kuːpəreɪt] vi récupérer; (from illness) se rétablir

recur [rɪ'kɜː*] vi se reproduire; (symptoms) réapparaître; **~rence** n répétition f, réapparition f; **~rent** adj périodique, fréquent(e)

recycle vt recycler

red [red] n rouge m; (POL: pej) rouge m/f ♦ adj rouge; (hair) roux(rousse); **in the ~** (account) à découvert; (business) en déficit; **~ carpet treatment** n réception f en grande pompe; **R~ Cross** n Croix-Rouge f; **~currant** n groseille f (rouge); **~den** vt, vi rougir; **~dish** adj rougeâtre; (hair) qui tirent sur le roux

redeem [rɪ'diːm] vt (debt) rembourser; (sth in pawn) dégager; (fig, also REL) racheter; **~ing** adj (feature) qui sauve, qui rachète (le reste)

redeploy [riːdɪ'plɔɪ] vt (resources) réorganiser

redevelopment [riːdɪ'veləpmənt] n rénovation f, reconstruction f

red: **~-haired** ['hɛəd] adj roux(rousse); **~-handed** ['hændɪd] adj: **to be caught ~-handed** être pris(e) en flagrant délit or la main dans le sac; **~head** [-'hed] n roux(rousse); **~ herring** n (fig) diversion f, fausse piste; **~-hot** [-'hɒt] adj chauffé(e) au rouge, brûlant(e)

redirect [riːdaɪ'rekt] vt (mail) faire suivre

red light n: **to go through a ~** (AUT) brûler un feu rouge; **red-light district** n quartier m des prostituées

redo ['riː'duː] (irreg) vt refaire

redolent ['redəulənt] adj: **~ of** qui sent; (fig) qui évoque

redress [rɪ'dres] n réparation f ♦ vt redresser

Red Sea n: **the ~** la mer Rouge

redskin ['redskɪn] n Peau-Rouge m/f

red tape n (fig) paperasserie (administrative)

reduce [rɪ'djuːs] vt réduire; (lower) abaisser; **"~ speed now"** (AUT) "ralentir"; **reduction** [rɪ'dʌkʃən] n réduction f; (discount) rabais m

redundancy [rɪ'dʌndənsɪ] (BRIT) n licenciement m, mise f au chômage

redundant [rɪ'dʌndənt] adj (BRIT: worker) mis(e) au chômage, licencié(e); (detail, object) superflu(e); **to be made ~** être licencié(e), être mis(e) au chômage

reed [riːd] n (BOT) roseau m; (MUS: of clarinet etc) hanche f

reef [riːf] n (at sea) récif m, écueil m

reek [riːk] vi: **to ~ (of)** puer, empester

reel [riːl] n bobine f; (FISHING) moulinet m; (CINEMA) bande f; (dance) quadrille écossais ♦ vi (sway) chanceler; **~ in** vt (fish, line) ramener

ref [ref] (inf) n abbr (= referee) arbitre m

refectory [rɪ'fektərɪ] n réfectoire m

refer [rɪ'fɜː*] vt: **to ~ sb to** (inquirer: for information, patient: to specialist) adresser qn à; (reader: to text) renvoyer qn à; (dispute, decision): **to ~ sth to** soumettre qch à ♦ vi: **~ to** (allude to) parler de, faire allusion à; (consult) se reporter à

referee [refə'riː] n arbitre m; (TENNIS) juge-arbitre m; (BRIT: for job application) répondant(e)

reference ['refrəns] n référence f, renvoi m; (mention) allusion f, mention f; (for job application: letter) références, lettre f de recommandation; **with ~ to** (COMM: in letter) me référant à, suite à; **~ book** n ouvrage m de référence

refill [vb 'riː'fɪl, n 'riː'fɪl] vt remplir à nouveau; (pen, lighter etc) recharger ♦ n (for pen etc) recharge f

refine [rɪ'faɪn] vt (sugar, oil) raffiner; (taste) affiner; (theory, idea) fignoler (inf); **~d** adj (person, taste) raffiné(e)

reflect [rɪ'flekt] vt (light, image) réfléchir, refléter; (fig) refléter ♦ vi (think) réfléchir, méditer; **it ~s badly on him** cela le discrédite; **it ~s well on him** c'est tout à son honneur; **~ion** [rɪ'flekʃən] n réflexion f; (image) reflet m; (criticism): **~ion on** critique f de; atteinte f à; **on ~ion** réflexion faite

reflex ['riːfleks] adj réflexe ♦ n réflexe m; **~ive** [rɪfleksɪv] adj (LING) réfléchi(e)

reform [rɪ'fɔːm] n réforme f ♦ vt réformer; **R~ation** [refə'meɪʃən] n: **the R~ation** la Réforme; **~atory** (US) n ≈ centre m d'éducation surveillée

refrain [rɪ'freɪn] vi: **to ~ from doing** s'abstenir de faire ♦ n refrain m

refresh [rɪ'freʃ] vt rafraîchir; (subj: sleep) reposer; **~er course** (BRIT) n cours m de recyclage; **~ing** adj (drink) rafraîchissant(e); (sleep) réparateur(trice); **~ments** npl rafraîchissements mpl

refrigerator [rɪ'frɪdʒəreɪtə*] n réfrigérateur m, frigidaire m (®)

refuel ['riː'fjuəl] vi se ravitailler en carburant

refuge ['refjuːdʒ] n refuge m; **to take ~ in** se réfugier dans

refugee [refju'dʒiː] n réfugié(e)

refund [n 'riː'fʌnd, vb rɪ'fʌnd] n remboursement m ♦ vt rembourser

refurbish [ri:'fɜ:bɪʃ] vt remettre à neuf

refusal [ri'fju:zəl] n refus m; **to have first ~ on** avoir droit de préemption sur

refuse[1] [ri'fju:z] vt, vi refuser

refuse[2] ['refju:s] n ordures fpl, détritus mpl; **~ collection** n ramassage m d'ordures

regain [ri'geɪn] vt regagner; retrouver

regal ['ri:gəl] adj royal(e)

regard [ri'gɑ:d] n respect m, estime f, considération f ♦ vt considérer; **to give one's ~s to** faire ses amitiés à; **"with kindest ~s"** "bien amicalement"; **as ~s, with ~ to = regarding**; **~ing** prep en ce qui concerne; **~less** adv quand même; **~less of** sans se soucier de

régime [reɪ'ʒi:m] n régime m

regiment [n 'redʒɪmənt, vb 'redʒɪment] n régiment m; **~al** [redʒɪ'mentl] adj d'un or du régiment

region ['ri:dʒən] n région f; **in the ~ of** (fig) aux alentours de; **~al** adj régional(e)

register ['redʒɪstə*] n registre m; (also: electoral ~) liste électorale ♦ vt enregistrer; (birth, death) déclarer; (vehicle) immatriculer; (POST: letter) envoyer en recommandé; (subj: instrument) marquer ♦ vi s'inscrire; (at hotel) signer le registre; (make impression) être (bien) compris(e); **~ed** adj (letter, parcel) recommandé(e); **~ed trademark** n marque déposée; **registrar** [redʒɪs'trɑ:*] n officier m de l'état civil; **registration** [redʒɪs'treɪʃən] n enregistrement m; (BRIT AUT: also: ~ number) numéro m d'immatriculation

registry ['redʒɪstrɪ] n bureau m de l'enregistrement; **~ office** (BRIT) n bureau m de l'état civil; **to get married in a ~ office** ≈ se marier à la mairie

regret [ri'gret] n regret m ♦ vt regretter; **~fully** adv à or avec regret

regular ['regjʊlə*] adj régulier(ère); (usual) habituel(le); (soldier) de métier ♦ n (client etc) habitué(e); **~ly** adv régulièrement

regulate ['regjʊleɪt] vt régler; **regulation** [regjʊ'leɪʃən] n (rule) règlement m; (adjustment) réglage m

rehabilitation ['ri:həbɪlɪ'teɪʃən] n (of offender) réinsertion f; (of addict) réadaptation f

rehearsal [ri'hɜ:səl] n répétition f

rehearse [ri'hɜ:s] vt répéter

reign [reɪn] n règne m ♦ vi régner

reimburse [ri:ɪm'bɜ:s] vt rembourser

rein [reɪn] n (for horse) rêne f

reindeer ['reɪndɪə*] n, pl inv renne m

reinforce [ri:ɪn'fɔ:s] vt renforcer; **~d concrete** n béton armé; **~ments** npl (MIL) renfort(s) m(pl)

reinstate ['ri:ɪn'steɪt] vt rétablir, réintégrer

reject [n 'ri:dʒekt, vb ri'dʒekt] n (COMM) article m de rebut ♦ vt refuser; (idea) reje-

ter; **~ion** ['ri:dʒekʃən] n rejet m, refus m

rejoice [ri'dʒɔɪs] vi: **to ~ (at or over)** se réjouir (de)

rejuvenate [ri'dʒu:vɪneɪt] vt rajeunir

relapse [ri'læps] n (MED) rechute f

relate [ri'leɪt] vt (tell) raconter; (connect) établir un rapport entre ♦ vi: (connect) **this ~s to** cela se rapporte à; **to ~ to sb** entretenir des rapports avec qn; **~d** adj apparenté(e); **relating to** prep concernant

relation [ri'leɪʃən] n (person) parent(e); (link) rapport m, lien m; **~ship** n rapport m, lien m; (personal ties) relations fpl, rapports; (also: family ~ship) lien de parenté

relative ['relətɪv] n parent(e) ♦ adj relatif(ive); **all her ~s** toute sa famille; **~ly** adv relativement

relax [ri'læks] vi (muscle) se relâcher; (person: unwind) se détendre ♦ vt relâcher; (mind, person) détendre; **~ation** [ri:læk'seɪʃən] n relâchement m; (of mind) détente f, relaxation f; (recreation) détente, délassement m; **~ed** adj détendu(e); **~ing** adj délassant(e)

relay ['ri:leɪ] n (SPORT) course f de relais ♦ vt (message) retransmettre, relayer

release [ri'li:s] n (from prison, obligation) libération f; (of gas etc) émission f; (of film etc) sortie f; (new recording) disque m ♦ vt (prisoner) libérer; (gas etc) émettre, dégager; (free: from wreckage etc) dégager; (TECH: catch, spring etc) faire jouer; (book, film) sortir; (report, news) rendre public, publier

relegate ['relɪgeɪt] vt reléguer; (BRIT: SPORT): **to be ~d** descendre dans une division inférieure

relent [ri'lent] vi se laisser fléchir; **~less** adj implacable; (unceasing) continuel(le)

relevant ['reləvənt] adj (question) pertinent(e); (fact) significatif(ive); (information) utile; **~ to** ayant rapport à, approprié à

reliable [ri'laɪəbl] adj (person, firm) sérieux(euse), fiable; (method, machine) fiable; (news, information) sûr(e); **reliably** adv: **to be reliably informed** savoir de source sûre

reliance [ri'laɪəns] n: **~ (on)** (person) confiance f (en); (drugs, promises) besoin m (de), dépendance f (de)

relic ['relɪk] n (REL) relique f; (of the past) vestige m

relief [ri'li:f] n (from pain, anxiety etc) soulagement m; (help, supplies) secours m(pl); (ART, GEO) relief m

relieve [ri'li:v] vt (pain, patient) soulager; (fear, worry) dissiper; (bring help) secourir; (take over from: gen) relayer; (: guard) relever; **to ~ sb of sth** débarrasser qn de qch; **to ~ o.s.** se soulager

religion [ri'lɪdʒən] n religion f; **religious** [ri'lɪdʒəs] adj religieux(euse); (book) de piété

relinquish [ri'lɪŋkwɪʃ] vt abandonner;

(plan, habit) renoncer à

relish ['relɪʃ] *n* (CULIN) condiment *m*; *(enjoyment)* délectation *f* ♦ *vt* *(food etc)* savourer; **to ~ doing** se délecter à faire

relocate ['riːləʊ'keɪt] *vt* installer ailleurs ♦ *vi* déménager, s'installer ailleurs

reluctance [rɪ'lʌktəns] *n* répugnance *f*

reluctant [rɪ'lʌktənt] *adj* peu disposé(e), qui hésite; **~ly** *adv* à contrecœur

rely on [rɪlaɪ] *vt fus* (be dependent) dépendre de; *(trust)* compter sur

remain [rɪ'meɪn] *vi* rester; **to ~** rester *m*; **~ing** *adj* qui reste; **~s** *npl* restes *mpl*

remand [rɪ'mɑːnd] *n*: **on ~** en détention préventive ♦ *vt*: **to be ~ed in custody** être placé(e) en détention préventive; **~ home** *(BRIT)* *n* maison *f* d'arrêt

remark [rɪ'mɑːk] *n* remarque *f*, observation *f* ♦ *vt* (faire) remarquer, dire; **~able** *adj* remarquable

remedial [rɪ'miːdɪəl] *adj* *(tuition, classes)* de rattrapage; **~ exercises** gymnastique corrective

remedy ['remədɪ] *n*: **~ (for)** remède *m* (contre *or* à) ♦ *vt* remédier à

remember [rɪ'membə*] *vt* se rappeler, se souvenir de; *(send greetings)*: **~ me to him** saluez-le de ma part; **remembrance** [rɪ'membrəns] *n* souvenir *m*; mémoire *f*

remind [rɪ'maɪnd] *vt*: **to ~ sb of** rappeler à qn; **to ~ sb to do** faire penser à qn à faire, rappeler à qn qu'il doit faire; **~er** *n* *(souvenir)* souvenir *m*; *(letter)* rappel *m*

reminisce [remɪ'nɪs] *vi*: **to ~ (about)** évoquer ses souvenirs (de)

reminiscent [remɪ'nɪsnt] *adj*: **to be ~ of** rappeler, faire penser à

remiss [rɪ'mɪs] *adj* négligent(e)

remission [rɪ'mɪʃən] *n* *(of illness, sins)* rémission *f*; *(of debt, prison sentence)* remise *f*

remit [rɪ'mɪt] *vt* *(send: money)* envoyer; **~tance** *n* paiement *m*

remnant ['remnənt] *n* reste *m*, restant *m*; *(of cloth)* coupon *m*; **~s** *npl* *(COMM)* fins *fpl* de série

remorse [rɪ'mɔːs] *n* remords *m*; **~ful** *adj* plein(e) de remords; **~less** *adj* *(fig)* impitoyable

remote [rɪ'məʊt] *adj* éloigné(e), lointain(e); *(person)* distant(e); *(possibility)* vague; **~ control** *n* télécommande *f*; **~ly** *adv* au loin; *(slightly)* très vaguement

remould ['riːməʊld] *(BRIT)* *n* *(tyre)* pneu rechapé

removable [rɪ'muːvəbl] *adj* *(detachable)* amovible

removal [rɪ'muːvəl] *n* *(taking away)* enlèvement *m*; suppression *f*; *(BRIT: from house)* déménagement *m*; *(from office: dismissal)* renvoi *m*; *(of stain)* nettoyage *m*; *(MED)* ablation *f*; **~ van** *(BRIT)* *n* camion *m* de déménagement

remove [rɪ'muːv] *vt* enlever, retirer; *(employee)* renvoyer; *(stain)* faire partir; *(abuse)* supprimer; *(doubt)* chasser

render ['rendə*] *vt* rendre; **~ing** *n* *(MUS etc)* interprétation *f*

rendezvous *n* rendez-vous *m inv*

renew [rɪ'njuː] *vt* renouveler; *(negotiations)* reprendre; *(acquaintance)* renouer; **~able** *adj* *(energy)* renouvelable; **~al** *n* renouvellement *m*; reprise *f*

renounce [rɪ'naʊns] *vt* renoncer à

renovate ['renəveɪt] *vt* rénover; *(art work)* restaurer

renown [rɪ'naʊn] *n* renommée *f*; **~ed** *adj* renommé(e)

rent [rent] *n* loyer *m* ♦ *vt* louer; **~al** *n* *(for television, car)* (prix *m* de) location *f*

rep [rep] *n abbr* = **representative**; = **repertory**

repair [rɪ'pɛə*] *n* réparation *f* ♦ *vt* réparer; **in good/bad ~** en bon/mauvais état; **~ kit** *n* trousse *f* de réparation

repatriate [riː'pætrɪeɪt] *vt* rapatrier

repay [riː'peɪ] *(irreg)* *vt* *(money, creditor)* rembourser; *(sb's efforts)* récompenser; **~ment** *n* remboursement *m*

repeal [rɪ'piːl] *n* *(of law)* abrogation *f* ♦ *vt* *(law)* abroger

repeat [rɪ'piːt] *n* *(RADIO, TV)* reprise *f* ♦ *vt* répéter; *(COMM: order)* renouveler; *(SCOL: a class)* redoubler ♦ *vi* répéter; **~edly** *adv* souvent, à plusieurs reprises

repel [rɪ'pel] *vt* repousser; **~lent** *adj* repoussant(e) ♦ *n*: **insect ~lent** insectifuge *m*

repent [rɪ'pent] *vi*: **to ~ (of)** se repentir (de); **~ance** *n* repentir *m*

repertory ['repətərɪ] *n* *(also: ~ theatre)* théâtre *m* de répertoire

repetition [repə'tɪʃən] *n* répétition *f*

repetitive [rɪ'petɪtɪv] *adj* *(movement, work)* répétitif(ive); *(speech)* plein(e) de redites

replace [rɪ'pleɪs] *vt* *(put back)* remettre, replacer; *(take the place of)* remplacer; **~ment** *n* *(substitution)* remplacement *m*; *(person)* remplaçant(e)

replay ['riːpleɪ] *n* *(of match)* match rejoué *m*; *(of tape, film)* répétition *f*

replenish [rɪ'plenɪʃ] *vt* *(glass)* remplir (de nouveau); *(stock etc)* réapprovisionner

replica ['replɪkə] *n* réplique *f*, copie exacte

reply [rɪ'plaɪ] *n* réponse *f* ♦ *vi* répondre; **~ coupon** *n* coupon-réponse *m*

report [rɪ'pɔːt] *n* rapport *m*; *(PRESS etc)* reportage *m*; *(BRIT: also: school ~)* bulletin *m* (scolaire); *(of gun)* détonation *f* ♦ *vt* rapporter, faire un compte rendu de; *(PRESS etc)* faire un reportage sur; *(bring to notice: occurrence)* signaler ♦ *vi* *(make a ~)* faire un rapport *(or* un reportage); *(present o.s.)*: **to ~ (to sb)** se présenter (chez qn); *(be responsible to)*: **to ~ to sb** être sous les ordres de qn; ~ **card** (*US, SCOTTISH*) n bulletin m scolaire; ~**edly** adv: **she is ~edly living in ...** elle habiterait ...; **he ~edly told them to ...** il leur aurait ordonné de ...; ~**er** n reporter m

repose [rɪ'pəʊz] n: **in ~** en or au repos

represent [reprɪ'zent] vt représenter; (*view, belief*) présenter, expliquer; (*describe*): **to ~ sth as** présenter or décrire qch comme; ~**ation** [reprɪzen'teɪʃən] n représentation f; ~**ations** npl (*protest*) démarche f; ~**ative** n représentant(e); (*US: POL*) député m ♦ adj représentatif(ive), caractéristique

repress [rɪ'pres] vt réprimer; ~**ion** [rɪ'preʃən] n répression f

reprieve [rɪ'priːv] n (*LAW*) grâce f; (*fig*) sursis m, délai m

reprisal [rɪ'praɪzəl] n: ~**s** npl représailles fpl

reproach [rɪ'prəʊtʃ] vt: **to ~ sb with sth** reprocher qch à qn; ~**ful** adj de reproche

reproduce [riːprə'djuːs] vt reproduire ♦ vi se reproduire; **reproduction** [riːprə'dʌkʃən] n reproduction f

reproof [rɪ'pruːf] n reproche m

reptile ['reptaɪl] n reptile m

republic [rɪ'pʌblɪk] n république f; ~**an** adj républicain(e)

repudiate [rɪ'pjuːdɪeɪt] vt répudier, rejeter

repulsive [rɪ'pʌlsɪv] adj repoussant(e), répulsif(ive)

reputable ['repjʊtəbl] adj de bonne réputation; (*occupation*) honorable

reputation [repjʊ'teɪʃən] n réputation f

reputed [rɪ'pjuːtɪd] adj (*supposed*) supposé(e); ~**ly** adv d'après ce qu'on dit

request [rɪ'kwest] n demande f; (*formal*) requête f ♦ vt: **to ~ (of or from sb)** demander (à qn); ~ **stop** (*BRIT*) n (*for bus*) arrêt facultatif

require [rɪ'kwaɪə*] vt (*need: subj: person*) avoir besoin de; (: *thing, situation*) demander; (*want*) exiger; (*order*): **to ~ sb to do sth/sth of sb** exiger que qn fasse qch/qch de qn; ~**ment** n exigence f; besoin m; condition requise

requisite ['rekwɪzɪt] n chose f nécessaire ♦ adj requis(e), nécessaire; **toilet ~s** accessoires mpl de toilette

requisition [rekwɪ'zɪʃən] n: ~ **(for)** demande f (de) ♦ vt (*MIL*) réquisitionner

rescue ['reskjuː] n (*from accident*) sauvetage m; (*help*) secours mpl ♦ vt sauver; ~ **party** n équipe f de sauvetage; ~**r** n sauveteur m

research [rɪ'səːtʃ] n recherche(s) f(pl) ♦ vt faire des recherches sur

resemblance [rɪ'zembləns] n ressemblance f

resemble [rɪ'zembl] vt ressembler à

resent [rɪ'zent] vt être contrarié(e) par; ~**ful** adj irrité(e), plein(e) de ressentiment; ~**ment** n ressentiment m

reservation [rezə'veɪʃən] n (*booking*) réservation f; (*doubt*) réserve f; (*for tribe*) réserve; **to make a ~ (in a hotel/a restaurant/on a plane)** réserver or retenir une chambre/une table/une place

reserve [rɪ'zəːv] n réserve f; (*SPORT*) remplaçant(e) ♦ vt (*seats etc*) réserver, retenir; ~**s** npl (*MIL*) réservistes mpl; **in ~** en réserve; ~**d** adj réservé(e)

reshuffle ['riːʃʌfl] n: **Cabinet ~** (*POL*) remaniement ministériel

residence ['rezɪdəns] n résidence f; ~ **permit** (*BRIT*) n permis m de séjour

resident ['rezɪdənt] n résident(e) ♦ adj résidant(e); ~**ial** [rezɪ'denʃəl] adj (*area*) résidentiel(le); (*course*) avec hébergement sur place; ~**ial school** n internat m

residue ['rezɪdjuː] n reste m; (*CHEM, PHYSICS*) résidu m

resign [rɪ'zaɪn] vt (*one's post*) démissionner de ♦ vi démissionner; **to ~ o.s. to** se résigner à; ~**ation** [rezɪg'neɪʃən] n (*of post*) démission f; (*state of mind*) résignation f; ~**ed** adj résigné(e)

resilient [rɪ'zɪlɪənt] adj (*material*) élastique; (*person*) qui réagit, qui a du ressort

resist [rɪ'zɪst] vt résister à; ~**ance** n résistance f

resolution [rezə'luːʃən] n résolution f

resolve [rɪ'zɒlv] n résolution f ♦ vt (*problem*) résoudre ♦ vi: **to ~ to do** résoudre or décider de faire

resort [rɪ'zɔːt] n (*town*) station f; (*recourse*) recours m ♦ vi: **to ~ to** avoir recours à; **in the last ~** en dernier ressort

resound [rɪ'zaʊnd] vi: **to ~ (with)** retentir or résonner (de); ~**ing** [rɪ'zaʊndɪŋ] adj retentissant(e)

resource [rɪ'sɔːs] n ressource f; ~**s** npl (*supplies, wealth etc*) ressources; ~**ful** adj ingénieux(euse), débrouillard(e)

respect [rɪs'pekt] n respect m ♦ vt respecter; ~**s** npl (*compliments*) respects, hommages mpl; **with ~ to** en ce qui concerne; **in this ~** à cet égard; ~**able** adj respectable; ~**ful** adj respectueux(euse)

respite ['respaɪt] n répit m

resplendent [rɪs'plendənt] adj resplendissant(e)

respond [rɪs'pɒnd] vi répondre; (*react*) réagir; **response** [rɪs'pɒns] n réponse f; réaction f

responsibility [rɪspɒnsə'bɪlɪtɪ] n responsabilité f

responsible [rɪs'pɒnsəbl] adj (*liable*): ~ **(for)** responsable (de); (*person*) digne de confiance; (*job*) qui comporte des responsabilités

responsive [rɪs'pɒnsɪv] adj qui réagit; (*person*) qui n'est pas réservé(e) or indifférent(e)

rest [rest] n repos m; (*stop*) arrêt m, pause f; (*MUS*) silence m; (*support*) support m,

appui *m*; (*remainder*) reste *m*, restant *m* ♦
vi se reposer; (*be supported*): **to ~ on** appuyer *or* reposer sur; (*remain*) rester ♦ *vt*
(*lean*): **to ~ sth on/against** appuyer qch
sur/contre; **the ~ of them** les autres; **it ~s
with him to ...** c'est à lui de ...
restaurant ['restərɒŋ] *n* restaurant *m*; **~
car** (*BRIT*) *n* wagon-restaurant *m*
restful ['restful] *adj* reposant(e)
restive ['restiv] *adj* agité(e), impatient(e);
(*horse*) rétif(ive)
restless ['restləs] *adj* agité(e)
restoration [restə'reiʃən] *n* restauration *f*;
restitution *f*; rétablissement *m*
restore [ri'stɔː*] *vt* (*building*) restaurer; (*sth
stolen*) restituer; (*peace, health*) rétablir; **to
~ to** (*former state*) ramener à
restrain [ris'trein] *vt* contenir; (*person*): **to
~ (from doing)** retenir (de faire); **~ed** *adj*
(*style*) sobre; (*manner*) mesuré(e); **~t** *n*
(*restriction*) contrainte *f*; (*moderation*) retenue *f*
restrict [ris'trikt] *vt* restreindre, limiter;
~ion [ris'trikʃən] *n* restriction *f*, limitation *f*
rest room (*US*) *n* toilettes *fpl*
result [ri'zʌlt] *n* résultat *m* ♦ *vi*: **to ~ in**
aboutir à, se terminer par; **as a ~ of** à la
suite de
resume [ri'zjuːm] *vt, vi* (*work, journey*) reprendre
résumé ['reizjuːmei] *n* résumé *m*; (*US*) curriculum vitae *m*
resumption [ri'zʌmpʃən] *n* reprise *f*
resurgence [ri'sɜːdʒəns] *n* (*of energy, activity*) regain *m*
resurrection [rezə'rekʃən] *n* résurrection *f*
resuscitate [ri'sʌsiteit] *vt* (*MED*) réanimer
retail [*n, adj* 'riːteil, *vb* 'riːteil] *adj* de *or* au
détail ♦ *adv* au détail; **~er** ['riːteilə*] *n* détaillant(e); **~ price** *n* prix *m* de détail
retain [ri'tein] *vt* (*keep*) garder, conserver;
~er *n* (*fee*) acompte *m*, provision *f*
retaliate [ri'tælieit] *vi*: **to ~ (against)** se
venger (de); **retaliation** [ritæli'eiʃən] *n* représailles *fpl*, vengeance *f*
retarded [ri'tɑːdid] *adj* retardé(e)
retch [retʃ] *vi* avoir des haut-le-cœur
retentive [ri'tentiv] *adj*: **~ memory** excellente mémoire
retina ['retinə] *n* rétine *f*
retire [ri'taiə*] *vi* (*give up work*) prendre sa
retraite; (*withdraw*) se retirer, partir; (*go to
bed*) (aller) se coucher; **~d** *adj* (*person*) retraité(e); **~ment** *n* retraite *f*; **retiring**
[ri'taiəriŋ] *adj* (*shy*) réservé(e); (*leaving*) sortant(e)
retort [ri'tɔːt] *vi* riposter
retrace [ri'treis] *vt*: **to ~ one's steps** revenir sur ses pas
retract [ri'trækt] *vt* (*statement, claws*) rétracter; (*undercarriage, aerial*) rentrer, escamoter

retrain ['riː'trein] *vt* (*worker*) recycler
retread ['riːtred] *n* (*tyre*) pneu rechapé
retreat [ri'triːt] *n* retraite *f* ♦ *vi* battre en
retraite
retribution [retri'bjuːʃən] *n* châtiment *m*
retrieval [ri'triːvəl] *n* (*see vb*) récupération
f; réparation *f*
retrieve [ri'triːv] *vt* (*sth lost*) récupérer; (*situation, honour*) sauver; (*error, loss*) réparer;
~r *n* chien *m* d'arrêt
retrospect ['retrəuspekt] *n*: **in ~** rétrospectivement, après coup; **~ive** [retrəu'spektiv]
adj rétrospectif(ive); (*law*) rétroactif(ive)
return [ri'tɜːn] *n* (*going or coming back*) retour *m*; (*of sth stolen etc*) restitution *f*; (*FINANCE: from land, shares*) rendement *m*,
rapport *m* ♦ *cpd* (*journey*) de retour; (*BRIT:
ticket*) aller et retour; (*match*) retour ♦ *vi*
(*come back*) revenir; (*go back*) retourner ♦
vt rendre; (*bring back*) rapporter; (*send
back; also: ball*) renvoyer; (*put back*) remettre; (*POL: candidate*) élire; **~s** *npl* (*COMM*)
recettes *fpl*; (*FINANCE*) bénéfices *mpl*; **in ~
(for)** en échange (de); **by ~ (of post)** par
retour (du courrier); **many happy ~s (of
the day)!** bon anniversaire!
reunion [riː'juːnjən] *n* réunion *f*
reunite ['riːjuː'nait] *vt* réunir
rev [rev] *n abbr* (*AUT*: = *revolution*) tour *m*
♦ *vt* (*also: ~ up*) emballer
revamp ['riː'væmp] *vt* (*firm, system etc*)
réorganiser
reveal [ri'viːl] *vt* (*make known*) révéler; (*display*) laisser voir; **~ing** *adj* révélateur(trice);
(*dress*) au décolleté généreux *or* suggestif
revel ['revl] *vi*: **to ~ in sth/in doing** se délecter de qch/à faire
revelry ['revlri] *n* festivités *fpl*
revenge [ri'vendʒ] *n* vengeance *f*; **to take
~ on** (*enemy*) se venger sur
revenue ['revənjuː] *n* revenu *m*
reverberate [ri'vɜːbəreit] *vi* (*sound*) retentir, se répercuter; (*fig: shock etc*) se propager
reverence ['revərəns] *n* vénération *f*, révérence *f*
Reverend ['revərənd] *adj* (*in titles*): **the ~
John Smith** (*Anglican*) le révérend John
Smith; (*Catholic*) l'abbé (John) Smith; (*Protestant*) le pasteur (John) Smith
reversal [ri'vɜːsl] *n* (*of opinion*) revirement
m; (*of order*) renversement *m*; (*of direction*)
changement *m*
reverse [ri'vɜːs] *n* contraire *m*, opposé *m*;
(*back*) dos *m*, envers *m*; (*of paper*) verso *m*;
(*of coin; also: setback*) revers *m*; (*AUT: also:
~ gear*) marche *f* arrière ♦ *adj* (*order, direction*) opposé(e), inverse ♦ *vt* (*order, position*) changer, inverser; (*direction, policy*)
changer complètement de; (*decision*) annuler; (*roles*) renverser; (*car*) faire marche arrière avec ♦ *vi* (*BRIT: AUT*) faire marche ar-

rière; **he ~d (the car) into a wall** il a embouti un mur en marche arrière; **~d charge call** (*BRIT*) n (*TEL*) communication f en PCV; **reversing lights** (*BRIT*) npl (*AUT*) feux mpl de marche arrière or de recul

revert [rɪ'vɜːt] vi: **to ~ to** revenir à, retourner à

review [rɪ'vjuː] n revue f; (of book, film) critique f, compte rendu; (of situation, policy) examen m, bilan m ♦ vt passer en revue; faire la critique de; examiner; **~er** n critique m

revile [rɪ'vaɪl] vt injurier

revise [rɪ'vaɪz] vt réviser, modifier; (manuscript) revoir, corriger ♦ vi (study) réviser; **revision** [rɪ'vɪʒən] n révision f

revival [rɪ'vaɪvəl] n (recovery) rétablissement m; (of faith) renouveau m

revive [rɪ'vaɪv] vt (person) ranimer; (custom) rétablir; (economy) relancer; (hope, courage) raviver, faire renaître; (play) reprendre ♦ vi (person) reprendre connaissance; (: from ill health) se rétablir; (hope etc) renaître; (activity) reprendre

revoke [rɪ'vəʊk] vt révoquer; (law) abroger

revolt [rɪ'vəʊlt] n révolte f ♦ vi se révolter, se rebeller ♦ vt révolter, dégoûter; **~ing** adj dégoûtant(e)

revolution [revə'luːʃən] n révolution f; (of wheel etc) tour m, révolution; **~ary** adj révolutionnaire ♦ n révolutionnaire m/f

revolve [rɪ'vɒlv] vi tourner

revolver [rɪ'vɒlvə*] n revolver m

revolving [rɪ'vɒlvɪŋ] adj tournant(e); (chair) pivotant(e); **~ door** n (porte f à) tambour m

revulsion [rɪ'vʌlʃən] n dégoût m, répugnance f

reward [rɪ'wɔːd] n récompense f ♦ vt: **to ~ (for)** récompenser (de); **~ing** adj (fig) qui (en) vaut la peine, gratifiant(e)

rewind [riː'waɪnd] (irreg) vt (tape) rembobiner

rewire [riː'waɪə*] vt (house) refaire l'installation électrique de

rheumatism ['ruːmətɪzəm] n rhumatisme m

Rhine [raɪn] n: **the ~** le Rhin

rhinoceros [raɪ'nɒsərəs] n rhinocéros m

Rhone [rəʊn] n: **the ~** le Rhône

rhubarb ['ruːbɑːb] n rhubarbe f

rhyme [raɪm] n rime f; (verse) vers mpl

rhythm ['rɪðəm] n rythme m

rib [rɪb] n (ANAT) côte f

ribbon ['rɪbən] n ruban m; **in ~s** (torn) en lambeaux

rice [raɪs] n riz m; **~ pudding** n riz au lait

rich [rɪtʃ] adj riche; (gift, clothes) somptueux(euse) ♦ npl: **the ~** les riches mpl; **~es** npl richesses fpl; **~ly** adv richement; (deserved, earned) largement

rickets ['rɪkɪts] n rachitisme m

rickety ['rɪkɪtɪ] adj branlant(e)

rickshaw ['rɪkʃɔː] n pousse-pousse m inv

rid [rɪd] (pt, pp rid) vt: **to ~ sb of** débarrasser qn de; **to get ~ of** se débarrasser de

riddle ['rɪdl] n (puzzle) énigme f ♦ vt: **to be ~d with** être criblé(e) de; (fig: guilt, corruption, doubts) être en proie à

ride [raɪd] (pt rode, pp ridden) n promenade f, tour m; (distance covered) trajet m ♦ vi (as sport) monter (à cheval), faire du cheval; (go somewhere: on horse, bicycle) aller (à cheval or bicyclette etc); (journey: on bicycle, motorcycle, bus) rouler ♦ vt (a certain horse) monter; (distance) parcourir, faire; **to take sb for a ~** (fig) faire marcher qn; **to ~ a horse/bicycle** monter à cheval/à bicyclette; **~r** n cavalier(ère); (in race) jockey m; (on bicycle) cycliste m/f; (on motorcycle) motocycliste m/f

ridge [rɪdʒ] n (of roof, mountain) arête f; (of hill) faîte m; (on object) strie f

ridicule ['rɪdɪkjuːl] n ridicule m; dérision f

ridiculous [rɪ'dɪkjʊləs] adj ridicule

riding ['raɪdɪŋ] n équitation f; **~ school** n manège m, école f d'équitation

rife [raɪf] adj répandu(e); **~ with** abondant(e) en, plein(e) de

riffraff ['rɪfræf] n racaille f

rifle ['raɪfl] n fusil m (à canon rayé) ♦ vt vider, dévaliser; **~ through** vt (belongings) fouiller; (papers) feuilleter; **~ range** n champ m de tir; (at fair) stand m de tir

rift [rɪft] n fente f, fissure f; (fig: disagreement) désaccord m

rig [rɪg] n (also: oil ~: at sea) plate-forme pétrolière ♦ vt (election etc) truquer; **~ out** (BRIT) vt: **to ~ out as/in** habiller en/de; **~ up** vt arranger, faire avec des moyens de fortune; **~ging** n (NAUT) gréement m

right [raɪt] adj (correctly chosen: answer, road etc) bon(bonne); (true) juste, exact(e); (suitable) approprié(e), convenable; (just) juste, équitable; (morally good) bien inv; (not left) droit(e) ♦ n (what is morally right) bien m; (title, claim) droit m; (not left) droite f ♦ adv (answer) correctement, juste; (treat) bien, comme il faut; (not on the left) à droite ♦ vt redresser ♦ excl bon!; **to be ~** (person) avoir raison; (answer) être juste or correct(e); (clock) à l'heure (juste); **by ~s** en toute justice; **on the ~** à droite; **to be in the ~** avoir raison; **~ now** en ce moment même; tout de suite; **~ in the middle** en plein milieu; **~ away** immédiatement; **~ angle** n (MATH) angle droit; **~eous** ['raɪtʃəs] adj droit(e), vertueux(euse); (anger) justifié(e); **~ful** adj légitime; **~-handed** adj (person) droitier(ère); **~-hand man** n bras droit m; **~-hand side** n côté droit; **~ly** adv (with reason) à juste titre; **~ of way** n droit m de passage; (AUT)

priorité f; ~-**wing** adj (POL) de droite
rigid ['rɪdʒɪd] adj rigide; (principle, control) strict(e)
rigmarole ['rɪgmərəʊl] n comédie f
rigorous ['rɪgərəs] adj rigoureux(euse)
rile [raɪl] vt agacer
rim [rɪm] n bord m; (of spectacles) monture f; (of wheel) jante f
rind [raɪnd] n (of bacon) couenne f; (of lemon etc) écorce f, zeste m; (of cheese) croûte f
ring [rɪŋ] (pt **rang**, pp **rung**) n anneau m; (on finger) bague f; (also: wedding ~) alliance f; (of people, objects) cercle m; (of spies) réseau m; (of smoke etc) rond m; (arena) piste f, arène f; (for boxing) ring m; (sound of bell) sonnerie f ♦ vi (telephone, bell) sonner; (person: by telephone) téléphoner; (also: ~ out: voice, words) retentir; (ears) bourdonner ♦ vt (BRIT: TEL: also: ~ up) téléphoner à, appeler; (bell) faire sonner; **to ~ the bell** sonner; **to give sb a ~** (BRIT: TEL) appeler qn; ~ **back** (BRIT) vt, vi téléphoner; ~ **off** (BRIT) vi (TEL) raccrocher; ~ **up** (BRIT) vt (TEL) appeler; ~**ing** n (of telephone) sonnerie f; (of bell) tintement m; (in ears) bourdonnement m; ~**ing tone** (BRIT) n (TEL) sonnerie f; ~**leader** n (of gang) chef m, meneur m
ringlets ['rɪŋlɪts] npl anglaises fpl
ring road (BRIT) n route f de ceinture; (motorway) périphérique m
rink [rɪŋk] n (also: ice ~) patinoire f
rinse [rɪns] vt rincer
riot ['raɪət] n émeute f; (of flowers, colour) profusion f ♦ vi faire une émeute, manifester avec violence; **to run ~** se déchaîner; ~**ous** adj (mob, assembly) séditieux(euse), déchaîné(e); (living, behaviour) débauché(e); (party) très animé(e); (welcome) délirant(e)
rip [rɪp] n déchirure f ♦ vt déchirer ♦ vi se déchirer; ~**cord** ['rɪpkɔːd] n poignée f d'ouverture
ripe [raɪp] adj (fruit) mûr(e); (cheese) fait(e); ~**n** vt mûrir ♦ vi mûrir
ripple ['rɪpl] n ondulation f; (of applause, laughter) cascade f ♦ vi onduler
rise [raɪz] (pt **rose**, pp **risen**) n (slope) côte f, pente f; (hill) hauteur f; (increase: in wages: BRIT) augmentation f; (: in prices, temperature) hausse f, augmentation f; (fig: to power etc) ascension f ♦ vi s'élever, monter; (prices, numbers) augmenter; (waters) monter; (sun; person: from chair, bed) se lever; (also: ~ up: tower, building) s'élever; (: rebel) se révolter; se rebeller; (in rank) s'élever; **to give ~ to** donner lieu à; **to ~ to the occasion** se montrer à la hauteur; **rising** adj (increasing: number, prices) en hausse; (tide) montant(e); (sun, moon) levant(e)
risk [rɪsk] n risque m ♦ vt risquer; **at ~ en**

danger; **at one's own ~** à ses risques et périls; ~**y** adj risqué(e)
rissole ['rɪsəʊl] n croquette f
rite [raɪt] n rite m; **last ~s** derniers sacrements; **ritual** ['rɪtjʊəl] adj rituel(le) ♦ n rituel m
rival ['raɪvəl] adj, n rival(e); (in business) concurrent(e) ♦ vt (match) égaler; ~**ry** n rivalité f, concurrence f
river ['rɪvə*] n rivière f; (major, also fig) fleuve m ♦ cpd (port, traffic) fluvial(e); **up/down ~** en amont/aval; ~**bank** n rive f, berge f
rivet ['rɪvɪt] n rivet m ♦ vt (fig) river, fixer
Riviera [rɪvɪ'ɛərə] n: **the (French)** ~ la Côte d'Azur; **the Italian** ~ la Riviera (italienne)
road [rəʊd] n route f; (in town) rue f; (fig) chemin, voie f; **major/minor** ~ route principale or à priorité/voie secondaire; ~ **accident** n accident m de la circulation; ~**block** n barrage routier; ~**hog** n chauffard m; ~ **map** n carte routière; ~ **safety** n sécurité routière; ~**side** n bord m de la route, bas-côté m; ~**sign** n panneau m de signalisation; ~**way** n chaussée f; ~ **works** npl travaux mpl (de réfection des routes); ~**worthy** adj en bon état de marche
roam [rəʊm] vi errer, vagabonder
roar [rɔː*] n rugissement m; (of crowd) hurlements mpl; (of vehicle, thunder, storm) grondement m ♦ vi rugir; hurler; gronder; **to ~ with laughter** éclater de rire; **to do a ~ing trade** faire des affaires d'or
roast [rəʊst] n rôti m ♦ vt (faire) rôtir; (coffee) griller, torréfier; ~ **beef** n rôti m de bœuf, rosbif m
rob [rɔb] vt (person) voler; (bank) dévaliser; **to ~ sb of sth** voler or dérober qch à qn; (fig: deprive) priver qn de qch; ~**ber** n bandit m, voleur m; ~**bery** n vol m
robe [rəʊb] n (for ceremony etc) robe f; (also: bath~) peignoir m; (US) couverture f
robin ['rɔbɪn] n rouge-gorge m
robust [rəʊ'bʌst] adj robuste; (material, appetite) solide
rock [rɔk] n (substance) roche f, roc m; (boulder) rocher m; (US: small stone) caillou m; (BRIT: sweet) ≈ sucre m d'orge ♦ vt (swing gently: cradle) balancer; (: child) bercer; (shake) ébranler, secouer ♦ vi (se) balancer; être ébranlé(e) or secoué(e); **on the ~s** (drink) avec des glaçons; (marriage etc) en train de craquer; ~ **and roll** n rock (and roll) m, rock'n'roll m; ~-**bottom** adj (fig: prices) sacrifié(e); ~**ery** n (jardin m de) rocaille f
rocket ['rɔkɪt] n fusée f; (MIL) fusée, roquette f
rocking chair ['rɔkɪŋ-] n fauteuil m à bascule

rocking horse n cheval m à bascule
rocky ['rɒkɪ] adj (hill) rocheux(euse); (path) rocailleux(euse)
rod [rɒd] n (wooden) baguette f; (metallic) tringle f; (TECH) tige f; (also: fishing ~) canne f à pêche
rode [rəʊd] pt of **ride**
rodent ['rəʊdənt] n rongeur m
rodeo ['rəʊdɪəʊ] (US) n rodéo m
roe [rəʊ] n (species: also: ~ deer) chevreuil m; (of fish, also: hard ~) œufs mpl de poisson; **soft** ~ laitance f
rogue [rəʊg] n coquin(e)
role [rəʊl] n rôle m
roll [rəʊl] n rouleau m; (of banknotes) liasse f; (also: bread ~) petit pain; (register) liste f; (sound: of drums etc) roulement m ♦ vt rouler; (also: ~ up: string) enrouler; (: sleeves) retrousser; (: ~ out: pastry) étendre au rouleau, abaisser ♦ vi rouler; ~ **about** vi rouler ça et là; (person) se rouler par terre; ~ **around** vi = **roll about**; ~ **by** vi (time) s'écouler, passer; ~ **in** vi (mail, cash) affluer; ~ **over** vi se retourner; ~ **up** vi (inf: arrive) arriver, s'amener ♦ vt rouler; ~ **call** n appel m; ~**er** n rouleau m; (wheel) roulette f; (for road) rouleau compresseur; ~**er coaster** n montagnes fpl russes; ~**er skates** npl patins mpl à roulettes; ~**ing** ['rəʊlɪŋ] adj (landscape) onduleux(euse); ~**ing pin** n rouleau m à pâtisserie; ~**ing stock** n (RAIL) matériel roulant
ROM [rɒm] n abbr (= read only memory) mémoire morte
Roman ['rəʊmən] adj romain(e); ~ **Catholic** adj, n catholique (m/f)
romance [rəʊ'mæns] n (love affair) idylle f; (charm) poésie f; (novel) roman m à l'eau de rose
Romania [rəʊ'meɪnɪə] n Roumanie f; ~**n** adj roumain(e) ♦ n Roumain(e); (LING) roumain m
Roman numeral n chiffre romain
romantic [rəʊ'mæntɪk] adj romantique; sentimental(e)
Rome [rəʊm] n Rome
romp [rɒmp] n jeux bruyants ♦ vi (also: ~ about) s'ébattre, jouer bruyamment; ~**ers** ['rɒmpəz] npl barboteuse f
roof [ru:f] (pl ~s) n toit m ♦ vt couvrir (d'un toit); **the** ~ **of the mouth** la voûte du palais; ~**ing** n toiture f; ~ **rack** n (AUT) galerie f
rook [rʊk] n (bird) freux m; (CHESS) tour f
room [ru:m] n (in house) pièce f; (also: bed~) chambre f (à coucher); (in school etc) salle f; (space) place f; ~**s** npl (lodging) meublé m; "~**s to let** (BRIT) or "~**s for rent**" (US) "chambres à louer"; **single/double** ~ chambre pour une personne/deux personnes; **there is** ~ **for improvement** cela lais-

se à désirer; ~**ing house** (US) n maison f or immeuble m de rapport; ~**mate** n camarade m/f de chambre; ~ **service** n service m des chambres (dans un hôtel); ~**y** adj spacieux(euse); (garment) ample
roost [ru:st] vi se jucher
rooster ['ru:stə*] n (esp US) coq m
root [ru:t] n (BOT, MATH) racine f; (fig: of problem) origine f, fond m ♦ vi (plant) s'enraciner; ~ **about** vi (fig) fouiller; ~ **for** vt fus encourager, applaudir; ~ **out** vt (find) dénicher
rope [rəʊp] n corde f; (NAUT) cordage m ♦ vt (tie up or together) attacher; (climbers: also: ~ together) encorder; (area: ~ off) interdire l'accès de; (divide off) séparer; **to know the** ~**s** (fig) être au courant, connaître les ficelles; ~ **in** vt (fig: person) embringuer
rosary ['rəʊzərɪ] n chapelet m
rose [rəʊz] pt of **rise** ♦ n rose f; (also: ~**bush**) rosier m; (on watering can) pomme f
rosé ['rəʊzeɪ] n rosé m
rosebud ['rəʊzbʌd] n bouton m de rose
rosemary ['rəʊzmərɪ] n romarin m
roster ['rɒstə*] n: **duty** ~ tableau m de service
rostrum ['rɒstrəm] n tribune f (pour un orateur etc)
rosy ['rəʊzɪ] adj rose; **a** ~ **future** un bel avenir
rot [rɒt] n (decay) pourriture f; (fig: pej) idioties fpl ♦ vt, vi pourrir
rota ['rəʊtə] n liste f, tableau m de service; **on a** ~ **basis** par roulement
rotary ['rəʊtərɪ] adj rotatif(ive)
rotate [rəʊ'teɪt] vt (revolve) faire tourner; (change round: jobs) faire à tour de rôle ♦ vi (revolve) tourner; **rotating** adj (movement) tournant(e)
rote [rəʊt] n: **by** ~ machinalement, par cœur
rotten ['rɒtn] adj (decayed) pourri(e); (dishonest) corrompu(e); (inf: bad) mauvais(e), moche; **to feel** ~ (ill) être mal fichu(e)
rotund [rəʊ'tʌnd] adj (person) rondelet(te)
rough [rʌf] adj (cloth, skin) rêche, rugueux(euse); (terrain) accidenté(e); (path) rocailleux(euse); (voice) rauque, rude; (person, manner: coarse) rude, fruste; (: violent) brutal(e); (district, weather) mauvais(e); (sea) houleux(euse); (plan etc) ébauché(e); (guess) approximatif(ive) ♦ n (GOLF) rough m; **to** ~ **it** vivre à la dure; **to sleep** ~ (BRIT) coucher à la dure; ~**age** n fibres fpl alimentaires; ~**-and-ready** adj rudimentaire; ~ **copy,** ~**draft** n brouillon m; ~**ly** adv (handle) rudement, brutalement; (speak) avec brusquerie; (make) grossièrement; (approximately) à peu près, en gros
roulette [ru:'let] n roulette f

Roumania [ruːˈmeɪnɪə] *n* = Romania

round [raʊnd] *adj* rond(e) ♦ *n* (*BRIT: of toast*) tranche *f*; (*duty: of policeman, milkman etc*) tournée *f*; (: *of doctor*) visites *fpl*; (*game: of cards, in competition*) partie *f*; (*BOXING*) round *m*; (*of talks*) série *f* ♦ *vt* (*corner*) tourner ♦ *prep* autour de ♦ *adv*: **all ~** tout autour; **the long way ~** (par) le chemin le plus long; **all the year ~** toute l'année; **it's just ~ the corner** (*fig*) c'est tout près; **~ the clock** 24 heures sur 24; **to go ~ to sb's (house)** aller chez qn; **go ~ the back** passez par derrière; **to go ~ a house** visiter une maison, faire le tour d'une maison; **enough to go ~** assez pour tout le monde; **~ of ammunition** cartouche *f*; **~ of applause** ban *m*, applaudissements *mpl*; **~ of drinks** tournée *f*; **~ of sandwiches** sandwich *m*; **~ off** *vt* (*speech etc*) terminer; **~ up** *vt* rassembler; (*criminals*) effectuer une rafle et; (*price, figure*) arrondir (au chiffre supérieur); **~about** *n* (*BRIT: AUT*) rond-point *m* (à sens giratoire); (: *at fair*) manège *m* (de chevaux de bois) ♦ *adj* (*route, means*) détourné(e); **~ers** *n* (*game*) sorte de baseball; **~ly** *adv* (*fig*) tout net, carrément; **~-shouldered** *adj* au dos rond; **~ trip** *n* (voyage *m*) aller et retour *m*; **~up** *n* rassemblement *m*; (*of criminals*) rafle *f*

rouse [raʊz] *vt* (*wake up*) réveiller; (*stir up*) susciter; provoquer; éveiller.

rousing [ˈraʊzɪŋ] *adj* (*welcome*) enthousiaste

rout [raʊt] *n* (*MIL*) déroute *f*

route [ruːt] *n* itinéraire *m*; (*of bus*) parcours *m*; (*of trade, shipping*) route *f*; **~ map** (*BRIT*) *n* (*for journey*) croquis *m* d'itinéraire

routine [ruːˈtiːn] *adj* (*work*) ordinaire, courant(e); (*procedure*) d'usage ♦ *n* (*habits*) habitudes *fpl*; (*pej*) train-train *m*; (*THEATRE*) numéro *m*

rove [rəʊv] *vt* (*area, streets*) errer dans

row[1] [rəʊ] *n* (*line*) rangée *f*; (*of people, seats, KNITTING*) rang *m*; (*behind one another: of cars, people*) file *f* ♦ *vi* (*in boat*) ramer; (*as sport*) faire de l'aviron ♦ *vt* (*boat*) faire aller à la rame *or* à l'aviron; **in a row** (*fig*) d'affilée

row[2] [raʊ] *n* (*noise*) vacarme *m*; (*dispute*) dispute *f*, querelle *f*; (*scolding*) réprimande *f*, savon *m* ♦ *vi* se disputer, se quereller

rowboat [ˈrəʊbəʊt] (*US*) *n* canot *m* (à rames)

rowdy [ˈraʊdɪ] *adj* chahuteur(euse); (*occasion*) tapageur(euse)

rowing [ˈrəʊɪŋ] *n* canotage *m*; (*as sport*) aviron *m*; **~ boat** (*BRIT*) *n* canot *m* (à rames)

royal [ˈrɔɪəl] *adj* royal(e); **R~ Air Force** (*BRIT*) *n* armée de l'air britannique

royalty [ˈrɔɪəltɪ] *n* (*royal persons*) (membres *mpl* de la) famille royale; (*payment: to author*) droits *mpl* d'auteur; (: *to inventor*) royalties *fpl*

rpm *abbr* (*AUT: = revs per minute*) tr/mn

RSVP *abbr* (= *répondez s'il vous plaît*) R.S.V.P.

Rt Hon. *abbr* (*BRIT: = Right Honourable*) titre donné aux députés de la Chambre des communes

rub [rʌb] *vt* frotter; frictionner; (*hands*) se frotter ♦ *n* (*with cloth*) coup *m* chiffon *or* de torchon; **to give sth a ~** donner un coup de chiffon *or* de torchon à; **to ~ sb up** (*BRIT*) or **to ~ sb** (*US*) **the wrong way** prendre qn à rebrousse-poil; **~ off** *vi* partir; **~ off on** *vt fus* déteindre sur; **~ out** *vt* effacer

rubber [ˈrʌbə*] *n* caoutchouc *m*; (*BRIT: eraser*) gomme *f* (à effacer); **~ band** *n* élastique *m*; **~ plant** *n* caoutchouc *m* (*plante verte*)

rubbish [ˈrʌbɪʃ] *n* (*from household*) ordures *fpl*; (*fig: pej*) camelote *f*; (: *nonsense*) bêtises *fpl*, idioties *fpl*; **~ bin** (*BRIT*) *n* poubelle *f*; **~ dump** *n* décharge publique, dépotoir *m*

rubble [ˈrʌbl] *n* décombres *mpl*; (*smaller*) gravats *mpl*; (*CONSTR*) blocage *m*

ruby [ˈruːbɪ] *n* rubis *m*

rucksack [ˈrʌksæk] *n* sac *m* à dos

rudder [ˈrʌdə*] *n* gouvernail *m*

ruddy [ˈrʌdɪ] *adj* (*face*) coloré(e); (*inf: damned*) sacré(e), fichu(e)

rude [ruːd] *adj* (*impolite*) impoli(e); (*coarse*) grossier(ère); (*shocking*) indécent(e), inconvenant(e)

ruffian [ˈrʌfɪən] *n* brute *f*, voyou *m*

ruffle [ˈrʌfl] *vt* (*hair*) ébouriffer; (*clothes*) chiffonner; (*fig: person*): **to get ~d** s'énerver

rug [rʌg] *n* petit tapis; (*BRIT: blanket*) couverture *f*

rugby [ˈrʌgbɪ] *n* (*also: ~ football*) rugby *m*

rugged [ˈrʌgɪd] *adj* (*landscape*) accidenté(e); (*features, character*) rude

rugger [ˈrʌgə*] (*BRIT: inf*) *n* rugby *m*

ruin [ˈruːɪn] *n* ruine *f* ♦ *vt* ruiner; (*spoil, clothes*) abîmer; (*event*) gâcher; **~s** *npl* (*of building*) ruine(s)

rule [ruːl] *n* règle *f*; (*regulation*) règlement *m*; (*government*) autorité *f*, gouvernement *m* ♦ *vt* (*country*) gouverner; (*person*) dominer ♦ *vi* commander; (*LAW*) statuer; **as a ~** normalement, en règle générale; **~ out** *vt* exclure; **~d** *adj* (*paper*) réglé(e); **~r** *n* (*sovereign*) souverain(e); (*for measuring*) règle *f*; **ruling** *adj* (*party*) au pouvoir; (*class*) dirigeant(e) ♦ *n* (*LAW*) décision *f*

rum [rʌm] *n* rhum *m*

Rumania [ruːˈmeɪnɪə] *n* = Romania

rumble [ˈrʌmbl] *vi* gronder; (*stomach, pipe*) gargouiller

rummage ['rʌmɪdʒ] *vi* fouiller
rumour ['ruːmə*] (*US* rumor) *n* rumeur *f*, bruit *m* (qui court) ♦ *vt*: **it is ~ed that** le bruit court que
rump [rʌmp] *n* (*of animal*) croupe *f*; (*inf: of person*) postérieur *m*; **~ steak** *n* rumsteck *m*
rumpus ['rʌmpəs] (*inf*) *n* tapage *m*, chahut *m*
run [rʌn] (*pt* ran, *pp* run) *n* (*fast pace*) (*pas m* de) course *f*; (*outing*) tour *m or* promenade *f* (en voiture); (*distance travelled*) parcours *m*, trajet *m*; (*series*) suite *f*, série *f*; (*THEATRE*) série de représentations; (*SKI*) piste *f*; (*CRICKET, BASEBALL*) point *m*; (*in tights, stockings*) maille filée, échelle *f* ♦ *vt* (*operate: business*) diriger; (: *competition, course*) organiser; (: *hotel, house*) tenir; (*race*) participer à; (*COMPUT*) exécuter; (*to pass: hand, finger*) passer; (*water, bath*) faire couler; (*PRESS: feature*) publier ♦ *vi* courir; (*flee*) s'enfuir; (*work: machine, factory*) marcher; (*bus, train*) circuler; (*continue: play*) se jouer; (: *contract*) être valide; (*flow: river, bath; nose*) couler; (*colours, washing*) déteindre; (*in election*) être candidat, se présenter; **to go for a ~** faire un peu de course à pied; **there was a ~ on ...** (*meat, tickets*) les gens se sont rués sur ...; **in the long ~** à longue échéance; à la longue; **on the ~** en fuite; **I'll ~ you to the station** je vais vous emmener *or* conduire à la gare; **to ~ a risk** courir un risque; **~ about** *vi* (*children*) courir çà et là; **~ across** *vt fus* (*find*) trouver par hasard; **~ around** *vi* = **run about**; **~ down** *vt* (*production*) réduire progressivement; (*factory*) réduire progressivement la production de; (*AUT*) renverser; (*criticize*) critiquer, dénigrer; **to be ~ down** (*person: tired*) être fatigué(e) *or* à plat; **~ in** (*BRIT*) *vt* (*car*) roder; **~ into** *vt fus* (*meet: person*) rencontrer par hasard; (: *trouble*) se heurter à; (*collide with*) heurter; **~ off** *vi* s'enfuir ♦ *vt* (*water*) laisser s'écouler; (*copies*) tirer; **~ out** *vi* (*person*) sortir en courant; (*liquid*) couler; (*lease*) expirer; (*money*) être épuisé(e); **~ out of** *vt fus* se trouver à court de; **~ over** *vt* (*AUT*) écraser ♦ *vt fus* (*revise*) revoir, reprendre; **~ through** *vt fus* (*recapitulate*) reprendre; (*play*) répéter; **~ up** *vt*: **to ~ up against** (*difficulties*) se heurter à; **to ~ up a debt** s'endetter; **~away** *adj* (*horse*) emballé(e); (*truck*) fou(folle); (*person*) fugitif(ive); (*teenager*) fugueur(euse)
rung [rʌŋ] *pp of* **ring** ♦ *n* (*of ladder*) barreau *m*
runner ['rʌnə*] *n* (*in race: person*) coureur(euse); (: *on sledge*) patin *m*; (*for drawer etc*) coulisseau *m*; **~ bean** (*BRIT*) *n* haricot *m* (à rames); **~-up** *n* second(e)

running ['rʌnɪŋ] *n* course *f*; (*of business, organization*) gestion *f*, direction *f* ♦ *adj* (*water*) courant(e); **to be in/out of the ~ for sth** être/ne pas être sur les rangs pour qch; **6 days ~** 6 jours de suite; **~ commentary** *n* commentaire détaillé; **~ costs** *npl* frais *mpl* d'exploitation
runny ['rʌnɪ] *adj* qui coule
run-of-the-mill ['rʌnəvðə'mɪl] *adj* ordinaire, banal(e)
runt [rʌnt] (*also pej*) *n* avorton *m*
run-up ['rʌnʌp] *n*: **~ to sth** (*election etc*) période *f* précédant qch
runway ['rʌnweɪ] *n* (*AVIAT*) piste *f*
rupee [ruː'piː] *n* roupie *f*
rupture ['rʌptʃə*] *n* (*MED*) hernie *f*
rural ['ruərəl] *adj* rural(e)
rush [rʌʃ] *n* (*hurry*) hâte *f*, précipitation *f*; (*of crowd, COMM: sudden demand*) ruée *f*; (*current*) flot *m*; (*of emotion*) vague *f*; (*BOT*) jonc *m* ♦ *vt* (*hurry*) transporter *or* envoyer d'urgence ♦ *vi* se précipiter; **~ hour** *n* heures *fpl* de pointe
rusk [rʌsk] *n* biscotte *f*
Russia ['rʌʃə] *n* Russie *f*; **~n** *adj* russe ♦ *n* Russe *m/f*; (*LING*) russe *m*
rust [rʌst] *n* rouille *f* ♦ *vi* rouiller
rustic ['rʌstɪk] *adj* rustique
rustle ['rʌsl] *vi* bruire, produire un bruissement ♦ *vt* (*paper*) froisser; (*US: cattle*) voler
rustproof ['rʌstpruːf] *adj* inoxydable
rusty ['rʌstɪ] *adj* rouillé(e)
rut [rʌt] *n* ornière *f*; (*ZOOL*) rut *m*; **to be in a ~** suivre l'ornière, s'encroûter
ruthless ['ruːθləs] *adj* sans pitié, impitoyable
rye [raɪ] *n* seigle *m*; **~ bread** *n* pain de seigle

S s

Sabbath ['sæbəθ] *n* (*Jewish*) sabbat *m*; (*Christian*) dimanche *m*
sabotage ['sæbətɑːʒ] *n* sabotage *m* ♦ *vt* saboter
saccharin(e) ['sækərɪn] *n* saccharine *f*
sachet ['sæʃeɪ] *n* sachet *m*
sack [sæk] *n* (*bag*) sac *m* ♦ *vt* (*dismiss*) renvoyer, mettre à la porte; (*plunder*) piller, mettre à sac; **to get the ~** être renvoyé(e), être mis(e) à la porte; **~ing** *n* (*material*) toile *f* à sac; (*dismissal*) renvoi *m*

sacrament ['sækrəmənt] *n* sacrement *m*
sacred ['seɪkrɪd] *adj* sacré(e)
sacrifice ['sækrɪfaɪs] *n* sacrifice *m* ♦ *vt* sacrifier
sad [sæd] *adj* triste; (*deplorable*) triste, fâcheux(euse)
saddle ['sædl] *n* selle *f* ♦ *vt* (*horse*) seller; **to be ~d with sth** (*inf*) avoir qch sur les bras; **~bag** *n* sacoche *f*
sadistic [sə'dɪstɪk] *adj* sadique
sadly *adv* tristement; (*unfortunately*) malheureusement; (*seriously*) fort
sadness ['sædnəs] *n* tristesse *f*
s.a.e. *n abbr* = **stamped addressed envelope**
safe [seɪf] *adj* (*out of danger*) hors de danger, en sécurité; (*not dangerous*) sans danger; (*unharmed*) indemne; (*journey*) bon voyage!; (*cautious*) prudent(e); (*sure: bet etc*) assuré(e) ♦ *n* coffre-fort *m*; ~ **from** à l'abri de; ~ **and sound** sain(e) et sauf(sauve); (**just**) **to be on the ~ side** pour plus de sûreté, par précaution; **~-conduct** *n* sauf-conduit *m*; **~-deposit** *n* (*vault*) dépôt *m* de coffres-forts; (*box*) coffre-fort *m*; **~guard** *n* sauvegarde *f*, protection *f* ♦ *vt* sauvegarder, protéger; **~keeping** *n* bonne garde; **~ly** *adv* (*assume, say*) sans risque d'erreur; (*drive, arrive*) sans accident; ~ **sex** *n* rapports *mpl* sexuels sans risque, sexe *m* sans risques
safety ['seɪftɪ] *n* sécurité *f*; ~ **belt** *n* ceinture *f* de sécurité; ~ **pin** *n* épingle *f* de sûreté *or* de nourrice; ~ **valve** *n* soupape *f* de sûreté
sag [sæg] *vi* s'affaisser; (*hem, breasts*) pendre
sage [seɪdʒ] *n* (*herb*) sauge *f*; (*person*) sage *m*
Sagittarius [sædʒɪ'tɛərɪəs] *n* le Sagittaire
Sahara [sə'hɑːrə] *n*: **the ~ (Desert)** le (désert du) Sahara
said [sed] *pt, pp of* **say**
sail [seɪl] *n* (*on boat*) voile *f*; (*trip*): **to go for a ~** faire un tour en bateau ♦ *vt* (*boat*) manœuvrer, piloter ♦ *vi* (*travel: ship*) avancer, naviguer; (*set off*) partir, prendre la mer; (*sport*) faire de la voile; **they ~ed into Le Havre** ils sont entrés dans le port du Havre; ~ **through** *vi, vt fus* (*fig*) réussir haut la main; ~ **boat** (*US*) *n* bateau *m* à voiles, voilier *m*; **~ing** (*sport*) voile *f*; **to go ~ing** faire de la voile; **~ing boat** *n* bateau *m* à voiles, voilier *m*; **~ing ship** *n* grand voilier; **~or** *n* marin *m*, matelot *m*
saint [seɪnt] *n* saint(e)
sake [seɪk] *n*: **for the ~ of** pour (l'amour de), dans l'intérêt de; par égard pour
salad ['sæləd] *n* salade *f*; ~ **bowl** *n* saladier *m*; ~ **cream** (*BRIT*) *n* (sorte de) mayonnaise *f*; ~ **dressing** *n* vinaigrette *f*
salary ['sælərɪ] *n* salaire *m*

sale [seɪl] *n* vente *f*; (*at reduced prices*) soldes *mpl*; **"for ~"** "à vendre"; **on ~** en vente; **on ~ or return** vendu(e) avec faculté de retour; **~room** *n* salle *f* des ventes; **~s assistant** *n* vendeur(euse); **~s clerk** (*US*) *n* vendeur(euse); **~sman** (*irreg*) *n* vendeur *m*; (*representative*) représentant *m* de commerce; **~swoman** (*irreg*) *n* vendeuse *f*; (*representative*) représentante *f* de commerce
sallow ['sæləʊ] *adj* cireux(euse)
salmon ['sæmən] *n inv* saumon *m*
saloon [sə'luːn] *n* (*US*) bar *m*; (*BRIT: AUT*) berline *f*; (*ship's lounge*) salon *m*
salt [sɔːlt] *n* sel *m* ♦ *vt* saler; ~ **cellar** *n* salière *f*; **~water** *adj* de mer; **~y** *adj* salé(e)
salute [sə'luːt] *n* salut *m* ♦ *vt* saluer
salvage ['sælvɪdʒ] *n* (*saving*) sauvetage *m*; (*things saved*) biens sauvés *or* récupérés ♦ *vt* sauver, récupérer
salvation [sæl'veɪʃən] *n* salut *m*; **S~ Army** *n* armée *f* du Salut
same [seɪm] *adj* même ♦ *pron*: **the ~** le(la) même, les mêmes; **the ~ book as** le même livre que; **at the ~ time** en même temps; **all** *or* **just the ~** tout de même, quand même; **to do the ~** faire de même, en faire autant; **to do the ~ as sb** faire comme qn; **the ~ to you!** à vous de même!; (*after insult*) toi-même!
sample ['sɑːmpl] *n* échantillon *m*; (*blood*) prélèvement *m* ♦ *vt* (*food, wine*) goûter
sanctimonious [sæŋktɪ'məʊnɪəs] *adj* moralisateur(trice)
sanction ['sæŋkʃən] *n* approbation *f*, sanction *f*
sanctity ['sæŋktɪtɪ] *n* sainteté *f*, caractère sacré
sanctuary ['sæŋktjʊərɪ] *n* (*holy place*) sanctuaire *m*; (*refuge*) asile *m*; (*for wild life*) réserve *f*
sand [sænd] *n* sable *m* ♦ *vt* (*furniture: also*: ~ **down**) poncer
sandal ['sændl] *n* sandale *f*
sand: **~box** (*US*) *n* tas *m* de sable; **~castle** *n* château *m* de sable; **~paper** *n* papier *m* de verre; **~pit** (*BRIT*) *n* (*for children*) tas *m* de sable; **~stone** *n* grès *m*
sandwich ['sænwɪdʒ] *n* sandwich *m*; **cheese/ham ~** sandwich au fromage/jambon; ~ **course** (*BRIT*) *n* cours *m* de formation professionnelle
sandy ['sændɪ] *adj* sablonneux(euse); (*colour*) sable *inv*, blond roux *inv*
sane [seɪn] *adj* (*person*) sain(e) d'esprit; (*outlook*) sensé(e), sain(e)
sang [sæŋ] *pt of* **sing**
sanitary ['sænɪtərɪ] *adj* (*system, arrangements*) sanitaire; (*clean*) hygiénique; ~ **towel** (*US* = **napkin**) *n* serviette *f* hygiénique
sanitation [sænɪ'teɪʃən] *n* (*in house*) installations *fpl* sanitaires; (*in town*) système *m* sanitaire; ~ **department** (*US*) *n* service *m*

de voirie

sanity ['sænɪtɪ] n santé mentale; (*common sense*) bon sens

sank [sæŋk] pt of **sink**

Santa Claus [sæntə'klɔːz] n le père Noël

sap [sæp] n (*of plants*) sève f ♦ vt (*strength*) saper, miner

sapling ['sæplɪŋ] n jeune arbre m

sapphire ['sæfaɪə*] n saphir m

sarcasm ['sɑːkæzəm] n sarcasme m, raillerie f

sardine [sɑː'diːn] n sardine f

Sardinia [sɑː'dɪnɪə] n Sardaigne f

sash [sæʃ] n écharpe f

sat [sæt] pt, pp of **sit**

satchel ['sætʃəl] n cartable m

satellite ['sætəlaɪt] n satellite m; ~ **dish** n antenne f parabolique; ~ **television** n télévision f par câble

satin ['sætɪn] n satin m ♦ adj en or de satin, satiné(e)

satisfaction [sætɪs'fækʃən] n satisfaction f; **satisfactory** [sætɪs'fæktərɪ] adj satisfaisant(e)

satisfy ['sætɪsfaɪ] vt satisfaire, contenter; (*convince*) convaincre, persuader; ~**ing** adj satisfaisant(e)

Saturday ['sætədeɪ] n samedi m

sauce [sɔːs] n sauce f; ~**pan** n casserole f

saucer ['sɔːsə*] n soucoupe f

saucy ['sɔːsɪ] adj impertinent(e)

Saudi ['saʊdɪ]: ~ **Arabia** n Arabie Saoudite; ~ **(Arabian)** adj saoudien(ne)

sauna ['sɔːnə] n sauna m

saunter ['sɔːntə*] vi: **to** ~ **along/in/out** etc marcher/entrer/sortir etc d'un pas nonchalant

sausage ['sɒsɪdʒ] n saucisse f; (*cold meat*) saucisson m; ~ **roll** n ≈ friand m

savage ['sævɪdʒ] adj (*cruel, fierce*) brutal(e), féroce; (*primitive*) primitif(ive), sauvage ♦ n sauvage m/f

save [seɪv] vt (*person, belongings*) sauver; (*money*) mettre de côté, économiser; (*time*) (faire) gagner; (*keep*) garder; (*COMPUT*) sauvegarder; (*SPORT: stop*) arrêter; (*avoid: trouble*) éviter ♦ vi (*also:* ~ **up**) mettre de l'argent de côté ♦ n (*SPORT*) arrêt m (du ballon) ♦ prep sauf, à l'exception de

saving ['seɪvɪŋ] n économie f ♦ adj: **the** ~ **grace of sth** ce qui rachète qch; ~**s** npl (*money saved*) économies fpl; ~**s account** n compte m d'épargne; ~**s bank** n caisse f d'épargne

saviour ['seɪvjə*] (*US* **savior**) n sauveur m

savour ['seɪvə*] (*US* **savor**) vt savourer; ~**y** (*US* **savory**) adj (*dish: not sweet*) salé(e)

saw [sɔː] (*pt* ~**ed**, *pp* ~**ed** or **sawn**) vt scier ♦ n (*tool*) scie f ♦ pt of **see**; ~**dust** n sciure f; ~**mill** n scierie f; ~**n-off** adj: ~**n-off shotgun** carabine f à canon scié

saxophone ['sæksəfəʊn] n saxophone m

say [seɪ] (*pt, pp* **said**) n: **to have one's** ~ dire ce qu'on a à dire ♦ vt dire; **to have a** or **some** ~ **in sth** avoir voix au chapitre; **could you** ~ **that again?** pourriez-vous répéter ce que vous venez de dire?; **that goes without** ~**ing** cela va sans dire, cela va de soi; ~**ing** n dicton m, proverbe m

scab [skæb] n croûte f; (*pej*) jaune m

scaffold ['skæfəʊld] n échafaud m; ~**ing** n échafaudage m

scald [skɔːld] n brûlure f ♦ vt ébouillanter

scale [skeɪl] n (*of fish*) écaille f; (*MUS*) gamme f; (*of ruler, thermometer etc*) graduation f, échelle (graduée); (*of salaries, fees etc*) barème m; (*of map, also size, extent*) échelle ♦ vt (*mountain*) escalader; ~**s** npl (*for weighing*) balance f; (*also: bathroom* ~) pèse-personne m inv; **on a large** ~ sur une grande échelle, en grand; ~ **of charges** tableau m des tarifs; ~ **down** vt réduire

scallop ['skɒləp] n coquille f Saint-Jacques; (*SEWING*) feston m

scalp [skælp] n cuir chevelu ♦ vt scalper

scamper ['skæmpə*] vi: **to** ~ **away** or **off** détaler

scampi ['skæmpɪ] npl langoustines (frites), scampi mpl

scan [skæn] vt scruter, examiner; (*glance at quickly*) parcourir; (*TV, RADAR*) balayer ♦ n (*MED*) scanographie f

scandal ['skændl] n scandale m; (*gossip*) ragots mpl

Scandinavian [skændɪ'neɪvɪən] adj scandinave

scant [skænt] adj insuffisant(e); ~**y** adj peu abondant(e), insuffisant(e); (*underwear*) minuscule

scapegoat ['skeɪpgəʊt] n bouc m émissaire

scar [skɑː*] n cicatrice f ♦ vt marquer (d'une cicatrice)

scarce ['skeəs] adj rare, peu abondant(e); **to make o.s.** ~ (*inf*) se sauver; ~**ly** adv à peine; **scarcity** n manque m, pénurie f

scare ['skeə*] n peur f, panique f ♦ vt effrayer, faire peur à; **to** ~ **sb stiff** faire une peur bleue à qn; **bomb** ~ alerte f à la bombe; ~ **away** vt faire fuir; ~ **off** vt = **scare away**; ~**crow** n épouvantail m; ~**d** adj: **to be** ~**d** avoir peur

scarf [skɑːf] (*pl* ~**s** or **scarves**) n (*long*) écharpe f; (*square*) foulard m

scarlet ['skɑːlət] adj écarlate; ~ **fever** n scarlatine f

scary ['skeərɪ] (*inf*) adj effrayant(e)

scathing ['skeɪðɪŋ] adj cinglant(e), acerbe

scatter ['skætə*] vt éparpiller, répandre; (*crowd*) disperser ♦ vi se disperser; ~**brained** adj écervelé(e), étourdi(e)

scavenger ['skævɪndʒə*] n (*person: in bins etc*) pilleur m de poubelles

scene [siːn] n scène f; (*of crime, accident*) lieu(x) m(pl); (*sight, view*) spectacle m, vue f; ~**ry** ['si:nərɪ] n (THEATRE) décor(s) m(pl); (landscape) paysage m; **scenic** ['si:nɪk] adj (picturesque) offrant de beaux paysages or panoramas

scent [sent] n parfum m, odeur f; (track) piste f

sceptical ['skeptɪkəl] (US **skeptical**) adj sceptique

schedule ['ʃedju:l, (US) 'skedju:l] n programme m, plan m; (of trains) horaire m; (of prices etc) barème m, tarif m ♦ vt prévoir; **on** ~ à l'heure (prévue); à la date prévue; **to be ahead of/behind** ~ avoir de l'avance/du retard; ~**d flight** n vol régulier

scheme [ski:m] n plan m, projet m; (dishonest plan, plot) complot m, combine f; (arrangement) arrangement m, classification f; (pension ~ etc) régime m ♦ vi comploter, manigancer; **scheming** ['ski:mɪŋ] adj rusé(e), intrigant(e) ♦ n manigances fpl, intrigues fpl

scholar ['skɒlə*] n érudit(e); (pupil) boursier(ière); ~**ly** adj érudit(e), savant(e); ~**ship** n (knowledge) érudition f; (grant) bourse f (d'études)

school [sku:l] n école f; (secondary ~) collège m, lycée m; (US: university) université f; (in university) faculté f ♦ cpd scolaire; ~**book** n livre m scolaire or de classe; ~**boy** n écolier m; (secondary) collégien m, lycéen m; ~**children** npl écoliers mpl; collégiens mpl, lycéens mpl; ~**days** npl années fpl de scolarité; ~**girl** n écolière f; (secondary) collégienne f, lycéenne f; ~**ing** n instruction f, études fpl; ~**master** n (primary) instituteur m; (secondary) professeur m; ~**mistress** n institutrice f; professeur m; ~**teacher** n instituteur(trice); professeur m

sciatica [saɪˈætɪkə] n sciatique f

science ['saɪəns] n science f; ~ **fiction** n science-fiction f; **scientific** [saɪənˈtɪfɪk] adj scientifique; **scientist** ['saɪəntɪst] n scientifique m/f; (eminent) savant m

scissors ['sɪzəz] npl ciseaux mpl

scoff [skɒf] vt (BRIT: inf: eat) avaler, bouffer ♦ vi: **to** ~ **(at)** (mock) se moquer (de)

scold [skəuld] vt gronder

scone [skɒn] n sorte de petit pain rond au lait

scoop [sku:p] n pelle f (à main); (for ice cream) boule f à glace; (PRESS) scoop m; ~ **out** vt évider, creuser; ~ **up** vt ramasser

scooter ['sku:tə*] n (also: motor ~) scooter m; (toy) trottinette f

scope [skəup] n (capacity: of plan, undertaking) portée f, envergure f; (: of person) compétence f, capacités fpl; (opportunity) possibilités fpl; **within the** ~ **of** dans les limites de

scorch [skɔ:tʃ] vt (clothes) brûler (légèrement), roussir; (earth, grass) dessécher, brûler

score [skɔ:*] n score m, décompte m des points; (MUS) partition f; (twenty) vingt ♦ vt (goal, point) marquer; (success) remporter ♦ vi marquer des points; (FOOTBALL) marquer un but; (keep ~) compter les points; ~**s of** (very many) beaucoup de, un tas de (fam); **on that** ~ sur ce chapitre, à cet égard; **to** ~ **6 out of 10** obtenir 6 sur 10; ~ **out** vt rayer, barrer, biffer; ~**board** n tableau m

scorn ['skɔ:n] n mépris m, dédain m

Scorpio ['skɔ:pɪəu] n le Scorpion

Scot [skɒt] n Écossais(e)

Scotch [skɒtʃ] n whisky m, scotch m

scotch vt (plan) faire échouer; (rumour) étouffer

scot-free ['skɒt'fri:] adv: **to get off** ~ s'en tirer sans être puni(e)

Scotland ['skɒtlənd] n Écosse f

Scots [skɒts] adj écossais(e); ~**man** (irreg) n Écossais; ~**woman** (irreg) n Écossaise f

Scottish ['skɒtɪʃ] adj écossais(e)

scoundrel ['skaundrəl] n vaurien m

scour ['skauə*] vt (search) battre, parcourir

scourge [skɜ:dʒ] n fléau m

scout [skaut] n (MIL) éclaireur m; (also: boy ~) scout m; **girl** ~ (US) guide f, ~ **around** vi explorer, chercher

scowl [skaul] vi se renfrogner, avoir l'air maussade; **to** ~ **at** regarder de travers

scrabble ['skræbl] vi (also: ~ around: search) chercher à tâtons; (claw): **to** ~ **(at)** gratter ♦ n: **S~** (R) Scrabble m (R)

scram [skræm] (inf) vi ficher le camp

scramble ['skræmbl] n (rush) bousculade f, ruée f ♦ vi: **to** ~ **up/down** grimper/descendre tant bien que mal; **to** ~ **out** sortir or descendre à toute vitesse; **to** ~ **through** se frayer un passage (à travers); **to** ~ **for** se bousculer or se disputer pour (avoir); ~**d eggs** npl œufs brouillés

scrap [skræp] n bout m, morceau m; (fight) bagarre f; (also: ~ iron) ferraille f ♦ vt jeter, mettre au rebut; (fig) abandonner, laisser tomber ♦ vi (fight) se bagarrer; ~**s** npl (waste) déchets mpl; ~**book** n album m; ~ **dealer** n marchand m de ferraille

scrape [skreɪp] vt, vi gratter, racler ♦ n: **to get into a** ~ s'attirer des ennuis; **to** ~ **through** réussir de justesse; **to** ~ **together** vt (money) racler ses fonds de tiroir pour réunir

scrap: ~ **heap** n: **on the** ~ **heap** (fig) au rancart or rebut; ~ **merchant** (BRIT) n marchand m de ferraille; ~ **paper** n papier m brouillon; ~**py** adj décousu(e)

scratch [skrætʃ] n égratignure f, rayure f; éraflure f; (from claw) coup m de griffe ♦ cpd: ~ **team** équipe de fortune or improvisée ♦ vt (rub) (se) gratter; (record) rayer; (paint etc) érafler; (with claw, nail) griffer ♦ vi (se) gratter; **to start from** ~ partir de zé-

ro; **to be up to** ~ être à la hauteur
scrawl [skrɔːl] *vi* gribouiller
scrawny ['skrɔːnɪ] *adj* décharné(e)
scream [skriːm] *n* cri perçant, hurlement *m*
♦ *vi* crier, hurler
screech [skriːtʃ] *vi* hurler; *(tyres)* crisser;
(brakes) grincer
screen [skriːn] *n* écran *m*; *(in room)* paravent *m*; *(fig)* écran, rideau *m* ♦ *vt (conceal)*
masquer, cacher; *(from the wind etc)* abriter, protéger; *(film)* projeter; *(candidates etc)*
filtrer; ~**ing** *n (MED)* test *m (or* tests) de
dépistage; ~**play** *n* scénario *m*
screw [skruː] *n* vis *f* ♦ *vt (also:* ~ *in)* visser;
~ **up** *vt (paper etc)* froisser; **to** ~ **up one's
eyes** plisser les yeux; ~**driver** *n* tournevis
m
scribble ['skrɪbl] *vt, vi* gribouiller, griffonner
script [skrɪpt] *n (CINEMA etc)* scénario *m*,
texte *m*; *(system of writing)* (écriture *f*)
script *m*
Scripture(s) ['skrɪptʃə*(z)] *n(pl) (Christian)*
Écriture sainte; *(other religions)* écritures
saintes
scroll [skrəʊl] *n* rouleau *m*
scrounge [skraʊndʒ] *(inf) vt:* **to** ~ **sth off**
or **from sb** taper qn de qch; ~**r** *(inf) n* parasite *m*
scrub [skrʌb] *n (land)* broussailles *fpl* ♦ *vt*
(floor) nettoyer à la brosse; *(pan)* récurer;
(washing) frotter; *(inf: cancel)* annuler
scruff [skrʌf] *n:* **by the** ~ **of the neck** par
la peau du cou
scruffy ['skrʌfɪ] *adj* débraillé(e)
scrum(mage) ['skrʌm(ɪdʒ)] *n (RUGBY)*
mêlée *f*
scruple ['skruːpl] *n* scrupule *m*
scrutiny ['skruːtɪnɪ] *n* examen minutieux
scuff [skʌf] *vt* érafler
scuffle ['skʌfl] *n* échauffourée *f*, rixe *f*
sculptor ['skʌlptə*] *n* sculpteur *m*
sculpture ['skʌlptʃə*] *n* sculpture *f*
scum [skʌm] *n* écume *f*, mousse *f*; *(pej:
people)* rebut *m*, lie *f*
scurrilous ['skʌrɪləs] *adj* calomnieux(euse)
scurry ['skʌrɪ] *vi* filer à toute allure; **to** ~
off détaler, se sauver
scuttle ['skʌtl] *n (also: coal* ~) seau *m* (à
charbon) ♦ *vt (ship)* saborder ♦ *vi (scamper):* **to** ~ **away** *or* **off** détaler
scythe [saɪð] *n* faux *f*
sea [siː] *n* mer *f* ♦ *cpd* marin(e), de (la)
mer; **by** ~ *(travel)* par mer, en bateau; **on
the** ~ *(boat)* en mer; *(town)* au bord de la
mer; **to be all at** ~ *(fig)* nager
complètement; **out to** ~ au large; *(out)* **at**
~ en mer; ~**board** *n* côte *f*; ~**food** *n*
fruits *mpl* de mer; ~**front** *n* bord *m* de
mer; ~**going** *adj (ship)* de mer; ~**gull** *n*
mouette *f*
seal [siːl] *n (animal)* phoque *m*; *(stamp)*

sceau *m*, cachet *m* ♦ *vt* sceller; *(envelope)*
coller; *(: with seal)* cacheter; ~ **off** *vt (forbid entry to)* interdire l'accès de
sea level *n* niveau *m* de la mer
sea lion *n* otarie *f*
seam [siːm] *n* couture *f*; *(of coal)* veine *f*,
filon *m*
seaman ['siːmən] *(irreg) n* marin *m*
seance ['seɪɑ̃s] *n* séance *f* de spiritisme
seaplane ['siːpleɪn] *n* hydravion *m*
search [sɜːtʃ] *n (for person, thing, COMPUT)*
recherche(s) *f(pl)*; *(LAW: at sb's home)* perquisition *f* ♦ *vt* fouiller; *(examine)* examiner
minutieusement; scruter ♦ *vi:* **to** ~ **for**
chercher; **in** ~ **of** à la recherche de; ~
through *vt fus* fouiller; ~**ing** *adj* pénétrant(e); ~**light** *n* projecteur *m*; ~ **party** *n*
expédition *f* de secours; ~ **warrant** *n*
mandat *m* de perquisition
sea: ~**shore** ['siːʃɔː*] *n* rivage *m*, plage *f*,
bord *m* de (la) mer; ~**sick** ['siːsɪk] *adj:* **to
be** ~**sick** avoir le mal de mer; ~**side**
['siːsaɪd] *n* bord *m* de la mer; ~**side resort**
n station *f* balnéaire
season ['siːzn] *n* saison *f* ♦ *vt* assaisonner,
relever; **to be in/out of** ~ être/ne pas être
de saison; ~**al** *adj (work)* saisonnier(ère);
~**ed** *adj (fig)* expérimenté(e); ~ **ticket** *n*
carte *f* d'abonnement
seat [siːt] *n* siège *m*; *(in bus, train: place)*
place *f*; *(buttocks)* postérieur *m*; *(of trousers)* fond *m* ♦ *vt* faire asseoir, placer;
(have room for) avoir des places assises
pour, pouvoir accueillir; ~ **belt** *n* ceinture
f de sécurité
sea: ~ **water** *n* eau *f* de mer; ~**weed**
['siːwiːd] *n* algues *fpl*; ~**worthy** ['siːwɜːðɪ]
adj en état de naviguer
sec. *abbr* = **second(s)**
secluded [sɪˈkluːdɪd] *adj* retiré(e), à l'écart
seclusion [sɪˈkluːʒən] *n* solitude *f*
second¹ [sɪˈkɒnd] *(BRIT) vt (employee)* affecter provisoirement
second² ['sekənd] *adj* deuxième, second(e)
♦ *adv (in race etc)* en seconde position ♦ *n*
(unit of time) seconde *f*; *(AUT:* ~ *gear)* seconde; *(COMM: imperfect)* article *m* de second choix; *(BRIT: UNIV)* licence *f* avec
mention ♦ *vt (motion)* appuyer; ~**ary** *adj*
secondaire; ~**ary school** *n* collège *m*, lycée *m*; ~**-class** *adj* de deuxième classe;
(RAIL) de seconde (classe) *(POST)* au tarif
réduit *(pej)* de qualité inférieure ♦ *adv*
(RAIL) en seconde; *(POST)* au tarif réduit;
~**hand** *adj* d'occasion; de seconde main;
~ **hand** *n (on clock)* trotteuse *f*; ~**ly** *adv*
deuxièmement; ~**ment** [sɪˈkɒndmənt]
(BRIT) n détachement *m*; ~**-rate** *adj* de
deuxième ordre, de qualité inférieure; ~
thoughts *npl* doutes *mpl*; **on** ~ **thoughts**
or (US) **thought** à la réflexion
secrecy ['siːkrəsɪ] *n* secret *m*

secret ['si:krət] *adj* secret(ète) ♦ *n* secret *m*; **in ~** en secret, secrètement, en cachette

secretary ['sekrətrı] *n* secrétaire *m/f*; (*COMM*) secrétaire général; **S~ of State (for)** (*BRIT: POL*) ministre *m* (de)

secretive ['si:krətıv] *adj* dissimulé

sectarian [sek'teərıən] *adj* sectaire

section ['sekʃən] *n* section *f*; (*of document*) section, article *m*, paragraphe *m*; (*cut*) coupe *f*

sector ['sektə*] *n* secteur *m*

secular ['sekjulə*] *adj* profane; laïque; séculier(ère)

secure [sı'kjuə*] *adj* (*free from anxiety*) sans inquiétude, sécurisé(e); (*firmly fixed*) solide, bien attaché(e) (*or* fermé(e) *etc*); (*in safe place*) en lieu sûr, en sûreté ♦ *vt* (*fix*) fixer, attacher; (*get*) obtenir, se procurer

security [sı'kjuərıtı] *n* sécurité *f*, mesures *fpl* de sécurité; (*for loan*) caution *f*, garantie *f*

sedan [sı'dæn] (*US*) *n* (*AUT*) berline *f*

sedate [sı'deıt] *adj* calme; posé(e) ♦ *vt* (*MED*) donner des sédatifs à

sedative ['sedıtıv] *n* calmant *m*, sédatif *m*

seduce [sı'dju:s] *vt* séduire; **seduction** [sı'dʌkʃən] *n* séduction *f*; **seductive** [sı'dʌktıv] *adj* séduisant(e); (*smile*) séducteur(trice); (*fig: offer*) alléchant(e)

see [si:] (*pt* **saw**, *pp* **seen**) *vt* voir; (*accompany*): **to ~ sb to the door** reconduire *or* raccompagner qn jusqu'à la porte ♦ *vi* voir ♦ *n* évêché *m*; **to ~ that** (*ensure*) veiller à ce que +*sub*, faire en sorte que +*sub*, s'assurer que; **~ you soon!** à bientôt!; **~ about** *vt fus* s'occuper de; **~ off** *vt* accompagner (à la gare *or* à l'aéroport *etc*); **~ through** *vt* mener à bonne fin ♦ *vt fus* voir clair dans; **~ to** *vt fus* s'occuper de, se charger de

seed [si:d] *n* graine *f*; (*sperm*) semence *f*; (*fig*) germe *m*; (*TENNIS*) tête *f* de série; **to go to ~** monter en graine; (*fig*) se laisser aller; **~ling** *n* jeune plant *m*, semis *m*; **~y** *adj* (*shabby*) minable, miteux/euse

seeing ['si:ıŋ] *conj*: **~ (that)** vu que, étant donné que

seek [si:k] (*pt, pp* **sought**) *vt* chercher, rechercher

seem [si:m] *vi* sembler, paraître; **there ~s to be ...** il semble qu'il y a ...; on dirait qu'il y a ...; **~ingly** *adv* apparemment

seen [si:n] *pp of* **see**

seep [si:p] *vi* suinter, filtrer

seesaw ['si:sɔ:] *n* (jeu *m* de) bascule *f*

seethe [si:ð] *vi* être en effervescence; **to ~ with anger** bouillir de colère

see-through ['si:θru:] *adj* transparent(e)

segment *n* segment *m*; (*of orange*) quartier *m*

segregate ['segrıgeıt] *vt* séparer, isoler

seize [si:z] *vt* saisir, attraper; (*take posses-*

sion of) s'emparer de; (*opportunity*) saisir; **~ up** *vi* (*TECH*) se gripper; **~ (up)on** *vt fus* saisir, sauter sur

seizure ['si:ʒə*] *n* (*MED*) crise *f*, attaque *f*; (*of power*) prise *f*

seldom ['seldəm] *adv* rarement

select [sı'lekt] *adj* choisi(e), d'élite ♦ *vt* sélectionner, choisir; **~ion** [sı'lekʃən] *n* sélection *f*, choix *m*

self [self] (*pl* **selves**) *n*: **the ~** le moi *inv* ♦ *prefix* auto-; **~-assured** *adj* sûr(e) de soi; **~-catering** (*BRIT*) *adj* avec cuisine, où l'on peut faire sa cuisine; **~-centred** (*US* **~-centered**) *adj* égocentrique; **~-confidence** *n* confiance *f* en soi; **~-conscious** *adj* timide, qui manque d'assurance; **~-contained** (*BRIT*) *adj* (*flat*) avec entrée particulière, indépendant(e); **~-control** *n* maîtrise *f* de soi; **~-defence** (*US* **~-defense**) *n* autodéfense *f*; (*LAW*) légitime défense *f*; **~-discipline** *n* discipline personnelle; **~-employed** *adj* qui travaille à son compte; **~-evident** *adj*: **to be ~-evident** être évident(e), aller de soi; **~-governing** *adj* autonome; **~-indulgent** *adj* qui ne se refuse rien; **~-interest** *n* intérêt personnel; **~-ish** *adj* égoïste; **~-ishness** *n* égoïsme *m*; **~-less** *adj* désintéressé(e); **~-pity** *n* apitoiement *m* sur soi-même; **~-possessed** *adj* assuré(e); **~-preservation** *n* instinct *m* de conservation; **~-respect** *n* respect *m* de soi, amour-propre *m*; **~-righteous** *adj* suffisant(e); **~-sacrifice** *n* abnégation *f*; **~-satisfied** *adj* content(e) de soi, suffisant(e); **~-service** *adj* libre-service, self-service; **~-sufficient** *adj* autosuffisant(e); (*person: independent*) indépendant(e); **~-taught** *adj* (*artist, pianist*) qui a appris par lui-même

sell [sel] (*pt, pp* **sold**) *vt* vendre ♦ *vi* se vendre; **to ~ at** *or* **for 10 F** se vendre 10 F; **~ off** *vt* liquider; **~ out** *vi*: **to ~ out (of sth)** (*use up stock*) vendre tout son stock (de qch); **the tickets are all sold out** il ne reste plus de billets; **~-by date** *n* date *f* limite de vente; **~er** *n* vendeur(euse), marchand(e); **~ing price** *n* prix *m* de vente

Sellotape ['seləuteıp] (®: *BRIT*) *n* papier collant *m*, scotch *m* (®)

selves [selvz] *npl of* **self**

semblance ['sembləns] *n* semblant *m*

semen ['si:mən] *n* sperme *m*

semester [sı'mestə*] *n* (*esp US*) semestre *m*

semi ['semı] *prefix* semi-, demi-; à demi, à moitié; **~circle** *n* demi-cercle *m*; **~colon** *n* point-virgule *m*; **~detached (house)** (*BRIT*) *n* maison jumelée *or* jumelle; **~final** *n* demi-finale *f*

seminar ['semına:*] *n* séminaire *m*

seminary ['semınərı] *n* (*REL: for priests*) séminaire *m*

semiskilled ['semɪ'skɪld] *adj*: ~ **worker** ouvrier(ère) spécialisé(e)

semi-skimmed milk *n* lait demi-écrémé

senate ['senɪt] *n* sénat *m*; **senator** *n* sénateur *m*

send [send] (*pt, pp* sent) *vt* envoyer; ~ **away** *vt* (*letter, goods*) envoyer, expédier; (*unwelcome visitor*) renvoyer; ~ **away for** *vt fus* commander par correspondance, se faire envoyer; ~ **back** *vt* renvoyer; ~ **for** *vt fus* envoyer chercher; faire venir; ~ **off** *vt* (*goods*) envoyer, expédier; (*BRIT: SPORT: player*) expulser *or* renvoyer du terrain; ~ **out** *vt* (*invitation*) envoyer (par la poste); (*light, heat, signal*) émettre; ~ **up** *vt* faire monter; (*BRIT: parody*) mettre en boîte, parodier; ~**er** *n* expéditeur(trice); ~**-off** *n*: a good ~**-off** des adieux chaleureux

senior ['siːnɪə*] *adj* (*high-ranking*) de haut niveau; (*of higher rank*): **to be ~ to sb** être le supérieur de qn; (*in older*): **she is 15 years his ~** elle est son aînée de 15 ans, elle est plus âgée que lui de 15 ans; ~ **citizen** *n* personne âgée; ~**ity** [siːnɪ'ɒrɪtɪ] *n* (*in service*) ancienneté *f*

sensation [sen'seɪʃən] *n* sensation *f*; ~**al** *adj* qui fait sensation; (*marvellous*) sensationnel(le)

sense [sens] *n* sens *m*; (*feeling*) sentiment *m*; (*meaning*) sens, signification *f*; (*wisdom*) bon sens ♦ *vt* sentir, pressentir; **it makes ~** c'est logique; ~**less** *adj* insensé(e), stupide; (*unconscious*) sans connaissance

sensible ['sensəbl] *adj* sensé(e), raisonnable; sage

sensitive ['sensɪtɪv] *adj* sensible

sensual ['sensjʊəl] *adj* sensuel(le)

sensuous ['sensjʊəs] *adj* voluptueux(euse), sensuel(le)

sent [sent] *pt, pp of* **send**

sentence ['sentəns] *n* (*LING*) phrase *f*; (*LAW: judgment*) condamnation *f*, sentence *f*; (*: punishment*) peine *f* ♦ *vt*: **to ~ sb to death/to 5 years in prison** condamner qn à mort/à 5 ans de prison

sentiment ['sentɪmənt] *n* sentiment *m*; (*opinion*) opinion *f*, avis *m*; ~**al** [sentɪ'mentl] *adj* sentimental(e)

sentry ['sentrɪ] *n* sentinelle *f*

separate [*adj* 'seprət, *vb* 'sepəreɪt] *adj* séparé(e), indépendant(e), différent(e) ♦ *vt* séparer; (*make a distinction between*) distinguer ♦ *vi* se séparer; ~**ly** *adv* séparément; ~**s** *npl* (*clothes*) coordonnés *mpl*; **separation** [sepə'reɪʃən] *n* séparation *f*

September [sep'tembə*] *n* septembre *m*

septic ['septɪk] *adj* (*wound*) infecté(e); ~ **tank** *n* fosse *f* septique

sequel ['siːkwəl] *n* conséquence *f*; séquelles *fpl*; (*of story*) suite *f*

sequence ['siːkwəns] *n* ordre *m*, suite *f*; (*film* ~) séquence *f*; (*dance* ~) numéro *m*

sequin ['siːkwɪn] *n* paillette *f*

serene [sə'riːn] *adj* serein(e), calme, paisible

sergeant ['sɑːdʒənt] *n* sergent *m*; (*POLICE*) brigadier *m*

serial ['sɪərɪəl] *n* feuilleton *m*; ~ **number** *n* numéro *m* de série

series ['sɪərɪz] *n inv* série *f*; (*PUBLISHING*) collection *f*

serious ['sɪərɪəs] *adj* sérieux(euse); (*illness*) grave; ~**ly** *adv* sérieusement; (*hurt*) gravement

sermon ['sɜːmən] *n* sermon *m*

serrated [se'reɪtɪd] *adj* en dents de scie

servant ['sɜːvənt] *n* domestique *m/f*; (*fig*) serviteur/servante

serve [sɜːv] *vt* (*employer etc*) servir, être au service de; (*purpose*) servir à; (*customer, food, meal*) servir; (*subj: train*) desservir; (*apprenticeship*) faire, accomplir; (*prison term*) purger ♦ *vi* (*be useful*): **to ~ as/for/to do** servir de/à/à faire ♦ *n* (*TENNIS*) service *m*; **it ~s him right** c'est bien fait pour lui; ~ **out**, ~ **up** *vt* (*food*) servir

service ['sɜːvɪs] *n* service *m*; (*AUT: maintenance*) révision *f*; (*CAR, washing machine*) réviser; **the S~s** les forces armées; **to be of ~ to sb** rendre service à qn; ~**able** *adj* pratique, commode; ~ **charge** (*BRIT*) *n* service *m*; ~**man** (*irreg*) *n* militaire *m*; ~ **station** *n* station-service *f*

serviette [sɜːvɪ'et] (*BRIT*) *n* serviette *f* (de table)

session ['seʃən] *n* séance *f*

set [set] (*pt, pp* set) *n* série *f*, assortiment *m*; (*of tools etc*) jeu *m*; (*RADIO, TV*) poste *m*; (*TENNIS*) set *m*; (*group of people*) cercle *m*, milieu *m*; (*THEATRE: stage*) scène *f*; (*: scenery*) décor *m*; (*MATH*) ensemble *m*; (*HAIRDRESSING*) mise *f* en plis ♦ *adj* (*fixed*) fixe, déterminé(e); (*ready*) prêt(e) ♦ *vt* (*place*) poser, placer; (*fix, establish*) fixer; (*: record*) établir; (*adjust*) régler; (*decide: rules etc*) fixer, choisir; (*task*) donner; (*exam*) composer ♦ *vi* (*sun*) se coucher; (*jam, jelly, concrete*) prendre; (*bone*) se ressouder; **to be ~ on doing** être résolu à faire; **to ~ the table** mettre la table; **to ~ (to music)** mettre en musique; **to ~ on fire** mettre le feu à; **to ~ free** libérer; **to ~ sth going** déclencher qch; **to ~ sail** prendre la mer; ~ **about** *vt fus* (*task*) entreprendre, se mettre à; ~ **aside** *vt* mettre de côté; (*time*) garder; ~ **back** *vt* (*in time*): **to ~ back (by)** retarder (de); (*cost*): **to ~ sb back £5** coûter 5 livres à qn; ~ **off** *vi* se mettre en route, partir ♦ *vt* (*bomb*) faire exploser; (*cause to start*) déclencher; (*show up well*) mettre en valeur, faire valoir; ~ **out** *vi* se mettre en route, partir ♦ *vt* (*arrange*) disposer; (*arguments*) présenter, exposer; **to ~ out to do**

entreprendre de faire, avoir pour but *or* intention de faire; ~ **up** *vt* (*organization*) fonder, créer; (*business*) (*hitch*) revers *m*, contretemps *m*; ~ **menu** *n* menu *m*

settee [se'ti:] *n* canapé *m*

setting ['setɪŋ] *n* cadre *m*; (*of jewel*) monture *f*; (*position: of controls*) réglage *m*

settle ['setl] *vt* (*argument, matter, account*) régler; (*problem*) résoudre; (*MED: calm*) calmer ♦ *vi* (*bird, dust etc*) se poser; (*also: ~ down*) s'installer, se fixer; (*calm down*) se calmer; **to ~ for sth** accepter qch, se contenter de qch; **to ~ on sth** opter *or* se décider pour qch; ~ **in** *vi* s'installer; ~ **up** *vi*: **to ~ up with sb** régler (ce que l'on doit à) qn; ~**ment** *n* (*payment*) règlement *m*; (*agreement*) accord *m*; (*village etc*) établissement *m*; hameau *m*; ~**r** *n* colon *m*

setup ['setʌp] *n* (*arrangement*) manière *f* dont les choses sont organisées; (*situation*) situation *f*

seven ['sevn] *num* sept; ~**teen** *num* dix-sept; ~**th** *num* septième; ~**ty** *num* soixante-dix

sever ['sevə*] *vt* couper, trancher; (*relations*) rompre

several ['sevrəl] *adj, pron* plusieurs *m/fpl*; ~ **of us** plusieurs d'entre nous

severance ['sevərəns] *n* (*of relations*) rupture *f*; ~ **pay** *n* indemnité *f* de licenciement

severe [sɪ'vɪə*] *adj* (*stern*) sévère, strict(e); (*serious*) grave, sérieux(euse); (*plain*) sévère, austère; **severity** [sɪ'verɪtɪ] *n* sévérité *f*; gravité *f*; rigueur *f*

sew [səu] (*pt* sewed, *pp* sewn) *vt, vi* coudre; ~ **up** *vt* (re)coudre

sewage ['sju:ɪdʒ] *n* vidange(s) *f(pl)*

sewer ['sjuə*] *n* égout *m*

sewing ['səuɪŋ] *n* couture *f*; (*item(s)*) ouvrage *m*; ~ **machine** *n* machine *f* à coudre

sewn [səun] *pp* of **sew**

sex [seks] *n* sexe *m*; **to have ~ with** avoir des rapports (sexuels) avec; ~**ist** *adj* sexiste; ~**ual** ['seksjuəl] *adj* sexuel(le); ~**y** ['seksɪ] *adj* sexy *inv*

shabby ['ʃæbɪ] *adj* miteux(euse), (*behaviour*) mesquin(e), méprisable

shack [ʃæk] *n* cabane *f*, hutte *f*

shackles ['ʃæklz] *npl* chaînes *fpl*, entraves *fpl*

shade [ʃeɪd] *n* ombre *f*; (*for lamp*) abat-jour *m inv*; (*of colour*) nuance *f*, ton *m* ♦ *vt* abriter du soleil, ombrager; **in the ~** à l'ombre; **a ~ too large/more** un tout petit peu trop grand/plus

shadow ['ʃædəu] *n* ombre *f* ♦ *vt* (*follow*) filer; ~ **cabinet** (*BRIT*) *n* (*POL*) cabinet parallèle formé par l'Opposition; ~**y** *adj* ombragé(e); (*dim*) vague, indistinct(e)

shady ['ʃeɪdɪ] *adj* ombragé(e); (*fig: dishonest*) louche, véreux(euse)

shaft [ʃɑ:ft] *n* (*of arrow, spear*) hampe *f*;

(*AUT, TECH*) arbre *m*; (*of mine*) puits *m*; (*of lift*) cage *f*; (*of light*) rayon *m*, trait *m*

shaggy ['ʃægɪ] *adj* hirsute; en broussaille

shake [ʃeɪk] (*pt* shook, *pp* shaken) *vt* secouer; (*bottle, cocktail*) agiter; (*house, confidence*) ébranler ♦ *vi* trembler; **to ~ one's head** (*in refusal*) dire *or* faire non de la tête; (*in dismay*) secouer la tête; **to ~ hands with sb** serrer la main à qn; ~ **off** *vt* secouer; (*pursuer*) se débarrasser de; ~ **up** *vt* secouer; ~**n** ['ʃeɪkn] *pp of* **shake**; **shaky** ['ʃeɪkɪ] *adj* (*hand, voice*) tremblant(e); (*building*) branlant(e), peu solide

shall [ʃæl] *aux vb*: **I ~ go** j'irai; ~ **I open the door?** j'ouvre la porte?; **I'll get the coffee, ~ I?** je vais chercher le café, d'accord?

shallow ['ʃæləu] *adj* peu profond(e); (*fig*) superficiel(le)

sham [ʃæm] *n* frime *f* ♦ *vt* simuler

shambles ['ʃæmblz] *n* (*muddle*) confusion *f*, pagaïe *f*, fouillis *m*

shame [ʃeɪm] *n* honte *f* ♦ *vt* faire honte à; **it is a ~ (that/to do)** c'est dommage (que +*sub*/de faire); **what a ~!** quel dommage!; ~**faced** *adj* honteux(euse), penaud(e); ~**ful** *adj* honteux(euse), scandaleux(euse); ~**less** *adj* éhonté(e), effronté(e)

shampoo [ʃæm'pu:] *n* shampooing *m* ♦ *vt* faire un shampooing à; ~ **and set** *n* shampooing *m* (et) mise *f* en plis

shamrock ['ʃæmrɔk] *n* trèfle *m* (*emblème de l'Irlande*)

shandy ['ʃændɪ] *n* bière panachée

shan't [ʃɑ:nt] = **shall not**

shanty town ['ʃæntɪ-] *n* bidonville *m*

shape [ʃeɪp] *n* forme *f* ♦ *vt* façonner, modeler; (*sb's ideas*) former; (*sb's life*) déterminer ♦ *vi* (*also: ~ up: events*) prendre tournure; (*: person*) faire des progrès, s'en sortir; **to take ~** prendre forme *or* tournure; -**shaped** *suffix*: **heart-shaped** en forme de cœur; ~**less** *adj* informe, sans forme; ~**ly** *adj* bien proportionné(e), beau(belle)

share [ʃɛə*] *n* part *f*; (*COMM*) action *f* ♦ *vt* partager; (*have in common*) avoir en commun; ~ **out** *vi* partager; ~**holder** *n* actionnaire *m/f*

shark [ʃɑ:k] *n* requin *m*

sharp [ʃɑ:p] *adj* (*razor, knife*) tranchant(e), bien aiguisé(e); (*point, voice*) aigu(guë); (*nose, chin*) pointu(e); (*outline, increase*) net(te); (*cold, pain*) vif(vive); (*taste*) piquant(e), âcre; (*MUS*) dièse; (*person: quickwitted*) vif(vive), éveillé(e); (*: unscrupulous*) malhonnête ♦ *n* (*MUS*) dièse *m* ♦ *adv* (*precisely*): **at 2 o'clock ~** à 2 heures pile *or* précises; ~**en** *vt* aiguiser; (*pencil*) tailler; ~**ener** *n* (*also: pencil ~ener*) taille-crayon(s) *m inv*; ~**-eyed** *adj* à qui rien n'échappe; ~**ly** *adv* (*turn, stop*) brusquement; (*stand out*) nettement; (*criticize, re-*

tort) sèchement, vertement

shatter ['ʃætə*] vt briser; (*fig: upset*) bouleverser; (: *ruin*) briser, ruiner ♦ vi voler en éclats, se briser

shave [ʃeɪv] vt raser ♦ vi se raser ♦ n: **to have a** ~ se raser; **~r** n (*also: electric* ~r) rasoir m électrique

shaving ['ʃeɪvɪŋ] n (*action*) rasage m; **~s** npl (*of wood etc*) copeaux mpl; **~ brush** n blaireau m; **~ cream** n crème f à raser; **~ foam** n mousse f à raser

shawl [ʃɔːl] n châle m

she [ʃiː] pron elle ♦ prefix: **~-cat** chatte f; **~-elephant** éléphant m femelle

sheaf [ʃiːf] (pl **sheaves**) n gerbe f; (*of papers*) liasse f

shear [ʃɪə*] (pt **~ed**, pp **shorn**) vt (*sheep*) tondre; **~ off** vi (*branch*) partir, se détacher; **~s** npl (*for hedge*) cisaille(s) f(pl)

sheath [ʃiːθ] n gaine f, fourreau m, étui m; (*contraceptive*) préservatif m

shed [ʃed] (pt, pp **shed**) n remise f, resserre f ♦ vt perdre; (*tears*) verser, répandre; (*workers*) congédier

she'd [ʃiːd] = **she had; she would**

sheen [ʃiːn] n lustre m

sheep [ʃiːp] n inv mouton m; **~dog** n chien m de berger; **~ish** adj penaud(e); **~skin** n peau f de mouton

sheer [ʃɪə*] adj (*utter*) pur(e), pur et simple; (*steep*) à pic, abrupt(e); (*almost transparent*) extrêmement fin(e) ♦ adv à pic, abruptement

sheet [ʃiːt] n (*on bed*) drap m; (*of paper*) feuille f; (*of glass, metal etc*) feuille, plaque f

sheik(h) [ʃeɪk] n cheik m

shelf [ʃelf] (pl **shelves**) n étagère f, rayon m

shell [ʃel] n (*on beach*) coquillage m; (*of egg, nut etc*) coquille f; (*explosive*) obus m; (*of building*) carcasse f ♦ vt (*peas*) écosser; (*MIL*) bombarder (d'obus)

she'll [ʃiːl] = **she will; she shall**

shellfish ['ʃelfɪʃ] n inv (*crab etc*) crustacé m; (*scallop etc*) coquillage m ♦ npl (*as food*) fruits mpl de mer

shell suit n survêtement m (*en synthétique froissé*)

shelter ['ʃeltə*] n abri m, refuge m ♦ vt abriter, protéger; (*give lodging to*) donner asile à ♦ vi s'abriter, se mettre à l'abri; **~ed housing** n foyers mpl (*pour personnes âgées ou handicapées*)

shelve [ʃelv] vt (*fig*) mettre en suspens or en sommeil; **~s** npl of **shelf**

shepherd ['ʃepəd] n berger m ♦ vt (*guide*) guider, escorter; **~'s pie** (BRIT) n ≈ hachis m Parmentier

sheriff ['ʃerɪf] (US) n shérif m

sherry ['ʃerɪ] n xérès m, sherry m

she's [ʃiːz] = **she is; she has**

Shetland ['ʃetlənd] n (*also: the* ~s, *the* ~

Islands) les îles fpl Shetland

shield [ʃiːld] n bouclier m; (*protection*) écran m de protection ♦ vt: **to** ~ (**from**) protéger (de or contre)

shift [ʃɪft] n (*change*) changement m; (*work period*) période f de travail; (*of workers*) équipe f, poste m ♦ vt déplacer, changer de place; (*remove*) enlever ♦ vi changer de place, bouger; **~less** adj (*person*) fainéant(e); **~ work** n travail m en équipe or par relais or par roulement; **~y** adj sournois(e); (*eyes*) fuyant(e)

shilly-shally ['ʃɪlɪʃælɪ] vi tergiverser, atermoyer

shimmer ['ʃɪmə*] vi miroiter, chatoyer

shin [ʃɪn] n tibia m

shine [ʃaɪn] (pt, pp **shone**) n éclat m, brillant m ♦ vi briller ♦ vt (*torch etc*): **to** ~ **on** braquer sur; (*polish: pt, pp* ~**d**) faire briller or reluire

shingle ['ʃɪŋgl] n (*on beach*) galets mpl; **~s** n (MED) zona m

shiny ['ʃaɪnɪ] adj brillant(e)

ship [ʃɪp] n bateau m; (*large*) navire m ♦ vt transporter (par mer); (*send*) expédier (par mer); **~building** n construction navale; **~ment** n cargaison f; **~per** n affréteur m; **~ping** n (*ships*) navires mpl; (*the industry*) industrie navale; (*transport*) transport m; **~wreck** n (*ship*) épave f; (*event*) naufrage m ♦ vt: **to be ~wrecked** faire naufrage; **~yard** n chantier naval

shire ['ʃaɪə*] (BRIT) n comté m

shirk [ʃɜːk] vt esquiver, se dérober à

shirt [ʃɜːt] n (*man's*) chemise f; (*woman's*) chemisier m; **in (one's)** ~ **sleeves** en bras de chemise

shit [ʃɪt] (*infl*) n, excl merde f (*l*)

shiver ['ʃɪvə*] n frisson m ♦ vi frissonner

shoal [ʃəʊl] n (*of fish*) banc m; (*fig: also:* ~s) masse f, foule f

shock [ʃɒk] n choc m; (ELEC) secousse f; (MED) commotion f, choc ♦ vt (*offend*) choquer, scandaliser; (*upset*) bouleverser; **~ absorber** n amortisseur m; **~ing** adj (*scandalizing*) choquant(e), scandaleux(euse); (*appalling*) épouvantable

shod [ʃɒd] pt, pp of **shoe**

shoddy ['ʃɒdɪ] adj de mauvaise qualité, mal fait(e)

shoe [ʃuː] (pt, pp **shod**) n chaussure f, soulier m; (*also: horse~*) fer m à cheval ♦ vt (*horse*) ferrer; **~lace** n lacet m (de soulier); **~ polish** n cirage m; **~ shop** n magasin m de chaussures; **~string** n (*fig*): **on a ~string** avec un budget dérisoire

shone [ʃɒn] pt, pp of **shine**

shoo [ʃuː] excl ouste!

shook [ʃʊk] pt of **shake**

shoot [ʃuːt] (pt, pp **shot**) n (*on branch, seedling*) pousse f ♦ vt (*game*) chasser; tirer; abattre; (*person*) blesser (or tuer) d'un coup de fusil (*or* de revolver); (*execute*) fusiller; (*arrow*) tirer; (*gun*) tirer un coup de; (*film*) tourner ♦ *vi* (*with gun, bow*): **to ~ (at)** tirer (sur); (*FOOTBALL*) shooter, tirer; **~ down** *vt* (*plane*) abattre; **~ in** *vi* entrer comme une flèche; **~ out** *vi* sortir comme une flèche; **~ up** *vi* (*fig*) monter en flèche; **~ing** *n* (*shots*) coups *mpl* de feu, fusillade *f*; (*HUNTING*) chasse *f*; **~ing star** *n* étoile filante

shop [ʃɔp] *n* magasin *m*; (*workshop*) atelier *m* ♦ *vi* (*also*: **go ~ping**) faire ses courses *or* ses achats; **~ assistant** (*BRIT*) *n* vendeur(euse); **~ floor** (*BRIT*) *n* (*INDUSTRY*: *fig*) ouvriers *mpl*; **~keeper** *n* commerçant(e); **~lifting** *n* vol *m* à l'étalage; **~per** *n* personne *f* qui fait ses courses, acheteur(euse); **~ping** *n* (*goods*) achats *mpl*, provisions *fpl*; **~ping bag** *n* sac *m* (à provisions); **~ping centre** (*US* **~ping center**) *n* centre commercial; **~-soiled** *adj* défraîchi(e), qui a fait la vitrine; **~ steward** (*BRIT*) *n* (*INDUSTRY*) délégué(e) syndical(e); **~ window** *n* vitrine *f*

shore [ʃɔ:*] *n* (*of sea, lake*) rivage *m*, rive *f* ♦ *vt*: **to ~ (up)** étayer; **on ~** à terre

shorn [ʃɔ:n] *pp of* **shear**

short [ʃɔ:t] *adj* (*not long*) court(e); (*soon finished*) court, bref(brève); (*person, step*) petit(e); (*curt*) brusque, sec(sèche); (*insufficient*) insuffisant(e); **to be/run ~ of sth** être à court de *or* manquer de qch; **in ~** bref; en bref; **~ of doing** ... à moins de faire ...; **everything ~ of** tout sauf; **it is ~ for** c'est l'abréviation *or* le diminutif de; **to cut ~** (*speech, visit*) abréger, écourter; **to fall ~ of** ne pas être à la hauteur de; **to run ~ of** arriver à court de, venir à manquer de; **to stop ~** s'arrêter net; **to stop ~ of** ne pas aller jusqu'à; **~age** *n* manque *m*, pénurie *f*; **~bread** *n* ≈ sablé *m*; **~change** *vt* ne pas rendre assez à; **~circuit** *n* court-circuit *m*; **~coming** *n* défaut *m*; **~(crust) pastry** (*BRIT*) *n* pâte brisée; **~cut** *n* raccourci *m*; **~en** *vt* raccourcir; (*text, visit*) abréger; **~fall** *n* déficit *m*; **~hand** (*BRIT*) *n* sténo(graphie) *f*; **~hand typist** (*BRIT*) *n* sténodactylo *m/f*; **~list** (*BRIT*) *n* (*for job*) liste *f* des candidats sélectionnés; **~-lived** *adj* de courte durée; **~ly** *adv* bientôt, sous peu; **~s** *npl*: **(a pair of) ~s** un short; **~-sighted** *adj* (*BRIT*) myope, (*fig*) qui manque de clairvoyance; **~-staffed** *adj* à court de personnel; **~ story** *n* nouvelle *f*; **~-tempered** *adj* qui s'emporte facilement; **~-term** *adj* (*effect*) à court terme; **~ wave** *n* (*RADIO*) ondes courtes

shot [ʃɔt] *pt, pp of* **shoot** ♦ *n* coup *m* (de feu); (*try*) coup, essai *m*; (*injection*) piqûre *f*; (*PHOT*) photo *f*; **he's a good/poor ~** il tire bien/mal; **like a ~** comme une flèche; (*very readily*) sans hésiter; **~gun** *n* fusil *m*

de chasse

should [ʃud] *aux vb*: **I ~ go now** je devrais partir maintenant; **he ~ be there now** il devrait être arrivé maintenant; **I ~ go if I were you** si j'étais vous, j'irais; **I ~ like to** j'aimerais bien, volontiers

shoulder [ʃəuldə*] *n* épaule *f* ♦ *vt* (*fig*) endosser, se charger de; **~ bag** *n* sac *m* à bandoulière; **~ blade** *n* omoplate *f*; **~ strap** *n* bretelle *f*

shouldn't [ʃudnt] = **should not**

shout [ʃaut] *n* cri *m* ♦ *vt* crier ♦ *vi* (*also*: **~ out**) crier, pousser des cris; **~ down** *vt* huer; **~ing** *n* cris *mpl*

shove [ʃʌv] *vt* pousser; (*inf*: *put*): **to ~ sth in** fourrer *or* ficher qch dans; **~ off** (*inf*) *vi* ficher le camp

shovel [ʃʌvl] *n* pelle *f*

show [ʃəu] (*pt* **~ed**, *pp* **shown**) *n* (*of emotion*) manifestation *f*, démonstration *f*; (*semblance*) semblant *m*, apparence *f*; (*exhibition*) exposition *f*, salon *m*; (*THEATRE, TV*) spectacle *m* ♦ *vt* montrer; (*film*) donner; (*courage etc*) faire preuve de, manifester; (*exhibit*) exposer ♦ *vi* se voir, être visible; **for ~** pour l'effet; **on ~** (*exhibits etc*) exposé(e); **~ in** *vt* (*person*) faire entrer; **~ off** *vi* (*pej*) crâner ♦ *vt* (*display*) faire valoir; **~ out** *vt* (*person*) reconduire (jusqu'à la porte); **~ up** *vi* (*stand out*) ressortir; (*inf*: *turn up*) se montrer ♦ *vt* (*flaw*) faire ressortir; **~ business** *n* le monde du spectacle; **~down** *n* épreuve *f* de force

shower [ʃauə*] *n* (*rain*) averse *f*; (*of stones etc*) pluie *f*, grêle *f*; (*also*: **~bath**) douche *f* ♦ *vi* prendre une douche, se doucher ♦ *vt*: **to ~ sb with** (*gifts etc*) combler qn de; **to have** *or* **take a ~** prendre une douche; **~proof** *adj* imperméable(e)

showing [ʃəuɪŋ] *n* (*of film*) projection *f*

show jumping *n* concours *m* hippique

shown [ʃəun] *pp of* **show**

show: **~-off** [ʃəuɔf] (*inf*) *n* (*person*) crâneur(euse), m'as-tu-vu(e); **~piece** *n* (*of exhibition*) trésor *m*; **~room** [ʃəurum] *n* magasin *m or* salle *f* d'exposition

shrank [ʃræŋk] *pt of* **shrink**

shrapnel [ʃræpnl] *n* éclats *mpl* d'obus

shred [ʃred] *n* (*gen pl*) lambeau *m*, petit morceau ♦ *vt* mettre en lambeaux, déchirer; (*CULIN*) râper; couper en lanières; **~der** *n* (*for vegetables*) râpeur *m*; (*for documents*) déchiqueteuse *f*

shrewd [ʃru:d] *adj* astucieux(euse), perspicace; (*businessman*) habile

shriek [ʃri:k] *vi* hurler, crier

shrill [ʃrɪl] *adj* perçant(e), aigu(guë), strident(e)

shrimp [ʃrɪmp] *n* crevette *f*

shrine [ʃraɪn] *n* (*place*) lieu *m* de pèlerinage

shrink [ʃrɪŋk] (*pt* **shrank**, *pp* **shrunk**) *vi* rétrécir; (*fig*) se réduire, diminuer; (*move*:

also: ~ *away*) reculer ♦ *vt* (*wool*) (faire) rétrécir ♦ *n* (*inf: pej*) psychiatre *m/f*, psy *mf*; **to ~ from (doing) sth** reculer devant (la pensée de faire) qch; ~**age** *n* rétrécissement *m*; ~**wrap** *vt* emballer sous film plastique

shrivel ['ʃrɪvl] *vt* (*also*: ~ *up*) ratatiner, flétrir ♦ *vi* se ratatiner, se flétrir

shroud [ʃraʊd] *n* linceul *m* ♦ *vt*: ~**ed in mystery** enveloppé(e) de mystère

Shrove Tuesday ['ʃrəʊv-] *n* (le) Mardi gras

shrub [ʃrʌb] *n* arbuste *m*; ~**bery** *n* massif *m* d'arbustes

shrug [ʃrʌg] *vt*, *vi*: **to ~ (one's shoulders)** hausser les épaules; ~ **off** *vt* faire fi de

shrunk [ʃrʌŋk] *pp of* **shrink**

shudder ['ʃʌdə*] *vi* frissonner, frémir

shuffle ['ʃʌfl] *vt* (*cards*) battre ♦ *vt*, *vi*: **to ~ (one's feet)** traîner les pieds

shun [ʃʌn] *vt* éviter, fuir

shunt [ʃʌnt] *vt* (*RAIL*) aiguiller

shut [ʃʌt] (*pt*, *pp* **shut**) *vt* fermer ♦ *vi* (se) fermer; ~ **down** *vt*, *vi* fermer définitivement; ~ **off** *vt* couper, arrêter; ~ **up** *vi* (*inf: keep quiet*) se taire ♦ *vt* (*close*) fermer; (*silence*) faire taire; ~**ter** *n* volet *m*; (*PHOT*) obturateur *m*

shuttle ['ʃʌtl] *n* navette *f*; (*also*: ~ *service*) (service *m* de) navette *f*

shuttlecock ['ʃʌtlkɒk] *n* volant *m* (*de badminton*)

shy [ʃaɪ] *adj* timide

sibling ['sɪblɪŋ] *n*: ~**s** enfants *mpl* de mêmes parents

Sicily ['sɪsɪlɪ] *n* Sicile *f*

sick [sɪk] *adj* (*ill*) malade; (*vomiting*): **to be ~** vomir; (*humour*) noir(e), macabre; **to feel ~** avoir envie de vomir, avoir mal au cœur; **to be ~ of** (*fig*) en avoir assez de; ~**bay** *n* infirmerie *f*; ~**en** *vt* écœurer; ~**ening** *adj* (*fig*) écœurant(e), dégoûtant(e)

sickle ['sɪkl] *n* faucille *f*

sick: ~ **leave** *n* congé *m* de maladie; ~**ly** *adj* maladif(ive), souffreteux(euse); (*causing nausea*) écœurant(e); ~**ness** *n* maladie *f*; (*vomiting*) vomissement(s) *m(pl)*; ~ **pay** *n* indemnité *f* de maladie

side [saɪd] *n* côté *m*; (*of lake, road*) bord *m*; (*team*) camp *m*, équipe *f* ♦ *adj* (*door, entrance*) latéral(e) ♦ *vi*: **to ~ with sb** prendre le parti de qn, se ranger du côté de qn; **by the ~ of** au bord de; ~ **by ~** côte à côte; **from ~ to ~** d'un côté à l'autre; **to take ~s (with)** prendre parti (pour); ~**board** *n* buffet *m*; ~**boards** (*BRIT*), ~**burns** *npl* (*whiskers*) pattes *fpl*; ~ **drum** *n* tambour plat; ~ **effect** *n* effet *m* secondaire; ~**light** *n* (*AUT*) veilleuse *f*; ~**line** *n* (*SPORT*) (ligne *f* de) touche *f*; (*fig*) travail *m* secondaire; ~**long** *adj* oblique; ~**saddle** *adv* en amazone; ~**show** *n* attrac-

tion *f*; ~**step** *vt* (*fig*) éluder; éviter; ~ **street** *n* (petite) rue transversale; ~**track** *vt* (*fig*) faire dévier de son sujet; ~**walk** (*US*) *n* trottoir *m*; ~**ways** *adv* de côté

siding ['saɪdɪŋ] *n* (*RAIL*) voie *f* de garage

sidle ['saɪdl] *vi*: **to ~ up (to)** s'approcher furtivement (de)

siege [siːdʒ] *n* siège *m*

sieve [sɪv] *n* tamis *m*, passoire *f*

sift [sɪft] *vt* (*fig*: *also*: ~ *through*) passer en revue; (*lit*: *flour etc*) passer au tamis

sigh [saɪ] *n* soupir *m* ♦ *vi* soupirer, pousser un soupir

sight [saɪt] *n* (*faculty*) vue *f*; (*spectacle*) spectacle *m*; (*on gun*) mire *f* ♦ *vt* apercevoir; **in ~** visible; **out of ~** hors de vue; ~**seeing** *n* tourisme *m*; **to go ~seeing** faire du tourisme

sign [saɪn] *n* signe *m*; (*with hand etc*) signe, geste *m*; (*notice*) panneau *m*, écriteau *m* ♦ *vt* signer; ~ **on** (*MIL*) s'engager; (*as unemployed*) s'inscrire au chômage; (*for course*) s'inscrire ♦ *vt* (*MIL*) engager; (*employee*) embaucher; ~ **over** *vt*: **to ~ sth over to sb** céder qch par écrit à qn; ~ **up** *vt* engager ♦ *vi* (*MIL*) s'engager; (*for course*) s'inscrire

signal ['sɪgnl] *n* signal *m* ♦ *vi* (*AUT*) mettre son clignotant ♦ *vt* (*person*) faire signe à; (*message*) communiquer par signaux; ~**man** (*irreg*) *n* (*RAIL*) aiguilleur *m*

signature ['sɪgnətʃə*] *n* signature *f*; ~ **tune** *n* indicatif musical

signet ring ['sɪgnət-] *n* chevalière *f*

significance [sɪg'nɪfɪkəns] *n* signification *f*; importance *f*; **significant** [sɪg'nɪfɪkənt] *adj* significatif(ive); (*important*) important(e), considérable

signpost ['saɪnpəʊst] *n* poteau indicateur

silence ['saɪləns] *n* silence *m* ♦ *vt* faire taire, réduire au silence; ~**r** *n* (*on gun, BRIT: AUT*) silencieux *m*

silent ['saɪlənt] *adj* silencieux(euse); (*film*) muet(te); **to remain ~** garder le silence, ne rien dire; ~ **partner** *n* (*COMM*) bailleur *m* de fonds, commanditaire *m*

silhouette [sɪluːˈet] *n* silhouette *f*

silicon chip ['sɪlɪkən-] *n* puce *f* électronique

silk [sɪlk] *n* soie *f* ♦ *cpd* de *or* en soie; ~**y** *adj* soyeux(euse)

silly ['sɪlɪ] *adj* stupide, sot(te), bête

silt [sɪlt] *n* vase *f*; limon *m*

silver ['sɪlvə*] *n* argent *m*; (*money*) monnaie *f* (en pièces d'argent); (*also*: ~*ware*) argenterie *f* ♦ *adj* d'argent, en argent; ~ **paper** (*BRIT*) *n* papier *m* d'argent *or* d'étain; ~-**plated** *adj* plaqué(e) argent; ~**smith** *n* orfèvre *m/f*; ~**y** *adj* argenté(e)

similar ['sɪmɪlə*] *adj*: ~ **(to)** semblable (à); ~**ly** *adv* de la même façon, de même

simile ['sɪmɪlɪ] *n* comparaison *f*

simmer ['sɪmə*] *vi* cuire à feu doux, mijoter

simple ['sɪmpl] *adj* simple; **simplicity** [sɪm'plɪsɪtɪ] *n* simplicité *f*; **simply** *adv* (*without fuss*) avec simplicité

simultaneous [sɪməl'teɪnɪəs] *adj* simultané(e)

sin [sɪn] *n* péché *m* ♦ *vi* pécher

since [sɪns] *adv, prep* depuis ♦ *conj* (*time*) depuis que; (*because*) puisque, étant donné que, comme; ~ **then, ever** ~ depuis ce moment-là

sincere [sɪn'sɪə*] *adj* sincère; ~**ly** *adv see* **yours; sincerity** [sɪn'serɪtɪ] *n* sincérité *f*

sinew ['sɪnju:] *n* tendon *m*

sinful ['sɪnful] *adj* coupable; (*person*) pécheur(eresse)

sing [sɪŋ] (*pt* **sang**, *pp* **sung**) *vt, vi* chanter

singe [sɪndʒ] *vt* brûler légèrement; (*clothes*) roussir

singer ['sɪŋə*] *n* chanteur(euse)

singing ['sɪŋɪŋ] *n* chant *m*

single ['sɪŋgl] *adj* seul(e), unique; (*unmarried*) célibataire; (*not double*) simple ♦ *n* (*BRIT: also:* ~ **ticket**) aller *m* (simple); (*record*) 45 tours *m*; ~ **out** *vt* choisir; (*distinguish*) distinguer; ~ **file** *n*: **in** ~ **file** en file indienne; ~-**handed** *adv* tout(e) seul(e), sans (aucune) aide; ~-**minded** *adj* résolu(e), tenace; ~-**room** *n* chambre *f* à un lit *or* pour une personne; ~**s** *n* (*TENNIS*) simple *m*; **singly** *adv* séparément

singular ['sɪŋgjulə*] *adj* singulier(ère), étrange; (*outstanding*) remarquable; (*LING*) (au) singulier, du singulier ♦ *n* singulier *m*

sinister ['sɪnɪstə*] *adj* sinistre

sink [sɪŋk] (*pt* **sank**, *pp* **sunk**) *n* évier *m* ♦ *vt* (*ship*) couler, faire sombrer; (*foundations*) creuser ♦ *vi* couler, sombrer; (*ground etc*) s'affaisser; (*also:* ~ **back**, ~ **down**) s'affaisser, se laisser retomber; **to** ~ **sth into** enfoncer qch dans; **my heart sank** j'ai complètement perdu courage; ~ **in** *vi* (*fig*) pénétrer, être compris(e)

sinner ['sɪnə*] *n* pécheur(eresse)

sinus ['saɪnəs] *n* sinus *m inv*

sip [sɪp] *n* gorgée *f* ♦ *vt* boire à petites gorgées

siphon ['saɪfən] *n* siphon *m*; ~ **off** *vt* siphonner; (*money: illegally*) détourner

sir [sɜ:*] *n* monsieur *m*; **S~ John Smith** sir John Smith; **yes** ~ oui, Monsieur

siren ['saɪərən] *n* sirène *f*

sirloin ['sɜ:lɔɪn] *n* (*also:* ~ **steak**) aloyau *m*

sissy ['sɪsɪ] (*inf*) *n* (*coward*) poule mouillée

sister ['sɪstə*] *n* sœur *f*; (*nun*) religieuse *f*, sœur; (*BRIT: nurse*) infirmière *f* en chef; ~-**in-law** *n* belle-sœur *f*

sit [sɪt] (*pt, pp* **sat**) *vi* s'asseoir; (*be sitting*) être assis(e); (*assembly*) être en séance, siéger; (*for painter*) poser ♦ *vt* (*exam*) passer,

se présenter à; ~ **down** *vi* s'asseoir; ~ **in on** *vt fus* assister à; ~ **up** *vi* s'asseoir; (*straight*) se redresser; (*not go to bed*) rester debout, ne pas se coucher

sitcom ['sɪtkɒm] *n abbr* (= *situation comedy*) comédie *f* de situation

site [saɪt] *n* emplacement *m*, site *m*; (*also: building* ~) chantier *m* ♦ *vt* placer

sit-in ['sɪtɪn] *n* (*demonstration*) sit-in *m inv*, occupation *f* (de locaux)

sitting ['sɪtɪŋ] *n* (*of assembly etc*) séance *f*; (*in canteen*) service *m*; ~ **room** *n* salon *m*

situated ['sɪtjueɪtɪd] *adj* situé(e)

situation [sɪtju'eɪʃən] *n* situation *f*; "~**s vacant**" (*BRIT*) "offres d'emploi"

six [sɪks] *num* six; ~**teen** *num* seize; ~**th** *num* sixième; ~**ty** *num* soixante

size [saɪz] *n* taille *f*; dimensions *fpl*; (*of clothing*) taille *f*; (*of shoes*) pointure *f*; (*fig*) ampleur *f*; (*glue*) colle *f*; ~ **up** *vt* juger, jauger; ~**able** *adj* assez grand(e); assez important(e)

sizzle ['sɪzl] *vi* grésiller

skate [skeɪt] *n* patin *m*; (*fish: pl inv*) raie *f* ♦ *vi* patiner; ~**board** *n* skateboard *m*, planche *f* à roulettes; ~**r** *n* patineur(euse); **skating** ['skeɪtɪŋ] *n* patinage *m*; **skating rink** *n* patinoire *f*

skeleton ['skelɪtn] *n* squelette *m*; (*outline*) schéma *m*; ~ **staff** *n* effectifs réduits

skeptical ['skeptɪkl] (*US*) *adj* = **sceptical**

sketch [sketʃ] *n* (*drawing*) croquis *m*, esquisse *f*; (*THEATRE*) sketch *m*, saynète *f* ♦ *vt* esquisser, faire un croquis *or* une esquisse de; ~ **book** *n* carnet *m* à dessin; ~**y** *adj* incomplet(ète), fragmentaire

skewer ['skjuə*] *n* brochette *f*

ski [ski:] *n* ski *m* ♦ *vi* skier, faire du ski; ~ **boot** *n* chaussure *f* de ski

skid [skɪd] *vi* déraper

ski: ~**er** ['ski:ə*] *n* skieur(euse); ~**ing** ['ski:ɪŋ] *n* ski *m*; ~ **jump** *n* saut *m* à skis

skilful ['skɪlful] (*US* **skillful**) *adj* habile, adroit(e)

ski lift *n* remonte-pente *m inv*

skill [skɪl] *n* habileté *f*, adresse *f*, talent *m*; (*requiring training: gen pl*) compétences *fpl*; ~**ed** *adj* habile, adroit(e); (*worker*) qualifié(e)

skim [skɪm] *vt* (*milk*) écrémer; (*glide over*) raser; , effleurer ♦ *vi*: **to** ~ **through** (*fig*) parcourir; ~**med milk** *n* lait écrémé

skimp [skɪmp] *vt* (*also:* ~ **on: work**) bâcler, faire à la va-vite; (: *cloth etc*) lésiner sur; ~**y** *adj* maigre; (*skirt*) étriqué(e)

skin [skɪn] *n* peau *f* ♦ *vt* (*fruit etc*) éplucher; (*animal*) écorcher; ~ **cancer** *n* cancer *m* de la peau; ~-**deep** *adj* superficiel(le); ~-**diving** *n* plongée sous-marine; ~**ny** *adj* maigre, maigrichon(ne); ~**tight** *adj* (*jeans etc*) collant(e), ajusté(e)

skip [skɪp] *n* petit bond *or* saut *m*; (*BRIT:*

container) benne f ♦ *vi* gambader, sautiller; *(with rope)* sauter à la corde ♦ *vt* sauter
ski pants *npl* fuseau *m* (de ski)
ski pole *n* bâton *m* de ski
skipper ['skɪpə*] *n* capitaine *m*; *(in race)* skipper *m*
skipping rope ['skɪpɪŋ-] *(BRIT)* n corde f à sauter
skirmish ['skɜːmɪʃ] *n* escarmouche f, accrochage *m*
skirt [skɜːt] *n* jupe f ♦ *vt* longer, contourner; ~**ing board** *(BRIT)* n plinthe f
ski slope *n* piste f de ski
ski suit *n* combinaison f (de ski)
skittle ['skɪtl] *n* quille f; **skittles** n *(game)* (jeu *m* de) quilles *fpl*
skive [skaɪv] *(BRIT: inf)* vi tirer au flanc
skulk [skʌlk] *vi* rôder furtivement
skull [skʌl] *n* crâne *m*
skunk [skʌŋk] *n* mouffette f
sky [skaɪ] *n* ciel *m*; ~**light** *n* lucarne f; ~**scraper** *n* gratte-ciel *m inv*
slab [slæb] *n (of stone)* dalle f; *(of food)* grosse tranche
slack [slæk] *adj (loose)* lâche, desserré(e); *(slow)* stagnant(e); *(careless)* négligent(e), peu sérieux(euse) *or* conscientieux(euse); ~**s** *npl (trousers)* pantalon *m*; ~**en** *vi* ralentir, diminuer ♦ *vt (speed)* réduire; *(grip)* relâcher; *(clothing)* desserrer
slag heap [slæg-] *n* crassier *m*
slag off *(BRIT: inf)* vt dire du mal de
slain [sleɪn] *pp of* **slay**
slam [slæm] *vt (door)* (faire) claquer; *(throw)* jeter violemment, flanquer *(fam)*; *(criticize)* démolir ♦ *vi* claquer
slander ['slɑːndə*] *n* calomnie f; diffamation f
slang [slæŋ] *n* argot *m*
slant [slɑːnt] *n* inclinaison f; *(fig)* angle *m*, point *m* de vue; ~**ed** *adj =* **slanting**; ~**ing** *adj* en pente, incliné(e); ~**ing eyes** yeux bridés
slap [slæp] *n* claque f, gifle f; tape f ♦ *vt* donner une claque *or* une gifle *or* une tape à; *(paint)* appliquer rapidement ♦ *adv (directly)* tout droit, en plein; ~**dash** *adj* fait(e) sans soin *or* à la va-vite; *(person)* insouciant(e), négligent(e); ~**stick** *n (comedy)* grosse farce, style *m* tarte à la crème; ~-**up** *(BRIT)* adj: a ~-**up meal** un repas extra *or* fameux
slash [slæʃ] *vt* entailler, taillader; *(fig: prices)* casser
slat [slæt] *n* latte f, lame f
slate [sleɪt] *n* ardoise f ♦ *vt (fig: criticize)* éreinter, démolir
slaughter ['slɔːtə*] *n* carnage *m*, massacre *m* ♦ *vt (animal)* abattre; *(people)* massacrer; ~**house** *n* abattoir *m*
slave [sleɪv] *n* esclave *m/f* ♦ *vi (also:* ~ *away)* trimer, travailler comme un forçat;

~**ry** *n* esclavage *m*; **slavish** *adj* servile
slay [sleɪ] *(pt* **slew**, *pp* **slain**) vt tuer
sleazy ['sliːzɪ] *adj* miteux(euse), minable
sledge [sledʒ] *n* luge f
sledgehammer *n* marteau *m* de forgeron
sleek [sliːk] *adj (hair, fur etc)* brillant(e), lisse; *(car, boat etc)* aux lignes pures *or* élégantes
sleep [sliːp] *(pt, pp* **slept**) n sommeil *m* ♦ *vi* dormir; *(spend night)* dormir, coucher; **to go to** ~ s'endormir; ~ **around** *vi* coucher à droite et à gauche; ~ **in** *vi (over~)* se réveiller trop tard; ~**er** *(BRIT)* n *(RAIL: train)* train-couchettes *m*; *(: berth)* couchette f; ~**ing bag** *n* sac *m* de couchage; ~**ing car** *n (RAIL)* wagon-lit *m*, voiture-lit f; ~**ing partner** *(BRIT)* n associé *m* commanditaire; ~**ing pill** *n* somnifère *m*; ~**less** *adj:* a ~**less night** une nuit blanche; ~**walker** *n* somnambule *m/f*; ~**y** *adj* qui a sommeil; *(fig)* endormi(e)
sleet [sliːt] *n* neige fondue
sleeve [sliːv] *n* manche f; *(of record)* pochette f
sleigh [sleɪ] *n* traîneau *m*
sleight [slaɪt] *n:* ~ **of hand** tour *m* de passe-passe
slender ['slendə*] *adj* svelte, mince; *(fig)* faible, ténu(e)
slept [slept] *pt, pp of* **sleep**
slew [sluː] *vi (also:* ~ *around)* virer, pivoter ♦ *pt of* **slay**
slice [slaɪs] *n* tranche f; *(round)* rondelle f; *(utensil)* spatule f, truelle f ♦ *vt* couper en tranches *(or* en rondelles)
slick [slɪk] *adj (skilful)* brillant(e) (en apparence); *(salesman)* qui a du bagout ♦ *n (also: oil* ~) nappe f de pétrole, marée noire
slide [slaɪd] *(pt, pp* **slid**) n *(in playground)* toboggan *m*; *(PHOT)* diapositive f; *(BRIT: also: hair* ~) barrette f; *(in prices)* chute f, baisse f ♦ *vt* (faire) glisser ♦ *vi* glisser; **sliding** ['slaɪdɪŋ] *adj (door)* coulissant(e); **sliding scale** *n* échelle f mobile
slight [slaɪt] *adj (slim)* mince, menu(e); *(frail)* frêle; *(trivial)* faible, insignifiant(e); *(small)* petit(e), léger(ère) *(before n)* ♦ *n* offense f, affront *m*; **not in the** ~**est** pas le moins du monde, pas du tout; ~**ly** *adv* légèrement, un peu
slim [slɪm] *adj* mince ♦ *vi* maigrir; *(diet)* suivre un régime amaigrissant
slime [slaɪm] *n (mud)* vase f; *(other substance)* substance visqueuse
slimming ['slɪmɪŋ] *adj (diet, pills)* amaigrissant(e); *(foodstuff)* qui ne fait pas grossir
sling [slɪŋ] *(pt, pp* **slung**) n *(MED)* écharpe f; *(for baby)* porte-bébé *m*; *(weapon)* fronde f, lance-pierre f ♦ *vt* lancer, jeter
slip [slɪp] *n* faux pas; *(mistake)* erreur f; étourderie f; bévue f; *(underskirt)* combinai-

son f; (of paper) petite feuille, fiche f ♦ vt (slide) glisser ♦ vi glisser; (decline) baisser; (move smoothly): **to ~ into/out of** se glisser or se faufiler dans/hors de; **to ~ sth on/off** enfiler/enlever qch; **to give sb the ~** fausser compagnie à qn; **a ~ of the tongue** un lapsus; **~ away** vi s'esquiver; **~ in** vt glisser ♦ vi (errors) s'y glisser; **~ out** vi sortir; **~ up** vi faire une erreur, gaffer; **~ped disc** n déplacement m de vertèbre

slipper ['slɪpə*] n pantoufle f

slippery ['slɪpərɪ] adj glissant(e)

slip road (BRIT) n (to motorway) bretelle f d'accès

slipshod ['slɪpʃɒd] adj négligé(e), peu soigné(e)

slip-up ['slɪpʌp] n bévue f

slipway ['slɪpweɪ] n cale f (de construction or de lancement)

slit [slɪt] (pt, pp **slit**) n fente f; (cut) incision f ♦ vt fendre; couper; inciser

slither ['slɪðə*] vi glisser; (snake) onduler

sliver ['slɪvə*] n (of glass, wood) éclat m; (of cheese etc) petit morceau, fine tranche

slob [slɒb] (inf) n rustaud(e)

slog [slɒg] (BRIT) vi travailler très dur ♦ n gros effort; tâche fastidieuse

slogan ['sləugən] n slogan m

slop [slɒp] vi (also: ~ **over**) se renverser; déborder ♦ vt répandre; renverser

slope [sləup] n pente f, côte f; (side of mountain) versant m; (slant) inclinaison f ♦ vi: **to ~ down** être or descendre en pente; **to ~ up** monter; **sloping** adj en pente; (writing) penché(e)

sloppy ['slɒpɪ] adj (work) peu soigné(e), bâclé(e); (appearance) négligé(e), débraillé(e)

slot [slɒt] n fente f ♦ vt: **to ~ sth into** encastrer or insérer qch dans

sloth [sləuθ] n (laziness) paresse f

slot machine (BRIT: vending machine) distributeur m (automatique); (for gambling) machine f à sous

slouch [slautʃ] vi avoir le dos rond, être voûté(e)

slovenly ['slʌvnlɪ] adj sale, débraillé(e); (work) négligé(e)

slow [sləu] adj lent(e); (watch): **to be ~** retarder ♦ adv lentement ♦ vt, vi (also: ~ **down**, ~ **up**) ralentir; **"~"** (road sign) "ralentir"; **~ly** adv lentement; **~ motion** n: **in ~ motion** au ralenti

sludge [slʌdʒ] n boue f

slue [slu:] (US) vi = **slew**

slug [slʌg] n limace f; (bullet) balle f

sluggish ['slʌgɪʃ] adj (person) mou(molle), lent(e); (stream, engine, trading) lent

sluice [slu:s] n (also: ~ **gate**) vanne f

slum [slʌm] n (house) taudis m

slump [slʌmp] n baisse soudaine, effondre-

ment m; (ECON) crise f ♦ vi s'effondrer, s'affaisser

slung [slʌŋ] pt, pp of **sling**

slur [slɜ:*] n (fig: smear): ~ **(on)** atteinte f (à); insinuation f (contre) ♦ vt mal articuler

slush [slʌʃ] n neige fondue; ~ **fund** n caisse noire, fonds secrets

slut [slʌt] (pej) n souillon f

sly [slaɪ] adj (person) rusé(e); (smile, expression, remark) sournois(e)

smack [smæk] n (slap) tape f; (on face) gifle f ♦ vt donner une tape à; (on face) gifler; (on bottom) donner la fessée à ♦ vi: **to ~ of** avoir des relents de, sentir

small [smɔːl] adj petit(e); ~ **ads** (BRIT) npl petites annonces; ~ **change** n petite or menue monnaie; ~ **fry** n (fig) menu fretin; **~holder** (BRIT) n petit cultivateur; ~ **hours** npl: **in the ~ hours** au petit matin; **~pox** n variole f; ~ **talk** n menus propos

smart [smɑːt] adj (neat, fashionable) élégant(e), chic inv; (clever) intelligent(e), astucieux(euse), futé(e); (quick) rapide, vif(vive), prompt(e) ♦ vi faire mal, brûler; (fig) être piqué(e) au vif; **~en up** vi devenir plus élégant(e), se faire beau(belle) ♦ vt rendre plus élégant(e)

smash [smæʃ] n (also: ~-up) collision f, accident m; (: ~ hit) succès foudroyant ♦ vt casser, briser, fracasser; (opponent) écraser; (SPORT: record) pulvériser ♦ vi se briser, se fracasser; s'écraser; **~ing** (inf) adj formidable

smattering ['smætərɪŋ] n: **a ~ of** quelques notions de

smear [smɪə*] n tache f, salissure f; trace f; (MED) frottis m ♦ vt enduire; (make dirty) salir; ~ **campaign** n campagne f de diffamation

smell [smel] (pt, pp **smelt** or **smelled**) n odeur f; (sense) odorat m ♦ vt sentir ♦ vi (food etc): **to ~ (of)** sentir (de); (pej) sentir mauvais

smelly ['smelɪ] adj qui sent mauvais, malodorant(e)

smile [smaɪl] n sourire m ♦ vi sourire

smirk [smɜːk] n petit sourire suffisant or affecté

smock [smɒk] n blouse f

smog [smɒg] n brouillard mêlé de fumée, smog m

smoke [sməuk] n fumée f ♦ vt, vi fumer; **~d** adj (bacon, glass) fumé(e); ~**r** n (person) fumeur(euse); (RAIL) wagon m fumeurs; ~ **screen** n rideau m or écran m de fumée; (fig) paravent m; **smoking** ['sməukɪŋ] n tabagisme m; **"no smoking"** (sign) "défense de fumer"; **to give up smoking** arrêter de fumer; **smoky** ['sməukɪ] adj enfumé(e); (taste) fumé(e)

smolder ['sməuldə*] (US) vi = **smoulder**

smooth [smuːð] adj lisse; (sauce) onctueux(euse); (flavour, whisky) moelleux(euse); (movement) régulier(ère), sans à-coups or heurts; (pej: person) doucereux(euse), mielleux(euse) ♦ vt (also: ~ out: skirt, paper) lisser, défroisser; (: creases, difficulties) faire disparaître

smother ['smʌðə*] vt étouffer

smoulder ['sməuldə*] (US **smolder**) vi couver

smudge [smʌdʒ] n tache f, bavure f ♦ vt salir, maculer

smug [smʌg] adj suffisant(e)

smuggle ['smʌgl] vt passer en contrebande or en fraude; ~**r** n contrebandier(ère); **smuggling** ['smʌglɪŋ] n contrebande f

smutty ['smʌtɪ] adj (fig) grossier(ère), obscène

snack [snæk] n casse-croûte m inv; ~ **bar** n snack(-bar) m

snag [snæg] n inconvénient m, difficulté f

snail [sneɪl] n escargot m

snake [sneɪk] n serpent m

snap [snæp] n (sound) claquement m, bruit sec; (photograph) photo f, instantané ♦ adj subit(e); fait(e) sans réfléchir ♦ vt (break) casser net; (fingers) faire claquer ♦ vi se casser net or avec un bruit sec; (speak sharply) parler d'un ton brusque; **to ~ shut** se refermer brusquement; ~ **at** vt fus (subj: dog) essayer de mordre; ~ **off** vi (break) casser net; ~ **up** vt sauter sur, saisir; ~**py** (inf) adj prompt(e); (slogan) qui a du punch; **make it ~py!** grouille-toi!, et que ça saute!; ~**shot** n photo f, instantané m

snare [snɛə*] n piège m

snarl [snɑːl] vi gronder

snatch [snætʃ] n (small amount): ~**es of** des fragments mpl or bribes fpl de ♦ vt saisir (d'un geste vif); (steal) voler

sneak [sniːk] (pt (US) also **snuck**) vi: **to ~ in/out** entrer/sortir furtivement or à la dérobée ♦ n (inf, pej: informer) faux jeton; **to ~ up on sb** s'approcher de qn sans faire de bruit; ~**ers** ['sniːkəz] npl tennis mpl or baskets mpl

sneer [snɪə*] vi ricaner; **to ~ at** traiter avec mépris

sneeze [sniːz] vi éternuer

sniff [snɪf] vi renifler ♦ vt renifler, flairer; (glue, drugs) sniffer, respirer

snigger ['snɪgə*] vi ricaner; pouffer de rire

snip [snɪp] n (cut) petit coup; (BRIT: inf: bargain) (bonne) occasion or affaire f ♦ vt couper

sniper ['snaɪpə*] n tireur embusqué

snippet ['snɪpɪt] n bribe(s) f(pl)

snivelling ['snɪvlɪŋ] adj larmoyant(e), pleurnicheur(euse)

snob [snɒb] n snob m/f; ~**bish** adj snob inv

snooker ['snuːkə*] n sorte de jeu de billard

snoop [snuːp] vi: **to ~ about** fureter

snooty ['snuːtɪ] adj snob inv

snooze [snuːz] n petit somme ♦ vi faire un petit somme

snore [snɔː*] vi ronfler

snorkel ['snɔːkl] n tuba m

snort [snɔːt] vi grogner; (horse) renâcler

snout [snaut] n museau m

snow [snəu] n neige f ♦ vi neiger; ~**ball** n boule f de neige; ~**bound** adj enneigé(e), bloqué(e) par la neige; ~**drift** n congère f; ~**drop** n perce-neige m or f; ~**fall** n chute f de neige; ~**flake** n flocon m de neige; ~**man** (irreg) n bonhomme m de neige; ~**plough** (US ~**plow**) n chasse-neige m inv; ~**shoe** n raquette f (pour la neige); ~**storm** n tempête f de neige

snub [snʌb] vt repousser, snober ♦ n rebuffade f; ~**-nosed** adj au nez retroussé

snuff [snʌf] n tabac m à priser

snug [snʌg] adj douillet(te), confortable; (person) bien au chaud

snuggle ['snʌgl] vi: **to ~ up to sb** se serrer or se blottir contre qn

———————————— KEYWORD

so [səu] adv **1** (thus, likewise) ainsi; **if** ~ **is** oui; ~ **do or have I** moi aussi; **it's 5 o'clock - ~ it is!** il est 5 heures - en effet! or c'est vrai!; **I hope/think** ~ je l'espère/le crois; ~ **far** jusqu'ici, jusqu'à maintenant; (in past) jusque-là

2 (in comparisons etc: to such a degree) si, tellement; ~ **big (that)** si or tellement grand (que); **she's not ~ clever as her brother** elle n'est pas aussi intelligente que son frère

3: ~ **much** adj, adv tant (de); **I've got ~ much work** j'ai tant de travail; **I love you ~ much** je vous aime tant; ~ **many** tant (de)

4 (phrases): **10 or** ~ à peu près or environ 10; ~ **long!** (inf: goodbye) au revoir!, à un de ces jours!

♦ conj **1** (expressing purpose): ~ **as to do** pour faire or afin de faire; ~ **(that)** pour que or afin que +sub

2 (expressing result) donc, par conséquent; ~ **that** si bien que, de (telle) sorte que

————————————

soak [səuk] vt faire tremper; (drench) tremper ♦ vi tremper; ~ **in** vi être absorbé(e); ~ **up** vt absorber

soap [səup] n savon m; ~**flakes** npl paillettes fpl de savon; ~ **opera** n feuilleton télévisé; ~ **powder** n lessive f; ~**y** adj savonneux(euse)

soar [sɔː*] vi monter (en flèche), s'élancer; (building) s'élancer

sob [sɒb] n sanglot m ♦ vi sangloter

sober ['səubə*] adj qui n'est pas (or plus) ivre; (serious) sérieux(euse), sensé(e); (colour, style) sobre, discret(ète); ~ **up** vt dessoûler (*inf*) ♦ *vi* dessoûler (*inf*)

so-called ['səu'kɔːld] *adj* soi-disant *inv*

soccer ['sɒkə*] *n* football *m*

social ['səuʃəl] *adj* social(e); (*sociable*) sociable ♦ *n* (petite) fête; ~ **club** *n* amicale *f*, foyer *m*; ~**ism** *n* socialisme *m*; ~**ist** *adj* socialiste ♦ *n* socialiste *m/f*; ~**ize** *vi*: **to** ~**ize (with)** lier connaissance (avec); parler (avec); ~ **security** (*BRIT*) *n* aide sociale; ~ **work** *n* assistance sociale, travail social; ~ **worker** *n* assistant(e) social(e)

society [sə'saiəti] *n* société *f*; (*club*) société, association *f*; (*also*: high ~) (haute) société, grand monde

sociology [səusi'ɒlədʒi] *n* sociologie *f*

sock [sɒk] *n* chaussette *f*

socket ['sɒkit] *n* cavité *f*; (*BRIT*: *ELEC*: *also*: wall ~) prise *f* de courant

sod [sɒd] *n* (*of earth*) motte *f*; (*BRIT*: *inf!*) con *m* (*!*); salaud *m* (*!*)

soda ['səudə] *n* (*CHEM*) soude *f*; (*also*: ~ water) eau *f* de Seltz; (*US*: *also*: ~ pop) soda *m*

sodden ['sɒdn] *adj* trempé(e); détrempé(e)

sofa ['səufə] *n* sofa *m*, canapé *m*

soft [sɒft] *adj* (*not rough*) doux(douce); (*not hard*) doux; mou(molle); (*not loud*) doux, léger(ère); (*kind*) doux, gentil(le); ~ **drink** *n* boisson non alcoolisée; ~**en** ['sɒfn] *vt* (r)amollir; (*fig*) adoucir; atténuer ♦ *vi* se ramollir; s'adoucir; s'atténuer; ~**ly** *adv* doucement; gentiment; ~**ness** *n* douceur *f*; ~ **spot** *n*: **to have a** ~ **spot for sb** avoir un faible pour qn; ~**ware** ['sɒftwɛə*] *n* (*COMPUT*) logiciel *m*, software *m*

soggy ['sɒgi] *adj* trempé(e); détrempé(e)

soil [sɔil] *n* (*earth*) sol *m*, terre *f* ♦ *vt* salir; (*fig*) souiller

solace ['sɒləs] *n* consolation *f*

solar ['səulə*] *adj* solaire; ~ **panel** *n* panneau *m* solaire; ~ **power** *n* énergie *f* solaire

sold [səuld] *pt*, *pp* of **sell**

solder ['səuldə*] *vt* souder (*au fil à souder*) ♦ *n* soudure *f*

soldier ['səuldʒə*] *n* soldat *m*, militaire *m*

sole [səul] *n* (*of foot*) plante *f*; (*of shoe*) semelle *f*; (*fish*: *pl inv*) sole *f* ♦ *adj* seul(e), unique

solemn ['sɒləm] *adj* solennel(le); (*person*) sérieux(euse), grave

sole trader *n* (*COMM*) chef *m* d'entreprise individuelle

solicit [sə'lisit] *vt* (*request*) solliciter ♦ *vi* (*prostitute*) racoler

solicitor [sə'lisitə*] *n* (*for wills etc*) ≈ notaire *m*; (*in court*) ≈ avocat *m*

solid ['sɒlid] *adj* solide; (*not hollow*) plein(e), compact(e), massif(ive); (*entire*): **3** ~ **hours** 3 heures entières ♦ *n* solide *m*

solidarity [sɒli'dæriti] *n* solidarité *f*

solitary ['sɒlitəri] *adj* solitaire; ~ **confinement** *n* (*LAW*) isolement *m*

solo ['səuləu] *n* solo *m* ♦ *adv* (*fly*) en solitaire; ~**ist** *n* soliste *m/f*

soluble ['sɒljubl] *adj* soluble

solution [sə'luːʃən] *n* solution *f*

solve [sɒlv] *vt* résoudre

solvent ['sɒlvənt] *adj* (*COMM*) solvable ♦ *n* (*CHEM*) (dis)solvant *m*

─────── KEYWORD ───────

some [sʌm] *adj* **1** (*a certain amount or number of*): ~ **tea/water/ice cream** du thé/de l'eau/de la glace; ~ **children/apples** des enfants/pommes

2 (*certain: in contrasts*): ~ **people say that ...** il y a des gens qui disent que ...; ~ **films were excellent, but most ...** certains films étaient excellents, mais la plupart ...

3 (*unspecified*): ~ **woman was asking for you** il y avait une dame qui vous demandait; **he was asking for** ~ **book (or other)** il demandait un livre quelconque; ~ **day** un de ces jours; ~ **day next week** un jour la semaine prochaine

♦ *pron* **1** (*a certain number*) quelques-un(e)s, certain(e)s; **I've got** ~ (*books etc*) j'en ai (quelques-uns); ~ (**of them**) **have been sold** certains ont été vendus

2 (*a certain amount*) un peu; **I've got** ~ (*money, milk*) j'en ai un peu

♦ *adv*: ~ **10 people** quelque 10 personnes, 10 personnes environ

some: ~**body** ['sʌmbədi] *pron* = **someone**; ~**how** ['sʌmhau] *adv* d'une façon ou d'une autre; (*for some reason*) pour une raison ou une autre; ~**one** ['sʌmwʌn] *pron* quelqu'un; ~**place** ['sʌmpleis] (*US*) *adv* = **somewhere**

somersault ['sʌməsɔːlt] *n* culbute *f*, saut périlleux ♦ *vi* faire la culbute *or* un saut périlleux; (*car*) faire un tonneau

something ['sʌmθiŋ] *pron* quelque chose; ~ **interesting** quelque chose d'intéressant

sometime ['sʌmtaim] *adv* (*in future*) un de ces jours, un jour ou l'autre; (*in past*): ~ **last month** au cours du mois dernier

some: ~**times** ['sʌmtaimz] *adv* quelquefois, parfois; ~**what** ['sʌmwɒt] *adv* quelque peu, un peu; ~**where** ['sʌmwɛə*] *adv* quelque part

son [sʌn] *n* fils *m*

song [sɒŋ] *n* chanson *f*; (*of bird*) chant *m*

son-in-law ['sʌninlɔː] *n* gendre *m*, beau-fils *m*

sonny ['sʌni] (*inf*) *n* fiston *m*

soon [suːn] *adv* bientôt; (*early*) tôt; ~ **afterwards** peu après; **as** ~ **as possible** dès possible, aussitôt possible; *see also* **as**; ~**er** *adv* (*time*) plus tôt; (*preference*): **I would** ~**er do** j'aimerais autant *or* je préférerais faire; ~**er or later** tôt ou tard

soot [sut] *n* suie *f*

soothe [su:ð] vt calmer, apaiser

sophisticated [sə'fistikeitid] adj raffiné(e); sophistiqué(e); (machinery) hautement perfectionné(e), très complexe

sophomore ['sɒfəmɔː*] (US) n étudiant(e) de seconde année

sopping ['sɒpiŋ] adj (also: ~ wet) complètement trempé(e)

soppy ['sɒpi] (pej) adj sentimental(e)

soprano [sə'prɑːnəu] n (singer) soprano m/f

sorcerer ['sɔːsərə*] n sorcier m

sore [sɔː*] adj (painful) douloureux(euse), sensible ♦ n plaie f; **~ly** adv (tempted) fortement

sorrow ['sɒrəu] n peine f, chagrin m

sorry ['sɒri] adj désolé(e); (condition, excuse) triste, déplorable; ~! pardon!, excusez-moi!; ~? pardon?; **to feel ~ for sb** plaindre qn

sort [sɔːt] n genre m, espèce f, sorte f ♦ vt (also: ~ out) trier; classer; ranger; (: problems) résoudre, régler; **~ing office** n bureau m de tri

SOS n abbr (= save our souls) S.O.S. m

so-so ['səu'səu] adv comme ci comme ça

sought [sɔːt] pt, pp of **seek**

soul [səul] n âme f; **~-destroying** adj démoralisant(e); **~ful** adj sentimental(e); (eyes) expressif(ive)

sound [saund] adj (healthy) en bonne santé, sain(e); (safe, not damaged) solide, en bon état; (reliable, not superficial) sérieux(euse), solide; (sensible) sensé(e) ♦ adv: **~ asleep** profondément endormi(e) ♦ n son m; bruit m; (GEO) détroit m, bras m de mer ♦ vt (alarm) sonner ♦ vi sonner, retentir; (fig: seem) sembler (être); **to ~ like** ressembler à; ~ **out** vt sonder; **~ barrier** n mur m du son; **~ effects** npl bruitage m; **~ly** adv (sleep) profondément; (beat) complètement, à plate couture; **~proof** adj insonorisé(e); **~track** n (of film) bande f sonore

soup [su:p] n soupe f, potage m; **in the ~** (fig) dans le pétrin; ~ **plate** n assiette creuse or à soupe; **~spoon** n cuiller f à soupe

sour ['sauə*] adj aigre; **it's ~ grapes** (fig) c'est du dépit

source [sɔːs] n source f

south [sauθ] n sud m ♦ adj sud inv, du sud ♦ adv au sud, vers le sud; **S~ Africa** n Afrique f du Sud; **S~ African** adj sudafricain(e) ♦ n Sud-Africain(e); **S~ America** n Amérique f du Sud; **S~ American** adj sud-américain(e) ♦ n Sud-Américain(e); **~-east** n sud-est m; **~erly** ['sʌðəli] adj du sud; au sud; **~ern** ['sʌðən] adj (du sud) sud; méridional(e); **S~ Pole** n Pôle m Sud; **~ward(s)** adv vers le sud; **~-west** n sudouest m

souvenir [suːvə'niə*] n (objet) souvenir m

sovereign ['sɒvrin] n souverain(e)

soviet ['səuviət] adj soviétique; **the S~ Union** l'Union f soviétique

sow[1] [sau] n truie f

sow[2] [səu] (pt ~**ed**, pp **sown**) vt semer; **~n** [səun] pp of **sow**[2]

soya ['sɔiə] (US **soy**) n: ~ **bean** graine f de soja; ~ **sauce** sauce f de soja

spa [spɑː] n (town) station thermale; (US: also: health ~) établissement m de cure de rajeunissement etc

space [speis] n espace m; (room) place f, espace; (length of time) laps m de temps ♦ cpd spatial(e) ♦ vt (also: ~ out) espacer; **~craft** n engin spatial; **~man** (irreg) n astronaute m, cosmonaute m; **~ship** n = **spacecraft**; **~woman** (irreg) n astronaute f, cosmonaute f; **spacing** n espacement m

spade [speid] n (tool) bêche f, pelle f; (child's) pelle; **~s** npl (CARDS) pique m

Spain [spein] n Espagne f

span [spæn] n (of bird, plane) envergure f; (of arch) portée f; (in time) espace m de temps, durée f ♦ vt enjamber, franchir; (fig) couvrir, embrasser

Spaniard ['spænjəd] n Espagnol(e)

spaniel ['spænjəl] n épagneul m

Spanish ['spæniʃ] adj espagnol(e) ♦ n (LING) espagnol m; **the ~** npl les Espagnols mpl

spank [spæŋk] vt donner une fessée à

spanner ['spænə*] (BRIT) n clé f (de mécanicien)

spar [spɑː*] n espar m ♦ vi (BOXING) s'entraîner

spare [speə*] adj de réserve, de rechange; (surplus) de or en trop, de reste ♦ n (part) pièce f de rechange, pièce détachée ♦ vt (do without) se passer de; (afford to give) donner, accorder; (refrain from hurting) épargner; **to ~** (surplus) en surplus, de trop; ~ **part** n pièce f de rechange, pièce détachée; ~ **time** n moments mpl de loisir, temps m libre; ~ **wheel** n (AUT) roue f de secours; **sparing** ['speəriŋ] adj: **to be sparing with** ménager; **sparingly** adv avec modération

spark [spɑːk] n étincelle f; **~(ing) plug** n bougie f

sparkle ['spɑːkl] n scintillement m, éclat m ♦ vi étinceler, scintiller; **sparkling** ['spɑːkliŋ] adj (wine) mousseux(euse), pétillant(e); (water) pétillant(e); (fig: conversation, performance) étincelant(e), pétillant(e)

sparrow ['spærəu] n moineau m

sparse [spɑːs] adj clairsemé(e)

spartan ['spɑːtən] adj (fig) spartiate

spasm ['spæzəm] n (MED) spasme m; **~odic** [spæz'mɒdik] adj (fig) intermittent(e)

spastic ['spæstik] n handicapé(e) moteur

spat [spæt] pt, pp of **spit**

spate [speit] n (fig): **a ~ of** une avalanche or un torrent de

spatter ['spætə*] vt éclabousser
spawn [spɔːn] vi frayer ♦ n frai m
speak [spiːk] (pt **spoke**, pp **spoken**) vt parler; (truth) dire ♦ vi parler; (make a speech) prendre la parole; **to ~ to sb/of** or **about sth** parler à qn/de qch; **~ up!** parle plus fort!; **~er** n (in public) orateur m; (also: loud~er) haut-parleur m; **the S~er** (BRIT POL) le président de la chambre des Communes; (US POL) le président de la chambre des Représentants
spear [spɪə*] n lance f ♦ vt transpercer; **~head** vt (attack etc) mener
spec [spek] (inf) n: **on ~** à tout hasard
special ['speʃəl] adj spécial(e); **~ist** n spécialiste m/f; **~ity** n spécialité f; **~ize** vi: **to ~ize (in)** se spécialiser (dans); **~ly** adv spécialement, particulièrement; **~ty** (esp US) n = **speciality**
species ['spiːʃiːz] n inv espèce f
specific [spə'sɪfɪk] adj précis(e); particulier(ère); (BOT, CHEM etc) spécifique; **~ally** adv expressément, explicitement; **~ation** n (TECH) spécification f; (requirement) stipulation f
specimen ['spesɪmɪn] n spécimen m, échantillon m; (of blood) prélèvement m
speck [spek] n petite tache, petit point; (particle) grain m; **~led** ['spekld] adj tacheté(e), moucheté(e)
specs [speks] (inf) npl lunettes fpl
spectacle ['spektəkl] n spectacle m; **~s** npl (glasses) lunettes fpl
spectacular [spek'tækjulə*] adj spectaculaire
spectator [spek'teɪtə*] n spectateur(trice)
spectrum ['spektrəm] (pl **spectra**) n spectre m
speculation [spekju'leɪʃən] n spéculation f
speech [spiːtʃ] n (faculty) parole f; (talk) discours m, allocution f; (manner of speaking) façon f de parler, langage m; (enunciation) élocution f; **~less** adj muet(te)
speed [spiːd] n vitesse f; (promptness) rapidité f ♦ vi: **to ~ along/past** etc aller/passer etc à toute vitesse; **at full** or **top ~** à toute vitesse or allure; **~ up** vi aller plus vite, accélérer ♦ vt accélérer; **~boat** n vedette f, hors-bord m inv; **~ily** adv rapidement, promptement; **~ing** n (AUT) excès m de vitesse; **~ limit** n limitation f de vitesse, vitesse maximale permise; **~ometer** [spɪ'dɒmɪtə*] n compteur m (de vitesse); **~way** n (SPORT: also: ~way racing) épreuve(s) f(pl) de vitesse de motos; **~y** adj rapide, prompt(e)
spell [spel] (pt, pp **spelt** (BRIT) or **~ed**) n (also: magic ~) sortilège m, charme m; (period of time) (courte) période ♦ vt (in writing) écrire, orthographier; (aloud) épeler; (fig) signifier; **to cast a ~ on sb** jeter un sort à qn; **he can't ~** il fait des fautes d'or-

thographe; **~bound** adj envoûté(e), subjugué(e); **~ing** n orthographe f
spend [spend] (pt, pp **spent**) vt (money) dépenser; (time, life) passer; consacrer; **~thrift** n dépensier(ère)
sperm [spɜːm] n sperme m
spew [spjuː] vt (also: ~ out) vomir
sphere [sfɪə*] n sphère f
spice [spaɪs] n épice f
spick-and-span ['spɪkən'spæn] adj impeccable
spicy ['spaɪsɪ] adj épicé(e), relevé(e); (fig) piquant(e)
spider ['spaɪdə*] n araignée f
spike [spaɪk] n pointe f; (BOT) épi m
spill [spɪl] (pt, pp **spilt** or **~ed**) vt renverser; répandre ♦ vi se répandre; **~ over** vi déborder
spin [spɪn] (pt **spun** or **span**, pp **spun**) n (revolution of wheel) tour m; (AVIAT) (chute f en) vrille f; (trip in car) petit tour, balade f ♦ vt (wool etc) filer; (wheel) faire tourner ♦ vi filer; (turn) tourner, tournoyer; **~ out** vt faire durer
spinach ['spɪnɪtʃ] n épinard m; (as food) épinards
spinal ['spaɪnl] adj vertébral(e), spinal(e); **~ cord** n moelle épinière
spindly ['spɪndlɪ] adj grêle, filiforme
spin-dryer ['spɪn'draɪə*] (BRIT) n essoreuse f
spine [spaɪn] n colonne vertébrale; (thorn) épine f; **~less** adj (fig) mou(molle)
spinning ['spɪnɪŋ] n (of thread) filature f; **~ top** n toupie f; **~ wheel** n rouet m
spin-off ['spɪnɒf] n avantage inattendu; sous-produit m
spinster ['spɪnstə*] n célibataire f, vieille fille (péj)
spiral ['spaɪərl] n spirale f ♦ vi (fig) monter en flèche; **~ staircase** n escalier m en colimaçon
spire ['spaɪə*] n flèche f, aiguille f
spirit ['spɪrɪt] n esprit m; (mood) état m d'esprit; (courage) courage m, énergie f; **~s** npl (drink) spiritueux mpl, alcool m; **in good ~s** de bonne humeur; **~ed** adj vif(vive), fougueux(euse), plein(e) d'allant; **~ual** ['spɪrɪtjuəl] adj spirituel(le); (religious) religieux(euse)
spit [spɪt] (pt, pp **spat**) n (for roasting) broche f; (saliva) salive f ♦ vi cracher; (sound) crépiter
spite [spaɪt] n rancune f, dépit m ♦ vt contrarier, vexer; **in ~ of** en dépit de, malgré; **~ful** adj méchant(e), malveillant(e)
spittle ['spɪtl] n salive f; (of animal) bave f; (spat out) crachat m
splash [splæʃ] n (sound) plouf m; (of colour) tache f ♦ vt éclabousser ♦ vi (also: ~ about) barboter, patauger
spleen [spliːn] n (ANAT) rate f

splendid ['splendıd] adj splendide, superbe, magnifique

splint [splınt] n attelle f, éclisse f

splinter ['splıntə*] n (wood) écharde f; (glass) éclat m ♦ vi se briser, se fendre

split [splıt] (pt, pp split) n fente f, déchirure f; (fig: POL) scission f ♦ vt diviser; (work, profits) partager, répartir ♦ vi (divide) se diviser; ~ **up** vi (couple) se séparer, rompre; (meeting) se disperser

splutter ['splʌtə*] vi bafouiller; (spit) postillonner

spoil [spɔıl] (pt, pp spoilt or ~ed) vt (damage) abîmer; (mar) gâcher; (child) gâter; ~**s** npl butin m; (fig: profits) bénéfices npl; ~**sport** n trouble-fête m, rabat-joie m

spoke [spəʊk] pt speak ♦ n (of wheel) rayon m; ~**n** ['spəʊkn] pp of speak; ~**sman** ['spəʊksmən] (irreg) n porte-parole m inv; ~**swoman** ['spəʊkswʊmən] (irreg) n porte-parole m inv

sponge [spʌndʒ] n éponge f; (also: ~ cake) ≈ biscuit m de Savoie ♦ vt éponger ♦ vi: to ~ **off** or **on** vivre aux crochets de; ~ **bag** (BRIT) n trousse f de toilette

sponsor ['spɒnsə*] n (RADIO, TV, SPORT) sponsor m; (for application) parrain m, marraine f; (BRIT: for fund-raising event) donateur(trice) ♦ vt sponsoriser; parrainer; faire un don à; ~**ship** n sponsoring m; parrainage m; dons mpl

spontaneous [spɒn'teınıəs] adj spontané(e)

spooky ['spu:kı] (inf) adj qui donne la chair de poule

spool [spu:l] n bobine f

spoon [spu:n] n cuiller f; ~**feed** vt nourrir à la cuiller; (fig) mâcher le travail à; ~**ful** n cuillerée f

sport [spɔːt] n sport m; (person) chic type(fille) ♦ vt arborer; ~**ing** adj sportif(ive); to **give sb a** ~**ing chance** donner sa chance à qn; ~ **jacket** (US) n = **sports jacket**; ~**s car** n voiture f de sport; ~**s jacket** (BRIT) n veste f de sport; ~**sman** (irreg) n sportif m; ~**smanship** n esprit sportif, sportivité f; ~**swear** n vêtements mpl de sport; ~**swoman** (irreg) n sportive f; ~**y** adj sportif(ive)

spot [spɒt] n tache f; (dot: on pattern) pois m; (pimple) bouton m; (place) endroit m, coin m; (RADIO, TV: in programme: for person) numéro m; (: for activity) rubrique f; (small amount): a ~ **of** un peu de ♦ vt (notice) apercevoir, repérer; **on the** ~ sur place, sur les lieux; (immediately) sur-le-champ; (in difficulty) dans l'embarras; ~ **check** n sondage m, vérification ponctuelle; ~**less** adj immaculé(e); ~**light** n projecteur m; ~**ted** adj (fabric) à pois; ~**ty** adj (face, person) boutonneux(euse)

spouse [spaʊz] n époux(épouse)

spout [spaʊt] n (of jug) bec m; (of pipe) orifice m ♦ vi jaillir

sprain [spreın] n entorse f, foulure f ♦ vt: to ~ **one's ankle** etc se fouler or se tordre la cheville etc

sprang [spræŋ] pt of **spring**

sprawl [sprɔːl] vi s'étaler

spray [spreı] n jet m (en fines gouttelettes); (from sea) embruns mpl; (container) vaporisateur m; (for garden) pulvérisateur m; (aerosol) bombe f; (of flowers) petit bouquet ♦ vt vaporiser, pulvériser; (crops) traiter

spread [spred] (pt, pp spread) n (distribution) répartition f, (CULIN) pâte f à tartiner; (inf: meal) festin m ♦ vt étendre, étaler; répandre; (wealth, workload) distribuer ♦ vi (disease, news) se propager; (also: ~ out: stain) s'étaler; ~ **out** vi (people) se disperser; ~**eagled** ['spredi:gld] adj étendu(e) bras et jambes écartés; ~**sheet** n (COMPUT) tableur m

spree [spri:] n: to go on a ~ faire la fête

sprightly ['spraıtlı] adj alerte

spring [sprıŋ] (pt sprang, pp sprung) n (leap) bond m, saut m; (coiled metal) ressort m; (season) printemps m; (of water) source f ♦ vi (leap) bondir, sauter; **in** ~ au printemps; **to** ~ **from** provenir de; ~ **up** vi (problem) se présenter, surgir; (plant, buildings) surgir de terre; ~**board** n tremplin m; ~**clean(ing)** n grand nettoyage de printemps; ~**time** n printemps m

sprinkle ['sprıŋkl] vt: to ~ **water** etc on, ~ **with water** etc asperger d'eau etc; to ~ **sugar** etc on, ~ **with sugar** etc saupoudrer de sucre etc; ~**r** ['sprıŋklə*] n (for lawn) arroseur m; (to put out fire) diffuseur m d'extincteur automatique d'incendie

sprint [sprınt] n sprint m ♦ vi courir à toute vitesse; (SPORT) sprinter

sprout [spraʊt] vi germer, pousser; ~**s** npl (also: Brussels ~s) choux mpl de Bruxelles

spruce [spru:s] n inv épicéa m ♦ adj net(te), pimpant(e)

sprung [sprʌŋ] pp of **spring**

spry [spraı] adj alerte, vif(vive)

spun [spʌn] pt, pp of **spin**

spur [spɜ:*] n éperon m; (fig) aiguillon m ♦ vt (also: ~ on) éperonner; aiguillonner; **on the** ~ **of the moment** sous l'impulsion du moment

spurious ['spjʊərıəs] adj faux(fausse)

spurn [spɜ:n] vt repousser avec mépris

spurt [spɜ:t] n (of blood) jaillissement m; (of energy) regain m, sursaut m ♦ vi jaillir, gicler

spy [spaı] n espion(ne) ♦ vi: to ~ **on** espionner, épier; (see) apercevoir; ~**ing** n espionnage m

sq. abbr = **square**

squabble ['skwɒbl] vi se chamailler

squad [skwɒd] *n* (*MIL, POLICE*) escouade *f*, groupe *m*; (*FOOTBALL*) contingent *m*

squadron ['skwɒdrən] *n* (*MIL*) escadron *m*; (*AVIAT, NAUT*) escadrille *f*

squalid ['skwɒlɪd] *adj* sordide

squall [skwɔ:l] *n* rafale *f*, bourrasque *f*

squalor ['skwɒlə*] *n* conditions *fpl* sordides

squander ['skwɒndə*] *vt* gaspiller, dilapider

square [skwɛə*] *n* carré *m*; (*in town*) place *f* ♦ *adj* carré(e); (*inf: ideas, tastes*) vieux jeu *inv* ♦ *vt* (*arrange*) régler; arranger; (*MATH*) élever au carré ♦ *vi* (*reconcile*) concilier; **all ~ quitte**; **à égalité**; **a ~ meal** un repas convenable; **2 metres ~** (de) 2 mètres sur 2; **2 ~ metres** 2 mètres carrés; **~ly** *adv* carrément

squash [skwɒʃ] *n* (*BRIT: drink*): **lemon/ orange ~** citronnade *f*/orangeade *f*; (*US: marrow*) courge *f*; (*SPORT*) squash *m* ♦ *vt* écraser

squat [skwɒt] *adj* petit(e) et épais(se), ramassé(e) ♦ *vi* (*also: ~ down*) s'accroupir; **~ter** *n* squatter *m*

squawk [skwɔ:k] *vi* pousser un *or* des gloussement(s)

squeak [skwi:k] *vi* grincer, crier; (*mouse*) pousser un petit cri

squeal [skwi:l] *vi* pousser un *or* des cri(s) aigu(s) *or* perçant(s); (*brakes*) grincer

squeamish ['skwi:mɪʃ] *adj* facilement dégoûté(e)

squeeze [skwi:z] *n* pression *f*; (*ECON*) restrictions *fpl* de crédit ♦ *vt* presser; (*hand, arm*) serrer; **~ out** *vt* exprimer

squelch [skweltʃ] *vi* faire un bruit de succion

squid [skwɪd] *n* calmar *m*

squiggle ['skwɪgl] *n* gribouillis *m*

squint [skwɪnt] *vi* loucher ♦ *n*: **he has a ~** il louche, il souffre de strabisme

squirm [skwɜ:m] *vi* se tortiller

squirrel ['skwɪrəl] *n* écureuil *m*

squirt [skwɜ:t] *vi* jaillir, gicler

Sr *abbr* = **senior**

St *abbr* = **saint; street**

stab [stæb] *n* (*with knife etc*) coup *m* (de couteau *etc*); (*of pain*) lancée *f*; (*inf: try*): **to have a ~ at (doing) sth** s'essayer à (faire) qch ♦ *vt* poignarder

stable ['steɪbl] *n* écurie *f* ♦ *adj* stable

stack [stæk] *n* tas *m*, pile *f* ♦ *vt* (*also: ~ up*) empiler, entasser

stadium ['steɪdɪəm] *n* (*pl* **stadia** *or* **~s**) stade *m*

staff [stɑ:f] *n* (*workforce*) personnel *m*; (*BRIT: SCOL*) professeurs *mpl* ♦ *vt* pourvoir en personnel

stag [stæg] *n* cerf *m*

stage [steɪdʒ] *n* scène *f*; (*platform*) estrade *f* ♦ *n*; (*profession*): **the ~** le théâtre; (*point*) étape *f*, stade *m* ♦ *vt* (*play*) monter, mettre en scène; (*demonstration*) organiser; **in ~s**

par étapes, par degrés; **~coach** *n* diligence *f*; **~ manager** *n* régisseur *m*

stagger ['stægə*] *vi* chanceler, tituber ♦ *vt* (*person: amaze*) stupéfier; (*hours, holidays*) étaler, échelonner; **~ing** *adj* (*amazing*) stupéfiant(e), renversant(e)

stagnate [stæg'neɪt] *vi* stagner, croupir

stag party *n* enterrement *m* de vie de garçon

staid [steɪd] *adj* posé(e), rassis(e)

stain [steɪn] *n* tache *f*; (*colouring*) colorant *m* ♦ *vt* tacher; (*wood*) teindre; **~ed glass window** *n* vitrail *m*; **~less steel** *n* acier *m* inoxydable, inox *m*; **~ remover** *n* détachant *m*

stair [stɛə*] *n* (*step*) marche *f*; **~s** *npl* (*flight of steps*) escalier *m*; **~case** *n* escalier *m*; **~way** *n* = **staircase**

stake [steɪk] *n* pieu *m*, poteau *m*; (*BETTING*) enjeu *m*; (*COMM: interest*) intérêts *mpl* ♦ *vt* risquer, jouer; **to be at ~** être en jeu; **to ~ one's claim (to)** revendiquer

stale [steɪl] *adj* (*bread*) rassis(e); (*food*) pas frais(fraîche); (*beer*) éventé(e); (*smell*) de renfermé; (*air*) confiné(e)

stalemate ['steɪlmeɪt] *n* (*CHESS*) pat *m*; (*fig*) impasse *f*

stalk [stɔ:k] *n* tige *f* ♦ *vt* traquer ♦ *vi*: **to ~ out/off** sortir/partir d'un air digne

stall [stɔ:l] *n* (*BRIT: in street, market etc*) éventaire *m*, étal *m*; (*in stable*) stalle *f* ♦ *vt* (*AUT*) caler; (*delay*) retarder ♦ *vi* (*AUT*) caler; (*fig*) essayer de gagner du temps; **~s** *npl* (*BRIT: in cinema, theatre*) orchestre *m*

stallion ['stælɪən] *n* étalon *m* (*cheval*)

stalwart ['stɔ:lwət] *adj* dévoué(e); fidèle

stamina ['stæmɪnə] *n* résistance *f*, endurance *f*

stammer ['stæmə*] *n* bégaiement *m* ♦ *vi* bégayer

stamp [stæmp] *n* timbre *m*; (*rubber ~*) tampon *m*; (*mark, also fig*) empreinte *f* ♦ *vi* (*also: ~ one's foot*) taper du pied ♦ *vt* (*letter*) timbrer; (*with rubber ~*) tamponner; **~ album** *n* album *m* de timbres(-poste); **~ collecting** *n* philatélie *f*

stampede [stæm'pi:d] *n* ruée *f*

stance [stæns] *n* position *f*

stand [stænd] (*pt, pp* **stood**) *n* (*position*) position *f*; (*for taxis*) station *f* (de taxis); (*music ~*) pupitre *m* à musique; (*COMM*) étalage *m*, stand *m*; (*SPORT*) tribune *f* ♦ *vi* être *or* se tenir (debout); (*rise*) se lever, se mettre debout; (*be placed*) se trouver; (*remain: offer etc*) rester valable; (*BRIT: in election*) être candidat(e), se présenter ♦ *vt* (*place*) mettre, poser; (*tolerate, withstand*) supporter; (*treat, invite to*) offrir (*treat, invite*), payer; **to make** *or* **take a ~** prendre position; **to ~ at** (*score, value etc*) être de; **to ~ for parliament** (*BRIT*) se présenter aux élections législatives; **~ by** *vi* (*be ready*) se tenir prêt(e) ♦ vt fus (opinion) s'en tenir à; (person) ne pas abandonner, soutenir; ~ **down** vi (withdraw) se retirer; ~ **for** vt fus (signify) représenter, signifier; (tolerate) supporter, tolérer; ~ **in for** vt fus remplacer; ~ **out** vi (be prominent) ressortir; ~ **up** vi (rise) se lever, se mettre debout; ~ **up for** vt fus défendre; ~ **up to** vt fus tenir tête à, résister à

standard ['stændəd] n (level) niveau (voulu); (norm) norme f, étalon m; (criterion) critère m; (flag) étendard m ♦ adj (size etc) ordinaire, normal(e); courant(e); (text) de base; ~**s** npl (morals) morale f, principes mpl; ~ **lamp** n (BRIT) lampadaire m; ~ **of living** n niveau m de vie

stand-by ['stændbaɪ] n remplaçant(e); **to be on** ~ se tenir prêt(e) (à intervenir); être de garde; ~ **ticket** n (AVIAT) billet m stand-by

stand-in ['stændɪn] n remplaçant(e)

standing ['stændɪŋ] adj debout inv; (permanent) permanent(e) ♦ n réputation f, rang m, standing m; **of many years'** ~ qui dure or existe depuis longtemps; ~ **joke** n vieux sujet de plaisanterie; ~ **order** n (BRIT) n (at bank) virement m automatique, prélèvement m bancaire; ~ **room** n places fpl debout

standoffish [-'ɒfɪʃ] adj distant(e), froid(e)

standpoint ['stændpɔɪnt] n point m de vue

standstill ['stændstɪl] n: **at a** ~ paralysé(e); **to come to a** ~ s'immobiliser, s'arrêter

stank [stæŋk] pt of **stink**

staple ['steɪpl] n (for papers) agrafe f ♦ adj (food etc) de base ♦ vt agrafer; ~**r** n agrafeuse f

star [stɑ:*] n étoile f; (celebrity) vedette f ♦ vi: **to** ~ **(in)** être la vedette (de) ♦ vt (CINEMA etc) avoir pour vedette; **the** ~**s** npl l'horoscope m

starboard ['stɑ:bəd] n tribord m

starch [stɑ:tʃ] n amidon m; (in food) fécule f

stardom ['stɑ:dəm] n célébrité f

stare [stɛə*] n regard m fixe ♦ vi: **to** ~ **at** regarder fixement

starfish ['stɑ:fɪʃ] n étoile f de mer

stark [stɑ:k] adj (bleak) désolé(e), morne ♦ adv: ~ **naked** complètement nu(e)

starling ['stɑ:lɪŋ] n étourneau m

starry ['stɑ:rɪ] adj étoilé(e); ~**-eyed** adj (innocent) ingénu(e)

start [stɑ:t] n commencement m, début m; (of race) départ m; (sudden movement) sursaut m; (advantage) avance f, avantage m ♦ vt commencer; (found) créer; (engine) mettre en marche ♦ vi partir, se mettre en route; (jump) sursauter; **to** ~ **doing** or **to do sth** se mettre à faire qch; ~ **off** vi commencer; (leave) partir; ~ **up** vi commencer; (car) démarrer ♦ vt (business) créer; (car) mettre en marche; ~**er** n (AUT)

démarreur m; (SPORT: official) starter m; (BRIT: CULIN) entrée f; ~**ing point** n point m de départ

startle ['stɑ:tl] vt faire sursauter; donner un choc à; **startling** adj (news) surprenant(e)

starvation [stɑ:'veɪʃən] n faim f, famine f; **starve** [stɑ:v] vi mourir de faim; être affamé(e) ♦ vt affamer

state [steɪt] n état m; (POL) État ♦ vt déclarer, affirmer; **the S**~**s** npl (America) les États-Unis mpl; **to be in a** ~ être dans tous ses états; ~**ly** adj majestueux(euse), imposant(e); ~**ment** n déclaration f; ~**sman** (irreg) n homme m d'État

static ['stætɪk] n (RADIO, TV) parasites mpl ♦ adj statique

station ['steɪʃən] n gare f; (police ~) poste m de police ♦ vt placer, poster

stationary ['steɪʃənərɪ] adj à l'arrêt, immobile

stationer ['steɪʃənə*] n papetier(ère); ~**'s (shop)** n papeterie f; ~**y** n papier m à lettres, petit matériel de bureau

stationmaster ['steɪʃənmɑ:stə*] n (RAIL) chef m de gare

station wagon (US) n break m

statistic [stə'tɪstɪk] n statistique f; ~**s** n (science) statistique f

statue ['stætjuː] n statue f

status ['steɪtəs] n position f, situation f; (official) statut m; (prestige) prestige m; ~ **symbol** n signe extérieur de richesse

statute ['stætjuːt] n loi f, statut m; **statutory** adj statutaire, prévu(e) par un article de loi

staunch [stɔːntʃ] adj sûr(e), loyal(e)

stave off [steɪv] vt (attack) parer; (threat) conjurer

stay [steɪ] n (period of time) séjour m ♦ vi rester; (reside) loger; (spend some time) séjourner; **to** ~ **put** ne pas bouger; **to** ~ **with friends** loger chez des amis; **to** ~ **the night** passer la nuit; ~ **behind** vi rester en arrière; ~ **in** vi (at home) rester à la maison; ~ **on** vi rester; ~ **out** vi (of house) ne pas rentrer; ~ **up** vi (at night) ne pas se coucher; ~**ing power** n endurance f

stead [sted] n: **in sb's** ~ à la place de qn; **to stand sb in good** ~ être très utile à qn

steadfast ['stedfɑst] adj ferme, résolu(e)

steadily ['stedɪlɪ] adv (regularly) progressivement; (firmly) fermement; (: walk) d'un pas ferme; (fixedly: look) sans détourner les yeux

steady ['stedɪ] adj stable, solide, ferme; (regular) constant(e), régulier(ère); (person) calme, pondéré(e) ♦ vt stabiliser; (nerves) calmer; **a** ~ **boyfriend** un petit ami

steak [steɪk] n (beef) bifteck m, steak m; (fish, pork) tranche f

steal [stiːl] (pt **stole**, pp **stolen**) vt voler ♦ vi voler; (move secretly) se faufiler, se dé-

placer furtivement
stealth [stelθ] *n*: by ~ furtivement
steam [sti:m] *n* vapeur *f* ♦ *vt* (*CULIN*) cuire à la vapeur ♦ *vi* fumer; ~ **engine** *n* locomotive *f* à vapeur; ~**er** *n* (bateau *m* à) vapeur *m*; ~**ship** *n* = **steamer**; ~**y** *adj* embué(e), humide
steel [sti:l] *n* acier *m* ♦ *adj* d'acier; ~**works** *n* aciérie *f*
steep [sti:p] *adj* raide, escarpé(e); (*price*) excessif(ive)
steeple [sti:pl] *n* clocher *m*
steer [stɪə*] *vt* diriger; (*boat*) gouverner; (*person*) guider, conduire ♦ *vi* tenir le gouvernail; ~**ing** *n* (*AUT*) conduite *f*; ~**ing wheel** *n* volant *m*
stem [stem] *n* (*of plant*) tige *f*; (*of glass*) pied *m* ♦ *vt* contenir, arrêter, juguler; ~ **from** *vt fus* provenir de, découler de
stench [stentʃ] *n* puanteur *f*
stencil [stensl] *n* stencil *m*; (*pattern used*) pochoir *m* ♦ *vt* polycopier
stenographer [ste'nɒgrəfə*] (*US*) *n* sténographe *m/f*
step [step] *n* pas *m*; (*stair*) marche *f*; (*action*) mesure *f*, disposition *f* ♦ *vi*: **to** ~ **forward/back** faire un pas en avant/arrière, avancer/reculer; ~**s** *npl* (*BRIT*) = **stepladder**; **to be in/out of** ~ (**with**) (*fig*) aller dans le sens (de)/être déphasé(e) (par rapport à); ~ **down** *vi* (*fig*) se retirer, se désister; ~ **up** *vt* augmenter; intensifier; ~**brother** *n* demi-frère *m*; ~**daughter** *n* belle-fille *f*; ~**father** *n* beau-père *m*; ~**ladder** (*BRIT*) *n* escabeau *m*; ~**mother** *n* belle-mère *f*; ~**ping stone** *n* pierre *f* de gué; (*fig*) tremplin *m*; ~**sister** *n* demi-sœur *f*; ~**son** *n* beau-fils *m*
stereo [steɪrɪəʊ] *n* (*sound*) stéréo *f*; (*hi-fi*) chaîne *f* stéréo ♦ *adj* (*also*: ~**phonic**) stéréo(phonique)
sterile [sterail] *adj* stérile; **sterilize** [sterɪlaɪz] *vt* stériliser
sterling [stɜ:lɪŋ] *adj* (*silver*) de bon aloi, fin(e) ♦ *n* (*ECON*) livres *fpl* sterling *inv*; **a pound** ~ une livre sterling
stern [stɜ:n] *adj* sévère ♦ *n* (*NAUT*) arrière *m*, poupe *f*
stew [stju:] *n* ragoût *m* ♦ *vt*, *vi* cuire (à la casserole)
steward [stju:əd] *n* (*on ship, plane, train*) steward *m*; ~**ess** *n* hôtesse *f* (de l'air)
stick [stɪk] (*pt, pp* **stuck**) *n* bâton *m*; (*walking* ~) canne *f* ♦ *vt* (*glue*) coller; (*inf: put*) mettre, fourrer; (: *tolerate*) supporter; (*thrust*): **to** ~ **sth into** planter or enfoncer qch dans ♦ *vi* (*become attached*) rester collé(e) or fixé(e); (*be unmoveable: wheels etc*) se bloquer; (*remain*) rester; ~ **out** *vi* dépasser, sortir; ~ **up** *vi* = **stick out**; ~ **up for** *vt fus* défendre; ~**er** *n* auto-collant *m*; ~**ing plaster** *n* sparadrap *m*, pansement

adhésif
stickler [stɪklə*] *n*: **to be a** ~ **for** être pointilleux(euse) sur
stick-up [stɪkʌp] (*inf*) *n* braquage *m*, hold-up *m inv*
sticky [stɪkɪ] *adj* poisseux(euse); (*label*) adhésif(ive); (*situation*) délicat(e)
stiff [stɪf] *adj* raide; rigide; dur(e); (*difficult*) difficile, ardu(e); (*cold*) froid(e), distant(e); (*strong, high*) fort(e), élevé(e) ♦ *adv*: **to be bored/scared/frozen** ~ s'ennuyer à mort/être mort(e) de peur/froid; ~**en** *vi* se raidir; ~ **neck** *n* torticolis *m*
stifle [staɪfl] *vt* étouffer, réprimer
stigma [stɪgmə] *n* stigmate *m*
stile [staɪl] *n* échalier *m*
stiletto [stɪ'letəʊ] (*BRIT*) *n* (*also*: ~ **heel**) talon *m* aiguille
still [stɪl] *adj* immobile ♦ *adv* (*up to this time*) encore, toujours; (*even*) encore; (*nonetheless*) quand même, tout de même; ~**born** *adj* mort-né(e); ~ **life** *n* nature morte
stilt [stɪlt] *n* (*for walking on*) échasse *f*; (*pile*) pilotis *m*
stilted [stɪltɪd] *adj* guindé(e), emprunté(e)
stimulate [stɪmjʊleɪt] *vt* stimuler
stimulus [stɪmjʊləs] (*pl* **stimuli**) *n* stimulant *m*; (*BIOL, PSYCH*) stimulus *m*
sting [stɪŋ] (*pt, pp* **stung**) *n* piqûre *f*; (*organ*) dard *m* ♦ *vt*, *vi* piquer
stingy [stɪndʒɪ] *adj* avare, pingre
stink [stɪŋk] (*pt* **stank**, *pp* **stunk**) *n* puanteur *f* ♦ *vi* puer, empester; ~**ing** (*inf*) *adj* (*fig*) infect(e), vache; **a** ~**ing** ... un(e) foutu(e) ...
stint [stɪnt] *n* part *f* de travail ♦ *vi*: **to** ~ **on** lésiner sur, être chiche sur
stir [stɜ:*] *n* agitation *f*, sensation *f* ♦ *vt* remuer ♦ *vi* remuer, bouger; ~ **up** *vt* (*trouble*) fomenter, provoquer
stirrup [stɪrəp] *n* étrier *m*
stitch [stɪtʃ] *n* (*SEWING*) point *m*; (*KNITTING*) maille *f*; (*MED*) point de suture; (*pain*) point de côté ♦ *vt* coudre, piquer; (*MED*) suturer
stoat [stəʊt] *n* hermine *f* (avec son pelage d'été)
stock [stɒk] *n* réserve *f*, provision *f*; (*COMM*) stock *m*; (*AGR*) cheptel *m*, bétail *m*; (*CULIN*) bouillon *m*; (*descent, origin*) souche *f*; (*FINANCE*) valeurs *fpl*, titres *mpl* ♦ *adj* (*fig: reply etc*) classique ♦ *vt* (*have in* ~) avoir, vendre; ~**s and shares** valeurs (mobilières), titres; **in/out of** ~ en stock *or* en magasin/épuisé(e); **to take** ~ **of** (*fig*) faire le point de; ~ **up** *vi*: **to** ~ **up** (**with**) s'approvisionner (en); ~**broker** [stɒkbrəʊkə*] *n* agent *m* de change; ~ **cube** *n* bouillon-cube *m*; ~ **exchange** *n* Bourse *f*
stocking [stɒkɪŋ] *n* bas *m*

stock: ~ **market** n Bourse f, marché financier; ~ **phrase** n cliché m; ~**pile** n stock m, réserve f ♦ vt stocker, accumuler; ~**taking** (BRIT) n (COMM) inventaire m

stocky ['stɒkɪ] adj trapu(e), râblé(e)

stodgy ['stɒdʒɪ] adj bourratif(ive), lourd(e)

stoke [stəʊk] vt (fire) garnir, entretenir; (boiler) chauffer

stole [stəʊl] pt of **steal** ♦ n étole f

stolen ['stəʊlən] pp of **steal**

stolid ['stɒlɪd] adj impassible, flegmatique

stomach ['stʌmək] n estomac m; (abdomen) ventre m ♦ vt digérer, supporter; ~**ache** n mal m à l'estomac or au ventre

stone [stəʊn] n pierre f; (pebble) caillou m, galet m; (in fruit) noyau m; (MED) calcul m; (BRIT: weight) = 6,348 kg ♦ adj de or en pierre ♦ vt (person) lancer des pierres sur, lapider; ~-**cold** adj complètement froid(e); ~-**deaf** adj sourd(e) comme un pot; ~**work** n maçonnerie f

stood [stʊd] pt, pp of **stand**

stool [stuːl] n tabouret m

stoop [stuːp] vi (also: have a ~) être voûté(e); (: ~ down: bend) se baisser

stop [stɒp] n arrêt m; halte f; (in punctuation: also: full ~) point m ♦ vt arrêter, bloquer; (break off) interrompre; (also: put a ~ to) mettre fin à ♦ vi s'arrêter; (rain, noise etc) cesser, s'arrêter; **to ~ doing sth** cesser or arrêter de faire qch; **to ~ dead** vi s'arrêter net; ~ **off** vi faire une courte halte; ~ **up** vt (hole) boucher; ~**gap** n (person) bouche-trou m; (measure) mesure f intérimaire; ~**over** n halte f, (AVIAT) escale f; ~**page** ['stɒpɪdʒ] n (strike) arrêt de travail; (blockage) obstruction f; ~**per** ['stɒpə*] n bouchon m; ~ **press** n nouvelles fpl de dernière heure; ~**watch** ['stɒpwɒtʃ] n chronomètre m

storage ['stɔːrɪdʒ] n entreposage m; ~ **heater** n radiateur m électrique par accumulation

store [stɔː*] n (stock) provision f, réserve f; (depot) entrepôt m; (BRIT: large shop) grand magasin; (US) magasin m ♦ vt emmagasiner; (information) enregistrer; ~**s** npl (food) provisions fpl; **in ~** en réserve; ~ **up** vt mettre en réserve; accumuler; ~**room** n réserve f, magasin m

storey ['stɔːrɪ] (US **story**) n étage m

stork [stɔːk] n cigogne f

storm [stɔːm] n tempête f; (thunder~) orage m ♦ vi (fig) fulminer ♦ vt prendre d'assaut; ~**y** adj orageux(euse)

story ['stɔːrɪ] n histoire f; récit m; (US) = **storey**; ~**book** n livre m d'histoires or de contes

stout [staʊt] adj solide; (fat) gros(se), corpulent(e) ♦ n bière brune

stove [stəʊv] n (for cooking) fourneau m; (: small) réchaud m; (for heating) poêle m

stow [stəʊ] vt (also: ~ away) ranger; ~**away** n passager(ère) clandestin(e)

straddle ['strædl] vt enjamber, être à cheval sur

straggle ['strægl] vi être (or marcher) en désordre; (houses) être disséminé(e)

straight [streɪt] adj droit(e); (hair) raide; (frank) honnête, franc(franche); (simple) simple ♦ adv (directly) droit; (drink) sec, sans eau; **to put** or **get** ~ (fig) mettre au clair; ~ **away**, ~ **off** (at once) tout de suite; ~**en** vt ajuster; (bed) arranger; ~**en out** vt (fig) débrouiller; ~-**faced** adj impassible; ~**forward** adj simple; (honest) honnête, direct(e)

strain [streɪn] n tension f; pression f; (physical) effort m; (mental) tension (nerveuse); (breed) race f ♦ vt (stretch: resources etc) mettre à rude épreuve, grever; (hurt: back etc) se faire mal à; (vegetables) égoutter; ~**s** npl (MUS) accords mpl, accents mpl; **back** ~ tour m de rein; ~**ed** adj (muscle) froissé(e); (laugh etc) forcé(e), contraint(e); (relations) tendu(e); ~**er** n passoire f

strait [streɪt] n (GEO) détroit m; ~**s** npl: **to be in dire ~s** avoir de sérieux ennuis (d'argent); ~**jacket** n camisole f de force; ~-**laced** adj collet monté inv

strand [strænd] n (of thread) fil m, brin m; (of rope) toron m; (of hair) mèche f; ~**ed** adj en rade, en plan

strange [streɪndʒ] adj (not known) inconnu(e); (odd) étrange, bizarre; ~**ly** adv étrangement, bizarrement; see also **enough**; ~**r** n inconnu(e); (from another area) étranger(ère)

strangle ['stræŋgl] vt étrangler; ~**hold** n (fig) emprise totale, mainmise f

strap [stræp] n lanière f, courroie f, sangle f; (of slip, dress) bretelle f

strapping ['stræpɪŋ] adj costaud(e)

strategic [strə'tiːdʒɪk] adj stratégique

strategy ['strætədʒɪ] n stratégie f

straw [strɔː] n paille f; **that's the last ~!** ça, c'est le comble!

strawberry ['strɔːbərɪ] n fraise f

stray [streɪ] adj (animal) perdu(e), errant(e); (scattered) isolé(e) ♦ vi s'égarer; ~ **bullet** n balle perdue

streak [striːk] n bande f, filet m; (in hair) raie f ♦ vt zébrer, strier ♦ vi: **to ~ past** passer à toute allure

stream [striːm] n ruisseau m; courant m, flot m; (of people) défilé ininterrompu, flot ♦ vt (SCOL) répartir par niveau ♦ vi ruisseler; **to ~ in/out** entrer/sortir à flots; ~**er** ['striːmə*] n serpentin m; (banner) banderole f; ~**lined** ['striːmlaɪnd] adj aérodynamique; (fig) rationalisé(e)

street [striːt] n rue f; ~**car** (US) n tramway m; ~ **lamp** n réverbère m; ~ **plan** n plan m (des rues); ~**wise** (inf) adj futé(e), réaliste

strength [streŋθ] n force f; (of girder, knot etc) solidité f; **~en** vt fortifier; renforcer; consolider

strenuous ['strenjʊəs] adj vigoureux(euse), énergique

stress [stres] n (force, pressure) pression f; (mental strain) tension (nerveuse), stress m; (accent) accent m ♦ vt insister sur, souligner

stretch [stretʃ] n (of sand etc) étendue f ♦ vi s'étirer; (extend): **to ~ to** or **as far as** s'étendre jusqu'à ♦ vt tendre, étirer; (fig) pousser (au maximum); **~ out** vi s'étendre ♦ vt (arm etc) allonger, tendre; (spread) étendre

stretcher ['stretʃə*] n brancard m, civière f

strewn [struːn] adj: **~ with** jonché(e) de

stricken ['strɪkən] adj (person) très éprouvé(e); (city, industry etc) dévasté(e); **~ with** (disease etc) frappé(e) or atteint(e) de

strict [strɪkt] adj strict(e)

stride [straɪd] (pt **strode**, pp **stridden**) n grand pas, enjambée f ♦ vi marcher à grands pas

strife [straɪf] n conflit m, dissensions fpl

strike [straɪk] (pt, pp **struck**) n grève f; (of oil etc) découverte f; (attack) raid m ♦ vt frapper; (oil etc) trouver, découvrir; (deal) conclure ♦ vi faire grève; (attack) attaquer; (clock) sonner; **on** (workers) en grève; **~ a match** frotter une allumette; **~ down** vt terrasser; **~ up** vt (MUS) se mettre à jouer; **to ~ up a friendship with** se lier d'amitié avec; **to ~ up a conversation (with)** engager une conversation (avec); **~r** n gréviste m/f; (SPORT) buteur m; **striking** ['straɪkɪŋ] adj frappant(e), saisissant(e); (attractive) éblouissant(e)

string [strɪŋ] (pt, pp **strung**) n ficelle f; (row: of beads) rang m; (: of onions) chapelet m; (MUS) corde f ♦ vt: **to ~ out** échelonner; **the ~s** npl (MUS) les instruments mpl à cordes; **to ~ together** enchaîner; **to pull ~s** (fig) faire jouer le piston; **~ bean** n haricot vert; **~(ed) instrument** n (MUS) instrument m à cordes

stringent ['strɪndʒənt] adj rigoureux(euse)

strip [strɪp] n bande f ♦ vt (undress) déshabiller; (paint) décaper; (also: **~ down**: machine) démonter ♦ vi se déshabiller; **~ cartoon** n bande dessinée

stripe [straɪp] n raie f, rayure f; (MIL) galon m; **~d** adj rayé(e), à rayures

strip lighting (BRIT) n éclairage m au néon or fluorescent

stripper ['strɪpə*] n strip-teaseur(euse) f

strive [straɪv] (pt **strove**, pp **striven**) vi: **to ~ to do/for sth** s'efforcer de faire/ d'obtenir qch

strode [strəʊd] pt of **stride**

stroke [strəʊk] n coup m; (SWIMMING)

nage f; (MED) attaque f ♦ vt caresser; **at a ~** d'un (seul) coup

stroll [strəʊl] n petite promenade ♦ vi flâner, se promener nonchalamment; **~er** (US) n (pushchair) poussette f

strong [strɒŋ] adj fort(e); vigoureux(euse); (heart, nerves) solide; **they are 50 ~** ils sont au nombre de 50; **~hold** n bastion m; **~ly** adv fortement, avec force; vigoureusement; solidement; **~room** n chambre forte

strove [strəʊv] pt of **strive**

struck [strʌk] pt, pp of **strike**

structural ['strʌktʃərəl] adj structural(e); (CONSTR: defect) de construction; (damage) affectant les parties portantes

structure ['strʌktʃə*] n structure f; (building) construction f

struggle ['strʌgl] n lutte f ♦ vi lutter, se battre

strum [strʌm] vt (guitar) jouer (en sourdine) de

strung [strʌŋ] pt, pp of **string**

strut [strʌt] n étai m, support m ♦ vi se pavaner

stub [stʌb] n (of cigarette) bout m, mégot m; (of cheque etc) talon m ♦ vt: **to ~ one's toe** se cogner le doigt de pied; **~ out** vt écraser

stubble ['stʌbl] n chaume m; (on chin) barbe f de plusieurs jours

stubborn ['stʌbən] adj têtu(e), obstiné(e), opiniâtre

stuck [stʌk] pt, pp of **stick** ♦ adj (jammed) bloqué(e), coincé(e); **~-up** (inf) adj prétentieux(euse)

stud [stʌd] n (on boots etc) clou m; (on collar) bouton m de col; (earring) petite boucle d'oreille; (of horses: also: **~ farm**) écurie f, haras m; (also: **~ horse**) étalon m ♦ vt (fig): **~ded with** parsemé(e) or criblé(e) de

student ['stjuːdənt] n étudiant(e) ♦ adj estudiantin(e); d'étudiant; **~ driver** (US) n (conducteur(trice) débutant(e)

studio ['stjuːdɪəʊ] n studio m, atelier m; (TV etc) studio

studious ['stjuːdɪəs] adj studieux(euse), appliqué(e); (attention) soutenu(e); **~ly** adv (carefully) soigneusement

study ['stʌdɪ] n étude f; (room) bureau m ♦ vt étudier; (examine) examiner ♦ vi étudier, faire ses études

stuff [stʌf] n chose(s) f(pl); affaires fpl, trucs mpl; (substance) substance f ♦ vt rembourrer; (CULIN) farcir; (inf: push) fourrer; **~ing** n bourre f, rembourrage m; (CULIN) farce f; **~y** adj (room) mal ventilé(e) or aéré(e); (ideas) vieux jeu inv

stumble ['stʌmbl] vi trébucher; **to ~ across** or **on** (fig) tomber sur; **stumbling block** n pierre f d'achoppement

stump [stʌmp] n souche f; (of limb) moignon m ♦ vt: **to be ~ed** sécher, ne pas sa-

voir que répondre
stun [stʌn] vt étourdir; abasourdir
stung [stʌŋ] pt, pp of **sting**
stunk [stʌŋk] pp of **stink**
stunning adj (news etc) stupéfiant(e); (girl etc) éblouissant(e)
stunt [stʌnt] n (in film) cascade f, acrobatie f; (publicity ~) truc m publicitaire ♦ vt retarder, arrêter(r) ~**ed** adj rabougri(e); (growth) retardé(e); ~**man** (irreg) n cascadeur m
stupendous [stjuˈpendəs] adj prodigieux(euse), fantastique
stupid [ˈstjuːpɪd] adj stupide, bête; ~**ity** [stjuːˈpɪdɪtɪ] n stupidité f, bêtise f
sturdy [ˈstɜːdɪ] adj robuste, solide
stutter [ˈstʌtə*] vi bégayer
sty [staɪ] n (for pigs) porcherie f
stye [staɪ] n (MED) orgelet m
style [staɪl] n style m; (distinction) allure f, cachet m, style; **stylish** [ˈstaɪlɪʃ] adj élégant(e), chic inv
stylus [ˈstaɪləs] (pl **styli** or ~**es**) n (of record player) pointe f de lecture
suave [swɑːv] adj doucereux(euse), onctueux(euse)
sub... [sʌb] prefix sub..., sous-; ~**conscious** adj subconscient(e); ~**contract** vt sous-traiter
subdue [səbˈdjuː] vt subjuguer, soumettre; ~**d** adj (light) tamisé(e); (person) qui a perdu de son entrain
subject [n ˈsʌbdʒɪkt, vb səbˈdʒekt] n sujet m; (SCOL) matière f ♦ vt: **to ~ to** soumettre à; exposer à; **to be ~ to** (law) être soumis(e) à; (disease) être sujet(te) à; ~**ive** [səbˈdʒektɪv] adj subjectif(ive); ~ **matter** n (content) contenu m
sublet [ˈsʌbˈlet] vt sous-louer
submarine [sʌbməˈriːn] n sous-marin m
submerge [səbˈmɜːdʒ] vt submerger ♦ vi plonger
submission [səbˈmɪʃən] n soumission f; **submissive** [səbˈmɪsɪv] adj soumis(e)
submit [səbˈmɪt] vt soumettre ♦ vi se soumettre
subnormal [ˈsʌbˈnɔːməl] adj au-dessous de la normale
subordinate [səˈbɔːdɪnət] adj subalterne ♦ n subordonné(e)
subpoena [səˈpiːnə] n (LAW) citation f, assignation f
subscribe [səbˈskraɪb] vi cotiser; **to ~ to** (opinion, fund) souscrire à; (newspaper) s'abonner à; être abonné(e) à; ~**r** n (to periodical, telephone) abonné(e); **subscription** [səbˈskrɪpʃən] n (to magazine etc) abonnement m
subsequent [ˈsʌbsɪkwənt] adj ultérieur(e), suivant(e); conséculif(ive); ~**ly** adv par la suite
subside [səbˈsaɪd] vi (flood) baisser; (wind,

feelings) tomber; ~**nce** [sʌbˈsaɪdəns] n affaissement m
subsidiary [səbˈsɪdɪərɪ] adj subsidiaire; accessoire ♦ n (also: ~ company) filiale f
subsidize [ˈsʌbsɪdaɪz] vt subventionner; **subsidy** [ˈsʌbsɪdɪ] n subvention f
substance [ˈsʌbstəns] n substance f
substantial [səbˈstænʃəl] adj substantiel(le); (fig) important(e); ~**ly** adv considérablement; (in essence) en grande partie
substantiate [səbˈstænʃɪeɪt] vt étayer, fournir des preuves à l'appui de
substitute [ˈsʌbstɪtjuːt] n (person) remplaçant(e); (thing) succédané m ♦ vt: **to ~ sth/sb** for substituer qch/qn à, remplacer par qch/qn
subterranean [sʌbtəˈreɪnɪən] adj souterrain(e)
subtitle [ˈsʌbtaɪtl] n (CINEMA) sous-titre m
subtle [ˈsʌtl] adj subtil(e)
subtotal [sʌbˈtəutl] n total partiel
subtract [səbˈtrækt] vt soustraire, retrancher; ~**ion** n soustraction f
suburb [ˈsʌbɜːb] n faubourg m; **the ~s** npl la banlieue; ~**an** [səˈbɜːbən] adj de banlieue, suburbain(e); ~**ia** [səˈbɜːbɪə] n la banlieue
subway [ˈsʌbweɪ] n (US: railway) métro m; (BRIT: underpass) passage souterrain
succeed [səkˈsiːd] vi réussir ♦ vt succéder à; **to ~ in doing** réussir à faire; ~**ing** adj (following) suivant(e)
success [səkˈses] n succès m; réussite f; ~**ful** adj (venture) couronné(e) de succès; **to be ~ful (in doing)** réussir (à faire); ~**fully** adv avec succès
succession [səkˈseʃən] n succession f; **3 days in ~** 3 jours de suite
successive [səkˈsesɪv] adj successif(ive); consécutif(ive)
such [sʌtʃ] adj tel(telle); (of that kind): ~ **a book** un livre de ce genre, un livre pareil, un tel livre; (so much): ~ **courage** un tel courage ♦ adv si; ~ **books** des livres de ce genre, des livres pareils, de tels livres; ~ **a long trip** un si long voyage; ~ **a lot of** tellement or tant de; ~ **as** (like) tel que, comme; **as** ~ en tant que tel, à proprement parler; ~**-and-such** adj tel ou tel
suck [sʌk] vt sucer; (breast, bottle) téter; ~**er** n ventouse f; (inf) poire f
suction [ˈsʌkʃən] n succion f
sudden [ˈsʌdn] adj soudain(e), subit(e); **all of a ~** soudain, tout à coup; ~**ly** adv brusquement, tout à coup, soudain
suds [sʌdz] npl eau savonneuse
sue [suː] vt poursuivre en justice, intenter un procès à
suede [sweɪd] n daim m
suet [suɪt] n graisse f de rognon
suffer [ˈsʌfə*] vt souffrir, subir; (bear) tolérer, supporter ♦ vi souffrir; ~**er** n (MED)

malade *m/f*; **~ing** *n* souffrance(s) *f(pl)*

sufficient [sə'fɪʃənt] *adj* suffisant(e); **~ money** suffisamment d'argent; **~ly** *adv* suffisamment, assez

suffocate ['sʌfəkeɪt] *vi* suffoquer; étouffer

sugar ['ʃugə*] *n* sucre *m* ♦ *vt* sucrer; **~ beet** *n* betterave sucrière; **~ cane** *n* canne *f* à sucre

suggest [sə'dʒest] *vt* suggérer, proposer; *(indicate)* dénoter; **~ion** *n* suggestion *f*

suicide ['suɪsaɪd] *n* suicide *m*; *see also* **commit**

suit [su:t] *n (man's)* costume *m*, complet *m*; *(woman's)* tailleur *m*, ensemble *m*; *(LAW)* poursuite(s) procès *m*; *(CARDS)* couleur *f* ♦ *vt* aller à; convenir à; *(adapt)*: **to ~ sth to** adapter or approprier qch à; **well ~ed** *(couple)* faits l'un pour l'autre, très bien assortis; **~able** *adj* qui convient; approprié(e); **~ably** *adv* comme il se doit *(or se devait etc)*, convenablement

suitcase ['su:tkeɪs] *n* valise *f*

suite [swi:t] *n (of rooms, also MUS)* suite *f*; *(furniture)*: **bedroom/dining room ~** *(ensemble m de)* chambre *f* à coucher/salle *f* à manger

suitor ['su:tə*] *n* soupirant *m*, prétendant *m*

sulfur ['sʌlfə*] *(US)* *n* = **sulphur**

sulk [sʌlk] *vi* bouder; **~y** *adj* boudeur(euse), maussade

sullen ['sʌlən] *adj* renfrogné(e), maussade

sulphur ['sʌlfə*] *(US* **sulfur**) *n* soufre *m*

sultana [sʌl'tɑːnə] *n (CULIN)* raisin (sec) de Smyrne

sultry ['sʌltrɪ] *adj* étouffant(e)

sum [sʌm] *n* somme *f*; *(SCOL etc)* calcul *m*; **~ up** *vt, vi* résumer

summarize ['sʌməraɪz] *vt* résumer

summary ['sʌmərɪ] *n* résumé *m*

summer ['sʌmə*] *n* été *m* ♦ *adj* d'été, estival(e); **~house** *n (in garden)* pavillon *m*; **~time** *n* été *m*; **~ time** *n (by clock)* heure *f* d'été

summit ['sʌmɪt] *n* sommet *m*

summon ['sʌmən] *vt* appeler, convoquer; **~ up** *vt* rassembler, faire appel à; **~s** *n* citation *f*, assignation *f*

sump [sʌmp] *(BRIT)* *n (AUT)* carter *m*

sun [sʌn] *n* soleil *m*; **in the ~** au soleil; **~bathe** *vi* prendre un bain de soleil; **~burn** *n* coup de soleil; **~burned** *adj* = **sunburnt**; **~burnt** *adj (tanned)* bronzé(e)

Sunday ['sʌndeɪ] *n* dimanche *m*; **~ school** *n* ≈ catéchisme *m*

sundial ['sʌndaɪəl] *n* cadran *m* solaire

sundown ['sʌndaʊn] *n* coucher *m* du *(or* de) soleil

sundries ['sʌndrɪz] *npl* articles divers

sundry ['sʌndrɪ] *adj* divers(e), différent(e) ♦ **all and ~** tout le monde, n'importe qui

sunflower ['sʌnflaʊə*] *n* tournesol *m*

sung [sʌŋ] *pp of* **sing**

sunglasses ['sʌnglɑːsɪz] *npl* lunettes *fpl* de soleil

sunk [sʌŋk] *pp of* **sink**

sun: **~light** ['sʌnlaɪt] *n (lumière f du)* soleil *m*; **~lit** *adj* ensoleillé(e); **~ny** *adj* ensoleillé(e); **~rise** *n* lever *m* du *(or* de) soleil; **~ roof** *n (AUT)* toit ouvrant; **~set** *n* coucher *m* du *(or* de) soleil; **~shade** *n (over table)* parasol *m*; **~shine** *n (lumière f du)* soleil *m*; **~stroke** *n* insolation *f*; **~tan** *n* bronzage *m*; **~tan lotion** *n* lotion *f* or lait *m* solaire; **~tan oil** *n* huile *f* solaire

super ['su:pə*] *(inf)* *adj* formidable

superannuation ['su:pərænju'eɪʃən] *n (contribution)* cotisations *fpl* pour la pension

superb [su:'pɜːb] *adj* superbe, magnifique

supercilious [su:pə'sɪlɪəs] *adj* hautain(e), dédaigneux(euse)

superficial [su:pə'fɪʃəl] *adj* superficiel(le)

superimpose [su:pərɪm'pəʊz] *vt* superposer

superintendent [su:pərɪn'tendənt] *n* directeur(trice); *(POLICE)* ≈ commissaire *m*

superior [su'pɪərɪə*] *adj, n* supérieur(e); **~ity** [supɪərɪ'ɒrɪtɪ] *n* supériorité *f*

superlative [su:'pɜːlətɪv] *n (LING)* superlatif *m*

superman ['su:pəmæn] *(irreg)* *n* surhomme *m*

supermarket ['su:pəmɑːkɪt] *n* supermarché *m*

supernatural [su:pə'nætʃərəl] *adj* surnaturel(le)

superpower ['su:pəpaʊə*] *n (POL)* superpuissance *f*

supersede [su:pə'si:d] *vt* remplacer, supplanter

superstitious [su:pə'stɪʃəs] *adj* superstitieux(euse)

supervise ['su:pəvaɪz] *vt* surveiller; diriger; **supervision** [su:pə'vɪʒən] *n* surveillance *f*; contrôle *m*; **supervisor** ['su:pəvaɪzə*] *n* surveillant(e); *(in shop)* chef *m* de rayon

supine ['su:paɪn] *adj* couché(e) or étendu(e) sur le dos

supper ['sʌpə*] *n* dîner *m*; *(late)* souper *m*

supple ['sʌpl] *adj* souple

supplement [*n* 'sʌplɪmənt, *vb* sʌplɪ'ment] *n* supplément *m* ♦ *vt* compléter; **~ary** *adj* supplémentaire; **~ary benefit** *(BRIT)* *n* allocation *f* (supplémentaire) d'aide sociale

supplier [sə'plaɪə*] *n* fournisseur *m*

supply [sə'plaɪ] *vt (provide)* fournir; *(equip)*: **to ~ (with)** approvisionner or ravitailler (en); fournir (en) provision *f*, réserve *f*; *(~ing)* approvisionnement *m*; **supplies** *npl (food)* vivres *mpl*; *(MIL)* subsistances *fpl*; **~ teacher** *(BRIT)* *n* suppléant(e)

support [sə'pɔːt] *n (moral, financial etc)*

soutien *m*, appui *m*; (*TECH*) support *m*, soutien ♦ *vt* soutenir, supporter; (*financially*) subvenir aux besoins de; (*uphold*) être pour, être partisan de, appuyer; **~er** *n* (*POL etc*) partisan(e); (*SPORT*) supporter *m*

suppose [sə'pəʊz] *vt* supposer; imaginer; **to be ~d to do** être censé(e) faire; **~dly** [sə'pəʊzɪdlɪ] *adv* soi-disant; **supposing** [sə'pəʊzɪŋ] *conj* si, à supposer que +*sub*

suppress [sə'pres] *vt* (*revolt*) réprimer; (*information*) supprimer; (*yawn*) étouffer; (*feelings*) refouler

supreme [sʊ'priːm] *adj* suprême

surcharge ['sɜːtʃɑːdʒ] *n* surcharge *f*

sure [ʃʊə*] *adj* sûr(e); (*definite, convinced*) sûr, certain(e); **~!** (*of course*) bien sûr!; **~ enough** effectivement; **to make ~ of sth** s'assurer de *or* vérifier qch; **to make ~ that** s'assurer *or* vérifier que; **~ly** *adv* sûrement; certainement

surety ['ʃʊərətɪ] *n* caution *f*

surf [sɜːf] *n* (*waves*) ressac *m*

surface ['sɜːfɪs] *n* surface *f* ♦ *vt* (*road*) poser un revêtement sur ♦ *vi* remonter à la surface; faire surface; **~ mail** *n* courrier *m* par voie de terre (*or* maritime)

surfboard ['sɜːfbɔːd] *n* planche *f* de surf

surfeit ['sɜːfɪt] *n*: **a ~ of** un excès de; une indigestion de

surfing ['sɜːfɪŋ] *n* surf *m*

surge [sɜːdʒ] *n* vague *f*, montée *f* ♦ *vi* déferler

surgeon ['sɜːdʒən] *n* chirurgien *m*

surgery ['sɜːdʒərɪ] *n* chirurgie *f*; (*BRIT: room*) cabinet *m* (de consultation); (: *also*: **~ hours**) heures *fpl* de consultation

surgical ['sɜːdʒɪkəl] *adj* chirurgical(e); **~ spirit** (*BRIT*) *n* alcool *m* à 90°

surly ['sɜːlɪ] *adj* revêche, maussade

surname ['sɜːneɪm] *n* nom *m* de famille

surplus ['sɜːpləs] *n* surplus *m*, excédent *m* ♦ *adj* en surplus, de trop; (*COMM*) excédentaire

surprise [sə'praɪz] *n* surprise *f*; (*astonishment*) étonnement *m* ♦ *vt* surprendre; (*astonish*) étonner; **surprising** [sə'praɪzɪŋ] *adj* surprenant(e), étonnant(e); **surprisingly** *adv* (*easy, helpful*) étonnamment

surrender [sə'rendə*] *n* reddition *f*, capitulation *f* ♦ *vi* se rendre, capituler

surreptitious [sʌrəp'tɪʃəs] *adj* subreptice, furtif(ive)

surrogate ['sʌrəgɪt] *n* substitut *m*; **~ mother** *n* mère porteuse *or* de substitution

surround [sə'raʊnd] *vt* entourer; (*MIL etc*) encercler; **~ing** *adj* environnant(e); **~ings** *npl* environs *mpl*, alentours *mpl*

surveillance [sɜː'veɪləns] *n* surveillance *f*

survey [*n* 'sɜːveɪ, *vb* sɜː'veɪ] *n* enquête *f*, étude *f*; (*in housebuying etc*) inspection *f*, (rapport *m* d')expertise *f*; (*of land*) levé *m* ♦ *vt* enquêter sur; inspecter; (*look at*) embras-

ser du regard; **~or** [sə'veɪə*] *n* (*of house*) expert *m*; (*of land*) (arpenteur *m*) géomètre *m*

survival [sə'vaɪvəl] *n* survie *f*; (*relic*) vestige *m*

survive [sə'vaɪv] *vi* survivre; (*custom etc*) subsister ♦ *vt* survivre à; **survivor** [sə'vaɪvə*] *n* survivant(e); (*fig*) battant(e)

susceptible [sə'septəbl] *adj*: **~ (to)** sensible (à); (*disease*) prédisposé(e) (à)

suspect [*n, adj* 'sʌspekt, *vb* səs'pekt] *adj, n* suspect(e) ♦ *vt* soupçonner, suspecter

suspend [səs'pend] *vt* suspendre; **~ed sentence** *n* condamnation *f* avec sursis; **~er belt** *n* porte-jarretelles *m inv*; **~ers** *npl* (*BRIT*) jarretelles *fpl*; (*US*) bretelles *fpl*

suspense [səs'pens] *n* attente *f*, incertitude *f*; (*in film etc*) suspense *m*

suspension [səs'penʃən] *n* suspension *f*; (*of driving licence*) retrait *m* provisoire; **~ bridge** *n* pont suspendu

suspicion [səs'pɪʃən] *n* soupçon(s) *m(pl)*

suspicious [səs'pɪʃəs] *adj* (*suspecting*) soupçonneux(euse), méfiant(e); (*causing suspicion*) suspect(e)

sustain [səs'teɪn] *vt* soutenir; (*food etc*) nourrir, donner des forces à; (*suffer*) subir; recevoir; **~able** *adj* (*development, growth etc*) viable; **~ed** *adj* (*effort*) soutenu(e), prolongé(e)

sustenance ['sʌstɪnəns] *n* nourriture *f*; (*money*) moyens *mpl* de subsistance

swab [swɒb] *n* (*MED*) tampon *m*

swagger ['swægə*] *vi* plastronner

swallow ['swɒləʊ] *n* (*bird*) hirondelle *f* ♦ *vt* avaler; **~ up** *vt* engloutir

swam [swæm] *pt of* **swim**

swamp [swɒmp] *n* marais *m*, marécage *m* ♦ *vt* submerger

swan [swɒn] *n* cygne *m*

swap [swɒp] *vt*: **to ~ (for)** échanger (contre), troquer (contre)

swarm [swɔːm] *n* essaim *m* ♦ *vi* fourmiller, grouiller

swarthy ['swɔːðɪ] *adj* basané(e), bistré(e)

swastika ['swɒstɪkə] *n* croix gammée

swat [swɒt] *vt* écraser

sway [sweɪ] *vi* se balancer, osciller ♦ *vt* (*influence*) influencer

swear [swɛə*] (*pt* **swore**, *pp* **sworn**) *vt, vi* jurer; **~word** *n* juron *m*, gros mot

sweat [swet] *n* sueur *f*, transpiration *f* ♦ *vi* suer

sweater ['swetə*] *n* tricot *m*, pull *m*

sweaty ['swetɪ] *adj* en sueur, moite *or* mouillé(e) de sueur

Swede [swiːd] *n* Suédois(e)

swede [swiːd] (*BRIT*) *n* rutabaga *m*

Sweden ['swiːdn] *n* Suède *f*; **Swedish** ['swiːdɪʃ] *adj* suédois(e) ♦ *n* (*LING*) suédois *m*

sweep [swiːp] (*pt, pp* **swept**) *n* coup *m* de

balai; (*also: chimney ~*) ramoneur *m* ♦ *vt* balayer; (*subj: current*) emporter ♦ *vi* (*hand, arm*) faire un mouvement; (*wind*) souffler; ~ **away** *vt* balayer; entraîner; emporter; ~ **past** *vi* passer majestueusement *or* rapidement; ~ **up** *vi* balayer; ~**ing** *adj* (*gesture*) large; circulaire; a ~**ing statement** une généralisation hâtive

sweet [swi:t] *n* (*candy*) bonbon *m*; (*BRIT: pudding*) dessert *m* ♦ *adj* doux(douce); (*not savoury*) sucré(e); (*fig: kind*) gentil(le); (*baby*) mignon(ne); ~**corn** *n* maïs *m*; ~**en** *vt* adoucir; (*with sugar*) sucrer; ~**heart** *n* amoureux(euse); ~**ness** *n* goût sucré; douceur *f*; ~**pea** *n* pois *m* de senteur

swell [swel] (*pt* ~**ed**, *pp* **swollen** *or* ~**ed**) *n* (*of sea*) houle *f* ♦ *adj* (*US: inf: excellent*) chouette ♦ *vi* grossir, augmenter; (*sound*) s'enfler; (*MED*) enfler; ~**ing** *n* (*MED*) enflure *f*; (*lump*) grosseur *f*

sweltering ['sweltərɪŋ] *adj* étouffant(e), oppressant(e)

swept [swept] *pt, pp of* **sweep**

swerve [swɜːv] *vi* faire une embardée *or* un écart; dévier

swift [swɪft] *n* (*bird*) martinet *m* ♦ *adj* rapide, prompt(e)

swig [swɪg] (*inf*) *n* (*drink*) lampée *f*

swill [swɪl] *vt* (*also: ~ out, ~ down*) laver à grande eau

swim [swɪm] (*pt* **swam**, *pp* **swum**) *n*: **to go for a** ~ aller nager *or* se baigner ♦ *vi* nager; (*SPORT*) faire de la natation; (*head, room*) tourner ♦ *vt* traverser (à la nage); (*a length*) faire (à la nage); ~**mer** *n* nageur(euse); ~**ming** *n* natation *f*; ~**ming cap** *n* bonnet *m* de bain; ~**ming costume** (*BRIT*) *n* maillot *m* (de bain); ~**ming pool** *n* piscine *f*; ~**ming trunks** *npl* caleçon *m or* slip *m* de bain; ~**suit** *n* maillot *m* (de bain)

swindle ['swɪndl] *n* escroquerie *f*

swine [swaɪn] (*inf!*) *n inv* salaud *m* (*!*)

swing [swɪŋ] (*pt, pp* **swung**) *n* balançoire *f*; (*movement*) balancement *m*, oscillations *fpl*; (*MUS: also rhythm*) rythme *m*; (*change: in opinion etc*) revirement *m* ♦ *vt* balancer, faire osciller; (*also: ~ round*) tourner, faire virer ♦ *vi* se balancer, osciller; (*also: ~ round*) virer, tourner; **to be in full** ~ battre son plein; ~ **bridge** *n* pont tournant; ~ **door** (*US* ~**ing door**) *n* porte battante

swingeing ['swɪndʒɪŋ] (*BRIT*) *adj* écrasant(e); (*cuts etc*) considérable

swipe [swaɪp] (*inf*) *vt* (*steal*) piquer

swirl [swɜːl] *vi* tourbillonner, tournoyer

swish [swɪʃ] *vi* (*tail*) remuer; (*clothes*) froufrouter

Swiss [swɪs] *adj* suisse ♦ *n inv* Suisse *m/f*

switch [swɪtʃ] *n* (*for light, radio etc*) bouton *m*; (*change*) changement *m*, revirement *m* ♦ *vt* changer; ~ **off** *vt* éteindre; (*engine*) arrêter; ~ **on** *vt* allumer; (*engine, machine*)

mettre en marche; ~**board** *n* (*TEL*) standard *m*

Switzerland ['swɪtsələnd] *n* Suisse *f*

swivel ['swɪvl] *vi* (*also: ~ round*) pivoter, tourner

swollen ['swəʊlən] *pp of* **swell**

swoon [swuːn] *vi* se pâmer

swoop [swuːp] *n* (*by police*) descente *f* ♦ *vi* (*also: ~ down*) descendre en piqué, piquer

swop [swɒp] *vt* = **swap**

sword [sɔːd] *n* épée *f*; ~**fish** *n* espadon *m*

swore [swɔː*] *pt of* **swear**

sworn [swɔːn] *pp of* **swear** ♦ *adj* (*statement, evidence*) donné(e) sous serment

swot [swɒt] *vi* bûcher, potasser

swum [swʌm] *pp of* **swim**

swung [swʌŋ] *pt, pp of* **swing**

syllable ['sɪləbl] *n* syllabe *f*

syllabus ['sɪləbəs] *n* programme *m*

symbol ['sɪmbəl] *n* symbole *m*

symmetry ['sɪmɪtrɪ] *n* symétrie *f*

sympathetic [sɪmpə'θetɪk] *adj* compatissant(e); bienveillant(e), compréhensif(ive); (*likeable*) sympathique; ~ **towards** bien disposé(e) envers

sympathize ['sɪmpəθaɪz] *vi*: **to ~ with sb** plaindre qn; (*in grief*) s'associer à la douleur de qn; **to ~ with sth** comprendre qch; ~**r** *n* (*POL*) sympathisant(e)

sympathy ['sɪmpəθɪ] *n* (*pity*) compassion *f*; **sympathies** *npl* (*support*) soutien *m*; **left-wing etc sympathies** penchants *mpl* à gauche *etc*; **in ~ with** (*strike*) en *or* par solidarité avec; **with our deepest ~** en vous priant d'accepter nos sincères condoléances

symphony ['sɪmfənɪ] *n* symphonie *f*

symptom ['sɪmptəm] *n* symptôme *m*; indice *m*

syndicate ['sɪndɪkət] *n* syndicat *m*, coopérative *f*

synonym ['sɪnənɪm] *n* synonyme *m*

synopsis [sɪ'nɒpsɪs, *pl* -siːz] (*pl* **synopses**) *n* résumé *m*

syntax ['sɪntæks] *n* syntaxe *f*

synthetic [sɪn'θetɪk] *adj* synthétique

syphon ['saɪfən] *n, vb* = **siphon**

Syria ['sɪrɪə] *n* Syrie *f*

syringe [sɪ'rɪndʒ] *n* seringue *f*

syrup ['sɪrəp] *n* sirop *m*; (*also: golden ~*) mélasse raffinée

system ['sɪstəm] *n* système *m*; (*ANAT*) organisme *m*; ~**atic** [sɪstə'mætɪk] *adj* systématique; méthodique; ~ **disk** *n* (*COMPUT*) disque *m* système; ~**s analyst** *n* analyste fonctionnel(le)

T t

ta [tɑː] (BRIT: inf) excl merci!

tab [tæb] n (label) étiquette f; (on drinks can etc) languette f; **to keep ~s on** (fig) surveiller

tabby ['tæbɪ] n (also: ~ cat) chat(te) tigré(e)

table ['teɪbl] n table f ♦ vt (BRIT: motion etc) présenter; **to lay** or **set the ~** mettre le couvert or la table; **~cloth** ['-klɒθ] n nappe f; **~ d'hôte** ['tɑːbl'dəʊt] adj (meal) à prix fixe; **~ lamp** n lampe f de table; **~mat** ['teɪblmæt] n (for plate) napperon m, set m; (for hot dish) dessous-de-plat m inv; **~ of contents** n table f des matières; **~spoon** ['teɪblspuːn] n cuiller f de service; (also: ~spoonful: as measurement) cuillerée f à soupe

table football n baby-foot m.

tablet ['tæblət] n (MED) comprimé m; (of stone) plaque f

table tennis n ping-pong m ®, tennis m de table

table wine n vin m de table

tabloid ['tæblɔɪd] n quotidien m populaire

tabulate ['tæbjʊleɪt] vt (data, figures) présenter sous forme de table(s)

tack [tæk] n (nail) petit clou ♦ vt clouer; (fig) direction f; (BRIT: stitch) faufiler ♦ vi tirer un or des bord(s)

tackle ['tækl] n matériel m, équipement m; (for lifting) appareil m de levage; (RUGBY) plaquage m ♦ vt (difficulty, animal, burglar etc) s'attaquer à; (person: challenge) s'expliquer avec; (RUGBY) plaquer

tacky ['tækɪ] adj collant(e); (pej: of poor quality) miteux(euse)

tact [tækt] n tact m; **~ful** adj plein(e) de tact

tactical ['tæktɪkəl] adj tactique

tactics ['tæktɪks] npl tactique f

tactless ['tæktləs] adj qui manque de tact

tadpole ['tædpəʊl] n têtard m

taffy ['tæfɪ] n (US) (bonbon m au) caramel m

tag [tæg] n étiquette f; **~ along** vi suivre

tail [teɪl] n queue f; (of shirt) pan m ♦ vt (follow) suivre, filer; **~s** npl habit m; **~ away, ~ off** vi (in size, quality etc) baisser peu à peu; **~back** (BRIT) n (AUT) bouchon m; **~ end** n bout m, fin f; **~gate** n (AUT) hayon m arrière

tailor ['teɪlə*] n tailleur m; **~ing** n (cut) coupe f; **~-made** adj fait(e) sur mesure; (fig) conçu(e) spécialement

tailwind ['teɪlwɪnd] n vent m arrière inv

tainted ['teɪntɪd] adj (food) gâté(e); (water, air) infecté(e); (fig) souillé(e)

take [teɪk] (pt took, pp taken) vt prendre; (gain: prize) remporter; (require: effort, courage) demander; (tolerate) accepter, supporter; (hold: passengers etc) contenir; (accompany) emmener, accompagner; (bring, carry) apporter, emporter; (exam) passer, se présenter à; **to ~ sth from** (drawer etc) prendre qch dans; (person) prendre qch à; **I ~ it that ...** je suppose que ...; **~ after** vt fus ressembler à; **~ apart** vt démonter; **~ away** vt enlever; (carry off) emporter; **~ back** vt (return) rendre, rapporter; (one's words) retirer; **~ down** vt (building) démolir; (letter etc) prendre, écrire; **~ in** vt (deceive) tromper, rouler; (understand) comprendre, saisir; (include) comprendre, inclure; (lodger) prendre; **~ off** vi (AVIAT) décoller ♦ vt (go away) s'en aller; (remove) enlever; **~ on** vt (work) accepter, se charger de; (employee) prendre, embaucher; (opponent) accepter de se battre contre; **~ out** vt (invite) emmener, sortir; (remove) enlever; **to ~ sth out of sth** (drawer, pocket etc) prendre qch dans qch; **~ over** vt (business) reprendre ♦ vi: **to ~ over from sb** prendre la relève de qn; **~ to** vt fus (person) se prendre d'amitié pour; (thing) prendre goût à; **~ up** vt (activity) se mettre à; (dress) raccourcir; (occupy: time, space) prendre, occuper; **to ~ sb up on an offer** accepter la proposition de qn; **~away** (BRIT) adj (food) à emporter ♦ n (shop, restaurant) qui vend des plats à emporter; **~off** n (AVIAT) décollage m; **~over** n (COMM) rachat m; **takings** ['teɪkɪŋz] npl (COMM) recette f

talc [tælk] n (also: ~um powder) talc m

tale [teɪl] n (story) conte m, histoire f; (account) récit m; **to tell ~s** (fig) rapporter

talent ['tælənt] n talent m, don m; **~ed** adj doué(e), plein(e) de talent

talk [tɔːk] n (a speech) causerie f, exposé m; (conversation) discussion f, entretien m; (gossip) racontars mpl ♦ vi parler; **~s** npl (POL etc) entretiens mpl; **to ~ about** parler de; **to ~ sb into/out of doing** persuader qn de faire/ne pas faire; **to ~ shop** parler métier or affaires; **to ~ over** vt discuter (de); **~ative** ['tɔːkətɪv] adj bavard(e); **~ show** n causerie (télévisée or radiodiffusée)

tall [tɔːl] adj (person) grand(e); (building, tree) haut(e); **to be 6 feet ~** ≈ mesurer 1 mètre 80; **~ story** n histoire f invraisemblable

tally ['tælɪ] n compte m ♦ vi: **to ~ (with)** correspondre (à)

talon ['tælən] n griffe f; (of eagle) serre f

tame [teɪm] *adj* apprivoisé(e); *(fig: story, style)* insipide

tamper ['tæmpə*] *vi*: **to ~ with** toucher à

tampon ['tæmpɔn] *n* tampon *m* (hygiénique *or* périodique)

tan [tæn] *n (also: sun~)* bronzage *m* ♦ *vt, vi* bronzer ♦ *adj (colour)* brun roux *inv*

tang [tæŋ] *n* odeur *(or* saveur) piquante

tangent ['tændʒənt] *n (MATH)* tangente *f*; **to go off at a ~** *(fig)* changer de sujet

tangerine [tændʒə'riːn] *n* mandarine *f*

tangle ['tæŋgl] *n* enchevêtrement *m*; **to get in(to) a ~** s'embrouiller

tank [tæŋk] *n (water ~)* réservoir *m*; *(for fish)* aquarium *m*; *(MIL)* char *m* d'assaut, tank *m*

tanker ['tæŋkə*] *n (ship)* pétrolier *m*, tanker *m*; *(truck)* camion-citerne *m*

tantalizing ['tæntəlaɪzɪŋ] *adj (smell)* extrêmement appétissant(e); *(offer)* terriblement tentant(e)

tantamount ['tæntəmaʊnt] *adj*: **~ to** qui équivaut à

tantrum ['tæntrəm] *n* accès *m* de colère

tap [tæp] *n (on sink etc)* robinet *m*; *(gentle blow)* petite tape ♦ *vt* frapper *or* taper légèrement; *(resources)* exploiter, utiliser; *(telephone)* mettre sur écoute; **on ~** *(fig: resources)* disponible; **~-dancing** ['tæpdɑːnsɪŋ] *n* claquettes *fpl*

tape [teɪp] *n* ruban *m*; *(also: magnetic ~)* bande *f* (magnétique); *(cassette)* cassette *f*; *(sticky)* scotch *m* ♦ *vt (record)* enregistrer; *(stick with ~)* coller avec du scotch; **~ deck** *n* platine *f* d'enregistrement; **~ measure** *n* mètre *m* à ruban

taper ['teɪpə*] *n* cierge *m* ♦ *vi* s'effiler

tape recorder *n* magnétophone *m*

tapestry ['tæpɪstri] *n* tapisserie *f*

tar [tɑː*] *n* goudron *m*

target ['tɑːgɪt] *n* cible *f*; *(fig)* objectif *m*

tariff ['tærɪf] *n (COMM)* tarif *m*; *(taxes)* tarif douanier

tarmac ['tɑːmæk] *n (BRIT: on road)* macadam *m*; *(AVIAT)* piste *f*

tarnish ['tɑːnɪʃ] *vt* ternir

tarpaulin [tɑː'pɔːlɪn] *n* bâche (goudronnée)

tarragon ['tærəgən] *n* estragon *m*

tart [tɑːt] *n (CULIN)* tarte *f*; *(BRIT: inf: prostitute)* putain *f* ♦ *adj (flavour)* âpre, aigrelet(te); **~ up** *(BRIT: inf)* vt *(object)* retaper; **to ~ o.s. up** se faire beau(belle), s'attifer *(pej)*

tartan ['tɑːtən] *n* tartan *m* ♦ *adj* écossais(e)

tartar ['tɑːtə*] *n (on teeth)* tartre *m*; **~(e) sauce** *n* sauce *f* tartare

task [tɑːsk] *n* tâche *f*; **to take sb to ~** prendre qn à partie; **~ force** *n (MIL, POLICE)* détachement spécial

tassel ['tæsəl] *n* gland *m*; pompon *m*

taste [teɪst] *n* goût *m*; *(fig: glimpse, idea)* idée *f*, aperçu *m* ♦ *vt* goûter ♦ *vi*: **to ~ of** *or* **like** *(fish etc)* avoir le *or* un goût de; **you can ~ the garlic (in it)** on sent bien l'ail; **can I have a ~ of this wine?** puis-je goûter un peu de ce vin?; **in good/bad ~** de bon/mauvais goût; **~ful** *adj* de bon goût; **~less** *adj (food)* fade; *(remark)* de mauvais goût; **tasty** ['teɪsti] *adj* savoureux(euse), délicieux(euse)

tatters ['tætəz] *npl*: **in ~** en lambeaux

tattoo [tə'tuː] *n* tatouage *m*; *(spectacle)* parade *f* militaire ♦ *vt* tatouer

tatty *(BRIT: inf)* *adj (clothes)* frippé(e); *(shop, area)* délabré(e)

taught [tɔːt] *pt, pp* of **teach**

taunt [tɔːnt] *n* raillerie *f* ♦ *vt* railler

Taurus ['tɔːrəs] *n* le Taureau

taut [tɔːt] *adj* tendu(e)

tax [tæks] *n (on goods etc)* taxe *f*; *(on income)* impôts *mpl*, contributions *fpl* ♦ *vt* taxer; imposer; *(fig: patience etc)* mettre à l'épreuve; **~able** *adj (income)* imposable; **~ation** [tæk'seɪʃən] *n* taxation *f*; impôts *mpl*, contributions *fpl*; **~ avoidance** *n* dégrèvement fiscal; **~ disc** *n (AUT)* vignette *f* (automobile); **~ evasion** *n* fraude fiscale; **~-free** *adj* exempt(e) d'impôts

taxi ['tæksi] *n* taxi *m* ♦ *vi (AVIAT)* rouler (lentement) au sol; **~ driver** *n* chauffeur *m* de taxi; **~ rank** *(BRIT) n* station *f* de taxis; **~ stand** *n* = taxi rank

tax: **~ payer** *n* contribuable *m/f*; **~ relief** *n* dégrèvement fiscal; **~ return** *n* déclaration *f* d'impôts *or* de revenus

TB *n abbr* = **tuberculosis**

tea [tiː] *n* thé *m*; *(BRIT: snack: for children)* goûter *m*; **high ~** *(BRIT)* collation combinant goûter et dîner; **~ bag** *n* sachet *m* de thé; **~ break** *(BRIT) n* pause-thé *f*

teach [tiːtʃ] *(pt, pp* **taught**) *vt*: **to ~ sb sth, ~ sth to sb** apprendre qch à qn; *(in school etc)* enseigner qch à qn enseigner; **~er** *n (in secondary school)* professeur *m*; *(in primary school)* instituteur(trice); **~ing** *n* enseignement *m*

tea cosy *n* cloche *f* à thé

teacup ['tiːkʌp] *n* tasse *f* à thé

teak [tiːk] *n* teck *m*

team [tiːm] *n* équipe *f*; *(of animals)* attelage *m*; **~work** *n* travail *m* d'équipe

teapot ['tiːpɔt] *n* théière *f*

tear[1] [tɛə*] *(pt* **tore**, *pp* **torn**) *n* déchirure *f* ♦ *vt* déchirer ♦ *vi* se déchirer; **~ along** *vi (rush)* aller à toute vitesse; **~ up** *vt (sheet of paper etc)* déchirer, mettre en morceaux *or* pièces

tear[2] [tɪə*] *n* larme *f*; **in ~s** en larmes; **~ful** *adj* larmoyant(e); **~ gas** *n* gaz *m* lacrymogène

tearoom ['tiːrʊm] *n* salon *m* de thé

tease [tiːz] *vt* taquiner; *(unkindly)* tourmenter

tea set *n* service *m* à thé

teaspoon ['tiːspuːn] *n* petite cuiller; (*also:*
~*ful: as measurement*) ≈ cuillerée *f* à café
teat [tiːt] *n* tétine *f*
teatime ['tiːtaɪm] *n* l'heure *f* du thé
tea towel (*BRIT*) *n* torchon *m* (à vaisselle)
technical ['tɛknɪkəl] *adj* technique; ~**ity**
[tɛknɪ'kælɪtɪ] *n* (*detail*) détail *m* technique;
(*point of law*) vice *m* de forme; ~**ly** *adv*
techniquement; (*strictly speaking*) en théorie
technician [tɛk'nɪʃən] *n* technicien(ne)
technique [tɛk'niːk] *n* technique *f*
technological [tɛknə'lɒdʒɪkəl] *adj* technologique; **technology** [tɛk'nɒlədʒɪ] *n* technologie *f*
teddy (bear) ['tɛdɪ-] *n* ours *m* en peluche
tedious ['tiːdɪəs] *adj* fastidieux(euse)
tee [tiː] *n* (*GOLF*) tee *m*
teem [tiːm] *vi*: **to ~ (with)** grouiller (de); **it
is ~ing (with rain)** il pleut à torrents
teenage ['tiːneɪdʒ] *adj* (*fashions etc*) pour
jeunes, pour adolescents; (*children*) adoles-
cent(e); ~**r** *n* adolescent(e)
teens [tiːnz] *npl*: **to be in one's ~** être
adolescent(e)
tee-shirt ['tiːʃəːt] *n* = T-shirt
teeter ['tiːtə*] *vi* chanceler, vaciller
teeth [tiːθ] *npl of* **tooth**
teethe [tiːð] *vi* percer ses dents
teething ring ['tiːðɪŋ-] *n* anneau pour bébé
qui perce ses dents
teething troubles *npl* (*fig*) difficultés initiales
teetotal ['tiː'təʊtl] *adj* (*person*) qui ne boit
jamais d'alcool
telegram ['tɛlɪgræm] *n* télégramme *m*
telegraph ['tɛlɪgrɑːf] *n* télégraphe *m*; ~
pole *n* poteau *m* télégraphique
telephone ['tɛlɪfəʊn] *n* téléphone *m* ♦ *vt*
(*person*) téléphoner à; (*message*) téléphon-
ner; **on the ~** au téléphone; **to be on the
~** (*BRIT: have a ~*) avoir le téléphone; ~
booth (*BRIT*) *n* = **telephone box**; ~ **box**
n cabine *f* téléphonique; ~ **call** *n* coup *m*
de téléphone, appel *m* téléphonique; ~
directory *n* annuaire *m* (du téléphone); ~
number *n* numéro *m* de téléphone; **tele-
phonist** [tə'lɛfənɪst] (*BRIT*) *n* téléphoniste
m/f
telescope ['tɛlɪskəʊp] *n* télescope *m*
television ['tɛlɪvɪʒən] *n* télévision *f*; **on ~** à
la télévision; ~ **set** *n* (poste *f* de) télévision *m*
telex ['tɛlɛks] *n* télex *m*
tell [tɛl] (*pt, pp* **told**) *vt* dire; (*relate: story*)
raconter; (*distinguish*): **to ~ sth from** distinguer qch de ♦ *vi* (*talk*): **to ~ (of)** parler
(de); (*have effect*) se faire sentir, se voir; **to
~ sb to do** dire à qn de faire; ~ **off** *vt* réprimander, gronder; ~**er** *n* (*in bank*) cais-
sier(ère); ~**ing** *adj* (*remark, detail*) révéla-
teur(trice); ~**tale** *adj* (*sign*) éloquent(e), ré-
vélateur(trice)

telly ['tɛlɪ] (*BRIT: inf*) *n abbr* (= *television*)
télé *f*
temp [tɛmp] *n abbr* (= *temporary*) (secrétaire *f*) intérimaire *f*
temper ['tɛmpə*] *n* (*nature*) caractère *m*;
(*mood*) humeur *f*; (*fit of anger*) colère *f* ♦ *vt*
(*moderate*) tempérer, adoucir; **to be in a ~**
être en colère; **to lose one's ~** se mettre
en colère
temperament ['tɛmprəmənt] *n* (*nature*)
tempérament *m*; ~**al** [tɛmpərə'mɛntl] *adj*
capricieux(euse)
temperate ['tɛmpərət] *adj* (*climate, country*)
tempéré(e)
temperature ['tɛmprɪtʃə*] *n* température *f*;
to have *or* run a ~ avoir de la fièvre
temple ['tɛmpl] *n* (*building*) temple *m*;
(*ANAT*) tempe *f*
temporary ['tɛmpərərɪ] *adj* temporaire,
provisoire; (*job, worker*) temporaire
tempt [tɛmpt] *vt* tenter; **to ~ sb into
doing** persuader qn de faire; ~**ation**
[tɛmp'teɪʃən] *n* tentation *f*
ten [tɛn] *num* dix
tenacity [tə'næsɪtɪ] *n* ténacité *f*
tenancy ['tɛnənsɪ] *n* location *f*; état *m* de
locataire
tenant ['tɛnənt] *n* locataire *m/f*
tend [tɛnd] *vt* s'occuper de ♦ *vi*: **to ~ to do**
avoir tendance à faire
tendency ['tɛndənsɪ] *n* tendance *f*
tender ['tɛndə*] *adj* tendre; (*delicate*) déli-
cat(e); (*sore*) sensible ♦ *n* (*COMM: offer*)
soumission *f* ♦ *vt* offrir
tenement ['tɛnəmənt] *n* immeuble *m*
tenet ['tɛnət] *n* principe *m*
tennis ['tɛnɪs] *n* tennis *m*; ~ **ball** *n* balle *f*
de tennis; ~ **court** *n* (court *m* de) tennis;
~ **player** *n* joueur(euse) de tennis; ~
racket *n* raquette *f* de tennis; ~ **shoes** *npl*
(chaussures *fpl* de) tennis *mpl*
tenor ['tɛnə*] *n* (*MUS*) ténor *m*
tenpin bowling (*BRIT*) *n* bowling *m* (à
dix quilles)
tense [tɛns] *adj* tendu(e) ♦ *n* (*LING*) temps
m
tension ['tɛnʃən] *n* tension *f*
tent [tɛnt] *n* tente *f*
tentative ['tɛntətɪv] *adj* timide, hésitant(e);
(*conclusion*) provisoire
tenterhooks ['tɛntəhʊks] *npl*: **on ~** sur des
charbons ardents
tenth [tɛnθ] *num* dixième
tent peg *n* piquet *m* de tente
tent pole *n* montant *m* de tente
tenuous ['tɛnjʊəs] *adj* ténu(e)
tenure ['tɛnjʊə*] *n* (*of property*) bail *m*; (*of
job*) période *f* de jouissance
tepid ['tɛpɪd] *adj* tiède
term [tɜːm] *n* terme *m*; (*SCOL*) trimestre *m*
♦ *vt* appeler; ~**s** *npl* (*conditions*) conditions
fpl; (*COMM*) tarif *m*; **in the short/long ~** à

court/long terme; **to come to ~s with**
(*problem*) faire face à
terminal ['tɜːmɪnl] *adj* (*disease*) dans sa
phase terminale; (*patient*) incurable ♦ *n*
(*ELEC*) borne *f*; (*for oil, ore etc, COMPUT*)
terminal *m*; (*also:* air ~) aérogare *f*; (*BRIT:
also: coach ~*) gare routière
terminate ['tɜːmɪneɪt] *vt* mettre fin à;
(*pregnancy*) interrompre
terminus ['tɜːmɪnəs] (*pl* **termini**) *n* terminus *m inv*

terrace ['terəs] *n* terrasse *f*; (*BRIT: row of
houses*) rangée *f* de maisons (*attenantes*);
the ~s *npl* (*: SPORT*) les gradins *mpl*; **~d**
adj (*garden*) en terrasses
terracotta ['terə'kɔtə] *n* terre cuite
terrain [te'reɪn] *n* terrain *m* (*sol*)
terrible ['terɪbl] *adj* terrible, atroce;
(*weather, conditions*) affreux(euse), épouvantable; **terribly** ['terɪblɪ] *adv* terriblement; (*very badly*) affreusement mal
terrier ['terɪə*] *n* terrier *m* (*chien*)
terrific [tə'rɪfɪk] *adj* fantastique, incroyable,
terrible; (*wonderful*) formidable, sensation-
nel(le)
terrify ['terɪfaɪ] *vt* terrifier
territory ['terɪtərɪ] *n* territoire *m*
terror ['terə*] *n* terreur *f*; **~ism** *n* terrorisme *m*; **~ist** *n* terroriste *m/f*
terse [tɜːs] *adj* (*style*) concis(e); (*reply*)
sec(sèche)
Terylene ['terɪliːn] ⓇR) *n* tergal *m* ⓇR)
test [test] *n* (*trial, check*) essai *m*; (*of courage etc*) épreuve *f*; (*MED*) examen *m*;
(*CHEM*) analyse *f*; (*SCOL*) interrogation *f*;
(*also: driving ~*) (examen du) permis *m* de
conduire ♦ *vt* essayer; mettre à l'épreuve;
examiner; analyser; faire subir une interrogation à
testament ['testəmənt] *n* testament *m*; **the
Old/New T~** l'Ancien/le Nouveau Testament
testicle ['testɪkl] *n* testicule *m*
testify ['testɪfaɪ] *vi* (*LAW*) témoigner, déposer; **to ~ to sth** attester qch
testimony ['testɪmənɪ] *n* témoignage *m*;
(*clear proof*): **to be (a) ~ to** être la preuve
de
test: **~ match** *n* (*CRICKET, RUGBY*) match
international; **~ pilot** *n* teste *m* d'essai; **~
tube** *n* éprouvette *f*
tetanus ['tetənəs] *n* tétanos *m*
tether ['teðə*] *vt* attacher ♦ *n*: **at the end
of one's ~** à bout (de patience)
text [tekst] *n* texte *m*; **~book** *n* manuel *m*
textile *n* textile *m*
texture ['tekstʃə*] *n* texture *f*; (*of skin, paper etc*) grain *m*
Thames [temz] *n*: **the ~** la Tamise
than [ðæn, ðən] *conj* que; (*with numerals*):
more ~ 10/once plus de 10/d'une fois; **I
have more/less ~ you** j'en ai plus/moins

que toi; **she has more apples ~ pears** elle
a plus de pommes que de poires
thank [θæŋk] *vt* remercier, dire merci à; **~s**
npl (*gratitude*) remerciements *mpl* ♦ *excl*
merci!; **~ you (very much)** merci (beaucoup); **~s to** grâce à; **~ God!** Dieu merci!;
~ful: **~ful (for)** reconnaissant(e) (de);
~less *adj* ingrat(e); **T~sgiving (Day)** *n*
jour *m* d'action de grâce (*fête américaine*)

— *KEYWORD*

that [ðæt] *adj* (*demonstrative: pl those*) ce,
cet *+vowel or h mute*, *f* cette; **~ man/
woman/book** cet homme/cette femme/ce
livre; (*not this*) cet homme-là/cette femme-
là/ce livre-là; **~ one** celui-là(celle-là)

♦ *pron* **1** (*demonstrative: pl those*) ce; (*not
this one*) cela, ça; **who's ~?** qui est-ce?;
what's ~? qu'est-ce que c'est?; **is ~ you?**
c'est toi?; **I prefer this to ~** je préfère ceci
à cela or ça; **~'s what he said** c'est or voilà ce qu'il a dit; **~ is (to say)** c'est-à-dire, à
savoir

2 (*relative: subject*) qui; (*: object*) que; (*: indirect*) lequel(laquelle), lesquels(lesquelles)
pl; **the book ~ I read** le livre que j'ai lu;
the books ~ are in the library les livres
qui sont dans la bibliothèque; **all ~ I have**
tout ce que j'ai; **the box ~ I put it in** la
boîte dans laquelle je l'ai mis; **the people
~ I spoke to** les gens auxquels or à qui
j'ai parlé

3 (*relative: of time*) où; **the day ~ he came**
le jour où il est venu

♦ *conj* que; **he thought ~ I was ill** il pen-
sait que j'étais malade

♦ *adv* (*demonstrative*): **I can't work ~
much** je ne peux pas travailler autant que
cela; **I didn't know it was ~ bad** je ne savais pas que c'était si *or* aussi mauvais; **it's
about ~ high** c'est à peu près de cette
hauteur

---

thatched [θætʃt] *adj* (*roof*) de chaume; **~
cottage** chaumière *f*
thaw [θɔː] *n* dégel *m* ♦ *vi* (*ice*) fondre;
(*food*) dégeler ♦ *vt* (*: also: ~ out*) (faire) dégeler

— *KEYWORD*

the [ðiː, ðə] *def art* **1** (*gen*) le, la *f*, l' *+vo-
wel or h mute*, les *pl*; **~ boy/girl/ink** le
garçon/la fille/l'encre; **~ children** les enfants; **~ history of the world** l'histoire du
monde; **give it to ~ postman** donne-le au
facteur; **to play ~ piano/flute** jouer du
piano/de la flûte; **~ rich and ~ poor** les riches et les pauvres

2 (*in titles*): **Elizabeth ~ First** Elisabeth
première; **Peter ~ Great** Pierre le Grand

3 (*in comparisons*): **~ more he works, ~
more he earns** plus il travaille, plus il ga-

gne de l'argent

theatre ['θɪətə*] n théâtre m; (also: lecture ~) amphi(théâtre) m; (MED: also: operating ~) salle f d'opération; **~-goer** n habitué(e) du théâtre; **theatrical** [θɪ'ætrɪkəl] adj théâtral(e)
theft [θeft] n vol m (larcin)
their [δεə*] adj leur; (pl) leurs; see also **my**; **~s** pron le(la) leur; (pl) les leurs; see also **mine¹**
them [δεm, δəm] pron (direct) les; (indirect) leur; (stressed, after prep) eux(elles); see also **me**
theme [θi:m] n thème m; ~ **park** n parc m (d'attraction) à thème; ~ **song** n chanson principale
themselves [δəm'selvz] pl pron (reflexive) se; (emphatic, after prep) eux-mêmes(elles-mêmes); see also **oneself**
then [δεn] adv (at that time) alors, à ce moment-là; (next) puis, ensuite; (and also) et puis ♦ conj (therefore) alors, dans ce cas ♦ adj: **the ~ president** le président d'alors or de l'époque; **by ~** (past) à ce moment-là; (future) d'ici là; **from ~ on** dès lors
theology [θɪ'ɒlədʒɪ] n théologie f
theoretical [θɪə'retɪkəl] adj théorique
theorize ['θɪəraɪz] vi faire des théories
theory ['θɪərɪ] n théorie f
therapy ['θerəpɪ] n thérapie f

────── *KEYWORD*

there [δεə*] adv **1**: ~ **is**, ~ **are** il y a; ~ **are 3 of them** (people, things) il y en a 3; ~ **has been an accident** il y a eu un accident
2 (referring to place) là, là-bas; **it's ~** c'est là(-bas); **in/on/up/down** ~ là-dedans/là-dessus/là-haut/en bas; **he went ~ on Friday** il y est allé vendredi; **I want that book ~** je veux ce livre-là; ~ **he is!** le voilà!
3: ~, ~ (esp to child) allons, allons!

thereabouts [δεərə'baʊts] adv (place) par là, près de là; (amount) environ, à peu près
thereafter [δεər'ɑːftə*] adv par la suite
thereby [δεə'baɪ] adv ainsi
therefore ['δεəfɔː*] adv donc, par conséquent
there's ['δεəz] = **there is**; **there has**
thermal ['θɜːml] adj (springs) thermal(e); (underwear) en thermoiactyl ®; (COMPUT: paper) thermosensible; (: printer) thermique
thermometer [θə'mɒmɪtə*] n thermomètre m
Thermos ['θɜːməs] ® n (also: ~ **flask**) thermos m or f inv ®
thermostat ['θɜːməʊstæt] n thermostat m
thesaurus [θɪ'sɔːrəs] n dictionnaire m des synonymes

these [δiːz] pl adj ces; (not "those"): ~ **books** ces livres-ci ♦ pl pron ceux-ci(celles-ci)
thesis ['θiːsɪs] (pl **theses**) n thèse f
they [δeɪ] pl pron ils(elles); (stressed) eux(elles); ~ **say that ...** (it is said that) on dit que ...; **~'d** = ~ **had**; ~ **would**; **~'ll** = **they shall**; ~ **will**; **~'re** = ~ **are**; **~'ve** = **they have**
thick [θɪk] adj épais(se); (stupid) bête, borné(e) ♦ n: **in the ~ of** au beau milieu de, en plein cœur de; **it's 20 cm ~** il/elle a 20 cm d'épaisseur; **~en** vi s'épaissir ♦ vt (sauce etc) épaissir; **~ness** n épaisseur f; **~set** adj trapu(e), costaud(e); **~skinned** adj (fig) peu sensible
thief [θiːf] (pl **thieves**) n voleur(euse)
thigh [θaɪ] n cuisse f
thimble ['θɪmbl] n dé m (à coudre)
thin [θɪn] adj mince; (skinny) maigre; (soup, sauce) peu épais(se), clair(e); (hair, crowd) clairsemé(e) ♦ vt: **to ~ (down)** (sauce, paint) délayer
thing [θɪŋ] n chose f; (object) objet m; (contraption) truc m; (mania): **to have a ~ about** être obsédé(e) par; **~s** npl (belongings) affaires fpl; **poor ~!** le(la) pauvre!; **the best ~ would be to** le mieux serait de; **how are ~s?** comment ça va?
think [θɪŋk] (pt, pp **thought**) vi penser, réfléchir; (believe) penser ♦ vt (imagine) imaginer; **what did you ~ of them?** qu'avez-vous pensé d'eux?; **to ~ about sth/sb** penser à qch/qn; **I'll ~ about it** je vais y réfléchir; **to ~ of doing** avoir l'idée de faire; **I ~ so/not** je crois or pense que oui/non; **to ~ well of** avoir une haute opinion de; ~ **over** vt bien réfléchir à; ~ **up** vt inventer, trouver; ~ **tank** n groupe m de réflexion
thinly adv (cut) en fines tranches; (spread) en une couche mince
third [θɜːd] num troisième ♦ n (fraction) tiers m; (AUT) troisième (vitesse) f; (BRIT: SCOL: degree) ≈ licence f sans mention; **~ly** adv troisièmement; ~ **party insurance** (BRIT) n assurance f au tiers; **~-rate** adj de qualité médiocre; **the T~ World** n le tiers monde
thirst [θɜːst] n soif f; **~y** adj (person) qui a soif, assoiffé(e); (work) qui donne soif; **to be ~y** avoir soif
thirteen ['θɜː'tiːn] num treize
thirty ['θɜːtɪ] num trente

────── *KEYWORD*

this [δɪs] adj (demonstrative: pl **these**) ce, cet +vowel or h mute, cette f; ~ **man/woman/book** cet homme/cette femme/ce livre; (not that) cet homme-ci/cette femme-ci/ce livre-ci; ~ **one** celui-ci(celle-ci)
♦ pron (demonstrative: pl **these**) ce; (not that

one) celui-ci(celle-ci), ceci; **who's ~?** qui est-ce?; **what's ~?** qu'est-ce que c'est?; **I prefer ~ to that** je préfère ceci à cela; **~ is what he said** voici ce qu'il a dit; **~ is Mr Brown** (*in introductions*) je vous présente Mr Brown; (*in photo*) c'est Mr Brown; (*on telephone*) ici Mr Brown
♦ *adv* (*demonstrative*): **it was about ~ big** c'était à peu près de cette grandeur *or* grand comme ça; **I didn't know it was ~ bad** je ne savais pas que c'était si *or* aussi mauvais

thistle ['θɪsl] *n* chardon *m*
thorn [θɔːn] *n* épine *f*
thorough ['θʌrə] *adj* (*search*) minutieux(euse); (*knowledge, research*) approfondi(e); (*work, person*) consciencieux(euse); (*cleaning*) à fond; **~bred** *n* (*horse*) pursang *m inv*; **~fare** *n* route *f*; **"no ~fare"** "passage interdit"; **~ly** *adv* minutieusement; en profondeur; à fond; (*very*) tout à fait
those [ðəuz] *pl adj* ces; (*not "these"*): **~ books** ces livres-là ♦ *pl pron* ceux-là(celles-là)
though [ðəu] *conj* bien que +*sub*, quoique +*sub* ♦ *adv* pourtant
thought [θɔːt] *pt, pp of* **think** ♦ *n* pensée *f*; (*idea*) idée *f*; (*opinion*) avis *m*; **~ful** *adj* (*deep in thought*) pensif(ive); (*serious*) réfléchi(e); (*considerate*) prévenant(e); **~less** *adj* étourdi(e); qui manque de considération
thousand ['θauzənd] *num* mille; **two ~** deux mille; **~s of** des milliers de; **~th** *num* millième
thrash [θræʃ] *vt* rouer de coups; donner une correction à; (*defeat*) battre à plate couture; **~ about, ~ around** *vi* se débattre; **~ out** *vt* débattre de
thread [θred] *n* fil *m*; (*of screw*) pas *m*, filetage *m* ♦ *vt* (*needle*) enfiler; **~bare** *adj* râpé(e), élimé(e)
threat [θret] *n* menace *f*; **~en** *vi* menacer ♦ *vt*: **to ~en sb with sth/to do** menacer qn de qch/de faire
three [θriː] *num* trois; **~-dimensional** *adj* à trois dimensions; **~-piece suit** *n* complet *m* (avec gilet); **~-piece suite** *n* salon *m* comprenant un canapé et deux fauteuils assortis; **~-ply** *adj* (*wool*) trois fils *inv*
thresh [θreʃ] *vt* (*AGR*) battre
threshold ['θreʃhəuld] *n* seuil *m*
threw [θruː] *pt of* **throw**
thrift [θrɪft] *n* économie *f*; **~y** *adj* économe
thrill [θrɪl] *n* (*excitement*) émotion *f*, sensation forte; (*shudder*) frisson *m* ♦ *vt* (*audience*) électriser; **to be ~ed** (*with gift etc*) être ravi(e); **~er** *n* film *m* (*or roman m or pièce f*) à suspense; **~ing** *adj* saisissant(e),

palpitant(e)
thrive [θraɪv] (*pt ~d*, **throve**, *pp ~d*) *vi* pousser, se développer; (*business*) prospérer; **he ~s on it** cela lui réussit; **thriving** ['θraɪvɪŋ] *adj* (*business, community*) prospère
throat [θrəut] *n* gorge *f*; **to have a sore ~** avoir mal à la gorge
throb [θrɒb] *vi* (*heart*) palpiter; (*engine*) vibrer; **my head is ~bing** j'ai des élancements dans la tête
throes [θrəuz] *npl*: **in the ~ of** au beau milieu de
throne [θrəun] *n* trône *m*
throng [θrɒŋ] *n* foule *f* ♦ *vt* se presser dans
throttle ['θrɒtl] *n* (*AUT*) accélérateur *m* ♦ *vt* étrangler
through [θruː] *prep* à travers; (*time*) pendant, durant; (*by means of*) par, par l'intermédiaire de; (*owing to*) à cause de ♦ *adj* (*ticket, train, passage*) direct(e) ♦ *adv* à travers; **to put sb ~ to sb** (*BRIT: TEL*) passer qn à qn; **to be ~** avoir la communication; (*esp US: have finished*) avoir fini; **to be ~ with sb** (*relationship*) avoir rompu avec qn; **"no ~ road"** (*BRIT*) "impasse"; **~out** [θruː'aut] *prep* (*place*) partout dans; (*time*) durant tout(e) le(la) ♦ *adv* partout
throve [θrəuv] *pt of* **thrive**
throw [θrəu] (*pt* **threw**, *pp* **thrown**) *n* jet *m*; (*SPORT*) lancer *m* ♦ *vt* lancer, jeter; (*SPORT*) lancer; (*rider*) désarçonner; (*fig*) décontenancer; **to ~ a party** donner une réception; **~ away** *vt* jeter; **~ off** *vt* se débarrasser de; **~ out** *vt* jeter; (*reject*) rejeter; (*person*) mettre à la porte; **~ up** *vi* vomir; **~away** *adj* à jeter; (*remark*) fait(e) en passant; **~-in** *n* (*SPORT*) remise *f* en jeu
thru [θruː] (*US*) = **through**
thrush [θrʌʃ] *n* (*bird*) grive *f*
thrust [θrʌst] (*pt, pp* **thrust**) *n* (*TECH*) poussée *f* ♦ *vt* pousser brusquement; (*push in*) enfoncer
thud [θʌd] *n* bruit sourd
thug [θʌg] *n* voyou *m*
thumb [θʌm] *n* (*ANAT*) pouce *m*, arrêter une voiture; **to ~ a lift** faire de l'auto-stop; **~ through** *vt* (*book*) feuilleter; **~tack** *n* (*US*) punaise *f* (*clou*)
thump [θʌmp] *n* grand coup; (*sound*) bruit sourd ♦ *vt* cogner sur ♦ *vi* cogner, battre fort
thunder ['θʌndə*] *n* tonnerre *m* ♦ *vi* tonner; (*train etc*): **to ~ past** passer dans un grondement *or* un bruit de tonnerre; **~bolt** *n* foudre *f*; **~clap** *n* coup *m* de tonnerre; **~storm** *n* orage *m*; **~y** *adj* orageux(euse)
Thursday ['θɜːzdeɪ] *n* jeudi *m*
thus [ðʌs] *adv* ainsi
thwart [θwɔːt] *vt* contrecarrer
thyme [taɪm] *n* thym *m*
tiara [tɪ'ɑːrə] *n* (*woman's*) diadème *m*

tick [tɪk] n (sound: of clock) tic-tac m; (mark) coche f; (ZOOL) tique f; (BRIT: inf): **in a ~** dans une seconde ♦ vi faire tic-tac ♦ vt (item on list) cocher; **~ off** vt (item on list) cocher; (person) réprimander, attraper; **~ over** vi (engine) tourner au ralenti; (fig) aller or marcher doucement

ticket ['tɪkɪt] n billet m; (for bus, tube) ticket m; (in shop: on goods) étiquette f; (for library) carte f; (parking ~) papillon m, p.-v. m; **~ collector** n contrôleur(euse); **~ office** n guichet m, bureau m de vente des billets

tickle ['tɪkl] vt, vi chatouiller; **ticklish** adj (person) chatouilleux(euse); (problem) épineux(euse)

tidal ['taɪdl] adj (force) de la marée, (estuary) à marée; **~ wave** n raz-de-marée m inv

tidbit ['tɪdbɪt] (US) n = **titbit**

tiddlywinks ['tɪdlɪwɪŋks] n jeu m de puce

tide [taɪd] n marée f; (fig: of events) cours m ♦ vt: **to ~ sb over** dépanner qn; **high/low ~** marée haute/basse

tidy ['taɪdɪ] adj (room) bien rangé(e); (dress, work) net(te), soigné(e); (person) ordonné(e), qui a de l'ordre ♦ vt (also: **~ up**) ranger

tie [taɪ] n (string etc) cordon m; (BRIT: also: neck~) cravate f; (fig: link) lien m; (SPORT: draw) égalité f de points; match nul ♦ vt (parcel) attacher; (ribbon, shoelaces) nouer ♦ vi (SPORT) faire match nul; finir à égalité de points; **to ~ sth in a bow** faire un nœud à or avec qch; **to ~ a knot in sth** faire un nœud à qch; **~ down** vt (fig): **~ sb down (to)** contraindre qn (à accepter); **to be ~d down** (by relationship) se fixer; **~ up** vt (parcel) ficeler; (dog, boat) attacher; (prisoner) ligoter; (arrangements) conclure; **to be ~d up** (busy) être pris(e) or occupé(e)

tier [tɪə*] n gradin m; (of cake) étage m

tiger ['taɪgə*] n tigre m

tight [taɪt] adj (rope) tendu(e), raide; (clothes) étroit(e), très juste; (budget, programme, bend) serré(e); (control) strict(e), sévère; (inf: drunk) ivre, rond(e) ♦ adv (squeeze) très fort; (shut) hermétiquement, bien; **~en** vt (rope) tendre; (screw) resserrer; (control) renforcer ♦ vi se tendre, se resserrer; **~fisted** adj avare; **~ly** adv (grasp) bien, très fort; **~rope** n corde f raide; **~s** (BRIT) npl collant m

tile [taɪl] n (on roof) tuile f; (on wall or floor) carreau m; **~d** adj en tuiles; carrelé(e)

till [tɪl] n caisse f (enregistreuse) ♦ vt (land) cultiver ♦ prep, conj = **until**

tiller ['tɪlə*] n (NAUT) barre f (du gouvernail)

tilt [tɪlt] vt pencher, incliner ♦ vi pencher, être incliné(e)

timber ['tɪmbə*] n (material) bois m (de construction); (trees) arbres mpl

time [taɪm] n temps m; (epoch: often pl) époque f, temps m; (by clock) heure f; (moment) moment m; (occasion, also MATH) fois f; (MUS) mesure f ♦ vt (race) chronométrer; (programme) minuter; (visit) fixer; (remark etc) choisir le moment de; **a long ~** un long moment, longtemps; **for the ~ being** pour le moment; **4 at a ~** 4 à la fois; **from ~ to ~** de temps en temps; **at ~s** parfois; **in ~** (soon enough) à temps; (after some ~) avec le temps, à la longue; (MUS) en mesure; **in a week's ~** dans une semaine; **in no ~** en un rien de temps; **any ~** n'importe quand; **on ~** à l'heure; **5 ~s 5** 5 fois 5; **what ~ is it?** quelle heure est-il?; **to have a good ~** bien s'amuser; **~ bomb** n bombe f à retardement; **~ lag** (BRIT) n décalage m; (in travel) décalage horaire; **~less** adj éternel(le); **~ly** adj opportun(e); **~ off** n temps m libre; **~r** n (TECH) minuteur m; (in kitchen) compte-minutes m inv; **~scale** n délais mpl; **~-share** n maison f (or appartement m) en multipropriété; **~ switch** (BRIT) n minuteur m; (for lighting) minuterie f; **~table** n (RAIL) (indicateur m) horaire m; (SCOL) emploi m du temps; **~ zone** n fuseau m horaire

timid ['tɪmɪd] adj timide; (easily scared) peureux(euse)

timing ['taɪmɪŋ] n minutage m; chronométrage m; **the ~ of his resignation** le moment choisi pour sa démission

timpani ['tɪmpənɪ] npl timbales fpl

tin [tɪn] n étain m; (also: **~ plate**) fer-blanc m; (BRIT: can) boîte f (de conserve); (for storage) boîte f; **~foil** n papier m d'étain or aluminium

tinge [tɪndʒ] n nuance f ♦ vt: **~d with** teinté(e) de

tingle ['tɪŋgl] vi picoter; (person) avoir des picotements

tinker ['tɪŋkə*] n (gipsy) romanichel m; **~ with** vt fus bricoler, rafistoler

tinkle ['tɪŋkl] vi tinter

tinned [tɪnd] (BRIT) adj (food) en boîte, en conserve

tin opener [-'əʊpnə*] (BRIT) n ouvre-boîte(s) m

tinsel ['tɪnsəl] n guirlandes fpl de Noël (argentées)

tint [tɪnt] n teinte f; (for hair) shampooing colorant m; **~ed** adj (hair) teint(e); (spectacles, glass) teinté(e)

tiny ['taɪnɪ] adj minuscule

tip [tɪp] n (end) bout m; (gratuity) pourboire m; (BRIT: for rubbish) décharge f; (advice) tuyau m ♦ vt (waiter) donner un pourboire à; (tilt) incliner; (overturn: also: **~ over**) r[...] verser; (empty: **~ out**) déverser; **~** [...]

(*hint*) tuyau *m*; ~**ped** (BRIT) *adj* (*cigarette*) (à bout) filtre *inv*

tipsy ['tɪpsɪ] (*inf*) *adj* un peu ivre, éméché(e)

tiptoe ['tɪptəʊ] *n*: **on** ~ sur la pointe des pieds

tiptop ['tɪp'tɒp] *adj*: **in** ~ **condition** en excellent état

tire ['taɪə*] *n* (US) = **tyre** ♦ *vt* fatiguer ♦ *vi* se fatiguer; ~**d** *adj* fatigué(e); **to be** ~**d of** en avoir assez de, être las(lasse) de; ~**less** *adj* (*person*) infatigable; (*efforts*) inlassable; ~**some** *adj* ennuyeux(euse); **tiring** ['taɪərɪŋ] *adj* fatigant(e)

tissue ['tɪʃuː] *n* tissu *m*; (*paper handkerchief*) mouchoir *m* en papier, kleenex *m* (®); ~ **paper** *n* papier *m* de soie

tit [tɪt] *n* (*bird*) mésange *f*; **to give** ~ **for tat** rendre la pareille

titbit ['tɪtbɪt] *n* (*food*) friandise *f*; (*news*) potin *m*

title ['taɪtl] *n* titre *m*; ~ **deed** *n* (LAW) titre (constitutif) de propriété; ~ **role** *n* rôle principal

titter ['tɪtə*] *vi* rire (bêtement)

TM *abbr* = **trademark**

─────────── KEYWORD ───────────

to [tuː, tə] *prep* **1** (*direction*) à; ~ **go France/Portugal/London/school** aller en France/au Portugal/à Londres/à l'école; ~ **go** ~ **Claude's/the doctor's** aller chez Claude/le docteur; **the road** ~ **Edinburgh** la route d'Édimbourg

2 (*as far as*) (jusqu')à; ~ **count** ~ **10** compter jusqu'à 10; **from 40** ~ **50 people** de 40 à 50 personnes

3 (*with expressions of time*): **a quarter** ~ **5** 5 heures moins le quart; **it's twenty** ~ **3** il est 3 heures moins vingt

4 (*for, of*) de; **the key** ~ **the front door** la clé de la porte d'entrée; **a letter** ~ **his wife** une lettre (adressée) à sa femme

5 (*expressing indirect object*) à; ~ **give sth** ~ **sb** donner qch à qn; ~ **talk** ~ **sb** parler à qn

6 (*in relation to*) à; **3 goals** ~ **2** 3 (buts) à 2; **30 miles** ~ **the gallon** ≈ 9,4 litres aux cent (km)

7 (*purpose, result*): ~ **come** ~ **sb's aid** venir au secours de qn, porter secours à qn; ~ **sentence sb** ~ **death** condamner qn à mort; ~ **my surprise** à ma grande surprise

♦ *with vb* **1** (*simple infinitive*): ~ **go/eat** aller/manger

2 (*following another vb*): ~ **want/try/start** ~ **do** vouloir/essayer de/commencer à faire

3 (*with vb omitted*): **I don't want** ~ je ne ~ux pas

...rpose, result) pour; **I did it** ~ **help** ...'ai fait pour vous aider

...ent to relative clause): **I have**

things ~ **do** j'ai des choses à faire; **the main thing is** ~ **try** l'important est d'essayer

6 (*after adjective etc*): **ready** ~ **go** prêt(e) à partir; **too old/young** ~ ... trop vieux/jeune pour ...

♦ *adv*: **push/pull the door** ~ tirez/poussez la porte

toad [təʊd] *n* crapaud *m*

toadstool *n* champignon (vénéneux)

toast [təʊst] *n* (CULIN) pain grillé, toast *m*; (*drink, speech*) toast ♦ *vt* (CULIN) faire griller; (*drink to*) porter un toast à; ~**er** *n* grille-pain *m inv*

tobacco [tə'bækəʊ] *n* tabac *m*; ~**nist** [tə'bækənɪst] *n* marchand(e) de tabac; ~**nist's (shop)** *n* (bureau *m* de) tabac *m*

toboggan [tə'bɒgən] *n* toboggan *m*; (*child's*) luge *f*

today [tə'deɪ] *adv* (*also fig*) aujourd'hui ♦ *n* aujourd'hui *m*

toddler ['tɒdlə*] *n* enfant *m/f* qui commence à marcher, bambin *m*

to-do [tə'duː] *n* (*fuss*) histoire *f*, affaire *f*

toe [təʊ] *n* doigt *m* de pied, orteil *m*; (*of shoe*) bout *m* ♦ *vt*: **to** ~ **the line** (*fig*) obéir, se conformer; ~**nail** *n* ongle *m* du pied

toffee ['tɒfɪ] *n* caramel *m*; ~ **apple** (BRIT) *n* pomme caramélisée

toga ['təʊgə] *n* toge *f*

together [tə'geðə*] *adv* ensemble; (*at same time*) en même temps; ~ **with** avec

toil [tɔɪl] *n* dur travail, labeur *m* ♦ *vi* peiner

toilet ['tɔɪlət] *n* (BRIT: *lavatory*) toilettes *fpl* ♦ *cpd* (*accessories etc*) de toilette; ~ **paper** *n* papier *m* hygiénique; ~**ries** ['tɔɪlətrɪz] *npl* articles *mpl* de toilette; ~ **roll** *n* rouleau *m* de papier hygiénique; ~ **water** *n* eau *f* de toilette

token ['təʊkən] *n* (*sign*) marque *f*, témoignage *m*; (*metal disc*) jeton *m* ♦ *adj* (*strike, payment etc*) symbolique; **book/record** ~ (BRIT) chèque-livre/-disque *m*; **gift** ~ *n* bon-cadeau *m*

told [təʊld] *pt, pp of* **tell**

tolerable ['tɒlərəbl] *adj* (*bearable*) tolérable; (*fairly good*) passable

tolerant ['tɒlərnt] *adj*: ~ **(of)** tolérant(e) (à l'égard de)

tolerate ['tɒləreɪt] *vt* supporter, tolérer

toll [təʊl] *n* (*tax, charge*) péage *m* ♦ *vi* (*bell*) sonner; **the accident** ~ **on the roads** le nombre des victimes de la route

tomato [tə'mɑːtəʊ] (*pl* ~**es**) *n* tomate *f*

tomb [tuːm] *n* tombe *f*

tomboy ['tɒmbɔɪ] *n* garçon manqué

tombstone ['tuːmstəʊn] *n* pierre tombale

tomcat ['tɒmkæt] *n* matou *m*

tomorrow [tə'mɒrəʊ] *adv* (*also fig*) demain ♦ *n* demain *m*; **the day after** ~ après-demain; ~ **morning** demain matin

ton [tʌn] *n* tonne *f* (*BRIT* = 1016kg; *US* = 907kg); (*metric*) tonne (= 1000 kg); ~**s of** (*inf*) des tas de

tone [təʊn] *n* ton *m* ♦ *vi* (*also*: ~ **in**) s'harmoniser; ~ **down** *vt* (*colour, criticism*) adoucir; (*sound*) baisser; ~ **up** *vt* (*muscles*) tonifier; ~-**deaf** *adj* qui n'a pas d'oreille

tongs [tɒŋz] *npl* (*for coal*) pincettes *fpl*; (*for hair*) fer *m* à friser

tongue [tʌŋ] *n* langue *f*; ~ **in cheek** ironiquement; ~-**tied** *adj* (*fig*) muet(te); ~ **twister** *n* phrase *f* très difficile à prononcer

tonic ['tɒnɪk] *n* (*MED*) tonique *m*; (*also*: ~ *water*) tonic *m*, Schweppes *m* (®)

tonight [tə'naɪt] *adv, n* cette nuit; (*this evening*) ce soir

tonsil ['tɒnsl] *n* amygdale *f*; ~**litis** *n* angine *f*

too [tuː] *adv* (*excessively*) trop; (*also*) aussi; ~ **much** *adv* trop de ♦ *adj* trop; ~ **many** trop de; ~ **bad!** tant pis!

took [tʊk] *pt of* **take**

tool [tuːl] *n* outil *m*; ~ **box** *n* boîte *f* à outils

toot [tuːt] *n* (*of car horn*) coup *m* de klaxon; (*of whistle*) coup de sifflet ♦ *vi* (*with car horn*) klaxonner

tooth [tuːθ] *n* (*pl* **teeth**) *n* (*ANAT, TECH*) dent *f*; ~**ache** *n* mal *m* de dents; ~**brush** *n* brosse *f* à dents; ~**paste** *n* (*pâte f*) dentifrice *m*; ~**pick** *n* cure-dent *m*

top [tɒp] *n* (*of mountain, head*) sommet *m*; (*of page, ladder, garment*) haut *m*; (*of box, cupboard, table*) dessus *m*; (*lid: of box, jar*) couvercle *m*; (*: of bottle*) bouchon *m*; (*toy*) toupie *f* ♦ *adj* du haut; (*in rank*) premier(ère); (*best*) meilleur(e) ♦ *vt* (*exceed*) dépasser; (*be first in*) être en tête de; **on** ~ **of** sur; (*in addition to*) en plus de; **from** ~ **to bottom** de fond en comble; ~ **up** (*US* ~ **off**) *vt* (*bottle*) remplir; (*salary*) compléter; ~ **floor** *n* dernier étage; ~ **hat** *n* haut-de-forme *m*; ~-**heavy** *adj* (*object*) trop lourd(e) du haut

topic ['tɒpɪk] *n* sujet *m*, thème *m*; ~**al** *adj* d'actualité

top: ~**less** ['tɒpləs] *adj* (*bather etc*) aux seins nus; ~-**level** ['tɒp'levl] *adj* (*talks*) au plus haut niveau; ~**most** ['tɒpməʊst] *adj* le(la) plus haut(e)

topple ['tɒpl] *vt* renverser, faire tomber ♦ *vi* basculer; tomber

top-secret ['tɒp'siːkrət] *adj* top secret(ète)

topsy-turvy ['tɒpsɪ'tɜːvɪ] *adj, adv* sens dessus dessous

torch [tɔːtʃ] *n* torche *f*; (*BRIT: electric*) lampe *f* de poche

tore [tɔː*] *pt of* **tear**[1]

torment [*n* 'tɔːment, *vb* tɔː'ment] *n* tourment *m* ♦ *vt* tourmenter; (*fig: annoy*) harce-

ler

torn [tɔːn] *pp of* **tear**[1]

tornado [tɔː'neɪdəʊ] (*pl* ~**es**) *n* tornade *f*

torpedo [tɔː'piːdəʊ] (*pl* ~**es**) *n* torpille *f*

torrent ['tɒrənt] *n* torrent *m*

tortoise ['tɔːtəs] *n* tortue *f*; ~**shell** *adj* en écaille

torture ['tɔːtʃə*] *n* torture *f* ♦ *vt* torturer

Tory ['tɔːrɪ] (*BRIT POL*) *adj* tory, conservateur(trice) ♦ *n* tory *m/f*, conservateur(trice)

toss [tɒs] *vt* lancer, jeter; (*pancake*) faire sauter; (*head*) rejeter en arrière; **to** ~ **a coin** jouer à pile ou face; **to** ~ **up for sth** jouer qch à pile ou face; **to** ~ **and turn** (*in bed*) se tourner et se retourner

tot [tɒt] *n* (*BRIT: drink*) petit verre; (*child*) bambin *m*

total ['təʊtl] *adj* total(e) ♦ *n* total *m* ♦ *vt* (*add up*) faire le total de, additionner; (*amount to*) s'élever à; ~**ly** ['təʊtəlɪ] *adv* totalement

totter ['tɒtə*] *vi* chanceler

touch [tʌtʃ] *n* contact *m*, toucher *m*; (*sense, also skill: of pianist etc*) toucher *m* ♦ *vt* toucher; (*tamper with*) toucher à; **a** ~ **of** (*fig*) un petit peu de; une touche de; **to get in** ~ **with** prendre contact avec; **to lose** ~ (*friends*) se perdre de vue; ~ **on** *vt fus* (*topic*) effleurer, aborder; ~ **up** *vt* (*paint*) retoucher; ~-**and-go** *adj* incertain(e); ~**down** *n* atterrissage *m*; (*on sea*) amerrissage *m*; (*US: FOOTBALL*) touché-en-but *m*; ~**ed** *adj* (*moved*) touché(e); ~**ing** *adj* touchant(e), attendrissant(e); ~**line** *n* (*SPORT*) (ligne *f* de) touche *f*; ~**y** *adj* (*person*) susceptible

tough [tʌf] *adj* dur(e); (*resistant*) résistant(e), solide; (*meat*) dur, coriace; (*firm*) inflexible; (*task*) dur, pénible; ~**en** *vt* (*character*) endurcir; (*glass etc*) renforcer

toupee ['tuːpeɪ] *n* postiche *m*

tour ['tʊə*] *n* voyage *m*; (*also: package* ~) voyage organisé; (*of town, museum*) tour *m*, visite *f*; (*by artist*) tournée *f* ♦ *vt* visiter

tourism ['tʊərɪzm] *n* tourisme *m*

tourist ['tʊərɪst] *n* touriste *m/f* ♦ *cpd* touristique; ~ **office** *n* syndicat *m* d'initiative

tournament ['tʊənəmənt] *n* tournoi *m*

tousled ['taʊzld] *adj* (*hair*) ébouriffé(e)

tout [taʊt] *vi*: **to** ~ **for** essayer de raccrocher, racoler (*also: ticket* ~) revendeur *m* de billets

tow [təʊ] *vt* remorquer; (*caravan, trailer*) tracter; "**on** (*BRIT*) **or in** (*US*) ~" (*AUT*) "véhicule en remorque"

toward(s) [tə'wɔːd(z)] *prep* vers; (*of attitude*) envers, à l'égard de; (*of purpose*) pour

towel ['taʊəl] *n* serviette *f* (de toilette); ~**ling** *n (fabric)* tissu éponge *m*; ~ **rail** (*US* ~ **rack**) *n* porte-serviettes *m inv*

tower ['taʊə*] *n* tour *f*; ~ **block** (*BRIT*) *n* tour *f* (d'habitation); ~**ing** *adj* très haut(e), imposant(e)

town [taʊn] *n* ville *f*; **to go to** ~ aller en ville; *(fig)* y mettre le paquet; ~ **centre** *n* centre *m* de la ville, centre-ville *m*; ~ **council** *n* conseil municipal; ~ **hall** *n* ≈ mairie *f*; ~ **plan** *n* plan *m* de ville; ~ **planning** *n* urbanisme *m*

towrope ['təʊrəʊp] *n* (câble *m* de) remorque *f*

tow truck *(US)* *n* dépanneuse *f*

toy [tɔɪ] *n* jouet *m*; ~ **with** *vt fus* jouer avec; *(idea)* caresser

trace [treɪs] *n* trace *f* ♦ *vt* (*draw*) tracer, dessiner; *(follow)* suivre la trace de; *(locate)* retrouver; **tracing paper** *n* papier-calque *m*

track [træk] *n* (*mark*) trace *f*; *(path: gen)* chemin *m*, piste *f*; (: *of bullet etc*) trajectoire *f*; (: *of suspect, animal*) piste; *(RAIL)* voie ferrée, rails *mpl*; *(on tape, SPORT)* piste; *(on record)* plage *f* ♦ *vt* suivre la trace *or* la piste de; **to keep** ~ **of** suivre; ~ **down** *vt* (*prey*) trouver et capturer; *(sth lost)* finir par retrouver; ~ **suit** *n* survêtement *m*

tract [trækt] *n* *(GEO)* étendue *f*, zone *f*; *(pamphlet)* tract *m*

traction ['trækʃən] *n* traction *f*; *(MED)*: **in** ~ en extension

tractor ['træktə*] *n* tracteur *m*

trade [treɪd] *n* commerce *m*; *(skill, job)* métier *m* ♦ *vi* faire du commerce ♦ *vt* (*exchange*): **to** ~ **sth (for sth)** échanger qch (contre qch); ~ **in** *vt* *(old car etc)* faire reprendre; ~ **fair** *n* foire(-exposition) commerciale; ~**-in price** *n* prix *m* à la reprise; ~**mark** *n* marque *f* de fabrique; ~ **name** *n* nom *m* de marque; ~**r** *n* commerçant(e), négociant(e); ~**sman** *(irreg)* *n* *(shopkeeper)* commerçant; ~ **union** *n* syndicat *m*; ~ **unionist** *n* syndicaliste *m/f*

tradition [trə'dɪʃən] *n* tradition *f*; ~**al** *adj* traditionnel(le)

traffic ['træfɪk] *n* trafic *m*; *(cars)* circulation *f* ♦ *vi*: **to** ~ **in** (*pej: liquor, drugs*) faire le trafic de; ~ **circle** *(US)* *n* rond-point *m*; ~ **jam** *n* embouteillage *m*; ~ **lights** *npl* feux *mpl* (de signalisation); ~ **warden** *n* contractuel(le)

tragedy ['trædʒədɪ] *n* tragédie *f*

tragic ['trædʒɪk] *adj* tragique

trail [treɪl] *n* *(tracks)* trace *f*, piste *f*; *(path)* chemin *m*, piste; *(of smoke etc)* traînée *f* ♦ *vt* traîner, tirer; *(follow)* suivre ♦ *vi* traîner; *(in game, contest)* être en retard; ~ **behind** *vi* traîner, être à la traîne; ~**er** *n* *(AUT)* remorque *f*; *(US)* caravane *f*; *(CINEMA)* bande-annonce *f*; ~**er truck** *(US)* *n* (camion *m*) semi-remorque *m*

train [treɪn] *n* train *m*; *(in underground)* rame *f*; *(of dress)* traîne *f* ♦ *vt* *(apprentice, doctor etc)* former; *(sportsman)* entraîner; *(dog)* dresser; *(memory)* exercer; *(point: gun etc)*: **to** ~ **sth on** braquer qch sur ♦ *vi* sui-

vre une formation; *(SPORT)* s'entraîner; **one's** ~ **of thought** le fil de sa pensée; ~**ed** *adj* qualifié(e), qui a reçu une formation; *(animal)* dressé(e); ~**ee** *n* stagiaire *m/f*; *(in trade)* apprenti(e); ~**er** *n* *(SPORT: coach)* entraîneur(euse); (: *shoe*) chaussure *f* de sport; *(of dogs etc)* dresseur(euse); ~**ing** *n* formation *f*; entraînement *m*; **in** ~**ing** *(SPORT)* à l'entraînement; *(fit)* en forme; ~**ing college** *n* école professionnelle; *(for teachers)* ≈ école normale; ~**ing shoes** *npl* chaussures *fpl* de sport

traipse [treɪps] *vi*: **to** ~ **in/out** entrer/sortir d'un pas traînant

trait [treɪ(t)] *n* trait *m* (de caractère)

traitor ['treɪtə*] *n* traître *m*

tram ['træm] *(BRIT)* *n* *(also:* ~*car)* tram(way) *m*

tramp [træmp] *n* *(person)* vagabond(e), clochard(e); *(inf: pej: woman)*: **to be a** ~ être coureuse ♦ *vi* marcher d'un pas lourd

trample ['træmpl] *vt*: **to** ~ **(underfoot)** piétiner

trampoline ['træmpəliːn] *n* trampoline *m*

tranquil ['træŋkwɪl] *adj* tranquille; ~**lizer** *(US* ~**izer)** *n* *(MED)* tranquillisant *m*

transact [træn'zækt] *vt* *(business)* traiter; ~**ion** *n* transaction *f*

transatlantic ['trænzət'læntɪk] *adj* transatlantique

transfer [*n* 'trænsfə*, *vt* træns'fɜː*] *n* *(gen, also SPORT)* transfert *m*; *(POL: of power)* passation *f*; *(picture, design)* décalcomanie *f*; (: *stick-on*) autocollant *m* ♦ *vt* transférer; passer; **to** ~ **the charges** *(BRIT: TEL)* téléphoner en P.C.V.

transform [træns'fɔːm] *vt* transformer

transfusion [træns'fjuːʒən] *n* transfusion *f*

transient ['trænzɪənt] *adj* transitoire, éphémère

transistor [træn'zɪstə*] *n* *(ELEC, also:* ~ *radio)* transistor *m*

transit ['trænzɪt] *n*: **in** ~ en transit

transitive ['trænzɪtɪv] *adj* *(LING)* transitif(ive)

transit lounge *n* salle *f* de transit

translate [trænz'leɪt] *vt* traduire; **translation** [trænz'leɪʃən] *n* traduction *f*; **translator** [trænz'leɪtə*] *n* traducteur(trice)

transmission [trænz'mɪʃən] *n* transmission *f*

transmit [trænz'mɪt] *vt* transmettre; *(RADIO, TV)* émettre

transparency [træns'pærənsɪ] *n* *(of glass etc)* transparence *f*; *(BRIT: PHOT)* diapositive *f*; **transparent** [træns'pærənt] *adj* transparent(e)

transpire [træns'paɪə*] *vi* *(turn out)*: **it** ~**d that ...** on a appris que ...; *(happen)* arriver

transplant [*vb* træns'plɑːnt, *n* 'trænsplɑːnt] *vt* transplanter; *(seedlings)* repiquer ♦ *n* *(MED)* transplantation *f*

transport [*n* 'trænspɔːt, *vb* træns'pɔːt] *n* transport *m*; (*car*) moyen *m* de transport, voiture *f* ♦ *vt* transporter; ~**ation** [trænspɔː'teɪʃən] *n* transport *m*; (*means of* ~) moyen *m* de transport; ~ **café** (*BRIT*) *n* ≈ restaurant *m* de routiers

trap [træp] *n* (*snare, trick*) piège *m*; (*carriage*) cabriolet *m* ♦ *vt* prendre au piège; (*confine*) coincer; ~ **door** *n* trappe *f*

trapeze [trə'piːz] *n* trapèze *m*

trappings ['træpɪŋz] *npl* ornements *mpl*; attributs *mpl*

trash [træʃ] (*pej*) *n* (*goods*) camelote *f*; (*nonsense*) sottises *fpl*; ~ **can** (*US*) *n* poubelle *f*

trauma ['trɔːmə] *n* traumatisme *m*; ~**tic** *adj* traumatisant(e)

travel ['trævl] *n* voyage(s) *m(pl)* ♦ *vi* voyager; (*news, sound*) circuler, se propager ♦ *vt* (*distance*) parcourir; ~ **agency** *n* agence *f* de voyages; ~ **agent** *n* agent *m* de voyages; ~**ler** (*US* ~**er**) *n* voyageur(euse); ~**ler's cheque** (*US* ~**er's check**) *n* chèque *m* de voyage; ~**ling** (*US* ~**ing**) *n* voyage(s) *m(pl)*; ~ **sickness** *n* mal *m* de la route (*or* de mer *or* de l'air)

travesty ['trævəstɪ] *n* parodie *f*

trawler ['trɔːlə*] *n* chalutier *m*

tray [treɪ] *n* (*for carrying*) plateau *m*; (*on desk*) corbeille *f*

treacherous *adj* (*person, look*) traître(esse); (*ground, tide*) dont il faut se méfier

treachery ['tretʃərɪ] *n* traîtrise *f*

treacle ['triːkl] *n* mélasse *f*

tread [tred] (*pt* **trod**, *pp* **trodden**) *n* pas *m*; (*sound*) bruit *m* de pas; (*of tyre*) chape *f*, bande *f* de roulement ♦ *vi* marcher; ~ **on** *vt fus* marcher sur

treason ['triːzn] *n* trahison *f*

treasure ['treʒə*] *n* trésor *m* ♦ *vt* (*value*) tenir beaucoup à

treasurer ['treʒərə*] *n* trésorier(ère)

treasury ['treʒərɪ] *n*: **the T**~, (*US*) **the T**~ **Department** le ministère des Finances

treat [triːt] *n* petit cadeau, petite surprise ♦ *vt* traiter; **to** ~ **sb to sth** offrir qch à qn

treatment ['triːtmənt] *n* traitement *m*

treaty ['triːtɪ] *n* traité *m*

treble ['trebl] *adj* triple ♦ *vt, vi* tripler; ~ **clef** *n* (*MUS*) clé *f* de sol

tree [triː] *n* arbre *m*

trek [trek] *n* (*long*) voyage; (*on foot*) (*longue*) marche, tirée *f*

tremble ['trembl] *vi* trembler

tremendous [trə'mendəs] *adj* (*enormous*) énorme, fantastique; (*excellent*) formidable

tremor ['tremə*] *n* tremblement *m*; (*also: earth* ~) secousse *f* sismique

trench [trentʃ] *n* tranchée *f*

trend [trend] *n* (*tendency*) tendance *f*; (*of events*) cours *m*; (*fashion*) mode *f*; ~**y** *adj* (*idea, person*) dans le vent; (*clothes*) dernier

cri *inv*

trepidation [trepɪ'deɪʃən] *n* vive agitation *or* inquiétude *f*

trespass ['trespəs] *vi*: **to** ~ **on** s'introduire sans permission dans; **"no** ~**ing"** "propriété privée", "défense d'entrer"

trestle ['tresl] *n* tréteau *m*

trial ['traɪəl] *n* (*LAW*) procès *m*, jugement *m*; (*test: of machine etc*) essai *m*; ~**s** *npl* (*unpleasant experiences*) épreuves *fpl*; **to be on** ~ (*LAW*) passer en jugement; **by** ~ **and error** par tâtonnements; ~ **period** *n* période *f* d'essai

triangle ['traɪæŋgl] *n* (*MATH, MUS*) triangle *m*

tribe [traɪb] *n* tribu *f*; ~**sman** (*irreg*) *n* membre *m* d'une tribu

tribunal [traɪ'bjuːnl] *n* tribunal *m*

tributary ['trɪbjutərɪ] *n* (*river*) affluent *m*

tribute ['trɪbjuːt] *n* tribut *m*, hommage *m*; **to pay** ~ **to** rendre hommage à

trice [traɪs] *n*: **in a** ~ en un clin d'œil

trick [trɪk] *n* (*magic* ~) tour *m*; (*joke, prank*) tour, farce *f*; (*skill, knack*) astuce *f*, truc *m*; (*CARDS*) levée *f* ♦ *vt* attraper, rouler; **to play a** ~ **on sb** jouer un tour à qn; **that should do the** ~ ça devrait faire l'affaire; ~**ery** *n* ruse *f*

trickle ['trɪkl] *n* (*of water etc*) filet *m* ♦ *vi* couler en un filet *or* goutte à goutte

tricky ['trɪkɪ] *adj* difficile, délicat(e)

tricycle ['traɪsɪkl] *n* tricycle *m*

trifle ['traɪfl] *n* bagatelle *f*; (*CULIN*) ≈ diplomate *m* ♦ *adv*: **a** ~ **long** un peu long

trifling ['traɪflɪŋ] *adj* insignifiant(e)

trigger ['trɪgə*] *n* (*of gun*) gâchette *f*; ~ **off** *vt* déclencher

trim [trɪm] *adj* (*house, garden*) bien tenu(e); (*figure*) svelte ♦ *n* (*haircut etc*) légère coupe; (*on car*) garnitures *fpl* ♦ *vt* (*cut*) couper légèrement; (*NAUT: a sail*) gréer; (*decorate*): **to** ~ (**with**) décorer (de); ~**mings** *npl* (*CULIN*) garniture *f*

trinket ['trɪŋkɪt] *n* bibelot *m*; (*piece of jewellery*) colifichet *m*

trip [trɪp] *n* voyage *m*; (*excursion*) excursion *f*; (*stumble*) faux pas ♦ *vi* faire un faux pas, trébucher; (*go lightly*) marcher d'un pas léger; **on a** ~ en voyage; ~ **up** *vi* trébucher ♦ *vt* faire un croc-en-jambe à

tripe [traɪp] *n* (*CULIN*) tripes *fpl*; (*pej: rubbish*) idioties *fpl*

triple ['trɪpl] *adj* triple

triplets ['trɪplɪts] *npl* triplés(ées)

triplicate ['trɪplɪkɪt] *n*: **in** ~ en trois exemplaires

tripod ['traɪpɒd] *n* trépied *m*

trite [traɪt] (*pej*) *adj* banal(e)

triumph ['traɪʌmf] *n* triomphe *m* ♦ *vi*: **to** ~ (**over**) triompher (de)

trivia ['trɪvɪə] (*pej*) *npl* futilités *fpl*

trivial ['trɪvɪəl] *adj* insignifiant(e); (*common-*

place) banal(e)
trod [trɒd] *pt of* **tread**
trodden ['trɒdn] *pp of* **tread**
trolley ['trɒlɪ] *n* chariot *m*
trombone [trɔm'bəʊn] *n* trombone *m*
troop [truːp] *n* bande *f*, groupe *m* ♦ *vi*: ~ **in/out** entrer/sortir en groupe; ~**s** *npl* (*MIL*) troupes *fpl*; (: *men*) hommes *mpl*, soldats *mpl*; ~**ing the colour** (*BRIT*) *n* (*ceremony*) le salut au drapeau
trophy ['trəʊfɪ] *n* trophée *m*
tropic ['trɒpɪk] *n* tropique *m*; ~**al** *adj* tropical(e)
trot [trɒt] *n* trot *m* ♦ *vi* trotter; **on the** ~ (*BRIT*: *fig*) d'affilée
trouble ['trʌbl] *n* difficulté(s) *f(pl)*, problème(s) *m(pl)*; (*worry*) ennuis *mpl*, soucis *mpl*; (*bother*, *effort*) peine *f*; (*POL*) troubles *mpl*; (*MED*): **stomach** *etc* ~ troubles gastriques *etc* ♦ *vt* (*disturb*) déranger, gêner; (*worry*) inquiéter ♦ *vi*: **to** ~ **to do** prendre la peine de faire; ~**s** *npl* (*POL etc*) troubles *mpl*; (*personal*) ennuis, soucis; **to be in** ~ avoir des ennuis; (*ship*, *climber etc*) être en difficulté; **what's the** ~? qu'est-ce qui ne va pas?; ~**d** *adj* (*person*) inquiet(ète); (*epoch*, *life*) agité(e); ~**maker** *n* élément perturbateur, fauteur *m* de troubles; ~**shooter** *n* (*in conflict*) médiateur *m*; ~**some** *adj* (*child*) fatigant(e), difficile; (*cough etc*) gênant(e)
trough [trɒf] *n* (*also*: *drinking* ~) abreuvoir *m*; (: *feeding* ~) auge *f*; (*depression*) creux *m*
trousers ['traʊzəz] *npl* pantalon *m*; **short** ~ culottes courtes
trout [traʊt] *n inv* truite *f*
trowel ['traʊəl] *n* truelle *f*; (*garden tool*) déplantoir *m*
truant ['truːənt] (*BRIT*) *n*: **to play** ~ faire l'école buissonnière
truce [truːs] *n* trêve *f*
truck [trʌk] *n* camion *m*; (*RAIL*) wagon *m* à plate-forme; ~ **driver** *n* camionneur *m*; ~ **farm** (*US*) *n* jardin maraîcher
trudge [trʌdʒ] *vi* marcher lourdement, se traîner
true [truː] *adj* vrai(e); (*accurate*) exact(e); (*genuine*) vrai, véritable; (*faithful*) fidèle; **to come** ~ se réaliser
truffle ['trʌfl] *n* truffe *f*
truly ['truːlɪ] *adv* vraiment, réellement; (*truthfully*) sans mentir; *see also* **yours**
trump [trʌmp] *n* (*also*: ~ *card*) atout *m*; ~**ed up** *adj* inventé(e) (de toutes pièces)
trumpet ['trʌmpɪt] *n* trompette *f*
truncheon ['trʌntʃən] (*BRIT*) *n* bâton *m* (d'agent de police); matraque *f*
trundle ['trʌndl] *vt, vi*: **to** ~ **along** rouler lentement et bruyamment)
trunk [trʌŋk] *n* (*of tree*, *person*) tronc *m*; (*of elephant*) trompe *f*; (*case*) malle *f*; (*US:*

AUT) coffre *m*; ~**s** *npl* (*also*: *swimming* ~*s*) maillot *m or* slip *m* de bain
truss [trʌs] *n* (*MED*) bandage *m* herniaire ♦ *vt*: **to** ~ (**up**) (*CULIN*) brider, trousser
trust [trʌst] *n* confiance *f*; (*responsibility*) charge *f*; (*LAW*) fidéicommis *m* ♦ *vt* (*rely on*) avoir confiance en; (*hope*) espérer; (*entrust*): **to** ~ **sth to sb** confier qch à qn; **to take sth on** ~ accepter qch les yeux fermés; ~**ed** *adj* en qui l'on a confiance; ~**ee** *n* (*LAW*) fidéicommissaire *m/f*; (*of school etc*) administrateur(trice); ~**ful**, ~**ing** *adj* confiant(e); ~**worthy** *adj* digne de confiance
truth [truːθ, *pl* truːðz] *n* vérité *f*; ~**ful** *adj* (*person*) qui dit la vérité; (*answer*) sincère
try [traɪ] *n* essai *m*, tentative *f*; (*RUGBY*) essai *m* ♦ *vt* (*attempt*) essayer, tenter; (*test: sth new*: *also*: ~ *out*) essayer, tester; (*LAW: person*) juger; (*strain*) éprouver ♦ *vi* essayer; **to have a** ~ essayer; **to** ~ **to do** essayer de faire; (*seek*) chercher à faire; ~ **on** *vt* (*clothes*) essayer; ~**ing** *adj* pénible
T-shirt ['tiːʃɜːt] *n* tee-shirt *m*
T-square ['tiːskwɛə*] *n* équerre *f* en T, té *m*
tub [tʌb] *n* cuve *f*; (*for washing clothes*) baquet *m*; (*bath*) baignoire *f*
tubby ['tʌbɪ] *adj* rondelet(te)
tube [tjuːb] *n* tube *m*; (*BRIT: underground*) métro *m*; (*for tyre*) chambre *f* à air
TUC *n abbr* (*BRIT*: = *Trades Union Congress*) confédération *f* des syndicats britanniques
tuck [tʌk] *vt* (*put*) mettre; ~ **away** *vt* cacher, ranger; ~ **in** *vt* rentrer; (*child*) border ♦ *vi* (*eat*) manger (de bon appétit); ~ **up** *vt* (*child*) border; ~ **shop** (*BRIT*) *n* boutique *f* à provisions (*dans une école*)
Tuesday ['tjuːzdeɪ] *n* mardi *m*
tuft [tʌft] *n* touffe *f*
tug [tʌg] *n* (*ship*) remorqueur *m* ♦ *vt* tirer (sur); ~**-of-war** *n* lutte *f* à la corde; (*fig*) lutte acharnée
tuition [tjuː'ɪʃən] *n* (*BRIT*) leçons *fpl*; (: *private* ~) cours particuliers; (*US: school fees*) frais *mpl* de scolarité
tulip ['tjuːlɪp] *n* tulipe *f*
tumble ['tʌmbl] *n* (*fall*) chute *f*, culbute *f* ♦ *vi* tomber, dégringoler; **to** ~ **to sth** (*inf*) réaliser qch; ~**down** *adj* délabré(e); ~ **dryer** (*BRIT*) *n* séchoir *m* à air chaud
tumbler ['tʌmblə*] *n* (*glass*) verre (droit), gobelet *m*
tummy ['tʌmɪ] (*inf*) *n* ventre *m*
tumour ['tjuːmə*] (*US tumor*) *n* tumeur *f*
tuna ['tjuːnə] *n inv* (*also*: ~ *fish*) thon *m*
tune [tjuːn] *n* (*melody*) air *m* ♦ *vt* (*MUS*) accorder; (*RADIO, TV, AUT*) régler; **to be in/out of** ~ (*instrument*) être accordé/désaccordé; (*singer*) chanter juste/faux; **to be in/out of** ~ **with** (*fig*) être en accord/

désaccord avec; ~ **in** vi (RADIO, TV): **to ~ in (to)** se mettre à l'écoute (de); ~ **up** vi (musician) accorder son instrument; ~**ful** adj mélodieux(euse); ~**r** n: **piano ~r** accordeur m (de pianos)

tunic ['tjuːnɪk] n tunique f

Tunisia [tjuːˈnɪzɪə] n Tunisie f

tunnel ['tʌnl] n tunnel m; (in mine) galerie f ♦ vi percer un tunnel

turbulence ['tɜːbjʊləns] n (AVIAT) turbulence f

tureen [tjʊˈriːn] n (for soup) soupière f; (for vegetables) légumier m

turf [tɜːf] n gazon m; (clod) motte f (de gazon) ♦ vt gazonner; ~ **out** (inf) vt (person) jeter dehors

turgid ['tɜːdʒɪd] adj (speech) pompeux(euse)

Turk [tɜːk] n Turc(Turque) m(f)

Turkey ['tɜːkɪ] n Turquie f

turkey ['tɜːkɪ] n dindon m, dinde f

Turkish ['tɜːkɪʃ] adj turc(turque) ♦ n (LING) turc m

turmoil ['tɜːmɔɪl] n trouble m, bouleversement m; **in** ~ en émoi, en effervescence

turn [tɜːn] n tour m; (in road) tournant m; (of mind, events) tournure f; (performance) numéro m; (MED) crise f, attaque f ♦ vt tourner; (collar, steak) retourner; (change): **to ~ sth into** changer qch en ♦ vi (object, wind, milk) tourner; (person: look back) se (re)tourner; (reverse direction) faire demi-tour; (become) devenir; (age) atteindre; **to ~ into** se changer en; **a good** ~ un service; **it gave me quite a** ~ ça m'a fait un coup; **"no left ~"** (AUT) "défense de tourner à gauche"; **it's your** ~ c'est (à) votre tour; **in** ~ à son tour; à tour de rôle; **to take** ~**s (at)** se relayer (pour or à); ~ **away** vi se détourner ♦ vt (applicants) refuser; ~ **back** vi revenir, faire demi-tour ♦ vt (person, vehicle) faire faire demi-tour à; (clock) reculer; ~ **down** vt (refuse) rejeter, refuser; (reduce) baisser; (fold) rabattre; ~ **in** vi (inf: go to bed) aller se coucher ♦ vt (fold) rentrer; ~ **off** vi (from road) tourner ♦ vt (light, radio etc) éteindre; (tap) fermer; (engine) arrêter; ~ **on** vt (light, radio etc) allumer; (tap) ouvrir; (engine) mettre en marche; ~ **out** vt (light, gas) éteindre; (produce) produire ♦ vi (voters, troops etc) se présenter; **to** ~ **out to be ...** s'avérer ..., se révéler ...; ~ **over** vi (person) se retourner ♦ vt (object) retourner; (page) tourner; ~ **round** vi faire demi-tour; (rotate) tourner; ~ **up** vi (person) arriver, se pointer (inf); (lost object) être retrouvé(e) ♦ vt (collar) remonter; (radio, heater) mettre plus fort; ~**ing** n (in road) tournant m; ~**ing point** n (fig) tournant m, moment décisif

turnip ['tɜːnɪp] n navet m

turnout ['tɜːnaʊt] n (of voters) taux m de participation

turnover ['tɜːnəʊvə*] n (COMM: amount of money) chiffre m d'affaires; (: of goods) roulement m; (of staff) renouvellement m, changement m

turnpike ['tɜːnpaɪk] n (US) autoroute f à péage

turnstile ['tɜːnstaɪl] n tourniquet m (d'entrée)

turntable ['tɜːnteɪbl] n (on record player) platine f

turn-up ['tɜːnʌp] n (BRIT) (on trousers) revers m

turpentine ['tɜːpəntaɪn] n (also: **turps**) (essence f de) térébenthine f

turquoise ['tɜːkwɔɪz] n (stone) turquoise f ♦ adj turquoise inv

turret ['tʌrɪt] n tourelle f

turtle ['tɜːtl] n tortue marine or d'eau douce; ~**neck (sweater)** n (BRIT) pullover m à col montant; (US) pullover à col roulé

tusk [tʌsk] n défense f

tussle ['tʌsl] n bagarre f, mêlée f

tutor ['tjuːtə*] n (in college) directeur(trice) d'études; (private teacher) précepteur(trice); ~**ial** [tjuːˈtɔːrɪəl] n (SCOL) (séance f de) travaux mpl pratiques

tuxedo [tʌkˈsiːdəʊ] (US) n smoking m

TV ['tiːˈviː] n abbr (= television) télé f

twang [twæŋ] n (of instrument) son vibrant; (of voice) ton nasillard

tweed [twiːd] n tweed m

tweezers ['twiːzəz] npl pince f à épiler

twelfth [twelfθ] num douzième

twelve [twelv] num douze; **at** ~ **(o'clock)** à midi; (midnight) à minuit

twentieth ['twentɪɪθ] num vingtième

twenty ['twentɪ] num vingt

twice [twaɪs] adv deux fois; ~ **as much** deux fois plus

twiddle ['twɪdl] vt, vi: **to** ~ **(with) sth** tripoter qch; **to** ~ **one's thumbs** (fig) se tourner les pouces

twig [twɪg] n brindille f ♦ vi (inf) piger

twilight ['twaɪlaɪt] n crépuscule m

twin [twɪn] adj, n jumeau(elle) ♦ vt jumeler; ~**(-bedded) room** n chambre f à deux lits

twine [twaɪn] n ficelle f ♦ vi (plant) s'enrouler

twinge [twɪndʒ] n (of pain) élancement m; **a** ~ **of conscience** un certain remords; **a** ~ **of regret** un pincement au cœur

twinkle ['twɪŋkl] vi scintiller; (eyes) pétiller

twirl [twɜːl] vt faire tournoyer ♦ vi tournoyer

twist [twɪst] n torsion f, tour m; (in road) virage m; (in wire, flex) tortillon m; (in story) coup m de théâtre ♦ vt tordre; (weave) entortiller; (roll around) enrouler; (fig) déformer ♦ vi (road, river) serpenter

twit [twɪt] (inf) n crétin(e)

twitch [twɪtʃ] n (pull) coup sec, saccade f;

(*nervous*) tic *m* ♦ *vi* se convulser; avoir un tic

two [tu:] *num* deux; **to put ~ and ~ together** (*fig*) faire le rapprochement; **~-door** *adj* (*AUT*) à deux portes; **~-faced** (*pej*) *adj* (*person*) faux(fausse); **~fold** *adv*: **to increase ~fold** doubler; **~-piece (suit)** *n* (*man's*) costume *m* (deux-pièces); (*woman's*) (tailleur *m*) deux-pièces *m inv*; **~-piece (swimsuit)** *n* (maillot *m* de bain) deux-pièces *m inv*; **~some** *n* (*people*) couple *m*; **~-way** *adj* (*traffic*) dans les deux sens

tycoon [taɪˈkuːn] *n*: (**business**) ~ gros homme d'affaires

type [taɪp] *n* (*category*) type *m*, genre *m*, espèce *f*; (*model, example*) type *m*, modèle *m*; (*TYP*) type, caractère *m* ♦ *vt* (*letter etc*) taper (à la machine); **~-cast** *adj* (*actor*) condamné(e) à toujours jouer le même rôle; **~face** *n* (*TYP*) œil *m* de caractère; **~script** *n* texte dactylographié; **~writer** *n* machine *f* à écrire; **~written** *adj* dactylographié(e)

typhoid [ˈtaɪfɔɪd] *n* typhoïde *f*

typical [ˈtɪpɪkəl] *adj* typique, caractéristique

typing [ˈtaɪpɪŋ] *n* dactylo(graphie) *f*

typist [ˈtaɪpɪst] *n* dactylo *m/f*

tyrant [ˈtaɪərnt] *n* tyran *m*

tyre [taɪə*] (*US* **tire**) *n* pneu *m*; ~ **pressure** *n* pression *f* (de gonflage)

U u

U-bend [ˈjuːˈbend] *n* (*in pipe*) coude *m*

ubiquitous *adj* omniprésent(e)

udder [ˈʌdə*] *n* pis *m*, mamelle *f*

UFO [ˈjuːfəʊ] *n abbr* (= *unidentified flying object*) ovni *m*

Uganda [juːˈgændə] *n* Ouganda *m*

ugh [ɜːh] *excl* pouah!

ugly [ˈʌglɪ] *adj* laid(e), vilain(e); (*situation*) inquiétant(e)

UK *n abbr* = **United Kingdom**

ulcer [ˈʌlsə*] *n* ulcère *m*; (*also*: **mouth ~**) aphte *f*

Ulster [ˈʌlstə*] *n* Ulster *m*; (*inf*: *Northern Ireland*) Irlande *f* du Nord

ulterior [ʌlˈtɪərɪə*] *adj*: ~ **motive** arrière-pensée *f*

ultimate [ˈʌltɪmət] *adj* ultime, final(e); (*authority*) suprême; **~ly** *adv* en fin de compte; finalement

ultrasound [ˈʌltrəˈsaʊnd] *n* ultrason *m*

umbilical cord [ʌmˈbɪlɪkl-] *n* cordon ombilical

umbrella [ʌmˈbrelə] *n* parapluie *m*; (*for sun*) parasol *m*

umpire [ˈʌmpaɪə*] *n* arbitre *m*; (*TENNIS*) juge *m* de chaise

umpteen [ˈʌmptiːn] *adj* je ne sais combien de; **~th** *adj*: **for the ~th time** pour la nième fois

UN *n abbr* = **United Nations**

unable [ʌnˈeɪbl] *adj*: **to be ~ to** ne pas pouvoir, être dans l'impossibilité de; (*incapable*) être incapable de

unaccompanied [ˈʌnəˈkʌmpənɪd] *adj* (*child, lady*) non accompagné(e); (*song*) sans accompagnement

unaccountably [ˈʌnəˈkaʊntəblɪ] *adv* inexplicablement

unaccustomed [ˈʌnəˈkʌstəmd] *adj*: **to be ~ to sth** ne pas avoir l'habitude de qch

unanimous [juːˈnænɪməs] *adj* unanime; **~ly** *adv* à l'unanimité

unarmed [ʌnˈɑːmd] *adj* (*without a weapon*) non armé(e); (*combat*) sans armes

unashamed [ʌnəˈʃeɪmd] *adj* effronté(e), impudent(e)

unassuming [ʌnəˈsjuːmɪŋ] *adj* modeste, sans prétentions

unattached [ʌnəˈtætʃt] *adj* libre, sans attaches; (*part*) non attaché(e), indépendant(e)

unattended [ˈʌnəˈtendɪd] *adj* (*car, child, luggage*) sans surveillance

unattractive [ʌnəˈtræktɪv] *adj* peu attrayant(e); (*character*) peu sympathique

unauthorized [ˈʌnˈɔːθəraɪzd] *adj* non autorisé(e), sans autorisation

unavoidable [ʌnəˈvɔɪdəbl] *adj* inévitable

unaware [ˈʌnəˈweə*] *adj*: **to be ~ of** ignorer, être inconscient(e) de; **~s** *adv* à l'improviste, au dépourvu

unbalanced [ˈʌnˈbælənst] *adj* déséquilibré(e); (*report*) peu objectif(ive)

unbearable [ʌnˈbeərəbl] *adj* insupportable

unbeatable [ʌnˈbiːtəbl] *adj* imbattable

unbeknown(st) [ˈʌnbɪˈnəʊn(st)] *adv*: ~ **to me/Peter** à mon insu/l'insu de Peter

unbelievable [ʌnbɪˈliːvəbl] *adj* incroyable

unbend [ʌnˈbend] (*irreg*) *vi* se détendre ♦ *vt* (*wire*) redresser, détordre

unbiased [ʌnˈbaɪəst] *adj* impartial(e)

unborn [ʌnˈbɔːn] *adj* à naître, qui n'est pas encore né(e)

unbreakable [ʌnˈbreɪkəbl] *adj* incassable

unbroken [ˈʌnˈbrəʊkən] *adj* intact(e); (*fig*) continu(e), ininterrompu(e)

unbutton [ʌnˈbʌtn] *vt* déboutonner

uncalled-for [ʌnˈkɔːldfɔː*] *adj* déplacé(e), injustifié(e)

uncanny [ʌnˈkænɪ] *adj* étrange, troublant(e)

unceasing [ʌnˈsiːsɪŋ] *adj* incessant(e), continu(e)

unceremonious ['ʌnserɪ'məʊnɪəs] *adj* (*abrupt, rude*) brusque

uncertain [ʌn'sɜːtn] *adj* incertain(e); (*hesitant*) hésitant(e); **in no ~ terms** sans équivoque possible; **~ty** *n* incertitude *f*, doute(s) *m(pl)*

unchecked ['ʌn'tʃekt] *adv* sans contrôle *or* opposition

uncivilized ['ʌn'sɪvɪlaɪzd] *adj* (*gen*) non civilisé(e); (*fig: behaviour etc*) barbare; (*hour*) indu(e)

uncle ['ʌŋkl] *n* oncle *m*

uncomfortable [ʌn'kʌmfətəbl] *adj* inconfortable, peu confortable; (*uneasy*) mal à l'aise, gêné(e); (*unpleasant*) désagréable

uncommon [ʌn'kɒmən] *adj* rare, singulier(ère), peu commun(e)

uncompromising [ʌn'kɒmprəmaɪzɪŋ] *adj* intransigeant(e), inflexible

unconcerned [ʌnkən'sɜːnd] *adj*: **to be ~ (about)** ne pas s'inquiéter (de)

unconditional ['ʌnkən'dɪʃənl] *adj* sans conditions

unconscious [ʌn'kɒnʃəs] *adj* sans connaissance, évanoui(e); (*unaware*): **~ of** inconscient(e) de ♦ *n*: **the ~** l'inconscient *m*; **~ly** *adv* inconsciemment

uncontrollable ['ʌnkən'trəʊləbl] *adj* indiscipliné(e); (*temper, laughter*) irrépressible

unconventional [ʌnkən'venʃənl] *adj* peu conventionnel(le)

uncouth [ʌn'kuːθ] *adj* grossier(ère), fruste

uncover [ʌn'kʌvə*] *vt* découvrir

undecided ['ʌndɪ'saɪdɪd] *adj* indécis(e), irrésolu(e)

under ['ʌndə*] *prep* sous; (*less than*) (de) moins au-dessous de; (*according to*) selon, en vertu de ♦ *adv* au-dessous; en dessous; **~ there** là-dessous; **~ repair** en (cours de) réparation

under: **~age** *adj* (*person*) qui n'a pas l'âge réglementaire; **~carriage** *n* (*AVIAT*) train *m* d'atterrissage; **~charge** *vt* ne pas faire payer assez à; **~coat** *n* (*paint*) couche *f* de fond; **~cover** *adj* secret(ète), clandestin(e); **~current** *n* courant *or* sentiment sousjacent; **~cut** (*irreg*) *vt* vendre moins cher que; **~dog** *n* opprimé *m*; **~done** *adj* (*CULIN*) saignant(e); (*pej*) pas assez cuit(e); **~estimate** *vt* sous-estimer; **~fed** *adj* sous-alimenté(e); **~foot** *adv* sous les pieds; **~go** (*irreg*) *vt* subir; (*treatment*) suivre; **~graduate** *n* étudiant(e) (qui prépare la licence); **~ground** *n* (*BRIT: railway*) métro *m*; (*POL*) clandestinité *f* ♦ *adj* souterrain(e); (*fig*) clandestin(e) ♦ *adv* dans la clandestinité, clandestinement; **~growth** *n* broussailles *fpl*, sous-bois *m*; **~hand(ed)** *adj* (*fig: behaviour, method etc*) en dessous; **~lie** (*irreg*) *vt* être à la base de; **~line** *vt* souligner; **~ling** (*pej*) *n* sous-fifre *m*, subalterne *m*; **~mine** *vt* saper, miner; **~neath**

['ʌndə'niːθ] *adv* (en) dessous ♦ *prep* sous, au-dessous de; **~paid** *adj* sous-payé(e); **~pants** *npl* caleçon *m*, slip *m*; **~pass** (*BRIT*) *n* passage souterrain; (*on motorway*) passage inférieur; **~privileged** ['ʌndə'prɪvɪlɪdʒd] *adj* défavorisé(e), économiquement faible; **~rate** *vt* sous-estimer; **~shirt** (*US*) *n* tricot *m* de corps; **~shorts** (*US*) *npl* caleçon *m*, slip *m*; **~side** *n* dessous *m*; **~skirt** (*BRIT*) *n* jupon *m*

understand [ʌndə'stænd] (*irreg: like stand*) *vt, vi* comprendre; **I ~ that ...** je me suis laissé dire que ...; je crois comprendre que ...; **~able** *adj* compréhensible; **~ing** *adj* compréhensif(ive) ♦ *n* compréhension *f*; (*agreement*) accord *m*

understatement ['ʌndəsteɪtmənt] *n*: **that's an ~** c'est (bien) peu dire, le terme est faible

understood [ʌndə'stʊd] *pt, pp of* **understand** ♦ *adj* entendu(e); (*implied*) sousentendu(e)

understudy ['ʌndəstʌdɪ] *n* doublure *f*

undertake [ʌndə'teɪk] (*irreg*) *vt* entreprendre; se charger de; **to ~ to do sth** s'engager à faire qch

undertaker ['ʌndəteɪkə*] *n* entrepreneur *m* des pompes funèbres, croque-mort *m*

undertaking [ʌndə'teɪkɪŋ] *n* entreprise *f*; (*promise*) promesse *f*

undertone ['ʌndətəʊn] *n*: **in an ~** à mi-voix

under: **~water** ['ʌndə'wɔːtə*] *adv* sous l'eau ♦ *adj* sous-marin(e); **~wear** ['ʌndəwɛə*] *n* sous-vêtements *mpl*; (*women's only*) dessous *mpl*; **~world** ['ʌndəwɜːld] *n* (*of crime*) milieu *m*, pègre *f*; **~writer** ['ʌndəraɪtə*] *n* (*INSURANCE*) assureur *m*

undies ['ʌndɪz] (*inf*) *npl* dessous *mpl*, lingerie *f*

undiplomatic [ʌndɪplə'mætɪk] *adj* peu diplomatique

undo [ʌn'duː] (*irreg*) *vt* défaire; **~ing** *n* ruine *f*, perte *f*

undoubted [ʌn'daʊtɪd] *adj* indubitable, certain(e); **~ly** *adv* sans aucun doute

undress ['ʌn'dres] *vi* se déshabiller

undue ['ʌndjuː] *adj* indu(e), excessif(ive)

undulating ['ʌndjʊleɪtɪŋ] *adj* ondoyant(e), onduleux(euse)

unduly ['ʌn'djuːlɪ] *adv* trop, excessivement

unearth ['ʌn'ɜːθ] *vt* déterrer; (*fig*) dénicher

unearthly [ʌn'ɜːθlɪ] *adj* (*hour*) indu(e), impossible

uneasy [ʌn'iːzɪ] *adj* mal à l'aise, gêné(e); (*worried*) inquiet(ète); (*feeling*) désagréable; (*peace, truce*) fragile

uneconomic(al) [ʌniːkə'nɒmɪk(l)] *adj* peu économique

uneducated [ʌn'ɛdjukeɪtɪd] *adj* (*person*) sans instruction

unemployed ['ʌnɪm'plɔɪd] *adj* sans travail, en *or* au chômage ♦ *n*: **the ~** les chômeurs *mpl*; **unemployment** ['ʌnɪm'plɔɪmənt] *n* chômage *m*

unending [ʌn'endɪŋ] *adj* interminable, sans fin

unerring ['ʌn'ɜːrɪŋ] *adj* infaillible, sûr(e)

uneven ['ʌn'iːvən] *adj* inégal(e); irrégulier(ère)

unexpected [ʌnɪk'spektɪd] *adj* inattendu(e), imprévu(e); **~ly** *adv* (*arrive*) à l'improviste; (*succeed*) contre toute attente

unfailing ['ʌn'feɪlɪŋ] *adj* inépuisable; infaillible

unfair ['ʌn'feə*] *adj*: **~ (to)** injuste (envers)

unfaithful ['ʌn'feɪθful] *adj* infidèle

unfamiliar [ʌnfə'mɪlɪə*] *adj* étrange, inconnu(e); **to be ~ with** mal connaître

unfashionable [ʌn'fæʃnəbl] *adj* (*clothes*) démodé(e); (*place*) peu chic *inv*

unfasten ['ʌn'fɑːsn] *vt* défaire; détacher; (*open*) ouvrir

unfavourable ['ʌn'feɪvərəbl] (*US* **unfavorable**) *adj* défavorable

unfeeling [ʌn'fiːlɪŋ] *adj* insensible, dur(e)

unfinished [ʌn'fɪnɪʃt] *adj* inachevé(e)

unfit ['ʌn'fɪt] *adj* en mauvaise santé; pas en forme; (*incompetent*): **~ (for)** impropre (à); (*work, service*) inapte (à)

unfold ['ʌn'fəuld] *vt* déplier ♦ *vi* se dérouler

unforeseen ['ʌnfɔː'siːn] *adj* imprévu(e)

unforgettable [ʌnfə'getəbl] *adj* inoubliable

unfortunate [ʌn'fɔːtʃnət] *adj* malheureux(euse); (*event, remark*) malencontreux(euse); **~ly** *adv* malheureusement

unfounded ['ʌn'faundɪd] *adj* sans fondement

unfriendly [ʌn'frendlɪ] *adj* inamical(e), peu aimable

ungainly [ʌn'geɪnlɪ] *adj* gauche, dégingandé(e)

ungodly [ʌn'gɒdlɪ] *adj* (*hour*) indu(e)

ungrateful [ʌn'greɪtful] *adj* ingrat(e)

unhappiness [ʌn'hæpɪnəs] *n* tristesse *f*, peine *f*

unhappy [ʌn'hæpɪ] *adj* triste, malheureux(euse); **~ about** *or* **with** (*arrangements etc*) mécontent(e) de, peu satisfait(e) de

unharmed ['ʌn'hɑːmd] *adj* indemne, sain(e) et sauf(sauve)

unhealthy [ʌn'helθɪ] *adj* malsain(e); (*person*) maladif(ive)

unheard-of [ʌn'hɜːdɒv] *adj* inouï(e), sans précédent

unhurt [ʌn'hɜːt] *adj* indemne

unidentified [ʌnaɪ'dentɪfaɪd] *adj* non identifié(e); *see also* **UFO**

uniform ['juːnɪfɔːm] *n* uniforme *m* ♦ *adj* uniforme

uninhabited [ʌnɪn'hæbɪtɪd] *adj* inhabité(e)

unintentional [ʌnɪn'tenʃənəl] *adj* involontaire

union ['juːnjən] *n* union *f*; (*also: trade ~*) syndicat *m* ♦ *cpd* du syndicat, syndical(e); **U~ Jack** *n* drapeau du Royaume-Uni

unique [juː'niːk] *adj* unique

unison ['juːnɪsn] *n*: **in ~** (*sing*) à l'unisson; (*say*) en chœur

unit ['juːnɪt] *n* unité *f*; (*section: of furniture etc*) élément *m*, bloc *m*; **kitchen ~** élément de cuisine

unite [juː'naɪt] *vt* unir ♦ *vi* s'unir; **~d** *adj* uni(e); unifié(e); (*effort*) conjugué(e); **U~d Kingdom** *n* Royaume-Uni *m*; **U~d Nations (Organization)** *n* (Organisation *f* des) Nations unies; **U~d States (of America)** *n* États-Unis *mpl*

unit trust (*BRIT*) *n* fonds commun de placement

unity ['juːnɪtɪ] *n* unité *f*

universal [juːnɪ'vɜːsəl] *adj* universel(le)

universe ['juːnɪvɜːs] *n* univers *m*

university [juːnɪ'vɜːsɪtɪ] *n* université *f*

unjust ['ʌn'dʒʌst] *adj* injuste

unkempt ['ʌn'kempt] *adj* négligé(e), débraillé(e); (*hair*) mal peigné(e)

unkind [ʌn'kaɪnd] *adj* peu gentil(le), méchant(e)

unknown ['ʌn'nəun] *adj* inconnu(e)

unlawful [ʌn'lɔːful] *adj* illégal(e)

unleaded [ʌn'ledɪd] *adj* (*petrol, fuel*) sans plomb

unleash ['ʌn'liːʃ] *vt* (*fig*) déchaîner, déclencher

unless [ən'les] *conj*: **~ he leaves** à moins qu'il ne parte

unlike ['ʌn'laɪk] *adj* dissemblable, différent(e) ♦ *prep* contrairement à

unlikely [ʌn'laɪklɪ] *adj* improbable; invraisemblable

unlimited [ʌn'lɪmɪtɪd] *adj* illimité(e)

unlisted [ʌn'lɪstɪd] (*US*) *adj* (*TEL*) sur la liste rouge

unload ['ʌn'ləud] *vt* décharger

unlock ['ʌn'lɒk] *vt* ouvrir

unlucky [ʌn'lʌkɪ] *adj* (*person*) malchanceux(euse); (*object, number*) qui porte malheur; **to be ~** (*person*) ne pas avoir de chance

unmarried ['ʌn'mærɪd] *adj* célibataire

unmistak(e)able [ʌnmɪs'teɪkəbl] *adj* indubitable; qu'on ne peut pas ne pas reconnaître

unmitigated [ʌn'mɪtɪgeɪtɪd] *adj* non mitigé(e), absolu(e), pur(e)

unnatural [ʌn'nætʃrəl] *adj* non naturel(le); (*habit*) contre nature

unnecessary ['ʌn'nesəsərɪ] *adj* inutile, superflu(e)

unnoticed [ʌn'nəutɪst] *adj*: **(to go** *or* **pass) ~** (passer) inaperçu(e)

UNO ['juːnəu] *n abbr* = **United Nations Organization**

unobtainable ['ʌnəb'teɪnəbl] *adj* impossible à obtenir

unobtrusive [ˌʌnəb'truːsɪv] *adj* discret(ète)

unofficial [ˌʌnə'fɪʃl] *adj* (*news*) officieux(euse); (*strike*) sauvage

unorthodox [ʌn'ɔːθədɒks] *adj* peu orthodoxe; (*REL*) hétérodoxe

unpack ['ʌn'pæk] *vi* défaire sa valise ♦ *vt* (*suitcase*) défaire; (*belongings*) déballer

unpalatable [ʌn'pælətəbl] *adj* (*meal*) mauvais(e); (*truth*) désagréable (à entendre)

unparalleled [ʌn'pærəleld] *adj* incomparable, sans égal

unpleasant [ʌn'pleznt] *adj* déplaisant(e), désagréable

unplug ['ʌn'plʌg] *vt* débrancher

unpopular [ʌn'pɒpjʊlə*] *adj* impopulaire

unprecedented [ʌn'presɪdəntɪd] *adj* sans précédent

unpredictable [ʌnprɪ'dɪktəbl] *adj* imprévisible

unprofessional [ʌnprə'feʃənl] *adj*: ~ **conduct** manquement *m* aux devoirs de la profession

unqualified ['ʌn'kwɒlɪfaɪd] *adj* (*teacher*) non diplômé(e), sans titres; (*success, disaster*) sans réserve, total(e)

unquestionably [ʌn'kwestʃənəblɪ] *adv* incontestablement

unravel [ʌn'rævəl] *vt* démêler

unreal ['ʌn'rɪəl] *adj* irréel(le); (*extraordinary*) incroyable; ~**istic** [ʌnrɪə'lɪstɪk] *adj* irréaliste; peu réaliste

unreasonable [ʌn'riːznəbl] *adj* qui n'est pas raisonnable

unrelated [ʌnrɪ'leɪtɪd] *adj* sans rapport; sans lien de parenté

unrelenting [ʌnrɪ'lentɪŋ] *adj* implacable

unreliable [ʌnrɪ'laɪəbl] *adj* sur qui (*or* quoi) on ne peut pas compter, peu fiable

unremitting [ʌnrɪ'mɪtɪŋ] *adj* inlassable, infatigable, acharné(e)

unreservedly [ʌnrɪ'zɜːvɪdlɪ] *adv* sans réserve

unrest [ʌn'rest] *n* agitation *f*, troubles *mpl*

unroll [ʌn'rəʊl] *vt* dérouler

unruly [ʌn'ruːlɪ] *adj* indiscipliné(e)

unsafe [ʌn'seɪf] *adj* (*in danger*) en danger; (*journey, car*) dangereux(euse)

unsaid ['ʌn'sed] *adj*: **to leave sth** ~ passer qch sous silence

unsatisfactory ['ʌnsætɪs'fæktərɪ] *adj* peu satisfaisant(e)

unsavoury ['ʌn'seɪvərɪ] (*US* **unsavory**) *adj* (*fig*) peu recommandable

unscathed [ʌn'skeɪðd] *adj* indemne

unscrew ['ʌn'skruː] *vt* dévisser

unscrupulous [ʌn'skruːpjʊləs] *adj* sans scrupules

unsettled ['ʌn'setld] *adj* perturbé(e); instable

unshaven ['ʌn'ʃeɪvn] *adj* non *or* mal rasé(e)

unsightly [ʌn'saɪtlɪ] *adj* disgracieux(euse), laid(e)

unskilled ['ʌn'skɪld] *adj*: ~ **worker** manœuvre *m*

unspeakable [ʌn'spiːkəbl] *adj* indicible; (*awful*) innommable

unstable [ʌn'steɪbl] *adj* instable

unsteady [ʌn'stedɪ] *adj* mal assuré(e), chancelant(e), instable

unstuck ['ʌn'stʌk] *adj*: **to come** ~ se décoller; (*plan*) tomber à l'eau

unsuccessful ['ʌnsək'sesful] *adj* (*attempt*) infructueux(euse), vain(e); (*writer, proposal*) qui n'a pas de succès; **to be** ~ (*in attempting sth*) ne pas réussir; ne pas avoir de succès; (*application*) ne pas être retenu(e)

unsuitable ['ʌn'suːtəbl] *adj* qui ne convient pas, peu approprié(e); inopportun(e)

unsure [ʌn'ʃʊə*] *adj* pas sûr(e); **to be** ~ **of o.s.** manquer de confiance en soi

unsuspecting [ʌnsə'spektɪŋ] *adj* qui ne se doute de rien

unsympathetic ['ʌnsɪmpə'θetɪk] *adj* (*person*) antipathique; (*attitude*) peu compatissant(e)

untapped ['ʌn'tæpt] *adj* (*resources*) inexploité(e)

unthinkable [ʌn'θɪŋkəbl] *adj* impensable, inconcevable

untidy [ʌn'taɪdɪ] *adj* (*room*) en désordre; (*appearance, person*) débraillé(e); (*person: in character*) sans ordre, désordonné

untie ['ʌn'taɪ] *vt* (*knot, parcel*) défaire; (*prisoner, dog*) détacher

until [ən'tɪl] *prep* jusqu'à; (*after negative*) avant ♦ *conj* jusqu'à ce que +*sub*; (*in past, after negative*) avant que +*sub*; ~ **he comes** jusqu'à ce qu'il vienne, jusqu'à son arrivée; ~ **now** jusqu'à présent, jusqu'ici; ~ **then** jusque-là

untimely [ʌn'taɪmlɪ] *adj* inopportun(e); (*death*) prématuré(e)

untold ['ʌn'təʊld] *adj* (*story*) jamais raconté(e); (*wealth*) incalculable; (*joy, suffering*) indescriptible

untoward [ʌntə'wɔːd] *adj* fâcheux(euse), malencontreux(euse)

unused[1] [ʌn'juːzd] *adj* (*clothes*) neuf(neuve)

unused[2] [ʌn'juːst] *adj*: **to be unused to sth/to doing sth** ne pas avoir l'habitude de qch/de faire qch

unusual [ʌn'juːʒʊəl] *adj* insolite, exceptionnel(le), rare

unveil [ʌn'veɪl] *vt* dévoiler

unwanted [ʌn'wɒntɪd] *adj* (*child, pregnancy*) non désiré(e); (*clothes etc*) à donner

unwelcome [ʌn'welkəm] *adj* importun(e); (*news*) fâcheux(euse)

unwell ['ʌn'wel] *adj* souffrant(e); **to feel** ~ ne pas se sentir bien

unwieldy [ʌn'wiːldɪ] *adj* (*object*) difficile à

manier; (*system*) lourd(e)

unwilling ['ʌn'wɪlɪŋ] *adj*: **to be ~ to do** ne pas vouloir faire; **~ly** *adv* à contrecœur, contre son gré

unwind ['ʌn'waɪnd] (*irreg*) *vt* dérouler ♦ *vi* (*relax*) se détendre

unwise [ʌn'waɪz] *adj* irréfléchi(e), imprudent(e)

unwitting [ʌn'wɪtɪŋ] *adj* involontaire

unworkable [ʌn'wɜːkəbl] *adj* (*plan*) impraticable

unworthy [ʌn'wɜːðɪ] *adj* indigne

unwrap ['ʌn'ræp] *vt* défaire; ouvrir

unwritten ['ʌn'rɪtn] *adj* (*agreement*) tacite

KEYWORD

up [ʌp] *prep*: **he went ~ the stairs/the hill** il a monté l'escalier/la colline; **the cat was ~ a tree** le chat était dans un arbre; **they live further ~ the street** ils habitent plus haut dans la rue
♦ *adv* **1** (*upwards, higher*): **~ in the sky/the mountains** (là-haut) dans le ciel/les montagnes; **put it a bit higher ~** mettez-le un peu plus haut; **~ there** là-haut; **~ above** au-dessus
2: **to be ~** (*out of bed*) être levé(e); (*prices*) avoir augmenté *or* monté
3: **~ to** (*as far as*) jusqu'à; **~ to now** jusqu'à présent
4: **to be ~ to** (*depending on*): **it's ~ to you** c'est à vous de décider; (*equal to*): **he's not ~ to it** (*job, task etc*) il n'en est pas capable; (*inf*: *be doing*): **what is he ~ to?** qu'est-ce qu'il peut bien faire?
♦ *n*: **~s and downs** hauts et bas *mpl*

---

up-and-coming [ʌpənd'kʌmɪŋ] *adj* plein(e) d'avenir *or* de promesses

upbringing ['ʌpbrɪŋɪŋ] *n* éducation *f*

update [ʌp'deɪt] *vt* mettre à jour

upgrade *vt* (*house*) moderniser; (*job*) revaloriser; (*employee*) promouvoir

upheaval [ʌp'hiːvəl] *n* bouleversement *m*; branle-bas *m*; crise *f*

uphill ['ʌp'hɪl] *adj* qui monte; (*fig*: *task*) difficile, pénible ♦ *adv* (*face, look*) en amont; **to go ~** monter

uphold [ʌp'həʊld] (*irreg*) *vt* (*law, decision*) maintenir

upholstery [ʌp'həʊlstərɪ] *n* rembourrage *m*; (*cover*) tissu *m* d'ameublement; (*of car*) garniture *f*

upkeep ['ʌpkiːp] *n* entretien *m*

upon [ə'pɒn] *prep* sur

upper ['ʌpə*] *adj* supérieur(e); du dessus ♦ *n* (*of shoe*) empeigne *f*; **~-class** *adj* de la haute société, aristocratique; **~ hand** *n*: **to have the ~ hand** avoir le dessus; **~most** *adj* le(la) plus haut(e); **what was ~most in my mind** ce à quoi je pensais surtout

upright ['ʌpraɪt] *adj* droit(e); vertical(e);

(*fig*) droit, honnête

uprising ['ʌpraɪzɪŋ] *n* soulèvement *m*, insurrection *f*

uproar ['ʌprɔː*] *n* tumulte *m*; (*protests*) tempête *f* de protestations

uproot [ʌp'ruːt] *vt* déraciner

upset [*n* 'ʌpset, *vb, adj* ʌp'set] (*irreg*: *like* **set**) *n* bouleversement *m*; (*stomach ~*) indigestion *f* ♦ *vt* (*glass etc*) renverser; (*plan*) déranger; (*person*: *offend*) contrarier; (: *grieve*) faire de la peine à; bouleverser ♦ *adj* contrarié(e); peiné(e); (*stomach*) dérangé(e)

upshot ['ʌpʃɒt] *n* résultat *m*

upside-down ['ʌpsaɪd'daʊn] *adv* à l'envers; **to turn ~** mettre sens dessus dessous

upstairs ['ʌp'steəz] *adv* en haut ♦ *adj* (*room*) du dessus, d'en haut ♦ *n*: **the ~** l'étage *m*

upstart ['ʌpstɑːt] (*pej*) *n* parvenu(e)

upstream ['ʌp'striːm] *adv* en amont

uptake ['ʌpteɪk] *n*: **to be quick/slow on the ~** comprendre vite/être lent à comprendre

uptight ['ʌp'taɪt] (*inf*) *adj* très tendu(e), crispé(e)

up-to-date ['ʌptə'deɪt] *adj* moderne; (*information*) très récent(e)

upturn ['ʌptɜːn] *n* (*in luck*) retournement *m*; (*COMM*: *in market*) hausse *f*

upward ['ʌpwəd] *adj* ascendant(e); vers le haut; **~(s)** *adv* vers le haut; **~(s) of 200** 200 et plus

urban ['ɜːbən] *adj* urbain(e)

urbane [ɜː'beɪn] *adj* urbain(e), courtois(e)

urchin ['ɜːtʃɪn] *n* polisson *m*

urge [ɜːdʒ] *n* besoin *m*; envie *f*; forte envie, désir *m* ♦ *vt*: **to ~ sb to do** exhorter qn à faire, pousser qn à faire; recommander vivement à qn de faire

urgency ['ɜːdʒənsɪ] *n* urgence *f*; (*of tone*) insistance *f*

urgent ['ɜːdʒənt] *adj* urgent(e); (*tone*) insistant(e), pressant(e)

urinal *n* urinoir *m*; (*vessel*) urinal *m*

urine ['jʊərɪn] *n* urine *f*

urn [ɜːn] *n* urne *f*; (*also: tea ~*) fontaine *f* à thé

US *n abbr* = **United States**

us [ʌs] *pron* nous; *see also* **me**

USA *n abbr* = **United States of America**

use [*n* juːs, *vb* juːz] *n* emploi *m*, utilisation *f*, usage *m*; (*usefulness*) utilité *f* ♦ *vt* se servir de, utiliser, employer; **in ~** en usage; **out of ~** hors d'usage; **to be of ~** servir, être utile; **it's no ~** ça ne sert à rien; **she ~d to do it** elle le faisait (autrefois), elle avait coutume de le faire; **~d to**: **to be ~d to** avoir l'habitude de, être habitué(e) à; **~ up** *vt* finir, épuiser, consommer; **~d** *adj* (*car*) d'occasion; **~ful** *adj* utile; **~fulness** *n* utilité *f*; **~less** *adj* inutile; (*person*: *hope-*

less) nul(le); ~**r** *n* utilisateur(trice), usager *m*; ~**r-friendly** *adj* (*computer*) convivial(e), facile d'emploi

usher ['ʌʃə*] *n* (*at wedding ceremony*) placeur *m*; ~**ette** [ʌʃə'ret] *n* (*in cinema*) ouvreuse *f*

usual ['juːʒuəl] *adj* habituel(le); **as** ~ comme d'habitude; ~**ly** *adv* d'habitude, d'ordinaire

utensil [juːˈtensl] *n* ustensile *m*

uterus ['juːtərəs] *n* utérus *m*

utility [juːˈtɪlɪtɪ] *n* utilité *f*; (*also: public* ~) service public; ~ **room** *n* buanderie *f*

utmost ['ʌtməust] *adj* extrême, le(la) plus grand(e) ♦ *n*: **to do one's** ~ faire tout son possible

utter ['ʌtə*] *adj* total(e), complet(ète) ♦ *vt* (*words*) prononcer, proférer; (*sounds*) émettre; ~**ance** *n* paroles *fpl*; ~**ly** *adv* complètement, totalement

U-turn ['juːˈtɜːn] *n* demi-tour *m*

V v

v. *abbr* = **verse; versus; volt;** (= *vide*) voir

vacancy ['veɪkənsɪ] *n* (*BRIT: job*) poste vacant; (*room*) chambre *f* disponible

vacant ['veɪkənt] *adj* (*seat etc*) libre, disponible; (*expression*) distrait(e); ~ **lot** (*US*) *n* terrain inoccupé; (*for sale*) terrain à vendre

vacate [vəˈkeɪt] *vt* quitter

vacation [vəˈkeɪʃən] *n* vacances *fpl*

vaccinate ['væksɪneɪt] *vt* vacciner

vacuum ['vækjum] *n* vide *m*; ~ **cleaner** *n* aspirateur *m*; ~-**packed** *adj* emballé(e) sous vide

vagina [vəˈdʒaɪnə] *n* vagin *m*

vagrant ['veɪgrənt] *n* vagabond(e)

vague [veɪg] *adj* vague, imprécis(e); (*blurred: photo, outline*) flou(e); ~**ly** *adv* vaguement

vain [veɪn] *adj* (*useless*) vain(e); (*conceited*) vaniteux(euse); **in** ~ en vain

valentine ['væləntaɪn] *n* (*also:* ~ *card*) carte *f* de la Saint-Valentin; (*person*) bien-aimé(e) (*le jour de la Sainte-Valentin*)

valiant ['vælɪənt] *adj* vaillant(e)

valid ['vælɪd] *adj* valable; (*document*) valable, valide

valley ['vælɪ] *n* vallée *f*

valour ['vælə*] (*US* **valor**) *n* courage *m*

valuable ['væljuəbl] *adj* (*jewel*) de valeur; (*time, help*) précieux(euse); ~**s** *npl* objets *mpl* de valeur

valuation [væljuˈeɪʃən] *n* (*price*) estimation *f*; (*quality*) appréciation *f*

value ['væljuː] *n* valeur *f* ♦ *vt* (*fix price*) évaluer, expertiser; (*appreciate*) apprécier; ~ **added tax** (*BRIT*) *n* taxe *f* à la valeur ajoutée; ~**d** *adj* (*person*) estimé(e); (*advice*) précieux(euse)

valve [vælv] *n* (*in machine*) soupape *f*, valve *f*; (*MED*) valve, valvule *f*

van [væn] *n* (*AUT*) camionnette *f*

vandal ['vændl] *n* vandale *m/f*; ~**ism** *n* vandalisme *m*; ~**ize** ['vændəlaɪz] *vt* saccager

vanguard ['vængɑːd] *n* (*fig*): **in the** ~ **of** à l'avant-garde de

vanilla [vəˈnɪlə] *n* vanille *f*

vanish ['vænɪʃ] *vi* disparaître

vanity ['vænɪtɪ] *n* vanité *f*

vantage point ['vɑːntɪdʒ-] *n* bonne position

vapour ['veɪpə*] (*US* **vapor**) *n* vapeur *f*; (*on window*) buée *f*

variable ['vɛərɪəbl] *adj* variable; (*mood*) changeant(e)

variance ['vɛərɪəns] *n*: **to be at** ~ (**with**) être en désaccord (avec); (*facts*) être en contradiction (avec)

varicose ['værɪkəus] *adj*: ~ **veins** varices *fpl*

varied ['vɛərɪd] *adj* varié(e), divers(e)

variety [vəˈraɪətɪ] *n* variété *f*; (*quantity*) nombre *m*, quantité *f*; ~ **show** *n* (spectacle *m* de) variétés *fpl*

various ['vɛərɪəs] *adj* divers(e), différent(e); (*several*) divers, plusieurs

varnish ['vɑːnɪʃ] *n* vernis *m* ♦ *vt* vernir

vary ['vɛərɪ] *vt, vi* varier, changer

vase [vɑːz] *n* vase *m*

Vaseline ['væsɪliːn] (®) *n* vaseline *f*

vast [vɑːst] *adj* vaste, immense; (*amount, success*) énorme

VAT [væt] *n abbr* (= *value added tax*) TVA *f*

vat [væt] *n* cuve *f*

vault [vɔːlt] *n* (*of roof*) voûte *f*; (*tomb*) caveau *m*; (*in bank*) salle *f* des coffres; chambre forte ♦ *vt* (*also:* ~ *over*) sauter (d'un bond)

vaunted ['vɔːntɪd] *adj*: **much-vaunted** tant vanté(e)

VCR *n abbr* = **video cassette recorder**

VD *n abbr* = **venereal disease**

VDU *n abbr* = **visual display unit**

veal [viːl] *n* veau *m*

veer [vɪə*] *vi* tourner; virer

vegetable ['vedʒətəbl] *n* légume *m* ♦ *adj* végétal(e)

vegetarian [vedʒɪˈtɛərɪən] *adj, n* végétarien(ne)

vehement ['viːɪmənt] *adj* violent(e), impétueux(euse); (*impassioned*) ardent(e)

vehicle ['viːɪkl] *n* véhicule *m*

veil [veɪl] *n* voile *m*

vein [veɪn] *n* veine *f*; *(on leaf)* nervure *f*

velocity [vɪ'lɒsɪtɪ] *n* vitesse *f*

velvet ['velvɪt] *n* velours *m*

vending machine ['vendɪŋ-] *n* distributeur *m* automatique

veneer [və'nɪə*] *n* *(on furniture)* placage *m*; *(fig)* vernis *m*

venereal [vɪ'nɪərɪəl] *adj*: ~ **disease** maladie vénérienne

Venetian blind [vɪ'ni:ʃən-] *n* store vénitien

vengeance ['vendʒəns] *n* vengeance *f*; **with a** ~ *(fig)* vraiment, pour de bon

venison ['venɪsn] *n* venaison *f*

venom ['venəm] *n* venin *m*

vent [vent] *n* conduit *m* d'aération; *(in dress, jacket)* fente *f* ♦ *vt* *(fig: one's feelings)* donner libre cours à

ventilator ['ventɪleɪtə*] *n* ventilateur *m*

ventriloquist [ven'trɪləkwɪst] *n* ventriloque *m/f*

venture ['ventʃə*] *n* entreprise *f* ♦ *vt* risquer, hasarder ♦ *vi* s'aventurer, se risquer

venue ['venju:] *n* lieu *m*

verb [vɜ:b] *n* verbe *m*; ~**al** *adj* verbal(e); *(translation)* littéral(e)

verbatim [vɜ:'beɪtɪm] *adj, adv* mot pour mot

verdict ['vɜ:dɪkt] *n* verdict *m*

verge [vɜ:dʒ] *n* *(BRIT)* bord *m*, bas-côté *m*; **"soft ~s"** *(: AUT)* "accotement non stabilisé"; **on the** ~ **of doing** sur le point de faire; ~ **on** *vt fus* approcher de

verify ['verɪfaɪ] *vt* vérifier; *(confirm)* confirmer

vermin ['vɜ:mɪn] *npl* animaux *mpl* nuisibles; *(insects)* vermine *f*

vermouth ['vɜ:məθ] *n* vermouth *m*

versatile ['vɜ:sətaɪl] *adj* polyvalent(e)

verse [vɜ:s] *n* *(poetry)* vers *mpl*; *(stanza)* strophe *f*; *(in Bible)* verset *m*

version ['vɜ:ʃən] *n* version *f*

versus ['vɜ:səs] *prep* contre

vertical ['vɜ:tɪkəl] *adj* vertical(e) ♦ *n* verticale *f*

vertigo ['vɜ:tɪgəu] *n* vertige *m*

verve [vɜ:v] *n* brio *m*; enthousiasme *m*

very ['verɪ] *adv* très ♦ *adj*: **the** ~ **book which** le livre même que; **the** ~ **last** le tout dernier; **at the** ~ **least** tout au moins; ~ **much** beaucoup

vessel ['vesl] *n* *(ANAT, NAUT)* vaisseau *m*; *(container)* récipient *m*

vest [vest] *n* *(BRIT)* tricot *m* de corps; *(US: waistcoat)* gilet *m*

vested interest ['vestɪd-] *n* *(COMM)* droits acquis

vet [vet] *n abbr* *(BRIT: = veterinary surgeon)* vétérinaire *m/f* ♦ *vt* examiner soigneusement

veteran ['vetərn] *n* vétéran *m*; *(also: war ~)* ancien combattant

veterinarian [vetrə'neərɪən] *(US)* *n* = **veterinary surgeon**

veterinary surgeon ['vetrɪnərɪ-] *(BRIT)* *n* vétérinaire *m/f*

veto ['vi:təu] *(pl ~es)* *n* veto *m* ♦ *vt* opposer son veto à

vex [veks] *vt* fâcher, contrarier; ~**ed** *adj* *(question)* controversé(e)

via ['vaɪə] *prep* par, via

viable ['vaɪəbl] *adj* viable

vibrate [vaɪ'breɪt] *vi* vibrer

vicar ['vɪkə*] *n* pasteur *m* *(de l'Église anglicane)*; ~**age** *n* presbytère *m*

vicarious [vɪ'keərɪəs] *adj* indirect(e)

vice [vaɪs] *n* *(evil)* vice *m*; *(TECH)* étau *m*

vice- *prefix* vice-

vice squad *n* ≈ brigade mondaine

vice versa ['vaɪsɪ'vɜ:sə] *adv* vice versa

vicinity [vɪ'sɪnɪtɪ] *n* environs *mpl*, alentours *mpl*

vicious ['vɪʃəs] *adj* *(remark)* cruel(le), méchant(e); *(blow)* brutal(e); *(dog)* méchant(e), dangereux(euse); *(horse)* vicieux(euse); ~ **circle** *n* cercle vicieux

victim ['vɪktɪm] *n* victime *f*

victor ['vɪktə*] *n* vainqueur *m*

Victorian [vɪk'tɔ:rɪən] *adj* victorien(ne)

victory ['vɪktərɪ] *n* victoire *f*

video ['vɪdɪəu] *cpd* vidéo *inv* ♦ *n* *(~ film)* vidéo *f*; *(also: ~ cassette)* vidéocassette *f*; *(: ~ cassette recorder)* magnétoscope *m*; ~ **tape** *n* bande *f* vidéo *inv*; *(cassette)* vidéocassette *f*

vie [vaɪ] *vi*: **to** ~ **with** rivaliser avec

Vienna [vɪ'enə] *n* Vienne

Vietnam [vjet'næm] *n* Viêt-nam *m*, Vietnam *m*; ~**ese** [vjetnə'mi:z] *adj* vietnamien(ne) ♦ *n inv* Vietnamien(ne); *(LING)* vietnamien *m*

view [vju:] *n* vue *f*; *(opinion)* avis *m*, vue ♦ *vt* voir, regarder; *(situation)* considérer; *(house)* visiter; **in full** ~ **of** sous les yeux de; **in** ~ **of the weather/the fact that** étant donné le temps/que; **in my** ~ à mon avis; ~**er** *n* *(TV)* téléspectateur(trice); ~**finder** *n* viseur *m*; ~**point** *n* point *m* de vue

vigorous ['vɪgərəs] *adj* vigoureux(euse)

vile [vaɪl] *adj* *(action)* vil(e); *(smell, food)* abominable; *(temper)* massacrant(e)

villa ['vɪlə] *n* villa *f*

village ['vɪlɪdʒ] *n* village *m*; ~**r** *n* villageois(e)

villain ['vɪlən] *n* *(scoundrel)* scélérat *m*; *(BRIT: criminal)* bandit *m*; *(in novel etc)* traître *m*

vindicate ['vɪndɪkeɪt] *vt* *(person)* innocenter; *(action)* justifier

vindictive [vɪn'dɪktɪv] *adj* vindicatif(ive), rancunier(ère)

vine [vaɪn] *n* vigne *f*; *(climbing plant)* plante grimpante

vinegar ['vɪnɪgə*] n vinaigre m
vineyard ['vɪnjəd] n vignoble m
vintage ['vɪntɪdʒ] n (year) année f, millésime m; ~ **car** n voiture f d'époque; ~ **wine** n vin m de grand cru
viola [vɪ'əulə] n (MUS) alto m
violate ['vaɪəleɪt] vt violer
violence ['vaɪələns] n violence f
violent ['vaɪələnt] adj violent(e)
violet ['vaɪələt] adj violet(te) ♦ n (colour) violet m; (plant) violette f
violin [vaɪə'lɪn] n violon m; ~**ist** n violoniste m/f
VIP n abbr (= very important person) V.I.P. m
virgin ['vɜːdʒɪn] n vierge f ♦ adj vierge
Virgo ['vɜːgəu] n la Vierge
virile ['vɪraɪl] adj viril(e)
virtually ['vɜːtjuəlɪ] adv (almost) pratiquement
virtual reality n (COMPUT) réalité virtuelle
virtue ['vɜːtjuː] n vertu f; (advantage) mérite m, avantage m; **by** ~ **of** en vertu or en raison de; **virtuous** ['vɜːtjuəs] adj vertueux(euse)
virus ['vaɪərəs] n (also: COMPUT) virus m
visa ['viːzə] n visa m
visibility [vɪzɪ'bɪlɪtɪ] n visibilité f
visible ['vɪzəbl] adj visible
vision ['vɪʒən] n (sight) vue f, vision f; (foresight, in dream) vision
visit ['vɪzɪt] n visite f; (stay) séjour m ♦ vt (person) rendre visite à; (place) visiter; ~**ing hours** npl (in hospital etc) heures fpl de visite; ~**or** n visiteur(euse); (to one's house) visite f, invité(e)
visor ['vaɪzə*] n visière f
vista ['vɪstə] n vue f
visual ['vɪzjuəl] adj visuel(le); ~ **aid** n support visuel; ~ **display unit** n console f de visualisation, visuel m; ~**ize** ['vɪzjuəlaɪz] vt se représenter, s'imaginer
vital ['vaɪtl] adj vital(e); (person) plein(e) d'entrain; ~**ly** adv (important) absolument; ~ **statistics** npl (fig) mensurations fpl
vitamin ['vɪtəmɪn] n vitamine f
vivacious [vɪ'veɪʃəs] adj animé(e), qui a de la vivacité
vivid ['vɪvɪd] adj (account) vivant(e); (light, imagination) vif(vive); ~**ly** adv (describe) d'une manière vivante; (remember) de façon précise
V-neck ['viː'nek] n décolleté m en V
vocabulary [vəu'kæbjulərɪ] n vocabulaire m
vocal ['vəukəl] adj (noise) vocal(e); (articulate) qui sait s'exprimer; ~ **cords** npl cordes vocales
vocation [vəu'keɪʃən] n vocation f; ~**al** adj professionnel(le)
vociferous [vəu'sɪfərəs] adj bruyant(e)
vodka ['vɒdkə] n vodka f
vogue [vəug] n: **in** ~ en vogue f

voice [vɔɪs] n voix f ♦ vt (opinion) exprimer, formuler
void [vɔɪd] n vide m ♦ adj nul(le); ~ **of** vide de, dépourvu(e) de
volatile ['vɒlətaɪl] adj volatil(e); (person) versatile; (situation) explosif(ive)
volcano [vɒl'keɪnəu] (pl ~**es**) n volcan m
volition [və'lɪʃən] n: **of one's own** ~ de son propre gré
volley ['vɒlɪ] n (of gunfire) salve f; (of stones etc) grêle f, volée f; (of questions) multitude f, série f; (TENNIS etc) volée f; ~**ball** n volley(-ball) m
volt [vəult] n volt m; ~**age** n tension f, voltage m
volume ['vɒljuːm] n volume m
voluntarily adv volontairement
voluntary ['vɒləntərɪ] adj volontaire; (unpaid) bénévole
volunteer [vɒlən'tɪə*] n volontaire m/f ♦ vt (information) fournir (spontanément) ♦ vi (MIL) s'engager comme volontaire; **to** ~ **to do** se proposer pour faire
vomit ['vɒmɪt] vt, vi vomir
vote [vəut] n vote m, suffrage m; (cast) voix f, vote; (franchise) droit m de vote ♦ vt (elect): **to be** ~**d chairman** etc être élu président etc; (propose): **to** ~ **that** proposer que ♦ vi voter; ~ **of thanks** discours m de remerciement; ~**r** n électeur(trice); **voting** ['vəutɪŋ] n scrutin m, vote m
voucher ['vautʃə*] n (for meal, petrol, gift) bon m
vouch for [vautʃ] vt fus se porter garant de
vow [vau] n vœu m, serment m ♦ vi jurer
vowel ['vauəl] n voyelle f
voyage ['vɔɪdʒ] n voyage m par mer, traversée f; (by spacecraft) voyage
vulgar ['vʌlgə*] adj vulgaire
vulnerable ['vʌlnərəbl] adj vulnérable
vulture ['vʌltʃə*] n vautour m

W w

wad [wɒd] n (of cotton wool, paper) tampon m; (of banknotes etc) liasse f
waddle ['wɒdl] vi se dandiner
wade [weɪd] vi: **to** ~ **through** marcher dans, patauger dans; (fig: book) s'évertuer à lire
wafer ['weɪfə*] n (CULIN) gaufrette f
waffle ['wɒfl] n (CULIN) gaufre f; (inf) verbiage m, remplissage m ♦ vi parler pour ne

rien dire, faire du remplissage
waft [wɑːft] *vt* porter ♦ *vi* flotter
wag [wæg] *vt* agiter, remuer ♦ *vi* remuer
wage [weɪdʒ] *n* (*also*: ~s) salaire *m*, paye *f* ♦ *vt*: **to ~ war** faire la guerre; **~ earner** *n* salarié(e); **~ packet** *n* (enveloppe *f* de) paye *f*
wager ['weɪdʒə*] *n* pari *m*
waggle ['wægl] *vt, vi* remuer
wag(g)on ['wægən] *n* (*horse-drawn*) chariot *m*; (*BRIT: RAIL*) wagon *m* (de marchandises)
wail [weɪl] *vi* gémir; (*siren*) hurler
waist [weɪst] *n* taille *f*; **~coat** (*BRIT*) *n* gilet *m*; **~line** *n* (tour *m* de) taille *f*
wait [weɪt] *n* attente *f* ♦ *vi* attendre; **to keep sb ~ing** faire attendre qn; **to ~ for** attendre; **I can't ~ to ...** (*fig*) je meurs d'envie de ...; **~ behind** *vi* rester (à attendre); **~ on** *vt fus* servir; **~er** *n* garçon *m* (de café), serveur *m*; **~ing** *n*: "no ~ing" (*BRIT: AUT*) "stationnement interdit"; **~ing list** *n* liste *f* d'attente; **~ing room** *n* salle *f* d'attente; **~ress** *n* serveuse *f*
waive [weɪv] *vt* renoncer à, abandonner
wake [weɪk] (*pt* **woke**, ~**d**, *pp* **woken**, ~**d**) *vt* (*also*: ~ **up**) réveiller ♦ *vi* (*also*: ~ **up**) se réveiller ♦ *n* (*for dead person*) veillée *f* mortuaire; (*NAUT*) sillage *m*
Wales [weɪlz] *n* pays *m* de Galles; **the Prince of ~** le prince de Galles
walk [wɔːk] *n* promenade *f*; (*short*) petit tour; (*gait*) démarche *f*; (*path*) chemin *m*; (*in park etc*) allée *f* ♦ *vi* marcher; (*for pleasure, exercise*) se promener ♦ *vt* (*distance*) faire à pied; (*dog*) promener; **10 minutes' ~ from** à 10 minutes à pied de; **from all ~s of life** de toutes conditions sociales; **~ out** *vi* (*audience*) sortir, quitter la salle; (*workers*) se mettre en grève; **~ out on** (*inf*) *vt fus* quitter, plaquer; **~er** *n* (*person*) marcheur(euse); **~ie-talkie** *n* talkie-walkie *m*; **~ing** *n* marche *f* à pied; **~ing shoes** *npl* chaussures *fpl* de marche; **~ing stick** *n* canne *f*; **~out** *n* (*of workers*) grève-surprise *f*; **~over** (*inf*) *n* victoire *f* or examen *m* etc facile; **~way** *n* promenade *f*, cheminement *m* piéton
wall [wɔːl] *n* mur *m*; (*of tunnel, cave etc*) paroi *m*; **~ed** *adj* (*city*) fortifié(e); (*garden*) entouré(e) d'un mur, clos(e)
wallet ['wɒlɪt] *n* portefeuille *m*
wallflower ['wɔːlflaʊə*] *n* giroflée *f*; **to be a ~** (*fig*) faire tapisserie
wallop ['wɒləp] (*BRIT: inf*) *vt* donner un grand coup à
wallow ['wɒləʊ] *vi* se vautrer
wallpaper ['wɔːlpeɪpə*] *n* papier peint ♦ *vt* tapisser
walnut ['wɔːlnʌt] *n* noix *f*; (*tree, wood*) noyer *m*
walrus ['wɔːlrəs] (*pl* ~ *or* ~**es**) *n* morse *m*

waltz [wɔːlts] *n* valse *f* ♦ *vi* valser
wan [wɒn] *adj* pâle; triste
wand [wɒnd] *n* (*also*: **magic ~**) baguette *f* (magique)
wander ['wɒndə*] *vi* (*person*) errer; (*thoughts*) vagabonder, errer ♦ *vt* errer dans
wane [weɪn] *vi* (*moon*) décroître; (*reputation*) décliner
wangle ['wæŋgl] (*BRIT: inf*) *vt* se débrouiller pour avoir; carotter
want [wɒnt] *vt* vouloir; (*need*) avoir besoin de ♦ *n*: **for ~ of** par manque de, faute de; **~s** *npl* (*needs*) besoins *mpl*; **to ~ to do** vouloir faire; **to ~ sb to do** vouloir que qn fasse; **~ed** *adj* (*criminal*) recherché(e) par la police; **"cook ~ed"** "on recherche un cuisinier"; **~ing** *adj*: **to be found ~ing** ne pas être à la hauteur
wanton ['wɒntən] *adj* (*gratuitous*) gratuit(e); (*promiscuous*) dévergondé(e)
war [wɔː*] *n* guerre *f*; **to make ~ (on)** faire la guerre à
ward [wɔːd] *n* (*in hospital*) salle *f*; (*POL*) canton *m*; (*LAW: child*) pupille *m/f*; **~ off** *vt* (*attack, enemy*) repousser, éviter
warden ['wɔːdən] *n* gardien(ne); (*BRIT: of institution*) directeur(trice); (: *also*: **traffic ~**) contractuel(le); (*of youth hostel*) père *m* or mère *f* aubergiste
warder ['wɔːdə*] (*BRIT*) *n* gardien *m* de prison
wardrobe ['wɔːdrəʊb] *n* (*cupboard*) armoire *f*; (*clothes*) garde-robe *f*; (*THEATRE*) costumes *mpl*
warehouse ['wɛəhaʊs] *n* entrepôt *m*
wares [wɛəz] *npl* marchandises *fpl*
warfare ['wɔːfɛə*] *n* guerre *f*
warhead ['wɔːhed] *n* (*MIL*) ogive *f*
warily ['wɛərɪlɪ] *adv* avec prudence
warm [wɔːm] *adj* chaud(e); (*thanks, welcome, applause, person*) chaleureux(euse); **it's ~** il fait chaud; **I'm ~** j'ai chaud; **~ up** *vi* (*person, room*) se réchauffer; (*water*) chauffer; (*athlete*) s'échauffer ♦ *vt* (*food*) (faire) réchauffer, (faire) chauffer; (*engine*) faire chauffer; **~-hearted** *adj* affectueux(euse); **~ly** *adv* chaudement; chaleureusement; **~th** *n* chaleur *f*
warn [wɔːn] *vt* avertir, prévenir; **to ~ sb (not) to do** conseiller à qn de (ne pas) faire; **~ing** *n* avertissement *m*; (*notice*) avis *m*; (*signal*) avertisseur *m*; **~ing light** *n* avertisseur lumineux; **~ing triangle** *n* (*AUT*) triangle *m* de présignalisation
warp [wɔːp] *vi* (*wood*) travailler, se déformer ♦ *vt* (*fig: character*) pervertir
warrant ['wɒrənt] *n* (*guarantee*) garantie *f*; (*LAW: to arrest*) mandat *m* d'arrêt; (: *to search*) mandat de perquisition
warranty ['wɒrəntɪ] *n* garantie *f*
warren ['wɒrən] *n* (*of rabbits*) terrier *m*; (*fig: of streets etc*) dédale *m*

warrior ['wɒrɪə*] n guerrier(ère)
Warsaw ['wɔːsɔː] n Varsovie
warship ['wɔːʃɪp] n navire m de guerre
wart [wɔːt] n verrue f
wartime ['wɔːtaɪm] n: **in ~** en temps de
guerre
wary ['wɛərɪ] adj prudent(e)
was [wɒz, wəz] pt of **be**
wash [wɒʃ] vt laver ♦ vi se laver; (sea): **to
~ over/against sth** inonder/baigner qch ♦
n (clothes) lessive f; (~ing programme) lavage m; (of ship) sillage m; **to have a ~** se
laver, faire sa toilette; **to give sth a ~** laver qch; **~ away** vt (stain) enlever au lavage; (subj: river etc) emporter; **~ off** vi partir
au lavage; **~ up** vi (BRIT) faire la vaisselle;
(US) se débarbouiller; **~able** adj lavable;
~basin (US **~bowl**) n lavabo m; **~cloth**
(US) n gant m de toilette; **~er** n (TECH)
rondelle f, joint m; **~ing** n (dirty) linge m;
(clean) lessive f; **~ing machine** n machine
f à laver; **~ing powder** (BRIT) n lessive f
(en poudre); **~ing-up** n vaisselle f; **~ing-
up liquid** n produit m pour la vaisselle;
~-out (inf) n désastre m; **~room** (US) n
toilettes fpl
wasn't ['wɒznt] = **was not**
wasp [wɒsp] n guêpe f
wastage ['weɪstɪdʒ] n gaspillage m; (in
manufacturing, transport etc) pertes fpl, déchets mpl; **natural ~** départs naturels
waste [weɪst] n gaspillage m; (of time) perte
f; (rubbish) déchets mpl; (also: household
~) ordures fpl ♦ adj (leftover): **~ material**
déchets mpl; (land, ground: in city) à
l'abandon ♦ vt gaspiller; (time, opportunity)
perdre; **~s** npl (area) étendue f désertique;
~ away vi dépérir; **~ disposal unit**
(BRIT) n broyeur m d'ordures; **~ful** adj gas-
pilleur(euse); (process) peu économique; **~
ground** (BRIT) n terrain m vague; **~paper
basket** n corbeille f à papier; **~ pipe** n
(tuyau m de) vidange f
watch [wɒtʃ] n montre f; (act of ~ing) surveillance f; guet m; (MIL: guards) garde f;
(NAUT: guards, spell of duty) quart m ♦ vt
(look at) observer; (: match, programme, TV)
regarder; (spy on, guard) surveiller; (be
careful of) faire attention à ♦ vi regarder;
(keep guard) monter la garde; **~ out** vi faire attention; **~dog** n chien m de garde;
(fig) gardien(ne); **~ful** adj attentif(ive), vigi-
lant(e); **~maker** n horloger(ère); **~man**
(irreg) n see **night**; **~strap** n bracelet m de
montre
water ['wɔːtə*] n eau f ♦ vt (plant, garden)
arroser ♦ vi (eyes) larmoyer; (mouth): **it
makes my mouth ~** j'en ai l'eau à la bouche; **in British ~s** dans les eaux territoria-
les britanniques; **~ down** vt (milk) couper
d'eau; (fig: story) édulcorer; **~colour** (US
~color) n aquarelle f; **~cress** n cresson m

(de fontaine); **~fall** n chute f d'eau; **~
heater** n chauffe-eau m; **~ing can** n arrosoir m; **~ lily** n nénuphar m; **~line** n
(NAUT) ligne f de flottaison; **~logged** adj
(ground) détrempé(e); **~ main** n canalisation f d'eau; **~melon** n pastèque f;
~proof adj imperméable; **~shed** n (GEO)
ligne f de partage des eaux; (fig) moment m
critique, point décisif; **~skiing** n ski m
nautique; **~tight** adj étanche; **~way** n
cours m d'eau navigable; **~works** n (building) station f hydraulique; **~y** adj (coffee,
soup) trop faible; (eyes) humide, lar-
moyant(e)
watt [wɒt] n watt m
wave [weɪv] n vague f; (of hand) geste m,
signe m; (RADIO) onde f; (in hair) ondulation f ♦ vi faire signe de la main; (flag) flotter au vent; (grass) ondoyer ♦ vt (handkerchief) agiter; (stick) brandir; **~length** n
longueur f d'ondes
waver ['weɪvə*] vi vaciller; (voice) trembler;
(person) hésiter
wavy ['weɪvɪ] adj ondulé(e); onduleux(euse)
wax [wæks] n cire f; (for skis) fart m ♦ vt cirer; (car) lustrer; (skis) farter ♦ vi (moon)
croître; **~works** npl personnages mpl de
cire ♦ n musée m de cire
way [weɪ] n chemin m, voie f; (distance)
distance f; (direction) chemin, direction f;
(manner) façon f, manière f; (habit) habitude f, façon; **which ~? - this ~** par où? -
par ici; **on the ~** (en route) en route; **to be
on one's ~** être en route; **to go out of
one's ~ to do** (fig) se donner du mal pour
faire; **to be in the ~** bloquer le passage;
(fig) gêner; **to lose one's ~** perdre son
chemin; **under ~** en cours; **in a ~** dans un
sens; **in some ~s** à certains égards; **no ~!**
(inf) pas question!; **by the ~ ...** à propos
...; **"~ in"** (BRIT) "entrée"; **"~ out"** (BRIT)
"sortie"; **the ~ back** le chemin du retour;
"give ~" (BRIT: AUT) "cédez le passage";
~lay [weɪ'leɪ] (irreg) vt attaquer
wayward ['weɪwəd] adj capricieux(euse),
entêté(e)
we [wiː] pl pron nous
weak [wiːk] adj faible; (health) fragile;
(beam etc) peu solide; **~en** vi faiblir, décliner ♦ vt affaiblir; **~ling** n (physically) gringalet m; (morally etc) faible m/f; **~ness** n
faiblesse f; (fault) point m faible; **to have a
~ness for** avoir un faible pour
wealth [welθ] n (money, resources) riches-
se(s) f(pl); (of details) profusion f; **~y** adj riche
wean [wiːn] vt sevrer
weapon ['wepən] n arme f
wear [wɛə*] (pt **wore**, pp **worn**) n (use)
usage m; (deterioration through use) usure f;
(clothing): **sports/baby~** vêtements mpl de
sport/pour bébés ♦ vt (clothes) porter; (put

on) mettre; (*damage: through use*) user ♦ *vi* (*last*) faire de l'usage; (*rub etc through*) s'user; **town/evening** ~ tenue *f* de ville/soirée; ~ **away** *vt* user, ronger ♦ *vi* (*inscription*) s'effacer; ~ **down** *vt* user; (*strength, person*) épuiser; ~ **off** *vi* disparaître; ~ **out** *vt* user; (*person, strength*) épuiser; ~ **and tear** *n* usure *f*

weary ['wɪərɪ] *adj* (*tired*) épuisé(e); (*dispirited*) las(lasse); abattu(e) ♦ *vi*: **to** ~ **of** se lasser de

weasel ['wiːzl] *n* (ZOOL) belette *f*

weather ['weðə*] *n* temps *m* ♦ *vt* (*tempest, crisis*) essuyer, réchapper à, survivre à; **under the** ~ (*fig: ill*) mal fichu(e); ~**-beaten** *adj* (*person*) hâlé(e); (*building*) dégradé(e) par les intempéries; ~**cock** *n* girouette *f*; ~ **forecast** *n* prévisions *fpl* météorologiques, météo *f*; ~ **man** (*irreg: inf*) *n* météorologue *m*; ~ **vane** *n* = ~**cock**

weave [wiːv] (*pt* **wove**, *pp* **woven**) *vt* (*cloth*) tisser; (*basket*) tresser; ~**r** *n* tisserand(e)

web [web] *n* (*of spider*) toile *f*; (*on foot*) palmure *f*; (*fabric, also fig*) tissu *m*

wed [wed] (*pt, pp* **wedded**) *vt* épouser ♦ *vi* se marier

we'd [wiːd] = **we had; we would**

wedding ['wedɪŋ] *n* mariage *m*; **silver/golden** ~ (**anniversary**) noces *fpl* d'argent/d'or; ~ **day** *n* jour *m* du mariage; ~ **dress** *n* robe *f* de mariée; ~ **ring** *n* alliance *f*

wedge [wedʒ] *n* (*of wood etc*) coin *m*, cale *f*; (*of cake*) part *f* ♦ *vt* (*fix*) caler; (*pack tightly*) enfoncer

Wednesday ['wenzdeɪ] *n* mercredi *m*

wee [wiː] *adj* (SCOTTISH) petit(e); tout(e) petit(e)

weed [wiːd] *n* mauvaise herbe ♦ *vt* désherber; ~**killer** *n* désherbant *m*; ~**y** *adj* (*man*) gringalet

week [wiːk] *n* semaine *f*; **a** ~ **today/on Friday** aujourd'hui/vendredi en huit; ~**day** *n* jour *m* de semaine; (COMM) jour ouvrable; ~**end** *n* week-end *m*; ~**ly** *adv* une fois par semaine, chaque semaine ♦ *adj* hebdomadaire ♦ *n* hebdomadaire *m*

weep [wiːp] (*pt, pp* **wept**) *vi* (*person*) pleurer; ~**ing willow** *n* saule pleureur

weigh [weɪ] *vt, vi* peser; **to** ~ **anchor** lever l'ancre; ~ **down** *vt* (*person, animal*) écraser; (*fig: with worry*) accabler; ~ **up** *vt* examiner

weight [weɪt] *n* poids *m*; **to lose/put on** ~ maigrir/grossir; ~**ing** *n* (*allowance*) indemnité *f*, allocation *f*; ~**lifter** *n* haltérophile *m*; ~**y** *adj* lourd(e); (*important*) de poids, important(e)

weir [wɪə*] *n* barrage *m*

weird [wɪəd] *adj* bizarre

welcome ['welkəm] *adj* bienvenu(e) ♦ *n* accueil *m* ♦ *vt* accueillir; (*also: bid* ~) souhaiter la bienvenue à; (*be glad of*) se réjouir de; **thank you - you're** ~! merci - de rien *or* il n'y a pas de quoi!

weld [weld] *vt* souder; ~**er** *n* soudeur(euse)

welfare ['welfɛə*] *n* (*well-being*) bienêtre *m*; (*social aid*) assistance sociale; ~ **state** *n* Etat-providence *m*; ~ **work** *n* travail social

well [wel] *n* puits *m* ♦ *adv* bien ♦ *adj*: **to be** ~ aller bien ♦ *excl* eh bien!; bon!; enfin!; **as** ~ aussi, également; **as** ~ **as** (*in addition to*) en plus de; ~ **done!** bravo!; **get** ~ **soon** remets-toi vite!; **to do** ~ bien réussir; (*business*) prospérer; ~ **up** *vi* monter

we'll [wiːl] = **we will; we shall**

well: ~**-behaved** ['welbɪ'heɪvd] *adj* sage, obéissant(e); ~**-being** ['welbiːŋ] *n* bien-être *m*; ~**-built** ['wel'bɪlt] *adj* (*person*) bien bâti(e); ~**-deserved** *adj* (bien) mérité(e); ~**-dressed** *adj* bien habillé(e); ~**-heeled** (*inf*) *adj* (*wealthy*) nanti(e)

wellingtons ['welɪŋtənz] *npl* (*also*: **wellington boots**) bottes *fpl* de caoutchouc

well: ~**-known** ['wel'nəʊn] *adj* (*person*) bien connu(e); ~**-mannered** ['wel'mænəd] *adj* bien élevé(e); ~**-meaning** ['wel'miːnɪŋ] *adj* bien intentionné(e); ~**-off** ['wel'ɒf] *adj* aisé(e); ~**-read** ['wel'red] *adj* cultivé(e); ~**-to-do** ['weltə'duː] *adj* aisé(e); ~**-wishers** ['welwɪʃəz] *npl* amis *mpl* et admirateurs *mpl*; (*friends*) amis *mpl*

Welsh [welʃ] *adj* gallois(e) ♦ *n* (LING) gallois *m*; **the** ~ *npl* (*people*) les Gallois *mpl*; ~**man** (*irreg*) *n* Gallois *m*; ~ **rarebit** *n* toast *m* au fromage; ~**woman** (*irreg*) *n* Galloise *f*

went [went] *pt of* **go**

wept [wept] *pt, pp of* **weep**

were [wɜː*] *pt of* **be**

we're [wɪə*] = **we are**

weren't [wɜːnt] = **were not**

west [west] *n* ouest *m* ♦ *adj* ouest *inv*, de *or* à l'ouest ♦ *adv* à *or* vers l'ouest; **the W~** *n* l'Occident *m*, l'Ouest; **the W~ Country** (BRIT) *n* le sud-ouest de l'Angleterre; ~**erly** *adj* (*wind*) d'ouest; (*point*) à l'ouest; ~**ern** *adj* occidental(e), de *or* à l'ouest ♦ *n* (CINEMA) western *m*; **W~ Indian** *adj* antillais(e) ♦ *n* Antillais(e); **W~ Indies** *npl* Antilles *fpl*; ~**ward(s)** *adv* vers l'ouest

wet [wet] *adj* mouillé(e); (*damp*) humide; (*soaked*) trempé(e); (*rainy*) pluvieux(euse) ♦ *n* (BRIT: POL) modéré *m* du parti conservateur; **to get** ~ se mouiller; "~ **paint**" "attention peinture fraîche"; ~ **blanket** *n* (*fig*) rabat-joie *m inv*; ~ **suit** *n* combinaison *f* de plongée

we've [wiːv] = **we have**

whack [wæk] *vt* donner un grand coup à

whale [weɪl] *n* (ZOOL) baleine *f*

wharf [wɔːf] (*pl* **wharves**) *n* quai *m*

---

what [wɒt] *adj* quel(le); ~ **size is he?** quelle taille fait-il?; ~ **colour is it?** de quelle couleur est-ce?; ~ **books do you need?** quels livres vous faut-il?; ~ **a mess!** quel désordre!

♦ *pron* **1** *(interrogative)* que, *prep* +quoi; ~ **are you doing?** que faites-vous?, qu'est-ce que vous faites?; ~ **is happening?** qu'est-ce qui se passe?, que se passe-t-il?; ~ **are you talking about?** de quoi parlez-vous?; ~ **is it called?** comment est-ce que ça s'appelle?; ~ **about me?** et moi?; ~ **about doing ...?** et si on faisait ...?

2 *(relative: subject)* ce qui; *(: direct object)* ce que; *(: indirect object)* ce +*prep* +quoi, ce dont; **I saw** ~ **you did/was on the table** j'ai vu ce que vous avez fait/ce qui était sur la table; **tell me** ~ **you remember** dites-moi ce dont vous vous souvenez

♦ *excl (disbelieving)* quoi!, comment!

---

whatever [wɒt'evə*] *adj:* ~ **book** quel que soit le livre que *(or* qui) +*sub*; n'importe quel livre ♦ *pron:* **do** ~ **is necessary** faites (tout) ce qui est nécessaire; ~ **happens** quoi qu'il arrive; **no reason** ~ pas la moindre raison; **nothing** ~ rien du tout

whatsoever [wɒt'səuevə*] *adj* = **whatever**

wheat [wiːt] *n* blé *m*, froment *m*

wheedle ['wiːdl] *vt:* **to** ~ **sb into doing sth** cajoler *or* enjôler qn pour qu'il fasse qch; **to** ~ **sth out of sb** obtenir qch de qn par des cajoleries

wheel [wiːl] *n* roue *f*; *(also: steering* ~*)* volant *m*; *(NAUT)* gouvernail *m* ♦ *vt (pram etc)* pousser ♦ *vi (birds)* tournoyer; *(also:* ~ *round: person)* virevolter; ~**barrow** *n* brouette *f*; ~**chair** *n* fauteuil roulant; ~ **clamp** *n (AUT)* sabot *m* (de Denver)

wheeze [wiːz] *vi* respirer bruyamment

---

when [wen] *adv* quand; ~ **did he go?** quand est-ce qu'il est parti?

♦ *conj* **1** *(at, during, after the time that)* quand, lorsque; **she was reading** ~ **I came in** elle lisait quand *or* lorsque je suis entré

2 *(on, at which):* **on the day** ~ **I met him** le jour où je l'ai rencontré

3 *(whereas)* alors que; **I thought I was wrong** ~ **in fact I was right** j'ai cru que j'avais tort alors qu'en fait j'avais raison

---

whenever [wen'evə*] *adv* quand donc ♦ *conj* quand; *(every time that)* chaque fois que

where [wεə*] *adv, conj* où; **this is** ~ c'est là que; ~**abouts** ['wεərə'bauts] *adv* où donc ♦ *n:* **nobody knows his** ~**abouts** personne ne sait où il se trouve; ~**as** [wεər'æz] *conj* alors que; ~**by** *adv* par lequel *(or* laquelle *etc)*; ~**upon** *adv* sur quoi

wherever [wεər'evə*] *adv* où donc ♦ *conj* où que +*sub*

wherewithal ['wεəwɪðɔːl] *n* moyens *mpl*

whet [wet] *vt* aiguiser

whether ['weðə*] *conj* si; **I don't know** ~ **to accept or not** je ne sais pas si je dois accepter ou non; **it's doubtful** ~ il est peu probable que +*sub*; ~ **you go or not** que vous y alliez ou non

---

which [wɪtʃ] *adj* **1** *(interrogative: direct, indirect)* quel(le); ~ **picture do you want?** quel tableau voulez-vous?; ~ **one?** lequel(laquelle)?

in ~ **case** auquel cas

♦ *pron* **1** *(interrogative)* lequel(laquelle), lesquels(lesquelles) *pl;* **I don't mind** ~ peu importe lequel; ~ *(of these)* **are yours?** lesquels sont à vous?; **tell me** ~ **you want** dites-moi lesquels *or* ceux que vous voulez

2 *(relative: subject)* qui; *(: object)* que, *prep* +lequel(laquelle); **the apple** ~ **you ate**/~ **is on the table** la pomme que vous avez mangée/qui est sur la table; **the chair on** ~ **you are sitting** la chaise sur laquelle vous êtes assis; **the book of** ~ **you spoke** le livre dont vous avez parlé; **he knew,** ~ **is true/I feared** il le savait, ce qui est vrai/ce que je craignais; **after** ~ après quoi

---

whichever [wɪtʃ'evə*] *adj:* **take** ~ **book you prefer** prenez le livre que vous préférez, peu importe lequel; ~ **book you take** quel que soit le livre que vous preniez

whiff [wɪf] *n* bouffée *f*

while [waɪl] *n* moment *m* ♦ *conj* pendant que; *(as long as)* tant que; *(whereas)* alors que; bien que +*sub*; **for a** ~ pendant quelque temps; ~ **away** *vt (time)* (faire) passer

whim [wɪm] *n* caprice *m*

whimper ['wɪmpə*] *vi* geindre

whimsical ['wɪmzɪkəl] *adj (person)* capricieux(euse); *(look, story)* étrange

whine [waɪn] *vi* gémir, geindre

whip [wɪp] *n* fouet *m*; *(for riding)* cravache *f*; *(POL: person)* chef de file assurant la discipline dans son groupe parlementaire ♦ *vt* fouetter; *(eggs)* battre; *(move quickly)* enlever *(or* sortir) brusquement; ~**ped cream** *n* crème fouettée; ~**-round** *(BRIT) n* collecte *f*

whirl [wɜːl] *vt* faire tourbillonner; faire tournoyer ♦ *vi* tourbillonner; *(dancers)* tournoyer; ~**pool** *n* tourbillon *m*; ~**wind** *n* tornade *f*

whirr [wɜː*] *vi (motor etc)* ronronner; *(: louder)* vrombir

whisk [wɪsk] *n (CULIN)* fouet *m* ♦ *vt* fouetter; *(eggs)* battre; **to** ~ **sb away** *or* **off** emmener qn rapidement

whiskers ['wɪskəz] *npl* (*of animal*) moustaches *fpl*; (*of man*) favoris *mpl*

whisky ['wɪskɪ] (*IRELAND, US* **whiskey**) *n* whisky *m*

whisper ['wɪspə*] *vt, vi* chuchoter

whistle ['wɪsl] *n* (*sound*) sifflement *m*; (*object*) sifflet *m* ♦ *vi* siffler

white [waɪt] *adj* blanc(blanche); (*with fear*) blême ♦ *n* blanc *m*; (*person*) blanc(blanche); ~ **coffee** (*BRIT*) *n* café *m* au lait, (café) crème *m*; ~ **collar worker** *n* employé(e) de bureau; ~ **elephant** *n* (*fig*) objet dispendieux et superflu; ~ **lie** *n* pieux mensonge; ~ **paper** *n* (*POL*) livre blanc; ~**wash** *n* blanchir à la chaux; (*fig*) blanchir ♦ *n* (*paint*) blanc *m* de chaux

whiting ['waɪtɪŋ] *n inv* (*fish*) merlan *m*

Whitsun ['wɪtsn] *n* la Pentecôte

whittle ['wɪtl] *vt*: **to ~ away, ~ down** (*costs*) réduire

whizz [wɪz] *vi*: **to ~ past** *or* **by** passer à toute vitesse; ~ **kid** (*inf*) *n* petit prodige

who [hu:] *pron* qui; ~**dunit** [hu:'dʌnɪt] (*inf*) *n* roman policier

whoever [hu:'evə*] *pron*: ~ **finds it** celui(celle) qui le trouve(, qui que ce soit), quiconque le trouve; **ask ~ you like** demandez à qui vous voulez; ~ **he marries** quelle que soit la personne qu'il épouse; ~ **told you that?** qui a bien pu vous dire ça?

whole [həʊl] *adj* (*complete*) entier(ère), tout(e); (*not broken*) intact(e), complet(ète) ♦ *n* (*all*): **the ~** la totalité de, tout(e) le(la); (*entire unit*) tout *m*; **the ~ of the town** la ville tout entière; **on the ~, as a ~** dans l'ensemble; ~**food(s)** *n(pl)* aliments complets; ~**hearted** *adj* sans réserve(s); ~**meal** (*BRIT*) *adj* (*bread, flour*) complet(ète); ~**sale** (*vente f en*) gros *m* ♦ *adj* (*price*) de gros; (*destruction*) systématique ♦ *adv* en gros; ~**saler** *n* grossiste *m/f*; ~**some** *adj* sain(e); ~**wheat** *adj* = ~**meal**; **wholly** ['həʊlɪ] *adv* entièrement, tout à fait

whom [hu:m] *pron* **1** (*interrogative*) qui; ~ **did you see?** qui avez-vous vu?; **to ~ did you give it?** à qui l'avez-vous donné?

2 (*relative*) que, *prep* + qui; **the man ~ I saw/to ~ I spoke** l'homme que j'ai vu/à qui j'ai parlé

whooping cough ['hu:pɪŋ-] *n* coqueluche *f*

whore [hɔ:*] (*inf: pej*) *n* putain *f*

whose [hu:z] *adj* **1** (*possessive: interrogative*): ~ **book is this?** à qui est ce livre?; ~ **pencil have you taken?** à qui est le crayon que vous avez pris?, c'est le crayon de qui

que vous avez pris?; ~ **daughter are you?** de qui êtes-vous la fille?

2 (*possessive: relative*): **the man ~ son you rescued** l'homme dont *or* de qui vous avez sauvé le fils; **the girl ~ sister you were speaking to** la fille à la sœur de qui *or* de laquelle vous parliez; **the woman ~ car was stolen** la femme dont la voiture a été volée

♦ *pron* à qui; ~ **is this?** à qui est ceci?; **I know ~ it is** je sais à qui c'est

why [waɪ] *adv* pourquoi ♦ *excl* eh bien!, tiens!; **the reason ~** la raison pour laquelle; **tell me ~** dites-moi pourquoi; ~ **not?** pourquoi pas?; ~**ever** *adv* pourquoi donc, mais pourquoi

wicked ['wɪkɪd] *adj* mauvais(e), méchant(e); (*crime*) pervers(e); (*mischievous*) malicieux(euse)

wicket ['wɪkɪt] *n* (*CRICKET*) guichet *m*; terrain *m* (*entre les deux guichets*)

wide [waɪd] *adj* large; (*area, knowledge*) vaste, très étendu(e); (*choice*) grand(e) ♦ *adv*: **to open ~** ouvrir tout grand; **to shoot ~** tirer à côté; ~**angle lens** *n* objectif *m* grand angle; ~**awake** *adj* bien éveillé(e); ~**ly** *adv* (*differing*) radicalement; (*spaced*) sur une grande étendue; (*believed*) généralement; (*travel*) beaucoup; ~**n** *vt* élargir ♦ *vi* s'élargir; ~ **open** *adj* grand(e) ouvert(e); ~**spread** *adj* (*belief etc*) très répandu(e)

widow ['wɪdəʊ] *n* veuve *f*; ~**ed** *adj* veuf(veuve); ~**er** *n* veuf *m*

width [wɪdθ] *n* largeur *f*

wield [wi:ld] *vt* (*sword*) manier; (*power*) exercer

wife [waɪf] (*pl* **wives**) *n* femme *f*, épouse *f*

wig [wɪg] *n* perruque *f*

wiggle ['wɪgl] *vt* agiter, remuer

wild [waɪld] *adj* sauvage; (*sea*) déchaîné(e); (*idea, life*) fou(folle); (*behaviour*) extravagant(e), déchaîné(e); ~**s** *npl* (*remote area*) régions *fpl* sauvages; **to make a ~ guess** émettre une hypothèse à tout hasard; ~**erness** ['wɪldənəs] *n* désert *m*, région *f* sauvage; ~**goose chase** *n* (*fig*) fausse piste; ~**life** *n* (*animals*) faune *f*; ~**ly** *adv* (*behave*) de manière déchaînée; (*applaud*) frénétiquement; (*hit, guess*) au hasard; (*happy*) follement

wilful ['wɪlful] (*US* **willful**) *adj* (*person*) obstiné(e); (*action*) délibéré(e)

will [wɪl] (*vt: pt, pp* **willed**) *aux vb* **1** (*forming future tense*): **I ~ finish it tomorrow** je le finirai demain; **I ~ have finished it by tomorrow** je l'aurai fini d'ici demain; ~ **you do it? - yes I ~/no I won't** le ferez-vous? - oui/non

2 (*in conjectures, predictions*): **he ~** *or* **he'll**

be there by now il doit être arrivé à l'heure qu'il est; that ~ be the postman ça doit être le facteur
3 (*in commands, requests, offers*): ~ **you be quiet!** voulez-vous bien vous taire!; ~ **you help me?** est-ce que vous pouvez m'aider?; ~ **you have a cup of tea?** voulez-vous une tasse de thé?; **I won't put up with it!** je ne le tolérerai pas!
♦ *vt*: **to** ~ **sb to do** souhaiter ardemment que qn fasse; **he ~ed himself to go on** par un suprême effort de volonté, il continua
♦ *n* volonté *f*; testament *m*

willing ['wɪlɪŋ] *adj* de bonne volonté, serviable; **he's** ~ **to do it** il est disposé à le faire, il veut bien le faire; ~**ly** *adv* volontiers; ~**ness** *n* bonne volonté
willow ['wɪləʊ] *n* saule *m*
willpower ['wɪl'paʊə*] *n* volonté *f*
willy-nilly ['wɪlɪ'nɪlɪ] *adv* bon gré mal gré
wilt [wɪlt] *vi* dépérir; (*flower*) se faner
wily ['waɪlɪ] *adj* rusé(e)
win [wɪn] (*pt, pp* **won**) *n* (*in sports etc*) victoire *f* ♦ *vt* gagner; (*prize*) remporter; (*popularity*) acquérir ♦ *vi* gagner; ~ **over** *vt* convaincre; ~ **round** (*BRIT*) *vt* = ~ **over**
wince [wɪns] *vi* tressaillir
winch [wɪntʃ] *n* treuil *m*
wind[1] [wɪnd] *n* (*also MED*) vent *m*; (*breath*) souffle *m* ♦ *vt* (*take breath*) couper le souffle à
wind[2] [waɪnd] (*pt, pp* **wound**) *vt* enrouler; (*wrap*) envelopper; (*clock, toy*) remonter ♦ *vi* (*road, river*) serpenter; ~ **up** *vt* (*clock*) remonter; (*debate*) terminer, clôturer
windfall ['wɪndfɔːl] *n* coup *m* de chance
winding ['waɪndɪŋ] *adj* (*road*) sinueux(euse); (*staircase*) tournant(e)
wind instrument *n* (*MUS*) instrument *m* à vent
windmill ['wɪndmɪl] *n* moulin *m* à vent
window ['wɪndəʊ] *n* fenêtre *f*; (*in car, train, also:* ~ **pane**) vitre *f*; (*in shop etc*) vitrine *f*; ~ **box** *n* jardinière *f*; ~ **cleaner** *n* (*person*) laveur(euse) de vitres; ~ **ledge** *n* rebord *m* de la fenêtre; ~ **pane** *n* vitre *f*, carreau *m*; ~**-shopping** *n*: **to go** ~**-shopping** faire du lèche-vitrines; ~**sill** *n* (*inside*) appui *m* de la fenêtre; (*outside*) rebord *m* de la fenêtre
windpipe ['wɪndpaɪp] *n* trachée *f*
wind power *n* énergie éolienne
windscreen ['wɪndskriːn] *n* pare-brise *m inv*; ~ **washer** *n* lave-glace *m inv*; ~ **wiper** *n* essuie-glace *m inv*
windshield ['wɪndʃiːld] (*US*) *n* = **windscreen**
windswept ['wɪndswept] *adj* balayé(e) par le vent; (*person*) ébouriffé(e)
windy ['wɪndɪ] *adj* venteux(euse); **it's** ~ il y a du vent
wine [waɪn] *n* vin *m*; ~ **bar** *n* bar *m* à vin;

~ **cellar** *n* cave *f* à vin; ~ **glass** *n* verre *m* à vin; ~ **list** *n* carte *f* des vins; ~ **waiter** *n* sommelier *m*
wing [wɪŋ] *n* aile *f*; ~**s** *npl* (*THEATRE*) coulisses *fpl*; ~**er** *n* (*SPORT*) ailier *m*
wink [wɪŋk] *n* clin *m* d'œil ♦ *vi* faire un clin d'œil; (*blink*) cligner des yeux
winner ['wɪnə*] *n* gagnant(e)
winning ['wɪnɪŋ] *adj* (*team*) gagnant(e); (*goal*) décisif(ive); ~**s** *npl* gains *mpl*
winter ['wɪntə*] *n* hiver *m*; **in** ~ en hiver; ~ **sports** *npl* sports *mpl* d'hiver; **wintry** ['wɪntrɪ] *adj* hivernal(e)
wipe [waɪp] *n*: **to give sth a** ~ donner un coup de torchon (*or* de chiffon *or* d'éponge) à qch ♦ *vt* essuyer; (*erase: tape*) effacer; ~ **off** *vt* enlever; ~ **out** *vt* (*debt*) éteindre, amortir; (*memory*) effacer; (*destroy*) anéantir; ~ **up** *vt* essuyer
wire ['waɪə*] *n* fil *m* (de fer); (*ELEC*) fil électrique; (*TEL*) télégramme *m* ♦ *vt* (*house*) faire l'installation électrique de; (*also:* ~ **up**) brancher; (*person: send telegram to*) télégraphier à; ~**less** ['waɪəlɪs] (*BRIT*) *n* poste *m* de radio; **wiring** ['waɪərɪŋ] *n* installation *f* électrique
wiry ['waɪərɪ] *adj* noueux(euse), nerveux(euse); (*hair*) dru(e)
wisdom ['wɪzdəm] *n* sagesse *f*; (*of action*) prudence *f*; ~ **tooth** *n* dent *f* de sagesse
wise [waɪz] *adj* sage, prudent(e); (*remark*) judicieux(euse) ♦ *suffix*: ...**wise**: **timewise** *etc* en ce qui concerne le temps *etc*; ~**crack** *n* remarque *f* ironique
wish [wɪʃ] *n* (*desire*) désir *m*; (*specific desire*) souhait *m*, vœu *m* ♦ *vt* souhaiter, désirer, vouloir; **best** ~**es** (*on birthday etc*) meilleurs vœux; **with best** ~**es** (*in letter*) bien amicalement; **to** ~ **sb goodbye** dire au revoir à qn; **he** ~**ed me well** il m'a souhaité bonne chance; **to** ~ **to do/sb to do** désirer *ou* vouloir faire/que qn fasse; **to** ~ **for** souhaiter; ~**ful** *adj*: **it's** ~**ful thinking** c'est prendre ses désirs pour des réalités
wistful ['wɪstful] *adj* mélancolique
wit [wɪt] *n* (*gen pl*) intelligence *f*, esprit *m*; (*presence of mind*) présence *f* d'esprit; (*wittiness*) esprit; (*person*) homme/femme *f* d'esprit
witch [wɪtʃ] *n* sorcière *f*; ~**craft** *n* sorcellerie *f*

────── KEYWORD

with [wɪð, wɪθ] *prep* **1** (*in the company of*) avec; (*at the home of*) chez; **we stayed** ~ **friends** nous avons logé chez des amis; **I'll be** ~ **you in a minute** je suis à vous dans un instant
2 (*descriptive*): **a room** ~ **a view** une chambre avec vue; **the man** ~ **the grey hat/blue eyes** l'homme au chapeau gris/

aux yeux bleus
3 (*indicating manner, means, cause*): ~
tears in her eyes les larmes aux yeux; **to
walk** ~ **a stick** marcher avec une canne;
red ~ **anger** rouge de colère; **to shake** ~
fear trembler de peur; **to fill sth** ~ **water**
remplir qch d'eau
4: **I'm** ~ **you** (*I understand*) je vous suis; **to
be** ~ **it** (*inf: up-to-date*) être dans le vent

withdraw [wɪθ'drɔ:] (*irreg*) *vt* retirer ♦ *vi* se
retirer; ~**al** *n* retrait *m*; ~**al symptoms**
npl (*MED*): **to have** ~**al symptoms** être en
état de manque; ~**n** *adj* (*person*) renfer-
mé(e)
wither ['wɪðə*] *vi* (*plant*) se faner
withhold [wɪθ'həʊld] (*irreg*) *vt* (*money*) retenir; **to** ~ (**from**) (*information*) cacher (à);
(*permission*) refuser (à)
within [wɪð'ɪn] *prep* à l'intérieur de ♦ *adv* à
l'intérieur; ~ **his reach** à sa portée; ~
sight of en vue de; ~ **a kilometre of** à
moins d'un kilomètre de; ~ **the week**
avant la fin de la semaine
without [wɪð'aʊt] *prep* sans; ~ **a coat** sans
manteau; ~ **speaking** sans parler; **to go** ~
sth se passer de qch
withstand [wɪθ'stænd] (*irreg*) *vt* résister à
witness ['wɪtnəs] *n* (*person*) témoin *m* ♦ *vt*
(*event*) être témoin de; (*document*) attester
l'authenticité de; **to bear** ~ (**to**) (*fig*) attester; ~ **box** *n* barre *f* des témoins; ~ **stand**
(*US*) *n* = ~ **box**
witticism ['wɪtɪsɪzəm] *n* mot *m* d'esprit.
witty ['wɪtɪ] *adj* spirituel(le), plein(e) d'esprit
wives [waɪvz] *npl of* **wife**
wizard ['wɪzəd] *n* magicien *m*
wk *abbr* = **week**
wobble ['wɒbl] *vi* trembler; (*chair*) branler
woe [wəʊ] *n* malheur *m*
woke [wəʊk] *pt of* **wake**
woken ['wəʊkən] *pp of* **wake**
wolf [wʊlf, *pl* wʊlvz] (*pl* **wolves**) *n* loup *m*
woman ['wʊmən] (*pl* **women**) *n* femme *f*;
~ **doctor** *n* femme *f* médecin; ~**ly** *adj* fé-
minin(e)
womb [wu:m] *n* (*ANAT*) utérus *m*
women ['wɪmɪn] *npl of* **woman**; ~**'s lib**
(*inf*) *n* MLF *m*; **W**~**'s (Liberation) Movement** *n* mouvement *m* de libération de la
femme
won [wʌn] *pt, pp of* **win**
wonder ['wʌndə*] *n* merveille *f*, miracle *m*;
(*feeling*) émerveillement *m* ♦ *vi*: **to** ~
whether/why se demander si/pourquoi; **to**
~ **at** (*marvel*) s'émerveiller de; **to** ~ **about**
songer à; **it's no** ~ (**that**) il n'est pas étonnant (que +*sub*); ~**ful** *adj* mer-
veilleux(euse)
won't [wəʊnt] = **will not**
woo [wu:] *vt* (*woman*) faire la cour à;

(*audience etc*) chercher à plaire à
wood [wʊd] *n* (*timber, forest*) bois *m*; ~
carving *n* sculpture *f* en or sur bois; ~**ed**
adj boisé(e); ~**en** *adj* en bois; (*fig*) raide;
inexpressif(ive); ~**pecker** *n* pic *m* (*oiseau*);
~**wind** *n* (*MUS*): **the** ~**wind** les bois *mpl*;
~**work** *n* menuiserie *f*, ~**worm** *n* ver *m*
du bois
wool [wʊl] *n* laine *f*; **to pull the** ~ **over
sb's eyes** (*fig*) en faire accroire à qn; ~**len**
(*US* ~**en**) *adj* de or en laine; (*industry*) lai-
nier(ère); ~**lens** *npl* (*clothes*) lainages *mpl*;
~**ly** (*US* ~**y**) *adj* laineux(euse); (*fig: ideas*)
confus(e)
word [wɜ:d] *n* mot *m*; (*promise*) parole *f*;
(*news*) nouvelles *fpl* ♦ *vt* rédiger, formuler;
in other ~**s** en d'autres termes; **to break/
keep one's** ~ manquer à sa parole/tenir
parole; ~**ing** *n* termes *mpl*; libellé *m*; ~
processing *n* traitement *m* de texte; ~
processor *n* machine *f* de traitement de
texte
wore [wɔ:*] *pt of* **wear**
work [wɜ:k] *n* travail *m*; (*ART, LITERATU-
RE*) œuvre *f* ♦ *vi* travailler; (*mechanism*)
marcher, fonctionner; (*plan etc*) marcher;
(*medicine*) agir ♦ *vt* (*clay, wood etc*) travailler; (*mine etc*) exploiter; (*machine*) faire
marcher *or* fonctionner; (*miracles, wonders
etc*) faire; **to be out of** ~ être sans emploi;
to ~ **loose** se défaire, se desserrer; ~ **on**
vt fus travailler à; (*principle*) se baser sur;
(*person*) (essayer d')influencer; ~ **out** *vi*
(*plans etc*) marcher ♦ *vt* (*problem*) résoudre;
(*plan*) élaborer; **it** ~**s out at £100** ça fait
100 livres; ~ **up** *vt*: **to get** ~**ed up** se mettre dans tous ses états; ~**able** *adj* (*solution*)
réalisable; ~**aholic** [wɜ:kə'hɒlɪk] *n* bourreau *m* de travail; ~**er** *n* travailleur(euse),
ouvrier(ère); ~**force** *n* main-d'œuvre *f*;
~**ing class** *n* classe ouvrière; ~**ing-class**
adj ouvrier(ère); ~**ing order** *n*: **in** ~**ing order** en état de marche; ~**man** (*irreg*) *n* ouvrier *m*; ~**manship** *n* (*skill*) métier *m*, habileté *f*; ~**s** *n* ♦ *npl*
(*of clock, machine*) mécanisme *m*; ~ **sheet**
n (*COMPUT*) feuille *f* de programmation;
~**shop** *n* atelier *m*; ~ **station** *n* poste *m*
de travail; ~**-to-rule** (*BRIT*) *n* grève *f* du
zèle
world [wɜ:ld] *n* monde *m* ♦ *cpd* (*champion*)
du monde; (*power, war*) mondial(e); **to
think the** ~ **of sb** (*fig*) ne jurer que par
qn; ~**ly** *adj* de ce monde; (*knowledgeable*)
qui a l'expérience du monde; ~**wide** *adj*
universel(le)
worm [wɜ:m] *n* ver *m*
worn [wɔ:n] *pp of* **wear** ♦ *adj* usé(e); ~-
out (*object*) complètement usé(e); (*person*) épuisé(e)
worried ['wʌrɪd] *adj* inquiet(ète)
worry ['wʌrɪ] *n* souci *m* ♦ *vt* inquiéter ♦ *vi*

s'inquiéter, se faire du souci

worse [wɜːs] *adj* pire, plus mauvais(e) ♦ *adv* plus mal ♦ *n* pire *m*; **a change for the ~** une détérioration; **~n** *vt, vi* empirer; **~ off** *adj* moins à l'aise financièrement; (*fig*): **you'll be ~ off this way** ça ira moins bien de cette façon

worship ['wɜːʃɪp] *n* culte *m* ♦ *vt* (*God*) rendre un culte à; (*person*) adorer; **Your W~** (*BRIT: to mayor*) Monsieur le maire; (: *to judge*) Monsieur le juge

worst [wɜːst] *adj* le(la) pire, le(la) plus mauvais(e) ♦ *adv* le plus mal ♦ *n* pire *m*; **at ~** au pis aller

worth [wɜːθ] *n* valeur *f* ♦ *adj*: **to be ~** valoir; **it's ~ it** cela en vaut la peine, ça vaut la peine; **it is ~ one's while (to do)** on gagne (à faire); **~less** *adj* qui ne vaut rien; **~while** *adj* (*activity, cause*) utile, louable

worthy [wɜːðɪ] *adj* (*person*) digne; (*motive*) louable; **~ of** digne de

---
KEYWORD
---

would [wʊd] *aux vb* **1** (*conditional tense*): **if you asked him he ~ do it** si vous le lui demandiez, il le ferait; **if you had asked him he ~ have done it** si vous le lui aviez demandé, il l'aurait fait
2 (*in offers, invitations, requests*): **~ you like a biscuit?** voulez-vous *or* voudriez-vous un biscuit?; **~ you close the door please?** voulez-vous fermer la porte, s'il vous plaît?
3 (*in indirect speech*): **I said I ~ do it** j'ai dit que je le ferais
4 (*emphatic*): **it WOULD have to snow today!** naturellement il neige aujourd'hui! *or* il fallait qu'il neige aujourd'hui!
5 (*insistence*): **she ~n't do it** elle n'a pas voulu *or* elle a refusé de le faire
6 (*conjecture*): **it ~ have been midnight** il devait être minuit
7 (*indicating habit*): **he ~ go there on Mondays** il y allait le lundi

would-be ['wʊdbiː] (*pej*) *adj* soi-disant
wouldn't ['wʊdnt] = **would not**
wound[1] [wuːnd] *n* blessure *f* ♦ *vt* blesser
wound[2] [waʊnd] *pt, pp* of **wind**[2]
wove [wəʊv] *pt* of **weave**
woven ['wəʊvən] *pp* of **weave**
wrap [ræp] *vt* (*also: ~ up*) envelopper, emballer; (*wind*) enrouler; **~per** *n* (*BRIT: of book*) couverture *f*; (*on chocolate*) emballage *m*, papier *m*; **~ping paper** *n* papier *m* d'emballage; (*for gift*) papier cadeau
wrath [rɒθ] *n* courroux *m*
wreak [riːk] *vt*: **to ~ havoc (on)** avoir un effet désastreux (sur)
wreath [riːθ, *pl* riːðz] (*pl* ~**s**) *n* couronne *f*
wreck [rek] *n* (*ship*) épave *f*; (*vehicle*) véhicule accidenté; (*pej: person*) loque humaine

♦ *vt* démolir; (*fig*) briser, ruiner; **~age** *n* débris *mpl*; (*of building*) décombres *mpl*; (*of ship*) épave *f*

wren [ren] *n* (*ZOOL*) roitelet *m*
wrench [rentʃ] *n* (*TECH*) clé *f* (à écrous); (*tug*) violent mouvement de torsion; (*fig*) déchirement *m* ♦ *vt* tirer violemment sur, tordre; **to ~ sth from** arracher qch à *or* de
wrestle ['resl] *vi*: **to ~ (with sb)** lutter (avec qn); **~r** *n* lutteur(euse); **wrestling** *n* lutte *f*; (*also: all-in wrestling*) catch *m*
wretched ['retʃɪd] *adj* misérable; (*inf*) maudit(e)
wriggle ['rɪgl] *vi* (*also: ~ about*) se tortiller
wring [rɪŋ] (*pt, pp* **wrung**) *vt* tordre; (*wet clothes*) essorer; (*fig*): **to ~ sth out of sb** arracher qch à qn
wrinkle ['rɪŋkl] *n* (*on skin*) ride *f*; (*on paper etc*) pli *m* ♦ *vt* plisser ♦ *vi* se plisser
wrist [rɪst] *n* poignet *m*; **~watch** *n* montre-bracelet *f*
writ [rɪt] *n* acte *m* judiciaire
write [raɪt] (*pt* **wrote**, *pp* **written**) *vt, vi* écrire; (*prescription*) rédiger; **~ down** *vt* noter; (*put in writing*) mettre par écrit; **~ off** *vt* (*debt*) passer aux profits et pertes; (*project*) mettre une croix sur; **~ out** *vt* écrire; **~ up** *vt* rédiger; **~-off** *n* perte totale; **~r** *n* auteur *m*, écrivain *m*
writhe [raɪð] *vi* se tordre
writing ['raɪtɪŋ] *n* écriture *f*; (*of author*) œuvres *fpl*; **in ~** par écrit; **~ paper** *n* papier *m* à lettres
wrong [rɒŋ] *adj* (*incorrect: answer, information*) faux(fausse); (*inappropriate: choice, action etc*) mauvais(e); (*wicked*) mal; (*unfair*) injuste ♦ *adv* mal ♦ *n* tort *m* ♦ *vt* faire du tort à, léser; **you are ~ to do it** tu as tort de le faire; **you are ~ about that, you've got it ~** tu te trompes; **what's ~?** qu'est-ce qui ne va pas?; **to go ~** (*person*) se tromper; (*plan*) mal tourner; (*machine*) tomber en panne; **to be in the ~** avoir tort; **~ful** *adj* injustifié(e); **~ly** *adv* mal, incorrectement; **~ side** *n* (*of material*) envers *m*
wrote [rəʊt] *pt* of **write**
wrought [rɔːt] *adj*: **~ iron** fer forgé
wrung [rʌŋ] *pt, pp* of **wring**
wry [raɪ] *adj* désabusé(e)
wt. *abbr* = **weight**

X Y Z

Xmas ['eksməs] *n abbr* = **Christmas**
X-ray ['eks'reɪ] *n* (*ray*) rayon *m* X; (*photo*)

radio(graphie) f
xylophone ['zaɪləfəʊn] n xylophone m
yacht [jɒt] n yacht m; voilier m; ~**ing** n yachting m, navigation f de plaisance; ~**sman** (irreg) n plaisancier m
Yank(ee) [jæŋk(ɪ)] (pej) n Amerloque m/f
yap [jæp] vi (dog) japper
yard [jɑːd] n (of house etc) cour f; (measure) yard m (= 91,4 cm); ~**stick** n (fig) mesure f, critères mpl
yarn [jɑːn] n fil m; (tale) longue histoire
yawn [jɔːn] n bâillement m ♦ vi bâiller; ~**ing** adj (gap) béant(e)
yd. abbr = **yard(s)**
yeah [jeə] (inf) adv ouais
year [jɪə*] n an m, année f; to be 8 ~**s old** avoir 8 ans; an eight-~-**old child** un enfant de huit ans; ~**ly** adj annuel(le) ♦ adv annuellement
yearn [jɜːn] vi: to ~ for sth aspirer à qch, languir après qch; to ~ to do aspirer à faire
yeast [jiːst] n levure f
yell [jel] vi hurler
yellow ['jeləʊ] adj jaune
yelp [jelp] vi japper; glapir
yeoman ['jəʊmən] (irreg) n: ~ **of the guard** hallebardier m de la garde royale
yes [jes] adv oui; (answering negative question) si ♦ n oui m; to say/answer ~ dire/répondre oui
yesterday ['jestədeɪ] adv hier ♦ n hier m; ~ **morning/evening** hier matin/soir; all **day** ~ toute la journée d'hier
yet [jet] adv encore; déjà ♦ conj pourtant, néanmoins; **it is not finished** ~ ce n'est pas encore fini or toujours pas fini; **the best** ~ le meilleur jusqu'ici or jusque-là; as ~ jusqu'ici, encore
yew [juː] n if m
yield [jiːld] n production f, rendement m; rapport m ♦ vt produire, rendre, rapporter; (surrender) céder ♦ vi céder; (US: AUT) céder la priorité
YMCA n abbr (= Young Men's Christian Association) YMCA m
yoghourt ['jɒgət] n yaourt m
yog(h)urt ['jɒgət] n = **yoghourt**
yoke [jəʊk] n joug m
yolk [jəʊk] n jaune m (d'œuf)

you [juː] pron **1** (subject) tu; (polite form) vous; (plural) vous; → **French enjoy your food** vous autres Français, vous aimez bien manger; ~ **and I will go** toi et moi or vous et moi, nous irons
2 (object: direct, indirect) te, t' +vowel; vous; **I know** ~ je te or vous connais; **I gave it to** ~, je vous l'ai donné, je te l'ai donné
3 (stressed) toi; vous; **I told YOU to do it**

c'est à toi or vous que j'ai dit de le faire
4 (after prep, in comparisons) toi; vous; **it's for** ~ c'est pour toi or vous; **she's younger than** ~ elle est plus jeune que toi or vous
5 (impersonal: one) on; **fresh air does** ~ **good** l'air frais fait du bien; ~ **never know** on ne sait jamais

you'd [juːd] = **you had**; **you would**
you'll [juːl] = **you will**; **you shall**
young [jʌŋ] adj jeune ♦ npl (of animal) petits mpl; (people): **the** ~ les jeunes, la jeunesse; ~**er** adj (brother etc) cadet(te); ~**ster** n jeune m (garçon m); (child) enfant m/f
your ['jɔː*] adj ton(ta), tes pl; (polite form, pl) votre, vos pl; see also **my**
you're ['jʊə*] = **you are**
yours [jɔːz] pron le(la) tien(ne), les tiens(tiennes); (polite form, pl) le(la) vôtre, les vôtres; ~ **sincerely/faithfully/truly** veuillez agréer l'expression de mes sentiments les meilleurs; see also **mine¹**
yourself [jɔː'self] pron (reflexive) te; (: polite form) vous; (after prep) toi; vous; (emphatic) toi-même; vous-même; see also **oneself**; **yourselves** pl pron vous; (emphatic) vous-mêmes
youth [juːθ, pl juːðz] n jeunesse f; (young man: pl youths) jeune homme m; ~ **club** n centre m de jeunes; ~**ful** adj jeune; (enthusiasm) de jeunesse, juvénile; ~ **hostel** n auberge f de jeunesse
you've [juːv] = **you have**
YTS (BRIT) n abbr (= Youth Training Scheme) ≈ TUC m
Yugoslav adj yougoslave ♦ n Yougoslave m/f; ~**ia** n Yougoslavie f
yuppie ['jʌpɪ] (inf) n yuppie m/f
YWCA n abbr (= Young Women's Christian Association) YWCA m

zany ['zeɪnɪ] adj farfelu(e), loufoque
zap [zæp] vt (COMPUT) effacer
zeal [ziːl] n zèle m, ferveur f; empressement m
zebra ['ziːbrə] n zèbre m; ~ **crossing** (BRIT) n passage clouté or pour piétons
zero ['zɪərəʊ] n zéro m
zest [zest] n entrain m, élan m; (of orange) zeste m
Zimbabwe [zɪm'bɑːbwɪ] n Zimbabwe m
zinc [zɪŋk] n zinc m
zip [zɪp] n (also: ~ **fastener**) fermeture f éclair (®) ♦ vt (: ~ **up**) fermer avec une fermeture éclair (®); ~ **code** (US) n code postal; ~**per** (US) n = **zip**
zodiac ['zəʊdɪæk] n zodiaque m
zone [zəʊn] n zone f
zoo [zuː] n zoo m
zoom [zuːm] vi: to ~ **past** passer en trombe; ~ **lens** n zoom m
zucchini [zuː'kiːnɪ] n(pl) courgette(s) f(pl)

Grammar

Using the Grammar

The Grammar section deals systematically and comprehensively with all the information you will need in order to communicate accurately in French. The user-friendly layout explains the grammar point on a left-hand page, leaving the facing page free for illustrative examples. The bracketed numbers, (→1) etc, direct you to the relevant example in every case.

The Grammar section also provides invaluable guidance on the danger of translating English structures by identical structures in French. Use of Numbers and Punctuation are important areas covered towards the end of the section. Finally, the index lists the main words and grammatical terms in both English and French.

Abbreviations

ctd.	continued	**p(p)**	page(s)	**qu**	quelqu'un
fem.	feminine	**perf.**	perfect	**sb**	somebody
infin.	infinitive	**plur.**	plural	**sing.**	singular
masc.	masculine	**qch**	quelque chose	**sth**	something

4 CONTENTS

6 VERBS

Simple Tenses: formation

In French the simple tenses are:

Present	(→ **1**)
Imperfect	(→ **2**)
Future	(→ **3**)
Conditional	(→ **4**)
Past Historic	(→ **5**)
Present Subjunctive	(→ **6**)
Imperfect Subjunctive	(→ **7**)

They are formed by adding endings to a verb stem. The endings show the number and person of the subject of the verb (→ **8**)

The stem and endings of regular verbs are totally predictable. The following sections show all the patterns for regular verbs. For irregular verbs see pp. 74 ff.

Regular Verbs

There are three regular verb patterns (called conjugations), each identifiable by the ending of the infinitive:

● First conjugation verbs end in **-er** e.g. **donner** to give

● Second conjugation verbs end in **-ir** e.g. **finir** to finish

● Third conjugation verbs end in **-re** e.g. **vendre** to sell

These three conjugations are treated in order on the following pages.

Continued

1 je donne
I give, I am giving, I do give

2 je donnais
I gave, I was giving, I used to give

3 je donnerai
I shall give, I shall be giving

4 je donnerais
I should/would give, I should/would be giving

5 je donnai
I gave

6 (que) je donne
(that) I give/gave

7 (que) je donnasse
(that) I gave

8 je donne   I give
nous donnons   we give
je donnerais   I would give
nous donnerions   we would give

Simple Tenses: First Conjugation

● The stem is formed as follows:

TENSE	FORMATION	EXAMPLE
Present		
Imperfect		
Past Historic	infinitive minus **-er**	**donn-**
Present Subjunctive		
Imperfect Subjunctive		
Future	infinitive	**donner-**
Conditional		

● To the appropriate stem add the following endings:

		PRESENT (→1)	IMPERFECT (→2)	PAST HISTORIC (→3)
sing.	1st person	-e	-ais	-ai
	2nd person	-es	-ais	-as
	3rd person	-e	-ait	-a
plur.	1st person	-ons	-ions	-âmes
	2nd person	-ez	-iez	-âtes
	3rd person	-ent	-aient	-èrent

		PRESENT SUBJUNCTIVE (→4)	IMPERFECT SUBJUNCTIVE (→5)
sing.	1st person	-e	-asse
	2nd person	-es	-asses
	3rd person	-e	-ât
plur.	1st person	-ions	-assions
	2nd person	-iez	-assiez
	3rd person	-ent	-assent

		FUTURE (→6)	CONDITIONAL (→7)
sing.	1st person	-ai	-ais
	2nd person	-as	-ais
	3rd person	-a	-ait
plur.	1st person	-ons	-ions
	2nd person	-ez	-iez
	3rd person	-ont	-aient

1 PRESENT		**2** IMPERFECT		**3** PAST HISTORIC	
je	donne	je	donnais	je	donnai
tu	donnes	tu	donnais	tu	donnas
il	donne	il	donnait	il	donna
elle	donne	elle	donnait	elle	donna
nous	donnons	nous	donnions	nous	donnâmes
vous	donnez	vous	donniez	vous	donnâtes
ils	donnent	ils	donnaient	ils	donnèrent
elles	donnent	elles	donnaient	elles	donnèrent

4 PRESENT SUBJUNCTIVE		**5** IMPERFECT SUBJUNCTIVE	
je	donne	je	donnasse
tu	donnes	tu	donnasses
il	donne	il	donnât
elle	donne	elle	donnât
nous	donnions	nous	donnassions
vous	donniez	vous	donnassiez
ils	donnent	ils	donnassent
elles	donnent	elles	donnassent

6 FUTURE		**7** CONDITIONAL	
je	donnerai	je	donnerais
tu	donneras	tu	donnerais
il	donnera	il	donnerait
elle	donnera	elle	donnerait
nous	donnerons	nous	donnerions
vous	donnerez	vous	donneriez
ils	donneront	ils	donneraient
elles	donneront	elles	donneraient

Simple Tenses: Second Conjugation

● The stem is formed as follows:

TENSE	FORMATION	EXAMPLE
Present		
Imperfect		
Past Historic	infinitive minus **-ir**	**fin-**
Present Subjunctive		
Imperfect Subjunctive		
Future	infinitive	**finir-**
Conditional		

● To the appropriate stem add the following endings:

		PRESENT (→**1**)	IMPERFECT (→**2**)	PAST HISTORIC (→**3**)
sing.	1st person	-is	-issais	-is
	2nd person	-is	-issais	-is
	3rd person	-it	-issait	-it
plur.	1st person	-issons	-issions	-îmes
	2nd person	-issez	-issiez	-îtes
	3rd person	-issent	-issaient	-irent

		PRESENT SUBJUNCTIVE (→**4**)	IMPERFECT SUBJUNCTIVE (→**5**)
sing.	1st person	-isse	-isse
	2nd person	-isses	-isses
	3rd person	-isse	-ît
plur.	1st person	-issions	-issions
	2nd person	-issiez	-issiez
	3rd person	-issent	-issent

		FUTURE (→**6**)	CONDITIONAL (→**7**)
sing.	1st person	-ai	-ais
	2nd person	-as	-ais
	3rd person	-a	-ait
plur.	1st person	-ons	-ions
	2nd person	-ez	-iez
	3rd person	-ont	-aient

1	PRESENT	**2**	IMPERFECT	**3**	PAST HISTORIC
je	finis	je	finissais	je	finis
tu	finis	tu	finissais	tu	finis
il	finit	il	finissait	il	finit
elle	finit	elle	finissait	elle	finit
nous	finissons	nous	finissions	nous	finîmes
vous	finissez	vous	finissiez	vous	finîtes
ils	finissent	ils	finissaient	ils	finirent
elles	finissent	elles	finissaient	elles	finirent

4	PRESENT SUBJUNCTIVE	**5**	IMPERFECT SUBJUNCTIVE
je	finisse	je	finisse
tu	finisses	tu	finisses
il	finisse	il	finît
elle	finisse	elle	finît
nous	finissions	nous	finissions
vous	finissiez	vous	finissiez
ils	finissent	ils	finissent
elles	finissent	elles	finissent

6	FUTURE	**7**	CONDITIONAL
je	finirai	je	finirais
tu	finiras	tu	finirais
il	finira	il	finirait
elle	finira	elle	finirait
nous	finirons	nous	finirions
vous	finirez	vous	finiriez
ils	finiront	ils	finiraient
elles	finiront	elles	finiraient

Simple Tenses: Third Conjugation

● The stem is formed as follows:

TENSE	FORMATION	EXAMPLE
Present		
Imperfect		
Past Historic	infinitive minus **-re**	**vend-**
Present Subjunctive		
Imperfect Subjunctive		
Future	infinitive minus **-e**	**vendr-**
Conditional		

● To the appropriate stem add the following endings:

		PRESENT (→**1**)	IMPERFECT (→**2**)	PAST HISTORIC (→**3**)
sing.	1st person	**-s**	**-ais**	**-is**
	2nd person	**-s**	**-ais**	**-is**
	3rd person	**–**	**-ait**	**-it**
plur.	1st person	**-ons**	**-ions**	**-îmes**
	2nd person	**-ez**	**-iez**	**-îtes**
	3rd person	**-ent**	**-aient**	**-irent**

		PRESENT SUBJUNCTIVE (→**4**)	IMPERFECT SUBJUNCTIVE (→**5**)
sing.	1st person	**-e**	**-isse**
	2nd person	**-es**	**-isses**
	3rd person	**-e**	**-ît**
plur.	1st person	**-ions**	**-issions**
	2nd person	**-iez**	**-issiez**
	3rd person	**-ent**	**-issent**

		FUTURE (→**6**)	CONDITIONAL (→**7**)
sing.	1st person	**-ai**	**-ais**
	2nd person	**-as**	**-ais**
	3rd person	**-a**	**-ait**
plur.	1st person	**-ons**	**-ions**
	2nd person	**-ez**	**-iez**
	3rd person	**-ont**	**-aient**

1 PRESENT		**2** IMPERFECT		**3** PAST HISTORIC	
je	vend**s**	je	vend**ais**	je	vend**is**
tu	vend**s**	tu	vend**ais**	tu	vend**is**
il	vend	il	vend**ait**	il	vend**it**
elle	vend	elle	vend**ait**	elle	vend**it**
nous	vend**ons**	nous	vend**ions**	nous	vend**îmes**
vous	vend**ez**	vous	vend**iez**	vous	vend**îtes**
ils	vend**ent**	ils	vend**aient**	ils	vend**irent**
elles	vend**ent**	elles	vend**aient**	elles	vend**irent**

4 PRESENT SUBJUNCTIVE		**5** IMPERFECT SUBJUNCTIVE	
je	vend**e**	je	vend**isse**
tu	vend**es**	tu	vend**isses**
il	vend**e**	il	vend**ît**
elle	vend**e**	elle	vend**ît**
nous	vend**ions**	nous	vend**issions**
vous	vend**iez**	vous	vend**issiez**
ils	vend**ent**	ils	vend**issent**
elles	vend**ent**	elles	vend**issent**

6 FUTURE		**7** CONDITIONAL	
je	vend**rai**	je	vend**rais**
tu	vend**ras**	tu	vend**rais**
il	vend**ra**	il	vend**rait**
elle	vend**ra**	elle	vend**rait**
nous	vend**rons**	nous	vend**rions**
vous	vend**rez**	vous	vend**riez**
ils	vend**ront**	ils	vend**raient**
elles	vend**ront**	elles	vend**raient**

First Conjugation Spelling Irregularities

Before certain endings, the stems of some '**-er**' verbs may change slightly.

Below, and on subsequent pages, the verb types are identified, and the changes described are illustrated by means of a representative verb.

Verbs ending:	**-cer**
Change:	**c** becomes **ç** before **a** or **o**
Tenses affected:	Present, Imperfect, Past Historic, Imperfect Subjunctive, Present Participle
Model:	**lancer** *to throw* (→ **1**)

● Why the change occurs:
  A cedilla is added to the **c** to retain its soft [s] pronunciation before the vowels **a** and **o**

Verbs ending:	**-ger**
Change:	**g** becomes **ge** before **a** or **o**
Tenses affected:	Present, Imperfect, Past Historic, Imperfect Subjunctive, Present Participle
Model:	**manger** *to eat* (→ **2**)

● Why the change occurs:
  An **e** is added after the **g** to retain its soft [ʒ] pronunciation before the vowels **a** and **o**

Continued

1   *INFINITIVE*   *PRESENT PARTICIPLE*
          lancer   **lançant**

          PRESENT   *IMPERFECT*
          je lance   **je lançais**
          tu lances   **tu lançais**
          il/elle lance   **il/elle lançait**
          nous lançons   nous lancions
          vous lancez   vous lanciez
          ils/elles lancent   **ils/elles lançaient**

          PAST HISTORIC   *IMPERFECT SUBJUNCTIVE*
          je lançai   **je lançasse**
          tu lanças   **tu lançasses**
          il/elle lança   **il/elle lançât**
          nous lançâmes   **nous lançassions**
          vous lançâtes   **vous lançassiez**
          ils/elles lancèrent   **ils/elles lançassent**

2   *INFINITIVE*   *PRESENT PARTICIPLE*
          manger   **mangeant**

          PRESENT   *IMPERFECT*
          je mange   **je mangeais**
          tu manges   **tu mangeais**
          il/elle mange   **il/elle mangeait**
          nous mangeons   nous mangions
          vous mangez   vous mangiez
          ils/elles mangent   **ils/elles mangeaient**

          PAST HISTORIC   *IMPERFECT SUBJUNCTIVE*
          je mangeai   **je mangeasse**
          tu mangeas   **tu mangeasses**
          il/elle mangea   **il/elle mangeât**
          nous mangeâmes   **nous mangeassions**
          vous mangeâtes   **vous mangeassiez**
          ils/elles mangèrent   **ils/elles mangeassent**

First Conjugation Spelling Irregularities (ctd.)

Verbs ending	**-eler**
Change:	**-l** doubles before **-e**, **-es**, **-ent** and throughout the Future and Conditional tenses
Tenses affected:	Present, Present Subjunctive, Future, Conditional
Model:	**appeler** *to call* (→ **1**)

● Exceptions: **geler** *to freeze* **peler** *to peel* } like **mener** (p. 18)

Verbs ending	**-eter**
Change:	**-t** doubles before **-e**, **es**, **-ent** and throughout the Future and Conditional tenses
Tenses affected:	Present, Present Subjunctive, Future, Conditional
Model:	**jeter** *to throw* (→ **2**)

● Exceptions: **acheter** *to buy* **haleter** *to pant* } like **mener** (p. 18)

Verbs ending	**-yer**
Change:	**y** changes to **i** before **-e**, **-es**, **-ent** and throughout the Future and Conditional tenses
Tenses affected:	Present, Present Subjunctive, Future, Conditional
Model:	**essuyer** *to wipe* (→ **3**)

● The change described is optional for verbs ending in **-ayer** e.g. **payer** *to pay*, **essayer** *to try*

Continued

1 *PRESENT (+ SUBJUNCTIVE)*

	j'**appelle**
tu	**appelles**
il/elle	**appelle**
nous	appelons
	(appelions)
vous	appelez
	(appeliez)
ils/elles	**appellent**

FUTURE

	j'**appellerai**
tu	**appelleras**
il	**appellera** *etc.*

CONDITIONAL

	j'**appellerais**
tu	**appellerais**
il	**appellerait** *etc.*

2 *PRESENT (+ SUBJUNCTIVE)*

je	**jette**
tu	**jettes**
il/elle	**jette**
nous	jetons
	(jetions)
vous	jetez
	(jetiez)
ils/elles	**jettent**

FUTURE

je	**jetterai**
tu	**jetteras**
il	**jettera** *etc.*

CONDITIONAL

je	**jetterais**
tu	**jetterais**
il	**jetterait** *etc.*

3 *PRESENT (+ SUBJUNCTIVE)*

	j'**essuie**
tu	**essuies**
il/elle	**essuie**
nous	essuyons
	(essuyions)
vous	essuyez
	(essuyiez)
ils/elles	**essuient**

FUTURE

	j'**essuierai**
tu	**essuieras**
il	**essuiera** *etc.*

CONDITIONAL

	j'**essuierais**
tu	**essuierais**
il	**essuierait** *etc.*

First Conjugation Spelling Irregularities (ctd.)

Verbs ending	**mener, peser, lever** etc
Change:	**e** changes to **è**, before **-e**, **-es**, **-ent** and throughout the Future and Conditional tenses
Tenses affected:	Present, Present Subjunctive, Future, Conditional
Model:	**mener** *to lead* (→ **1**)

Verbs like:	**céder, régler, espérer** etc
Change:	**é** changes to **è** before **-e**, **-es**, **-ent**
Tenses affected:	Present, Present Subjunctive
Model:	**céder** *to yield* (→ **2**)

1   *PRESENT (+ SUBJUNCTIVE)*

je	**mène**
tu	**mènes**
il/elle	**mène**
nous	menons
	(menions)
vous	menez
	(meniez)
ils/elles	**mènent**

FUTURE

je	**mènerai**
tu	**mèneras**
il	**mènera** *etc.*

CONDITIONAL

je	**mènerais**
tu	**mènerais**
il	**mènerait** *etc.*

2   *PRESENT (+ SUBJUNCTIVE)*

je	**cède**
tu	**cèdes**
il/elle	**cède**
nous	cédons
	(cédions)
vous	cédez
	(cédiez)
ils/elles	**cèdent**

The Imperative

The imperative is the form of the verb used to give commands or orders. It can be used politely, as in English 'Shut the door, please'.

The imperative is the same as the present tense **tu**, **nous** and **vous** forms without the subject pronouns:

donne*	**finis**	**vends**
give	*finish*	*sell*

*The final 's' of the present tense of first conjugation verbs is dropped, except before **y** and **en** (→ **1**)

donnons	**finissons**	**vendons**
let's give	*let's finish*	*let's sell*

donnez	**finissez**	**vendez**
give	*finish*	*sell*

● The imperative of irregular verbs is given in the verb tables, pp. 74 ff.

● Position of object pronouns with the imperative:
in POSITIVE commands: they follow the verb and are attached to it by hyphens (→ **2**)
in NEGATIVE commands: they precede the verb and are not attached to it (→ **3**)

● For the order of object pronouns, see p. 170

● For reflexive verbs – e.g. **se lever** *to get up* – the object pronoun is the reflexive pronoun (→ **4**)

1 Compare: **Tu donnes de l'argent à Paul**
         You give (some) money to Paul
 and: **Donne de l'argent à Paul**
         Give (some) money to Paul

2 **Excusez-moi**
Excuse me
Crois-nous
Believe us
Attendons-la
Let's wait for her/it

Envoyons-les-leur
Let's send them to them
Expliquez-le-moi
Explain it to me
Rends-la-lui
Give it back to him/her

3 **Ne me dérange pas**
Don't disturb me
Ne les négligeons pas
Let's not neglect them
Ne leur répondez pas
Don't answer them

Ne leur en parlons pas
Let's not speak to them about it
N'y pense plus
Don't think about it any more
Ne la lui rends pas
Don't give it back to him/her

4 **Lève-toi**
Get up
Dépêchons-nous
Let's hurry
Levez-vous
Get up

Ne te lève pas
Don't get up
Ne nous affolons pas
Let's not panic
Ne vous levez pas
Don't get up

Compound Tenses: formation

In French the compound tenses are:

Perfect	(→ **1**)
Pluperfect	(→ **2**)
Future Perfect	(→ **3**)
Conditional Perfect	(→ **4**)
Past Anterior	(→ **5**)
Perfect Subjunctive	(→ **6**)
Pluperfect Subjunctive	(→ **7**)

They consist of the past participle of the verb together with an auxiliary verb. Most verbs take the auxiliary **avoir**, but some take **être** (see p. 28).

Compound tenses are formed in exactly the same way for both regular and irregular verbs, the only difference being that irregular verbs may have an irregular past participle.

The Past Participle

For all compound tenses you need to know how to form the past participle of the verb. For regular verbs this is as follows:
● 1st conjugation: replace the **-er** of the infinitive by **-é** (→ **8**)
● 2nd conjugation: replace the **-ir** of the infinitive by **-i** (→ **9**)
● 3rd conjugation: replace the **-re** of the infinitive by **-u** (→ **10**)

● See p. 50 for agreement of past participles.

Continued

with **avoir**	with **être**
1 **j'ai donné** I gave, have given	**je suis tombé** I fell, have fallen
2 **j'avais donné** I had given	**j'étais tombé** I had fallen
3 **j'aurai donné** I shall have given	**je serai tombé** I shall have fallen
4 **j'aurais donné** I should/would have given	**je serais tombé** I should/would have fallen
5 **j'eus donné** I had given	**je fus tombé** I had fallen
6 **(que) j'aie donné** (that) I gave, have given	**(que) je sois tombé** (that) I fell, have fallen
7 **(que) j'eusse donné** (that) I had given	**(que) je fusse tombé** (that) I had fallen

8 **donner** → **donné**
   to give   given

9 **finir** → **fini**
   to finish   finished

10 **vendre** → **vendu**
    to sell   sold

Compound Tenses: formation (ctd.)

Verbs taking the auxiliary avoir

Perfect tense:	the present tense of **avoir** plus the past participle (→ **1**)
Pluperfect tense:	the imperfect tense of **avoir** plus the past participle (→ **2**)
Future Perfect:	the future tense of **avoir** plus the past participle (→ **3**)
Conditional Perfect:	the conditional of **avoir** plus the past participle (→ **4**)
Past Anterior:	the past historic of **avoir** plus the past participle (→ **5**)
Perfect Subjunctive:	the present subjunctive of **avoir** plus the past participle (→ **6**)
Pluperfect Subjunctive:	the imperfect subjunctive of **avoir** plus the past participle (→ **7**)

● For how to form the past participle of regular verbs see p. 22. The past participle of irregular verbs is given for each verb in the verb tables, pp. 74 ff.

● The past participle must agree in number and in gender with any preceding direct object (see p. 50)

Continued

1 *PERFECT*
j'ai donné   nous avons donné
tu as donné   vous avez donné
il/elle a donné   ils/elles ont donné

2 *PLUPERFECT*
j'avais donné   nous avions donné
tu avais donné   vous aviez donné
il/elle avait donné   ils/elles avaient donné

3 *FUTURE PERFECT*
j'aurai donné   nous aurons donné
tu auras donné   vous aurez donné
il/elle aura donné   ils/elles auront donné

4 *CONDITIONAL PERFECT*
j'aurais donné   nous aurions donné
tu aurais donné   vous auriez donné
il/elle aurait donné   ils/elles auraient donné

5 *PAST ANTERIOR*
j'eus donné   nous eûmes donné
tu eus donné   vous eûtes donné
il/elle eut donné   ils/elles eurent donné

6 *PERFECT SUBJUNCTIVE*
j'aie donné   nous ayons donné
tu aies donné   vous ayez donné
il/elle ait donné   ils/elles aient donné

7 *PLUPERFECT SUBJUNCTIVE*
j'eusse donné   nous eussions donné
tu eusses donné   vous eussiez donné
il/elle eût donné   ils/elles eussent donné

Compound Tenses: formation (ctd.)

Verbs taking the auxiliary être

Perfect tense: the present tense of **être** plus the past participle (→ **1**)

Pluperfect tense: the imperfect tense of **être** plus the past participle (→ **2**)

Future Perfect: the future tense of **être** plus the past participle (→ **3**)

Conditional Perfect: the conditional of **être** plus the past participle (→ **4**)

Past Anterior: the past historic of **être** plus the past participle (→ **5**)

Perfect Subjunctive: the present subjunctive of **être** plus the past participle (→ **6**)

Pluperfect Subjunctive: the imperfect subjunctive of **être** plus the past participle (→ **7**)

● For how to form the past participle of regular verbs see p. 22. The past participle of irregular verbs is given for each verb in the verb tables, pp. 74 ff.

● For agreement of past participles, see p. 50

● For a list of verbs and verb types that take the auxiliary **être**, see p. 28

Continued

1 *PERFECT*
je suis tombé(e)
tu es tombé(e)
il est tombé
elle est tombée

nous sommes tombé(e)s
vous êtes tombé(e)(s)
ils sont tombés
elles sont tombées

2 *PLUPERFECT*
j'étais tombé(e)
tu étais tombé(e)
il était tombé
elle était tombée

nous étions tombé(e)s
vous étiez tombé(e)(s)
ils étaient tombés
elles étaient tombées

3 *FUTURE PERFECT*
je serai tombé(e)
tu seras tombé(e)
il sera tombé
elle sera tombée

nous serons tombé(e)s
vous serez tombé(e)(s)
ils seront tombés
elles seront tombées

4 *CONDITIONAL PERFECT*
je serais tombé(e)
tu serais tombé(e)
il serait tombé
elle serait tombée

nous serions tombé(e)s
vous seriez tombé(e)(s)
ils seraient tombés
elles seraient tombées

5 *PAST ANTERIOR*
je fus tombé(e)
tu fus tombé(e)
il fut tombé
elle fut tombée

nous fûmes tombé(e)s
vous fûtes tombé(e)(s)
ils furent tombés
elles furent tombées

6 *PERFECT SUBJUNCTIVE*
je sois tombé(e)
tu sois tombé(e)
il soit tombé
elle soit tombée

nous soyons tombé(e)s
vous soyez tombé(e)(s)
ils soient tombés
elles soient tombées

7 *PLUPERFECT SUBJUNCTIVE*
je fusse tombé(e)
tu fusses tombé(e)
il fût tombé
elle fût tombée

nous fussions tombé(e)s
vous fussiez tombé(e)(s)
ils fussent tombés
elles fussent tombées

Compound Tenses (ctd.)

The following verbs take the auxiliary être

● Reflexive verbs (see p. 30) (→ **1**)

● The following intransitive verbs (i.e. verbs which cannot take a direct object), largely expressing motion or a change of state:

aller	*to go* (→ **2**)	**passer**	*to pass*
arriver	*to arrive; to happen*	**rentrer**	*to go back/in*
descendre	*to go/come down*	**rester**	*to stay* (→ **5**)
devenir	*to become*	**retourner**	*to go back*
entrer	*to go/come in*	**revenir**	*to come back*
monter	*to go/come up*	**sortir**	*to go/come out*
mourir	*to die* (→ **3**)	**tomber**	*to fall*
naître	*to be born*	**venir**	*to come* (→ **6**)
partir	*to leave* (→ **4**)		

● Of these, the following are conjugated with **avoir** when used transitively (i.e. with a direct object):

descendre	*to bring/take down*
entrer	*to bring/take in*
monter	*to bring/take up* (→ **7**)
passer	*to pass; to spend* (→ **8**)
rentrer	*to bring/take in*
retourner	*to turn over*
sortir	*to bring/take out* (→ **9**)

● Note that the past participle must show an agreement in number and gender whenever the auxiliary is **être** EXCEPT FOR REFLEXIVE VERBS WHERE THE REFLEXIVE PRONOUN IS THE INDIRECT OBJECT (see p. 50)

1 **je me suis arrêté(e)**
  I stopped
  tu t'es levé(e)
  you got up

  elle s'est trompée
  she made a mistake
  ils s'étaient battus
  they had fought (one another)

2 **elle est allée**
  she went

3 **ils sont morts**
  they died

4 **vous êtes partie**
  you left (*addressing a female person*)
  vous êtes parties
  you left (*addressing more than one female person*)

5 **nous sommes resté(e)s**
  we stayed

6 **elles étaient venues**
  they [female] had come

7 **Il a monté les valises**
  He's taken up the cases

8 **Nous avons passé trois semaines chez elle**
  We spent three weeks at her place

9 **Avez-vous sorti la voiture?**
  Have you taken the car out?

Reflexive Verbs

A reflexive verb is one accompanied by a reflexive pronoun, e.g. **se lever** *to get up*; **se laver** *to wash (oneself)*. The pronouns are:

PERSON	SINGULAR	PLURAL
1st	**me (m')**	**nous**
2nd	**te (t')**	**vous**
3rd	**se (s')**	**se (s')**

The forms shown in brackets are used before a vowel, an **h** 'mute', or the pronoun **y** (→ **1**)

● In positive commands, **te** changes to **toi** (→ **2**)

● The reflexive pronoun 'reflects back' to the subject, but it is not always translated in English (→ **3**)
The plural pronouns are sometimes translated as *one another*, *each other* (the 'reciprocal' meaning) (→ **4**)
The reciprocal meaning may be emphasised by **l'un(e) l'autre (les un(e)s les autres)** (→ **5**)

● Simple tenses of reflexive verbs are conjugated in exactly the same way as those of non-reflexive verbs except that the reflexive pronoun is always used. Compound tenses are formed with the auxiliary **être**. A sample reflexive verb is conjugated in full on pp. 34 and 35.

For agreement of past participles, see p. 32

Position of Reflexive Pronouns

● In constructions other than the imperative affirmative the pronoun comes before the verb (→ **6**)

● In the imperative affirmative, the pronoun follows the verb and is attached to it by a hyphen (→ **7**)

Continued

1 **Je m'ennuie**
I'm bored
Elle s'habille
She's getting dressed
Ils s'y intéressent
They are interested in it
2 **Assieds-toi**
Sit down
Tais-toi
Be quiet
3 **Je me prépare**
I'm getting (myself) ready
Nous nous lavons
We're washing (ourselves)
Elle se lève
She gets up
4 **Nous nous parlons**
We speak to each other
Ils se ressemblent
They resemble one another
5 **Ils se regardent l'un l'autre**
They are looking at each other
6 **Je me couche tôt**
I go to bed early
Comment vous appelez-vous?
What is your name?
Il ne s'est pas rasé
He hasn't shaved
Ne te dérange pas pour nous
Don't put yourself out on our account
7 **Dépêche-toi**
Hurry (up)
Renseignons-nous
Let's find out
Asseyez-vous
Sit down

Reflexive Verbs (ctd.)

Past Participle Agreement

● In most reflexive verbs the reflexive pronoun is a DIRECT object pronoun (→ **1**)

● When a direct object accompanies the reflexive verb the pronoun is then the INDIRECT object (→ **2**)

● The past participle of a reflexive verb agrees in number and gender with a direct object which *precedes* the verb (usually, but not always, the reflexive pronoun) (→ **3**)
The past participle does not change if the direct object follows the verb (→ **4**)

Here are some common reflexive verbs:

s'en aller	*to go away*	**se hâter**	*to hurry*
s'amuser	*to enjoy oneself*	**se laver**	*to wash (oneself)*
s'appeler	*to be called*	**se lever**	*to get up*
s'arrêter	*to stop*	**se passer**	*to happen*
s'asseoir	*to sit (down)*	**se promener**	*to go for a walk*
se baigner	*to go swimming*	**se rappeler**	*to remember*
se blesser	*to hurt oneself*	**se ressembler**	*to resemble each other*
se coucher	*to go to bed*	**se retourner**	*to turn round*
se demander	*to wonder*	**se réveiller**	*to wake up*
se dépêcher	*to hurry*	**se sauver**	*to run away*
se diriger	*to make one's way*	**se souvenir de**	*to remember*
s'endormir	*to fall asleep*	**se taire**	*to be quiet*
s'ennuyer	*to be/get bored*	**se tromper**	*to be mistaken*
se fâcher	*to get angry*	**se trouver**	*to be (situated)*
s'habiller	*to dress (oneself)*		

Continued

1 **Je m'appelle**
   I'm called (*literally: I call myself*)
   Asseyez-vous
   Sit down (*literally: Seat yourself*)
   Ils se lavent
   They wash (themselves)

2 **Elle se lave les mains**
   She's washing her hands (*literally: She's washing to herself the hands*)
   Je me brosse les dents
   I brush my teeth
   Nous nous envoyons des cadeaux à Noël
   We send presents to each other at Christmas

3 **'Je me suis endormi' s'est-il excusé**
   'I fell asleep', he apologized
   Pauline s'est dirigée vers la sortie
   Pauline made her way towards the exit
   Ils se sont levés vers dix heures
   They got up around ten o'clock
   Elles se sont excusées de leur erreur
   They apologised for their mistake
   Est-ce que tu t'es blessée, Cécile?
   Have you hurt yourself, Cécile?

4 **Elle s'est lavé les cheveux**
   She (has) washed her hair
   Nous nous sommes serré la main
   We shook hands
   Christine s'est cassé la jambe
   Christine has broken her leg

Reflexive Verbs (ctd.)

Conjugation of: **se laver** *to wash (oneself)*

| SIMPLE TENSES

PRESENT
  je me lave　　　　　　**nous nous lavons**
  tu te laves　　　　　　　**vous vous lavez**
  il/elle se lave　　　　　**ils/elles se lavent**

IMPERFECT
  je me lavais　　　　　　**nous nous lavions**
  tu te lavais　　　　　　　**vous vous laviez**
  il/elle se lavait　　　　**ils/elles se lavaient**

FUTURE
  je me laverai　　　　　　**nous nous laverons**
  tu te laveras　　　　　　**vous vous laverez**
  il/elle se lavera　　　　**ils/elles se laveront**

CONDITIONAL
  je me laverais　　　　　**nous nous laverions**
  tu te laverais　　　　　**vous vous laveriez**
  il/elle se laverait　　**ils/elles se laveraient**

PAST HISTORIC
  je me lavai　　　　　　　**nous nous lavâmes**
  tu te lavas　　　　　　　**vous vous lavâtes**
  il/elle se lava　　　　　**ils/elles se lavèrent**

PRESENT SUBJUNCTIVE
  je me lave　　　　　　　**nous nous lavions**
  tu te laves　　　　　　　**vous vous laviez**
  il/elle se lave　　　　　**ils/elles se lavent**

IMPERFECT SUBJUNCTIVE
  je me lavasse　　　　　**nous nous lavassions**
  tu te lavasses　　　　　**vous vous lavassiez**
  il/elle se lavât　　　　　**ils/elles se lavassent**

Reflexive Verbs (ctd.)

Conjugation of: **se laver** *to wash (oneself)*

II *COMPOUND TENSES*

PERFECT
   je me suis lavé(e)   nous nous sommes lavé(e)s
   tu t'es lavé(e)   vous vous êtes lavé(e)(s)
   il/elle s'est lavé(e)   ils/elles se sont lavé(e)s

PLUPERFECT
   je m'étais lavé(e)   nous nous étions lavé(e)s
   tu t'étais lavé(e)   vous vous étiez lavé(e)(s)
   il/elle s'était lavé(e)   ils/elles s'étaient lavé(e)s

FUTURE PERFECT
   je me serai lavé(e)   nous nous serons lavé(e)s
   tu te seras lavé(e)   vous vous serez lavé(e)(s)
   il/elle se sera lavé(e)   ils/elles se seront lavé(e)s

CONDITIONAL PERFECT
   je me serais lavé(e)   nous nous serions lavé(e)s
   tu te serais lavé(e)   vous vous seriez lavé(e)(s)
   il/elle se serait lavé(e)   ils/elles se seraient lavé(e)s

PAST ANTERIOR
   je me fus lavé(e)   nous nous fûmes lavé(e)s
   tu te fus lavé(e)   vous vous fûtes lavé(e)(s)
   il/elle se fut lavé(e)   ils/elles se furent lavé(e)s

PERFECT SUBJUNCTIVE
   je me sois lavé(e)   nous nous soyons lavé(e)s
   tu te sois lavé(e)   vous vous soyez lavé(e)(s)
   il/elle se soit lavé(e)   ils/elles se soient lavé(e)s

PLUPERFECT SUBJUNCTIVE
   je me fusse lavé(e)   nous nous fussions lavé(e)s
   tu te fusses lavé(e)   vous vous fussiez lavé(e)(s)
   il/elle se fût lavé(e)   ils/elles se fussent lavé(e)s

The Passive

In the passive, the subject *receives* the action (e.g. *I was hit*) as opposed to *performing* it (e.g. *I hit him*). In English the verb 'to be' is used with the past participle. In French the passive is formed in exactly the same way, i.e.:

a tense of **être** + past participle

The past participle agrees in number and gender with the subject (→1)

A sample verb is conjugated in the passive voice on pp. 38 and 39.

● The indirect object in French cannot become the subject in the passive:

in **quelqu'un m'a donné un livre** the indirect object **m'** cannot become the subject of a passive verb (unlike English: *someone gave me a book→I was given a book*)

● The passive meaning is often expressed in French by:
  – **on** plus a verb in the active voice (→2)
  – a reflexive verb (see p. 30) (→3)

1 Philippe a été récompensé
Phillip has been rewarded
Cette peinture est très admirée
This painting is greatly admired
Ils le feront pourvu qu'ils soient payés
They'll do it provided they're paid
Les enfants seront félicités
The children will be congratulated
Cette mesure aurait été critiquée si ...
This measure would have been criticized if ...
Les portes avaient été fermées
The doors had been closed

2 On leur a envoyé une lettre
They were sent a letter
On nous a montré le jardin
We were shown the garden
On m'a dit que ...
I was told that ...

3 Ils se vendent 30 francs (la) pièce
They are sold for 30 francs each
Ce mot ne s'emploie plus
This word is no longer used

The Passive (ctd.)

Conjugation of: **être aimé** *to be liked*

PRESENT
> **je suis aimé(e)**   **nous sommes aimé(e)s**
> **tu es aimé(e)**   **vous êtes aimé(e)(s)**
> **il/elle est aimé(e)**   **ils/elles sont aimé(e)s**

IMPERFECT
> **j'étais aimé(e)**   **nous étions aimé(e)s**
> **tu étais aimé(e)**   **vous étiez aimé(e)(s)**
> **il/elle était aimé(e)**   **ils/elles étaient aimé(e)s**

FUTURE
> **je serai aimé(e)**   **nous serons aimé(e)s**
> **tu seras aimé(e)**   **vous serez aimé(e)(s)**
> **il/elle sera aimé(e)**   **ils/elles seront aimé(e)s**

CONDITIONAL
> **je serais aimé(e)**   **nous serions aimé(e)s**
> **tu serais aimé(e)**   **vous seriez aimé(e)(s)**
> **il/elle serait aimé(e)**   **ils/elles seraient aimé(e)s**

PAST HISTORIC
> **je fus aimé(e)**   **nous fûmes aimé(e)s**
> **tu fus aimé(e)**   **vous fûtes aimé(e)(s)**
> **il/elle fut aimé(e)**   **ils/elles furent aimé(e)s**

PRESENT SUBJUNCTIVE
> **je sois aimé(e)**   **nous soyons aimé(e)s**
> **tu sois aimé(e)**   **vous soyez aimé(e)(s)**
> **il/elle soit aimé(e)**   **ils/elles soient aimé(e)s**

IMPERFECT SUBJUNCTIVE
> **je fusse aimé(e)**   **nous fussions aimé(e)s**
> **tu fusses aimé(e)**   **vous fussiez aimé(e)(s)**
> **il/elle fût aimé(e)**   **ils/elles fussent aimé(e)s**

The Passive (ctd.)

Conjugation of: **être aimé** *to be liked*

PERFECT
j'ai été aimé(e)   **nous avons été aimé(e)s**
tu as été aimé(e)   **vous avez été aimé(e)(s)**
il/elle a été aimé(e)   **ils/elles ont été aimé(e)s**

PLUPERFECT
j'avais été aimé(e)   **nous avions été aimé(e)s**
tu avais été aimé(e)   **vous aviez été aimé(e)(s)**
il/elle avait été aimé(e) **ils/elles avaient été aimé(e)s**

FUTURE PERFECT
j'aurai été aimé(e)   **nous aurons été aimé(e)s**
tu auras été aimé(e)   **vous aurez été aimé(e)(s)**
il/elle aura été aimé(e)   **ils/elles auront été aimé(e)s**

CONDITIONAL PERFECT
j'aurais été aimé(e)   **nous aurions été aimé(e)s**
tu aurais été aimé(e)   **vous auriez été aimé(e)(s)**
il/elle aurait été aimé(e) **ils/elles auraient été aimé(e)s**

PAST ANTERIOR
j'eus été aimé(e)   **nous eûmes été aimé(e)s**
tu eus été aimé(e)   **vous eûtes été aimé(e)(s)**
il/elle eut été aimé(e)   **ils/elles eurent été aimé(e)s**

PERFECT SUBJUNCTIVE
j'aie été aimé(e)   **nous ayons été aimé(e)s**
tu aies été aimé(e)   **vous ayez été aimé(e)(s)**
il/elle ait été aimé(e)   **ils/elles aient été aimé(e)s**

PLUPERFECT SUBJUNCTIVE
j'eusse été aimé(e)   **nous eussions été aimé(e)s**
tu eusses été aimé(e)   **vous eussiez été aimé(e)(s)**
il/elle eût été aimé(e)   **ils/elles eussent été aimé(e)s**

Impersonal Verbs

Impersonal verbs are used only in the infinitive and in the third person singular with the subject pronoun **il**, generally translated *it*.

e.g. **il pleut**
it's raining
il est facile de dire que ...
it's easy to say that ...

The most common impersonal verbs are:

INFINITIVE	CONSTRUCTIONS
s'agir	**il s'agit de** + noun (→**1**)
	it's a question/matter of something,
	it's about something
	il s'agit de + infinitive (→**2**)
	it's a question/matter of doing; somebody must do
falloir	**il faut** + noun object (+ indirect object) (→**3**)
	(somebody) needs something, something is necessary (to somebody)
	il faut + infinitive (+ indirect object) (→**4**)
	it is necessary to do
	il faut que + subjunctive (→**5**)
	it is necessary to do, somebody must do
grêler	**il grêle**
	it's hailing
neiger	**il neige**
	it's snowing
pleuvoir	**il pleut** (→**6**)
	it's raining
tonner	**il tonne**
	it's thundering
valoir mieux	**il vaut mieux** + infinitive (→**7**)
	it's better to do
	il vaut mieux que + subjunctive (→**8**)
	it's better to do/that somebody does

Continued

1 **Il ne s'agit pas d'argent**
   It isn't a question/matter of money
   De quoi s'agit-il?
   What is it about?
   Il s'agit de la vie d'une famille au début du siècle
   It's about the life of a family at the turn of the century

2 **Il s'agit de faire vite**
   We must act quickly

3 **Il faut du courage pour faire ça**
   One needs courage to do that; Courage is needed to do that
   Il me faut une chaise de plus
   I need an extra chair

4 **Il faut partir**
   It is necessary to leave; We/I/You must leave*
   Il me fallait prendre une décision
   I had to make a decision

5 **Il faut que vous partiez**
   You have to leave/You must leave
   Il faudrait que je fasse mes valises
   I should have to/ought to pack my cases

6 **Il pleuvait à verse**
   It was raining heavily/It was pouring

7 **Il vaut mieux refuser**
   It's better to refuse; You/He/I had better refuse*
   Il vaudrait mieux rester
   You/We/She had better stay*

8 **Il vaudrait mieux que nous ne venions pas**
   It would be better if we didn't come; We'd better not come

   The translation here obviously depends on context

Impersonal Verbs (ctd.)

The following verbs are also commonly used in impersonal constructions:

INFINITIVE	CONSTRUCTIONS
avoir	**il y a** + noun (→**1**)
	there is/are
être	**il est** + noun (→**2**)
	it is; there are (very literary style)
	il est + adjective + **de** + infinitive (→**3**)
	it is
faire	**il fait** + adjective of weather (→**4**)
	it is
	il fait + noun depicting weather/dark/light etc.
	it is (→**5**)
manquer	**il manque** + noun (+ indirect object) (→**6**)
	there is/are ... missing, something is
	missing/lacking
paraître	**il paraît que** + subjunctive (→**7**)
	it seems/appears that
	il paraît + indirect object + **que** + indicative (→**8**)
	it seems/appears to somebody that
rester	**il reste** + noun (+ indirect object) (→**9**)
	there is/are ... left, (somebody) has something left
sembler	**il semble que** + subjunctive (→**10**)
	it seems/appears that
	il semble + indirect object + **que** + indicative (→**11**)
	it seems/appears to somebody that
suffire	**il suffit de** + infinitive (→**12**)
	it is enough to do
	il suffit de + noun (→**13**)
	something is enough, it only takes something

Continued

1 **Il y a du pain (qui reste)**
  There is some bread (left)
  Il n'y avait pas de lettres ce matin
  There were no letters this morning
2 **Il est dix heures**
  It's ten o'clock
  Il est des gens qui ...
  There are (some) people who ...
3 **Il était inutile de protester**
  It was useless to protest
  Il est facile de critiquer
  Criticizing is easy
4 **Il fait beau/mauvais**
  It's lovely/horrible weather
5 **Il faisait du soleil/du vent**
  It was sunny/windy
  Il fait jour/nuit
  It's light/dark
6 **Il manque deux tasses**
  There are two cups missing; Two cups are missing
  Il manquait un bouton à sa chemise
  His shirt had a button missing
7 **Il paraît qu'ils partent demain**
  It appears they are leaving tomorrow
8 **Il nous paraît certain qu'il aura du succès**
  It seems certain to us that he'll be successful
9 **Il reste deux miches de pain**
  There are two loaves left
  Il lui restait cinquante francs
  He/She had fifty francs left
10 **Il semble que vous ayez raison**
  It seems that you are right
11 **Il me semblait qu'il conduisait trop vite**
  It seemed to me (that) he was driving too fast
12 **Il suffit de téléphoner pour réserver une place**
  You need only phone to reserve a seat
13 **Il suffit d'une seule erreur pour tout gâcher**
  One single error is enough to ruin everything

The Infinitive

The infinitive is the form of the verb found in dictionary entries meaning 'to ...', e.g. **donner** *to give*, **vivre** *to live*.

There are three main types of verbal construction involving the infinitive:

- with no linking preposition (→**1**)
- with the linking preposition **à** (→**2**)
  (see also p. 64)
- with the linking preposition **de** (→**3**)
  (see also p. 64)

Verbs followed by an infinitive with no linking preposition

- **devoir, pouvoir, savoir, vouloir** and **falloir** (i.e. modal auxiliary verbs: p. 52) (→**1**)
- **valoir mieux:** see Impersonal Verbs, p. 40
- verbs of seeing or hearing e.g. **voir** *to see*, **entendre** *to hear* (→**4**)
- intransitive verbs of motion e.g. **aller** *to go*, **descendre** *to come/go down* (→**5**)
- **envoyer** *to send* (→**6**)
- **faillir** (→**7**)
- **faire** (→**8**)
- **laisser** *to let, allow* (→**9**)
- The following common verbs:

adorer	*to love*	
aimer	*to like, love*	(→**10**)
aimer mieux	*to prefer*	(→**11**)
compter	*to expect*	
désirer	*to wish, want*	(→**12**)
détester	*to hate*	(→**13**)
espérer	*to hope*	(→**14**)
oser	*to dare*	(→**15**)
préférer	*to prefer*	
sembler	*to seem*	(→**16**)
souhaiter	*to wish*	

Continued

1 **Voulez-vous attendre?**
Would you like to wait?
2 **J'apprends à nager**
I'm learning to swim
3 **Essayez de venir**
Try to come
4 **Il nous a vus arriver**   **On les entend chanter**
He saw us arriving   You can hear them singing
5 **Allez voir Nicolas**
Go and see Nicholas
Descends leur demander
Go down and ask them
6 **Je l'ai envoyé les voir**
I sent him to see them
7 **J'ai failli tomber**
I almost fell
8 **Ne me faites pas rire!**
Don't make me laugh!
J'ai fait réparer ma valise
I've had my case repaired
9 **Laissez-moi passer**
Let me pass
10 **Il aime nous accompagner**
He likes to come with us
11 **J'aimerais mieux le choisir moi-même**
I'd rather choose it myself
12 **Elle ne désire pas venir**
She doesn't wish to come
13 **Je déteste me lever le matin**
I hate getting up in the morning
14 **Espérez-vous aller en vacances?**
Are you hoping to go on holiday?
15 **Nous n'avons pas osé y retourner**
We haven't dared go back
16 **Vous semblez être inquiet**
You seem to be worried

The Infinitive: Set Expressions

The following are set in French with the meaning shown:

aller chercher	*to go for, to go and get*	(→**1**)
envoyer chercher	*to send for*	(→**2**)
entendre dire que	*to hear it said that*	(→**3**)
entendre parler de	*to hear of/about*	(→**4**)
faire entrer	*to show in*	(→**5**)
faire sortir	*to let out*	(→**6**)
faire venir	*to send for*	(→**7**)
laisser tomber	*to drop*	(→**8**)
vouloir dire	*to mean*	(→**9**)

The Perfect Infinitive

● The perfect infinitive is formed using the auxiliary verb **avoir** or **être** as appropriate with the past participle of the verb (→**10**)

● The perfect infinitive is found:
  – following the preposition **après** *after* (→**11**)
  – following certain verbal constructions (→**12**)

1 **Va chercher tes photos**
   Go and get your photos
   Il est allé chercher Alexandre
   He's gone to get Alexander
2 **J'ai envoyé chercher un médecin**
   I've sent for a doctor
3 **J'ai entendu dire qu'il est malade**
   I've heard it said that he's ill
4 **Je n'ai plus entendu parler de lui**
   I didn't hear anything more (said) of him
5 **Fais entrer nos invités**
   Show our guests in
6 **J'ai fait sortir le chat**
   I've let the cat out
7 **Je vous ai fait venir parce que ...**
   I sent for you because ...
8 **Il a laissé tomber le vase**
   He dropped the vase
9 **Qu'est-ce que cela veut dire?**
   What does that mean?
10 **avoir fini**
   to have finished
   être allé   **s'être levé**
   to have gone   to have got up
11 **Après avoir pris cette décision, il nous a appelé**
   After making/having made that decision, he called us
   Après être sorties, elles se sont dirigées vers le parking
   After leaving/having left, they headed for the car park
   Après nous être levé(e)s, nous avons lu les journaux
   After getting up/having got up, we read the papers
12 **pardonner à qn d'avoir fait**
   to forgive sb for doing/having done
   remercier qn d'avoir fait
   to thank sb for doing/having done
   regretter d'avoir fait
   to be sorry for doing/having done

The Present Participle

Formation

● 1st conjugation
  Replace the **-er** of the infinitive by **-ant** (→**1**)

  – Verbs ending in **-cer**: **c** changes to **ç** (→**2**)
  – Verbs ending in **-ger**: **g** changes to **ge** (→**3**)

● 2nd conjugation
  Replace the **-ir** of the infinitive by **-issant** (→**4**)

● 3rd conjugation
  Replace the **-re** of the infinitive by **-ant** (→**5**)

● For irregular present participles, see irregular verbs, p. 74 ff.

Uses

The present participle has a more restricted use in French than in English.

● Used as a verbal form, the present participle is invariable. It is found:
  – on its own, where it corresponds to the English present participle (→**6**)
  – following the preposition **en** (→**7**)
  Note, in particular, the construction:
  verb + **en** + present participle
  which is often translated by an English phrasal verb, i.e. one followed by a preposition like *to run down, to bring up* (→**8**)

● Used as an adjective, the present participle agrees in number and gender with the noun or pronoun (→**9**)

● Note, in particular, the use of **ayant** and **étant** – the present participles of the auxiliary verbs **avoir** and **être** – with a past participle (→**10**)

Continued

1 **donner** → **donnant**
  to give   giving
2 **lancer** → **lançant**
  to throw   throwing
3 **manger** → **mangeant**
  to eat   eating
4 **finir** → **finissant**
  to finish finishing
5 **vendre** → **vendant**
  to sell   selling
6 **David, habitant près de Paris, a la possibilité de . . .**
  David, living near Paris, has the opportunity of . . .
  Elle, pensant que je serais fâché, a dit '. . .'
  She, thinking that I would be angry, said '. . .'
  Ils m'ont suivi, criant à tue-tête
  They followed me, shouting at the top of their voices
7 **En attendant sa sœur, Richard s'est endormi**
  While waiting for his sister, Richard fell asleep
  Téléphone-nous en arrivant chez toi
  Telephone us when you get home
  En appuyant sur ce bouton, on peut . . .
  By pressing this button, you can . . .
  Il s'est blessé en essayant de sauver un chat
  He hurt himself trying to rescue a cat
8 **sortir en courant**
  to run out (*literally: to go out running*)
  avancer en boîtant
  to limp along (*literally: to go forward limping*)
9 **le soleil couchant**   **une lumière éblouissante**
  the setting sun   a dazzling light
  ils sont déroutants   **elles étaient étonnantes**
  they are disconcerting   they were surprising
10 **Ayant mangé plus tôt, il a pu . . .**
   Having eaten earlier, he was able to . . .
   Etant arrivée en retard, elle a dû . . .
   Having arrived late, she had to . . .

Past Participle Agreement

Like adjectives, a past participle must sometimes agree in number and gender with a noun or pronoun. For the rules of agreement, see below.
Example: **donné**

	MASCULINE	FEMININE
SING.	donné	donnée
PLUR.	donnés	données

● When the masculine singular form already ends in **-s**, no further **s** is added in the masculine plural, e.g. **pris** *taken*

Rules of Agreement in Compound Tenses

● When the auxiliary verb is **avoir**
The past participle remains in the masculine singular form, unless a direct object precedes the verb. The past participle then agrees in number and gender with the preceding direct object (→**1**)

● When the auxiliary verb is **être**
The past participle of a non-reflexive verb agrees in number and gender with the subject (→**2**)
The past participle of a reflexive verb agrees in number and gender with the reflexive pronoun, if the pronoun is a direct object (→**3**)
No agreement is made if the reflexive pronoun is an indirect object (→**4**)

The Past Participle as an adjective
The past participle agrees in number and gender with the noun or pronoun (→**5**)

1 **Voici le livre que vous avez demandé**
   Here's the book you asked for
   Laquelle avaient-elles choisie?
   Which one had they chosen?
   Ces amis? Je les ai rencontrés à Edimbourg
   Those friends? I met them in Edinburgh
   Il a gardé toutes les lettres qu'elle a écrites
   He has kept all the letters she wrote
2 **Est-ce que ton frère est allé à l'étranger?**
   Did your brother go abroad?
   Elle était restée chez elle
   She had stayed at home
   Ils sont partis dans la matinée
   They left in the morning
   Mes cousines sont revenues hier
   My cousins came back yesterday
3 **Tu t'es rappelé d'acheter du pain, Georges?**
   Did you remember to buy bread, George?
   Martine s'est demandée pourquoi il l'appelait
   Martine wondered why he was calling her
   'Lui et moi nous nous sommes cachés' a-t-elle dit
   'He and I hid,' she said
   Les vendeuses se sont mises en grève
   Shop assistants have gone on strike
   Vous vous êtes brouillés?
   Have you fallen out with each other?
   Les ouvrières s'étaient entraidées
   The workers had helped one another
4 **Elle s'est lavé les mains**
   She washed her hands
   Ils se sont parlé pendant des heures
   They talked to each other for hours
5 **à un moment donné**   **la porte ouverte**
   at a given time   the open door
   ils sont bien connus   **elles semblent fatiguées**
   they are well-known   they seem tired

Modal Auxiliary Verbs

● In French, the modal auxiliary verbs are: **devoir**, **pouvoir**, **savoir**, **vouloir** and **falloir**.

● They are followed by a verb in the infinitive and have the following meanings:

devoir
to have to, must (→**1**)
to be due to (→**2**)
in the conditional/conditional perfect:
should/should have, ought/ought to have (→**3**)

pouvoir
to be able to, can (→**4**)
to be allowed to, can, may (→**5**)
indicating possibility: *may/might/could* (→**6**)

savoir
to know how to, can (→**7**)

vouloir
to want/wish to (→**8**)
to be willing to, will (→**9**)
in polite phrases (→**10**)

falloir
to be necessary: see Impersonal Verbs, p. 40

1 **Je dois leur rendre visite**
I must visit them
Elle a dû partir
She (has) had to leave
Il a dû regretter d'avoir parlé
He must have been sorry he spoke

2 **Vous devez revenir demain**
You're due (to come) back tomorrow
Je devais attraper le train de neuf heures mais ...
I was (supposed) to catch the nine o'clock train but ...

3 **Je devrais le faire**
I ought to do it
J'aurais dû m'excuser
I ought to have apologised

4 **Il ne peut pas lever le bras**
He can't raise his arm
Pouvez-vous réparer cette montre?
Can you mend this watch?

5 **Puis-je les accompagner?**
May I go with them?

6 **Il peut encore changer d'avis**
He may change his mind yet
Cela pourrait être vrai
It could/might be true

7 **Savez-vous conduire?**
Can you drive?
Je ne sais pas faire une omelette
I don't know how to make an omelette

8 **Elle veut rester encore un jour**
She wants to stay another day

9 **Ils ne voulaient pas le faire**
They wouldn't do it/They weren't willing to do it
Ma voiture ne veut pas démarrer
My car won't start

10 **Voulez-vous boire quelque chose?**
Would you like something to drink?

Use of Tenses

The Present

● Unlike English, French does not distinguish between the simple present (e.g. *I smoke, he reads,* we live) and the continuous present (e.g. *I am smoking, he is reading, we are living*) (→ **1**)

● To emphasise continuity, the following constructions may be used:
être en train de faire } *to be doing* (→ **2**)
être à faire

● French uses the present tense where English uses the perfect in the following cases:
  – with certain prepositions of time – notably **depuis** *for/since* – when an action begun in the past is continued in the present (→ **3**)
  Note, however, that the perfect is used as in English when the verb is negative or the action has been completed (→ **4**)
  – in the construction **venir de faire** *to have just done* (→ **5**)

The Future

The future is generally used as in English, but note the following:

● Immediate future time is often expressed by means of the present tense of **aller** plus an infinitive (→ **6**)

● In time clauses expressing future action, French uses the future where English uses the present (→ **7**)

The Future Perfect

● Used as in English to mean *shall/will have done* (→ **8**)

● In time clauses expressing future action, where English uses the perfect tense (→ **9**)

Continued

1 **Je fume**   I smoke OR I am smoking
  Il lit   He reads OR He is reading
  Nous habitons   We live OR We are living
2 **Il est en train de travailler**
  He's (busy) working
3 **Paul apprend à nager depuis six mois**
  Paul's been learning to swim for six months (*and still is*)
  Je suis debout depuis sept heures
  I've been up since seven
  Il y a longtemps que vous attendez?
  Have you been waiting long?
  Voilà deux semaines que nous sommes ici
  That's two weeks we've been here (now)
4 **Ils ne se sont pas vus depuis des mois**
  They haven't seen each other for months
  Elle est revenue il y a un an
  She came back a year ago
5 **Elisabeth vient de partir**
  Elizabeth has just left
6 **Tu vas tomber si tu ne fais pas attention**
  You'll fall if you're not careful
  Il va manquer le train
  He's going to miss the train
  Ça va prendre une demi-heure
  It'll take half an hour
7 **Quand il viendra vous serez en vacances**
  When he comes you'll be on holiday
  Faites-nous savoir aussitôt qu'elle arrivera
  Let us know as soon as she arrives
8 **J'aurai fini dans une heure**
  I shall have finished in an hour
9 **Quand tu auras lu ce roman, rends-le-moi**
  When you've read the novel, give it back to me
  Je partirai dès que j'aurai fini
  I'll leave as soon as I've finished

Use of Tenses (ctd.)

The Imperfect
● The imperfect describes:
  – an action (or state) in the past without definite limits in time (→ **1**)
  – habitual action(s) in the past (often translated by means of *would* or *used to*) (→ **2**)
● French uses the imperfect tense where English uses the pluperfect in the following cases:
  – with certain prepositions of time – notably **depuis** *for/ since* – when an action begun in the remoter past was continued in the more recent past (→ **3**)
    Note, however, that the pluperfect *is* used as in English, when the verb is negative or the action has been completed (→ **4**)
  – in the construction **venir de faire** *to have just done* (→ **5**)

The Perfect
● The perfect is used to recount a completed action or event in the past. Note that this corresponds to a perfect tense or a simple past tense in English (→ **6**)

The Past Historic
● Only ever used in *written, literary* French, the past historic recounts a completed action in the past, corresponding to a simple past tense in English (→ **7**)

The Past Anterior
This tense is used instead of the pluperfect when a verb in another part of the sentence is in the past historic. That is
● in time clauses, after conjunctions like: **quand**, **lorsque** *when*, **dès que**, **aussitôt que** *as soon as*, **après que** *after* (→ **8**)
● after **à peine** *hardly, scarcely* (→ **9**)

The Subjunctive
● In spoken French, the present subjunctive generally replaces the imperfect subjunctive. See also pp. 58 ff.

1 **Elle regardait par la fenêtre**
   She was looking out of the window
   Il pleuvait quand je suis sorti de chez moi
   It was raining when I left the house
   Nos chambres donnaient sur la plage
   Our rooms overlooked the beach

2 **Dans sa jeunesse il se levait à l'aube**
   In his youth he got up at dawn
   Nous causions des heures entières
   We would talk for hours on end
   Elle te taquinait, n'est-ce pas?
   She used to tease you, didn't she?

3 **Nous habitions à Londres depuis deux ans**
   We had been living in London for two years (*and still were*)
   Il était malade depuis 1985
   He had been ill since 1985
   Il y avait assez longtemps qu'il le faisait
   He had been doing it for quite a long time

4 **Voilà un an que je ne l'avais pas vu**
   I hadn't seen him for a year
   Il y avait une heure qu'elle était arrivée
   She had arrived one hour before

5 **Je venais de les rencontrer**
   I had just met them

6 **Nous sommes allés au bord de la mer**
   We went/have been to the seaside
   Il a refusé de nous aider
   He (has) refused to help us
   La voiture ne s'est pas arrêtée
   The car didn't stop/hasn't stopped

7 **Le roi mourut en 1592**
   The king died in 1592

8 **Quand il eut fini, il se leva**
   When he had finished, he got up

9 **A peine eut-il parlé qu'on frappa à la porte**
   He had scarcely spoken when there was a knock at the door

The Subjunctive: when to use it

(For how to form the subjunctive see pp. 6 ff.)

● After certain conjunctions

quoique **bien que**	*although* (→ **1**)
pour que **afin que**	*so that* (→ **2**)
pourvu que	*provided that* (→ **3**)
jusqu'à ce que	*until* (→ **4**)
avant que (. . . ne)	*before* (→ **5**)
à moins que (. . . ne)	*unless* (→ **6**)
de peur que (. . . ne) **de crainte que (. . . ne)**	*for fear that, lest* (→ **7**)

Note that the **ne** following the conjunctions in examples **5** to **7** has no translation value. It is often omitted in spoken informal French.

● After the conjunctions

de sorte que **de façon que** **de manière que**	*so that* (indicating a *purpose*) (→ **8**)

When these conjunctions introduce a *result* and not a *purpose*, the subjunctive is not used (→ **9**)

● After impersonal constructions which express necessity, possibility etc

il faut que **il est nécessaire que**	*it is necessary that* (→ **10**)
il est possible que	*it is possible that* (→ **11**)
il semble que	*it seems that* (→ **12**)
il vaut mieux que	*it is better that* (→ **13**)
il est dommage que	*it's a pity that* (→ **14**)

Continued

1 **Bien qu'il fasse beaucoup d'efforts, il est peu récompensé**
Although he makes a lot of effort, he isn't rewarded for it

2 **Demandez un reçu afin que vous puissiez être remboursé**
Ask for a receipt so that you can get a refund

3 **Nous partirons ensemble pourvu que Sylvie soit d'accord**
We'll leave together provided Sylvie agrees

4 **Reste ici jusqu'à ce que nous revenions**
Stay here until we come back

5 **Je le ferai avant que tu ne partes**
I'll do it before you leave

6 **Ce doit être Paul, à moins que je ne me trompe**
That must be Paul, unless I'm mistaken

7 **Parlez bas de peur qu'on ne vous entende**
Speak softly lest anyone hears you

8 **Retournez-vous de sorte que je vous voie**
Turn round so that I can see you

9 **Il refuse de le faire de sorte que je dois le faire moi-même**
He refuses to do it so that I have to do it myself

10 **Il faut que je vous parle immédiatement**
I must speak to you right away / It is necessary that I speak . . .

11 **Il est possible qu'ils aient raison**
They may be right / It's possible that they are right

12 **Il semble qu'elle ne soit pas venue**
It appears that she hasn't come

13 **Il vaut mieux que vous restiez chez vous**
It's better that you stay at home

14 **Il est dommage qu'elle ait perdu cette adresse**
It's a shame / a pity that she's lost the address

The Subjunctive: when to use it (ctd.)

● After verbs of:
　– 'wishing'
　vouloir que ⎫
　désirer que ⎬ *to wish that, want (→ 1)*
　souhaiter que ⎭

　– 'fearing'
　craindre que ⎫
　avoir peur que ⎬ *to be afraid that (→ 2)*

Note that **ne** in the first phrase of example 2 has no translation value. It is often omitted in spoken informal French.

　– 'ordering', 'forbidding', 'allowing'
　ordonner que *to order that (→ 3)*
　défendre que *to forbid that (→ 4)*
　permettre que *to allow that (→ 5)*

　– opinion, expressing uncertainty
　croire que ⎫
　penser que ⎬ *to think that (→ 6)*
　douter que *to doubt that (→ 7)*

　– emotion (e.g. regret, shame, pleasure)
　regretter que *to be sorry that (→ 8)*
　être content/surpris etc **que**
　to be pleased/ surprised etc that (→ 9)

● After a superlative (→ 10)

● After certain adjectives expressing some sort of 'uniqueness'
dernier ... qui/que	*last ... who/that*	⎫
premier ... qui/que	*first ... who/that*	⎬ (→ 11)
meilleur ... qui/que	*best ... who/that*	
seul ⎱ ... **qui/que**	*only ... who/that*	⎭
unique ⎰		

Continued

1 **Nous voulons qu'elle soit contente**
  We want her to be happy (*literally: We want that she is happy*)
  Désirez-vous que je le fasse?
  Do you want me to do it?

2 **Il craint qu'il ne soit trop tard**
  He's afraid it may be too late
  Avez-vous peur qu'il ne revienne pas?
  Are you afraid that he won't come back?

3 **Il a ordonné qu'ils soient désormais à l'heure**
  He has ordered that they be on time from now on

4 **Elle défend que vous disiez cela**
  She forbids you to say that

5 **Permettez que nous vous aidions**
  Allow us to help you

6 **Je ne pense pas qu'ils soient venus**
  I don't think they came

7 **Nous doutons qu'il ait dit la vérité**
  We doubt that he told the truth

8 **Je regrette que vous ne puissiez pas venir**
  I'm sorry that you cannot come

9 **Je suis content que vous les aimiez**
  I'm pleased that you like them

10 **la personne la plus sympathique que je connaisse**
  the nicest person I know
  l'article le moins cher que j'aie jamais acheté
  the cheapest item I have ever bought

11 **Voici la dernière lettre qu'elle m'ait écrite**
  This is the last letter she wrote to me
  David est la seule personne qui puisse me conseiller
  David is the only person who can advise me

The Subjunctive: when to use it (ctd.)

● After   **si (...) que**   *however (...)*   (→ **1**)
              qui que   *whoever*   (→ **2**)
              quoi que   *whatever*   (→ **3**)

  ● After **que** in the following:
    – to form the 3rd person imperative or to express a wish (→ **4**)
    – when **que** has the meaning *if*, replacing **si** in a clause (→ **5**)
    – when **que** has the meaning *whether* (→ **6**)

● In relative clauses following certain types of indefinite and negative construction (→ **7/8**)

● In set expressions (→ **9**)

1 **si courageux qu'il soit**
  however brave he may be
  si peu que ce soit
  however little it is

2 **Qui que vous soyez, allez-vous-en!**
  Whoever you are, go away!

3 **Quoi que nous fassions, ...**
  Whatever we do, ...

4 **Qu'il entre!**
  Let him come in!
  Que cela vous serve de leçon!
  Let that be a lesson to you!

5 **S'il fait beau et que tu te sentes mieux, nous irons ...**
  If it's nice and you're feeling better, we'll go ...

6 **Que tu viennes ou non, je ...**
  Whether you come or not, I ...

7 **Il cherche une maison qui ait deux caves**
  He's looking for a house which has two cellars
  (*subjunctive used since such a house may or may not exist*)
  J'ai besoin d'un livre qui décrive l'art du mime
  I need a book which describes the art of mime
  (*subjunctive used since such a book may or may not exist*)

8 **Je n'ai rencontré personne qui la connaisse**
  I haven't met anyone who knows her
  Il n'y a rien qui puisse vous empêcher de ...
  There's nothing that can prevent you from ...

9 **Vive le roi!**
  Long live the king!
  Que Dieu vous bénisse!
  God bless you!

Verbs governing à and de

The following lists (pp. 64 to 72) contain common verbal constructions using the prepositions **à** and **de**

Note the following abbreviations:

infin.	infinitive
perf. infin.	perfect infinitive*
qch	quelque chose
qn	quelqu'un
sb	somebody
sth	something

*For formation see p. 46

accuser qn de qch/de + perf. infin.	*to accuse sb of sth/of doing, having done* (→**1**)
accoutumer qn à qch/à + infin.	*to accustom sb to sth/to doing*
acheter qch à qn	*to buy sth from sb/for sb* (→**2**)
achever de + infin.	*to end up doing*
aider qn à + infin.	*to help sb to do* (→**3**)
s'amuser à + infin.	*to have fun doing*
s'apercevoir de qch	*to notice sth* (→**4**)
apprendre qch à qn	*to teach sb sth*
apprendre à + infin.	*to learn to do* (→**5**)
apprendre à qn à + infin.	*to teach sb to do* (→**6**)
s'approcher de qn/qch	*to approach sb/sth* (→**7**)
arracher qch à qn	*to snatch sth from sb* (→**8**)
(s')arrêter de + infin.	*to stop doing* (→**9**)
arriver à + infin.	*to manage to do* (→**10**)
assister à qch	*to attend sth, be at sth*
s'attendre à + infin.	*to expect to do* (→**11**)
blâmer qn de qch/de + perf. infin.	*to blame sb for sth/for having done* (→**12**)
cacher qch à qn	*to hide sth from sb* (→**13**)
cesser de + infin.	*to stop doing* (→**14**)

Continued

1 **Il m'a accusé d'avoir menti**
He accused me of lying

2 **Marie-Christine leur a acheté deux billets**
Marie-Christine bought two tickets from/for them

3 **Aidez-moi à porter ces valises**
Help me to carry these cases

4 **Il ne s'est pas aperçu de son erreur**
He didn't notice his mistake

5 **Elle apprend à lire**
She's learning to read

6 **Je lui apprends à nager**
I'm teaching him/her to swim

7 **Elle s'est approchée de moi, en disant '…'**
She came up to me, saying '…'

8 **Le voleur lui a arraché l'argent**
The thief snatched the money from him/her

9 **Arrêtez de faire du bruit!**
Stop being (so) noisy!

10 **Je n'arrive pas à le comprendre**
I can't understand it

11 **Est-ce qu'elle s'attendait à le voir?**
Was she expecting to see him?

12 **Je ne la blâme pas de l'avoir fait**
I don't blame her for doing it

13 **Cache-les-leur!**
Hide them from them!

14 **Est-ce qu'il a cessé de pleuvoir?**
Has it stopped raining?

Verbs governing à and de (ctd.)

changer de qch	*to change sth* (→ **1**)
se charger de qch/de + infin.	*to see to sth/undertake to do*
chercher à + infin.	*to try to do*
commander à qn de + infin.	*to order sb to do* (→ **2**)
commencer à/de + infin.	*to begin to do* (→ **3**)
conseiller à qn de + infin.	*to advise sb to do* (→ **4**)
consentir à qch/à + infin.	*to agree to sth/to do* (→ **5**)
continuer à/de + infin.	*to continue to do*
craindre de + infin.	*to be afraid to do/of doing*
décider de + infin.	*to decide to* (→ **6**)
se décider à + infin.	*to make up one's mind to do*
défendre à qn de + infin.	*to forbid sb to do* (→ **7**)
demander qch à qn	*to ask sb sth/for sth* (→ **8**)
demander à qn de + infin.	*to ask sb to do* (→ **9**)
se dépêcher de + infin.	*to hurry to do*
dépendre de qn/qch	*to depend on sb/sth*
déplaire à qn	*to displease sb* (→ **10**)
désobéir à qn	*to disobey sb* (→ **11**)
dire à qn de + infin.	*to tell sb to do* (→ **12**)
dissuader qn de + infin.	*to dissuade sb from doing*
douter de qch	*to doubt sth*
se douter de qch	*to suspect sth*
s'efforcer de + infin.	*to strive to do*
empêcher qn de + infin.	*to prevent sb from doing* (→ **13**)
emprunter qch à qn	*to borrow sth from sb* (→ **14**)
encourager qn à + infin.	*to encourage sb to do* (→ **15**)
enlever qch à qn	*to take sth away from sb*
enseigner qch à qn	*to teach sb sth*
enseigner à qn à + infin.	*to teach sb to do*
entreprendre de + infin.	*to undertake to do*
essayer de + infin.	*to try to do* (→ **16**)
éviter de + infin.	*to avoid doing* (→ **17**)

Continued

1 **J'ai changé d'avis/de robe**
I changed my mind/my dress
Il faut changer de train à Toulouse
You have to change trains at Toulouse

2 **Il leur a commandé de tirer**
He ordered them to shoot

3 **Il commence à neiger**
It's starting to snow

4 **Il leur a conseillé d'attendre**
He advised them to wait

5 **Je n'ai pas consenti à l'aider**
I haven't agreed to help him/her

6 **Qu'est-ce que vous avez décidé de faire?**
What have you decided to do?

7 **Je leur ai défendu de sortir**
I've forbidden them to go out

8 **Je lui ai demandé l'heure**
I asked him/her the time
Il lui a demandé un livre
He asked him/her for a book

9 **Demande à Alain de le faire**
Ask Alan to do it

10 **Leur attitude lui déplaît**
He/She doesn't like their attitude

11 **Ils lui désobéissent souvent**
They often disobey him/her

12 **Dites-leur de se taire**
Tell them to be quiet

13 **Le bruit m'empêche de travailler**
The noise is preventing me from working

14 **Puis-je vous emprunter ce stylo?**
May I borrow this pen from you?

15 **Elle encourage ses enfants à être indépendants**
She encourages her children to be independent

16 **Essayez d'arriver à l'heure**
Try to arrive on time

17 **Il évite de lui parler**
He avoids speaking to him/her

Verbs governing à and de (ctd.)

s'excuser de qch/de + (perf.) infin.	*to apologise for sth/for doing, having done* (→ **1**)
exceller à + infin.	*to excel at doing*
se fâcher de qch	*to be annoyed at sth*
feindre de + infin.	*to pretend to do* (→ **2**)
féliciter qn de qch/de + (perf.) infin.	*to congratulate sb on sth/on doing, having done* (→ **3**)
se fier à qn	*to trust sb* (→ **4**)
finir de + infin.	*to finish doing* (→ **5**)
forcer qn à + infin.	*to force sb to do*
habituer qn à + infin.	*to accustom sb to doing*
s'habituer à + infin.	*to get/be used to doing* (→ **6**)
se hâter de + infin.	*to hurry to do*
hésiter à + infin.	*to hesitate to do*
interdire à qn de + infin.	*to forbid sb to do* (→ **7**)
s'intéresser à qn/qch/à + infin.	*to be interested in sb/sth/in doing* (→ **8**)
inviter qn à + infin.	*to invite sb to do* (→ **9**)
jouer à (+ sports, games)	*to play* (→ **10**)
jouer de (+ musical instruments)	*to play* (→ **11**)
jouir de qch	*to enjoy sth* (→ **12**)
jurer de + infin.	*to swear to do*
louer qn de qch	*to praise sb for sth*
manquer à qn	*to be missed by sb* (→ **13**)
manquer de qch	*to lack sth*
manquer de + infin.	*to fail to do* (→ **14**)
se marier à qn	*to marry sb*
se méfier de qn	*to distrust sb*
menacer de + infin.	*to threaten to do* (→ **15**)
mériter de + infin.	*to deserve to do* (→ **16**)
se mettre à + infin.	*to begin to do*
se moquer de qn/qch	*to make fun of sb/sth*
négliger de + infin.	*to fail to do*

Continued

1 **Je m'excuse d'être (arrivé) en retard**
   I apologise for being (arriving) late
2 **Elle feint de dormir**
   She's pretending to be asleep
3 **Je l'ai félicitée d'avoir gagné**
   I congratulated her on winning
4 **Je ne me fie pas à ces gens-là**
   I don't trust those people
5 **Avez-vous fini de lire ce journal?**
   Have you finished reading this newspaper?
6 **Il s'est habitué à boire moins de café**
   He got used to drinking less coffee
7 **Il a interdit aux enfants de jouer avec des allumettes**
   He's forbidden the children to play with matches
8 **Elle s'intéresse beaucoup au sport**
   She's very interested in sport
9 **Il m'a invitée à danser**
   He asked me to dance
10 **Elle joue au tennis et au hockey**
   She plays tennis and hockey
11 **Il joue du piano et de la guitare**
   He plays the piano and the guitar
12 **Il jouit d'une santé solide**
   He enjoys good health
13 **Tu manques à tes parents**
   Your parents miss you
14 **Je ne manquerai pas de le lui dire**
   I'll be sure to tell him/her about it
15 **Elle a menacé de démissionner tout de suite**
   She threatened to resign at once
16 **Ils méritent d'être promus**
   They deserve to be promoted

Verbs governing à and de (ctd.)

nuire à qch	*to harm sth* (→ **1**)
obéir à qn	*to obey sb*
obliger qn à + infin.	*to oblige sb to do* (→ **2**)
s'occuper de qch/qn	*to look after sth/sb* (→ **3**)
offrir de + infin.	*to offer to do* (→ **4**)
omettre de + infin.	*to fail to do*
ordonner à qn de + infin.	*to order sb to do* (→ **5**)
ôter qch à qn	*to take sth away from sb*
oublier de + infin.	*to forget to do*
pardonner qch à qn	*to forgive sb for sth*
pardonner à qn de + perf. infin.	*to forgive sb for having done* (→ **6**)
parvenir à + infin.	*to manage to do*
se passer de qch	*to do/go without sth* (→ **7**)
penser à qn/qch	*to think about sb/sth* (→ **8**)
permettre qch à qn	*to allow sb sth*
permettre à qn de + infin.	*to allow sb to do* (→ **9**)
persister à + infin.	*to persist in doing*
persuader qn de + infin.	*to persuade sb to do* (→ **10**)
se plaindre de qch	*to complain about sth*
plaire à qn	*to please sb* (→ **11**)
pousser qn à + infin.	*to urge sb to do*
prendre qch à qn	*to take sth from sb* (→ **12**)
préparer qn à + infin.	*to prepare sb to do*
se préparer à + infin.	*to get ready to do*
prier qn de + infin.	*to beg sb to do*
profiter de qch/de + infin.	*to take advantage of sth/of doing*
promettre à qn de + infin.	*to promise sb to do* (→ **13**)
proposer de + infin.	*to suggest doing* (→ **14**)
punir qn de qch	*to punish sb for sth* (→ **15**)
récompenser qn de qch	*to reward sb for sth*
réfléchir à qch	*to think about sth*
refuser de + infin.	*to refuse to do* (→ **16**)

Continued

1 **Ce mode de vie va nuire à sa santé**
This lifestyle will damage her health
2 **Il les a obligés à faire la vaisselle**
He made them do the washing-up
3 **Je m'occupe de ma nièce**
I'm looking after my niece
4 **Stuart a offert de nous accompagner**
Stuart has offered to go with us
5 **Les soldats leur ont ordonné de se rendre**
The soldiers ordered them to give themselves up
6 **Est-ce que tu as pardonné à Charles de t'avoir menti?**
Have you forgiven Charles for lying to you?
7 **Nous nous sommes passés d'électricité pendant plusieurs jours**
We did without electricity for several days
8 **Je pense souvent à toi**
I often think about you
9 **Permettez-moi de continuer, s'il vous plaît**
Allow me to go on, please
10 **Elle nous a persuadés de rester**
She persuaded us to stay
11 **Est-ce que ce genre de film lui plaît?**
Does he/she like this kind of film?
12 **Je lui ai pris son baladeur**
I took his personal stereo from him
13 **Ils ont promis à Pascale de venir**
They promised Pascale that they would come
14 **J'ai proposé de les inviter**
I suggested inviting them
15 **Il a été puni de sa malhonnêteté**
He has been punished for his dishonesty
16 **Il a refusé de coopérer**
He has refused to cooperate

Verbs governing à and de (ctd.)

regretter de + perf. infin.	*to regret doing, having done (→ 1)*
remercier qn de qch/de + perf. infin.	*to thank sb for sth/for doing, having done (→ 2)*
renoncer à qch/à + infin.	*to give sth up/give up doing*
reprocher qch à qn	*to reproach sb with/for sth (→ 3)*
résister à qch	*to resist sth (→ 4)*
résoudre de + infin.	*to resolve to do*
ressembler à qn/qch	*to look/be like sb/sth (→ 5)*
réussir à + infin.	*to manage to do (→ 6)*
rire de qn/qch	*to laugh at sb/sth*
risquer de + infin.	*to risk doing (→ 7)*
servir à qch/à + infin.	*to be used for sth/for doing (→ 8)*
se servir de qch	*to use sth; to help oneself to sth (→ 9)*
songer à + infin.	*to think of doing*
se souvenir de qn/qch/de + perf. infin.	*to remember sb/sth/doing, having done (→ 10)*
succéder à qn	*to succeed sb*
survivre à qn	*to outlive sb (→ 11)*
tâcher de + infin.	*to try to do (→ 12)*
tarder à + infin.	*to delay doing (→ 13)*
tendre à + infin.	*to tend to do*
tenir à + infin.	*to be keen to do (→ 14)*
tenter de + infin.	*to try to do (→ 15)*
se tromper de qch	*to be wrong about sth (→ 16)*
venir de* + infin.	*to have just done (→ 17)*
vivre de qch	*to live on sth*
voler qch à qn	*to steal sth from sb*

*See also Use of Tenses, pp. 54 and 56

1 **Je regrette de ne pas vous avoir écrit plus tôt**
  I'm sorry for not writing to you sooner
2 **Nous les avons remerciés de leur gentillesse**
  We thanked them for their kindness
3 **On lui reproche son manque d'enthousiasme**
  They're reproaching him for his lack of enthusiasm
4 **Comment résistez-vous à la tentation?**
  How do you resist temptation?
5 **Elles ressemblent beaucoup à leur mère**
  They look very like their mother
6 **Vous avez réussi à me convaincre**
  You've managed to convince me
7 **Vous risquez de tomber en faisant cela**
  You risk falling doing that
8 **Ce bouton sert à régler le volume**
  This knob is (used) for adjusting the volume
9 **Il s'est servi d'un tournevis pour l'ouvrir**
  He used a screwdriver to open it
10 **Vous vous souvenez de Lucienne?**
  Do you remember Lucienne?
  Il ne se souvient pas de l'avoir perdu
  He doesn't remember losing it
11 **Elle a survécu à son mari**
  She outlived her husband
12 **Tâchez de ne pas être en retard!**
  Try not to be late!
13 **Il n'a pas tardé à prendre une décision**
  He was not long in taking a decision
14 **Elle tient à le faire elle-même**
  She's keen to do it herself
15 **J'ai tenté de la comprendre**
  I've tried to understand her
16 **Je me suis trompé de route**
  I took the wrong road
17 **Mon père vient de téléphoner**   **Nous venions d'arriver**
  My father's just phoned   We had just arrived

Irregular Verbs

The verbs listed opposite and conjugated on pp. 76 to 131 provide the main patterns for irregular verbs. The verbs are grouped opposite according to their infinitive ending (except **avoir** and **être**), and are shown in the following tables in alphabetical order.

In the tables, the most important irregular verbs are given in their most common simple tenses, together with the imperative and the present participle.

The auxiliary (**avoir** or **être**) is also shown for each verb, together with the past participle, to enable you to form all the compound tenses, as on pp. 24 and 26.

● For a fuller list of irregular verbs, the reader is referred to Collins Gem French Verb Tables, which shows you how to conjugate some 2000 French verbs.

Continued

avoir
être

'-er': aller
envoyer

'-ir': acquérir
bouillir
courir
cueillir
dormir
fuir
haïr
mourir
ouvrir
partir
sentir
servir
sortir
tenir
venir
vêtir

'-oir': s'asseoir
devoir
falloir
pleuvoir
pouvoir
recevoir
savoir
valoir
voir
vouloir

'-re': battre
boire
connaître
coudre
craindre
croire
croître
cuire
dire
écrire
faire
lire
mettre
moudre
naître
paraître
plaire
prendre
résoudre
rire
rompre
suffire
suivre
se taire
vaincre
vivre

acquérir *to acquire* Auxiliary: **avoir**

PAST PARTICIPLE
acquis

PRESENT PARTICIPLE
acquérant

IMPERATIVE
acquiers
acquérons
acquérez

PRESENT

	j'acquiers
tu	acquiers
il	acquiert
nous	acquérons
vous	acquérez
ils	acquièrent

FUTURE

	j'acquerrai
tu	acquerras
il	acquerra
nous	acquerrons
vous	acquerrez
ils	acquerront

PRESENT SUBJUNCTIVE

	j'acquière
tu	acquières
il	acquière
nous	acquérions
vous	acquériez
ils	acquièrent

IMPERFECT

	j'acquérais
tu	acquérais
il	acquérait
nous	acquérions
vous	acquériez
ils	acquéraient

CONDITIONAL

	j'acquerrais
tu	acquerrais
il	acquerrait
nous	acquerrions
vous	acquerriez
ils	acquerraient

PAST HISTORIC

	j'acquis
tu	acquis
il	acquit
nous	acquîmes
vous	acquîtes
ils	acquirent

aller *to go*   Auxiliary: **être**

PAST PARTICIPLE
allé

PRESENT PARTICIPLE
allant

IMPERATIVE
va
allons
allez

PRESENT

je	**vais**
tu	**vas**
il	**va**
nous	allons
vous	allez
ils	**vont**

IMPERFECT

	j'allais
tu	allais
il	allait
nous	allions
vous	alliez
ils	allaient

FUTURE

	j'irai
tu	**iras**
il	**ira**
nous	**irons**
vous	**irez**
ils	**iront**

CONDITIONAL

	j'irais
tu	**irais**
il	**irait**
nous	**irions**
vous	**iriez**
ils	**iraient**

PRESENT SUBJUNCTIVE

	j'aille
tu	**ailles**
il	**aille**
nous	allions
vous	alliez
ils	**aillent**

PAST HISTORIC

	j'allai
tu	allas
il	alla
nous	allâmes
vous	allâtes
ils	allèrent

s'asseoir *to sit down*   Auxiliary: être

PAST PARTICIPLE
assis

PRESENT PARTICIPLE
s'asseyant

IMPERATIVE
assieds-toi
asseyons-nous
asseyez-vous

PRESENT

je	m'assieds *or* assois
tu	t'assieds *or* assois
il	s'assied *or* assoit
nous	nous asseyons *or* assoyons
vous	vous asseyez *or* assoyez
ils	s'asseyent *or* assoient

IMPERFECT

je	m'asseyais
tu	t'asseyais
il	s'asseyait
nous	nous asseyions
vous	vous asseyiez
ils	s'asseyaient

FUTURE

je	m'assiérai
tu	t'assiéras
il	s'assiéra
nous	nous assiérons
vous	vous assiérez
ils	s'assiéront

CONDITIONAL

je	m'assiérais
tu	t'assiérais
il	s'assiérait
nous	nous assiérions
vous	vous assiériez
ils	s'assiéraient

PRESENT SUBJUNCTIVE

je	m'asseye
tu	t'asseyes
il	s'asseye
nous	nous asseyions
vous	vous asseyiez
ils	s'asseyent

PAST HISTORIC

je	m'assis
tu	t'assis
il	s'assit
nous	nous assîmes
vous	vous assîtes
ils	s'assirent

avoir *to have*   Auxiliary: **avoir**

PAST PARTICIPLE
eu

PRESENT PARTICIPLE
ayant

IMPERATIVE
aie
ayons
ayez

PRESENT		*IMPERFECT*	
	j'ai		j'avais
tu	as	tu	avais
il	a	il	avait
nous	avons	nous	avions
vous	avez	vous	aviez
ils	ont	ils	avaient

FUTURE		*CONDITIONAL*	
	j'aurai		j'aurais
tu	auras	tu	aurais
il	aura	il	aurait
nous	aurons	nous	aurions
vous	aurez	vous	auriez
ils	auront	ils	auraient

PRESENT SUBJUNCTIVE		*PAST HISTORIC*	
	j'aie		j'eus
tu	aies	tu	eus
il	ait	il	eut
nous	ayons	nous	eûmes
vous	ayez	vous	eûtes
ils	aient	ils	eurent

battre *to beat*   Auxiliary: **avoir**

PAST PARTICIPLE
battu

PRESENT PARTICIPLE
battant

IMPERATIVE
bats
battons
battez

PRESENT		IMPERFECT	
je	**bats**	je	battais
tu	**bats**	tu	battais
il	**bat**	il	battait
nous	battons	nous	battions
vous	battez	vous	battiez
ils	battent	ils	battaient

FUTURE		CONDITIONAL	
je	battrai	je	battrais
tu	battras	tu	battrais
il	battra	il	battrait
nous	battrons	nous	battrions
vous	battrez	vous	battriez
ils	battront	ils	battraient

PRESENT SUBJUNCTIVE		PAST HISTORIC	
je	batte	je	battis
tu	battes	tu	battis
il	batte	il	battit
nous	battions	nous	battîmes
vous	battiez	vous	battîtes
ils	battent	ils	battirent

boire *to drink*   Auxiliary: **avoir**

PAST PARTICIPLE
bu

PRESENT PARTICIPLE
buvant

IMPERATIVE
bois
buvons
buvez

PRESENT

je	bois
tu	bois
il	boit
nous	**buvons**
vous	**buvez**
ils	**boivent**

IMPERFECT

je	**buvais**
tu	**buvais**
il	**buvait**
nous	**buvions**
vous	**buviez**
ils	**buvaient**

FUTURE

je	boirai
tu	boiras
il	boira
nous	boirons
vous	boirez
ils	boiront

CONDITIONAL

je	boirais
tu	boirais
il	boirait
nous	boirions
vous	boiriez
ils	boiraient

PRESENT SUBJUNCTIVE

je	**boive**
tu	**boives**
il	**boive**
nous	**buvions**
vous	**buviez**
ils	**boivent**

PAST HISTORIC

je	**bus**
tu	**bus**
il	**but**
nous	**bûmes**
vous	**bûtes**
ils	**burent**

bouillir *to boil*   Auxiliary: **avoir**

PAST PARTICIPLE
  bouilli

IMPERATIVE
  bous
  bouillons
  bouillez

PRESENT PARTICIPLE
  bouillant

PRESENT		IMPERFECT	
je	**bous**	je	**bouillais**
tu	**bous**	tu	**bouillais**
il	**bout**	il	**bouillait**
nous	**bouillons**	nous	**bouillions**
vous	**bouillez**	vous	**bouilliez**
ils	**bouillent**	ils	**bouillaient**

FUTURE		CONDITIONAL	
je	bouillirai	je	bouillirais
tu	bouilliras	tu	bouillirais
il	bouillira	il	bouillirait
nous	bouillirons	nous	bouillirions
vous	bouillirez	vous	bouilliriez
ils	bouilliront	ils	bouilliraient

PRESENT SUBJUNCTIVE		PAST HISTORIC	
je	**bouille**	je	bouillis
tu	**bouilles**	tu	bouillis
il	**bouille**	il	bouillit
nous	**bouillions**	nous	bouillîmes
vous	**bouilliez**	vous	bouillîtes
ils	**bouillent**	ils	bouillirent

connaître *to know*

Auxiliary: **avoir**

PAST PARTICIPLE
connu

PRESENT PARTICIPLE
connaissant

IMPERATIVE
connais
connaissons
connaissez

PRESENT

je	**connais**
tu	**connais**
il	connaît
nous	**connaissons**
vous	**connaissez**
ils	**connaissent**

IMPERFECT

je	**connaissais**
tu	**connaissais**
il	**connaissait**
nous	**connaissions**
vous	**connaissiez**
ils	**connaissaient**

FUTURE

je	connaîtrai
tu	connaîtras
il	connaîtra
nous	connaîtrons
vous	connaîtrez
ils	connaîtront

CONDITIONAL

je	connaîtrais
tu	connaîtrais
il	connaîtrait
nous	connaîtrions
vous	connaîtriez
ils	connaîtraient

PRESENT SUBJUNCTIVE

je	**connaisse**
tu	**connaisses**
il	**connaisse**
nous	**connaissions**
vous	**connaissiez**
ils	**connaissent**

PAST HISTORIC

je	**connus**
tu	**connus**
il	**connut**
nous	**connûmes**
vous	**connûtes**
ils	**connurent**

coudre *to sew*   Auxiliary: **avoir**

PAST PARTICIPLE
  cousu

PRESENT PARTICIPLE
  cousant

IMPERATIVE
  couds
  cousons
  cousez

PRESENT		*IMPERFECT*	
je	couds	**je**	**cousais**
tu	couds	**tu**	**cousais**
il	coud	**il**	**cousait**
nous	**cousons**	**nous**	**cousions**
vous	**cousez**	**vous**	**cousiez**
ils	**cousent**	**ils**	**cousaient**

FUTURE		*CONDITIONAL*	
je	coudrai	je	coudrais
tu	coudras	tu	coudrais
il	coudra	il	coudrait
nous	coudrons	nous	coudrions
vous	coudrez	vous	coudriez
ils	coudront	ils	coudraient

PRESENT SUBJUNCTIVE		*PAST HISTORIC*	
je	**couse**	**je**	**cousis**
tu	**couses**	**tu**	**cousis**
il	**couse**	**il**	**cousit**
nous	**cousions**	**nous**	**cousîmes**
vous	**cousiez**	**vous**	**cousîtes**
ils	**cousent**	**ils**	**cousirent**

courir *to run*   Auxiliary: **avoir**

PAST PARTICIPLE
couru

PRESENT PARTICIPLE
courant

IMPERATIVE
cours
courons
courez

PRESENT

je	cours
tu	cours
il	court
nous	courons
vous	courez
ils	courent

IMPERFECT

je	courais
tu	courais
il	courait
nous	courions
vous	couriez
ils	couraient

FUTURE

je	courrai
tu	courras
il	courra
nous	courrons
vous	courrez
ils	courront

CONDITIONAL

je	courrais
tu	courrais
il	courrait
nous	courrions
vous	courriez
ils	courraient

PRESENT SUBJUNCTIVE

je	coure
tu	coures
il	coure
nous	courions
vous	couriez
ils	courent

PAST HISTORIC

je	courus
tu	courus
il	courut
nous	courûmes
vous	courûtes
ils	coururent

craindre *to fear*

Auxiliary: **avoir**

PAST PARTICIPLE
craint

PRESENT PARTICIPLE
craignant

IMPERATIVE
crains
craignons
craignez

PRESENT

je	**crains**
tu	**crains**
il	**craint**
nous	**craignons**
vous	**craignez**
ils	**craignent**

IMPERFECT

je	**craignais**
tu	**craignais**
il	**craignait**
nous	**craignions**
vous	**craigniez**
ils	**craignaient**

FUTURE

je	craindrai
tu	craindras
il	craindra
nous	craindrons
vous	craindrez
ils	craindront

CONDITIONAL

je	craindrais
tu	craindrais
il	craindrait
nous	craindrions
vous	craindriez
ils	craindraient

PRESENT SUBJUNCTIVE

je	**craigne**
tu	**craignes**
il	**craigne**
nous	**craignions**
vous	**craigniez**
ils	**craignent**

PAST HISTORIC

je	**craignis**
tu	**craignis**
il	**craignit**
nous	**craignîmes**
vous	**craignîtes**
ils	**craignirent**

Verbs ending in **-eindre** and **-oindre** are conjugated similarly

croire *to believe*   Auxiliary: **avoir**

PAST PARTICIPLE
cru

IMPERATIVE
crois
croyons
croyez

PRESENT PARTICIPLE
croyant

PRESENT		*IMPERFECT*	
je	crois	**je**	**croyais**
tu	crois	**tu**	**croyais**
il	**croit**	**il**	**croyait**
nous	**croyons**	**nous**	**croyions**
vous	**croyez**	**vous**	**croyiez**
ils	croient	**ils**	**croyaient**

FUTURE		*CONDITIONAL*	
je	croirai	je	croirais
tu	croiras	tu	croirais
il	croira	il	croirait
nous	croirons	nous	croirions
vous	croirez	vous	croiriez
ils	croiront	ils	croiraient

PRESENT SUBJUNCTIVE		*PAST HISTORIC*	
je	croie	**je**	**crus**
tu	croies	**tu**	**crus**
il	croie	**il**	**crut**
nous	**croyions**	**nous**	**crûmes**
vous	**croyiez**	**vous**	**crûtes**
ils	croient	**ils**	**crurent**

croître *to grow*   Auxiliary: **avoir**

PAST PARTICIPLE
crû

PRESENT PARTICIPLE
croissant

IMPERATIVE
croîs
croissons
croissez

PRESENT		IMPERFECT	
je	**croîs**	je	**croissais**
tu	**croîs**	tu	**croissais**
il	croît	il	**croissait**
nous	**croissons**	nous	**croissions**
vous	**croissez**	vous	**croissiez**
ils	**croissent**	ils	**croissaient**

FUTURE		CONDITIONAL	
je	croîtrai	je	croîtrais
tu	croîtras	tu	croîtrais
il	croîtra	il	croîtrait
nous	croîtrons	nous	croîtrions
vous	croîtrez	vous	croîtriez
ils	croîtront	ils	croîtraient

PRESENT SUBJUNCTIVE		PAST HISTORIC	
je	**croisse**	je	**crûs**
tu	**croisses**	tu	**crûs**
il	**croisse**	il	**crût**
nous	**croissions**	nous	**crûmes**
vous	**croissiez**	vous	**crûtes**
ils	**croissent**	ils	**crûrent**

cueillir *to pick*   Auxiliary: **avoir**

PAST PARTICIPLE
cueilli

PRESENT PARTICIPLE
cueillant

IMPERATIVE
cueille
cueillons
cueillez

PRESENT
je	**cueille**
tu	**cueilles**
il	**cueille**
nous	**cueillons**
vous	**cueillez**
ils	**cueillent**

IMPERFECT
je	**cueillais**
tu	**cueillais**
il	**cueillait**
nous	**cueillions**
vous	**cueilliez**
ils	**cueillaient**

FUTURE
je	**cueillerai**
tu	**cueilleras**
il	**cueillera**
nous	**cueillerons**
vous	**cueillerez**
ils	**cueilleront**

CONDITIONAL
je	**cueillerais**
tu	**cueillerais**
il	**cueillerait**
nous	**cueillerions**
vous	**cueilleriez**
ils	**cueilleraient**

PRESENT SUBJUNCTIVE
je	**cueille**
tu	**cueilles**
il	**cueille**
nous	**cueillions**
vous	**cueilliez**
ils	**cueillent**

PAST HISTORIC
je	cueillis
tu	cueillis
il	cueillit
nous	cueillîmes
vous	cueillîtes
ils	cueillirent

cuire *to cook*   Auxiliary: **avoir**

PAST PARTICIPLE
cuit

IMPERATIVE
cuis
cuisons
cuisez

PRESENT PARTICIPLE
cuisant

PRESENT

je	cuis
tu	cuis
il	**cuit**
nous	**cuisons**
vous	**cuisez**
ils	**cuisent**

IMPERFECT

je	**cuisais**
tu	**cuisais**
il	**cuisait**
nous	**cuisions**
vous	**cuisiez**
ils	**cuisaient**

FUTURE

je	cuirai
tu	cuiras
il	cuira
nous	cuirons
vous	cuirez
ils	cuiront

CONDITIONAL

je	cuirais
tu	cuirais
il	cuirait
nous	cuirions
vous	cuiriez
ils	cuiraient

PRESENT SUBJUNCTIVE

je	**cuise**
tu	**cuises**
il	**cuise**
nous	**cuisions**
vous	**cuisiez**
ils	**cuisent**

PAST HISTORIC

je	**cuisis**
tu	**cuisis**
il	**cuisit**
nous	**cuisîmes**
vous	**cuisîtes**
ils	**cuisirent**

---

nuire *to harm*, conjugated similarly, but past participle **nui**

devoir *to have to; to owe*   Auxiliary: **avoir**

PAST PARTICIPLE
dû

IMPERATIVE
dois
devons
devez

PRESENT PARTICIPLE
devant

PRESENT		*IMPERFECT*	
je	**dois**	je	**devais**
tu	**dois**	tu	**devais**
il	**doit**	il	**devait**
nous	**devons**	nous	**devions**
vous	**devez**	vous	**deviez**
ils	**doivent**	ils	**devaient**

FUTURE		*CONDITIONAL*	
je	**devrai**	je	**devrais**
tu	**devras**	tu	**devrais**
il	**devra**	il	**devrait**
nous	**devrons**	nous	**devrions**
vous	**devrez**	vous	**devriez**
ils	**devront**	ils	**devraient**

PRESENT SUBJUNCTIVE		*PAST HISTORIC*	
je	**doive**	je	**dus**
tu	**doives**	tu	**dus**
il	**doive**	il	**dut**
nous	**devions**	nous	**dûmes**
vous	**deviez**	vous	**dûtes**
ils	**doivent**	ils	**durent**

dire *to say, tell*   Auxiliary: **avoir**

PAST PARTICIPLE
dit

IMPERATIVE
dis
disons
dites

PRESENT PARTICIPLE
disant

PRESENT		*IMPERFECT*	
je	dis	**je**	**disais**
tu	dis	**tu**	**disais**
il	**dit**	**il**	**disait**
nous	**disons**	**nous**	**disions**
vous	**dites**	**vous**	**disiez**
ils	**disent**	**ils**	**disaient**

FUTURE		*CONDITIONAL*	
je	dirai	je	dirais
tu	diras	tu	dirais
il	dira	il	dirait
nous	dirons	nous	dirions
vous	direz	vous	diriez
ils	diront	ils	diraient

PRESENT SUBJUNCTIVE		*PAST HISTORIC*	
je	**dise**	**je**	**dis**
tu	**dises**	**tu**	**dis**
il	**dise**	**il**	**dit**
nous	**disions**	**nous**	**dîmes**
vous	**disiez**	**vous**	**dîtes**
ils	**disent**	**ils**	**dirent**

---

interdire *to forbid*, conjugated similarly, but 2nd person plural of the present tense is **vous interdisez**

dormir *to sleep*   Auxiliary: **avoir**

PAST PARTICIPLE
dormi

IMPERATIVE
dors
dormons
dormez

PRESENT PARTICIPLE
dormant

PRESENT			*IMPERFECT*	
je	**dors**		**je**	**dormais**
tu	**dors**		**tu**	**dormais**
il	**dort**		**il**	**dormait**
nous	**dormons**		**nous**	**dormions**
vous	**dormez**		**vous**	**dormiez**
ils	**dorment**		**ils**	**dormaient**

FUTURE			*CONDITIONAL*	
je	dormirai		je	dormirais
tu	dormiras		tu	dormirais
il	dormira		il	dormirait
nous	dormirons		nous	dormirions
vous	dormirez		vous	dormiriez
ils	dormiront		ils	dormiraient

PRESENT SUBJUNCTIVE			*PAST HISTORIC*	
je	**dorme**		je	dormis
tu	**dormes**		tu	dormis
il	**dorme**		il	dormit
nous	**dormions**		nous	dormîmes
vous	**dormiez**		vous	dormîtes
ils	**dorment**		ils	dormirent

écrire *to write*   Auxiliary: **avoir**

PAST PARTICIPLE
écrit

PRESENT PARTICIPLE
écrivant

IMPERATIVE
écris
écrivons
écrivez

PRESENT
	j'écris
tu	écris
il	écrit
nous	**écrivons**
vous	**écrivez**
ils	**écrivent**

IMPERFECT
	j'écrivais
tu	**écrivais**
il	**écrivait**
nous	**écrivions**
vous	**écriviez**
ils	**écrivaient**

FUTURE
	j'écrirai
tu	écriras
il	écrira
nous	écrirons
vous	écrirez
ils	écriront

CONDITIONAL
	j'écrirais
tu	écrirais
il	écrirait
nous	écririons
vous	écririez
ils	écriraient

PRESENT SUBJUNCTIVE
	j'écrive
tu	**écrives**
il	**écrive**
nous	**écrivions**
vous	**écriviez**
ils	**écrivent**

PAST HISTORIC
	j'écrivis
tu	**écrivis**
il	**écrivit**
nous	**écrivîmes**
vous	**écrivîtes**
ils	**écrivirent**

envoyer *to send*   Auxiliary: **avoir**

PAST PARTICIPLE
envoyé

IMPERATIVE
envoie
envoyons
envoyez

PRESENT PARTICIPLE
envoyant

PRESENT
     j'envoie
tu envoies
il envoie
nous envoyons
vous envoyez
ils envoient

IMPERFECT
     j'envoyais
tu envoyais
il envoyait
nous envoyions
vous envoyiez
ils envoyaient

FUTURE
     j'enverrai
tu enverras
il enverra
nous enverrons
vous enverrez
ils enverront

CONDITIONAL
     j'enverrais
tu enverrais
il enverrait
nous enverrions
vous enverriez
ils enverraient

PRESENT SUBJUNCTIVE
     j'envoie
tu envoies
il envoie
nous envoyions
vous envoyiez
ils envoient

PAST HISTORIC
     j'envoyai
tu envoyas
il envoya
nous envoyâmes
vous envoyâtes
ils envoyèrent

être *to be*   Auxiliary: **avoir**

PAST PARTICIPLE
été

IMPERATIVE
sois
soyons
soyez

PRESENT PARTICIPLE
étant

PRESENT
je	**suis**
tu	**es**
il	**est**
nous	**sommes**
vous	**êtes**
ils	**sont**

IMPERFECT
	j'**étais**
tu	**étais**
il	**était**
nous	**étions**
vous	**étiez**
ils	**étaient**

FUTURE
je	**serai**
tu	**seras**
il	**sera**
nous	**serons**
vous	**serez**
ils	**seront**

CONDITIONAL
je	**serais**
tu	**serais**
il	**serait**
nous	**serions**
vous	**seriez**
ils	**seraient**

PRESENT SUBJUNCTIVE
je	**sois**
tu	**sois**
il	**soit**
nous	**soyons**
vous	**soyez**
ils	**soient**

PAST HISTORIC
je	**fus**
tu	**fus**
il	**fut**
nous	**fûmes**
vous	**fûtes**
ils	**furent**

faire *to do; to make*   Auxiliary: **avoir**

PAST PARTICIPLE
fait

PRESENT PARTICIPLE
faisant

IMPERATIVE
fais
faisons
faites

PRESENT
je	fais
tu	fais
il	**fait**
nous	**faisons**
vous	**faites**
ils	**font**

FUTURE
je	**ferai**
tu	**feras**
il	**fera**
nous	**ferons**
vous	**ferez**
ils	**feront**

PRESENT SUBJUNCTIVE
je	**fasse**
tu	**fasses**
il	**fasse**
nous	**fassions**
vous	**fassiez**
ils	**fassent**

IMPERFECT
je	**faisais**
tu	**faisais**
il	**faisait**
nous	**faisions**
vous	**faisiez**
ils	**faisaient**

CONDITIONAL
je	**ferais**
tu	**ferais**
il	**ferait**
nous	**ferions**
vous	**feriez**
ils	**feraient**

PAST HISTORIC
je	**fis**
tu	**fis**
il	**fit**
nous	**fîmes**
vous	**fîtes**
ils	**firent**

falloir *to be necessary*   Auxiliary: **avoir**

PAST PARTICIPLE
  fallu

IMPERATIVE
  not used

PRESENT PARTICIPLE
  not used

PRESENT
  il   faut

IMPERFECT
  il   fallait

FUTURE
  il   faudra

CONDITIONAL
  il   faudrait

PRESENT SUBJUNCTIVE
  il   faille

PAST HISTORIC
  il   fallut

fuir *to flee*   Auxiliary: **avoir**

PAST PARTICIPLE
  fui

IMPERATIVE
  fuis
  fuyons
  fuyez

PRESENT PARTICIPLE
  fuyant

PRESENT
je	fuis
tu	fuis
il	fuit
nous	**fuyons**
vous	**fuyez**
ils	**fuient**

IMPERFECT
je	**fuyais**
tu	**fuyais**
il	**fuyait**
nous	**fuyions**
vous	**fuyiez**
ils	**fuyaient**

FUTURE
je	fuirai
tu	fuiras
il	fuira
nous	fuirons
vous	fuirez
ils	fuiront

CONDITIONAL
je	fuirais
tu	fuirais
il	fuirait
nous	fuirions
vous	fuiriez
ils	fuiraient

PRESENT SUBJUNCTIVE
je	**fuie**
tu	**fuies**
il	**fuie**
nous	**fuyions**
vous	**fuyiez**
ils	**fuient**

PAST HISTORIC
je	fuis
tu	fuis
il	fuit
nous	fuîmes
vous	fuîtes
ils	fuirent

haïr *to hate*   Auxiliary: **avoir**

PAST PARTICIPLE
haï

PRESENT PARTICIPLE
haïssant

IMPERATIVE
hais
haïssons
haïssez

PRESENT		*IMPERFECT*	
je	hais	**je**	**haïssais**
tu	hais	**tu**	**haïssais**
il	hait	**il**	**haïssait**
nous	**haïssons**	**nous**	**haïssions**
vous	**haïssez**	**vous**	**haïssiez**
ils	**haïssent**	**ils**	**haïssaient**

FUTURE		*CONDITIONAL*	
je	haïrai	je	haïrais
tu	haïras	tu	haïrais
il	haïra	il	haïrait
nous	haïrons	nous	haïrions
vous	haïrez	vous	haïriez
ils	haïront	ils	haïraient

PRESENT SUBJUNCTIVE		*PAST HISTORIC*	
je	**haïsse**	**je**	**haïs**
tu	**haïsses**	**tu**	**haïs**
il	**haïsse**	**il**	**haït**
nous	**haïssions**	**nous**	**haïmes**
vous	**haïssiez**	**vous**	**haïtes**
ils	**haïssent**	**ils**	**haïrent**

lire *to read*   Auxiliary: **avoir**

PAST PARTICIPLE
lu

PRESENT PARTICIPLE
lisant

IMPERATIVE
lis
lisons
lisez

PRESENT
je	lis
tu	lis
il	**lit**
nous	**lisons**
vous	**lisez**
ils	**lisent**

IMPERFECT
je	**lisais**
tu	**lisais**
il	**lisait**
nous	**lisions**
vous	**lisiez**
ils	**lisaient**

FUTURE
je	lirai
tu	liras
il	lira
nous	lirons
vous	lirez
ils	liront

CONDITIONAL
je	lirais
tu	lirais
il	lirait
nous	lirions
vous	liriez
ils	liraient

PRESENT SUBJUNCTIVE
je	**lise**
tu	**lises**
il	**lise**
nous	**lisions**
vous	**lisiez**
ils	**lisent**

PAST HISTORIC
je	**lus**
tu	**lus**
il	**lut**
nous	**lûmes**
vous	**lûtes**
ils	**lurent**

mettre *to put*   Auxiliary: **avoir**

PAST PARTICIPLE
mis

PRESENT PARTICIPLE
mettant

IMPERATIVE
mets
mettons
mettez

PRESENT		IMPERFECT	
je	**mets**	je	mettais
tu	**mets**	tu	mettais
il	**met**	il	mettait
nous	mettons	nous	mettions
vous	mettez	vous	mettiez
ils	mettent	ils	mettaient

FUTURE		CONDITIONAL	
je	mettrai	je	mettrais
tu	mettras	tu	mettrais
il	mettra	il	mettrait
nous	mettrons	nous	mettrions
vous	mettrez	vous	mettriez
ils	mettront	ils	mettraient

PRESENT SUBJUNCTIVE		PAST HISTORIC	
je	mette	**je**	**mis**
tu	mettes	**tu**	**mis**
il	mette	**il**	**mit**
nous	mettions	**nous**	**mîmes**
vous	mettiez	**vous**	**mîtes**
ils	mettent	**ils**	**mirent**

moudre *to grind*   Auxiliary: **avoir**

PAST PARTICIPLE
moulu

PRESENT PARTICIPLE
moulant

IMPERATIVE
mouds
moulons
moulez

PRESENT
je	mouds
tu	mouds
il	moud
nous	**moulons**
vous	**moulez**
ils	**moulent**

FUTURE
je	moudrai
tu	moudras
il	moudra
nous	moudrons
vous	moudrez
ils	moudront

PRESENT SUBJUNCTIVE
je	**moule**
tu	**moules**
il	**moule**
nous	**moulions**
vous	**mouliez**
ils	**moulent**

IMPERFECT
je	**moulais**
tu	**moulais**
il	**moulait**
nous	**moulions**
vous	**mouliez**
ils	**moulaient**

CONDITIONAL
je	moudrais
tu	moudrais
il	moudrait
nous	moudrions
vous	moudriez
ils	moudraient

PAST HISTORIC
je	**moulus**
tu	**moulus**
il	**moulut**
nous	**moulûmes**
vous	**moulûtes**
ils	**moulurent**

mourir to die   Auxiliary: **être**

PAST PARTICIPLE
mort

IMPERATIVE
meurs
mourons
mourez

PRESENT PARTICIPLE
mourant

PRESENT
je	**meurs**
tu	**meurs**
il	**meurt**
nous	**mourons**
vous	**mourez**
ils	**meurent**

IMPERFECT
je	**mourais**
tu	**mourais**
il	**mourait**
nous	**mourions**
vous	**mouriez**
ils	**mouraient**

FUTURE
je	**mourrai**
tu	**mourras**
il	**mourra**
nous	**mourrons**
vous	**mourrez**
ils	**mourront**

CONDITIONAL
je	**mourrais**
tu	**mourrais**
il	**mourrait**
nous	**mourrions**
vous	**mourriez**
ils	**mourraient**

PRESENT SUBJUNCTIVE
je	**meure**
tu	**meures**
il	**meure**
nous	**mourions**
vous	**mouriez**
ils	**meurent**

PAST HISTORIC
je	**mourus**
tu	**mourus**
il	**mourut**
nous	**mourûmes**
vous	**mourûtes**
ils	**moururent**

naître *to be born*   Auxiliary: **être**

PAST PARTICIPLE
né

PRESENT PARTICIPLE
naissant

IMPERATIVE
nais
naissons
naissez

PRESENT

je	**nais**
tu	**nais**
il	naît
nous	**naissons**
vous	**naissez**
ils	**naissent**

FUTURE

je	naîtrai
tu	naîtras
il	naîtra
nous	naîtrons
vous	naîtrez
ils	naîtront

PRESENT SUBJUNCTIVE

je	**naisse**
tu	**naisses**
il	**naisse**
nous	**naissions**
vous	**naissiez**
ils	**naissent**

IMPERFECT

je	**naissais**
tu	**naissais**
il	**naissait**
nous	**naissions**
vous	**naissiez**
ils	**naissaient**

CONDITIONAL

je	naîtrais
tu	naîtrais
il	naîtrait
nous	naîtrions
vous	naîtriez
ils	naîtraient

PAST HISTORIC

je	naquis
tu	naquis
il	naquit
nous	naquîmes
vous	naquîtes
ils	naquirent

ouvrir *to open*   Auxiliary: **avoir**

PAST PARTICIPLE
ouvert

IMPERATIVE
ouvre
ouvrons
ouvrez

PRESENT PARTICIPLE
ouvrant

PRESENT
	j'ouvre
tu	**ouvres**
il	**ouvre**
nous	**ouvrons**
vous	**ouvrez**
ils	**ouvrent**

IMPERFECT
	j'ouvrais
tu	**ouvrais**
il	**ouvrait**
nous	**ouvrions**
vous	**ouvriez**
ils	**ouvraient**

FUTURE
	j'ouvrirai
tu	ouvriras
il	ouvrira
nous	ouvrirons
vous	ouvrirez
ils	ouvriront

CONDITIONAL
	j'ouvrirais
tu	ouvrirais
il	ouvrirait
nous	ouvririons
vous	ouvririez
ils	ouvriraient

PRESENT SUBJUNCTIVE
	j'ouvre
tu	**ouvres**
il	**ouvre**
nous	**ouvrions**
vous	**ouvriez**
ils	**ouvrent**

PAST HISTORIC
	j'ouvris
tu	ouvris
il	ouvrit
nous	ouvrîmes
vous	ouvrîtes
ils	ouvrirent

---

offrir *to offer*, **souffrir** *to suffer* are conjugated similarly

paraître *to appear*   Auxiliary: **avoir**

PAST PARTICIPLE
paru

PRESENT PARTICIPLE
paraissant

IMPERATIVE
parais
paraissons
paraissez

PRESENT		*IMPERFECT*	
je	**parais**	je	**paraissais**
tu	**parais**	tu	**paraissais**
il	paraît	il	**paraissait**
nous	**paraissons**	nous	**paraissions**
vous	**paraissez**	vous	**paraissiez**
ils	**paraissent**	ils	**paraissaient**

FUTURE		*CONDITIONAL*	
je	paraîtrai	je	paraîtrais
tu	paraîtras	tu	paraîtrais
il	paraîtra	il	paraîtrait
nous	paraîtrons	nous	paraîtrions
vous	paraîtrez	vous	paraîtriez
ils	paraîtront	ils	paraîtraient

PRESENT SUBJUNCTIVE		*PAST HISTORIC*	
je	**paraisse**	je	**parus**
tu	**paraisses**	tu	**parus**
il	**paraisse**	il	**parut**
nous	**paraissions**	nous	**parûmes**
vous	**paraissiez**	vous	**parûtes**
ils	**paraissent**	ils	**parurent**

partir *to leave*   Auxiliary: **être**

PAST PARTICIPLE
parti

IMPERATIVE
pars
partons
partez

PRESENT PARTICIPLE
partant

PRESENT

je	**pars**
tu	**pars**
il	**part**
nous	**partons**
vous	**partez**
ils	**partent**

IMPERFECT

je	**partais**
tu	**partais**
il	**partait**
nous	**partions**
vous	**partiez**
ils	**partaient**

FUTURE

je	partirai
tu	partiras
il	partira
nous	partirons
vous	partirez
ils	partiront

CONDITIONAL

je	partirais
tu	partirais
il	partirait
nous	partirions
vous	partiriez
ils	partiraient

PRESENT SUBJUNCTIVE

je	**parte**
tu	**partes**
il	**parte**
nous	**partions**
vous	**partiez**
ils	**partent**

PAST HISTORIC

je	partis
tu	partis
il	partit
nous	partîmes
vous	partîtes
ils	partirent

plaire *to please*   Auxiliary: **avoir**

PAST PARTICIPLE
plu

PRESENT PARTICIPLE
plaisant

IMPERATIVE
plais
plaisons
plaisez

PRESENT
je	plais
tu	plais
il	**plaît**
nous	**plaisons**
vous	**plaisez**
ils	**plaisent**

IMPERFECT
je	**plaisais**
tu	**plaisais**
il	**plaisait**
nous	**plaisions**
vous	**plaisiez**
ils	**plaisaient**

FUTURE
je	plairai
tu	plairas
il	plaira
nous	plairons
vous	plairez
ils	plairont

CONDITIONAL
je	plairais
tu	plairais
il	plairait
nous	plairions
vous	plairiez
ils	plairaient

PRESENT SUBJUNCTIVE
je	**plaise**
tu	**plaises**
il	**plaise**
nous	**plaisions**
vous	**plaisiez**
ils	**plaisent**

PAST HISTORIC
je	**plus**
tu	**plus**
il	**plut**
nous	**plûmes**
vous	**plûtes**
ils	**plurent**

pleuvoir *to rain*   Auxiliary: **avoir**

PAST PARTICIPLE
plu

IMPERATIVE
not used

PRESENT PARTICIPLE
pleuvant

PRESENT
   il   pleut
	IMPERFECT
	   il pleuvait

FUTURE
   il   pleuvra
	CONDITIONAL
	   il pleuvrait

PRESENT SUBJUNCTIVE
   il   pleuve
	PAST HISTORIC
	   il plut

pouvoir *to be able to*   Auxiliary: **avoir**

PAST PARTICIPLE
pu

IMPERATIVE
not used

PRESENT PARTICIPLE
pouvant

PRESENT

je	**peux***
tu	**peux**
il	**peut**
nous	**pouvons**
vous	**pouvez**
ils	**peuvent**

IMPERFECT

je	**pouvais**
tu	**pouvais**
il	**pouvait**
nous	**pouvions**
vous	**pouviez**
ils	**pouvaient**

FUTURE

je	**pourrai**
tu	**pourras**
il	**pourra**
nous	**pourrons**
vous	**pourrez**
ils	**pourront**

CONDITIONAL

je	**pourrais**
tu	**pourrais**
il	**pourrait**
nous	**pourrions**
vous	**pourriez**
ils	**pourraient**

PRESENT SUBJUNCTIVE

je	**puisse**
tu	**puisses**
il	**puisse**
nous	**puissions**
vous	**puissiez**
ils	**puissent**

PAST HISTORIC

je	**pus**
tu	**pus**
il	**put**
nous	**pûmes**
vous	**pûtes**
ils	**purent**

*In questions: **puis-je?**

prendre *to take*   Auxiliary: **avoir**

PAST PARTICIPLE
pris

IMPERATIVE
prends
prenons
prenez

PRESENT PARTICIPLE
prenant

PRESENT
je	prends
tu	prends
il	prend
nous	**prenons**
vous	**prenez**
ils	**prennent**

IMPERFECT
je	**prenais**
tu	**prenais**
il	**prenait**
nous	**prenions**
vous	**preniez**
ils	**prenaient**

FUTURE
je	prendrai
tu	prendras
il	prendra
nous	prendrons
vous	prendrez
ils	prendront

CONDITIONAL
je	prendrais
tu	prendrais
il	prendrait
nous	prendrions
vous	prendriez
ils	prendraient

PRESENT SUBJUNCTIVE
je	**prenne**
tu	**prennes**
il	**prenne**
nous	**prenions**
vous	**preniez**
ils	**prennent**

PAST HISTORIC
je	**pris**
tu	**pris**
il	**prit**
nous	**prîmes**
vous	**prîtes**
ils	**prirent**

recevoir *to receive* Auxiliary: **avoir**

PAST PARTICIPLE
reçu

IMPERATIVE
reçois
recevons
recevez

PRESENT PARTICIPLE
recevant

PRESENT		IMPERFECT	
je	**reçois**	je	**recevais**
tu	**reçois**	tu	**recevais**
il	**reçoit**	il	**recevait**
nous	**recevons**	nous	**recevions**
vous	**recevez**	vous	**receviez**
ils	**reçoivent**	ils	**recevaient**

FUTURE		CONDITIONAL	
je	**recevrai**	je	**recevrais**
tu	**recevras**	tu	**recevrais**
il	**recevra**	il	**recevrait**
nous	**recevrons**	nous	**recevrions**
vous	**recevrez**	vous	**recevriez**
ils	**recevront**	ils	**recevraient**

PRESENT SUBJUNCTIVE		PAST HISTORIC	
je	**reçoive**	je	**reçus**
tu	**reçoives**	tu	**reçus**
il	**reçoive**	il	**reçut**
nous	**recevions**	nous	**reçûmes**
vous	**receviez**	vous	**reçûtes**
ils	**reçoivent**	ils	**reçurent**

résoudre *to solve*   Auxiliary: **avoir**

PAST PARTICIPLE
résolu

IMPERATIVE
résous
résolvons
résolvez

PRESENT PARTICIPLE
résolvant

PRESENT		*IMPERFECT*	
je	**résous**	je	**résolvais**
tu	**résous**	tu	**résolvais**
il	**résout**	il	**résolvait**
nous	**résolvons**	nous	**résolvions**
vous	**résolvez**	vous	**résolviez**
ils	**résolvent**	ils	**résolvaient**

FUTURE		*CONDITIONAL*	
je	résoudrai	je	résoudrais
tu	résoudras	tu	résoudrais
il	résoudra	il	résoudrait
nous	résoudrons	nous	résoudrions
vous	résoudrez	vous	résoudriez
ils	résoudront	ils	résoudraient

PRESENT SUBJUNCTIVE		*PAST HISTORIC*	
je	**résolve**	je	**résolus**
tu	**résolves**	tu	**résolus**
il	**résolve**	il	**résolut**
nous	**résolvions**	nous	**résolûmes**
vous	**résolviez**	vous	**résolûtes**
ils	**résolvent**	ils	**résolurent**

rire *to laugh*   Auxiliary: **avoir**

PAST PARTICIPLE
ri

PRESENT PARTICIPLE
riant

IMPERATIVE
ris
rions
riez

PRESENT
je	ris
tu	ris
il	**rit**
nous	rions
vous	riez
ils	rient

FUTURE
je	rirai
tu	riras
il	rira
nous	rirons
vous	rirez
ils	riront

PRESENT SUBJUNCTIVE
je	rie
tu	ries
il	rie
nous	riions
vous	riiez
ils	rient

IMPERFECT
je	riais
tu	riais
il	riait
nous	riions
vous	riiez
ils	riaient

CONDITIONAL
je	rirais
tu	rirais
il	rirait
nous	ririons
vous	ririez
ils	riraient

PAST HISTORIC
je	**ris**
tu	**ris**
il	**rit**
nous	**rîmes**
vous	**rîtes**
ils	**rirent**

rompre *to break*   Auxiliary: **avoir**

PAST PARTICIPLE
rompu

IMPERATIVE
romps
rompons
rompez

PRESENT PARTICIPLE
rompant

PRESENT
je	romps
tu	romps
il	**rompt**
nous	rompons
vous	rompez
ils	rompent

IMPERFECT
je	rompais
tu	rompais
il	rompait
nous	rompions
vous	rompiez
ils	rompaient

FUTURE
je	romprai
tu	rompras
il	rompra
nous	romprons
vous	romprez
ils	rompront

CONDITIONAL
je	romprais
tu	romprais
il	romprait
nous	romprions
vous	rompriez
ils	rompraient

PRESENT SUBJUNCTIVE
je	rompe
tu	rompes
il	rompe
nous	rompions
vous	rompiez
ils	rompent

PAST HISTORIC
je	rompis
tu	rompis
il	rompit
nous	rompîmes
vous	rompîtes
ils	rompirent

savoir *to know*　　　　　　　　　Auxiliary: **avoir**

PAST PARTICIPLE
su

PRESENT PARTICIPLE
sachant

IMPERATIVE
sache
sachons
sachez

PRESENT

je	**sais**
tu	**sais**
il	**sait**
nous	**savons**
vous	**savez**
ils	**savent**

IMPERFECT

je	**savais**
tu	**savais**
il	**savait**
nous	**savions**
vous	**saviez**
ils	**savaient**

FUTURE

je	**saurai**
tu	**sauras**
il	**saura**
nous	**saurons**
vous	**saurez**
ils	**sauront**

CONDITIONAL

je	**saurais**
tu	**saurais**
il	**saurait**
nous	**saurions**
vous	**sauriez**
ils	**sauraient**

PRESENT SUBJUNCTIVE

je	**sache**
tu	**saches**
il	**sache**
nous	**sachions**
vous	**sachiez**
ils	**sachent**

PAST HISTORIC

je	**sus**
tu	**sus**
il	**sut**
nous	**sûmes**
vous	**sûtes**
ils	**surent**

sentir *to feel; to smell* Auxiliary: **avoir**

PAST PARTICIPLE
senti

PRESENT PARTICIPLE
sentant

IMPERATIVE
sens
sentons
sentez

PRESENT		IMPERFECT	
je	**sens**	je	**sentais**
tu	**sens**	tu	**sentais**
il	**sent**	il	**sentait**
nous	**sentons**	nous	**sentions**
vous	**sentez**	vous	**sentiez**
ils	**sentent**	ils	**sentaient**

FUTURE		CONDITIONAL	
je	sentirai	je	sentirais
tu	sentiras	tu	sentirais
il	sentira	il	sentirait
nous	sentirons	nous	sentirions
vous	sentirez	vous	sentiriez
ils	sentiront	ils	sentiraient

PRESENT SUBJUNCTIVE		PAST HISTORIC	
je	**sente**	je	sentis
tu	**sentes**	tu	sentis
il	**sente**	il	sentit
nous	**sentions**	nous	sentîmes
vous	**sentiez**	vous	sentîtes
ils	**sentent**	ils	sentirent

servir *to serve*   Auxiliary: **avoir**

PAST PARTICIPLE
  servi

PRESENT PARTICIPLE
  servant

IMPERATIVE
  sers
  servons
  servez

PRESENT

je	**sers**
tu	**sers**
il	**sert**
nous	**servons**
vous	**servez**
ils	**servent**

IMPERFECT

je	**servais**
tu	**servais**
il	**servait**
nous	**servions**
vous	**serviez**
ils	**servaient**

FUTURE

je	servirai
tu	serviras
il	servira
nous	servirons
vous	servirez
ils	serviront

CONDITIONAL

je	servirais
tu	servirais
il	servirait
nous	servirions
vous	serviriez
ils	serviraient

PRESENT SUBJUNCTIVE

je	**serve**
tu	**serves**
il	**serve**
nous	**servions**
vous	**serviez**
ils	**servent**

PAST HISTORIC

je	servis
tu	servis
il	servit
nous	servîmes
vous	servîtes
ils	servirent

sortir *to go/come out*   Auxiliary: **être**

PAST PARTICIPLE
sorti

PRESENT PARTICIPLE
sortant

IMPERATIVE
sors
sortons
sortez

PRESENT

je	**sors**
tu	**sors**
il	**sort**
nous	**sortons**
vous	**sortez**
ils	**sortent**

FUTURE

je	sortirai
tu	sortiras
il	sortira
nous	sortirons
vous	sortirez
ils	sortiront

PRESENT SUBJUNCTIVE

je	**sorte**
tu	**sortes**
il	**sorte**
nous	**sortions**
vous	**sortiez**
ils	**sortent**

IMPERFECT

je	**sortais**
tu	**sortais**
il	**sortait**
nous	**sortions**
vous	**sortiez**
ils	**sortaient**

CONDITIONAL

je	sortirais
tu	sortirais
il	sortirait
nous	sortirions
vous	sortiriez
ils	sortiraient

PAST HISTORIC

je	sortis
tu	sortis
il	sortit
nous	sortîmes
vous	sortîtes
ils	sortirent

suffire *to be enough*

Auxiliary: **avoir**

PAST PARTICIPLE
suffi

PRESENT PARTICIPLE
suffisant

IMPERATIVE
suffis
suffisons
suffisez

PRESENT

je	suffis
tu	suffis
il	suffit
nous	**suffisons**
vous	**suffisez**
ils	**suffisent**

IMPERFECT

je	**suffisais**
tu	**suffisais**
il	**suffisait**
nous	**suffisions**
vous	**suffisiez**
ils	**suffisaient**

FUTURE

je	suffirai
tu	suffiras
il	suffira
nous	suffirons
vous	suffirez
ils	suffiront

CONDITIONAL

je	suffirais
tu	suffirais
il	suffirait
nous	suffirions
vous	suffiriez
ils	suffiraient

PRESENT SUBJUNCTIVE

je	**suffise**
tu	**suffises**
il	**suffise**
nous	**suffisions**
vous	**suffisiez**
ils	**suffisent**

PAST HISTORIC

je	**suffis**
tu	**suffis**
il	**suffit**
nous	**suffîmes**
vous	**suffîtes**
ils	**suffirent**

suivre *to follow*   Auxiliary: **avoir**

PAST PARTICIPLE
suivi

IMPERATIVE
suis
suivons
suivez

PRESENT PARTICIPLE
suivant

PRESENT
je	**suis**
tu	**suis**
il	**suit**
nous	suivons
vous	suivez
ils	suivent

IMPERFECT
je	suivais
tu	suivais
il	suivait
nous	suivions
vous	suiviez
ils	suivaient

FUTURE
je	suivrai
tu	suivras
il	suivra
nous	suivrons
vous	suivrez
ils	suivront

CONDITIONAL
je	suivrais
tu	suivrais
il	suivrait
nous	suivrions
vous	suivriez
ils	suivraient

PRESENT SUBJUNCTIVE
je	suive
tu	suives
il	suive
nous	suivions
vous	suiviez
ils	suivent

PAST HISTORIC
je	suivis
tu	suivis
il	suivit
nous	suivîmes
vous	suivîtes
ils	suivirent

se taire *to stop talking*

Auxiliary: **être**

PAST PARTICIPLE
tu

PRESENT PARTICIPLE
se taisant

IMPERATIVE
tais-toi
taisons-nous
taisez-vous

PRESENT

je	me tais
tu	te tais
il	se tait
nous	**nous taisons**
vous	**vous taisez**
ils	**se taisent**

IMPERFECT

je	**me taisais**
tu	**te taisais**
il	**se taisait**
nous	**nous taisions**
vous	**vous taisiez**
ils	**se taisaient**

FUTURE

je	me tairai
tu	te tairas
il	se taira
nous	nous tairons
vous	vous tairez
ils	se tairont

CONDITIONAL

je	me tairais
tu	te tairais
il	se tairait
nous	nous tairions
vous	vous tairiez
ils	se tairaient

PRESENT SUBJUNCTIVE

je	**me taise**
tu	**te taises**
il	**se taise**
nous	**nous taisions**
vous	**vous taisiez**
ils	**se taisent**

PAST HISTORIC

je	**me tus**
tu	**te tus**
il	**se tut**
nous	**nous tûmes**
vous	**vous tûtes**
ils	**se turent**

tenir *to hold*   Auxiliary: **avoir**

PAST PARTICIPLE
tenu

PRESENT PARTICIPLE
tenant

IMPERATIVE
tiens
tenons
tenez

PRESENT		*IMPERFECT*	
je	**tiens**	je	**tenais**
tu	**tiens**	tu	**tenais**
il	**tient**	il	**tenait**
nous	**tenons**	nous	**tenions**
vous	**tenez**	vous	**teniez**
ils	**tiennent**	ils	**tenaient**

FUTURE		*CONDITIONAL*	
je	**tiendrai**	je	**tiendrais**
tu	**tiendras**	tu	**tiendrais**
il	**tiendra**	il	**tiendrait**
nous	**tiendrons**	nous	**tiendrions**
vous	**tiendrez**	vous	**tiendriez**
ils	**tiendront**	ils	**tiendraient**

PRESENT SUBJUNCTIVE		*PAST HISTORIC*	
je	**tienne**	je	**tins**
tu	**tiennes**	tu	**tins**
il	**tienne**	il	**tint**
nous	**tenions**	nous	**tînmes**
vous	**teniez**	vous	**tîntes**
ils	**tiennent**	ils	**tinrent**

vaincre *to defeat*   Auxiliary: **avoir**

PAST PARTICIPLE
vaincu

IMPERATIVE
vaincs
vainquons
vainquez

PRESENT PARTICIPLE
vainquant

PRESENT
je	vaincs
tu	vaincs
il	vainc
nous	**vainquons**
vous	**vainquez**
ils	**vainquent**

IMPERFECT
je	**vainquais**
tu	**vainquais**
il	**vainquait**
nous	**vainquions**
vous	**vainquiez**
ils	**vainquaient**

FUTURE
je	vaincrai
tu	vaincras
il	vaincra
nous	vaincrons
vous	vaincrez
ils	vaincront

CONDITIONAL
je	vaincrais
tu	vaincrais
il	vaincrait
nous	vaincrions
vous	vaincriez
ils	vaincraient

PRESENT SUBJUNCTIVE
je	**vainque**
tu	**vainques**
il	**vainque**
nous	**vainquions**
vous	**vainquiez**
ils	**vainquent**

PAST HISTORIC
je	**vainquis**
tu	**vainquis**
il	**vainquit**
nous	**vainquîmes**
vous	**vainquîtes**
ils	**vainquirent**

valoir *to be worth*   Auxiliary: **avoir**

PAST PARTICIPLE
valu

IMPERATIVE
vaux
valons
valez

PRESENT PARTICIPLE
valant

PRESENT
je	**vaux**
tu	**vaux**
il	**vaut**
nous	**valons**
vous	**valez**
ils	**valent**

IMPERFECT
je	**valais**
tu	**valais**
il	**valait**
nous	**valions**
vous	**valiez**
ils	**valaient**

FUTURE
je	**vaudrai**
tu	**vaudras**
il	**vaudra**
nous	**vaudrons**
vous	**vaudrez**
ils	**vaudront**

CONDITIONAL
je	**vaudrais**
tu	**vaudrais**
il	**vaudrait**
nous	**vaudrions**
vous	**vaudriez**
ils	**vaudraient**

PRESENT SUBJUNCTIVE
je	**vaille**
tu	**vailles**
il	**vaille**
nous	**valions**
vous	**valiez**
ils	**vaillent**

PAST HISTORIC
je	**valus**
tu	**valus**
il	**valut**
nous	**valûmes**
vous	**valûtes**
ils	**valurent**

venir *to come*   Auxiliary: **être**

PAST PARTICIPLE
venu

PRESENT PARTICIPLE
venant

IMPERATIVE
viens
venons
venez

PRESENT		*IMPERFECT*	
je	viens	je	venais
tu	viens	tu	venais
il	vient	il	venait
nous	venons	nous	venions
vous	venez	vous	veniez
ils	viennent	ils	venaient

FUTURE		*CONDITIONAL*	
je	viendrai	je	viendrais
tu	viendras	tu	viendrais
il	viendra	il	viendrait
nous	viendrons	nous	viendrions
vous	viendrez	vous	viendriez
ils	viendront	ils	viendraient

PRESENT SUBJUNCTIVE		*PAST HISTORIC*	
je	vienne	je	vins
tu	viennes	tu	vins
il	vienne	il	vint
nous	venions	nous	vînmes
vous	veniez	vous	vîntes
ils	viennent	ils	vinrent

vêtir *to dress*   Auxiliary: **avoir**

PAST PARTICIPLE
vêtu

PRESENT PARTICIPLE
vêtant

IMPERATIVE
vêts
vêtons
vêtez

PRESENT		*IMPERFECT*	
je	**vêts**	**je**	**vêtais**
tu	**vêts**	**tu**	**vêtais**
il	**vêt**	**il**	**vêtait**
nous	**vêtons**	**nous**	**vêtions**
vous	**vêtez**	**vous**	**vêtiez**
ils	**vêtent**	**ils**	**vêtaient**

FUTURE		*CONDITIONAL*	
je	vêtirai	je	vêtirais
tu	vêtiras	tu	vêtirais
il	vêtira	il	vêtirait
nous	vêtirons	nous	vêtirions
vous	vêtirez	vous	vêtiriez
ils	vêtiront	ils	vêtiraient

PRESENT SUBJUNCTIVE		*PAST HISTORIC*	
je	**vête**	je	vêtis
tu	**vêtes**	tu	vêtis
il	**vête**	il	vêtit
nous	**vêtions**	nous	vêtîmes
vous	**vêtiez**	vous	vêtîtes
ils	**vêtent**	ils	vêtirent

vivre *to live*   Auxiliary: **avoir**

PAST PARTICIPLE
vécu

PRESENT PARTICIPLE
vivant

IMPERATIVE
vis
vivons
vivez

PRESENT		IMPERFECT	
je	**vis**	je	vivais
tu	**vis**	tu	vivais
il	**vit**	il	vivait
nous	vivons	nous	vivions
vous	vivez	vous	viviez
ils	vivent	ils	vivaient

FUTURE		CONDITIONAL	
je	vivrai	je	vivrais
tu	vivras	tu	vivrais
il	vivra	il	vivrait
nous	vivrons	nous	vivrions
vous	vivrez	vous	vivriez
ils	vivront	ils	vivraient

PRESENT SUBJUNCTIVE		PAST HISTORIC	
je	vive	**je**	**vécus**
tu	vives	**tu**	**vécus**
il	vive	**il**	**vécut**
nous	vivions	**nous**	**vécûmes**
vous	viviez	**vous**	**vécûtes**
ils	vivent	**ils**	**vécurent**

voir *to see*   Auxiliary: **avoir**

PAST PARTICIPLE
  vu

PRESENT PARTICIPLE
  voyant

IMPERATIVE
  vois
  voyons
  voyez

PRESENT		IMPERFECT	
je	**vois**	je	**voyais**
tu	**vois**	tu	**voyais**
il	**voit**	il	**voyait**
nous	**voyons**	nous	**voyions**
vous	**voyez**	vous	**voyiez**
ils	**voient**	ils	**voyaient**

FUTURE		CONDITIONAL	
je	**verrai**	je	**verrais**
tu	**verras**	tu	**verrais**
il	**verra**	il	**verrait**
nous	**verrons**	nous	**verrions**
vous	**verrez**	vous	**verriez**
ils	**verront**	ils	**verraient**

PRESENT SUBJUNCTIVE		PAST HISTORIC	
je	**voie**	je	**vis**
tu	**voies**	tu	**vis**
il	**voie**	il	**vit**
nous	**voyions**	nous	**vîmes**
vous	**voyiez**	vous	**vîtes**
ils	**voient**	ils	**virent**

vouloir *to wish, want*   Auxiliary: **avoir**

PAST PARTICIPLE
voulu

PRESENT PARTICIPLE
voulant

IMPERATIVE
veuille
veuillons
veuillez

PRESENT

je	**veux**
tu	**veux**
il	**veut**
nous	**voulons**
vous	**voulez**
ils	**veulent**

IMPERFECT

je	**voulais**
tu	**voulais**
il	**voulait**
nous	**voulions**
vous	**vouliez**
ils	**voulaient**

FUTURE

je	**voudrai**
tu	**voudras**
il	**voudra**
nous	**voudrons**
vous	**voudrez**
ils	**voudront**

CONDITIONAL

je	**voudrais**
tu	**voudrais**
il	**voudrait**
nous	**voudrions**
vous	**voudriez**
ils	**voudraient**

PRESENT SUBJUNCTIVE

je	**veuille**
tu	**veuilles**
il	**veuille**
nous	**voulions**
vous	**vouliez**
ils	**veuillent**

PAST HISTORIC

je	**voulus**
tu	**voulus**
il	**voulut**
nous	**voulûmes**
vous	**voulûtes**
ils	**voulurent**

The Gender of Nouns

In French, all nouns are either masculine or feminine, whether denoting people, animals or things. Unlike English, there is no neuter gender for inanimate objects and abstract nouns.

Gender is largely unpredictable and has to be learnt for each noun. However, the following guidelines will help you determine the gender for certain types of nouns.

● Nouns denoting male people and animals are usually – but not always – masculine, e.g.

un homme	**un taureau**
a man	*a bull*
un infirmier	**un cheval**
a (male) nurse	*a horse*

● Nouns denoting female people and animals are usually – but not always – feminine, e.g.

une fille	**une vache**
a girl	*a cow*
une infirmière	**une brebis**
a nurse	*a ewe*

● Some nouns are masculine OR feminine depending on the sex of the person to whom they refer, e.g.

un camarade	**une camarade**
a (male) friend	*a (female) friend*
un Belge	**une Belge**
a Belgian (man)	*a Belgian (woman)*

● Other nouns referring to either men or women have only one gender which applies to both, e.g.

un professeur	**une personne**	**une sentinelle**
a teacher	*a person*	*a sentry*
un témoin	**une victime**	**une recrue**
a witness	*a victim*	*a recruit*

● Sometimes the ending of the noun indicates its gender. Shown below are some of the most important to guide you:

Masculine endings

-age	**le courage** *courage*, **le rinçage** *rinsing* EXCEPTIONS: **une cage** *a cage*, **une image** *a picture*, **la nage** *swimming*, **une page** *a page*, **une plage** *a beach*, **une rage** *a rage*
-ment	**le commencement** *the beginning* EXCEPTION: **une jument** *a mare*
-oir	**un couloir** *a corridor*, **un miroir** *a mirror*
-sme	**le pessimisme** *pessimism*, **l'enthousiasme** *enthusiasm*

Feminine endings

-ance, anse	**la confiance** *confidence*, **la danse** *dancing*
-ence, -ense	**la prudence** *caution*, **la défense** *defence* EXCEPTION: **le silence** *silence*
-ion	**une région** *a region*, **une addition** *a bill* EXCEPTIONS: **un pion** *a pawn*, **un espion** *a spy*
-oire	**une baignoire** *a bath(tub)*
-té, -tié	**la beauté** *beauty*, **la moitié** *half*

● Suffixes which differentiate between male and female are shown on pp. 134 and 136

● The following words have different meanings depending on gender:

le crêpe	*crêpe*	**la crêpe**	*pancake*
le livre	*book*	**la livre**	*pound*
le manche	*handle*	**la manche**	*sleeve*
le mode	*method*	**la mode**	*fashion*
le moule	*mould*	**la moule**	*mussel*
le page	*page(boy)*	**la page**	*page* (in book)
le physique	*physique*	**la physique**	*physics*
le poêle	*stove*	**la poêle**	*frying pan*
le somme	*nap*	**la somme**	*sum*
le tour	*turn*	**la tour**	*tower*
le voile	*veil*	**la voile**	*sail*

Gender: the formation of feminines

As in English, male and female are sometimes differentiated by the use of two quite separate words, e.g.

mon oncle	**ma tante**
my uncle	*my aunt*
un taureau	**une vache**
a bull	*a cow*

There are, however, some words in French which show this distinction by the form of their ending

● Some nouns add an **e** to the masculine singular form to form the feminine (→ **1**)

● If the masculine singular form already ends in **-e**, no further **e** is added in the feminine (→ **2**)

● Some nouns undergo a further change when **e** is added. These changes occur regularly and are shown on p. 136

Feminine forms to note

MASCULINE	FEMININE	
un âne	**une ânesse**	*donkey*
le comte	**la comtesse**	*count/countess*
le duc	**la duchesse**	*duke/duchess*
un Esquimau	**une Esquimaude**	*Eskimo*
le fou	**la folle**	*madman/madwoman*
le Grec	**la Grecque**	*Greek*
un hôte	**une hôtesse**	*host/hostess*
le jumeau	**la jumelle**	*twin*
le maître	**la maîtresse**	*master/mistress*
le prince	**la princesse**	*prince/princess*
le tigre	**la tigresse**	*tiger/tigress*
le traître	**la traîtresse**	*traitor*
le Turc	**la Turque**	*Turk*
le vieux	**la vieille**	*old man/old woman*

Continued

1 un ami
   a (male) friend
   un employé
   a (male) employee
   un Français
   a Frenchman

   une amie
   a (female) friend
   une employée
   a (female) employee
   une Française
   a Frenchwoman

2 un élève
   a (male) pupil
   un collègue
   a (male) colleague
   un camarade
   a (male) friend

   une élève
   a (female) pupil
   une collègue
   a (female) colleague
   une camarade
   a (female) friend

Regular feminine endings

MASC. SING.	FEM. SING.	
-f	-ve	(→ 1)
-x	-se	(→ 2)
-eur	-euse	(→ 3)
-teur	⎰ -teuse	(→ 4)
	⎱ -trice	(→ 5)

Some nouns double the final consonant before adding **e**:

MASC. SING.	FEM. SING.	
-an	-anne	(→ 6)
-en	-enne	(→ 7)
-on	-onne	(→ 8)
-et	-ette	(→ 9)
-el	-elle	(→ 10)

Some nouns add an accent to the final syllable before adding **e**:

MASC. SING.	FEM. SING.	
-er	-ère	(→ 11)

Pronunciation and feminine endings

This is dealt with on p. 244.

1 **un sportif**
  a sportsman
  un veuf
  a widower

 une sportive
 a sportswoman
 une veuve
 a widow

2 **un époux**
  a husband
  un amoureux
  a man in love

 une épouse
 a wife
 une amoureuse
 a woman in love

3 **un danseur**
  a dancer
  un voleur
  a thief

 une danseuse
 a dancer
 une voleuse
 a thief

4 **un menteur**
  a liar
  un chanteur
  a singer

 une menteuse
 a liar
 une chanteuse
 a singer

5 **un acteur**
  an actor
  un conducteur
  a driver

 une actrice
 an actress
 une conductrice
 a driver

6 **un paysan**
  a countryman

 une paysanne
 a countrywoman

7 **un Parisien**
  a Parisian

 une Parisienne
 a Parisian (woman)

8 **un baron**
  a baron

 une baronne
 a baroness

9 **le cadet**
  the youngest (child)

 la cadette
 the youngest (child)

10 **un intellectuel**
   an intellectual

 une intellectuelle
 an intellectual

11 **un étranger**
   a foreigner
   le dernier
   the last (one)

 une étrangère
 a foreigner
 la dernière
 the last (one)

The formation of plurals

● Most nouns add **s** to the singular form (→ **1**)

● When the singular form already ends in **-s**, **-x** or **-z**, no further **s** is added (→ **2**)

● For nouns ending in **-au**, **-eau** or **-eu**, the plural ends in **-aux**, **-eaux** or **-eux** (→ **3**)

Exceptions:	**pneu**	*tyre*	(plur: **pneus**)
	bleu	*bruise*	(plur: **bleus**)

● For nouns ending in **-al** or **-ail**, the plural ends in **-aux** (→ **4**)

Exceptions:	**bal**	*ball*	(plur: **bals**)
	festival	*festival*	(plur: **festivals**)
	chandail	*sweater*	(plur: **chandails**)
	détail	*detail*	(plur: **détails**)

● Forming the plural of compound nouns is complicated and you are advised to check each one individually in a dictionary

Irregular plural forms

● Some masculine nouns ending in **-ou** add **x** in the plural. These are:

bijou	*jewel*	**genou**	*knee*	**joujou**	*toy*
caillou	*pebble*	**hibou**	*owl*	**pou**	*louse*
chou	*cabbage*				

● Some other nouns are totally unpredictable. Chief among these are:

SINGULAR	PLURAL
œil *eye*	**yeux**
ciel *sky*	**cieux**
Monsieur *Mr.*	**Messieurs**
Madame *Mrs.*	**Mesdames**
Mademoiselle *Miss*	**Mesdemoiselles**

Pronunciation of plural forms

This is dealt with on p. 244

1 **le jardin**   **les jardins**
  the garden   the gardens
  une voiture   **des voitures**
  a car   (some) cars
  l'hôtel   **les hôtels**
  the hotel   the hotels

2 **un tas**   **des tas**
  a heap   (some) heaps
  une voix   **des voix**
  a voice   (some) voices
  le gaz   **les gaz**
  the gas   the gases

3 **un tuyau**   **des tuyaux**
  a pipe   (some) pipes
  le chapeau   **les chapeaux**
  the hat   the hats
  le feu   **les feux**
  the fire   the fires

4 **le journal**   **les journaux**
  the newspaper   the newspapers
  un travail   **des travaux**
  a job   (some) jobs

The Definite Article

	WITH MASC. NOUN	WITH FEM. NOUN	
SING.	le (l')	la (l')	the
PLUR.	les	les	the

● The gender and number of the noun determines the form of the article (→ **1**)

● **le** and **la** change to **l'** before a vowel or an **h** 'mute' (→ **2**)

● For uses of the definite article see p. 142

● **à + le/la (l'), à + les**

	WITH MASC. NOUN	WITH FEM. NOUN	
SING.	au (à l')	à la (à l')	(→ **3**)
PLUR.	aux	aux	

● The definite article combines with the preposition **à**, as shown above. You should pay particular attention to the masculine singular form **au**, and both plural forms **aux**, since these are not visually the sum of their parts

● **de + le/la (l'), de + les**

	WITH MASC. NOUN	WITH FEM. NOUN	
SING.	du (de l')	de la (de l')	(→ **4**)
PLUR.	des	des	

● The definite article combines with the preposition **de**, as shown above. You should pay particular attention to the masculine singular form **du**, and both plural forms **des**, since these are not visually the sum of their parts

Continued

MASCULINE	FEMININE
1 **le train**	**la gare**
the train	the station
le garçon	**la fille**
the boy	the girl
les hôtels	**les écoles**
the hotels	the schools
les professeurs	**les femmes**
the teachers	the women
2 **l'acteur**	**l'actrice**
the actor	the actress
l'effet	**l'eau**
the effect	the water
l'ingrédient	**l'idée**
the ingredient	the idea
l'objet	**l'ombre**
the object	the shadow
l'univers	**l'usine**
the universe	the factory
l'hôpital	**l'heure**
the hospital	the time
3 **au cinéma**	**à la bibliothèque**
at/to the cinema	at/to the library
à l'employé	**à l'infirmière**
to the employee	to the nurse
à l'hôpital	**à l'hôtesse**
at/to the hospital	to the hostess
aux étudiants	**aux maisons**
to the students	to the houses
4 **du bureau**	**de la réunion**
from/of the office	from/of the meeting
de l'auteur	**de l'Italienne**
from/of the author	from/of the Italian woman
de l'hôte	**de l'horloge**
from/of the host	of the clock
des Etats-Unis	**des vendeuses**
from/of the United States	from/of the saleswomen

Uses of the definite article

While the definite article is used in much the same way in French as it is in English, its use is more widespread in French. Unlike English the definite article is also used:

● with abstract nouns, except when following certain prepositions (→ **1**)

● in generalisations, especially with plural or uncountable* nouns (→ **2**)

● with names of countries (→ **3**)
Exceptions: no article with countries following **en** *to/in* (→ **4**)

● with parts of the body (→ **5**)
'Ownership' is often indicated by an indirect object pronoun or a reflexive pronoun (→ **6**)

● in expressions of quantity/rate/price (→ **7**)

● with titles/ranks/professions followed by a proper name (→ **8**)

● The definite article is NOT used with nouns in apposition (→ **9**)

*An uncountable noun is one which cannot be used in the plural or with an indefinite article, e.g. **l'acier** *steel*, **le lait** *milk*

1 Les prix montent
Prices are rising
L'amour rayonne dans ses yeux
Love shines in his eyes
BUT   **avec plaisir**   **sans espoir**
          with pleasure   without hope

2 Je n'aime pas le café
I don't like coffee
Les enfants ont besoin d'être aimés
Children need to be loved

3 le Japon   la France   l'Italie   les Pays-Bas
    Japan   France   Italy   The Netherlands

4 aller en Ecosse   Il travaille en Allemagne
    to go to Scotland   He works in Germany

5 Tournez la tête à gauche
Turn your head to the left
J'ai mal à la gorge
My throat is sore, I have a sore throat

6 La tête me tourne
My head is spinning
Elle s'est brossé les dents
She brushed her teeth

7 40 francs le mètre/le kilo/la douzaine/la pièce
40 francs a metre/a kilo/a dozen/each
rouler à 80 km à l'heure
to go at 50 m.p.h.
payé à l'heure/au jour/au mois
paid by the hour/by the day/by the month

8 le roi Georges III   le capitaine Darbeau
    King George III   Captain Darbeau
    le docteur Rousseau   Monsieur le président
    Dr. Rousseau   Mr. Chairman/President

9 Victor Hugo, grand écrivain du dix-neuvième siècle
Victor Hugo, a great author of the nineteenth century
Joseph Leblanc, inventeur et entrepreneur, a été le premier ...
Joseph Leblanc, an inventor and entrepreneur, was the first ...

The Partitive Article

The partitive article has the sense of *some* or *any*, although the French is not always translated in English.

Forms of the partitive

	WITH MASC. NOUN	WITH FEM. NOUN	
SING.	**du (de l')**	**de la (de l')**	*some, any*
PLUR.	**des**	**des**	*some, any*

- The gender and number of the noun determines the form of the partitive (→ **1**)

- The forms shown in brackets are used before a vowel or an **h** 'mute' (→ **2**)

- **des** becomes **de** (**d'** + vowel) before an adjective (→ **3**), unless the adjective and noun are seen as forming one unit (→ **4**)

- In negative sentences **de** (**d'** + vowel) is used for both genders, singular and plural (→ **5**)
  Exception: after **ne ... que** *only*, the positive forms above are used (→ **6**)

1 **Avez-vous du sucre?**
Have you any sugar?
J'ai acheté de la farine et de la margarine
I bought (some) flour and margarine
Il a mangé des gâteaux
He ate some cakes
Est-ce qu'il y a des lettres pour moi?
Are there (any) letters for me?

2 **Il me doit de l'argent**   **C'est de l'histoire ancienne**
He owes me (some) money   That's ancient history

3 **Il a fait de gros efforts pour nous aider**
He made a great effort to help us
Cette région a de belles églises
This region has some beautiful churches

4 **des grandes vacances**   **des jeunes gens**
summer holidays   young people

5 **Je n'ai pas de nourriture/d'argent**
I don't have any food/money
Vous n'avez pas de timbres/d'œufs?
Have you no stamps/eggs?
Je ne mange jamais de viande/d'omelettes
I never eat meat/omelettes
Il ne veut plus de visiteurs/d'eau
He doesn't want any more visitors/water

6 **Il ne boit que du thé/de la bière/de l'eau**
He only drinks tea/beer/water
Je n'ai que des problèmes avec cette machine
I have nothing but problems with this machine

The Indefinite Article

	WITH MASC. NOUN	WITH FEM. NOUN	
SING.	un	une	a
PLUR.	des	des	some

● **des** is also the plural of the partitive article (see p. 144)

● In negative sentences, **de** (**d'** + vowel) is used for both singular and plural (→ **1**)

● The indefinite article is used in French largely as it is in English EXCEPT:

 – there is no article when a person's profession is being stated (→ **2**) The article *is* present however, following **ce** (**c'** + vowel) (→ **3**)

 – the English article is not translated by **un/une** in constructions like *what a surprise, what an idiot* (→ **4**)

 – in structures of the type given in example **5** the article **un/une** is used in French and not translated in English (→ **5**)

1 **Je n'ai pas de livre / d'enfants**
   I don't have a book / (any) children

2 **Il est professeur**   **Ma mère est infirmière**
   He's a teacher   My mother's a nurse

3 **C'est un médecin**
   He's / She's a doctor
   Ce sont des acteurs
   They're actors

4 **Quelle surprise!**   **Quel dommage!**
   What a surprise!   What a shame!

5 **avec une grande sagesse / un courage admirable**
   with great wisdom / admirable courage
   Il a fait preuve d'un sang-froid incroyable
   He showed incredible coolness
   Un produit d'une qualité incomparable
   A product of incomparable quality

Adjectives

Most adjectives agree in number and in gender with the noun or pronoun.

The formation of feminines

● Most adjectives add an **e** to the masculine singular form (→ **1**)

● If the masculine singular form already ends in **-e**, no further **e** is added (→ **2**)

● Some adjectives undergo a further change when **e** is added. These changes occur regularly and are shown on p. 150

● Irregular feminine forms are shown on p. 152

The formation of plurals

● The plural of both regular and irregular adjectives is formed by adding an **s** to the masculine or feminine singular form, as appropriate (→ **3**)

● When the masculine singular form already ends in **-s** or **-x**, no further **s** is added (→ **4**)

● For masculine singulars ending in **-au** and **-eau**, the masculine plural is **-aux** and **-eaux** (→ **5**)

● For masculine singulars ending in **-al**, the masculine plural is **-aux** (→ **6**)

>   Exceptions: **final** (masculine plural **finals**)
>   **fatal** (masculine plural **fatals**)
>   **naval** (masculine plural **navals**)

Pronunciation of feminine and plural adjectives
This is dealt with on p. 244

1 **mon frère aîné**
my elder brother
le petit garçon
the little boy
un sac gris
a grey bag
un bruit fort
a loud noise

    ma sœur aînée
my elder sister
la petite fille
the little girl
une chemise grise
a grey shirt
une voix forte
a loud voice

2 **un jeune homme**
a young man
l'autre verre
the other glass

    une jeune femme
a young woman
l'autre assiette
the other plate

3 **le dernier train**
the last train
une vieille maison
an old house
un long voyage
a long journey
la rue étroite
the narrow street

    les derniers trains
the last trains
de vieilles maisons
old houses
de longs voyages
long journeys
les rues étroites
the narrow streets

4 **un diplomate français**
a French diplomat
un homme dangereux
a dangerous man

    des diplomates français
French diplomats
des hommes dangereux
dangerous men

5 **le nouveau professeur**
the new teacher
un chien esquimau
a husky (Fr. = an Eskimo dog)

    les nouveaux professeurs
the new teachers
des chiens esquimaux
huskies (Fr. = Eskimo dogs)

6 **un ami loyal**
a loyal friend
un geste amical
a friendly gesture

    des amis loyaux
loyal friends
des gestes amicaux
friendly gestures

Regular feminine endings

MASC. SING.	FEM. SING.	EXAMPLES	
-f	-ve	neuf, vif	(→ 1)
-x	-se	heureux, jaloux	(→ 2)
-eur	-euse	travailleur, flâneur	(→ 3)
-teur	{ -teuse	flatteur, menteur	(→ 4)
	{ -trice	destructeur, séducteur	(→ 5)

Exceptions:
    bref: see p. 152
    doux, faux, roux, vieux: see p. 152
    extérieur, inférieur, intérieur, meilleur, supérieur: all add **e** to
    the masculine
    enchanteur: fem. = ᴜnchanteresse

MASC. SING.	FEM. SING.	EXAMPLES	
-an	-anne	paysan	(→ 6)
-en	-enne	ancien, parisien	(→ 7)
-on	-onne	bon, breton	(→ 8)
-as	-asse	bas, las	(→ 9)
-et*	-ette	muet, violet	(→ 10)
-el	-elle	annuel, mortel	(→ 11)
-eil	-eille	pareil, vermeil	(→ 12)

Exception:
    ras: fem. = **rase**

MASC. SING.	FEM. SING.	EXAMPLES	
-et*	-ète	secret, complet	(→ 13)
-er	-ère	étranger, fier	(→ 14)

*Note that there are two feminine endings for masculine adjectives
ending in -**et**.

1 **un résultat positif**
a positive result

une attitude positive
a positive attitude

2 **d'un ton sérieux**
in a serious tone (of voice)

une voix sérieuse
a serious voice

3 **un enfant trompeur**
a deceitful child

une déclaration trompeuse
a misleading statement

4 **un tableau flatteur**
a flattering picture

une comparaison flatteuse
a flattering comparison

5 **un geste protecteur**
a protective gesture

une couche protectrice
a protective layer

6 **un problème paysan**
a farming problem

la vie paysanne
country life

7 **un avion égyptien**
an Egyptian plane

une statue égyptienne
an Egyptian statue

8 **un bon repas**
a good meal

de bonne humeur
in a good mood

9 **un plafond bas**
a low ceiling

à voix basse
in a low voice

10 **un travail net**
a clean piece of work

une explication nette
a clear explanation

11 **un homme cruel**
a cruel man

une remarque cruelle
a cruel remark

12 **un livre pareil**
such a book

en pareille occasion
on such an occasion

13 **un regard inquiet**
an anxious look

une attente inquiète
an anxious wait

14 **un goût amer**
a bitter taste

une amère déception
a bitter disappointment

Adjectives with irregular feminine forms

MASC. SING.	FEM. SING.		
aigu	aiguë	*sharp; high-pitched*	(→ 1)
ambigu	ambiguë	*ambiguous*	
beau (bel)*	belle	*beautiful*	
bénin	bénigne	*benign*	
blanc	blanche	*white*	
bref	brève	*brief, short*	(→ 2)
doux	douce	*soft; sweet*	
épais	épaisse	*think*	
esquimau	esquimaude	*Eskimo*	
faux	fausse	*wrong*	
favori	favorite	*favourite*	(→ 3)
fou (fol)*	folle	*mad*	
frais	fraîche	*fresh*	(→ 4)
franc	franche	*frank*	
gentil	gentille	*kind*	
grec	grecque	*Greek*	
gros	grosse	*big*	
jumeau	jumelle	*twin*	(→ 5)
long	longue	*long*	
malin	maligne	*malignant*	
mou (mol)*	molle	*soft*	
nouveau (nouvel)*	nouvelle	*new*	
nul	nulle	*no*	
public	publique	*public*	(→ 6)
roux	rousse	*red-haired*	
sec	sèche	*dry*	
sot	sotte	*foolish*	
turc	turque	*Turkish*	
vieux (vieil)*	vieille	*old*	

*This form is used when the following word begins with a vowel or an **h** 'mute' (→ 7)

1 **un son aigu**
a high-pitched sound

une douleur aiguë
a sharp pain

2 **un bref discours**
a short speech

une brève rencontre
a short meeting

3 **mon sport favori**
my favourite sport

ma chanson favorite
my favourite song

4 **du pain frais**
fresh bread

de la crème fraîche
fresh cream

5 **mon frère jumeau**
my twin brother

ma sœur jumelle
my twin sister

6 **un jardin public**
a (public) park

l'opinion publique
public opinion

7 **un bel appartement**
a beautiful flat
le nouvel inspecteur
the new inspector
un vieil arbre
an old tree

un bel habit
a beautiful outfit
un nouvel harmonica
a new harmonica
un vieil hôtel
an old hotel

Comparatives and Superlatives

Comparatives
These are formed using the following constructions:

plus ... (que)	*more ... (than)*	(→ **1**)
moins ... (que)	*less ... (than)*	(→ **2**)
aussi ... que	*as ... as*	(→ **3**)
si ... que*	*as ... as*	(→ **4**)

*used mainly after a negative

Superlatives
These are formed using the following constructions:

le/la/les plus ... (que)	*the most ... (that)*	(→ **5**)
le/la/les moins ... (que)	*the least ... (that)*	(→ **6**)

● When the possessive adjective is present, two constructions are possible (→ **7**)
● After a superlative the preposition **de** is often translated as *in* (→ **8**)
● If a clause follows a superlative, the verb is in the subjunctive (→ **9**)

Adjectives with irregular comparatives/superlatives

ADJECTIVE	COMPARATIVE	SUPERLATIVE
bon	**meilleur**	**le meilleur**
good	*better*	*the best*
mauvais	**pire** OR	**le pire** OR
bad	**plus mauvais**	**le plus mauvais**
	worse	*the worst*
petit	**moindre*** OR	**le moindre*** OR
small	**plus petit**	**le plus petit**
	smaller;	*the smallest*;
	lesser	*the least*

*used only with abstract nouns

● Comparative and superlative adjectives agree in number and in gender with the noun, just like any other adjective (→ **10**)

1 **une raison plus grave**
   a more serious reason
   Elle est plus petite que moi
   She is smaller than me
2 **un film moins connu**
   a less well-known film
   C'est moins cher qu'il ne pense
   It's cheaper than he thinks
3 **Robert était aussi inquiet que moi**
   Robert was as worried as I was
   Cette ville n'est pas aussi grande que Bordeaux
   This town isn't as big as Bordeaux
4 **Ils ne sont pas si contents que ça**
   They aren't as happy as all that
5 **le guide le plus utile**   **la voiture la plus petite**
   the most useful guidebook   the smallest car
   les plus grandes maisons
   the biggest houses
6 **le mois le moins agréable**   **la fille la moins forte**
   the least pleasant month   the weakest girl
   les moins belles peintures
   the least attractive paintings
7 **Mon désir le plus cher** }
   Mon plus cher désir   } **est de voyager**
   My dearest wish is to travel
8 **la plus grande gare de Londres**
   the biggest station in London
   l'habitant le plus âgé du village/de la région
   the oldest inhabitant in the village/in the area
9 **la personne la plus gentille que je connaisse**
   the nicest person I know
10 **les moindres difficultés**
   the least difficulties
   la meilleure qualité
   the best quality

Demonstrative Adjectives

	MASCULINE	*FEMININE*	
SING.	**ce (cet)**	**cette**	*this; that*
PLUR.	**ces**	**ces**	*these; those*

● Demonstrative adjectives agree in number and gender with the noun (→ **1**)

● **cet** is used when the following word begins with a vowel or an **h** 'mute' (→ **2**)

● For emphasis or in order to distinguish between people or objects, **-ci** or **-là** is added to the noun: **-ci** indicates proximity (usually translated *this*) and **là** distance (*that*) (→ **3**)

1 **Ce stylo ne marche pas**
This/That pen isn't working
Comment s'appelle cette entreprise?
What's this/that company called?
Ces livres sont les miens
These/Those books are mine
Ces couleurs sont plus jolies
These/Those colours are nicer

2 **cet oiseau**
this/that bird
cet article
this/that article
cet homme
this/that man

3 **Combien coûte ce manteau-ci?**
How much is this coat?
Je voudrais cinq de ces pommes-là
I'd like five of those apples
Est-ce que tu reconnais cette personne-là?
Do you recognize that person?
Mettez ces vêtements-ci dans cette valise-là
Put these clothes in that case
Ce garçon-là appartient à ce groupe-ci
That boy belongs to this group

Interrogative Adjectives

	MASCULINE	FEMININE	
SING.	quel?	quelle?	what?; which?
PLUR.	quels?	quelles?	what?; which?

● Interrogative adjectives agree in number and gender with the noun (→ 1)

● The forms shown above are also used in indirect questions (→ 2)

Exclamatory Adjectives

	MASCULINE	FEMININE	
SING.	quel!	quelle!	what (a)!
PLUR.	quels!	quelles!	what!

● Exclamatory adjectives agree in number and gender with the noun (→ 3)

● For other exclamations, see p. 214

1 Quel genre d'homme est-ce?
What type of man is he?
Quelle est leur décision?
What is their decision?
Vous jouez de quels instruments?
What instruments do you play?
Quelles offres avez-vous reçues?
What offers have you received?
Quel vin recommandez-vous?
Which wine do you recommend?
Quelles couleurs préférez-vous?
Which colours do you prefer?

2 Je ne sais pas à quelle heure il est arrivé
I don't know what time he arrived
Dites-moi quels sont les livres les plus intéressants
Tell me which books are the most interesting

3 Quel dommage!
What a pity!
Quelle idée!
What an idea!
Quels beaux livres vous avez!
What fine books you have!
Quelles jolies fleurs!
What nice flowers!

Possessive Adjectives

WITH SING. NOUN		WITH PLUR. NOUN	
MASC.	FEM.	MASC./FEM.	
mon	ma (mon)	mes	my
ton	ta (ton)	tes	your
son	sa (son)	ses	his; her; its
notre	notre	nos	our
votre	votre	vos	your
leur	leur	leurs	their

● Possessive adjectives agree in number and gender with the noun, NOT WITH THE OWNER (→ 1)

● The forms shown in brackets are used when the following word begins with a vowel or an **h** 'mute' (→ 2)

● **son**, **sa**, **ses** have the additional meaning of *one's* (→ 3)

1 **Catherine a oublié son parapluie**
Catherine has left her umbrella
Paul cherche sa montre
Paul's looking for his watch
Mon frère et ma sœur habitent à Glasgow
My brother and sister live in Glasgow
Est-ce que tes voisins ont vendu leur voiture?
Did your neighbours sell their car?
Rangez vos affaires
Put your things away

2 **mon appareil-photo**
my camera
ton histoire
your story
son erreur
his/her mistake
mon autre sœur
my other sister

3 **perdre son équilibre**
to lose one's balance
présenter ses excuses
to offer one's apologies

Position of Adjectives

● French adjectives usually follow the noun (→ **1**)

● Adjectives of colour or nationality *always* follow the noun (→ **2**)

● As in English, demonstrative, possessive, numerical and interrogative adjectives precede the noun (→ **3**)

● The adjectives **autre** *other* and **chaque** *each, every* precede the noun (→ **4**)

● The following common adjectives can precede the noun:

beau	*beautiful*	**jeune**	*young*
bon	*good*	**joli**	*pretty*
court	*short*	**long**	*long*
dernier	*last*	**mauvais**	*bad*
grand	*great*	**petit**	*small*
gros	*big*	**tel**	*such (a)*
haut	*high*	**vieux**	*old*

● The meaning of the following adjectives varies according to their position:

	BEFORE NOUN	AFTER NOUN	
ancien	*former*	*old, ancient*	(→ **5**)
brave	*good*	*brave*	(→ **6**)
cher	*dear (beloved)*	*expensive*	(→ **7**)
grand	*great*	*tall*	(→ **8**)
même	*same*	*very*	(→ **9**)
pauvre	*poor (wretched)*	*poor (not rich)*	(→ **10**)
propre	*own*	*clean*	(→ **11**)
seul	*single, sole*	*on one's own*	(→ **12**)
simple	*mere, simple*	*simple, easy*	(→ **13**)
vrai	*real*	*true*	(→ **14**)

● Adjectives following the noun are linked by **et** (→ **15**)

1 **le chapitre suivant**
the following chapter
l'heure exacte
the right time

2 **une cravate rouge**
a red tie
un mot français
a French word

3 **ce dictionnaire**
this dictionary
mon père
my father

le premier étage
the first floor
deux exemples
two examples

quel homme?
which man?

4 **une autre fois**
another time
chaque jour
every day

5 **un ancien collègue**
a former colleague
l'histoire ancienne
ancient history

6 **un brave homme**
a good man
un homme brave
a brave man

7 **mes chers amis**
my dear friends
une robe chère
an expensive dress

8 **un grand peintre**
a great painter
un homme grand
a tall man

9 **la même réponse**
the same answer
vos paroles mêmes
your very words

10 **cette pauvre femme**
that poor woman
une nation pauvre
a poor nation

11 **ma propre vie**
my own life
une chemise propre
a clean shirt

12 **une seule réponse**
a single reply
une femme seule
a woman on her own

13 **un simple regard**
a mere look
un problème simple
a simple problem

14 **la vraie raison**
the real reason
les faits vrais
the true facts

15 **un acte lâche et trompeur**
a cowardly, deceitful act
un acte lâche, trompeur et ignoble
a cowardly, deceitful and ignoble act

Personal Pronouns

SUBJECT PRONOUNS

PERSON	SINGULAR	PLURAL
1st	**je (j')**	**nous**
	I	*we*
2nd	**tu**	**vous**
	you	*you*
3rd (masc.)	**il**	**ils**
	he; it	*they*
(fem.)	**elle**	**elles**
	she; it	*they*

je changes to **j'** before a vowel, an **h** 'mute', or the pronoun **y** (→ **1**)

● **tu/vous**
Vous, as well as being the second person plural, is also used when addressing one person. As a general rule, use **tu** only when addressing a friend, a child, a relative, someone you know very well, or when invited to do so. In all other cases use **vous**. For singular and plural uses of **vous**, see example **2**.

● **il/elle; ils/elles**
The form of the 3rd person pronouns reflects the number and gender of the noun(s) they replace, referring to animals and things as well as to people. **Ils** also replaces a combination of masculine and feminine nouns (→ **3**)

● Sometimes stressed pronouns replace the subject pronouns, see p. 172

Continued

1 J'arrive!
I'm just coming!
J'en ai trois
I've got 3 of them
J'hésite à le déranger
I hesitate to disturb him
J'y pense souvent
I often think about it

2 Compare: **Vous êtes certain, Monsieur Leclerc?**
                 Are you sure, Mr Leclerc?
   and: **Vous êtes certains, les enfants?**
                 Are you sure, children?
   Compare: **Vous êtes partie quand, Estelle?**
                 When did you leave, Estelle?
   and: **Estelle et Sophie – vous êtes parties quand?**
                 Estelle and Sophie – when did you leave?

3 Où logent ton père et ta mère quand ils vont à Rome?
Where do your father and mother stay when they go to Rome?
Donne-moi le journal et les lettres quand ils arriveront
Give me the newspaper and the letters when they arrive

Personal Pronouns (ctd.)

DIRECT OBJECT PRONOUNS

PERSON	SINGULAR	PLURAL
1st	**me (m')**	**nous**
	me	*us*
2nd	**te (t')**	**vous**
	you	*you*
3rd (masc.)	**le (l')**	**les**
	him; it	*them*
(fem.)	**la (l')**	**les**
	her; it	*them*

The forms shown in brackets are used before a vowel, an **h** 'mute', or the pronoun **y** (→ **1**)

● In positive commands **me** and **te** change to **moi** and **toi** except before **en** or **y** (→ **2**)

● **le** sometimes functions as a 'neuter' pronoun, referring to an idea or information contained in a previous statement or question. It is often not translated (→ **3**)

Position of direct object pronouns
● In constructions other than the imperative affirmative the pronoun comes before the verb (→ **4**)
The same applies when the verb is in the infinitive (→ **5**)
In the imperative affirmative, the pronoun follows the verb and is attached to it by a hyphen (→ **6**)

● For further information, see Order of Object Pronouns, p. 170

Reflexive Pronouns
These are dealt with under reflexive verbs, p. 30

Continued

1 **Il m'a vu**
He saw me
Je ne t'oublierai jamais
I'll never forget you
Ça l'habitue à travailler seul
That gets him/her used to working on his/her own
Je veux l'y accoutumer
I want to accustom him/her to it

2 **Avertis-moi de ta décision** → **Avertis-m'en**
Inform me of your decision   Inform me of it

3 **Il n'est pas là. – Je le sais bien.**
He isn't there. – I know that.
Aidez-moi si vous le pouvez
Help me if you can
Elle viendra demain. – Je l'espère bien.
She'll come tomorrow. – I hope so.

4 **Je t'aime**
I love you
Les voyez-vous?
Can you see them?
Elle ne nous connaît pas
She doesn't know us
Est-ce que tu ne les aimes pas?
Don't you like them?
Ne me faites pas rire
Don't make me laugh

5 **Puis-je vous aider?**
May I help you?

6 **Aidez-moi**   **Suivez-nous**
Help me   Follow us

Personal Pronouns (ctd.)

INDIRECT OBJECT PRONOUNS

PERSON	SINGULAR	PLURAL
1st	**me (m′)**	**nous**
2nd	**te (t′)**	**vous**
3rd (masc.)	**lui**	**leur**
(fem.)	**lui**	**leur**

me and **te** change to **m′** and **t′** before a vowel or an **h** 'mute' (→**1**)

● In positive commands, **me** and **te** change to **moi** and **toi** except before **en** (→**2**)

● The pronouns shown in the above table replace the preposition **à** + noun, where the noun is a person or an animal (→**3**)

● The verbal construction affects the translation of the pronoun (→**4**)

Position of indirect object pronouns
● In constructions other than the imperative affirmative, the pronoun comes before the verb (→**5**)
The same applies when the verb is in the infinitive (→**6**)
In the imperative affirmative, the pronoun follows the verb and is attached to it by a hyphen (→**7**)

● For further information, see Order of Object Pronouns, p. 170

Reflexive Pronouns
These are dealt with under reflexive verbs, p. 30

Continued

1 **Tu m'as donné ce livre**
   You gave me this book
   Ils t'ont caché les faits
   They hid the facts from you

2 **Donnez-moi du sucre**   → **Donnez-m'en**
   Give me some sugar   Give me some
   Garde-toi assez d'argent   → **Garde-t'en assez**
   Keep enough money for   Keep enough for yourself
   yourself

3 **J'écris à Suzanne**   → **Je lui écris**
   I'm writing to Suzanne   I'm writing to her
   Donne du lait au chat   → **Donne-lui du lait**
   Give the cat some milk   Give it some milk

4 **arracher qch à qn**   to snatch sth from sb:
       Un voleur m'a arraché mon porte-monnaie
       A thief snatched my purse from me
   promettre qch à qn   to promise sb sth:
       Il leur a promis un cadeau
       He promised them a present
   demander à qn de faire   to ask sb to do:
       Elle nous avait demandé de revenir
       She had asked us to come back

5 **Elle vous a écrit**   **Vous a-t-elle écrit?**
   She's written to you   Has she written to you?
   Il ne nous parle pas
   He doesn't speak to us
   Est-ce que cela ne vous intéresse pas?
   Doesn't it interest you?
   Ne leur répondez pas
   Don't answer them

6 **Voulez-vous leur envoyer l'adresse?**
   Do you want to send them the address?

7 **Répondez-moi**   **Donnez-nous la réponse**
   Answer me   Tell us the answer

Personal Pronouns (ctd.)

Order of object pronouns

● When two object pronouns of different persons come before the verb, the order is: indirect before direct, i.e.

me			le	
te	}	before	la	(→ **1**)
nous			les	
vous				

● When two 3rd person object pronouns come before the verb, the order is: direct before indirect, i.e.

le			lui	
la	}	before	leur	(→ **2**)
les				

● When two object pronouns come after the verb (i.e. in the imperative affirmative), the order is: direct before indirect, i.e.

			moi	
			toi	
le			lui	
la	}	before	nous	(→ **3**)
les			vous	
			leur	

● The pronouns **y** and **en** (see pp. 176 and 174) always come last (→ **4**)

Continued

1 **Dominique vous l'envoie demain**
  Dominique's sending it to you tomorrow
  Est-ce qu'il te les a montrés?
  Has he shown them to you?
  Ne me le dis pas
  Don't tell me (it)
  Il ne veut pas nous la prêter
  He won't lend it to us

2 **Elle le leur a emprunté**
  She borrowed it from them
  Je les lui ai lus
  I read them to him/her
  Ne la leur donne pas
  Don't give it to them
  Je voudrais les lui rendre
  I'd like to give them back to him/her

3 **Rends-les-moi**
  Give them back to me
  Donnez-le-nous
  Give it to us
  Apportons-les-leur
  Let's take them to them

4 **Donnez-leur-en**
  Give them some
  Je l'y ai déposé
  I dropped him there
  Ne nous en parlez plus
  Don't speak to us about it any more

Personal Pronouns (ctd.)

STRESSED OR DISJUNCTIVE PRONOUNS

PERSON	SINGULAR	PLURAL
1st	**moi**	**nous**
	me	*us*
2nd	**toi**	**vous**
	you	*you*
3rd (masc.)	**lui**	**eux**
	him; it	*them*
(fem.)	**elle**	**elles**
	her; it	*them*
('reflexive')	**soi**	
	oneself	

● These pronouns are used:
  – after prepositions (→ **1**)
  – on their own (→ **2**)
  – following **c'est**, **ce sont** *it is* (→ **3**)
  – for emphasis, especially where contrast is involved (→ **4**)
  – when the subject consists of two or more pronouns (→ **5**)
  – when the subject consists of a pronoun and a noun (→ **6**)
  – in comparisons (→ **7**)
  – before relative pronouns (→ **8**)

● For particular emphasis **-même** (singular) or **-mêmes** (plural) is
  added to the pronoun (→ **9**)

moi-même	*myself*	**nous-mêmes**	*ourselves*
toi-même	*yourself*	**vous-même**	*yourself*
lui-même	*himself; itself*	**vous-mêmes**	*yourselves*
elle-même	*herself; itself*	**eux-mêmes**	*themselves*
soi-même	*oneself*	**elles-mêmes**	*themselves*

1 **Je pense à toi**
   I think about you
   C'est pour elle
   This is for her
   Venez avec moi
   Come with me

   Partez sans eux
   Leave without them
   Assieds-toi à côté de lui
   Sit beside him
   Il a besoin de nous
   He needs us

2 **Qui a fait cela? – Lui.**
   Who did that? – He did.
   Qui est-ce qui gagne? – Moi
   Who's winning? – Me

3 **C'est toi, Simon? – Non, c'est moi, David.**
   Is that you, Simon? – No, it's me, David
   Qui est-ce? – Ce sont eux.
   Who is it? – It's them.

4 **Ils voyagent séparément: lui par le train, elle en autobus**
   They travel separately: he by train and she by bus
   Toi, tu ressembles à ton père, eux pas
   You look like your father, *they* don't
   Il n'a pas l'air de s'ennuyer, lui!
   He doesn't look bored!

5 **Lui et moi partons demain**
   He and I are leaving tomorrow
   Ni vous ni elles ne pouvez rester
   Neither you nor they can stay

6 **Mon père et elle ne s'entendent pas**
   My father and she don't get on

7 **plus jeune que moi**
   younger than me

   Il est moins grand que toi
   He's smaller than you (are)

8 **Moi, qui étais malade, je n'ai pas pu les accompagner**
   I, who was ill, couldn't go with them
   Ce sont eux qui font du bruit, pas nous
   They're the ones making the noise, not us

9 **Je l'ai fait moi-même**
   I did it myself

The pronoun en

● **en** replaces the preposition **de** + noun (→ **1**)
  The verbal construction can affect the translation (→ **2**)

● **en** also replaces the partitive article (*English* = *some, any*) + noun
  (→ **3**)

In expressions of quantity **en** represents the noun (→ **4**)

● Position:
  en comes before the verb, except in positive commands when it
  follows and is attached to the verb by a hyphen (→ **5**)

● **en** follows other object pronouns (→ **6**)

1 Il est fier de son succès → **Il en est fier**
  He's proud of his success   He's proud of it
  Elle est sortie du cinéma → **Elle en est sortie**
  She came out of the cinema   She came out (of it)
  Je suis couvert de peinture → **J'en suis couvert**
  I'm covered in paint   I'm covered in it
  Il a beaucoup d'amis → **Il en a beaucoup**
  He has lots of friends   He has lots (of them)
2 avoir besoin de qch   to need sth:
      J'en ai besoin
      I need it/them
  avoir peur de qch   to be afraid of sth:
      J'en ai peur
      I'm afraid of it/them
3 Avez-vous de l'argent? → **En avez-vous?**
  Have you any money?   Do you have any?
  Je veux acheter des timbres → **Je veux en acheter**
  I want to buy some stamps   I want to buy some
4 J'ai deux crayons → **J'en ai deux**
  I've two pencils   I've two (of them)
  Combien de sœurs as-tu? – J'en ai trois.
  How many sisters do you have? – I have three.
5 Elle en a discuté avec moi
  She discussed it with me
  En êtes-vous content?
  Are you pleased with
  it/them?
  Je veux en garder trois
  I want to keep three of them
  N'en parlez plus
  Don't talk about it any more
  Prenez-en   **Soyez-en fier**
  Take some   Be proud of it/them
6 Donnez-leur-en   **Il m'en a parlé**
  Give them some   He spoke to me about it

The pronoun y

● **y** replaces the preposition **à** + noun (→ **1**)
  The verbal construction can affect the translation (→ **2**)

● **y** also replaces the prepositions **dans** and **sur** + noun (→ **3**)

● **y** can also mean *there* (→ **4**)

● Position:
  y comes before the verb, except in positive commands when it follows and is attached to the verb by a hyphen (→ **5**)

● **y** follows other object pronouns (→ **6**)

1 Ne touchez pas à ce bouton → **N'y touchez pas**
Don't touch this switch   Don't touch it
Il participe aux concerts → **Il y participe**
He takes part in the concerts   He takes part (in them)

2 penser à qch   to think about sth:
  J'y pense souvent
  I often think about it
consentir à qch   to agree to sth:
  Tu y as consenti?
  Have you agreed to it?

3 Mettez-les dans la boîte → **Mettez-les-y**
Put them in the box   Put them in it
Il les a mis sur les étagères → **Il les y a mis**
He put them on the shelves   He put them on them
**J'ai placé de l'argent sur ce
compte** → **J'y ai placé de l'argent**
I've put money into this   I've put money into it
account

4 Elle y passe tout l'été
She spends the whole summer there

5 Il y a ajouté du sucre
He added sugar to it
Elle n'y a pas écrit son nom
She hasn't written her name on it
Comment fait-on pour y aller?
How do you get there?
N'y pense plus!
Don't give it another thought!
Restez-y   **Réfléchissez-y**
Stay there   Think it over

6 Elle m'y a conduit   **Menez-nous-y**
She drove me there   Take us there

Indefinite Pronouns

aucun(e)	*none, not any*	(→**1**)
certain(e)s	*some, certain*	(→**2**)
chacun(e)	*each (one)*	
	everybody	(→**3**)
on	*one, you*	
	somebody	
	they, people	(→**4**)
	we (informal use)	
personne	*nobody*	(→**5**)
plusieurs	*several*	(→**6**)
quelque chose	*something; anything*	(→**7**)
quelques-un(e)s	*some, a few*	(→**8**)
quelqu'un	*somebody; anybody*	(→**9**)
rien	*nothing*	(→**10**)
tout	*all; everything*	(→**11**)
tous (toutes)	*all*	(→**12**)
l'un(e) . . . l'autre	*(the) one . . . the other*	
les un(e)s . . . les autres	*some . . . others*	(→**13**)

● **aucun(e), personne, rien**
When used as subject or object of the verb, these require the word **ne** placed immediately before the verb. Note that **aucun** further needs the pronoun **en** when used as an object (→**14**)

● **quelque chose, rien**
When qualified by an adjective, these pronouns require the preposition **de** before the adjective (→**15**)

1 **Combien en avez-vous? – Aucun**
How many have you got? – None

2 **Certains pensent que ...**
Some (people) think that ...

3 **Chacune de ces boîtes est pleine**   **Chacun son tour!**
Each of these boxes is full   Everybody in turn!

4 **On voit l'église de cette fenêtre**
You can see the church from this window
À la campagne on se couche tôt
In the country they/we go to bed early
Est-ce qu'on lui a permis de rester?
Was he/she allowed to stay?

5 **Qui voyez-vous? – Personne**
Who can you see? – Nobody

6 **Ils sont plusieurs**
There are several of them

7 **Mange donc quelque chose!**   **Tu as vu quelque chose?**
Eat something!   Did you see anything?

8 **Je connais quelques-uns de ses amis**
I know some of his/her friends

9 **Quelqu'un a appelé**   **Tu as vu quelqu'un?**
Somebody called (out)   Did you see anybody?

10 **Qu'est-ce que tu as dans la main? – Rien**
What have you got in your hand? – Nothing

11 **Il a tout gâché**   **Tout va bien**
He has spoiled everything   All's well

12 **Tu les as tous?**   **Elles sont toutes venues**
Do you have all of them?   They all came

13 **Les uns sont satisfaits, les autres pas**
Some are satisfied, (the) others aren't

14 **Je ne vois personne**   **Rien ne lui plaît**
I can't see anyone   Nothing pleases him/her
Aucune des entreprises ne veut ...   **Il n'en a aucun**
None of the companies wants ...   He hasn't any (of them)

15 **quelque chose de grand**   **rien d'intéressant**
something big   nothing interesting

Relative Pronouns

qui *who; which*
que *who(m); which*

These are subject and direct object pronouns that introduce a clause and refer to people or things.

	PEOPLE	THINGS
SUBJECT	**qui** (→1)	**qui** (→3)
	who, that	*which, that*
DIRECT OBJECT	**que (qu')** (→2)	**que (qu')** (→4)
	who(m), that	*which, that*

● **que** changes to **qu'** before a vowel (→2/4)
● You cannot omit the object relative pronoun in French as you can in English (→2/4)

After a preposition:
● When referring to people, use **qui** (→5)
    Exceptions: after **parmi** *among* and **entre** *between* use **lesquels/lesquelles** (see below) (→6)
● When referring to things, use forms of **lequel**:

	MASCULINE	FEMININE	
SING.	**lequel**	**laquelle**	*which*
PLUR.	**lesquels**	**lesquelles**	*which*

The pronoun agrees in number and gender with the noun (→7)

● After the prepositions **à** and **de, lequel** and **lesquel(le)s** contract as follows:

> à + lequel → auquel
> à + lesquels → auxquels   (→8)
> à + lesquelles → auxquelles
>
> de + lequel → duquel
> de + lesquels → desquels   (→9)
> de + lesquelles → desquelles

Continued

1 **Mon frère, qui a vingt ans, est à l'université**
My brother, who's twenty, is at university

2 **Les amis que je vois le plus sont . . .**
The friends (that) I see most are . . .
Lucienne, qu'il connaît depuis longtemps, est . . .
Lucienne, whom he has known for a long time, is . . .

3 **Il y a un escalier qui mène au toit**
There's a staircase which leads to the roof

4 **La maison que nous avons achetée a . . .**
The house (which) we've bought has . . .
Voici le cadeau qu'elle m'a envoyé
This is the present (that) she sent me

5 **la personne à qui il parle**
the person he's talking to
la personne avec qui je voyage
the person with whom I travel
les enfants pour qui je l'ai acheté
the children for whom I bought it

6 **Il y avait des jeunes, parmi lesquels Robert**
There were some young people, Robert among them
les filles entre lesquelles j'étais assis
the girls between whom I was sitting

7 **le torchon avec lequel il l'essuie**
the cloth he's wiping it with
la table sur laquelle je l'ai mis
the table on which I put it
les moyens par lesquels il l'accomplit
the means by which he achieves it
les pièces pour lesquelles elle est connue
the plays for which she is famous

8 **le magasin auquel il livre ces marchandises**
the shop to which he delivers these goods

9 **les injustices desquelles il se plaint**
the injustices he's complaining about

Relative Pronouns (ctd.)

quoi   *which, what*

● When the relative pronoun does not refer to a specific noun, **quoi** is used after a preposition (→**1**)

dont   *whose, of whom, of which*

● **dont** often (but not always) replaces **de qui, duquel**, **de laquelle**, and **desquel(le)s** (→**2**)

● It cannot replace **de qui**, **duquel** etc in the construction preposition + noun + **de qui/duquel** (→**3**)

Continued

1 **C'est en quoi vous vous trompez**
  That's where you're wrong
  A quoi, j'ai répondu '...'
  To which I replied, '...'

2 **la femme dont (= de qui) la voiture est garée en face**
  the woman whose car is parked opposite
  un prix dont (= de qui) je suis fier
  an award I am proud of
  un ami dont (= de qui) je connais le frère
  a friend whose brother I know
  les enfants dont (= de qui) vous vous occupez
  the children you look after
  le film dont (= duquel) il a parlé
  the film of which he spoke
  la fenêtre dont (= de laquelle) les rideaux sont tirés
  the window whose curtains are drawn
  des livres dont (= desquels) j'ai oublié les titres
  books whose titles I've forgotten
  les maladies dont (= desquelles) il souffre
  the illnesses he suffers from

3 **une personne sur l'aide de qui on peut compter**
  a person whose help one can rely on
  les enfants aux parents de qui j'écris
  the children to whose parents I'm writing
  la maison dans le jardin de laquelle il y a ...
  the house in whose garden there is ...

Relative Pronouns (ctd.)

ce qui, ce que   *that which, what*
These are used when the relative pronoun does not refer to a specific noun, and they are often translated as *what* (literally: *that which*)

> **ce qui**   is used as the subject (→**1**)
> **ce que***   is used as the direct object (→**2**)
>
> ***que** changes to **qu'** before a vowel (→**2**)

● Note the construction
> **tout ce qui** }
> **tout ce que** }   *everything/all that*   (→**3**)

● **de + ce que → ce dont** (→**4**)

● preposition + **ce que → ce** + preposition + **quoi** (→**5**)

● When **ce qui, ce que** etc, refers to a previous CLAUSE the translation is *which* (→**6**)

1 **Ce qui m'intéresse ne l'intéresse pas forcément**
  What interests me doesn't necessarily interest him
  Je n'ai pas vu ce qui s'est passé
  I didn't see what happened

2 **Ce que j'aime c'est la musique classique**
  What I like is classical music
  Montrez-moi ce qu'il vous a donné
  Show me what he gave you

3 **Tout ce qui reste c'est ...**
  All that's left is ...
  Donnez-moi tout ce que vous avez
  Give me everything you have

4 **Il risque de perdre ce dont il est si fier**
  He risks losing what he's so proud of
  Voilà ce dont il s'agit
  That's what it's about

5 **Ce n'est pas ce à quoi je m'attendais**
  It's not what I was expecting
  Ce à quoi je m'intéresse particulièrement c'est ...
  What I'm particularly interested in is ...

6 **Il est d'accord, ce qui m'étonne**
  He agrees, which surprises me
  Il a dit qu'elle ne venait pas, ce que nous savions déjà
  He said she wasn't coming, which we already knew

Interrogative Pronouns

qui?   *who?; whom?*
que?   *what?*
quoi?   *what?*

These pronouns are used in direct questions.
The form of the pronoun depends on:

      – whether it refers to people or to things
      – whether it is the subject or object of the verb, or if it comes
        after a preposition

Qui and **que** have longer forms, as shown in the tables below.

● Referring to people:

SUBJECT	**qui?**	
	qui est-ce qui?	(→**1**)
	who?	
OBJECT	**qui?**	
	qui est-ce que*?	(→**2**)
	who(m)?	
AFTER	**qui?**	
PREPOSITIONS	*who(m)?*	(→**3**)

● Referring to things:

SUBJECT	**qu'est-ce qui?**	(→**4**)
	what?	
OBJECT	**que*?**	
	qu'est-ce que*?	(→**5**)
	what?	
AFTER	**quoi?**	
PREPOSITIONS	*what?*	(→**6**)

*****que** changes to **qu'** before a vowel (→**2, 5**)

Continued

1 **Qui vient?**
  Qui est-ce qui vient?
  Who's coming?

2 **Qui vois-tu?**
  Qui est-ce que tu vois?
  Who(m) can you see?
  Qui a-t-elle rencontré?
  Qui est-ce qu'elle a rencontré?
  Who(m) did she meet?

3 **De qui parle-t-il?**
  Who's he talking about?
  Pour qui est ce livre?
  Who's this book for?
  A qui avez-vous écrit?
  To whom did you write?

4 **Qu'est-ce qui se passe?**
  What's happening?
  Qu'est-ce qui a vexé Paul?
  What upset Paul?

5 **Que faites-vous?**
  Qu'est-ce que vous faites?
  What are you doing?
  Qu'a-t-il dit?
  Qu'est-ce qu'il a dit?
  What did he say?

6 **A quoi cela sert-il?**
  What's that used for?
  De quoi a-t-on parlé?
  What was the discussion about?
  Sur quoi vous basez-vous?
  What do you base it on?

Interrogative Pronouns (ctd.)

qui   *who; whom*
ce qui   *what*
ce que   *what*
quoi   *what*

These pronouns are used in indirect questions.
The form of the pronoun depends on:

- whether it refers to people or to things
- whether it is the subject or object of the verb, or if it comes after a preposition

● Referring to people: use **qui** in all instances (→**1**)

● Referring to things:

SUBJECT	**ce qui** *what*	(→**2**)
OBJECT	**ce que*** *what*	(→**3**)
AFTER *PREPOSITIONS*	**quoi** *what*	(→**4**)

***que** changes to **qu'** before a vowel (→**3**)

1 **Demande-lui qui est venu**
   Ask him who came
   Je me demande qui ils ont vu
   I wonder who they saw
   Dites-moi qui vous préférez
   Tell me who you prefer
   Elle ne sait pas à qui s'adresser
   She doesn't know who to apply to
   Demandez-leur pour qui elles travaillent
   Ask them who they work for

2 **Il se demande ce qui se passe**
   He's wondering what's happening
   Je ne sais pas ce qui vous fait croire que ...
   I don't know what makes you think that ...

3 **Raconte-nous ce que tu as fait**
   Tell us what you did
   Je me demande ce qu'elle pense
   I wonder what she's thinking

4 **On ne sait pas de quoi vivent ces animaux**
   We don't know what these animals live on
   Je vais lui demander à quoi il fait allusion
   I'm going to ask him what he's hinting at

Interrogative Pronouns (ctd.)

lequel?, laquelle?; lesquels?, lesquelles?

	MASCULINE	FEMININE	
SING.	**lequel?**	**laquelle?**	*which (one)?*
PLUR.	**lesquels?**	**lesquelles?**	*which (ones)?*

● The pronoun agrees in number and gender with the noun it refers to (→**1**)

● The same forms are used in indirect questions (→**2**)

● After the prepositions **à** and **de**, **lequel** and **lesquel(le)s** contract as follows:

> **à + lequel? → auquel?**
> **à + lesquels? → auxquels?**
> **à + lesquelles? → auxquelles?**
>
> **de + lequel? → duquel?**
> **de + lesquels? → desquels?**
> **de + lesquelles? → desquelles?**

1 **J'ai choisi un livre. – Lequel?**
  I've chosen a book. – Which one?
  Laquelle de ces valises est la vôtre?
  Which of these cases is yours?
  Amenez quelques amis. – Lesquels?
  Bring some friends. – Which ones?
  Lesquelles de vos sœurs sont mariées?
  Which of your sisters are married?

2 **Je me demande laquelle des maisons est la leur**
  I wonder which is their house
  Dites-moi lesquels d'entre eux étaient là
  Tell me which of them were there

Possessive Pronouns

SINGULAR

MASCULINE	FEMININE	
le mien	la mienne	*mine*
le tien	la tienne	*yours*
le sien	la sienne	*his; hers; its*
le nôtre	la nôtre	*ours*
le vôtre	la vôtre	*yours*
le leur	la leur	*theirs*

PLURAL

MASCULINE	FEMININE	
les miens	les miennes	*mine*
les tiens	les tiennes	*yours*
les siens	les siennes	*his; hers; its*
les nôtres	les nôtres	*ours*
les vôtres	les vôtres	*yours*
les leurs	les leurs	*theirs*

● The pronoun agrees in number and gender with the noun it replaces, NOT WITH THE OWNER (→**1**)

● Alternative translations are *my own, your own* etc; **le sien, la sienne** etc. may also mean *one's own* (→**2**)

● After the prepositions **à** and **de** the articles **le** and **les** are contracted in the normal way (see p. 140):

> **à + le mien → au mien**
> **à + les miens → aux miens**   (→**3**)
> **à + les miennes → aux miennes**
>
> **de + le mien → du mien**
> **de + les miens → des miens**   (→**4**)
> **de + les miennes → des miennes**

1 **Demandez à Carole si ce stylo est le sien**
Ask Carol if this pen is hers
Quelle équipe a gagné – la leur ou la nôtre?
Which team won – theirs or ours?
Mon stylo marche mieux que le tien
My pen writes better than yours
Richard a pris mes affaires pour les siennes
Richard mistook my belongings for his
Si tu n'as pas de disques, emprunte les miens
If you don't have any records, borrow mine
Nos maisons sont moins grandes que les vôtres
Our houses are smaller than yours

2 **Est-ce que leur entreprise est aussi grande que la vôtre?**
Is their company as big as your own?
Leurs prix sont moins élevés que les nôtres
Their prices are lower than our own
Le bonheur des autres importe plus que le sien
Other people's happiness matters more than one's own

3 **Pourquoi préfères-tu ce manteau au mien?**
Why do you prefer this coat to mine?
Quelles maisons ressemblent aux leurs?
Which houses resemble theirs?

4 **Leur car est garé**
Their coach is parked
Vos livres sont au-dessus des miens
Your books are on top of mine

Demonstrative Pronouns

celui, celle; ceux, celles

	MASCULINE	FEMININE	
SING.	**celui**	**celle**	*the one*
PLUR.	**ceux**	**celles**	*the ones*

● The pronoun agrees in number and gender with the noun it replaces (→**1**)

● Uses:
  – preceding a relative pronoun, meaning *the one(s) who/which* (→**1**)
  – preceding the preposition **de**, meaning *the one(s) belonging to, the one(s) of* (→**2**)
  – with **-ci** and **-là**, for emphasis or to distinguish between two things:

	MASCULINE	FEMININE		
SING.	**celui-ci**	**celle-ci**	*this (one)*	(→**3**)
PLUR.	**ceux-ci**	**celles-ci**	*these (ones)*	

	MASCULINE	FEMININE		
SING.	**celui-là**	**celle-là**	*that (one)*	(→**3**)
PLUR.	**ceux-là**	**celles-là**	*those (ones)*	

  – an additional meaning of **celui-ci/celui-là** etc. is *the former/the latter*

Continued

1 Lequel? – Celui qui parle à Anne
Which man? – The one who's talking to Anne
Quelle robe désirez-vous? – Celle qui est en vitrine
Which dress do you want? – The one which is in the window
Est-ce que ces livres sont ceux qu'il t'a donnés?
Are these the books that he gave you?
Quelles filles? – Celles que nous avons vues hier
Which girls? – The ones we saw yesterday
Cet article n'est pas celui dont vous m'avez parlé
This article isn't the one you spoke to me about

2 Ce jardin est plus grand que celui de mes parents
This garden is bigger than my parents' (garden)
Est-ce que ta fille est plus âgée que celle de Gabrielle?
Is your daughter older than Gabrielle's (daughter)?
Je préfère les enfants de Paul à ceux de Roger
I prefer Paul's children to Roger's (children)
Comparez vos réponses à celles de votre voisin
Compare your answers with your neighbours (answers)
les montagnes d'Écosse et celles du pays de Galles
the mountains of Scotland and those of Wales

3 Quel tailleur préférez-vous: celui-ci ou celui-là?
Which suit do you prefer: this one or that one?
Cette chemise a deux poches mais celle-la n'en a pas
This shirt has two pockets but that one has none
Quels œufs choisirais-tu: ceux-ci ou ceux-là?
Which eggs would you choose: these (ones) or those (ones)?
De toutes mes jupes, celle-ci me va le mieux
Of all my skirts, this one fits me best

Demonstrative Pronouns (ctd.)

ce (c') *it, that*

● Usually used with **être**, in the expressions **c'est**, **c'était**, **ce sont** etc. (→**1**)

● Note the spelling **ç** when followed by the letter **a** (→**2**)

● Uses:
  – to identify a person or object (→**3**)
  – for emphasis (→**4**)
  – as a neuter pronoun, referring to a statement, idea etc. (→**5**)

ce qui, ce que, ce dont   etc.: see Relative Pronouns (p. 184), Interrogative Pronouns (p. 188)

cela, ça *it, that*

● **cela** and **ça** are used as 'neuter' pronouns, referring to a statement, an idea, an object (→**6**)

● In everyday spoken language **ça** is used in preference to **cela**

ceci *this* (→**7**)

● **ceci** is not used as often as 'this' in English; **cela**, **ça** are often used where we use 'this'

1 **C'est...**
  It's/That's ...

  C'était moi
  It was me

2 **Ç'a été la cause de ...**
  It has been cause of ...

3 **Qui est-ce?**
  Who is it?; Who's this/that?; Who's he/she?
  C'est lui/mon frère/nous
  It's/That's him/my brother/us
  C'est une infirmière*
  She's a nurse
  Qu'est-ce que c'est?
  What's this/that?
  C'est une agrafeuse
  It's a stapler

  Ce sont eux
  It's them
  Ce sont des professeurs*
  They're teachers
  Qu'est-ce que c'est que ça?
  What's that?
  Ce sont des trombones
  They're paper clips

4 **C'est moi qui ai téléphoné**
  It was me who phoned
  Ce sont les enfants qui importent le plus
  It's the children who matter most

5 **C'est très intéressant**
  That's/It's very interesting
  Ce serait dangereux
  That/It would be dangerous

6 **Ça ne fait rien**
  It doesn't matter
  A quoi bon faire ça?
  What's the use of doing that?
  Cela ne compte pas
  That doesn't count
  Cela demande du temps
  It/That takes time

7 **A qui est ceci?**
  Whose is this?

  Ouvrez-le comme ceci
  Open it like this

*See pp. 146 and 147 for the use of the article when stating a person's
profession

Adverbs

Formation

● Most adverbs are formed by adding **-ment** to the feminine form of the adjective (→**1**)

● **-ment** is added to the *masculine* form when the masculine form ends in **-é**, **-i** or **-u** (→**2**)
Exception: **gai** (→**3**)
Occasionally the **u** changes to **û** before **-ment** is added (→**4**)

● If the adjective ends in **-ant** or **-ent**, the adverb ends in **-amment** or **-emment** (→**5**)
Exceptions: **lent**, **présent** (→**6**)

Irregular Adverbs

ADJECTIVE		ADVERB		
aveugle	*blind*	**aveuglément**	blindly	
bon	*good*	**bien**	well	(→**7**)
bref	*brief*	**brièvement**	briefly	
énorme	*enormous*	**énormément**	enormously	
exprès	*express*	**expressément**	expressly	(→**8**)
gentil	*kind*	**gentiment**	kindly	
mauvais	*bad*	**mal**	badly	(→**9**)
meilleur	*better*	**mieux**	better	
pire	*worse*	**pis**	worse	
précis	*precise*	**précisément**	precisely	
profond	*deep*	**profondément**	deeply	(→**10**)
traître	*treacherous*	**traîtreusement**	treacherously	

Adjectives used as adverbs

Certain adjectives are used adverbially. These include: **bas, bon, cher, clair, court, doux, droit, dur, faux, ferme, fort, haut, mauvais** and **net** (→**11**)

1 *MASC/FEM. ADJECTIVE*   *ADVERB*

heureux/heureuse fortunate   **heureusement** fortunately

franc/franche frank   **franchement** frankly

extrême/extrême extreme   **extrêmement** extremely

2 *MASC. ADJECTIVE*   *ADVERB*

désespéré desperate   **désespérément** desperately

vrai true   **vraiment** truly

résolu resolute   **résolument** resolutely

3 gai cheerful   **gaiement** *OR* **gaîment** cheerfully

4 continu continuous   **continûment** continuously

5 constant constant   **constamment** constantly

courant fluent   **couramment** fluently

évident obvious   **évidemment** obviously

fréquent frequent   **fréquemment** frequently

6 lent slow   **lentement** slowly

présent present   **présentement** presently

7 Elle travaille bien

She works well

8 Il a expressément défendu qu'on parte

He has expressly forbidden us to leave

9 Un emploi mal payé

A badly paid job

10 J'ai été profondément ému

I was deeply moved

11 parler bas/haut

to speak softly/loudly

coûter cher

to be expensive

voir clair

to see clearly

travailler dur

to work hard

chanter faux

to sing off key

sentir bon/mauvais

to smell nice/horrible

Position of Adverbs

● When the adverb accompanies a verb in a simple tense, it generally follows the verb (→ 1)
● When the adverb accompanies a verb in a compound tense, it generally comes between the auxiliary verb and the past participle (→ 2)
  Some adverbs, however, follow the past participle (→ 3)
● When the adverb accompanies an adjective or another adverb it generally precedes the adjective/adverb (→ 4)

Comparatives of Adverbs

These are formed using the following constructions:

plus ... (que)	*more ... (than)*	(→ **5**)
moins ... (que)	*less ... (than)*	(→ **6**)
aussi ... que	*as ... as*	(→ **7**)
si ... que*	*as ... as*	(→ **8**)

*used mainly after a negative

Superlatives of Adverbs

These are formed using the following constructions:

le plus ... (que)	*the most ... (that)*	(→ **9**)
le moins ... (que)	*the least ... (that)*	(→ **10**)

Adverbs with irregular comparatives/superlatives

ADVERB	COMPARATIVE	SUPERLATIVE
beaucoup	**plus**	**le plus**
a lot	*more*	*(the) most*
bien	**mieux**	**le mieux**
well	*better*	*(the) best*
mal	**pis** OR	**le pis** OR
	plus mal	**le plus mal**
badly	*worse*	*(the) worst*
peu	**moins**	**le moins**
little	*less*	*(the) least*

1 **Il dort encore**
He's still asleep

Je pense souvent à toi
I often think about you

2 **Ils sont déjà partis**
They've already gone
J'ai presque fini
I'm almost finished

J'ai toujours cru que …
I've always thought that …
Il a trop mangé
He's eaten too much

3 **On les a vus partout**
We saw them everywhere

Elle est revenue hier
She came back yesterday

4 **un très beau chemisier**
a very nice blouse
beaucoup plus vite
much faster

une femme bien habillée
a well-dressed woman
peu souvent
not very often

5 **plus vite**
more quickly
Elle chante plus fort que moi
She sings louder than I do

plus régulièrement
more regularly

6 **moins facilement**
less easily

moins souvent
less often

Nous nous voyons moins fréquemment qu'auparavant
We see each other less frequently than before

7 **Faites-le aussi vite que possible**
Do it as quickly as possible
Il en sait aussi long que nous
He knows as much about it as we do

8 **Ce n'est pas si loin que je pensais**
It's not as far as I thought

9 **Marianne court le plus vite**
Marianne runs fastest
Le plus tôt que je puisse venir c'est samedi
The earliest that I can come is Saturday

10 **C'est l'auteur que je connais le moins bien**
It's the writer I'm least familiar with

Common adverbs and their usage

assez	*enough; quite*	(→ **1**) See also below
aussi	*also, too; as*	(→ **2**)
autant	*as much*	(→ **3**) See also below
beaucoup	*a lot; much*	(→ **4**) See also below
bien	*well; very*	(→ **5**) See also below
	very much; 'indeed'	
combien	*how much; how many*	(→ **6**) See also below
comme	*how; what*	(→ **7**)
déjà	*already; before*	(→ **8**)
encore	*still; yet*	(→ **9**)
	more; even	
moins	*less*	(→ **10**) See also below
peu	*little, not much; not very*	(→ **11**) See also below
plus	*more*	(→ **12**) See also below
si	*so; such*	(→ **13**)
tant	*so much*	(→ **14**) See also below
toujours	*always; still*	(→ **15**)
trop	*too much; too*	(→ **16**) See also below

● **assez, autant, beaucoup, combien** etc. are used in the construction *adverb* + **de** + *noun* with the following meanings:

assez de	*enough*	(→**17**)
autant de	*as much; as many*	
	so much; so many	
beaucoup de	*a lot of*	
combien de	*how much; how many*	
moins de	*less; fewer*	(→**17**)
peu de	*little, not much; few,*	
	not many	
plus de	*more*	
tant de	*so much; so many*	
trop de	*too much; too many*	

● **bien** can be followed by a partitive article (see p. 144) plus a noun to mean *a lot of; a good many* (→ **18**)

1 **Avez-vous assez chaud?**   **Il est assez tard**
Are you warm enough?   It's quite late

2 **Je préfère ça aussi**   **Elle est aussi grande que moi**
I prefer it too   She is as tall as I am

3 **Je voyage autant que lui**
I have as much as him

4 **Tu lis beaucoup?**   **C'est beaucoup plus loin?**
Do you read a lot?   Is it much further?

5 **Bien joué!**   **Je suis bien content que ...**
Well played!   I'm very pleased that ...
Il s'est bien amusé   **Je l'ai bien fait**
He enjoyed himself very much   I DID do it

6 **Combien coûte ce livre?**   **Vous êtes combien?**
How much is this book?   How many of you are there?

7 **Comme tu es jolie!**   **Comme il fait beau!**
How pretty you look!   What lovely weather!

8 **Je l'ai déjà fait**   **Êtes-vous déjà allé en France?**
I've already done it   Have you been to France before?

9 **J'en ai encore deux**   **Elle n'est pas encore là**
I've still got two   She isn't there yet
Encore du café, Alain?   **Encore mieux!**
More coffee, Alan?   Even better!

10 **Travaillez moins**   **Je suis moins étonné que toi**
Work less   I'm less surprised than you are

11 **Elle mange peu**   **C'est peu important**
She doesn't eat very much   It's not very important

12 **Il se détend plus**   **Elle est plus timide que Sophie**
He relaxes more   She is shyer than Sophie

13 **Simon est si charmant**   **une si belle vue**
Simon is so charming   such a lovely view

14 **Elle l'aime tant**   She loves him so much

15 **Il dit toujours ça!**   **Tu le vois toujours?**
He always says that!   Do you still see him?

16 **J'ai trop mangé**   **C'est trop cher**
I've eaten too much   It's too expensive

17 **assez d'argent/de livres**   **moins de temps/d'amis**
enough money/books   less time/fewer friends

18 **bien du mal/des gens**   a lot of harm/a good many people

On the following pages you will find some of the most frequent uses of prepositions in French. Particular attention is paid to cases where usage differs markedly from English. It is often difficult to give an English equivalent for French prepositions, since usage *does* vary so much between the two languages.

In the list below, the broad meaning of the preposition is given on the left, with examples of usage following.

Prepositions are dealt with in alphabetical order, except **à**, **de** and **en** which are shown first.

à

at	**lancer qch à qn**	*to throw sth at sb*
	il habite à St. Pierre	*he lives at St. Pierre*
	à 5 francs (la) pièce	*(at) 5 francs each*
	à 100 km à l'heure	*at 100 km per hour*
in	**à la campagne**	*in the country*
	à Londres	*in London*
	au lit	*in bed* (also *to bed*)
	un livre à la main	*with a book in his/her hand*
on	**un tableau au mur**	*a picture on the wall*
to	**aller au cinéma**	*to go to the cinema*
	donner qch à qn	*to give sth to sb*
	le premier/dernier à faire	*the first/last to do*
	demander qch à qn	*to ask sb sth*
from	**arracher qch à qn**	*to snatch sth from sb*
	acheter qch à qn	*to buy sth from sb*
	cacher qch à qn	*to hide sth from sb*
	emprunter qch à qn	*to borrow sth from sb*
	prendre qch à qn	*to take sth from sb*
	voler qch à qn	*to steal sth from sb*

descriptive	**la femme au chapeau vert**	*the woman with the green hat*
	un garçon aux yeux bleus	*a boy with blue eyes*
manner, means	**à l'anglaise**	*in the English manner*
	fait à la main	*handmade*
	à bicyclette / cheval	*by bicycle/on horseback* (BUT note other forms of transport used with **en** and **par**)
	à pied	*on foot*
	chauffer au gaz	*to heat with/by gas*
	à pas lents	*with slow steps*
	cuisiner au beurre	*to cook with butter*
time, date: *at, in*	**à minuit**	*at midnight*
	à trois heures cinq	*at five past three*
	au 20ème siècle	*in the 20th century*
	à Noël / Pâques	*at Christmas/Easter*
distance	**à 6 km d'ici**	*(at a distance of) 6 km from here*
	à deux pas de chez moi	*just a step from my place*
destined for	**une tasse à thé**	*a teacup* (compare **une tasse de thé**)
	un service à café	*a coffee service*
after certain adjectives	**son écriture est difficile à lire**	*his writing is difficult to read* (compare the usage with **de**, p. 206)
	prêt à tout	*ready for anything*
after certain verbs *Continued*	see p. 64	

de

from	**venir de Londres** **du matin au soir** **du 21 juin au 5 juillet** **de 10 à 15**	*to come from London* *from morning till night* *from 21st June till 5th July* *from 10 to 15*
belonging to, *of*	**un ami de la famille** **les vents d'automne**	*a family friend* *the autumn winds*
contents, composition, material	**une boîte d'allumettes** **une tasse de thé** **une robe de soie**	*a box of matches* *a cup of tea* (compare **une tasse à thé**) *a silk dress*
manner	**d'une façon irrégulière** **d'un coup de couteau**	*in an irregular way* *with the blow of a knife*
quality	**la société de consommation** **des objets de valeur**	*the consumer society* *valuable items*
comparative + a number	**il y avait plus/moins de cent personnes**	*there were more/fewer than a hundred people*
after superlatives: *in*	**la plus/moins belle ville du monde**	*the most/least beautiful city in the world*
after certain adjectives	**surpris de voir** **il est difficile d'y accéder**	*surprised to see* *access is difficult* (compare the usage with **à**, p. 205)
after certain verbs	see p. 64	

en

place: *to, in, on*	**en ville**	*in/to town*
	en pleine mer	*on the open sea*
	en France	*in/to France* (note that masculine countries use **à**)
dates, months: *in*	**en 1923**	*in 1923*
	en janvier	*in January*
transport	**en voiture**	*by car*
	en avion	*by plane* (but note usage of **à** and **par** in other expressions)
language	**en français**	*in French*
duration	**je le ferai en trois jours**	*I'll do it in three days* (i.e. *I'll take 3 days to do it*: compare **dans trois jours**)
material	**un bracelet en or**	*a bracelet made of gold* (note that the use of **en** stresses the material more than the use of **de**)
	consister en	*to consist of*
in the manner of, like a	**parler en vrai connaisseur**	*to speak like a real connoisseur*
	déguisé en cowboy	*dressed up as a cowboy*
+ present participle	**il l'a vu en passant devant la porte**	*he saw it as he came past the door*

Continued

avant

before	**il est arrivé avant toi**	*he arrived before you*
+ infinitive (add **de**)	**je vais finir ça avant de manger**	*I'm going to finish this before eating*
preference	**la santé avant tout**	*health above all things*

chez

at the home of	**chez lui/moi** **être chez soi** **venez chez nous**	*at his/my house* *to be at home* *come round to our place*
at/to a shop	**chez le boucher**	*at/to the butcher's*
in a person, *among* a group of people or animals	**ce que je n'aime pas chez lui c'est son ...** **chez les fourmis**	*what I don't like in him is his ...* *among ants*

dans

position	**dans une boîte**	*in(to) a box*
circumstance	**dans son enfance**	*in his childhood*
future time	**dans trois jours**	*in three days' time* (compare **en trois jours**, p. 207)

depuis

since: time place	**depuis mardi** **il pleut depuis Paris**	*since Tuesday* *it's been raining since Paris*
for	**il habite cette maison depuis 3 ans**	*he's been living in this house for 3 years* (NOTE TENSE)

dès

past time	**dès mon enfance**	*since my childhood*
future time	**je le ferai dès mon retour**	*I'll do it as soon as I get back*

entre

between	**entre 8 et 10**	*between 8 and 10*
among	**Jean et Pierre, entre autres**	*Jean and Pierre, among others*
reciprocal	**s'aider entre eux**	*to help each other (out)*

d'entre

of, among	**trois d'entre eux**	*three of them*

par

agent of passive: *by*	**renversé par une voiture**	*knocked down by a car*
	tué par la foudre	*killed by lightning*
weather conditions	**par un beau jour d'été**	*on a lovely summer's day*
by (means of)	**par un couloir/sentier**	*by a corridor/path*
	par le train	by train (but see also **à** and **en**)
	par l'intermédiaire de M. Duval	*through Mr. Duval*
distribution	**deux par deux**	*two by two*
	par groupes de dix	*in groups of ten*
	deux fois par jour	*twice a day*

Continued

pour

for	c'est pour vous	it's for you
	c'est pour demain	it's for tomorrow
	une chambre pour 2 nuits	a room for 2 nights
	pour un enfant, il se débrouille bien	for a child he manages very well
	il part pour l'Espagne	he's leaving for Spain
	il l'a fait pour vous	he did it for you
	il lui a donné 50 francs pour ce livre	he gave him 50 francs for this book
	je ne suis pas pour cette idée	I'm not for that idea
	pour qui me prends-tu?	who do you take me for?
	il passe pour un idiot	he's taken for a fool
+ infinitive: (in order) to	elle se pencha pour le ramasser	she bent down to pick it up
	c'est trop fragile pour servir de siège	it's too fragile to be used as a seat
to(wards)	être bon/gentil pour qn	to be kind to sb
with prices, time	pour 200 francs d'essence	200 francs' worth of petrol
	j'en ai encore pour une heure	I'll be another hour (at it) yet

sans

without	sans eau	without water
	sans ma femme	without my wife
+ infinitive	sans compter les autres	without counting the others

sauf

except (for)	**tous sauf lui**	all except him
	sauf quand il pleut	except when its raining
barring	**sauf imprévu**	barring the unexpected
	sauf avis contraire	unless you hear to the contrary

sur

on	**sur le siège**	on the seat
	sur l'armoire	on top of the wardrobe
	sur le mur	on (top of) the wall (if the meaning is *hanging on the wall* use **à**, p. 204)
	sur votre gauche	on your left
	être sur le point de faire	to be on the point of doing
on (to)	**mettez-le sur la table**	put it on the table
proportion: out of; by	**8 sur 10**	8 out of 10
	un automobiliste sur 5	one motorist in 5
	la pièce fait 2 mètres sur 3	the room measures 2 metres by 3

Conjunctions

There are conjunctions which introduce a main clause, such as **et** *and*, **mais** *but*, **si** *if*, **ou** *or* etc., and those which introduce subordinate clauses like **parce que** *because*, **pendant que** *while*, **après que** *after* etc. They are all used in much the same way as in English, but the following points are of note:

● Some conjunctions in French require a following subjunctive, see p. 58

● Some conjunctions are 'split' in French like *both ... and, either ... or* in English:

et ... et	*both ... and*	(→ **1**)
ni ... ni ... ne	*neither ... nor*	(→ **2**)
ou (bien) .. ou (bien)	*either ... or (else)*	(→ **3**)
soit ... soit	*either ... or*	(→ **4**)

● **si** + **il(s)** → **s'il(s)** (→ **5**)

● **que**
  – meaning *that* (→ **6**)
  – replacing another conjunction (→ **7**)
  – replacing **si**, see p. 62
  – in comparisons, meaning *as, than* (→ **8**)
  – followed by the subjunctive, see p. 62

● **aussi** *so, therefore*: the subject and verb are inverted if the subject is a pronoun (→ **9**)

1 **Ces fleurs poussent et en été et en hiver**
These flowers grow in both summer and winter

2 **Ni lui ni elle ne sont venus**
Neither he nor she came
Ils n'ont ni argent ni nourriture
They have neither money nor food

3 **Elle doit être ou naïve ou stupide**
She must be either naïve or stupid
Ou bien il m'évite ou bien il ne me reconnaît pas
Either he's avoiding me or else he doesn't recognise me

4 **Il faut choisir soit l'un soit l'autre**
You have to choose either one or the other

5 **Je ne sais pas s'il vient/s'ils viennent**
I don't know if he's coming/if they're coming
Dis-moi s'il y a des erreurs
Tell me if there are any mistakes
Votre passeport, s'il vous plaît
Your passport, please

6 **Il dit qu'il t'a vu**
He says (that) he saw you
Est-ce qu'elle sait que vous êtes là?
Does she know that you're here?

7 **Quand tu seras plus grand et que tu auras une maison à toi, ...**
When you're older and you have a house of your own, ...
Comme il pleuvait et que je n'avais pas de parapluie, ...
As it was raining and I didn't have an umbrella, ...

8 **Ils n'y vont pas aussi souvent que nous**
They don't go there as often as we do
Il les aime plus que jamais
He likes them more than ever
L'argent est moins lourd que le plomb
Silver is lighter than lead

9 **Ceux-ci sont plus rares, aussi coûtent-ils cher**
These ones are rarer, so they're expensive

Word Order

Word order in French is largely the same as in English, except for the following. Most of these have already been dealt with under the appropriate part of speech, but are summarised here along with other instances not covered elsewhere.

- Object pronouns nearly always come before the verb (→ **1**)
  For details, see pp. 166 to 170

- Certain adjectives come after the noun (→ **2**)
  For details, see p. 162

- Adverbs accompanying a verb in a simple tense usually follow the verb (→ **3**)
  For details, see p. 200

- After **aussi** *so, therefore*, **à peine** *hardly*, **peut-être** *perhaps*, the verb and subject are inverted (→ **4**)

- After the relative pronoun **dont** *whose* (→ **5**)
  For details, see p. 182

- In exclamations, **que** and **comme** do not affect the normal word order (→ **6**)

- Following direct speech:
  - the *verb + subject* order is inverted to become *subject + verb* (→ **7**)
  - with a pronoun subject, the verb and pronoun are linked by a hyphen (→ **8**)
  - when the verb ends in a vowel in the 3rd person singular, **-t-** is inserted between the pronoun and the verb (→ **9**)

For word order in negative sentences, see p. 216
For word order in interrogative sentences, see pp. 220 and 222

1 **Je les vois!**   **Il me l'a donné**
   I can see them!   He gave it to me
2 **une ville française**   **du vin rouge**
   a French town   some red wine
3 **Il pleut encore**   **Elle m'aide quelquefois**
   It's still raining   She sometimes helps me
4 **Il vit tout seul, aussi fait-il ce qu'il veut**
   He lives alone, so he does what he likes
   A peine la pendule avait-elle sonné trois heures que ...
   Hardly had the clock struck three when ...
   Peut-être avez-vous raison
   Perhaps you're right
5 Compare: **un homme dont je connais la fille**
                  a man whose daughter I know
   and: **un homme dont la fille me connaît**
                  a man whose daughter knows me

   If the person (or object) 'owned' is the *object* of the verb, the order is:
   dont + verb + noun (1st sentence)
   If the person (or object) 'owned' is the *subject* of the verb, the order is:
   dont + noun + verb (2nd sentence)

   Note also: **l'homme dont elle est la fille**
                  the man whose daughter she is
6 **Qu'il fait chaud!**   **Que je suis content de vous**
   How warm it is!   **voir!**
                         How pleased I am to see you!

   Comme c'est cher   **Que tes voisins sont gentils!**
   How expensive it is!   How kind your neighbours are!
7 **'Je pense que oui' a dit Luc**   **'Ça ne fait rien' répondit Jean**
   'I think so,' said Luke   'It doesn't matter,' John replied
8 **'Quelle horreur!' me suis-je exclamé**
   'How awful!' I exclaimed
9 **'Pourquoi pas?' a-t-elle demandé**
   'Why not?' she asked
   'Si c'est vrai,' continua-t-il '...'
   'If it's true,' he went on '...'

Negatives

ne ... pas	*not*
ne ... point (literary)	*not*
ne ... rien	*nothing*
ne ... personne	*nobody*
ne ... plus	*no longer, no more*
ne ... jamais	*never*
ne ... que	*only*
ne ... aucun(e)	*no*
ne ... nul(le)	*no*
ne ... nulle part	*nowhere*
ne ... ni	*neither ... nor*
ne ... ni ... ni	*neither ... nor*

● **Word order**

- In simple tenses and the imperative:
    ne precedes the verb (and any object pronouns) and the second
    element follows the verb (→ **1**)

- In compound tenses:
    i **ne ... pas, ne ... point, ne ... rien, ne ... plus, ne ...
       jamais, ne ... guère** follow the pattern:
       ne + auxiliary verb + **pas** + past participle (→ **2**)
    ii **ne ... personne, ne ... que, ne ... aucun(e), ne ... nul(le),
       ne ... nulle part, ne ... ni (... ni)** follow the pattern:
       ne + auxiliary verb + past participle + **personne** (→ **3**)

- With a verb in the infinitive:
    ne ... pas, ne ... point (etc. see i above) come together (→ **4**)

● For use of **rien, personne** and **aucun** as pronouns, see p. 178

Continued

1 **Je ne fume pas**
I don't smoke
Ne changez rien
Don't change anything
Je ne vois personne
I can't see anybody
Nous ne nous verrons plus
We won't see each other any more
Il n'arrive jamais à l'heure
He never arrives on time
Il n'avait qu'une valise
He only had one suitcase
Je n'ai reçu aucune réponse
I have received no reply
Il ne boit ni ne fume
He neither drinks nor smokes
Ni mon fils ni ma fille ne les connaissaient
Neither my son nor my daughter knew them
2 **Elle n'a pas fait ses devoirs**
She hasn't done her homework
Ne vous a-t-il rien dit?
Didn't he say anything to you?
Ils n'avaient jamais vu une si belle maison
They had never seen such a beautiful house
Tu n'as guère changé
You've hardly changed
3 **Je n'ai parlé à personne**
I haven't spoken to anybody
Il n'avait mangé que la moitié du repas
He had only eaten half the meal
Elle ne les a trouvés nulle part
She couldn't find them anywhere
Il ne l'avait ni vu ni entendu
He had neither seen nor heard him
4 **Il essayait de ne pas rire**
He was trying not to laugh

Negatives (ctd.)

● Combination of negatives.

These are the most common combinations of negative particles:

ne ... plus jamais	(→ **1**)
ne ... plus personne	(→ **2**)
ne ... plus rien	(→ **3**)
ne ... plus ni ... ni ...	(→ **4**)
ne ... jamais personne	(→ **5**)
ne ... jamais rien	(→ **6**)
ne ... jamais que	(→ **7**)
ne ... jamais ni ... ni ...	(→ **8**)
(ne ... pas) non plus	(→ **9**)

non and **pas**

● **non** *no* is the usual negative response to a question (→ **10**)

It is often translated as *not* (→ **11**)

● **pas** is generally used when a distinction is being made, or for emphasis (→ **12**)

It is often translated as *not* (→ **13**)

1 **Je ne le ferai plus jamais**
   I'll never do it again

2 **Je ne connais plus personne à Rouen**
   I don't know anybody in Rouen any more

3 **Ces marchandises ne valaient plus rien**
   Those goods were no longer worth anything

4 **Ils n'ont plus ni chats ni chiens**
   They no longer have either cats or dogs

5 **On n'y voit jamais personne**
   You never see anybody there

6 **Ils ne font jamais rien d'intéressant**
   They never do anything interesting

7 **Je n'ai jamais parlé qu'à sa femme**
   I've only ever spoken to his wife

8 **Il ne m'a jamais ni écrit ni téléphoné**
   He has never either written to me or phoned me

9 **Ils n'ont pas d'enfants et nous non plus**
   They don't have any children and neither do we
   Je ne les aime pas – Moi non plus
   I don't like them – Neither do I; I don't either

10 **Vous voulez nous accompagner? – Non**
   Do you want to come with us? – No (I don't)

11 **Tu viens ou non?**
   Are you coming or not?
   J'espère que non
   I hope not

12 **Ma sœur aime le ski, moi pas**
   My sister likes skiing, I don't

13 **Qui a fait ça? – Pas moi!**
   Who did that? – Not me!
   Est-il de retour? – Pas encore
   Is he back? – Not yet
   Tu as froid? – Pas du tout
   Are you cold? – Not at all

Question forms: direct

There are four ways of forming direct questions in French:

- by inverting the normal word order so that
  pronoun subject + verb → verb + pronoun subject.
  A hyphen links the verb and pronoun (→ **1**)

  - When the subject is a noun, a pronoun is inserted after the verb and linked to it by a hyphen (→ **2**)

  - When the verb ends in a vowel in the third person singular, **-t-** is inserted before the pronoun (→ **3**)
- by maintaining the word order *subject + verb*, but by using a rising intonation at the end of the sentence (→ **4**)

- by inserting **est-ce que** before the construction *subject + verb* (→ **5**)

- by using an interrogative word at the beginning of the sentence, together with inversion *or* the **est-ce que** form above (→ **6**)

1 **Aimez-vous la France?**
   Do you like France?
   Est-ce possible?
   Is it possible?
   Part-on tout de suite?
   Are we leaving right away?

   Avez-vous fini?
   Have you finished?
   Est-elle restée?
   Did she stay?

2 **Tes parents sont-ils en vacances?**
   Are your parents on holiday?
   Jean-Benoît est-il parti?
   Has Jean-Benoît left?

3 **A-t-elle de l'argent?**
   Has she any money?
   La pièce dure-t-elle longtemps?
   Does the play last long?
   Mon père a-t-il téléphoné?
   Has my father phoned?

4 **Il l'a fini**
   He's finished it
   Robert va venir
   Robert's coming

   Il l'a fini?
   Has he finished it?
   Robert va venir?
   Is Robert coming?

5 **Est-ce que tu la connais?**
   Do you know her?
   Est-ce que tes parents sont revenus d'Italie?
   Have your parents come back from Italy?

6 **Quel train** { **prends-tu?**
                    est-ce que tu prends?
   What train are you getting?
   Lequel { **est-ce que ta sœur préfère?**
               ta sœur préfère-t-elle?
   Which one does your sister prefer?
   Quand { **êtes-vous arrivé?**
              est-ce que vous êtes arrivé?
   When did you arrive?
   Pourquoi { **ne sont-ils pas venus?**
                 est-ce qu'ils ne sont pas venus?
   Why haven't they come?

Question forms: indirect

An indirect question is one that is 'reported', e.g. he asked me *what the time was*, tell me *which way to go*. Word order in indirect questions is as follows:

● *interrogative word + subject + verb* (→ **1**)

● when the subject is a noun, and not a pronoun, the subject and verb are often inverted (→ **2**)

n'est-ce pas

This is used wherever English would use *isn't it?, don't they?, weren't we?, is it?* etc. tagged on to the end of a sentence (→ **3**)

oui and si

Oui is the word for *yes* in answer to a question put in the affirmative (→ **4**)
Si is the word for *yes* in answer to a question put in the negative or to contradict a negative statement (→ **5**)

1 **Je me demande s'il viendra**
  I wonder if he'll come
  Je ne sais pas à quoi ça sert
  I don't know what it's for
  Dites-moi quel autobus va à la gare
  Tell me which bus goes to the station
  Il m'a demandé combien d'argent j'avais
  He asked me how much money I had

2 **Elle ne sait pas à quelle heure commence le film**
  She doesn't know what time the film starts
  Je me demande où sont mes clés
  I wonder where my keys are
  Elle nous a demandé comment allait notre père
  She asked us how our father was
  je ne sais pas ce que veulent dire ces mots
  I don't know what these words mean

3 **Il fait chaud, n'est-ce pas?**
  It's warm, isn't it?
  Vous n'oublierez pas, n'est-ce pas?
  You won't forget, will you?

4 **Tu l'as fait? – Oui**
  Have you done it? – Yes (I have)

5 **Tu ne l'as pas fait? – Si**
  Haven't you done it? – Yes (I have)

Numbers

Cardinal (*one, two etc.*)		Ordinal (*first, second etc.*)	
zéro	0		
un (une)	1	premier (première)	1er, 1ère
deux	2	deuxième, second(e)	2ème
trois	3	troisième	3ème
quatre	4	quatrième	4ème
cinq	5	cinquième	5ème
six	6	sixième	6ème
sept	7	septième	7ème
huit	8	huitième	8ème
neuf	9	neuvième	9ème
dix	10	dixième	10ème
onze	11	onzième	11ème
douze	12	douzième	12ème
treize	13	treizième	13ème
quatorze	14	quatorzième	14ème
quinze	15	quinzième	15ème
seize	16	seizième	16ème
dix-sept	17	dix-septième	17ème
dix-huit	18	dix-huitième	18ème
dix-neuf	19	dix-neuvième	19ème
vingt	20	vingtième	20ème
vingt et un (une)	21	vingt et unième	21ème
vingt-deux	22	vingt-deuxième	22ème
vingt-trois	23	vingt-troisième	23ème
trente	30	trentième	30ème
quarante	40	quarantième	40ème
cinquante	50	cinquantième	50ème
soixante	60	soixantième	60ème
soixante-dix	70	soixante-dixième	70ème
soixante et onze	71	soixante-onzième	71ème
soixante-douze	72	soixante-douzième	72ème
quatre-vingts	80	quatre-vingtième	80ème
quatre-vingt-un (une)	81	quatre-vingt-unième	81ème
quatre-vingt-dix	90	quatre-vingt-dixième	90ème
quatre-vingt-onze	91	quatre-vingt-onzième	91ème

Numbers (ctd.)

Cardinal		Ordinal	
cent	100	centième	100ème
cent un (une)	101	cent unième	101ème
cent deux	102	cent deuxième	102ème
cent dix	110	cent dixième	110ème
cent quarante-deux	142	cent quarante-deuxième	142ème
deux cents	200	deux centième	200ème
duex cent un (une)	201	deux cent unième	201ème
duex cent deux	202	deux cent-deuxième	202ème
trois cents	300	trois centième	300ème
quatre cents	400	quatre centième	400ème
cinq cents	500	cinq centième	500ème
six cents	600	six centième	600ème
sept cents	700	sept centième	700ème
huit cents	800	huit centième	800ème
neuf cents	900	neuf centième	900ème
mille	1000	millième	1000ème
mille un (une)	1001	mille unième	1001ème
mille deux	1002	mille deuxième	1002ème
deux mille	2000	deux millième	2000ème
cent mille	100.000	cent millième	100.000ème
un million	1.000.000	millionième	1.000.000ème
deux millions	2.000.000	deux millionième	2.000.000ème

Fractions		Others	
un demi, une demie	½	zéro virgule cinq	0,5
un tiers	⅓	un virgule trois	1,3
deux tiers	⅔	dix pour cent	10%
un quart	¼	deux plus deux	2 + 2
trois quarts	¾	deux moins deux	2 − 2
un cinquième	⅕	deux fois deux	2 × 2
cinq et trois quarts	5¾	deux divisé par deux	2 ÷ 2

Note the use of points with large numbers and commas with fractions, i.e. the opposite of English usage.

Numbers: Other Uses

● **-aine** denoting approximate numbers:

une douzaine (de pommes)	about a dozen (apples)
une quinzaine (d'hommes)	about fifteen (men)
des centaines de personnes	hundreds of people
BUT: **un millier (de voitures)**	about a thousand (cars)

● measurements:

vingt mètres carrés	20 square metres
vingt mètres cubes	20 cubic metres
un pont long de quarante mètres	a bridge 40 metres long
avoir trois mètres de large/de haut	to be 3 metres wide/high

● miscellaneous:

Il habite au dix	He lives at number 10
C'est au chapitre sept	It's in chapter 7
(C'est) à la page 17	(It's) on page 17
(Il habite) au septième étage	(He lives) on the 7th floor
Il est arrivé le septième	He came in 7th
échelle au vingt-cinq millième	scale 1:25,000

Telephone numbers

Je voudrais Edimbourg trois cent trente, vingt-deux, dix
I would like Edinburgh 330 22 10

Je voudrais le soixante-cinq, treize, vingt-deux, zéro deux
Could you get me 65 13 22 02

Poste trois cent trente-cinq
Extension number 335

Poste vingt-deux, trente-trois
Extension number 22 33

N.B. In French, telephone numbers are broken down into groups of two or three numbers (never four), and are not spoken separately as in English. They are also written in groups of two or three numbers.

The calendar

Dates

Quelle est la date d'aujourd'hui?
Quel jour sommes-nous? } What's the date today?

C'est ...
Nous sommes ... } It's the ...

    le premier février   1st of February
    le deux février   2nd of February
    le vingt-huit février   28th of February

Il vient le sept mars   He's coming on the 7th of March

N.B. Use cardinal numbers except for the first of the month.

Years

Je suis né en 1971
I was born in 1971

le douze février { **dix-neuf cent soixante et onze**
                  { **mil neuf cent soixante et onze**
(on) 12th February 1971

N.B. There are two ways of expressing the year (see last example).
Note the spelling of **mil** *one thousand* in dates.

Other expressions

dans les années cinquante	during the fifties
au vingtième siècle	in the twentieth century
en mai	in May
lundi (quinze)	on Monday (the 15th)
le lundi	on Mondays
dans dix jours	in 10 days' time
il y a dix jours	10 days ago

The Time

Quelle heure est-il?   *What time is it?*
Il est ...   *It's ...*

00.00	**minuit** *midnight, twelve o'clock*
00.10	**minuit dix, zéro heure dix**
00.15	**minuit et quart, zéro heure quinze**
00.30	**minuit et demi, zéro heure trente**
00.45	**une heure moins (le) quart, zéro heure quarante-cinq**

01.00	**une heure du matin** *one a.m., one o'clock in the morning*
01.10	**une heure dix (du matin)**
01.15	**une heure et quart, une heure quinze**
01.30	**une heure et demie, une heure trente**
01.45	**deux heures moins (le) quart, une heure quarante-cinq**
01.50	**deux heures moins dix, une heure cinquante**
01.59	**deux heures moins une, une heure cinquante-neuf**

12.00	**midi, douze heures** *noon, twelve o'clock*
12.30	**midi et demi, douze heures trente**

13.00	**une heure de l'après-midi, treize heures** *one p.m., one o'clock in the afternoon*
01.30	**une heure et demie (de l'après-midi), treize heures trente**

19.00	**sept heures du soir, dix-neuf heures** *seven p.m., seven o'clock in the evening*
19.30	**sept heures et demie (du soir), dix-neuf heures trente**

A quelle heure venez-vous? – A sept heures
What time are you coming? – At seven o'clock
Les bureaux sont fermés de midi à quatorze heures
The offices are closed from twelve until two
à deux heures du matin/de l'après-midi
at two o'clock in the morning/afternoon, at two a.m./p.m.
à sept heures du soir
at seven o'clock in the evening, at seven p.m.
à cinq heures précises *or* **pile**
at five o'clock sharp
vers neuf heures
about nine o'clock
peu avant/après midi
shortly before/after noon
entre huit et neuf heures
between eight and nine o'clock
Il est plus de trois heures et demie
It's after half past three
Il faut y être à dix heures au plus tard/au plus tôt
You have to be there by ten o'clock at the latest/earliest
Ne venez pas plus tard que onze heures moins le quart
Come no later than a quarter to eleven
Il en a pour une demi-heure
He'll be half an hour (at it)
Elle est restée sans connaissance pendant un quart d'heure
She was unconscious for a quarter of an hour
Je les attends depuis une heure
I've been waiting for them for an hour/since one o'clock
Ils sont partis il y a quelques minutes
They left a few minutes ago
Je l'ai fait en vingt minutes
I did it in twenty minutes
Le train arrive dans une heure
The train arrives in an hour('s time)
Combien de temps dure ce film?
How long does this film last?

Beware of translating word for word. While on occasion this is quite possible, quite often it is not. The need for caution is illustrated by the following:

● English phrasal verbs (i.e. verbs followed by a preposition) e.g. *to run away*, *to fall down* are often translated by one word in French (→ **1**)

● English verbal constructions often contain a preposition where none exists in French, or vice versa (→ **2**)

● Two or more prepositions in English may have a single rendering in French (→ **3**)

● A word which is singular in English may be plural in French, or vice versa (→ **4**)

● French has no equivalent of the possessive construction denoted by --'s/--'s (→ **5**)
See also *at/in/to*, p. 234

Specific problems

-ing

This is translated in a variety of ways in French:

● *to be . . .-ing* is translated by a simple verb (→ **6**)
    Exception: when a physical position is denoted, a past participle is used (→ **7**)

● in the construction *to see/hear sb . . .-ing*, use an infinitive or **qui** + verb (→ **8**)

-ing can also be translated by:
    – an infinitive (→ **9**)
        (see p. 44)
    – a perfect infinitive (→ **10**)
        (see p. 46)
    – a present participle (→ **11**)
        (see p. 48)
    – a noun (→ **12**)
Continued

1 **s'enfuir**   **tomber**   **céder**
to run away   to fall down   to give in

2 **payer**   **regarder**   **écouter**
to pay for   to look at   to listen to
obéir à   **nuire à**   **manquer de**
to obey   to harm   to lack

3 **s'étonner de**   **satisfait de**
to be surprised at   satisfied with
voler qch à   **apte à**
to steal sth from   capable of; fit for

4 **les bagages**   **ses cheveux**
the luggage   his/her hair
le bétail   **mon pantalon**
the cattle   my trousers

5 **la voiture de mon frère**   **la chambre des enfants**
my brother's car   the children's bedroom
(*literally: ... of my brother*)   (*literally: ... of the children*)

6 **Il part demain**   **Je lisais un roman**
He's leaving tomorrow   I was reading a novel

7 **Elle est assise là-bas**   **Il était couché par terre**
She's sitting over there   He was lying on the ground

8 **Je les vois** { **venir** / **qui viennent** } I can see them coming

Je l'ai entendue { **chanter** / **qui chantait** } I heard her singing

9 **J'aime aller au cinéma**   **Arrêtez de parler!**
I like going to the cinema   Stop talking!
Au lieu de répondre   **Avant de partir**
Instead of answering   Before leaving

10 **Après avoir ouvert la boîte, il ...**
After opening the box, he ...

11 **Etant plus timide que moi, elle ...**
Being shyer than me, she ...

12 **Le ski me maintient en forme**
Skiing keeps me fit

to be

● Generally translated by **être** (→ **1**)
   When physical location is implied, **se trouver** may be used (→ **2**)

● In set expressions, describing physical and emotional conditions,
   avoir is used:

avoir chaud/froid	*to be warm/cold*
avoir faim/soif	*to be hungry/thirsty*
avoir peur/honte	*to be afraid/ashamed*
avoir tort/raison	*to be wrong/right*

● Describing the weather, e.g. *what's the weather like?*, *it's windy/sunny*, use **faire** (→ **3**)

● For ages, e.g. *he is 6*, use **avoir** (→ **4**)

● For state of health, e.g. *he's unwell, how are you?*, use **aller** (→ **5**)

it is, it's

● Usually **il/elle est**, when referring to a noun (→ **6**)

● For expressions of time, also use **il est** (→ **7**)

● To describe the weather, e.g. *it's windy*, see above

● In the construction: *it is difficult/easy to do sth*, use **il est** (→ **8**)

● In all other constructions, use **c'est** (→ **9**)

there is/there are

● Both are translated by **il y a** (→ **10**)

can, be able

● Physical ability is expressed by **pouvoir** (→ **11**)

● If the meaning is *to know how to*, use **savoir** (→ **12**)

● *Can* + a 'verb of hearing or seeing etc.' in English is not translated in French (→ **13**)

1 **Il est tard**
It's late

C'est peu probable
It's not very likely

2 **Où se trouve la gare?**
Where's the station?

3 **Quel temps fait-il?**
What's the weather like?

Il fait beau/mauvais/du vent
It's lovely/miserable/windy

4 **Quel âge avez-vous?**
How old are you?

J'ai quinze ans
I'm fifteen

5 **Comment allez-vous?**
How are you?

Je vais très bien
I'm very well

6 **Où est mon parapluie? – Il est là, dans le coin**
Where's my umbrella? – It's there, in the corner
Descends la valise si elle n'est pas trop lourde
Bring down the case if it isn't too heavy

7 **Quelle heure est-il? – Il est sept heures et demie**
What's the time? – It's half past seven

8 **Il est difficile de répondre à cette question**
It's difficult to reply to this question

9 **C'est moi qui ne l'aime pas**
It's me who doesn't like him
C'est Charles/ma mère qui l'a dit
It's Charles/my mother who said so
C'est ici que je les ai achetés
It's here that I bought them
C'est parce que la poste est fermée que . . .
It's because the post office is closed that . . .

10 **Il y a quelqu'un à la porte**
There's somebody at the door
Il y a cinq livres sur la table
There are five books on the table

11 **Pouvez-vous atteindre cette étagère?**
Can you reach up to that shelf?

12 **Elle ne sait pas nager**
She can't swim

13 **Je ne vois rien**
I can't see anything

Il les entendait
He could hear them

to (see also below)

● Generally translated by **à** (→ **1**)
(See p. 204)

● In time expressions, e.g. *10 to 6*, use **moins** (→ **2**)

● When the meaning is *in order to*, use **pour** (→ **3**)

● Following a verb, as in *to try to do*, *to like to do*, see pp. 44 and 64

● *easy/difficult/impossible* etc. *to do*:
The preposition used depends on whether a specific noun is referred to (→ **4**) or not (→ **5**)

at/in/to

● With feminine countries, use **en** (→ **6**)
With masculine countries, use **au** (**aux** with plural countries) (→ **7**)

● With towns, use **à** (→ **8**)

● *at/to the butcher's/grocer's* etc.: use **à** + noun designating the shop, or **chez** + noun designating the shopkeeper (→ **9**)

● *at/to the dentist's/doctor's* etc.: use **chez** (→ **10**)

● *at/to ...'s/...s' house*: use **chez** (→ **11**)

1 **Donne le livre à Patrick**
Give the book to Patrick

2 **dix heures moins cinq**   **à sept heures moins le quart**
five to ten   at a quarter to seven

3 **Je l'ai fait pour vous aider**
I did it to help you
Il se pencha pour nouer son lacet
He bent down to tie his shoelace

4 **Ce livre est difficile à lire**
This book is difficult to read

5 **Il est difficile de comprendre leurs raisons**
It's difficult to understand their reasons

6 **Il est allé en France/en Suisse**
He has gone to France/to Switzerland
un village en Norvège/en Belgique
a village in Norway/in Belgium

7 **Etes-vous allé au Canada/au Danemark/aux Etats-Unis?**
Have you been to Canada/to Denmark/to the United States?
une ville au Japon/au Brésil
a town in Japan/in Brazil

8 **Il est allé à Vienne/à Bruxelles**
He has gone to Vienna/to Brussels
Il habite à Londres/à Genève
He lives in London/in Geneva
Ils logent dans un hôtel à St. Pierre
They're staying in a hotel at St. Pierre

9 **Je l'ai acheté** { **à l'épicerie** / **chez l'épicier** }   I bought it at the grocer's

Elle est allée { **à la boulangerie** / **chez le boulanger** }   She's gone to the baker's

10 **J'ai un rendez-vous chez le dentiste**
I've an appointment at the dentist's
Il est allé chez le médecin
He has gone to the doctor's

11 **chez Christian**   **chez les Pagot**
at/to Christian's house   at/to the Pagots' house

General Points

● Activity of the lips
The lips play a very important part in French. When a vowel is described as having 'rounded' lips, the lips are slightly drawn together and pursed, as when an English speaker expresses exaggerated surprise with the vowel 'ooh!'. Equally, if the lips are said to be 'spread', the corners are pulled firmly back towards the cheeks, tendng to reveal the front teeth.

In English, lip position is not important, and vowel sounds tend to merge because of this. In French, the activity of the lips means that every vowel sound is clearly distinct from every other.

● No diphthongs
A diphthong is a glide between two vowel sounds in the same syllable. In English, there are few 'pure' vowel sounds, but largely diphthongs instead. Although speakers of English may *think* they produce one vowel sound in the word 'day', in fact they use a diphthong, which in this instance is a glide between the vowels [e] and [ɪ]: [deɪ]. In French the tension maintained in the lips, tongue and the mouth in general prevents diphthongs occurring, as the vowel sound is kept constant throughout. Hence the French word corresponding to the above example, 'dé', is pronounced with no final [ɪ] sound, but is phonetically represented thus: [de].

● Consonants
In English, consonants are often pronounced with a degree of laxness that can result in their practically disappearing altogether although not strictly 'silent'. In a relaxed pronunciation of a word such as 'hat', the 't' is often scarcely heard, or is replaced by a 'glottal stop' (a sort of jerk in the throat). This never occurs in French, where consonants are always given their full value.

Pronunciation of Consonants

Some consonants are pronounced almost exactly as in English: [b, p, f, v, g, k, m, w].
Most others are similar to English, but slight differences should be noted.

EXAMPLES	*HINTS ON PRONUNCIATION*
[d] **d**in**d**e	
[t] **t**en**t**e	The tip of the tongue touches the upper front teeth and not the roof of the mouth as in English
[n] **n**on**n**e	
[l] **L**il**l**e	
[s] tou**s ç**a	The tip of the tongue is down behind the bottom front teeth, lower than in English
[z] **z**éro ro**s**e	
[ʃ] **ch**ose ta**ch**e	Like the *sh* of English *shout*
[ʒ] **j**e **g**ilet bei**g**e	Like the *s* of English *measure*
[j] **y**eux pai**ll**e	Like the *y* of English *yes*

Three consonants are not heard in English:

[ʀ] **r**are veni**r**	*R* is often silent in English, e.g. fa*r*m. In French the [ʀ] is never silent, unless it follows an **e** at the end of a word e.g. cherch**er**. To pronounce it, try to make a short sound like gargling. Similar, too, to the Scottish pronunciation of lo*ch*
[ŋ] vi**gn**e a**gn**eau	Similar to the *ni* of Spa*ni*ard
[ɥ] h**u**ile l**u**eur	Like a very rapid [y] (see p. 239) followed immediately by the next vowel of the word

Pronunciation of Vowels

EXAMPLES	HINTS ON PRONUNCIATION
[a] **patte** pl**at a**mour	Similar to the vowel in English *pat*
[ɑ] **bas** p**â**te	Longer than the sound above, it resembles the English exclamation of surprise *ah!* Similar, too, to the English vowel in *car* without the final *r* sound
[ɛ] l**ai**t jou**et** m**e**rci	Similar to the English vowel in *pet*. Beware of using the English diphthong [eɪ] as in *pay*
[e] **é**t**é** jou**er**	A pure vowel, again quite different from the diphthong in English *pay*
[ə] l**e** pr**e**mier	Similar to the English sound in butt*er* when the *r* is not pronounced
[i] **i**c**i** v**ie** l**y**cée	The lips are well spread towards the cheeks while uttering this sound. Shorter than the English vowel in *see*
[ɔ] m**o**rt h**o**mme	The lips are well rounded while producing a sound similar to the *o* of English *cot*
[o] m**o**t d**ô**me **eau**	A pure vowel with strongly rounded lips; quite different from the diphthong in English *bone, low*

[u] gen**ou** r**ou**e	A pure vowel with strongly rounded lips. Similar to the English *ooh!* of surprise
[y] r**ue** vê**tu**	Often the most difficult for English speakers to produce: round your lips and try to pronounce [i] (see above). There is no [j] sound (see p. 237) as there is in English *pure*
[œ] s**œur** b**eu**rre	Similar to the vowel in English *fir* or *murmur*, but without the *r* sound and with the lips more strongly rounded
[ø] p**eu** d**eux**	To pronounce this, try to say [e] (see above) with the lips strongly rounded

Nasal Vowels

These are spelt with a vowel followed by a 'nasal' consonant – **n** or **m**. The production of nasal vowels really requires the help of a teacher or a recording of the sound. However, to help you, the vowel is pronounced by allowing the air from the lungs to come partly down the nose and partly through the mouth, and the **n** or **m** is not pronounced at all.

[ɑ̃] l**ent** s**ang** d**ans**

[ɛ̃] mat**in** pl**ein**

[ɔ̃] n**on** p**ont**

[œ̃] br**un un** parf**um**

In each case, the vowel shown in the phonetic symbol is pronounced as described above, but air is allowed to come through the nose as well as the mouth

From Spelling to Sounds

Although it may not seem so at first sight, there are some fairly precise 'rules' which can help you to know how to pronounce French words from their spelling.

Vowels

SPELLING	PRONOUNCED	EXAMPLES
a, à	[a]	ch**a**tte, t**a**ble
a, â	[ɑ]	p**â**te, p**a**s
e, é	[e]	**é**t**é**, march**er**
e, é, ê	[ɛ]	fen**ê**tre, f**er**mer, ch**è**re
e	[ɔ]	d**ou**ble, fenêtr**e**
i, î, y	[i]	l**i**t. ab**î**mer, lyc**ée**
o, ô	[o]	p**o**t, tr**o**p, d**ô**me
o	[ɔ]	s**o**tte, **o**range
u, û	[y]	batt**u**, f**û**t, p**u**r

Vowel Groups

There are several groups of vowels in French spelling which are regularly pronounced in the same way:

ai	[ɛ] or [e]	m**ai**son, march**ai**, f**ai**re
ail	[aj]	port**ail**
ain, aim, (c)in, im	[ɛ̃]	p**ain**, f**aim**, fr**ein**, **im**pair
au	[o]	**au**berge, land**au**
an, am, en, em	[ɑ̃]	pl**an**, **am**ple, **en**trer, t**em**ps
eau	[o]	bat**eau**, **eau**
eu	[œ] or [ø]	f**eu**, p**eu**r
euil(le), ueil	[œj]	f**euille**, rec**ueil**
oi, oy	[wa]	v**oi**re, v**oy**age
on, om	[ɔ̃]	t**on**, c**om**pter
ou	[u]	hib**ou**, **ou**til
œu	[œ]	s**œu**r, c**œu**r
ue	[y]	r**ue**
un, um	[œ̃]	br**un**, parf**um**

Added to these are the many groups of letters occurring at the end of words, where their pronunciation is predictable, bearing in mind the tendency (see p. 242) of final consonants to remain silent:

TYPICAL WORDS	*PRONUNCIATION OF FINAL SYLLABLE*
pas, mât, chat	[ɑ] or [a]
marcher, marchez **marchais, marchait,** **baie, valet, mes, fumée**	[e] or [ɛ]
nid	[i]
chaud, vaut, faux, **sot, tôt, Pernod, dos, croc**	[o]
bout, bijoux, sous, boue	[u]
fut, fût, crus, crûs	[y]
queue, heureux, bleus	[ø]
en, vend, vent, **an, sang, grand, dans**	[ã]
fin, feint, frein, vain	[ɛ̃]
on, pont, fond, avons	[ɔ̃]
brun, parfum	[œ̃]

Continued

From Spelling to Sounds (ctd.)

Consonants

● Final consonants are usually silent (→**1**)

● **n** or **m** at the end of a syllable or word are silent, but they have the effect of 'nasalizing' the preceding vowel(s) (see p. 239 on Nasal Vowels)

● The letter **h** is either 'silent' ('mute') or 'aspirate' when it begins a word. When silent, the word behaves as though it started with a vowel and takes a liaison with the preceding word where appropriate.
When the **h** is aspirate, no liaison is made (→**2**)
There is no way of predicting which words start with which sort of **h** – this simply has to be learnt with each word

● The following consonants in spelling have predictable pronunciations: b, d, f, k, l, p, r, t, v, w, x, y, z. Others vary:

SPELLING	PRONOUNCED	ENGLISH EXAMPLES	
c + a, o, u	[k]	can, cot, cut	(→**3**)
+ l, r		class, cram	
c + e, i, y	[s]	ceiling, ice	(→**4**)
ç + a, o, u	[s]	ceiling, ice	(→**5**)
ch	[ʃ]	shop, lash	(→**6**)
g + a, o, u	[g]	gate, got, gun	(→**7**)
+ l, r		glass, gramme	
g + e, i, y	[ʒ]	leisure	(→**8**)
gn	[ɲ]	companion, onion	(→**9**)
j	[ʒ]	measure	(→**10**)
q, qu	[k]	quay, kit	(→**11**)
s between vowels:	[z]	rose	(→**12**)
elsewhere	[s]	sit	
th	[t]	Thomas	(→**13**)
t in **-tion**	[s]	sit	(→**14**)

1 **éclat**
   [ekla]
   chaud
   [ʃo]

   nez
   [ne]
   aider
   [ɛde]

2 silent **h**:
   des hôtels
   [de zotɛl]

   aspirate **h**:
   des haricots
   [de aʀiko]

3 **café**
   [kafe]
   classe
   [klas]

   côte
   [kot]
   croûte
   [kʀut]

   culture
   [kyltyʀ]

4 **ceci**
   [səsi]

   cil
   [sil]

   cycliste
   [siklist]

5 **ça**
   [sɑ]

   garçon
   [gaʀsɔ̃]

   déçu
   [desy]

6 **chat**
   [ʃa]

   riche
   [ʀiʃ]

7 **gare**
   [gaʀ]
   glaise
   [glɛz]

   gourde
   [guʀd]
   gramme
   [gʀam]

   aigu
   [ɛgy]

8 **gemme**
   [ʒɛm]

   gilet
   [ʒilɛ]

   gymnaste
   [ʒimnast]

9 **vigne**
   [viɲ]

   oignon
   [ɔɲɔ̃]

10 **joli**
    [ʒɔli]

    Jules
    [ʒyl]

11 **quiche**
    [kiʃ]

    quitter
    [kite]

12 **sable**
    [sablə]

    maison
    [mɛzɔ̃]

13 **théâtre**
    [teatʀ]

    Thomas
    [tɔma]

14 **nation**
    [nasjɔ̃]

    action
    [aksjɔ̃]

Feminine Forms and Pronunciation

● For adjectives and nouns ending in a vowel in the masculine, the addition of an **e** to form the feminine does not alter the pronunciation (→**1**)

● If the masculine ends with a silent consonant, generally **-d**, **-s**, **-r** or **-t**, the consonant is sounded in the feminine (→**2**)
This also applies when the final consonant is doubled before the addition of the feminine **e** (→**3**)

● If the masculine ends in a nasal vowel and a silent **n**, e.g. **-an**, **-on**, **-in**, the vowel is no longer nasalized and the **-n** is pronounced in the feminine (→**4**)
This also applies when the final **-n** is doubled before the addition of the feminine **e** (→**5**)

● Where the masculine and feminine forms have totally different endings (see pp. 136 and 150), the pronunciation of course varies accordingly (→**6**)

Plural Forms and Pronunciation

● The addition of **s** or **x** to form regular plurals generally does not affect pronunciation (→**7**)

● Where liaison has to be made, the final **-s** or **-x** of the plural form is pronounced (→**8**)

● Where the masculine singular and plural forms have totally different endings (see pp. 138 and 148), the pronunciation of course varies accordingly (→**9**)

● Note the change in pronunciation in the following nouns:

SINGULAR		PLURAL		
bœuf	[bœf]	**bœufs**	[bø]	*ox/oxen*
œuf	[œf]	**œufs**	[ø]	*egg/eggs*
os	[ɔs]	**os**	[o]	*bone/bones*

ADJECTIVES		NOUNS	
1 joli [ʒɔli]	→ **jolie** [ʒɔli]	**un ami** [ami]	→ **une amie** [ami]
déçu [desy]	→ **déçue** [desy]	**un employé** [ãplwaje]	→ **une employée** [ãplwaje]
2 chaud [ʃo]	→ **chaude** [ʃod]	**un étudiant** [etydjã]	→ **une étudiante** [etydjãt]
français [fRãsɛ]	→ **française** [fRãsɛz]	**un Anglais** [ãglɛ]	→ **une Anglaise** [ãglɛz]
inquiet [ɛ̃kjɛ]	→ **inquiète** [ɛ̃kjɛt]	**un étranger** [etRãʒe]	→ **une étrangère** [etRãʒɛR]
3 violet [vjɔlɛ]	→ **violette** [vjɔlɛt]	**le cadet** [kadɛ]	→ **la cadette** [kadɛt]
gras [gRɑ]	→ **grasse** [gRɑs]		→
4 plein [plɛ̃]	→ **pleine** [plɛn]	**le souverain** [suvRɛ̃]	→ **la souveraine** [suvRɛn]
fin [fɛ̃]	→ **fine** [fin]	**Le Persan** [pɛRsã]	→ **la Persane** [pɛRsan]
brun [bRœ̃]	→ **brune** [bRyn]	**le voisin** [vwazɛ̃]	→ **la voisine** [vwazin]
5 canadien [kanadjɛ̃]	→ **canadienne** [kanadjɛn]	**le paysan** [peizã]	→ **la paysanne** [peizan]
breton [bRətɔ̃]	→ **bretonne** [bRətɔn]	**le baron** [baRɔ̃]	→ **la baronne** [baRɔn]
6 vif [vif]	→ **vive** [viv]	**le veuf** [vœf]	→ **la veuve** [vœv]
traître [tRɛtRɛ]	→ **traîtresse** [tRɛtRɛs]	**le maître** [mɛtRə]	→ **la maîtresse** [mɛtRɛs]
7 beau [bo]	→ **beaux** [bo]	**la maison** [mɛzɔ̃]	→ **les maisons** [mɛzɔ̃]
8 des anciens élèves [de zãsjɛ̃ zelɛv]			
de beaux arbres [də bo zaRbR(ə)]			
9 amical [amikal]	→ **amicaux** [amiko]	**un journal** [ʒuRnal]	→ **des journaux** [ʒuRno]

The Alphabet

A, a	[ɑ]	**J, j**	[ʒi]	**S, s**	[ɛs]
B, b	[be]	**K, k**	[ka]	**T, t**	[te]
C, c	[se]	**L, l**	[ɛl]	**U, u**	[y]
D, d	[de]	**M, m**	[ɛm]	**V, v**	[ve]
E, e	[ə]	**N, n**	[ɛn]	**W, w**	[dubləve]
F, f	[ɛf]	**O, o**	[o]	**X, x**	[iks]
G, g	[ʒe]	**P, p**	[pe]	**Y, y**	[igʀɛk]
H, h	[aʃ]	**Q, q**	[ky]	**Z, z**	[zɛd]
I, i	[i]	**R, r**	[ɛr]		

Capital letters are used as in English *except* for the following:

● adjectives of nationality
  e.g. **une ville espagnole**   **un auteur français**
      a Spanish town   a French author

● languages
  e.g. **Parlez-vous anglais?**   **Il parle français et allemand**
      Do you speak English?   He speaks French and German

● days of the week:
lundi	Monday
mardi	Tuesday
mercredi	Wednesday
jeudi	Thursday
vendredi	Friday
samedi	Saturday
dimanche	Sunday

● months of the year:
janvier	January	**juillet**	July
février	February	**août**	August
mars	March	**septembre**	September
avril	April	**octobre**	October
mai	May	**novembre**	November
juin	June	**décembre**	December

The following index lists comprehensively both grammatical terms and key words in French and English contained in this book.